Rhetoric, Religion and the Civil Rights Movement 1954–1965

Studies in Rhetoric and Religion 1

EDITORIAL BOARD

Rhetoric, Religion and the Civil Rights Movement 1954–1965

Davis W. Houck

David E. Dixon

EDITORS

B
_____

Baylor University Press
Waco, Texas

Book Design by Helen Lasseter

Cover Design by Cynthia Dunne, Blue Farm Graphics

Permission acknowledgments are to be found on page 973 and are a continuation of the copyright page.

Library of Congress Cataloging-in-Publication Data

Rhetoric, religion, and the civil rights movement, 1954-1965 / Davis W. Houck, David E. Dixon, editors.
    p. cm. -- (Studies in rhetoric and religion ; 1)
    Includes index.
    ISBN-13: 978-1-932792-54-6 (pbk. : alk. paper)
    1. African Americans--Civil rights--History--20th century--Sources. 2. Civil rights movements--United States--History--20th century--Sources. 3. United States--Race relations--History--20th century--Sources. 4. Civil rights--Religious aspects--Christianity--History--20th century--Sources. 5. Race relations--Religious aspects--Christianity--History--20th century--Sources. 6. Rhetoric--Political aspects--United States--History--20th century--Sources. 7. Speeches, addresses, etc., American. 8. Sermons, American. I. Houck, Davis W. II. Dixon, David E.

E185.61.R48 2006
323.1196'073--dc22

2006021173

Printed in the United States of America on acid-free paper, with a minimum of 30% pcw recycled content.

Dedication

To Raymond Fleming and H. Stephen Whitaker: Freedom fighters and friends—who fought so that I didn't have to.

AND

Out of gratitute for the world emerging from our contributors' sacrifice, in the hope I can keep that world spinning for Nick, Jano, and Nora until they can shoulder it on their own.

And they were saints in that most effective and telling way: sanctified by leading ordinary lives in a completely supernatural manner, sanctified by obscurity, by usual skills, by common tasks, by routine, but skills, tasks, routine which received a supernatural form from grace within, and from the habitual union of their souls with God in deep faith and charity.

— Thomas, Merton, *The Seven Storey Mountain*

Contents

1965

PREFACE

In a project of this scope and ambition, we have amassed many, many debts. These debts range from doing archival research and transcribing audio recordings to our contributors' family members sharing memories and resources. To say that we have been blessed is a considerable understatement. And so we say thank you to the many people who so graciously helped us assemble this book: Jim and Barbara Houck, Abraham Iqbal Khan, Greg Dorchak, Jim Kimble, Devery Anderson, Wendy Shay, Rev. Edwin King, Dave Dennis, Charles McLaurin, Will D. Campbell, Laurie and Happy Lee, Gail Parker, Marc Periou, Luther Brown, Paul D. Pearson, Michelle Deardorff, Kay Mills, Ray Bonis, Chad Underwood, Burt Altman, Anne Prichard, Charlotte Grimes, Robert Graetz, Everett Tilson, Amy M. Fitzgerald, Leah Reeb, Dale Patterson, Anita and Ralph Stutzman, Cornelia Akins Taylor, Elaine Hall, Peter Filardo, Sean O'Rourke, James Lawson, Emily Paige Pusser, Margaret Holmes, Charles Mason, Ryan Crowder, Kristen E. Fischer, Meredith M. Duncan, Allison L. Jarrett, Carolyn G. Thompson, Laney Harris, Julius van de Laar, Clarence Taylor, James Findlay, David Chappell, Paul Harvey, David Beito, Kathryn Koczwara, Katherine A. Dickens, James Quillen, Dimitar Simidchiev, Cora Vander Broek, Christian Dupont, Michael Plunkett, Tim West, Laura Clark Brown, Barbara D. Porter, Karen Jefferson, Andrea Jackson, Frances O'Donnell, Landon Scott Bell, Ilya Ruvinsky, Teresa M. Burk, Diane Pike, Brian DeShazor, Kathleen Manwaring, Theodore Myles, Branch B. Rickey III, Terry Goddard, Chana Lee, Naomi Nelson, Bruna Abram, Alan Breitler, Kenneth Chandler, Sharman Hartson, Marlene Patterson, Aimee Morgan, Andrew Manis, Beth Bidlack, Joyce Glaise, Patrick J. Stevens, Steve Lucht, Julian Bond, Jan O'Connell, James L. Hudson, Cammie East Cowan, Byron East, Philip Ensley, Gloria Swayzee, Rev. Wilson Kilgore, Lee Emerson, Bruce Prescott, Sara Evans, J. Claude Evans, Jr., Rev. J. Claude Evans, Sr., Maxilla Evans, Mabel Harris, Bob Crossman, Marcia Crossman, Rev. James R. Bullock, Jr., Rev. Theodore M. Hesburgh, Mary Fisher, Rev. Donald W. Shriver, Jr., Lynn Slawson, Adam Clayton Powell III, Yvonne Arnold, Roger Wilkins, Russ Enzor, Chet Weigle, Marna Weston, John Nichols, Gayraud Wilmore, Lilly Byrd, Carlos E. Martin, Molly Carnes, John T. Spike, Roger Boyle, Patton Boyle, George A. Chauncey, Sr., George A. Chauncey, Jr., Dunbar H. Ogden III, Charles Wittenstein, Bishop Charles Mason Ford, Martin Shelton, and Dr. R. Catherine Cohen.

Several institutions and archives have been most helpful in facilitating this project; they include: Florida State University, St. Joseph's College, the M.I.T. Alumni Association, the Columbia University Alumni Association, the Smithsonian Institution, Harvard University, the University of Virginia, Virginia Commonwealth University, Syracuse University, the University of Florida, Bellarmine University, the University of Minnesota, the Pacifica Radio Archives, the Library of Congress, Bethune-Cookman College, Vanderbilt University, the University of Southern Mississippi, Bangor Theological Seminary, the University of North Carolina, Chapell Hill, Florida A&M University, the King Center, and the Southern Regional Council.

A bit closer to home, we'd like to thank the congregants at Pisgah United Methodist Church in Tallahassee, the Missions of the Precious Blood at St. Joseph's College and the Adult Bible Fellowship Class led by Brian Hall at Trinity Evangelical Church in Mishawaka, Indiana.

A special thank you goes out to our families, for enduring this project cheerfully along with us. Would that they, and all of our readers, draw inspiration from its many lessons.

A very special and talented group of Florida State students were instrumental in creating both the headnotes and the bibliography; they are: Lauren Antista, Liza Arias, Veronica Bayo, Sarah Cruz, Melissa Dewey, Kate Ficarotta, Evan Goldberg, Carlos Gonzalez, Mary Hice, Toni Hyde, Tammy Jacobs, Bill Lawson, Kelly Lesso, Alison McEachin, Nicole Maestri, Jason Parker, Amanda Powell, Padrah Reichman, Jennifer Santoro, Shelly Sobol, Lori Swift, Beth Walker, Mary White, Charles Yhap, and Jacob Zipfel.

We are greatly indebted to the talented and hardworking staff at Baylor University Press, particularly, Helen Lasseter, Diane Smith, and Jordan Foreman. Finally, to Baylor University Press director Carey Newman and series editor Martin J. Medhurst, a special thank you for believing in this project and for encouraging it at every stage of development.

DWH
Tallahassee

DED
Mishawaka

INTRODUCTION

Since time immemorial rhetoric and religion have conspired to cocreate reality. Nowhere was this cocreation more central than in the American civil rights movement of the mid-twentieth century. Many leaders of that movement were ordained clergy; others were lay ministers or faithful congregants. All used the resources of rhetoric to move a nation. As we document throughout this volume, both Old and New Testament renderings and reappropriations were used to make the civil rights movement move. The story of captivity and slavery; the chosen people's wandering in the wilderness; the prophetic warnings of judgment and promises of justice; the Parable of the Good Samaritan; the many examples from Christ's ministry, including his final plea for unity; the Apostle Paul's seemingly endless quest to unite Jew and Gentile—these and many other biblical resources are at the core of the rhetoric of the civil rights movement. And it was not just black ministers thundering from pulpits in prominent urban churches; it was also the white southern minister imploring intransigent congregants weaned on Jim Crow as well as local black activists raised on the redemptive promises of righteous suffering.

All scholarship emerges from certain historiographical currents, and ours is no different. Prior to June 2004, we might have been inclined to disagree with David L. Chappell. In his book, *A Stone of Hope: Prophetic Religion and the Death of Jim Crow*, Chappell argues that a vital factor—perhaps *the* factor—in understanding the successes of the civil rights movement is religion, or what he terms "the irrational traditions of prophetic, revivalistic religion."[1] Our initial disagreement with Chappell's thesis had less to do with some sort of rhetorical atheism than a simple, experiential fact: we'd never heard that tradition. Aside from the civil rights documentaries and anniversaries so freighted and weighted with the voice of Dr. Martin Luther King, Jr., the religious sounds of the movement remained elusive. Where were the sounds or video recordings of a Lawrence Campbell, a Cleveland Jordan, an Ed King, or a Dave Dennis? And perhaps far more fundamental, how does a claim of rhetorical success—since prophecy is a fundamentally rhetorical business—get warranted on the desiccated bones of faded texts?

---

[1] David L. Chappell, *A Stone of Hope: Prophetic Religion and the Death of Jim Crow* (Chapel Hill: University of North Carolina Press, 2004), 179.

In other words, we wanted to hear the words that moved a region and a nation. Experience has taught us that even the speech voted the best American speech of the twentieth century—King's "I Have a Dream"—appears less impressive on paper and its power lies largely in its performance.

What then of Campbell, Jordan, King, and Dennis? Furthermore, who are these four? At the Archives Center of the National Museum of American History is the Moses Moon Collection. Moon, formerly Alan Ribback of Chicago, escaped the north in 1963 and 1964 and brought his sound recording equipment south. At the invitation of Student Nonviolent Coordinating Committee (SNCC) executive secretary Jim Forman, Moon recorded civil rights meetings across the Deep South—from Jackson, Hattiesburg, Greenwood, and Indianola, Mississippi to Selma, Alabama and Americus, Georgia. Moon also recorded meetings in the upper South, in Danville, Virginia and Washington, D.C. With nearly 80 hours of audiotape, the collection is most unique. Only the unprocessed Guy and Candy Carawan collection at the University of North Carolina, Chapel Hill contains a similar quantity and type of materials.[3]

Listening to the Moon collection, we became believers. As we listened to the tapes with headphones in the reading room of the Archives Center, patrons wondered about us. The looks were less hostile and more bemused: why were these fellows singing, laughing, tapping, and even excitedly high-fiving each other? This was not decorous archival behavior. And so it was not. We came away from the Moon collection not only bursting with 22-hours of recorded material, but with the realization that civil rights was fundamentally a religious affair. And how could it not be? No amount of Aristotelian rationalism or Enlightenment exegesis on natural rights could persuade a black Indianola, Mississippi tenant farmer to go down to the county courthouse and try to register to vote. It was decidedly not in his best "material" interest to make that trip. While the local White Citizens Council might call in a loan, or the plantation owner might terminate his employment, a local peckerwood or a clandestine Klavern might pay him an unannounced evening visit. But to "redish," in the Mississippi

---

[2] For the top 100 American speeches of the twentieth century, see Stephen E. Lucas and Martin J. Medhurst, *Words of a Century: The Top 100 American Speeches, 1900–1999* (New York: Oxford University Press, forthcoming). King's "I Have a Dream" speech was the clear winner for top speech.

[3] While the tapes remain unprocessed, a detailed finding aide is available online at http://www.lib.unc.edu/mss/inv/htm/20008.html. In his award-winning book on civil rights in Mississippi, Charles M. Payne quotes from several speeches in the collection; see *I've Got the Light of Freedom: The Organizing Tradition and the Mississippi Freedom Struggle* (Berkeley: University of California Press, 1995).

vernacular, was not primarily about political self-interest so much as it was a Divine Call to personhood, a faithful enactment of God's Plan, and a fulfillment of a uniquely American promise. No, the brave soul who was seeking the franchise in Sunflower County had most likely been filled with the Spirit during a local civil rights meeting.[4] How do we know? We listened to the meetings.

And what of Campbell, Jordan, King, and Dennis? Only the most serious civil rights scholars might know of Campbell and Jordan. Lawrence Campbell was a local minister who helped lead the Danville (VA) Christian Progressive Association (DCPA), while Cleveland Jordan was a fourth-grade educated civil rights activist and farmer who lived in Greenwood, Mississippi. Moon recorded both. Edwin King and Dave Dennis are more widely known. Both were major players in the Council of Federal Organizations (COFO) as well as local movements in Mississippi. Moon recorded both. And in recording these four men and scores of others, Moon has allowed scholars to bear witness to the fact that it was local southerners—black and white—who made the movement move. Dr. King got the headlines, the awards, and the adulation; but the Ed Kings did the daily dirty work so essential to the movement's many successes.[5]

The Moon collection filled us with the Spirit, too. And we set out to locate other documents—textual, video, and audio—that articulate the Judeo-Christian foundations of the modern civil rights movement. Even as historians have raced far ahead in civil rights scholarship, many primary sources remain largely hidden away in private collections and archives around the country. And so, in addition to providing primary source evidence for the claims of Chappell and others, claims about the primacy of rhetoric and religion to the modern civil rights movement, we also heed the call of our own field (rhetorical studies) to recover and reclaim the oratorical text.

Martin J. Medhurst, along with several other prominent rhetoricians, has repeatedly made the plea for a type of public address scholarship grounded in primary sources.[6] And scholars have gone to the archives,

---

[4] Instead of an alter call, movement leaders would typically ask at the close of a meeting for a show of hands of people willing to volunteer for movement work. That work could involve a march, a picket line, registering to vote and even going to jail. But importantly, the point was to act immediately on the Spirit, to translate the singing, the praying, and the oratory into collective action.

[5] For a profile of Reverend Edwin King as well as support for Chappell's position on the central role of religion to the movement, see Charles Marsh, *God's Long Summer: Stories of Faith and Civil Rights* (Princeton: Princeton University Press, 1999), 116–51.

[6] See, for example, the following works by Martin J. Medhurst, "Public Address and Significant Scholarship: Four Challenges to the Rhetorical Renaissance," in *Texts in Context*, ed. Michael C. Leff and Fred J. Kauffeld (Davis, CA: Hermagoras Press, 1989), 29–42; "The

leading not only to a revitalized field of inquiry, but to a vastly more prolific and interdisciplinary one as well. In a field once dominated by case
studies that illustrated theoretical points, theory is now incidental to the
careful historical and critical rendering of important episodes in public
address. In like manner scholars of public discourse have made public the
call for the "recovery" of significant texts in the history of public address.
Without such significant texts, scholarship runs the risk of stagnation if
not decay. As a consequence, rhetorical scholars are not only publishing
groundbreaking studies of heretofore unknown or forgotten speeches, but
they are also providing, in many cases for the first time, a contemporary
audience for those speeches. Thus, while the "great speeches" are finally
getting their due, so too are those forgotten moments of public persuasion.
While much work remains to be done, that project has started and is moving forward.[7]

Our project has indeed been a fascinating "recovery." From Bangor,
Maine to Los Angeles, California, we have searched diligently for the
speeches presented here. Unfortunately, many important and likely eloquent speeches during pivotal moments of the movement have been lost
forever. One such voice is Fannie Lou Hamer, the Mississippi sharecropper-
turned-civil rights activist. So commanding was her eloquence that president Lyndon Johnson preempted her nationally televised speech before
the Credentials Committee at the 1964 Democratic National Convention
with a presidential press conference. Never before had a Mississippi sharecropper with a sixth grade education moved the world's most powerful
man to act—and with dispatch. While a small handful of Hamer's speeches
survive, the oral tradition, so pervasive among rural and uneducated peoples, militates against recovery. Hamer's friend and fellow activist, Victoria
Gray Adams, long an activist in and around Hattiesburg, tells a revealing anecdote. Appearing together on a local radio program in Clarksdale,
Mississippi, both Gray and Hamer spoke from a prepared text. After the
program Hamer said, "Gray, I messed that up." To which Gray responded,

---

Academic Study of Public Address: A Field in Transition," in *Landmark Essays on American
Public Address*, ed. Martin J. Medhurst (Davis, CA: Hermagoras Press, 1993), xi–xliii;
"The Rhetorical Renaissance: A Battlefield Report," *Southern Communication Journal* 63
(1998): 309–14; "The Contemporary Study of Public Address: Renewal, Recovery, and
Reconfiguration," *Rhetoric & Public Affairs* 4 (2001): 495–511. For the field's earliest call
for primary source-based scholarship, see William Norwood Brigance, "Whither Research?"
Quarterly Journal of Speech 19 (1933): 552–61.

[7] Lucas and Medhurst's *Words of a Century* is exemplary in this regard. Texas A&M
University Press' Library of Presidential Rhetoric is a planned 50-volume series in which
each volume is devoted to careful historical and critical analysis of individual presidential
addresses. To date four volumes have been published and several more are in press.

"You don't need a script. Whenever you get a script, just go through it and see what they want you [t]o say and then put it aside. And she said, 'Do you think that's so?' And I said, 'I know it's so. I've seen you before. And you don't need a script.'"[8] And so she did not, as her 1964 speech near her home in Ruleville, transcribed and printed here, makes abundantly clear. But for every Fannie Lou Hamer, there are scores of other activists, white and black, whose speeches were never recorded nor transcribed.

Two other black activists deserve mention in this context. One of the events that catalyzed the nascent civil rights movement was the murder of Emmett Till in the Mississippi Delta during the summer of 1955. That murder, the ensuing trial, and the massive media coverage made unfortunate celebrities of Till's mother, Mamie Till-Bradley and Till's great uncle, Moses Wright, also known as "preacher" for occasionally appearing in the pulpit at the tiny Church of Christ near his home. The NAACP, seeking to capitalize on the coverage, sponsored a West Coast speaking tour for Wright, the man who had the audacity to rise literally and point the finger publicly at a white man in a Mississippi courtroom. We searched feverishly in the Library of Congress for his speeches. Notoriously vigilant for remarks made in its name, the NAACP's papers contained everything but speeches: promotional fliers, descriptions of events, monies generated, but no texts. We remain hopeful that Moses Wright did not go to his grave without some testimony of his attempts to redeem his grand-nephew's sacrifice.

We had similar results with Methodist minister, James Lawson. Working with both SNCC and the Southern Christian Leadership Conference (SCLC), Lawson helped train a generation of important activists, including John Lewis, Diane Nash, and James Bevel. Still an activist, Lawson continues to conduct nonviolent workshops from the Holman Methodist Church in Los Angeles. We are grateful to Reverend Lawson for being a staunch supporter of this project. Along with many others, we also eagerly anticipate the day when he makes available his considerable archive of speeches and first-hand experiences. No doubt he will enable historians to attain a far more nuanced understanding of the movement he was so instrumental in shaping.

We take rhetoric to be a most serious matter. A much-maligned term since at least Plato's ambivalent pronouncements through the lips of his mentor Socrates, rhetoric was central to the civil rights movement. Civil rights historians such as Paul Harvey, Andrew M. Manis, and Jane Daily have begun to take the study of rhetoric seriously; movement rhetoric, though "difficult to articulate," ought to be positioned at the very center

---

[8] Quoted in Kay Mills, *This Little Light of Mine: The Life of Fannie Lou Hamer* (New York: Plume, 1994), 44.

of civil rights inquiry.[9] Why? Euphemisms such as "leadership," "grassroots organizing," and "local activism" carry the historian's imprimatur, but such disciplinary god-terms obscure the singular fact that strategic words and actions lie at the heart of the movement's successes. Activists sought public means through which to move a nation to change its private attitudes and its public institutions. Speeches represent but one important sliver of the rhetorical constellation: sit-ins, boycotts, marches, pray-ins, wade-ins, public letters, songs, and, of course, the televised images of vicious attacks caught on film at places like Birmingham and Selma were all part of the persuasive mosaic that changed the nation. Is it any wonder that the first thing racist thugs typically went after were the presses' cameras? Perhaps SCLC was better attuned to the publicity angle than were other organizations; Birmingham, as a city, after all, was targeted after the problems experienced in Albany, Georgia, in part because of the threat of violence and the proximity to major media. The two were not unrelated.[10]

What often gets lost in this transactional and instrumental model of rhetoric is the source. That is, as Richard Gregg's work on the "ego-function" of protest rhetoric demonstrates, participating in the movement uniquely emboldened the participants.[11] Going to jail for one's beliefs is, among many things, a powerful act of self-affirmation and definition. So, too, speaking at a civil rights rally is constitutive of identity in the most profound ways. For so many black southerners, such identities had been carefully, if not brutally, suppressed by a white supremacy premised on maintaining identities of inferiority among blacks. Staying in one's "place" was less about geography and much more about how identity inflects geography. Thus is social equality shot through with the rhetorical.

Our aims, then, are two. First, we seek to offer empirical evidence for the oft-stated claim that the Judeo-Christian religion was the rhetorical hinge on which the movement pivoted. In addition, we hope to illustrate not just the "what" of such rhetoric, but also the "how": How did speakers attempt to move audience members from within the weighty Judeo-

---

[9] Paul Harvey, *Freedom's Coming: Religious Culture and the Shaping of the South from the Civil War through the Civil Rights Era* (Chapel Hill: University of North Carolina Press, 2005); Andrew M. Manis, *Southern Civil Religions in Conflict: Civil Rights and the Culture Wars*, 2d ed. (Macon, GA: Mercer University Press, 2002); and Jane Dailey, "Sex, Segregation, and the Sacred after Brown," *The Journal of American History* 91 (2004): 119–44.

[10] For an analysis of the visual rhetoric of Birmingham and Selma, see Sasha Torres, *Black, White and in Color: Television and Black Civil Rights* (Princeton: Princeton University Press, 2003). For an expanded discussion of the rhetorical dimensions of the civil rights movement, see Davis W. Houck, "Ed King's Jaw—Or, Reading, Writing and Embodying Civil Rights," *Rhetoric & Public Affairs* 7 (2004): 69–90.

[11] Richard B. Gregg, "The Ego-Function of the Rhetoric of Protest," *Philosophy and Rhetoric* 4 (1971): 71–91.

Christian corpus? Second, we seek to recover many of the heretofore lost voices and texts of the movement in order to appreciate the full rhetorical diversity of the movement's many participants as well as to offer new avenues of historical and critical inquiry. That said, we are not turning our back on such stalwarts as King, A. Philip Randolph, Adam Clayton Powell, and Thomas Merton. To do so would be to bear false witness, or at least to distort what constitutes "the movement."[12]

We would also point out that "Judeo-Christian" does not necessarily denote a place or a denomination. Aldon Morris, among others, has demonstrated how important the black church was to movement organizing; the Klan knew it too, as its reign of terror during Freedom Summer destroyed more than 40 churches in Mississippi alone.[13] But catch-all categories such as the "black church" or "white Southern Baptists" move us far afield of the particularities and contingencies of a given rhetorical situation. Surely churches and denominations mattered to the civil rights movement; far more important, however, were the individual voices and symbolic actions themselves.

We need to say a word, as well, about the way in which we have periodized the movement. Most periodizing schemes are necessary fictions, ours included. But by beginning in 1954 and ending in 1965, we have simply borrowed from the civil rights orthodoxy.[14] Of course civil rights activists were active long before 1954 and long after 1965.[15] Insofar as a

---

[12] We use the terms "civil rights movement" and "black freedom movement" interchangeably. We would emphasize, along with many other scholars, that the singular form of "movement" is altogether misleading. While most organizations had similar ends, the means were often very different and certainly not subject to a unifying national presence or set of objectives.

[13] Aldon D. Morris, *The Origins of the Civil Rights Movement: Black Communities Organizing for Change* (New York: Free Press, 1986). For a more regional history of the role of the black church, see Johnny E. Williams, *African American Religion and the Civil Rights Movement in Arkansas* (Jackson: University Press of Mississippi, 2003).

[14] For excellent overviews of civil rights historiography and some of the difficult problems related to periodization, see Steven F. Lawson, "Freedom Then, Freedom Now," in *Civil Rights Crossroads: Nation, Community, and the Black Freedom Struggle* (Lexington: The University Press of Kentucky, 2001), 3–28; John Dittmer, "The Civil Rights Movement," in *The African American Experience: An Historiographical and Bibliographical Guide*, ed. Arvarh E. Strickland and Robert E. Weems, Jr. (Westport, Conn.: Greenwood, 2001), 352–67; and Jeanne Theoharis and Komozi Woodard, "Introduction," in *Groundwork: Local Black Freedom Movements in America*, ed. Theoharis and Woodard (New York: New York University Press, 2005), 1–16.

[15] For recent trends in civil rights scholarship pre-Brown, see Charles M. Payne and Adam Green, eds., *Time Longer Than Rope: A Century of African American Activism, 1850–1950* (New York: New York University Press, 2003); and Glenn Feldman, ed., *Before Brown: Civil Rights and White Backlash in the Modern South* (Tuscaloosa: University of Alabama Press, 2004).

movement is often defined by the resistance that it provokes, the cataclysm of the Supreme Court's unanimous *Brown* decision on May 17, 1954 emboldened freedom fighters just as it did members of what would become the White Citizens Councils. It also emboldened many church denominations to act for the first time—or at least engage in symbolic action. That is, Baptists, Methodists, Presbyterians, and others now had the authority of law as well as the longstanding authority of Scripture to speak out against segregation. However, as we illustrate throughout the book, the deed of integration often lagged far behind the word. As for our "ending" the movement in 1965, many before us have argued that this marks the end of a key legislative phase of the movement with passage of the Voting Rights Act. And while many date the radicalization of the movement and its "Black Power" phase to 1966 and the Meredith March, we would hasten to add that the repudiation of the Mississippi Freedom Democratic Party (MFDP) at the Democratic National Convention in 1964 also revealed to many activists the limits of civil rights activism within traditional political channels. In the words of SNCC activist John Lewis, that moment of repudiation in Atlantic City "was the turning point of the civil rights movement."[16] In sum, then, does the civil rights movement pre- and post-date 1954 and 1965? Yes. We use this 12-year period as a window into the struggle for black civil rights.[17]

Within that window, we have selected speeches situated in civil rights orthodoxy: pivotal moments such as *Brown*, the death of Emmett Till, Little Rock, the student sit-ins, the integration of Ole' Miss, the murder of Medgar Evers, the March on Washington, the Sixteenth Street Baptist Church bombing, Freedom Summer, and the Selma marches all get hearings. So, too, do lesser known moments involving such topics as school integration in Charlotte, the Freedom Vote in Mississippi, voter registration across the South, protests in Danville, Virginia, and local white congregations scattered across the South grappling with the demise of their Way of Life.

Our aims and time frame, of course, strongly influence what speeches we have selected for inclusion. Obviously many prosegregationists, northern and southern used biblical warrants to ground racial separatism and the status quo. We might well remember in this regard that Edgar Ray

[16] John Lewis and Michael D'Orso, *Walking with the Wind: A Memoir of the Movement* (San Diego: Harcourt, 1998), 291.

[17] In his award-winning book, *Local People*, John Dittmer begins his story of civil rights in Mississippi immediately after World War II as sustained civil rights protest in the state commenced with black soldiers returning from the battlefield; see *Local People: The Struggle for Civil Rights in Mississippi* (Urbana: University of Illinois Press, 1994), 1–18.

Killen, the man convicted of manslaughter in 2005 in the deaths of Andrew Goodman, James Chaney, and Mickey Schwerner, was known by his Klan cronies as "Preacher" for his occasional Sunday homilies.[18] Similarly, many fence-sitters, perhaps best typified by the clergy addressed in King's famous Birmingham jail rejoinder, used the Scriptures to advocate a ponderous gradualism in which "extremists" on both sides were roundly condemned for their provocations. We leave it for others to document these stances.[19] We are concerned exclusively with racial progressives arguing for integration, the franchise, and social and economic equality.

Several other considerations have guided our selection. We have privileged many regional and local voices, those leaders—clergy and lay—who were instrumental in helping their communities protest, define, and negotiate civil rights related issues. These same leaders often helped to contextualize the national movement for a local audience. We have also included national leaders speaking to both national and local concerns. Several eulogies have been included, as martyrdom was an ever-present reality for movement participants. We have tried to stray from a rigid quantity quotient: "unless the Judeo-Christian tradition manifests itself x times in a speech, we won't include it." Instead, we have looked carefully at how the Scriptures or an understanding of them were employed for strategic rhetorical effect and whether those attempts tell us something important. And while we make no claim to measuring those effects, we can get a clearer picture of how Judeo-Christian texts, teachings, and traditions were inculcated into a persuasive message.

We have also strived to achieve some sense of diversity in selecting various speakers. As the reader will duly note, relatively few women are represented here.[20] This is not for lack of effort. Many familiar names are not

---

[18] See, for example, Marsh's chapters on Sam Bowers and Douglas Hudgins; Marsh, *God's Long Summer*.

[19] Chappell claims that a "booming subfield" involves the documentary history of the opposition to the civil rights movement; see Chappell, "Civil Rights: Grassroots, High Politics, Or Both?" *Reviews in American History* 32 (2004): 571. In this context see the work of W. Stuart Towns, particularly his anthology, *Public Address in the Twentieth-Century: The Evolution of a Region* (Westport, Conn.: Praeger, 1999).

[20] Despite the lack of primary source materials, beginning in the 1990s, scholars have detailed the important movement work of many women. See for example, Vicki L. Crawford, Jacquelyn Anne Rouse, and Barbara Woods, eds., *Women in the Civil Rights Movement: Trailblazers and Torchbearers, 1941–1965* (Brooklyn: Carlson, 1990); Lynne Olson, *Freedom's Daughters* (New York: Scribner, 2001); Gail S. Murray, ed., *Throwing Off the Cloak of Privilege: White Southern Women Activists in the Civil Rights Era* (Gainesville: University Press of Florida, 2004); and Bettye Collier-Thomas and V. P. Franklin, eds., *Sisters in the Struggle: African American Women in the Civil Rights-Black Power Movement* (New York: New York University Press, 2001). For scholarship on individual female civil rights activists, see Barbara Ransby, *Ella Baker and the Black Freedom Movement: A Radical*

here: Septima Clark, Annie Devine, Gloria Richardson, Annelle Ponder, Ruby Doris Smith Robinson, Rosa Parks, Diane Nash, Victoria Gray Adams, Dorothy Height, Jo Anne Robinson, Virginia Durr, Amelia Boynton, and Prathia Hall, to say nothing of the myriad local women whose names are not familiar at all. Would that we might someday recover their eloquence, so abundantly evident in the movement they helped shape and lead. Even so, we have included speeches by Ella Baker, Mary McLeod Bethune, Sarah Patton Boyle, Fannie Lou Hamer, Mildred Bell Johnson, and Mamie Till-Bradley.

We also feature many white southern clergy, in part because of a historiographical bias we have noted. In *A Stone of Hope*, for example, Chappell largely pits black against white—black civil rights religious leadership versus pro-segregation white religious leadership. That makes for a good story. It also excludes numerous brave white southern clergy who were trying to lead typically recalcitrant all-white congregations to a more enlightened understanding of race relations.[21] Many lost their jobs or were reassigned elsewhere. Some received votes of no-confidence. Others were denied monies promised to their congregation. In nearly all cases, being a white progressive in the southern pulpit between 1954 and 1965 came at a high cost. Through our research on so many largely unknown clergy, we have met many of these brave and outspoken men or their families that survive them. Often their ministries, lives, and family relationships were defined by just one pro-civil rights message from the pulpit. Many did not attempt a second.

Democratic Vision (Chapel Hill: University of North Carolina Press, 2003); Chana Kai Lee, *For Freedom's Sake: The Life of Fannie Lou Hamer* (Urbana: University of Illinois Press, 1999); and Cynthia Griggs Fleming, *Soon We Will Not Cry: The Liberation of Ruby Doris Smith Robinson* (Lanham, Md.: Rowman & Littlefield, 1998). For memoirs, see Mamie Till-Mobley and Christopher Benson, *Death of Innocence: The Story of a Hate Crime That Changed America* (New York: Random House, 2003); Pauli Murray, *Pauli Murray: The Autobiography of a Black Activist, Feminist, Lawyer, Priest and Poet* (Knoxville: University of Tennessee Press, 1989); Hollinger F. Barnard, ed., *Outside the Magic Circle: The Autobiography of Virginia Foster Durr* (Tuscaloosa: University of Alabama Press, 1985); Dorothy I. Height, *Open Wide the Freedom Gates: A Memoir* (New York: Public Affairs, 2003); Daisy Bates, *The Long Shadow of Little Rock: A Memoir* (Fayetteville: University of Arkansas Press, 1987); Jo Ann Robinson, *The Montgomery Bus Boycott and the Women Who Started It: The Memoir of Jo Ann Gibson Robinson* (Knoxville: University of Tennessee Press, 1987).

[21] For challenges to Chappell's thesis, see John M. Giggie, "The Third Great Awakening: Religion and the Civil Rights Movement," *Reviews in American History* 22 (2005): 254–62; Harvey, *Freedom's Coming*; Michael B. Friedland, *Lift Up Your Voice Like a Trumpet: White Clergy and the Civil Rights and Antiwar Movements, 1954–1973* (Chapel Hill: University of North Carolina Press, 1998); Manis, *Southern Civil Religions in Conflict*; and Dailey, "Sex, Segregation, and the Sacred after Brown," 119–44.

Of course the black clergy is also represented in our selections. SCLC stalwarts such as Ralph David Abernathy, Fred Shuttlesworth, Wyatt Tee Walker, and James Bevel are featured; but materials could not be located for such important leaders as Hosea Williams, C. K. Steele, Joseph Lowery, and James Orange. Dr. King's sole appearance is less about importance and more about copyright costs. For those seeking more of his materials, Clayborne Carson's Martin Luther King Jr. Papers Project at Stanford recently published its fifth volume of a planned 14-volume set. But it should be emphasized that not all black clergy were in favor of the movement's aims; in fact, a majority of black churches did not actively participate in the civil rights movement.[22] Many even refused to offer their sanctuaries for meetings for fear of retaliation; thus did James Bevel deliver a speech in Savannah, Georgia at a popular local nightspot.

Our speaker biases then are clear: Rhetorical ecumenism rather than a narrow "great speaker" approach to the black freedom movement guides our selection. But we need to say much more about what we have somewhat loosely designated as the Judeo-Christian tradition and its relationship to our subject. We would emphasize that the sermonic form does not define and delimit the generic parameters of our topic. We have certainly included many Sunday sermons that draw on both Old and New Testament Scriptures. But we have also included many speeches given at various civil rights related rallies and meetings that, on the surface, have no overt links with a religious service or tradition. Rather than the occasion stipulating a Judeo-Christian appeal, many speakers ground their calls for change less on the nation's secular governing traditions and more on the ministry of Jesus Christ. In other words, speech setting and Judeo-Christian content are highly variable.

And yet Christ's earthly ministry, as recorded in the gospels, represents but one locus of powerful appeals in the civil rights revolution. Many black ministers, for example, borrow from the Old Testament by focusing on the parallels between an Egypt of past captivity and suffering, and a Canaan of divine prosperity and freedom. The idea of a chosen people, hardened by years of slavery, left to wander in a desolate wilderness, resonated powerfully with many black Americans. Powerful, and plentiful,

---

[22] Adam Fairclough notes, for example, that during the Birmingham campaign of 1963, only 20 out of 250 black ministers were involved; see Fairclough, "The Preachers and the People: The Origins and Early Years of the Southern Christian Leadership Conference, 1955–1959," *Journal of Southern History* 52 (1986): 426; for additional work on the Birmingham clergy, see Glenn T. Eskew, "'The Classes and the Masses': Fred Shuttlesworth's Movement and Birmingham's Black Middle Class," in *Birmingham Revolutionaries: The Reverend Fred Shuttlesworth and the Alabama Christian Movement for Human Rights*, eds., Marjorie L. White and Andrew M. Manis (Macon, GA: Mercer University Press, 2000), 31–47.

too, are references to Paul's teaching, particularly his letter to the churches of Galatia and his famous call for unity: "There is no longer Jew and Greek, There is no longer slave or free, There is no longer male and female; for all of you are one in Christ Jesus" (3:28). And yet for many movement activists, biblical teaching was less an adjunct or series of lessons and more of an organic whole with any freedom-seeking people. That is, the Scriptures were often not so much a historical or philosophical support for civil rights as they were the animating, constitutive force behind it. God called the movement into being and not vice-versa. As such, to participate in the movement was to be an agent of God's will and divine plan. Dr. King's "beloved community" was a heaven-on-earth, not a pie-in-the-sky eternity rendered apolitical by a misreading of the beatitudes.

But Scripture can be summoned not only to motivate but also to indict. That indictment, of course, culminates in guilt—an emotion not unfamiliar to many Baptists and Catholics, among others. The charge of not following God's explicit command to "love thy neighbor as thyself" was employed relentlessly by activists. These same activists often went a step further in calling out their listeners for claiming belief in one thing while doing another. The hypocrite, profoundly rendered by Christ in the figure of the Pharisee, was a powerful and familiar archetype that was often aimed at the black middle-class church. In a few instances, speakers would even argue that sins against a brother's civil rights indicated a lack of salvation; forgiveness was not the point, truly accepting God's call was.

We should also emphasize that the civil rights movement was perhaps above all else a nonviolent movement. It was not a movement that retaliated in deed or word, or sanctioned any other sort of response to provocation other than turning the other cheek. To suffer righteously represents the apotheosis of New Testament doctrine translated into deed; a quiet, well-mannered and well-dressed witness, willing to sacrifice everything for racial equality bodied forth Christ's own suffering. And for those who bore witness to such suffering, shame would indeed prove a catalyzing force for civil rights progress. To bear witness and not act was to be complicitous in the humiliation. While several speakers in this volume articulate the Christian premises of nonviolent protest, others explicitly link violence with a non-Christian witness that could both antagonize bigots and encourage a white press that was only too willing to hyperbolize rock-throwing into a "Negro riot."

There is no one specific way, then, that the Judeo-Christian teachings and traditions manifest themselves in discourse on or about the civil rights movement. To have favored a specific type of discourse or a specific teaching or tradition would badly misrepresent the myriad ways in which they appear. Readers will find entire civil rights speeches based on a single Bible verse. Readers will also find speeches in which religion is referenced relatively sparingly. The point is to note not only that religion was used, but to observe how such use has designs on a listener. The rhetorical mosaic that emerges by the close of the book is one we find convincing—and one that also profoundly convicts.

We should also emphasize that our selections are not doctrinally driven. Methodists, Baptists, Presbyterians, Catholics, Jews, Church of God in Christ, Disciples of Christ, Unitarians, and Lutherans, and even a few agnostics, all get a hearing in what follows. There are many very fine institutional and church histories that document how different denominations responded to and participated in the civil rights movement.[23] Others have detailed how organizations such as the National Council of Churches were involved with the movement.[24] We leave it for others to record doctrinal rhetorical patterns. We did not find any.

A third difficult choice, in addition to speakers and speeches, involves organization. Just how does one organize 130 different speeches spread over a 12-year period? Or better yet, how should they be organized? We initially tinkered with the idea of themes such as speeches devoted to James Meredith's integration of Ole Miss or speeches related to the murder of Unitarian minister James Reeb. We also considered grouping speeches by type, such as sermons, eulogies, and commencement addresses. And we also considered a denominational organization in which faith traditions would serve as organizing principles. For better or worse, and borrowing a page from Foner and Branham's fine anthology *Lift Every Voice*, we have opted for a chronological organization; thus,

---

[23] For Jews and civil rights see Mark K. Bauman and Berkley Kalin, eds., *The Quiet Voices: Southern Rabbis and Black Civil Rights* (Tuscaloosa: University of Alabama Press, 1997); for Methodists see Peter C. Murray, *Methodists and the Crucible of Race 1930–1975* (Columbia: University of Missouri Press, 2004), and Donald E. Collins, *When the Church Bell Rang Racist: The Methodist Church and the Civil Rights Movement in Alabama* (Macon, GA: Mercer University Press, 1998); for Southern Baptists, see Mark Newman, *Getting Right With God: Southern Baptists and Desegregation, 1945–1995* (Tuscaloosa: University of Alabama Press, 2001); for Presbyterians, see Joel L. Alvis, Jr., *Religion & Race: Southern Presbyterians, 1946–1983* (Tuscaloosa: University of Alabama Press, 1994); for Catholics see John T. McGreevy, "Racial Justice and the People of God: The Second Vatican Council, the Civil Rights Movement, and American Catholics," *Religion and American Culture* 4 (1994): 221–54. For one of the few books dedicated to the activism of a single church, see Houston Bryan Roberson, *Fighting the Good Fight: The Story of the Dexter Avenue King Memorial Baptist Church, 1865–1977* (New York: Routledge, 2005).

[24] James F. Finley, *Church People in the Struggle: The National Council of Churches and the Black Freedom Movement, 1950–1970* (New York: Oxford University Press, 1993); and Mark Newman, *Divine Agitators: The Delta Ministry and Civil Rights in Mississippi* (Athens: University of Georgia Press, 2004).

we begin with a speech delivered by Mordecai Johnson on January 10, 1954 and we conclude with an address by Kelly Miller Smith given on December 26, 1965.[25]

Every speech is preceded by a brief biocritical headnote in which important biographical, critical, and contextual details are highlighted. Where germane, we have also specified where readers can locate a given speaker's archived papers. Several entries have only brief biographical sketches because our research turned up very little that was germane to our purpose. In many cases, we resorted to phone calls and e-mails in trying to locate various speakers and their families. Such contacts typically resulted in warm and supportive conversations; it is clear that the movement still moves so many of its advanced guard.

Unlike many speech anthologies, we have published only those speeches with a complete transcript. In this emphasis we have something of the rhetorical purist in us: to publish an excerpt is to demean, however subtly, the larger whole. That said, in working with the Moses Moon collection, several speeches had breaks in the audiotape caused either by equipment malfunctions or running out of audiotape. However, such breaks have not done grave violence to any speech we have included. In translating sounds into written words, we have also tried to maintain the vernacular that any given speaker employed. We have no desire to anglicize a Fannie Lou Hamer, Dave Dennis, or a Dick Gregory—not when so much of the rhetorical power of their message comes from their purposeful adoption (and simultaneous renunciation) of a given vernacular. Of course this sensibility makes for a lot of serrated red lines in Microsoft Word; Ebonic-friendly the program is not. We also have a new appreciation for punctuation and paragraph form, matters normally excluded in the oral tradition. As for the printed speeches we have included, the only changes we have made involve spelling. Where relevant and identifiable, we have also included last names and occasionally places in brackets to help specify a given person or place. Where a speaker has used emphasis, we have noted it with italics. We also recognize a very important shortcoming of printed speeches: we have not been able to authenticate them via a sound recording. This is a shortcoming we are forced to accept.

---

[25] Philip S. Foner, and Robert James Branham, eds., *Lift Every Voice: African-American Oratory, 1787–1900* (Tuscaloosa: University of Alabama Press, 1998).

Finally, it is our fervent hope that these speeches, taken either singly or together, will stand less as static monuments to a movement and more as dynamic moments in a volatile context. As rhetoric must be, the speeches are but partial representations and instantiations of that volatility. As monuments, these speeches don't ask merely for praise and adulation; false idols all the same. But as dynamic moments in civil rights history, the speeches invite our interaction and our engagement, our passions and our sympathies.

1954

⸙

1954

§1 Dr. Mordecai Wyatt Johnson

Dr. Mordecai Johnson was born on January 12, 1890 in Paris, Tennessee. His parents, Wyatt and Carolyn, were former slaves. He received his bachelor's degree from the University of Chicago. He also studied at Harvard and Rochester Theological Seminary. In 1911 he joined the faculty at Morehouse College. Johnson was pastor of the Second Baptist Church in Mumford, New York and the First Baptist Church of Charleston, West Virginia. He married Anna Ethelyn Gardner in 1916. The two had three sons and two daughters. In 1926 he began his 34-year presidency at Howard University. He was the first African American to serve in this capacity. In 1928 Johnson received his Doctorate of Divinity from Gammon Theological Seminary. He died in 1976.

Dr. Johnson was considered a gifted speaker. Martin Luther King, Jr. credited one of his lectures on Mahatma Gandhi as a source of his belief in nonviolent resistance. Some speculate that Dr. Johnson's greatest contribution to the cause of civil rights was his role in transforming Howard University's Law School into an assembly line producing some of the finest civil rights attorneys and law professors in the nation. Charles Howard Houston, who Johnson appointed to lead the law school in 1929, was a key architect of the *Brown v. Board of Education* decision that ended school segregation.

In this very interesting pre-*Brown* speech, Dr. Johnson begins with God and rhetoric: "We have no power whatsoever to force a program of any kind. We have only the power to persuade. But the obligation to persuade is upon us today as if God Himself had made us an assignment." Clearly sensing the changing political and racial winds, Johnson tells his Emancipation Day listeners that they must work for but two things: desegregation and equal job opportunities. Southerners fear such fundamental changes, claims Johnson, for the simple reason that they have no confidence; they have no practice with democracy. Southern states, he argues, have practical experience with neither democracy nor Christianity. He believes that Christian values, once introduced, will inevitably lead Southerners to a soul searching reform.

In the remainder of the speech, Johnson moves to foreign affairs, specifically the battle for the political allegiances of millions of the worlds' colored population. His reasoning is a fairly simple Cold War racial calculus: continue to deny rights in your own country, and the world will look to the Communists and Russia. Blacks can help defeat the Communist menace by voting for only those politicians who support desegregation. Of course Johnson's exhortation begs the question for many blacks: voting would not be an option for them for another 11 years.

Emancipation Day Address
Bethel AME Church, Baltimore, Maryland
January 10, 1954

Mr. Grandmaster, Willard Allen, Governor McKeldin, Dr. Byrd, distinguished guests, ladies, and gentlemen:

I am very happy for the privilege of being here today under the auspices of this great society.

My father was a member of this society, and I can remember that when I was a boy there were two things he held dear and kept close to his heart: One was his church and the other was the Masons. He let me see all the books and apparatus connected with the church, but what he had to do with the Masons, he kept locked up in a drawer. I don't know why. But I do know that he held it to be a highly constructive society, and he felt that its principles were such that they deserved the all-but-religious devotion of his life.

I had anticipated that His Excellency, Governor McKeldin, would be here today. He was with us a few Sundays ago, not as governor, but as a religious man. We enjoyed him greatly, and he had said that he would be here today.

But I did not anticipate what is really joyous to me: that we should have on this platform the representatives of the two great political parties of America and of this state. I rejoice that this is so. I do not hesitate at all. I was going to talk to the colored people about our program for the future. I am going right on and say just what I had planned to say from the very beginning, because I have long ago made it a habit to have no thought and no program in relation to the colored people that I wouldn't be willing to lay on the table with anybody present.

What I think is highly significant is the remarkable development the southern states have undergone. Only eighty-eight years after emancipation of the slaves, we have on this platform in a great southern city the representatives of both the great political parties of America. They are bidding for the allegiance of all the citizens and have frankly and seriously come out here today to be present with the colored minority. That very fact tells us we have passed through a great dark period in the South. We are through it and are in another period.

There was a time when this gathering could not have been done in the South, when men would have feared to do it. But there is no fear here today. There was a time when both political parties would have thought it useless to be present—even though they had been in existence here—because they would have assumed to begin with that the colored man would have voted for only one of them. But there is no party in America that can assume this today.

The most important political fact about the colored man today is that his vote is incalculable. Nobody knows where he is going to cast it next time. Because the colored man has at last come to the place where he has a program of his own, a political program of his own that he proposes to work for. He will work with the political party only in the proportion to which it helps him with his program.

Increasingly, we have come to know what that program is. Our political power, which we must not underestimate the necessity of developing, depends in my judgment, on the strength, intellectual power, and cohesive power with which we hold to this nonpartisan program of ours, and about which we propose to become partisan, only in proportion as either one of the parties helps us carry it out.

It is most important to have this program, and it is extremely important that we try to get both parties to stand for this program. I believe that the time has come in the history of this nation when the discussions made by these two political parties regarding the colored man and his relationship to the majority in these southern states not only is going to determine the future of the colored man, but also is going to determine the future of the leadership of the world.

I believe that the decisions made by the Republican Party and the Democratic Party on the question of segregation in institutions of public life and on the question of fair employment for the colored man not only will determine the future of the colored man but also will determine whether or not this nation will succeed in leading this world—or whether her leadership in this world is going to be superseded.

We are a very humble people. At best, we constitute a tenth of the population of this country. We have no power whatsoever to force a program of any kind. We have only the power to persuade. But the obligation to persuade is upon us today as if God Himself had made us an assignment. We ought to be as near as we can, as clear as we can, about what it is that we want.

In all humility and with a spirit unembittered, I want to tell you what I think we must work for. It isn't going to be in ten points either—just two.

We must—when I say must, I mean must—believe that we are commanded by the Eternal God to work for the complete elimination of segregation in every institution of the public life. We must leave no doubt that desegregation is what we want.

We want the complete elimination of segregation from education. We are suing to get that now, and it is our sweet, calm purpose to continue to sue either until we get it or until the courts of the land and both the Republican Party and the Democratic Party openly adopt desegregation as the fundamental pattern of this nation.

We must fight against segregation in parks, public places, swimming pools, hotels, railroad trains, and all avenues of public employment. We must not only be permitted to enter there but also be permitted to enter and to stay there as individuals on the basis of our merit as men, regardless of our color.

Now, politically, that is as far as we can go with our battle against segregation, but our prayer goes further than that. We want the white people of the South, in their hearts, to take an entirely new attitude toward us as individual human beings. Up to this time, they have been willing to receive everything from us—our labor, our love, our suffering on the battlefield—and they have received these things with a loyalty that is as unsullied and beautiful as any majority ever had coming, enslaving a minority since the foundation of this world, as they have not failed to testify. This is true.

In return, they have given us segregation in the schools, segregation in the streets, segregation in the graveyard, and segregation in the churches. The Christian Church, which they operate, operates in a field of consent that takes segregation for granted. That is why we left their church.

This is the only thing that we must let the white people know: in every other thing, they segregated us, but in religion, we segregated ourselves. In addition to the segregation that they have given in all the areas of public life, they have uniformly met our persons and the persons of our wives and our children with personal condescension and contempt.

We can't legislate that. We cannot enforce anything, but in our prayers not only do we want them to get rid of external segregation, but also we want them to substitute their contempt with respect and love for the persons of our children and our wives and our homes. There is no need for them to tell us that we have that, because we don't. If we say that we want anything less from them, we are liars and the truth is not in us.

Further, we want to get rid of segregation in all institutions of public life, and we want to get rid of segregation in their hearts. We long for the day when the highest aristocrat of Maryland upon meeting the humblest colored charwoman, the mother of a child, may be driven by his heart to lift his hat.

We may not get that respect this year. We may not get it next year, but if it takes a thousand years, we shall never be satisfied until we get it.

Now, that was number one.

Point number two is akin and part of desegregation, but it is so important that I'll separate it. We want white people to give us the same opportunity to work in these southern states that they give to their own children.

There is no need to try to deceive us. Eighty years ago—and that is one thing we admire about them—they stick to the policies they have made. Eighty years ago the leaders of these states made up their minds that they were going to confine colored labor to two or three categories: agricultural labor, domestic and menial labor, and such managerial semiskilled labor as they found they couldn't do without. They were going to reserve all unskilled labor in these states, so far as possible, for us. That they have succeeded in doing for eighty years. You go into the national capital and you see it. You go into all the department stores and no colored clerks, no colored buyers, no colored administrative officers, no colored managers but plenty of janitors, plenty of delivery boys. You go into the banks, and there is not a single black face in a skilled position in a single bank in the capital of this nation, unless it is in a colored bank. The banking fraternity has successfully excluded colored persons from any form of apprenticeship in the learning of banking.

Those southern leaders have effectively excluded us from all employment. One of the things that causes me great enjoyment is development of the industrial enterprise in the southern states. I think there is nothing in this country more remarkable than the development of textiles and other forms of manufacturing in these states.

Sometimes we colored people would do well not only to think about our own progress since the Civil War, but also to stop and think about the remarkable progress that the southern white people themselves have made and the progress that they have made in the industrialization of the South and the transformation of the one group cotton system to diversified agriculture. It is one of the most remarkable developments in the history of the world.

But with all that development, they have successfully excluded the colored man from all scientific and technical employment in these manufacturing establishments. You see colored people sweeping the floors, delivering the goods, and stoking the engines, but no colored skilled operators, no scientific and technical intelligence, and no managerial intelligence.

This not an accident. It is a deliberate policy. Today not only are they doing that, but also they are building down here plants that used to exist in the North, on condition that those plants subscribe to that doctrine before they come.

This is one of the most tragic aspects of our life in America. We colored people must know that if the South continues to be loyal to that policy, it can weaken us on every other front and, by that front alone, break our backbone and bring us down to a caste based on color, from which we shall have no power to recover.

The most important single platform in America, so far as we are concerned, is to break down this policy and build the South to the place where it will employ the individual colored man in any capacity whatsoever on the basis of his ability as an individual human being.

Now we must stick to that program. If we don't stick to both sides of it, we aren't fit to be Americans. There is no decent white man in America who will respect us or should respect us if we want anything less than that in the South and all over the country.

If I had time, I would point out remarkable progress. I would say that the progress that we colored people have made in the past fifteen years has been more significant than all the progress that we have made in all the other seventy years since the emancipation of the slaves.

One of the most beautiful things about that progress is the way in which certain Southerners have cooperated. Even while the progress has come, apparently, against the will of southern leadership, it has been received with a dignity and restraint and fine feeling that is beautiful to look upon.

But we have not turned the corner. Unless we can turn the corner on these two fundamental things now—first the elimination of segregation from every area of the public life and by all means, and second the elimination of this wretched policy of economic segregation—we colored people are not yet free.

That is only the introduction of what I want to say. There is, as you may expect it to be (it is not abnormal), a fundamental fear in these southern states to deal with this thing. It is a good thing that we colored people should recognize the naturalness of that fear.

The South has never had any experience with democracy. It does not, therefore, have the confidence in dealing with these matters that would come out of a long experience of democracy. That fear would especially arise in such a state as South Carolina, presided over by Mr. James Byrnes. It would be especially strong in a state like Mississippi and Alabama. For 250 years—do you realize it—these states have not had any democracy? They don't know any more about democracy than what they have read.

There has never been a two-party system in those states. Not for 250 years have the white citizens of those states ever had a chance to cast a real vote between two parties. In every presidential election, every candidate for the presidency passes by those states. Not only does he not go down there and make any speeches, but also he does not even ride through there on the back end of a Pullman platform and wave his flag.

He knows there is no use to do that—those people down there either voted for him or against him before they were born, and there is no way for him to change it now. So those states don't know anything about democracy.

They also know very little about Christianity, because they haven't experimented with it. We have to distinguish between being a Christian and being religious. We don't have any experience much with that distinction, because Christianity is of a radical, universal ethic. It is founded upon the conviction of the sacred and inviolable worth of every human individual. Any group of people, people who have never experimented with that, wouldn't know anything about Christianity except what they read.

We know what it is, as Jesus Himself said, only when we do it. "He that willeth to do the will shall know," said Jesus, "whether I speak of myself or whether it is God that speaketh through me."

In general, what I have said about Mississippi and Alabama and Louisiana is characteristic of the former slave states as a whole. We are just now making a tentative effort to experiment with democracy.

I have just been invited to sponsor a statewide campaign for the YMCA in Washington with Mr. Eisenhower and Mr. Spencer and others. I wrote a long letter and respectfully declined. And, in declining, I said this, "Out of the deepest conviction, I can no longer endorse any Christian institution that bases its life upon the assumption of a segregated social order. I am convinced that this Christianity is a liability to Protestantism, a liability to Christianity itself, and a curse to the Western world."

These hesitations are normal, and we don't discount the human being because he has them.

Take Mr. Byrnes (Governor James Byrnes of South Carolina). I have known Mr. Byrnes for twenty-seven years. He has been against everything that I have held precious in my life. But you can't, by that means, hate Mr. Byrnes. He's a southern boy—and nearly every southern boy in the last generation was born on the bottom of life.

He has come up intellectually to the height where he is capable of being not only governor of the state of South Carolina, but also Secretary of State of the greatest nation on earth and a member of the Supreme Court of the United States.

You cannot withhold a certain profound admiration from any southern boy who rises that high in the world. And you cannot fail to be glad that he was able to win that victory. You wish that, along with that victory, he could have won a victory in his heart.

After rising to that height in the world, he is probably the greatest enemy that we have. I may add, with all reverence, that in my judgment he is one of the chief and most dangerous enemies to the world of democracy now in existence in the world. I'll tell you why in a minute. And I say that with love. I wouldn't harm a hair on his head. I have no thought, even in the middle of night when I am alone, about him that his wife or his children or he would ever fear, because I know that he is suffering from one of the greatest diseases that can come upon human life.

His own Heavenly Father has blinded Mr. Byrnes so that he cannot see. In the most critical period in the life of this nation—when it needs nothing in this world so much as vigorous courage on this whole question of race, he is trying to lead us down a road that, if we would follow him as a nation, would destroy our leadership. That road would take the leadership of this country clearly out of Western civilization.

So I want you to see how natural it is that we should be oppressed, because the South has had no experience on the basis of which she could go confidently ahead. But as the South goes ahead in these two main directions that I have stated here today (and I believe, under God, she must go ahead), she can walk only by faith.

The time must come, when the South, in her political and economical leadership, must really go into the prayer room alone and raise the question with herself as to whether she really believes in one God and one human family. She must consider whether she is willing to reach a course of action in this world on the basis of a belief. She must understand that this is the only course of action God will permit to succeed.

Now I have probably already spoken too long, but I want to leave the framework of what I have said.

There are 2.4 billion people in this world today. We are so close together that any one of us in this room could get up and in twenty-four hours we could be sitting down, shaking hands, and eating dinner with any other group of human beings in this world. We are so indisputably associated that we never will get any further apart. As a matter of fact, the jet planes have put us only twenty-four hours apart, and we will never be separated.

This is going to startle you colored people—us colored people. Two-thirds of all the human beings in this world are colored. They are either black or brown or yellow. Only one-third of the human beings in this world are white. Two-thirds are black and brown and yellow.

A few months ago, I went over to India. There are 400 million people in India, and I was astonished. It looked to me, as I got off the plane in Calcutta, that this little group of colored people had overflowed and flooded the world—400 million. If any of you colored people in here—we colored people—look in a mirror and are not satisfied with the way we look, it isn't on account of this color. Some colored people are the most beautiful creatures God ever made on this earth.

Somebody said to me, "Dr. Johnson, do you believe in intermarriage?" I said, "Oh, yes. I believe the human race is one race. I believe in it. But now, personally, if you're asking me what my program is, I want to say to you, that I didn't marry the little brown skin woman that I married because she is colored. I married her after meeting two or three million women in the world, and because I think she is the most beautiful, sweetest, and most gracious creature the Lord ever made. If she should ever throw me over, I know ten other colored women by name in the United States I'd like to speak to privately. And since I have been to India, I raise that up to 100.

I repeat, three-quarters of all human beings are black and brown and yellow. In this multicolored world, the United States is the most powerful nation that ever existed. And you and I are voting members of that nation and candidates to be on the roll of the Republican and Democratic Parties to determine their policies.

The second most powerful nation in that world is Soviet Russia. That is extraordinary, because fifty years ago, that nation was made up, mostly, of freed serfs who came out of serfdom practically the same time we came out of slavery. They had no learning, no money, no skills, and no capacity for organization. Yet inside of thirty years they had organized themselves, built up the second most powerful nation in the world in a military fashion, and launched a program of economical and spiritual force on a worldwide scale, which in less than thirty years has 808 million followers. An additional 800 million people have not yet made up their minds which of these sides they are going to be on.

All but about 10 percent of that second 800 million are colored. The white people are divided. Not all the white people are on our side. The Russian white people; the white people of Latvia, Estonia, Lithuania, Poland, Czechoslovakia, Bulgaria, Romania, and Albania; a considerable portion of the white people of France; and almost enough Italians to control the Italian government are on the other side. Also on the other side are 450 million colored people in China.

On our side are some white people of the United States and Canada. Also on our side are the people who are technically from South and Central America and who are so much mixed up with colored people that they don't have any segregation down there among not quite as many as 450 million colored people.

The colored people, who are on our side, are divided into two parts: They are the colored people who are free and are on our side because they want to be, and the colored people who are on our side because our allies have their feet on those people's necks and they cannot get out. Also there are 600 million to 800 million colored people who used to have their necks under the feet of our allies. They are now free and nobody knows but God whose side they are going to be on. I want to tell you where they are. If you take a map and stretch it up and then let your finger rest on Afghanistan, just to the south of the western part of Pakistan, through India up through east Pakistan and down through Africa, you will see where they are.

They have no military power adequate to defend themselves from Russia and China. They have an undefended border of 2,500 miles. They have all been under the heels of imperial Britain or France or Holland. They have suffered from the same kind of segregation, the same kind of discrimination in employment, and the same kind of political domination that we have suffered from in this country.

Now let me say this to us southerners, all of us. We must not believe that this system of segregation and discrimination we have here affecting the colored people is peculiar to ourselves and is purely domestic.

Segregation is the product of the colonial system. Colored people are here because the British and the Dutch and the Portuguese and the whites—the great colonial powers—brought us here, sold us, and made more money off our souls than they made off anything else in their trade.

When they quit enslaving us, they began to operate the whole of the continent of Africa on this basis. You don't have to take my word for it; look at Africa today. Look at South Africa, where the Boers, who are Protestant Christians, are operating their relationships against the millions of black Africans in exactly the same way that Maryland is operating her relationship to colored people in this state. The French in Tunisia are doing exactly the same thing. The Belgians in the Congo don't talk about it much, but they are doing the same thing. The folks in North Africa are doing the same thing.

All the 200 million colored people in Africa, except the people of Abyssinia and Liberia, are being politically dominated, economically and socially segregated, and exploited by the European colonial process. Those colonialists are the same as the people who sold us into slavery, and they are doing that now. Fifteen years ago the British had 400 million black and brown and yellow people under their control in India, dominating them politically and making no offer to set up a democracy. Britain exploited them economically to such an extent that today the British have left 300 million peasants in India who make only $48 a year, only $24 of which they have to use for their families after they have paid their taxes and their rents. Certainly those people, all of them, know what economic segregation is, what political domination is, and what difficulties they are having today because they have suffered it for over 200 years.

Now what chance have we to get those colored peoples to come on our side? We've got to win! We've got to win those very people. If we lose India alone, we're losing 400 million at one shot. That will give the Communists the control over half of this human race. And on what condition do you think they'll come on our side? Tentatively, the Indians are on the British side. Very soon there will be but one power in this world that is capable of winning those people for the democratic side. That power is the one to which we belong, the United States of America.

What will the United States of America undertake with her military power? And I may say this now that the British and the French and the Dutch are so powerless that not only can they not regain India and China by themselves, but also they cannot hold Africa by themselves. Their military is now so reduced that they have to give up the colonial system entirely unless the United States of America supports them with her military forces.

The great question in this world at this hour—the most important question in this world at this hour—is this: Is the United States of America going to use her military power to support the political domination, the economic and social segregation, and the humiliation of the people of Africa and to undertake to restore the colonial system in India and China? Nobody knows. We haven't answered that question, and the people over there—550 million of them—are scared to death about that question.

They don't want to be Communists. They are just as scared of Communism as we are. But they are not going to run from Communism into the control of a new nation that segregates and humiliates them and robs them of equal opportunity to earn a living. You will see, therefore, that when the Republican and Democratic Parties are raising the question as to whether they are going to be for or against the continued segregation of the colored man in Maryland, Georgia, and Alabama, and whether they are going to maintain this system of unfair employment practices, they are not merely answering that question in relation to the colored man. They are answering it in the sight of Eternal God, and they are answering it for Africa, India, and China. Now that's where we are. Don't take my word for it.

It is a terrible thing to be in politics today. The leaders of the Republican and Democratic Parties have got to decide whether they are going to stay in their corners, or whether they are going to override segregation and set the colored man free. Now I'm through. We colored people should be as politically active in the next five years as we can conceive it to be possible. We must ask every candidate for governor, every candidate for Senator, and every candidate for public office in the state or nation these specific questions. If the answer is "No," we must prayerfully and lovingly vote those candidates down. If the answer is "Yes," we must support them because in them and them alone is all salvation. We cannot leave them alone to decide the salvation of our country.

I want to give you some encouragement before I sit down. I want to show you who is on our side, and this is very significant. In the past government, the President of the United States was on our side. The greatest progress that the colored people have ever made since the Civil War was made under the leadership of President Harry Truman. He was the only President since the Civil War who has unequivocally and repeatedly declared himself to be in favor of absolute equality of opportunity in every respect for the colored man. And he risked his political life and lost it.

It looks as if the present President of the United States is on our side. He is at least tiptoeing a little bit and is a little tentative. It looks as if he might be on our side if he is pushed a little more.

The biggest organization in the world outside of the Communist Party is the Roman Catholic Church. The Roman Catholic Church is against segregation and is on our side.

Now here is something remarkable. The Episcopal Church has lately come up on our side. I am not talking about the American Episcopal Church; I am talking about the Church of England. The Church of England is just like a coin on one side of which you see "In God We Trust" and on the other side, "Glory Be to the King." The Episcopal Church is the religious experience of the British Empire whose bishops are appointed by the king. Its rectors are supported by the state taxes.

For years the Church of England has been sprinkling holy water and blessings. It was so in favor of segregation in India that it segregated Mahatma Gandhi.

The entire Episcopal faculty of a southern theological seminary in the United States resigned because the Board of Trustees would not receive a colored man into that school. Now the faculty hadn't read anything new in the New Testament. It's the same New Testament that they had been looking at for 250 years.

I could give you a list of ten more things but I'm going to give you only one.

The British are on our side. When you see the Roman Catholic Church, the Episcopal Church, and the British Commonwealth on anybody's side together, you will know that God is on the loose and something new is taking place in this world.

The greatest question in the world is this: Where in the United States of America is this new determination? You know who will decide that. It will be decided by the Democratic and Republican Parties in Maryland and in the South. If you say "No," it won't be done. It was the fear that they would say, "No," that made Thomas Jefferson, the greatest southern president whom we ever had, say, "When I look at slavery and remember that God is just, I tremble for my country."

The Republican and Democratic Parties in the South have it in their power to cement the world leadership in this country. If they undertake to support the continued segregation of the colored people in the public life, and if this support is continued, depriving the colored man of equal opportunities in employment, then there will be nothing for the darker people of this world to hope for. They can't depend on us for leadership. They—and you—will have to look somewhere else. There is nowhere else for them to look but to the Communists and to Russia. My God, my fellow men, don't force them to make that choice.

§2 Charles P. Bowles

On the Sunday following the U.S. Supreme Court's ruling in *Brown v. Board of Education*, Charles P. Bowles addressed his congregants at the Dilworth Methodist Church in Charlotte, North Carolina. A graduate of Duke Divinity School and a pastor at Dilworth since 1949, Bowles gives this sermon less as an encomium for the decision and more as a warning to the South. Bowles notes that "the world is saying as it watches us with critical eyes, 'Make your democracy work at home if you expect it to work elsewhere.'" In the midst of the Cold War, Bowles warns that of 60 million babies born 10 years ago, only 17 million of them were white; moreover, in such a racial context, "it will be difficult to go against communism which knows no race or creed." The demographics aren't without consequence: "I have said that heretofore racial prejudice was immoral. Now it is suicidal. We must care now for selfish reasons, if for no other." Malcolm X would later make a similar point following the successes of the Bandung Conference in 1955. So while Reverend Bowles might privately celebrate the *Brown* decision with his family, and while the decision has scriptural warrant in the story of the Good Samaritan, the logic is clear: abide by the Supreme Court's decision lest we allow our prejudices to tilt the balance in the Communist's favor.

———————

A Cool Head and a Warm Heart (Luke 10:25-37)

Dilworth Methodist Church, Charlotte, North Carolina
May 23, 1954

It has happened! The Supreme Court has spoken, and segregation of the races in public schools has been declared unconstitutional.

How are we to react as Christians—as followers of the Man of Galilee who told the story of our Scripture this morning? I have the feeling that if he were here this morning, he too would begin his remarks with that story. Yes, if we like the lawyer of old would ask him, "Who is my neighbor or brother?" he would answer as he did then by telling this story. The issue is squarely before us, and we must decide if we are to act as Christian citizens— citizens of the Kingdom first, and then citizens of a great democracy.

After I had selected my topic, "Keep a *cool* head and a *warm* heart," and had given it to my secretary for the bulletin, I noticed an editorial in one of our fine newspapers entitled: "Cool Heads, Calm Emotions Needed as South Moves toward New Era." Certainly we are going to need cool heads—all of us. The editorial listed four reasons for disappointment over the ruling, but then added: "But the court has spoken, and with a unanimous voice. Non-segregation in education will become the law of the land as soon as the formal decree is issued, and we want no more civil wars. . . . Somehow the south must keep the sweep of history in perspective, must use its intelligence coolly and dispassionately, and must find the resources for giving all its children equality of education."

The fact that the decision was unanimous should help us keep a cool head. A five-to-four opinion with a strongly convincing dissent would have kept alive the flames of contention over the legal issues. With the legal question settled so decisively, we can give ourselves now to the working out of the methods which will protect the rights and equities of all citizens without unnecessarily offending sensitivities that have developed from generations of a segregated society.

We do not need to be too hasty in our decisions and pronouncements. The matter is by no means settled. There is a built-in delay in the Supreme Court ruling. The interested parties have until October 1 to file briefs, and the court will not hear arguments until October 12. This affords a time lag of five months, and it should tend to dissuade southerners of strong opinions and high emotions from giving voice to hasty thoughts and taking impulsive action.

This issue confronts the south with a chance to prove its real greatness. Let us remember that our nation met its first great challenge under Washington when we won our independence. We met our second challenge under Lincoln when we saved the Union and became forever indissolubly united. Our third great challenge is nothing less than the moral leadership of the free world. That is our tremendous challenge today, and the world is saying as it watches us with critical eyes, "Make your democracy work at home if you expect it to work elsewhere." Years ago we talked about making the world safe for democracy. Our challenge today is to make democracy safe for the world.

This is a real challenge to our nation, but the burden rests with us in the south. Of the fifteen million Negroes in our population, ten and one-half million are in the seventeen so-called southern states and the District of Columbia. So it is with us that the severe adjustment will have to be made. If it works, we are the ones who will have to see that it works.

Having said this I want to hasten to add that I am highly pleased with the restraint with which the ruling has been received. Governor Byrnes of

South Carolina, who had made some rather drastic suggestions as to what would be done in his state, won the approbation of our President when, though he was "shocked by the decision," he said, "I earnestly urge all our people, white and colored, to exercise restraint and preserve order." On the other hand we have the bitter and vitriolic denunciations of Governor Herman Talmadge of Georgia, who flatly says, "There will be no mixed schools while I am governor." I was heartened to learn that Dr. Garinger, superintendent of Charlotte city schools, said: "Both our white and Negro citizens will face this problem fairly and honestly in an effort to work out a satisfactory solution. . . . I think Charlotte is a Christian city and a law-abiding city, and we can be expected to do what the law of the land directs. . . . I believe we have among our white and Negro citizens people who will face this fairly and honestly and meet the situation in such a way that it can be solved to everybody's satisfaction."

The thing which heartened me most was the fact that so many positive suggestions were being made so soon after the decision was handed down. Having lived in Greensboro for twelve years, I was proud to see that the school board of that city took one of the first affirmative official actions on the ruling made by a southern school body. The Greensboro board has told its superintendent, Ben Smith, to start studying "ways and means for complying with" the Supreme Court decision. D. E. Hudgins, chairman of the board and the man who introduced the resolution, said its adoption "would let the community, the state, the south—and if necessary the nation—know that we propose to live under the rule of law. . . . We must not fight or attempt to circumvent it."

You will be pleased to know that Phil Van Every, mayor of our city, has called for the appointment of a commission composed of white and Negro citizens to study positive ways of implementing the decision of the Supreme Court.

We realize that a decisive hour has struck for our nation and for the south which is so vitally involved. One commentator ably says: "The decision of the Supreme Court on segregation should cause no lamentations. Man-made law will not change the fundamental character of the Negro. His own courageous struggle evidences that. There are those who believe that the Negro leaders, who have a chance now to be "big men," will choose rather the course that will lead to enduring greatness as they help to bridge this difficult gap. This delicate and very human situation can be handled with ultimate satisfaction, but only if it is handled first with statesmanship and charity. No tragic upheaval will result unless, in this hour of decision, each race seeks self-defeating victory through non-compromising action."

Now let me turn to each of you personally. Let me urge you, before you criticize too strongly, to be sure you are informed, that you know what you are talking about. Be sure that you are not acting merely on your prejudices rather than on rational judgment. And be sure that you are acting from a warm heart of love—the warm heart of our Master who told the story of the Good Samaritan.

We can best understand our responsibility if we do what I suggested in a sermon not long ago—put ourselves in the place of the children of the other race and see what damage the feeling of inferiority would do to us. Then we cannot help looking at this problem not only with cool heads, but also with warm, compassionate hearts.

If we keep a warm heart we must look at this issue in the light of our Christian intelligence and not in the light of our prejudices. On the day after the decision was handed down, I spoke at a men's club meeting. The man sitting next to me—an average American and an average Methodist—said this: "I know it is not Christian to be opposed to segregation, but I am opposed to it just the same." He represents the thought of many Christians in our churches. We know what is right, but we prefer to follow our prejudices rather than to be right.

If we keep a warm heart we will not give ourselves over to the pernicious practice of name-calling. How damaging to our morals it is to stoop to this! It damages the "caller" more than the "called." It always has. It is a sign of weakness. When the enemies of Jesus could not answer him, there was nothing left for them to do but to call names—"wine-bibber," "gluttonous man," "blasphemer," "friend of sinners"—and when this did not avail they crucified him. You see this kind of procedure may lead to violent action.

Furthermore, we must not give over to the hysteria of hate. When we look at this problem in the light of the past and in the light of our prejudices, it is difficult not to surrender to such hysteria. But in the name of him who said, "Love your enemies," I charge you not to yield. If you were to think of a great deal that has happened in the past and many things you can imagine that might happen in the future, it might be hard for some of you not to hate. But in the name of him who looked down from a cross and said "Father forgive . . ," do not give over to it. We cannot build a world of lasting brotherhood and peace through hate. We must show the world that a Christian democracy can and will work. This is the supreme hour of our nation.

As I said earlier, the third great challenge of our nation is nothing less than the moral leadership of the world. We are now faced with a decision that will have global repercussions in this regard. As one of our Negro citizens said, "Christianity and democracy have been given a great place in America through the elimination of segregation in public schools, and communism has lost a talking point."

There is no question but that "we have suffered under the taunts of foreign enemies who have proclaimed that we did not live up to our protestations of true democracy." This action of the Supreme Court will help to free us from that charge. There is no secret of the fact that things have gone rather badly for us at Geneva. The whole difficulty, according to competent observers, hinged on the color question. There is grave concern in the world now as to the domination of the white race. We are definitely in the minority, and unless we prove our democracy it will be difficult to go against communism which knows no race or creed.

You have heard me say that ten years ago the number of babies born in the world per year was 60 million, and the number is much higher now. Of this 60 million, 43 million were colored—red, yellow, brown and black—while only 17 million of them were white. You can see what this does to the ratio of population. I have said that heretofore racial prejudice was immoral. Now it is suicidal. We must care now for selfish reasons, if for no other. But we must do more than that. We must care because it is right; it is God's way as revealed by the Teller of the story of the Good Samaritan.

Let us remember then that we cannot *force* democracy on the world. We must *demonstrate* it. We must make real and vital the principle of human brotherhood upon which democracy is founded. The first thing propounded in our Declaration of Independence was this basic truth: "We hold these truths to be self-evident, that all men are created equal." Christian democracy is based on that principle, coupled with our basic Christian concept as found in the New Testament: "He made from one every nation of men to live on all the face of the earth."

The great common denominator for the solution of the problems of the world is this great principle of Jesus—human brotherhood. But if we exert the moral influence the world so greatly needs at this decisive and challenging hour, we must demonstrate that principle right here at home. We must face the third great challenge that has confronted our nation, and face it squarely. If we do not, it will present a situation, to quote another, "which will make Gabriel on that last day feel that his trumpet need make no announcement."

As the rest of the world looks at the Christian church today, it has a right to say, "Physician, heal yourself." I fear Gardner Taylor was right when he said: "There is more segregation at 11 o'clock on Sunday morning when we stand to sing, 'In Christ there is no East or West,' than at any time in the week in the market place, the sports arena or the gambling casino." That hurts, doesn't it? But it is true that organized baseball, television, radio, the Red Cross and many secular movements have gone ahead of the church on this matter.

Tuesday morning as the Bowles family sat at breakfast we were talking about this highly controversial issue. Then my wife read the devotional in the *Christian Family*. The closing Scripture was the last verse of our responsive reading this morning: "Let the words of my mouth and the meditation of my heart be acceptable in thy sight, O Lord, my rock and my redeemer." I said, "Children, that's it! That's what we need." Could I have given better advice to my family? Can I give better advice to my church family?

§3 Reverend A. Powell Davies

From his birth in Birkenhead, England on June 5, 1902, to his untimely death in 1957, Reverend A. Powell Davies led an active life as a minister, speaker, author, and activist. Growing up in a large family in a small suburb of Liverpool, England, Davies experienced energetic conversations and debates. His early love for engaging listeners spurred his later involvement with political and social movements. Davies's spiritual vocation actually began in his native country of England as a Methodist minister. After completing his theological studies at the University of London, Davies and his wife, Muriel, moved to the United States in 1928. His religious career changed paths after converting and being ordained a Unitarian minister in 1933. After serving the Community Church of Summit, New Jersey for 11 years, Davies completed his earthly ministry at the All Souls Church in Washington, D.C., serving the church for 13 years.

Rev. A. Powell Davies's expansive and unconventional activism promoted his reputation as a renowned social and political advocate. From his pulpit Davies emphasized America's leadership role in promoting its founding principles and he applied religion to public and social issues. In his magazine articles and books he addressed and critiqued national and international affairs. Reverend Davies not only defended the rights of the majority but all classes of oppressed people. He preached frequently on his intense opposition to prejudice. Davies's nonjudgmental attitude even extended to his defense of atheists and the promotion that all campuses across the nation should include at least one on the faculty. This unusual approach to civil equality attracted many new members prompting the greatest influx of participating congregations of the Unitarian faith in Washington, D.C. In 1950 All Souls accepted African Americans as full members for the first time. Such was Davies's influence that his untimely death at age 55 prompted three sitting Supreme Court justices to attend his funeral service. His papers are housed at the Andover-Harvard Theological Library in Cambridge, Massachusetts; the Meadville/Lombard School Library in Chicago, Illinois, and at the Davies Memorial Unitarian Universalist Church in Camp Springs, Maryland.

In his sermon from the All Souls pulpit on the Supreme Court's *Brown v. Board of Education* decision, Rev. Davies puts race into a universal context. He maintains that intolerance and bigotry are local, regional, state, and national problems. Davies's honest analysis of racism as an international and almost ageless problem gives him validation for chipping away at the very foundation of prejudice. He asserts that equality is a necessity, mandated in the United States by the Declaration of Independence and guaranteed by the founders' fealty to natural law. And yet, the nation's moral codes do not reflect the founding leaders' fundamental principles.

The high court's *Brown* ruling, restored the founders' original intent. That ruling correctly interpreted the meaning of the American Revolution. Reverend Davies closes his sermon by invoking the story of the Good Samaritan and Jesus' closing command to do likewise. That command compels us to respect our unified being as one race.

––––––––

The Supreme Court Decision

All Souls Church (Unitarian), Washington, D.C.
May 23, 1954

If you believe—as I do—that mankind is now in the crucial stage of a race between morality and disaster, you will often be depressed at the trend of events. Too much that is happening is lowering the moral level and increasing the pace at which we seem to be careening towards catastrophe. At times, the scene takes on an aspect of nightmarish unreality. Can it be, you wonder, that people are willing to act in such utter disregard of what has come to be their situation? Do they *know*—have they ever really absorbed it?—the awesome nature of the problems they must solve if they are not to perish?

Do they know that these problems are not merely military? Do they realize that two-thirds of the earth's population, none of it white-skinned, is on the march, determined to put an end to hunger and destitution, oppression and misery? Or are they taken in by the propaganda that tells them that all this is manufactured in Moscow? *That*, of course, is what they are *invited* to believe: that the Asians and the Africans—and perhaps some of the South Americans—have been so poisoned by Communist propaganda that they have come to think that famines can be ended, that epidemics can be controlled, that parasitic oppressions can be overthrown, and that human life, even in Asia and Africa, can have dignity.

What our people have been blind to, here in America, is that it is our own success—our success in raising the standard of life of ordinary people—that is the incitement everywhere in the world to seek a similar advancement. It is likewise our own Revolution—not the Communist one—that has given the backward peoples a basis to go upon. What is necessary, so far as Americans are concerned, is that the moral principles upon which their own nation was founded shall be applied—and boldly—to the problems of a world of ferment and transition. It is the only way, tolerable to Americans, by which the problems of mankind can be brought towards solution.

Our great principle, for instance, that all men are endowed with equal natural rights holds more promise for world security than any other principle ever enunciated. It is the only possible basis for a world community of free people. There is no other foundation—none whatever—for a peaceful world society that includes all races. And quite obviously, a world society, whether peaceful or otherwise, *must* include all races. But unless it is to be a society ruled by tyranny, and therefore foredoomed to the dissensions which, in the presence of the modern weapons, must end up in disaster, it *must* be a *free* society of *equal* peoples.

Nothing is more short-sighted than to think of the race problem as a local problem, or a problem of certain states in the American South, or even as an American national problem: it is an all-inclusive problem of the modern age. We have been slow—dangerously slow—in seeing the problem in its true dimensions. But others have seen it. Hitler, for instance, saw it, and proposed to deal with it with brutal cynicism. There shall be, he said, a master-race, the Germans; at the next highest level will come the other white races, under German guidance and dominion; the lower levels will be composed of the non-white races, enslaved for the advantage of those at the top. The Japanese at one time had a similar plan for the Orient. The Communists, although they promise an eventual equality, would enslave the entire world under a privileged bureaucracy—and it would be foolish not to see that this bureaucracy would harden into a permanent class of overlords, though, of course, it might be interracial.

At any rate, the Communists do have a plan, and one of universal scope, and they know that the race problem is of paramount importance. But we have not seen the situation half as plainly. We still hear, in the United States, that the race question is something conjured up by agitators; or that it is kept alive by visionary idealists. If such people would leave it alone, we are told, the difficulties would subside. Or perhaps that is what we *used* to be told. Today, if you have anything but the most negative views on race, you are liable to be called a Communist. This is pitiful, indeed, for it means, to the minds of those who use the epithet, that the only people who want race problems solved are the Communists.

Now, let us state a very simple fact—so simple that it seems odd that there should be any need to state it. The race problem does not arise because of agitators or even because of idealists who are not agitators; the race problem arises because mankind is composed of a number of different races. The primitive reaction to this fact is one of hostility. Whatever is different is potentially dangerous: it is necessary to be defensive against it. Sometimes, this has meant annihilation of people of one race by people of another. Sometimes, it has meant enslavement. But always, as any two races have remained in contact, there has been increasing comprehension of each other; and always they have mingled. Nevertheless, down to now, the primitive reaction has never been subdued—not entirely—by a civilized recognition of realities. The fact of the oneness of humanity, although religion has extolled it, has been acknowledged without being observed. High morality, like true rationality, has been available but has not been used. And race attitudes have remained very largely primitive.

At the time, however, that the United States was founded, it was well understood, at least by some among the founders, that the human equality they were adopting as a principle should be applied universally, and therefore without racial reservations. Jefferson and John Adams both wanted an immediate end of Negro slavery. Unfortunately, their wish did not prevail. But the principle was declared, and the declaration was unequivocal.

There are those who say that if this is what was intended, it was intended only by the few. The conscience of the many did not require it. This is a plausible objection—if we do not stop to notice what would need to have been the alternatives. First, could the Declaration of Independence have avoided a statement on the equality of human rights? The answer is that it could *not*: some such statement was a political necessity. There were many who did not like it but the temper of the times meant that it had to go in. It is true that Jefferson had his difficulties; the opposition was formidable. Yet, he represented—and knew that he represented—the new spirit of the age. He spoke for an authentic revolution. Very well, then, the clause had to go in. The next question is, why was it not phrased: "All *white* men are endowed by their Creator with certain inalienable rights"?

The answer is obvious: it would have destroyed the entire principle of *natural* rights which was being asserted. Later, of course, a case was made out, not only in legislatures but from pulpits, that the rights of white men and the rights of Negroes were not the same. But this could not have been done, I think, at the time of the Revolution. You cannot found a nation upon a labored argument. It has to be—as it was—something that can be called self-evident. And to the American Revolutionaries the equal rights of all—as *natural* rights—did seem self-evident.

But it had to be *all*. The whole revolutionary impulse required it. The conscience of the time required it. The equal rights of *some* men while excluding others could never have been said to be endowed by man's Creator. And they would not have been self-evident.

So the declaration was unreserved and unequivocal. But it was in conflict with the man-made facts. White Americans were ceaselessly aware of the conflict; gradually, the outer world became aware of it, too. The American Declaration caused a surge of hope wherever it became known, but the American performance brought resentment and dismay. Within the United States, little by little, the principle nevertheless wrote itself into the Constitution—but not without an agonizing struggle. In the conscience of the world outside—a world drawing smaller and nearer—this struggle had continuing impact.

It was noticed how hard we labored to retain the principle and yet avoid its implications. After all, the principle itself we could not abandon: it was the *basis* of American democracy. So we enunciated such doctrines as "separate but equal," refusing to see that when you put your fellow-man in a category apart, you are denying that he is your equal. You are saying to him, "I will give you something as good as I am keeping for myself, if only you will stay away from me; for although I know I have a duty to you, you are offensive to me." That—in simple, honest words, words which it was important never to speak—was what was meant by "separate but equal."

Last week, the Supreme Court, to its everlasting honor, set us free from this hypocrisy. In a decision as historic as any ever rendered, it gave unqualified effect to the most basic of our founding principles. It correctly interpreted the meaning of the American Revolution. It spoke for the conscience of the Founding Fathers: as it did also for the conscience of Americans from then till now. It was the *right* decision, restoring to us something of our self-esteem.

And it was also constructive—nothing has been more so—in our relations with the world outside. At a time when our prestige has been declining and other nations have been doubtful of our leadership, this decision reaffirms American morality. We are willing to be true to our principles.

It is not the case, of course, that the decision has been universally popular. Right decisions seldom are. But it is remarkable—and reassuring—to see the extent to which those who do not like the decision nevertheless acknowledge it as the law of the land and are prepared to abide by it.

All this is good. Here is something that is *not* depressing, but points towards hope and gives us courage.

A decision, however, no matter how enlightened, is that and nothing more until we have begun to carry it out. And in carrying it out, everything depends upon what is in the hearts of the people. Yes, and in their minds as well. We must think clearly if we are to act wisely. And if we do, we shall see, however reluctantly, that although we can make great gains in meeting the problems of race relationship, we are not likely within a short time to bring them to complete solution. Indeed, as to this, we should understand that the full solution of race problems will only come when the races are indistinguishable. In short, as long as there are races there will be race problems. In the same way that as long as there are young and old there will be problems between the generations, and as long as there are men and women there will be problems between the sexes. This, I was at pains to point out in a sermon I preached from this pulpit in January, 1946, at a time when you felt much more lonely if you happened to believe as I did and felt the need to speak out about it. I said then, and I repeat now, that it is important to reckon with realities, one of which is that wherever there are differences there are problems. But the problems can be lessened. We can become more mature in dealing wisely with them. We can grow in character and in breadth of humanity as understanding depends and we increasingly act upon it.

Our individual attitudes are vital. In the changes to be brought about, here in the District of Columbia as much as anywhere, the part that each of us will play will be a part of what is good or bad in the total situation. And here we have to make—each of us, as individuals, I mean—a personal decision. I was thinking of this requirement near the end of last week when I chanced to take up from my desk a printed copy of an address by Dr. Murray D. Lincoln, the President of CARE, which has done so much for overseas relief, much of it through individuals. We are all of us, says Dr. Lincoln, a part of the world crisis, and we all have responsibility. And then he says this: "We must answer the question, 'Am I a part of the problem or part of the solution?'"

I can think of no better way of putting what must be for each of us an individual decision. Certainly, that is the question to be answered first. "Am I part of the problem?" I may deplore the problem but do my views, my attitude, the things I say, the tensions I allow myself to feel, yes—even my prejudices—do these make me part of the problem: the problem that other people are working hard to solve? If they do, must I not ask myself whether I am not being foolish and unworthy? Since the problem is here and attempts must be made to meet it, of what use is my attitude, my opposition, my refractoriness? And is it something that can give me self-respect? Am *I* part of the problem?

But then, there is another way of being part of the problem, too. Do I stand aside from it, not actively impeding anyone else but not doing anything constructive myself, either? If so, I am part of the burden, no matter how passive, that other people are carrying. And so, I am part of the problem.

It is a very searching question, isn't it? The kind that it is not easy to forget. And I hope that you will *not* forget it; I hope it will keep recurring to you over and over again. I hope it will *worry* you, and although I don't like to see people suffer, I hope it will upset you if necessary until you do something that puts you on the right side. "Are you part of the problem or part of the solution?"

To be part of the solution, you must be willing to do all you can to help. In this area, in the period immediately before us, this will be, not something vague and general, but definite, palpable things.

I said earlier that we are in a race between morality and disaster. You must not think of this as rhetoric. It is literally true. Only as the moral level rises—the level of justice and benevolence, truth and righteousness—can we *be* the people who will have the vision, the purpose and the resolution to survive. Yes, and only as we reach this level can we come towards national unity. You cannot unite a nation upon the basis of mistrust and bitterness, suspicion and prejudice. A low moral level means dissension and disunity, which, in turn, mean catastrophe. Moreover, at a low moral level, we shall not do what is needed in the world, and the situation will go against us.

That is what I mean by a race between morality and disaster. And we do, each of us, have something to do with whether this race is won or lost. I think we have something to do with it when we define our attitude to the issues we have taken up, this morning: we have something to do with it when we speak and when we act.

That, after all, is the thing that is decisive. I have always been impressed by the story of the young man who came to Jesus to have a discussion—academic, he hoped—of the vexed question as to who was his neighbor. It was a question much canvassed at the time, and one to which was given a great variety of theoretical answers. "I know I should love my neighbor as myself," said the young man, " but my trouble is one of definition: who *is* my neighbor?"

And you will remember that Jesus told him the story of the Good Samaritan, and then made him decide which of the three, the priest, the Levite, or the despised Samaritan was a true neighbor to the man who had been robbed, and lay by the side of the road. The young man, no matter how he felt about this story, seems to have made a prompt decision. The Samaritan, he said, was quite clearly the good neighbor. And then Jesus, for whom theory had only limited charm, greatly surprised the young man. "Go," said Jesus, "and do thou likewise."

And the command still remains. As it always will until we acknowledge from our hearts that here is only one race—the human race—and that the neighbors of each of us are all of us, everywhere throughout the world.

§4 Frank P. Graham

Frank Porter Graham was born in Fayetteville, North Carolina on October 14, 1886. He was raised in a Scottish Presbyterian family where education was paramount. Graham received his B.A. from the University of North Carolina at Chapel Hill in 1909. Graham pursed a law degree, yet he never practiced law. In 1914 he decided to teach history at the university as his life's work. In 1916 he received an M.A. in history from Columbia University. Feeling the call of duty when the United States entered into World War I, he joined the Marines as a private and was discharged as a lieutenant in 1919. He resumed his teaching career at UNC in 1920 and rose rapidly through the ranks. In 1930 he assumed the presidency of the university.

The thirties marked the beginning of Graham's political career. He figured prominently in more than 150 political organizations. He remained president of the university while pursuing his political assignments, including his appointment to the Committee on Civil Rights by President Truman in 1946. In 1949 he was appointed to the U.S. Senate to fill a vacancy, yet in 1950 he did not survive the Democratic primary runoff. From 1951 to 1970 he was employed by the United Nations, where he was a successful mediator. Graham died on February 16, 1972 in Chapel Hill. His papers are housed in the Southern Historical Collection at the University of North Carolina.

Graham was a political liberal, a vocal advocate of racial desegregation and freedom of education. While serving on the Committee on Civil Rights in 1946, he was one of two southerners on the committee. He supported recommendations to eliminate segregation, the poll tax, the white primary, and other forms of discrimination. He felt that education (secular, religious, and democratic) would end segregation.

Graham's speech to the Council of Christian Relations as part of the Board of Church Extension, urged the active support of the Presbyterian Church in accepting the unanimous Supreme Court decision to declare all state segregation laws unconstitutional. He notes that although states, with a big push from churches and schools, might have moved the South to desegregate, federal law trumps those who had the first chance and did not use it. Graham emphasizes that the Presbyterian Church enjoys the religious, civic, and moral responsibility to support the unanimous decision of the Supreme Court, the newly established law of the land in all states. Graham touches on the fact that the Presbyterians have had a leading role in American history since helping to bring on the American Revolution, and should continue this trend.

Council of Christian Relations, 94th General Assembly of the Presbyterian Church, Montreat, North Carolina

May 29, 1954

Under God, the Father of all, and in loyalty to the teachings and saving mission of Jesus Christ, Son of man, Son of God and Brother of all, the Council of Christian Relations, as part of the work of the Board of Church Extension, in advance of the decision of the Supreme Court, prepared its unanimous recommendations against segregation in the Presbyterian Church in the United States. Though not a member of the Council, as a simple layman in humility and hope, I make this statement in support of the Council.

In the wide Southern region, in which have prevailed the bi-racial customs of centuries and the mores of many millions of people, four main groups of members of our Church have had their different approaches toward working out the complex problem of the races:

1. A large group of white members of our Church long held that the bi-racial structure in the states with the largest approximation to equality in numbers of the two races, was the wise basis for the peaceful cooperation and advance of both races.

2. Another large group of white members, growing in numbers, have considered, with increasing conviction, that segregation is unchristian, undemocratic and, in its spiritual exclusion, morally damaging to both the privileged and the disinherited. The members of this group have sought within the states and with the gradually increasing influence of religion, the humane spirit of education, and the principles of democracy in the minds and hearts of the people, to prepare the way by progressive stages for the voluntary religions, political, educational and economic integration of peoples, without discrimination, as equal members of the spiritual communion and as equal citizens of the commonwealth, without recourse to federal compulsory power.

3. A large group of colored members have sincerely and happily preferred to have their own separate congregations, officers and ministers. They will doubtless continue for some time to have their own churches as they freely choose.

4. Another group of colored members of our Southern Church, recently rapidly increasing in numbers, have, with deepening conviction, held that segregation is a stigma of inequality and against the basic teachings of Christianity, the fundamentals of democracy and the purposes of humane education. The members of this group held that segregation should be abolished outright in the churches and progressively within the states with recourse to federal action if the states lagged in their progress. Many of them will, with welcome, join integrated churches.

All these points of view no doubt, among others, were presented by the ablest attorneys to the United States Supreme Court. I trust I may be pardoned a simple personal reference. With the faith that the bi-racial structure should, and would, give way in time under the impact of the increasing influence of vital religion, dynamic democracy, scientific and social studies, the rising humane spirit, and the freedom and dignity of man, I have long held that the basic solution of the problem of the races should wisely be worked out within the states through religious, democratic and humane influences in the minds and hearts of the people. This view was based on the faith that successive generations of college youth as leaders in churches, business and industry, labor, and in farm, professional, women, and civic organizations would challenge the mores and change the laws of the states. It was hoped that the churches would meet the challenge of the President's Commission on Civil Rights and lead the way. But, even the churches, for the most part, which were not under the prohibition of state laws, and which could have provided the example and preachments, lagged in the leadership which would have given effective meaning to this view.

The Court considered such a view among weightier views but unanimously decided that the time had now come to declare unconstitutional the long-standing Plessy "separate but equal doctrine" as a denial by the states of the "equal protection of the laws" guaranteed by the 14th Amendment, as applied to the states, and as a denial of the "liberty" federally guaranteed to all persons by the "due process of law" clause of the 5th Amendment, as applied to the District of Columbia.

The Court is composed of members of both major parties and of citizens from all sections of the country. They heard most distinguished counsel present all pertinent facts, factors, varying points of view and differing interpretations of the constitution and the laws involved in the five cases. After fair hearings and re-hearings in open court and long consideration of all the issues, the Court came to a unanimous decision. Those of us who favored working out the problem through progressive stages within the states now have the religious, civic, and moral responsibility and opportunity of supporting the unanimous decision of our highest umpire, under God, as the new established supreme law of the land in all the states.

The Court was aware that the Southern states, which had appropriated much less than twelve million dollars for the operation of all their public schools in 1875, appropriated much more than twelve thousand million dollars for the operation of the public schools in 1954; that, overall, the length of the school year, the college training of teachers, and the number of students per teacher, were approximating equality for the separate schools in the Southern states; and that Negro teachers in the public schools of Virginia, North Carolina and Tennessee have longer training and receive larger salaries than the white teachers. The Court favorably knew that the Southern people, without a Marshall Plan, had risen from the ruins, as unconquerable in spirit amid the almost universal poverty and desolation of defeat as they had been brave against the heavy odds of a long and exhausting war. They also sympathetically knew that many millions of Negroes in the South in the decades of their sorrows and joys, frustrations, struggles and hopes, with the goodwill of millions of their white fellow Southerners, had made incomparable progress against the heaviest odds, revealing with patient work, prayer and faith, laughter and song, the innate capacities of a great people to make their rich and enduring economic, political, intellectual contributions to the meaning and making of America.

The Court was doubtless aware that the Southern people invested proportionately more of their income in the public schools than the people of the non-South, and, with one-sixth of the financial ability, educated one-third of the nation's children, who were to become citizens of the nation as well as of the states. With all this progress, the Southern schools in per pupil expenditure were at the bottom of the nation, the rural schools were at the bottom in the South, and the Negro schools were the lowest of all.

Let those of us who favored the approach of the increasing influence of religion and education within the states seek to understand the position of the Court. The Court knew that a number of states and many communities, with all their commendable progress, lagged behind the recently enlarging conception both of the meaning of equal opportunity and of the moral damage of discrimination not only to those discriminated against but also to those who discriminated.

The Court was aware of the need of the regeneration of the principles of the American Declaration of Independence, the Gettysburg Address and the Atlantic Charter. World-wide revolutionary movements were moving fast from crisis to larger crisis involving all the 2,500,000,000 people who interdependently inhabit man's little home on the earth, two-thirds of whom are colored. Amid the lag of states and communities, the onrush of totalitarian tyranny and consequent fear, the wavering of hundreds of millions of people, and the crisis of democracy in a desperate world—amid all these came the need for the reassertion that human freedom and equality of opportunity are the historic and living sources of the American people's faith in themselves, the world's faith in America and America's moral influence and power in the world. The lamp of liberty, shining from the clear windows of the New World, which has long lit up the earth with the hope of great declarations and heroic actions of faith in civil liberties and programs for the general welfare, again sends its rays across the seas and the lands, authentic and prophetic with the humane hopes of all people for freedom and equality before God and under the law.

It is not out of place to recall here in Montreat, North Carolina, in these Southern surroundings of Presbyterianism and Americanism, that Presbyterians had a forward part (1) in bringing on the American Revolution; (2) in the founding and building of the Republic; (3) in westward expansion; (4) in resisting the nullification of laws of the land by the states; (5) in holding that "public office is a public trust," due the respect of all citizens in all the states; (6) in the adjudication and administration of equal justice under law; and (7) in the national leadership of "the new freedom" and the self-determination of peoples and the world leadership of the new internationalism for justice and peace among nations.

It is also timely to recall that Washington, Jefferson, John Marshall, Jackson, Lincoln and Wilson were born in Southern states, and that Chief Justice Fred Vinson, a Southerner, led a unanimous Court in setting up standards of equality that made it impossible for separate graduate and professional schools to qualify as equal, and that three Southerners joined

Chief Justice Warren in leading a unanimous Court in extending the application of the unconstitutionality of "the separate but equal doctrine" to the public schools.

As the people of both races grapple with the fulfillment of this epochal decision, it is well that the people of all sections share with the people of the South some understanding of the stubborn problem in the communities where large and approximately equal numbers of the two races give complexity to age-old customs and new tensions in an age of fear and hope. The race problem is not the vicious creation or exclusive monopoly of Southern people. In this wide world there have been, and still are, varying degrees of tensions between white people and yellow people, yellow people and brown people, brown people and black people, and black people and white people. In spite of the findings of scientific and social studies regarding the preconceptions of race, pigmentation of skin and the cephalic index, some of the indices of the degree of the persisting tensions are (1) the degree of the visibility of the differences; (2) the size and approximation of the numbers of the different races in the same community; (3) the differences in history, culture and opportunities; and (4) the competition for jobs between the low income groups of both races . . . [the South needs] to cooperate with calmness against hysteria, with knowledge against rumor, with faith against fear and violence, and with firmness against nullification.

The mores of centuries and of millions of people do not end suddenly with the compulsion of power. Decisions of courts only become real and effective by acceptance in the minds and hearts of the people. It is in more than a thousand school communities that committees of both races from churches, farm, civic, business, labor, patriotic and women's organizations, must work wisely, resolutely and cooperatively for carrying out the law of the land in good faith.

Many Southerners who worked steadfastly for equalization of the separate schools will now work sincerely for the acceptance of integration. Some who worked against equalization now work against integration. Demagogues will seek to exploit racial tensions and fears to the damage of the South in America and of America in the world. The churches must be on guard against setbacks in the program in the relation of the races and must become the spiritual outposts of the present advance. The church must stand clearly and firmly against any movement for nullification. Boards of Trustees of state institutions and schools, who have held that the legislatures and a majority of the people would more likely accept decisions of the Supreme Court in genuinely contested cases rather than acts of administrators contrary to the then constitutionally established law of the land in the Southern states, should now accept the fact that the Supreme Court, after a genuine contest, has declared all the state segregation laws unconstitutional and therefore against the law of the land as now deter-mined by a unanimous Court. Implementation should promptly begin in all the states of the South, first in the communities of the smallest propor-tion in the number of Negro children and progressively in the communities with the larger proportions, for the wise, faithful and effective fulfillment of the decision of the Court.

When the bi-racial structure was required by state laws and upheld by the Supreme Court, members of the churches rendered unto Caesar the things that are Caesar's. Though the churches were not under prohibitions by the laws of the states, yet the churches, in their racially separated congre-gations, lagged in rendering unto God the things that are God's in the com-munion and brotherhood of the Churches of Christ. Now is the time of the Church's great opportunity to use its influence and its commitments to the teachings of Jesus so that the decision of the Court will, in the deep South and in communities of highest potential, result not in an intensification of the problem but in cooperative adjustments for permanent progress.

Humility in the presence of complex and stubborn problems, soul-searching, fasting and prayer, the understanding heart, spiritual commu-nion, and the sense of human brotherhood are deeply needed in this hour. The churches, which should have led the way, must not now lag behind the states. This is the great responsibility of the churches, under God, and this is the high opportunity of the Church, in the spirit and mission of Jesus, to stand forth and work with understanding, sympathy, and spiritual guid-ance for the wise acceptance of the law of the land under the Fatherhood of one God in the brotherhood of all people.

Conflicts of sections, pride of position, threats of nullification, counter-threats of the use of federal power, and hazards of setbacks in the progress in the relation of the races, must give way to humility of spirit, the under-standing of sections, the cooperation of both races and all groups in the local school communities in working out the effective ways and stages of carrying out the law of the land. It is the adjustments made by the people in the local school communities which will give substances to the decision of the Court and make it another direction post in the difficult and unresting climb of the Southern people toward a nobler South in what has often been their historic role as a creative and cooperative part of an increasingly freer and fairer America for themselves and all their children.

Across two thousand years we hear a voice saying above the tumult and the fears of the times, "Let not your heart be troubled neither let it be afraid." He drew no lines of color, race or region when He said, "I and the Father are one and ye are my brethren ... Our Father give us this day our daily bread ... Man cannot live by bread alone ... Know the truth and the truth shall make you free ... Suffer the children to come unto me and forbid them not for such is the Kingdom of Heaven . . . I am come that you might have life and have it more abundantly . . . He that loses his life shall find it." He crossed the line of custom and caste and chose as the example of the good neighbor the Samaritan beyond the pale. He lived, taught, ministered, suffered and died for people of every status, race, color, creed and religion.

In the free minds, loyal hearts and devout faith of millions of Southern people of both races will live and grow the unfulfilled teachings of our religion, the freedom to struggle for freedom, and the faith of the American dream with the message of brotherhood and hope in an age of tension and fear. This is one of the historic tides in the affairs of churches, states and peoples of the earth, whose global currents encompass, in this atomic age, the peoples of both hemispheres with meaning, the future of human freedom, the hope of peace, and the fate of civilization. Let us thank God for the opportunity which has come in this hour of history to this Assembly of the Presbyterian Church in the United States. The action of the Presbyterian Church now, regarding the recommendations of this Council and the action of the Baptist, Methodist, Episcopal, Lutheran, Christian, Congregational, Quaker, Catholic and all other churches in the national, regional and local communities, will become decisions which make laws live in the minds and hearts of the people, without which laws lose their living meaning. God grant that the Church will not fail the times but will rise both to the responsibility of the moral power in the equal freedom of a fairer America and to the opportunity for the moral greatness in the equal brotherhood of the Kingdom of God.

§5 Mary McLeod Bethune

Mary McLeod Bethune was one of the most important educators and political leaders of her time. Born during Reconstruction on July 10, 1875 in Maysville, South Carolina, Bethune was the fifteenth of seventeen children, born of two former slaves, Samuel and Patsy McLeod. Bethune's childhood consisted of schooling and working in her family's cotton fields. Her mother instilled early in her daughter's mind that God did not discriminate based on color. She attended Maysville Presbyterian Mission School, the town's one-room schoolhouse, and later attended Scotia Seminary in Concord, North Carolina. Bethune graduated in 1894, and received a scholarship to Dwight Moody's Institute for Home and Foreign Missions in Chicago. In 1898 she married Albertus Bethune. They had one child, Albert McLeod Bethune, born the following year.

Bethune's education career began as she returned to her grade school in Maysville to begin teaching. In 1904 Bethune founded a school in Daytona, Florida for African American girls; she and her students baked pies to gain the financial resources for the school, Daytona Normal and Industrial Institute for Negro Girls. She also solicited money for the school by having her students sing

Negro spirituals to white, northern tourists in their hotels. The school thrived and eventually merged with an all boys school to form Bethune-Cookman College. Bethune served as president until 1942.

While education was her lifelong vocation, Bethune was also active politically. She was president of the Florida Federation of Colored Women and vice president of the NAACP. She also worked with the Association of American Colleges, the National Urban League, and the League of Women. Bethune was appointed to the planning committee under the National Youth Association and was a nationally renowned consultant. She was director of Negro Affairs in the National Youth Administration (1936–1944), the national commander of the Women's Army for National Defense, and she was a consultant to the U.S. secretary of war to help select the first female officer candidates. She was an advisor to President Franklin Roosevelt on child welfare, education, and home ownership; and because of her milestones in equality, she served as a member of Roosevelt's "black cabinet." Internationally she consulted on interracial affairs and understanding at a charter conference of the United Nations and was awarded two medals: the Haitian Medal of Honor and Merit (the country's highest honor), and the Liberian Commander of the Order of the Star of Africa. Ironically, her original intent was to become an African missionary, but thought a black woman would not be allowed such an opportunity. Bethune died on May 18, 1955 at her home in Daytona Beach.

In this address less than one month after the historic *Brown* decision, Bethune tells the audience that America has discovered a new freedom with the Supreme Court decision. But with this new freedom and blessing from God come great responsibilities and even greater opportunities. She reminds her listeners that the point of the *Brown* decision is not merely to go to school with white children. Rather, *Brown* represents an opportunity to cultivate oneself in an optimal environment. The challenge just now is leadership: who has the courage, the understanding and the faith to harvest the fruit in a post-*Brown* world? Bethune closes her speech with a lengthy story about Chileans and Argentines in an early twentieth century land dispute. Once settled, the countries dedicated a statue of Jesus Christ and placed it on one of the disputed boundary lines to serve as a constant reminder of their mutual peace. So, too, does Bethune urge her listeners to build Christian landmarks to guide our evolving values. The dark irony of her example looms quietly in the twenty-first-century subtext: the United Kingdom served as the neutral party between the two southern nations in conflict. The allure of Las Malvinas would surely have made such a solution impossible in some eras. Progress can always end. Retrogression, too, is an option.

––––––––

Full Integration—America's Newest Challenge

Detroit, Michigan
June 11, 1954

When first I heard of the Supreme Court Decision, I lifted my voice to utter the first inspiration of my heart—and I said,

"Let the people praise Thee, O God!
Let ALL the people praise thee."

That pronouncement should have been met with praises to God, not only from those who enjoyed the new freedom but from all of America. For America that moment, under God

"had a new birth of freedom"
"and our government of the people, by the people and for the people shall NOT perish from the earth."

The immortal Lincoln was a prophet whose words have re-echoed down through the years since that memorable occasion of the dedication of the National Cemetery at Gettysburg, November 19, 1863.

But I do not come to you to dedicate a cemetery. I do not come to keep a rendezvous with death. I come to you so that we together may keep a rendezvous with LIFE. And to say to you that this opportunity to enjoy the rich ripe fruits of democracy is a challenge to all of us. We now have, as Mrs. Roosevelt said to a group of young graduates this year, an opportunity—a responsibility—yes, even a privilege—to make our freedom real.

It is significant to me that exactly fifty years after I started my venture in this field of education that this marvelous new door has opened. For fifty years we have been harrowing the soil, cultivating the land, planting the seeds of service and learning. Should we be startled at the fruit we have reaped? Even those of us who have toiled to bring this seed to flower are awe-stricken with the sense of its reality.

I want to congratulate you who have set aside a special occasion to think upon this responsibility that you must assume as you stand upon the threshold of your larger future. Now is the acceptable time for us to confirm our common faith in the already existing enterprises for full integration and to use every possible resource in forging ahead to fulfill every immediate opportunity for making it work.

"We are not here to dream to drift
We have hard work to do and loads to lift
Shun not the struggle, FACE IT!
Tis God's Gift."

Oh, my stalwart Americans—let us be strong in this undertaking remembering always that you are giving not only America a new birth of freedom—but you are giving our world a chance to believe in the brotherhood of man and the possibility that men of varying creeds and nationalities may share this life together in peace and goodwill.

During this last year of my life, I have had many relationships that are international and far reaching. In every instance I have thought of the people as interesting, beautiful, charming, wonderful. It has never occurred to me that they were strikingly different from myself. I have always found them sharing common experiences which have made our meeting fruitful and memorable. On the local and national scenes this same fact is true. God has enriched me with the power to enjoy people, without labeling them for their color or their national backgrounds. I love people. Inherent in the fundamental principles which were established by our forefathers before they put into words the CONSTITUTION, there was the essence of democratic living which gave to each man the worthiness of his person and the dignity of his personality. One of the challenges of our new task is that every one may enjoy self-realization. We belittle our opportunity when we say, "Now is our chance to go to school with white people." That is not the point at all. We want the chance to realize our fullest and best selves in the richest and most inspiring environments under the best guidance that can be made available. Such goodness is not available to all the people when the funds available for such abundance must be allotted for the same thing in fractional proportions. All of our people are free or none are free.

In his last address, which he did not live to speak, Franklin Delano Roosevelt wrote words which were his political testament. He said:

> "We are faced with the pre-eminent fact that if civilization is to survive, we must cultivate the science of human relationship—the ability of people of all kinds to live together and work together in the same world, at peace."

The world has looked to America for the leadership in that issue of peace through better human relations. The door to the fulfillment of Roosevelt's utterance has just been opened. The challenge is that we must work zealously to discover the ways to put to work our knowledge of the science of human relationships. We know the facts. Now we must practice what we know or we are doomed as a civilization.

The fact that our leaders were able to make this pronouncement portrays our readiness to act upon it. The fruit is ripe to harvest. I pray you then, friends, who among you is prepared to lead us in the harvesting[?] The challenge of the hour is leadership. Let us discover those who have the abilities and the skills; whose hearts are filled with the understanding and the faith; whose courage is unswerving whose service motives are worthy of emulation. Let us discover them, I say, and put all that we have in confidence and cooperation and goodwill behind them so that they may be able to lead us to the fullest realization of our goals. All of the challenges to full integration depend upon the kind of education and ground work we do from this point on. We are often reminded by leaders outside the field of education, that the educative process is slow. H. G. Wells warned our world that if our processes of training did not change, our civilization was already doomed. The works of science and technology have far surpassed our understanding. Human beings change slowly. Some of us still recite the age old adage:

> "Be not the first by whom the new is tried
> Nor yet the last to lay the old aside."

But in the words of a newer philosophy,

> "Time makes ancient good uncouth."

We must be upward and doing if we would keep abreast with truth. So it is today my earnest plea that we work cooperatively and with great precision toward the dissemination of the truths that will undergird the realization of a full integration. What are the facts? Who can best give them to the people? When and where are the best places? What organized groups already have the platforms and the facilities that we need? It all means that we lay aside our own bigotries and littleness and with an open mind prepare the people to accept the new responsibilities. Let us pray for the illumination of our minds and our hearts and then let us set to work with a master will to achieve.

The tools are in our hands. All the people love art, literature, music, for in them is full release and harmony. They are the therapies for wounded minds and broken spirits. The world is hungry for the love which can be brought to the people through the avenues of life. They turn away anger, subside fears and kill evils.

You must work too to discover the common needs which may become the common tasks of many people. You know what they are but you have not taken time to put the variety of peoples at work together upon them. These now are your responsibilities. More than ever now we need to know what the gifts and powers of the people are so that we may use them for the common good.

May I close with that thrilling story of the Christ of the Andes: Far, far away to the south of our United States, on the other side of the equator at the farthest end of South America, are the countries of Chile and Argentina. While we are picking roses and shooting firecrackers on the Fourth of July, they are shivering in winter; and they have their roses and warm weather at Christmas. Now the Argentine Republic is on the Atlantic Ocean side of South America and Chile on the Pacific side and the Andes mountains rise between them. They are very very high mountains—so high that the snow never melts on their tops, but stays there both summer and winter—as on our Rocky Mountains in the United States. Really they are the southern end of our Rocky Mountains. Since the mountains are so high, so snowy and rocky and very steep, you can see how hard it would be for a surveyor to scramble up on top and that is how it happened that no one could really discover where the boundary line between the two countries really ought to be. So they just took it for granted. So it happened that the rulers of the two countries at one time began to squabble about how much belonged to one or the other. Each one went to work building big war ships and lots of guns and fortresses and gathering together armies of soldiers; and the poor people of the land who did not care at all about where the boundary was had to pay for it all and see their families suffer and fight and die. Finally when things were at their worst, the women and the clergymen of the country made up their minds to try to put a stop to it. The good Bishop of Argentina went around and pleaded for peace and tried to show the people the foolishness of war. He told them that even after the fighting would be over, they would not then know to whom the land and the waterways belonged. He pleaded with the people to accept Christ and peace. Bishop Jara of Chile did the same thing among his people. Finally they agreed to let the King of England be their judge. Finally they agreed and made treaties of peace. When the question arose as to what they should do with their forts, warships, guns and other implements of war, they began to realize what a waste had been allowed because of their ignorance.

In the meantime, a beautiful statue of Christ had been made by a young sculptor of Argentina from bronze cannons which had been taken at the time Argentina was fighting against Spain for her independence. The cannon was melted into a great figure of Christ more than 25 feet high with one hand stretched out to bless the two peaceful countries and the other holding a cross. One hundred thousand dollars were raised, mostly by the women of both countries to pay for this wonderful statue. On the 25th day of May in 1903, the day the treaty of peace was signed, the Presidents of Chile and Argentina were called to see this great statue. One of the brave women asked that this statue be placed on the highest accessible pinnacle of the Andes on one of the disputed boundary lines. This was granted and with great effort the huge statue was carried to this special place and erected. There was great joy among the people. Hundreds toiled up the steep road the night before the great unveiling and prayed their prayers and sung their hymns of thanksgiving. Chileans and Argentineans met and watched in breathless silence as the cover was taken off and the lovely face of Christ looked upon them—and He seemed to speak to them . . . "Blessed are the peacemakers; for they shall be called the children of God. . . . " In their hearts hundreds of them exclaimed: "Peace! Good will to men." The statue still stands there and on the granite at the base are these words: "Sooner shall these mountains crumble to dust than Argentines and Chileans break the peace which at the feet of Christ the Redeemer they have sworn to maintain."

My friends, let us erect Jesus Christ and His great principles of living so that all of the people of our land may see the values of creating the abundant life—not just for themselves, but for others.

§6 Dr. Benjamin E. Mays

Benjamin Elijah Mays was the youngest child born to former slaves and tenant farmers on August 1, 1894 in Epworth, South Carolina. A precocious child, Mays graduated as valedictorian of his high school class. A Phi Beta Kappa graduate of Bates College in 1920 and an expert debater, he married Ellen Harvin that same year. She died in 1923 from complications in surgery. Mays taught mathematics at Morehouse College in the early 1920s, where he also coached intercollegiate debate. He received his Masters in 1925 and his Doctorate in 1935, both from the University of Chicago. In 1921 he became an ordained minister and pastor of Shiloh Baptist Church in Atlanta and remained there until 1924.

Two years later, Mays married his second wife Sadie Gray. After teaching English at South Carolina State College, Mays was commissioned for a study of Negro churches in America, which he entitled *The Negro's Church* (1933). He held many positions including president of the Tampa Urban League (1926–1928), the national student secretary for Young Men's Christian Associations (1928–1930), and dean of Howard University's school of religion (1934–1940). Later he became the president of Morehouse College (1940–1967) and a visiting professor at Michigan State University (1968–1969). It was at Morehouse that the young Martin Luther King, Jr., came under Mays's considerable influence. Mays was president of the United Negro College Fund from 1958 to 1961, chair of the Atlanta Board of Education from 1970 to 1081, and a trustee of the Danforth Foundation and National Fund for Medical Education.

His national and international interest in religion was manifest when he became a delegate and committee member of the World Council of Churches (1948–1953) and led the Baptist World Alliance Assembly (1950). Mays worked with the advisory council for the U.S. Committee for the United Nations (1959), the Peace Corps (1961), and was a member of the U.S. National Commission for UNESCO (1962). His contributions to education (through his eight publications and two weekly columns in the *Pittsburgh Courier* and the *Journal of Negro Education*, fundraising tactics, positions held, and vision) backed by strong religious influence earned him 23 awards and 46 honorary degrees. His influence is seen in the speeches and actions of key members of the civil rights movement such as King and Maynard Jackson, the first African American mayor of Atlanta. Mays died in 1984. His papers are housed at the Moorland-Spingarn Research Center at Howard University in Washington, D.C.; the University of South Carolina in Columbia; and Morehouse College in Atlanta, Georgia.

Mays's eloquence and debate background are evident in his well-known 1954 address to the World Council of Churches. Mays systematically refutes the notion that segregation is warranted by the Scriptures, both Old and New Testaments; by ancient, medieval, and modern church history; and by modern science. As Mays makes clear, racial segregation in the church is a product of modern western imperialism: "Race and color did not count in the early existence of the Protestant church. It was when modern western imperialism began to explore and exploit the colored peoples of Africa, Asia, and America, that the beginning of segregation and discrimination based on color and race was initiated." The Commission's findings suggested but one conclusion: if "we preach a universal gospel that demands that our deeds reflect our theory," then segregation would be "sheer hypocrisy." Mays closes by calling for a Pentecost in 1954, whereby the conviction of the Holy Spirit will lead to a reconciliation between belief and action.

The Church Amidst Ethnic and Racial Tensions

Second Assembly, World Council of Churches, Evanston, Illinois
August 21, 1954

Within the past quarter of a century, Christians have been forced to think about the bearing of their faith upon the problem of racial discrimination and upon the meaning of races in human history. Wars involving all mankind, the rise of atheistic communism, the development of the Nordic theory of racial superiority, the struggles of the colored people everywhere for freedom, and a new emphasis on the meaning of the Gospel in our time have made us embarrassedly aware of the wide gulf that frequently exists between our Gospel and our practice.

The Jerusalem Conference in 1928 prepared an extensive volume on the subject. Subsequent ecumenical conferences have devoted considerable time to the general topic, "The Christian and Race": Oxford and Edinburgh in 1937; Madras in 1938, Amsterdam in 1948. It suffices to say that in all of these ecumenical bodies, segregation in the Church of Christ based on race and color has been strongly condemned.

Your present Commission has critically examined these documents and has benefited greatly by them. We have tried to build substantially on the work of previous scholars, and we believe we have dug new foundations. Since the Church gets its authority from the Bible, we have searched the Scriptures anew—both the Old and the New Testaments—to see whether there is anything there to justify our modern policy of segregation based on race, color, or ethnic origins.

The members of your Commission, supported by the best Biblical scholars, conclude that anyone who seeks shelter in the Bible for his defense of racial segregation in the Church is living in a glass house, which is neither rock nor bulletproof. In the Old Testament, the lines are definitely and sharply drawn, but they are drawn along religious and not along racial lines.

For example, when Moses exhorted the Jews not to intermarry with the people in the land they were to possess, he did so on neither racial nor ethnic grounds. In Deuteronomy 7:2-4, this fact is made plain:

> When the Lord your God gives them over to you and you defeat them; then you must utterly destroy them; you shall make no covenant with them, and show no mercy to them. You shall not make marriages with them, giving daughters to their sons or taking their daughters for your sons. For they would turn away your sons from following me, to serve other gods, then the anger of the Lord would be kindled against you, and he would destroy you quickly.

The objection to mixing is religious—not related to race, color, or ethnic group. Ancient Israel was held together by religion and not by race, just as the Jews today are held together by religion and culture. In fact, the nations that surrounded Israel belonged to the same racial stock as Israel. The Moabites shared Israel's language, the Edomites were tied to Israel by bonds of blood, and the Canaanites lived in the same country. But as long as they served their own gods, they were not accepted by Israel. On the other hand, the Gibeonites, who accepted Israel's God, ultimately became Israelites.

The drastic action of Ezra, on the return of the Jews to Jerusalem, in decreeing that the Jews had to put away their foreign wives, was not made on racial grounds. It resulted from an honest belief that they had trespassed against God by marrying wives of foreign religions. We search in vain, therefore, if we expect to find in the Old Testament support for our kind of racial or color segregation. The truth is that the Jews did not constitute a pure strain, and throughout its history, Israel made proselytes from other nations and races.

When we turn to the New Testament, it is equally clear that separateness was based on religion and culture, not on the grounds of race or ethnic origin. Your Commission points out once more that from the beginning of his career, Jesus proclaimed a religion that was supra-racial, supra-national, supra-cultural, and supra-class. His doctrine of God as father embraces the human race and makes us all children of the same God. God is our Father, and we are his children. When we pray "Our Father, which art in Heaven," we acknowledge our kinship in Him. And His concern for all His children is so great that the very hairs on their heads are numbered. Each is precious in His sight. To deny the universalism in the teachings of Christ is to deny the very genius of Christianity.

It is not surprising, therefore, that Hitler wanted nothing to do with Christ and nothing to do with the Christian religion, because they are antipathetic to everything that he stood for. His doctrine of Nordic superiority cannot stand up against the doctrine of the fatherhood of God and the brotherhood of man, nor against the brilliant account of Peter and Cornelius—a Jew and a Gentile standing face to face, confronted with the same Christ and with the same God—nor against the story of the good Samaritan. It was a Samaritan, a member of another race, who responded helpfully and sympathetically to the Jew's needs, thus dramatizing forever the fact that anyone who is in need is your neighbor and that neighborliness cuts across race and class. Jesus challenged the proud Jews to do as well as the despised Samaritan in displaying love and dispensing mercy across racial and cultural lines.

Jesus declared that he found greater faith in a Roman Centurion than he had found in all Israel. On another occasion he declared, ". . . Many will come from the east and west, and will recline with Abraham, and Isaac, and Jacob, in the Kingdom of Heaven; but the sons of the Kingdom will be cast into the outer darkness" (Matthew 8:11-12). Speaking in the Synagogue at Nazareth, Jesus made his audience angry when he reminded them that Elijah had been sent not to the widows of Israel in the time of famine, but only to the Gentile women of Sarepta, and that Elisha did not cure the Hebrew leper, but only the Gentile Naaman. The position of Jesus on this point is so clear that he who runs can read and understand.

Some Jewish Christians insisted that, in order to benefit by the Gospel of Christ, one had to be born a Jew or become a Jew by accepting the rite of circumcision and being adopted into the Jewish people; but they were not arguing against Gentiles on the basis of race. Any foreigner who accepted circumcision and who was so adopted was readily accepted. Here we must draw a sharp distinction between Jewish segregation and ours. The kind of segregation or exclusiveness practiced by the Jews generally, and by the Jewish Christians differed widely from modern segregation based on caste, color, and race. A non-Jew could become a member of a local Jewish group. He could qualify by meeting the conditions. But in our time, when segregation is based on race or color, there is nothing one can do to qualify. One cannot qualify even when he accepts the same creed, practices the same ritual, prays to the same God, and partakes of the same culture. Segregation based on color or race makes it impossible for the Christian of color to qualify; for one cannot change his color and he cannot change his race. And this restriction is tantamount to penalizing one for being what God made him and tantamount to saying to God, "You make a mistake, God, when you made peoples of different races and colors."

According to Acts, the Spirit descended on the people on the day of Pentecost, fifty days after the resurrection. The disciples and the people got a new sense of power, and they interpreted this to mean that the Holy

Spirit was present. At Pentecost, a new community was created. The church was born. Jews and proselytes gathered together, and representatives of some fifteen different nations were assembled. Acts 2:1 makes this point clear, "When the day of Pentecost had come, they were all together in one place." There they were: Parthians, Medes and Elamites; the dwellers in Mesopotamia, Judea, Cappadocia, Pontus, Asia, Phrygia, Pamphylia, Egypt, and the part of Libya about Cyrene; strangers from Rome, Jews and proselytes, Cretans and Arabians. In their own tongues, the proselytes heard of the mighty and glorious deeds of God.

Peter admitted in his encounter with Cornelius that it was unlawful for a Jew to associate with one of another nation. He told the group at Caesarea, "You yourselves know how unlawful it is for a Jew to associate with or visit anyone of another nation; but God has shown me that I should not call any man common or unclean" (Acts 10:28). Continuing, Peter proclaimed the great universal truth: "Truly I perceive that God shows no partiality, but in every nation anyone who fears him and does what is right is acceptable to him" (Acts 10:34-35).

Paul carried this universal note further than Peter. Paul saw instantly that these differences could not establish the true church and could not further the missionary enterprise. He took the position that a Gentile did not have to become a Jew in order to be a Christian. The Jewish law had been fulfilled in Christ and had been superseded by Him. In Galatians 3:28, Paul declared: "There is neither Jew nor Greek, there is neither slave nor free, there is neither male nor female; for you are all one in Christ Jesus." Again in Romans 10:12, we are told: "For there is no difference between the Jew and the Greek: for the same Lord over all is rich unto all that call upon him."

Paul set aside racial heritage, social status, and sex. In Christ all divisions are unified, and racial and ethnic groups become one. He declared on Mars Hill, "God that made the world and all things therein, seeing that he is Lord of heaven and earth . . . hath made of one blood all nations of men for to dwell on all the face of the earth" (Acts 17:24, 26). Thus, centuries before science discovered that all men are of one blood, that truth was apprehended by men of faith. My distinguished colleague, B. J. Marais, sought the thinking of the fourteen leading theologians of Europe on this subject, including Emil Brunner and Karl Barth. They all agree that we can find no justification in the Bible for a segregated church based on race or ethnic origin. This universalism in the Gospel is climaxed and attested to by the fact that Christ died for all mankind. So if there are those among us who seek support in the Bible for segregated churches based on color, race, caste, or ethnic origin, they must turn elsewhere for support.

Your Commission has gone further. We have delved into church history: ancient, medieval, and modern. We have sought to find out what the churches have practiced through the centuries in their worship and fellowship. New Testament scholars and church historians all agree that since its inception, the Christian Church has had in its membership people of different nations, races, and even colors. Nowhere in the early church do we find distinctions drawn on the basis of country or race. James (2:1-6) condemns the separation of cultural and social groups in the local church. The fact that the early church drew no distinctions based on race or color, and that Christians were often described as a "new people" or a "third race," drawn from many racial or ethnic groups, is attested by Tertullian, Origen, Ignatius, Hermas, Barnabas, Clement, and others. Their position is sustained by later scholars—Harnack and Ramsay, Cadoux and Moffat, Griffin, and Latourette. We seek in vain for signs of segregation based on race and color in the church of the first centuries of the Christian era.

What was true of the early church was true of the church of the Middle Ages. In both the ancient and the medieval church, the basis of membership was faith in Jesus Christ, our Lord. The basis of membership was faith, not race; Christ, not color; creedal acceptance and not nationality. The creeds of Christendom have always been formulated and enforced in terms of certain beliefs about God, Jesus, man, sin, and salvation, never on theories about race or ethnic groups. In summarizing this fact, Marais says: "In the extensive literature of the history of the Church till after the Reformation, we look in vain for any sign of a crucial basis for admission to the congregation." If color, race, or cultural background was a condition of membership in the local congregation of the early church or the local church of the Middle Ages, our survey does not reveal it.

It seems clear, then, that the color or racial bar in the church is a modern thing. It was not, in fact, until the seventeenth century that the outlines of the modern race problem began to emerge. It is the modern church that again crucifies the body of Christ on the racial cross. Race and color did not count in the early existence of the Protestant Church. It was when modern western imperialism began to explore and exploit the colored peoples of Africa, Asia, and America, that the beginning of segregation and discrimination based on color and race was initiated. It was then that color was associated with "inferiority," and whiteness with "superiority." Our Commission writes: "The broad pattern of major racial group tensions which trouble the world today had its historical origins in the period of European overseas exploration and expansion into America, Asia and Africa. The resulting exploration of one group by another, involving groups differing in race, varied in the three countries. But the same general relation of asserted superiority and inferiority developed between the white world and the colored world. Color became first the symbol, and then the accepted characteristic of the intergroup tensions."

Your Commission concludes, therefore, that the modern church can find no support for this practice of segregation based on race, color, or ethnic origin in the Bible, no basis for it in the ancient and medieval churches, and none for it in the various theologies of the Catholic and Protestant churches.

Your Commission has probed beyond the church and the Bible. We have sought to find out what support modern science gives for segregation and discrimination. We could quote scientist after scientist on the question of whether there is or is not an inherent superiority which one race possesses over the another. Forty or fifty years ago, scientists were divided on the subject. Also, men argued that some groups were biologically superior to others. Hundreds of volumes were written to justify a denial of equal opportunity to some peoples on the ground that they were inferior and that God had made them that way. But now there is no disagreement among the top scientists of the earth. As a recent UNESCO publication points out: "In matters of race, the only characteristics which anthropologists have so far been able to use effectively as a basis for classification are physical (anatomical and physiological). Available scientific knowledge provides no basis for believing that the groups of mankind differ in their innate capacity for intellectual and emotional development. Some biological differences between human beings within a single race may be as great as or greater than the same biological differences between races." In another connection, the United Nations publication speaks for modern science on race: "All of us believed that the biological differences found amongst human racial groups can in no case justify the views of racial inequality which have been based on ignorance and prejudice, and that all of the differences which we know can well be disregarded for all ethical human purposes." At long last, science has caught up with religion, for it was Paul who declared on Mars Hill nineteen centuries ago, that God made of one blood all nations of men.

If the church can find no support in science for ethnic and racial tension, none in the Bible for segregation based on race or color, none in the practices of the ancient and medieval churches, and none in Christian theologies, the questions naturally arise: How can segregation and discrimination in the church be justified? What can the churches do to put themselves in line with the gospel, the practices of the ancient and medieval churches, and in line with the findings of modern science? If the modern churches cannot practice full Christian fellowship in worship and membership, how can they preach the prophetic word to secular organizations that discriminate on grounds of race, color, and caste? To answer these questions, is our task at Evanston. It is to these problems that the Commission on the Church Amidst Ethnic and Racial Tensions will address itself.

There is one aspect of this subject which we often overlook. Usually the question is, what does discrimination or segregation do to the person segregated, to the disadvantaged person? It is conceded that segregation and discrimination hurt the pride of the person discriminated against, that they retard his mental, moral, and physical development, and that they rob society of what the disadvantaged group might contribute to enrich humanity. We agree that imposed separateness breeds ill-will and hatred, that it develops in the segregated a feeling of inferiority to the extent that he never knows what his capabilities are. His mind is never free to develop unrestricted. The ceiling and not the sky is the limit of his striving.

But we seldom realize what discrimination does to the person who practices it. It scars not only the soul of the segregated but the soul of the segregator as well. When we build fences to keep others out, erect barriers to keep others down, deny to them the freedom which we ourselves enjoy and cherish most, we keep ourselves in, hold ourselves down, and the barriers we erect against others become prison bars to our own souls. We cannot grow to the mental and moral stature of free men if we view life with prejudiced eyes, for thereby we shut our minds to truth and reality, which are essential to spiritual, mental, and moral growth. The time we should spend in creative activity we waste on small things which dwarf the mind and stultify the soul. It is both economically and psychologically wasteful. So it is not clear who is damaged more—the person who inflicts the discrimination or the person who suffers it, the man who is held down or the man who holds him down, the segregated or the segregator. Your Commission will wrestle with this problem.

The churches are called upon to recognize the urgency of the present situation. Even if we laid no claim to a belief in democracy, if the whole world were at peace internationally, if atheistic communism had never developed, if fascism had never been born and Nazism were wholly unknown, a non-segregated church and social and economic justice for all men are urgent because we preach a universal gospel that demands that our deeds reflect our theory. To proclaim one thing and act another is sheer hypocrisy. It weakens the influence of the church, not only in its own fellowship but throughout the world. It hampers our efforts to evangelize Africa and Asia. It is not communism, not fascism, not the struggle between East and West, but the gospel itself which demands interracial justice and an unsegregated church. We should move interracially in the church, not from fear of communism but from "our concern for our brother for whom Christ died." It has always been the responsibility of the church and the Gospel to plow new ground, smash traditions, break the mores, and make new creatures. Such was the role of the Hebrew prophets, of Jesus and Paul, of the early church, of Savonarola and Martin Luther, of Livingstone and Albert Schweitzer.

In the Commission, we will wrestle with the ever-present questions, "To what extent is the church to be governed by expedience? Is it wise to live up to the gospel we preach, or is it wiser to conform to the mandates of a secular society? Shall the church obey the laws of the state when they violate the laws of love, or the law of God which commands us to love one another? What should be the attitude of the churches toward laws that are obviously unjust and discriminatory? Obey them? Seek to change them? Violate them?"

Finally, the task before the Commission and the Assembly is to show how the theme of the Assembly, *Christian Hope*, is related to racial and ethnic tensions, not only in the past days but in the present days. The major problem will not be to demonstrate from the Bible and church history that it is only in modern times that race has become a basis for church membership. The task will be to show how the gospel of Christ can be presented and lived so as to make new creatures of men and women in the area of race, and bring hope and abundant life to all men—not only beyond history but in history. We refuse to believe that God is limited in history and that we must wait until the end of history before his mighty works can be performed.

We have known for centuries what the Bible says about race. We have known for a long time that the early church and the church of the Middle Ages did not segregate on the basis of race and ethnic origin. We know that there is no scientific basis for our treating one group as inferior to another. The gospel on race has been proclaimed for nineteen centuries. One world conference after another has condemned racial separation in the church. Yet segregation remains the great scandal in the church, especially in the United States and South Africa. The local churches permit secular bodies such as the state and federal courts, the United Nations, big league baseball, professional boxing, colleges and universities, the public schools, and theaters to initiate social change in the area of race. But even when secular bodies initiate the change, local churches, Negro and white, follow slowly or not at all. It will be a sad commentary on our life and time if future historians can write that the last bulwark of segregation based on race and color in the United States and South Africa was God's church.

We have plenty of light on the subject, but like Pilate of old we lack the will and moral courage to act on the light we have and the knowledge we possess. Clearly, knowledge is not enough. Paul knew this centuries ago when he said in essence: "I find myself doing that which I know I ought not to do and I find myself failing to do that which I know I ought to do."

We quote Tennyson:

> Let knowledge grow from more to more,
> But more of reverence in us dwell;
> That mind and soul, according well,
> May make one music as before,
> But vaster.

Drinkwater likewise deserves to be used in this context when he profoundly wrote:

> Knowledge we ask not—Knowledge Thou hast lent,
> But, Lord, the will—there lies our bitter need,
> Give us to build above the deep intent
> The deed, the deed.

Here at Evanston, the church will want to know how to deal with race within its own membership, the local congregation. The question will be— how can the local church so exemplify the spirit of Christ in Christian fellowship that the world will be compelled to follow its example?

At this Assembly, the people will want to know whether the church has any responsibility as an organized group for the alleviation of racial injustice in social, political, and economic life. What is the church's responsibility as an organized group? What is the responsibility of the individual Christian? What is the church's duty toward assisting the individual to fulfill his Christian task in his daily vocations? Above all, we should ask ourselves the question: Can there be a Pentecost in 1954?

If there can be a Pentecost in 1954, the individual Christian will be responsive to the Gospel, and he will act on his Christian convictions. There is no dichotomy between what we believe and what we do. We do what we believe. If an atheistic communist can act on his belief, a Christian can act on his. If a communist is willing to suffer for his convictions, go to jail, and die for them, surely the followers of Christ's God can suffer for theirs. The true believer, like Peter, Paul, and Jesus, is not a slave to his environment. He can rise above it and transform it. He will testify to the unity in Christ by his daily deeds.

If there is to be a modern Pentecost, the church must do likewise in its worship and membership. It must also encourage its members to exemplify in their vocations this supra-racial unity in Christ. Being thus convicted, all Christians here in Evanston will take appropriate steps in their respective congregations to make it possible for the will of God to operate to the end that all churches will be opened in membership and worship to all who serve and love the Lord. For the church is God's creation, not man's, and it belongs to God. And in God's domain, all men are equal.

§7 Dr. J. R. Brokhoff

On December 19, 1913 John Rudolph Brokhoff was born in Pottsville, Pennsylvania. He received an A.B. degree from Muhlenberg College in 1935, an M.A. from the University of Pennsylvania and an M.Div. from Philadelphia Lutheran Seminary in 1938. That same year, Brokhoff was ordained as a Lutheran minister. He received an honorary doctorate from Muhlenberg in 1951. Dr. Brokhoff served churches in Pennsylvania, North Carolina, Virginia, and Georgia before becoming a professor at Candler School of Theology, Emory University in 1965. An active scholar, Brokhoff's theological work is still held in high esteem.

In addition to his work as a pastor, professor, and writer, Dr. Brokhoff served as president of the Christian Council of Atlanta from 1950 to 1952. He was president of the Mecklenburg Minister's Association in Charlotte, North Carolina from 1960 to 1961. He also served as secretary of the Protestant Radio-TV Center in Atlanta, Georgia from 1948 to 1954 and as a board member of the Academy of Preachers in Philadelphia, Pennsylvania from 1982 to 1984. Brokhoff authored several books. In 1966 he received the George Washington Medal from the Freedom Foundation of Valley Forge, Pennsylvania. He retired from Emory in 1979. Brokhoff died 24 years later in 2003 on December 8. His papers are housed at the Pitts Theological Library at Emory University in Atlanta, Georgia.

Dr. J. R. Brokhoff delivers a powerful speech before his Atlanta congregants, seeking to upend much of the contemporary thought on Christians and their role as catalysts for change. Brokhoff argues against common perceptions of Christ. Jesus did not meekly go along with the social norms and conditions of his time, as witnessed repeatedly in the New Testament. Jesus did not shirk from the responsibilities of what he knew he must do in the pursuit of justice and his calling. He went forth, making waves, and his example challenges us to do the same—even if we are called Communists. We must not shirk the responsibility we bear for the actions demanded of us. Brokhoff insists that if we love Christ and call ourselves Christians we must do as Christ did. We must open our hearts and minds. We must be kind to our enemies and those from whom social norms tell us we must separate ourselves. We cannot hide behind a façade of what is socially acceptable. If it was good enough for Christ, it is good enough for us. Only in directly confronting and solving the great social evils of our time can we truly follow Christ as Christians. One such evil is the "racial situation in our country." Christ compels the church to disturb her segregated nation and world.

The Disturbing Christ

Lutheran Church of the Redeemer, Atlanta, Georgia
August 22, 1954

"And he entered the temple and began to drive out those who sold . . ."
~ Luke 19:45

In an address some years ago to the American Sociological Society Professor Ross of Wisconsin University said, "There may come a time in the career of every sociologist when it is his solemn duty to raise hell." This may sound to you rather blunt and crude, but what he was implying was that Sociologists who are ever studying the problems of society should reach a point where they can no longer take a balcony-look upon these social problems but must do something about them.

There came a time to raise hell in Jesus' career. It is described in today's gospel lesson of the cleansing of the temple. This was not the first time Jesus saw the money-changers in the temple. He went to the temple at least once each year and saw all the corruption, commercialism, and graft that took place under the guise of religion. He preached against the conditions. He warned the religious leaders of the practice but nothing was ever done. Finally Jesus loses patience and begins to raise sand. On his face is not a beatific smile but the fury of God. His hands are not tenderly laid upon a child's head but they are gripping a whip which he caused to fall upon the backs of the money-changers. Tables are over-turned. All is violence chaos and bedlam. And Jesus is the cause of it.

This is not the popular but the forgotten side of Jesus. We usually think of Jesus as "tender, meek, and mild" and we love to sing about a tender Shepherd leading us. That is one side of Jesus' character, it is true, but there is another side, a disturbing Christ who challenges every evil.

In today's gospel account of the cleansing of the temple we see the disturbing Christ of yesterday. He challenged the status quo of his society. His three year public ministry was filled with controversy, tension, and strife. It can be said of Jesus as was said of St. Paul that wherever he went there was either a revival or a riot. Jesus upset smug ideas, overturned customs, and defied ancient practices.

Jesus disturbed the religious forces of his day, because they were superficial and downright evil. In public Jesus denounced the religious leaders, the Pharisees for being hypocrites, and called them sepulchers full of dead bones and offspring of snakes. Moreover, Jesus disturbed the interpretation of the Mosaic laws then in vogue. In the Sermon on the Mount, Jesus said, "Ye have heard it was said of old . . . But I say unto you." He changed the interpretation and meaning of the Ten Commandments. This naturally upset the religious authorities of the day. Again, Jesus upset the religious practices of his day. The Sabbath was most sacred; it was considered the keystone of the Decalogue. But Jesus violated it by healing on the Sabbath and permitting his Disciples to pluck and eat corn. He turned the law upside down when he said, "The Sabbath was made for man and not man for the Sabbath." He aroused the wrath of the Pharisees by teaching that the spirit of the Law was greater than the letter. He pointed out to the

Pharisees' disgust that true greatness was not in pomp and position but in humility and service.

Turmoil existed in Jesus' day because he broke down the artificial barriers erected by men. He was the center of the storm because he had a barrierless love which made him cross all human barriers between classes and races. One of those barriers was social. As in our day so in Jesus', the better classes would not associate with the lower. There was no social equality. But Jesus refused to stay in his place. He went to sinners and publicans to help and win them. He went so far as to call a publican, Matthew, to be one of his inner circle of followers. He went into the home of a notorious sinner, Zaccheus. He talked, and laughed, and ate with them as though they were equals.

Jesus' love took him across the national barriers of his day. In his day, there were Jews and Gentiles, Romans and Israelites. Rome had an army of occupation in Palestine to keep order and to collect taxes. As can be expected, the Jews hated their conquerors. Yet Jesus did not share their hatred. The gospels tell us of a certain centurion who came to him for help in curing his servant. In the course of the conversation, the centurion displayed great confidence in Jesus' ability to heal. At the close of the interview, Jesus said to his fellow Jews that not in all Israel did he find such great faith. Think of the meaning of that statement! The Jews claimed they were the chosen people of God. They were raised on the true faith and had the Law of Moses. Yet here was a heathen, a non-Israelite, and Jesus said this despised Roman had more faith than any Jew. No wonder Jesus disturbed the people of his day!

Jesus furthermore aroused animosity by his disregard of their racial barriers. As in our day, the Jews had racial distinctions and prejudice. There were Jews and Samaritans. The Jews considered the Samaritans as half-breeds, inferior people. They would have no relations with them. If a Samaritan came down one side of the street, the Jew would cross the street to avoid him. The Jew would not walk or talk with a Samaritan, but would only spit on him. Jesus' wonderful love of all men would not permit him to share in this attitude. His attitude was revealed in John 4 where you will find an account of Jesus' interview with a Samaritan woman at a well. Being thirsty, Jesus asked the woman for a drink. This startled her, for this was perhaps the first time in her life that a Jew ever spoke to her. The prejudice of the day is explained by John when he says that the Jews have no dealings with the Samaritans. Jesus crossed the racial barrier to reach and win a woman living in sin.

Why was Jesus this disturbing person? Here it must be made very clear that Jesus was no rabble-rouser, trouble-maker, or devotee of violence. As you well know, there are many people today who love strife and confusion.

There are trouble-makers who love to stir up people, create chaos, and to pit one man against another. These are in most cases "little" people suffering from an inferiority complex. They think that by spreading false rumors or talking about people behind their backs they can tear people down and by doing that they will build themselves up. Jesus was not one of this type. He suffered from no inferiority complex. He was so humble that no one was any lower. He was so great that he had no personal aspirations for popularity.

There are certain trouble-makers who promote strife to profit by the chaos. The best example of this type is modern Communists. Their strategy is to pit one race against another as in the South where they are trying to arouse hostility between whites and blacks. They also get into labor unions to foment trouble between labor and management. They are active in colonial nations to arouse the dispossessed to revolt against their leaders. They claim they are the champions of the people who shall receive freedom, democracy, and a higher standard of living. When they succeed in splitting a country with dissension, they move in and seize power. Then all their promises evaporate in thin air. Now, no one could ever accuse Jesus of having this purpose in mind by disturbing the status quo. What did he get out of his work? When his family tried to apologize for his teaching which was so radical as to be embarrassing, they said he was out of his mind. His country branded him a traitor. The church of his day proclaimed him a heretic. His own people erected a cross and nailed him to it. No, Jesus' only reason for disturbing his generation was his love for God and man. He, like God, could not tolerate evil. He knew perfectly that man's sins would find him out and would bring him nothing but misery and death. He disturbed his countrymen that though upset they would repent and live.

Today's gospel account of the cleansing of the temple presents us with the disturbing Christ of today. This is not stretching a point, because in the New Testament we read, "Jesus Christ the same yesterday, today, and forever." If Christ was a disturber in his day, he is the same for our day. He challenges the modern status quo through the church and true Christians. The real revolutionaries of the 20th century are not the Communists but true Christians. Jesus' teachings are as radical as they can be. When Christians attempt to put them into modern living, they become social reformers and are considered radicals. True Christian living today is dangerous living. Jesus called his followers the salt of the earth, and Archbishop Berggrav reminds us that Christians are "Dangerous salt." One reason for the danger to Christians in being truly Christian is the world's accusation that such a Christian is a Communist. It happens often that Communists and Christians are defying the same social evils and working toward greater social, economic, and political justice. But the big difference between the two is that Communists do it to gain political power and Christians have no other motive than to help mankind live a fuller, better life. The worst punishment that can be given to a person today is to be tagged a Communist when he is nothing but a sincere Christian. This was illustrated in the case of Bishop Oxnam who had to defend himself and his social pioneering before a Congressional investigating committee. Nevertheless, true Christians are the spokesmen today of a disturbing Christ.

On the contemporary scene Jesus disturbs our world by disturbing us as individuals. His perfection and purity disturb us when we sin. He enlightens our conscience which aggravates us when we do wrong. Whenever we stoop to sin, Jesus approaches us like Nathan the prophet who pointed his finger at David after his adultery and said, "Thou art the man." Christ will not let a man sin and be comfortable. The only way to sin and enjoy it is to get rid of Christ.

He disturbs us individually by giving us a vision of what he wants us to be. Someone said the only hell we need is a vision of what we were meant to be. When we look at Christ we see in him what we ought to be. His beauty and love make us see our ugliness and worldliness. When we look into his eyes, we are reminded of his high expectations: "Love God with all thy heart . . . Love your neighbor as yourself . . . Love your enemies . . . Forgive not seven but seventy times seven." These things we should be doing. Here he shows the manner of man each of us should be. That high calling, that challenging vision makes us dissatisfied with ourselves by saying, "You should be better than you are."

Jesus' personality disturbs us. There is something about Jesus that will not let us be at peace until we surrender to him. Lloyd Douglas teaches that lesson in "The Robe." The soldier who won Jesus' garment had no rest by day or night. He was distraught and upset. He wandered from place to place seeking peace. His calm came only when he surrendered to the One who wore the robe. The same message was dramatically given by Francis Thompson's poem, "Hound of Heaven." God is portrayed as a mighty hound racing down the path of life pursuing a sinner. God in his love desires man for himself. Man runs as fast as he can to escape God. Finally man drops in exhaustion and surrenders. Then God says, "Whom couldst thou find to love ignoble thee, save me, save only me?" Perfect peace means perfect surrender to God. Christ will have nothing less than our all, and he will not let us alone until we dedicate our whole selves to him.

Through the church today Christ is disturbing our society for its social evils. Are we brave enough today to face these issues in the light of Christ's teaching and example?

Let us begin with the racial situation in our country. There was a time when we could dismiss the subject by saying segregation was the law of the land. The recent Supreme Court decision changed that, and every law still existing enforcing segregation is unconstitutional. The church is disturbed today because it is the most segregated organization in America, and the church's pronouncements against segregation are disturbing the non-Christian forces of our land. The church is disturbed, for the World Council of Churches meeting in Evanston heard that segregation in the church is the scandal of the church. We know many Christians and non-Christians are being disturbed by Christ on this issue, because of their hot-headed protests and their public vitriolic statements.

Let's put this issue on a local level as it affects this congregation. A negro from a bi-racial Lutheran congregation up north moves to our city and calls. He says, "I am a United Lutheran, but there is no colored United Lutheran church in Atlanta. I love the Lutheran church and want to remain one. Would you permit me to become a member of your church?" There is the whole racial question in our laps. What shall we do? Will Christ let us say "No" or say nothing which is the equivalent of saying "No"? If the Bible declares all men are equal, that God is no respecter of persons, that every person is a precious soul to be saved, that prejudice and discrimination are sin—shall we say "No"? Christ is disturbing us, for a "No" does not satisfy our consciences.

Take another area of our social status today. Here too Christ is disturbing us. Within a 100 miles of our city we have an abominable situation of dope, white slavery, alcohol, graft, and political murder. The big question is why the churches of Columbus and Phoenix City have not raised their voices long before the National Guard had to take over the situation? Christ is disturbing us for our indifference and lack of interest in the social sores of our communities.

What shall we Americans do about the miserable conditions abroad? The secular press reports that China is now suffering from the worst flood in a century. Millions of acres are inundated. Millions of people are sure to starve and die of disease. Shall we send over or at least offer some of our surplus foods? Then we think of Korea, and again of Indochina, and of the Communist terror, and we instinctively say, "Let them starve and die." But Christ who said "Love your enemies" will not let us be content with that answer. We are reminded of the Scriptures, "If thine enemy hunger, feed him." Christ is challenging us to take our God-given surplus and save even our enemies.

Another problem in our society is denominationalism. In the grass roots of our churches we still have too much narrow sectarianism. Folks sincerely think that only they have the whole truth and others will never be saved unless they change churches. Jonathan Swift put it in a few liners:

"We are God's chosen few,
All others will be damned;
There is no place in heaven for you,
We can't have heaven crammed!"

The World Council of Churches' meeting at this present moment is Christ's protest to that isolationism. In his last great earthly prayer Jesus prayed that all his children might be one. Is our Denominationalism according to his will? Are we in the spirit and mind of Christ when we insist that our church alone is the true church and all other churches are false? Christ is disturbing us to be more cooperative, more tolerant, more helpful to each other.

Today's gospel presents us with a disturbing Christ. But do we want this type of Christ? Some in Jesus' day did not. The people who lost their swine when the demons of a maniac caused them to run into the sea asked Jesus to please leave their vicinity. They would rather have a maniac living naked among the tombs of the cemetery and their pigs than to have no maniac and no pigs.

When Jesus was buried, his enemies thought they were rid of the Troubler. Pilate told them to make the stone as sure as they could and gave them soldiers to keep him forever in the tomb. A modern author, feeling the same, writes, "I helped roll the stone to keep him there to trouble me no more."

Perhaps we do not want this kind of Christ, but would rather have One who tenderly says, "Come unto me . . . and I will give you rest." The trouble with this is that no one can [have] a part of Christ. All of him must be taken or none at all. The disturbing Christ is a part of the peace-giving Christ. Shall we accept this Christ today or turn away from him? Once a large number of followers turned away from Jesus because he offended them with his speech and then Jesus asked his 12, "Will ye also go away?" Peter answered nobly: "Lord, to whom shall we go? Thou hast the words of eternal life." May God grant us grace today to answer the disturbing Christ with the same words.

§8 William Lloyd Imes

William Lloyd Imes was born on December 29, 1889 in Memphis, Tennessee, to Benjamin A. Imes, a minister, and his wife, Elizabeth Wallace Imes. He attended Fisk University where he received both a B.A. and an M.A. In 1912 he traveled to New York City to study at the Union Theological Seminary, from which he received a B.D. In 1915, Imes earned an M.A. from Columbia University. In the same year he married Grace Virginia Frank; the couple had three children. Lincoln University conferred an honorary Doctor of Divinity on Imes in 1929. In 1915 Imes was ordained as a Presbyterian minister, and pastored several churches throughout the Northeast, including St. James Church in New York City. In 1943 he became President of Knoxville College in Tennessee. After four years there, he became director of social and adult education for the New York State Council of Churches. Imes retired from public life in 1958 even as he remained active in church affairs. He passed away in 1986. His papers are housed at Syracuse University in Syracuse, New York.

Less than five months after the Supreme Court's *Brown* decision, Reverend William Lloyd Imes takes aim at the Church's woeful performance in integrating its own house. To continue to do nothing is to betray "our own Gospel." That gospel, Imes instructs, as recounted in Christ's Sermon on the Mount and the Pentecost Assembly of the early church as described in Acts, is unequivocal on the subject of race: integration is a Christian inheritance. The matter is really quite simple: "Either we do, or we do not, practice the Gospel which we preach. If we preach it, we dare not deny it in practice, unless we admit our failure and sin." The advantages of an integrated church are many, claims Imes, notably, sharing talents, enriching our personal and social lives—even enlivening the worship service. Even so, the church remains largely a social club of exclusivity, and until we conquer the "paralysis of wills" and act upon the will of God, the church will remain in its glass house.

The Challenge of Integration as Regards the Church

Alumni Seminary Convocation, Lincoln University, Lincoln University, Pennsylvania
October 5, 1954

On May 17, 1954, an epoch-making decision was announced by press, radio, and other media of modern communication—the Supreme Court of the United States had decided that racial segregation in public schools is not in accordance with our National Constitution, and that those states who still clung to the outmoded "separate but equal" doctrine of the late nineteenth century should now make plans to integrate the student bodies which are separated because of race or color.

We of the U.S.A. have known for a long time, and all too well, that our nation has been seriously and regrettably divided on this question. The special and open segregationists have been very largely those of the seventeen southeastern states, but there have also been those cases in "border" states, and a few far western states (especially southwestern), where school segregation has been practiced, both public and private. It is not a happy nor an inspiring picture. When we look at it from the standpoint of the Declaration of Independence, the Constitution, the Bill of Rights, the Emancipation Proclamation, we must admit that continued segregation of races in education is something of a monstrosity and a nightmare, in the light of our progress in humanitarian and scientific fields. Even humanity and science, not to mention religion, cry out against such reaction.

But, much as we lament and regret racial segregation in education, are not we of religion and the church very much like those who live in the proverbial "glass houses"? We have not ourselves had really and truly *de-segregated* churches; and, only in recent years, very recent, to be honest, that our church and inter-church bodies took official and definite stands on this question. I recall being present at Columbus, Ohio, in a meeting of the Federal Council of Churches, in 1946, at which a positive and definite declaration was made on racial segregation in the church. There was in this the open and frank confession that the church itself had not set the example in its local and daily practice, of non-segregation. How, then, could it speak to the secular world regarding the evil of segregation? Here was a dilemma of terrifying magnitude, and one on which the Christian Church simply could not afford to keep silent! Either we of the Church must bear witness by faith and practice in this matter, or we would stand self-accused of betrayal of our own Gospel! For, the Christian faith, by all its history and interpretation, has always stood for the sovereignty of God and the fellowship of the saints!

Let us put this conviction in a slightly different form: *Worship* is our attitude toward God—it is giving God His *worth*. Literally, it is *worth-ship*. The correlative of this is man's right relation toward his fellow man; we call this relation *fellowship*. These two ideals are interdependent both in theory and practice. No worship? Then no fellowship! No fellowship, then no worship! The classical instance of this teaching is found in Jesus' statement: "If thou bring thy gift to the altar, and there rememberest that thy brother hath ought against thee, leave there thy gift before the altar and go thy way; first be reconciled to thy brother, and then come and offer thy gift." ·

The whole basis for this is laid deeply in the entire ministry of the Master, and it comes to a magnificent climax in the Sermon on the Mount, from which this quotation is made. It is also laid in the basis of Early Church history, with the Book of Acts as a sourcebook: "Parthians, and Medes, and Elamites, and the dwellers in Mesopotamia, and in Judea, and Cappadocia, in Pontus and Asia, Phrygia, and Pamphilia, in Egypt, and in the parts of Libya and Cyrene, and strangers of Rome, Jews and proselytes, Cretes, and Arabians, we do hear them speak in our tongues the wonderful word of God." This vivid description of the Pentecost Assembly of the Early Church tells its own forthright story of the integration of many races, classes and dialects. And, as if to make the matter of racial integration more explicit, the record is given of Peter, first great leader of the Church in Jerusalem, and following Pentecost. Peter's conversion from narrow Jewish exclusiveness and from racial and religious prejudices is told in Chapters 10, 11 and 15 of Acts. The New Testament Church is definitely founded on the principle of integration of *all believers*, regardless of race, language or custom.

This inheritance of an integrated church is, therefore, clearly from the Apostolic Age. Nothing could be more true to the established Christian tradition than this. The spirit of God was given at Pentecost not to a segregated, but an *unsegregated* Church. Even its intense Jewishness, quite as troublesome in the first century as our color-prejudice in the twentieth, could not submerge this principle, nor its practice.

Why we should have to struggle so in this twentieth century to re-establish this age-long principle, and to work earnestly to endeavor to put it into practice, is one of the vexing and persistent problems of both our secular and our church life. It will hardly excuse us to point to the examples of war, politics, and education, in all of which we have confessedly come up short. *Religion* is the *one experience* in which we have no excuse for not living up to the highest ethical standards. Either we do, or we do not, practice the Gospel which we preach. If we preach it, we dare not deny it in practice, unless we admit our failure and sin. And, if we do so confess our shortcomings, the next move is that of seeking the forgiveness of God, and the restitution of the right human relationship that will confirm and carry out the behests of the Gospel.

If one is seeking an explanation for our lack of integration in the church it might be well found in the facts of our divided *nationalism*, *racism*, and *class-structure* in the modern world. This merely explains, however, and does not excuse. Our Christian ethic is quite plain and uncompromising on the point of absolute brotherhood. Either it is exactly that, or it is *not Christian!* "One is your Master, even Christ, and all ye are brethren."

There are obvious advantages of integration. Many different groups, races, classes, can and do bring various gifts and talents to the common store of human good. While it is true that any one group tends to magnify its own culture and contribution, yet it is also true that it is not too hard a task, nor too great a step to take, to undertake the use *of our love for our own* as a bridge to cross over, to understand and appreciate the values we find in the contributions of others. To be quite specific on this point, as regards our American scene, the emotional warmth and exuberance of the Afro-American tradition in religion, reminiscent of the camp-meeting, revival, and similar experiences might well bring a new glow into the common religious life, if brought helpfully into contact with the more sedate and intellectually-oriented types of worship. Conversely, the Euro-American stocks, who have brought their particular theologies and liturgies into American church life, might helpfully balance and supplement the emotional and artistic contribution of the Afro-American tradition. That this could well be done is brought out in the Welsh revival experience in modern England in which the pronounced emotional fervor of the people of Wales came into vital contact with the more intellectual approach of the Established Church, and certain non-conformists who leaned heavily toward a theological and creedal expression of religion. Integration on the religious level is really very much like that of education and cultural and economic levels. It is not easy to achieve, because of our prejudices and selfishnesses, but once the barrier is broken, it is perfectly amazing how much we see of the advantages of a multi-cultural order, with its enrichment of the personal and social life. The Afro-American religious folk-songs, affectionately called spirituals, have brought a new insight into American religious thought; similarly, Welsh hymnody has greatly ennobled and assisted religious life and work in the England of both yesterday and today.

Integration in religious life in America has had to take the same hurdle that all other areas which touch sensitive social relationships have experienced. We have been hesitant about it for many reasons, most of them utterly unworthy of really religious people. Far too much emphasis has been placed upon the Church as a sort of *social club*, into which the people of a certain *class*, or *race*, or other like nature would gather, and with the kind of exclusiveness, it was never too easy for churchmen to practice the brotherhood they so loudly preached. We are now witnessing what that same kind of attempt at exclusiveness, based upon race, has accomplished in the public educational field. It is hard to keep from laughing outright, but, on second thought, it is pathetic beyond any human power to describe, that in the current fight in a neighboring state, Delaware, in one of two sections of the more racially prejudiced communities of the state, they should be saying out loud that they are organizing a NAAWP as a counter-weapon against the NAACP. The very fact that, all this country over, only isolated cases like the Church of all Nations in San Francisco, and the Community Church of New York, we have actually integrated both our clergy and congregations of worshippers on the unit local level, makes us of the Church think twice before we condemn too harshly such reaction as that just described in some of Delaware's public school districts.

All in all, The Church is moving toward integration, but it is doing it with timid and hesitant steps. There is conviction in our hearts, but there is also a certain paralysis in our wills. We need, desperately, a vision of the social order in which the will of God and the welfare of *all* his children will become the dominant motives which impel us. We have denominational and interdenominational bodies that have made brave and splendid pronouncements; we have achieved at least a respectable beginning of a real ecumenical movement, as witness the Second Assembly of the World Council of Churches recently meeting in Evanston, with its moving demonstration of international and interracial fellowship across many creedal lines. But the goal of genuine fellowship and worship with perfect freedom and integration at the local level is still ahead of us. It is a goal worth achieving. It will help both the man farthest up and the man farthest down, for the Lord is the Maker of them all.

1955

1955

§9 Sarah Patton Boyle

Sarah Patton Boyle was born on May 9, 1906 in Albemarle County, Virginia to Robert Williams, an Episcopal clergyman, and Jane Patton. A cousin to General George S. Patton, she married E. Roger Boyle, a drama professor at the University of Virginia in 1932. By late 1953, Mrs. Boyle had published more than one hundred articles for newspapers, magazines, and religious publications on the issue of integration. In 1962 "Patty" Boyle authored a memoir entitled *The Desegregated Heart*, which explains her transformation from a traditional white southern aristocratic woman to a civil rights activist. Key to that transformation was the admission of Gregory Swanson, an African American attorney, to the University of Virginia Law School in 1950. Subsequently, she befriended T. J. Sellers, the editor of Charlottesville's black newspaper, *The Tribune*. So outspoken was Boyle on civil rights that on August 29, 1956, the Ku Klux Klan burned a cross on her front yard. She was the first white person to serve on the Charlottesville NAACP chapter's board of directors.

A self-proclaimed "naive idealist," Boyle thought that by discussing the intentions of Jesus and by setting an example, she could encourage southern whites to support racial equality. Martin Luther King, Jr. in his famous "Letter from Birmingham Jail," credited Boyle for explaining the moral importance of faith in the fight for racial justice. In June 1964 Boyle was arrested in St. Augustine, Florida, during a civil rights demonstration at the Monson Motor Lodge. Boyle retired from active participation in the freedom movement in 1967. In 1983 twenty-one years after the publication of her first book, Boyle authored *The Desert Blooms: A Personal Adventure in Growing Old Creatively*. She died in 1994. On May 8, 2001, the City of Charlottesville honored Boyle for her civil rights work. A bronze plaque with her name was placed on the Drewary Brown Bridge recognizing her as a "bridge builder." Her papers are housed at the University of Virginia.

In this very brief speech before the Calvary Christian Church, Sarah Patton Boyle takes up the "great white southern fear": interracial marriage. An integrated society, she promises, will not lead to increased intermarriage. Why? Experience shows us that, even without segregation of criminals, poor white trash, gangsters, pick-pockets and sex fiends, we don't worry about our daughters marrying the aforementioned deviants. Note that Boyle, like so many white southerners of her day, assumes a very specific gendered relationship—the old canard of black men marrying white women. Experience and commonsense also reveal that integration will not lead to more intermarriages, as observed in the real world example of New York City. Boyle also subtly expands her case for racial integration by arguing that blacks would not seek social equality with whites, nor would they seek to "storm our private lives." The point Boyle drives home, though, is about choice: "And yet to them [blacks] it makes all the difference between manhood and submanhood if they are the ones who are allowed to make the choice." Place, when navigated by choice rather than by Jim Crow mandate, engenders "the freedom and self respect of a whole people," a "small concession to the dark, beloved Children of the God who gave us his Son."

———————

Calvary Christian Church, Covington, Virginia
February 13, 1955

Although, some find passages in the Old Testament which seem to support segregation, none can look squarely at the life and teachings of Jesus and believe that he would support segregation if he were here today.

Nearly all Christian people, therefore, would like to see integration if they could be sure that no harm would come of it. Many, however, have very real fears which they are entitled to have allayed.

Probably the greatest of them is that intermarriage will increase. This fear has virtually no foundation. I shall try to show you why.

Do you realize that there is no segregation of paroled criminals? Yet you don't—unless you're neurotic—worry over the possibility of your daughters marrying one. There's no segregation of poor white trash either, yet you don't, I hope, worry about the possibility of your daughter's marrying one of these. There's no segregation of gangsters, or pickpockets, or even sex fiends—if they don't happen to be serving a term.

Unless we want to have a nervous collapse from pondering on possible in-laws, we simply have to assume that our children will use a modicum of common sense in the selection of life partners. Concerning integration, this common sense must be assumed, too—by colored parents, as well as white. For it's as inadvisable for a Negro to marry a white as for a white to marry a Negro. Unhappiness lies in wait in either case.

In every locality where there are no laws against intermarriage there's ample proof that our young people of both races have better judgment than we think.

Take New York City, for example. There are no segregation laws of any kind there. And the city's Negro population is so large that if they were all gathered together in one section they would make a black city approximately twice the size of Richmond, Virginia. Yet interracial couples are so rare, even in and near Harlem, that people turn around and look at them on the street.

The simple truth is that when persons are completely free to choose whom they will, each automatically seeks his own kind, both in social intercourse and in marriage. This is true not only of racial groups, but even of nationalities. We find such gatherings as Little Italy, Germantown, and so on, in every city where any minority is large for it to be practical to herd together. This is for the obvious, uncomplicated reason that they are simply more congenial with their own.

Experiences all over the country show that we and our colored Christian brothers can easily meet in church, in school and in business day after day, and yet each go our own separate ways in other matters by free and mutual choice.

We wouldn't fear that Negroes will storm our private lives if only we would give them a chance to do so. For they are far more uncomfortable with us than the most bigoted among us is with them. You see, they have been indoctrinated in the belief that we regard them as stupid and crude and unfit to associate with.

Would you enjoy a gathering in which you thought the people felt this way about you? The boldest of you might go among such people a few times, just to prove to yourself and others that you could, and were not afraid. But after proving this, you would stay away simply because you couldn't possibly enjoy yourself under such conditions. Our colored neighbors are sensitive human beings like ourselves, and they too stay away of their own accord.

I know this not only from study and investigation but from personal experience. For over four years my home has been thrown open to Negro guests. I have repeatedly urged many of the colored people of my community to stop by for tea with me any time. They always joyfully exclaim that they surely will. Yet in those four years only two have ever called without a specific, definite and urgent invitation, and each of these two has called only once.

And yet to them it makes all the difference between manhood and submanhood if they are the ones who are allowed to make the choice. It makes all the difference between their having a sense of belonging and a sense of rejection if they are invited. It makes all the difference between their feeling that they are first class citizens, and that they are second [class] citizens in our democracy if they can go where they choose instead of where we choose.

Isn't this a very little thing for us to do for the freedom and self respect of a whole people? I know that we of the South are not so small natured and so cold hearted that we will not give even this small concession to the dark, beloved children of the God who gave us his Son.

And now I shall ask you to pray with me, for I have a favorite prayer that I want to share with you.

> O, Lord, make me an instrument of thy peace;
> Where there is hatred, let me sow love;
> Where there is injury, pardon;

Where there is discord, union;
Where there is doubt, faith.

O, Divine Master,
Grant that I shall not seek so much to be consoled as to console;
To be understood as to understand;
To be loved as to love.

§10 Sarah Patton Boyle

Sarah Patton Boyle's biography appears in the introduction to her February 13, 1955 speech to Calvary Christian Church. Boyle begins the speech below to the Covington Ministerial Association with the radical premise that courage might not be a Christian virtue. Recounting her only violent encounter with a racist, Boyle learned, "I knew that one could face an angry mob without even the beginning of fear if one loved them like this. Courage is not needed in the house of love, for fear is not there." Boyle likens the transformative act of loving an enemy to alchemy, though a decidedly Christ-centered concoction. In so doing, we become "not the doers but only the means by which it [loving enemies] is done."

For a relatively short speech, Boyle packs it with personal stories of the church and race relations. Several contain a similar theme: the image we have of the white southerner often does not square with reality. Even in "the bosom of Mississippi" one can find a white Methodist minister willing to open his church to an integrated women's group. But even the most virulent racist must be loved—in the same way and to the same extent as "those whom they oppress." And by showing "Christian leadership" and love to all peoples, we can remedy a "situation which the conscience of no just person can condone." Just as love glows in us, so too will "it glow in the living soul of every man."

––––––––––

Covington Ministerial Association, Covington, Virginia
February 13, 1955

"If ye have faith as a grain of mustard seed, ye shall say unto this mountain, Remove hence to yonder place; and it shall remove; and nothing shall be impossible unto you."
~Matthew 17:20

People often tell me, "I know that segregation is un-Christian, but I simply haven't the courage to make a stand against it in the South."

I doubt if any of us has the courage—if we allow ourselves to think in terms of courage. For when we consider how much we personally might lose, and what a trivial gain for the cause could be achieved by our puny voices, the sacrifice appears foolhardy.

But did it ever occur to you that perhaps courage is a pagan virtue?

Jesus and the apostles never stressed courage. They by-passed the whole area of courage, for Christianity is a religion of by-passes.

They focused their attention on two short cuts to all good things. These are faith and love. When we take these routes we by-pass every mountain, torrent and chasm which lies in our way. By love and faith we can travel easily and joyously to our goal through the rugged country of our time.

I was one of many who spoke last November at the Public Education Hearing in Richmond. Waiting my turn, as I looked out over an audience of 2,000, most of whom would not agree with me, I knew that I was too frightened to speak. Only through concentration on loving them, I decided, could I escape terror of them.

When my turn came this concentration resulted in a strange and good feeling of having dispelled my individual personality. The truth alone was tangible. I was only the channel through which it came. The feeling continued even after I stopped speaking.

As I left the auditorium, I suffered the only violent, face to face attack which I have experienced in nearly five years of defending minority rights. A woman, white around the mouth with rage, confronted me and demanded to know why I was "trying to mongrelize the race."

Looking into her hate-blazing face something which was not mine flowed out of me, enveloping us both. I felt suddenly closer to her than in our dearest moments we feel to our dearest ones. I was a mother and she was a heart-torn, desperate child.

This was the alchemy of which Jesus spoke. This is how the loving of enemies is done—not of ourselves but by a supreme act of not being ourselves, so that we are not the doers but only the means by which it is done.

Suddenly I knew that one could face an angry mob without even the beginning of fear if one loved them like this. Courage is not needed in the house of love, for fear is not there.

I think that Jesus' admonition, "Love your enemies!" is the most practical suggestion ever offered, for it disintegrates fear, and it makes defeat impossible.

Perhaps in this age the by-pass of faith is even less traveled than the by-pass of love. This is serious, because we can neutralize even love by lack of faith in it. Most of us obviously believe that hate can triumph over love. If Jesus had believed this he could not have risen from the dead.

Actually, our faith in hate is not only un-Christian, but also idiotic, for the chief strength of the powers of darkness lies in their ability to bluff us. Their mirages dissolve before the man who continues to walk straight ahead. My own researches and experiences have convinced me that well over three fourths of our "barriers" to brotherhood are the entirely imaginary offspring of our faith in evil.

Three years ago the president of an interracial organization in a southern town gravely assured me that the only place where his group could have a supper meeting was the Unitarian church.

"Are you sure?" I wanted to know. "Have you asked the other ministers?"

"Well, not point blank, but they've made it pretty clear that it's no use asking."

I got his permission to inquire [about] "point blank," then telephoned the Episcopal minister. Having carefully explained the nature and aims of the group, I asked if the next supper meeting could be held at his church.

"Just a minute and I'll see if that date's open," he told me.

It was.

Next I called the Presbyterian minister. "We have a rule," he said stiffly, "that before an organization is given permission to use the facilities of the church, the Session must pass on it. It meets tomorrow. I'll present this case."

Aw-aw, I thought, and next day asked myself if it was any use embarrassing us both by demanding to know a verdict which his chilly, hurried voice had already foretold would be negative. But setting my jaw, I called him.

In the same chilly, hurried voice he said: "We voted unanimously to welcome the gathering. I knew we would."

The one remaining minister was Baptist, who said, "Of course, why of course. We like to encourage that kind of thing."

I'm not trying to imply that one never meets opposition from the clergy. Rather I am trying to show that the images of our fellow beings which we carry in our own minds give us far more trouble in the struggle for integration than real live southerners do. Indeed the ministers themselves are beset by these false images—or devils, as they might have been called in the early church.

In the bosom of Mississippi there nestles a certain town with two Methodist churches. A few years ago "The Women's Society of Christian Service" decided to hold their annual meeting there, and the chairman of the committee on arrangements asked one of the ministers if his church would play host to the group, including meals. He graciously agreed, but retracted when told that there were colored members.

Personally, of course, he would like to welcome them all, he said, but his congregation would be in uttermost rebellion. You just couldn't force the people in matters of this kind, he pointed out, and eating together was the very last thing . . . You only stirred up trouble if you went too far, you know. He would, however, be glad to arrange meals for colored members in the homes of Negroes in the town.

But the chairman of the committee had faith that people are people, rather than merely personifications of prejudice. So she declined to sink sadly into the white-washed tomb of what "you can't do in the South." She turned instead to the pastor of the other church, who said:

"How can we send missionaries abroad and not do this at home? We shall be privileged to welcome your colored members to our table."

Few modern people are able to believe that faith can move mountains but it shouldn't be too much to ask that they believe that it can move people. At any rate this minister's people justified his faith in them, for they welcomed their dark sisters as daughters of the King.

If this happened in Mississippi, don't you think it would be likely to happen anywhere that the minister reached out to his people in faith and love?

However, this alchemy will not work unless the act is wholly Christian. A partly Christian act is not strong enough to carry the powerful current of God's will. And an act is not wholly Christian unless it is performed in love and faith toward all people, and not merely toward a chosen group. If a minister or other Christian leader would bring the shine of brotherhood into his church, his heart must go out to the prejudiced equally as to the oppressed. For they also are God's struggling children upon whom He sends His rain and His love.

Not enough of our Christian leaders grasp the basic truth that you cannot win people to brotherly love without first loving them, even as God first loved us. How many of the very best of us, ministers or laymen, have really mastered the difficult art of turning away from sin but never from the sinner?

And yet unless we can pour down upon the hostile and the prejudiced the same love which we pour upon those whom they oppress, we can't hope to alter that prejudice by anything we say or do. This, I am convinced, is a spiritual law which we must learn or defeat our ends.

Conforming to this law is one of the most difficult things that I know. I certainly don't claim to be one of those who can do it. But I do say that on those rare occasions when I, or others have succeeded in conforming to it, it certainly works.

Several years ago in the so-called "black belt" of Virginia a Negro couple applied for membership in a certain protestant church. I'm afraid that the average southern minister would have regretfully explained that he could not accept them because his white parishioners had not yet learned brotherhood. But this rector was a minister of God rather than a minister of mores, and he welcomed his new members from his heart, having faith in his white parishioners because he loved them, too.

Did any person in his large parish let him down? ONE did. She greeted him at the door with this firm declaration: "You'll have to choose between us. I can't stand having Negroes in our own church."

"I'm sorry," he told her with the same heartfelt sympathy he would have expressed if she had confided that she had tuberculosis. "You know you can count on my prayers. But I'm afraid you can't take communion with us until you feel better. You see, our service specifies that you must be in love and charity with your neighbors."

Did she leave the church? No. Each Sunday at 11 she is faithfully in her pew, but the last report I heard, she was still driving 25 miles on Good Friday and Christmas Eve to take communion in another church.

I often think that while our ministers follow what they believe to be the un-Christian will of the people, most of the people await only Christian leadership to help them out of a situation which the conscience of no just person can condone. Like Peter, we deny Christ in fear of our fellow men. It is time for us to go out and weep!

Three years ago I was assigned to a panel for an unrehearsed discussion of the pros and cons of integration before an all white audience. The panel was instructed to meet for an hour in private to learn each other's general approach before we had the public discussion.

I knew that one member of the opposition was a witty, brilliant and uncompromising bigot. His method was to bait and ridicule. If we weren't careful, I knew he would make all his good-willed opponents look like sentimental fools.

Only God could handle such a situation, so I decided to give God a free hand by refusing to resist this evil and by yielding myself wholly to faith and love. I forced myself to assume that the bigot was seeking honest information when he baited me, and that his ridicule was good humored wit. I chuckled right along with him when he made fun of my ideals, admitting that they did sound pretty naïve but insisting that when put into practice they nevertheless somehow worked.

After twitting and baiting me on this and that angle for several minutes without succeeding in arousing the anger he was trying to provoke, he finally said: "But how can any southerner ever bring himself to call a nigger Mr.?"

Determined to treat even this as an honest question, I replied: "I'm glad you asked that because it's so easily answered. We think we will feel silly calling Negroes Mr. because we have never really known any who weren't working for us or for our friends, and most people don't call their household help Mr., even if he is white.

"But when we move out into the colored community and find ourselves talking about public affairs to a colored man whose education, intelligence and courtesy obviously are superior to our own, as very often happens to me, we suddenly discover that we would feel even sillier addressing him as Jim than we would feel addressing him as Mr. Parker. After that it's quite easy."

To my complete surprise the bigot replied, "Mrs. Boyle, I'm glad that you like Negroes." He then went on to ask me questions which really were honest, and to crack jokes which really were good humored. The game of faith I had been playing suddenly had come true.

When we appeared before the audience it continued to come true. The bigot turned his wit on himself for his bigotry and on all other southerners, who, like himself, couldn't adjust to changing times. I think that he did more to undermine prejudice and to make it seem ridiculous that day than I and my supporters did.

I believe that if we will only fasten our faith on the power of love, and know that as love glows in us so does it glow in the living soul of every man, we can say to the mountain of prejudice, "Remove hence!" and it will remove, and nothing will be impossible to us.

§11 William Lloyd Imes

William Lloyd Imes's biography appears at the introduction of his October 5, 1954 address to alumni at Lincoln University. In the following sermon, Reverend Imes engages in the common practice of celebrating Abraham Lincoln's birthday as part of a life with political and divine meaning. Imes begins his Lincoln Day sermon by identifying two men separated in life by thousands of years but drawn inexorably together by their common name and by their unflinching duty to God. His understanding of Abraham Lincoln's ethical conduct was that the Civil War president led a life in obedience to God. Perhaps more importantly, Lincoln had "the sense of being sent of God." Imes offers a brief biography of Lincoln, informed by Dr. John D. Long's *The Life of Lincoln*, in which key events are but manifestations of a divine will working outs its details. That will finds its full rhetorical expression and culmination in Lincoln's devotion to biblical study. The climactic moment in Imes's sermon is the "Slave Question" and Lincoln's "righteousness" in handling it. "Good politics" could also be "good morals," notes Imes, such that even the politically expedient Emancipation Proclamation did not make "his act any less decent, or righteous, or Christ-like in its dealing with his fellow-men."

––––––––

Abraham Then, and Now: Religion and the Pioneer
First Presbyterian Church, Hammonds Port, New York
February 14, 1955

"By faith, Abraham, went out, not knowing whither he went."
Letter to the Hebrews, 11:8

"Abe was the son of pioneers. He did not live in the backwoods, but in the front woods. It is always the more vigorous people who march in advance of the rest."
John D. Long, in *Life of Lincoln*, p. 35.

One does not need an unduly long stretch of imagination to envision the parallel between the ancient Abraham of our Bible and the modern Abraham of our now historic nineteenth century America. Both were pioneers in every sense of the world. They were plain, simple men first of all, and because of that they became great men! No man is great merely by force of circumstances alone; there must be in him the great desire to be of service to the age in which he lives. And one's greatness is surely not a thing to be grasped like a prize; it is rather an opportunity, like the alluring light of a far-off but certain beacon, which holds one steady and true on his course, until the harbor is attained.

The ancient Abraham was called the father of the faithful. He believed humbly and utterly in God. He came out of an externally great civilization; Ur of the Chaldees was a centre of culture in its day. Not quite like that in external surroundings was the scene of our modern Abraham's emergence, but, in its essential and spiritual basis, it was, nevertheless, a background of far more than log cabin days, and frontier hardships. Abraham Lincoln, by the grace of God, and by the dint of his hardy life and pioneer ancestry, came of the best stock of this new world, regardless of race. We sometimes look with condescension upon his birth and upbringing. We ought to look with real pride upon his beginnings. Lowly as they were, they were the matrix of the new world. And there is where all greatness starts, whether in palace or in hut. A world of divine discontent is the necessary world for those who would fulfill God's destiny for humankind. A Ruskin might have the comforts of a home of wealth and utmost cultural opportunity, yet spiritually it became a frontier beyond which its hero ever was wont to go forth. A Lincoln might have that humble cabin in Knob Creek Valley in Kentucky for his apparently negligible chance in making life worthwhile, yet that same spirit of restless devotion to something far beyond the common and the material drove him resistlessly forth. "There was a man sent from God whose name was John," sings our most poetically gifted writer of the New Testament, and well may we paraphrase, "There were two Abrahams sent from God, one from Ur, millennia before Christ, and the other from Knob Creek, millennia after Christ." And every man or woman who has sought to fulfill his life thoroughly and well, is by that same token sent from God. Indeed, true religion is the acceptance of this task and commission—that one has the sense of being sent of God.

There are many lives of Lincoln. What figure in all American history is more attractive than this? Small wonder that from the exhaustive records of Nicolay and Hay, Lamon and Herndon, down to comparatively recent works like the very readable and instructive *Life of Lincoln* by the late Dr. John D. Long, from which one of our texts is taken, we have all possible access to a great mass of detail, interpretation, and insight into the character of this most widely-known, and most sincerely loved of all Americans. Not even the "Father of his country," the renowned Washington, can begin to compare with the sheer loveableness of him whom we delight to call "Savior of his country," Lincoln.

Our biographer, Dr. Long is not content to give mere anecdotes of the great Lincoln. Those would be attractive and interesting enough in themselves, but they are merely the scaffolding upon which we follow and work with the builder until he reveals what God has wrought in the architecture of human life. Now we see our hero in his Kentucky cabin, then in his new Indiana home, his young manhood strength vying with other backwoodsmen. Now we see the grief of the family of Thomas Lincoln when Nancy Hanks, that lovely character, was laid to rest in a rude frontier burial ground; then later we see Abe and the others fending for themselves while our hero becomes ferryman on the Ohio River, storekeeper, militiaman, postmaster at New Salem in Illinois, politician and man of affairs, never ashamed of his humble beginnings and never afraid to help the lowliest folk like himself. If ever there was a man who took the deepest concern in human beings, and lived life to the full in that regard, surely that man was honest Abe.

His sense of humor is not only droll and inimitable; it is so full of that plain earthiness and common mother-wit that it compels our admiration. Faced with his own utter ignorance of military tactics when he enlisted in the Black Hawk exploit, he came to a turnstile when drilling a company of men needing to get through. "Fall out, and then fall in again on the other side," was the command which was military nonsense, of course, but the grandest of common sense. Any one except a man of real humility and courage like Abe would have let his being a captain in that frontier outfit go straight to his head. But he confessed that he was not only ignorant of soldierly practice, but that he actually in all that campaign had never even seen a battle or engagement of any sort! Fancy the pompous individual who would have told embellished tales of their imagined heroism: Think of all the lesser men who would have used that chance to gain some cheap favor for their own advancement! In all this, as in every part of his career, Lincoln measured himself by the average needs and aspirations of all his fellows. He had no need to make himself great; he *was* great! Well did he say, "God must have loved the common people, for he made so many of them." And he was never ashamed to consider himself among those common people!

Let us turn now to that insistent call of God which is the prelude to every great event in human history. I refer to Lincoln's deepest concern with books; not of course merely with his pitifully few volumes in his own library, but with that world of the spirit which is manifest physically in documents that we call books, because they embody the finest strivings of humanity to know the ultimate values of life—the things that really count. From his boyhood up Lincoln had always loved learning. And he knew that one of the sure pathways to learning was by the method of reading. Fortunately had he possessed some of the trivialities among books which masquerade as literature in our day, I doubt if he would have given much heed to them. Here was rather his choice: when he knew he was interested in the law, he chose Blackstone, and borrowed his books from his more fortunate neighbors and friends, when unable to buy them; when he saw the excellence of the English style of some others, he steeped his mind in Shakespeare, and read with avidity what that great master had to say of human nature; and who of us has any doubt where he got his great sense of moral idealism, and his undeniable faith in a "power that makes for righteousness." Well, you and I know full well that the Bible was his great source of inspiration here, and anyone who dares to doubt this needs only to turn to his great state papers again and again to note the richness of biblical allusions and parallels. To argue here would be to weaken the point and indeed is unnecessary. The Bible is, whatever its hostile critics may say, the foundation of our best literary style, and of our moral sense of values. "Young man, sell your bed and buy books!" said a great Scottish preacher in the last generation, and well did he voice that which Lincoln and all other great men have done. They literally sold their ease and sloth and replaced it with the hard work of learning. No easy road is this, but it is veritably the King's Highway to the greatest ends of life.

Politics and the Slave Question formed the next great part of Lincoln's career. Now, many biographers and historians have taken quite the natural path, the line of least resistance here. They have tried to explain Lincoln as merely one more man of Whiggish persuasion, with a bit more humanity than was to be expected by one of that party, in that he dared to oppose slavery. But you cannot so explain our hero satisfactorily. Fortunately, Dr. Long does not belong to that group of arm-chair biographers who cannot see beneath the surface. He shows clearly, with ample illustrations, the method and the motive of Abraham Lincoln of Illinois in attacking what was the monumental struggle of that day: *the political character of the slave-power*. He saw its determination to whip the North into line, even though

the mercantile North had no economic interest in slavery, and only tolerated it because it was busy with its industry and finance, and wished to
keep on as good terms with the feudal agrarianism of the South as possible. Less astute politicians than he could not and did not see this point.
Lincoln not only saw it, but used his insight into the desperate character
of this situation to explain it in such political terms that he made his adversaries not only appear ridiculous, but actually inhuman. The climax of
this came in the so-called Lincoln-Douglas debates, which set all the Mid-
West of that day agog with excitement. Bent on pinning his pro-slavery
opponent down with an unanswerable argument, a dilemma on which he
must impale himself whichever horn he took, Lincoln compelled Douglass
to admit that he (Douglas) would allow the settlers of any new territory
to decide as to whether theirs should be free or slave territory before such
a territory should be organized into statehood. Here was master-strategy,
and having been completely routed in this conflict, Douglass, whose littleness was unfortunately as much of mind as body (he was known familiarly
as "The Little Giant") faded into obscurity, and is only remembered today
because of his connection with the great Savior of our nation.

One cannot tell a man's life in terms of his public career alone. We are
measured by the quieter areas in which we live just as much as by all the
pomp and circumstances that may be our lot. We well know that Lincoln
himself did not care for the glory that surrounds public life, and the
apparently necessary glamour that lights up the scene of men and affairs.
Accordingly, even when his public office career began in Illinois, first as
State Legislator, then later as national congressman, he shunned as much of
this artificial life as he could. Mrs. Lincoln, that fiery dark-haired Southern
beauty, who made him a devoted wife in spite of the variance in their dis-
positions, had a hard time to get her incurably domestic companion to put
on any style at all; the great politician preferred to lie on his back in their
library in Springfield, and prop his long stilts of legs up the back of the
nearest chair. What a cheerful and homely scene, even if it did vex Mary

Lincoln saw exactly what all great souls have ever seen: that righteousness in dealing with public questions is the best policy, and from the days
of Abraham of Ur with the Lot and Sodom question, or of Paul the Apostle
and the Gentile question, down to the mid-nineteenth century America
and the slave-power question, there is no road of expediency or compromise with wrong that can possibly win more than passing favor. The side of
righteousness and human justice, whether to Gentile, or Jew, to Negro or
Aryan is one eternal matter in the hands of God, and he who fights against
honor and justice to any of God's children, must inevitably come against
God Himself. To Lincoln this course was good politics, and thank God, it
is always good morals.

Todd Lincoln! Or one cannot help with a smile [to] recall Lincoln's dialog with the Springfield ice-man who served them; it appears that this vendor had been scolded by Mrs. Lincoln, and declared to Mr. Lincoln that he wouldn't stand for it and was going to quit:

"Why, man," Lincoln drawled, "is that all she did? Why she's been scolding me for the last ten years, and I ain't quit her yet."

Such bites of personal life are infinitely precious, for they reveal the true gold of character beneath the surface of an outward reticent life, and they show why he was the great man, who, when destiny and duty called in thundering tones, was able to answer clearly and unafraid. The long and lanky man who ambled down the streets of that mid-western town in its horse-and-buggy days was as much at home when taking his little son by the hand, as he was when mounting the platform at his inaugural, or telling with unforgettable pathos and wisdom the lesson of the Gettysburg battlefield.

All in all, it was a magnificent life! And strangely enough, even if truly enough, its climax came in this personal relationship which he carried out into his gigantic task of dealing with the war-torn nation that was split on both the questions of the slave-power and of state-sovereignty. President Lincoln dealt with *all* the nation, both its loyal part, and its misguided and disloyal part, with the tolerant kindness that was intensely personal. And if Southerners who may grow angry at this charge of mine think I am belittling them, let them know that I too, am a Southerner by birth, and Lincoln, himself, was nothing if not a Southerner! In this area of controversy, also, comes the much-mooted question as to whether Lincoln really intended to free the slaves, or whether he would have kept the slave in chains if he could have kept the nation united without such a measure as the Emancipation Proclamation. Well, what if the answer is yes? Lincoln did say that the emancipation of the slave was a war measure, and was a political measure determined to insure the unity of the nation! Does that make it any the less an act of heroism? If his bold stroke of undeniable genius did have in it a large amount of political sagacity and cleverness, does that make his act any less decent, or righteous, or Christlike in its dealing with the fellow-men? Surely, the answer here is "No."

From that moment on, the moment of his supreme decision, our modern Abraham trod his wine-press alone, but for the presence of One who walked with his ancient and shadowy prototype who dared to venture forth from Ur, and dared later to pray for an unrepentant Sodom; One walked with Him who trod the lonely way to Golgotha when his own received him not. After his enemies had done their worst, and the assassins bullet had found its mark, a worldly-wise politician made a sentimental remark by the Emancipator's bedside, "Now he belongs to the ages," and that was but a partial truth. He always belonged to the ages! He never belonged to the pettiness and pretense of any time or system or party. He belonged and belongs with all who have ever dared to be pilgrims of truth, and forerunners of the ever-coming Kingdom of God's grace in Christ.

§12 Dr. James Hudson

James Hudson was born in 1904 in Birmingham, Alabama. He met with misfortune at the tender age of seven when he was injured in a playground accident. The general lack of access to medical care for African Americans caused him unnecessarily to lose an arm. At 17 he attended Morehouse College in Atlanta, graduating in 1926. Upon graduation, he was ordained as a minister and then subsequently attended the Colgate-Rochester School of Religion, receiving his divinity degree in 1931. Reverend Hudson worked as a chaplain in Baker, Louisiana, at Leland College until 1946 when he attended Boston University earning a doctoral degree focusing on civil disobedience. He moved to Tallahassee where he joined the faculty at Florida Agricultural and Mechanical University (FAMU) as the chaplain. Hudson created FAMU's department of philosophy and religion the following year. Throughout his time in Tallahassee, Hudson worked closely with Reverend Charles Kenzie Steele, a close friend of his; the two worked on a wide variety of civil rights protests and boycotts in Tallahassee. Hudson remained active in the community even after his retirement from FAMU in 1973. He died in 1980, a month after the death of Reverend Steele. His papers are housed at Florida A&M University in Tallahassee, Florida.

Reverend Hudson participated enthusiastically in the civil rights struggles in Tallahassee throughout the 1950s and 1960s. His most notable involvement was his organizational work during the Tallahassee bus boycott. The impetus for the boycott dates to May 26, 1956 with the arrest of two FAMU students, Wilhelmina Jakes and Carrie Paterson. Similar to the Montgomery bus boycott, then in its six month, a car pool system worked so well that the city passed a law making it illegal. Hudson went to jail for his role even as FAMU president George W. Gore, Jr. urged students and faculty not to participate. Also like Montgomery, the leaders of the bus boycott created a new organization, the Inter Civic Council (ICC), an organization born in the black church. Hudson, Steele, and others did much to draw attention to the plight of African Americans in Florida's capital. City by city such work created and sustained the civil rights movement.

In this brief address on world racial brotherhood, "the essence of the teachings of Jesus," Dr. Hudson recommends "four simple routes": recognizing differences to the extent of seeing God's plan in diversity; acknowledging the contributions and achievements of others and even sharing those achievements across racial lines; recognition of the interdependence of humankind; and practicing the golden rule of doing unto others as you would have them do unto you. "When each man becomes a brother," Hudson closes, the "cruelty of the world will surely end."

Toward World Brotherhood

February 26, 1955

Radclyffe Hall, author of *The Well of Loneliness*, makes the following statement:

> "There is something that mankind can never destroy in spite of an un-reasoning will to destruction, and this is its own idealism, that integral part of its very being. The aging and cynical may make wars, but the young and the idealistic must fight them, and thus there are bound to come quick reactions, blind impulses not always comprehended. Men will curse as they kill, yet accomplish deeds of self-sacrifice, giving their lives for others; poets will write with their pens dipped in blood, yet will not write of death but of life eternal; strong and courteous friendships will be born, to endure in the face of enmity and destruction. And so persistent is this urge to the ideal, above all in the presence of great di-saster, that mankind, the willful destroyer of beauty, must immediately strive to create new beauties lest it perish from its own desolation."

I cite this passage because I think it expresses so beautifully the apparent incompatibility between man's ideals on the one hand, and his actions, on the other.

The ideal of Brotherhood is a Christian ideal. It represents the es-sence of the teachings of Jesus. On every turn Jesus was teaching this sim-ple ideal. "Who is my neighbor?" Jesus answers with the parable of the Good Samaritan. "What? You a Jew, and you ask me for a drink—me, a Samaritan! The Jews have nothing to do with each other." Jesus responded with the offer of the "living water of life." Listen to this clarification of the Law and the Prophets: "Whatsoever ye would that men do unto you, do ye likewise unto them."

Let us suggest four simple routes toward the Christian ideal of Brotherhood—steps which individuals, races, or nations can take with as-surance that their lives are directed toward a Christian ideal: this ideal of Brotherhood.

A first step toward World Brotherhood is the recognition of the fact of differences in the scheme of things. All about us, everywhere we see in the Divine plan sharp and emphatic differences. We see beauty evolve from contrast—the red rose deepening in hue when placed against a foliage of green leaves; the melody of a great hymn swelling from the blending of dif-ferent voices—the soprano, the tenor, the contralto, and the bass.

If we are to move toward World Brotherhood we must attempt to rec-ognize, to respect, and make the world safe for differences. This means that we must be tolerant—not just to tolerate, but an active effort to let others be themselves, the positive and cordial effort to understand another's beliefs, practices and habits without necessarily sharing or accepting them. We must be willing to accept another for what he is and as he is. We must seek that peace of mind which enables us to live and to be fit to live with.

A second step toward World Brotherhood is the recognition of the contributions and achievements of others. The late Dr. James Weldon Johnson suggested a very practical way of bettering Negro-White relationships. He suggested that if each Negro, through conversation and personal letters, kept before his White friends the contributions of the Negro to America that the White may begin to have a greater appreciation of the Negro.

Let us take pride not in a false assumption of superiority to any other people but in our friendly knowledge of all the other peoples of the world.

A third step in the direction of World Brotherhood is a recognition of the interdependence of man.

The Rev. Mr. Carlton Lee, who was our Religious Emphasis Week Speaker, told a story of Boss Ed Crump of Memphis. Mr. Crump wanted to clean up the city. He decided to go to a woman's club to accomplish the job. The women accepted the responsibility. They planted flowers; put on a campaign to see that garbage pails were well covered. The campaign was a success. Then the group came to Mr. Crump to report, one woman was selected to report. She said to him: "Mr. Crump, we have cleaned up and beautified the city. We have gotten rid of all the flies except the colored flies."

Here is a picture of the spectacle of man's action. Flies have no respect for race, or nation or creed. These women overlooked the fact that these very colored flies may bring diseased germs from the colored section of the city to the white section. The beauty and sanitation of Memphis may include the colored flies. I am my brother's keeper. The condition of my neighbor's home is a determining factor in the value of mine.

A fourth and final step toward the Christian Ideal of Brotherhood is a profound belief in, and, a determined will to practice the Golden Rule. This simply means to love all men. The Greeks had three words for the word love. Eros, meaning sensual lust; our word erotic comes from this word. Philia, meaning intimate affection or brotherly love, the word source of the name of the city of Philadelphia, the city of brotherly love. The third and noblest word is agape. This means understanding, redeeming, creative and good will. "Whatsoever ye would that men do unto you, even so do ye unto them." "Love your enemies." Look upon all men, near and far, as sons of God, to practice understanding and creative good will to all men as human beings—that is the Christian Ideal toward which we must move.

In the words of Governor Thomas E. Dewey, "To recognize that any infringement on the rights of any is an infringement on the rights of all"—that is a basic condition of World Brotherhood. To accept another as myself, to accept him as he is and for what he is—that is Brotherhood. To recognize the basic human needs in all men and to render unto them the same condition I want for myself—that is Brotherhood. To give to others the rights and respect I want for myself; to respect all people—that is Brotherhood. Brotherhood is personal; it involves attitudes, how we feel toward others; it involves action, how we act in relation to others—that is Brotherhood.

"America, America. God shed his grace on Thee, and crown thy good with Brotherhood from sea to shining sea."

When man sees man just as a man and not his skin, creed, or color Justice will be given to every man as you would a brother. The blood that was spilled on the battlefield has just one common color. The cruelty of the world will surely end when each man becomes a brother.

§13 Mary McLeod Bethune

Mary McLeod Bethune's biography appears in the introduction to her speech of June 11, 1954. In the following speech, Spiritual Rearmament, given less than two months before her death, an existential Bethune proves the importance of appealing to those who seem, in retrospect, under-addressed within the civil rights movement—women. This is a vital call to action that acknowledges women as able and necessary to the cause of desegregation, claiming the only path towards stable future generations to come requires proper use of the God-given talents of women as a collective force. Specifically she names three tasks: education (soul revival sans the tempting lure of materialism); looking to God so he may provide a prudential purpose, hence provoking action and leadership in the community; and finally living acceptingly and harmoniously with all people. She appeals to both sexes, however, when she claims the solution to the inclusive, universal want of purpose within identity can be found only through heavenly means. Her consistent, driving confidence in their impending success through God's able-bodied masses uniquely empowers this speech. Bethune's is a quintessentially American confidence as she excoriates "an outstanding churchman" for urging the preservation of "racial heritage." Bethune thunders: "What racial heritage do we have other than that which belongs to every American? For we are Americans."

———

Spiritual Rearmament
Narcissus Literary Club, Dothan, Alabama
March 20, 1955

Young women like you are a great inspiration to me. When I look upon you, my heart warms with feelings of pride and joy, and then I am grateful that as I lay down the torch of work and achievement, there are strong ones like you to take it up and blaze new and better trails than I have been able to do. Another very surging thought possesses me as I think about you. You are a mighty potential. Oh what can God do with all of your loves, your faiths, your courage, your zeal, your spiritual, moral and mental energies, your powers of thought and achievement, your all. He would soon re-arm the entire world with those armors of strength and usefulness that would hasten the kingdom upon the earth.

And as we stand today upon the threshold of a new world order, think of what your opportunity *is*—to be ambassadors of a true and workable plan for human brotherhood and world peace.

> "Be strong! Say not the days are evil,
> Whose to blame, and fold your hands in acquiesce.
> O Shame!
> Stand up, speak out and bravely,
> In God's Name,
> Be Strong!
> Be Strong! It matters not how deep entrenched
> the wrong,
> How hard the battle goes,
> The day how long.
> Faint not! Fight on!
> Tomorrow comes the song,
> Be strong!

Even as we repeat those marvelous words, we know that the saying of them is not sufficient. They have a martial air, and they are inspiring. They give us the fight spirit. But they pour out a challenge which calls for action. It is my deep desire and daily prayer that I may awaken women, strong women, efficient, capable women to shoulder the tasks that must be shouldered if we are to usher in a new day for our children and our children's children.

The first task—after conviction—is to become informed. I speak to you of spiritual re-armament. We have spent our time and our money on material things. We have fattened our bodies and filled our homes with one luxury and then another. All the while we have never taken time to give our souls a feast. Our inner selves are weak and flabby and undeveloped. We must become strong on the inside. We begin by reading and studying to know the truth—the truth that shall free us from the bondages that still hold us fast. There is at Tuskegee Institute a great monument to Booker

T. Washington. It shows that devoted leader pulling away the veil of ignorance from the face of his people. Ignorance still lurks around us and hinders our progress. We must *study* to show ourselves approved for the opportunities we hope to grasp. Our spiritual re-armament begins with the glowing truths that make us free. We are free to find ways of showing to all people that God is revealing to man, how those things which some have tried to label as racial traits and peculiarities, are human traits and are common to mankind regardless of race or color or creed.

I heard an outstanding churchman plead with a group a few weeks ago, asking them to preserve their racial heritage and their simple philosophies. What racial heritage do we have other than that which belongs to every American? For we are Americans. But how do you know? What do you propose to say out of the depths of unfed, dwarf-like souls about what makes your American heritage, except as you read and study and know what is true and listen to the voice of God, so that He may reveal unto you the ways of speaking and acting and thinking which will make you effective workmen for His cause in this world? It is one thing to pray, "Thy kingdom come on earth" and it is another thing to get out and bring in the kingdom through the courage of conviction, the knowledge of people, the ability to speak fearlessly and inspiringly to that end.

The second great task is that you go to God for the endowment of yourselves that you may become active as leaven in the mass of people who seek leadership and guidance. Frank Buchman, a great prophet of our times, has said that "The lesson the world most needs is the art of listening to God." He remembers an incident in his life which impressed this need on his mind. A general once sent him a postcard, during an international conference, with the picture of a man on it. The thought below was this, "God gave a man two ears and one mouth. Why don't you listen twice as much as you talk?" Here is the secret. God's endowment for us comes through listening to Him and hearing Him speak to us so that His guidance enriches us and fills us with a purpose and the glowing experiences which will help us to make that purpose a reality. As we face the issues of desegregation and the many new relationships involved, you and I are conscious for the need of a rich spiritual endowment that will govern our wills and control our thoughts and actions so that they may be channeled into the right ways.

The third great task is spreading fellowship, goodwill and social acceptance, among people. I am always happy that God has given me such a wonderful love for people. I enjoy hearing them tell of their experiences. I like to be with them in a variety of experiences. "The fellowship of kindred souls" *is* wonderful. Through people we are able to see and to know God better. Because this world is made up of such a wonderful variety of people, we must learn the use of our spiritual powers in helping people to get along with each other and helping them to use the wonders of God's world creatively and for the good of mankind rather than for his destruction and downfall. Where tensions exist between groups, or frustrations destroy goodwill between persons, the very structure of our human family is undermined. When these doubtful conditions destroy our faith in each other we lose the very powers that make us human beings capable of God's endowment and His guidance. How beautiful a thing it is for people to dwell together in unity!

The spread of our spiritual growth goes from breast to breast and from group to group. In order that we may be ready to assume our roles when the time comes, young women and young men, older women and older men should be meeting together in small groups all around our wonderful southland, sharing and understanding and building up the bridges and securing the relationships that will give success to our efforts. Now is the time to do this. We are obligated to our generation to build the kinds of mutual respect among us that will mean human brotherhood. We will recognize in others the precious qualities which we love and enjoy. We will become tolerant of weakness in others because we feel weakness in ourselves. We will enjoy the use of our talents in the unfolding of our creative selves together. We will be humble in the awe we feel as we see deep meanings revealed and merit achieved and creative growth demonstrated. Those things which are destructive, hateful and shameful to the realization of mankind's miracle powers will be set aside and we will lay the firm foundations of freedom, truth, love and mutual understanding.

§14 Roy Wilkins

Roy Wilkins was born August 30, 1901 in St. Louis, Missouri. Throughout his childhood, Wilkins lived in a largely integrated section of St. Paul, Minnesota; most of his playmates, close friends, and teachers were white. His experiences growing up in an integrated society allowed him to see the positive effects of integration. While attending the University of Minnesota, Wilkins's interest in advocacy led him to pursue an education in journalism and community affairs. While matriculating, Wilkins served as a secretary with a local chapter of the National Association for the Advancement of Colored People (NAACP). Graduating with a bachelor's degree in sociology in 1923, Wilkins began his career as a reporter and editor, first with Minnesota papers and later with the *Kansas City Call*.

Not long after marrying Aminda Badeau in 1934, he was appointed editor of the NAACP's national magazine, *The Crisis;* he replaced the legendary W. E. B. DuBois. While working with the NAACP, Wilkins organized a boycott of segregated theaters and advocated nonviolent political action to achieve equal rights for

African Americans. Aside from his work with the NAACP, Wilkins also worked as a consultant for the War Department on the subjects of training and placement of African Americans in the military. In 1949, after being appointed acting secretary of the NAACP, Wilkins served as chairman of the National Emergency Civil Rights Mobilization. Throughout his career as a civil rights activist, Wilkins lobbied for federal antilynching laws, pushed the government to desegregate military facilities, and fought to eliminate employment discrimination. Because of his ceaseless dedication, Wilkins was often referred to as the "Senior Statesman of the Civil Rights Movement," or more simply as "Mr. Civil Rights." He was awarded the U.S. Medal of Freedom in 1968 and the Joseph Prize for Human Rights in 1975 for his many achievements for civil rights. He retired from the NAACP in 1977. Roy Wilkins died on September 9, 1981 at the age of 80. Wilkins's papers are housed at the Library of Congress and at Rust College in Holly Springs, Mississippi.

As vice-president of the Regional Council of Negro Leadership and an NAACP activist, the Reverend George W. Lee, a 52-year old clergyman from Belzoni, Mississippi was a marked man. Called by some as a "tan-skinned, stumpy spell binder," Lee had been urging his fellow black Mississippians to register to vote— this despite death threats and intimidation from local White Citizens' Councils. On the night of May 7, 1955, driving alone in Belzoni, a convertible approached Lee's car from behind. Shots were fired. Despite buckshot taking off the lower half of his face, Lee managed to pull himself from the wreckage. He died on the way to the hospital. The following day, the Jackson *Clarion-Ledger* titled its article on Lee's death, "Negro Leader Dies in Odd Accident."

That Roy Wilkins came to Belzoni for Lee's memorial meeting says a great deal about the importance of the minister's work; as head of the largest black civil rights organization in the country, Wilkins's presence was much in demand. In addition to eulogizing Lee for his civil rights activism, Wilkins uses the occasion for a lengthy discussion of voting in Mississippi. What was the meaning of a mere 20,000 registered Negro voters? "It means that Mississippi does not have a government system that gives representation to all the people, only to a small part of them."

Wilkins also addresses the issue of segregation in public schools and deftly lists several states, such as Missouri and Kansas, in which school integration is working quite well. Throughout his speech, Wilkins lists the accomplishments of the NAACP and the reasons why the organization is such a powerful force in the civil rights movement. Wilkins prophesies correctly that the murder of Rev. George W. Lee might never be solved. To date, no one has ever been indicted. So, too, Wilkins prophesies about Mississippi's future: in August, Brookhaven's Lamar Smith would be gunned down on the courthouse lawn; two weeks later, Emmett Till would be tortured and killed. He closes the speech by advising his audience that the road ahead to peaceful relations between whites and blacks will be a difficult one, but through hard work, faith, and courage, the prize is attainable.

Memorial Meeting for Rev. George W. Lee of Belzoni, Shot and Killed by Persons Unknown on May 7, 1955

Belzoni, Mississippi
May 22, 1955

In a sense, I suppose, I am returning to Mississippi, for although it is not my native state, my father and mother were born here, in Holly Springs. My father left with his bride as soon as he was married and went to St. Louis, where I was born. He never told me why he left, but I can guess. I came here in 1932 for the NAACP, dressed as a laborer, to investigate working conditions on the levee-building project and roamed along the river north from Greenville to Friar's Point and Tunica. I returned in 1953 and spoke for our state meeting of the NAACP at Indianola.

It was not too good then, but at least we did not have the White Councils that we have today. One daily paper has called them "manicured Ku Klux Klans." Hodding Carter, the Greenville editor, wrote an article for *Look* Magazine in which he said they "could get out of hand," and apparently from what happened on May 7, they have. That great Southern daily paper, the Montgomery, Alabama *Advertiser*, has called the White Council program "economic thuggery."

Its victims are Negro Americans who simply want what other men want and who lawfully try to get it. The White Councils are trying to turn back the clock, to make the seas be still, to command the tides of the ocean not to come in to the shore. They will fail. Such efforts have always failed. "Time marches on" is a slogan, but it is also true. No man or men, not even the government of Mississippi, can hold it back.

Meanwhile we have troubles, heartache, despair, death, and murder. In this hour I am reminded of David's supplication to the Lord in the 143rd Psalm, third verse: "For the enemy hath persecuted my soul; he hath smitten my life down to the ground; he hath made me dwell in darkness, as those that have been long dead." " . . . he hath smitten my life down to the ground . . . "

The life of George W. Lee was "smitten down to the ground" and with it we were smitten down, each one of us, in Mississippi and out of it. We—all of us—are "made to dwell in darkness," a darkness similar to that which covers "those that have been long dead."

We pay tribute to a man today, a good citizen, a minister of the church, one who believed not only in the life hereafter, but the life here. Some ministers, you know, always talk about what we will have in heaven. Reverend Lee believed in heaven, too, but he believed that all God's children should have something down here on this earth as well.

What did he believe we should have? Well, knowing that in the sight of God, all men are equal, he believed in equality here on earth, even here in Mississippi. He wanted for himself and his people the same things that all other people have.

He believed we should not only pray for this equality, but work for it. He joined the National Association for the Advancement of Colored People because our Association works for equality of opportunity, because it does not believe prejudice is right, because it does not believe in discrimination and segregation.

This is the kind of minister every minister should be. He should be a man who helps his people with their burdens in this life and does not confine himself to telling them to be patient and wait for what is coming in the "by and by."

Reverend Lee did not just tell the people what they ought to do. He gave them an example: he did these things himself. He fought for equality and first-class citizenship himself, and he then asked them to follow him.

Reverend Lee was shot because he thought he ought to vote just like other Americans. Someone threatened him and told him he should withdraw his name from the registration lists. He refused to do this because he was an American and Americans have the right to vote.

The people who try to keep Negroes from voting forget that Americans have always fought for the right to vote. The thirteen colonies fought the Revolutionary War and won their freedom from England because they did not want to be taxed without representation in the English Parliament that passed the tax laws.

You remember the Boston Tea Party when the Americans dumped the tea in Boston Harbor because of the tax. Today in Mississippi, Negro citizens are being taxed without representation. They want to vote on the men who are elected to the legislature. They want to vote on the men elected to Congress. They want to vote on the candidates for Governor and other state and local offices.

There is nothing wrong about this. It is real Americanism. The founders of our country set up a nation to be governed by the consent of the people. When you seek to have a voice in the government that makes the laws by which you live, you are being 100 percent American.

In Mississippi there is a real reason for your effort to vote. The 1950 census shows the total population of the state as 2,178,914, of which 1,188,429 were white and 990,354 were colored. The white margin was only 198,075. Negroes are very close to being half the population, but I don't have to tell you that they get very much less than half the benefits. Although there were 710,000 whites of voting age and 497,000 Negroes, only 285,000 votes were cast in the 1952 election. How many of these were Negro we do not know, but we do know that Negro registration was only about 20,000. So, Negroes had practically no vote of consequence in 1952, and now they are trying to take even that little from you.

To see how the Mississippi system works let us compare one district here with one district in California in the election of a Congressman. In your first district here, where Representative Thomas Abernethy was elected, the population is 365,000. In the first district in California, where Representative Hubert B. Scudder was elected, the population is also 365,000.

But only 51,600 votes were cast in Abernethy's district, whereas 175,200 votes were cast in Scudder's district. Three and one-half times as many people voted in the California district as voted in your first district here. Other examples could be cited from Michigan, Illinois, Ohio and other states, all showing the same thing.

What does it mean? It means that Mississippi does not have a government system that gives representation to all the people, only to a small part of them. It means that not only Negroes, but tens of thousands of whites are prevented from voting. What our forefathers fought for in the Revolutionary War has not yet come to pass in Mississippi.

How is this made to work, especially as far as Negroes are concerned? Well, it works first of all through threats and terror, and even murder—as in the case of Reverend Lee. Negroes are "persuaded" not to pay their poll tax or to register. Or they are "persuaded" to tear up their poll tax receipts or to remove their names from the registration lists. Reverend Lee refused to be "persuaded," so he is dead.

Then they use a registration system which has some tests for citizens. You have to fill out a blank and explain what a section of the state constitution means. After you do that you are required to write out a statement (and I read here from the printed registration form) "a statement setting forth your understanding of the duties and obligations of citizenship under a constitutional form of government."

That is the one. That is the catch-all. If you get by that one to the satisfaction of the registrar you not only can vote, but you are a genius.

But even this does not satisfy some people. No sooner had Governor White signed the bill than there was clamor for its repeal. The head of the registrar's organization is quoted by a Jackson daily paper as saying that the new system made it hard to explain—with a written record in the files—why a Negro was disqualified and a white man passed. "There are," he is reported as saying, "some things you don't want known."

These are methods we condemn, not only because of what they do to us as a group, but because of what they do to the American democratic system. America was not founded to permit one little group to rule over the rest of the people—ordering them around, kicking them around, and shooting them down. Indeed, it was founded to get rid of just that, because that was the system in Europe from which the First Americans ran away and came to a new land.

The people who kick Negroes around are kicking America around.

At the present time, of course, everyone is excited about the Supreme Court decision that racial segregation in the public school is unconstitutional. Judging from the actions of your state, no one is more excited than Mississippi. Last summer the Governor and his advisors thought they had the thing licked. They would get the Negroes together and get them to ask for "voluntary" segregation. So they got ninety Negro leaders from all over the state to come to Jackson. Mind you, these were not men and women from New York and Chicago and Detroit. They were "home grown"—from Mississippi. When they got in the room with Governor White and his committee, eighty-nine of the ninety turned thumbs down on "voluntary" segregation.

The Governor said he was "stunned." Well, my friends, he could have avoided being stunned. His advisors, black and white, gave him the wrong information. For, make no mistake about it: the vast majority of Negroes, deep down in their hearts, do not want segregated schools, or segregated anything else.

They want to be treated exactly as other groups are treated. They want the same freedom to go and come, to do, and to enjoy, that others have. We could have told the Governor, but he would not listen to us. He had to find out the hard and embarrassing way. All credit to the honesty and courage of the eighty-nine men and women who stood up and told the truth.

The truth is that most Southern white people do not know what Negroes really want because we tell them only what we think they want to hear, or what will get us by in a particular situation.

Despite this demonstration of last summer, I see in the papers that a certain Negro editor in Mississippi has asked Congressman C. C. Diggs, Jr., of Detroit, Michigan, one of our three Negro Congressmen in Washington, to sponsor a resolution having Congress recognize "voluntary segregation."

This editor is wasting his breath, his writing paper, and his postage because Congressman Diggs will not give such a resolution a first thought, much less a second one. How can any man ask his people to accept "voluntary segregation?" How can any man ask for his people any less than that which other men have? What kind of thinking is this?

We may have to endure—for a time—segregation and discrimination that is thrust upon us, but in God's name, do we have to ask for it?

We all know that segregation means inequality. We know there is no such thing as "separate but equal." As far as schools are concerned, the Supreme Court has said, "separate schools are inherently unequal." This Negro editor is trying to say that we as a race should take less than the Supreme Court says we should have.

Our Association intends to continue the campaign to implement the Court's decision. We know that if our children are to have an equal chance in this world they must have an education equal to that of other children. If they don't get it, they have lost the race of life before they even start. We believe that in spite of all the shouting, segregated schools will be abolished. We believe there are white people in Mississippi who want to see this done and that they will work to bring it about. We know that elsewhere in the South there are white people who want to obey the Supreme Court and the same must be true in Mississippi.

In Texas, Negroes and whites are going to college and junior college together without friction and in good will. In Texas there is one town which has gone ahead and sent Negro children to a white elementary school. Nothing has happened. In Arkansas Negro children and whites are going to the same high school in two towns.

Of course, you know what has happened in Missouri and Kansas and parts of Delaware and West Virginia. The schools are mixed and there has been no trouble. Also in the nation's capital. There are many signs that soon there will be desegregation in Oklahoma, Kentucky, Tennessee, and North Carolina. Also in many parts of Texas.

What has happened there can happen in Mississippi. This is part of what Reverend Lee believed in and died for: equality of opportunity for children to get the education to which they are entitled as Americans.

It will be good for children of both races to go to school together. It will be good for Negroes and it will be good for whites; it will be good for our country. One of the troubles in our relations between the races has been our lack of knowledge of each other. You can't really know people if they live on one side of town and you on the other; if they go to one school and you to another; if they attend one church and you another. You may see them every day, but you do not know them, you do not understand them.

When we misunderstand each other all sorts of trouble can develop. There is the old story that Negro children can't learn like white children. Well, they can when they get the chance. A few weeks ago the Attorney General of Virginia told the United States Supreme Court that Negro children could not learn like whites and that all white children in Virginia were smarter than the smartest Negro children.

But just last week it was announced that a Negro girl in Virginia had taken a nation-wide test for a scholarship and had come out with the highest mark!

Segregation hurts both white and colored people; it harms all our youngsters, white and black. The sooner we get rid of it the better off our nation will be. Lillian Smith, the distinguished white Georgia author, puts it this way in her book *Now is the Time:* "We know that men cannot do without each other. Animals may go it alone. Men cannot do so. Genius or retarded child or ordinary man, sick or well, rich or poor, white or colored, Westerner or Asian—however different or alike we may be, we need each other. We belong together."

We meet today not in hatred of any man or men. Our Association is not anti-white; it is pro-American. It works legally, under the United States Constitution and the laws generally. It does things in the American way. It does not advocate violence, but it does advise Negroes to stand up for their rights and work to get them in every legitimate way.

Many white people are members of the NAACP. Many more are sympathetic to its program. Right here in the South there are white people who are against segregation. There are white people who agree with the United States Supreme Court and think that segregated schools are unconstitutional and should be abolished.

We are not fighting people. We are fighting ideas—ideas that all Negroes are inferior and therefore should not have the same citizenship rights as other Americans. President Eisenhower has said America cannot have second-class citizens. We can all join him in that sentiment. What we want is first-class citizenship—all the rights and privileges that other Americans have.

I would not be honest if I told you that the way ahead is easy. It is not. I cannot tell you that you will not have difficulties, disappointments, and heartaches. You will have all of these. I cannot tell you that we can solve the Reverend Lee murder or that we will be able to bring the guilty ones to justice. You and I must demand this in every legitimate way. From here you have written your Governor. From our national office we have placed the matter before the Department of Justice in Washington. I pledge you that we shall not let up. We must use every method open to us to persuade the regular law enforcement machinery to function and uphold the law.

It is a shameful thing that a minister of the cloth should be shot down in cold blood for no crime whatsoever. The sheriff, who at first thought it was not murder, now says he is convinced it was murder. We can hope and pray that he will go on from there to find the murderers.

But regardless of the troubles along the way, one thing is certain: we shall win the prizes we desire; we shall satisfy the dreams of our fathers and the aspirations of our hearts. For our children—and all children, there will be a better world.

For the struggles ahead we will need courage and faith and work.

You can work by joining the National Association for the Advancement of Colored People. It has a 45-year record of service and accomplishment. It has state organizations in Texas, Arkansas, Oklahoma, Louisiana, Mississippi, Georgia, Alabama, North and South Carolina, Florida, and Virginia, as well as in Tennessee and Kentucky. Let no one tell you that this is a "Northern" organization of "outsiders." It is a national organization spread over the entire country and into Alaska, and it can be as strong in battle as you make it with your memberships.

We set up a state office in Jackson in January with Medgar Evers as state secretary. Dr. A. H. McCoy is state president. We expect to stay for the duration—until victory is won.

As you work you must maintain your courage and faith in the face of temporary setbacks. This crusade is not for the weak or the faint-hearted. Neither is it for the traitors, the turncoats, the Uncle Toms. From the ninth chapter of the gospel according to St. Luke, we have these words: "And Jesus said unto him, No man, having put his hand to the plough, and looking back, is fit for the kingdom of God."

Draw your strength from the righteousness of our cause and from the love of our Heavenly Father. Remember always what Paul wrote to the Galatians: "Stand fast, therefore, in the liberty wherewith Christ hath made us free, and be not entangled again with the yoke of bondage. . . Let us not be weary in well-doing: for in due season we shall reap, if we faint not."

§15 Albert D'Orlando

Albert D'Orlando was born in 1915 in Boston, Massachusetts. He received his M.Th. from Tufts University and was ordained as a Unitarian in 1945. He ministered to two small churches in New Hampshire until 1950. Upon his arrival in New Orleans that year he began to integrate his church, and continued to serve the congregation and the broader community for nearly 50 more years. Reverend D'Orlando was the epitome of what intransigent segregationists hated—a Bostonian Yankee who came south to tell others how to live their lives. He joined others to establish a Louisiana chapter of the ACLU in 1956. In 1958 he testified before the House of Representatives' Un-American Activities Committee. He used all available resources to support as many ground-breaking civil rights advances as he could, including the integration of Tulane University and public schools. He also came to the aid of children convicted under Napoleonic law for criminal anarchy following sit-ins and other peaceful protests. He routinely received death threats. Disgruntled Klansmen firebombed his home and church. In 1966 Reverend D'Orlando received the Holmes-Weatherly Award for his social activism.

After retiring from the pulpit in 1981, he remained active in various campaigns for social justice. He died on February 28, 1998 at the age of 83. He is survived by a wife and a daughter. His papers are housed at the Andover-Harvard Theological Library in Cambridge, Massachusetts.

Reverend D'Orlando is a persistent voice during the tumultuous events rolling through the apartheid South. In his sermon given just two days after the verdict in the Emmett Till murder trial, he urges members of the congregation to follow the pragmatic lead of Rabbi Feibelman, who points out the wastefulness of pooling resources to slow the inevitable march of integration. The world needs more "do-gooders," claims D'Orlando, people who willingly disturb the peace, trespass on sacred ground and assault human complacency. Jesus was a "do-gooder," as was Dorothea Dix, Albert Schweitzer, and many who fought for women's rights and suffrage for the poor. But D'Orlando warns that time is running out for the good people. A new spirit, a creative power, is needed in each of us to achieve the beloved community. Unless and until the "good people" speak out against injustices such as that of the Till verdict, the entire South will stand indicted in the court of public opinion—and with good reason.

————

Do We Still Need Do-Gooders?

Universalist Unitarian Church, New Orleans, Louisiana
September 25, 1955

This morning we are begging the question. Do we still need "do-gooders"? Do we still need people? Do we still need life?

It is not for us to say whether or not we still need people—or life—although it is within the scope of our power to deal a heavy blow to the continuity of life. But, we do believe that as long as people shall inhabit this earth there will be a need for "do-gooders." As long as people are people there will be problems to solve in human relationships; problems arising out of demands for improving the welfare of all the people, as well as those primarily affecting the well-being of groups of people. As long as this shall be true we will have need of those whose penetrating insight and wisdom enables them to see clear through to the heart of a problem, to evaluate its effect on people—on human beings—then to work with unceasing energy toward its solution.

At the very outset it must be acknowledged that not everybody can be a "do-gooder." It is not that everybody wants to be one, for if this were so then we would be so pure as not to have need for any. It is not for everybody to fall within this select circle because the qualifications are so demanding that it isn't everyman (or woman) who dares to accept the challenge.

Perhaps the chief characteristic of such a person is that he is a disturber of the peace. In almost every situation we may cite, a refusal to face facts has resulted in a kind of peaceful existence which would tend to give the impression that "God is in his Holy Temple, and all is right with the world."

Beneath that outward appearance there is human suffering awaiting some form of alleviation.

Another characteristic of the "do-gooder" is that he not only trespasses on "forbidden ground," but he commits assault and battery on human complacency. It is as though he happens upon a sign reading "Private: Do Not Enter"; but beyond the sign he sees several individuals in distress, all the while they are being watched by a large group of people who are powerless to do anything because of the sign. By committing the unpardonable sin of trespassing he offers the most devastating blow to their complacency.

What it all adds up to is that by disturbing the peace, by trespassing on forbidden ground, and by committing assault and battery on human complacency, the "do-gooder" stands as the conscience of people, who—at least in terms of human relationships—have apparently been successful in suppressing this aspect of their humanity. As we well know, people don't like to have the peace disturbed, they don't like to have anybody trespass upon their private domain, they don't like to have their complacency attacked, they don't like to have their conscience aroused.

Rabbi Julian Feibelman of Temple Sinai was recently distinguished by having been characterized as a "do-gooder." He had appeared before the School Board of this city to request that the Board give serious consideration to the formulation of a plan designed to implement the Supreme Court Decision on Segregation. In his preliminary statement given prior to the presentation of a petition signed by 179 of our citizens—many of whom are members of this church—Rabbi Feibelman questioned the propriety of appropriating public funds to defend segregation in the schools. It is now a matter of record that the school board has retained an attorney at a fee of $25,000.00 plus a $150.00 per diem fee on business taking him outside the city. Because of this it was suggested to the Board that inasmuch as everybody admits that eventually we will have integration, why not put both our public money and our collective energy to the formulation of a positive, constructive, plan by which this may be achieved in the good spirit of human cooperation.

The logic that motivates this thinking is quite clear. If we wish to build a house we cannot hope that it will blossom of its own. The house must have a foundation: but, before the foundation is prepared, *it must have a plan*. This plan is usually conceived in the mind of one who is trained to think in such terms, then it is carefully drawn to the last detail. So too, in the building of good relationships in the community: this is something that will not blossom of its own. We do not start by ignoring it: we start by acknowledging that it is anticipated as the way men must live together— then we go on to develop our plan.

In all fairness to the situation it should be pointed out that this is desired by far more of our population than the 179 who signed the petition. Rabbi Feibelman so well stated it—he was merely the spokesman for a small, informal group, that had no intention of constituting an organization. Its position was merely to suggest that serious thought be given to a pressing social matter.

What actually happened is that by virtue of opening up a subject hitherto ignored, this spokesman did disturb the peace, he did trespass on forbidden ground, he did attack the complacency of the community, and he did represent the aroused conscience of those who would adopt the ostrich technique. And so, it was said of him that he was a "do-gooder," the implication being that he had been motivated by a compassion arising out of his professional interest in religion, but that he had no real understanding of the problem he would solve. In other words, he is just an "Ivory-Towerist" who just doesn't quite know the score.

The least that can be said about this is that he is in good company: he is in a class with reformers of all time whose opposition stemmed from a frustration at being unable to cope with an aroused conscience. Sooner or later they have all become targets for terms bearing derogatory connotations. One is reminded of another term coined a little over a century ago. In 1841 Emerson observed that the history of the world had never seen such scope as at that hour. It seemed to him that every human institution was being questioned: Christianity, the laws, commerce, schools, the farm, the laboratory. The plea was for Emancipation, women's rights, public education, temperance, and universal peace. In the midst of such an exciting period Bronson Alcott came forth with his own description of the "do-gooders" who had stimulated all the activity: he called the, "*The Lord's Chore Boys.*"

It would appear that over the years we have developed two attitudes toward the "do-gooders." There is the one we have already mentioned: that they are "Ivory-Towerists" who don't know the score. The other attitude is that they ought to become affiliated with some social service agency, where their talents may be used to good advantage.

With regard to the first, there has never been a better example than that offered by the life of Jesus. Here was one who was said to have lived in an "Ivory-Tower." Because he didn't seem to understand that one shouldn't associate with sinners, he went out of his way to give them some assurance that their life was not to be wasted away. He championed the poor, the merciful, the ones who had been persecuted for righteousness sake. He rebuked the scribes and the Pharisees, and he broke with the customs that had arisen to distort the law. Make no mistake about it: he lived in an "Ivory Tower," far above the coming and the going of his community.

He occupied a vantage point from which he might view with a critical eye the constant degeneration of human relationships of the times in which he lived. Then, when he was satisfied that he understood his people and when he was satisfied that he understood himself, he became an aroused conscience; one that could not be tolerated. For 2,000 years now his teachings have continued to provide fuel for humanitarian enterprises. If the clergy—of all denominations and religions—have demonstrated that the "social gospel" may open the human mind to human needs, then it cannot be that they belong to the "Ivory Tower" mentality. They have seen it as their duty to point the way to new and significant relationships as the basis for the world they would create.

Our second attitude toward "do-gooders" would seem to suggest that social agencies of the community provide our answer to the method of solving our social problems. We have done well in our communities to organize a number of agencies whose function it is to cope with a variety of problems. The least contact with any of them reveals at once the tremendous load being carried. (Parenthetically, I might speak a word for the Community Chest, and the United Fund, which support this work. It deserves our full support in the drive scheduled to begin next week.) But, *the more basic function of social agencies is to acknowledge the existence of a social problem.* While they are all doing a Herculean job there isn't one agency that has the funds or the personnel to explore into the basic cause of the problem itself. The cause remains untouched, awaiting the amelioration of human relationships in the community.

Nevertheless, one factor must be noted. It is that "do-gooders" of the past have recognized the social problem and have attempted to reach it through various channels. Consequently, they have been treated differently according to the period in which they have lived. When Dorothea Dix discovered neglected victims of mental disorder lying chained, frozen and starved in cellars and jails she was stimulated to provide the care they needed. Nobody understood what she was doing; nobody seemed to understand the kind of care these people needed. She did this long before Freud came along to provide the scientific background to enable us all to understand. Today, psychiatry can tell us by name the emotional status of almost any among us; it can prescribe treatment for those who need it and want it. When Dorothea Dix did it in her own way, she did it out of a profound human understanding of human values, and out of a conviction that it was necessary to arouse the social conscience to a similar point of view.

When we think about the present situation and the present role of the "do-gooder," it should be no surprise to us that he has met with opposition.

This has been the reaction to the introduction of almost every new idea, which at one time may have seemed to have been quite revolutionary, but which we now take so much for granted. Indeed, we go so far as to say that these are things to which we are entitled. As James Russell Lowell reminds us in his essay on "Democracy": "Not a change for the better in our human housekeeping has ever taken place that wise and good men have not opposed it."

When Robert Raike in 1780 saw the condition of the mill children on the streets of Gloucester, in England, he organized the first Sunday School. This was opposed by many ministers, bishops, and laymen as a desecration of the Sabbath, and because the lower classes should not be taught above their station.

When Horace Mann suggested a program of Universal Public Education it was denounced as opening the way to discontent and decay. It was said that providing free education to all would cause the children of the poor to grow up lazy. Furthermore, it would be government interference in the relations of parent and child.

From time to time we have been reminded that it was Lucy Stone, Julia Ward Howe, Susan B. Anthony, and Margaret Fuller, who were among those responsible for bringing to women the rights they now enjoy. Whenever such reference is made the male members among us may have a tendency to gloat at their generosity in having granted these rights. But, what is almost entirely forgotten is how recent has been the granting of similar rights to the men themselves. A look into the more or less recent past reveals that the proponents of manhood suffrage met with an organized resistance by the forces in power.

Daniel Webster, Justice Stony, James Madison and Chief Justice Marshall all joined together to warn against the dangers of rule by "King Numbers," that is by what they described as the "speckled population of the large cities and towns, comprising . . . every kindred and tongue." They insisted that only property holders had a sense of responsibility needed for wielding political power wisely.In the words of the eminent New York jurist, Chancellor Kent, "Universal suffrage jeopardizes property and puts it into the power of the poor and the profligate to control the affluent." "I hope," he implored, that "we shall not carry desolation through all the departments of the fabric erected by our fathers."

In spite of this plea the "do-gooders" continued to arouse the public conscience to the point where suffrage was finally achieved.

The times have changed, but the times have not changed. Gains have been made, but gains have not been made. Our attitudes in human relationships have not taken a new turn. We continue to oppose the kind of social development that is inevitable, with the identical rationalizations that have been used to oppose every measure of reform through the years. Always it is said that we must hold down a segment of the population "because it is not ready for progress; because it has no sense of responsibility." *Always, our rationalization is but a feeble defense of our own vested interests.*

When I reached this point in the preparation of the sermon, word came from Sumner, Mississippi, that the jury in the Till murder case had voted for acquittal of the defendants. We ought not to let this pass without notice, particularly on an occasion when our plea is for a universal recognition of human dignity. It is not for us to re-indict the defendants, nor do we suggest that the trial was anything but fair. Nevertheless, when one reads in the newspaper the remarks uttered by the foreman of the jury, following the announcement of acquittal, then one can only conclude that there was never any serious intention—at least on the part of the jury—to bring these men to justice. When this person—speaking for the jury—can ridicule some of the witnesses, then say that important testimony was ignored as irrelevant, we are hard put to it to understand the unwritten code that takes precedence over the state law. These men have won their freedom, but the state of Mississippi has now assumed the role of defendant in the court of public opinion: a court by the way which is always in session and in which the defendant is given every opportunity to prove that his attitude has changed. It is more unfortunate that in this case it is an entire region rather than only one state which is on trial.

When we travel to different parts of the country on our summer vacations, it is with the knowledge that wherever we go we will be questioned about the South. We may not like it—you may not like it—but the simple fact is that the good people of this area are maligned by the actions of a Mississippi jury. We tell our friends that this is contrary to the human spirit expressed by the good people of the South, that the good people are a large majority of the entire population, that they too are sorry at every miscarriage of justice. And, we who live here day in and day out—we know that this is true. But, we also know that time is running out on us; that the good people must soon speak out, they must soon stand up and be counted as a demonstration of their good faith. The time is long since past when we can leave it all to the Hodding Carter's, the Lillian Smith's, the Ralph McGill's, or, on a local level, to Rabbi Feibelman. We need leaders, people who can see through to the heart of a matter, disturbers of the peace who are willing to show the way, *but we also need a new spirit in the heart of each of us.* We need an understanding of what Schweitzer defines as the "human spirit" as the basis for achieving the beloved community. Can the "human spirit" do it? Listen to the words of Schweitzer himself:

We must not underestimate its strength. Through human history this strength has made itself manifest. It is to the strength of the human mind that we owe the humanitarianism that is at the origin of all progress towards a higher way of life. When we are animated by humanitarianism we are faithful to ourselves and we are capable of creation. When the contrary state of mind takes hold of us, we are unfaithful to ourselves and a prey to errors of every kind.

How strange it is that in an age when we anticipate with bated breath the next mechanical gadget designed to make life easier, we look with cynicism at the inventions of those who would make life more meaningful; those who are animated by humanitarianism—who are faithful for all mankind and who are capable of creation. An interesting aspect of this is that the kind of opposition now expressed toward the inventors of ideas and methods in human relations was also expressed in the last century toward many of the mechanical inventions typical of that period.Until men learned to accept the idea of invention, the inventors were looked upon as men who lived in an "Ivory Tower"; idealists who were somewhat removed from reality. During this present century we have learned to relax our attitudes in this direction; nay, we are anxious to know about the next remarkable discovery. And just when it seems that discovery in one particular field has been completely exhausted, up comes another to render obsolete those of the past.

Several years ago automobile driving was made easier by the introduction of the "Hydro-matic Drive." Now there was open the possibility of driving a car without being annoyed with the necessity of shifting from one gear to another. Now, it was to be automatic; only that shifting was still required if one wished to go backward rather than forward. Just a few days ago I noticed in an advertisement sponsored by one of the major producers of automobiles, that there is a new twist on this hydromatic-drive. No longer will it be necessary to bother with a gear shift of any description.Now, one need only to press a button and to step on the accelerator.

We urge manufacturers to continue with their inventions; to bring forth cars with safety equipment, rubber fenders, shatterproof glass, and safety belts to hold us at the time of an accident. But, with all the safety equipment we demand we still refuse to come to grips with the one foremost factor in all accidents—the human being behind the wheel. It is here that a new attitude is needed; a new attitude toward one's responsibility to others who share the road. We have our federal, state, and local laws regulating the rights and responsibilities of all our citizens: from time to time we review the laws—we ask that they be written to guarantee greater safety to the individual. But, still there is needed a new attitude on the part of those who sit in the jury box when issues are at stake. It is here that a new attitude is needed toward one's responsibility to others who share the privilege of life.

Similarly, on the larger scale of human relationships; we have our social agencies, our courts, and our diplomats. But, what is desperately needed is an acceptance of those inventions brought forth by the "do-gooder"; inventions which touch the heart, and which influence the human spirit. During the days and months immediately ahead we shall be experiencing a change in the human relationships expressed on a national and on an international level. Plenty of tensions and problems remain, but there has come a lessening of suspicion and an increase in hope. Diplomats are more friendly than they have been, leaders of governments have met together at "summit" level, committees are investigating the injustices of investigating committees, the State Department is passing out passports more freely. How do we evaluate this development?

Improved feeling does not necessarily mean that all the problems have been solved: it means simply that certain difficulties have been overcome, that basic differences need not drive people apart—rather that they may live together in one world notwithstanding philosophical and ideological conflict, and that by calling an end to the cold war there is provided an opportunity for the realization of this hope. It is this identical principle which will soon function here in the city of New Orleans—when we shall call an end to the cold war creating divisions in our community and in our schools—which will see the realization of the hope in us all.

For ourselves we see that we too have a part to play: we come to church to be reminded of great figures such as Jesus, the Buddha, Isaiah and Socrates; men who patiently and effectively brought to bear upon human life the creative power of what this morning we are calling the "human spirit." We come to rediscover in our own and in each other's abilities to think and to hope, to worship and to work together, those qualities which draw us into a unit, and which inspire us to act individually for the common good.

One final quote from Schweitzer: "I am convinced, intellectually convinced, that the human spirit in our time is capable of creating a new attitude of mind. This conviction persuades me to affirm that more than one truth has long remained dormant and ineffective for no other reason than that nobody had imagined that it could ever have any application to reality."

> "May the strength of the lighted mind and the dedicated heart be ours today and on the morrow as we find fulfillment in the common tasks of brotherhood and of peace." (Amen)

§16 Dr. T. R. M. Howard

Theodore Roosevelt Howard was born on March 2, 1908 in Murray, Kentucky. As a child he witnessed extreme poverty, violence, and racial discrimination within his small neighborhood of Pooltown. Despite these hardships, Howard was a brilliant boy and at the age of twelve he became determined that one day he would be a doctor. Howard quickly found a mentor for his precocious aspirations. Dr. William Herbert Mason recognized young Howard's potential and offered him several small jobs around his hospital. Their relationship flourished as Howard's intelligence and diligence matured. In 1924 Howard applied to Oakwood Junior College in Huntsville, Alabama with the promise of financial assistance and a letter of recommendation from Mason. Just before graduating from Oakwood in 1929, Howard legally changed his named to Theodore Roosevelt Mason Howard as a tribute to his mentor.

T. R. M. Howard, as he would later be called, prospered as a physician and political activist. In the early 1940s, Howard moved to the all black town of Mound Bayou, Mississippi, as chief surgeon at the Knights and Daughters of Tabor Hospital. Throughout the 1950s, Howard was on the leading edge of civil rights activism, especially in the rich alluvial plain known as the Mississippi Delta. In 1951 Howard founded the Regional Council of Negro Leadership (RCNL) in Cleveland, Mississippi; the organization challenged Jim Crow laws and advocated citizenship rights for local African Americans. While Howard became well known and respected for his brave activism among many civil rights workers, he has yet to receive due credit for his pioneering work in perhaps the most lethal place in 1950's America, the Mississippi Delta. So hated by Mississippi white supremacists, one story goes, Howard escaped the state only by feigning his own death in a casket-carrying hearse. Fleeing to Chicago, as had so many southern blacks before him, Howard opened a very controversial abortion clinic. Profligate in both his charity, his spending, and his womanizing, Howard died on May 1, 1976 at the age of 68, deep in debt. According to David and Linda Royster Beito, Howard fathered at least eight children from nearly as many mothers.

Immediately after the Emmett Till murder trial concluded in late September 1955, the NAACP sponsored a northern speaking tour for many of the principals in the case, including Howard and Till's mother, Mamie Till-Bradley. Ostensibly to catalyze black and white outrage over the not-guilty verdict, as well as to raise money, one of the first speeches Howard gave was to a Baltimore audience of 2,500. Held at the Sharp Street Methodist Church, Howard's lengthy oration amounts to an extensive, if anecdotal, primer on Mississippi racial politics. Perhaps not surprisingly, the charismatic and witty raconteur, was warmly received.

Importantly, Howard places the Till murder and trial in the context of post-*Brown* Mississippi, a closed society willing to kill to keep its way of life. In this context Till is but the lineal martyr of Reverend George W. Lee and Lamar Smith, two black activists gunned down in May and August 1955. In telling an insider's account of the murder and trial, Howard privileges the testimony of Carolyn Bryant and Willie Reed. Bryant, the wife of defendant Roy Bryant, was allegedly groped and whistled at by the 14-year old Chicago boy. Reed proved to be Howard's key find. Employing several black journalists, most notably the *Cleveland Call and Post's* James Hicks, Howard was able to track down, and get to testify, at least one Delta black who allegedly saw the murder victim on the morning of the abduction. Despite the 18-year old's testimony, Mamie Till-Bradley would later impugn the quality of his testimony (see her speech of October 29, 1955).

Howard closes his speech by adding a challenge to the standard request for generous contributions to the NAACP. He calls upon the black clergy to leave the comfort of their robes, Sunday dinners, and heavenly mansions: "I wish to challenge the great church of America this afternoon to a new crusade. For 92 years now, the average preacher has kept his people's minds on the long, white robes, the golden slippers, the mansions in the sky, and the diet of milk and honey." The net effect of such otherworldly preaching, claims Howard, is that "people are content to spend their time here living in a cabin, poorly clothed, and poorly fed, satisfied with any and all types of treatment, ever looking forward to the golden slippers, the long white robes, and the milk and honey, and the mansions in the sky." Presaging many of Dr. King's challenges to the clergy, the earth belonged to the Lord, too, Howard reminds his listeners. "The Christian, as a Heaven-bound pilgrim, must realize that he can't live here and board in Heaven."

Terror Reigns in Mississippi

Sharp Street Methodist Church, Baltimore, Maryland
October 2, 1955

I want to thank the Rev. Mr. Nixon for that introduction. I'm just sorry that I didn't bring my wife, Reverend, so she could have heard that introduction. Around home sometimes she seems to think I'm just a little boy. If she could have heard that introduction, I believe that she would have been convinced that maybe I had grown into manhood.

When I was called only a few days ago and asked if it would be possible for me to be here in Baltimore this afternoon, I hesitated after I was told the thing that you wanted me to do here, because I hardly felt that a country doctor could fill such an important part on your program.

But after I said that I would come, I was made to think of one of our greatest Baptist speakers down at the Shadrack Mechack Baptist Church at Puckiner, Mississippi, where the Rev. Solomon D. Jones has served as pastor for the last 37 and a half years. A financial drive was staged a few weeks ago to replace a room on the church, which had been blown away by a recent Mississippi storm. The Rev. Mr. Jones thought that he would invite the members of the First Baptist Church, white, in this little town to assist in the financial drive. He invited the pastor of that church to deliver the sermon, and he had hoped that a number of the white members would come over for this occasion. The pastor did come and bring a number of his members with him, and when he rose to speak, he took as his subject, "Servants, Obey Your Masters." He proceeded to give them a sermon on white superiority and how they should remain humble and shouldn't pay any attention to recent decisions of the Supreme Court of the United States. The preacher ended his sermon by saying, "Dear colored brothers and sisters, you know one of these days we're all going up to heaven. You good colored people are not going to have streets of gold to walk on like the white people. The Lord's going to provide good cabins for you on the back streets of Heaven." Then he took his seat.

As he sat down, the Rev. Mr. Jones caught the eye of Deacon Anthony D. Smith and asked him to lead in a word of prayer. Well, sir, Deacon Smith had gotten so mad during the white preacher's sermon that he didn't even want to address God properly. After thanking God for everything, he said, "Now, Lord, it 'pears to me that some of our white preachers here in Mississippi ain't been study'n your word right, talkin' 'bout us black folks ain't gonna walk no streets 'o gold. Oh Lord, oh, God, please teach this white preacher and all these white brethren that when we colored folks get up in Heaven, we'll walk where we damned please!"

Ladies and Gentlemen, the reason that there is so much disturbance in Mississippi today is that the colored people in Mississippi have decided since the deacon's prayer that we don't want to wait until we get to Heaven to walk where we please. We want to do it right here in this present world.

As I told a group in Mississippi last night, I'm from what is considered the "Iron Curtain state of Mississippi," where the governor is considering calling another special session of the Legislature to try and impeach the Supreme Court of the United States and to try and have the words "Desegregate" and "Integration" removed from the English language. In fact, Mississippi would have liked to secede from the Union on the afternoon of May 17, 1954, if there had been any place for her to go.

But there was only one place for Mississippi to go on that afternoon, and since Theodore Bilbo went there a few years ago, he sent word back that there were a lot of Mississippians down there. The word is out in Mississippi that Bilbo, through the spirit world, sent a message to Gov. Hugh White several months ago and told him that he wished that he would change the way that they were treating colored people in Mississippi. He said he wanted him to treat them better, to give them the right to vote and to give them a human being's chance before the courts. This message disturbed Governor White very much and he sought to send a message back inquiring why Bilbo had had such a change of heart so far as the colored Mississippians were concerned. Bilbo sent this message back: Bilbo said, you know, they have a colored fireman down here on 24-hour duty and he's keeping it hot all the time!

As a minority group in this nation, we are, indeed, fortunate that we live in a nation whose watchwords are liberty, freedom and democracy. It is of historical interest this afternoon in view of all the things that are happening in my Mississippi, to note that when the Pilgrim Fathers set foot upon the shores of America in 1620, they laid the foundation of our national government upon the bedrock of liberty, freedom and democracy. It is with interest this afternoon that we note that in all of our wars we have gone into them from Mississippi, South Carolina and Georgia. We have decided in Mississippi that we are tired of dying for something on Heartbreak Ridge in Korea that we can't vote for in Belzoni, Mississippi.

The decision of the Supreme Court of the United States of America outlawing segregation in the public schools on May 17, 1954 caught the entire South, especially Mississippi, unprepared for this decision. The State of Mississippi sought to find some way around the decision of the Supreme Court. The Governor and the State Legislature felt that if they took the colored people of the state into their confidence (I might explain just here that as most of you know, the population in Mississippi is about equally divided between whites and colored citizens). At the present time, we have a few more whites in the state than we have colored people because of the large number of colored people who have left the state during the last 30 years.

At the present time, we have approximately 1,230,000 whites and we have approximately one million colored people. So, the governor felt that the easiest way out would be to work out some plan he called "voluntary segregation." That is if we can just get the colored people of the state to go along with us on a voluntary basis, then we can say to the President of the United States, we can say to the Congress of the United States, we can say to the Supreme Court of the United States and we can say to the world, that the colored people in Mississippi don't want this thing which you are calling for.

It's an interesting thing, my friends; I don't care whether it's in Maryland or whether it's in Mississippi, when certain white parties get something that they want to put over on colored people, they can always find an "Uncle Tom," who will serve their purpose. So the Governor of Mississippi had seven of his handpicked boys called in and he revealed to them that we are now ready to accept the theory of separate but equal. You know, all of us fooled ourselves for a number of years in believing that there was such a thing as a separate but equal theory in education. We all know today that there is no such thing as separate but equal facilities where a matter as vital as the education of our children is involved.

The Governor, in addressing these seven colored leaders, forgot that since the Mississippi constitutional convention of 1890, Mississippi had separate but equal provisions for education for colored children of the state. He had forgotten all about that provision in the laws of the State of Mississippi until he felt the sharp leg of the Supreme Court of the United States of America. After the Governor (Prolonged applause as Gloria Lockerman entered the auditorium) I know that we all feel very proud as we see our little spelling champion, little Gloria Lockerman. After the Governor had talked to this group of seven men about this plan, they were anxious to please the Governor. They told him that they were sure that 95 percent of the colored people of Mississippi would go along with the plan of voluntary segregation in public schools.

When the people of Mississippi read what these leaders had promised the Governor, they became so indignant that they wanted to use some of Mississippi's methods of violence on the leaders who had sold them down the river. There was so much protest that the governor decided that maybe he had better call 100 of the people's chosen leaders to find out what they thought about his plan of voluntary segregation. This meeting was called in the executive mansion in Jackson on July 30 of last year.

I'm happy today to tell you that 99 persons out of that 100 stood and shouted in one voice that we want no part of segregation and discrimination in Mississippi or any other place. My heart was filled and overcome with joy. I thanked God that at last we are coming of age in Mississippi.

That very afternoon, the governor of Mississippi called a special session of the Mississippi Legislature. Three things were done at this special session that are of importance to each of us. I want to tell you about them. First of all, they had seen from this demonstration that the day had passed and forever gone when a few handpicked leaders could stand before the executives of the state and express incorrectly the desires of the overwhelming majority of the people. They had also found out that if they urged voluntary segregation in Mississippi, colored people would not accept it. Therefore, they passed a constitutional amendment to abolish the public schools in Mississippi should the colored people seek integration.

And I am happy to tell you this afternoon that since we have had the May 1 decision of the Supreme Court, whereby it was necessary for the colored residents in the various school districts to file separate petitions where they wanted integration, we have had five communities to send in their petitions. We let Mississippi and the world know that we want the same kind of democracy in Mississippi that's given to the rest of this country. The first of these petitions was filed in Vicksburg. We have a courageous, young funeral director there by the name of George Jefferson who is chairman of the local branch of the NAACP. As soon as this petition was filed, the

Ku Klux Klan proceeded to burn a cross in the front of his funeral home. George called up the sheriff of the county and said: "Mr. Sheriff, they have burned a cross in front of my funeral home. I'm sure that you and every-body in Vicksburg know where my wife and my family live. I understand that they are going out there to burn a cross. And, Mr. Sheriff, I just want to tell you, that Mississippi requires separate ambulances for transportation of colored and white persons and inasmuch as the white hearse can't carry a colored man and a colored hearse can't carry a white man, I'm telling you that when that group comes out to my home to burn a cross, I have already got my colored ambulance standing by. I want you to send a white hearse along because somebody's going to be hauled away." It's needless for me to tell you that the cross in front of George Jefferson's home had not been burned up until last night.

The next thing that this Legislature decided to do was to pass an amend-ment that would make it impossible for any more colored people to register and vote in the State of Mississippi, notwithstanding the fact that we have a million colored residents in Mississippi. Up to this point, we have only about 25,000 colored registered voters in the State of Mississippi. They are fearful that, as the colored citizens have been aroused during the past three or four years, they must tighten the restrictions on voting lest Mississippi might be sending a colored representative to Congress.

These are the things that colored people have to do in order to register to vote in Mississippi: They must go before the circuit court clerk. The cir-cuit court clerk picks out a portion of the Mississippi constitution and asks the individual to read it. He must pronounce every word correctly; a grade of 99 will not pass him to vote. He must make 100. If he reads the passage well, then the clerk may ask him to spell any word in it. After doing that, the individual is passed a sheet of paper and asked to write an essay on "What is meant by a constitutional form of government." The lawyers present this afternoon will agree with me that even a lawyer might flunk such a test.

Now, you should know some things about the educational level of the individuals called upon to give this test to prospective voters in Mississippi. Let me just give you this story. In the month of February, we had a young serviceman wounded in Korea. He was in hospitals for a long time and came back to Mound Bayou, Miss., to recuperate. Before going back to be mus-tered out of the Army, it was time for registration. He decided he would go down to the courthouse and register. He found the clerk to be an old boy-hood playmate. The clerk talked, asked him about his experiences in Korea and then he said "Well, George, what can I do for you?" The young man said, "Mr. Smith, I came down to register." Mr. Smith rubbed his neck and said, "Well, George, you know it's kinda hard but I must turn you down." Said the soldier, "You mean I've almost died for something I can't vote for here in Mississippi?"Mr. Smith said, "Well, George that is a little hard." Then Mr. Smith look around and said, "Listen here, George, you know that organization, that NAACP? It's been making a lot of fuss down here about the 14th Amendment." He said, "Now it ain't nobody in here but you and me and if you can give me the 14th amendment to the Constitution, I'm going to let you register. Do you know that amendment?"

It's been a long time since George was in school. He wasn't sure that even the circuit court clerk knew the 14th Amendment either, so George said, "Yes sir, Mr. Smith, I know that 14th amendment." "Well," he said, "Well George, give me the 14th amendment." George said: "Four score and seven years ago our fathers brought forth on this continent a new nation." Mr. Smith said, "Don't say no more, George, that's the 14th amendment and it's all right."

Now the third thing that was done during this special session of the Legislature was to organize the modern version of the Ku Klux Klan of the Southland, this group calling itself the Citizens' Council. They announced to the world what they plan to do and I want to give you their plans at this time. First of all, any colored person who says that he wants to vote or that he wants his children to go to a mixed school in Mississippi is to be classed as a "troublemaker." If he works for white people, he is to be immediately fired; if he lives in a house that doesn't belong to him and does belong to a white person, he is to be asked to move; if he is a cotton farmer and has cotton that has to be ginned before he sells it, none of the gins in the community are to accept his cotton. If he has notes at the bank where he is supposed to pay installments over a five-year period that bank note is to be declared then "due" and he must pay in full or lose his property. Such a colored person is not to borrow money at any of the banks or at any of the agencies in the community.

Now ladies and gentlemen, I'm not telling you about conditions behind the iron curtain, I'm telling you what's happening to the colored citizen who desires to be a first-class citizen in Mississippi, U.S.A., in this year of our Lord, 1955. They have carried out those threats. Just a few days ago, I had a patient from Belzoni, the county seat, a county where the Rev. George W. Lee was killed, and I'll tell you more about that a little bit later.

But this fellow came to me and he said, "You know, Doctor, on my little 120-acre farm, I have picked 16 bales of cotton and I have them stored in an old house on the place. The only reason I have it stored there is because in my county none of the gins will process my cotton. You see, after the cotton is taken out of the field, the very first thing you want to do is to get it to a gin. The gin will send it to a federal compress and the federal compress will give a receipt for it, so that if anything happens to it the federal compress is responsible, and the individual is not responsible." He said,

"I'm fearful that somebody is going to set a match to that house and burn up the cotton that I have stored there." And then he said, "I'll lose my farm because I won't have money to meet my notes this month."

I said to him, "Brother Tilghman, what's the trouble down there?" He said, "Well, you know, I registered two years ago to become a voter in Humphrey County and that's one of the 60 counties in Mississippi where colored people have not voted since the days of Reconstruction." And he said each of those gin owners told him that if he would go to the court-house and scratch his name off the registration list, they would process his cotton. But so long as he remained a registered voter of Humphrey County there's not a gin in that county that would accept it.

Ladies and gentlemen, as I looked into the eyes of this man, a man about fifty years of age and saw the tears streaming down his cheeks because he wanted to be a man in the United States of America and because he was being deprived of his constitutional rights, I was made to say: "Oh, God, how long will such a condition exist in these United States of America?" But he had no other choice. He went the next morning and scratched his name off the list because he didn't want to lose the farm and the home that his father had worked and slaved for. He had three children in school at Alcorn College in Mississippi. If he wanted those children to go to school, he had to strike his name off the list in order to get his cotton ginned in Belzoni, Mississippi.

These are some of the terrific trials that our people are having to un-dergo in Mississippi. At the meeting of the Mississippi Regional Council of colored leaders on April 29 of this year, we had our young Congressman Charles C. Diggs as principal speaker. And I want to say to you in this con-nection, I have just spent the week with Charles Diggs, who left his business in Detroit to come down (I won't call it a trial) to the Roman holiday that we had over in Sumner, Mississippi. I want to say that Charles C. Diggs, as congressman from the 13th Congressional District of Michigan, is the brightest light we have had in Congress since the days of Reconstruction.

It was at this meeting, in my annual message as president of that orga-nization, I told more than 20,000 of my fellow Mississippians that as soon as the Citizens Council (white) had found out that their economic pres-sure was failing, that they were going to start a well organized campaign of violence and that we might as well prepare ourselves for it.

I want to thank many of you and to thank the friends and the liberal organizations throughout America for the help which you have given us to resist this economic pressure in Mississippi. I cannot stand here and tell you this afternoon that we have succeeded completely, because every day, just as with this farmer that I just told you about, it's raising its ugly head in many different ways.

Economic pressure, where the [sic] most of the security rests with the other fellow, is an awful thing to witness. But I must say the drive which was sponsored by the NAACP, to put money in the Tri-State bank in Memphis, has helped any number of colored people in the state of Mississippi to hold up their heads and be men. They would have had to hang their heads in the dust had it not been possible for them to get loans and aid from the Tri-State bank in Memphis, Tennessee.

On the 7th of May, in the city of Belzoni, Mississippi, violence raised its ugly head in the very worst way that it could raise it. There we had a militant minister of the gospel, Rev. George W. Lee, a man who two years before that time, had gone with us before a grand jury and had testified that the sheriff of that county would not let colored people pay their poll tax. We won our fight there. The sheriff was ordered to receive these poll taxes. In Mississippi, you have to pay poll tax for two years before you can vote. So on the 7th of last May, colored people who had paid their poll tax for two years were now qualified to vote for the first time since the days of Reconstruction.

In Humphrey County are 17,500 colored residents and approximately 11,000 whites. The whites decided that colored residents were not going to vote. They made a number of threats. They broke into the Elks Club just two weeks before the storm and left a number of nasty notes saying what was going to happen to colored people if they voted. The Rev. Mr. Lee, in his sermon on the Sunday morning before his death the following Saturday night, had talked to his people because they were frightened. Some went to the courthouse and took their names off the list, as the white people had asked them to do.

This worried the Rev. Mr. Lee and that Sunday morning he preached the greatest sermon of his long and illustrious career. In that sermon he reviewed the history of the colored American's part in working for freedom and democracy as Americans. He ended by saying: "If God gives me grace, and if I'm living on the second day of May, I'm going to march boldly to the courthouse and register."

The sermon spread through the county. As he walked along the streets during the next week, men who had spoken to him for 25 years looked the other way as he walked past. On May 7, at 11:35, as he was on his way to his home, a Mercury convertible with three men in it rolled up beside him and the left side of his face was blown away.

I am sorry to tell you this afternoon that the investigation of the Federal Bureau of Investigation until this day has not revealed the killers. It's getting to be a strange thing that nothing happens when colored people are murdered in the South. The Federal Bureau of Investigation, with all of its knowledge, with all its power, can never work out who the killer is when a colored person in the South is the victim. Something is wrong somewhere and I believe that there is enough wrong that the President of the United States, the Attorney General, and J. Edgar Hoover, himself, must be called into a conference to see why southern investigators of the department can never solve the crime when there's a black man involved.

In the Lee case there were eyewitnesses. The Chinese who sold the buck-shot has even identified the man to whom he sold it. But nothing has come from the law enforcement officers of Humphrey County and the Federal Bureau of Investigation.

Terror reigns in Mississippi. Hodding Carter of Greenville, Mississippi, in an article in *Look Magazine* in March of this year wrote under the heading "A Wave of Terror Threatens the South." I'm here to tell you this afternoon that the wave of terror no longer threatens the South, but the wave of terror is in the South.

The next individual to be shot down in this wave of terror was Lamar Smith of Brookhaven, Mississippi. I talked with Lamar Smith on the 29th of April when he was in Mound Bayou to attend our great meeting. He told me of some of the difficulties that they were having in his county trying to vote. He was very much concerned about this and later at our NAACP memorial meeting in Belzoni, after the death of the Rev. Mr. Lee, Lamar Smith brought a carload of people from his native Brookhaven to be there for the memorial service. Little did he think at that time that the next martyr to the cause would be himself. Lamar Smith was shot down on the courthouse grounds of Brookhaven.

There were some 30 to 40 witnesses standing around when he was shot down. But, do you know, just the other day, the grand jury met on his case and failed to bring in a true bill, because none of the individuals who saw Lamar Smith shot down would open their mouths. I declare to you this afternoon a wave of terror is in Mississippi.

During the last few weeks there hasn't been a day that has passed that many of you have not thought about little Emmett Till. Emmett Till was just an average American boy. On August 20, after his great uncle had paid him a visit in Chicago, it was decided that Emmett and his cousin would return home with his great uncle for a two week vacation on the farm. All of you know how a boy loves to romp and play on the farm. Around Money, Mississippi, there are a number of our best lakes, where a little boy 14 years of age can enjoy fishing.

The boy went down to Money, Mississippi. The nearest store was two and eight tenths miles from his great uncle's home. The boys went to the little store in the afternoon to buy bubble gum and chewing gum and candy. I talked with a 16 year old cousin who was right there with Emmett and was on the porch of the store watching other colored people play checkers while Emmett was on the inside of the store. He told me that Emmett went in the store to buy bubble gum. The little fellow had once had Infantile Paralysis and there was a stammer in his voice. As he came out of the store, he said to the storekeeper, "Goodbye."

The boys who were on the porch of the store, teasing like boys do said, "You said goodbye to that lady." They said, "Don't you know colored people don't say goodbye to white women in the South? They just don't do that." One of the boys said, "What did you think about the lady?" And not being able to express himself very well, he whistled, whew-whew, like that, in reply to what they said, meaning that she was good looking.

Now I want to say to you people, I have talked with five of the eight or nine persons who were present and, incidentally, Mrs. Bryant admitted on the stand in Sumner the other day that there were eight or nine colored people on the outside. But she got on that stand and tried to playwrite. When she asked the boy for the money, she said the little boy caught her hand and tried to put his arms around her. I wish that the reporters who are here this afternoon would please tell the entire South that that old lie they've been telling all these countries is getting so old that it ought to stink even to them!

Every time they get ready to lynch a colored person in the South, it's got to be about some white woman. I wish you'd also tell them that the colored man is satisfied with his women, and my great desire this afternoon is that the Mississippi white man would be as satisfied with his own women as I am with mine.

However, the colored people on that porch have told me that they don't believe that Mrs. Bryant even heard the boy say goodbye or heard his whistle. There was some two-bit person sitting there who wanted 50 cents worth of credit; that individual told Mr. Bryant that a boy from Chicago, a northern boy, whistled at his wife. If she had heard that whistle, what was the excuse for waiting four days before he went down there?

The incident happened on Wednesday, and it was 2 o'clock Sunday morning, August 28, when they went to the great uncle's home and took the little boy out. There was plenty of evidence in this case that the State of Mississippi didn't make any effort to get. It was last Sunday night that I was passing a group of eyewitnesses. They got word to me that they had evidence that they wanted to give me. They wanted me to get the evidence to the proper authorities. They didn't want the people where they lived, on those plantations, to know anything about this evidence. I wondered for a while about meeting those eyewitnesses because you know I live dangerously in Mississippi.

For the past six months I've had two guards about my home on 24-hour duty, not trying to protect me, but to protect my wife and my two children.

I've had guards around my hospital and I have two other individuals to go with me wherever I go throughout the State of Mississippi. I don't know if this counts for much, but I do want somebody to know at least where I take my last step.

After this news came, I kept the rendezvous with these people. They told me there was an 18-year old youth by the name of William Reed who was on his way to the store to get something for his grandma to cook for Sunday morning breakfast. It was 6 o'clock when a green 1955 Chevrolet truck with a white top passed by him. He noticed that there were four white men on the front seat. One of them he recognized as J. W. Milam, one of the defendants in this case.

He noticed that there were three colored men sitting on the side of the pickup truck and that there was a younger colored person sitting on the floor of the truck with his back against the cab of the truck. Noting they were strangers in the little community, he looked around to see who it was, and as he turned around as the truck was going away from him, he looked right into the face of little Emmett Till. He recognized him because of the first picture that came out in the paper.

He carried the paper to his grandmother and grandfather and said, "There's the little boy." He had to go past a barn on the way to the store. As he neared the barn he heard somebody cry , "Lord have mercy, mama save me." He heard someone pushed down, and he heard cursing and heard blows. He rushed on past the barn. He went on up to Aunt Mandy's house, stopped there and asked Aunt Mandy, "Who are they beating to death down there at little children, crawling all over the barn?" [sic]

Aunt Mandy was cutting bacon for breakfast. She threw down the bacon, rushed to the window and said, "Lord have mercy, I didn't know they were beating anybody." He said, "It's something going on down to the barn." She listened at the window, but she couldn't hear anything. She emptied the water out of the bucket and said, "Son go and get Aunt Mandy a bucket of water and see if they are beatin' somebody up there." The boy said, "I don't want to go back by myself." But it so happened that there was another man there. He said, "I'll go to the well with you, they won't think anything of us coming to get a bucket of water."

As they neared the well, they heard the little boy hollering and they could hear the licks. As they were standing there getting the water, they heard the cries getting fainter, fainter and fainter until there were no more cries. Two minutes later all four of the white men came out the barn. A little bit later, a tractor, standing near the storeroom, was moved out of its stall and a pickup truck was run into it. A minute later, the witnesses saw them put a bundle on the truck, throw a tarpaulin over it, and drive away.

I attended the trial of the alleged killers. When they wanted to use the restroom, I saw them stroll to the restroom. And I saw their little children, crawling all over them, holding their arms around their necks. Those 12 Mississippi jurymen sat there looking at them. I knew from the very first day of the trial that there would be no conviction. I know the way of the Mississippi white man. I am saying today that I don't believe that they could have gotten 12 white men anywhere in the State of Mississippi who would have convicted these men.

Men in Mississippi realize that they are on trial. They want the rest of America and the world to know that the colored Mississippian has no rights that the Mississippi white man must respect. I want to say to you this afternoon, don't get all worked up about this kidnapping trial. It will surprise me if the kidnapping part of it ever goes on trial. I won't be surprised if you pick up your newspaper in just a day or two and notice that those men are out on bond. There's going to be a lot of maneuvering when they get out on bond.

These, ladies and gentlemen, are some of the things that are taking place in Mississippi. And then you'll say to me, Dr. Howard, what are you going to do in Mississippi? What's the Mississippi colored citizens going to do about this? You say they ought to feel terribly disturbed. But I want to say to you that this is no hour to be disturbed, my fellow citizens. Someone said a long time ago that the darkest hours are just before dawn.

I wish that you could go with me back in the swamps on the plantations of Mississippi and see these eager young colored people who come forward to shake a hand and say, "Dr. Howard, I'm with you. I'm with you." I am reminded that my grandfather was born in northern Mississippi. He told me a long time ago, as a little boy on a plantation, that just before the end of the Civil War he had begun to feel something. It was something that works like religion. He didn't explain what it was, but he said there was something in there that made me feel that the war would soon be over and I would soon be free.

Now, ladies and gentlemen, in Mississippi, I know what my old grandfather was talking about. There's something in Mississippi, everywhere, that makes us know that this reign of terror and the undemocratic practices of the South will soon be over and we'll all soon be free. I never speak before a group where there are so many young people but my heart goes out to them. I know, and you must know, that there is a brighter day for them.

In fact, when I tell the youth of the South, that there is a better day coming, I'm reminded of that ancient discourse of Socrates on "Good Government." When a student said, "Socrates, I do not believe that there is such a City of God anywhere on earth." Socrates replied: "Whether such a city exists in Heaven or will exist on earth, the wise man will live up to the manner of that city, having nothing to do with any other, and in so living will set his own house in order."

I'm thankful, ladies and gentlemen, for the remarkable part that the NAACP has played in bringing about this new day. I'm talking to some of you this afternoon who have said in your hearts, well, I don't know whether the NAACP is needed any longer. I want to say to you this afternoon that as long as there is one colored person in the swamps of Mississippi who is not receiving justice, the NAACP will be needed.

A number of you have come out of the Deep South. You feel that since you reached Baltimore everything is all right. You don't have to worry about what's going on in Mississippi. The NAACP, through the FEPC, has made it possible for you to have good jobs and you're making more money than you've ever made in your life. Everything's all right. As soon as restrictive covenants were declared illegal, many of you moved from where you have had to live all your days and you're living in better neighborhoods. Some of you have had to pay as much as $500 to get credit, but you haven't given $2 for membership in the NAACP.

The only organization that the Mississippi white man is afraid of is the NAACP. Down there, we have got to starve trying to vote. Many of you Baltimoreans do not walk two blocks to register. Wake up, Baltimore! So long as there is oppression, violence and death in Mississippi, you can't enjoy your comforts and be satisfied.

Thurgood Marshall sent out an SOS call the other day, stating that they do not have money to do the job in Mississippi that needs to be done. I pray to God that Mrs. Jackson will telephone Thurgood Marshall in the morning and tell him that the citizens of Baltimore placed on the table $5,000 in cash to help carry into court one of these school cases in Mississippi. They're going to make us carry these school districts into court one by one and it's going to cost about $5,000 to carry one of these Federal cases into Federal court.

I hope that when I return to Mississippi on tomorrow, I can tell my people that the good citizens of Baltimore didn't come up with 50 cents and 1 dollar. My God in Heaven, if you can pay $7.50 for a fifth of you know what, then what person here can not buy at least $10 worth of citizenship?

There are four things we must have in Mississippi to be prepared for an integrated society. First, we must have equality in education. We must not be satisfied until every child in America is privileged to go to the same school and receive the same type of education. In Mississippi, they're still saying that it will never happen here! I'm telling you, it will happen there!

Secondly, we must have the unrestricted ballot. It is a shame on our American democracy that in Mississippi, where we have a million colored citizens we have fewer than 25,000 qualified voters.

Thirdly, we must have money. The colored people in the South don't handle an awful lot of money. We must fight for fair employment at such wages we can keep some of them in our savings. We must remember that while we are fighting to end segregation, we're not fighting to lose our identity as people.

I'll have to say, ministers of the gospel, that it is not encouraging to me that the religious songs we like to sing best are songs like: "Take all of this world, but give me Jesus." "A tent or a cottage or why should I care, they're building a cottage for me over there." I wish to challenge the great church of America this afternoon to a new crusade. For 92 years now, the average preacher has kept his people's minds on the long, white robes, the golden slippers, the mansions in the sky and the diet of milk and honey. The psychological effect of this type of preaching has been that the people are content to spend their time here living in a cabin, poorly clothed and poorly fed, satisfied with any and all types of treatment, ever looking forward to the golden slippers, the long white robes and milk and honey, and the mansions in the sky.

While the Kingdom of Heaven must be made as realistic as possible today, the minister must tell his people that there is something for him to do while he is waiting for his wing measurements. We must be taught that the same Bible which outlines the diet and the wearing apparel of the Kingdom of Heaven also states that the earth, of which Maryland is part, is the Lord's and the fullness thereof: that the gold and the silver is the Lord's and that the cattle upon a thousand hills belong to the Lord.

We often confess to have more religion than anybody else. We certainly do more preaching, more praying, more moaning and groaning than any other people. Yet the average Christian has less faith than anybody. I cannot believe that the great God that we serve cares any more for a soul wrapped up in a white skin than He does for a soul wrapped up in a black skin. I know, as a student of medical science, that in the anatomical structure and physiological functioning of the body which God has given the human race, made after His own image, the only basic difference is in the pigment of the skin and the texture of the hair.

The Christian, as a Heaven-bound pilgrim, must realize that he can't live here and board in Heaven. Therefore, the preacher must talk to us more about the rights we've enjoyed here in this present world.

Finally, we must have the religion of Jesus Christ in an integrated society. Religion and democracy have been cooperating forces in American life. Thomas Jefferson wrote into the Declaration of Independence that "all men are created equal and are endowed by their Creator with certain inalienable rights." This democratic statement was a religious affirmation and an acknowledgment of God as Creator. We are, indeed, fortunate that we have the hope and the belief that God created all men equal. Jesus said, "I came that ye might have life and life more abundantly."

All over the world, in South Africa, in India, in China and in Mississippi, people are crying for the more abundant life—but you say to me this afternoon, "Dr. Howard, what is life?" A few years ago, while attending a career conference at Tennessee State University, a young man with many problems came to me. He said, "Dr. Howard, I want you to give me your definition of life." I said, "Young man, to me life is a one way tunnel connecting two appendages. Life's beginning starts in mystery and its ending is in controversy. Theologians and scholars and philosophers have argued for years trying to rescue this thing we call life from the unknown."

I know not, ladies and gentlemen, how long this conflict will last; I don't know how long I will be able to continue my work in this city, but I'm going to leave this with you. Armed with the Constitution of the United States of America, armed with the decision of the Supreme Court of the United States of America, with the NAACP standing behind me and with God dictating my every move, I shall stay in Mississippi.

I have reached the point of no return. I must stay in Mississippi, and fight until the fires of Theodore G. Bilbo shall know that the time has come, in God's own way, when all second-class citizenship shall be done away with within these United States of America.

I am sorry that my oppressed people in Mississippi can't hear your applause.

§17 Mamie Till-Bradley

Mamie Elizabeth Carthan was born in Webb, Mississippi in Tallahatchie County in 1921. At two, her family moved to Argo, a small town just outside of Chicago. At the age of thirty-four, she would return to Tallahatchie County for the murder trial of her only child.

Carthan married Louis Till in 1940. On July 25, 1941 she gave birth to a son, Emmett Louis Till. Her husband died during World War II, not from war wounds. Rather he was executed on July 2, 1945 upon conviction of raping two Italian women and murdering another. She married "Pink" Bradley in 1951. The two later divorced. In 1957 she married for a third and final time, to Gene Mobley. He preceded her in death in 2000.

Mamie Till became a heroine of the civil rights movement for her brave actions in the summer and fall of 1955. Following the brutal slaying of her child, she not only had his body shipped back to Chicago, but she opened the casket, allowing any and all to see what "Mississippi has done to my son." Photographs of the corpse were soon published in prominent magazines and newspapers such as the *Chicago Defender*, the *Pittsburgh Courier*, *Jet Magazine*, and the NAACP's *Crisis*. No mainstream white newspaper or magazine published the graphic photographs. Mamie

Till also traveled to Sumner, Mississippi, site of the trial, to testify on her son's behalf. Immediately after the trial, in cooperation with the NAACP, she spoke to packed venues across the country about her ordeal. In November 1955 she parted company with the NAACP over misunderstandings regarding compensation for a scheduled west coast speaking tour. Her uncle, Mose Wright, went in her place.

In 1956 Mamie Till entered Chicago Teacher's College, graduating cum laude in 1960. Until her retirement in 1983, she taught in the Chicago public school system. She also founded the Emmett Till Players, a traveling group of young students who would recite from memory Dr. King's rhetorical masterpieces. She completed her memoir, *Death of Innocence: The Story of the Hate Crime That Changed America*, with Christopher Benson before her death on January 6, 2003. She was 81.

On October 29, 1955, less than five weeks after her son's murder trial ended in a not guilty verdict for J. W. Milam and Roy Bryant, Mamie Till addressed a standing-room only crowd at a Baltimore NAACP rally held at Bethel AME Church. The climax of the address comes midway when she graphically recounts identifying her son's body in a Chicago morgue. Further detail of the gruesome identification appears in her memoir. Like Dr. T. R. M. Howard's October 2, Baltimore speech, Mamie Till underscores Willie Reed's dramatic eyewitness testimony—only to emphasize Reed's ineffectual presence in court caused by Mississippi's system of educational apartheid.

Throughout the address the presence of God is invoked to provide a guiding telos to the murder and trial; that is, she understands this incredible burden as a gift from God to aid in the cause of civil rights. Mamie Till often "thanked God that he felt that I was worthy to have a son that was worthy to die for such a worthy cause." And, more secularly, "I have invested a son in freedom and I'm determined that his death isn't in vain." At the close of her address, and also like Dr. Howard, Till calls on her listeners to make a sacrifice—of automobiles and fine clothes—for the NAACP and its mission. With such a sacrifice, "we can make this world one we'll be proud of." In addition to Till's religious undertones, she also provides a rhetorical archetype for monotheistic traditions that re visit a common theme. The Christian God and Abraham must be willing to give up their sons. Some day, as well, people from all three monotheistic traditions must come to grips with the desertion of Ishmael with a few days' food in the desert. Till's remarkable strength and good will provides an admirable ethic.

I Want You to Know What They Did to My Boy

Bethel AME Church, Baltimore, Maryland

October 29, 1955

During the last two months, I have found it very necessary to talk to God quite a few times.

When I first found out that Emmett was kidnapped, I was just so upset and so shocked I didn't know what to do. So, having been dependent on my mother most of my life, the first thing that I did was to call her. I thought that when I got to mother's house, she could take care of everything. She could handle it. This would be another burden that I could dump on her. When I got to mother's house, she had started making numerous telephone calls and she had found out nothing.

We stood there. We sat there. We waited for two or three days trying to find out what had happened to Emmett. During these two or three days, I looked at my mother and saw that she was failing. I was sitting at the telephone one night. I saw her walk through the dining room toward the front room. She weakened as she got there, and fell to the floor. I noticed as she passed me, I was getting stronger as she was getting weaker. It kind of startled me.

When she fell, I jumped up to run in there and put my hand on her and all of a sudden it seemed that something told me that if you touch her, you'll take her strength so fast, it'll kill her. So I stood there. I asked the others to let her alone. She'll be all right, I said and turned around and took my seat at the telephone.

I had been answering the phone night and day, taking messages and trying to send messages. And that's when I realized, for the first time in my life, I was going to have to stand up on my feet and be a woman. A real one.

And I started praying to God to give me strength. Because I just thought that I could never have anything that mama couldn't handle or daddy couldn't take care of. As long as I had them, there was no point to exert myself too much. But with mother there and with father there, there was still something that I had to do that nobody else could do. I sat at the phone. I sent the messages out. I tried to get through to Mississippi. Ladies and gentlemen, the hardest thing in the world that I have ever tried to do is get a call into Mississippi and get information out.

We remark about the Iron Curtain in Russia, but there's a cotton curtain in Mississippi that must have a steel lining. When you make a telephone call, I don't know who signals whom, but the person that you want to talk to doesn't want to talk if the call is coming from Chicago. The people that you always knew as being great, wonderful leaders, suddenly had nothing whatsoever to say. We called the home of the man on whose plantation my uncle has worked for 40 years. The man said he was too old to hear. He didn't have a pencil. He didn't know where the paper was. He was just in a helpless condition. He couldn't even call anybody to the phone who could take the message.

In fact there was nobody there. I thought what a shame for all of those people to go out and leave that helpless old man at that telephone. But just about the time that the crops were gathered in and they start weighing up to find what they are going to pay their sharecroppers, this old man gets very active. He loses all that helplessness. He's able to answer telephones.

He's able to make calls. He's able to go over and tell a poor sharecropper that he only cleared $10 this year, that his bills ran rather high. There is no accounting system down around these farms. They just have to take what the white man says.

Now before I get too far, I want to stop and point out and to make clear that our job here tonight is not to stir up a whole lot of racism. We're not trying to start a race riot. Instead we're only trying to pin point and to focus on the conditions that are existing in this country, the conditions that make this no true democracy. Standing up here tonight and talking to you white people and to you colored people, I want to say we're not trying to start trouble, we're trying to end trouble. The trouble is down there where a man can't look at a man and judge him for himself but must judge him by his color.

Many of us have been in homes where the mother and the father battle each other constantly. A neighbor doesn't have to walk in there and break up that home, it breaks up itself. Well, that's just what's going to happen here in these United States if the white man and the black man fight one another day in and day out. Foreign powers won't have to come over here to destroy us. We'll just stand here and disintegrate. I'm kind of proud of being a part of a great nation. I wouldn't want to think that my nation was getting behind. Sure we have progressed so far in the past. I think we can do better now because we have more to work with.

The average person now is intelligent. We get a chance to go to school to learn how to love our neighbors and love one another, to respect a man for what he is worth and represents. Why should we just let a few states upset all of that? Why should we let them put us back in the dark ages? I don't want to go back there. I received letters from some well-wishers. They weren't intentional well-wishers, however: they were hate letters. They were letters telling me that you've had a show already, why don't you sign off.

They wrote me: I'm glad that it was your n—- boy that was killed; that'll show some more smart kids in Chicago that they can't come down in Mississippi and get away with what they get away with in Chicago. I would like to tell those people tonight, that if it hadn't been for those letters, I probably wouldn't be standing here. I want them to know that every one of those letters gave me a new determination to stand up and fight that much harder. I do realize that those people are going to have to be taught. As long as they exist, and as long as their minds stay dirty, we're going to have a little harder time progressing and advancing. I also know that if I'm upsetting just one of them, then I feel that I'm doing a pretty good job.

We sat at our telephone trying to get through to Mississippi and get these different messages in and out. Finally we had to resort to telegrams. I wired my uncle some money and told him to do the best he could. I would wait for a reply, but the answer that I asked for never did come back and we went through hours and hours and hours of such torture. And finally on Wednesday, with the presses working and everybody working the news finally came through. Emmett Till's body had been found in Mississippi. The news came through a girl friend of mine. She knew that she should have called earlier, but just didn't feel that she should break the news.

So when she called she was reluctant to talk. She didn't want to talk to me at all. But I insisted that she give me the message. Whatever it was, I could take it. She did, and I wrote down what she told me. As I sat there, I suddenly divided into two different people. One was handling the telephone. The other was standing off telling the others what to do, or helping me to keep myself under control. And this second person told me you don't have time to cry now—you might not have time to cry tomorrow. You can't cry at anytime. Don't worry about that because there's something you've got to do. There are a whole lot of people out there that are going to do the crying for you.

If I should even cry the rest of my life there wouldn't be enough tears for Emmett Till. For Emmett Till was just an ordinary boy like your ordinary boys and girls you have here. He had made his mark in a way because his heart was generous and the people in the neighborhood liked him. He was a well-mannered child. He wasn't on a higher level than anybody else. He was just Mr. John Doe. Emmett Louis Till, an American. He didn't realize that because he was colored, he was at a disadvantage. He had been taught that you are what you are taught to be and what you make yourself because that's the way I had trained him.

He never guessed that a "yes" or a "no" answer would cost him his life. When I found out that Emmett had been discovered we got ourselves together, held ourselves in check a little while and started making these other calls back to Mississippi. To our surprise, we found that it wasn't going to be an easy job to get his body shipped back here. The sheriff at Money had ordered my uncle Mose to immediately bury that body. He had also called a colored undertaker who rushed to the scene with a box, a box covered with some gray flannel material. They picked up that body from the river bank and threw it in that box. They herded it away to the cemetery.

He started making telephone calls down to Money. They had promised that they would let my uncle know if they happened to find Bo, or if any word came through about him. But somehow they forgot to do that. He had the presence of mind to get a sheriff and go down there. By the time he got there, the funeral had been preached and 2 men were digging a grave to bury my son's body. He told them they would have to stop. "I have to take that body up north." The sheriff was rather surprised or maybe he wasn't. I don't know what the situation was at that time. But my uncle had the presence of mind to call a white undertaker and ask him if he would handle that body, embalm it and fix it for shipment.

The colored undertaker told my uncle, "I'll tell you the truth. I don't dare let that body stay in my establishment over night." He said if he did, "I wouldn't have any place in the morning and perhaps I wouldn't be alive by morning." This colored man took the body to the white undertaker. The white undertaker looked at him and shook his head and said "I'll do the best I can with one provision. I'll handle this body and prepare it for ship-ment provided you promise me that this seal will never be broken and that nobody will ever review that body."

My uncle didn't have time to stand up there and argue with anybody about anything. He agreed. And he had every intention of carrying out that promise. When I met that body at the station that fatal Friday morn-ing, I was overcome with grief. To think that I had sent a fine 14-year-old boy to Money, Mississippi, to spend an innocent two weeks vacation and at the end of 7 days, he came back to me in a pine box. That was enough to make anybody cry. Well, we went on to the undertaker's parlor. Mr. Rayner picked up the body and escorted us to his establishment. We waited while he opened the casket.

He came to me and said, "Now, Mrs. Bradley, I want to talk to you. As a friend of the family, I would advise you not to open that box." I said, "Mr. Rayner, I'm sorry, that's all that I will ever be able to do for Bo now is to look at him and pay my last respects." I said if I die, it doesn't make any difference. I don't have too much to live for anyway.

So Mr. Rayner looked at me and he shook his head and said, Well, if that's the way you want it, that's the way it'll have to be." So with my fa-ther on one side, and my friend on the other we made a few steps to that casket. The first thing that greeted us when we walked into the parlor was a terrible odor. I think I'll carry that odor with me to my grave. But out of the newspaper accounts and all the other stories I had heard I wasn't prepared for what I saw. When I got up to that casket, and looked over in there, something happened to me that is akin to getting religion. I have seen people shout. I have seen them jerk. I have seen them lose control of themselves and be very happy. And then again I've seen them very sad.

But it hit me from the head and the feet at the same time. And it met in the middle and straightened me up. I looked at my arms because it felt that every bone had turned to steel. I wanted to know was the change physical, was it noticeable. Then after examining myself, I looked in the casket again, and I said, "Oh my God!"

What I saw looked like it came from out of space. It didn't look like anything that we could dream, imagine in a funny book or any place else. It just didn't look like it was for real. And I had to stand up there and find my boy. I couldn't find him in five minutes, because that was not the Emmett that I had sent to Mississippi. The first thing that struck my attention was a big gash in his forehead. It was big enough for me to stick my hands through. I said they must have done this with an ax.

I saw something that I imagine was his brains down there. Then I looked over here and I saw a gash that was so large you could look right through and tell that every tooth in the back had been knocked out. And Emmett left home with a beautiful set of teeth. One of the most beautiful sets that I have ever seen. I had worried with those teeth and bothered him about them. I would have known his teeth anywhere. But Emmett didn't have any back teeth at all, he just had about 6 perhaps, right across the front.

I could tell because his mouth had been choked open. His tongue was out. His lips were twisted and his teeth were bared just like a snarling dog's. And I said, "Oh my God!" I had to keep calling on Him in order to stand there. And then I looked at his nose. There was another hole. I noticed that somebody even had the nerve to put a bullet in his brain. I wondered why they wasted a bullet because surely it wasn't necessary.

I stopped then, and put all of these pieces together, and it wasn't exactly an easy job. But after I took them one by one, I said that's Emmett's nose, the bottom part here, you couldn't mistake that. And I said, that's his forehead, because it was very prominent. And I looked at his one eye over here, that was bulging out. His eyes were very light in color, and I said that certainly is his eye. And then I looked over here where it seemed that the right eye had been picked out with a nut picker, so I couldn't really go by that.

I decided to examine his ears because he had very large ears, larger than an ordinary person. That's when I found out that part of the ear was gone, and the entire back of the head had been knocked out. I said, "Mr. Rayner, I can't see very well." I said, "Will you take this body out of this box and let me look at the left-hand side, because it's not too much to go by on the right-hand side?" And the man really looked at me like I was crazy. He just shook his head and said you sit down and I'll do it, but I'd rather for you to go home and come back."

I said, "All right. I'll do that. I'll bring you some clothes to put on Bo" because they didn't dress him. He was covered in white powder when he got here, because nobody was to see him anyway. I sent the clothes to the parlor and went back a little while later. Mr. Rayner had laid the body out on a slab. That's when I walked around to the left-hand side of him and looked. It looked as if somebody had taken a criss-cross knife and gone insane on the left side of his face. It was beat into a pulp.

I told Mr. Rayner, if you will have the wake here, I said I would like for as many people to walk in here and see this thing as want to come. As long as we cover these things up, they're going to keep on happening. I said,

I'm pulling the lid off of this one. Nothing else worse than this could ever happen to me—my personal feelings don't matter, it's those other boys and girls out there that we're going to have to look out for. And the more people that walk by Emmett and look at what happened to this 14-year-old boy, the more people will be interested in what happens to their children. Now, maybe, I didn't say those exact words. I doubt if I did. But I do know that I wanted the world to see what had happened to my boy.

We went on home and we had our funeral Saturday as we had planned. While that body was at the funeral parlor, they tell me that 50,000 people walked by that night. They had to close the parlor up at 1:30 a.m. because windows were being broken and the place was just in a shambles. You couldn't move traffic for blocks around. I asked Rev. Roberts if he would be good enough to let me move the body to his church and have the funeral there. Rev. Roberts said yes. Not only that, he said, "I will open the doors so that the people can continue the wake until the time of the funeral." We went in there Saturday and had our funeral and there were so many people locked outside of that church. I guess they must have stood for 8 blocks or more.

I told Rev. Roberts the funeral isn't over until the remains have been viewed. If you will let us have our funeral and go home, you tell those people out there they won't be turned away, they can see, too. Rev. Roberts was very cooperative. He said, "Yes, Mrs. Bradley. I'll throw these doors open 24 hours a day." I said if we don't bury him today, which was Saturday, we can't bury Sunday or Monday, because it's a holiday. I figured on Tuesday we would proceed to the cemetery. Those people walked 24 hours a day. They walked for blocks. They were 6 abreast and I'm told that the traffic was tied up from Saturday afternoon until Tuesday at the close of the funeral. People were interested. They wanted to know what was happening. One would go out and tell another and more than 600,000 people looked at Emmett Louis (Bobo) Till.

When they walked in that church, they had one feeling. But when they looked down in that casket, they got another. Men fainted and women fainted. I'm told that one out of every ten went to their knees and had to be carried out. Those 600,000 people were stirred up so much until the newspapers in Chicago got stirred too. And other people became stirred. And that's why you're out here tonight, because they reached you. We went back to the church on Tuesday and took Emmett to the cemetery.

We have a little town near Chicago, called Argo, and that's where Emmett was practically born and raised. The people out there, the school system and everything, is mostly white. You might find five or six colored children in a class of 130 pupils in high school. You might find eight or nine children in a class of 40 in the grade school. The children out there don't realize that I'm black and you're white. That's where I was educated incidentally. I never discovered I was colored until I was a pretty big girl. I just didn't know. It hadn't occurred to me that I was darker than some of the other people that were in the class. I was graded strictly according to my ability to perform and I was never looked down on.

For that reason I cherish my white friends and my colored friends, because I have no reason to be standoffish or to feel inferior to any of them. They treated me the way I treated them. These schools in Argo, Illinois, turned out en masse. Every school, public and Catholic, in Argo, Summit and Bedford Park turned out to pay tribute to Emmett Louis Till. Most of the people didn't know Emmett. Just a few of them did. Not only that, but the police and everybody cooperated to the fullest extent. We had a 100-police escort to the cemetery. They stopped traffic. They stopped transportation. They stopped everything to let Emmett Till's body be moved. When we got to the cemetery, there were approximately 50 or more cars waiting. I'm sure that there were 200 in the procession that left Chicago. Not only did they take us there on an uninterrupted journey, but they brought us back to my door the same way.

I had the privilege of hearing Adam Clayton Powell speak several nights ago, and I listened to him tell about the situation existing over in Africa and other places. He said those people have decided they're going to have freedom regardless of the amount of blood they have to spill. You can't scare a man whose life expectancy is only 28 years. In some countries that's as long as they expect to live. They're starved to death, they're hungry and everything else. How can you scare them with an atom bomb or a hydrogen bomb? There comes a time when you get beyond fear—fear doesn't mean anything. You're going to die one way or the other so you might as well die fighting. So, those poor ignorant people over there have stood up and asserted themselves. They have said that we are going to die trying to do better. We're not going to just sit here and waste away or idle away and let somebody kick us around 'till we die. And they have gotten very good results.

If those ignorant unlearned people can stand up and take a stand, how can we who have been exposed to education, exposed to all of the good things sit down and let somebody just walk up and say I'm not going to give it to you and you're not going to have it. We can't sit here and wait for somebody to come and hand it to us on a silver platter. That's not going to happen. I don't think there are very many people who have ever had somebody walk up and say here's a Cadillac. I think you deserve it, you've waited patiently for it. When you wanted it, you went out and worked pretty hard.

I think my freedom is worth more to me than a Cadillac, because if I have the Cadillac and can't drive it, I don't need it anyway. I have invested a son in freedom and I'm determined that his death isn't in vain. When I was talking to God and pleading with Him and asking why did You let it be my boy, it was as if He spoke to me and said:—"Without the shedding of innocent blood, no cause is won." And I turned around then and thanked God that He felt that I was worthy to have a son that was worthy to die for such a worthy cause.

I don't say that I'm not regretting it. I don't say that I'm accepting it gleefully or happily. It's a terrible thing to have to accept, but still I'm glad that He made me able to accept it. And also I have stopped, I wondered, and even asked myself how am I making it; how am I doing the things that I am doing, why is it that I'm still in my right mind? The answer always comes back to me that there is a God up there. He's looking down here.

My constant prayer through this ordeal, hasn't been so much for myself. I haven't prayed too much for Mamie, because I think God's looking out after me. But I have prayed to Him rather to keep me aware of what I am doing and why I am doing it. Don't let me get my feet off the ground, my head way up in the air and just start thinking, that I am great because there are no great people really. We are only as great as the least one can become. We're going to have to stop worrying about am I too good to associate with you, or this and that and the other. Instead we are all going to have to realize that we are all very, very small. We are very tiny as individuals. But together we can't be beat. If we stand up and unite ourselves together for a common cause, there is nothing that can stand before us—not just colored people but white people altogether. The colored people can't do it by themselves and the white can't do it by themselves.

As long as we are awakening, I don't think we're going to stand to be held back. I don't believe that the average good, white person wants us to be held back. We can read where our race has contributed innumerable things to the progress of America. Without that rich resource to be tapped and things that we are able to contribute, America herself would not be as great as she is. So I want to stand up now and I want you to stand up, too, and demand our place. Then after we get it, walk in it and respect it. We'll have to be very dignified. The day is gone that we're nobodys; we are all somebodys, and together, I can't tell you how great we are as somebodys.

I would like to touch briefly on the trial in Mississippi. The Mississippi trial was really an ordeal. When I started down there, I'm not going to tell anybody I was brave and raring to go. If there had been any other way I don't think I would have gone. And without the people and the press standing behind me, I still probably would not have made it. My father came from Detroit, my mother was in Chicago already. She was telling me, she said, if you go it will be over my dead body. Other relatives and friends were calling up and saying please don't go. I really didn't want [you] to go. I was convinced that I shouldn't go, but then I had a dream, and it seemed like to me my place was in Mississippi, that I had more business in Mississippi than anybody down there.

I called my father in Detroit the day before I was getting ready to leave, and I said Dad, we're going to Mississippi. He said, "what?" I said, yes, we're going tomorrow, so get here as quickly as you can, and if you're here by a certain time, we'll leave together, if not, I'll have to go without you. I don't think I would have left though until he got there. When we first mentioned going to Mississippi, we got so much response until I knew we would just have to hire an Illinois Central train to take all the people to Mississippi.

But about three hours before plane time, we started making calls to check on the people who wanted to go. Suddenly so many ailments cropped up. There were ingrown toenails and migraine headaches. The Chicago police department said it had no jurisdiction. They couldn't send anybody. Detective agencies with big strong detectives weren't authorized to go to Mississippi. So I looked around. I said, well, it's just me and my dad and Mr. Mooty. I said we'll take God and that will be enough. So that's the way we flew to Memphis, Tennessee. And He was there, because we could feel Him in the plane. He was there.

We got there. We went on down to Mississippi. It was the second day of the trial and it was just about 10 o'clock in the morning, when we go to the courtroom. I was surprised to see the number of colored people milling around there. I had thought maybe their bosses would have told them that they better not go to the trial. But they were there. When we got out of the car, I noticed that there were several television outfits there. There were the newsmen and they were looking for us, and they were right there on guard to see to it, to watch us with the eyes of the camera, to see to it that nothing happened.

When we walked in the courtroom, the judge had made the announcement that if anybody took any pictures, they would be thrown out. But when we walked in there, those white reporters, and those colored reporters, evidently forgot what the judge had said, because they stood on chairs, they stood on tables, they stood on railings, even on one another and took pictures. So the trial had to be recessed.

We can have another recess down in Mississippi, if we let them know that they are not going to lynch people, they are not going to make slaves of our men and women down there. We can have another recess, and it can be just as effective as the one, when I walked in the courtroom.

They settled down and they had what they called the trial. Little vendors were going around selling cases of pop. Mr. Milam and Mr. Bryant went to the washroom unescorted without handcuffs. They had their children on their laps and they spanked them playfully. They hugged their wives and kissed their mothers. They were just privileged characters. Then we had this jury that looked like, well I just can't really tell you what they looked like. But the way that they looked at us, you'd have thought we came from outer space.

The big question in their mind was, what business did we have down there. It was Mississippi's problem and Mississippi was going to handle it. But without the newspapers and the press news agencies, there never would have been a trial in Mississippi. That was forced on them. It was bitter gall in their mouths. They even released an article to the citizens around there. I won't try to quote it. In substance it meant that we know that you're being tried. We know that this is getting under your skin, but for God's sake try to take it. You have a right to get up and blow somebody's head off if you want to because they are certainly down here disrupting your life. But just wait two days: we'll have this over, and you can just go right on back to lynching and doing whatever you want to do. That was just the feeling of the whole town. We knew that they were only holding off, because they didn't dare latch on.

After the summaries were made, it wasn't hard to tell within a few days which way the trial was going. In fact when we got there, the prosecutor told me Tuesday that we should have it over with by Wednesday afternoon. What they hadn't figured on was that Dr. T. R. M. Howard, the NAACP and the colored press were going to get together and dig up some more witnesses. They hadn't figured on that at all. But those people went around down there and got this information. On Tuesday evening, they told the District Attorney that they had eye witnesses to this murder and they would like to have the court recess until they could produce them.

Thursday and Friday they went on the stand. Little Willie Reed stood up there and told how he saw Emmett Till in the back of a truck that Mr. Milam was in. He describes how there were four white men in the cab and four colored men in the back. One of these four colored people, he said, was my boy. He was sitting on the floor of the truck. He recognized him from a picture that he saw in the newspaper. He said that he saw this truck because he had gotten up early that Sunday morning to go and get himself some cigarettes. Well I don't think God necessarily teaches us to smoke. I think it might have been God's will that Willie Reed ran out of cigarettes and just happened to want to get up at 6 o'clock Sunday morning and go to the store.

Willie Reed saw Mr. Bryant when he got out of the truck and go in the same store, come out, get in the truck and drive away. It just happened that Willie Reed lived on the farm of Mr. Milam's brother. So he went on back to his house and when he got to the house, he saw the truck was there. And he also heard a lot of noise out of the barn. He heard a voice screaming. He heard a boy crying for his life, calling for his mother and calling on God. He heard him begging for mercy and he heard the blows that were being struck on the body.

Willie Reed asked a friend, "who is that they're beating up over there," but he didn't know. So Willie came back to a pump, which was approximately 400 feet from where the beating was going on. He also saw Mr. Milam walk up to the pump with a gun still around his waist. It was the same gun he had had when he went to my uncle's house and took the boy out of bed. He saw that man and recognized him. He even spoke to him. Mr. Milam went back to the barn. They tell me that this confusion must have lasted about an hour or better. Pretty soon there was no more noise. They pulled this tractor out of this barn and backed the truck into the barn. When the truck came out, there were only four white men in the cab. There were no colored people to be seen. I know what happened to one of those colored people. There was a tarpaulin over the back of the truck.

We don't know how long they were in there. Maybe it was one, maybe it was two hours, maybe it was more. But for the life of me I don't see how Emmett Till could have screamed that long because any one of those blows on his head would have surely killed him. But then I imagine the body can take a lot of punishment. And his body was badly beaten and because the skin even popped and rolled off. The second skin was all that was left on Emmett's body.

After little Willie Reed got up on that stand, he was questioned by the prosecuting attorney. It was then the need for desegregation really stood forth. Willie Reed had a story, but he couldn't tell it. It was locked inside of him. It would have taken education to put the key in the lock and turn it loose. Every word that was gotten from Willie had to be pulled out word by word. That's because Willie is 18 years old and has probably been to school only 3 years. What he learned in school was not enough really to have gone to the trouble to go there every day.

That's why you are going to have to integrate those schools and make it possible for those children to talk and know what they see and be able to tell it. When the defense got up and questioned Willie, they tore his story all apart. He didn't even know how far he was from the barn. They said, well, would you say you were 5000 feet? Little Willie would say "yes, I guess so," but he didn't know how far 5000 feet were. We all know that you can't see anything from that distance. But they didn't ask him 500 feet, 5 feet, or yards. No, they put it at the impossible distance, because they knew that Little Willie wouldn't be able to defend himself.

They threw that testimony out. Little Willie Reed was not a good witness. He was standing too far away. Moses Wright said that the men walked in his house, took the boy out of the bed. The defense got up, they said that anybody could have walked in Moses Wright's house and said Mr. Preacher, let me in, this is Mr. Bryant. Perhaps Mr. Bryant had an enemy who was playing a joke on him. And so far as Mr. Milam is concerned, there are a lot of tall, fat, baldheaded men in Mississippi and it didn't necessarily have to be him.

In other words they were saying that Moses Wright was too big a fool to know who he saw come in his house. So that tore that testimony down. When I got up on the stand, they realized immediately that I wasn't exactly a fool. Then they turned around and made a very bad person out of me. They questioned me as to the insurance I had, and then they proved to the satisfaction of that jury, that I sent Bobo down there and had Uncle Mose get him killed, so I could collect the insurance. And the jury was satisfied. That explanation pleased them very much. Well I had a 10 cent policy and a 15 cent policy and I don't think that's enough for me to get my son killed, because it wasn't enough to bury him. Well, the trial proceeded. The men said they took Emmett and that they questioned Emmett. He wasn't the right boy, so they turned him loose. Yet and still Emmett Till has never turned up at home. I had proved beyond a shadow of a doubt that that was my son. The ring that he had on his finger was the one that the Army sent me with his father's personal effects. The ring was made in Casablanca and there was only one of that kind because it was a hand made ring.

They did give Moses Wright credit for being smart after all. They said that Moses, being a preacher recognized the possibility of starting something, when Emmett was taken from his house. But knowing that Emmett was going to be turned loose up the road a piece, he rushed out to meet him. That perhaps he knocked him in the head, threw him in the bushes or buried him or maybe, he put him on the train and sent him home. Then he took this ring off Bo's finger, and contacted the NAACP down there. They got together and went out in Tallahatchie River and got them a body, put this ring on the finger, put this gin mill fan around the neck and dropped it over there very conveniently so that they could find it a few days later.

And you'd be surprised how the jury fell for that story. It was just a plot to disgrace Mississippi. But they didn't try to explain whose body it was. It seems that bodies are pretty plentiful down there. And the only point that they were trying to prove is that the body, that I had, did not belong to me. The county doctor took the stand. He said that when he went down to the river bank and examined the body, he couldn't tell if it was a colored or white man.

Then the sheriff stood up on the stand. He too couldn't tell if it was a colored or white man. Yet and still he called a colored undertaker. The man was black enough for nobody to wonder if he was white or black. You might not know it, but down in Mississippi you don't call a colored undertaker to handle a white body. If there is any doubt in your mind whatsoever, you call a white undertaker because a white man or a black man can get his brains blown out if he makes the mistake of giving a white corpse to a colored undertaker. That you just don't do.

Well another mistake that Mississippi made. They held the inquest. They sent me three death certificates signed by the same doctor that couldn't tell whether the body was that of a colored or white man. He testified that Emmett Louis Till had died on such and such a date, "colored" age 14, born the 25th of July, 1941, in Chicago, Illinois. There was the paper in black and white that this was my body. They sent me the death certificate. The insurance policy paid off on the basis of those death certificates. Yet and still when we got down to the Mississippi trial, it couldn't possibly be my boy. I think they should be a little more careful before they start signing these death certificates. But I knew because I stood up there and looked. I found what I was looking for.

Somebody has to sacrifice for a cause. With the sacrifice of a few of our automobiles and some of our fine clothes, we can make this world one that we'll be proud of. I don't think that freedom is so far away that we are not going to enjoy it. I think that pretty soon this thing is going to be over. In fact, it's over now, we just haven't realized it. The tooth has been pulled out, but the jaw is still swollen.

It's just a matter of time before it's going to go down. If we all get together and support the NAACP, that has fought so hard to make things come to where they are now, then I do believe that we are right over the hill to victory. Pray for me, pray for your organization and above all, don't forget the NAACP.

Thank you.

§18 Reverend Robbins Ralph

The Reverend Robbins Ralph (1907–2002) lived a long life heavily involved in the ministry. Coming from a long line of Congregationalist ministers, Ralph attended Beloit College and Yale Divinity School before serving churches in Vermont, New Hampshire, Massachusetts, and Florida. Reverend Ralph also held the position of conference minister of the Florida Congregational Christian Conference for 19 years.

In his sermon to his Madeira Beach, Florida congregants, Ralph lays out a powerful indictment against the cruel forces of discrimination in a speech dripping with righteous sarcasm. Ralph begins his speech discussing the reasons that he is glad that he has been born white. One by one he lists out freedoms and privileges that are available to him and denied to blacks based purely on the color of one's skin. Reverend Ralph discusses how this blatant discrimination touches every aspect of life from the serious to the mundane. From cars to homes to schools, nothing is free from the taint of racial discrimination. And it's a good thing, Reverend Ralph facetiously argues. The white man within him enjoys the temptation of power and ostensible superiority. However, he quickly shows that this seductive thought is decidedly wrong. It is a wrong against our fellow man but more importantly it is a wrong committed against God. Reverend Ralph explains that to be true to his faith and to God, he must reject these immoral feelings of superiority over other races. The burdens of racial discrimination placed upon blacks are a responsibility shared by us all. Only by fighting for their rights can we remove the blood from our collective hands. Only by helping in their struggle can we secure the blessings of God upon ourselves and our nation "... not (as) a white man's country not (as) a black man's country but (as) God's country. For all men are His children." This sermon was reprinted in two parts by the *Tri-State Defender*, a black newspaper published in Memphis.

I'm Glad I Was Born White, Since This Is A White Man's World
Church-by-the-Sea, Madeira Beach, Florida
October 1955

I'm glad I was born white, since this is a white man's world. There are lots of reasons. I can go into any kind of a store, for example, a clothing store, and be fitted for a suit. My wife can try on a dress in any dress shop in any city in the country. We can board a bus or train or boat, if we can pay for the ticket, and we can occupy any seat that is available, and no questions asked.

I'm glad I am a white man. I can go to any theatre, and choose my own seat. If I were a Negro I could not do that. I enjoy baseball, and when I go to the park, all I have to have is one dollar and I can enter the main gate and go anywhere I choose in the great [shaded] grandstand. The Negroes have to sit on bleachers out in the sun. I'm glad I'm a white man.

I'm glad my children have the privileges and advantages of freedom. The public schools that have been open to them are fine schools. They could attend any private school or college in the country to which I could afford to send them and for which they are intellectually qualified. They may apply for any job in the country, and the only requirement is that they have the ability to perform the work. And that they be white. I'm glad my children are white, since this is a white man's world.

One of my sons turned out to have a good deal of musical ability. He specialized in the clarinet. He played with the high school orchestra then joined the St. Petersburg, Florida Symphony orchestra and worked up to first clarinet. When the road show, "South Pacific" came to St. Petersburg for a week they needed a clarinetist and he played with the orchestra and earned as much in a week as I earned in a week as a minister. We were proud of him. And glad he was white. If he had been a Negro, he could have played in the Negro high school band—and that is good—but not in the city's symphony or in "South Pacific."

I'm glad our family is white, since this is a white man's world.

And yet I'm not altogether glad that I'm a white man. There is something on my mind. Since this is a white man's world, I rather naturally get the impression that I'm a better man than the Negro . . . More intelligent, more cultured.

Take the matter of money, for example. I know how to use money fairly wisely. I don't spend it as fast as I get it, and then go on relief when it is gone. I don't own a television set because I can't afford it. I don't drive a Cadillac because, for my money, there are other values in life more important. But the Negroes who live in tumble down shacks have forests of TV towers over their quarters. They love to drive flashy and powerful cars. Their cultural scale is obviously lower than mine. Or so I am tempted to think.

And yet, something bothers me. It just happens that I like to live in an adequate and modern house, set on a spacious, landscaped lot, in a pleasant neighborhood. How do I know what I would do if this privilege were denied me? How do I know what I would do if I had to live in the narrow confines of a crowded slum? If it were impossible for me to go out and buy, or build, or rent the kind of house I like? If I could not go to the better churches, could not spend my money at the better theatres, could not play golf at the country club? I imagine I'd get a television set as soon as I could manage the down payment. Would I be able to keep up the payments? I don't know. If a white man and I work together in a certain place and the employer has to let one of us go, I'll be the one laid off. I can't be sure of the future anyway. I might as well enjoy TV while I can. And if they have to take the set back to the store, so what?

And as for the Cadillac, this is the white man's world. And in the white man's world a Cadillac is a symbol of success, achievement of power and prestige. Since I happen to be a white man, there are also other ways in which I can satisfy the urge to be somebody; other ways in which I can prove myself successful. I don't need a Cadillac. But if these other avenues were closed to me, if I could not have a good house to live in, if I could not hob-nob with the best people; if I could walk through the hotel dining room as a waiter but not as a diner; if I could go out on the Municipal pier with a broom to sweep the floor but not with a pole to catch the fish; if my wife could go into the homes of the rich and elegant to serve tea but not to take tea, you know, I think a Cadillac might be tempting.

No, I'm not altogether happy about being a white man in a white man's world. This world gives me the impression that I'm a better man. But the horrible and disturbing thought is that it may be wrong? The cards are stacked in my favor. Maybe I'm an inferior person, and don't know it.

I'm not entirely happy about my children being white. I suppose, like any fond father, I thought my boy was the best clarinetist his age in town. But how do I know? There were hundreds of youngsters who never had a chance to show. Maybe I'm unconsciously afraid that I'm not a better man. Maybe I'm not really sure my boy is such a superior musician. Maybe I'm afraid a black boy might beat him out. Is that why I'm glad he's white? May God have mercy on me.

We went to see "South Pacific," even though the price was steep. It was worth the price of admission just to hear one certain song in that play. A song that goes like this:

> You've got to be taught to hate and hear,
> You've got to be taught from year to year,
> It's got to be drummed in your dear little ear,
> You've got to be carefully taught.
> You've got to be taught to be afraid   .
> Of people whose eyes are queerly made,
> Of people whose skin is a different shade,
> You've got to be carefully taught.
> You've got to be taught before it's too late,
> Before you are six or seven or eight.
> To hate the people your relatives hate;
> You've got to be carefully taught.

We white people have been taught, carefully taught, by the culture in which we live, that we are the superior race. It has been drummed into our dear little ear until we believe it. The only trouble is, it just possibly isn't so.

No, I'm not entirely happy about being a white man in a white man's world. There is something gnawing on my conscience. It is on my conscience that I and my sort are depressing my brother and his children. His children can't go where mine can. His children can't do the things my children can do. There are doors that close. When we elevate ourselves by stepping on the colored race, by the same act we send the colored race down. When we deceive ourselves into notions of innate and God given superiority, by the same token we sometimes force upon the Negro a sense of inferiority which dooms him to live way below his best. If he is sensitive (and he is human), some get crushed. Why push in where you obviously are not wanted? You can always go back to shantytown, the television, the Cadillac. For excitement and adventure you can always turn to moonshine, liquor and the bolita game.

And I am the white man who sends him there. I am not altogether happy about myself. My conscience is bothering me. May God have mercy on my soul.

I love this church, and the people in it. I love them very greatly. Could I come to church some Sunday morning with a Negro friend and could we worship quietly together? I don't know. We had better be doing some thinking and some praying about these things.

July 4 was Independence Day, the 179th anniversary of the American Declaration of Independence. We look with pride on the struggle carried on by our spiritual ancestors in the founding of a nation freed not only from a caste-ridden nobility, freed from the over-lordship of an aristocracy born above the common man. We need to be reminded that less than two centuries ago, in most of the world, 90 per cent of the people, regardless of race, were thought to be unworthy to be educated, unworthy to vote. People like you and me, children like yours and mine, were not good enough to go to school, at least with the silk-clad children of the aristocrats. It was folly to think of educating common people like us. What was the point of it? What did we know of the finer things of life? Your ancestors and mine were born for the heavy work, the dirty work, the servile work. We had no business aspiring to greatness or achievement in art or science or music or business or politics. It would only soil our usefulness to let such notions get into our heads.

But we repudiated that kind of thinking in this country. This was to be not a rich man's country, not the aristocrat's country, but the common man's country. But it is still a white man's country. The revolution is not yet finished. The struggle for freedom, for justice, for equality of opportunity is not yet won.

At present, it is still a white man's country, the American Negro today being where all our ancestors were 200 years ago, where all women were 100 years ago. We do not well to boast of freedom until the last battle has been fought and won.

I happen to be white. I want to be a Christian. The white man part of me is satisfied with the way things are. The Christian part of me is restless and unhappy and guilty and ashamed. The Christian part of me will not be at ease until this is not a white man's country nor a black man's country but God's country. For all men are His children.

I beg your pardon if I have spoken in such a way as to disturb your thinking. I beg God's pardon if I have not.

§19 Sarah Patton Boyle

Sarah Patton Boyle's biography appears in the introduction to her February 13, 1955 sermon at Calvary Christian Church. In this fascinating speech/sermon before the Council of Church Women in Charlottesville, Sarah Patton Boyle uses strategic ambiguity to convict her fellow Christian women. She never uses the terms race, civil rights, black, or Negro to convey her message that white Christians must minister to the needs of the black community. The best clue we have that the speech is indeed about race is Boyle's use of the phrase "those of us who hold ourselves apart." Delicately, through indirection, Boyle convicts her audience that to feed all of God's sheep is not to separate or segregate: "Bidding ourselves apart is not loving our neighbors, is not feeding his sheep, is not regarding all men as a part of ourselves and of Him."

Feed My Sheep

Council of Church Women, Charlottesville, Virginia
November 4, 1955

Jesus used words and concepts symbolically as well as literally. When He said, "Beware the leaven of the Pharisees," and his disciples thought He meant material bread, He rebuked them, saying, "Do you not even yet understand?"

We are sending our Parcels for Peace in the Christian spirit, knowing that they are not only to assuage the bodily pangs of distressed peoples, but also to assuage the enervating soul hunger, chill and sickness which can spring from feeling rejected, isolated and unloved.

Just as in our communion services the material and tangible are used to symbolize what is of even more value, so to inert, material help we add the living bread of love, acceptance and concern. In doing so we give to our foreign brothers strength to endure and to overcome their own material lacks. For as Christians we know that without this inner strength bodily welfare can never be enough.

It's of this bread of greater value that I shall speak today, for it is this above all other which we as Christians are obligated to offer to all in need.

Most of us, I think, sincerely try to do this. Our failures spring more from lack of understanding than from un-Christian intent. Few of us harden our hearts against the known needs of others. Rather, awareness of their needs escapes us.

Some years ago the Harvard School of Business carried on an 18-year research program to determine the factors which enable man to work efficiently. Can you guess what was uncovered as the chief factor in the productivity of workers?

Most of us would probably guess improved facilities and surroundings, shorter hours, better tools, or better pay. But the 18 years of intensive and careful research revealed that it is none of these things.

The greatest stimulus to individual productivity was found to be a sense of belonging. Next came recognition, then approval. The list of human needs for efficient work was long, and physical facilities of all kinds were low on the list.

About eight years ago a discerning teacher of retarded children made psychological history by raising the I.Q.'s of her pupils, in some cases, I believe, more than 20%, simply by filling approximately these same needs.

I think psychiatrists are unanimous in the opinion that the average person can be almost destroyed as a happy and useful citizen by withdrawing from him a sense of approval, and refusing him recognition and respect. Indeed, much of the rehabilitation of wrecked personalities consists in the psychiatrist himself offering the patient this daily bread for which so many people ache with hunger.

We who could be instruments of the Almighty must remember that like the love of God which must be poured down upon us before we can love either God or man, these gifts of acceptance, approval and respect must be offered to us before we can become fully worthy of them.

Some years ago I had a job in which the person working immediately over me had the fixed idea that I was exceedingly stupid. I could literally feel my alertness draining off through the funnel of her conviction. Never in my life have I fumbled more, made more idiotic errors or forgot as much as I did during the period when her hollow belief was affixed to my mind.

Happily, a mutual friend came to my rescue and by some hoax or legerdemain convinced my boss that she had underrated my I.Q. I knew nothing about this until later, but she had hardly more than entered the room next morning than I felt suddenly able to think and function properly. For in her face and manner I read a new attitude of respect, approval and acceptance of me as worthy of fellowship with herself.

No wonder he who says to his brother, "Thou Fool!" is in desperate danger. If we believe that our brother doesn't meet our standards of efficiency or morals, the action called for is that we fall on our knees and ask forgiveness of the God who made us all of one blood.

We cannot shirk our personal responsibility for real or imagined weaknesses of any neighbor, no matter how distant, and no matter how near. For if he lacks what we have, it is only because somewhere along the line we have not fed the Lord's sheep, nor guided them to the storehouses of our supply.

We are members one of another in a more literal sense than we realize. In every contact with others we give or withhold their daily bread. Not a day passes that we lack the opportunity to strengthen or to drain some one, both in the world community and in our own. Our responsibility as members of the body of Christ is more immediate and overwhelming than most of us pause to grasp.

People starve upon the doorsteps of our hearts, and every single one of those who starve is Jesus Christ himself! The time has come when Christians can no longer evade the thunderous, flaming words of God which roar down the centuries like a forest fire to over take us: "IN AS MUCH AS YE HAVE DONE IT UNTO THE LEAST OF THESE, YE HAVE DONE IT UNTO ME!"

Can we, as church women, fail to consider modern dilemmas in the light of these blazing words? Have we any choice but to fall on our knees and rend our hearts in penitence? Haven't we sometimes even been guilty of fearing that if we follow the Lord's way that our educational and moral standards may suffer? Dare we call ourselves Christians if we cannot summon even that modicum of faith?

Is there any standard higher than the one which Jesus set? "Love thy neighbor . . . Feed my sheep . . .Whatever you do to any man you do to me." Is there any standard which we would rather our children would [sic] maintain than this? Surely we don't believe in the depths of us that our standards might be lowered by doing what the Lord bids us to do?

Many of us today are stuffing scriptural quotations into the holes in our consciences, but I've yet to meet a God revering man or woman who will stand up and say, "Jesus would endorse our efforts to hold ourselves apart." Bidding ourselves apart is not loving our neighbors, is not feeding his sheep, is not regarding all men as a part of ourselves and of him.

Yet it is true that we're all one with each other and with him. And the more we struggle to follow his way the more aware of this truth we become.

Those of us who have been in a position where many others were aligned against us know that our chief enemy is not any one who attacks us, but an overwhelming lethargy and weariness, such as you might feel if you had just donated, not one but two pints of blood. Our daily bread of acceptance, of fellowship, of approval is cut off, and we are weak with hunger.

Yet many who have had this experience have made an exciting discovery. And that is that there is a way to get our daily bread directly from the Father. It is simply by launching ourselves on the exciting Christian truth, "Give and ye shall receive." If we turn and give to those who repudiate us the understanding and acceptance which they have withheld from us, our strength rushes back as into a vacuum.

Suddenly we know what Jesus meant when He said, "And if the house be worthy, let your peace come upon it; but if it be not worthy, let your peace return to you." For when we offer goodwill to enemies if they accept it, it blesses them, and they in turn bless us. But if they reject it, somehow mysteriously it returns and pours down upon us the blessings which were meant for them. There rises within us an indestructible fellowship with themselves, with mankind and with God which swallows up our loneliness like a wave.

And echoing down the centuries St. Paul's discovery is rediscovered in us: "I am persuaded that neither death nor life . . . nor things present, not things to come . . . nor anything . . . shall be able to separate us from the love of God."

Nothing, nothing at all but our own rejection of him can separate us from his love. But He told us in one of the clearest and most unmistakable passages in the entire Bible that each time we reject another human being, we reject Him.

In our home, in our town, in our nation, in our world, our brothers faint for the sustaining bread of a sense of belonging, of our approval, of our respect, and they thirst for the living waters of Christian love. Both those of us who hold ourselves apart and those who ache with rejection should remember that we cannot give without receiving. For this is the law [for] which Jesus died that we might learn.

I always like to close my talks with a portion of the peace prayer of St. Francis of Assisi. Please join me in praying it aloud.

> O Lord,
> Make me an instrument
> Of thy peace.
> Where there is hatred
> Let me sow love;
> Where there is injury,
> Pardon;
> Where there is discord,
> Union;
> Where there is doubt,
> Faith.
>
> Oh Divine Master,
> Grant that I
> Shall not so much seek
> To be consoled
> As to console;
> To be understood
> As to understand;
> To be loved
> As to love. AMEN.

1956

1956

§20 Branch Rickey

Wesley "Branch" Rickey pioneered the integration of Major League Baseball. Born on December 20, 1881 in Stockdale, Ohio, Rickey had a mediocre career as a catcher for several professional franchises. An Ohio Wesleyan University graduate, the Cincinnati Reds dropped Rickey after he refused to play Sundays. Shortly thereafter, Rickey moved into baseball's executive office. For nearly half a century, Rickey oversaw the administrative efforts of the St. Louis Cardinals, Brooklyn Dodgers, and Pittsburgh Pirates. He was one of baseball's great innovators, introducing the minor league farm system, spring training facilities, and a number of training devices, such as the batting cage. Branch Rickey's fame, though, stems from a decision he made during his tenure as General Manager of the Brooklyn Dodgers. In 1945, acting on his idealism and his managerial acumen, he signed Negro League star Jackie Robinson to a professional contract, thereby beginning the process of Major League Baseball's integration. An innovator until the end, Rickey died on December 9, 1965.

Jackie Robinson was a star athlete long before he broke baseball's color barrier. Born in Cairo, Georgia on January 31, 1919 his resume included athletic competition at both Pasadena Community College and UCLA. During his time at UCLA, Robinson became the school's first athlete to letter in four different sports. After a two-year stint in the army—Robinson was honorably discharged in 1944 following an unsuccessful court-martial attempt for insubordination—he returned to baseball by signing a one-year contract with the Kansas City Monarchs of the Negro League. His success in Kansas City led Dodgers' General Manager Branch Rickey to the Midwest. Upon meeting Rickey, Robinson said, "But if Mr. Rickey hadn't signed me, I wouldn't have played another year in the black league. It was too difficult. The travel was brutal. Financially, there was no reward. It took everything you make to live off." Rickey signed Robinson to a major league contract, and in 1947 Robinson won the National League Rookie of the Year Award. This was the first of many achievements for Robinson, who ended his career with six World Series appearances and a league Most Valuable Player award. Robinson was elected to the Baseball Hall of Fame in 1962, the first black player to "integrate" Cooperstown, New York as well. Very active in the civil rights movement, Robinson served on the board of the NAACP until 1967. Grieved by the death of his oldest son in an automobile accident in 1971, Robinson soon succumbed to complications from diabetes on October 24, 1972. A wife and two children survive him. In 1997 Major League Baseball retired his number 42 forever and made April 15, Jackie Robinson Day.

Rickey begins his speech to the Atlanta One Hundred Percent Wrong Club banquet by examining several problems that barricade Negroes from entering Major

League Baseball. He characterizes them as primary objectives undertaken in his decision to employ Jackie Robinson. His decision to integrate professional baseball is contingent on off-the-field considerations. Quite simply, only a strong and courageous man could overcome criticisms and racism from whites and blacks alike to break the color barrier. Religion also played a part. In a *Look* magazine photo caption, Rickey had earlier remarked, "I cannot face my God much longer knowing that His black creatures are held separate and distinct from His white creatures in the game that has given me all that I can call my own." Rickey depicts his relationship with God as a compelling and motivating force behind his desire to break baseball's color barrier. His past experiences with men of strong Christian faith guide him toward certain answers he seeks. For Branch Rickey, his association with the church instilled in him that what he was doing was inherently right, possibly even the will of God. He concludes his address by detailing four solutions to America's racial dilemmas: proximity, cultural interactions, a middle class, and a recognition that "all men are equal in the sight of God."

"One Hundred Percent Wrong Club"
Atlanta, Georgia
January 20, 1956

Dr. May, gentlemen, ladies and gentlemen. My plane doesn't leave until tomorrow at 10:35 A.M. and I haven't a thing to do between now and then but to talk if I get the chance, and I feel like talking.

I asked Mr. Lawson and several others today about my time limit, and I think I was rather insistent upon it, and I never did get a time limit and I just concluded that I would talk as long as I pleased. I don't know what time you gentlemen have engagements for tomorrow morning's work but I want to talk about a thing or two.

I feel a little remote; the speaking spot is not as close as I would like it. I should like to feel that each one of you were my guests tonight at my own home, and that I could talk to you just as I would if you were there. And I am going to try to maintain that attitude of mine from my remarks that I am very close to you and whether you may agree with what I have to say or not, you will know that I am trying to be intimately confidential and frank about my remarks.

Now I could talk at some length, of course, about the problem of hiring a negro ball player after an experience of 25 years in St. Louis, where at the end I had no stock at all in the club and no Negro was permitted to buy his way into the grandstand during that entire period of my residence in St. Louis. The only place a Negro could witness a ball game in St. Louis was to buy his way into the bleachers,—the pavilion. With an experience of that kind in back of me, and having had sort of a "bringing up" that was a bit contrary to that regime, milieu in St. Louis, I went to Brooklyn.

Within the first month in Brooklyn, I approached what I considered the number one problem in the hiring of a Negro in professional baseball in this country. Now that is a story and that could be a fairly long speech. Namely, ownership. Ownership must be in line with you, and I was at that time an employee, not at that time a part owner of the club. And when ownership was passed, then five other things presented themselves. This is not my speech. I am just giving you this as a preliminary. But I want to get out of the road of this thing, and have you say that, well, I wish he had talked about that thing.

The second thing was to find the right man as a player. I spent $25,000 in all the Caribbean countries, in Puerto Rico, Cuba, employed two scouts, one for an entire year in Mexico, to find that the greatest Negro players were in our own country.

Then I had to get the right man off the field. I couldn't come with a man to break down a tradition that had in it centered and concentrated all the prejudices of a great many people north and south unless he was good. He must justify himself upon the positive principle of merit. He must be a great player. I must not risk an excuse of trying to do something in the sociological field, or in the race field, just because of sort of a "holier than thou." I must be sure that the man was good on the field, but more dangerous to me, at that time, and even now, is the wrong man off the field. It didn't matter to me so much in choosing a man off the field that he was temperamental, righteously subject to resentments. I wanted a man of exceptional intelligence, a man who was able to grasp and control the responsibilities of himself to his race and could carry that load. That was the greatest danger point of all. Really greater than the number five in the whole six.

Number one was ownership, number two is the man on the field, number three the man off the field. And number four was my public relations, transportation, housing, accommodations here, embarrassments, feasibility. That required investigation and therein lies the speech. And the Cradle of Liberty in America was the last place to make and to give us generous considerations.

And the fifth one was the Negro race itself, over-adulation, mass attendance, dinners, of one kind or another of such a public nature that it would have a tendency to create a solidification of the antagonisms and misunderstandings, over-doing it. And I want to tell you that the committee of 32—it was called, in Greater New York—eminent Negro citizens, and Judge Kazansky, and my secretary and myself, those 32 men organized all eight cities in the National League and did a beautiful job of it. And for two years not one of those things was attempted or done and I never had any embarrassments in Brooklyn. They did have a great trainload of people go to see you play in Montreal and Buffalo and other places, and I tried to stop that but I was too late.

But the greatest danger, the greatest hazard, I felt was the Negro race itself. Not people of this crowd any more than you would find antagonisms organized in a white crowd of this caliber either. Those of less understanding, those of a lower grade of education frankly. And that job was done beautifully under the leadership of a fine judge in New York who became a Chairman of an Executive Committee. That story has never been told. The meetings we had, two years of investigations, the Presidents of two of the Negro colleges, the publisher of the *Pittsburgh Courier*, a very helpful gentleman he was to me, a professor of sociology in New York University, and a number of others, the LaGuardia Committee on Anti-Discrimination, Tom Dewey's Committee in support of the Quinn-Ives Law in New York state.

And sixth was the acceptance by his colleagues, by his fellow players. And that one I could not handle in advance. The other five over a period of two and one-half years, I worked very hard on it. I felt that the time was ripe, that there wouldn't be any reaction on the part of a great public if a man had superior skill, if he had intelligence and character and had patience and forbearance, and "could take it" as it was said here. I didn't make a mistake there. I have made mistakes, lots of mistakes.

A man of exceptional courage, and exceptional intelligence, a man of basically fine character, and he can thank his forbearers for a lot of it. He comes from the right sort of home, and I knew all this, and when somebody, somewhere, thinks in terms of a local athletic club not playing some other club because of the presence on the squad of a man of color. I am thinking that if an exhibition game were to be played in these parts against a team on whose squad was Jackie Robinson, even leaving out all of the principles of fair play, all the elements of equality and citizenship, all the economic necessities connected with it, all the violations of the whole form and conceptions of our Government from its beginning up to now, leave it all out of the picture, he would be depriving some of the citizens of his own community, some wonderful boys, from seeing an exhibition of skill and technique, and the great, beautiful, graciousness of a slide, the like of which they could not see from any other man in this country. And that's not fair to a local constituency.

I am wondering, I am compelled to wonder, how it can be. And at the breakfast, recently, when a morning paper's story was being discussed and my flaxen hair daughter said to me, "He surely didn't say it." I thought, yes it is understandable. It is understandable. And when a great United States Senator said to me some few days after that, "Do you know that the headlines in Egypt are terribly embarrassing to our State Department?" And then he told me, in part, a story whose utter truthfulness I have no reason to doubt, about the tremendous humiliation—"The Land of the Free and the Home of the Brave"—"where we are talking about extending to all civilizations, tremendous and beautiful freedoms, and the unavoidable, hypocritical position it puts us in internationally," "How could anybody do it," said my daughter.

That night we had a family discussion. It lasted a long time. My five daughters were there, mother was there, auntie was there, four sons-in-law were there; it was Christmas time. And I said to them what I want to say to you tonight. It is understandable that an American with a certain background, certain exposures in the field of education, would represent a more or less a plausible inheritance in regard to the assimilation, the relationship, the acceptance in our current life of the Negro.

The whole thing as a difference between the acceptance in Brazil, for instance, Spanish and Portuguese countries, and the British West Indies and America, a very remarkable thing, but understood by all historians and all writers on the subject. Portugal was the first one to import slaves from Africa, took them into Portugal. It was the last one to give up the slave trade. 19,000,000 go into one country alone in South America, imported slaves over a period of over four hundred years. Now, slavery antedated Negro slavery, oh many years, really thousands of years, before any Negro was taken out of Africa. It was an accident, a misfortune, a thing that could be remedied. All slavery throughout the centuries preceded African importation of slaves. It was the result of war, it was a result of debt. There were several things that led to it, but always there was manumition in front of the man. Freedom obtainable. And the laws going back clear beyond Seneca, and Cicero refers to it, all the way through all those centuries, manumition was a comparatively easy thing. The law of that time, all of it, Plato, the Roman jurisprudence is based upon it, that you can become free. You may be a slave today, you can be a Moor, you can be a Greek, you can be a man of high intelligence. Slavery was a matter of accident or misfortune. And the Spanish Law, the Latin nations inherited that law both in its enactment and in its interpretation were favorable to manumition, making men free. It was not a matter of color at all and the law supported that and the importation of slaves into South America, and all of South America, into Mexico earlier, a few were there subsequently, and in all the Caribbean countries which are now predominant, all of it came in the line of probable manumition, so that when, say, 90% of all the slaves who had been slaves came to be free in Brazil, for example. Then would come in the other importations and the other men who were slaves. There was a group of qualified free men to take care of the small number, 10%, who were slaves. That was Latin America.

They had no problems such as we had here in the south following the Civil War, where there was nobody to take care of a great number of free men and no previous free men in the colored race to adapt themselves to those conditions. And, of course, there was disgraceful governmental conduct. Now the difference, miracle that it is, mystery that it is, and yet greed at the bottom of it the slave trade was immensely profitable—Liverpool was—I was going to say, was built out of it, and America followed suit on it. And whereas the law that men are equal long before, I say, the Negro came into the picture.

The church has always, and it has been a tendency of the Christian church too to undertake to establish the equality of all men in the sight of God. And to the extent which that prevailed to that extent it became inevitable that all men should ultimately become free. That was the greatest force in the world, to give every man moral stature. Of course the Emancipation Proclamation by Lincoln made the southern Negro slave free, but it never did make the white man morally free. He remained a slave to his inheritances. And some are even today.

I believe that a man can play baseball as coming to him from a call from God.

I was in Cleveland at a dinner when I was a youngster, just out of college, and a man in Cleveland who was called, editorially in the Cleveland *Plain Dealer*, on the occasion of his death, the foremost citizen of Cleveland, George Shurtliffe was his name. I never had met him except at that luncheon that day up there in the cupola of that building, 12 or 13 gentlemen around the table, and I was asked to take a job, a certain job that I had never thought about taking. And I didn't feel that I was qualified for the job, and I didn't know whether I wanted it; I was quite ill at ease about it, but the strengthened force of the men who were asking me to take it was influential with me. And we had this dinner and Mr. Shurtliffe was asked to come.

He was identified with the organization in some capacity, and when we had just about finished the meal, I was sitting the second one on the left side of the table and he was down yonder at the end, he said to me, "Branch," he said, "do you believe in the call of God?" No, his first question was, "if you thought God wanted you to do something would you do it?"

I said, "if I knew what God wanted me to do, I think any boy would."

He said, "do you believe in the call of God?" I didn't answer.

He said, "do you know what the call of God is?"

I said, "I don't know that I do," but I said, "I don't think it is a little bird that comes and sits on your ear and whispers and says to you go do this."

He said, "I think you are right."

"Well," I said, "Bishop Basford said that to me and it's not original," but I said, "I don't. . . ."

He said, "would you like to know what I think it is?"

And I said, "I would," because he was a distinguished man.

He said that the first thing in the call of God is aptitude. God doesn't want any man to do something that he can't do. He made me define the word in front of those gentlemen.

He said, the second thing in the call of God is the advice of his friends, and he made me tell him all my friends and we got down from the 8,000 people that had seen that professional football game that fall where I had made a touchdown, I was a great big fellow, and I couldn't name all those 8,000. I thought they were all my friends. They gave nine rahs with my name on the end of it and it got down to the place where I named my father and mother and then the girl that I had announced I was going to marry. He accepted her. And that made two and then he took a professor in school after questioning me about it. And then he took a boyhood friend that I had grown up with way down in the hills of southern Ohio, a country boy. He said, no man has more than a handful of real friends under adversity. He said, they are God's angels: go talk to them. God speaks to men through his friends. Be careful who your friends are. The second thing he said.

And the third thing, he said, was opportunity. He said, when you are prepared to do something and your friends all tell you that you should do it and then the chance comes to do it, he said, that's where God shows His face. Now, he said to me, and I didn't quite know what the word meant when he said it. And he said there may be some sophistry about that. But whether there was or not, I have used it often. And I have thought about it in connection with ball players. What should they be doing in this thing that emphasizes the physical over the mental or spiritual or whatnot. And what are the weaknesses of opportunity in the field? What are the great chances for moral deterioration on the part of great men who go into this thing where they have been under hours of labor previously and now have leisure time, the most damnable thing in the world.

Leisure in the hands of the man who has no creativeness: lots of young men don't have it. That thing that can write great symphonies that can write great tragedies in this use of time. I have often wondered where God may come into the picture. There are some boys who shouldn't be playing ball. This chap, and others; it's a wonderful thing to have a family background and to have something you can hold on to that is basic and firm and strong.

Character is a great thing to have in an athlete, a team. It's a great thing. And when I wonder if there is any condonation, any explanation, anything that can be done to make an extenuating circumstance out of something that violates the right of a part of our citizenship throughout the country when I know that the Man of 1900 years ago spent His life and died for the sake of freedom, the right to come, to go, to see, to think, to believe, to act. It is to be understood, but it is too profoundly regretted.

Education is a slow process. It may solve it. It is inevitable that this thing comes to fruition. Too many forces are working fast. This so called little Robinson—we call it the "Robinson Experiment"—tremendous as it will be for Jackie to have so placed himself in relation not only to his own people in this country, but to his whole generation and to all America that he will leave the mark of fine sportsmanship and fine character. That is something that he must guard carefully. He has a responsibility there.

Frank Tannenbaum, in his book on Slave and Citizen, he is a professor of Latin American history in Columbia University, points out—I think it is the bible on the subject—it really is. I'm not sure, I'm not sure that legislators ought to drive against a prominent and very antagonistic minority. I'm not sure that they should drive F.E.C. too fast too far. I'm not sure that the 18th Amendment might repeat itself. That you would have an organization of glued antagonisms that would be able to delay the solution of a problem that is now in my judgment fast being solved, and when you once gain an eminence you do not have to recede from it. The educational process is something.

Four things, says Tannenbaum, is solving this question, with an unrealized rapidity. First, proximity. Clay Hopper, Jackie's first manager. I've never told it in public. I've never allowed it to be printed if I could help it, took me by the lapels of my coat as he sat there sweating in his underclothes watching a game over on the inside park at Daytona Beach. And this boy had made a great play in the fourth inning and I had remarked about it and the two of us sitting there together, and this boy coming from—I shouldn't have given his name—forget the name and I will tell you the story. I'll deny that he ever said it. He took me by the front of my coat when in the seventh inning Jackie made one of those tremendous remarkable plays that very few people can make: went toward first base, made a slide, stabbed the ball, came with it in his left hand glove and as he turned with the body control that's almost inconceivable and cut off the runner at second base on a force play. I took Clay and I put my hand on his shoulder and I said, "Did you ever see a play to beat it?"

Now this fellow comes from Greenwood, Mississippi. And he would forgive me, I am sure, because of the magnificent way that he came through on it. He took me and shook me and his face that far from me and he said, "do you really think that a 'nigger' is a human being, Mr. Rickey?" That's what he said. That's what that fellow said. I have never answered him until this minute.

And six months later he came into my office after the year at Montreal when he was this boy's manager. He didn't want him to be sent to him.

And he said to me, "I want to take back what I said to you last spring." He said, "I'm ashamed of it." "Now," he said, "you may have plans for him to be on your club," and he was, "but," he said, "if you don't have plans to have him on the Brooklyn club," he said, "I would like to have him back in Montreal." And then he told me that he was not only a great ball player good enough for Brooklyn, but he said that he was a fine gentleman. Proximity. Proximity, says Tannenbaum, will solve this thing if you can have enough of it. But that is a limited thing, you see.

And the second thing, says Tannenbaum, is the cultural inter-twining through the arts, through literature, through painting, through singing, through the professions, where you stabbed through the horizontal strata of social makeup, and you make vertical thrusts in that cultural inter-twining. That inevitably will help solve this problem, and be believed with rapidity.

And third, the existence in our democracy here of a middle class, the middle class in Great Britain, the middle class in probably every country, I think, that makes secure, if anything does, a democracy such as we know. This group here like this, these groups throughout America of all colors. That existence in this country will bring it about surely and faster than people know.

And fourth, the recognition of the moral stature of all men, that all humans are equal. This thing of freedom has been bought at a great price. That all men are equal in the sight of God. That all law must recognize that men are equal, all humans are equal by nature. The same pains, and the same joys, and in our country the same food, the same dress, the same religion, the same language, the same everything. And perhaps quite as questionable an ancestry civically in this country on the part of the black men as we can trace many of the forbearers in the white race of the other settlers of this country.

Gentlemen, it is inconceivable to me that in view of domestic tranquility and home understanding that anywhere, anytime, anybody, can question the right of citizens of this country for equal economic opportunity under the law. How can it be? And how can anyone in official authority, where more attention is given to remarks than would come from an ordinary civilian, be so unremindful of his country's relationship that he could bring us into and disgrace [us] internationally.

These four things I mention will work, I think, in due time with a sureness that will make possibly the very next generation wonder and look back, as I said that you quoted me in Cincinnati, I had forgotten that I had ever said it, look back with incredulity upon everything that was a problem to us today in this country, and will wonder what the issue was all about. I am completely color-blind. I know that America is, it's been proven Jackie is more interested in the grace of a man's swing, in the dexterity of his cutting a base, and his speed afoot, in his scientific body control, in his excellence as a competitor on the field. America, wide and broad, and in Atlanta, and in Georgia, will become instantly more interested in those marvelous, beautiful qualities than they are in the pigmentation of a man's skin, or indeed in the last syllable of his name. Men are coming to be regarded of value based upon their merits, and God hasten the day when Governors of our States will become sufficiently educated that they will respond to those views.

§21 Reverend Paul N. Carnes

Paul N. Carnes was born on February 1, 1921 in Jeffersonville, Indiana. He graduated Phi Beta Kappa from Indiana University and he received his theological degree, with honors, from Harvard. Carnes served as a second lieutenant in World War II and was a prisoner of war in Tunisia from 1942 to 1945. After the war he married Freda Wolf. After finishing his theological training at Harvard, he served as minister to several Unitarian congregations, including the First Unitarian Church of Youngstown and the First Unitarian Church of Memphis, from 1954 to 1958. While in Youngstown, Carnes was president of the city's Interracial Committee. He would later serve as the Unitarian Universalist Association's president from 1977 to 1979. Unitarians have served as the shadow voice of Christianity since the Council of Nicea condemned Arianist non-trinitarian heresies of universal salvation in 325 A.D. More recently they have spoken out against sixteenth-century church-sponsored executions of non-trinitarians (both Catholic and Protestant), and twentieth century discrimination based on race.

During Carnes's brief four year ministry in Memphis, he received death threats for advocating home sales in his neighborhood to blacks. From 1968 through the mid-1970s, the Unitarian Black Affairs Council came to dramatic confrontations at the UUA General Assembly which included at least one incidence of spitting between leaders bitterly divided over the virtues of black empowerment versus integration. During Carnes's presidency, the assembly resolved to recognize the 25th anniversary of *Brown v. Board of Education*, having navigated Brown's turbulent aftermath. The neighborhood near 1283 Inman St. (Memphis), where the Carnes family lived, has maintained its middle class composition, and is now predominantly African American. Carnes died at his home in Boston on March 17, 1979. His papers are housed at the Andover-Harvard Theological Library in Cambridge, Massachusetts.

In his address to Memphis Unitarians, Carnes makes deft use of Floyd Hunter's community power structure theory, arguing that black and white elites have to find moderates among them to steer Memphis through a potentially chaotic storm. He gently reminds his congregation that there are reasonable people searching for the right path, and connects rationality to the commonsensical need for gradualism. He is also flexible, and does not care whether the multiracial elite pact stays within the formal sphere of a mayoral commission or if people have to create their own venues to steer Memphis. But Carnes is firm that Uncle Tom-ism cannot steer the city through its present dangerous "drift." While Carnes frequently adopts the voice of the racial moderate, his consistent support of the NAACP and condemnation of segregationists suggests a progressivism that dared not speak its name for a white man in the Deep South.

———————

Drifting is Dangerous
First Unitarian Church, Memphis, Tennessee
February 26, 1956

I have not as yet made any statements from this pulpit in direct reference to the relationship between the historic decisions of the Supreme Court of the United States and the community in which we live. The most obvious reason is that this is hardly a matter which is likely to be settled by any amount of homiletic oratory. Frankly, I have generally been content to adopt a "wait and see" attitude so far as the community implications of the Supreme Court decisions are concerned.

Two things, however, now lead me to beg your attention for the general consideration of "The Problem," i.e., desegregation. The first thing is that I am convinced that the policy of "drift" which we are following as a city could, in the long run, be as dangerous as the policies of open opposition to the Supreme Court accepted by some of our sister states in the South. A policy of further drift would be dangerous because it creates a responsible leadership vacuum. And where there is no responsible leadership, people become insecure. In their insecurity they turn to those who do offer leadership, even if this leadership is irresponsible. This is not an opinion I read in a book. This is a conclusion I have come to after observing life in Memphis during the past six months.

It is being held that the relationship between the racial groups in Memphis is deteriorating. Of this I am not convinced. What is deteriorating is the general attitude toward bettering race relations. This has resulted in an increased size, and voice, and organizational strength of groups who either in sophisticated or ignorant terms deny the reality of the 20th Century.

The most militant and extreme of these groups are composed of the disinherited, the down-trodden, the unsuccessful entrepreneur, and are almost pathological in their hatred. But they are also composed of some really fine people who are amenable to reason, who want to do the right thing, but who are frankly afraid. They are afraid that some unseen power is going to wipe away all barriers between the races tomorrow—and that tomorrow should be underlined. They really seek order out of the seeming increasing chaos, but no one offers them this. They really seek the truth, patiently and sympathetically explained, but no one is telling them the truth. But there is shouted at them the propaganda of the extreme, and in the absence of truth, this they believe. Many of them honestly believe that the United States Government, the State Governor, the Communists, the Churches and their ministers are engaged in one great plot to give their daughters over to interracial marriage. And yet, most of them would accept a rational plan of desegregation if it were instituted on a moderate basis and dictated by men of prestige and responsibility. They form the extremist among the white people and their number is increasing. They can also form a mob if they are not given responsible leadership.

In some states the situation seems to have reached a point of no return and things will simply have to get worse before they get better, for the governments of the states are implementing and exploiting the fears of the people. Such, however, is not the situation in Memphis—at least not yet.

At the other extreme stand certain elements in the NAACP. I say certain elements. The national leaders of the NAACP have been fairly restrained, considering their position. They have the law on their side. After years of struggle they see the dawning of their victory over legalized segregation. On the other hand, the national leaders cannot exercise complete control over the local branches. Any local branch may go into court at any time it sets up a suitable case. Some of the lesser leaders of the NAACP have made unfortunate public statements which, more than their actual actions, lead them to be regarded as extremists. Yet the policy of "drift" gives greater power and prestige to the extremist aspect of the NAACP, for these can say to their people that only they can get them the rights which are rightly and constitutionally theirs.

However, it is not only because I believe that a further policy of drift will be chaotic to human relations in Memphis that I speak this morning. I speak because there is a possibility that this policy can be reversed and the pattern of fear and tension be reversed if the right men in the right places will do the right things—and, I might add, for the right reasons. The papers have carried stories of the formation of a new group of "Moderates" in Memphis. This group is composed of some of the business and professional leaders of the city. These men have an opportunity to be the answer to our civic need. But whether or not they are the answer depends on whether they are prepared to make sense out of moderation. Whether or not they are going to make sense out of moderation will depend on how they are going to answer three questions—and on their answers may depend MEMPHIS FORWARD or MEMPHIS BACKWARD.

Question 1: Are these men prepared to accept the cold, and perhaps for many of them unpleasant, facts of life, and state clearly and unequivocally that the decisions of the Supreme Court represent not only the law of the land but also the law of Memphis and their own law? If they answer Yes, then moderation applies to methods of implementation of these decisions, and it can make sense.

Only an idiot would demand the immediate elimination of all segregation. We are all gradualists. The important question is, gradually doing what? Some people just gradually like to do nothing from now to eternity. Others know that the decisions of the Supreme Court are going to be expanded and enforced, but they would like to see the implementation of these decisions gradual enough to create the minimum possible social upheaval consistent with progress.

But in the latter case, the goal is clear and unquestioned. Compromise does not apply to this goal; only to methods of approach. And let us not live in a world of dreams, a world in which more and more people find themselves living. The decisions of the Supreme Court are going to be enforced. It may take many legal battles, but in the end they will be enforced. It is only a question of whether they are to be implemented and enforced by reasonable men or as the result of the unnecessary and perhaps sanguinary battles between irrational extremists. Mr. Quill Cope, Tennessee State Education Commissioner has put it clearly when he said, "Most of our citizens and school authorities prefer to think of the Supreme Court decision as something that never happened. These decisions illustrate what happens when educators and leaders do not take proper steps to resolve the problem which faces them." And other decisions will follow, as night follows day, unless local community leadership assumes sincere responsibility.

It would seem that we are extremely fortunate in that this new organization has faced this issue and has answered in the affirmative. The use of the words "Constitution" and "law" in their Statement of Purpose would lead us to believe that we can take hope that they are not going to be a group which will hide either evasion or inactivity under the cloak of moderation and non-violence.

It should be pointed out that responsible citizens can hold moderation in implementation. Such a position would rally the really well-intentioned and law abiding citizens of our city and this is the majority, the overwhelmingly large majority. But there can be no moderate position possible in opposition to the principle of desegregation.

Yes, one can have interposition and evasion become a fight between the NAACP and the rabid segregationists, and the moderates will find themselves pushed either to one side or the other. When that happens, we are lost. But it hasn't happened yet. And these men can prevent it, first by upholding the decisions of the Supreme Court, and then by seeking to implement them—by moderation.

This brings us to the second question. The moderates must be more than a discussion group. What we need is not only the establishment of law, but the establishment of policy in view of the law. There is no reason why we as a community should throw all of the responsibility for policy on either the Courts or the City Government. There has already been enough buck-passing. Let this group of moderates, if they want moderation to make sense, draw up some sort of plan for desegregation which, through give and take, compromise and horse-trading, can gain the support of the public. This would reverse the present pitiful policy of drift.

The problem of desegregation is not restricted solely to the schools. It is comprehensive. It involves parks and playgrounds, golf courses, the zoo, the libraries, and a host of other public facilities. Let a plan be formed. Make it a ten-year plan—a twenty-year plan. But let it have some point of departure. Maybe this year the zoo. Maybe next year the libraries. But let it start! Only thus can moderation—only thus can gradualism, really—be justified and make sense.

There is yet one other question on which the success of moderation depends. Will this group include the moderates of both races? If it does, it can make sense. If it does not, even with the best intent, it can hardly succeed. Community relations in this city involve two races. They can be harmonized only by the two working together. There is a thing we must realize. A great many Negroes may make all sorts of public statements against the NAACP, but most of them go on paying their dues, quite willing for that organization to be their official and active spokesman. And whether we like it or not, the NAACP is no longer going to allow race relations to be a one-sided affair. I am not saying whether this is good or bad. It is a fact of life, plain to all who have eyes, who can stand to see the truth.

Here again, it would seem that this newly organized group is prepared to face this issue and make sense. It is reported that Negroes will be asked to join and will be among the directors. I trust these men enough to believe that this intention is in good faith—that this does not mean that a single hand-picked Negro whose opinions can be trusted to coincide with whatever is expected will be made as director as proof of the bi-racial character of the group.

What a magnificent thing it would be in this wonderful city of ours here in the Mid-South if we could see the leading and responsible citizens of both races coming together to discuss on equal terms as equal members of the same organization the problems arising with the removal of the traditional barriers of segregation.

What an opportunity these men have! What a contribution to the future of our city they can make! We care not how long or hard the course if there is hope in our journey. And this is what these men can give, particularly to the Negroes who for so long have had so little to say about their life in their city.

Actually, what is needed in our community in this hour is a Mayor's Commission composed of the responsible leading business and professional men from both races to set the pace in our human relations. This is not a novel thing. Many large cities have them. Such a commission could not only perform the above mentioned tasks, but could also work to improve the relations between the races through open discussions, public forums, education, teacher and police training, and a host of other techniques which lift race relations above the level of hatred, fanaticism and propaganda. But I'll settle, in lieu of such a commission, for a group of "moderates" who will make sense.

I do not know what instigated the formation of this new organization. I only know that their's is the hour if they will but seize it. The NAACP has done a magnificent job in bringing the issue of discrimination out from under the rug where it has been swept for so many years. But as far as Memphis is concerned its function has been achieved: its principles have been established. We now need strategists rather than tacticians; diplomats rather than soldiers. As a consequence, the future of our city should lie neither in the hands of the NAACP nor those who would seek to lift higher and set deeper the walls of segregation. Yet this is what will happen unless law and moderation be mingled with progress.

We are extremely fortunate that men of position and good-will have arisen with the vision to see our need. It will not be easy for them. It is never easy for the moderate, for he is going to be opposed by extremes of both sides. But joyful can be his task for he is doing what history and the majority of his fellow citizens will judge as right. If, however, these men are deluding us, then let their shame be as bitter as our disappointment. I do not believe they are. I am assuming that we can trust both their present words and actions, and as long as we can do this, they deserve our wholehearted defense and support.

We face a choice. It can almost be put in a formula. The extremists in the end place their determination against change and ultimately this means an acceptance of lawlessness. We need, on the other hand, men of affairs who will place their acceptance on change and their determination on peace and progress. If the men who will call themselves moderates will do this; if they will do it together with the leaders of the Negro race; and if together they will give us a plan and a policy, they will not only reverse our present policy of drift, but they will also have raised a standard to which all men of good will can repair—not only in Memphis, not only in the South, but through the length and breadth of our country. If such be the case, we can sing with the prophet of old. "They shall not labour in vain, nor bring forth for trouble; for they are the seed of the blessed of the Lord, and their offspring with them." Isaiah 65:23

§22 Dr. J. R. Brokhoff

Dr. J. R. Brokhoff's biographical information appears in the introduction to his August 22, 1954 sermon in Atlanta, Georgia. In the following sermon on tolerance to parishioners of St. Mark's Lutheran Church in Charlotte, Brokhoff begins with sacred and secular violence: James and John wishing to cast down fire on the Samaritans, the murder of Emmett Till and Autherine Lucy's attempts to integrate the University of Alabama. "More than any other lesson," states Brokhoff, "America needs this lesson on tolerance." The key term does not mean indifference, nor yet racial merger or compulsion. Rather, tolerance admits of recognizing and respecting difference. As far as practicing tolerance, Brokhoff urges his listeners to see humanity in universal terms. We are children of God first, human beings second, and Americans third. Seeing our neighbors in any of the three categories is to practice tolerance. We must also be willing to uphold the rights of all people and to practice love, even to those with whom we differ.

───────────

A Lesson on Tolerance

St. Mark's Lutheran Church, Charlotte, North Carolina

March 7, 1956

John answered, "Master, we saw a man casting out demons in your name, and we forbade him, because he does not follow with us." But Jesus said to him, "Do not forbid him; for he that is not against you is for you." "When the days drew near for him to be received up, he set his face to go to Jerusalem. And he sent messengers ahead of him, who went and entered a village of the Samaritans, to make ready for him; but the people would not receive him, because his face was set toward Jerusalem. And when the disciples James and John saw it, they said, "Lord, do you want us to bid fire come down from heaven and consume them?" But he turned and rebuked them. —Luke 9:49-55

More than any other lesson, America needs this lesson on tolerance. In the South particularly, race relations is our most pressing problem today. We are on the verge of violence. In recent months a Till lad was murdered in Mississippi and a riot took place on the campus of the University of Alabama when a Miss Lucy, a Negress, attended classes. There is more race consciousness, more hatred and racial prejudice among both whites and blacks than in a century. We have come to the sad state of affairs when a state senator of Alabama says in commenting upon the riot at the University of Alabama: "Yesterday was a great day in Alabama. There is a time to get mad and raise hell."

Jesus faced intolerance in his own day among his own followers. John felt bitter about a man casting out demons in Jesus' name. In a spirit of intolerance, he wanted to stop the man, but Jesus would have no part in it.

Later, when Jesus was going to Jerusalem with his disciples, he was not given a welcome by the people. The people felt that if Jesus was not going to stay with them to teach and heal them, there was no use of showing him any hospitality. This enraged the "Sons of Thunder" that they wanted to liquidate the people by calling down fire from heaven upon them. Jesus turned on them and rebuked them for their intolerance. As Jesus had no sympathy for prejudice in his day, he has none with our intolerance today. He would rebuke us for it. Today he wants to teach us a lesson in tolerance.

As a teacher would, Jesus wants to define the word, tolerance, in order that we may understand him and each other. In the spirit of Christ, we can say that tolerance should not be defined as indifference. Those who interchange tolerance with indifference are usually people who have no convictions. They are lukewarm and minimize differences to the point where they do not exist. For example, some say that they can get along with any religious group, because we all believe in the same God and have the same goal. That is not true. To base tolerance on ignorance is nothing but false tolerance. Dr. Stewart Herman, Director of Latin American Affairs of the Lutheran World Federation, reported to the recent annual convention of the National Lutheran Council that Uruguay was the most tolerant of the South American nations toward Protestantism and at the same time was the most indifferent country toward Christianity. Tolerance in that country is no credit to it. Tolerance results when we believe and yet respect the beliefs of others.

Tolerance does not mean, moreover, amalgamation or merger. Those who think so conclude that those who believe in tolerance must work toward mixing all groups until they are indistinguishable from each other. Intermarriage of the races is one aspect of the problem. It is not tolerance for one group or race or religion to lose its identity by merging into another group. Each race has its own traditions, culture, and genius. Each race should be proud of its past and hopeful of its future. There is no virtue in conformity; it is nothing but monotony and death. It would be a terrible thing if all of us thought and lived alike. The genius of America is that we have many races and cultures. America is stronger because of our differences. God, I am sure, does not intend for us all to be one race. There are many kinds of fish. God made the nations and the races. It is not His will that we should become one conglomerate race by a false idea of tolerance. Tolerance means that we have a right to be different, and each race should be proud of its own contribution.

Tolerance is also not compulsory integration of groups, nations, or races. If integration is desired and natural, integration of the races is praiseworthy. But, segregation in itself is not evil or sinful. Only enforced segregation is such. There is a natural segregation that bears no taint of evil. It is the product of the old saying, "Birds of a feather flock together." It is the principle that like attracts like. In Atlanta you can find such a case of natural segregation. The Morningside area is approximately 90% Jewish. They have congregated in this suburb by choice. They wanted to live with the people who had the same religion, same racial background, some customs, and interests. They wanted their children to go to school with children of the same culture. Why is not this perfectly satisfactory because it is voluntary and desired? Do we not practice the same when we choose our friends? We do not go with any "Tom, Dick or Harry." We are careful that our children choose the right kind of associates. We even move in certain neighborhoods that our children will meet the right kind of people. Just because we choose our friends and have social contacts with certain people rather than with other people does not say that we are prejudiced or intolerant. It is simply a matter of personal taste and preference. Because of our background, interests, and training we are happier, more satisfied when we are with a certain group. Tolerance admits this natural segregation. It does not demand that people be forced to associate with each other simply because we want to be "democratic" or tolerant.

This leads us to see what tolerance is. We are tolerant when we recognize our differences and yet agree to be different. In tolerance, we will live in the same community as good neighbors practicing goodwill and brotherhood. That is easier said than done. Imagine Senator Eastland of Mississippi living amicably next to the Executive Secretary of the NAACP! When that occurs, you may be thinking, the millennium will have occurred. It reminds us of the picture of the millennium given by the Old Testament when it says that the lion and the lamb will lie down beside each other in peace.

It is not enough to know what tolerance is. We must learn how to become tolerant of those who differ from us. One way to be tolerant is to possess a universal perspective of mankind. Intolerance is narrow and sectional. For example, we must see that we are first of all Americans, and sectionalists, second. At an ice hockey show, the difference was pointed out in a dramatic way. The game opened with the National Anthem. Of course, the thousands present stood solemnly. Not a word was said, not a handclap was given when it was finished. Immediately there followed "Dixie." This was welcomed with rebel calls, shouting, singing, and thunderous clapping. It was plain to see where the loyalty of that group was. There is a symptom of intolerance.

If we would see ourselves as Americans first, and regionalists second, we would have a different attitude in the South concerning Federal Law. The Constitution is for all 48 states. The Supreme Court's decisions are for all Americans. A law is a law and must be obeyed by all. The Southern States are childish and foolish when they try to block the Supreme Court's decision on desegregation in public schools by passing laws of Interposition.

Democracy is at stake in the issue. Democracy demands obedience from all citizens whether or not they like a particular law. A principle of Democracy is that the opposing minority goes along with the majority until it can persuade by peaceful means that the majority is wrong. Unless we hold to this principle, we shall have nothing but anarchy and chaos.

We should see also that we are human beings first and members of a particular race second. The human race is greater than a particular race. All of us belong to the human family. We have basically the same needs and feelings. Injustice is just as terrible for the white race as for the black. Color and race are superficial markings of a basic human nature. The color of one's skin, the texture of the hair, the thickness of the lips, the bend of the nose, the features of the face are simply externals that mean almost nothing. The thing that counts is what is in us. One man at a circus was selling balloons of all colors—red, white, black, yellow, green, blue. To attract attention he would let a balloon go to the sky. A colored boy was entranced by the ascending balloons. He asked the man, "Mister, will the black ones also go up?" The man answered with tact and wisdom, "My boy, it's not the color that makes them go up but what's inside them." There is an unforgettable lesson. The externals mean nothing. Inside we are human beings, and what we are inside makes us important enough to be tolerated.

Again, we must see ourselves as children of God first, and human beings, second. If we are children of God, we have God as our Father. If He is our Father, we cannot avoid being brothers one with another. It is not hard to get men to believe that God made each of us. We have a common Creator. This makes every man precious and of infinite value. God considers each man regardless of race or religion of extreme worth. He has no favorites. Now, the fact of brotherhood naturally follows. Here is the crux of our race relations problem. There is no hope of acting like brothers unless we know and believe we are truly brothers through God's fatherhood. We will not act what we are until we know and believe what we are. Race relations then is basically a spiritual problem.

If we are brothers with all men everywhere, tolerance is one aspect of our concern for our brothers. From the beginning of the human race, man has tried to dodge the responsibility of brotherhood. We still ask with Cain, "Am I my brother's keeper?" The answer is emphatically "Yes." We must be concerned about the condition and welfare of our brothers of every race and creed. Once a set of parents permitted a boy and his younger brother to go to a circus. When the day was about over and the boys did not return, they began to worry about them. At dusk, the older boy came home and as he approached he said, "Dad, the circus was wonderful!" The father asked, "Where is your brother?" The lad: "You should have seen the elephants. They were as big as mountains!" "Boy, where is your brother?" "And the giraffes! You never in your life saw such a long neck!" "Boy, where is your brother?" "And the clowns were so funny." The father now took his son by the shoulders and shaking him, shouted, "Lad, where is your brother?" We are so much like that today in our race relations with people of other races. We talk about the superficial things of the color, hair, and features, and forget to be concerned about their welfare in body, mind, and soul.

To become tolerant, second, we must recognize and uphold the rights of all men. We agree now that each man as made by God has infinite value and has inherent rights: life, liberty, and happiness. Tolerance calls for recognizing and upholding such rights. It is gross intolerance to deprive men of these rights or to make men feel they are less than God's children. To do this, men use force to subjugate and to deprive men who differ from them of their rights. Tolerance could be summed up in these words: "Live and let live."

Out of intolerance grows a desire to use force to compel men to conform to us. This Jesus refused to do. John wanted to stop the man casting out demons by using force. Again, when the people of the Samaritan village would not believe in or respect Jesus, the Disciples wanted to make them believe by calling down fire on their heads. Jesus refused the use of force. He told Peter outside the Garden of Gethsemane to put up his sword. Jesus rebuked the suggestion that he use force to make men believe in him or to comply to his standards.

The attempt to use force in present day race relations is one of the major causes of our violence. There is, on the one hand, an attempt to use force to guarantee segregation. This causes the Negro to feel deeply resentful. He does not want to be forced into a back seat or to a separate entrance just because he is different from the majority. We can understand his bitterness if we would put ourselves in his place. The best thing we could do would be to remove our laws of segregation and trust in natural segregation which would follow.

On the other hand, force is being used to establish segregation. This too is being done by law. We had the Supreme Court decision outlawing segregation in public schools. This is being enforced by lesser courts. The NAACP is forcing the issue by taking the matter to the courts. This is being thrust on a people, 80% of whom are against desegregation. Southern people are not ready for this radical social change. We ought to know that no people can be forced to change its habits and customs over night. The tragedy of the matter is that we have lost much of what we gained in recent decades when quietly and peacefully integration was taking place. For instance, in the last few years 1,000 Negroes were admitted to 100 White colleges which formerly would not take Negroes. Something as fundamental as racial relations can be changed only by education and the influence of the gospel. This demands time—much time and even more patience.

Today, the issue is being pushed to the breaking point of violence by extremists—the White Citizens Councils and the NAACP. Both are fanatical and both are using force. Here is where the great body of Christian people must step in. It is not the Christian position to take sides on the issue. Our mission at the present moment is to be peacemakers. We need to urge calm, peace, patience, and reason. We should try to get a moratorium on the issue for at least two years. Men's aroused zeal and passionate prejudice must have time to cool off that we may approach the problem rationally and in good spirits.

A third way to get tolerance is by practicing love toward those with whom we differ. Love knows no boundaries or barriers. When Edith Cavell in the First World War ministered to suffering German soldiers as well as her countrymen, she was executed as a traitor. Later the mistake was recognized, and on the base of a memorial statue, these words were placed: "Patriotism is not Enough." Love crosses racial barriers, too. Two colored boys once asked a grocer for 3 pennies. He gave them, and in a few days the boys brought them back. He did not want to take them back, but was told this story. The boys had an Italian friend whose parents were too poor to buy him his school lunch. They worked before and after school shining shoes to get the money for his lunches. One day they lacked three pennies. Later they earned a little more than needed and now they wanted to return the pennies. Love knows no racial barriers.

What are we going to do with the minority which differs from us. Surely we cannot send the Negroes back to Africa. Our Christian sense of morality would not let us liquidate 10 million black people like the Communists executed millions in China and Russia. We must learn to live with them in peace. A man once had trouble with dandelions in his lawn. He wrote to the Department of Agriculture for a formula to get rid of them. He sprayed the formula on his lawn, but more dandelions than ever sprang up. He asked for another formula, but even more dandelions came. In wrath, he wrote a critical letter and demanded a formula that would solve the problem. The Department wrote back: "The only fool-proof formula we know for getting rid of dandelions is, 'Learn to love dandelions.'" We must learn to love people of other races. Then we will accept them as neighbors and as fellow Americans.

It is urgent that we learn this lesson on tolerance before it is too late. We are living in the midst of a growing hatred and prejudice among the races, especially in the South. Now is the time for Christians to stand up and speak out for tolerance. When they do—and only when they do—will we be able to live out our lives in quietness and harmony based on goodwill and tolerance.

§23 Horace Mann Bond

Horace Mann Bond was born in 1904. In 1923 he received a bachelor's degree from Lincoln University. The noted educator took his M.A. and Ph.D. from the University of Chicago. Early in his academic career, Bond served as a key teacher and administrator at Fisk University and Dillard University. Between 1939 and 1957 Bond served as university president at Fort Valley State College, and Lincoln University. In 1957 Bond became dean of the School of Education at Atlanta University. Throughout his tenure in academia, Bond worked to abolish segregation while continually trying to improve the education of African American students. His influence as an educator and renowned sociologist is still seen in his articles, addresses, and his innovative critiques of intelligence and aptitude testing.

Horace Mann Bond was not the only member of his family to embrace the civil rights movement and the daunting task of desegregation. His legacy was carried on through his son, Julian Bond, who would later become an antiwar activist, an important member of the Student Nonviolent Coordinating Committee (SNCC), a controversial member of Congress, and president of the NAACP. Their tireless struggle for the advancement of black civil rights and interracial understanding underscored the research of Horace Mann Bond that stressed the impact of geographic and socio-economic factors on academic achievement. Bond died on December 21, 1972. His wife, Julia Washington Bond, and famous son Julian survive him.

Bond utilizes religion, politics, philosophy, and education to create a uniquely eloquent speech that, at its core, is a repentant tribute to an interracial incident involving a white man on death row, Johnnie Birchfield. Bond comes to Montgomery, most notably, to be a witness to history "in the grand manner." The Montgomery Bus Boycott was just then four months old. Bond moves through history to establish the contemporary ideal of "American freedom," as he reflects on the influence of classic and modern theological and political champions. All people are connected through God, and although lacking in perfection, have the ability to progress in the continual effort for social change. Bond remains the unwavering teacher, and by drawing from his own flaws of prejudice, reminds the proverbial members of the congregation that racism is a deep-rooted and prevalent problem in this nation. Despite his candid admission that the problem is persistent, Bond reiterates that the cause is not lost and freedom will prevail because of its foundation in the fundamental American principle of equality. Bond's substantial use of faith-based allusions indicates his belief in the power of prayer and religious guidance throughout the tumultuous campaign.

A Cigarette for Johnnie Birchfield
State Teachers Association, Montgomery, Alabama
March 22, 1956

My subject is, "A Cigarette for Johnnie Birchfield." I announce that subject, and assure you that, sooner or later, I intend to talk to the point of it. But first I must tell you why I am here; and this, in itself, is a long tale.

I was overjoyed to get your kind invitation to come to Montgomery, but uncertain as to whether I could do so. This uncertainty, I assure you, was altogether because of reasons of health. My health has not been so good in recent months, and it seemed extremely doubtful, if a trip to Montgomery, just at this season of the year, would be likely—(in spite of the ancient and well deserved reputation of these parts for salubrity of climate)—to contribute, restore, or improve my chances for living out the Biblical three-score-and-ten span promised by the Psalmist.

But then I reflected how much Montgomery had endeared itself to me in my youth, as a kind, urbane, and forgiving city. When I lived here, in the year 1927–1928, and during successive assignments as a researcher and summer school teacher, I had frequent occasion to reflect on the broad, liberal policies of the City Government—from the policeman on his beat, to His Honor in City Hall; all displayed commendable tolerance toward the frailties of human nature, and the misdeeds of evil-doers. In those days, the Tract was "wide open"; I do not know how it is now, but I shall never forget what an education it then was to me—a poor, ignorant, somewhat inno-cent boy reared in a narrow Christian home—to see (always from a dis-tance, I assure you!) those bright lights burning on Holt and its back streets and alleys, knowing that, fortunately, this was not for me; both because of my upbringing, and because those lights illumined a world dedicated to "joy" that was segregated, that it might also be "inter-racial."

When I did decide to come, it was for several reasons. Firstly, I was young, in Montgomery, 29 years ago; and one can never quite forget the pleasant memories of a stretch of one's youth spent amidst a veritable plethora of pretty girls; and I see there are still a lot of pretty girls in Montgomery!

Secondly, I wanted to come, to see this strange thing that was hap-pening in this town, according to the newspapers. By trade, I have been a historian, and my specialty has been the history of Alabama. I have written, literally, hundreds of thousands of words, trying to tell the story of the his-tory of this State; its mid-position in the Lower South gives that history an uncommon significance both for the entire Southern section, and for the Nation, and so for the world.

Now history is being made; and I saw it as my privilege, to visit one spot on earth while History, in the grand manner, was in process of being made. While thanking your Committee for inviting me, I reflected that I had, really, little to bring to this Association, or to this city, beyond a deep and lively curiosity, to view History in the making.

We hear a great deal, these days, about "outside agitators"; and about "gradualism." I can scarcely qualify as an "outside agitator," even if I wished to be one; but I must confess to being, if not the original gradualist, at least one of more than twenty years of standing. I am scarcely from the "outside," since I was born in Tennessee, lived in Kentucky, Alabama, and Georgia, as a youth; and, for years, worked and researched all over the very Deep South.

I say, again, that I am an old time "gradualist." On my arrival here this morning, I got from this Library a copy of a book on education I published in 1934—twenty-two years ago. I wanted to check up on some proposals for education that I then made. I turned to the pages where I discussed the future, and read with interest the confident proposal I then made. I had it all neatly figured out, whereby the South could achieve an equality of educational expenditures for whites and Negroes—and, of course, in a seg-regated system—between 1933 and 1953. My scheme was very simple, and would have been painless; I proposed that there be added, to the expendi-ture for each Negro child, per capita, just 50 cents more, each year, than was added to the expenditures for each white child; and estimated that in cities like Birmingham, Nashville, even Montgomery, this would have done the trick, neatly and effectively, in the twenty year period that began in 1933, and ended in 1953.

But no one paid any attention to my little book—in fact, few ever read it—and now, looking back, I think it is just as well; indeed, it is better, so.

The only moral is, that I now see myself a failure as a prophet, or, rather, as a prophet whose predictions have been outridden by History. As an "ed-ucational expert," I now see my work deserving a flunking mark; and the shape of things in 1956 out of all recognition as compared to my confident plans made in 1933.

This was no reason, to burden your association with my presence at this meeting.

But I had still a third reason, and that is the real reason why I came; and with gratitude. It was, to bring, "A Cigarette for Johnny Birchfield."

You've never heard of Johnnie Birchfield. Let me tell you how I knew him; and why I bring, tonight, a cigarette for him, and his memory.

I met Johnnie Birchfield for the first and last time, just twenty-eight years ago. I met him in the death cell at Kilby Prison, where I had gone, with the Reverend Williams, prison chaplain, to comfort two condemned prisoners in their last moments here on earth. One of the men was Charlie Washington, a Negro, from Birmingham; he had been convicted of killing a motor policeman, and the entire squad had come down from Birmingham to see him die.

The other prisoner was Johnnie Birchfield. He was a young white man from the hills of Eastern Alabama. Neither Charlie Washington, nor Johnnie Birchfield, had ever had much of an education; the first, because he was a Negro; the second, because he was a white boy from an Alabama white county. Both men had committed heinous crimes, and the Law, in all its majesty, was taking its just, but terrible, course.

Regardless of Justice, and Law; regardless, even, of Murder; it is not an easy thing to see human beings die, especially when they are young; and never had their full and complete chance; and when they die at the hands of a State that, somewhere, never quite did for such people what its Constitution and laws have pledged themselves to do for them. As I sang and prayed with Charlie Washington, and Johnnie Birchfield, that night twenty-eight years ago, there came to me an overwhelming realization of the responsibility each individual citizen owes to every other human being; and to his God.

Just before the last moment, they let the men out of their cells, to sing together in the corridor. Charlie Washington was on my left, and Johnnie Birchfield was on my right; and, between us, we held one hymn-book.

I can remember, as though it were tonight, Charlie Washington's black thumb on that hymn-book page; and Johnnie Birchfield's pink-white thumb, holding the other page. And I can remember the song we sang, together.

> I've wandered far away from home
> The paths of Sin too long I've roamed;
> Lord, I'm coming home.
>
> Coming home, coming home,
> Never more to roam;
> Open wide the gates of love;
> Lord, I'm coming home.
>
> I've wasted many precious years;
> Lord, I'm coming home;
> And now repent in bitter tears.
> Lord, I'm coming home.
>
> Coming home, coming home,
> Never more to roam,
> Open wide the gates of love,
> Lord, I'm coming home.

It struck me, that after we passed the first, and familiar verse, neither Charlie Washington, nor Johnnie Birchfield, could very well read the other verses; they had to follow me and the other chaplains.

This I could never forget. It may not have made any difference, if the State had given each of the men an education up to the Ph.D. level; they might yet have fallen into the toils of the law. But somehow, the society in which both had lived, was so contrived, that neither ever got much of any kind of education at all; the black man, because he was black; and the white boy, because he was a white boy from an Alabama hill county. Somehow it seemed then, as it still seems, a monstrous injustice, that it should be so; and that the monstrosity belongs to each and every human being who, living in such a society, knows the truth, but does not voice it.

And there was something else I can never forget.

In one of the interludes between song, and prayer; and prayer, and song; Johnnie Birchfield asked me for a cigarette.

Now, I had cigarettes in my pocket. I could have given Johnnie Birchfield a cigarette. But for some strange reason, that I yet cannot explain, I told Johnnie Birchfield that I didn't have a cigarette. It may have been mental shock; it may have been a sub-conscious shame at having so wicked a thing as a cigarette on my person, in this dread place of death that was also something like a Holy of Holies, for Men were here being consecrated to their Maker—or maybe it was just because Johnnie Birchfield was white—and I was Negro.

For whatever reason, I did the ultimate unkindness; I didn't give Johnnie Birchfield, who was scheduled to die in thirty minute, a cigarette.

Now that is why I am really here tonight.

Out of the remorse of twenty-eight years of regret; and into a world and state and city inhabited by the ghosts of Charlie Washingtons, and Johnnie Birchfields past, living, and yet to die; I bring a cigarette of love, to the memory of Johnnie Birchfield.

Your theme is, "Meeting our Crisis through Education: State, Nation, World." It may be well for us to realize that the Past is always Prologue; and that each new crisis may be understood, and its solution intelligently planned, only when we understand the history of the social crises that perennially afflict all mankind; and the history, likewise, of the solutions men have advanced to meet each new crisis.

There are three great sources of American educational traditions.

One, of course, is that ancient ethic and religion, Judaism, that first gave to human beings the notion that there was one God, and, therefore, the idea that all of the children of the One God must be brothers, since God was the Father of all mankind. Noble as it was, Judaism suffered limitations because its followers developed the theory that theirs was a singular God to a singularly chosen people. But the great, basic idea, flowered as Christianity, and the expansion of the idea that all men, of whatever race or condition, are truly children of one God, and, therefore, are brothers.

As the root of Judaism branched into Christianity, the third great tap source of our American educational heritage was the Enlightenment, that 18th Century philosophical movement, created by men like Locke and Rousseau, who developed a system of rationalism that deeply affected the history of this Nation. You know that this year we are celebrating the two hundred and fiftieth anniversary of Benjamin Franklin's birth; it is less well known that this universal sage and philosopher derived his conception of the natural rights of man from the Philosophers of the Enlightenment in France, and England, with whom he held commerce, as did Thomas Jefferson, the author of our Declaration of Independence. The very cornerstone of our American faith is, that "all men are created equal; and are endowed by their Creator, with certain unalienable rights." This was Judaism; this was the genius of Christianity; this was the genius of the 18th Century and of our American Revolution, each root leading upward to create a new nation and start its growth toward eventual realization of its ideals.

Both Thomas Jefferson and Franklin had to accept compromises, in the making of our American Constitution, and on the slave question. Thomas Jefferson faced difficulties, not from his Virginia constituents; for Virginia was on the brink of emancipating its slaves, as New York and Pennsylvania were then just doing. Jefferson, and Franklin, had to accept compromise because of the lower Southern colonies; South Carolina, and Georgia, in particular. But they did what they could to make a Federal Nation; they left intact in the basic constitutional documents, their sublime convictions, in good hope that some day, these principles might be realized; and each died in the great Faith they had made perpetual part of this Nation's great, founding documents; Franklin, in 1790; ten days after publishing his last letter, one to the newspapers, ridiculing a South Carolina Congressman who had defended human slavery; Jefferson, in 1826, emancipating his slaves, and leaving behind the tragic prophecy that he foresaw calamity for his country, should slavery be retained.

The American Faith is a noble one; one of its difficulties is that it encourages the belief in perpetual progress, rising ever upward. We have a noble creed; but we are also human; and human beings can never go steadily onward, and upward, without occasional relapses.

So was it with the American creed of human equality. As promulgated in 1776, with our Declaration of Independence; and made into a Constitution in 1789; the fervor of first things then seemed to promise immediate realization. This was the period when the New England and the Middle States did abolish slavery; and when the mid-South States moved strongly in that direction. Few recall that Virginia, repeatedly, failed only by a vote or two of abolishing slavery, the latest date being 1818, when a bill to abolish slavery in Virginia failed of passage only by a vote of 21-20. Sentiment in North Carolina, likewise, was strong.

Perhaps because of the economic changes that made slavery profitable; perhaps because of the almost inevitable tendency of human beings, to find it difficult to sustain permanently the high note and plane and of initial conviction; there was a reaction in the 1830s. Virginia, that only a few years before had nearly abolished slavery, now passed the harshest legislation to enforce the institution; and Virginia was followed by severe "Black Codes" adopted in the other Slave States.

The reaction, in terms of the bright, high hopes of the Revolutionary period, was almost complete; but there were still small voices stirring in the land. These were the voices of men, principally in New England, but also including many in the South; for one of the first published voices of the abolitionist movement was that of Elihu Embree, printed at Greenville, Tennessee. A great portion of the migration from North and South Carolina, across the mountains and up to the Middle West, was of men who could not bring themselves to continue to live in a slave state.

These "abolitionists" have now, in many quarters, a bad name; they are called "fanatics," "wild-eyed radicals," "troublemakers." But they never said anything more radical than what Thomas Jefferson wrote into our Declaration of Independence; their "radicalism," their "trouble making," consisted in voicing, in a different intellectual climate, the words Benjamin Franklin and Thomas Jefferson had enunciated fifty years before.

They were, then, peculiarly American, drawing their inspiration from sources that, likewise, were peculiarly American. We remember that the year 1848, in Europe was a time of great, but unsuccessful, revolutionary movements; the period of the Birth of Karl Marx's and Engel's, "Communist Manifesto." Communism had its birth in a social and political system where Revolution was defeated by bloody force of arms; and where the people had no tradition of individual freedom through law.

We have another tradition in America. It is, indeed, the great American tradition; the hope, and, indeed, certain faith, that social and political change can be effected through democratic procedures and policies. The "abolitionists" founded their Faith on the processes and theory of Christian Democracy.

And yet, they fought what in their times seemed to be, indeed, a "Lost Cause." The height of the work of the abolitionists was carried on from 1838 to 1854; and included in their ranks were Lucretia Mott, who worked, also, for the emancipation of women; the good poet, Whittier; Theodore Weld, the eloquent evangel who married Angelina Grimke, the South Carolina aristocrat who turned her back on slavery; Henry Barnard, who founded the National Education Association, and the first American Normal School; and Horace Mann himself, who left his secure job, as superintendent of Education in Massachusetts, to enter Congress on an anti-slavery platform.

The cause seemed lost; but it was planted by Horace Mann at Antioch College—now nobly represented in Montgomery by Mrs. Martin King;

and at Oberlin College, where, in 1834, was formed the first higher institution in America that opened its doors to two despised classes; women, and Negroes. The men who founded Oberlin founded also, the American Missionary Association; and even before the Civil War had begun, tried to establish an inter-racial college at Berea, in Kentucky, a slave state.

It should be remembered, that Berea was reconstituted after the Civil War; and continued to flourish as an institution, in the South, interracial in trustee board, faculty, and student body, until the Kentucky Day Law was passed in 1904, and upheld by the Supreme Court in 1907. It was in this decision that the great Kentucky jurist, Justice Harlan, repeated his famous dissent from Plessy vs. Ferguson of 1896; "The Constitution of the United States is Color Blind."

The theory of absolute human equality seemed briefly assured, after the Civil War; but by 1876, had again become a lost cause. Here in Alabama, it had its advocates. One was Peyton Finley, Negro, a member of the State Board of Education during Reconstruction.

It should be interesting to recall Peyton Finley's efforts. He pointed out to his contemporaries, in 1871, on the Board, that Negroes had been refused admission to the University of Alabama; why, then, not establish a University for the Negroes? Due to his insistency, this was finally done; and the "Alabama Colored People's University" was established at Marion; the parent of this Alabama State College of the present time.

And, in 1875, a great Alabama Superintendent of Education, a Democrat, and a Conservative, said of this school, "The normal school at Marion is designed to become a University for the colored race in the State; and it is not doubted that its facilities for furnishing the higher education to this race will be amplified as the demand therefore becomes apparent."

John K. McKleroy was, of course, perfectly sincere, and honest, but it did not turn out that way. There arose, in this State, and elsewhere in the South, a generation that knew not Joseph; nor remembered any of the promises made to Negroes when Reconstruction was ended. It is a striking commentary on "Gradualism"; but also, on how causes are lost over many generations, as well as years.

From 1890 to 1920, the cause seemed really lost. This was the period in which William Burns Paterson, and J. W. Beverly and George W. Trenholm struggled manfully to keep this institution alive, as its name was degraded through the years, and the yearly appropriation reduced from $25,000 to $15,000 to $10,000 and then to $4,000 a year.

But the cause was not really lost. The seed had been planted; the same seed of the faith in equal creation of mankind, that Thomas Jefferson had implanted in our Declaration of Independence; that Henry Barnard and Horace Mann had planted in American education; that had been nursed in the tiny colleges, that almost seemed to lie dormant; but where men like DuBois, James Weldon Johnson, Walter White, Thurgood Marshall, Charles Houston, James Nabrit, and the rest had been cradled, and given the great vision of human equality.

I think, some day, our histories will show that these men saved America; and so, saved the world. Theirs was the old—the oldest—American tradition, of human freedom.

The world has always learned the hard way, the inexorable lesson of the corruptions wrought by power, and wealth. Human beings are so constituted, that the quickest poison is that of exercising unchecked power over one's fellow men. The little band of men, and women, who in the 1830s, kept alive the apparently "lost cause" of absolute human equality, were the anti-body that preserved the health of this Nation, and armed it for its "time of troubles" when the 20th Century brought conflict with powerful and fanatic Fascist and Communist totalitarian States.

So have served the men, and women, in our generation, who have lived, and placed their lives in jeopardy, to keep this Nation true to its original aims. It is a thrilling fact, that the stone the builder rejected, now providentially turns itself into the chief cornerstone upon which this Nation's pretensions rest in its struggle for survival in a world yet dangerously constituted.

But here, in this city, we are seeing a high human drama, when the talent we have received from the 19th Century, and from the 18th Century, undergoes even a further refinement. A great many of the radical abolitionist of the 19th century were pacifists; such a one was Garrison. But a substantial number did believe in force, and the recapturing of human rights and equality through the application of force, to meet force.

It is a majestic thing, that here, before our eyes, is being added a fourth dimension to a noble heritage. For here we see the ancient heritage of the ancient Judaistic notion, that all men are the children of one God; consummated courageously and lovingly with the even greater heritage, of the Son of God who was also the Prince of Peace.

It is a historic time, and a historic place, for here, for the very first time in the history of these United States of America, have we witnessed thousands of American citizens exemplifying the principle of peaceful resistance to what their religious conviction and their basic American civil documents tell them is an outrage to human dignity.

This is love among the ashes of many lost human causes. This is the majesty of the common man, who thereby makes himself, and his fellows, an uncommon man. In this wicked, worried world, no application of force and violence has ever permanently won a cause. Here in Montgomery, we see being written hourly, daily, a new chapter in the history of the human race.

That is why I call this talk to you, "A Cigarette for Johnnie Birchfield." Not all of the electric chairs in the world reach to the roots of a soil wherein are grown Charlie Washington's, and Johnnie Birchfield's.

Having long felt that teachers like yourself are carriers of a great tradition, I now feel that great tradition has now been immeasurably enriched, by history being made here in Montgomery, Alabama. The lesson taught reaches to the heart, and, I hope, to your heart, and through your heart, to the heart of the hundreds of thousands of children you teach. It is an opportunity that never until this day has come, in the history of the entire teaching profession since time began.

None of us is perfect, nor ever will be. Still, man stumbles along the road to perfection. One man, or a dozen, or twenty, hit upon a great idea in a German, an Italian, an American laboratory; and, presto! by their genius the whole world is imperiled.

Here in Montgomery, one man; and a dozen; and a hundred; and a thousand; and fifty thousand; stumble upon another, but even more powerful, idea. And, Presto! by their simple genius and faith, the whole world is, prospectively, saved from immolation.

It is in the faith that this is so, that I bring here, tonight, a Cigarette for Johnnie Birchfield; and sing with him, whether in the corridors of Kilby Penitentiary, or in this Hall, and anywhere in the world where human beings are distressed of heart, imperiled of life, uneasy of their destiny:

> I've wandered far away from Home;
> The paths of Sin too long I've roamed;
> Lord, I'm coming home.
>
> Coming home, coming home;
> Never to roam;
> Open wide the gates of love;
> Lord, I'm coming home.

§24 Dr. James Hudson

James Hudson's biography appears at the introduction to his speech of February 26, 1955. Reverend Hudson begins the following Palm Sunday sermon to Howard University students and faculty with the predicament facing the Jews of Jesus' time. For them, they all sought freedom—salvation from Roman rule. Several different groups represented different paths they could take. Some advocated armed struggle. Others contended that acquiescence was their only way to survive. Still others said they should put up with Roman rule and just wait it out. On whom should the Jews have relied? Hudson argues that Jesus was their only true hope, as the Reverend details.

Jesus rode into Jerusalem riding a horse but certainly not one fit for battle. People praised him; however, he did not have any lasting widespread public support. What did Jesus represent? Jesus, more than anything, was the embodiment of how each of us should approach life and faith. He listened to God. Jesus did not represent anything of himself, but the one beyond him—God the father. Freedom, salvation, and victory are found not in our own resources, but in our marching to the tune that God plays for us. "Men take different strides in life. They set their marching according to the distant drum beats they hear. It seems to me that as Jesus rode on that memorable Palm Sunday he set his soul to the beat of a drummer in the sky. . . . This is the victory that over-cometh the world."

Was Reverend Hudson speaking directly to the nascent civil rights movement? Or, was he merely giving a Palm Sunday homily on the meaning of Jesus' entry into Jerusalem? Hudson provides the subtle answer early in the sermon: "The world is in revolution and we as a nation are at the crossroads of history. . . . At home there is also a crisis the stage setting of which has been provided by a series of judgments rendered by the highest body of Jurisprudence in our country. The unfolding logic of 'all men' at the heart of democracy is causing quite a disclosure of those who give democracy lip service and lip service alone." By the close of the sermon, Hudson clarifies Christ's lessons for would-be activists: "The predicament of Palm Sunday is our willingness to vocalize, but our unwillingness to implement sentiment into concrete reality." As Hudson would soon discover, his opportunity to "implement sentiment" would occur in two short months, when he helped organize the Tallahassee bus boycott.

————————

Where to Look for Victory

Howard University, Washington, D.C.

March 25, 1956

Charles Dickens opened his *Tale of Two Cities* with these memorable words, "It was the best of times, it was the worst of times. It was the age of wisdom, it was the age of foolishness. It was the epoch of belief, it was the epoch of credulity. It was the spring of hope, it was the winter of despair."

I am thinking this morning of still another city—the ancient city of Jerusalem. Perhaps one can say of Jerusalem, near the close of Jesus' ministry, that it was the city of hope; it was likewise the city of despair. Truly the times were a weird combination of wisdom and foolishness, belief and disbelief, hope and despair.

The big question before the people during those days was "Where Do We Look For Victory?" Barabas, the zealot, had led many patriotic Jews in revolt against Roman authority. The answer he gave was force, violence, or revolution. Some sought the leadership of the Schoolmen of the day—the Sanhedrin. Their answer was that victory will come through knowledge, a judicious accounting of tradition. Sadly enough, the scholar class was preoccupied with minutiae and priggishness over the inherited law. It was remarked of them that not one would use even one finger to lift the burdens from the backs of the people. Rather they would add to their burdens.

Still another group—the Essenes—were advocating quiet withdrawal from the social scene and the cultivation of piety and an inner peace of soul. "This," they said, "is Where to Look for Victory."

The Herodians too had their formula. They wanted conciliation and compromise with the ruling power. Some of them were outright quislings who connived with the enemy.

What could Jesus say to his generation faltering in one of the worst dilemmas in all of Jewish history? The modern world is in a dilemma. Perhaps I should say dilemmas. Our dilemmas are compounded. Our ancient profession of faith has been democracy and self determination of the peoples of the earth. We were born in a rebellion against tyranny. We have been welded together in a common plea for the expression of man's inalienable rights. Yet, today we find ourselves making common cause with certain world powers who seek to maintain their last stand of colonialism and imperialism. We are caught between the ideal on the one hand and expedience on the other. The world is in revolution and we as a nation are at the crossroads of history. The whole world is in a revolution. To use Toynbee's word, This Is *Crisis*. At home there is also a crisis the stage setting of which has been provided by a series of judgments rendered by the highest body of Jurisprudence in our country. The unfolding logic of "all men" at the heart of democracy is causing quite a disclosure of those who give democracy lip service and lip service alone. In the midst of these momentous problems that face us individually and collectively I shall be bold enough to set the traditional story of Christ's marching into Jerusalem and to argue wisely or unwisely that it has relevance for our times. This much is true—"Where Do We Look For Victory?" is a *vital* question.

Jesus made a dramatic figure in his march from Bethphage to Jerusalem. Speculation ran high in the effort to interpret the meaning of the incident. Jesus could hardly have been intent on Revolution. He rode upon a colt and not a war horse. The ritualistic shouts of "Hosanna" constituted no serious appeal for an unarmed innocent to seize physical power in revolt against Caesar. The intellectuals did not see in him the scholar type calling for research on an already heavy accumulation of legal erudition. The procession was hardly a mass movement. Were the indifferent and inert witnessing the dramatizing of a movement that was to become great enough to sweep Caesar from his throne? Some, no doubt, went on discussing among themselves the price of wheat, and if you permit it, the Dow Jones Stock Report, and the Roman occupation as if nothing had happened. Indeed they reflected that the world will be the same tomorrow and tomorrow and tomorrow.

Hegel, the German philosopher, is said to have remarked when Napolean rode past him—"There goes the spirit of the age—the Zeitgeist." What of Jesus passing by? Was he the spirit of all ages—the personification of the world spirit—the spirit of all times—the "Weltzeit"? Or was he indeed the spirit of no times?

In Jesus we have strangely enough a paradox of meekness and majesty. Perhaps a few caught the "wonder of his soul." But the majority, although having eyes, could not see. The open secret was closed to them who were not wise enough to see it. The triumphal march was realistically the prelude to the cross. Royalty and death go together as Jesus saw them. They kill the prophets and those who are sent unto them. A Hymn writer has put it boldly. "Ride on, ride on in majesty. In lowly pomp ride on to die." The awful realism is that any modern city would treat Jesus the same way he was treated by Jerusalem. A few hailing him and fewer still understanding him. Isn't it strange that there are those today in church and state who, whatever lip service they would pay to Christ, would think it worse than unfortunate if many people should take him seriously? The Reverend M. L. King of Montgomery is apparently taking Jesus seriously in his effort to secure justice for people of color. What is this unheard of before that the unarmed make war, and the slain hath the gain?

They spread their garments in the way. Some saw in him their ideal of the triumph of the good life and cast branches from trees and their garments in his path as he rode by. There is great symbolism here. *Everyman* has *something in his life* to which he will *freely bow* down in utter devotion. Some will bow down and throw their garments in reverence before the gadgets and material conveniences of life. The strategy of the West has been its mastery over the physical world and a precise handling of nature. We have become preoccupied with life's instrumentality. The magnificent obsession of the west has been with the *Concrete*. Some will bow down before the pleasures of life and confess that Bacchus and his associates are the gods of creation. Is it a car, a bank account, a house? Is it power? Let no one fool himself. Every man has an object of devotion, a lord enthroned before whom he will throw himself in surrender. Is it the Highest to which you surrender?

In *The Man Who Saw through Heaven*, the Reverend Hubert Diana is a representation of not a few modern men who have seen through the heaven of common folk theology. Like the Reverend Diana they have subsequently created a man deity, a material mindless nature with sensate worlds twirling around its materialistic fingers. Poor Reverend Diana dies virtually a blind captive of the world of physical things. We do not have to go to Africa to see

Reverend Diana. He is on every American street. There is no use in looking to him for victory. His frustration is pathetic. If in looking through heaven we see another heaven grander still we shall know for ourselves where victory begins. In one great chorus the prophets speak with conviction when they say—"I saw a new heaven and a new earth." Speaking a farewell to his son Laertes in Shakespeare's *Hamlet*, Polonius says, "This above all to thine ownself be true, and it must follow as the night, the day, Thou canst not then be false to any man." The son you know is about to go from Denmark to France. This new heaven of *self devotion to be best* is for Polonius the way to victory over life. O Polonius, thou giveth us a great lesson.

There were mixed opinions about Jesus as he rode to Jerusalem. For some it was—is this the Messiah? Others felt convinced that he was the Messiah. "Blessed is he that cometh in the name of the Lord." Each one of us has to make his *journey* from a question mark about Jesus or about life to an exclamation about life, and affirmation about life. Each man has to make it for himself. That journey can *never* be made by thought alone. It must be made by action and deeds, by concrete devotion in service. This is where we find the victory.

Jesus wept over Jerusalem when he saw that in her condition of conflict, hatred, and revolution she was neglecting the things of the spirit that would make her "fit for eternity." She was missing her great opportunity. Her soul was narrow and Jesus saw that the world would cave in on her. Edna St. Vincent Millay has put this condition of soul in the unforgettable *Lines of the Renascence*, the last stanza of which I share with you. "The world stands out on either side no wider than the heart is wide; above the world is stretched the sky, no higher than the soul is high. The heart can push the sea and land farther away on either hand; the soul can split the sky in two, and let the face of God shine through. But East and West will pinch the heart that cannot keep them pushed apart; and he whose soul is flat, the *sky* will cave in on him by and by."

Roman soldiers under Titus leveled Jerusalem leaving hardly one stone upon another. Call it history or prediction matters little. The road to victory is not the sword, but *militant reconciling love*. It was in allegiance to this new kingdom of love that Jesus rested his case. Gibran condemns all of us when he says of man in his relation to Christ: "Man would dream your dreams, but he would not wake to your dawn which is his greater dream. He would see with your vision; But he would not drag his heavy feet to your throne."

The *predicament of Palm Sunday* is our willingness to vocalize, but our unwillingness to implement sentiment into concrete reality. Reinhold Niebuhr in his book *Does Civilization Need Religion?* comments as follows: "The soul gains its highest *triumph* by renouncing the world, but renunciation is premature if a futile, and yet not futile effort, is not made to make the natural world conform to the needs of human character. Man must work out his destiny both as a *child of nature* and as a *servant of the absolute.*"

Years after the Palm Sunday march to Jerusalem a devoted disciple of Jesus, the Elder John, sought to nourish his spirit upon the memory of his experience of comradeship with the Master and broke forth in a proclamation. "This is the victory that over-cometh the world, even our faith" (I John 5:4). When we today behold Jesus who is both a child of nature and a servant of the absolute we find ourselves certain of where to look for victory.

In Henry David Thoreau's *A Rhapsody on Sound*, we hear him say as he reflects upon the *drum beats* from an insignificant drummer in the night: "The simple sounds related us to the stars. Aye, there was a logic in them so convincing that the combined sense of mankind could never make me doubt their conclusions." Men take different strides in life. They set their marching according to the distant drum beats they hear. It seems to me that as Jesus rode on that memorable Palm Sunday He set his soul to the beat of a drummer in the sky.

"In the beauty of the lilies Christ was born across the sea with a glory in his bosom that transfigured you and me. As He died to make man holy, let us die to make men free. Our God is marching on. Glory, Glory, Hallelujah! Our God is marching on."

This is the victory that over-cometh the world.

§25 Dr. T. R. M. Howard

Dr. T. R. M. Howard's biography appears in the introduction to his October 2, 1955 speech in Baltimore, Maryland.

In this speech before a northern NAACP audience, which had something of an uneasy relationship with the RCNL, Howard demonstrates his considerable rhetorical skill. Known as a captivating orator, Howard's chief weapon is in demonstrating the hypocrisy of American democratic theory and American democratic practice. And yet, as Howard notes, "we have not lost faith in our American democracy. The fact that there has been no violence on the part of Negroes in Mississippi in retaliation for the violence heaped upon us is everlasting proof that the religion of Jesus the Christ and American democracy has done more for the Negro in Mississippi than it has done for our White brother." Howard and his Mississippi supporters were willing to believe in America's civil religion—even if southern whites were not.

Part of Howard's rhetorical mission before a northern audience is also to raise awareness of Mississippi's racial violence and the legislative mechanics of state-sponsored racism. The former involved the under-publicized murders of Reverend George W. Lee of Belzoni and Lamar Smith of Brookhaven; far more knew about the Emmett Till murder and trial. The latter was ably illustrated by absurd voter registration tests in which applicants had to read and interpret perfectly the state constitution—to a white registrar. But the point Howard draws is not a regional one. Rather, "A chain is not stronger than its weakest links; as long as Mississippi, South Carolina, and Georgia are weak links in the chain of American Democracy, our whole democracy is weak." The inferential subtext lays bare the rusted chain of American Christianity.

Mississippi's Challenge in this Grave Hour
NAACP Civil Rights Rally, New York, New York
May 24, 1956

Mr. Chairman, Ladies and Gentlemen:

I wish to thank the Program Committee for inviting me to appear on this program. I come to you from the State which gave America Theodore G. Bilbo and the present Chairman of the Senate Judiciary Committee, James O. Eastland. I come from a State where the Governor is thinking about calling a Special Session of the State Legislature to have the letters N and A and C and P removed from the alphabet used in the Mississippi schools and to have the words Desegregate and Integrate removed from the English language. I come from the State where the White Citizens Council or the modern K.K.K. was born. I come from the State that would have liked to have seceded from the Union again on the afternoon of May 17th, 1954 if there would have been any place for Mississippi to have gone on that afternoon. But there was only one place that she could have gone and since the infamous Mississippian, Bilbo was giving them so much trouble down there, Hell just refused to let Mississippi move in.

As I journeyed from my home in Mississippi, U.S.A., the very last outpost of American Democracy, I wondered what I might say to this vast group of American citizens to cause you to double your efforts in fighting for complete freedom, liberty and democracy for all American citizens, regardless of Race, Creed, or Color.

We know that our theory of American Democracy is the greatest philosophy of government that has been given to man since the dawn of creation. We, who accept the simple truths of our American Democracy, profess faith in the intrinsic dignity of all humanity without stopping to think whether it is white humanity, black humanity, Jewish humanity, Catholic humanity, Latin American humanity, or oriental humanity; we profess faith in the reasonableness, the integrity, and the sense of moral and spiritual responsibilities in the human personality. Our basic concept of American Democracy takes on the plain principle of faith in the equality of man, in the right of all men to a free, a full and abundant life, socially, politically, economically and spiritually. Our American concept of democracy also declares that every man must have the freedom of opportunity to release the potentialities for greatness and for good that are implanted within man so that a form of wealth is created in artistic, scientific, cultural and economic contributions which is possible of distribution to all men in more abundant and richer living.

The historic edit of the Supreme Court of the U.S.A. on May 17th, 1954 declaring segregation in the public schools of America a serious violation of our American concept of democracy, has been met with mingled emotions throughout our nation. In the deep South it has been met with open hostility. In my state, Mississippi, the reaction has been most violent. No state official in Mississippi has said, up until this very hour, that ten years from now or a hundred years from now that they would comply with the decision of the Supreme Court. They are still saying: "We will never comply." In an all out effort to discourage the Negro people of Mississippi from demanding first-class citizenship, a state constitutional amendment has been enacted to abolish the public schools of the state, rather than comply with the Supreme Court's decision.

They have also enacted another state constitutional amendment which is aimed at preventing the Negro from voting in Mississippi. The Negro who tries to qualify to vote in Mississippi today is given a reading test. He must be able to read any part of the Mississippi Constitution that he is called upon to read, and he must be able to write an acceptable Essay on "What is meant by a Constitutional Form of Government." A grade of 99 will not pass the applicant; he must make 100% in order to vote in Mississippi, U.S.A. today. It will be of interest to you patriotic American citizens to know that today, 93 years after the signing of the Emancipation Proclamation, that Negroes are allowed to vote in only 22 of Mississippi's 82 counties, and yet Mississippi's Congressional Representation is based on the total population. We have 986,000 Negroes in Mississippi today with less than nineteen thousand registered Negro voters in the entire state. The frightful methods of intimidation and the dastardly boldness of the wholesale disfranchisement of the Negro citizen in Mississippi, and the total disregard for the 14th and 15th amendment of our Federal Constitution by Mississippi, is the blackest spot on our American Democracy today.

Fellow Americans, how can we go to Geneva and before other Deliberate International Bodies and talk about free elections in Germany or any other place in the world, so long as we have a Mississippi with the conditions that exist there today? Rev. George W. Lee of Belzoni, Miss. and Mr. Lamar Smith of Brookhaven, Miss. have been murdered in Mississippi during 1955 for the simple reason that they wanted to vote in Mississippi, U.S.A. Until this day, no one has been brought to justice for the death of these men.

Our so-called judicial system in Mississippi is without parallel in the annals of American history. The entire civilized world was shocked and is still stunned over the kidnapping and lynching of 14 year old Emmett Till, and the subsequent freeing of the murderers by a Mississippi court. As I sat through this trial down at Sumner, Mississippi, and saw the worst miscarriage of justice in the history of American crimes, I was made to call upon the judge of all mankind and ask of him: "How long, oh God, will we have a double standard of justice in this democracy, one standard for the White American and another for the Negro?" A chain is not stronger than its weakest links; as long as Mississippi, South Carolina, and Georgia are weak links in the chain of American Democracy, our whole democracy is weak.

But, you say to me: "Dr. Howard, that is the South and her problem." My answer is that it is not a southern problem, it is an American problem.

Go with me if you please, any Sunday morning to the churches in the hamlets, villages, towns, and cities of the nation. Here we find a cross section of American men and women, who in addition to their profession of Christian faith have suffered three wars in this generation to preserve democratic ideas—among which is the principle that all men are created free and equal and are endowed with certain inalienable rights to life, liberty, and the pursuit of happiness—these men and women sit in their segregated churches worshipping in a feeling of virtue, the God who commands that man love his brother, while denying church membership as a positive policy because they cannot conceive of a personal level of an association with fellow men who are not of the same race or color or creed.

Go with me any week day morning into the offices of our nation where jobs are denied to Catholics, to Jews, to Negroes, to Latin Americans and to Orientals, and there we find many professed Christians, many patriotic Americans formulating these policies which promote these rejections.

These violations of our American profession of faith in our Democracy cannot help but reflect themselves in our national and foreign policy.

A consideration of these facts to which I have called your attention in this brief message should not beget pessimism, but as patriotic American citizens these facts should cause us to realize that race prejudice is the greatest enemy that faces our American Democracy today and these facts should stimulate resolutions in all of us to work and fight until these enemies from within, which are undermining our Democracy, are destroyed.

Notwithstanding all of the economic pressure, terror and violence that has been heaped upon us in Mississippi, we have not lost faith in our American Democracy. The fact that there has been no violence on the part of Negroes in Mississippi in retaliation for the violence heaped upon us is everlasting proof that the religion of Jesus the Christ and American Democracy has done more for the Negro in Mississippi than it has done for our white brother. We are not afraid—we have sent our courageous Negro soldiers to the ends of the earth to fight, bleed, and die for a democracy that they did not know anything about in Mississippi, and we have grown tired of dying for something in Korea that we cannot vote for in Money, Mississippi. We are on the march and the Citizens Councils, with all the Eastlands and Talmadges and Timmermans and James Byrnes, are not going to stop our triumphant march. Just after the Battle of Dunkirk, when the faith, hope and courage of the people of Great Britain were at their lowest ebb, there were cries of despair on every side and faint hearted men were saying: "Let us surrender now." That towering genius and courageous statesman Sir Winston Churchill said: "We shall go on to the end. We shall fight with growing confidence and growing strength; we shall defend our rights, whatever the cost may be, we shall fight on the beaches, we shall fight in the fields and in the streets, we shall fight in the hills, we shall never surrender, until in God's good time the new world, with all its power and might, steps forth to the rescue and the liberation of the old."

These words seem to fit my feeling as I conclude this message, armed with the Constitution of the United States of America, the Declaration of Independence, the Bill of Rights and the Decisions of the Supreme Court, and with God on our side, with your votes and your dollars we shall fight with every legal means until the Rebels of the entire South shall know that God's clock of time has struck the hour in this nation when all second class citizenship shall be cast into the depths of the sea.

Thank you.

§26 Roy Wilkins

Roy Wilkins's biography appears in the introduction to his May 22, 1955 speech in Belzoni, Mississippi.

Before the largest religious body of blacks in the United States, Roy Wilkins takes as his biblical text Paul's second letter to the Corinthians. In bearing about in our bodies the death and life of Jesus, Wilkins urges "above all" that the faith from Christ's dying would bring "new and abundant life for all people forever." That faith and promise were particularly acute in 1956 since "we are confronted with a great moral problem, a problem of how to do justice under our laws and our Constitution to those who heretofore have not had either justice or equality under those laws and that Constitution." Less a legal or a political problem, by defining segregation as a moral and thus a spiritual problem, Wilkins brings contemporary problems of race directly into the convention hall of this conservative group. And, whereas Wilkins had been critical of the black clergy's inactivity in previous addresses, in Denver he has nothing but praise: "the church and the ministers have stood like a rock. Not only have the Negro Churchmen (with but few exceptions) resisted all efforts to get them to take sides with the segregationists, but they have spearheaded an offensive action for decency." Wilkins singles out for special commendation Martin Luther King, Jr. "and others, for the part they have played in the bus protest of that city." Wilkins singles out for special derision the president of the United States, Dwight Eisenhower, who had said or done nothing in the school crises of Clinton, Tennessee and Mansfield, Texas. "Here is the one man who, without favoring your child or mine, could set a moral tone for the nation in this sorry mess, but he chooses to stand mute." Wilkins ends his address by asking for financial help amid "a great conspiracy to make time stand still and to maintain injustice on the throne." With state legislatures in Louisiana, Florida, Alabama and Mississippi appropriating large sums of money to fight desegregation and the work of the NAACP, Wilkins assures his Baptist listeners that God's will and the promise of America will win out over the "rulers of darkness."

Speech to the National Baptist Convention

Denver, Colorado
September 6, 1956

I appreciate greatly the opportunity to bring greetings to this great convention of Baptists from the national officers, board of directors, branches and members of the National Association for the Advancement of Colored People.

It is appropriate that this word be brought [to] you because of the cooperation and support which your members throughout the nation have rendered the cause and program of the NAACP through the years. The church has been a bulwark of strength in the NAACP crusade from the very first days of its existence. Pastors and lay leaders of many faiths and denominations were represented among those who signed the call to organize the NAACP in 1909.

All along the way the church has stood with the NAACP in the fight for justice and equality, which is another way of saying the kingdom of heaven on earth. As I have moved about this convention I have seen men who are leaders in our branches all over the country, men who are presidents, vice presidents, and members of executive committees of our units from coast to coast. I see men in whose church edifices we have been welcomed to hold our annual conventions, our state and local conferences, and our mass meetings on questions of the day. I see men who have gone to Washington, to state capitals, and to city council meetings to urge justice for our people. I see men who have raised funds from their congregations to help finance the crusade for first class citizenship, who are life members of the Association and who have urged their members to join the NAACP. In short, I see a leadership of the people which is concerned with man's opportunity and happiness here on earth, and which realizes that this is properly the business of God's church. For this understanding and aid we of the NAACP are grateful. Indeed, the gratitude is not limited to the NAACP, but comes forth, I am sure, from the people everywhere who are today sorely troubled in body and mind, and who desperately need vigorous, uncompromising, yet comforting and understanding guidance.

Our present-day plight is well described by Paul in his letter to the people of Corinth, in Second Corinthians, the fourth chapter, and the eighth through the tenth verses: "We are troubled on every side, yet not distressed; we are perplexed, but not in despair; persecuted, but not forsaken; cast down, but not destroyed. Always bearing about in the body the dying of the Lord Jesus, that the life also of Jesus might be made manifest in our body."

"Bearing about in the body the dying of the Lord Jesus"—the courage, the compassion, but above all, the faith of that dying, the faith that from that death there would arise a new and abundant life for all people forever. And, too, the following and necessary corollary: "that the life also of Jesus might be made manifest in our body"—that we might so learn to live that we, ourselves, each one of us, would exemplify the compassion and sacrifice, the courage and faith of the Savior.

Today all the people of our nation—white and black—need that compassion, that courage and that faith. For we are confronted with a great moral problem, a problem of how to do justice under our laws and our Constitution to those who heretofore have not had either justice or equality under those laws and that Constitution.

Desegregation is the question of the day. It is plaguing the soul of America as never before. Is it just that men, merely because of skin color, be separated off from their fellows by state-imposed law, and in this fashion, and by this process, denied their equality as citizens of their native land? The highest court in our country has said they shall not be so separated; that this separation, of itself, constitutes discrimination and a denial of equality of opportunity, and that it is contrary to the Constitution of the United States.

This decision of May 17, 1954, was rendered with respect to segregation in public education, and while it is true that it and other decisions dealing with public recreation and interstate travel directly affect the whole status of the Negro as a citizen, it would be well not to lose sight of the particular item of educational equality for our children.

Each year several millions of our children are literally crippled for the battle of life because they are denied access to the kind and quality of public education being offered to children who are not colored. This is the central fact to be remembered: these children are not being given a fair chance to become the kind of men and women they might become. In a world which is changing at lightning speed they are being held to a snail's pace. We are already in the electronic age and have now entered the atomic age. Our children are already behind. Every year, every semester they are made to wait before they can enjoy their rights is a year, a semester, off of their productive lives.

And they are being made to wait. The ruling of the Supreme Court is being flouted and defied in some states of the Deep South. Yet progress has been made in many areas and this progress is the best proof that other localities could at least make a beginning. Of the seventeen original states and the District of Columbia that had school segregation by law, only eight have made no move to desegregate on the elementary and secondary levels. Of these eight, three—Virginia, North Carolina and Louisiana—now have Negro students in their state universities and other institutions of higher learning. That means that only five states, South Carolina, Florida, Georgia, Alabama, and Mississippi, have made no move on any level to eliminate racially segregated education.

These five states are defying the nation's highest court and making a mockery of law and order and of the Constitution through the speeches of United States senators, the pronouncements and actions of governors, state legislatures, and political office holders of every description. The court's opinion is also being defied through the employment of economic pressures and violence. I am sure I do not have to review the long list of instances of economic pressures: of men and women being fired from their jobs, of tenant farmers and workers being thrown off the land, of mortgages being foreclosed or denied, of business men being refused credit and small merchants the delivery of goods by wholesalers.

Legislatures have passed laws barring NAACP members from state, county, or municipal employment. Teachers are a special target. The communist smear has been used—anyone who favors desegregation is automatically a communist. The NAACP has been barred by court order from operating in Louisiana and Alabama because it would not submit its membership list to the authorities in those states.

The record shows plainly what would happen to any member whose name became known to the authorities. Alabama asked, among other things, for the name and address of each member in the state. We offered everything else they asked for: records, financial statements, cancelled checks, payroll and employees in Alabama, office leases, etc. It would seem that anyone could determine from this information whether the NAACP was doing business in Alabama, which is what they said they wanted to determine. But no—they wanted the name and address of each member. These we refused to give and we have been fined $100,000. We are still in court on the question and will exhaust all legal weapons to protect our members.

However, attempted intimidation of the NAACP will not stop the movement toward freedom and equality. It will go on; it is going on at this very minute. And attempted intimidation of Negro teachers will not stop the movement; in fact, the teachers have stood firm, despite the threat to their jobs. Twenty-four of them in Elloree, South Carolina resigned their jobs rather than sign a statement that they did not belong to the NAACP. The businessmen are standing firm. The workers and farmers have not given in. Except for a few Uncle Toms here and there—and a mighty few at that—Negro Americans have presented a solid phalanx for equality.

And, of course, the church and the ministers have stood like a rock. Not only have the Negro churchmen (with but few exceptions) resisted all efforts to get them to take sides with the segregationists, but they have spearheaded and offensive action for decency. I cannot add to the world acclaim that has been heaped upon the ministers of Montgomery, Alabama, led by the Reverend Martin Luther King, Jr. and others, for the part they have played in the bus protest of that city.

Nor can anyone estimate the good which has come and will come out of the National Day of Prayer observance affected by your own great leader, Dr. J. H. Jackson, as support for the brave people of Montgomery. The people have been inspired as never before. A new sense of Christian dignity has been planted and the harvest cannot help but be that "the life of Jesus may be made manifest in our body."

And "our body" here means not merely our part of the population, but the whole of our people, white as well as colored. For the message of Montgomery is a message to men everywhere, a call to Christian living and redemption. It is for our adversaries as well as for us; it is for their spirits as well as for ours.

Well, having found all other methods producing no results, our opponents have come out with naked violence, with mobs and threats of the use of guns.

In the past week we have seen the shameful spectacle of mobs of grown men gathering to bar a dozen children by physical force from attending school, all this in defiance of a court order.

To the everlasting credit of Governor Frank Clement and the state government of Tennessee, and to the credit, also, of the responsible citizens of Clinton, Tennessee, the mob was halted and the children are continuing in school. Clinton, Tennessee illustrates the fact that where the people in charge are firm in their support of law and order, the hoodlums can be beaten. More than 100 Clinton white citizens were sworn in as deputies to keep the peace. The National Guard, sent by the governor to maintain order, did its job and carried out the will of the townspeople.

However, in Mansfield, Texas, where a court order also had been issued, Governor Allan Shivers did not measure up to the demands of his office. He did send in Texas Rangers, but he instructed them to move out any Negro child who applied to the Mansfield high school! The contrast between Tennessee and Texas is glaring indeed.

The segregationists have declared over and over again that they intend to use "all legal means" to block desegregation. The senators and congressmen who signed the Southern Manifesto used this phrase. Do they endorse the mobs at Clinton and Mansfield as "legal means"? Do they approve of the threat of guns at Mansfield as a "legal" method of maintaining segregation? These men and others like Senator James O. Eastland of Mississippi who have whipped up and given encouragement to defiance of the Supreme Court were the fathers of the riotous demonstrations of the past week. When men in high places advise lawlessness, the hoodlums take them at their word.

And speaking of men in high places, who has heard a word from the President of the United States? The newspapers, radio and television are full of riot accounts in his own land. Governors have called out troops. Men have been hung in effigy. A guardsman has been stabbed. All the nation is watching in shocked horror at men making war upon children and upon the Supreme Court of the United States, upon the bedrock of the constitutional protection of every citizen—and from the White House not a mumbling word. It is incredible, but true, that the President of the United States is assuming a "neutral" position in a contest in which his own Supreme Court is under attack, and in which lawlessness is running riot. Here is the one man who, without favoring your child or mine, could set a moral tone for the nation in this sorry mess, but he chooses to stand mute.

Well, we shall continue to pray and to work. I promise you that the NAACP will press the crusade for freedom, that we will give it all the skill and perseverance we have learned through forty-seven years of activity. This is a most crucial time in our history. We must have unity and dedication in our efforts. Every individual and every organized body among us must work together toward victory. Now is no time for jealousies and divisions. Now we must be as one.

We have had your cooperation in the past. We have had your encouragement. We have had your financial support, both from this convention, from state and local associations, and from individual churches and ministers. We have had your prayers and your guidance.

I know we will continue to have these in the struggles which are ahead, the struggles which will decide our destiny as a people. The forces which oppose us are strong, even though wicked. Our enemies, who are also the enemies of freedom, have interlocked themselves in a great conspiracy to make time stand still and to maintain injustice on the throne.

The Louisiana legislature appropriated $100,000 to fight desegregation. The Alabama legislature appropriated $150,000. Mississippi set up a new state bureau and a secret police system. Florida has appropriated $50,000 to investigate the NAACP. The White Citizens Councils and similar organizations have a minimum fee of $5.00 and a claimed membership of 250,000—a treasury of $750,000. No one knows how much money private businessmen and industries in the South have paid in to the cause. Millions of pamphlets and books are being distributed.

They cannot succeed, but it will take all our dedication of effort and money to defeat them. To borrow again from Paul, from his letter to the Ephesians, the sixth chapter and the eleventh and twelfth verses, let us: "Put on the whole armor of God, that ye may be able to stand against the wiles of the devil. For we wrestle not against flesh and blood, but against principalities, against powers, against the rulers of the darkness of this world, against spiritual wickedness in high places."

The rulers of darkness shall not prevail. Man—all men of every shade and circumstance everywhere—shall be free in both body and spirit. This is the promise of the great land of America; this is the pattern of God's will.

§27 Reverend D. Perry Ginn

D. Perry Ginn was born on December 21, 1928. He grew up in Georgia and was educated at the University of Georgia. Ordained in 1949, Ginn's early ministry took him to Hodgenville, Kentucky, where he preached this sermon on desegregation. Not long after, Ginn returned to the university, to pursue advanced degrees at the Southern Baptist Theological Seminary in Louisville, Kentucky. He eventually received his Th.D. in Old Testament studies. Ginn later served Baptist congregations in Princeton, Kentucky; Knoxville, Tennessee; Gainesville and Atlanta, Georgia. Although he formally retired in 2000, Ginn came out of retirement in 2004 to pastor the Valley Brook Baptist Church in Decatur, Georgia.

With the Supreme Court's *Brown* decision more than two years old, Ginn outlines for his congregants at First Baptist Church what their responsibility is to their church, their homes, and their schools in matters of desegregation. Those responsibilities are thoroughly grounded in New Testament scripture as Ginn takes his listeners through Acts, Romans, John, Galatians and Colossians to support his desegregation position. For the Christian, it's not enough just to be law abiding, as per Paul's command in Romans; rather, Christians must also seek out the active will of God as revealed in the Bible. And the Bible is quite clear, claims Ginn: Christian love is premised on an unselfish concern for others—regardless of skin color. To this, Baptists have been willfully blind, even as they follow the scriptures to the letter on other liturgical matters. Sadly, even "fight promoters and baseball managers have done more to secure equality for Negroes than has the Church of

Jesus Christ." Ginn closes his sermon by delineating the Christian's role in desegregating Hodgenville, from parents changing the atmosphere in their homes to children helping up black boys and girls on the playground. Perhaps most importantly, the doors of First Baptist must be flung wide open to all races.

———

Christians and Desegregation
First Baptist Church, Hodgenville, Kentucky
November 1956 (reprinted)

In May 1954 the Supreme Court declared that segregation in the public schools is unconstitutional. This decision came as a shock to those of us in the south, for it was a challenge to the traditional southern way of life. Now we face the problem of making integration work. With desegregation becoming an actuality in Hodgenville this year, a tremendous responsibility falls on every Christian in our community, and in particular upon the members of the First Baptist Church. We must come to grips with that responsibility if our testimony for Christ is to be vital.

We look to the Word of God, seeking to find therein help and guidance. In this matter of Christian responsibility and desegregation, the Bible gives a clarion call for decisive action. ·

One of the most explicit teachings of the Bible is that *it is the responsibility of every Christian to be a law-abiding citizen.* Paul teaches this in Romans 13:1-7. Here he stresses that the principle of government is God-given, and that for one to resist the governing authorities—that is, for one to refuse to obey the law of the land—is in actuality to resist a decree of God himself. Whether we like it or not, the law says that segregation is unconstitutional, and it is therefore our duty as Christians to obey.

The Scriptures give only one justification for refusal to obey the law. If a law is contrary to the will of God, is detrimental to the welfare of individuals, or is inherently evil, then the Christian must look to the higher authority of God. *Only* in such a case may the Christian re-echo the words of Peter: "We must obey God rather than men." In this matter of desegregation we cannot claim such a right. This decision of the court was fundamentally democratic, truly American and inherently Christian. To disobey and oppose such a law is to make mockery of all that Christianity stands for.

But our responsibility as Christians goes far beyond that of being mere law-abiding citizens. As true Christians, *it is our fundamental responsibility to follow the will of God as that will is revealed in holy Scripture.* We glibly call Jesus our Lord, yet in our attitudes and actions we often deny our words. As far as the segregation problem is concerned, it could easily be said of us today: "This people honors me with their lips, but their heart is far from me."

Consider the nature of the gospel we preach. We call John 3:16 the epitome of the gospel. This verse teaches that the gospel is for "whoever believes." Color is of no consequence with God. The same God is Father of white and colored, and they are brothers and sisters in Christ, united by a tie that is greater than color or race. The very nature of the gospel condemns racial prejudice, for all men are equally in need of the grace of God, equally worthy of salvation and equally members of the family of God.

The Bible, however, is much more pointed than this in its condemnation of prejudice. The teachings of the Scriptures are clear on the matter of the relationship between races, and any real Christian must accept their truth. Peter, like many of us, had difficulty in freeing his life from prejudice; but when God acted to show him the true meaning of the gospel (Acts 10), Peter had the courage to accept and to obey. The same is true of Paul. He was a strict Pharisee with a natural antipathy toward the gentiles until he met Christ. No statements of Scripture are more clear than those of Paul as he deals with the matter of the relationship between races and different types of people (Galatians 3:28; Romans 10:12; Colossians 3:11). He clearly teaches that prejudice has no rightful place in Christian experience.

Jesus taught the dignity and worth of every human personality, that every man is equally important to God. In the parable of the Good Samaritan, Jesus teaches that the very essence of Christianity is love in action for those in need, and no amount of orthodoxy in theology and zeal in labor can make up for lack of love.

The New Testament Christians believed with John that "God is love." They knew that prejudice makes this affirmation a lie. In Acts 15 we read of the conference they held to deal with the problem of "integration." This conference declared that gentiles should be received into the church without prejudice or discrimination thus laying down, 1900 years ago, the principle governing the Christian attitude in race relations.

The Bible throughout teaches the basic unity of the human race, and Paul declares that God "hath made of one blood all nations of men." I had nothing to do with the fact that I am white, just as the colored man had nothing to do with the fact that he is colored. If I say that because I am white I am therefore superior to the man who is colored, I make God unfair and call the Bible a lie. God made us as we are, and God is just, righteous, holy; God is love. Racial snobbery is the very antithesis of the true Christian spirit.

The prevailing characteristic of a Christian's life is love. This Christian love is the attitude of unselfish good will and abiding concern for the welfare of others. It is thus the royal law of a Christ-like life. As the sun does not inquire upon what it shall shine, or whom it shall warm, but shines and warms because this is its nature; so the Christian loves indiscriminately and without questioning, for this is the very nature of Christian love. Prejudice can have no place in a life filled with such love.

We Baptists believe the Bible to be the inspired revelation of the will of God. Loud and long we proclaim that it is our sole authority in matters of faith and practice. Yet in the matter of segregation we have conveniently closed our eyes to the truth. We are so orthodox in the matters of baptism and the Lord's Supper, so strictly biblical in our confessions of faith, but so poorly Christian in the practice of Christian love in race relations. We call ourselves "New Testament Christians," yet all the while we ignore the plain implication of the New Testament that one simply cannot be a New Testament Christian and hold prejudice in his heart. Thousands of our church members are fundamentally non-Christian in their attitude toward the race question. The saddest commentary on contemporary Christianity is the fact that fight promoters and baseball managers have done more to secure equality for the Negro than has the Church of Jesus Christ.

Jesus says that Christians are the salt of the earth and the light of the world. What he means is that the influence of Christians should be felt in all areas of life. In this matter of desegregation, therefore, *it is the responsibility of every Christian to use his influence to the end that the transition from segregation to integration be done in an orderly and Christian manner.* Each of us in our community has the responsibility of exerting a moral influence upon others in the promotion of law and order.

One area in particular where Christian parents and school leaders have a specific responsibility is in the local P.T.A. The parents of the Negro school children should be invited and urged to become members and to participate actively. As you and I are interested in the welfare of our children, so Negro parents are interested in the welfare of their children.

We parents can help by creating the proper atmosphere in our homes. Children are not born prejudiced. It is only when adults create the impression that to be white is to be superior and to be colored is to be inferior that racial prejudice is born. We parents must teach our children the basic principle of democracy: the dignity of every human life.

The actual success of integration in Hodgenville, however, will depend upon the young, for they always show themselves more tolerant and less prejudiced than adults. My word to the young people is this: Do not condescend to the colored young people. They want to be treated as full human beings, with the same rights, the same privileges and the same responsibilities that others have. Accept them on the same basis as others. When a Negro boy slips on the basketball court, be just as quick to help him to his feet as you would anyone else. For remember, the pain of a turned ankle is not determined by one's color. And when a Negro girl falls on the playground and skins her knees, be just as quick to help, for the blood of a colored girl is just as red as that of a white girl. In the classrooms and clubs, do not discriminate. Rather treat the colored young people as you treat others: no better, and by all means no worse.

One further word must be said. *It is the responsibility of every Christian, and the responsibility of the church as a whole, to set the proper example.* It is here that we have been sadly negligent. We have failed to lead the way in social progress. In the matter of statement of principle the Supreme Court has been the engine pulling the train, and the church, shameful to say, has been the caboose.

Perhaps we can redeem ourselves in some measure if we will take the lead in making integration work. The demand, however, is for more than mere words. People are not going to listen to our words if our actions deny what we say. The greatest scandal upon the church is that it is the most segregated institution in the entire United States. It is time that this scandal ceases. The gospel of Christ is for all who *will* believe; and the church that Christ founded should be open to all who *have* believed, regardless of race or color.

The most effective and courageous thing the First Baptist Church could do to set the proper example of Christian responsibility in desegregation would be to open its doors to anyone wishing to join, regardless of color of race. I could wish that the men and women of this church were so filled with the Spirit of Christ that such a decision would be made, and that such a decision would become alive through actual practice in evangelistic work. Difficult it is to be sure; but that it is the Christian thing to do, no doubt exists.

I trust that none of you will interpret my words as coming from one who has already attained in his own life these ideals. It grieves me to confess it, but my own life is not yet completely free from prejudice. As in any son of the south, prejudice was instilled in me from the time I was born. Anything that has been so indelibly written into one's consciousness as has been the belief in segregation as a way of life, is not easily erased. (And this is what the extreme groups do not understand.) It is my prayer, however, that by the grace of God prejudice will be purged from my life.

We have God's promise that his grace is sufficient. As we continue to grow in grace and knowledge of Jesus, prejudice will be conquered. Our task now is to acknowledge that prejudice is sinful, to keep our eyes firmly fixed on the ideals of Scripture, and to continue to grow until these ideals become realities in our lives. My plea to you this morning is that we together set ourselves to the task, that we recognize Christian responsibility, and that we busy ourselves in carrying out that responsibility.

Yes, my friends, integration will work in Hodgenville; because you and I, led and empowered by God, will make it work.

1957

§28 P. D. East

Percy Dale East dispels most stereotypes of southern racism with his persistent decency despite his suspect demographics. It would be comfortable to assume that the son of an itinerant white sawyer would suffer the socioeconomic stigma of his place to the point that he would need to lash out at the one caste below him. It would also be comfortable to assume that a man run out of the armed forces during World War II for shortcomings in discipline would lack the persistence to make more than a footnote in the civil rights movement. Cozier yet is the notion that a family man would neither fail at three marriages nor die of liver failure at age fifty. P. D. East dispels all these myths. He was born in Columbia, Mississippi on November 21, 1921. He was raised the adopted son of a roving saw miller and a boarding house mother, moving from camp to camp and surviving the stigma of his place in society with obnoxious èlan.

East attended Pearl River Junior College for a semester in 1939 before working in public transportation jobs. In 1942 he enlisted in the army, receiving a discharge after a year for his unsuitable demeanor. He returned to a former employer until 1947, when he took up journalism and writing at Mississippi Southern College (today, the University of Southern Mississippi). In 1951 he resigned his work with the rail line and began writing for Hattiesburg labor union newspapers. He founded the *Petal Paper* in 1953 as a forum for his acerbic wit and egalitarian ideals. The paper managed to survive until 1971, but cost him and his family more antagonism than we can imagine in the comfortable world P. D. East created. His public opinions on civil rights resulted in dogged threats, harassment, and eventual exile to Alabama. During Freedom Summer, his widow, Cammie East Cowan recalls, Klansmen put a $25,000 bounty on his head "back when that was an awful lot of money." Almost always deeply in debt and often prostrate from a bleeding stomach ulcer, East died on December 31, 1971 of complications from liver failure. His papers are housed at Boston University. His memoir, *The Magnolia Jungle: The Life, Times and Education of a Southern Editor* was published in 1960.

The theology implicit in the following address stems in part from the office of Samuel L. Gandy, the Howard- and Chicago-educated dean of Lawless Memorial Chapel at Dillard University who extends a speaking engagement invitation to the unordained journalist. In this chapel address to students, members of the faculty, and administrators at Dillard University in New Orleans, Louisiana, East employs the extended metaphor of a medical diagnosis from a roving snake oil peddler to weave an endearing and intelligent rhetorical garment. His motivations for sharing this conceit are loyalty to a childhood friend in a temporary saw-mill camp and to his four-year-old daughter, Karen. In some detail, East diagnoses the South's sickness and its addiction to snake oil. Part of his remedy involves a healthy dose of religion, even as most of his other remedies extend from the Judeo-Christian tradition.

But in addition to the religious authority conferred upon East by Dean Gandy, East supplements sacred traditions with commonsense decency. Christian traditions need such moral bedrock to make sense of why Paul returned Onesimus to his master, Philemon. The same traditions need similar moral bedrock to shape the sediment swirling about Peter's exhortation that slaves obey their masters. East's commitment to these foundational ideals cost him, his wives, and his children a traditional family. But like a quail flapping its wings to attract attention away from its young, he preserved for them and for us a secure future in a fairer, more orderly world than he knew.

––––––––

The South, Collectively, Is A Patient Most Ill

Dillard University, New Orleans, Louisiana
March 11, 1957

President Dent, Dean Gandy, Faculty Members, and Members of the Student Body: On this day, eight weeks ago, I received from Dean Gandy an invitation to speak here. Frankly, my first impulse was to decline as I have done on a few previous occasions.

That I did not decline is, of course, perfectly obvious. Though, the possibility does exist that we all would be better off had I declined.

The reasons I did not decline this invitation, I feel I should tell you, as best I can, at any rate. I accepted this invitation because I have an obligation—to me it's an obligation I cannot ignore, not even if I wanted and tried to. I am obligated to one person, and perhaps, in the final analysis the view I take is a selfish one. Even so, I think you'll agree that selfishness, such as one feels toward his own child, is permissible. This invitation was accepted by me because of the realization of the fact that to my daughter, who is just four years old, I am deeply and eternally, and I might add, gratefully, obligated.

The thought process by which I reached such a conclusion is of no great importance. Perhaps, as I said, it's just plain selfishness. But I will add this in my own defense, just a few other factors were involved . . . but the final obligation remained the same.

Going quite briefly into the thought process, provided that's what it was, is the fact that had my grandfather seen fit to have fulfilled his obligation to my father chances are I'd not have felt the obligation to be here today. Going further, had my own father seen fit to have fulfilled his obligation to me, the chances are I'd not have felt the necessity of being here.

They failed . . . and in so failing, they passed to me a problem which they may have solved, or at least, a problem on which they should have made an effort. They failed . . . and because they failed, I have a problem . . . selfish person that I am, I have no desire to pass it on to my child. My thought process draws a blank when I consider that what was good enough for grandpa is good enough for my own child. In plain language, it ain't worth a damn.

It is my desire to see my daughter live a life of happiness, a life in which a person is respected and accepted as a human being on the basis of his individual merit . . . a life in which she can devote her energies toward something productive, perhaps even creative . . . at any rate, my obligation to her is to provide the opportunity to build . . . not destroy, nor even to cling to what she has as if it were all there was in the world.

But if I fail to face up to the times in which I live, if I fail to face reality, then I am failing to give her the things which I want desperately for her to have. I see no point in making any excuses . . . on that point, and in that desire, I'm selfish . . . as a matter of fact, I'm just downright greedy.

In addition to the fact that I'm under an obligation to my child, aside from the fact that my forefathers failed to face up to their times, I am here because I am guilty of having failed to face up to my times . . . not only do I feel guilty about it, I am guilty of the sin of omission. I admit my guilt, and I'm ashamed. Nonetheless, facts are facts, and facing them is a part of the answer we all are seeking in these, our times.

The thing of which I feel such keen guilt is not for something I did, but for something I failed to do. And I might add, here and now, that the crime of omission is being committed more today, and by more persons, than ever before.

By birth, by custom, by tradition . . . and by no choice of my own, I'm a Southerner, having been born and reared in Mississippi. The earlier part of my life was spent living in various saw mill camps all over the southern part of the state.

One evening there was an incident in my Mother's house which I recall to this day quite vividly. In the center of the room there was a pot-bellied stove, glowing red on its diet of pine-knots. Around the room was gathered a group of saw mill workers, exchanging jokes of first one sort then another. The discussion turned to the high prices which prevailed during the First World War. One man told the story of a small Negro boy whom he'd seen come into a grocery store and ask for a ten-cent piece of salt meat. According to the narrator, the clerk in the store said to the child, "Well, boy, for a dime you can smell the knife I cut salt meat with."

This story brought a thunderous amount of laughter in my Mother's house . . . and I was ashamed. Most ashamed. I didn't know why . . . and to this very day I'm not sure that I could explain my shame. I just left the room . . . I left without saying a word. As I recall, I was about seven years old.

During this same period of my childhood, I had a friend at one of the camps in which I lived. He was my favorite playmate, and about my own age, but he had one drawback . . . it was later before I became aware of the drawback from which he suffered. Because of the accident of birth which caused my friend, Tee, to be colored, it was understood that I was superior. Everyone seems to have understood it . . . except me. I am honest in saying that such an idea never once crossed my mind.

There were some things which I failed to understand. And at the age of seven or eight my limited ability to reason was even less than it is today. I could never get into my mind why Tee couldn't charge a nickel's worth of candy at the store to his daddy if I could charge candy to my daddy. I didn't do much thinking about it . . . I could charge candy . . . so I did. I would buy a dime's worth and give half of it to Tee, which to me, seemed a fair thing to do for a friend. True, I bought the candy and shared with Tee as I would expect him to share with me, had the situation been reversed.

But what I failed to do was to speak up for a friend. I took the easy way out . . . and I was to learn later in life that most folks do things that way.

Anyway, having failed to speak up for Tee, I was failing to speak up for my daughter . . . but at the age of seven or eight it is a trifle difficult to project one's thinking almost three decades.

Nevertheless, I committed a sin by my silence . . . it was the sin of omission, about which I feel guilty even to this hour. I don't like to feel guilty . . . it takes a lot out of a person . . . it takes out a lot that could be used to produce, to make whatever contribution a person is capable of making to the society in which he lives . . . and all persons have that obligation . . . each to the other.

As I said earlier, I am a Mississippian, and I would like to add that I'm about to be a presumptuous one at this point. Also, I am a product of my times; too, I'm a victim of my environment. Finding myself in such circumstances, I recognize that I am living in an age of analysis, psycho and otherwise, believe me.

I think it is unquestionably true that all men, in the final analysis, seek the same end . . . peace of mind. Everything we know as human beings is aimed at that goal. With that fact in mind, I prefer to look on the South today as a physician, a many faceted physician I'd like to point out, as such a man of medicine would view a patient. Also, I would like to make it understood that the doctor is just as sick as the patient . . . there is but one notable difference between the two: the doctor knows he's sick and in so realizing, is making an effort to cure himself.

At this point I want to make most clear a fact or two. Like everyone else, I am victim to my own ego. I view the South as a patient. That means I am setting myself up as a doctor. And you wonder about my qualifications? I have none. I am without a union card to treat the ill. Perhaps, after all, I'm nothing more or less than an uncalled quack. But, suffering from these weaknesses of human nature, you will allow that I have confessed before committing my crime.

From my unqualified point of view, the South, collectively, is a patient most ill.

The patient suffers from a condition which has been growing on it for well over a century. The symptoms have taken many forms, but on close observation they all point to one direction. For the purpose of treatment, I would diagnose the case as that of a many faceted, highly complicated, malignancy condition.

Now, there are a number of schools of thought where patient treatment is concerned, as you well know. I'll not bother with going into them. Just let me tell you the school of thought to which I subscribe. I am of the empty gourd school. The theory, quite basically, is that to render a cure, first get out of the patient that which is causing his illness, to get it out of the patient and into an empty gourd is to bring about a cure. Naturally, we seal up the gourd after the cause is in it.

So much for the school of medicine to which I subscribe. The ultimate cure of the patient is our aim.

It is a known fact that one of the surest signs of illness is the everlasting insistence by the patient that he's not sick at all. It's everyone else, provided it's anyone, according to the patient. And under such circumstances it's a safe thing to consider the possibility that when everyone is ill, no one is ill . . . or, at any rate, to consider that the norm has lost its meaning.

And no matter how well qualified a doctor is, he has to have the help of the patient before he can effect a cure. The patient which is under consideration has been helpful to the uncalled quack, quite without his knowing it. He has sprung a leak at Montgomery; he has blown a gasket at Tuscaloosa; he split at various seams in other places . . . and at Clinton, Tennessee, he almost ruptured himself! These are symptoms which I have taken into account.

And I am convinced of the fact that the patient is in serious condition. But is the patient convinced? Does he admit his illness? Only time will tell.

But in arriving at a prescription for the patient, we should know a little about his history. First, let us find out if the patient has been taking anything about which we should know. The answer is in every history book; it's primarily a matter of reading the facts objectively. The patient has been taking a concoction known as snake oil. He's been getting it from snake oil peddlers who have been in the business for centuries. They're slick characters, and know their business. The peddlers of snake oil have made many a buck off the unsuspecting patient, but of more importance, from their point of view, is the fact that they have been able to keep the patient under their control by his having become addicted to their medication.

The patient likes snake oil. It deadens the pain from which he suffers . . . but it does nothing toward bringing about a cure. Having run a lab check on snake oil, I find the contents to be ego-centric thinking, used as a base, with equal parts of selfishness, conceit, arrogance, pride, and more than a trace of down-right stupidity . . . and as I said, it deadens the pain, but it also deadens the patient.

Now, how can the patient be taken off the medication to which he has become accustomed? That is the question . . . and to it I have no answers. The illness can be pointed out to the patient, but the final decision, as to whether the patient wants to be cured, is up to him. There are no laws to make a person take anything he doesn't want to. A patient has to want to be well before anything can be done for him. And there are inducements, the greatest of which is peace of mind . . . but that's quite an involved matter.

At this point, we have a brief history of the patient, and since we have made a diagnosis of the case, right or wrong remains yet to be seen, then our next step is to offer a new prescription.

I would prescribe for the patient under discussion a mixture of ingredients, to be compounded with exacting cure and accuracy by the patient himself. For the want of a better name, I'd call the prescription . . . BITTERS.

It's a nasty dose, admittedly, but if the diagnosis is correct, BITTERS will sooner or later bring about a cure . . . at least, in most cases. Of course, it is understood that to all things there are exceptions . . . that we must grant.

I may as well admit to the fact that the prescription of BITTERS is a trifle complicated. The ingredients are the same for each individual, true, but the actual dosage is dependent entirely on the patient himself. And further to complicate the matter, I remind you again of the fact that the patient insists he's not ill.

Since I am like the patient, a product of my times, a victim of my environment, and since I recognize the fact that I'm ill, I insist that my brother is also ill . . . to some degree at any rate. This insistence is, as I have already admitted, a weakness of human nature. I cannot overemphasize the importance of the fact that the patient admit his illness and that snake oil just might be an outmoded remedy to which his addiction is sapping from him his vital life blood. Without the recognition of this basic fact nothing short of surgery is going to help.

And I feel it only fair to remind the patient of the fact that the Federal Government has the necessary instruments to operate.

As to the prescription of BITTERS, I would use as a base a strong belief in God, and that all men, after all, are the children of God. I would not insist that any man be his brother's keeper, but I would insist that he include a generous helping of being his brother's brother.

Next, I would include a dash, but not too small, of objective thinking. The use of this ingredient would be to bring about a condition in the patient whereby he admits there are in this world a few things beside himself.

Next, I think might be the bitterest of all the ingredients . . . but it's a magic item, and quite rare, or at least used rarely, called tolerance. Use it freely . . . it has never been known to hurt anyone.

Further, I'd admit humility. Humility is included in the hope of offsetting a harmful effect from the extended use of snake oil. With it, perhaps, if used generously, it might get into the gourd an evil from which the patient has suffered long . . . false pride. I don't know but what I'd throw in a dash of shame, too.

Then, I would add generosity, compounded with a touch of liberalism. These items would be used in the hope of broadening the soul of the patient . . . aimed at making the soul less stingy and selfish.

After that, a dash of modesty in compound with a bucketful of decency . . . again, no patient has ever died from the use of these ingredients.

And then, add equal parts of patience, forbearance, forgiveness . . . and just any item on which we could lay our hands to help the patient keep his temper under control.

Another item, I think, should be a generous helping of temperance, badly needed in this prescription. The use of it should not be spared.

Then, in an effort to get a deadly evil out of the patient and into the gourd, I would add generosity, kindness, and consideration in abundance.

Last, in the hope of keeping the patient on the mend, to keep him from suffering a relapse, I would add a sufficient amount of diligence and industriousness to this prescription . . . it would be added with the suggestion that he keep busy producing or creating something beneficial to his fellowmen.

I admit readily to the fact that this is a very bitter dose . . . but it can be swallowed. And even if the patient isn't sick, provided I made a mistake in my diagnosis, the compound will most certainly do no harm to the patient.

I should think this to be a sufficiency of medical practice for one day . . . especially since the patient didn't send for the doctor. I confess to this, in reviewing what I've said, I may well be the quack who's peddling the snake oil . . . and, admittedly, my motive is a selfish one. I want my daughter to live a life of happiness . . . and to her I'm obligated.

Too, I say again, as confessed earlier, that I'm ill, being a product of my times. I admit to myself my illness, complicated malignancy further complicated by a feeling of guilt for what I've not done.

Selfish though it may be, but with the help of God I propose to speak up for my daughter's interest and well-being . . . that I promise to do so long as I breath the air of the earth . . . and in the event I can get the trouble out of myself and into an empty gourd, I don't know but what I won't speak a word or two for my friend, Tee.

It's about time . . . to that I think you'll agree.

Perhaps at this point I would do well to ask: Is there a doctor in the house?

§29 Reverend Martin Luther King, Jr.

Martin Luther King, Jr., was born Michael Luther King, Jr., on January 15, 1929 in Atlanta, Georgia. Born into a prominent religious family, "M.L." or "Little Mike," as he was called, quickly became a fixture at Ebenezer Baptist Church where his father, "Daddy" King pastored. A sensitive young boy with clear intellectual gifts, King entered Morehouse College as a 15-year old freshman. Later, in 1948, he began his matriculation at the Crozer Theological Seminary just outside of Philadelphia. It was at Crozer where King developed his precocious talents in pulpit oratory, taking nine courses in the subject. Such was his prowess that King packed the chapel and the classroom whenever he sermonized. Finishing at the top of his class at Crozer, King moved north and east to pursue his Ph.D. at Boston University in 1951.

Early the following year, King met and courted Coretta Scott, a music student at Boston's New England Conservatory of Music. The two married on June 18, 1953. Less than a year later, King began as pastor of Dexter Avenue Baptist Church in Montgomery, Alabama. If geography is destiny, then King's first call was providential: in December of 1955 Rosa Parks refused to give up her seat and Martin Luther King, Jr., accepted the presidency of the Montgomery Improvement Association (MIA). Before a national audience, King would lead black Montgomery to a historic desegregation of the city's buses. And a star was born.

King's resumé needs but a brief gloss here. Upon founding the Southern Christian Leadership Conference (SCLC) in 1957, King was in demand as a speaker throughout the country. King's star also attracted the demented. At a book signing on September 17, 1958, he was attacked by a knife-wielding, Izola Ware Curry. Had King so much as sneezed while the knife was stuck in his chest, a surgeon later told him, he could have punctured his aorta and died immediately. King's legendary problems with the F.B.I. and its conflicted leader, J. Edgar Hoover, also commenced in the late 1950s because of his association with the communist-tainted Bayard Rustin and Stanley Levison. King returned to Atlanta in 1960 as copastor of his father's church, Ebenezer Baptist. With the student sit-ins early in 1960, King, perhaps ironically, was finally swept into a movement he had helped to create. Rather than merely preaching about non-violence and disobedience, the student movement convinced King of the efficacy of nonviolent protest. That movement lured him from the pulpit to the streets. First in Atlanta, then in Albany, Birmingham,

Selma, Chicago, and Memphis, King would lead the movement's political, judicial, and spiritual revolution. For his efforts he was awarded the Nobel Peace Prize in 1964 and a posthumous legacy of Martin Luther King Day, celebrated every January. King was murdered on April 4, 1968 at the Lorraine Motel in Memphis where a museum stands as a tribute. His papers are housed at Boston University and at the King Center in Atlanta. He is survived by his wife and four children.

King delivered this address before a relatively small audience of clergy gathered on the Vanderbilt University campus. Organized by Vanderbilt Divinity School faculty member Everett Tilson, King juxtaposes the nation's many advances in science, technology, and economics with the "plague of racial conflict." That plague centers principally on the "evil" of segregation, a practice that not only promoted inequality but scarred the souls of both segregator and segregated. Racism substituted an "I-thou" relationship with an "I-it" relationship thereby rendering the black man a depersonalized object. Amidst such unjust and un-Christian practices, King calls on his fellow clergy to lead the assault on racial mores—an assault sanctioned by the Judeo-Christian tradition perhaps best typified in Christ's ministry.

King does not call for his listeners to engage in direct nonviolent resistance. He rather urges them to take the lead in desegregating God's house. He also calls for clergy to open lines of communication between the races and to pursue economic justice. Above all, clergy must be mindful of a theocentric rather than an anthropocentric world view, in which all ministers are finally accountable only to God. King closes his remarks by defining the "beloved community," a heaven here on earth whose means is agape love and whose end is reconciliation and redemption. To be "maladjusted" in the psychological vernacular of the day, is to follow the example of Amos, Lincoln, Jefferson, and finally Christ in establishing God's kingdom here on earth.

The Role of the Church in Facing the Nation's Chief Moral Dilemma
Conference on Christian Faith and Human Relations, Vanderbilt University, Nashville, Tennessee
April 25, 1957

There can be no gain saying of the fact America has brought the world to an awe-inspiring threshold of the future. As one studies the majestic sweep of American history, he cannot help but be astounded and fascinated by the tremendous progress that has been made in so many areas. The scientific and technological advances made by this Nation still astound and stagger the imagination. Through our technological genius, we have been able to construct skyscrapers in buildings with their prodigious towers steeping heavenward. Through our advances in medical science, we have been able to cure many dread plagues and diseases, and thereby prolong our lives and make for greater security and physical well-being. Through the scientific ingenuity of the Wright brothers, the airplane was invented.

With this instrument, we have been able to dwarf distance and place time in chains. Yes, we have been able to carve highways through the stratosphere. Through nuclear energy, we are delving into the mysteries of the creation of matter. Not only have we made great progress in the area of technology and science, but we have made unprecedented strides in the area of economic growth. We have been able to build the greatest system of production that the world has ever known. Our material wealth astounds the world, and has catapulted our Nation into the greatest political power on earth. All of this is a dazzling picture of U.S.A. 1957.

But there is another side of our national life which is not so bright. In the midst of all of our scientific and technological advances, we still suffer the plague of racial conflict. We have not learned the simple art of loving our neighbors, and respecting the dignity and worth of all human personality. Through our scientific genius, we have made of the world, a neighborhood, but through our moral and spiritual geniuses, we have failed to make of our own Nation a brotherhood. This is the chief moral dilemma of our Nation. This tragic dilemma which we now confront leaves the nation and the Church with a tremendous challenge. The broad universalism standing at the center of the Gospel makes brotherhood morally inescapable. Racial segregation is a blatant denial of the unity which we have in Christ. Segregation is a tragic evil which is utterly un-Christian. There are at least three reasons why segregation is evil. First, segregation inevitably makes for inequality. There was a time that we sought to live with segregation. In 1896, the Supreme Court of this Nation, through the famous Plessy v. Ferguson decision, established the doctrine of separate-but-equal as the law of the land. The enforcement of this Plessy doctrine ended up making for tragic inequality and ungodly exploitation. There was a strict enforcement of the "separate" with not the slightest intention to abide by the "equal." So the old Plessy doctrine ended up plunging the Negro across the abyss of exploitation where he experienced the bleakness of nagging justice.

But even if it had been possible to provide the Negro with equal facilities, in terms of external construction and quantitative distribution, we would still confront inequality. Even if it were possible to provide Negro children with the same number of schools and the same type of buildings as the white students possess, there would still be inequality in the sense that the students could not communicate with each other. Equality is not only a matter of quantity but of quality; not merely of mathematics and geometry, but of psychology. The Supreme Court was eminently correct in saying the separate facilities are inherently unequal.

A second reason why segregation is evil is because it scars the soul of both the segregator and the segregated. It gives the segregator a false sense of superiority, and it gives the segregated a false sense of inferiority. This is why every Negro parent must continually remind his child that he is somebody, for he is the victim of a system that forever stares him in the face saying "you are less than"—"you are not equal to." Segregation is evil because it brings about a tragic distortion of human personality.

A third reason why segregation is evil is the fact that it ends up depersonalizing the segregated. The segregator looks upon the segregated as a thing to be used, not a person to be respected. He is considered a mere cog in a vast economic machine. This is what makes segregation utterly un-Christian. It substitutes an "I-it" relationship for the "I-thou" relationship. The segregator relegates the segregated to the status of a thing, rather than elevate him to the status of a person. The philosophy of Christianity is strongly opposed to the underlying philosophy of segregation.

Therefore, every Christian is confronted with the basic responsibility of working courageously for a non-segregated society. The task of conquering segregation is an inescapable *must* confronting the Christian Churches. Much progress has been made toward the goal of a non-segregated society, but we are still far from the promised land. Segregation still persists as a reality.

The churches are called upon to recognize the urgent necessity of taking a forthright stand on this crucial issue. If we are to remain true to the Gospel of Jesus Christ, we cannot rest until segregation and discrimination are banished from every area of American life. It has always been the responsibility of the Church to broaden horizons, challenge the status quo, and break the mores when necessary. Such was the role of Amos and Jeremiah, of Jesus and Paul, of the early Church, of Savonarola and Martin Luther, of Livingstone and Schweitzer.

There are several specific things that the Church can do in making brotherhood a reality. First, the Church should try to get to the ideational roots of race hate. All race prejudice is based upon suspicion, fears, and misunderstandings, most of which are groundless. The popular mind urgently needs direction here. Not only is the mind left confused by certain frictions that arise out of the ordinary contact of diverse human groups, but we are afflicted by the activities of the professional hate groups, that is, through the activities of leaders of racist movements, who gain prominence and power by the dissemination of false ideas, and by deliberately appealing to the deepest hate responses within the human mind. These two forces—ordinary antagonisms and abnormally aroused fears—keep the popular mind in such a state of confusion and excitement that they are unconsciously led to acts of meanness and oppression.

The church can show the unreasonableness of these popular beliefs. It can show that the idea of a superior or inferior race is a myth that has been refuted by the best evidence of the anthropological sciences. It can show

that Negroes are not innately inferior in academic, health and moral standards [and] are products of environment, not of race. Slums and poverty
breed germs and immorality, whatever racial group may occupy them. It
can show that when given opportunities, Negroes do as well as anyone else.
It can show that the Negro is no worse and no better than any other element in the National population.

The Church can help by showing that Negroes do not want to dominate
the Nation. They simply want the right to live as first-class citizens, with
all the responsibilities that good citizenship entails. The Church can help
by showing that the continual outcry of inter-marriage is a tragic distortion of the real issue. It can show that the Negro's primary aim is to be the
white man's brother, and not his brother-in-law. Many Churchmen are already aware of these things, but the truth is so widely distorted by the hate
groups that it needs to be reiterated over and over again.

Another thing that the Church can do in the area of race relations, is to
keep men's minds and visions centered on God. As I said a moment ago,
many of the present problems which we confront can be explained in terms
of fear. So many irrational fears have cropped up around the question of
integration that have no basis in reality. I have come to see that we not only
have the job of freeing the Negro from the bondage of segregation, but we
also have the responsibility of freeing our white brother from the bondage
of crippling fears. One of the best ways to rid ourselves of fear is to center
·our lives in the will and purposes of God.

In dealing with the race problem our thinking is so often anthropocentric rather than theocentric. The question which is usually asked is—"What
will my neighbors think if I am too liberal on the race question"—"What
will my friends think if I am too friendly to Negroes." Somehow men forget
to ask the question—"What will God think." And so men live in fear because they are bogged down on the horizontal plane with only a modicum
of deviation to the vertical.

The Church must remind men, once more, that God is the answer, and
that man finds greater security in devoting his life to the eternal demands
of the Almighty God, than in giving his ultimate allegiance to the transitory evanescent demands of man. The Church must continually say to
Christians, "ye are a colony of heaven." This means that although we live in
the colony of time, our ultimate allegiance is to the empire of eternity. We
have a dual citizenry. We live both in time and eternity; both in heaven and
earth. Therefore, we owe our ultimate allegiance to God. It is this love for
God and devotion to his will that casteth out fear.

A third thing that the Church can do in attempting to solve the race
problem is to take the lead in strong Christian social action. It is not enough
for the Church to be active in the ideological direction; it must also move

out into the arena of social action. The first act in this area should be the Church's determination to purge its own body of discriminatory practices. Only by doing this can the Church be effective in its attack on outside evils. Most of the major denominations practice segregation in local Churches, in Church hospitals, Church schools, and other Church institutions. It is appalling, indeed, that 11 o'clock on Sunday morning, when we stand to sing "In Christ there is no East nor West" is the most segregated hour in Christian America. It is true that there has been progress in this area. Here and there Churches are courageously making attacks on this system. But in most cases the attacks are local and independent. They are not yet the work of the Church as a whole. So the Church has an internal problem that it must cure.

The Church must become increasingly active in social action outside itself. It must seek to keep channels of communication open between the Negro and white community. Men hate each other because they fear each other; they fear each other because they don't know each other; they don't know each other because they are separated from each other. And only by keeping the channels of communication open can we know each other.

In the area of social action the Church must take an active stand against the injustices that Negroes confront in city and county courts of many southern towns. Here the Negro is robbed openly with little hope of re-dress. He is fined and jailed often in defiance of law.

Another area in which the influence of the Church is much needed but little felt is that of the economic order. The disadvantages that Negroes suf-fer in this area are startling indeed. In many fields they cannot get jobs at all; in others they are employed at appallingly low rates. This is a tragic end. It is murder in the first degree. It is strangulation of the moral, physical, and cultural development of the victims. So long as these blatant inequali-ties exist in the economic order our nation can never come to its full moral, economic, and political maturity. As guardian of the moral and spiritual life of the community the Church cannot look with indifference upon this glaring evil.

I must say just a word concerning the dire need for sincere, dedicated, and courageous leadership from individual Christians. It is my profound hope that more leadership will come from the moderates in the white south. Unfortunately, the leadership from the white south today all too often stems from the closeminded reactionaries. But it is my firm belief that this closeminded, reactionary, recalcitrant group constitutes a numer-ical minority. There is in the white south more open-minded moderates than appears on the surface. These persons are silent today because of fear of social, political, and economic reprisals. God grant that the white moderates of the south will rise up courageously, without fear, and take over the leadership of the south in this tense period of transition.

The nation is looking to the white ministers of the south for much of this leadership. Every minister of the gospel has a mandate to stand up courageously for righteousness, to proclaim the eternal verities of the gospel, and to lead men from the desolate midnight of falsehood to the bright daybreak of truth. I am aware of the difficulties that many white ministers confront when they take a stand in the area of human relations. But in spite of these difficulties the Christian minister must remember that he is a citizen of two worlds. Not only must he answer to the mores, but he must give account to God. He must again and again hear the words of Paul ringing across the centuries: "Be not conformed to this world, but be ye transformed by the renewing of your mind."

I am not unmindful of the fact that many white ministers in the south have already acted. Many such ministers are here today. I have nothing but praise for those ministers of the gospel who have stood unflinchingly amid threats and intimidation, inconvenience and unpopularity, and even at times amid sheer physical danger. There is nothing, to my mind, more majestic and sublime than the determined courage of an individual willing to suffer and sacrifice for truth. For such noble servants of God there is the consolation of the words of Jesus: "Blessed are ye when men shall revile you and persecute and say all manner of evil against you, falsely, for my sake; rejoice and be exceedingly glad; for so persecuted they the prophets which were before you."

It is also necessary to stress the urgent need for strong, sincere, and dedicated leadership from the Negro community. In this period of transition and growing social change, there is a dire need for leaders who are calm and yet positive. This is no day for the rabble-rouser, whether he be Negro or white. We must realize that we are grappling with one of the most weighty social problems of the century, and in grappling with such a problem there is no place for misguided emotionalism. We need a leadership that will stress the necessity for keeping our hands clean as we struggle for freedom and justice. We must not struggle with falsehood, hate, malice, or violence. We must never become bitter. We must never succumb to the temptation of using violence in the struggle, for if this happens unborn generations will be the recipients of a long and desolate night of bitterness and our chief legacy to the future will be an endless reign of meaningless chaos. There is still a voice crying through the vista of time saying to every potential Peter, "put up your sword." History is replete with the bleached bones of nations and communities that failed to follow this command.

The Negro leader must stress the fact that the aim of the Negro should never be to defeat or humiliate the white man, but to win his friendship and understanding. We must make it clear that it is injustice which we seek to defeat and not persons who may happen to be unjust. We have before us the glorious opportunity to inject a new dimension of love into the veins of our civilization. Our motto must be, "Freedom and justice through love." Not through violence; not through hate; no not even through boycotts; but through love. As we struggle for freedom in America it may be necessary to boycott at times. But we must remember as we boycott that a boycott is not an end within itself; it is merely a means to awaken a sense of shame within the oppressor and challenge his false sense of superiority. But the end is reconciliation; the end is redemption; the end is the creation of the beloved community. It is this type of spirit and this type of love that can transform opposers into friends. The type of love that I stress here is not *eros*, a sort of esthetic or romantic love; not *philia*, a sort of reciprocal love between personal friends; but it is *agape* which is understanding goodwill for all men. It is an overflowing love which seeks nothing in return. It is the love of God working in the lives of men. This is the love that may well be the salvation of our civilization. God grant that the leadership of the Negro race will remain true to these basic principles. To paraphrase the words of Holland:

> God give us leaders!
> A time like this demands great leaders;
> Leaders whom the lust of office does not kill;
> Leaders whom the spoils of life cannot buy;
> Leaders who possess opinions and a will;
> Leaders who have honor; leaders who will not lie.
> Leaders who can stand before a demagogue and damn his treacher-
> ous flatteries without winking!
> Tall leaders, sun crowned, who live above the fog in public duty and
> private thinking.

There are certain technical words in the vocabulary of every academic discipline which tend to become stereotypes and cliches. Psychologists have a word which is probably used more frequently than any other word in modern psychology. It is the word "maladjusted." This word is the ringing cry of the new child psychology. Now in a sense all of us must live the well adjusted life in order to avoid neurotic and schizophrenic personalities. But there are some things in our social system to which I am proud to be maladjusted and to which I suggest that you too ought to be maladjusted. I never intend to adjust myself to the viciousness of mob-rule. I never intend to adjust myself to the evils of segregation and the crippling effects of discrimination. I never intend to adjust myself to the tragic inequalities of an economic system which take necessities from the many to give luxuries to the few. I never intend to become adjusted to the madness of militarism and the self-defeating method of physical violence. I call upon you to be maladjusted. The challenge to you is to be maladjusted—as maladjusted as the prophet Amos, who in the midst of the injustices of his day, could cry out in words that echo across the centuries, "Let judgment run down like waters and righteousness like a mighty stream"; as maladjusted as Lincoln, who had the vision to see that this nation could not survive half slave and half free; as maladjusted as Jefferson, who in the midst of an age amazingly adjusted to slavery could cry out, in words lifted to cosmic proportions, "All men are created equal, and are endowed by their creator with certain unalienable rights, that among these are Life, Liberty and the pursuit of Happiness." As maladjusted as Jesus who dared to dream a dream of the Fatherhood of God and the brotherhood of men. The world is in desperate need of such maladjustment.

In closing let me urge each of you to keep faith in the future. Let us realize that as we struggle for righteousness we do not struggle alone, but God struggles with us. The God that we worship is not some Aristotelian unmoved mover who contemplates merely upon himself; He is not merely a self-knowing God, but an other loving God. He is working through history for the establishment of his kingdom. There is an event at the center of our faith that reminds us of this. Just last Sunday we celebrated this event. It comes as an eternal reminder to us that Good Friday may occupy the throne for a day, but ultimately it must give way to the triumphant beat of the drums of Easter. Evil may so shape events that Caesar will occupy a palace and Christ a cross, but one day that same Christ will rise up and split history into A.D. and B.C., so that even the life of Caesar must be dated by his name. This is our hope. One day, by the grace of God, we will be able to sing, "the kingdoms of this world have become the kingdom of our Lord and his Christ and he shall reign forever and ever, Hallelujah, Hallelujah!"

§30 Reverend James A. Pike

James A. Pike, Episcopal bishop and one of the leading liberal church voices in the country, was born in Oklahoma City on Valentine's Day, 1913. Raised Roman Catholic, Pike attended the University of Santa Clara, where he drifted away from Catholicism and became agnostic. Pike earned his law degree from Yale, and served as an attorney for the Securities and Exchange Commission in Washington, D.C. Following his time in Washington, Pike served from 1943 to 1945 with Naval Intelligence during WWII. During his time in the service, Pike entered the Episcopal church and studied theology. He received his B.D. from Union Theological Seminary in 1951, and became the dean of the Cathedral of

St. John the Divine in New York City—the nation's largest Episcopal church. At St. John the Divine, Pike's fame spread, culminating in a weekly ABC talk show that aired from 1955 to 1961. Perhaps the biggest Protestant media celebrity in the country, Pike was appointed Bishop of California in 1958. He also pastored Grace Cathedral in San Francisco.

An outspoken advocate of civil rights, gay rights, and the women's movement, Pike turned to transcendentalism and other popular late 1960s preoccupations. In 1968 Pike resigned his post to form the Foundation for Religious Transition. On a trip with his wife to Qumran in the Judean desert in April 1969, Pike got lost and stranded. After a 10-hour trek his wife made it out alive. Pike's body was discovered five days later. His papers are housed at Syracuse University in Syracuse, New York.

In this curious and extended address on the subject of "Methodism's Ministry to the Total Community," Episcopalian James Pike offers a blistering critique of the "dreadful scandal" of the church. That scandal involves race—in the south, in the north, and abroad in South Africa. In any and all locales, the church, its leaders, and its members are running behind the secular culture on such essentials as freedom and equality. Even Communist countries are running ahead of the U.S. on having an enlightened policy on race vis-à-vis South Africa.

Pike articulates a curious blend of theology and myth with a story running from the Zoroastrians to the Persians to the Jews and then to Christians. It is a story of Good versus Evil and which side we choose. Not to choose a side is to choose the side of Evil. More important for Pike, in the Judeo-Christian tradition, Good has already won. The devil's wrath is thus great because the time is short. And in much of its human rights policy, the U.S. is "on the side of the devil." By contrast, Christians must adopt a "theology of courage" in which our first loyalties are not with the nation or the community but with the kingdom of God—and to bring that kingdom to fruition here on earth. Such a "blessed treason," Pike avers, will actually save the U.S. Finally, and back to the more local issue of race, Pike states that loyalty to the kingdom translates into real affection and love for its fellow members.

––––––––––

Report of the Interracial Leadership Conference
Detroit, Michigan
April 30, 1957

Tonight I feel much in the position of the preacher in one of our churches on a very hot summer day. As he looked out upon the great, vast number of empty seats and the very small attendance of the Church, he felt it was hardly worth preaching a sermon. So he preached the shortest sermon on record. He said, "A lot of people aren't here today because they think it is hot. Let them just wait. Amen."

The attendance here is fine. I tell the joke for quite another reason. This preacher's sermon was a good one. I think the trouble with it was the right people did not hear it. The people he preached it to were there. It is the ones that were not there that needed to hear it.

I think this is sometimes what is wrong with our preaching and thinking. We are talking to the faithful. We are playing the old records with the convinced, and the people who won't come here to hear it are the ones who need to hear it.

If what I say tonight is to the convinced—and I am sure it is, or you would not have come to give this time to so seriously working for this cause—I am simply trying to help you and help myself find better words to convince the other people to help us put our cause in a more convincing way, to alert people to the seriousness of the situation we are in, the dreadful scandal which the church itself presents to the world along with its glory, that we may come closer to the purpose for which this conference is called.

I am going to be very blunt. You can take more from me than the outsiders can. Let's face it. I am going to throw out a few actualities and then we will talk about them.

Two weeks ago, the trustees of a seminary of your church in a state in which the secular institutions of higher learning no longer segregate, voted officially through its trustees that the seminary remain segregated. People like this believe you are immoral if you drink and smoke and dance but that to discriminate against your fellow man is all right.

Now, I am not against Methodists. I can tell you a lot about our dirty linen, too.

We have been talking about the Godless universities and Godless public schools and how the Church has got the real message. We have been talking about the secularism of our times and yet all this evil generation is ahead of the Godly generation. The children of darkness, indeed, are ahead of the Church.

I am going to say something that is quite personal and I want you to understand me. What I am going to mention is not your fault. It points to something behind it that is the fault of all of us. It is something you do not even realize, because you do not sit up here. But the fact is you are not sitting there together in an interracial way. If you look carefully, it is a fake. With two or three exceptions you are grouped right through the room in groups of white people and groups of Negroes.

You do not mean to do that. You would not come here if you meant to do that. What is behind it is the real trouble. We would not solve the thing by my saying, "Let's all shift." The fact is that you represent parishes and churches that don't have a mixture of people in them and so the friends you know, the people you came here with, are the same color as you are and that is why you are sitting with them.

That is all right. Don't move. I believe in naturally being congenial with the people we know. That is perfectly all right. But, the Church is so deeply segregated in the North—I do not waste my time condemning the South anymore as we have plenty to work on here and they take it with better grace when we talk about ourselves—and our communities are so deeply segregated that we just do not know very many people of a different race in a way that would even entitle us to dislike them. I believe in the right to dislike people but you cannot even dislike people on a sound basis unless you know them. It is a patronizing kind of discrimination, speaking now for white people, that you have to like every Negro. Why should you? I don't like every white person. I will tell you that I love every white person. We are commanded to love everybody, that is, be concerned for them and seek to meet their needs but "liking" is something that cannot be commanded. So I do not see why I should like every Negro person at all. But I should be close enough to people of different races that I can make a real choice on an individual basis, saying, "I like that man for what he is, and I do not like that man for what he is, and I don't like him even if he is a Negro or a white man."

Our churches give very little opportunity for that. Thus while we must gather like this and talk about these things, I do agree with the person who spoke just before that we should not be here; this is all wrong. We should not be here talking about this at all, and let's hope the day comes when we are not. In the meanwhile we must. It is only by talking about it frankly and together that the day will come when we don't have to talk about it.

Years ago when I was first a minister, I was serving in Washington in a very segregated parish, St. John's opposite the White House. Down the way was a segregated Negro parish and so our clergy and the clergy of that Church got together and decided to form an informal discussion group made up of about ten families of each parish to meet in different homes to talk together and get acquainted. This was way back when people were not often doing this sort of thing.

What did we talk about? We sat down and talked about segregation and race relations. The result is that meeting after meeting we were all very much aware of the fact that some of us were colored and some of us were white. And then somebody got a bright idea. He said, "Let's stop talking about this for a while. Let's study St. John's Gospel together," which we did. And within three weeks several people confessed that something had happened to them, they were no longer noticing at all about color. They were just noticing that this fellow's comment was rather bright and this fellow's comment was rather dumb—which is the way we ought to judge things.

I will make one more personal comment. This is a good choir but you see this all-Negro choir, good as it is, expresses the fact of our segregation and for that reason I do not like it. This is one of the apologies made for segregation, that every group has its own distinctive gifts to give. Alright. That wonderful spiritual we know comes from the Negro heritage. We do not want to lose that.

Would it have hurt some white people to sing that spiritual with you and learn how to do it? It is not that we want to give up what has been contributed by the various groups. The same is true of the Church unity; I want the Methodist people to come in and be more Methodist than they are. After all, you people took the oven out of our Church. I don't want the Lutherans to become less Lutheran. I want them to bring their great tradition in for the benefit of the rest of them. I want all we have to be shared in the hearing and doing.

Well now, let's go a little further afield. You may not know about this. I am surprised how many Americans do not know this thing has happened and four times now. Each year a resolution is introduced into the United Nations for the continuation of the committee to keep an eye on the apartheid policy of the government of South Africa—a policy of determined segregation that goes so far (in the Bantu Education Act) as to say, in effect, that a Negro may not be educated in the liberal arts because he must not get notions. In other words, he must learn things that will make him a servant, tradesman or mechanic.

There is nothing wrong with that kind of work but to say that people because of their color may not elect to work out their future in the humanities or in a profession is going to the very limit because it is seeking to seal off the growth and development of a given group.

There is now before the parliament of South Africa a ruling which gives the ministers of the interior the authority to forbid integrated worship in any church in the country at his own whim. A little more about that later.

This is an international issue of consequence. Their policy is a violation of the Declaration of Human Rights. Second, it is that which will most make possible the growth of communism in Africa. I can tell you when a man becomes a communist it is when he has nothing to lose, when things could not be worse. I can put myself in the position of those who would try anything in their despair to throw off the yoke no matter how foolish, ideological, or unwise this thing is. So, we encourage communism when we make things bitter for a majority of the citizenry of any nation. We have something at stake here. That is why the United Nations has had this committee. They cannot force South Africa but they can at least keep before the world what is going on.

But notice this. Every year, inconsistently enough, every communist nation has voted for the resolution; that is, for the principles of Christian brotherhood, against the government of South Africa. Every Arab country has voted for the resolution. The state of Israel has voted for the resolution. But not one leading Christian nation has voted for the resolution. This nation and every other leading Christian nation has voted for South Africa in its racial discrimination policy.

Every year it has happened and it is your government. It is your state department that voted that way.

Now the crowning point and it really gets me started on my main point, I really have something to say and will get to it sooner or later. The crowning point is that our nation has been defeated each year on that. The communist nations have won against us.

What is the position of the patriotic American? How do you feel about that victory against our nation on that issue? Is it the job of the patriotic American to wrap himself in the American flag and say "My country right or wrong." Not for one minute. I am delighted that our nation was defeated each year and I hope we are always defeated each year and I hope we are always defeated when we are on the side of the devil.

Now this is the point that I want to get across to help us convince the people not here. We have done a lot of talking; not much is happening. The Church is way behind the secular Godless society on this testing point of Christian justice and love. I think we have to move people by a deeper theology not just by ethical exhortation, one which we can understand better by going back to an old myth. The Persians were the nicest captors that the Jews ever had and, therefore, the Jews paid a lot of attention to the Persian religion. Remember that, too, when it comes to Evangelism. Everything we talk about in the field of rights, the Church's honest action in the field of brotherhood, it is not social ethics, it is Evangelism. This person who stays out of the Church may have reasons for it that are not worthy sometimes but some of the reasons are reasons we created for him because often we have shown the outsider we do not mean what we say. That is the judgment on the Church and, therefore, our work in this field is Evangelism as well as good social ethics. In any case, they picked up from the Zoroastrian religion an important myth. What is a myth? A myth is not a fable. A myth is a picture language way of explaining something very complicated that you can not put in plain sentences. It is a way of explaining a contradiction by a big picture. The Zoroastrians were worried about the problem of evil. How is it if God is good and powerful that there is so much evil in the world? They worked out this answer: There are two Gods. Both of the Gods are final and ultimate. One, the God of Light, called Mazda (after the familiar electric light bulb!); the other, the God of Evil or Darkness. Surrounding each God there is a kingdom of angels, good angels and bad angels, and the two kingdoms are in eternal warfare.

Now where do we come in? First, we are the innocent bystanders. You know what happens when a couple of groups are fighting and you are standing there. But we have a choice. Here is the ethical challenge of the Zoroastrian religion. The question is, "What do you want to give your life to? You have the choice of dedicating it to augment the spiritual forces surrounding the God of Light or you can give it to augment the forces surrounding the God of Darkness." And, anticipating what Jesus later said in another way, "If you don't decide, you have decided. You are for the Darkness."

Now the Jews just took that picture right into their tradition and you will find it in various places in the Bible and in the Apocrypha, and you will find it influencing the imagery of Jesus. But when the Jews took this myth into their system of religion, they made a little change in the story. And this little change is very crucial. Instead of the great force of evil being an independent God, he is a fallen angel; meaning, evil is spoilt goodness. Evil is parasitical. It feeds on the good. It does not have an independent basis of its own. It has no future of its own. Only God and good have eternal future. Therefore, when the Jew or the Christian—the Christian took this over lock, stock, and barrel—when the Jew or the Christian decides for the Kingdom of Light, he decides for a sure thing.

We know there is no future in evil and that evil is already doomed and judged and that only good shall abide. Now, this same way of putting things is in a capsule form in that last book of the Bible which we call, the Revelation of St. John the Divine. This last book of the Bible was originally circulated around the Mediterranean as a subversive pamphlet. The Christians, you know, were illegal, and they met in the back streets, behind closed doors, in cells, and they formed a network, seeking to worm their way into the civil service, into the army, and eventually take over, which they did.

It was predicted they would overturn the world. They did not quite do that but they caused quite a commotion, anyway. And the problem of those early Christians was this: They saw their brethren being informed on. They were being arrested and thrown to the lions. And they needed their courage picked up. They needed to be told that this great big brassy empire was through already and that they were the future.

So we get the old story again. You know the words, of course. There was war in heaven and Michael and his angels fought and Satan, the old serpent, and his angels fought. And Satan was cast out of heaven and there was no place found there for him any more.

This means in the ultimate outcome of things that evil has no place. And, then a great song of praise goes up to the heavens which the scholars tell us is a remnant of an early Christian hymn. There is praise of those that have already died and are in heaven, the martyrs. They did not love life so much that they stuck by the state.

Then, another complaint about informers; the accuser of our brethren. We go down to the meeting of the practical problem. You see, this does not quite solve the problem yet because the Christians would say, "Well, if the devil is already doomed, if he has already been cast out, why is he having such a time of it for himself? He is getting along very well for a fellow who has been licked, you know."

So, there is this glorious text that I regard as one of the finest things in all the scriptures in terms of social action and courage, realistic and with an answer. "But, woe unto the earth; the Devil has come down among you, having great wrath." Why? "Because he knows he has but a short time." He knows he is through: hence, his wrath.

Now, we can not date the war in heaven. This is not history. This is grand cosmic picture language letting us know what the big issues are and what the outcome will be, and where we are now in it. These early Christians who stayed loyal found this pamphlet very cheering, indeed. You know the cryptic language of the last book of the Bible is because they were trying to get it by the authorities. It is deliberately ambiguous. Whenever they wanted to talk about Rome, their own government, they called it Babylon. When they wanted to talk about the emperor they wrote his name in numerology, 666. This pamphlet did not please the Senate Un-Roman activities at all; and there was a new outbreak of persecution because of the pamphlet. It came into our Bible finally in about the fourth century when things were put together in the New Testament. And this was selected presumably because it has a message to men of every age—and it does.

Here is the theology of courage I have been trying to develop. The Christian is a man who is not first of all loyal to his own community or to his own nation. He is loyal to the Kingdom of God which he sees as transcending its own nation, its mores, its customs, its selfish interest.

He knows that nations come and go. "Where are kings and empires now?" Anybody who reads his Bible knows that nations come and go. Our forefathers in this country did not ever say, "America forever." They believed in the Kingdom of God forever and they saw here a chance for it to be expressed. And, I can well see the day, as a Christian with my first loyalty to the Kingdom, when the whole history of this nation will have become a paragraph and a half in somebody's history book. But, the Kingdom of Heaven will still be going on; the Church of Jesus Christ will be going on. Where is the Roman Empire now? Yet the Kingdom, the Church, is still here. We're the same outfit right here in Detroit, two thousand years away.

Therefore, we have to get first things first. First to our nation: Decidedly not. But, does this make for poor patriotism? I don't think so. In fact, our

Bill of Rights itself was conceived by men whose thought was nurtured in these ways, who thought that the nation would be safer if there were within it people who had a higher loyalty than the nation and looked critically at what the nation was doing and sought to make the nation what it ought to be, and simply not be "yes men" about what the nation is.

I think that is a better patriotism. But in any case we are colonists here and a colonist tries to make the colony look like home. You know the old British colonial who went out in the jungle and built his club so it was just like London and got some scotch and water, too, before they even got guns. It had to be like home. The missionaries who went along built gothic-style churches. Why? They were homesick for that little church back home they knew and missed. And they wanted to make this place look like that.

I am not for colonialism except this one kind of divine colonialism. Our job is to try and make this place look like heaven which is our true citizenship. Now when we get thinking in those terms we then can see above the momentary majority interest of our own people or the foreign policy or lack of the same that seems to be expressed by our state department.

The thing that we will do is to hold on to a wholesome, constructive criterion that will help this nation abide and not lose its influence in the world by its own blindness. The nation with no critical citizens in it is doomed. It was the prophets that saved Israel because they were always carping. They were wonderful people to read about in the Bible but you would not have liked them very well as dinner companions. A pretty rough fellow that Amos. He called a spade a spade. Not apt to get elected to the Rotary Club or probably not even president of the Ministerial Association. But, the nation is safest with people like that around.

Our task as Christians is to keep the eternal perspective always in mind and then inform ourselves well enough as to the facts and issues that we can make some judgments for our time. And, it is not enough for the clergy to speak out on the issues.

I have been asked by laymen, "Why do you think you have to use the pulpit to speak on political and social issues?" My answer is: "Because you don't. If enough of you did, I would not have to. But your mouths are closed and as long as they are, since I have been ordained a prophet, I shall serve as a prophet."

The point is that all of us by virtue of our Christian calling are called to be prophets. There is no part in my ministry that does not belong to the laity as a whole. That is the reformed doctrine of ministry that was recovered at the Reformation. Everything that I am supposed to do, every layman is supposed to do also, or I am not supposed to do it.

And our Christian laymen have not been vigorously speaking out—as Christians—against evil in their community, nation, and world. Sometimes they do as "good people" but rarely as Christians.

I want to go back to the idea the early Christian Church had. They did not think that if they just worked hard enough they might improve things. No. This myth of "The War in Heaven" means that the victory has already been won and all you have to do is join your life to it so that your life becomes worthwhile. In other words, they knew there was a good day coming. They knew good will came through and we can help it come quicker by getting in and working. That is different from the humanitarian notion that if you get in and worked hard enough, you might change something.

The power and secret of the communists comes out of biblical thinking. Karl Marx was raised in a devout Jewish household. He became a Lutheran. He took from the Judeo-Christian faith that conviction that the course of history is inevitable and is going to come out in a victorious way. It is not a question of whether we work hard enough. He left God out and Spirit out of his system and materialized it in terms of the victory of the proletariat, the classless society, and so forth. But this he retained: The Communist does not give himself to something that is going to happen if he works hard enough. For him it is going to happen. If they who do not believe in eternal life can have that amount of power, why it is that we Christians who got the idea in the first place are not confident enough of our cause, the cause of the Kingdom of God, when we know we will see with our own eyes, as persons living forever, God's Holy Will prevail? Why is it that we have lost that punch and that courage that this atheistic outfit has sort of "stolen our stuff" has got?

We must revive that notion toward social concern and social action; the knowledge that we are citizens of The Kingdom. Then we would be independent and critical of majorities, crowns, state departments, communities, mores, even the Church, itself. (The Church is not the Kingdom: It is just another reformation idea. It can express the Kingdom of God; it can also express the Kingdom of Darkness sometimes.)

If we put loyalty to the Kingdom ahead of everything else and have confidence in the outcome, there is no evil in our nation or in the community that would not wither before that power. We were never stronger in numbers. Sixty-five percent of our people are now church people. In the so-called good old days, for example, 1867, only fifteen percent of the population were church members. So if we really got going we would be an army terrible with banners but we are not. A distinguished evangelist at a large dinner in advance of an evangelistic campaign put on the platform a mayor of a large southern city who said that though he was an elder at one time in his church, he got converted one night at a mission conducted in his city by the evangelist. Then he went on to say, "My whole life was changed."

If there had been provision for questions I would like to have asked: "Mr. Mayor, I am glad to hear your whole life has changed. Now I would like to know what you have since done about the segregation in your city?" To ask about the fruits of conversion is a good Methodist question. You don't teach a thing the rest of us don't believe but you highlighted something that the rest of us were forgetting to be sure; conversion is by grace and faith but if something does not happen in the "convert's" life and if he is not trying to better the community around him or in his church, you are rather suspicious as to whether he had the grace in the first place. That is Methodism.

That is why I am glad a fine limestone statue of John Wesley is in our cathedral. We regard him as a saint. That is quite a credit to us. I saw no statue of Martin Luther in St. Peter's of Rome when I was in Rome last summer. At least we know when we have had it.

That note is the one by which we have to judge ourselves. Then why doesn't more happen? How can the Church be segregated when the civil society—the world outside the Church—is more Christian in this regard than we are? Every theatre in this city is integrated. The "evil" theatre, you know with all its sinful movies, all these pictures, while we singing our holy hymns are divided up by color. I am not sure that God doesn't like the theatre better because the people are there together as fellow human beings.

Go down to the tougher part of this city. Look into some taverns and dives, places we don't condone. If the church were strong enough that would be cleaned up too. But, at least they are not segregated whereas the fine holy people are segregated and I don't know which place God likes best. I would not want to say.

He would like us together in Church and not in dives. That is clear. Yes, that is the way to solve that question. Let's have it His way. Let's be in Church and not in evil places; let's spend more time in religious education than in theatres but let's be together.

I want to turn to two or three things which bear on the principle and then I hope I have the wit to stop.

A few years ago, two years ago to be exact, the professor of English in a top-ranking eastern college happened to be of the greatest influence upon the students. He was an atheist and didn't mind saying so. The chaplain of the college decided he was more important to him than winning over dozens of students, because as the generations went on it would make more difference in the influence. He tried everything; socializing, serious talks, kidding, everything. He got nowhere at all. Finally he gave up and sort of remained a good friend. Then, one day, this professor came into the chaplain's office and said, "I want to become a Christian." The chaplain said, "Well, why?" The professor replied, "Here is why." He put down on the desk a whole file of newspaper clippings. He said, "On every issue that is of importance to me in the last two or three years, leaders of the Christian church have been the boldest and most courageous to speak out and I want to get on that team." He went on to say, "I will work out the theology later. Count me in now."

It is good evangelism when we are different than the world. When we look just like the world, the salt has lost its savor. Why should anyone come in the outfit if it is simply a reflection of the mores of the community we are in. We dare not be just a pale reflection of the society around us. Now the society around us by virtue of changes in constitutional interpretation and social movements is really moving on some of these things. All the more we stand in an embarrassing light when we are lagging behind the procession.

There is the strange paradox. We are not behind the procession in terms of speaking out. It was the social concern of the churches and the speaking out of this question of segregation for years and years that changed the climate of opinion and made possible the Supreme Court decisions on integration. I am a lawyer. I can tell you that these Supreme Court decisions are not a matter of cold logic. They reflect what is the best thinking of the people. So, the Church had a lot to do with the fact of that decision. But once the decision happened then the civil society got ahead of us in the terms of actual performance. That is the paradox we are in. I don't want to play down too much our contribution but I think it is important that we realize that our performance is not up to our own critique of secular society. But where we do speak out courageously and if martyrdom either literally or in terms of other forms or punishment occur, then we know there is the Church.

Remember when those two rather aggressive apostles were trying to "work their way up" in the Kingdom? He, Jesus, put it right to them. "Can ye drink the cup that I drink of?" That's the test. I don't like to see persecution. I don't like to see any Christian pastor or layman hurt anywhere but it would be a terrible thing if no Christian were being hurt anymore. It would really mean that we had totally conformed to the world.

The great Bishop of Johannesburg, South Africa, Ambrose Reeves, was sitting in my study on a Saturday night before he preached his sermon for us, and I read the script over. I said, "Bishop do you think you had better preach that tomorrow? Remember you are taking a plane right back Sunday night to Johannesburg." And I said, "I bet you get into trouble." He said, "I will preach it." He did—and he did get in trouble. It was in the Monday morning papers in Johannesburg, courtesy of AP. I understand that an editorial on Tuesday morning said that the man should never set foot in South African again. His house was shot at by rifles by a gang encouraged by the government. His house has been set on fire three times.

The law that I referred to which makes it a crime, if a Government Minister so declares, to have integrated worship has received a reply from all the churches in South Africa; except the Dutch Reformed which has worked out a theology on the whole to support segregation, a very interesting theology. It takes a very subtle mind to develop something like that but you know these theologians, but even they have a few courageous pastors who are very much against all this. Indeed a Negro minister was invited to speak before a large Dutch Reformed Congregation.

The rest of the Churches, every one of them, have said something like this: "We cannot obey such a law. We will not. We are aware of the penalties. We will face them." At our cathedral church in Capetown a huge sign was erected: "This cathedral is open to all races at all times for all services"—defying the government.

Now those people who want us to be so patriotic here and don't want the Church to speak out on anything and condemn us every time we try to speak out about it, should remember that we don't like patriotism of that type when it is in other nations. For example, we love to see Christians rebel against the Communists abroad.

Those church leaders in South Africa are traitors and, furthermore, clergy of my church and of yours are under indictment for treason at this very moment and I have been raising a little money as chairman of the South African Defense Fund to get some good counsel for the trial, and we are trying to feed the families of the accused. These clergy have not sold their souls to their nation: they are loyal to the Kingdom of God and that, I suppose, is treason.

I am afraid the Christian had to be a traitor. Yet, that kind of blessed treason is what saves the nation. That is the peculiar paradox. South Africa, by its own policy, will go headlong into doom. There is no question about it. You cannot with a tiny white minority keep the Nero majority in this condition. We know that. God will not have it so. He will not let us get away with things like this, nor will he let our nation get away with decisions on the side of the devil.

Where we have in our own foreign policy put our own interest to the fore over a long series of years now, and under both administrations, with no principle, we find ourselves losing friends. We find ourselves losing the confidence of our allies. We find people catching on to what we are. When we, by every means at our disposal, encourage people like the Hungarians to revolt and then when they do revolt, we say, "Well, we'll help pick up a few of the pieces for a while. Should we or shouldn't we take more refugees? We are not responsible. Perhaps you shouldn't have revolted just at this time. Probably was not wise."

We did not have enough integrity in our foreign policy to have one man sit down and think of this question: When we were distributing handbills about freedom and liberation, what would we do if they believed us? What were we prepared to do?

We are very afraid of offending Russia these days. You remember that Russia stayed out for some eight or nine days when the revolt began. We all wondered why. They were waiting to see what we would do. They found out. We would do nothing. The nationalist regime pleaded with us to get something through the United Nations like the UNEF, later established in Egypt. We got Britain and France out of the Middle East. We wouldn't dream of getting Russia out of Hungary, and Russia decided we were not any problem at all.

Then, the Houses of Bishops of my church and of the Roman Catholic Church happened to be meeting in about ten days. They came up with exactly the same statements. They both said some good and prophetic things about this but all they could recommend to us now is this: We should pray for the Hungarian people.

I believe in prayer but it's a tragedy that the only thing we can do after we have fanned the flame and had no fuel for the fire is to pray. A wise man said pray as though all depends on God and work as though all depends on yourself. That is the only kind of honest prayer there is.

Then when we refused to follow up any action against Russia, when she would not allow observers to enter the country, when we would not make a move for sanctions, then we decided to force our allies out of Egypt and have sanctions against Israel.

Don't make any mistake. That is what the President and the Secretary of State tried to convince the congressional leaders of. They told the President he could not do it so he took to the television that night. What did he say? He said, in effect, Russia is a nation governed by economic materialism. So, as to them, we will use moral sanctions. Israel has moral principles; so apparently, as to them, he was open to the idea of economic sanctions.

See peculiar logic there? That kind of illogic which does not carry through with principle, for the first time in this whole unhappy series of events, got defeated by a groundswell of public opinion which caught the simple ethical principle that you don't treat the little fellows different than you treat big fellows. It is about the same as the small car getting a ticket and the big car not getting a ticket. The people showed they did not like it and the decision was changed. But, on the Hungarian-Russian question the people were helpless.

Now the reason is, first, that we do not have enough people dedicated as Christians who do put the Kingdom first, the principle first, and transcend the nation in their thoughts. The best national interest in the long run is that we transcend national interest. When people find out we are playing our own game for our own interests, we lose something in the world that no amount of money gifts can buy.

The same week the U.S. voted against an investigation of South Africa. We beamed Christmas carols all over the world to show how religious we were and very few people in the states knew about our country's decision that we voted for the apartheid policy, in effect, whereas the non-Christian nations in the world voted against it. That was plastered all over the front pages of every paper in the communist orbit and in the nations where people are predominately of a different color than pure white—in the Southeast Asia group, in India. I am sorry we played those Christmas carols because it does not do the reputation of our Christ any good that we were saying we were Christians that week. I wished that week they had thought we were atheists. What we did undermined the effect of economic aid and of our public relations because these nations that we have been pushing around are proud people and we falsely interpret them as being like us in our own materialism. We assume all they want is our money and if they get it then they will be happy with us.

Now, unfortunately, that is about all we sometimes seem to want but they are not necessarily that way. They don't like us for that and some people said right away, "Aha, that appearing in their newspapers was all communist propaganda." Yes, I suppose so. But you can't complain too much about propaganda if what the propaganda says happens to be the truth, and you made it the truth by your own free decision as we have done.

So first our American people need to have a loyalty that transcends national interest, and second, we need to be well enough informed that we really affect public opinion among ourselves so that instead of all small talk at a social occasion, sometimes we can talk seriously about the news in the Middle East and the interpretation of the background, or about what is going on the segregation/integration front. We should spread the word so that an intelligent public opinion is formed. This is the way you get a grassroots support for what a group like this already stands for.

The national bodies issue resolutions. The resolutions of the Council of Bishops of the Methodist Church are wonderful and your conferences are excellent. The same with all the churches. Why is it on the grassroots level it does not seem to work like resolutions? That doesn't mean we should not have these good resolutions. We should. But, we have to get more people in the act than just the leaders and the spokesmen.

And, finally, there is called for a quality of life. That same conviction of an ultimate loyalty to the Kingdom has to come through in terms of real affection and love for the fellow-members of the Kingdom—not in some artificial way of church fellowship such as a slap on the back but real love for each individual regardless of race or color, so that we discern the person and know him and sense his peculiar gifts and care about them. And then we can extend from the circle of the parish this whole concern for the world so it is not an abstract concern but is something grounded in particular human relationships.

We have in our prayer book and I suspect it is in your Methodist ritual, this phrase in a prayer: "Whose service is perfect freedom." Archbishop Cranmer, the great reformer, translated the prayer from the Latin but he mistranslated it. Lovely as the sentiment he expressed is, the Latin original is more apt for our purposes here. The original is "Cui servire est regnare"—"Whom to serve is to reign." What it says to us is this: God and His Kingdom will win. If we are with the Kingdom, we will win with Him. If we are not with the Kingdom, God will win anyhow. That is the judgment. To have missed the boat because we need not worry about the Kingdom.

We should worry about ourselves because God's Kingdom has won from the beginning and in the meanwhile we are in a period of transition. That period of transition can be linked with what happened in the last World War when we finally established a beachhead at Anzio. When we established that beachhead, the war was over, really, but there was left a "clean-up" job.

The beachhead of the Kingdom is already established. It has already won. Evil is beaten but we are going through a long mopping up operation; hence I will close with the text with which I opened, "The devil has come down among you having great wrath, for he knows he has but a short time." Amen.

§31 Dr. Mordecai Wyatt Johnson

Dr. Mordecai Johnson's biography appears in the introduction to his January 10, 1954 sermon in Baltimore, Maryland.

Johnson's speech at the Prayer Pilgrimage on May 17, 1957 commemorates the third anniversary of the *Brown* decision. Before 30,000 people gathered at the Lincoln Memorial, Johnson and other speakers walked something of a rhetorical tightrope. That is, King and A. Philip Randolph wanted to hold the march as a protest of the Eisenhower administration's unwillingness to hear black grievances. But in order to bring the resources of the NAACP to bear on the event, King and Randolph had to persuade Roy Wilkins. They did so primarily by arguing that the march would function as a rally for the administration's voting rights bill. With Wilkins on board, the NAACP eventually convinced the administration, by badmouthing King, to allow the pilgrimage to use the Lincoln Memorial as its staging ground.

In praising the Supreme Court's *Brown* decision, Johnson is careful not to praise the administration. It was Eisenhower, just months before, who noted, "You can't legislate morality." The *Brown* decision would also be a "pathway," claims Johnson, which will enable "the [N]egro people in the United States [to] possess every civil and constitutional right that is in the Constitution for them." Johnson has special praise both for the NAACP and its work, and for "large groups of southern white people" who had integrated their schools. As for those white southerners who had not integrated, Johnson claims to understand their "fears" and "trembling." In his only nonconciliatory statement of the short address, Johnson states, "we are going to withdraw our cooperation from you in doing these unholy things, and we are going to do everything that we can, under the law and in the presence of God, to make you ashamed of those things, until you change them." Of course Johnson could not have known of the "unlawful" means civil rights protesters would soon use in their battle for equal rights.

Address at the Prayer Pilgrimage for Freedom
Washington, D.C.
May 17, 1957

Mr. Chairman, my brothers and sisters: This great gathering is one of the most inspiring gatherings on behalf of the cause of freedom that I have ever looked upon in all the 50 years of my public life.

I want to tell you how my heart is lifted up to look upon you, and to see the noble and self controlled and deliberate and prayerful manner in which you have answered the call of these pure-hearted leaders who have brought us here.

This gathering is but a suggestion of the power of cooperation that lies within us. We must never forget this day. It must be to us a symbol of what greater things now lie before us—when we respond to the call of pure-hearted leaders to work together for the great cause of freedom.

We have come here in this holy place, in front of the great memorial to Abraham Lincoln, to bring to remembrance, in gladness and in prayer, some great things that have been done in this place for the emancipation of the Negro people, for the blessing of the people of the south, and for the strengthening of the moral power and leadership of our country in the world.

We have come here in the presence of the memory of Abraham Lincoln and of the God and father of our people, who have brought us thus far from slavery to thank God for the Supreme Court decision abolishing segregation in the public schools and setting forth the principle for the first time in 60 years, that under the Constitution of the United States, it is not possible lawfully to classify a child on the basis of his race or color and then force that child to go to an inferior accommodation of education; but that under this law whatsoever accommodation for education is built, for any child whatsoever, belongs to every child of a citizen of the United States, whatever his race or creed or color may be. This is the greatest single act of government since the Emancipation Proclamation, opening up the pathway of freedom for the Negro people and for the child of every human being that comes under the flag of the Constitution of the United States.

If the United States adheres to this decision and the people of the United States follow it steadily, it will not be long before the Negro people in the United States will possess every civil and constitutional right that is in the Constitution for them. To this cause we dedicate ourselves and, upholding our hands before the living God, we call upon him to remember. May our right hand lose its cunning and our tongue cleave to the roof of our mouths if we ever give up until every one of these liberties is possessed by us.

We have come here to express before God our great thanks for the National Association for the Advancement of Colored People; for the great work that it has done in drawing us together and enabling us to work for these objectives, and for being the instrument through which this great decision has come to us.

In the presence of Abraham Lincoln, and the God and father of our people, we declare that there is no law that can be passed, no criticism that can be said, no suffering that we will not undergo, including imprisonment, to keep alive in this country this organization, in whom we have complete confidence.

In the second place we have come here to express our thanks to the living God that, for the first time in 60 years, we have seen large groups of southern white people responding to the Supreme Court decision, opening the doors of their schools to our children, teaching our children lovingly and thoughtfully, and making known their gladness that before they have died God has given them the privilege to do this.

We want the superintendent and teachers in the District of Columbia, the teachers in the northern part of Delaware, the Governor and the leaders of the state of Maryland, the Governor and the leaders of the state of Oklahoma, the Governor and the leaders of the state of West Virginia, the Governor and the leaders of Missouri, and those people who—though their governors and legislators have not yet joined them—in Texas, in North Carolina, and all over the south, who are glad that the Supreme Court of the United States has at last given them a law, under which they can do what their hearts have always wanted to do—to help the Negro people move toward freedom.

We want them to know how glad we are, and how thrilled we are, to the depths of our being, to observe the gladness with which they do what they're doing. We want to tell the people of the south, who have not yet responded to this decision: we understand the fears that may arise in your heart, and a trembling which you have when you move up to the place where you have got to change the way that you have been doing things for 250 years. We want to tell you that we are not impatient in the presence of your fears and your hesitations. We want to tell you that this young man, Dr. King, down in Montgomery, Alabama, who tells you that we have no hatred to you, is telling you the truth. We have nothing against you as persons. We do not want to take away from you one symptom of the prosperity that you have. We do not want to break down anything that you consider holy. The only thing that we want to do is to persuade you to change the things that you are doing that are unholy and that hurt us.

And now, in the presence of the memory of Abraham Lincoln and the God of our fathers, we want to tell you that from this time on we are going to withdraw our cooperation from you in doing these unholy things, and we are going to do everything that we can, under the law and in the presence of God, to make you ashamed of those things, until you change them.

Now, finally, we will rejoice over the meaning of this decision to our country. Long before the morning papers ever got this decision, the United States government had translated it into 42 languages and sent it around the world. Why did they do that? They knew that there were 1,350,000,000 black and brown and yellow people in India, in China and in Africa listening with the ears of their hearts to find what that decision was going to be. They dreaded a negative decision. And if that Supreme Court had decided that segregation in school houses was a just and righteous thing under the law and Constitution of the United States, their hearts would have sunk. They would have bewailed their fate before God, and before midnight the leadership of this world would have been wrapped up in Christmas paper with red ribbon and turned over to the Communist leadership of this world.

But when they heard that the United States of America said that under this Constitution no human child shall be segregated and discriminated against in public education with the approval of the government of the United States, they all broke out, like Madame Pandit of India, and said: there is the America that we could trust and that we could love. This Supreme Court decision on segregation in schools has done more than any act of the government of the United States since the Emancipation Proclamation to make the 1,350,000,000 free colored people of this world trust our country and turn their faces hopefully toward her leadership.

It is a wonderful thing that what went out that night was not propaganda, but a decision of the Supreme Court of the United States. In answer to the plea of the humblest minority in this country, it told the people of the world, this is the nature of American democracy; that without concealing their purposes in any way, without resorting to violence in any way, the humblest minority in this country can find an open pathway to liberty and human dignity by due process of law only. Isn't that wonderful?

It tells the world that embedded in the Constitution of the United States there is a moral principle which operates to produce a continuous revolution against any institution which injures human life.

So our prayer here today is: Oh, Eternal God, who gave us Thomas Jefferson and the Declaration of Independence, O Eternal God, who gave us Abraham Lincoln and the Emancipation Proclamation, O Eternal God, in these dark days who has given us the unanimous decision of the Supreme Court of the United States, give us faith to trust thee, give us power to work together, give us love for our enemies, and give us the strength never to give up until the victory is completely won.

§32 Representative Adam Clayton Powell

Adam Clayton Powell, Jr. was born on November 29, 1908 in New Haven, Connecticut. At six, he moved with his family to Harlem, where his father pastored the most prestigious African American church in New York City, Abyssinian Baptist Church. Ordained as a Baptist minister, Powell also received degrees from Colgate in 1930, Columbia in 1932 and Shaw in 1935. In 1937 the younger Powell succeeded his father in the pulpit at Abyssinian. Not content to be merely a pastor, however, Powell was elected in 1941 to the New York City Council. Four years later, Powell entered national politics with his election to the U.S. House of Representatives. In so doing he became the first black congressman from the northeast. He would hold the seat representing New York's 22nd district until defeated by a young Charles Rangel in 1970. Throughout his time in Washington, Powell was a loud and often singular voice on civil rights in the halls of Congress, leading desegregation battles in the public schools, the military and even in the nation's capital. Even though ethics violations dogged him in later years, Powell remained a fearless advocate for civil rights. Powell married three times and is survived by two sons. He died on April 4, 1972.

In his brief remarks before marchers gathered before the Lincoln Memorial, Powell is not content with mere encomium. He uses the occasion to lambaste both political parties for their "studied contempt" of the *Brown* decision and to call for a "third" force in American politics. Instead of Republican and Democrat hypocrisy, Powell's third force is non-partisan, led by Negro clergy, interdenominational, and engaged in direct mass action exemplified by Dr. King. Powell closes by proclaiming that if Eisenhower, Nixon, Johnson, and Rayburn won't speak with them, "God still speaks." And his speaking will lead to freedom.

Address at the Prayer Pilgrimage for Freedom
Washington, D.C.
May 17, 1957

I'd like to say that the helicopter which was flying around had Senator Eastland in it. But truthfully (this is true), Congressman Diggs and I called up the Pentagon and asked them to stop it and they did. That's the truth.

I want to pay homage to the elder statesman of our race, Mr. A. Philip Randolph, who originally conceived of the idea of a march on Washington back in the days when we were fighting to make America and the world safe for democracy but wouldn't give Negroes jobs, and due to Mr. A. Philip Randolph the FEPC was born. And I want to pay homage to him now.

I want to pay homage to Roy Wilkins and let America know, black and white, north and south, that we Negro people are 100 percent behind the NAACP.

And I want to pay homage to that brilliant young prophet that God has put in a particular spot at a particular time, the Reverend Mr. Martin Luther King.

We meet here today in front of the Abraham Lincoln Memorial because we are getting more from a dead Republican than we are getting from a live Democrat or a live Republican. We must face the basic dishonesty and increasing hypocrisy of both of our two political parties.

Only the politically free Supreme Court views the American scene against a background of morality and uncompromising legality. In the north and in the south, amongst Republicans and Democrats, we find a studied contempt of the law of the land and the Supreme Court decision.

Even the proponents of civil rights legislation in my House and in the Senate have made deals behind the scenes now to emasculate and water down the present minimum civil rights legislation if not to kill it completely in the Senate of the United States.

As for the executive branch, it refuses to exercise the massive majesty and prestige of its office and speak out as it should.

And so the Negro today finds himself caught between the horns of a dilemma. We're faced with a bi-partisan Jim Crow policy, and we're not going to have a successful bi-partisan foreign policy until we wipe out our bi-partisan Jim Crow policy.

Black Africa and brown Asia and white Europe don't trust the United States of America because they know that we are being ruled here by a group of bi-partisan double-dealing, double-talking hypocrites, Republican and Democrat.

On May 5 I begged the chairman of my party, Mr. Paul Butler, for the Democratic National Committee to speak out in favor of civil rights at the National Democratic Committee meeting here May 5. He didn't say a word concerning civil rights. I don't give a tinkers damn about tidelands oil and natural gas and flexible and rigid farm price supports and private versus public power. I'm concerned and you're concerned and the world is concerned and God is concerned with decent civil rights for all God's people.

Therefore, it's time for we Negroes to bring a third force into the American political scene. I'm sick and tired of Democrat and Republican. Yeah, I'm a Democrat—but before I was a Democrat I was a Negro, and before I was a Negro I was a child of God, and I'm sick and tired of this two party hypocrisy. It's time for we Negroes to introduce into the American political life a third force, a force that will be non-partisan but definitely political; a force that will be non-racial but at the same time led by our Negro clergy who have given the greatest spiritual witness of any group of Christians in this century in the United States. A force that will be nondenominational, inviting men of all faiths. It must be a force housed only in the churches, led only by the clergy, powered through prayer, and bringing about direct mass action through the unity of the people.

We should from this force learn to vote together, work together, pray together, love together, live together, walk together: Walk together, children, don't you get weary? Great camp meeting in the promised land.

The technique of the southern Dixiecrat today is to outlaw the NAACP in the south. They're going to do this for the sole purpose of preventing the NAACP from presenting cases to the courts in the south. This will be an insurmountable roadblock to prevent the NAACP from reaching the Supreme Court.

But through the third force of clergy-led, church-housed and praying people we can channel funds through the underground to the NAACP. We can take the cases to the courts ourselves using the NAACP. There isn't anybody in the south big enough to stop the march of our people, because we're on the side of right.

We shall go from here today to use the technique so greatly exemplified and proven by Martin Luther King. We shall go from here with massive unity, based on passive resistance. Both locally and nationally, wherever the need arises we shall use boycotts, pickets, work stoppage, slowdown, sit-down, strike—until we bring American bigotry to its knees. Through these techniques we can turn the tide from hypocrisy to honesty.

And we welcome and we will aid all church groups, both white and Jewish who will work with us. And I'm so happy to announce today that the National Council of Churches, through the Reverend Mr. Sweeny, who is here, has presented a resolution to Dr. King saying that the National

Council of Churches of Christ in America are 100 percent behind this movement today.

I believe that from this meeting now should go four wires. One to Eisenhower demanding an appointment with the President of the United States. Another to Nixon demanding an appointment with the Vice President. Another to Lyndon Johnson, head of the Democratic Party in the Senate, demanding an appointment with him, and another one to Sam Rayburn, demanding an appointment with him.

These wires should say that 25,000 Negroes and whites gathered here have served a mandate that they must be heard. But I tell you that if Eisenhower doesn't speak, God still speaks. If Nixon won't speak, God still speaks. If Lyndon Johnson won't speak, God still speaks. If Sam Rayburn doesn't speak, God still speaks. There is a God, who rules above with a hand of power and a heart of love, and if we're right he'll fight our battle and we'll be free some day.

§33 A. Philip Randolph

A. Philip Randolph was born on April 15, 1889 in Crescent City, Florida. The son of an A.M.E. minister, Randolph attended the Methodist Cookman Institute in Jacksonville, which later merged with Mary McLeod Bethune's school. In 1911 Randolph headed north for New York City, where he would make his name and career in black union organizing. Unlike other black leaders such as W. E. B. DuBois, Randolph was convinced that organizing the black working class was vital for securing civil rights. Also unlike DuBois, Randolph urged black men not to serve in World War I, which earned him the appellation "the most dangerous man in America" from president Woodrow Wilson. In 1925 Randolph founded the Brotherhood of Sleeping Car Porters, a union of black porters which became a formidable organization and made its founder famous.

Randolph is remembered primarily for three events. On June 25, 1941 Franklin Roosevelt signed Executive Order 8802, which effectively ended discrimination in the defense industries. Randolph had threatened a massive march on Washington if the president didn't sign the order. Similarly, on July 26, 1948 Henry Truman signed Executive Order 9981, which desegregated the armed forces. Randolph led and organized the protests leading to that order. Third, Randolph was the key mover behind the 1963 March on Washington for Jobs and Freedom, which was organized by his protégé, Bayard Rustin. In 1968 Randolph stepped down from the Brotherhood of Sleeping Car Porters, but maintained interest in civil rights and labor largely through the AFL-funded, A. Philip Randolph Institute. Randolph died on May 16, 1979 in New York City at the age of 90. His wife, Lucille, preceded him in death. His papers are housed at the Library of Congress in Washington, D.C.

In this brief address at the 1957 Prayer Pilgrimage, Randolph pledges support for the NAACP, praises Dr. King and the movement in Montgomery, urges

President Eisenhower to speak out for obedience to law and order, expresses indignation over the Klan and the White Citizens Councils, rejects the support of communists, and Randolph reaffirms his faith in America's constitutional system. This series of speech acts is underscored by Randolph's syllogistic reasoning on civil rights: civil rights are a moral and spiritual issue since they involve humans; we are human by virtue of being created by God; all God's children are equal; therefore we are all "equal before the laws of the state."

Address at the Prayer Pilgrimage for Freedom
Washington, D.C.
May 17, 1957

My honored colleagues and coworkers, the Reverend Dr. King and the Honorable Mr. Wilkins, Ministers of the Church and fellow Prayer Pilgrims for Freedom:

In the pattern of good American traditions, Negroes and whites, Jews and Gentiles, Protestants and Catholics, trade unionists, professional and educational leaders have assembled here in a great pilgrimage of prayer for freedom at the monument of Abraham Lincoln, the Great Emancipator, to tell the story of our long night of trial and trouble and our renewal of faith in and consecration to the sacred cause of a rebirth of freedom and human dignity.

Thus, we have come to memorialize the third anniversary of the historic United States Supreme Court decision for the desegregation of public schools, a veritable Emancipation Proclamation of the mind and the human spirit.

We have come to demonstrate the unity of the Negroes and their allies, labor, liberals and the Church, behind the civil rights bills now before Congress, in order that they might not be strangled to death by committee maneuverings and the filibuster.

We have gathered together to proclaim our uncompromising support of the fight of the National Association for the Advancement of Colored People for civil rights and democracy under the able, resourceful and constructive leadership of Roy Wilkins, Executive Secretary. This is the agency which has been chiefly responsible for civil rights decisions in the courts of our land to eliminate second-class citizenship based upon race or color.

We are here to tell those who worship the false gods of white supremacy in the South to keep their evil hands off the National Association for the Advancement of Colored People.

And we have come to warn the liberal, religious, educational, labor and business forces of the North of the grave danger of a spreading sentiment in some sections of the South to deny the right of existence to the National Association for the Advancement of Colored People. It is a matter of common historical knowledge that the denial of free, voluntary association for the achievement of lawful, social, political and economic objectives of a particular group in our national community will, like the contagion of disease, spread to other associations of citizens which, for the present, may not be the objects of persecution. In very truth, it may be the NAACP which is banned by irrational racial legislation today, but the ban may come to the Knights of Columbus, B'nai B'rith, the AFL-CIO, and some of the sections of The National Council of the Churches of Christ in the U.S.A., tomorrow.

We are here to make known our unqualified sanction of and cooperation with the magnificent, challenging and successful struggle against segregated buses in Montgomery, Alabama, the cradle of the old Confederacy, under the inspired leadership of a great church leader and prophet of our times, the Reverend Mr. Martin Luther King. This is one of the great sagas of the struggle for human decency and freedom, made effective by a veritable miracle of unity of some fifty thousand Negroes under the spiritual banner of love, non-cooperation with evil and non-violence.

We are assembled here to express our righteous indignation against and condemnation of the notorious Ku Klux Klan and White Citizens Councils. The revival of these agencies of hate and violence constitute a grave threat, not only to law and order in the South but to the democracy of our country, as well as a shock to the faith and confidence of peoples everywhere in the integrity of our moral leadership of the free world.

We have come to call upon President Eisenhower, our great national and world leader, who is undoubtedly possessed of a high sense of humanity, to speak out against the lawlessness, terror and fears that hang like a pall over the hearts of citizens of color in the South as a result of devastating bombings of their homes and churches, shooting and killing of citizens who have the courage to assert their constitutional rights, and the intimidation of white and colored people by cross burnings and the parades of hooded men and women.

As the highest expression of the moral and political authority of our country, we urge the President to help rebuild the shaken and shattered hopes of millions of Negroes and white peoples of the South, by raising his voice of counsel to the people to obey the laws of the land.

We have come to state our unshakable belief in the principles of human solidarity and the worth, value and dignity of the personality of every human being, regardless of race, color, religion, national origin or ancestry, and to point out the fallacy and mythology of the doctrine of white supremacy.

It is written in the Declaration of Independence of our country that all men are created equal and possess the inalienable right to life, liberty and the pursuit of happiness. These are natural human rights. They are God-given, not man-made. Every organ of Government and official of State are required by constitutional fiat and the moral law to uphold these rights, not to conspire with anti-democratic forces to deny, nullify, and destroy them.

Thus, civil rights have a moral and spiritual basis, for they are designed to implement and give reality and force to our human rights that exist as a result of our being human, and we are human because we have been created human beings by God. Since all men are the children of God, they are equal before God and should be equal before the laws of the state.

We are here to assert that the issue in the crisis of civil rights in our nation today does not involve opposition of Negroes to whites or whites to Negroes. There are leaders in certain circles who would like to make this the issue, but the real issue involves conflict between certain basic social and moral values, such as freedom against slavery, truth against error, justice against injustice, equality against inequality, love against hate, good against evil, the right to vote against disenfranchisement, law and order against mob rule.

One has only to witness this great demonstration of prayer pilgrims for freedom to note that they have come from various creeds, colors, countries, classes, callings and crafts.

We like to think that God is on the side of our American way of life but this will only be true to the extent that our American way of life is on the side of God, who said: "I am the way, the truth and the light." Hence, in the eyes of God there is neither black nor white, nor red nor yellow, nor Jew nor Gentile, nor barbarian nor Scythian, but all are brothers in Christ Jesus. "By this will all men know that you are my disciples, if you have love one for another."

We have come to assert our rejection of the promise and pattern and path to freedom by communists and communism as an illusion and a snare; a fraud and a menace, which can only lead to the dead end of chaos and confusion, frustration and fear, dictatorship, slavery and despair.

Finally, we have come to reaffirm our belief in and devotion and allegiance to the American constitutional system of government, within which citizens, though not fully free, are possessed of the priceless right to fight for their rights.

But, to the end of achieving these civil rights and giving strength and integrity to our democratic order of government, it is the obligation and responsibility of every citizen of color, wage earner and lover of liberty to exercise his constitutional right to register and vote. We suggest no party or person to vote for, but we call upon every Negro, especially, not only to register and vote himself, but to serve as a missionary to get his neighbors in every house, in every block, in every hamlet, village, city and state of our country to register and vote, that we may build the power to help save the soul of America and extend and maintain the free world for free men.

Be not dismayed by the frightful wave of violence and persecution against persons of color now sweeping the South. It is written in the stars that the old order of southern feudalism, with its remnants and vestiges of lynching, peonage, vagrancy laws, mob violence, Ku Klux Klan, anti-labor union practices expressed in right-to-work laws, widespread illiteracy, low wages, dying; its death will come as a result of the emergence of the dynamic impulse for freedom surging in the hearts of Negroes, together with the march of industrialization, urbanization, labor union organization, extension of education and the modernization of government through the spread of the ballot. These new forces will create and build a new South, free for the white and black masses to pursue a life of dignity and decency.

In conclusion, in the words of David, "I will lift up mine eyes unto the hills from whence cometh my help."

Yes, we have set our hands to the cause of a better and happier tomorrow for all men, and though we be beset by setbacks, persecution and trouble, the lot of all peoples who have won liberty and justice, may God grant that we may never falter.

§34 Reverend Fred L. Shuttlesworth

Fred Lee Robinson was born on March 18, 1922 in Mt. Meigs, Alabama. His last name changed when his mother, who was a maid for a local white family, married a coal miner, William Shuttlesworth. Though raised in the African Methodist Episcopal church, Shuttlesworth began attending a Baptist church in 1943. Within a few months the church's preacher was inviting the gifted young orator to give guest sermons. Called to the ministry, Shuttlesworth attended Cedar Grove Academy Bible College in Prichard, Alabama, outside Mobile. He left Mobile to enroll at Selma University where he earned the highest marks in school history. Shuttlesworth earned a bachelor's degree there, a master's in education at Alabama State College, and an advanced divinity degree at Birmingham Baptist College. Birmingham's First Baptist Church called Shuttlesworth in 1949, and it wasn't long before the "silk stocking" parish and the hardscrabble, fiery preacher were at odds. In the spring of 1953, Shuttlesworth became pastor of the working class Bethel Baptist Church, where he made his name—both locally and nationally—for his daring civil rights work.

Shuttlesworth's first major foray into civil rights activism came in July of 1955, when he petitioned Birmingham's city council to hire black police officers. His petition was ignored. In 1956 he founded the Alabama Christian Movement for

Human Rights (ACMHR) in response to the state of Alabama's successful litigation to shut down the NAACP. On Christmas night, local Klansmen blew up his parsonage. Shuttlesworth and family members miraculously survived. The following year, Shuttlesworth helped organize the better-known Southern Christian Leadership Conference (SCLC). During September of 1957, he was beaten with bicycle chains and baseball bats, caught by local television cameras, as he tried to enroll two of his daughters at an all-white elementary school. In March of 1960, Shuttlesworth was arrested after organizing a series of sit-ins at segregated department stores. He was also instrumental in securing safe-haven for the Freedom Riders in May 1961 after they were brutally beaten in a Birmingham bus depot.

But Shuttlesworth's lasting fame dates to April and May of 1963 when, with Martin Luther King, Jr. and the SCLC, he helped launch Project C ("confrontation"). Shuttlesworth convinced King and other leaders in SCLC, after the failures of Albany, Georgia, that Birmingham was the right place at the right time. Close to major media outlets and intimately aware of the brutality that awaited anyone who crossed police commissioner Theophilus Eugene "Bull" Connor, Shuttlesworth proved prophetic. Demonstrations were called off in May after white leaders offered partial concessions. Shuttlesworth was one of the many casualties of the violence of Project C, as he was blasted by a fire hose outside Sixteenth Street Baptist Church and spent several days in the hospital. In 1988 Shuttlesworth returned to Birmingham at the invitation of Mayor Richard Arrington to help lobby for a civil rights museum, where a statue of Shuttlesworth was erected when it opened in 1992. Since 1966, Shuttlesworth has pastored the Greater New Light Baptist Church in Cincinnati. More recently, the octogenarian serves as president of the SCLC. His papers are housed at the King Center in Atlanta, Georgia.

In his first annual message to the Alabama Christian Movement for Human Rights, Reverend Shuttlesworth offers encouragement even as he recounts the past year's brutality in Birmingham. Shuttlesworth exhorts his listeners that they must love, be nonviolent, and have faith that God will see them through these troubled waters. Always the scriptural polyglot, Shuttlesworth calls on Paul, Revelation, Isaiah, and Samuel in his message of reassurance. Similarly does he intermingle these sacred texts with the nation's sacred texts, thus creating a fusion of Christianity and Democracy—a fusion that runs throughout American history.

While Shuttlesworth aims most of his ire at segregation, he also leads his listeners to its fundamental assumption; not surprisingly, he situates that assumption within the confines of the church: "white skin becomes more important than white and pure hearts. The love of Segregation has taken precedence over the Love of God; thus it becomes relatively easy for some white men to sing Amazing Grace on Sunday morning in the choirs, and march at night in robes to burn crosses." Shuttlesworth closes on a personal note, making mention of the Christmas Day 1956 bombing of his parsonage. Perhaps more than any other event in his extraordinary life, that bombing continues to define his civil rights work in Birmingham; for it was on that night that Shuttlesworth felt the protective embrace of God.

A Faith for Difficult and Critical Times

First Annual Address to the Alabama Christian Movement for Human Rights,
Birmingham, Alabama
June 5, 1957

Acts 27:25, "Wherefore, sirs, be of good cheer. For I believe God, that it shall be even as it was told me."

Tonight, one year ago we met in Sardis Baptist Church to form an organization designed to strike forever from our lives the shackles and bonds of an outdated slave society, and to press forward in this our day for the full rights, opportunities, and privileges of first class citizenship. We met then in a critical time and under difficult circumstances. Men who had the power of the South in their hands were trying to kill our hopes for freedom, and to stamp out by judicial directive the spark of faith that had fired the hearts of the founding fathers. Without a legal arm of defense, it was thought that Negroes could not again, or would never again dare attack the vile god of Segregation, and that there would be no further clamor from us for our Rights. The voice then was that of the White Citizens Councils and the Ku Klux Klan, who because of the political prestige that Segregation had given them, were able to dictate to the legislature, the courts, and the seats of local government.

But they reckoned without the power of Almighty God, or forgot to remember that Faith works its best miracles under difficult and critical circumstances. For we arose up that historic night to keep our date with destiny. We stood together as one man—pledging each to the other our lives, our fortunes, our sacred honor. With massive voice from unafraid hearts, we cried out "Give us liberty or give us death." We possessed that night a "faith that would not shrink, though pressed by every foe."

We stood up like men of faith, with love in our hearts, but with determination in our breasts not only to defy and challenge Segregation practices and customs, but also to say to the "Uncle Toms" of yesterday, "get behind us Satan, for you are offensive to us. You have kept us behind long enough." No longer do we need to procrastinate and receive "pats" and "handouts." Find your crack and hide, for Negroes from henceforth will follow a leadership that will lead to the mountain top. Crumbs will no longer sustain us; we must have part of the loaf that is democracy. Some become angry and envious, and the politicians raved; but together we have marched for a whole year. Some felt that this was just another "stunt" by eager and misguided Negroes, and that it would—as had many things in the past—blow over in a fortnight. It was felt that "they're hot now but they'll cool off after a while."

But God was speaking to us and through us, and tonight the "stunt" is still going strong; stronger than ever before. For in spite of the slander we have withstood, the threats that we have heard, and the violence we have sustained, I am sure, positively sure, that nothing shall stop us until we cross the Segregation river and tread the shores in our day of unrestricted freedom.

Our inspiration for freedom is bringing us closer together, and thank God, has made us unafraid. Never before have we stuck together and never before have we spoken as one. We are a Christian Organization and therefore will not hate. We are not against white people or their valid interests, but we are for true Americanism. God will that we shall ever remain so.

Let us now consider the times and a faith for these times. Darkness never subdues itself; it must be overcome by light. Satan, the archenemy of love, mercy, and justice never gives up in his struggle to imprison men's minds and create confusion. Thus our times are as critical and dangerous as a year ago.

Southern hospitality has taken wings and Southern justice has taken a holiday. Justice is what the Councils and Klans want it to be. The Supreme Court of the U.S. is the object of official and judicial Southern scorn, and the Birmingham City Judge has opinioned as unconstitutional the 14th Amendment to the Constitution. All this despite Article 3 of the Constitution which states that "this Constitution and the laws made in pursuance thereof shall be the supreme law of the land . . . and the judges in every state shall be bound thereby." It would be the worst of tragedies and the height of folly for the Federal Government to remain silent while the authority of the Constitution is being superceded in four or five states of the South.

In the absence of a positive and forthright position from the Federal Government, the scene in the South today is one of defiance, subversion of the Constitution, a tendency to challenge all federal authority, and confusion. Our legislative halls ring with efforts to preserve Segregation, even to the threat of abolishing counties to prevent Negroes from effective voting. While jury trials are called for by Southern Spokesmen in Washington, juries are busy in Alabama turning loose criminals who sign confessions of bombing sacred churches and defenseless houses at night, and freeing Klansmen who confess to wearing weapons and engage in violent shootings. In our area alone, 21 bombings have occurred without the apprehension of one person. We stand in extreme danger for our lives day and night, and it seems that help is far away. They would like for us to think there is no hope.

It was also in a distressing situation when Paul uttered the exaltation found in the text. He was a prisoner on a ship headed for home. Being caught in the treacherous currents between the islands in the Aegean Sea the ship was exceedingly tossed with a tempestuous and windy sea. Efforts to lighten and relieve the situation failed; neither the sun nor stars was seen for several days, all hope seemed to fail, and they were on the verge of shipwreck. Human efforts gave way to faith, as in the previous night God's Angel visited Paul to tell him that Heaven was watching. And to the terrified sailors aboard the servant of God spoke words of faith: "Cheer up men, for I believe God." The ship will be lost, and you will be saved—some even by broken boards, but none will be lost. Cheer up men; have courage, keep faith; the voice said it would be alright. Men I believe God.

Ladies and gentlemen, we are tonight in deep and treacherous waters. Without trying to be either philosophical or pathetic I tell you in plain simple language that some men are yet trying to hold shut forever in our faces the doors of equal opportunity and privileges. But I read in Revelation that God would set before us an open door which no man could shut. And I believe God, that it shall be ever as he said.

Truth would compel us to admit that there is really no real freedom for us under Segregation. And the professed love for the Negro by the Southern White man is in fact not real love, which means mutual respect and admiration, but a kind of paternalism, such as master for a slave, or big man to a little friend, or as a helping hand to one in need. Nobody fully respects anyone whom he can control or maneuver at will. So long as the Negro is docile, quiet, and "in his place," back doors, back seats, specially marked inferior facilities, his big friend will be sweet and kind; but once in a front seat, or first class facility, this same friend becomes a raging enemy.

Segregation has become a way of life for Whites in the South. It is the real enemy we face, and Segregation laws are what we are fighting. It legislates that a white person is superior and a Negro inferior. It places all governmental and judicial positions in white hands so that the politician feels and acts as if "all power is in his hands." But Jesus said "all power is in his hands" and I believe God.

Segregation is a moral and social cancer which is corrupting the health of the whole Southern body. It is an evil which must be destroyed. It causes otherwise normal men to forget dignity and act like beasts in defense of its laws.

It causes men who live together all their lives to fear and be suspicious of each other all their lives. It makes color of skin the criteria for supremacy; thus the worst low class white can occupy a place above the best Negro; and white skin becomes more important than white and pure hearts. The love of Segregation has taken precedence over the Love of God; thus it becomes relatively easy for some white men to sing Amazing Grace on Sunday morning in the choirs, and march at night in robes to burn crosses. Segregation causes one standard of justice for Whites and another for Negroes. It was perhaps ironic that the same paper which reported the release by a jury of confessed church bombers in Montgomery also carried that of a 17-year old Negro boy getting 20 years for attempted rape.

And so the story goes all down the line. Segregation, not the white man, is the enemy we face. It has become the fundamental issue in the country. If Segregation lives then Democracy must die. Any system which must be supported by [. . .] cannot forever live.

And so tonight, we reaffirm our Faith in American Democracy, and pledge our continued resistance to Segregation and Discrimination. We must never retreat from this position no matter what the cost. There must be one law for all or there will be no peace. We are called upon by God to stand now like men. "Therefore be strong, and of good courage . . . and let us play the men for our people . . . and the Lord do that which seemeth Him good" (II Samuel 10:12).

A personal word, please. I speak tonight as a man of Faith. I have no magic wand to wave nor any quick solution by which the god of Segregation can be made to disappear. I offer myself—my life—to lead as God directs. My family and I—and Bethel Church—have tasted of the bitterest dregs of the vile cup of Segregation. But from the pitch black terrors we have learned a Faith which cannot be conquered. We have found out that there's a Man upstairs who is not asleep; a Man who was there Christmas night, even before the bomb exploded. Truly the Angel of the Lord encampeth round them that fear God.

Because we stand up in these times, we may, even as the early Christians, have to pass through the fire and run thru the waters. But I read in Isaiah 43:2, "When thou passest through the waters I will be with thee; and through the rivers, they shalt not overflow thee; when thou walkest through the fire, it shalt not burn thee, neither shalt the flame be kindled upon thee." Ladies and gentlemen, I believe God, that it shall be even as He said. Thus we say to the god of Segregation: "It may be that our God whom we serve will deliver us; but if not, we will not bow, nor serve any longer."

Let us go on knowing in our hearts that we hate no one, nor will we harm anyone. Let us persevere through this midnight of terror and madness, so that the American children of the future will not have to undergo these ordeals: and thus will rise up and call us blessed.

I know not what the future holds. It matters little who is elected or who comes and goes; we will follow Him who was born to be the Leader and

Savior of men. Be not dismayed whatever betides. God will take care of you
. . . A mighty fortress is our God . . . A bulwark never failing.

I close with these words which are my daily inspiration:

> "Lead kindly Light, amid the encircling gloom. The night
> Is dark, and I am so far from home.
> I do not ask to see the distance scene,
> One step ahead is enough for me.
> Guide me oh thou great Jehovah."

§35 Dr. Channing H. Tobias

Dr. Channing Heggie Tobias was born in Augusta, Georgia, on February 1, 1882.
He received a B.A. and B.D. from Paine College and Drew Theological Seminary,
respectively, in addition to an honorary Doctorate of Divinity from Gammon
Theological Seminary. Dr. Channing lived a long and fruitful life including a marriage to Mary Pritchard in 1908. The Tobias's had two daughters. With Mary's
death in 1949, Tobias remarried in 1951 to Eva Arnold.

Tobias's life was dedicated to improving the well-being of African Americans
and society more generally as evidenced by his work in the YMCA and in various
positions of public service. Before doing so, he taught biblical literature at Paine
College from 1905 to 1911 and then entered the YMCA in 1911 becoming the
student secretary of the International Committee of the YMCA for twelve years.
From 1923 until his retirement in 1953, Tobias served in numerous leadership positions within the YMCA and spent much of his time and effort trying to improve
the lives and opportunities for African Americans.

On the public service front, Tobias was appointed by President Truman to the
Committee on Civil Rights. Tobias became a member of the NAACP's board of
trustees and was eventually elected the chairman of the NAACP in 1953. Eleanor
Roosevelt related the following to *Ebony* magazine about his masterful handling
of a situation in 1951 as the alternate U.S. representative to the United Nations.
"The Russian delegate said, 'Mr. Tobias, you should not be here telling us about
our treatment of spies. You should be telling us about how your people are treated
in the United States.' He named every state in the Union, telling of its laws. Then
he mentioned Georgia. Dr. Tobias in his calm, learned way said: 'I was born in the
state of Georgia which has such bad laws. But today I represent my entire country
in the United Nations. I have never said that we do not have states with bad laws,
nor that we do not have states with good laws which are not enforced. I do say
that we have the opportunity to move forward and so I am proud to represent my
country—all 48 states.' Then Dr. Tobias went back to his original point, but there
was dead silence from the Russians. It was a most eloquent handling of what could
have been an embarrassing situation. If I had argued the point it would not have
had half the effect it had coming from him."

Tobias died on November 5, 1961 after a lengthy illness. His papers are housed at
the Kautz Family YMCA Archives at the University of Minnesota in Minneapolis.

Tobias begins his speech to the annual convention of the NAACP by noting the vicious attacks the NAACP has recently endured, not just by private individuals and organizations, but by state legislatures. He argues that the changing nature of these attacks are troubling, not just for African Americans but for the whole country. *Brown v. Board of Education* showed the success of the racial equality movement, and it has sent its opponents scrambling. The Civil Rights movement is achieving victories, and these successes are causing those who advocate segregation to increase their efforts greatly to stop them. Tobias forcefully makes the case that the Civil Rights movement must redouble it efforts. He lays out several points upon which they must focus their collective energies in order to achieve success in their fight for racial equality. Perhaps most interesting and most important, Tobias focuses on the rhetorical battle for the hearts and minds and dollars of the nation. That is, the real battle ahead is for the "people who are torn by inner conflict." Because of their religious beliefs and their political ideals, this group of Americans understands that segregation is wrong; it remains for groups like the NAACP to "convert the uncommitted millions." Tobias ends the speech with a rousing, evocative call to arms imploring all to contribute in every way they can to this great cause.

Address to the 48th Annual NAACP Convention

Detroit, Michigan
June 25, 1957

As we assemble here for our 48th annual convention, we are confronted with a grave and unprecedented crisis. As a militant organization committed to the elimination of racial discrimination and segregation, the National Association for the Advancement of Colored People has throughout its history incurred the wrath of those who would cling to the old ways, who refuse to recognize the trend of the times and who would turn the clock back to 1860.

We have had to contend with their angry denunciations, their hostility and their threats. We have answered them in the courts of the land, in the arena of public opinion, and in legislative halls. We have thrived and grown in spite of their hostility and opposition. And we are proud of our activities which have forced out into the open the genteel as well as the uncouth racists who reject the treasured Hebraic-Christian concepts of human brotherhood and defile the democratic ideal of the equality of all mankind. For nearly half-a-century we have survived the hate-inspired attacks of these elements. But now something new has been added.

For the first time, our Association, as an organization, has become the object of official state action designed to render it ineffective if not to destroy it. Heretofore, we have been assailed by private individuals and organizations who did not like what we stood for, who viewed with alarm the progress we have made, who cried out aloud for return to the old days when they feared no challenge to their outmoded way of life. But in 1956 we were, for the first time, under attack by the legislative and judicial systems of the southern states.

Court action was invoked to ban our activities in Louisiana, Alabama and Texas. Legislation was passed to cripple us in Virginia, South Carolina, Mississippi, Alabama, Tennessee and Arkansas. In Georgia, state officials resorted to administrative action in an effort to penalize the Association. Florida authorized $50,000 for a legislative committee to investigate the activities of our organization. Previously, the State of Louisiana had established a legislative committee for the same purpose. The intent of all this has been to harass, cripple and run the NAACP out of business throughout the South in the vain hope that the drive for desegregation would cease. This was official state action in contrast with the unofficial activities of private individuals in the earlier years of our organization.

And what precipitated this ill-considered onslaught upon our Association? Our objectives have not changed from the days when we were first organized. Our methods have remained essentially the same. We seek now, as always, the elimination of racial discrimination and segregation. We continue to pursue this goal within the framework of the American constitutional system. Why then did these states wait nearly 50 years before they unleashed their attacks upon our organization?

The answer is simple. It began with the historic decision of the United States Supreme Court, handed down on May 17, 1954, in response to suits filed by NAACP lawyers. That decision outlawed racial segregation in public education. These states became alarmed by the success of our program and the almost universal approbation of the Court's ruling. To give vent to their hatred and defiance they launched an all-out attack upon the NAACP which they held responsible for the decision.

But their attack is not against the NAACP alone. It is also against the United States Supreme Court. It is against constitutional government as we have conceived it in this country. It is against federal authority. Stripped of its camouflage and all of its pretensions, the revolt against the Supreme Court decision is a declaration of secession not only from the United States of America but in reality from the human race. The extremists of all sections of the country, the supporters and advocates of the anachronism of white supremacy, look upon themselves as a special breed of mankind, as a race apart not only from their dark-skinned neighbors but from mankind of whatever race, color, religion or nationality throughout the world. In seceding from the human race they have turned their backs upon the great tenets of our religious faith and upon the democratic ideals for which men have sacrificed their lives from the American Revolution down until the Hungarian revolt against Soviet totalitarianism. They would deny the principles of liberty upon which this government was founded and the teachings of love expounded by the lowly Nazarene. They would substitute instead, the crass and inhuman ideology of Hitler and Malan.

In all the strife and turmoil that this resistance to constituted authority has precipitated, we may be proud of the role of the National Association for the Advancement of Colored People and of the Negroes in the South as a group. Not only has our organization been under fierce attack, but Negro citizens generally throughout the region have been victimized by the brutal assault upon human decency. Not only Negroes, but white persons who have had the courage to face the fury of the mob and declare themselves Americans and Christians and members of the human race as over and beyond their incidental identification as southerners. They, too, have suffered. They have been reviled, pushed around and denied an opportunity to earn a living. We cannot pay too high a tribute to those white southerners who, breaking with the traditions of their homeland, have risked their standing in the community and their economic welfare in order to affirm their allegiance to the United States of America and the democratic ideals for which it stands. We thank God for them!

Five days after the unanimous May 17th decision was handed down, the NAACP held a regional conference in Atlanta. Unable to attend this important meeting, I sent a message to the conference as chairman of your Board of Directors in which I said, and here I quote: "It is important that calm reasonableness prevail, that the difficulties of adjustment be realized, and that, without any sacrifice of basic principles, the spirit of give and take characterize the discussions. Let it not be said of us that we took advantage of a sweeping victory to drive hard bargains or impose unnecessary hardships upon those responsible for working out the details of adjustment. God be with you in your deliberations."

In this spirit the conference formulated the Atlanta Declaration asserting, and again I quote: "We look upon this memorable decision not as a victory for Negroes alone but for the whole American people and as a vindication of America's leadership of the Free World." Further, at our convention last year the delegates passed a resolution instructing our state conferences and branches in those states where desegregation had been begun "to redouble their efforts to negotiate with their local school boards to secure desegregation within a reasonable time and to proceed with such negotiations as long as the local board is acting in good faith. In those states, legal action in the courts is only to be used as a last resort." In eight states, the resolution continued, "constructive negotiations having been found to be impossible, we instruct the national legal staff immediately to process and give the necessary legal assistance to all parents in these states who have appealed to us for legal assistance to end racial segregation in their local communities."

We submit that this has been a most reasonable approach to the admittedly difficult problem of desegregation in a region which had grown accustomed to separate facilities for the races over a period of half a century.

We have been, and still are, patient within reasonable limits. We have launched no blitzkrieg against the South. For years we have worked through the courts, through political action and through the mobilization of public opinion to get rid of racial inequities. We have succeeded in leveling one barrier after another in the face of dire predictions of disaster. The South today is a better and more democratic land than it was even as late as 1950, largely because of our efforts.

We have gone into no community and demanded that the public schools be desegregated overnight. We have from the beginning recognized administrative difficulties involved in a changeover. We have not believed that any of these difficulties was insurmountable. We have initiated court action only as a last resort. Instead, our branches have offered to sit down with local school boards and city authorities in communities throughout the region for the purpose of developing a plan of action to comply with the Supreme Court's ruling. We have been militant in that we insist that a beginning be made, but we have been reasonable in that we recognize the need to work out a plan to achieve desegregation as speedily as possible compatible with the maintenance of an orderly public school system. We reject any proposals of gradualism which mean *never*. We are ready at all times to consider reasonable programs to assure that no child is denied his constitutional right to an equal and unsegregated public education.

Commenting upon the role of the NAACP in the present crisis in the South, Albert E. Barnett, a white Southerner and a grandson of a Confederate officer, wrote as follows in *The Christian Century* of May 30, 1956 and I quote: "Orderly militancy is of the essence of patience; it is moderation, not immoderation. Usually it requires thirty minutes to matriculate as a student at the University of Alabama. Miss Autherine Lucy needed two years. That's going pretty slow, it seems to me. That she 'kept on keeping on' in expectant calmness shows how typically patient Negroes are—not that they are using coercive measures to end segregation 'overnight.' . . . As a Southerner I am thankful for the NAACP. Elsewhere today—as has happened throughout history—repressed minorities are seeking redress of grievances by torch, dagger and bombs, instruments that produce social chaos and involve loss of precious moral values. . . . The NAACP counsels patience and moderation and admirably illustrates both. It hires a good lawyer and takes its case to court. For 50 years it lived under the 'separate but equal' mandate of the Supreme Court, despite the fact that forces now decrying integration emphasized separateness and ignored equalization of school accommodations."

While the NAACP has been pursuing this course of moderate and constitutional action, the segregationists have been resorting to violence, economic pressures, intimidation, punitive legislative action, injunctions, subversive manifestos, secessionist resolutions of interposition and all manner of actions, whether openly illegal or cloaked in the raiment of legality, in order to circumvent, evade and defeat the ruling of the U.S. Supreme Court. Negro citizens have indulged in none of these. In the face of extreme provocation, they have remained calm but nevertheless firm. They have met violence with non-violence. In Montgomery, Alabama, under the inspired leadership of the youthful Dr. Martin Luther King, they dramatically and successfully invoked the power of Christian faith and love in combating evil. They have sought redress of their grievances in the halls of justice and in the court of public opinion. They have turned their backs on the counsel of despair and the siren song of subversive elements. They have demonstrated their faith in the democratic process. They have behaved as adults and not as spoiled children. This is a record to be proud of and I assure you that I am proud of our people who have withstood this acid test.

We are, as I said earlier, faced with a crisis, but it is not a crisis for the NAACP alone nor for the Negro as a race. It is a crisis for the nation. No one can escape its impact no matter how detached he may wish to be. It is as impossible today to stand on the sidelines as it was a hundred years ago when the nation faced the crisis over slavery. It is for the nation to determine whether we shall be a truly democratic, law-abiding community affording equal opportunity and equal rights for all or whether we shall have classes of citizenship with some persons, by virtue of their race and color, enjoying more privileges than others. Democracy is inclusive, never exclusive.

A century ago it was recognized that this nation could not endure half free and half slave. It is equally clear today that we cannot remain half integrated and half segregated. The United States Constitution governs us all. It is a constitution of equality, not inequality.

As important as is the role of the NAACP in this crisis and the role of Negroes generally, it is a decision which we cannot make by ourselves. Nor is it up to the South alone. It is a decision which the nation as a whole must make.

Our goal as an organization is to achieve equality of citizenship. We want to develop in our country a society in which no man is either favored or penalized because of his race or color. We want a society in which equality is a normal and accepted condition. Insofar as the Negro is a debtor to our country he already shares equally in responsibilities. He pays the same taxes as other citizens. He abides by the laws of the country. He serves in the armed forces. He is required to offer his life in defense of the country. He contributes his share to the national welfare. However, insofar as the government is debtor to the citizen, the Negro suffers discrimination. He is disadvantaged in economic opportunity. He is restricted in his living quarters. He is compelled to send his children to inferior schools. He is subjected to daily humiliation. He is denied representation in the government which formulates the laws and regulations under which he lives. He is a victim of taxation without representation. In another period, the people of this country rose in armed revolt against such denial of representation.

The most important problem facing this convention is the development of a plan of action to meet the present crisis and to make possible the achievement of the NAACP goal of equal rights for all Americans. We cannot do this by speeches alone nor by resolutions in and of themselves. We cannot do this in anger and frustration. We cannot do this with bitterness in our hearts. We can do this only in an atmosphere of calm reasonableness. Our words and resolutions achieve significance only as they are translated into deeds. We have a major responsibility in this and we must be prepared to discharge that responsibility as reasonable men and women.

Let us consider what steps we may take in order to reach our goal.

1.   We must work day and night to increase the vote, particularly in the South. I realize that this is not an easy task in that region. There are tricky registration requirements. There are election officials determined to keep the Negro vote down. There is a poll tax in five states. There are threats and intimidation. There are economic and personal hazards. But we must face all of these. As our political strength waxes, these difficulties will wane. Not only must we increase the number of voters but we must give leadership in the intelligent use of the ballot. Negro voters in the presidential election of 1956 demonstrated their awareness of the value of an intelligently cast ballot. The Negro vote cannot afford to be tied to any political party. It must remain independent and free to vote for candidates, irrespective of party, committed to our nation's democratic principles of equal opportunity and equal rights for all. Our Association has a responsibility not only to work for the enlargement of the Negro vote but, within the framework of our non-partisan policy, to give it guidance in the crucial elections ahead.

2.   We must continue our efforts to secure enactment of civil rights legislation implementing the constitutional guarantees of basic American freedoms. Foremost among these measures is the pending bill to protect the right to vote. Our prospects for such legislation will be greatly enhanced through effective political action in states where we now have a free ballot.

3.   The basic legal groundwork has been laid. However, appeals to the courts will continue where necessary. The separate but equal doctrine is dead. Segregation in any public facility, institution or service is now not only immoral, but also illegal. The battle ahead lies primarily in the area of public opinion. We know that there are benighted elements in this country which will oppose every step toward the achievement of a democratic society. These are the hopeless and unreachable elements. There is another group of white Americans who by their religious and political convictions and their basic sense of human decency are committed to our side. Many of these are members of our organization. Others work individually or in other organizations for our goals. These are our true and tried friends who by their deeds have proved that we can rely upon them. They have given the NAACP moral and financial support. Some of them are professional and intellectual workers. Some are trade unionists. Some are in business. Some are devout churchmen. All of them believe in the essential equality of all mankind.

But there is a third group which may well constitute the great bulk of white Americans: people who are torn by an inner conflict. These may be misled by the racists and bigots into believing that they have a stake in maintaining segregation. On the other hand, they recognize the immorality and illegality of segregation and its incompatibility with their religious beliefs and political ideals. They know in their heart of hearts that segregation is a denial of their basic convictions. They believe in honoring and abiding by the rulings of our highest court. They are loyal American citizens opposed to subversion either of the right or of the left. These are the people who in the long run will determine in what direction America will go. These are the people whom we must reach with our message, whom we must convince that it is not only morally right to support the Court's ruling but that it is in their best interest and in the best interest of the nation.

The task ahead is clear. We must work to convert the uncommitted millions of Americans, to intensify the support of our friends, and to negate the sinister influence of the Ku Klux Klan, the White Citizens Councils and organizations and persons of their stripe. This is a gigantic task which calls for social engineering on a massive scale. It involves much more than publicity in the press and on radio and television. These may be helpful, but they are not sufficient to bring about the social change which is our objective.

We need to know why certain people cling so tenaciously to the old ways, why they place such exaggerated value on so superficial a quality as skin color, and why they persist in looking backwards to a day which cannot be brought back without total disaster to the entire nation. We need to know these facts in order to improve our present efforts to modify attitudes and stimulate full acceptance of professions of Christian brotherhood and democratic rights.

Some people are motivated by their religious convictions; others by their respect for law and order. The patriotic appeal is effective with many persons. Still others may be influenced by the profit motive. All of these are factors to be considered in mapping a plan of action to win people to our way of thinking.

Segregation is obviously contrary to our fundamental religious teachings.

Without law and order there can be no stable government, no reliable protection for anybody's rights or property. Defiance of the Supreme Court ruling not only negates law and order but it also feeds the propaganda mills of our foes at home and abroad. No patriotic American will want to engage in activities which contribute to this anti-American propaganda. In the present world struggle our country needs the support of millions of colored peoples in Asia and Africa as well as of Europeans who believe in human dignity. But our prospects of winning their support are dangerously impaired by acts of hate-inspired violence here at home.

It is obvious, also, that segregation is fantastically wasteful. It is not only a scandalous public extravagance but it also endangers the market abroad for American-made products. Peoples who are made to believe that Americans hold them in contempt merely because they are non-white will not wish to purchase American goods when they can get these goods elsewhere. Nor will they want to sell their vitally essential raw materials to a country in which they may be insulted and humiliated solely because of their color. Prejudice is costly in terms of our national economy.

These are just some of the themes of a program of action needed to win friends for the cause of American democracy; that is, for the realization of the American ideal of human equality.

In order to continue and accelerate our programs of legal and political action and to expand our efforts to win public support, we will have to have far greater financial resources than we have struggled along with in past years. There is urgent need for substantial funds for court action, for registration and voting campaigns, for the development and execution of a vastly enlarged public relations program. Without such resources we will not be able to do the kind of job now required.

When I addressed our convention in St. Louis in 1953, I proposed a Fight for Freedom Fund to complete emancipation over a 10-year period ending in 1963, the centennial of Lincoln's Emancipation Proclamation. I then proposed that we undertake to raise one million dollars a year for 10 years or a total of ten million dollars. The delegates enthusiastically approved that proposal. We have not quite reached the million dollar mark any year but we have approached it and increased our financial resources considerably since 1953. But much has happened since that convention. We are confronted with a new and perilous situation stemming from the die-hard resistance to the Supreme Court's anti-segregation ruling in certain southern states. We must be prepared to meet this new development.

If we are to carry on an adequate program we will have to find ways and means of substantially increasing our annual income. It is now evident that a million dollars a year is not ammunition enough to fight those who apparently have unlimited tax and private funds to carry on their campaign of hate and violence. We have the resources within our race and among our white friends to raise adequate funds—to match our foes, dollar for dollar. We are encouraged by the increased contributions to our Association by colored citizens of better than average means. Our life membership campaign, under the direction of Mr. Kivie Kaplan of Boston and Dr. Benjamin Mays of Atlanta, has proved most fruitful. The work of Dr. Alf Thomas and his associates here in Detroit has set an example for our business and professional people throughout the country. Detroit has demonstrated what can be done to support the Fight for Freedom. More and more of our people are coming to realize that all of us, no matter how well off we may be individually, have a stake in this fight and have a responsibility to see it through.

I shall not undertake again to set a figure to cover the kind of program needed. I am convinced, however, that we cannot fully succeed on our present limited income.

We are most fortunate this year in having as chairman of our Fight for Freedom Fund drive Jackie Robinson who is giving of his time, energy and talent to help us achieve our goal. He has expressed great confidence that we will exceed our goal this year. This, we can surely do, if all of us devote ourselves as unselfishly to the task as Jackie Robinson is doing.

And finally, I could not conclude without a word of tribute to Roy Wilkins and the members of his staff who have given leadership to our organization in this most trying period. They have worked hard day and night and through weekends in the struggle against resurgent racism. While many of us are relaxing, they are working for us and for all America. They are on call 24 hours a day, seven days a week. The least we can do is to support their unselfish efforts with wholehearted cooperation.

We will win this fight but we need the moral and financial support of every American who believes in our American democracy. It is up to us through you, the delegates, through our branches, to reach these people, to activate them in this cause and to secure their moral support and financial contributions.

§36 Shad Polier

Shad Polier, an attorney dedicated to equality and humanitarianism, was born on March 18, 1906 in Aiken, South Carolina. Polier graduated from the University of South Carolina in 1926 with his B.S. He then attended Harvard University where he earned his LL.B., as well as, his LL.M. In 1930 Polier was admitted to the New York bar, and practiced law in New York City until his death in 1976. He also served as vice president of the American Jewish Congress and as chairman of the National Governing Council and of the Congress's Commission on Law and Social Action. In addition, Polier was actively involved in the NAACP, serving for more than 30 years on the executive committee of the organization's Legal and Educational Defense Fund.

Polier made evident his passion for civil rights throughout his life. In 1946 he prosecuted Columbia University's college of Physicians and Surgeons charging that the university's admissions process discriminated against Jewish and minority students. The state of New York's very first fair education practices law was passed due to Polier's actions. Again in New York, Polier fought to eliminate racial injustices in 1948 when he brought suit against the Metropolitan Life Insurance Company. The company owned an apartment development, Stuyvesant Town, which allegedly discriminated against blacks. Although the lower court supported the exclusion of blacks from the apartment development and the Supreme Court would not hear the case, the American Jewish Congress continued its drive for fair housing laws. Furthermore, Polier took part in the monumental court case, *Brown v. Board of Education*, which eliminated the legal basis for segregation in Kansas and 20 other states that enforced segregated classrooms. He, along with other members of the American Jewish Congress, filed briefs of *amici curiae*, supporting students' rights to obtain equal education. Polier died in 1976, survived by his wife, Justine Wise Polier. His papers are housed at the American Jewish Historical Society in Waltham, Massachusetts.

In his address to the NAACP, Polier begins with a striking parallel between Jews and blacks: their collective "walks to freedom." From ancient Egypt to modern-day Montgomery, Polier forges a powerful sense of identification between the two groups in his very first paragraph. Polier also emphasizes the American Jewish Congress's belief that true liberty and democracy can exist only when all citizens hold equal rights. While doing so, he also speaks out against state legislatures that attempted to weaken the NAACP's efforts to promote integration, specifically the rights to expression, assembly, and association. Polier assures his audience of the AJC's strong support and understanding of their struggle for civil liberty. He assures the NAACP that Jewish Americans have experienced the results of policies of silence on controversial issues, and nearly all are committed to a proactive policy regarding the fight for civil rights for blacks and all Americans.

Walk to Freedom

Address to the 48th Annual NAACP Convention, Detroit, Michigan
June 27, 1957

When the history of the present cold civil war is written, it will be recorded that its greatest and most successful battle was fought by an unarmed group of citizens in Montgomery, Alabama, who, employing the weapons of patience, forbearance and resolution, walked their way to freedom. This event is not without its precedent—a precedent going back almost 2800 years and accounting in part for my appearance before you this morning. 2800 years ago an enslaved people resolved to walk to freedom. Theirs was a mighty march. Among them were the timid who yearned for slavery in Egypt in preference to the ordeals and risks of emancipation. Among them were the fearful who, confronted by the obstacles to be overcome in achieving the promised land, preferred to stay where they were. But that walk to freedom set in motion the history of my own Jewish people and laid down the major tenets which have guided our ethics and our faith to this very day.

In associating themselves with the cause of full equality for all Americans, the vastly overwhelming portion of the Jewish community of America has acted not only out of its commitment to the democratic idea but in fulfillment of these historic and religious obligations.

I stand before you this morning to share with you some reflections by an American Jew on the significance of guaranteeing to the American Negro freedom, equality and the right of full participation in the promise of the American way of life. I cannot undertake to speak for all Jews because they, like you and all Americans, hold varied points of view. But I can speak for that great number of Jews in the American Jewish Congress who have asked me to convey to you their wishes for a successful convention and for the achievement of those basic goals which we in the AJC share in common.

The affinity of the American Jewish Congress, its close identification with the cause of the NAACP is one of long standing, embodying the life of both agencies. My father-in-law, Dr. Stephen Wise, founder and long-time president of the American Jewish Congress, had been even earlier a founder of the NAACP. 10 years later he joined in founding AJC. Long before I became associated with the work of the Congress, I myself had been a member of the NAACP. In 1952 the American Jewish Congress bestowed its most distinguished award and the prize of $1,000 to the NAACP and Thurgood Marshall for the work in which we were all then engaged, the presentation of the segregation cases to the Supreme Court of this country.

Neither you nor we, nor the history of this country, will be unmindful of the fact that two of the six major studies cited by the Supreme Court in its historic decision of May 1954 were conducted by the research department of the American Jewish Congress and that the social scientists of the Congress staff presented expert testimony on the evils of segregation in equal facilities before the Courts. We were grateful for the privilege of having been a footnote in history and a headline in the lives of millions of Americans.

So we come to this morning under the compulsion of history and as the natural consequence of a recent, continuing and intimate association. We are now at a moment when this association is threatened. For we would be underestimating the corrosive effect of the assault on the NAACP if we were to think of it merely as a threat to the integrity of an organization bearing those initials. The very association of like-minded groups and like-minded peoples is at stake. It is not the intention of the American Jewish Congress to permit reactionary elements in America to destroy this freedom of association which we have so dearly established. The delegates to this convention may have seen, and if they have not, should see, the detailed report just published by the American Jewish Congress entitled *The Assault on Freedom of Association*. We believe this to be the first and the most fully documented report on the legislative attack upon the NAACP in the South.

We realize that neither the NAACP nor the Negro community are the sole victims of this attack. Great religious movements are being torn asunder with Northern and Southern versions of what their faiths teach. The Jewish people, itself, though not directly involved in this conflict is directly affected by it. Ourselves a miniscule minority in Southern communities, we are subject not only to the prejudices of the community around us but to crushing economic and social pressures to hold the line of discrimination. Despite overt threats to the security of the Jewish community in the South, it is well to be able to report that as a whole the Jewish people in America demonstrate a greater sensitivity to and sympathy for the plight of their Negro brothers than does any other identifiable element of the American people.

Not all Jewish Americans who share the view of civil rights I have described express that view by joining the American Jewish Congress (a source of regret to me and my colleagues) or even by joining other Jewish organizations. Many express those views by joining the NAACP or the American Civil Liberties Union or Americans for Democratic Action or by engaging in political activity of one kind or another. Many, however, do feel with me that their views can and should be expressed specifically in terms of Jewish values. The firm position of the American Jewish Congress on racial equality and other basic constitutional liberties stems from and expresses the deeply held views of its members.

Nor are we alone in this. The *organized Jewish community* of today is united against racial segregation. Not a single responsible Jewish organization defends the institution of segregation and virtually all have spoken out against it. All accept not only the abstract justice of the cause of equality but also the practical argument that the fight against all forms of discrimination must be carried on by all groups on all fronts. There may be some variation in the vigor with which those principles are practiced but there is no significant public disagreement and very little internal disagreement.

In all this, I am talking of the *organized, vocal* part of the Jewish community. I do not mean for a moment that all Jewish Americans have rid themselves of the prejudices that pervade the population or that none of them engage in discrimination. Jews have prejudices and do vent them—against Negroes, Puerto Ricans, Asians and even other Jews. There is a job still to be done with these unfortunates—a job of education and correction. The approach will be the same as it is with other prejudiced Americans, another sad proof of the indivisibility of the problem.

Yet, in the South too, it can be said that the proportion of liberal anti-segregationists is higher among the Jewish community than in the white population as a whole. Southern Jews are not entirely lost to the message of the Jewish religious tradition and our people's history. No rabbi has disgraced his calling by describing segregation as the work of God. The number of Jews who have lent their names to the shameful work of the White Citizens Councils is extremely small. If the Jews of the South have fallen short in the present crisis, it has been by allowing themselves to be silenced. In this, we must admit, they are no worse than their white Christian neighbors.

A few, very few, Southern Jewish communities not only have embraced the program of silence for themselves but have sought to impose it on their Northern Jewish brethren. Falling into the trap of viewing non-Southern Americans, Jew and non-Jewish, as "outsiders," they have demanded of the American Jewish Congress and all other national organizations "an immediate cessation of any overt action . . . on behalf of the Negro."

Since I am here, it is not necessary for me to say that the American Jewish Congress has rejected this demand. We do not regard our activity as being "on behalf of the Negro." Whatever policies and activities we have pursued have been in support of constitutional rights guaranteed to all Americans. Our position on desegregation stems from our support of civil rights and liberties for all. It does not differ from the position we have taken in opposing discrimination against Jews or any other group in the community. We regard our opposition to segregation as the logical fulfill-ment of our obligations as American citizens under the Constitution.

The majority of American Jews bitterly recall that when Jews were being persecuted by the Nazis, many nations refrained from vigorous opposition to these barbarities because to do so would jeopardize their security. They re-call that then, too, there were voices that counseled silence because the situa-tion would be exacerbated if the Jews spoke out. As we know now, these were policies of disaster. Aside from considerations of conscience, the majority of American Jews do not want history to record that they helped destroy the de-mocracy they cherished by failing to speak out clearly against undemocratic treatment accorded to those of their fellow-citizens who are Negroes.

The current assault on the NAACP gives all these principles a deeper reality. We have said for years that discrimination against Negroes threat-ens not only the right of all to equality but also our basic constitutional liberties. Until recently, we have had little evidence to support that state-ment. Now, as soon as the struggle against segregation begins to make real progress, so that the oppressors begin to feel their position is really threat-ened—in short, when the fighting begins to get rough—the evidence is there for all to see. At once, other minorities express their fears that the aroused fury will spill over and inundate them also. At once, the right of freedom of expression is challenged and an all-out effort is launched to destroy the right to freedom of association.

The Southern states have taken a dangerous step away from democ-racy and toward totalitarianism. We who lost 6,000,000 under the Nazis have the obligation to speak out. A state that asserts the right to halt orga-nized peaceful efforts to change its laws and institutions, as a number of Southern states have, abandons its status as a free government. "If there is any fixed star in our constitutional constellation," said the United States Supreme Court in 1942, "it is that no official, high or petty, can prescribe what shall be orthodox in politics, nationalism, religion, or other matters of opinion." It is significant that these words, so apt here, were spoken in defense of religious liberty in a case having no apparent connection with interracial problems.

The unity of Americans in defense of all their liberties and the liberties of all is the only sure basis for democracy. That means freedom of assem-bly. With that kind of unity we can be sure of ultimate victory.

§37 Reverend Marion A. Boggs

Marion A. Boggs was born on September 21, 1894 in Liberty, South Carolina. Upon graduating from Davidson College in 1915, Boggs entered Union Theological Seminary in Richmond, Virginia, where he earned his B.D. in 1919. Three years later, Boggs married Leila Flippin Kabler. For 42 years Boggs served Presbyterian churches in Arkansas, including a 23-year tenure at Second Presbyterian in Little Rock, where he delivered this sermon. After retiring from the ministry in 1964 and moving to Pensacola, Florida, Boggs worked occasionally as interim pastor around the country. He died in 1983. His papers are housed at the Presbyterian Historical Society in Montreat, North Carolina.

An outspoken proponent of integration in Little Rock's public schools, Boggs delivered this sermon to his Second Presbyterian parishioners months before the September 1957 crisis that would focus world attention on Little Rock. According to Boggs, the test of "Christian citizenship" involved removing the stigma of inferiority left by segregation. Three reasons warranted its overthrow: segregation contradicts the "Christian doctrine of the dignity of man"; second, segregation contradicts "the spirit and purpose of American freedom"; and third, the colored peoples of the world resented such unjust laws, which would have a spillover on the church's (in)ability to continue its missionary enterprises. Boggs closes his sermon by answering five specific questions related to desegregation, intermarriage, black leaders, northern aggression, and the church's role in race relations.

The Crucial Test of Christian Citizenship
Second Presbyterian Church, Little Rock, Arkansas
July 1957 (reprinted)

Today instead of preaching a sermon I want to have a heart-to-heart talk with the members of my congregation on the subject of Christian Citizenship. I am doing this not only because our General Assembly has designated the year 1957 as a year of special emphasis on Christian Citizenship, but also because I am firmly convinced that the church of Jesus Christ must rise to its full height of moral and ethical leadership as we face certain problems in this field. For the church to remain silent when great problems of moral and ethical import are being debated and being decided, would, in my judgment, amount to cowardice and a neglect of urgent duty.

The whole question of our rights and privileges as American citizens is before us at this time. We have just observed the 181st Anniversary of our nation's independence, and I am quite sure every one of us had a special prayer of thanksgiving for the goodness of God in casting our lot in this free and enlightened and God-protected land. This year especially we shall continue to have these things in mind as we celebrate the 350th year of the first Permanent English Settlement at Jamestown and as we welcome the coming of Mayflower the Second into Plymouth Bay. Within a few weeks Her Majesty, the Queen of Britain, will pay us an official visit and help us with the celebration. If the dead are aware of what is going on among the living, I feel sure King George III will turn over in his grave when Her

Queenly Majesty sets foot on our shores, welcomed by the highest notables of our land.

All of the flag-waving and all of the pomp and pageantry has its place, but the question before the house of our American Democracy is this: "Are we prepared to remove from our minds the prejudices and from our statute books the legal hindrances that stand in the way of full citizenship for our Negro citizens?" It is not in our power, of course, to remove the hindrances that the Negroes impose upon themselves through crime or ignorance or immorality. That is something they must take into their own hands. But we can, if we will, remove the legal hindrances that stand in their way, and that is, for this generation, at least, the crucial test of Christian Citizenship.

After three years of careful study and statesman-like planning, the Little Rock School Board has worked out a plan looking toward gradual and orderly compliance with the Supreme Court's decision, declaring segregation laws in tax-supported schools unconstitutional. A limited number of Negro students who can meet the qualification will be admitted to the high school. This plan is, in my judgment, wise and sound, and I hope that the Little Rock people will be wise enough and patriotic enough to give the plan their full and unified support. This is the point where Christian Citizenship comes home to our doorstep and awaits our decision. The men and women on the School Board and those who have the management of our Public schools deserve our support, and I, for one, am pledging my support here and now. It is my hope also, that all the officers and all the members of Second Church will join me in this declaration of purpose.

Let us recall a little American History that has point and meaning here. The Freedom that we prize, and which most of us take too much for granted, has been achieved, not all of a sudden, but by slow, and painful and costly process. The Roman officer who was responsible for Paul's arrest had this to say about his Roman citizenship: "With a great price obtained I [honor] this citizenship." We Americans have not had to pay any particular sum of money for our freedom, but it has been achieved, nevertheless, at a costly price.

Take our Freedom of Religion for instance. In the early days of the colonies, religious freedom was almost unheard-of. In New England the Puritans were predominant, and they required conformity to the Congregational Church. Roger Williams was banished from the Massachusetts Colony in the year 1635 because of his non-conformist religious views. Francis Mackemie and John Hampton were arrested and imprisoned in New York in the year 1707 for preaching Presbyterian doctrines without the consent of the governor. It was 170 years after the settlement of Jamestown that the Virginia Statute guaranteeing religious freedom was enacted. Before that time Presbyterians and Baptists and Methodists, and all others except the Episcopalians, were only "tolerated," and were hedged about with various limitations.

Consider also the long struggle for the liberation of the slaves. Like the ancient civilizations of Greece and Rome, slavery was a constituent part of our economic system, and for the first 244 years of our nation's history there was a large section of our population to whom the privileges of citizenship were not extended. They were not considered as "people" but as "property." As it later developed, the whole slavery system was like dynamite laid underneath and all about the foundations of the democracy. Thomas Jefferson wrote a declaration against slavery into the first draft of the Declaration of Independence, but it was not permitted to stand. He saw that slavery was in itself a contradiction to the noble words of the Declaration, and already he saw the danger signals on the horizon. When the Constitution was framed and our American liberties were outlined and defined, the presence of slavery was an embarrassment, and compromise after compromise had to be made to keep the nation from shattering before we began our career as an independent nation. For seventy-five years the struggle was carried on for the peaceful and orderly emancipation of the slaves. Every plan that our leaders could devise was at one time or another proposed, but all to no avail. Tempers flared on both sides of the controversy. Then came the costly, tragic war, the wounds of which it will take more than a hundred years to heal—all for what purpose—to extend the rights of citizenship and freedom to all our people.

Why could we not have learned from History? Why could we not have found peaceful and lawful means of extending the blessings of freedom to all our people, instead of having liberty extended through blood and toil and wholesale destruction? Why could we not have learned that when we are claiming freedom for ourselves we are in a very strong position, and in a very weak position when we are denying that very freedom to others? Segregation by force of law is a vestige and a hangover from slavery days, and the sooner it is eliminated from our minds and from our statute books the better.

Let me now indicate three reasons why this stigma of inferiority should be removed from our American way of life.

In the first place, Segregation by Law should be eliminated because it is a direct contradiction to the Christian Doctrine of the Dignity of Man.

Our General Assembly was the first great Christian body in America to make this affirmation. The declaration was made in May 1954, only a few days after the Supreme Court's historic decision. Our Assembly declared that "enforced segregation of the races is discrimination which is out of harmony with Christian theology and ethics." When our Assembly was requested by certain groups to rescind that action the following year, the Assembly not only did not rescind, but rather confirmed and strengthened the resolution.

This declaration of our Assembly is amply supported by the whole tenor of scripture teaching. Passage after passage in the Bible confirms and supports this position. Did not Simon Peter, after his great vision on the housetop at Joppa, declare: "I perceive that God is no respecter of persons, but in every nation he that feareth God and worketh righteousness is accepted of Him." (Acts 10:34-35) The Apostle Paul crossed over all the ancient boundaries of race and nationality when he declared that in Christ the middle wall of separation dividing Jew from Gentile had been broken down, and that all had become one in Jesus Christ. (Ephesians 2:11-20) When, at a later time, Simon Peter, under pressure of Jewish prejudice, refused to eat with the Gentiles, Paul administered a stinging rebuke which was sustained by the New Testament Church. (Galatians 2:11-14)

According to the law of Christian love we are to do unto others as we would have them do unto us. How would you like to be segregated by law and thus branded as inferior every time you stepped on a bus or every time you made application for admission to a tax-supported institution of learning? One of our Negro helpers said a few years ago, "How would you like to be met with insults and humiliations everywhere you turn?" My friends, how would you answer that question? After all, it is so little for us to give and so much for them to receive.

The second reason why this legal disability should be removed is that it is in direct contradiction to the spirit and purpose of American freedom.

For the past three years we have had a veritable warfare of words and opinions over the Supreme Court's decision. I suppose that tons and tons of paper and barrels of printer's ink have been used in carrying on the warfare. As many uncomplimentary things have been said about the nine justices of the Supreme Court as have been said about all the umpires on all the ball diamonds of America in the past decade. Three of the nine justices are Presbyterians, one of them the son of a Presbyterian minister, and knowing Presbyterians to be a hardy and durable variety, I don't imagine they have lost too much sleep over the furor caused by their decision. Having heard so much about the opinion, pro and con, I decided it would be a good thing to read it for myself. I had heard that the justices had based their opinion, not on the law and the constitution, but on highly questionably psychological and sociological findings. I am not a lawyer nor a lawyer's son, but it seems quite plain to me that the main burden of their opinion rests squarely on the Fourteenth Amendment to the Constitution, which reads, in part: "All persons born or naturalized in the United States, and subject to the jurisdiction thereof, are citizens of the United States and of the state wherein they reside. No state shall make or enforce any law which shall abridge the privileges and immunities of citizens of the United States; nor shall any state deprive any person of life, liberty, or property without due process of law; nor deny any person within its jurisdiction the equal protection of the laws." It seems to me, therefore, that the Supreme Court has not undertaken to destroy the sovereignty of the several states, but rather to enforce, all across the board, the clear provisions of a constitutional amendment. That, according to my understanding, is what the Supreme Court is supposed to do.

But, as I said, I am no expert in the law. This I do know, however; The Declaration of Independence as well as the Constitution of the United States, embodies the spirit and purpose of American Freedom, and that great Declaration says: "We hold these truths to be self-evident, that all men are created equal; and are endowed by their Creator with certain unalienable rights; and that among these rights are life, liberty, and the pursuit of happiness." How can a human being pursue happiness with any hope of achieving it, if he is segregated from the society of his fellow-citizens at every turn?

A third reason why segregation by force of law should be ended in the United States of America is the rising tide of resentment against it throughout the world and the urgent necessity for continuing the Missionary Enterprise.

Not only is there a rising tide of resentment against segregation in the United States of America; that resentment burns like a consuming flame among the millions in Africa, in India, in Indonesia and the Far East. As we sit here in this quiet sanctuary of worship we can hardly imagine the revolutionary character of the age in which we are living. The first half century since 1900 has witnessed two colossal wars, making it the bloodiest half century since time began. Within the past 11 years 700 million people, or approximately one third of the human race, have achieved political independence, and many millions more are clamoring for it. Since the end of World War II half the people of the earth have changed their form of government. Since 1917, or within the past 40 years, approximately 800 million people have come under the sway of revolutionary, atheistic, and materialistic Communism. John Foster Dulles, our Secretary of State, calls this "the most frightening fact that history records." What is the reason for all this seething volcano of unrest? Among other things, it is the uprising of the world's disinherited multitudes, who are tired of being walked over and considered "second rate" by the rest of mankind. And what is more, this deep unrest and smoldering resentment comes to a burning focus in "segregation laws" that remain upon the statute books of the West.

What is the road away from revolution? What is the road to a peaceful world in the future? Woodrow Wilson, a Presbyterian Elder, answered it in the last great utterance of his great career. He said: "The road away from revolution is the maintenance in every field of action of the highest and purest standards of justice and right dealing." Why do we not become wise here in America? Why do we not willingly and gladly and immediately remove this galling irritant of segregation from the mind and heart of the colored peoples of the earth? If we would do this, we would rob the Communists of one of their sharpest weapons, and what is a great deal better, we would make friends of the colored peoples of the earth and pave the way for a continuance of the Missionary Enterprise. If we will not do this, our days of opportunity for evangelizing the people of color are strictly numbered. It is later than we think!

This brings to an end my heart-to-heart talk. Now let me ask and answer a few important questions.

First, Will not desegregation bring many problems in the deep South? Yes indeed. But refusal to comply with the Supreme Court's directive will create more problems, and will inflame the ones we now have. A straight line is the shortest distance between two points and the surest solution of every problem is to do right and face the consequences.

Question No. 2. Will not integration of the schools lead to intermarriage and miscegenation of the races? No. I do not believe it will. Purity of race is a principle of great importance to the Negro as well as to the whites. But the dangers of miscegenation are largely passed. That took place in slavery time, when many white masters freely and without shame mingled their blood with that of female slaves. This is why there is so much white blood in Negro veins today.

The third question: Are there not many misguided Negroes? Yes. There are Negro leaders who are making themselves obnoxious, but we must not be deflected from the right course either by the folly of our friends or by the malice of our enemies.

The fourth question: Are not the people of the North trying to cram this down our throats like they did during the days of reconstruction following the war? No. This is a nation-wide problem, with greater difficulties and complications in the South. There are some Northerners that think of themselves as specially commissioned of the Almighty to reform the South, but we must also remember that there are also some Southerners who are exceedingly difficult to get along with. My conviction is that this is a part of the enlightened Southerner's unfinished business; or better still, the unfinished business of all true Americans whether North, South, East or West.

The fifth and final question: Why do you as a Presbyterian Minister preach on this subject when you run the risk of offending some of your good members? There are some of our members who have already made up their minds and who will disregard everything I have said here this morning. That is their privilege. But there are also many loyal Presbyterians who want light and guidance from their Church on this difficult and complex question. They have a right as loyal Presbyterians to know what position their Church has taken, and why. It is my responsibility and duty to tell them. It is for these [reasons] that I have spoken today. May the Lord God give us light and guidance, and give us strength to follow where His word and Spirit lead.

§38 Reverend A. Powell Davies

Reverend A. Powell Davies's biography appears in the introduction to his May 23, 1954 sermon in Washington, D.C. In the sermon below, just four days before his untimely death, Reverend Davies delivers a blistering attack on the nation, its supposed leaders, and segregation's adherents. As with many of his sermons, Powell keeps one eye on the community and one eye on the world. Thus is Little Rock rendered a morality tale in the larger Cold War battle for the world's allegiances. A hypocritical nation, Davies warns, one that betrays its own sacred principles, "could become a contribution to our final tragedy—our isolation and defeat, perhaps even our annihilation in a world that is marshaled against us."

He offers scathing critique for perhaps the two men most at fault for the Little Rock crisis, Arkansas Governor Orval Faubus and President Dwight Eisenhower. Employing both mens' facial comportment, Davies sees what others might not: Faubus's clever cunning and Eisenhower's gullibility. Perhaps the most entertaining part of Davies's message is his *reductio ad absurdum* of a prevailing southern reluctance to accept legal changes "until people are ready for it in their hearts." From the Mormon polygamist and the pork-eating cannibal to the larcenist, Davies reaches but one conclusion: "we must advance in race relations in spite of race prejudice." And, until the racists finally "get that poison out of their hearts," "communist cynicism" will continue "to defeat Western hypocrisy."

The Meaning of Little Rock
All Souls Church, Washington, D.C.
September 22, 1957

The capital city of Arkansas is not large. It has a population of about 110,000, a little less than a quarter of which is Negro. It has about 20,000 children in its schools, of which in all there are 33. The state of Arkansas itself is not by usual measurements among the more important in the federal union. Its population is expected to decline in the near future while the population of most states swiftly rises. Yet Arkansas has been in many ways a good part of the country in which to live and Little Rock has been a pleasant city.

Compared with other cities of the South, Little Rock for the most part has been more liberal in its race relations. There are 8,000 registered Negro voters, public transportation is not segregated, there are clergy of both races in its ministerial associations. Until recently, it looked as though this liberal trend would quietly continue, and there was no reason to suppose that Little Rock would be on the front pages of the newspapers.

But in the last few weeks, events in this small city have become important, not only in the United States but throughout the world. It is not an importance that will do any good to Arkansas; nor will it benefit the disquieted nation of which that state is a member; it is a sordid and malignant importance and one that could easily in the end be tragic. To those of us who still hope that democracy may somehow win in the desperate struggle with communism, what has been happening in Little Rock has, for good reason, been profoundly disturbing. In plain words, it is a severe setback. The eyes of the world have been on Little Rock, not on Hungary or Syria, and people of all races and of many nations have seen clearly the American betrayal of American principles.

And in addition to what has happened, there is that which failed to happen. Where were the voices of protest? From the southern liberals particularly there has been a very loud silence. And in high places in the federal government voices have been modulated almost to a whisper, solicitously soothing, confidingly soft. We must be patient, it was said. We must be very gentle. We must try to adjust things; these are delicate matters.

Which, in the opinion of many, has been the wise course—as in its own measure, no doubt it is. But where was the voice of moral authority? Who, in the highest places, reminded the nation that a choice is being made between right and wrong? Where were the highly placed who spoke in ringing tones of the law they were sworn to uphold, and of the justice that must be equal among all the people?

The fact is—and it is time to state it plainly—that the present administration of the United States is morally soft. It is less concerned to do right than to look right—and to avoid unpleasantness. And so, as the Bible puts it, when "The trumpet gives an uncertain sound, who shall prepare for the battle?" (I Corinthians 14:8)

And again one thinks of another verse from the Bible: "Yet a little sleep, a little slumber, a little folding of the hands to sleep." (Proverbs 6:10) But the consequence of this, the same passage continues, is a sudden awakening to the imminence of disaster, as when one man opens his eyes and sees before him the menacing figure of an armed man.

I repeat: where are the voices that speak boldly for righteousness? What are we to think of political leaders who hide behind the Supreme Court, and who whisper, "Well, you know: it is the law. The justices have decreed it. We shall have to try sometime somehow to some extent to obey it." Implying that apart from the Supreme Court there might be no problem. Not actually saying, of course, that the decision of the Court was regrettable but permitting that view to be a sort of pleasantly hazy inference. One could wish that there were others highly placed who were as conscientious and courageous as were the members of the Supreme Court in that decision. One would like to hear words from the executive branch as honest and as forthright as those of the Chief Justice. Indeed, one may say that the United States is immensely fortunate in its Chief Justice. How proud we would be if any other man of equal national eminence were similarly endowed for the moral responsibilities of high office!

Ah! but we are told, the country must be given time. As though there had been not time to do anything about integrating the schools until the Supreme Court's decision! It is nearly a century now since Lee surrendered to Grant and the South was restored to the United States. What might have been done more slowly during that century must now be done much more rapidly for the simple reason that there are new urgencies in the world, the chief of which is that we are losing our struggle with the communists.

That is why Governor Faubus cuts such a sorry figure. He is not legally guilty of treason under our present laws but has nevertheless done more harm to the country than any man who ever appeared before the Un-American Activities Committee. I watched him last Sunday on television, which allows you to look at every movement of a man's eyes, every twitch of his mouth, every shadow that passes over his face. And Governor Faubus has a very interesting face. One that reveals his quiet amusement at his easy parrying of awkward questions—and sometimes at the discomfiture of his adversaries. Evidently, the Governor enjoys his own cleverness. And he *is* clever. Even the President of the United States seems to have been tricked by him. Though this, perhaps, was not difficult. The President is not a guileful man. He has a very different face from Governor Faubus's— an equally expressive face but in a much more open way. Whatever his faults, Mr. Eisenhower is not a man of unusual cunning. In this respect, he must rely upon other people. But last weekend I think he relied on them in vain. Governor Faubus outwitted the President's advisors as well as the President. For nothing came of the conference but white-washed notoriety for Governor Faubus—and the applause no doubt of his supporters.

It has been said that Governor Faubus is not acting alone, but that his maneuvers were secretly concerted by other leaders among the segregationists. If so, and I for one entertain this thought quite seriously, what we have is an attempt to discover whether the authority of the United States can be undermined by determined intransigence and whether artifice and subterfuge can nullify its laws.

Such a conspiracy should not be met with patience. It should be met promptly and with vigor. It should be utterly defeated. It should be morally censured and legally condemned. And there should be no assumption, whether in the federal administration or in the country at large that the people of the South are not willing to obey the nation's laws.

The people of Little Rock, it is quite plain, were fully adjusted to the beginnings of integration in their schools until Governor Faubus raised difficulties. Arkansas belongs only in part to the Old South; in at least equal part it belongs with the West. I have been there. I preached the commencement sermon at its university a few years ago, at a time when desegregation in that institution was just beginning. There are liberals in Arkansas. There are also conservatives who are far from being extremists. And there are many who, whatever their private opinions, are willing to obey the federal laws. There is nothing to prevent the gradual integration of the Little Rock schools except trouble that is caused by incitement.

And here we come to something that should be far more clearly understood. Far too much is being said about progress being impossible until people are ready for it in their hearts. We did not delay the prohibition of polygamy in Utah until the Mormons were ready for it in their hearts. We said, No matter how many wives a man may want in his heart he is only going to have one wife by United States law. And the law has prevailed.

One remembers also the story of the mission board in London, the members of which were much disturbed because in one of their mission-fields cannibals kept eating their missionaries. Clearly, it had to be stopped—but it was difficult to stop. Then, seeing the board to be in a quandary, one of its new members, a business man, spoke up. "This change," he said, "may have to be made gradually and in a business-like spirit of compromise. Let us send them some pork with the missionaries, but gradually more pork and less missionaries until they have learned to eat only pork and no missionaries. Then the problem will be solved."

But the board, whether a real one or apocryphal, clearly could not have agreed to wait until the cannibals gave up cannibalism "in their hearts!" And if you say this is an extreme illustration, the answer is that it lends useful emphasis to more moderate cases.

If obedience to the law must wait in the case of desegregation until people are ready for it in their hearts the same might be urged of many other provisions of the law. Would we be willing, for instance, for the same delay in the case of theft or larceny? Or do we not recognize that crime has to be suppressed by law-enforcement irrespective of whether some people are not yet ready for it in their hearts?

Let us understand the plain truth that what people have in their hearts is not one thing but many and that among these many things, any of them, good or bad, may be brought to the top. There are people in Arkansas, for example, who have race prejudice in their hearts; but they also have loyalty to the United States and a respect for law and order in their hearts. If they know that law and order will be enforced they will accept that fact, whether they like it or not. But if they are encouraged to think—as Governor Faubus has encouraged them to think—that law can be flouted and need not be obeyed, then race prejudice will be revived and will become uppermost in their hearts.

To talk of waiting until people are ready for something in their hearts is all nonsense—worse than that, it is false and maliciously misleading—when the circumstances are such as I have outlined. There are indeed things which cannot be accomplished without the people's fuller, more complete assent—there are international arrangements, for instance, for which, unfortunately, many people are not yet ready in their hearts and which cannot be brought about until they are—but desegregation of the public schools in the manner prescribed by the Supreme Court is *not* one of the things that call for such delay. There has been delay enough already. People will become more ready for desegregation in their hearts, not through postponement which merely keeps the flames of prejudice burning, but through obedience to the law—and through learning new and better ways by meeting the requirements of changing circumstances.

We must remember that people were not ready for the Constitution of the United States in their hearts at the time of its promulgation. Some of them assembled in mobs and burned it. But it was lawfully adopted by the lawful assemblies which the people had themselves elected and its wisdom and great value soon became evident.

For those who are opposed to desegregation, the wise course is to accept it as the law and adapt themselves to it. They should remind themselves that people are all the while adapting themselves to things they do not like. The man called to the armed services may not like military discipline: and it may seem just as disagreeable to him at the end of his service as at the beginning; but he has to adapt himself to its requirements.

What I am saying is that we must advance in race relations in spite of race prejudice. Such prejudice is lamentable and those who do not share it should do all they can to persuade those who are affected by it to give it up—and until they do give it up these unfortunate people will never know how great a relief it is to get that poison out of their hearts. But we cannot wait until this happens before going on with desegregation. Conditions in our own country will not wait; and even more pressing are conditions abroad. Communist cynicism will always defeat Western hypocrisy. Only when we are morally in the clear can we hope for victory.

Nor is there much use talking of ways of life that are difficult to change. When the United States was founded a changed way of life was its very foundation. It was a sharp break with the past. All men *free* and *equal* has been an American principle from the American beginning and the moral basis of the American way of life. If there are those who reject this principle, it is to them and to them alone that it might appropriately be said, "Then go back where you came from." (There is even a new "Mayflower" anchored near our shores that might be used to take back the more patrician of these Un-Americans! And other replicas might be provided, to be moored, for instance, in the vicinity of Jamestown and even in the Potomac River!) For the principle has long since been established: our way of life is democratic with equal rights for all. And the world is watching—but not patiently—to see how close we are willing to come to fitting our practice to our proclamations.

Of course, the world may have made up its mind. It may be too late. I don't know. I just hope not. Realistically, I have to remember the McCarthy phase and all the damage that was done us then in world opinion. And the damage is just as real after McCarthy's death as if he were still living. To use hackneyed words, "The evil that men do lives after them." And I may say that I have no use whatever for the untruthful eulogies of McCarthy that were mouthed this summer. I hope it was just misguided sentiment and not moral insensitivity. Yes, a lot of time has been lost and Americans are not much admired any more. And now there has been this Little Rock betrayal, this stupid senseless undermining of our cause—and I just don't know how much time there is left. As Governor McKeldin said yesterday, we may be able to mend things in Arkansas fairly swiftly but to mend the effect on the world is another matter.

Nor is it clear yet what is going to happen next in Arkansas. But let us be hopeful. Perhaps the good people of Little Rock, many of whom have been dazed and confused—and some of them dismayed—by the antics of their governor, will align themselves more boldly on the side of lawful desegregation. If they do, progress will at once be possible. It is interesting to recall that it is barely over a year ago since there was loud lamentation in our own fair city over the alleged lowering of academic standards through school desegregation. That there was a problem no informed person would dispute. But it was not such a problem as it was represented to be and it arose, not from desegregation, but from the schools having been segregated for much too long. In any case, the principal of the Theodore Roosevelt High School, which is predominantly Negro, was reported in last Sunday's *New York Times* as having announced that her school was now academically equal or nearly equal to the other high schools, predominantly white. In the period of one year such near-miracles had been accomplished as a gain of four years in arithmetic, and there were many other achievements.

How had it come about? Chiefly by the resolute determination and hard work of the teachers and by their success in getting pupil and parent cooperation. These teachers and their principal, Mrs. Alva C. Wells, are warmly to be congratulated. They have proved that it is possible. Not that there are no remaining problems. There are problems of many sorts. But they can and will be solved. The chief requirement in solving them—as in solving all problems of race-relationship—is the *will* to solve them. If the real intention is to obstruct, then there will be obstruction instead of solution. But once the intention is to *solve*, there will be solutions.

Let us hope it may be so at Little Rock. The meaning of events in that city these last few weeks, as I have said, is a very sad one for America and could become a contribution to our final tragedy—our isolation and defeat, perhaps even our annihilation in a world that is marshaled against us. It may seem that at worst we do not quite deserve that fate but such are the conditions that press in upon us. However, more of us than before may be beginning to understand the realities. Some of our political leaders are beginning to mention them. And there may still be time. If we achieve desegregation of our schools in the United States, together with other solutions of our problems of race-relationship, it could have a dramatic effect upon the world. The moral superiority of our way of life over that of the communists would be unmistakable. And we need moral superiority every bit as much as we need military superiority. Perhaps more. We shall surely lose without it. But with it we can win. The sordidness and moral debasement of communism would be seen in all the squalor of its dingy, miserable reality, and its cynical propaganda could do nothing to conceal it.

But we have to *practice* our moral principles before this can happen not merely make excuses while we talk about them. Let us then, each of us, to the full extent of his own opportunity, be dedicated to that end. Let our faith be stronger than our doubt, let our hope shine steadily through the darkness of our disappointment and dismay; while with courage and unfaltering resolution we press onward, diligent in the work that is given us to do.

§39 Marion A. Wright

Marion A. Wright was born on January 18, 1894 in Johnston, South Carolina. He attended the University of South Carolina, where he received his law degree in 1919. Prior to practicing corporate law in Conway, South Carolina, Wright taught public school and was a reporter for the *Columbia Record*. In 1916 he married Lelia Hauser. In Conway, he was chairman of the Illiteracy Commission, as well as a member of the American Civil Liberties Union. From 1951 to 1958 Wright served as president of the Southern Regional Council. He also served the council as vice president from 1958 to 1965. In the following years, Wright founded and became the first president of North Carolinians against the Death Penalty (NCADP). Wright continued to fight for desegregation and the abolition of the death penalty, the two most important issues in his life, until his death on February 14, 1983.

As president and vice president of the Southern Regional Council, Wright often delivered speeches and lectures on important human and civil rights issues, as he used his position to influence his audiences and promote equality. Wright also played a vital role on the board of directors for the American Civil Liberties Union, as he continued to speak out against segregation. His papers are housed at the Southern Historical Collection at the University of North Carolina in Chapel Hill, Winthrop University in Rock Hill, South Carolina, and the University of South Carolina in Columbia.

On September 4, 1957 more than three years after the Supreme Court's ruling in *Brown v. Board of Education*, Charlotte, North Carolina integrated its public schools. In this speech, not long after that historic desegregation, Marion Wright offers a diagnosis of the city's problems and some possible solutions. Several people are singled out by Wright: Emmett Till, John Kasper, and Dorothy Counts. Wright uses Till's death as an illustration of a larger point: what state officials say often gets translated into violent and even deadly actions. Wright also warns that noted racist John Kasper was trying to stir up such actions with his September 1st call on the courthouse steps to rise up against the city's school board and prevent integration. Dorothy Counts integrated Harding High School on September 4. Sadly would she withdraw four days later from the constant harassment, threats, spitting, and even the shattering of a back window of her parents' car. Wright is particularly attuned to media coverage of the school desegregation: "no longer is action undetected or its full significance unappreciated. So, the eyes of the world are upon Charlotte." In fact, a picture of Dorothy Counts amid a long line of hecklers would win the World Press Photo of the Year in 1957.

The problem of school desegregation, notes Wright, is not a political problem so much as a moral problem—and politicians are not well qualified to deal with moral problems. The church, however, is, and Wright calls it out for a policy of silence and inaction—which translates into approval for the status quo. Churches must move from making noble proclamations to allowing their doors to swing wide open.

Integration and Public Morals
Charlotte, North Carolina
November 1957 (reprinted)

I am sure you will appreciate my dilemma. For a week now I have been thinking about what might properly be said to Charlotte people concerning the integration of their schools. I read all the papers. I listened to all the broadcasts. There have been times within the past week when I felt great pride in what was happening here. That came one night as I heard a Voice of America broadcast to Asia. The Voice contrasted Charlotte with Little Rock, explaining that the real sentiment of this country was expressed here. There have been times when I felt shame, as I know you have. What may the Voice of America now say to Asians? How may it gloss over the dark truth?

Well, as the young people would put it, tonight we are all crazy, mixed-up kids. We may feel slight pride—though I am not sure why—but a sense of shame overwhelms us. We may as well be honest. North Carolina has failed Dorothy Counts as Alabama failed Autherine Lucy. They are both casualties of men's blind and unreasoning prejudices. Those prejudices have taken root and flourished because we who don't share them have failed. We did not fail this week or last week. We failed years ago, in our homes, our schools, our churches, in our contacts with people on the street, in all that we said and did—in not removing the scales from men's eyes, in not living up to our proud pretensions about equality before the law.

It would be highly presumptuous of me to attempt a post mortem. That would seem to be the first order of business for this city. In my ignorance of local conditions I may only add to confusion. Of one thing, however, we may be sure. Integration will not fail. The small and precarious bridgehead it holds in this city at the moment will be expanded. The question is whether or not Charlotte has irretrievably sacrificed its leadership among the cities of the South.

With the hot news of the hour beating in upon us, it seems almost academic to deal in generalities, to discuss principles rather than people and events. But we must realize that people come and go. New actors mount the stage. Events are transitory. Tomorrow and the next day there will be new headlines. People and events have significance only because they are involved with principles. Principles abide. So let us discuss them.

One of the clichés we hear most often is that the world is growing smaller. What we really mean is that the community is growing larger—not that the world is narrowing and contracting but that the community is expanding in significance and importance to the point that whatever it says and does—or even thinks—has impact and repercussion throughout the world. A boy named Emmett Till is foully murdered in Mississippi. The shot that blew out his brains is heard round the world. The city of Louisville, with dignity, firmness and rare statesmanship, integrates its schools. That incident too, makes headlines in Bombay and Cairo and Shanghai. No longer in public affairs is anything done in a dark corner; no longer is action undetected or its full significance unappreciated.

So, the eyes of the world are upon Charlotte.

It is well that a forum be provided for presentation of the affirmative side of the integration issue. The negative lacks neither facilities nor spokesmen. Has it not occurred to you as being somewhat unfortunate that discussion of an issue which is of deep concern to parents, teachers and sociologists and which has such pronounced moral and ethical overtones should have been left almost exclusively to the politicians? That the forum should have been, not the school, the Parent-Teacher Association or the church, but the hustings?

Now, there are two reasons why it would seem that the politicians should have no monopoly of discussion of this issue.

In the first place, they have a vested interest in the issue. For as long as any of us here can remember there have been in the South a substantial number of them—few in North Carolina—who have risen to power and retained it by exploiting the race question. In an earlier time when they were bolder and more forthright their shibboleth was white supremacy. More recently they have gone respectable. They no longer use the term. Instead they preach a paternalistic and trusteeship doctrine which must be fully as offensive to our Negro citizens as the ancient militance. They assume to play God to the Negro—tell him in effect, "we are your best friends and we will give you what is good for you." The basic assumption of the paternalistic school is still the innate superiority of the white man.

Such men, happily decreasing in number and influence under the impact of events, have, as I have said, a vested interest in keeping the segregation issue alive. Deprive them of it and their mental bankruptcy would be exposed. We exclude men who have an interest in a lawsuit from serving upon juries because their judgment may not be trusted where their interests are involved. The application to the political school under consideration is too obvious to require expression.

There is another reason why the opinions of political leaders have no peculiar sanctity. It is a field beyond their special competence. If the question involved were entirely political in nature, one might concede the expert qualifications of such leaders. But we are here dealing with a profoundly moral issue. There are involved our sense of fair play, the right of every child to be taught as and where other children are taught, the degree to which we live up to our expressed beliefs in the equality of men before the law, the obligation of men to discharge the citizen's first duty of observing the law.

With due deference, I see nothing in the careers of such men to give them authority superior to our own in the field of morals. What is it that they recommend?

They recommend that we *appear* to be following the mandate of the Supreme Court without actually doing so. They recommend stratagems, ruses, wiles, which everyone knows to be dishonest. They pretend to decentralize the schools, so that there is no apparent state control, necessitating a separate suit against each district rather than one against the state, while setting up Advisory Boards which issue confidential suggestions to school boards that they not comply with law.

In the bright lexicon of genuine statesmanship there is no such word as evasion. In the bright lexicon of honor there is no such word as misrepresentation. Of course, public ethics and morals lag behind individual ethics and morals.

Now, I am usually on the receiving end of admonitions given in church. These verbal chastisements have done me no harm, and—who knows?—may have done me good, even if the results are not apparent. I am sure you will not begrudge me this rare opportunity to strike back. With a feeling almost of awe at my presumption, I venture a few timid words on one duty of a church.

One problem of our times is to close this gap between private and public morals. Certainly, there should be no lowering of individual standards—they are low enough already. But is there any doubt that our public standards may stand a little elevation? I do not want any fuzziness to tincture what I say. I am speaking definitely about the integration of our schools.

More than three years have elapsed since a court, composed of white men, chosen by white men, construing a constitution written by white men, held that segregation in our public schools was unlawful. While in many areas of the South there has been ungrudging compliance with that decision, the course followed elsewhere is not a cause for pride. In the face of an issue and at a time when men should think deeply, speak frankly, act honorably, to what have we been subjected?

There have been two facets to our public policy. One is puerile attacks upon members of the Court and the NAACP, as though the dilemma which now confronts us might never have arisen but for some unholy conspiracy between the two. This blindly overlooks the fact that what has happened in the South is merely part of a world movement for full and complete emancipation of colored peoples. If our leaders feel that they may beat back this upsurge of democratic spirit, I suggest they get brooms, go to Wilmington and try sweeping back the tide. No one of us is going to be dragged, even kicking and screaming, back into the 18th century.

The other facet consists of the evasion and subterfuge I have mentioned. It would be an exercise in morbidity to catalog these accomplished and proposed maneuvers. Suffice it to say that the objective of all of them is to abet and encourage the citizen to fail in his first duty—observe the law.

My thesis is that presentation of these schemes to the public presents also a moral issue to the church. The church, by silence and inaction, by remaining supine, may condone, if not approve, such policy. If religion is actually to be a force in the lives of men, it cannot retreat when confronted by a moral crisis. To do so is to abdicate its authority in the field of ethics. When, later, it seeks to set up standards of conduct in other fields, it may be reminded of its failure in this particular area. More, it will be haunted and its effectiveness blunted by its own consciousness of failure.

Let me be quick to say that already this crisis has produced its own ecclesiastical martyrs. They have not met death or imprisonment. We are a little too subtle and refined for that. But ministers have been assaulted. Others have had their homes and churches bombed. Still others have been relieved of their pastorates. These men are the heroes of this age. Long after some of our public figures have been forgotten, the South, white and Negro, will still pay tribute to Reverend Martin Luther King.

Now, our political leaders without exception deplore violence such as this. They have no truck with the Ku Klux Klan. But my contention is that they set in motion forces which bred the Klan and the very violence they now condemn. What they advocate, in essence, is disrespect for law. They choose to limit such advocacy to one law—that relating to the public schools. But when you enter the area of disrespect there is no such thing as a limited infection. It spreads. What right have they to tell me what laws I shall observe? They choose to flout school law. I may with as much right choose to flout the law which protects life and property of the man who disagrees with me. They seek to get results by chicanery. Men less subtle and sophisticated may perforce get their results by violence. There may be more than a thread of connection between what governors and senators say and what men in Mississippi did to Emmett Till.

Certain governors, following the Supreme Court decisions, announce that a segregated school system must be preserved. They employ all of their cunning to develop methods—private schools with state subsidy, tuition grants, pupil assignment acts, local control, complicated legal steps to be taken by aggrieved parties, redistricting and all the rest of a list of odorous maneuvers. One by one these devices come before the court and are branded for what they are—transparent frauds.

When cunning and what passes for intelligence have failed, what is an *untutored* citizen to do? Well, he has his fists, doesn't he? He has dynamite. He has bombs. He has torches. There rings in his ears the voice of authority telling him segregation must be preserved. So he uses the only tools he knows.

Then how crocodile are the tears of the governor who weeps at violence!

Charlotte and North Carolina have been saved the orgies of violence which have gripped Little Rock and Nashville and other cities only because the citizens here have sufficient intelligence and force of character and loyalty to the constitution to resist the appeal of demagogues.

I am sure, too that these politicians could not have foreseen that their advocacy should have led to a state of public mind which would in certain parts of the South result in substantial curtailment of the right of free speech and opinion. Certainly from this blight, North Carolina is far more free than most southern states. But let us indulge in no vainglory. It can happen here—and will, unless we are vigilant. Teacher's oaths, requirement that they list their organizations, the proscribing of the NAACP, boycott of advocates of law observance, withdrawal of advertising from certain newspapers—all these present an imminent peril. They flow directly from the germinal idea of evading the law of the land.

There is no more alarming phenomenon of this age than this mass effort to control what men shall publicly say or print. Opinion is the life blood of democracy. Upon its free expression democracy thrives and grows. You will not have sound opinion unless men may freely express and exchange views—test them in the marketplace. Thought itself is actually inhibited where it cannot be freely expressed. For, where all *seem* to be thinking alike no one is *actually* thinking at all.

So, we observe elsewhere the already achieved results of the official policy of evading the law—results which I am sure were not in contemplation of those who fashioned the policy. Legal chicanery and subterfuge have sired economic boycott, suppression of thought, and raw violence.

I ask you, as reasonable men and women, if other results are not in prospect unless the policy is reversed. Thus far, the legal subterfuges relate only to integration of our schools; boycott, suppression of thought and violence are directed only against advocates of compliance with school law. Will they stop there? If the rights of one minority group may be thus assailed, what about the rights of others? The Jews, the Catholics, the labor unions—any group that doesn't have the power of government in its hands? The rights of none of us are safe unless the rights of all of us are safe.

I have been at some pains to point out where we have drifted under our present policy and whither we tend. Always the point must be conceded that, in comparison with certain other states, North Carolina has high standards of respectability. The hysteria and violence found elsewhere have *so far* not gripped this commonwealth.

Now, in recent weeks one event has occurred in North Carolina which demonstrates, in a small way, at least, the growing resolution of our people to act honorably and decently. I refer, of course, to the action of school boards of Charlotte, Greensboro and Winston-Salem. I am quite frank in saying that the action was of a more limited nature than some might have thought possible. But what one of us can say what he would have done if he had been a member of the board? Certainly, the pressure upon the boards to continue to drift must have been considerable. Certainly, moral courage was required to resist that pressure. And that is a quality sufficiently rare to deserve the commendation and gratitude of all good citizens. It has been heartening to those of us out in the provinces of North Carolina to observe that, almost without exception, from all responsible quarters, commendation and gratitude have been expressed. Here, at least, the strident accents of the John Kaspers have fallen upon deaf ears.

Practically all of us have come to agree, I think, that the shabbiest and sorriest figure of our times is the man who would drive lines of cleavage among men. We need not walls to separate men from each other but bridges to connect, not sundering but unifying influences. The greatest public servant of our day is the one who breaks down artificial barriers with which men have sought to create the illusion of their superiority to other men.

No one of us may be a Gandhi or a Schweitzer. We lack their mental and spiritual endowments. But every one of us, to the limits of such endowments as he has, may, on this continent, in North Carolina—yes, in Charlotte—partake of the spirit of these men, spend his life to the same noble purposes.

What may we do? It is easy enough to entertain great sentiments. Translating those sentiments into wise deeds presents our practical problem. Answers will suggest themselves to each individual. I propose only the more obvious.

The first goes to our states of mind. We should constantly remind ourselves that the Negro parent is knocking on our school doors only because he wants his child to have the best this city offers for the education of his children. I think we should greatly resent having someone else tell us we don't know what is good for our children. We should reject the easy hypothesis that the Negro child is better off in his own school. The courts say that is not true. Every student of human behavior says it is not true.

The one lay organization concerned with out schools is the Parent-Teacher Association. There should be no segregation in such groups. If revision of bylaws is necessary to accomplish integration, they should be revised. At any rate, simple democracy requires that the voices of all of us should be equally heard, the influence of all of us be equally felt, in improving the standards of education.

The same reasons require that there should be Negro representation on boards of trustees and all other official bodies concerned with our schools. This should be no mere token or nominal representation. The appointees should be able and vigorous exponents of the Negro point-of-view. The comfortable assumptions—hangover from slavery days—that we know what is best for the Negro and are qualified to act as trustees for him must be tossed out the window. All of our history has demonstrated their falsity.

We must bear in mind that the Negro children who attend, or will attend, white schools are exercising rights guaranteed to them by the Constitution. Everyone deserves protection in the exercise of his rights. We should inform our police officials that they have our full support in guarding the persons and property of Negro children and parents involved, and that they will be held accountable for failure to do so.

Parenthetically, let me concede that you are in much better position than I to appraise the conduct of your law enforcement officers. But from my remote observation post, the impression was acquired that they reflected great credit on your city. Promptness and firmness upon the part of police officers are cardinal factors in the school situation.

We should realize, too, that the one or two Negro children in white schools are under emotional stress. They are in a strange environment with few, if any, friends enduring the same ordeal. They experience the loneliness of all pioneers. White parents may mitigate the rigors of the experiment, reduce its bruises and abrasions, by counseling their children to show courtesy to, and deal generously with, the brave child of another color.

The white mother, feeling that she makes some sacrifice, undergoes some disagreeable experience, in sending her child to a school attended also by a Negro child, should reflect for a moment upon the anguish of the Negro mother. Sometimes she walks through hostile groups to reach the steps of the school—at actual risk of physical violence. Always she hands over her child to a white faculty and into an association bewilderingly unfamiliar, if not resentful and challenging. Only the profoundest maternal instincts and limitless ambition for her child sustain her in that hour.

Out of the welter of last week's events we caught for a moment the image of a white woman taking a small Negro girl by the hand and leading her to a taxi, telling the angry crowd all that was important to a mother, "she's just a little girl."

One knew in that instant that integration will not fail. The bravery and courage and noble ambition of Negro mothers and their children are matched by the tenderness and compassion of white mothers. They are matched also by the nobility of the white girls who took the new girl by the hand and gave her welcome. Such are the permanent, the irresistible, forces.

The churches play a crucial role. Their own racial barriers much be lowered if they are to assume leadership in this new adventure in brotherhood. The pious resolution, adopted at some convention, while excellent as a proclamation of principle, is not enough. The doors of the church should be swung wide, not merely cracked an inch. It should not be necessary for a Negro minister to go from Charlotte to Quebec in order to preach the gospel of Jesus Christ to white people.

Finally, none of us should approach this great social experience negatively, in the frame of mind that this is the law and we shall make the best of a bad bargain. It is the law and a good bargain to boot. In the discussion the emphasis has been placed upon the injuries inflicted upon the Negro by our segregation system. They are considerable and grievous. But the whites have suffered too.

If segregation, as the court has said, has engendered feelings of inferiority in the Negro, it has also engendered feelings of superiority in the white man. These feelings of superiority, resting upon no solid base, tend to make us arrogant and proud. We suffer from delusions of grandeur. Arrogance and pride are not virtues. Indeed, we are not told that the arrogant shall inherit the earth. We are not told that humility goeth before destruction.

Moreover, as a society we have not permitted the Negro to pull his share of the load. We have assigned him to menial tasks and resolutely barred his advancement. Hence, the more skilled, the more intelligent, the ablest, migrate. This waste of Negro potential places extra burdens upon the whites. If there is actually "a white man's burden," it is a burden of his own creation.

All of us in North Carolina have come to take great pride in Charlotte. We take your papers. We listen to your radio. We look at your TV. The commercial, industrial and financial primacy of your city is assured. No one minimizes the importance of such achievement. Thus, the achievements of a certain rich young ruler were beyond cavil.

Success in the great experiment here and now undertaken would be the brightest jewel in your crown. Less resolute communities would be heartened by your example. So you may lead this great state into the way of full and complete democracy.

1958

1958

§40 Reverend James R. Bullock

Reverend James R. Bullock received his B.D. from Union Seminary in Richmond, Virginia, and his doctorate from Edinburgh University. His cultural legacy is manifest in the churches he helped build. First Presbyterian Church of Gladewater, where he first served, is a small congregation in a town of about 6,000 people with at least 32 other churches. Canal Street Presbyterian (New Orleans), where he served in the mid-1940s, proudly claims as one of its accomplishments the founding of a Chinese Presbyterian congregation. It also displays the script over the entrance: "For Mine House Shall be Called an House of Prayer for All People." From 1947 to 1957 Bullock served Second Presbyterian in Houston, which merged with St. Matthew's Presbyterian to become Grace Presbyterian, which now offers *cursillos*, the Spanish term for short courses.

Reverend Bullock had just moved his family to Jackson, Tennessee when he delivered his speech on reconciliation. First Presbyterian Church of Jackson now proudly displays its S.I.G.N. (Service in God's Name) program, where people of all races volunteer side by side to build homes for people in need. But west Tennessee was not such a place in the 1950s. The church session (board) had voted to close its doors to African Americans. Bullock wrote a protest in the minutes of the session meeting, and welcomed civil rights activists into his church. He stayed with his Jackson congregation 18 years, while it slowly transformed its stance toward race. His son, Reverend James R. Bullock, Jr., notes that during this time his father "loved and preached his way through those segregated walls." The Presbytery of Memphis, the audience of the following address, consisted primarily of white male clergy and elders, but included some leaders from predominantly African American congregations as well. Participants came from a broad array of vocations.

Bullock begins his speech with historian Arnold Toynbee's optimistic conclusion that civilizations can survive perpetually by adjusting to the eternal. This adjustment to the eternal is reconciliation, or a restoration of fellowship between God and His creature. But malignant human relationships block eternal restoration. Paul's exhortations to the churches of Ephesus, Corinth, and Rome are important models for restoration for the rapidly changing southern congregation as is the beatitude of peacemaking. But the end of the speech turns to a realist approach to the context of enmity, and cautions fellow pastors and lay ministers that they will struggle against the persistence of indifference, selfishness, resentment and, guilt. Bullock is no ordinary country preacher as he breathes life into Arnold Toynbee, Henrik Ibsen, sacred Christian texts, and a nation still recovering from slavery, secession, and war.

As with many other white ministers preaching in the troubled South, Bullock's approach to race is understated, referenced but twice in the whole sermon. But

Bullock's message is quite clear: reconciliation of people to God and to each other knows no racial or class distinctions. No doubt this subtle approach to race and Christianity allowed Bullock—and many other southern ministers—to work on the problem even as their messages often lacked overt signifiers that might inflame prejudiced congregants.

———

The Ministry of Reconciliation

Presbytery of Memphis, Memphis, Tennessee
April 22, 1958

Arnold Toynbee, the great historian of civilization, was asked if Western civilization must inevitably perish as one after another of the great cultures of the past have failed. He replied: "No, in order to endure it has only to fulfill a basic condition, that is, become adjusted to the eternal." He was applying in the realm of the spiritual the same fundamental law which conditions the survival of all things. To endure, physical life must adjust to its environment by adaptation in food, clothing, shelter. Hence moral, social, political, spiritual life must adjust to the eternal if it is to endure. The historian and philosopher was touching upon the need for reconciliation, a need that is both personal and social, mundane and cosmic, present and eternal.

Man is forever facing some strain, some tension between himself and his environment, particularly between himself and his fellow human beings, between himself and his God. He may be imperfectly conscious of this enmity, only dimly aware that it is there, but life is disquieted none the less and consciously or unconsciously a man longs for peace, for reconciliation. It is a personal problem. As personal beings we need reconciliation with a personal God, from whom we have turned away in stubborn perversity and pride. Although we fail to realize it at times, estrangement from God means estrangement from our neighbors as well. The heart of reconciliation lies in the personal restoration of true fellowship between God and His creature. When that relationship is restored, then all other relationships straighten themselves out.

We need not labor the point concerning the need for reconciliation, but we need to be reminded of some aspects of it. The daily headlines, speaking of the snarled relationship between our nation and France over the pitiful conflict in North Africa, point to the widening chasm between the privileged and under-privileged nations of the earth. Closer home, but demanding just as much our concern, are the growing divisions between races and classes. Every minister knows from the personal confidences of his study how deep are the enmities which separate individuals, which bring chaotic strife to society, business relationships, the home. Underlying all this is the fact that many of us are living in a far country so far as God is concerned. The heart of our malignant relationships with our fellows is a malignant relationship to God.

With a rare sensitiveness born of a deep concern for men and with prophetic insight concerning an answer to man's greatest need, Paul made central in his message the doctrine of reconciliation. Sometimes a man in his writings is able in a single phrase to express the whole purpose of his life and to identify himself with a larger and more inclusive purpose. Surely this can be said concerning Paul's phrase, "the ministry of reconciliation." In it we catch a vision of the heart and soul of this man of God who did so much to bring the world of his day to Christ.

What did Paul mean by reconciliation? To him it was the key to God's attitude toward men, His will for their salvation, His work in Christ. "God was in Christ, reconciling the world to Himself, not counting their trespasses against them." To remove the enmity in the heart of man, to tear down the walls of estrangement between men and God, this Paul conceived to be the purpose of God in Christ.

With that purpose Paul identified himself and all Christians. To saved men God had entrusted the message of reconciliation. Triumphantly he asserts, "we are ambassadors for Christ, God making his appeal through us." So the reconciling love of God was to be mediated through members of Christ's church, both in life as well as in words. The supreme purpose of the church was to reconcile men to God.

Paul was well aware of the fact that one of the greatest obstacles separating men from God was their enmity toward each other. How often he appealed to the people of the churches to whom he wrote to put aside those things that separated them. To the Ephesians he wrote, "Do not grieve the Holy Spirit of God in whom you were sealed for the day of redemption. Let all bitterness and wrath and anger and clamor and slander be put away from you, with all malice, and be kind to one another, tenderhearted, forgiving one another, as God in Christ forgave you." How well he perceived that the fears and suspicions that were tearing these people apart were also grieving the Holy Spirit, alienating from God Himself! Consider other instances of this same concern.

When Paul wrote the First Letter to the Corinthians he greeted his friends in his usual manner and proceeded at once to his main purpose in writing, which was reconciliation. "I appeal to you brethren," he says, "by the name of the Lord Jesus Christ that all of you agree that there be no dissensions among you, but that you be united in the same mind and the same judgment. For it has been reported to me by Chloe's people that there is quarrelling among you, my brethren." And from this point he proceeds to counsel them concerning the serious rifts which had appeared in the church over their differences concerning personalities, moral and social problems, and questions of doctrine. Indeed the theme of the book might well be stated as "answering the problems of a divided church." The purpose of the apostle was fundamentally reconciliation.

In the same spirit Paul wrote to the Roman Church concerning the differences which had arisen in their congregation over vegetarianism and the observance of the Jewish Sabbath. In his counsel to this church he emphasized several principles:

First—that each man is responsible to God alone and must follow his conscientious convictions;

Second—that fellow Christians should respect each other's convictions;

Third—that each individual must have regard not only to his own conscientious scruples, but must examine carefully the effects of his acts upon others;

Fourth—above all, that Christians should live under God, as members of His kingdom. The strong should bear with the failings of the weak in all things, each striving not to please himself, but to "please his neighbor for his good, to edify him. For Christ did not please Himself."

The apostle climaxes his appeal for reconciliation with the ardent prayer: "May God of steadfastness and encouragement grant you to live in such harmony with one another, in accordance with Christ Jesus, that together you may with one voice glorify the God and father of our Lord Jesus Christ."

In this instance on reconciliation between men estranged Paul followed in the footsteps of Jesus who over and over again stressed the necessity for peace. "Blessed are the peacemakers," He said, "for they shall be called the children of God." The followers of Jesus are called to peace. They have found their peace in Christ through forgiveness. He is their peace. But they are told that if they have it they must make it. To that end they renounce all strife and division. In the cause of Christ they realize that nothing is gained by force. His is a peaceful kingdom and the ends are achieved by love and persuasion. To His church is committed the great task of reconciliation—of men to God through the preaching of the atonement—of men to men through the practice of self-sacrificial love. It is not simply the "peace-keepers" that Jesus blesses, those who purchase peace at any price, but those who actively reconcile and enlarge the area of human goodwill. By so doing they prove their moral kinship to the God of peace.

But in this whole question of reconciliation, of peace-making, we must be realistic, not sentimental in our approach to our task. It does no good to cry "Peace, peace, when there is no peace." So we must turn to another question. WHAT ARE THE SOURCES OF DISHARMONY? Why are men estranged from one another and from God? There are many reasons.

INDIFFERENCE is a prime cause. Men are estranged from God because He is not in their thoughts. The Psalmist in describing the wicked says, "All his thoughts are—there is no God." Some men are so far from God that they may lack a conscious sense of estrangement. God is to them an empty voice. They live as if He did not exist. C. S. Lewis in his description of Hell "The Great Divorce" pictures men as living in a great gray city at a tremendous distance from God—light years away! With keen insight Mr. Lewis describes those remote people as also living at tremendous distances from each other, so far that communication is impossible. Is not this one of the great reasons for our estrangement from our fellows—indifference, unconcern, the loss of all communication? It is easier to believe that men about whom we know nothing are evil men.

SELFISHNESS, which leads us to seek our own way in defiance of what we know in our heart of hearts is right, is another potent source of disharmony with God. How many forms it takes—like the many heads of the ancient hydra—self-will, self-indulgence, self-pity, self-complacency, self-righteousness, all having their root in human pride and wilfulness. You remember the legend of the hydra, how when one head was cut off another took its place? Such is our condition. How well Ibsen describes it in his play "Peer Gynt." Peer asks the keeper of the madhouse in Cairo if the people in his institution are beside themselves and receives this answer:

> "Outside? No, there you are strangely mistaken
> It's here, sir, that one is oneself with a vengeance;
> Each one shuts himself up in the barrel of self
> No one has tears for another's woes;
> No one has mind for another's ideas.
> We're our very selves in thought and tone."

So the selfishness which sets up high walls between us and God, builds the same barriers between us and our fellows.

RESENTMENT against God also enters into this picture of estrangement. The bitter people of this world blame God for the seeming hopelessness of life, its sorrows and evils. It springs from a blindness to the love of God. Sometimes it is blatant; sometimes it hides underneath a seemingly pious resignation. It may be derived from the resentment of childhood toward a domineering parent. It results in a man having a grievance against all creation, against God Himself.

But how similar is this emotion to the resentments which separate us from our fellows! These spring from envy of the positions, powers, possessions, endowments of others. It may grow out of a distaste for criticism, a rebellion against scorn and belittling. Some man makes us feel small and we hate him for it. Another succeeds where we fail and bitterness sets in.

GUILT is the natural end of all these causes of estrangement. It is a sense of moral failure, unworthiness, moral impotence. It comes like a shadow between the soul and God, like the moon coming between the earth and the sun in an eclipse, shutting out the light. Specious arguments do not help it. Absolving ourselves from responsibility for our wrong doing is merely self deception and cannot remove the load. It hangs around our neck like the dead albatross around the neck of the Ancient Mariner in Coleridge's poem, and only a miracle of grace can remove it.

As guilt separates from God, so it alienates men from each other. A man cannot bear to face a person he has wronged, a man whom he has robbed of possessions or reputation, a friend to whom he has been disloyal, a marriage partner to whom he has been untrue.

As we face such estrangement, how can we overcome these obstacles which bring enmity and strife? What is required for reconciliation? We are entrusted with this ministry of reconciliation as Christians, as a church. Our job is the transmission of the message in life as well as in word. We are to be the instruments of God's peace. When a man is reconciled to God he is also reconciled to God's way, the way of love, of sacrificial devotion. If he lives in this way, he becomes an instrument of God's peace, bringing men to peace with God and to peace with each other. He becomes one of the blessed peace makers whom Christ called the children of God. So the church is in truth a fellowship of reconciliation. Reconciliation is not easy. It is extremely costly. How great was the cost of God's reconciliation through Christ! Someone writing of the love of the Shepherd for His sheep says:

> "But none of the ransomed ever knew
> How deep were the waters crossed,
> And how dark was the night that the
> Lord passed through,
> Ere he found His sheep that was lost."

It required that depth of love to reconcile us to God. It will take that sort of love to reconcile men to each other. Jesus said "Love one another." We love our own homes, our wives, our families, our friends. We are ready to do almost anything to secure the happiness of our loved ones and ourselves. We cherish our own opinions and ways of living and we are at great pains to perpetuate these. But Jesus tells us to step out of our own door, to look beyond our own garden. He would have us bring within the compass of our love every life that we touch and those far away from us as well. He tells us that we may have to give up our cherished opinions and way of life.

We may have to endure suffering and scorn, but that is the way of the cross, the way of reconciliation.

The way of love requires faith, the assumption of risk. We can never be sure that our overtures of peace will be accepted or ever understood. God loved us even when we rejected Him. "When we were yet sinners Christ died for the ungodly." We may have to launch out into the deep, prepared for disappointment, failure. Ours may be a defeat like that of President Wilson when his great dream of a League of Nations was rejected by his own country; or, like that of Paul who was given harsh treatment by members of the Corinthian church he sought to reconcile. Nevertheless, we must take the venture of faith. The older Archbishop Temple said in Westminster Abbey many years ago "We are not adventurers in the spirit of love and therefore we are not winning the world to the way of Christ." He could say the same today.

The way of love requires understanding. Communication is a difficulty. Curiously enough, in a world where a whisper can be heard across the sea in a moment, we do not understand our neighbors. It has often been said "We rub elbows with many but rub hearts with few." I heard a radio news commentator say the other day "This is the age of the misunderstood." Nations, races, individuals do not understand each other. We shout at one another across chasms of ignorance, misinterpretation and suspicion when we ought to be listening patiently to each other, judging each other in the spirit of Christ and according to His standards, not ours.

In the last analysis, reconciliation of men to God and men to each other is not a task we undertake alone. We are but instruments of God. It is through the work of His Spirit that men find peace. "The fruit of the Spirit is . . . peace." When the Spirit works in our lives and in all relationships we shall surely make peace.

God has given to us this ministry of reconciliation. Surely in the Church of Christ today men should find peace and a "unity of Spirit," a unity which transcends our differences. Macaulay somewhere speaks of Westminster Abbey as "That temple of silence and reconciliation where the enmities of twenty generations lie buried . . . the great Abbey which has for many ages afforded a resting place to those whose minds and bodies have been shattered by the great hall." Men of many opinions do rest there together, many of them sworn enemies in life. It is significant that they rest in peace together only because they are dead! But there is something symbolic in the reflection of the historian. Where but in and through the church, the fellowship of Christ, can men find the peace for which their hearts long in this world? The fact that the visible church has not always been at peace, and that there have been and still are many divisions and dissensions, is simply a challenge to us to make peace as we exercise the ministry of reconciliation.

§41 Dr. J. R. Brokhoff

Dr. J. R. Brokhoff's biography appears in the introduction to his August 22, 1954 sermon in Atlanta, Georgia. In the following sermon before the congregants at St. Mark's Lutheran Church in Charlotte, Reverend Brokhoff preaches on the inevitability of God's will. He argues that in the quest for freedom and justice, God's will cannot be denied by human hands—at least not in the long term. As the early church of the first century spread the gospel, and the Protestant reformers of the sixteenth century spread the truth of a personal God, the movement for racial justice and equality would not be denied. Nor would the larger worldwide movement of colonized people be denied. Rhetorically Brokhoff's strategy before a potentially hostile audience is brilliant: deny human agency even while giving irresistible historical agency to the will of God. To oppose God, therefore, is to deny the historical sweep of a sovereign and just and inevitable providence: "Integration, as an aspect of God's movement for justice, is inevitable; it cannot be stopped . . . the cause of human justice cannot be stopped by any man. It is of God."

───────

Life's Inevitables—Three Things You Cannot Stop
St. Mark's Lutheran Church, Charlotte, North Carolina
August 17, 1958

"But if it is of God, you will not be able to overthrow them. You might even be found opposing God!" Acts 5:39

Our modern scientific age has filled us with bravado and self-confidence. We believe there is nothing we cannot do, no place where we cannot go, nothing we cannot stop. We can shoot for the moon or sail under the polar ice cap. The spirit of our age was expressed by the Seabees of the last war, "Miracles we do at once; the impossible takes a little longer." It is evident that we are very much like the Pharisee in the temple at prayer, "I thank Thee that I am not like other men. . . . I fast twice a week, I give tithes of all I possess." We need more the spirit of humility expressed by the publican who beat his breast saying, "God, be merciful to me a sinner."

We would get that humility if we would stop to realize how many things in life we cannot stop. Who can tell the dawn not to come? Who can stand by the sea and command the tide not to come in? Who is able to demand that the clock stop its tick-tock? Who can avoid death? These are some of the things in life that are inevitable. They give us no trouble. We accept them, adjust to them, cooperate with them.

However, our trouble comes when we try to stop other things that equally cannot be stopped. The city fathers of Jerusalem faced that situation at the time of the original disciples. The Christian movement was spreading and turning the world upside down. They thought they were finished with

Jesus when they nailed him to the cross. Now he came alive again in the preaching and work of the disciples. They tried to stop them. They commanded they stop preaching about him. They threatened them with death if they did not stop. They put them in prison. Every time, however, they found the movement broke out in a new place. They were stymied. At their wits' end they called in Gamaliel, their most renowned teacher, and asked for his advice. Being a very wise man, he gave them sane and sound counsel. He told them that if this Christian movement were of men, it like other religious movements would in due time die out of its own accord. But, "if it is of God, you will not be able to overthrow them. You might even be found opposing God!"

Gamaliel sensed the truth facing us this morning. Whatever is of God cannot be stopped. It is one of life's inevitables. You can curse, scold, threaten, and persecute the movement of God, but you cannot permanently thwart its forward progress. You and I cannot stop the ongoing purposes of God in society. If we try, we shall be found opposing God.

One of the on-going purposes of God is truth. God is truth. God is for truth. God supports truth. It cannot be killed, just as God cannot be killed. For a time it can be hidden and suppressed, but it will break out again in due time. Paul wrote to Timothy while fettered in prison, but Paul assured his spiritual son that the Word of God was not fettered. God's Word can never be bound.

Yet men try to stop the ultimate victory of truth. This was the case in the 16th century at the time when the great idea of the Bible, salvation by grace through faith alone, was rediscovered by the Protestant reformers. The established church did all in its power to wipe out the evangelical "heresy." They threatened, imprisoned, tortured, and persecuted. The harder they hit the new movement of truth, the farther in they drove the nail of Protestantism. Will Durant in his recent *History of the Reformation* tells of a French Protestant leader, Jean Leclerc. This wool carder of Meaux tore down a bishop's bull of indulgences. He was arrested and the Parliament of Paris sentenced him to be branded on the forehead. This did not deter him. He went to Metz where he smashed the images before which incense was to be offered. For this the Catholic authorities cut off his right hand, tore off his nose, and burned him alive. This is not an isolated case. It was repeated thousands of times to suppress the truth of the Scriptures. They failed. You cannot stop the march of truth. The Protestant faith still lives and continues to grow. As long as the Protestant church is a mouthpiece for God's Word, it shall never die and will continue to grow and spread until the whole world accepts the truth of God.

In our own day we find the modern church to some extent here and there opposing the gospel. It can be found in the criticism and lack of support given to the Billy Graham crusades. Some may not like Graham's preaching or his methods of mass evangelism. Therefore, they do not cooperate or support his crusades when they come to their cities. Is this movement of God or not? Who can deny that the gospel is not preached and that Christ is not upheld and exalted? Is it not true that the Bible is honored and expounded? No one can deny that Billy Graham's crusades make whole cities more religiously conscious than any other speaker or project. If this movement is of God to call men to repentance, than to oppose it is to work against God.

This truth applies to us personally. We cannot stop the truth in our own personal lives. For a time we may lie and get away with it. We may for years be living a lie, but some day the truth will out. Others may be successful at our expense because they have lied about us. But truth in this case is on our side, and God is behind the truth. Some day there will be a victory for truth, and those who hold to it will share in that victory. No man can permanently live a lie. He will perish with the lie, for we cannot stop the ultimate victory of truth.

Another on-going purpose of God in society is freedom. God made man free. He meant men to be free. There is an instinctive cry in every man's heart for freedom. Men cannot be permanently subordinated or suppressed. For a while men and nations can be exploited and enslaved. But there is a reckoning day coming. Freedom in human hearts will begin to burn and will not be put out until freedom is gained. This is because God is in and for freedom. We cannot be defeated.

In our world today we find this movement for national freedom in many nations. It is expressing itself in nationalism. Throughout the world the idea of freedom has caught fire, and the movement for national independence cannot be stopped. In the Near East and North Africa we have Arab nationalism which is now one of the primary concerns of the world. Students of Africa tell us about the rising masses of former colonial nations who now demand their freedom. The same is true in the East and Indonesia. Everywhere millions of men formerly suppressed and oppressed by larger, more powerful nations are coming to life and demanding freedom from slavery, both political and economic.

Our country is in the very midst of this movement. It is a very uncomfortable position, because we are caught between our allies in NATO and the rising masses demanding freedom. We are not espousing the cause of freedom for these people because the NATO powers, Britain, Belgium, and France, have some of these people under their rule. Since we say nothing because of expediency, the masses blame America for their troubles. Throughout the world today there is a terrible feeling of ill will against America.

If only we in America could catch the meaning of this truth this morning and would declare ourselves in support of freedom everywhere, overnight we would find America in the position of being the champion of human and national freedom. At this moment, such a stand would, no doubt, offend the NATO powers, but it would be temporary. These imperialist nations are slowly and inevitably going to lose their colonies. Nothing can stop the trend toward national independence. In the long run, America would be on the right side, because it would be on the side of freedom, which is of God.

We cannot stop the forward march of freedom. Men some day will be free. Why then do we not cooperate with God rather than oppose him by championing the cause of freedom everywhere regardless of whom we may offend by the stand? Have we Americans forgotten 1776? Did we not once cry out for freedom? How then can we stand idly by in this generation which cries for independence?

A third on-going purpose of God in society today is justice. The cause of justice among men cannot be stopped. This is due to the fact that God is associated with justice, for God himself is justice.

We are living at a time when there are all kinds of injustice in our society: religious, economic, political, and social injustices. These exist for a time, because evil men thwart the will of God by suppressing men and depriving them of their innate rights. But men cannot permanently keep millions as second-class citizens or force them to be subordinates through enforced segregation.

Today in our country we are face to face with racial injustice. There is a movement on foot, as you well know, to get justice for all races and classes in our country. This movement is called integration. Now, integration is not really the issue. It is only a symptom of the more basic movement for human justice. The movement now on foot cannot be stopped. Integration will some day be a fact in our country, because it is a movement of God's justice. Slowly but surely whether we like it or not, whether we oppose it or support it, integration is coming in American society. Already tremendous progress has been made. In 1957, 122,000 Negro pupils attended formerly all-white public schools.

It is true, however, that this movement of God can be hampered and delayed. We can pass state laws forbidding integration, and for a time the process will be held up. We can resort to violence and through it cause so much fear that people will be afraid to demand justice for themselves or others. There can be the use of troops to enforce segregation, but this is only a temporary emergency stop-gap. Indeed, there will be the Faubuses of Arkansas, the Capeharts of Alabama, the Talmadges of Georgia, and the Almonds of Virginia, but one day they will pass away. They can hold back the tide for a short while, but they are defeated before they begin. Any politician who bases his campaign upon the segregation issue may be elected today because of prejudice and fear held by the majority, but he is associated with a cause that has no future. Integration, as an aspect of God's movement for justice, is inevitable; it cannot be stopped. How it will come and how fast it should come and to what extent we Christians should have a part in the movement is another problem which we do not have time to discuss in this sermon. At this time let it be sufficient to know that the cause of human justice cannot be stopped by any man. It is of God.

In considering the justice of God, we must note that we cannot stop the consequences of violating God's justice. When we do wrong, we offend divine justice. And there is always a price to pay for it.

We may, for instance, do wrong and thereby start a chain reaction of innocent suffering on others. We may be sorry right after we have done it, but we cannot stop the consequences from being visited upon the innocent. Take this matter of words. We may tell a malicious story about a friend. The gossip begins to spread. Who can stop the story from going from person to person and getting larger and larger as it proceeds? A father once opened a bag of feathers in the high wind. He told his son to pick them up. After a while he returned and said it was impossible. The father said, "Let that be a lesson to you, son. The words you say are like the feathers. They go everywhere and you will never be able to get them back."

The same can be said for the deeds we do. We cannot avoid the evil consequences of our misdeeds. Judas Iscariot, as you know, sold Jesus to the Pharisees for 30 pieces of silver. After he turned Jesus over to his enemies, he realized how wrong he was. He came back with the money to the religious leaders and asked them to take back the money. He confessed that he betrayed innocent blood. But, he could not get the men to release Jesus. Judas started a process that would not stop until death. Though he was sorry for his betrayal, he could not stop the movement leading to the cross no matter how badly he wanted the evil movement stopped.

In our personal lives we cannot avoid the consequences of God's justice. Of course, some of us think we can. We proudly say, "I will get by" or "It won't happen to me," or "They won't catch me." Remember the words of Paul: "God is not mocked for whatever a man sows that he will also reap." There is the inevitable law of God. You cannot sow one thing and reap another, neither in kind or in quantity. Sow wild oats in your youth and you will reap a wild harvest of suffering and degradation. There is no avoiding this law of God's justice. The consequences of evil action cannot be stopped.

This applies to a nation. Last Sunday we meditated upon Jesus' appeal to Jerusalem to accept him that the city may have peace. Because they refused his offer, he foretold about the city's destruction. In 70 AD the Romans came and sacked the city. The people were either killed or expelled. That was the end of the city and Jewish nation. The consequence of not accepting Christ was inevitable. God's justice eventually came.

This is true with an individual life. Felix, you remember, was the Roman Governor at Caesarea before whom Paul appeared for trial. He often heard Paul privately tell about the gospel. Each time he pushed Paul off and delayed a decision about Christ by saying, "At a more convenient season I will hear you." For two years he unjustly held Paul in prison and refused to release Paul as an innocent man. He was hoping for a gift of money from Paul. Felix was an unusual man, because he was the first slave ever to become a Roman governor. He refused Christ and his way of life, and eventually he paid the consequences. He placed himself on the wrong side in a conflict between Gentiles and Jews. In the upheaval many lost their lives. He was released from his position, and only his brother's influence with Nero saved him from execution. Felix became a name of shame. Reject Christ and you cannot stop the consequences of defeat and death!

In our individual lives we cannot stop the consequences of violating God's justice. When we do wrong, the consequence is a disturbed conscience. It cannot be stopped. It keeps saying, "Shame on you! You know you have done wrong." We try to stop the voice. We may take to drinking until we are drunk, but when we get sober back comes the voice, "Shame on you! You know you have done wrong." We may take to losing ourselves in busyness. We fill our lives with as many appointments and tasks as possible to try to forget. Yet, at every time of silence such as before retiring or upon getting up in the morning, back comes that voice that gives us inner turmoil. Or, we may try to silence the cry of conscience by filling our lives with pleasures, and go out for fun and thrills. But between thrills, there is the voice that keeps saying, "You should be ashamed! You know you have done wrong."

There is only one thing to do in a case like that. Surrender to God. Turn to Him in repentance. Beg for his forgiveness. Then, the soul will be relieved of the agonizing cry of conscience through the infinite love and mercy of God.

These are the on-going purposes of God in our society today—truth, freedom, and justice. We cannot stop them! Crucify them and you glorify them. Bury them and you give them an Easter Day. Delay them and you make their ultimate victory the more overwhelming. Now we are confronted with a major proposition: are we for God or opposing Him? You might react by saying: "How preposterous! I love God. I believe in Him. Christ is my Savior. I am a Christian. Of course, I want to be on God's side." Yet it is possible to be unconsciously against God. Jesus once told his disciples that the day would come when they would be put to death by those who thought they were doing God's service.

How can we know whether or not we are supporting or opposing God in the world of today? The experience of Peter can help us here. One time he was asked to come to the home of a Gentile, Cornelius, to tell about the gospel. In his day there was as much religious and racial prejudice as there is today. Peter hesitated to go. Then he had a vision. He saw a large sheet full of clean and unclean animals being let down from heaven. He was commanded to kill and eat them. He objected because he protested that he never in his life ate anything unclean. The voice said, "What God has cleansed, you must not call common." Peter went to Cornelius and preached the gospel. After the event his critics condemned him for going to a Gentile home. Peter answered by telling about his vision and said, "Who was I that I could withstand God?"

Each of us needs a similar vision to see that the things of God cannot be stopped. We need this vision to pierce through our blind prejudice and bigotry. Then, when we see that the movements of truth, liberty, and justice are of God, we too shall ask, "Who was I that I could withstand God?"

§42 Reverend Fred L. Shuttlesworth

Fred L. Shuttlesworth's biography appears in the introduction to his June 5, 1957 speech in Birmingham, Alabama. In the following brief but fascinating address to the Fair Share Organization of Gary, Indiana, Reverend Shuttlesworth evokes a favorite image from the outset—that of the Holy War for freedom and the recruitment of God's soldiers. Always a fighting militant himself, Shuttlesworth peppers this address with the prophets of the Old Testament and the propagators of the New Testament. Addressed primarily to the black clergy, a class-conscious group notoriously slow to action in many instances, Shuttlesworth repeatedly commands them to action—merely talking about political action is not a substitute. That movement has no need of "Uncle Toms, Professor Toms and Classy Maes"; these folks simply need to "hush."

While Shuttlesworth had a well-earned reputation for involving his whole family in the movement, and for being somewhat progressive on gender issues, he excoriates black women for being "bob-tailed and bossy," for wearing "short hair or Sack dresses," and for "nakedness or scant clothing." Whites are looking for anything to make light of "Negro morals," thus old-fashioned decorum must prevail. But the black clergy also gets Shuttlesworth's invective: the gap between "the classes and the masses must be closed." Moreover, he thunders that "Our Ministers—our first line Soldiers of God—must now understand that Christian Religion is concerned with the whole social, economic, and political structure involving man." If "Heaven's Generals" are walled up in their studies or "just busy doing nothing," God's call will go unheeded. Shuttlesworth closes with a primer on persuasion: to lead the battle, all combatants must be "motivated by love, and never use violence as wrong weapons to gain your ends." To do battle nonviolently will win the victory in Gary, just as it will directly aid the cause in Birmingham.

———

Speech at the Meeting of the Fair Share Organization

Gary, Indiana
September 25, 1958

Mr. President, Officers, Members, Ladies and Gentlemen:

It is an extreme honor to be invited back to Gary again. If I did that much good before, I'm very happy, and remind you that there are three strikes in any ball game—and this is just my second strike. My subject is: "The Struggle And The Outcome."

Life is a struggle—a lasting, continuous struggle. The digging into a solution of one problem inevitably leads into another, and we find ourselves forever amid the contrasts of lights and darkness, of shadows and substances. Many people are confused in these days of crises as they find themselves standing at the crossroads of safety and danger, and standing on the dividing line between going someplace or forever ending up nowhere. They ask themselves, "Which way must I go? Or to what voice must I listen? How can I stay out of involvement? And when will problems cease?"

There is an answer to life's problems, and it is to be found only within him who has the blueprint of Life itself. He who knows all gave the answer to the conflict of human relations when he said, "As ye would that men should do unto you, do ye even so unto them—this is the law and the prophets." Small wonder that Paul when he viewed the engrossment and entanglement of his own life with incessant and sometimes seeming unsolvable problems; when he came face to face with the irreconcilable conflict of right and wrong, of man's inhumanity to man, he cried in agony, "O wretched man that I am. Who shall deliver me?" and, "When I desire to do good, evil is always present."

But in a much more sublime note, this same Paul was elevated into the glorious 7th heaven of Faith, and then he was able to see that God still rules this world, that the crises and heartaches of humanity are God's way to say to man's heart, "be still and know that I'm God," that both right and wrong are weighed in balances in his hands who scooped out the seas, and calleth the stars by name and number, that Wrong may be crowned King for an evil moment but Righteousness and truth are scheduled to be forever glorified by Eternity; it was there where Paul saw that a person or nation, who is Right may be utterly beset on every hand, and yet in all those things—trials, tribulations, pains, struggles—that righteous person or nation backed by the Almighty Hand would move then conquer, that Paul exclaimed, "Thanks be to God who giveth us the victory through our Lord Jesus Christ."

So my friends, Life is a struggle and is in a turmoil all over the globe at this hour. In our nation we are in ferment North, South, East and West—even here in the heart of the great Midwest, Gary, Indiana. And we are Strugglers, Fighters, all—both North and South: "It is but one fight, one glorious struggle to really make this nation to be One Nation, under God, indivisible, with Liberty and Justice for all." Since we are committed to the struggle and Victory is sure, then let us fully realize that there is no use jumping into any ocean unless one intends to swim; no use getting on any highway unless one has a place to go; no use forever staring wistfully at distant mountain peaks without putting forth some effort to reach them; no use continually talking about Liberty and Freedom while being content to live like half slaves; no use echoing the yearnings of our slave parents unless by these same yearnings we are constrained to be free; no use—absolutely no use talking about their sacred blood having been shed yesterday unless we are willing to rise up today and exact freedom as the price of their blood. Yes there's no use cursing the darkness of this day; let us—you here, and us in the South strive to create that light which will forever banish from these shores the light of segregation and second class citizenship.

I'm speaking now of fighting in the struggle, with the weapon of love, honesty, decency, fairplay, and the needed improvements we must make upon ourselves as a race. Our nation needs servants who are soldiers and fighters—yet statesmen. Uncle Toms, Professor Toms, and Classy Maes need to hide and hush. Our Negro Race needs honest men to come to the front to lead us—men who love people more than what they can gain from people; men who will serve the cause without making themselves all the cause; men who will seek to lift others rather than be lifted by others; men who will ask God like Paul, "Lord what will you have me to do?" before going out to lead others.

In this struggling fight we must have consecrated Teachers, Preachers, who in this hour, when our White brothers are scandalizing Negro Morals, will stand forthright and tell our women that ours must not become an age of bob-tailed and bossy women, and that neither short hair or Sack dresses is an aid to sanctity or morality, and that nakedness or scant clothing will not glorify womanhood in a dressed up age. Our pulpits and forums must be loud in declaring that neither goodness, virtue, or righteousness is purchased in a tavern; and that switchblade knives and 45's can never be the badge of American manhood or a standard of the type of courage we seek to exemplify.

Let me here urge our two classes of people who are able to do most and (in the South) are doing less, to step up to your rightful places in this struggle. Our professional people need to understand that the gap between the classes and the masses must be closed. The classes evolved up from the masses, and where would you go and what would you do without the masses? I remind you that no tree ever grows tall enough to leave its roots, and that a man's head, however high and lofty it perches atop the body, can never achieve the advent ages of communicating with heads in other places without the lowly and covered foot. Remember, the masses will do the main fighting in the Segregation fight; if you can't or won't actively join them, then support them with the finances you have because of them.

Our Ministers—the first line Soldiers of God—must now understand that Christian Religion is concerned with the whole social, economic, and political structure involving man. The gospel is concerned with how and whether men eat as well as how they act. All hell in the form of Discrimination has overflowed its banks and is flooding our people out of jobs, homes, food. The front lines now are the picket lines around Krogers in Gary. And where are Heaven's Generals? In their studies or closed offices, or just busy, doing nothing? My brethren, the day is already come when common people desire bread, and homes today, while they are still willing to work for golden slippers and Pie-in-the-sky-bye and bye. I remind that when God has a job to be done Faith always gets the contract; and God's men—filled with Holy fire—have always arose to answer God's call. In the Midianite desert Moses answered, and led God's people; in the hour when God's people needed a world wide vision, Isaiah answered "here am I." A timid Elijah was emboldened to tell Ahab his faults, and tell Jezebel that dogs would lick her blood. A weeping Jeremiah went to the dungeon for his people; and Amos who was neither a prophet nor prophet's son was inspired to cry "let justice run down as the waters, and righteousness as a mighty stream."

Yes, my fellow ministers, it is time for us to understand that our success is not to be measured by the fineness of our dwelling nor the luxuriousness of a Cadillac Car. And must any preacher be content to be in this day carried to the skies on flowery beds of ease—while even now, men are picketing for jobs, bombs are bursting, schools are being closed in our children's faces. No, we must fight! And we must lead the fight! And no horse ever pulled a wagon from behind. John the Baptist had neither a Cadillac nor a home, but Jesus called him a great soul. Paul renounced fame to become a "fool for Christ's sake."

A final word to the Crusading members of this Fair Share Organization. Fight on until there need be no more fighting. March, until all the gilded

Jericho walls of discrimination be removed from all stores and businesses. You will be accused of trying to put men out of business; simply reply that you are trying to put justice and fair play in business. You will be accused of disturbing the peace, but no skyscraper was ever erected before the ground underneath was disturbed. You will be called Communists, but so are all who dare ask for their rights; the scandalous name of "Christian" in early times meant the same thing. You will not be liked, but it is better anyway to be respected than liked. The Sanhedrin Council never learned to like Jesus Christ, and even broke with Saul when his changed name and actions went against their purposes. You will be called radicals, but so was Martin Luther, and Paul, and Jesus Christ.

Only let your actions be motivated by love, and never use violence as wrong weapons to gain your ends. Unfortunately some of our White Brothers have never learned that lying to Negroes, mistreating them, or even bombing their homes will never stop the March of Negroes to the shores of Freedom's Lake. We are utterly determined to work where men work, spend money where men appreciate it, live where men live, and act like men act. Do it quickly here in Gary, and you will help us directly in Birmingham and the South, where justice has declared an indefinite holiday, and most of the judges, jurymen, and officers are Klansmen.

Let our courage, our calmness, our prowess to do battle with unlimited forces, backed up by Hooded riders and bombers, be an inspiration to you in the North. If we are willing to die for America, you should be willing to walk and to give.

Our road has been strong, hard, and grievous our burdens. Without the force of law on our side, we have had to stand naked and defenseless before the Night Riders. Most of our office holders love Segregation more than God Almighty, but we do not despair. Like Paul, we see through the darkness a Victory; a day when all Americans will be Americans.

We have indeed suffered—and you must suffer. I'm a living witness—but America and its ideals are worth suffering for. We must yet suffer until the Rebel flag, now again flying in Dixie, be finally laid low, and Rebel yells give way to shouts for Old Glory. Through the darkness of our night, our light has pointed the way, and in loneliness our defense has proved sure—Lightnings have flashed, thunders have rolled, but our God is still our defense. Thanks be to God for Victory—Victory over Jim Crow, Victory over evil, Victory for America! Stand fast! Your victory is sure.

1959

1959

§43 Chester Bowles

Chester Bowles was born in Springfield, Massachusetts on April 5, 1901. He received his B.S. from Yale University in 1924. After a successful career in advertising, he turned to public service. He first served as general manager of the massive Office of Price Administration beginning in 1943. He later served as governor of Connecticut (1948 to 1950), U.S. ambassador to India (1951–1953 and 1963–1969), and as a congressman (1959–1960). In addition to these prominent positions, he also played important roles at the United Nations Educational, Scientific and Cultural Organization (UNESCO) (1946), and at the United Nations (1947–1951). Bowles also served as an advisor to Adlai Stevenson and John F. Kennedy. A lifelong Unitarian, Bowles was a vocal advocate for racial reconciliation and international accord. While he served as ambassador to India, for example, Bowles rode his bicycle to work and enrolled his children in public schools. He died on May 25, 1986 at the age of 85. His papers are housed at Yale University in New Haven, Connecticut.

The following speech to the Health and Welfare Council in 1959 uses numerous Christian images and texts woven into other persuasive appeals to construct a powerful interpretation of the U.S. Supreme Court's 1954 mandate that boards of education end racial segregation with "all deliberate speed."

The Health and Welfare Council was one of two prominent umbrella organizations to guide resources among non-profit agencies in the African American community in Washington, D.C. The intended audience is a group of philanthropists, such as Dr. Euphemia Lofton Haynes, a key figure in ending segregation in the District of Columbia.

Early in the speech, Bowles argues that Christian civilization, with its 2000 year history, has greater depth than the evolving social contract of the U.S. Constitution, which was not even 200 years old at the time. This greater depth, he argues, potentially gives firmer moral ground to new laws that are shocking to many, if long overdue. He believes that the ethical responsibility of Christians is to convince others of their deeper moral purpose, calling for conciliation to the extent possible within the framework of the Constitution. Moderates, he argues, have access to the moral authority of Christian civilization. Christians from Thomistic traditions have long embraced the Aristotelian mean. God spoke through Isaiah, inviting the unjust to "reason together" in order to reconcile their original sins. Bowles then turns to Jefferson's account of a creator who endows all humans with inalienable rights. Whether those thoughts are Christian or deist is a matter our nation has not resolved, and Bowles attempts to build bridges among those struggling for Jefferson's religious legacy.

315

Bowles closes the address by focusing on the role of Christian congregations as leaders in the more perfect union. Ministers, he points out, cannot easily fly in the face of their laymen's values. But the Christian ethic is one of Stoic sacrifice and martyrdom, and everyone shares responsibility. We are our brothers' keepers. This final exhortation reminds us that knowing ourselves requires that we look to the global community. Bowles invokes the moral example of Mahatma Ghandi, reminding us at the end that those who satisfy themselves with the "deliberate" without the "speed" are settling for a society of untouchables, be they descendants of slaves or racists.

A Fresh Look At Race Relations

Speech to Health and Welfare Council, Washington, D.C.
May 1959

With considerable hesitation, I have decided to take this occasion to discuss our most critical and embittering social problem—race relations.

This week is a particularly good time to take stock. Five years ago last Sunday our Supreme Court ruled that color alone could no longer bar any child from a public school.

It was a momentous occasion and we all felt it. Those who had long favored desegregation thought the struggle had been won. And most of those who opposed it assumed that the only question left unanswered was the timing and the technique. The fact itself was accepted by the vast majority of Americans—north, east, south, and west.

Since then, more than one-fourth of the bi-racial school districts in the 17 southern and border States which officially practiced school segregation have been nominally desegregated, usually in a quiet and healthy manner which has escaped the headlines. In this connection the record of the District of Columbia, which so many of you helped to write, has been historic.

But these five years also have been scarred with smoldering resentments, defiance of court orders, and outbreaks of violence.

These expressions of racial conflict have not been limited to our southern States. Nor are they symbolized merely by a deserted school in Little Rock.

On the contrary, the attempted bombing of an integrated high school in Hobbs, New Mexico, a white mob stoning a Negro home in Levittown, Pennsylvania, an outburst of racial gang war in Chicago—these are signs to give pause to all the participants in America's racial conflict.

In 1954 the Nation as a whole underestimated the significance and meaning of the Supreme Court's decision. Since then we have tragically missed opportunities for constructive action.

After several years of optimism and complacency it is now clear that integration is a bigger, more stubborn, more universal, and more important problem than many of us imagined. We know now that racial differences and discrimination go deeper than Supreme Court decisions, not to mention paratroopers, can reach.

All of us, North and South, Negro and white, need to think anew.

Where and how do we go from here?

For we must go on in fulfilling the promises of the Constitution and of our national conscience. We can pause for reappraisal, but we cannot stop or go back.

The problem is full of agony and, as in most great issues, no one side has a monopoly of truth. Each has its points which must be considered with both humility and tolerance. All of us need to be awakened from our dogmatism and from our clichés.

My remarks today will undoubtedly disappoint those who have taken extreme positions in this controversy. Yet my approach inevitably reflects my personal experience—as a longtime friend of the South, as a former Governor of a northern industrial State, as a former Administrator of a large Federal agency in the turmoil of wartime Washington, and as U.S. Ambassador to India, where I saw our difficulties as the dark-skinned two-thirds of the world see them.

I offer my views not as solutions, but as guidelines to the kind of national discussion which I think is long overdue.

1. We must recognize the problem of discrimination as a national, not a sectional one.

Half of all American Negroes now live in the North. There is now no northern city without its tensions and its shame.

Yet many northerners still smugly look at racial discrimination as a sectional problem. Thus they condemn what they consider to be the slow pace of integration in the South, while remaining indifferent or nearly so to the discrimination all around them.

There are 39 States outside the South. Only 19 have established Fair Employment Practices Commissions. In the other non-Southern States, there has been no legislative action on employment discrimination at all.

Since 1949, when we in Connecticut first authorized our State Commission on Civil Rights to prevent discrimination in publicly owned housing, there has been some progress elsewhere. Yet today only nine States outside the South have adopted anti-discrimination legislation affecting publicly assisted housing. In 30 other non-Southern States, no official action to end housing discrimination has occurred.

The great northern and western industrial cities are all drawing Negroes out of the South, and are all faced with the demoralization of city slum life that goes beyond race. There are five times as many Negroes in Chicago as in Birmingham, four times as many in Detroit as in New Orleans, six times as many in Los Angeles as in Miami.

In most northern cities the professed equal protection of the laws still hides extensive segregation in fact—by residential exclusion, and by the natural selection of poverty. In few of our major northern cities do more than 20 percent of the Negro students attend school with white children.

To be sure, some cities such as New Haven, Pittsburgh, and Washington are now taking far-reaching steps to rebuild themselves, including the slum clearance and human rehabilitation essential to the solution of racial conflicts.

Yet almost any northern community that honestly examines its own racial relations will realize how far it is from living up to its professed ideals. And once we see what is missing in our own cities and States, we will be less inclined to feel that it is enough to denounce the foolhardy actions of white extremists south of the Mason-Dixon line.

Nothing will speak more persuasively to the South than a better example among the too-ready critics farther North.

2.   The Constitution as interpreted by the Supreme Court will ultimately prevail.

The Constitution, after all, is color blind. The 14th amendment does require the end of racial discrimination in all parts of our public life. The universal declaration of human rights, endorsed overwhelmingly by the people of the world, affirms this as one of the first principles of world order.

Moreover, our Constitution will be enforced. The Supreme Court has ordered desegregation with all deliberate speed.

Negro litigants will see that this is complied with—and the new Negro arising in the South and elsewhere, will supply all the litigants necessary, no matter what pressures are organized to stop him.

There can be no question but that in parts of the South, school desegregation will continue for some time to be massively resisted. The courts, the Department of Justice, and the President have no choice but to enforce the Constitution, gradually, case by case, step by step.

The courts and the country obviously will accept very gradual steps in good faith compliance. But regardless of what party is in power, the observance of the law ultimately will prevail.

The great hope, however, is not for a reluctant and grudging acceptance of the inevitable force of the law. Rather, the hope is that recognition of historical necessity will encourage an increasing effort to bring the various elements in each community into harmony.

3.   We must supplement litigation with persuasion.

Of course the law itself is a powerful teacher. The end of segregation in the Armed Forces, in the Nation's Capital, and on interstate trains did more to convince many skeptics that integration in these areas made sense than any amount of talk could have done.

There appears to be a temptation, however, to rest on the oars of lawyers and judges and say that this is all now a matter of law and order.

The President seemed to say precisely this when he stressed that he has told no one, not even his wife, whether he thinks the Supreme Court desegregation decision was right or wrong.

But Court orders alone will not suffice to change the minds and hearts of people. Somehow those who seek to end racial prejudice must go deeper than statutes and Court decisions.

If this were merely a legal issue between those who believe in upholding the law and those who seek to circumvent it, then there would have been no issue until the Supreme Court acted in 1954. But this turns the problem upside down.

The Court acted because the constitutional guarantee of equality involves the deepest political principles of this Nation and because there was a moral issue presented which went to the heart of our Bill of Rights and our Christian civilization.

The law does not get its sanction merely because it is the law. It wins support because it embodies the moral purpose of society.

The task of our political leaders, and of all who want to establish equal rights is not only that of invoking and carrying out court decisions but also of convincing people that they are right.

That is why the proposal for an independent Federal agency like the "Community Relations Service" advocated by the Senate majority leader, Senator Lyndon Johnson, could be so important. Conciliation, provided it is consistent with the guarantees of the Constitution, is precisely what is needed to help the law.

As Senator Johnson himself has said: "Controversies involving civil rights have reached a point where they can be paralyzing to whole communities. But they are controversies which can be settled if the yawning chasm can be bridged (by keeping) open the channels of communication among our people."

4.   The new generation, white and Negro, must rise above the deep-seated prejudices of their elders.

The spectacle of Negro children in Little Rock, Clinton, Sturgis, Nashville, and the integrating cities of North Carolina walking quietly to and from school through jeering, angry mobs shocked most Americans, as it did people around the world.

When one remembers the fears of childhood—of changing to a new school, even when everyone is friendly and of the same race—one can imagine how those lonely Negro children felt in the midst of unfriendly white crowds.

Yet is not the old prophecy coming alive again? Are not the children leading us now?

In almost every city and town in the South where school integration has begun, the children are making out all right together. "If the grownups would just leave us alone, there would be no trouble," said a white student in Little Rock.

5.   White and Negro moderates both have an historic role to play.

Many white southerners are still content to say that the problem will take a long time to solve and that the Negro must be patient.

No thoughtful man expects a quick solution. But we cannot afford to forget that a lot of time has already passed.

It is now 96 years since emancipation, 183 years since a southerner wrote the declaration to which this Nation is dedicated.

That all men are created equal, that they are endowed by their Creator with certain inalienable rights, and that to secure these rights governments are instituted among men—these are not just the words of Thomas Jefferson. They are the political creed of this country. Yet the historic timetable for establishing these equal rights for all Americans has been gradual indeed.

The white southerner nevertheless has a case he can and should make. Generations of slavery, second-class Negro citizenship, inferior schools, houses and jobs are now plaguing us in the form of high rates of disease and crime and a low level of education in areas where Negroes predominate.

To be sure, such demoralization is also the state of much of the rural poor whites of the South and Puerto Ricans brought up and trapped in our congested urban slums.

But the Negro has been an outcast longest, has suffered most, and is now the most extreme example of a problem facing the whole country.

This argument is indeed a good reason for doing more than simply integrating the schools. It underscores the need for getting at the very conditions which produce the demoralization in the first place.

The demoralization of the Negro does endanger southern white society, just as the demoralization of any member of a community endangers that community.

Take a county where a depressed Negro population outnumbers the white two or three or four to one. If that Negro community is ill housed, ill fed, ill clad, if it is sick, ignorant, and angry, can a relatively well-off white minority be "safe" in any meaningful sense of the word?

Or take a big southern city. In half of the town is a Negro slum, breeding uneducated bitterness, juvenile crime and racial violence, what kind of community will this be for the white people who pretend to want to live there?

The new South that is now taking shape has no room for low and inhuman standards of life for anyone.

Instead of using demoralization as an excuse for doing nothing about integration, it should cause the southern moderate to insist that a vast amount more must be done in a number of fields.

We need a far-reaching program to end the demoralization of much of the Negro community and of the poor whites as well. By championing slum clearance and measures for adequate housing and public health, the white South might then be in a position to ask the Negroes, the courts, and the rest of the country to accept a realistic pace for school integration—perhaps beginning only in the first grade and at the college and university level, with a voluntary transfer system, with even segregation by sex in some areas where co-education adds to the fears about integration.

But by holding back, southern moderates leave the field not only to white demagogues but to future Negro demagogues.

So far Negro leadership has been on the whole remarkably intelligent and restrained and the Negro people have accepted its counsel. They have steadily offered the hand of friendship and compromise for acceptance by at least some substantial part of the white South.

A new Negro is standing up in the South and elsewhere. His expectations may not all be met. But some good and true men of the white South must meet him face to face, must sit down at roundtable conference, must talk with him and understand him.

Without such a minimum response, it is too much to expect that the majority of Negroes will forever stand by the moderate ministers of the Gospel and the well-trained lawyers who now speak for them.

6. I believe that the Christian Church must take the initiative in advancing a racial reconciliation.

Let's face it: In many churches in America, a minister who goes against the prevailing sentiment of his congregation risks his job as much as the politician who alienates his constituents.

But from the beginning of the Christian era, it has been the church's duty to prevail against erroneous opinions, even at the price of martyrdom. Surely the church today should be the last citadel against the public relations approach that has infected so much of American life.

Many bishops and ministers in the South have spoken against violence and in favor of law and order. But is this enough?

There will be violence, and the law will be frustrated, unless the two sides in the racial conflict now splitting every southern community begin to communicate again with each other, to find common remedies.

Is this not the time for the white and Negro ministers of every southern community to form a continuing roundtable conference dedicated to finding Christian solutions to the racial problems of their community?

For, after all, no country should be in a better position than the United States of America to solve this problem this way. Not only do we have nearly two centuries of democratic experience behind us, but the racial groups in this country, particularly in the South, have the great good fortune and blessing to share the identical Christian faith.

It is no coincidence that it was a white minister in the South, perhaps the most fervently religious section of our country, who said of the integration crisis: "There's just one question to ask: what would Christ do?"

In our hearts we know the final answer. We know that Christ came to demonstrate the fatherhood of God and the brotherhood of man. We know we are our brother's keeper.

We know too that we have done those things which we ought not to have done and left undone those things we ought to have done.

We know that the pride of race, the fear of the strange and the different is one of man's original sins and that it has not been fully erased from man's mind anywhere.

But we also know, as Lincoln said, that the Declaration of Independence "gave liberty not alone to the people of this country, but hope to all the world. It gave promise that in due time the weights would be lifted from the shoulders of all men, and that all should have an equal chance."

Our religious and democratic faith tells us to get on with this job like men.

7. Our capacity to deal with discrimination in America is a measure of our capacity to lead a worldwide revolution for freedom.

My own perspective on this problem has been, I confess, affected by looking at it for some time from the other side of the globe. As a former Ambassador to India, I know how spectacularly American prestige rose as a result of the Supreme Court desegregation decision.

While touring Africa four years ago I sensed again how vital a successful solution of our racial troubles is for our future relationship with the two-thirds of the world's people who are colored.

In the winter of 1957 in South Asia I saw the enthusiasm generated by the successful conclusion of the Negroes' bus boycott in Montgomery, Alabama. Later in the Soviet Union I saw the Communists take full propaganda advantage of the bombing of Negro churches in the same State.

Of course we can say that prejudice is as old as the hills and just as persistent. India, for instance, has known conflict and caste through centuries of struggle between Hindus and Moslems, Brahmans and untouchables.

In Algeria there is open warfare between the French minority and the Arab majority.

In all of Africa the outnumbered white man feels the stirring of the slumbering African masses.

Therefore as we Americans concentrate on a new effort on our own major social problem, we can take mild comfort from the awareness that our country does not stand alone in isolation as an immoral historic throwback to a bygone age of prejudice.

Having said this, I hasten to add what is merely the other side of this coin. The world community has a vested interest in the speed and effectiveness with which we end discrimination in the United States. Our own role in the world depends increasingly upon the same proposition.

As is true in so many other aspects of our national policy today, the world situation is requiring us to do the things which we should do anyway. No one but a cynic would argue that we should suddenly become interested in equal rights for Negroes merely because our propaganda position in the world would be helped by such progress.

Nevertheless, it remains more true today than it was in 1947, when one of our distinguished former Secretaries of State, Henry L. Stimson wrote: "No private program and no public policy, in any section of our national life can now escape from the compelling fact that if it is not framed with reference to the world, it is framed with perfect futility."

In closing, I should like to suggest that all of us, northerners and southerners, easterners and westerners, Negroes and white can learn much from a study of that incredible man, Mahatma Gandhi.

There were always two sides to Gandhi's program. One was direct resistance to unjust laws or practices. The other was constructive popular action to create the conditions of justice.

He began his career before the turn of the 20th century in the Union of South Africa where he went as a lawyer for some Indian traders.

In 1893, South Africa was a land run by some million Europeans who sat on top of some 5 million Africans who had almost no rights at all. In addition, were 100,000 Indians, most of whom had been recruited as cheap labor for the white plantations and mines.

Soon after he reached Pretoria, the young man of 24 invited all the Indians in the city to a meeting. He urged them to fight racial discrimination but without hating or hurting their opponents.

And since their aim was to reason with the whites, the first thing they should do, he said, was to consider the reasons given by the whites for their discrimination.

To the Indian merchants before him, known for slick dealing and sharp bargainings, he proposed complete truthfulness and more concern for the poor. He called on all Indians to do something to improve the unsanitary conditions in the Indian sections of town.

Why wait for legal victories for the necessary drain cleaning? he asked.

We can't blame the whites for all our troubles, he argued. Perhaps we can't by ourselves end all the poverty in which our people are trapped, but if those of us with some money and some education will join in, the slums can be cleaned up, freshened with a coat of paint and made habitable; the illiterate adults can be taught to read; volunteer schools can be provided for the children of the poor.

And he began to build the institutions to do these constructive tasks.

In 1913 he returned to India, after negotiating a settlement with Prime Minister Smuts who once jailed him but later came to say to him, "I am not worthy to stand in the shoes of so great a man." And for over 30 years in India, Gandhi pressed his constructive program of village improvement, the end of untouchability, and the reform of individual lives.

The bus boycott in Montgomery carried out with dignity and restraint represented an adaptation of Gandhian principles in democratic America.

"We are seeking to improve not the Negro of Montgomery but the whole of Montgomery," said Reverend Martin Luther King on the occasion of the formation of the Montgomery Improvement Association which conducted the boycott.

Instead of merely sitting by until the Supreme Court ruled bus segregation unconstitutional, the Negroes of Montgomery in amazing unity carried out a courageous, peaceful, direct action which took the nation by surprise.

The long-term effects of this Ghandian-type action on the white conscience may take time to register. But it had an immediate effect in changing the Negroes.

Perhaps the change is best reflected in the story of the old Negro woman who, when asked if her feet were not tired from plodding so many miles each day to work replied, "Brother, for a long time my feet has rested, but my soul's been tired. Now my feet are tired, but my soul is resting."

In this light, with good cheer, let us move ahead with all deliberate speed.

§44 Rabbi Max D. Davidson

In his capacity as president of the Synagogue Council of America, Rabbi Max D. Davidson addresses the 50th anniversary of the founding of the National Association for the Advancement of Colored People (NAACP). Davidson's brief message begins with a fundamental and scriptural identification between Jews and blacks. Noting that the Passover story begins with "Slaves were we to Pharoah," and that "God brought us out with a mighty hand and an outstretched arm," the two histories of an oppressed people ground Davidson's discourse. He first highlights several Old Testament passages that speak of unity and wonders aloud whether the verses are "in the Bible of some of these preachers." Clearly, those clergy who preach hate, violence, and superiority are misinterpreting the holy Scriptures. Second, Davidson asks how we can get back to a divine conception of man. His answer involved education—not so much for the "other fellow" but for "our own." That is, one educated Jewish child meant more than ten Ph.D. strangers. Yes, education involves sacrifice, but education will redeem "the great potential talents and skills" of millions of black children.

Address at the 50th Anniversary of the NAACP
Polo Grounds, New York
July 19, 1959

First of all, I suppose that I ought to submit my credentials for sitting on this platform. Well, years ago I was a substitute catcher on the third team and that may entitle me to be on the same program as Jackie Robinson.

The Synagogue Council of America, whom I have the honor to represent today, does not participate in this celebration as a mere gesture. We are, and have been, seriously and intensely concerned with social justice, human rights, and individual freedom—ideals that are deeply rooted in Jewish religious teaching and tradition. We are concerned, not because they are *your* rights or *our* rights, but because these are the rights of all of the children of men.

To participate in this dazzling day, to be a part, even a small part, of this inspiring spectacle, moves me deeply. There passes before my mind's eye the panorama of my own people's past, *our* history of suffering and oppression, our own search for *security* and peace.

There is one night in the year when we use a special prayer book, a special service for the festival of Passover. We gather our children around us and begin to tell the story of our people. And do you know how we begin?

Not with Abraham, not with Isaac and not with Jacob or Moses. *These* are literally the first words in that service: "Slaves were we to Pharaoh in Egypt." Yes, and we go on: "and God brought us out with a mighty hand and an outstretched arm." Because we have passed through 4,000 years of struggle, because we have had this experience, I have the temerity to speak to you on this dynamic day; and because I see here, in your presence and in your organization, "The mighty hand and the outstretched arm of the Almighty."

I do not know whether I ought to quote from the Bible. I sometimes hear and read about preachers who preach hate and not love, and I wonder what book they are using. When they advocate injustice and violence and call themselves superior, is it possible that they are using the same Bible, are they worshipping the same God that you and I worship?

The ancient rabbis used to study the words of the scripture, the same that you and I read and they debated the question of which is the most important verse in the Bible. One of them said, "Do justice, love mercy and walk humbly with thy God."

I wonder whether that verse is in the Bible of some of these preachers?

And another Pharisaic preacher said, "Have we not all one father, hath not one God made us all?" Isn't the prophet Malachi in their Bible?

And another said, "No, the most important verse is: 'And thou shalt love they neighbor as thyself.'" Have *they* taken a scissors and cut that verse from the Bible?

And another said, "This is the book of the generations of man."

And finally, "and God created man in His image"—*one* man so that none, tracing back his lineage, should ever be able to boast, "My ancestors were better than yours," "and God *created* man in His image," *one* man from whom we are all descended. How do we attain that divine, that God-given quality that man has taken away? I can only give you some of the answers that my people have discovered out of the pain and the cruelty and the injustice of the centuries.

We looked upon the ignorance and the narrowness of our oppressors and we came to the conclusion that education was the answer. When people learn more and know more, they will wipe away the grime and the scum of the ages. Then we had a sudden shock. We had to ask ourselves a new question: Are educated men and women free from prejudice, and college campuses the most hospitable field of welcome? Are the sophisticated and successful members of fashionable clubs, who come from the best schools, any closer to the call of brotherhood than the laborer who lives on the wrong side of the tracks?

Maybe our definition of education was wrong. The process of education had to be changed but we didn't have the time and we didn't have the power to do it. Then we turned around and said, in pursuance of a long tradition of learning: It's not the other fellow's education that will solve the problem but our own education. We'll change our little world by study. Let us *learn* and *know*.

Would it be out of place for me to say that one educated child of our own meant more to *us* than ten Ph.D.'s who were strangers? It's not easy, as you and we know. It means sacrifices. When you don't have an even chance for a job, when you don't get a decent wage, what do you do? You have to give up other things. I know my father did.

We mortgage the future for refrigerators, radio and TV sets and automobiles. Is it out of order to make the same kind of sacrifice for a child's education, to mortgage the future for the sake of the future as many of you are doing, as many of all of us have done.And it doesn't always work out as you plan it. Sometimes the child grows up and betrays his people. He's too good for the people who made him what he is. We've had plenty such, but it hasn't scared us and I know it doesn't scare you. Sometimes they develop self-hate and slink off into dark corners where they think none will recognize their birth and origin. This mustn't keep you or your children away from the Book or the candle of knowledge. Knowledge is the price and the opportunity, not of a chosen few but of all your children.

This is important, not for you alone but for me as a Jew to see that justice comes to 15,000,000 Americans. It is important to me as an American that the great potential talents and skills of these millions be enabled to serve the growth and welfare of America and of the world.

These were for you the first fifty years, the end of a cycle, and the beginning. The Fiftieth Year in the Bible was the Jubilee, when God's good green earth was turned back to all of his children, to whom the earth had been given.

May you march on triumphantly from this place and from this memorable moment on a journey of justice to another giant jubilee—and I hope I can be there.

§45 Reverend Colbert S. Cartwright

Colbert ("Bert") Scott Cartwright was born on August 7, 1924 in Coffeyville, Kansas. He received a B.A. from Washington University of St. Louis in 1946, and a B.D and M.S.T. at Yale in 1948 and 1950. Cartwright, like his father, was a Disciples of Christ minister. From 1950 to 1989, he served in churches in the South and Midwest. As minister of Pulaski Heights Christian Church in Little Rock, Arkansas from 1954 to 1963, Cartwright's racial consciousness emerged in the wake of enormous conflict at Little Rock. In September 1957 Central High School in Little Rock had to open its doors to the Little Rock Nine—African American students who qualified to attend the previously segregated high school. Governor Orval

Faubus welcomed the students with the Arkansas National Guard (ANG), ostensibly to guarantee their safety. In fact, the ANG arrived with instructions to keep the African American children out of Central High School. They had the help of an angry mob, which ridiculed, spat upon, and assaulted the African American students. President Eisenhower obtained a court order to remove the ANG and activated the 101st Airborne division of the U.S. Army to safeguard the students' integration of the school.

In the weeks preceding the dramatic integration of Central High School, Cartwright joined a group of 35 local ministers to sign a statement that the Arkansas Governor's separatist legislation was worrisome in light of biblical principles emphasizing the equality of all humans in God's sight. This was just the beginning of the battle for Cartwright and his congregation, which would diminish by some ten percent despite the fact that it had a reputation as a liberal church. Beyond the pulpit, Cartwright helped found the Arkansas Council on Human Relations and served as its president in 1956 and 1957. An active writer and speaker, Cartwright published several books and was a frequent guest at racial summits around the nation. He died in April 1996. His papers are housed at the University of Arkansas in Fayetteville.

In his sermon to the citizens of Little Rock, Reverend Cartwright calls upon his listeners to follow God's lead, and engage in a ministry of reconciliation. Based on Paul's letter to the Corinthians, Cartwright asks at the outset, just how is our community going to overcome its alienation and fragmentation? How can this racial strife be overcome? How can reconciliation begin? He offers several features of God's ministry of reconciliation: first, it must be unconditionally offered to all—regardless of race, color, or creed; second, love, righteousness, and justice must appear in the heart of the reconciled, since congeniality is not reconciliation; third, we must not hold the past against those with whom we seek to be reconciled; and, finally, each person must find his or her cross to bear in becoming a reconciled community. If it took a crucifixion to reconcile us with God, so too will it take pain and effort on our part.

The Ministry of Reconciliation

Little Rock, Arkansas
July 1959 (reprinted)

We who live in Little Rock are all deeply aware of our involvement in the turmoil of events which surround the controversy over desegregation of our public schools. We have experienced personally the fragmentation of our relatively peaceful community. Before our unbelieving eyes we have witnessed the splintering of white neighbor from white neighbor, Negro friend from Negro friend, white person from colored, and colored from white. No one of us has been left unaffected in our personal relations with others by the crisis in our city. We are all caught up in the monstrous tragedy of estrangement from each other.

Above all else we in Little Rock feel desperately a need for the healing of personal relations. We are weary of carrying the weighty burden of estrangement. We are tired of guarding our words and actions lest they by chance should provoke a violent response from another. We are saddened by the voices which were once friendly but now are cold or silent. We are heartsick over the lack of even the simplest levels of understanding between ourselves and those of the Negro race.

Down in the depths of our hearts we know we were created for fellowship with our neighbors, and this estrangement we are experiencing is contrary to our very natures. We were made to live in a community in which every person loves and respects and helps the other. We were created to love our neighbors as ourselves.

We find ourselves, then, living a nightmarish kind of existence which is contrary to what we know to be the good and proper life for human beings. From the depths of our souls we long for some means of binding up our broken relations, healing the wounds between man and man, and unifying our fragmented community. But where shall we find the means to achieve this?

Our Christian scriptures suggest an answer. Certainly as we study the pages of the Bible we find no simple prescriptions for solving the Little Rock crisis; but, nevertheless, we do find a profound word directed to our condition. The Bible speaks to us a message concerning reconciliation which, of course, is the antonym of "alienation." Our alienation must be counteracted by reconciliation.

Paul in writing to the church at Corinth speaks of reconciliation. Let us listen to a few sentences from Paul and then see how they might relate to our present predicament: "God . . . through Christ reconciled us to himself and gave us the ministry of reconciliation; that is, God was in Christ reconciling the world to himself, not counting their trespasses against them, and entrusting to us the message of reconciliation" (*II Corinthians* 5:18-19).

Let us note that Paul's emphasis is not upon our alienation from our fellow men, but upon man's alienation from God. Paul says: "God . . . through Christ reconciled us to himself . . ." To be sure he is making himself clear, Paul seeks to express the same thought a second time in slightly different words. "That is," Paul goes on to say, "God was in Christ reconciling the world to himself, not counting their trespasses against them . . ."

We come, then to God's Holy Word asking for help in our problem of estrangement from our fellow men, and we are told to consider the fact that God Himself has had to deal with this very same problem of estrangement. God, too, is directly involved in relations with people. God has found the whole world estranged from Him, and has Himself had to seek a means of bringing about reconciliation. God has dealt with this problem of estrangement long before we came upon the scene.

The Gospel itself is the story of how God has sought to bring about reconciliation between Himself and the world. All mankind has been ugly and harsh and insulting to God. The world has ignored Him, treated Him with indifference, and oftentimes deliberately gone against His wishes. A man would hardly treat a fellow human being with the contempt he often treats God.

And the world's attitude and actions toward God have estranged the world from God just as assuredly as they would shatter any human being's relations with another person. God, confronted with callous mistreatment, has also had His own problems of reconciliation. What should He do about these estranged relations with His people? The answer is written in the life of Jesus Christ, for as Paul says: "God . . . through Christ reconciled us to himself . . . That is, God, was in Christ reconciling the world to himself."

It is only as we come to an understanding of the way God has sought to reconcile the world to Himself that we shall discover how we ourselves are to seek reconciliation in our present crisis. Our efforts toward reconciliation must be like that of God's. As Paul reminds us, God "*gave* us the ministry of reconciliation." Reconciliation is not something we can define and construct as we please, but a gift of a specific form to be received and passed on as it is. Let us, then, consider the nature of this reconciliation which God has already expressed toward the world and which we ourselves must express to our fellow men.

First, let us see that Good seeks reconciliation with everyone regardless of creed or condition or color. As Paul expressed it to the Corinthian Christians: "God was in Christ reconciling the *world*." God sought to become reconciled with every living person. This was a tremendous surprise to the Jews of Jesus' day. They thought that, at best, God would seek to restore only Jews to His fellowship. They were sure that God would be like them, and have nothing to do with Gentiles. But they were plainly mistaken, for through Christ persons of various races and backgrounds began to be restored into God's fellowship, so that Paul could say: "There is neither Jew nor Greek, there is neither slave nor free, there is neither male nor female; for you are all one in Christ Jesus" (*Galatians* 3:28). So God began reconciling all sorts of people to Himself.

Just as God seeks to become reconciled to every person regardless of who he is, so this is the nature of the reconciling spirit which we must exhibit in our own dealings with others. Our attempts at reconciliation must include all kinds of persons in our own community. If we are to exhibit God-like reconciliation, we must have an outreaching love which seeks to express itself alike toward integrationist and segregationist, Negro and white, demagogue and statesman, white citizens council member and NAACP member. All of these, including ourselves, are a part of the world toward which God seeks to become reconciled. God seeks to enfold all of these with His love, and so must we.

There is no one in Little Rock who is exempted from our responsibility for seeking reconciliation. The list is as big as a census of mankind. "God was in Christ reconciling the world. . . ."

Moving on a step further, let us see that God's effort toward reconciliation is such that it seeks to create love and righteousness in the one to be reconciled. Sometimes we tend to equate reconciliation with a sentimental ignoring of other's faults in a brave effort to get along. Reconciliation is not to be equated with congeniality. It has a moral quality to it which cannot be ignored.

God did not come into the world through Christ with the proclamation that no one needed to change at all, but that it would be enough simply to be friendly with God. Jesus never said, "God doesn't care what you are doing or what you believe, but He just wants to get along with you." No. Jesus opened his ministry with a call to repentance, and insisted that only those could become reconciled to God who hungered and thirsted for righteousness. As James Moffatt has observed: "The God whom Jesus called men to love and imitate was not a "bon Dieu," genially tolerant of distinctions between truth and falsehood or between right and wrong, but a God whose love embraced moral severity and justice, and also, by its quality of 'holiness,' reacted sternly against those who degraded or misled human souls." Dr. Moffatt goes on to remark that "there have been few representations or misrepresentations of Christian love which have done more to discredit it than the identification of this spirit with an easy-going temper of mere good-nature." We must recall that, even as Jesus sought to be God's means of reconciliation, he found it necessary as a part of his ministry to denounce, expose, and oppose the scribes and Pharisees.

So, in our own ministry of reconciliation, our task is to reflect God's concern for justice and righteousness. Even as we seek to be reconciled with every person in our city, we do so on the basis of what is just and proper, not simply on the flimsy basis of "peace at any price" or congeniality. It is not our Christian duty to surrender the Gospel for the sake of keeping peace. We seek to bring about a kind of reconciliation which is based on God's eternal principles of love and justice.

Looking at God's kind of reconciliation we see that we must never surrender what we know is loving and just in order to be superficially at one with some of our neighbors. The ministry of reconciliation makes every effort to let God's love and justice become a basis for uniting all people. It seeks to accomplish this with a spirit free from vindictiveness and malice.

It refuses ever to become bitter toward those who will not themselves take steps toward reconciliation. At the heart of the ministry of reconciliation as seen in Jesus is an openness to every person of whatever condition, but at the same time a firmness as to the high demands upon which true fellowship can be had.

We must move on now to see that God's effort toward reconciliation is such that it continuously seeks to take the initiative in bringing all estrangement to an end. This was a fact which struck Paul again and again. He expresses it in his letter to the Corinthian Christians: "God was in Christ reconciling the world to himself, not counting their trespasses against them. . . ." God didn't let the world's sins against Him deter Him from making every effort on His own initiative to find reconciliation with the world. Although He has been sinned against, God acted as if the trespasses against Him had never taken place in so far as His steps toward reconciliation were concerned.

At this moment, as we are caught up in a multitude of estrangements, these words of God's reconciliation must become ours. There are many persons whom we feel have sinned against us. If we are to undertake a ministry of reconciliation, we must not hold their past actions against them, refusing to have anything to do with them. We must take the initiative, and seek to restore the lines of communication and understanding. God's kind of reconciliation knows nothing of waiting on the other person to take the first move. The first move is up to us. "God was in Christ reconciling the world to himself, not counting their trespasses against them. . . ."

Finally, let us see that at the heart of God's efforts toward reconciliation stands a cross. It was the cross that haunted Paul's life above all else. As Paul exclaimed to the Romans: "God shows his love for us in that while we were yet sinners Christ died for us" (*Romans* 5:8). God, Himself, took up a cross in order to bring about reconciliation.

How can we grasp this dimension of God's reconciling love?

Possibly a scene in Marc Connelly's moving play for Negro actors, "Green Pastures," expresses in all its naiveté and simplicity what God's cross of reconciliation means. At one point in the play "De Lawd" is fed up with the sinful ways of men. He stands at the window listening to the prayers and pleadings of His people in their bondage; then He calls to them in a loud and final voice of righteous anger: "I ain't comin'. I tell you I ain't comin' down no mo'!" He turns, walks across the floor with His hands gripped tightly behind His back, but somehow the matter is not quite settled. Plainly a battle is going on in the heart of "De Lawd." Finally He walks back to the window of heaven, looks down for a long, long time. In a little while you hear Him say: "I'm comin', chillun, I'm comin'." Gabriel has "De Lawd's" hat and cane all ready, and as "De Lawd" leaves, He says to Gabriel:

"Look after things up here, Gabriel. I'm goin' down to give 'em another chance. I'll see you Saturday night."

So the play moves on to the last scene, and someone is standing at the gates of heaven looking down from the battlements of the sky to a hill outside a city wall. "Look!" he cries. "Look! Dey's gonna make 'im carry dat cross up a hill. Dat's an awful burden for one man to carry."

It is an awful burden, but it is a part of the cost of reconciliation. It is a part of the cost of God's reconciliation as He seeks us; it is a part of the cost of our reconciliation with our fellow men as we seek to end the ugly estrangements in our city.

For a long time now most of us have tried to find some means of reconciliation, but our efforts usually fall short of bearing a cross. If God Himself could not find a way apart from a cross, how in God's name do we think we can? No. There's a cross here in Little Rock awaiting you and me. It undoubtedly takes as many forms as there are Christians, and yet, whatever the form, it is a part of God's cross. It is a part of God's cross of reconciliation.

We find, then, as we turn to the Bible in the midst of our estrangements that God, too, knows what it means to experience estrangement from others. He, most of all, knows its heartache and isolation. But He found a way toward reconciliation, and His way must become ours. Indeed, Paul reminds us that we ourselves are both ones who are being reconciled, and ones who at the same time are instruments of reconciliation. We are both the "reconciled" and the "ministers of reconciliation." We shall become reconciled one to another just to the degree that we channel God's reconciling spirit down through our own lives and out to touch the lives of our estranged neighbors.

§46 Reverend Carlos E. Martin

Carlos E. Martin received his B.A. from Hendricks College in 1953 and his B.D. from Southern Methodist University in 1956. As a young Methodist minister, Martin was called to St. Luke in Pine Bluff, where he served from 1957 to 1959. He later served Methodist churches throughout Arkansas, including Oak Lawn United Methodist Church in Hot Springs as well as St. Luke United Methodist Church in Little Rock. In Pine Bluff Martin was an active and outspoken proponent for school integration at Dollarway High School—so much so that he received hate mail and death threats from the local Klan and White Citizens Council.

In this sermon to his small congregation in Pine Bluff, Martin gives an excruciatingly personal account of what it is like to serve both man and God. On the surface, the speech does not appear to address directly the issue of race. A careful reading, though, reveals that Martin's ministerial role as a prophet and truth-teller are surrounded by terms that suggest the vexing matter of race. As with many southern ministers, while Martin steers clear of such overt markers as "integration," "segregation," "black and white," and "Little Rock," it is clear that race lies at the heart of this anguished message. That message redounds to: know whether you are in disagreement with the message of your minister or the message of your God. There is a rather consequential difference.

Of This Gospel I was Made a Minister

St. Luke Methodist Church, Pine Bluff, Arkansas
November 8, 1959

Whatever I may be this morning as a Christian minister, indeed whatever I may become in the future, I shall owe in large measure to the experiences as pastor of this church. God seems to have both a strange and frightening way of placing people in life. This morning as I preach to you I realize the heavy responsibility He has placed on me. I am often frightened at the things I do and say, but more often I am frightened at the things I did not say and do. When a man is thrust into a position either by external circumstances or by his own desire and choice, he must do some serious thinking about what his position means and the way in which he must conduct himself. In this spirit I come to you today.

It is regrettable that a man's effectiveness as a Minister of the Gospel is often judged—not by his faith, not by his zeal, not by the evidence of God in his own life, nor by his Love of The Christ—but by his ability to grease the wheels of church machinery. And I want to make it perfectly clear that I understand that in order for The Gospel to be proclaimed and heard there must be form, there must be order, there must be efficiency of church organization. But when the preservation of the machinery of church organization becomes the primary task of the minister he has lost much of His High and Holy Calling. The Minister must always be that agent of God who speaks of redemption. He is or should be that man of God who leads people from hate to love, from their selfishness and pride to meekness and humility before God, from their sins to righteousness, from their unbelief or disbelief to belief, from their faithlessness to faithfulness, from their narrowness and prejudice to an understanding and acceptance of the broad and high and loving purposes of God for His creation. The Minister will always understand that his position before both God and men as creative and productive, but sometimes even divisive. And though he must understand and love people above all else, except God, and he must listen to people, indeed he must live with them in their hurts and sins, sharing with them in both their joys and their sorrows, but he must not and cannot simply reflect the will of the populace. This Minister can never let the judgment of people become his own and for this reason he is not "democratic" in the common understanding of the word. Paul spoke of the authority which the Lord had given unto him. So it seems to me that the Minister of Christ's Church must never forget that his position and his authority is a derived one—but from God and not men. As Paul says in Galatians: "Am I now seeking the favor of men, or of God? Or am I trying to please men? If I were still pleasing men, I should not be a servant of Christ."

Thus, it is this relationship with God through Christ that distinguishes the Christian minister from secular leadership. Tragically, I must confess that quite often the secular leader will stand above the Christian minister, even in his unwillingness to bow before the will of wrong and evil. Often times the secular leader may be devoted to a cause which is beyond himself. Sometimes he is dedicated only for the purpose of his own selfishness and self-aggrandizement. And the Minister sometimes finds this to be true, nevertheless, if he is true to his Calling his is a relationship that is unique. This is not to say that he has any special immunity or exemption from the darts of men. This is not to say that he does not likewise stand with accountability to men as well as God. This is not to say that the Christian Minister is justified in all things before either God or men. This is to say that he should be something more than a pattern of respectability in the community.

As Dr. James Robinson has said in his book *Adventurous Preaching*, "many ministers are contributing to the pattern that society sets for them and thus they have begun to resemble appendages to that society." How tragic that we Ministers of the Gospel today have become more like the appendix of a book rather than the forward to it. The community, the state, and the nation rush by us and we draw comfort and solace in the fact that as they hurriedly pass by they tip their hats to us in a gesture of respect. More often than not we are by-passed altogether—and even when we are invited to all manner of social gatherings the hope is plainly evident to all but the most sensitive soul, that we shall not stay long enough to become a kill-joy. We are invited to ask the blessing, give the benediction at all sorts of gatherings. We are placed at head tables to decorate the banquet and often this appears to be some effort to appease the deity. We are tolerated because we are believed to bring respectability to all kinds of assemblies such as labor unions, political parties, patriotic rallies, football games, and sundry other gatherings which then proceed to go their own way without any further reference to the judgment of God.

On every hand I am told today that people no longer want to be "preached to"—they merely want somebody to hold a discussion group with them. Granted that in our day this would in many instances prove to be more helpful than listening to the words of many preachers, but this is tragic.

And this in itself raises the crucial question about the words of the Man of God. The grave temptation which he faces is that he may and often does identify God's will with his own. But, you know, there is no sure way of distinguishing between the two, save his knowledge and practice of scripture, his meekness and humility and his finite wisdom. Very often what the preacher says is likely to be an interpretation of his own ideas and it is all too easy to slip unconsciously from "Thus saith the Lord," to "Thus say I." This danger is always present with every sermon. BUT MY FRIENDS THIS IS THE AWFUL DECISION THAT YOU THE HEARERS MUST MAKE.

You may disagree with what I have to say—You may even disagree in those times when I make bold enough to say that "Thus saith the Lord"—because you may think it is false and not from God, but there is one thing I must caution you about. You had better be sure, awfully sure, that it is just the preacher with whom you disagree and not God Himself. And well you may disagree with what your Church has to say on moral issues, but there is one thing I must caution you about. You had better be sure, awfully sure, that you are just disagreeing with an institutionalized organization and not God Himself. My Friends this is the awful decision which you the laymen have to make. All too often even the preachers have helped you to avoid making this decision by saying it doesn't really matter whether you agree with the preacher or not. As if the minister stands to proclaim that his church stands for total abstinence and preaches with all his conviction this stand to his people, and then at the close he says, now for those who disagree with what I have said, it doesn't really matter. Yes you must decide whether it be of God, if it is the pastor, District Superintendent or Bishop who is speaking.

My right to say "Thus saith the Lord" was not conferred with my degree from seminary. Nor was it effected by a process of osmosis when the Bishop laid his hand on my head in ordination—granted my right to say it in The Methodist Church came in that manner, but my right to say "Thus saith the Lord" comes only in my own consecration of self to Him, a studied mind and a disciplined life. It comes only through my faithful listening to Him and by my willingness to show his love and bear His witness in His world. The prophets declared The Word of The Lord, but the prophets were men who listened for that Word by a constant attention to the life of their people. They looked into the faces of the hungry, the angry, the faithless, and the sinful just as I must do. They saw the pride, the selfishness, the injustice, and the oppression in their nations just as I must do. They were willing to risk seeing their specific judgments and predictions corrected by God and History. This I am also willing to do. And who can say that even the greatest of the prophets were always right in their predictions of what God would do? But they always pointed to the righteousness of God which was ever present, moving in mysterious ways upon the earth.

Of this I am certain, God does not need parrots of a society, a political, or an ecclesiastical system. He needs prophets, who though torn by many inner struggles and who sometimes may not be quite sure of themselves, yet who by their vigils of prayer and listening to His voice, stand to affirm, "This is the way, walk ye in it." God knows the awful agony in which I find myself, for I am always filled with mixed emotions. Indeed I am but sharing with you this morning some of these, and saying only that this is the journey of one man's soul. Sometimes I am filled with great joy, sometimes great sorrow. Sometimes I have great courage at other times I am filled with fear seeking for ways to escape. Sometimes I feel that nothing will ever daunt the burning message that I feel inside and yet at other times wishing that I might be the meanest man alive (indeed I am) and perhaps then I could be free of this gnawing inside. Sometimes I feel that it is completely hopeless and at other times standing with great hope and optimism.

Ah, to talk to people who are tragically alone, and speak to them about the Presence of One who says "I will never leave you nor forsake you," is great joy. To hold the hand of one whose greatest love in life now lying cold in death and speak to them the precious promises of God is great joy. To talk with people whose life is trapped in a glass jail of bottles and bars of cork and to tell them about one who can quench their thirst, is great joy. To look into the eyes of little children and youth eagerly seeking life and to be able to point them to the one who said, "I am the way and the truth and the Light," is indeed great joy. But there are those agonizing moments of fatigue and weariness and these almost crush me in despair until at last my head falls upon The Holy Book and I hear the inspired pages crinkle beneath the weight of my own weariness and voices speaking to me of old, "Father, if it be possible let this cup pass from, nevertheless not as I will, but Thy will be done." Under God, how can any minister of His ever rest easy or be altogether sure when he has been entrusted with these treasures?

Some of my minister friends have said to me, "your business is to save souls." They seem to infer that this will help me to escape these awful social problems of my day. These are my minister friends who are not too much concerned with preserving church machinery, but just "in saving souls." They may think that this is the better way to escape and perhaps it is. Some may be able to wash their hands as Pilate did of the responsibility of the blood of men that is all over them, I can't. Some may be able to close their minds so as not to become unduly distributed—some just play like it isn't there or if it is there if we'll just be quiet long enough it will all go away. I cannot do this, for if I do I shall crush the God-given role as prophet, proclaimer of God's love, justice, judgment, and mercy. I have no alternative but to speak up, disregarding personal danger and insecurity. And if this means that I must take issue with leadership in my church, my state, or my government, then I must do just that or bear the guilt of deserting my post as a responsible man before God. Whether it is racial strife or whatever it be, if it is a threat to undermine the purpose of God and harm any being he has made, I must stand foursquare on the Christian teaching of love, though the reward be persecution. But there is one thing I know, if martyrdom is for any man, never fear, it will find him. But you see one can be a martyr to many things, indeed one can be a martyr and be wrong. No man can choose this path deliberately, only God may set it before him and when he does the man himself must decide. For though one may not choose it he can sometimes escape it if he is willing to pay the price. While there are those who choose the safe way and insist on seeing the end of the path before they make any decisions, I can only venture from day to day from step to step, with nothing more to guide me than the Holy Spirit. No true service to God will ever find its real reward externally from without; its real reward is always intrinsic to itself. The servant finds joy in his service, not in the applause of others, therefore, this calls for neither justification nor defense before men. For he can hold his head high—not in arrogance but in (do I dare say it) humble pride and proud humility.

The Christian Minister as no other man should be the master of compromise on non-essentials, but he must not compromise on the essentials of the Gospel. He cannot retract his own experience of the Love of God. Compromise may be urged upon him in the interest of harmony and unity and he is often tempted to temper his position, but he has to decide whom he will obey. There are many pressure groups both within the church and without. I have been in The Methodist Church all my life and I know that most churches have their "influential laymen" who often do not want the Gospel preached if it deals with any controversy or might disturb the peace and tranquility of the congregation. They want only "good preaching" on things with which they can agree and which will not rock their little boats, and heaven help the preacher who crosses them, for most of the time his ecclesiastical superiors will not, for they have their little boats also. But sometimes in the Name of Christ boats must be rocked and sometimes they must be sunk.

I realize full well that the time comes when a Minister's effective word is finished with a people. Sometimes a phase of a man's ministry is finished, completed and he can only rest it in the hands of God. But this is for God to decide, for I have discovered one should not sell Him short so quickly. The hardest thing I have to face as a Christian Minister, is the fact that I am expendable, but Jesus reminds me of this quite often. People do not like to be told that their thinking is narrow, that they are guilty of prejudice when

God has decreed that they should love. Ah, these things they may know, but no matter how gently or how roughly they are confronted with them and reminded of them, they often turn on those who do the reminding. But the hope is, that even while they turn, they are beginning to re-think their own position. The Gospel has always been rejected by the masses of people, no matter how logical or persuasive the prophet may be. He can only sow the seed and leave the results to God.

The position of the Christian Minister is always paradoxical. He loves his people deeply; if he did not he would not bother to try and help them. Yet his proclamation which has its source in love, may and often does separate him from those whom he loves and serves. But he must be willing to forsake the plaudits of men, and even their goodwill in order to serve Him who has Called him. He knows that he holds a message that is like a Balm in Gilead, which when spread over the life of a person will heal, and yet he knows that he must not spread it upon those who need to be pierced by judgment and the demands of the gospel. It is distressing to hear a hate-filled propagandist; but it is even more distressing to hear Him call upon God to justify his hate. He needs to be pricked by the gospel message. And the mere fact that he says he believes in God and even believes that God will take care of him in extremities and that Christ died for him—these can be dangerous unless his own hatred is exposed for what it is—a denial of the God of Love. There is one thing I have learned in the past two years about this 13th Chapter of II Corinthians, namely, it must be something more than an academic assent to the great principle of Love; it must be the experience of my life. Sometimes I become angry and resentful at wrong and evil and sometimes I become angry at persons, but no sooner has this happened, until I am begging God to forgive me and coming to Him in repentance. For I know, "that though I speak with the tongue of men and of angels, but have not love, it profiteth nothing." And this causes me to preach on the very edge of desperation itself, but knowing that even there God will guide me. I ran across this pre-sermon prayer of Canon Bernard I. Bell: "Dear Lord, this sermon of mine isn't much good. But I've worked honestly on it and it's the best I can do—at least for the moment. I know that any good that comes from my sermon will be Your doing, not mine. Please help me to live, that I may become an increasingly uncluttered channel of your grace. To that end, may I think your own thoughts after you, and speak your own word. I love you and I love these people, among whom I've been called. That's that God. Amen."

And so the preacher rises to preach and dares to say "Thus saith the Lord." And those who hear him must decide. Perhaps as he returns to his study he will say, "God, I didn't do so well today, but next time I'll do better, Lord." And maybe he will and maybe he won't.

§47 Reverend Edward Hughes Pruden

Edward Hughes Pruden was born on August 30, 1903 in Chase City, Virginia. He was educated at the University of Richmond, Southern Baptist Theological Seminary, Yale University, and he received his Ph.D. from the University of Edinburgh. From 1936 to 1969 Reverend Pruden pastored the First Baptist Church in Washington, D.C. In that capacity, he preached frequently with President Truman in attendance. An active leader in many Baptist organizations, Pruden also served on the board of trustees at the University of Richmond. He died in April 1987.

Reverend Pruden begins and ends his sermon on race relations with an emphasis on humility; with it, God's will can become manifest. Pruden also notes that a preacher, at "his best," is a prophet of God. And while he does not explicitly claim this mantle, Pruden's appeals to humility, his background as a southerner, and his duty to God cultivate a credibility that even southern audiences might find hard to resist. Pruden reminds his listeners of five things: first, the Christian concept of man emphasizes human dignity and the sacredness of every personality, including men, women and children; second, religion requires that we embrace high ideals; third, it is not easy being a Christian, as Paul reminds us; fourth, it is impossible to put ourselves in another's place; and finally, as Paul found out, citizenship has its privileges, and our laws can guarantee human rights even if they cannot change the human heart.

────────

Christianity and Racial Tensions

First Baptist Church, Washington, D.C.
1959 (reprinted)

The subject with which we are dealing this morning is one which arouses deep emotional responses. We should therefore approach it in that spirit of love and humility to which Paul refers when he wrote: "For I say, through the grace given unto me, to every man that is among you, not to think of himself more highly than he ought to think; but to think soberly, according as God hath dealt to every man the measure of faith" (Romans 12:3); and "Do nothing from selfishness or conceit, but in humility count others better than yourselves" (Philippians 2:3).

I have no desire to be controversial. As is the case with most people, I much prefer to be affable and agreeable; to say the thing that will be acceptable to the largest possible number of people. That is human nature! The minister of Jesus Christ at his best, however, must be the prophet of God, and therefore is not at liberty to follow his own inclinations. He must study the current scene carefully and prayerfully, and then attempt by all possible means to bring the will of God to bear upon all contemporary problems.

The Church of Christ cannot afford to be silent amidst turmoil and discord. The question we ask this morning is the question Zedekiah, the king, asked of Jeremiah, in the long ago: "Is there any word from the Lord?" and Jeremiah answered: "There is." We, too, believe that God has a word for us in the midst of our national crisis. I have prayed very earnestly that He would speak that word through me today.

What I shall have to say is addressed to Christians—those who have acknowledged their need of a Savior, and are seeking that spiritual rebirth by which we become new creatures. To those who are not Christians, any plea for humility, patience and genuine brotherhood is to no avail. Paul said that *before* he became a Christian he loved certain things and hated other things; but *after* he became a Christian and received Christ into his heart, the things he once hated he now loved, and the things he once loved, he now hated.

Not only do I address myself to Christians, but I trust that I am speaking to Christians who recognize the incompleteness of their religious experience. Not one of us has attained to the fullness of the life in Christ. At a midweek service a number of years ago, we departed from our usual procedure and asked members of the congregation to share with us the problems they were facing, in the hope that we could help them through prayer and encouragement to find solutions to those problems. Finally, one of our older deacons got up and said: "I think some of you know how difficult I can be at times; and how hard it is to get along with me under certain circumstances. But," he said, "you should have seen me thirty years ago." And then he went on to say, in true humility, that while he had not reached the ultimate goal he was seeking, nevertheless, in the intervening years God had led him step by step into a more Christian spirit. All of us are incomplete, unfinished Christians. Let us keep this in mind regarding race relations and all other difficult problems with which the human spirit is confronted.

I am also speaking this morning as a Southerner whose grandfather was a slave-owner, and whose boyhood hero was Robert E. Lee. I am speaking, too, as a Southerner whose three children attend integrated schools. Two of them have had Negro teachers for whom they have great admiration and respect. And as a Southerner, I speak against the background of two specific declarations made by our Southern Baptist Convention, both of which accepted the Supreme Court decision as the law of the land and called upon all our people to conduct themselves in the spirit of Christ. I am also speaking against the background of the fact that all six of our Southern Baptist Theological Seminaries are integrated. Negro students are received in all of them.

As a Southerner, and as a Christian, I recognize that extremists on both sides of the question have created a great deal of trouble which might have been avoided. Politicians on both sides of the question have sought to make political capital out of it. And some individuals have seen in such a controversy a chance to put themselves in the limelight, and advance their own personal fortunes. Such things, however, should not deter men of good will from trying to discover spiritually constructive means by which such a problem can be solved.

Let me suggest that we keep several things in mind. Consider first, that *as Christians, all of us are committed to the spiritual principle of human dignity and the sacredness of personality*. I don't believe there is a Christian in the world who would deny these vital concepts. Even the Psalmist, before the time of Christ, asked the question, "What is man?" and answered his own question: "Thou hast made him a little lower than the angels, and hast crowned him with glory and honor." Not *some* men, but *all* men, are born into this exalted state. Wherever Christianity has gone, the dignity of man has been recognized and practiced. Women have been given opportunities and privileges they have never known before. Children have been recognized and protected as never before. Lepers and outcasts, who were looked upon as the scum of the earth, have been taken into the fellowship of the concerned and ministered to in love and mercy. *All* men have received a higher status because of the concept of man which comes to us out of our Christian faith. And this concept of man must influence our relationship with all sorts and conditions of men, regardless of race, color or nationality.

Our Lord told the story of the good Samaritan for the purpose of illustrating that our mercy and good will should be extended not only to an inner circle of congenial persons, but to those also who occupy areas far removed from our own. And when He spoke of children, He said: "Rather than offend one of these little ones, it were better for a man that a millstone were hanged about his neck, and that he were cast into the midst of the sea." Christ was not speaking only of *white* children!

In the second place, let us never forget that our religion requires of us more than one finds in others. Jesus said to the Hebrews: "What do you more than others?" the inference being that they were committed to certain spiritual ideals and principles, and therefore more was expected of them. The Christian can never sink to the level of the average, popular opinion of men. He must espouse and defend certain exalted ideals which come to him out of his faith, and which he cannot in honest deny. The Christian faith carries with it certain inescapable imperatives. It requires of us a certain quality of thought and spirit which is not to be found in others who do not share such a faith.

In the third place, let us remember that it isn't easy to be a Christian. Following Christ goes counter to many natural tendencies with which we were born. Following Christ sets us apart from the man in the street, who is untouched and uninfluenced by the Christian Gospel. Paul, speaking to the early Christians, said to some of them: "Are you not behaving like ordinary men?" the inference being that they had no right to behave like ordinary men, for they possessed an extraordinary faith and experience. It is *hard* to be a Christian!

And let us keep in mind, too, that our immediate reactions are hardly ever *entirely* Christian. Though we are professing Christians, we're still in the thick of the spiritual struggle between the spiritual man and the natural man. Paul bears testimony to this in a bit of spiritual autobiography, when he tells us: "What I *would* do, I do not, and what I would *not* do, I do." "Every day," he said, "I struggle to keep my body under." These words were not written before he became a Christian, but after he had received Christ into his heart. Never assume that your immediate reactions are wholly Christian, but test them and try them against the norm of the spirit and life of Jesus Christ.

Remember also that it is practically impossible to put ourselves in another's place. How easy it is to say, "If I were a Negro I would do this, and that, and the other; I would be patient, I would wait, I would not insist on anything"; but how do you *know* what you would do, since you are *not* a Negro? It is simple enough for us to say, "Why did this matter have to be hastened? We were making progress; one of these days it would all have been worked out calmly and peacefully." That reaction is fine for *us*, but suppose *your* child were being adversely affected; his self-respect being violated by the impact of a social order which treats him as a second-class citizen? Could you then be as patient as you are now? The Golden Rule is admired and quoted by all of us, but frequently we forget its practical application: "Do unto others as you would have them do unto you."

Still again, let us be assured that if we do what is right we can leave the consequences in the hands of God. We are reminded of the old story of the ship coming into the harbor in the midst of a great storm, when the waves cast it upon the rocks, and it was in danger of being beaten to pieces. The captain of the Coast Guard called his men together and said: "You must go out and bring the people in before they are drowned." One of the sailors said: "Captain, we may *reach* the ship, but I doubt if we'll ever get back." To which the captain replied: "That isn't your business. As a member of the Coast Guard, when people are in danger, it is your duty to go to them. Whether or not you get back is an entirely different matter altogether." Our duty as the children of God is plain. Any consequences which may follow in the wake of doing His will as we see it will be cared for in His own way by an infinite, merciful, wise God. We can afford to leave the consequences with Him.

Then, finally, while most of us believe that kindness and brotherhood cannot be legislated, nevertheless we must recognize that there are times when laws serve a most useful purpose in the area of guaranteeing human rights. When Paul was arrested in a Roman city, his captors were on the point of thrusting him into prison, subjecting him to severe persecution, and perhaps even death, when suddenly they were reminded that he was a Roman citizen, and that under Roman law he had certain rights which could not be violated. Instantly the Roman soldiers changed their attitude. They had no disposition to show Paul mercy; they were not inclined to be kind and thoughtful; but they were under law, and because they were under law, Paul got a fair trial and decent treatment.

We have labor laws in the United States to protect the working man. They would never have been necessary if Christian people had exerted their influence. But almost every advantage the laboring man has won has been under legal pressure; not because people were kind-hearted or generous. Now, of course, almost everybody agrees that these laws are just and right. In the beginning, however, they were vigorously opposed by almost everyone who occupied a place of leadership in the realm of industry. It would be better if we were governed by conscience and humanitarian impulses, but until the consciences of men have been touched by the Holy Spirit of God, and the humanitarian impulses of men are sufficient to guarantee to every man that which is due him, we shall need certain legal decrees by which all men are protected.

May God give us grace to live calmly in the midst of confusion; graciously in the midst of cruelty; and constructively in the midst of chaos. Peter, on the housetop at Joppa, saw the vision of God, and heard the words of the Almighty: "That which I have cleansed, call not though unclean." What every man needs is the ability to hear the voice of God, and to acquire the spirit of humility by which we may follow His will wherever it may lead. "Love suffereth long and is kind."

1960

1960

§48 Governor LeRoy Collins

Thomas LeRoy Collins, born March 10, 1909 was the 33rd governor of Florida. Ironically, while Collins remains best known for his open opposition to segregation, the Tallahassean entered the political spotlight in support of it. Collins found the idea of segregation immoral as well as socially and economically harmful, though his belief in lawful behavior left him conflicted. These clashing ideals led him to decisions that seemed inconsistent during his time in the Florida House (1934–1940) and the Florida Senate (1940–1942, 1946–1954). For example, he opposed poll tax repeals but wanted to unmask the KKK. In 1952 Collins began working with Governor Dan McCarty to pass legislation, but McCarty died mid-term in 1954, and his lawful successor and head of the Senate, Charley Johns, replaced all of McCarty's men with his own. Collins decided then to run against him for governor—and won a special election. His views on segregation became apparent in 1957, when the Last Resort Bill, which would have closed down public schools before integrating them, passed. It would have become law without Collins's veto. He delivered a pro-integration address in that same year during the Tallahassee bus boycott, avoiding violence at all costs.

In 1960, after a close defeat by Lyndon B. Johnson for the vice presidency, his hometown of Tallahassee started to heat up. Praised by the *St. Petersburg Times* as the greatest speech ever delivered by a Florida governor, Collins's race relations address could not have happened at a more volatile time. The South was in chaos after eight straight weeks of lunch counter sit-ins (with Tallahassee being in its fifth). The student-led sit-ins started famously on February 1, with the four freshmen from North Carolina A&T sitting in at a local Woolworth's. Sit-ins were also causing the legal and social disintegration of Tallahassee, resulting in students being beaten and sprayed with tear gas and fire hoses, boycotts, and riotous showdowns consisting of over a thousand protesters. On March 12, nearly 250 Florida A&M University (FAMU) students marched in protest over the arrest of 23 activists. Police used tear gas to disperse the marchers. Many students were injured in the chaos, including FAMU student-activist, Patricia Stephens (later Patricia Stephens Due), whose vision was permanently damaged. Restaurants were closed and roped off for fear of being overtaken, while dozens of police officers, deputies, highway patrolmen, and officers from other agencies patrolled the streets. White students were encouraged not to attend any meetings at which demonstrations were even discussed. To make matters worse, politicians in Florida were mostly silent or opposed to the issue of integration due to the upcoming election campaign. Collins's speech occurred at a time when his action was predicted to cost him his political career. More importantly, his broadcast sparked enough national controversy such that few southern politicians could afford to stay silent on the matter of desegregation.

Although his speech was received favorably, there was also hostile opposition to his views. After giving a speech promoting integration in Jacksonville, he found his windows splattered with eggs and burning crosses in his front yard. This did not stop him. He soon became the first director of the Community Relations Service, a part of the Civil Rights Act of 1964. Desegregation, however, was not his only project. As president of the National Association of Broadcasters, Collins condemned tobacco producers for youth targeted advertising. He was also elected undersecretary of commerce. He failed in a final run for the Senate in 1968 thanks to a series of highly politicized misunderstandings. After John F. Kennedy was assassinated, Collins delivered a speech blaming the radicals of the South, but he mistakenly blamed the entire South. Another incident occurred during the marches at Selma. President Johnson sent Collins to try to negotiate a deal, but before he could negotiate, Collins was photographed next to Martin Luther King Jr., and was quickly labeled a racial liberal and a participant in the march. Collins spent the last years of his life between his beach house in Carrabelle, Florida and his home in Tallahassee until his death on March 12, 1991. That same month the Florida Legislature named him Floridian of the Century.

Collins's radio address is an attempt to depolarize opinions on race relations through the use of law, logic, morals, and Christianity. That he employed a live radio-television feed on a Sunday evening to deliver his address is not without consequence. He begins his speech by noting the pressure to remain silent. But Collins defines his role of governor as representative to all, not as a means to advancing his political career. He starts to explain the state of the nation by describing demonstrations and how they escalated because of misconceptions, blaming both store owners (by describing the first sit-in in North Carolina) and rioters (by pointing out incidents of how recent riots in Tallahassee were caused and escalated by rumors). He describes examples in Tallahassee: people, including police, were gathering in the thousands for no reason other than hearsay. In another incident, black students were rumored to be planning a riot. Townspeople had seen baseball bats. The "riot" turned out to be a scheduled baseball game between FAMU and Tuskegee. Collins also argues that while store owners had a legal right to refuse service, and that people could legally demonstrate, law alone would not solve the problem on its own, because not all laws are reasonable. Collins goes on to tell the Hindu story of the Blind Man and the Elephant, a tale that shows the fallibility of views only partially formed. He then describes a Lent service he attended, quoting Scripture made famous by Abraham Lincoln to show that division leads to destruction—precisely the aim of communists. Equal opportunity, he says, is the basis of American democracy and Christianity, and the equity struggle is embedded in the American dream. He proposes solutions such as forming a new biracial committee to succeed the old Fabisinski committee and forming local committees, both steps toward integration. He claims, however, that the success of communities in general depends on reason. He ends his speech by paralleling the current situation with the pressure put on Pontius Pilate to crucify Jesus. Although Pontius Pilate refused to take part in the crucifixion, he gave in to the mob, reason notwithstanding. He equates Pilate's reluctance to act with the death of morality and the rise of mob rule. Finally, Governor Collins appeals to the moderates to lead with reason, not blind emotion.

———

Statewide TV-Radio Talk to the People of Florida on Race Relations
Jacksonville, Florida
March 20, 1960

Hello, everybody. I first want to thank station WFGA and all the other broadcasting stations throughout the state for giving me this opportunity of coming into your living room this afternoon and talking to you about some problems about which I am very gravely concerned and that affect every man, woman and child in our state.

First, though, let me say to all the people of Florida how deeply we feel regret about the losses and damages that very high waters have occasioned so many of our citizens. We hope that damages can be minimized as best as possible, and, of course, all of us stand by as neighbors to render whatever help we can to these citizens and friends.

I want to talk to you person to person about race relations. Frankly, I had a group of my friends come over to see me yesterday and they said very frankly, "Governor, we don't think you should make this broadcast you are talking about tomorrow afternoon." I asked why and they said, "Well, you have less than a year now to serve in this office and certainly you know that whatever you say is going to make some people mad, and we just don't see the reason why you should stick your neck out or become involved in a discussion of that very explosive issue."

Well, frankly, I don't follow that sort of logic. I believe this is a very grave and serious matter facing the people of this state, affecting all of us, and I think the people of this state expect their governor to have convictions, and I think the people of this state when their governor has convictions about a matter expect him to express those convictions directly to them.

Now that's the policy I've been following as your governor. I know many times that I have taken stands that many people have not approved of. But I still believe that I have the respect of the people of Florida because I believe those people have felt I was sincere in my positions on problems and needs. And I think when they have differed with me, they have come later to feel that there was considerable logic to the stand that I had taken in respect to such.

Now let me say this, I believe very deeply that I represent every man, woman and child in this state as governor, whether a person is black or white, rich or poor, or influential or not influential.

A governor, if he is worth his salt, has a deep responsibility to all of the people, and I feel that responsibility. I want to say this to you, too, that I am not a candidate for anything. It seems almost every time I speak out about anything these days and for some time past now, I am projected as being a candidate for vice president or as having some personal motive of some sort. Now that is absolutely untrue—there is nothing to that.

I believe that the face of Florida is not in its pine trees or in its palm trees or even in its orange trees, but in the people of this state. I believe that large star on our map of the United States that represents Florida stands for the people of Florida.

Now let me review briefly something of the history of this racial strife that we are contending with. It was last February 1, that four Negro college students from a North Carolina college went into a Woolworth store in Greensboro, N.C. They bought some tooth paste and other minor items at one of the counters, then turned over to the lunch counter and ordered a cup of coffee. The waitress there said, "I'm sorry, we do not serve colored people here." One of the students said, "Why I have just been served here. I bought a tube of tooth paste over there." She said, "Well, we serve you over there, but we do not serve you here."

That was the first of these demonstrations. Many followed there in Greensboro involving hundreds of people. They spread throughout North Carolina on to Virginia, to South Carolina, to all of the other states of the South, including Florida.

We have had many throughout our state and, unlike some people assume, not all of these demonstrations were sponsored by students; in fact, only a minority have been sponsored by students. But the worst of all has occurred, I think, as some of you know, in Tallahassee. And there it was largely sponsored by students from the Florida A&M University, our Negro institution, and from Florida State University.

The City of Tallahassee took a rigid and punitive position in respect to these demonstrations. And, of course, this gave the appearance of partiality or of non-objectivity and this caused the conditions to become aggravated and we finally developed conditions in Tallahassee of which I am frankly ashamed.

Yesterday and the day before there was a tenseness about the atmosphere in Tallahassee that was disgraceful.

We had armed patrolmen, state, county and city, patrolling every street and the wildest rumors imaginable going on there about what was going to happen.

First a hundred Negro citizens were going to be brought in to augment local forces, then it got as high as 6,000. Also it was rumored that we had large numbers of White Citizens Council members who were coming in to augment the white forces and that grew up into the thousands. Of course, all that proved to be completely untrue but our people got worried. They were calling me at night—widows asking me if I thought they would be safe in their homes.

Fear is an insidious and dangerous thing to behold. When I was going back to my office yesterday at noon the highway patrolman who was driving me said, "Governor, I just got word that a bus load of students—Negro students from Alabama—has just pulled into the A&M University campus and they've got a lot of baseball bats and they're going to join with local forces there and put on some sort of demonstration."

I called the president of the university when I got to the office and he said, "It is true, Governor, we do have a bus load just in. For a year now we have had a baseball game scheduled with Tuskegee, the institution up there in Alabama, and the boys are here with their bats to play the ball game." And they played the ball game.

There were wild rumors about runs on hardware stores for ammunition, axes, hammers, knives, screwdrivers, and everything else. A perfectly absurd situation—I'd say—to develop here in our free America, in our free Florida, and in our free Tallahassee.

But what is the legal situation about these so-called demonstrations?

First, I want to say this to everyone of you: that we are going to have law and order in this state.

I don't care who the citizen is, he is going to be protected in pursuing his legal rights in Florida.

And that goes for every place in Florida and everybody in Florida.

Now under our free enterprise system and under our laws a merchant now has the legal right to select the private patrons he serves. As long as that is the law he is going to be protected in that legal right.

The customer, of course, has the legal right to trade or not to trade with any man he wants to—and, of course, there is the right to demonstrate, and the people will be protected in that right, too.

But I want to call to your attention that the right to demonstrate in all cases is limited by the fact that if there is any clear and present danger that a demonstration will incite public disorder, it becomes unlawful. And, of course, that kind of condition may exist in one community and not in another.

Now we have applied that rule before. I called on our sheriffs two years ago to apply it against the Ku Klux Klan. While they were planning a perfectly lawful demonstration under normal circumstances, from the information we had about the way they were going to conduct that, I felt it would clearly incite disorder and danger, and so we called upon the sheriffs to prevent the demonstrations, and they did.

But actually, friends, we are foolish if we just think about resolving this thing on a legal basis. In the first place, our merchants have much more involved so far as their business prosperity is concerned—in this matter of having, or not having, racial tensions of this kind.

Boycotts can be extremely damaging to their businesses. And, of course, racial tensions bring about depression in business and in the business spirit of any community.

But aside from that we've got some moral rights, and we've got some principles of brotherhood that are involved in these issues that I want to talk with you about.

I'm amazed at how different people react differently about racial matters. My own mother and father, I found the other day, don't fully agree on how they feel about race relations. I know my own wife and I have disagreements from time to time about race relations.

So far as I am personally concerned, and as your governor, I don't mind saying that I think that if a man has a department store and he invites the public generally to come into his department store and trade, I think then it is unfair and morally wrong for him to single out one department and say he will not allow people with black skin to patronize that one department.

Now he may have a legal right to do that under our law, but I still don't think that he can square that with moral right and justice.

Now some of you will not agree with that. Strange attitudes develop in respect to race relations. We have a department store there at home, for example, that has a counter where ladies go and buy clothes patterns. Both white and colored, have been seated there, side by side, selecting patterns at that counter for over 20 years.

Our banks in Tallahassee—and I think everywhere else—have no discrimination whatever in respect to what windows their customers use. One of our banks has recently initiated a program of serving coffee to all of its customers between 10 and 11 o'clock in the morning. And that service is provided without any discrimination; there are no special or separate places to sit. That institution feels an obligation to treat all of its customers alike.

The whole thing reminds me a little of that old Hindu story about the Blind Men and the Elephant. They didn't know what an elephant was like and so they wanted to find out and one blind man went up and felt the elephant's side and he said, "The elephant is like a wall." Another one went up and he touched the tusk and said, "The elephant's like a spear." The other one went up and he felt a leg and said, "The elephant is like a tree." The other one went up and he felt the ear and said, "the elephant is like a fan." The other one went up and he felt the tail and said, "The elephant is like a rope." And so it went.

Each interpreted as he felt it, but at the same time none of them had any real conception of what an elephant was actually like. Now none of us have all the answers to this situation, friends. I think all of us are probably part right and part wrong.

We must have more tolerance, more understanding, more Christianity, less words and less demonstrations, I think, if we are going to find the right answer.

I went to church this morning before driving over to Jacksonville for this broadcast and I was amazed that the scripture—the gospel—for this third Sunday in Lent which the minister read includes this: These words from the Master: "But he, knowing their thoughts, said unto them, every kingdom divided against itself is brought to desolation; and a house divided against itself falleth."

How appropriate that scripture was to me on this day because I firmly believe, as I hope you will, that every state divided against itself, every city divided against itself, every nation divided against itself, is bound to come to desolation.

Now that is true for many reasons because when there is division there is suspicion, there is fear, there is distrust and ultimately there is hate and hate consumes and destroys.

Friends, we must find answers. There is absolutely nothing that can aid the Communists more at this time in establishing supremacy over the United States—and that appears to be their ambition—than racial strife in this country.

I made that statement the other day and somebody said to me, "Yes, I think you are right about that. We understand how it injures our nation for the word to be passed along about our racial strife, but all this could be eliminated if the colored people would just stay in their place."

Now friends, that's not a Christian point of view.

That's not a democratic point of view.

That's not a realistic point of view.

We can never stop Americans from struggling to be free.

We can never stop Americans from hoping and praying that some day in some way that ideal imbedded in our Declaration of Independence, that all men are created equal, somehow will become a reality, and not just an illusory distant goal.

How are we going to work and what are we going to do?

Next week I am going to announce the appointment of a state-wide bi-racial committee to succeed the so-called Fabisinski committee which has been working with race relations. You will recall our unfortunate loss of Judge Fabisinski.

Mr. Cody Fowler of Tampa has agreed to serve as chairman of this new committee. The other members will be announced next week. Mr. Fowler is an outstanding man and will bring to that service outstanding competence and commitment. He was the president of the American Bar Association and he has long worked with inter-racial programs in the City of Tampa and he was one of the early members of our old Fabisinski committee.

And I want local bi-racial committees to be formed all over this state. I appeal to our communities—all communities—here and now to establish among your citizens bi-racial committees, that can take up and consider grievances of a racial character and that can honestly, and sincerely, and with a determined effort, try to find solutions to these difficulties.

Now the fact that your community has not had any difficulties yet should not deter you from moving to form this committee now because sooner or later you will have such difficulties. We are confronted with a great need in our state to intelligently and reasonably act, and to do that we must have the cooperation of the people.

Florida needs you in this program.

We need more reason and less emotion. We need more love and less hate. We need more work and effort and less talk and less demonstrations.

Citizens, please do not fail this great challenge.

We are in the Easter season. About two years ago the distinguished play-wright, Robert Sherwood, wrote a play for Robert Montgomery and it was presented on television. The title of it was "The Trial of Pontius Pilate." The title intrigued me because I had always thought of the events of those fateful times as working around the trial of Jesus. I never had thought in terms of Pontius Pilate being on trial.

But Sherwood in a very logical and in a very reasonable way pointed out that Pontius Pilate was truly the man who was on trial.

Pontius was a great, big, strong, politician at the court of the Caesars in Rome. He was a comer. Everybody expected him to do great things and to be given great assignments. His wife was of his greatest boosters. She thought that he would be assigned as the procurator of Egypt which was the most desired post available at that time. But when the day came for Pontius Pilate to get his assignment, it was to the little insignificant country of Judea. Pontius was furious because he felt that his assignment did not measure up to his capacity.

But he went on, of course, and undertook it just the same. You remember how the events developed toward the time of the crucifixion. The Pharisees got Jesus and they were trying their best to pin something on him that the Romans, of course, would feel would authorize his execution. They were having a tough time of it and they were pounding on Pilate's door, and trying to convince him that he should have Jesus executed, and you remember those early days how Pilate said, "But what's wrong with the man? I don't see, I don't hear anything treasonable about his conduct. Why should you or we be so disturbed?"

And they said: "He's inciting people to riot and disorder. He's creating insurrection. He's a dangerous and he's an evil man." And Pontius said to them, "I was talking to a man who was with him down in the temple yesterday and I asked him about what this Jesus had said, and he reported that somebody showed Jesus a coin and asked him point blank: 'What do you say about Caesar?' And Jesus said in response to that, 'Render unto Caesar the things that are Caesar's and unto God the things that are God's.' Now what's wrong with that?" Pontius asked. The mob then reported that Jesus was "attracting a lot of people to follow him. He's creating distrust in your government and in your supervision. You've got to do something about it."

Pontius' wife, Claudia, came into the picture about that time and she said, "Pontius, think carefully about this thing. I was down on the street the other day and I saw this man teaching and I went up because I wanted to hear what he had to say and he said very distinctly that, 'I came not to establish a kingdom on earth, but a kingdom in Heaven.'"

And Pontius turned to the mob and said, "How could that be treasonable?" But they insisted, and about that time the growing cry of the mob outdoors could be heard. First it was a soft, "Crucify Him," and then it got stronger, "Crucify Him," and then it got stronger, "Crucify Him," and then something happened to big, strong, Pontius Pilate.

Hearing the cry of the mob, he went out on the balcony [and the] big man started getting smaller and smaller and smaller in size. And he said, "Bring me a bowl of water." And when he got the water, he washed his hands in it.

And he said to that crowd, "I will not let the blood of this righteous man be on my hands. I wash my hands of it. See to it yourself."

And they did see to it themselves. They crucified him.

Friends, we've got mobs beginning to form now, in this nation, in this Southland, and in this state. The time requires intelligent, careful, thorough study of big problems, and the reaching of solutions that are going to be reasonable and sound and make good sense.

We cannot let this matter and these issues be decided by the mobs, whether they are made up of white people or whether they are made up of black people.

In this state we have extremists on one side, and we have extremists on the other. And we've got the beginnings of a mob too.

But where are the people in the middle? Why aren't they talking? Why aren't they working? They must start working. They must start efforts that are going to bring about solutions if we are going to resolve these problems and clear up these troubles and keep our state growing, as our state should grow.

You remember the song of the brook? It said, "Bring me men to match my plains, men with empires in their vision and new eras in their brains."

We need men to match our mountains.

We've got to have men with new eras in their brains. We've got a state to build. We've got a nation to save. And we have a God to serve. Thank you.

§49 Reverend James Lawson

James Lawson, one of the most important figures in the entire civil rights movement, was born on September 22, 1928 in Uniontown, Pennsylvania. He grew up in Massillon, Ohio and attended Baldwin-Wallace College. A life-long pacifist, Lawson spent 14 months in jail for refusing the draft in 1951. Upon his release from prison, he traveled to a Methodist missionary organization in Nagpur, India where he studied Gandhi's Satyagraha, a method of nonviolent resistance. Back in the United States in 1955, Lawson entered the Graduate School of Theology at Oberlin College. It was at Oberlin that Lawson met Martin Luther King, who urged him to come south and help in the burgeoning civil rights movement.

Under the auspices of the Fellowship of Reconciliation, Lawson moved to Nashville and in 1959 began conducting workshops in nonviolent resistance to local college students. That fall, he and the students began "test runs" of resistance tactics at various Nashville stores. His students included such civil rights luminaries as Bernard Lafayette, John Lewis, Marion Barry, Diane Nash, and James Bevel. In late February of 1960, the Nashville sit-ins began in earnest, earning Lawson arrest and eventual expulsion from Vanderbilt Divinity School.

In 1962 Lawson became pastor of Centenary Methodist Church in Memphis, Tennessee. Six years later, it was Reverend Lawson who invited Dr. King to Memphis to help dramatize the sanitation workers' struggle against the city. King was murdered in Memphis on April 4. In 1974 Lawson moved west to become pastor at Holman United Methodist Church in Los Angeles, where he still conducts workshops in nonviolence. In 1996 Vanderbilt Divinity School honored Lawson with its Distinguished Alumnus Award.

Lawson is notoriously abstemious with his speeches. As a consequence, very few have ever been published. In this speech, given at the apogee of the student sit-in movement of 1960 at Shaw University, Lawson offers the movement a Christian foundation for its existence and warrants for action. Civil rights historians recognize that the Shaw conference was the birth of the Student Nonviolent Coordinating Committee (SNCC)—a group that would become the avant-garde of the freedom movement. The conference was coordinated by Ella Baker, a Shaw graduate and a former Executive Director of the Southern Christian Leadership

Conference (SCLC) who lobbied extensively for the students to have their own separate group. While King, Baker, and others spoke to the students assembled at Shaw, it was Lawson who catalyzed the students' enthusiasm and idealism with this radical address.

The "Christian student" will want to know what all the fuss is about. Just why are college students protesting in the south? "Is it just a lot of nonsense over a hamburger?" Lawson chronicles what the movement is not: it is not about him and his expulsion from Vanderbilt; it is not about police partiality and brutality; it is not about reforming the nation's laws; nor is it about integration. Rather, the student movement had far loftier ends: "The Christian favors the breaking down of racial barriers because the redeemed community of which he is already a citizen recognizes no barriers dividing humanity. The kingdom of God, as in heaven so on earth, is the distant goal of the Christian." The message of the movement is thus twofold. The sit-ins highlighted the moral and spiritual dimensions of the problem and the movement demanded prompt action. Lawson got into trouble with the NAACP and Roy Wilkins for his attack on the organization for its legal and fundraising emphases, earning the "'black bourgeois' club organ" epithet. Similarly, Lawson's ire extends to the black church: "The Negro church and its minister function as in an earlier day and not as God's agents to redeem society." Lawson closes his address with a ringing declaration that only "a radical Christian obedience" would "transform [the] evil" of segregation.

Speech at Shaw University
Raleigh, North Carolina
April 15, 1960

These are exciting times in which to live.

Reflect how over the last few weeks, the "sit-in" movement has leaped from campus to campus, until today hardly any campus remains unaffected. At the beginning of this decade, the student generation was "silent," "uncommitted," or "beatnik." But after only four months, these analogies largely used by adults appear as hasty clichés which should not have been used in the first place. The rapidity and drive of the movement indicates that all the while American students were simply waiting in suspension; waiting for that cause, that ideal, that event, that "actualizing of their faith" which would catapult their right to speak powerfully to their nation and world.

The witness of enthusiastic, but mature young men and women, audacious enough to dare the intimidations and violence of racial injustice, a witness not to be matched by any social effort either in the history of the Negro or in the history of the nation, has caused this impact upon us. In his own time, God has brought this to pass.

But as so frequently happens, these are also enigmatic moments. Enigmatic, for like man in every age who cannot read the signs of the times, many of us are not able to see what appears before us, or hear what is spoken from lunch counter stools, or understand what has been cried by jail cell bars.

Already the paralysis of talk, the disobedience of piety, the frustration of false ambition, and the insensitiveness of an affluent society yearn to diffuse the meaning and flatten the thrust of America's first major nonviolent campaign.

One great university equates the movement to simply another student fad similar to a panty raid, or long black stockings. Many merchants zealously smothering their Negro customers with courtesy for normal services, anticipated an early end to the unprecedented binge. Certainly no southern white person and few Negroes expected the collegiates to face the hoses, jails, mobs and tear gas with such dignity, fearlessness, and nonviolence. In fact, under any normal conditions, the mere threat of the law was sufficient to send the Negro scurrying into his ghetto. Even astute race reporters accentuate the protest element as the major factor.

Amid this welter of irrelevant and superficial reactions, the primary motifs of the movement, the essential message, the crucial issue raised are often completely missed. So the Christian student who has not yet given his support or mind to the movement might well want to know what the issue is all about. Is it just a lot of nonsense over a hamburger? Or is it far more?

To begin, let us note what the issue is not. Many people of good-will, especially Methodists and Nashvillians, have considered my expulsion from Vanderbilt University and the self-righteousness of the press attack as the focus of attention. But nothing could be further from the truth. The expulsion, three months before the completion of the Bachelor of Divinity degree, drastically alters certain immediate personal plans. The press attack tended to make me a symbol of the movement. But such incidents illustrate an ancient way of escaping an existential moment. Call him "the son of the devil," or one of the "men who turn the world upside down," and there are always the gullible who will "swallow the camel."

Police partiality is not the issue. Nashville has been considered one of those "good" cities where racial violence has not been tolerated. Yet, on a Saturday in February, the mystique of yet another popular myth vanished. For only police permissiveness invited young white men to take over store after store in an effort to further intimidate or crush the "sit-in." Law enforcement agents accustomed to viewing crime, were able to mark well-dressed students waiting to make purchases, as loitering on the lunch counter stools, but they were unable even to suspect and certainly not to see assault and battery. Thus potential customers, quietly asking for service, are disorderly, breaching the peace, inciting riots, while swaggering, vilifying, violent, defiant white young teenagers are law-abiding. The police of the nation have always wreaked brutality upon minority groups. So our Nashville experience is nothing new, or even unexpected. We hold nothing against these hard-pressed officers. Such partiality, however, is symptomatic of the diagnosis only—an inevitable by-product—another means of avoiding the encounter. But the "sit-in" does not intend to make such partiality the issue.

Already many well-meaning and notable voices are seeking to define the problem in purely legal terms. But if the students wanted a legal case, they had only to initiate a suit. But not a single city began in this fashion. No one planned to be arrested or desired such. The legal battles which will be fought as a consequence of many arrests never once touch on the matter of eating where you normally shop, or on segregation per se.

The apparent misuse of local laws requires new legal definitions which can only be made in the courts, under the judgment of the Constitution of the United States. Old laws and ordinances originally written to hamper labor have been revived to stop or crush the sit-in; disorderly conduct codes which could be used against almost every conceivable peaceful demonstration; conspiracy to block trade charges. Obviously these have no relation to the Bill of Rights and are but gimmicks designed to impede civil liberty.

Let us admit readily that some of the major victories gained for social justice have come through the courts, especially the Supreme Court, while other branches of government were often neglecting their primary function to sustain the American experiment. The Negro has been a law-abiding citizen as he has struggled for justice against many unlawful elements.

But the major defeats have occurred when we have been unable to convince the nation to support or implement the Constitution, when a court decision is ignored or nullified by local and state action. A democratic structure of law remains democratic, remains lawful only as the people are continuously persuaded to be democratic. Law is always nullified by practice and disdain unless the minds and hearts of a people sustain law.

When elements of good-will called for law and order during the crisis in Little Rock, their pleas fell on deaf ears. In many sections of the country where law no longer sustains and enforces segregation, the segregation persists because it is etched upon the habits of mind and emotions of both Negro and white. Separate but equal in transportation has by the Supreme Court been judged as impossible and unconstitutional. Yet in many cities like Nashville the buses more or less remain segregated.

Both Negro and white sustain the custom because their basic inner attitudes and fears remain unchanged. Eventually our society must abide by the Constitution and not permit any local law or custom to hinder freedom or justice. But such a society lives by more than law. In the same respect the sit-in movement is not trying to create a legal battle, but points to that which is more than law.

Finally, the issue is not integration. This is particularly true for the Christian oriented person. Certainly the students are asking in behalf of the entire Negro community and the nation that these eating counters become places of service for all persons. But it would be extremely short-sighted to assume that integration is the problem or the word of the "sit-in." To the extent to which the movement reflects deep Christian impulses, desegregation is a necessary next step. But it cannot be the end. If progress has not been at a genuine pace, it is often because the major groups seeking equal rights tactically made desegregation the end and not the means.

The Christian favors the breaking down of racial barriers because the redeemed community of which he is already a citizen recognizes no barriers dividing humanity. The Kingdom of God, as in heaven so on earth, is the distant goal of the Christian. That Kingdom is far more than the immediate need for integration.

Having tried to dispel the many smokescreens spewed to camouflage the purpose and intent of the "sit-in," let me now try as carefully as possible to describe the message of our movement. There are two facets to that message.

In the first instance, we who are demonstrators are trying to raise what we call the "moral issue." That is, we are pointing to the viciousness of racial segregation and prejudice and calling it evil or sin. The matter is not legal, sociological or racial, it is moral and spiritual. Until America (South and North) honestly accepts the sinful nature of racism, this cancerous disease will continue to rape all of us.

For many years Negroes and white have pretended that all was well. "We have good race relations." A city like Nashville has acquired national fame about its progress in desegregation. Yet when the "sit-ins" began, the underlying hatred and sin burst to the surface. A police department with a good reputation for impartiality swiftly became the tool of the disease always there. A mayor, elected with overwhelming Negro support, made the decisions which permitted mob rule. If Nashville had "good race relations," why did such violence explode? The fact is that we were playing make-believe that we were good. All the while Negro and white by pretension, deliberate cooperation and conscious attitudes shared in such a deluded world.

The South and the entire nation are implicated in the same manner. True, there has been progress. For example, lynching has virtually disappeared (although there are many signs that even it might break forth again with unprecedented fury); but the real lynching continues unabated—the lynching of souls, persons (white and Negro) violating its victims absolutely, stripping them of human traits. This actual lynching goes on every day even while we make-believe that lynching is a phenomenon of the past. What's more, the masses of people, including most moderates of both "races," are glibly unaware of the lynching.

The nonviolent movement would convict us all of sin. We assert, "Segregation (racial pride) is sin. God tolerates no breach of his judgment. We are an unhealthy people who contrive every escape from ourselves." Thus a simple act of neatly dressed, non-violent students with purchases in their pockets, precipitated anger and frustration. Many "good" people (white and Negro) said, "This is not the way. We are already making adequate progress." Nonsense! No progress is adequate so long as any man, woman or child of any ethnic group is still a lynch victim.

That the nonviolent effort has convicted us of sin, and thus appealed to consciences is attested by the new-found unity and direction now established in Negro communities in places like Durham and Nashville. Witness further the many white people who say, "I never thought the problem was so serious. I feel so ashamed." Many of these people now support the movement.

In the second instance, the nonviolent movement is asserting, "get moving. The pace of social change is too slow. At this rate it will be at least another generation before the major forms of segregation disappear. All of Africa will be free before the American Negro attains first-class citizenship. Most of us will be grandparents before we can live normal human lives."

The choice of the nonviolent method, "the sit-in," symbolizes both judgment and promise. It is a judgment upon middle-class conventional, half-way efforts to deal with radical social evil. It is specifically a judgment upon contemporary civil rights attempts. As one high school student from Chattanooga exclaimed, "We started because we were tired of waiting for you adults to act."

The sum total of all our current efforts to end segregation is not enough to do so. After many court decisions, the deeper south we go, the more token integration (and that only in public schools) we achieve. *Crisis* magazine becomes known as a "black bourgeois" club organ, rather than a forceful instrument for justice. Interracial agencies expect to end segregation with discussions and teas. Our best agency (the NAACP) accents fundraising and court action rather than developing our greatest resource, a people no longer the victims of racial evil who can act in a disciplined manner to implement the Constitution. The Negro church and minister function as in an earlier day and not as God's agents to redeem society.

But the sit-in is likewise a sign of promise: God's promise that if radically Christian methods are adopted the rate of change can be vastly increased. This is why nonviolence dominates the movement's perspective. Under Christian nonviolence, Negro students reject the hardship of disobedient passivity and fear, but embrace the hardship (violence and jail) of obedience. Such nonviolence strips the segregationalist power structure of its major weapon: the manipulation of law or law enforcement to keep the Negro in his place.

Furthermore, such an act attracts, strengthens and sensitizes the support of many white persons in the South and across the nation (the numbers who openly identify themselves with the "sit-in" daily grow).

Nonviolence in the Negro's struggle gains a fresh maturity. And the Negro gains a new sense of his role in molding a redeemed society. The "word" from the lunch counter stool demands a sharp re-assessment of our organized evil and a radical Christian obedience to transform that evil. Christian nonviolence provides both that re-assessment and the faith of obedience. The extent to which the Negro joined by many others apprehends and incorporates nonviolence determines the degree that the world will acknowledge fresh social insight from America.

§50 Everett Tilson

Everett Tilson was born in 1923 and raised in Seven Mile Ford, Virginia, a tiny village with a population of 277—none of whom was black. As a seventh grader, his teacher gave him a copy of *Uncle Tom's Cabin*; the book changed his life. A graduate of King College and Vanderbilt University, Tilson earned his doctorate in religious studies at Vanderbilt in 1952. He remained on faculty in the Divinity School for nine years. One of his students at Vanderbilt was a Methodist minister, James Lawson, a friend of Martin Luther King, Jr., a member of the Fellowship of Reconciliation, a pacifist organization, and a leader of a local group of students he was training in Gandhian nonviolence. Several of Lawson's students became prominent civil rights activists, including James Bevel, Diane Nash, John Lewis, Bernard Lafayette, and Marion Barry. These students, along with many others, commenced sit-in demonstrations and picketing in downtown Nashville during February 1960. On March 3, Lawson was expelled from the Divinity School by Chancellor B. Harvie Branscomb for leading a planned campaign of civil disobedience. Lawson was scheduled to graduate in May, just two months after the expulsion.

Following Lawson's expulsion, Tilson was one of the more outspoken of Vanderbilt's faculty. While his efforts to reinstate Lawson proved futile, he was not alone: 10 of the school's 16 faculty members resigned and 17 students withdrew. Shortly before the fracas, Tilson accepted a position at the Methodist Theological School (MTS) of Ohio in Delaware. Nearly three years before the Lawson contretemps, Tilson had made up his mind to leave the Divinity School, as Branscomb refused to authorize a promotion and raise requested for him in the dean's budget, ostensibly because of Tilson's activism on race. A faculty member until he retired in 1988, Tilson remained active in the movement, getting arrested in Jackson,

Mississippi in 1964 for attempting to integrate an Easter church service at the Capital Street Methodist Church, and making the historic march from Selma to Montgomery in 1965. Upon retirement, Tilson volunteered at MTS for five years, serving as dean, director of admissions and coordinator of alumni activities. Tilson was forced to resign in 1994 for supporting the invitation of a lesbian theologian to give several lectures at MTS. He and his wife Mary live in Delaware, Ohio.

Tilson delivered this speech before the Nashville Christian Leadership Council on April 25, 1960, just days before the city integrated its lunch counters. Expertly using parallel constructions, Tilson offers a devastating critique of "Christian segregation" by refuting the practice based on the Ten Commandments. Whereas most ministers waged war on segregation via a New Testament lens, Tilson uses the Old Testament law to compelling rhetorical effect. Tilson also goes beyond canonical Hebraic law to call into question just who was responsible for the recent bombing of Nashville lawyer Alexander Looby's home—an attack so big that it blew out 147 windows at nearby Meharry Medical College. Culpability for the brazen attack is widespread. Three and a half years later, Charles Morgan, Jr. would make a similar indictment in the aftermath of the Sixteenth Street Church Bombing in Birmingham.

―――――――

Segregation and the Ten Commandments
Nashville Christian Leadership Council, Mt. Olive Baptist Church, Nashville, Tennessee
April 25, 1960

Almost universally the churches officially condemn segregation. They do so, not on constitutional grounds, but because of the demands of their Lord. Our Christian churches do not oppose segregation because it is illegal; they oppose segregation because it is immoral. They do not oppose it because it is unconstitutional; they oppose it because it is unchristian. They do not oppose it because it breaches the ten amendments; they oppose it because it breaches the Ten Commandments.

Segregation breaches the first commandment: "You shall have no other gods before me." It substitutes race for God as the organizing center of life. It measures the worth and growth of human existence by an altogether human yardstick. And this, as we all know, is worse than immoral; it is idolatrous. Christian segregationists think they have an answer to this charge. In unqualified commitment to their race, they assure us, they have escaped that bondage to self which Christian faith sees as the root evil of human existence. But this assurance can hardly survive close scrutiny. Quite the contrary, segregation furnishes us with a center for the organization of our pride and ambition. No matter how physically weak, mentally dull, or morally obtuse they may be, so long as men of distinction wear a white skin, they can take pride in their common heritage with Al Capone and John Dillinger, not to mention John Kasper and Senator James Eastland.

Segregationists do not betray their self-centeredness in their hymn of praise to the white man; they do it by their private refrain: "Just think of it! I am a member of the Master Race!" They do not take pride in their race because it is white; they take pride in the white race because it is theirs. They do not idolize white skin because it is a mark of distinction; they make white skin a mark of distinction because possession is nine-tenths of idolatry. They idolize the white race because they belong to the white race. Because of their possession of the skin of the superior man's color, they can idolize themselves. Worse yet, thanks to the presence among them of other men of this same color, vocal altruism becomes a shield for covert egocentrism. Segregation does worse than put the god of race before the God of the universe. It puts the maker of me and mine before the Maker of heaven and earth.

Segregation breaches the second commandment: "You shall not make yourself a graven image, or any likeness of anything . . . in heaven above, . . . in the earth below, or . . . in the water under the earth." It turns a pale-face into a graven image, then bows down and worships "the likeness" of what is "in the earth below." If here I were to substitute the platform of the Marxists or the ritual of the Canaanites for the platform or the ritual of the Eastlands, the breach of the second commandment would become quite clear. We Americans have remarkable skill in uncovering and shattering the graven images of the Russians and the Canaanites. Unfortunately, we do not fare so well in the struggle against the graven image of Jefferson Davis. But the graven image is there, and it is exceedingly dangerous. What must be set down as one of the most ironic facts of our time is the readiness of the most blatant anti-Marxists among us to let segregation take the same place in our life that Communism occupies in the Kremlin.

Segregation breaches the third commandment: "You shall not take the name of the Lord your God in vain." It asks God to bless us in our refusal to identify our neighbor by the love of God. Bishop Nygren reminds us, "When it is said that God loves man, this is not a judgment on what man is like, but what God is like." By the same token, when the New Testament confronts us with the demand to love neighbor as self it tells us nothing at all about our neighbor. Nothing about the size of his fortune, nothing about the state of his soul, nothing about the color of his skin. It tells us only that our neighbor, whoever, wherever, and whatever he is, is beloved of God. And God loves our neighbor not because he is lovable, but because God is loving. If God's love for neighbor be blind love, value blind, creed blind, color blind, and our love be conscious love, value conscious, creed conscious, and color conscious, we should hardly be surprised at Jesus' stinging rebuke of our unctuous piety: "Not every one who says to me, 'Lord, Lord,' shall enter the kingdom of heaven, but he who does the will of my Father who is in heaven."

Segregation breaches the fourth commandment: "Remember the Sabbath day, to keep it holy." It sunders those whom God would join together. Instead of bringing Christians together because of a common faith, it keeps them apart despite a common faith. A local minister in a recent sermon on "The Almighty Race Question" illustrates the deep tragedy of the relation between segregation and the fourth commandment. The church bulletin which carries this sermon contained the following words of welcome: "Ours is a friendly church—visitors are always welcome." But the sermon makes it quite clear that this applies only to certain visitors. There the minister said: "It is . . . the opinion of the official board that . . . in this time of tension any member of our church desiring to bring . . . Negroes must previously have cleared the matter with the pastor-in-charge, securing a written note from him to the effect that it is permissible." And some people are shocked by the requirement of a pass book in South Africa.

Segregation breaches the fifth commandment: "Honor your father and your mother." It defines kinship in terms of blood rather than faith. That is not the way Jesus defined it. One day as Jesus was speaking, "a crowd said to him, 'Your mother and your brothers are outside, asking for you.' And he replied, 'Who are my mother and my brothers?' And looking around on those who sat about him, he said, 'Here are my mother and my brothers! Whoever does the will of God is my brother, and sister, and mother.'"

Segregation breaches the sixth commandment: "You shall not kill." It kills the noblest impulses in man. As Jesus so clearly saw, you can kill men without taking up the sword against them. The vitriolic tongues or pens of angry little men can be just as murderous as the sword or bomb in the hands of a maniac. Our Lord said: "You have heard . . . it . . . said 'You shall not kill; and whoever kills shall be liable to judgment.' But I say to you that every one who is angry with his brother shall be liable to judgment; whoever insults his brother shall be liable to judgment, and whoever says 'You fool,' shall be liable to the hell of fire."

If Mr. and Mrs. Alexander Looby had been killed in the explosion that rocked Nashville recently, who would have been responsible for their murder? A lot of people would have been responsible for their murder. The jails of Nashville could not begin to accommodate all the people who helped to set the stage for that crime. A whole host of Nashvillians aided and abetted the men who threw that bomb. All of us who have in any way insulted Negroes, we, as well as the droppers of the bomb, would have been guilty of this crime.

Here I do not refer alone to the merchants who turned "thumbs down" on the request of the Negroes for service at downtown lunch counters, thus forcing people to have to wage demonstrations for rights you and I take for granted. I do not refer alone to the people who in one breath hail as patriots the American revolutionaries who took up arms in protest against "taxation without representation," then in the next condemn Negroes as anarchists for sitting down in protest against "equal prices without equal privileges." I do not refer alone to the people who, though many of them know better, trace this whole movement to a few outside "agitators." I do not refer alone to the operators of local television stations who, in the midst of a controversial issue, fail to ask any Negro leader to interpret for Nashville the other side of this controversy. I do not refer alone to the churchman who, after two months of eloquent silence in Nashville, calls the church in Denver to speak with "a clear voice" on race relations, but even at that safe distance fails to say what it is the church ought to say with "a clear voice." I do not refer alone to the tea-and-cocktail experts on human relations who, between their semiannual teas with Negro friends, drink cocktails once a week with Christian segregationists. I do not refer alone to the whites who believe cultured Negroes ought to play the role of guinea pigs that we might be convinced one by one of their readiness for admission into high civilization, as if the burden of proof rested on the shoulders of the Negro to show to you and me that he is our equal. I do not refer alone to the moderates who, until the Negroes laid siege to the wall of segregation, said it must fall, then after reading a few objective editorials on the subject, decided that Nashville is not the place, now is not the time, and these are not the Negroes. I do not refer alone to the people who, when Northern industrialists show up at downtown restaurants, treat them as distinguished guests, yet insult Americans from Mississippi or South Carolina because of a difference in the pigmentation of their skin.

I refer to those of us who insult the Negro by failing to translate his quest into human terms. I refer to all of us who, when we see a Negro man directing his thirsty child away from a water fountain, his hungry wife away from a lunch counter, or his frail mother away from a comfortable seat, insult him by failing to exclaim, "But for the accident of birth there I go." I refer to all of us who, when we see a Negro mother leave her children alone while she goes to another part of the city to keep those of a white socialite, insult her by failing to say, "But for the accident of birth there goes my sister."

There are endless ways of smothering the life of the oppressed. One of the oldest and most common is simply to close our minds and hearts to the fact of their existence.

The relation of segregation to the seventh commandment, "You shall not commit adultery," cannot be stated quite so simply. But one fact lies beyond dispute: Segregation has not prevented the violation of the commandment against adultery on an interracial basis. Here we do not even have to redefine adultery, as Jesus did, in terms of the lustful look. Under segregation, as under integration, men and women of both races have broken the seventh commandment. To paraphrase Lincoln: The fact that some white men will not have the black woman as a wife does not keep them from using her as a mistress.

Segregation breaches the eighth commandment: "You shall not steal." It robs the white man, and it robs the Negro. It robs the white man of a chance to discover that it is not the race but the segregation of the Negro that keeps him, in all too many of his places, in slums and poverty. It robs him of a chance to discover that, beneath the skin, Negroes and whites share a common humanity: They rejoice alike at birth; they weep alike at death; they suffer alike in pain; they hope alike in marriage; and they dream alike as parents. But what segregation steals from the Negro, as pointed out in the report of the President's Committee on Civil Rights, is much more basic and elementary. It robs him of equal access to public facilities. It robs him of equal access to educational opportunities. It robs him of equal access to decent housing in good neighborhoods. It robs him of equal access to a typical workweek and favorable working conditions. It robs him of equal access to hospital facilities. It robs him of the respect and dignity due him as a human being.

Segregation breaches the ninth commandment: "You shall not bear false witness against your neighbor." Segregation bears false witness against the white man, and it bears false witness against the Negro. Segregation bears false witness against the white man by ascribing his advantages to extraneous considerations. If he has a stratospheric intelligence quotient it is traced not to his genius but to his race. If he enjoys superior economic advantages it is traced not to his industry but to his race. If he is especially good, it is traced not to the purity of his heart but to the whiteness of his skin. If such logic held, a Negro of virtue, wealth, or intelligence would be an impossibility.

Segregation prompts men to bear false witness against the Negro. If he lives in a slum the Negro is charged not with poverty, but laziness. If he works in a kitchen the reason is not discrimination, but limitation. If he fails as an engineer, the reason is not a lack of education, but a shortage of intelligence. If he goes to jail, the reason is not environment, but heredity. If this logic held, there would be no Negroes in engineering, kitchens, or slums. All Negroes would be behind bars.

Segregation has betrayed us into bearing false witness about both races. It has betrayed us into granting the white man undeserved advantages. It has betrayed us into denying the Negro basic rights. In short, thanks in part at least to segregation, we have broken the ninth commandment against members of both races.

Segregation breaches the tenth commandment: "You shall not covet . . . anything that is your neighbor's." It prompts the white man to covet what belongs to the Negro. The Universal Declaration of Human Rights asserts that all men have a right to protection against any "inhuman or degrading treatment," against "any discrimination," against any denial of "equal access to public service," against any refusal of "equal pay for equal work," against "any restriction of full participation in the cultural and scientific advancements and benefits of society." If true, we cannot deny the Negro, or any other person, his enjoyment of these rights without coveting what belongs to our neighbor. Therefore, insofar as segregation does involve men in the denial of these rights, by the same token it involves them in the breach of the tenth commandment.

The future of desegregation depends on our point of departure in times of crisis. How we answer the questions, "When do we start?" and, "How fast do we travel?" will hinge largely on the authority from whom we take our orders. If we take our cues from our neighbors' prejudices we shall move slowly and in all probability in the wrong direction at the wrong time for the wrong reason. But on the other hand, if we take our cues from God's commandments, who among us would dare answer, "Be patient, Lord, and I'll do what you say, but not here and not yet." It may be later than we think. This may be the hour for the tribe of Elijah to rise up and say to this generation: "How long will you go limping with two different opinions? If Jesus Christ is Lord follow him; but if Jim Crow, then follow him."

§51 Dr. Benjamin E. Mays

Benjamin Elijah Mays's biography appears in the introduction to his May 27, 1954 sermon in Evanston, Illinois. In the following commencement address to the graduates of historically black college, Florida A&M University (FAMU), Dr. Mays asks his listeners to reflect on what 341 years of "disability" have done to blacks—and he challenges them to overcome it in a mere quarter century. The catalogue of disability is long: it has made blacks see themselves as inferior; it has destroyed countless ambitions and aspirations; it has created an intellectual ghetto where blacks were expected to stay in their place; it has made blacks ashamed of their race and their history; it has made blacks politically impotent; and, perhaps most of all, these centuries of disability have "thrown us behind in education."

How can this long history of oppression be overcome? First, Mays encourages the graduates to acknowledge without bitterness that they are behind; second, the pace is too slow and education is taking too long; and perhaps most importantly, all must proceed as if on a mission from God: "Whatever we do, if we are to overcome the disabilities of 341 years in a quarter of a century, we must do it as if God called us into the world to do it. We cannot allow any sand to burn under our feet." Unlike the recent past, the future is indeed bright for black graduates, as "the sky and not the ceiling is beginning to be the limit." Finally Mays urges his audience to see their efforts in a much larger context than race: "it matters much what happens to the Christian Gospel and to Democracy. Either Democracy and Christianity will function in America or it will perish from the earth. In this great fight of ours, we fight not for ourselves alone, but for the United States."

The Challenge to Overcome The Major Disabilities of 341 Years in a Quarter of a Century

Florida A&M University, Tallahassee, Florida
May 28, 1960

I am using tonight a rather strange subject. I hope you will like it. If you do not agree with my proposal, you must give reasons for your disagreement in which case I will have stimulated you to think in order to justify your opposition. If you agree, I have convinced you. So, head or tail, I win. The subject is: *The Challenge to Overcome the Major Disabilities of 341 Years in a Quarter of a Century.*

The Negro's sojourn in the United States may be roughly divided into three eras; the era of slavery from 1619 to 1865; the second era from 1865 to May 17, 1954; and the third era may be called the era of desegregation, or as it is wrongly called integration beginning in 1954.

The slave era was the era of subhumanity, the era of depersonalization, when the Negro was not a human but property owned and sold like cattle, like mules and horses, cows and hogs, cats and dogs, sheep and goat. In this era, the Negro was not a citizen. He had no standing in law. The bodies of the slaves belonged to the masters and if they so desired, they possessed the bodies of the female slaves and there was considerable evidence to show that many of the masters did desire and did possess the bodies of the female slaves.

Slavery, like all great evils, had to be justified. Conscience had to be silenced if the system was to be perpetuated. And all experience proves that there is no sin, however colossal, that the human mind cannot justify, this making it easy for one to sleep at night without a disturbed conscience. Four arguments were advanced to justify, and to perpetuate this crime against God and humanity. The slave, they argued, is fundamentally, bio-logically, and inherently inferior. It was even argued that the slave had no soul and that he was incapable of being educated. If one can accept the fact that the object he holds, in subjection is inferior by nature, he has no pangs of conscience when he kicks it around.

Perhaps the strongest argument in support of slavery was the argument that slavery is God's will. God sent the Negro into the world for the ex-pressed purpose to hew wood, to draw water, to till soil, to pick cotton, and to cultivate tobacco. And one must never interfere with the designs of God. It was argued thirdly that civilization depended on slave labor and that the abolition of slavery would mean the collapse of civilization.

There was a fourth argument to support the slave system. It was the most insidious of them all. "It is good for the slave that he be a slave." This fourth argument reminds me of an old African proverb: "full belly child said to empty belly child, be of good cheer." How strange! It often happens that the one man at the top argues that it is good for the man at the bottom to be at the bottom. Slavery was our lot for 246 years.

Finally, the slaves themselves began to rebel, the system was unprofit-able to the north and the abolitionists began to denounce the system as inhuman and a sin against God. Four years of bloody war split the na-tion in twain, Lincoln issued his emancipation proclamation, the Civil War ended and four million Negroes came out singing—"thank God, free at last. Before I would be a slave, I would be buried in my grave and go home to my Lord and be saved."

But Lincoln's proclamation and the eventual emancipation were not adequate. The slave had to be humanized, made a citizen, guaranteed the equal protection of the law and given the ballot; hence, the enactment of the 13th, 14th and 15th Amendments.

The second era was the era of segregation. The real problem came with emancipation. As a slave, the Negro's status was definite and fixed. As a free man, he became a problem and was unwanted. Four solutions were sought to get rid of the newly emancipated people: first, colonize them—give them a separate state; second, send them back to Africa; thirdly, leave them alone and they will die out, they will not be able to compete in a civilized society; and fourthly, segregate them. Up to May 17, 1954, segregation was the only program the United States government and the governments of the South had advanced to solve the so-called Negro problem.

The privileges exercised by the Negro during the few brief years of re-construction were short-lived. So, the segregated era may be roughly desig-nated as the period embracing the years 1865 to May 17, 1954.

Even before emancipation, segregation had begun and it was practiced in God's church. Between 1864 and 1919, segregation had entrenched itself by law in every area of southern life. The Negro was segregated by law in the South and by custom in the north.

Though not usually considered so, segregation by law was another form of slavery and in many ways just as devastating. Segregation by law imposed by the strong upon the weak was the main objective. The first aim of segregation by law is to brand the segregated as inferior, pin a badge on him or print a sign on his back marked "inferior" so that the whole wide world would know that here is an object unfit to associate with other human beings. The second object of segregation is to instill in the mind of the segregated the idea that he is inferior so that he will walk and talk like an inferior and cringe and kowtow like an inferior. The third object of segregation was and is to set the segregated apart so that he will be denied the ballot, given inferior goods and services, assigned inferior jobs, provide inferior education and given inferior accommodations. It was not until May 17, 1954 that the back of this deadly sin, segregation, was broken. And it was not until we began to sue in federal courts that we began to move toward equality in education. So the period from 1619 to 1954 is 335 years. We speak of 341 years of disability because segregation is still an ever present evil.

Let us now briefly examine these 341 years of disability—246 years of slavery and 95 years of segregation—and see what they have done to the heart, mind, soul, will and body of the Negro people. Let us not deceive ourselves, let us not be naïve, these 341 years of disability have left their visible marks and scars upon the Negro. What have they done to you and me?

These 341 years of disability made millions of Negroes believe that they were inferior—so much that millions of Negroes, since 1865, accepted without protest, their inferior status, behaved like an inferior and cringed and kowtowed like an inferior. How could it be other wise? Economically suppressed, politically disfranchised, educationally illiterate, physically afraid and deliberately set apart so that everything in the environment said to the Negro, "you do not belong." "You are no body." Tell this to a people for three and a half centuries, you have a situation in which millions of men and women will never be able to stand erect and will never be able to walk the earth with dignity and pride.

These 341 years of disability destroyed the ambition of millions, crushed the potential genius of thousands and [?] out the nerves of aspirations of hundreds of thousands. Every Negro boy and girl knew before he was six that the ceiling and not the sky was the limit for him and that the best things in politics, economics, and education were not meant for the Negro. Potential scientists, statesmen, engineers, authors, artists, and philosophers were *still* born.

This created an intellectual ghetto in the Negro race. The few who aspired to be "somebody" never gazed beyond the accomplishments of the few successful Negroes they saw about them. I was considered an "uppity" boy when it was learned in my community that my ambition extended far beyond that of being a teacher in a four months school at $25 a month. In this ghetto competition was racial and still is to some extent. Negro professionals sought to be the most outstanding Negro teacher, the best Negro preacher, the finest Negro farmer, the leading Negro professional to compete beyond the race. In fact, it was considered dangerous to compete with white men less you be branded as trying to be white. Negroes were expected to stay in their subordinate place.

Furthermore, these years of disability made Negroes ashamed of their race. Many Negroes wanted to be anything except a Negro—a Mexican, a Chinese, an American Indian, a poor white man—anything except a Negro. For a long time, Negroes were proud of their ignorance of Negro history and wanted to hear nothing of their African ancestry.

These years of disability naturally made Negroes disbelieve in themselves. Even the most competent Negro needed the endorsement and approval of white people before Negroes would accept his competence. Negroes had little faith in Negro doctors, dentists, businessmen and lawyers. That which was white was best. Authority resided in a white skin.

These 341 years of disability have made us politically impotent. For a long time, we were, and in some places still are, voteless. We have little voice in the governments that rule us. There is not one Negro in a single legislature in the deep South and virtually none on city councils. Out of 437 Congressmen in the House of Representatives only four are Negroes. Normally there should be 47 Negroes in the House of Representatives. Not one Negro Senator out of a total of 100. No Negro has ever been a full member of the Cabinet. No Negro has ever sat as one of the nine justices of the Supreme Court. We have produced no governors.

It is true that we have come a long way in our economic quest. And yet despite the gains, we are at the bottom of the economic ladder. The average income in the Negro family is half or less than that in the average white family. Most of the Negro workers are common laborers and semi-skilled workers.

Most of all these years of disability have thrown us behind in education. By an large, we do not do well on national tests. A few of us do exceptionally well on these tests but most of us fall way behind the national average. We are 10 percent of the population, but we have less than 4 percent of the collegiate enrollment. Only a fraction of the one percent of all the Ph.D's in the United States are Negroes. Our percentage of Negro doctors, engineers, lawyers, chemists and physicists is miserably low. We cannot deny the fact that we have more than our share of disease, crime and delinquency. These are but a few of the disabilities resulting from 341 years of slavery and segregation.

Members of the graduating class, it is these disabilities we are challenged to overcome in twenty-five years. I challenge you because you are young. You will live twenty-five years. I may not.

Do I hear you say, "fantastic?" It is fantastic, but not impossible. I hear another say, "an empty dream." It does not have to be an empty dream. "Foolishness," says someone else. It is foolishness only to the lazy, the coward and the unimaginative. To men of faith and courage, we can overcome these disabilities in twenty-five years.

How can it be done? First of all, we must accept the fact without bitterness and without ill will that we are behind. Admit that we have come a long way under adverse circumstances but admit also that we have come a long way under adverse circumstances also that we have further to go than we have come. We cannot brag too much about the number of Negro Ph.D.'s and Phi Beta Kappas. The number is negligible. A few Negroes have accumulated a million dollars but to find them is like looking for a needle in a hay stack. There are hundreds of fine homes owned by Negroes and yet in 1950, 60 percent of all Negroes live in substandard houses.

We have done well in education and yet, there are hardly enough able Negro scholars to staff all the divisions of the University of Chicago. We have made fine progress in medicine. But too few Charles Drews. There are hardly enough Negro specialists to staff from top to bottom Presbyterian Hospital and Medical Center, New York. We have done might well in banking but there are not enough Negroes skilled in money and banking to take over the Chase National Bank. We are very successful in insurance and yet we do not have enough expertise in insurance to run from top to bottom the Metropolitan Life Insurance Company. To overcome these disabilities in twenty-five years, we must recognize the fact that we are behind and get on with the job. This truth must be drilled into our hearts and minds; "the group that starts behind in the great race of life must forever remain behind or run faster than the race in front."

These facts must be made clear to Negroes everywhere. There must be known in the classrooms, expounded in the churches, printed in the press, impressed upon youth in the home, made the theme of fraternities and sororities, and stamped indelibly upon the minds of parents and teachers. Our pace is too slow. We can run faster than we are running if we develop the will and the determination to do so. Our academic pace from the first grade through our colleges is entirely too slow. There is too much academic leisure in our colleges. Too little pursuit of excellence. Students read and study too little and teachers demand too little. We write too few books, too few articles, and do not do enough research.

Our teachers must be motivated to teach Negro students with a sense of mission, as if God the Father called them into the world for the expressed purpose to teach. For sometime yet, the vast majority of Negro students will be taught by Negro teachers. We must teach as the prophets prophesied: as Amos, who said: "When the eternal God speaks, who can but prophecy;" as Jeremiah, who explained, "the spirit of the Lord is upon me for he has anointed me to preach the Gospel to the poor;" as Paul, who declared, "I am ruined if I preach not the Gospel." We must teach, preach, do business, build bridges, practice medicine and plead for justice as the poets write poetry. It was John Bunyan who said: "I had to set aside the writing of sermons and other serious tracts in order to write *Pilgrim Progress* [sic]." It was Horace who explained: "I could not sleep at night because of the pressure of unwritten poetry." Whatever we do, if we are to overcome the disabilities of 341 years in a quarter of a century, we must do it as if God called us into the world to do it. We cannot allow any sand to burn under our feet.

If it takes the sacrificing of social privileges in order to become master teachers, in the name of the Lord God almighty, let us sacrifice social privileges. Most of the Negro students are not necessarily dumb. They are handicapped by the disabilities of three and a half centuries. If it takes more patience in order to open their minds, for God's sake let us develop patience. If it takes extra love and affection in order to get the student to see the light, let us love them and give them the affection they need.

We can say to students now what we have never been able to say to them before. We can motivate them by making it clear to them that the future for the competent never looked so bright as it does today. As competence broke the color bar in every other area of American life. There are too few chemists, physicists, mathematicians, engineers, and too few top-flight scholars for college and university. Too few dedicated ministers. The time is near and possible at hand when no industry will refuse to hire a first class physicist or chemist because his skin is black. The Government in the future can ill afford to refuse to place a first-class psychologist because he happens to be a Negro. We could not say that to Negro students twenty-five years ago. We can tell him that the sky and not the ceiling is beginning to be the limit.

Now that segregation is a decrepit old man, discredited everywhere, fighting a losing battle for his life, the Negro can now look unto the hills from whence cometh his help.

I do not mean to give you the impression that the battle for equality has been won. Far from it. But we can win it in twenty-five years, if we continue the battle for first-class citizenship. If we stop the program to desegregate America, segregation will take a new hold and it will fasten its tendencies upon us for another fifty years. The state legislatures placed these disabilities upon us but the Federal Government must remove them. The state governments will not. The battle for respect which we who are older have waged for decades and which Negro students are carrying on now with a new technique must be continued. As you leave these hallowed walls, some kind of leadership will be thrust upon you. Never rest until every qualified Negro in your community is a registered voter. We will be respected in proportion as we exercise the ballot and participate in government. A voteless people is a helpless people.

What we use to motivate students we must use to motivate ourselves. The day of racial competition is over. We can no longer aspire to be a leading Negro surgeon. Today the competition is world wide. Every surgeon competes with surgeons everywhere. Every scientist is in competition with scientists the world over. Every artist competes in the world market. Every business man competes with business men in the world market.

If we are to overcome the disabilities of 341 years in three-quarters of a century [sic], we must close ranks and look with contempt upon no man. We are no better than our fellows. Let us identify ourselves with all mankind—the high and the low, the great and the small, the learned and the unlearned, the rich and the poor, white and black, yellow and brown. No man of himself is better than his fellow.

If any man is more favorably circumstanced than another, it's an accident, it's by the grace of God. No child can choose his parents. They may be rich, they may be poor. He didn't choose them. No man can choose his mind. If lucky to have a brilliant mind, let him thank God but never boast about it. He might have been a moron. One cannot choose his race. If born white given privileges and opportunities by virtue of whiteness, let him not boast about it. He might have been born black. One cannot choose his nation. If born in rich America with a silver spoon in his mouth, let him thank God but never boast about it. But for the grace of God he might have been one of the starving millions of India.

Every man is a part of humanity. The fate of one is the fate of all. Birth, life and death. Do not look down upon this illiterate Negro living in the slums of Tallahassee and New York. Eugene Debbs was so right when he said: "As long as there is a poorer class, I am in it. As long as there is a criminal element, I am of it. As long as there is a man in jail, I am not free." John Donne was equally right when he said: "No man is an island, etc."

The white graduate may neglect the spiritual and the moral but the Negro student cannot and must not. In seeking to overcome the disabilities of 341 years in twenty-five years, we fight not for ourselves for it matters little what happens to Negroes. But it matters much what happens to the Christian Gospel and to Democracy. Either Democracy and Christianity will function in America or it will perish from the earth. In this great fight of ours, we fight not for ourselves alone, but for the United States.

Finally, if we are to overcome the disabilities of 341 years in a quarter of a century, let us create in ourselves a divine discontent, a divine restlessness, an eternal dissatisfaction with mediocrity. Let us declare war on the average. Let us seek status not in our cars, not in our houses, but seek it as leaders of thought, as experts who extend the bounds of knowledge in research, see it as authors of books and articles, as outstanding chemists, teachers, ministers, and builders. Let us declare war on mediocre, ordinary performance.

The satisfied life is the dying life. The satisfied teacher will never improve his teaching. The man who is satisfied with slum living will never move out of the slums. The minister who brags about his sermons and is satisfied with them will never preach better. The artist who is satisfied with his art will never paint a better picture. The physician who is satisfied with his skill will never be a greater surgeon.

Houses and land, stocks and bonds, silver and gold, will keep you living but only your ideals will keep you alive. Ideals of justice, love, good will, brotherhood and ideals in the pursuit of excellence. I close with two poems which I hope will challenge you to do your part to help us overcome the disabilities of 341 years in a quarter of a century.

> To every man there openeth a way,
> And ways, and a way.
> And the high soul climbs the higher way,
> And the low soul gropes the low,
> And in between, on the misty flats,
> The rest drift to and fro.
> But to every man there openeth
> A high way, and a low.
> And every man decideth the way
> His soul shall go.
> —John Oxenham

> God thought his life is but a wraith,
> Although we know not what we use,
> Although we grope with little faith,
> *Give me the heart to fight—and lose!*

> Every insurgent let me be,
> Make me more daring than devout;
> From sleek contentment keep me free,
> *And fill me with a buoyant doubt.*

Open my eyes to vision girt
With beauty, and with wonder lit –
But let me always see the dirt
The little ballads of the slums

From compromise and things half done,
Keep me, with stern and stubborn pride;
And when at last, the fight is won
God, keep me still unsatisfied.
—Louis Unter Meyer

§52 Dr. Frank P. Graham

Frank Porter Graham's biography appears in the introduction to his May 29, 1954 sermon in Montreat, North Carolina. In the following wide-ranging address on civil rights, Dr. Graham traces the genealogy of racism only to declare his hope that, in a new generation of students, the claims of racial superiority will be "found wanting." Two roadblocks remain to fulfilling the promise of the American Revolution: the misuse of States' rights to defy the Supreme Court's *Brown* decision; and, a monopoly on suffrage rights held by the privileged few. Graham moves next to the student youth movement, so famously begun on February 1st in North Carolina. The seeds of their revolt should not be a stranger to the state given its progressive past. Moreover, its foundation in the Judeo-Christian tradition and the Declaration of Independence make it an entirely American and noble protest. Simply put, the American Negro is "the most basically religious and the most fundamentally American of us all. In sitting down they were in their heritage and hope standing up for the American dream." Graham closes by hoping that this heritage and hope will save the world from its own thermo-nuclear ambitions.

––––––––––

Students "Standing Up" for the American Dream
North Carolina
July 1960 (reprinted)

Amid the responsibilities and opportunities of this age, people live in a world of tensions, revolutions and terrors. The hot fuses of colonialism, racialism and totalitarianism, implanted in the accelerating time-bombs of our dynamic global society, can blow this world to pieces. In a world made fatefully one during the last 500 years by the Commercial, the Industrial and the Atomic Revolutions in reinforcing succession, it is now thermo-nuclear axiom that the people in both hemispheres will survive or perish together by the determination, at this late hour, of their destiny on the earth.

Embedded in the Charter of the United Nations are the universal principles of the dignity of persons, the equality of races, the self-determination of peoples and the cooperation of nations for justice and peace on earth.

In this world of tensions between the races in both hemispheres, there is more need of perspective and understanding for the reduction and elimination of racial prejudice and injustice. Group prejudice and racial discrimination are not the original creation or private monopoly of any people. Consciousness of kind is and has long been a powerful force in human affairs. What was considered different in race, region, color and creed, was considered alien. What was considered alien was held to be dangerous.

The ages of history witnessed the successive classification of people as chosen and unchosen, superior and inferior, Jews and Gentiles, Greeks and barbarians, Romans and provincials, the civilized Mediterraneans and the uncivilized tribes of northern and western Europe, the celestial Chinese and uncelestial other people, the high caste and low caste people in India, the Anglo-Saxon and "the lesser breeds without the law." The conception of racial superiority reached its highest pretensions in the Nazism of Adolph Hitler.

The armed Fascist-Nazi ideology of Aryan superiority was defeated on the battlefield and the misconception of racial superiority based on color of the skin and the shape of the head was found wanting in the scientific researches and social studies of the universities. It has been hoped by many people in our own South that racial prejudice and discrimination would give way in the transmission to youthful generations of these findings and the growing appreciation of the common heritage and the hope of the human race, the rich exchange value of the high culture of diverse races, the different but high achievements of persons of all races as belonging to the individual rather than to the race, and the growing consciousness of the inter-dependent oneness of the freedom, well-being and peace of all people.

The lag in interracial justice in many communities, the on-rush of totalitarianism around the earth, and the advancing religious and democratic conception of the all inclusiveness of human freedom and dignity, were in the background of the decision of the Supreme Court in its widening interpretation of the meaning of "liberty" in the old Bill of Rights, as applying to all persons regardless of race in the District of Columbia, and the meaning of "equal protection of the laws," as applying to all persons regardless of race in the States of the United States.

Not as justification of racial injustices, but for more informed cooperation of the races for ending the wrongs and for more effective fulfillment of the new law of the land against racial segregation in the use of public facilities in our Southern States, four factors are found to be related to the persistence of racial tensions and the massive resistance to the acceptance of the law which changes old customs in these States. The four factors which are somewhat correlated to the extent of interracial tensions are: (1) the ratio of numbers; (2) the degree of the visibility of differences; (3) the differences in historical and cultural background; and (4) the economic competition of the low income groups of the different races.

These basic factors are more or less related to the varying degrees of tensions between yellow and brown, brown and black, and white and colored peoples around the earth. As we look down the centuries and across the world, the need becomes imperative for the people in churches, schools, business enterprises, labor unions and voluntary associations in all lands, to join in promoting the fulfillment of their own constitutional guarantees of human rights and the adoption of national covenants and the conventions in accordance with the Universal Declaration of Human Rights of the United Nations.

It was an American President who proclaimed to a warring world that one of the conditions of peace was the self determination of people, now asserted and applied by the colonial and colored peoples of the earth.

Across the tidal and delta lands, the mountains and rivers, the prairies and plains of our own America, and across the oceans and continents of the world, comes the call to the American people to be true to their own historic revolution and their own great Congressional declarations, Presidential proclamations and judicial decisions for the equal freedom, dignity and opportunity of all people regardless of region or race, color or creed, national origin or economic status.

In the unfolding of the faith and hopes of the American Revolution, two roadblocks have been thrown across the ways of their fulfillment: the misuse of the noble theory of States' rights and the political monopoly of suffrage rights held by exclusive groups of Americans.

States' rights, with its noble heritage from the Jamestown Assembly and Plymouth Rock, as the foundation stones of local self-government in America, was unsheathed by Jefferson in "the revolution of 1800" as the sword of liberty against the popular hysteria and federal tyranny of the Alien and Sedition laws. The theory of States' Rights, which had been the sword of liberty, became later in the South the shield of slavery, and after the Civil War, the weapon in the North for human exploitation and legal defense against Jane Addams' humane proposals for minimum wages and hours for women and children working in the heartless sweatshops of the great cities. In our time the theory of States' Rights has become the argument of massive resistance to the law of the land as interpreted by the Supreme Court outlawing discrimination in the use of public facilities for education, transportation and recreation.

One of the needs of the times is emphasis on a deepening of the growing conception of States' rights as States' responsibilities for the equal dignity and freedom of all persons in the States.

Tensions will decrease with the increasing awareness that the decision of the Supreme Court in no way abridges the basic personal rights of privacy and friendship and is not counter to the general predisposition of peoples, with full regard for human freedom and dignity to preserve their own racial identity with its multicultural enrichment of the vigor and variety of the meaning and progress of America.

A second barrier to the sharing of the American dream was the exclusive policy of our political monopoly from which, we learned in our history, were excluded in many States of the Union (1) Jews, (2) Catholics, (3) people without land and property, (4) Negroes and (5) women. In the insurgent epochs of Jeffersonian, Jacksonian, Lincolnian and Progressive democracy, the ballot box was increasingly opened to all adult Americans regardless of creed, property, color and sex. The barriers of the monopolistic political oligarchy gave way before the insurgent currents of our expanding and advancing American democracy.

The only remaining barriers—both of the poll tax, cumulative in its exclusions in six states, and of the procedures for registration, discriminatory in practices on account of race in many communities of some States—cannot much longer hold back the presently combining spiritual momentum of 2,000 years and the unresting democratic momentum of more than a century and a half of American history.

America has taught the colored youth the heritage and hopes of America and, in her heart of hearts, she would not have them deny that heritage or renounce that hope as they write a new chapter in the unfolding of the ideals of the American Revolution, renewing in their generation the resurgent springs of American democracy in need of fresh renewal from epoch to epoch.

The Negro youth movement began in a State which was both one of the original thirteen States and one of the eleven Confederate States. This Southern State was one of the first States to authorize its delegate to join in an American Declaration of Independence; abolished the poll tax in 1921; has long maintained a nine-month twelve-grade public school system for all children, urban and rural, white and colored; pays Negro teachers higher average salaries than white teachers. In a few communities Negroes have led the ticket for the town council and school board.

The story of the people of North Carolina, with all our faults and frustrations, struggles and hopes, is a part of the story of a people who, in the aftermath of war and desolation were, in their poverty and work, as unconquerable in the duties of defeat as they had been brave on the battlefields against the great odds of a long and exhausting war.

As part of the story of the risen South and an expanding America, it is a significant fact that although only one-tenth of the Negroes in the world are in the United States, more Negroes are in colleges and universities in the United States than in all the rest of the world, now becoming increasingly open to all.

Not that there were more racial discriminations, but that educated Negro youth were more aware in that State of persisting discriminations, the indigenous Negro youth movement had its origin in North Carolina. It was not inspired or instigated by any subversive or un-American influence unless the Judaic-Christian heritage and the ideals of the American Declaration of Independence have in our time become subversive and un-American.

This movement of the college youth in the South is a contemporary expression of the on-going ideals of the American Revolution and a local expression of the world-wide revolution of the colored, colonial and exploited peoples of the earth.

In their faith and hopes, the Negro people of the South and all our American States, are, in the depth of their spiritual heritage and in the height of their American hopes, the most basically religious and the most fundamentally American of us all. In sitting down they were in their heritage and hope standing up for the American dream. The colored and white youth of the Southern colleges and universities, who with Bibles in their hands, the national anthem on their lips and non-violence in their hearts, sought in the main, to make lawful petition that stores, which sold to the public, should provide for the same price the same quantity and quality of service to all.

They and their leaders seek to understand those who misunderstand and fear them; meet violence with non-violence; sorrow and wrongs with humor, laughter and songs; prejudice and indignities with love and brotherhood. It is their faith that the Cross, warm with the blood of human brotherhood, will yet triumph over all the burning crosses lighted with the hot oils of prejudice, privilege and power.

The movement of American college youth may carry in its currents not only a rebirth of freedom in America but a survival of freedom and people on earth through a spiritual revolution in the ideas, faith and hopes of the people of the world.

The physical descent of man must be reinforced with the spiritual ascent of man, an idea as old as 2,000 years and as young as the hopes of men, long considered impractical, has in the atomic age become the most practical and necessary idea of them all, the idea of the Fatherhood of one

God and the brotherhood of all the people of the world. The primitive inheritance stored in countless ages deep down in the subconscious nature of man, the absolutism of the nation-states and the absolutism of atomic power, may, with the combined potentials of their explosive forces, break through all international economic, political and cultural incrustations and controls. In this age of the precarious peace of deterrent terror, the panicked press of a button may end the human race. In the war of nations, the hydrogen fallout carried by the winds of the world, may extinguish life in the far corners of two hemispheres, as remnants of people make their last human huddle on the farthest islands and in the remotest igloos.

At this late hour, the alternative to a reluctant and inadequate international cooperation and a lagging universal brotherhood, may become an accelerating universal annihilation.

In this world, when the roads of human destiny fatefully cross in the downward drift toward universal annihilation and the upward struggle toward more effective international cooperation through the United Nations, may this assembly mean the rededication of us all to equal justice under law and human brotherhood under God in this age of mortal peril and immortal hope for all mankind.

§53 Reverend Edler Garnet Hawkins

Born in 1908 to Albert and Anna Hawkins, Edler Garnet Hawkins came of age in the Bronx. Under the tutelage of William Lloyd Imes, Hawkins attended Union Seminary in New York City. Ordained a Presbyterian minister, Hawkins was called to St. Augustine Presbyterian Church on the border of Harlem and the Bronx; he would pastor this church for nearly 30 years, transforming it in the process into a large, multicultural and activist body. In 1958 Hawkins was elected moderator of the New York presbytery; four years later he was elected the first black moderator by the general assembly of the United Presbyterian Church (U.S.A.). After resigning his pastorate at St. Augustine in 1970, Hawkins taught homiletics and church administration at Princeton Seminary. He was the first African American on the Seminary's faculty. Outside of the Presbyterian church, Hawkins was elected to the central committee of the World Council of Churches in 1974 and actively promoted its Programme to Combat Racism. Hawkins died in 1977. His papers are housed at the Robert Woodruff Library Atlanta University Center in Atlanta, Georgia.

Prima facie, this is not a sermon about race; yet in it we find exhortation by indirection: for the church to witness to the world about civil rights will require an extraordinary faith—the faith typified by the early church. To be ordinary in the extraordinary 1960s is to invite the wrath of God and to mingle easily with the prevailing culture. Hawkins calls upon his parishioners to get its "verticals straight"; if so, the "horizontals" will follow. The message could not have been missed from a black preacher preaching to black and Hispanic congregants: to be ordinary, to steer clear of the crises of the times, is to miss the Holy Spirit's call to activism.

Behaving Like Ordinary Men
St. Augustine Presbyterian Church, New York, New York
October 1960

There come those moments and times where we are called upon to look very seriously again at our faith, to see whether it is adequate for the particular moment in which we stand.

We are getting all kinds of analysis of these 60's into which we have entered. All sorts of speculation as to what these next ten years ahead will mean. There is general agreement that they will be ten crucial years, years of crisis. And if they are to be like this, then we need to bring in similar critical analysis to our faith—to see how it will match the times. And if the times are extraordinary, then we will need an extraordinary faith.

This is the way it was in the beginning. If you turn to any of the opening pages of the Book of Acts, the record reveals an extraordinary people. They are alive and responsive to the issues of their times. They came on the scene at an extraordinary time, and they were people to match the time. *"Those who came to turn the world upside down"*—this is the phrase that recognized them as extraordinary people. Some of them were so rash as to stand up to the rulers of that day and say *"We must obey God rather than man"*—nothing ordinary about that.

Indeed—when Paul, later, was to lay a very serious charge against the Christians at Corinth, he used this phrase, *"Are you not behaving like ordinary men?"* They had sunk from the high level of being Christ's people to that of ordinary men [. . .] charges that can be brought against a person's faith and life—that of becoming ordinary men and women.

This is always the greatest danger of the individual Christian and the Christian Church—of sinking to the ordinary level, at which there is no difference between you and the pattern of life around you.

Time magazine, some time ago, reported on a town in the western state of Washington, which was the hometown of a man who had trouble with the government, in a criminal proceeding, and of how the town was wrestling with a bad case of troubled conscience. The man's name is not important . . . the issue is a real one.

In the bustling days of normalcy the man was accepted and acclaimed as a leading civic luminary who had gone a "long way to make our town a good place in which to live and do business." But now that his light has dimmed the face of the moral disclosure of misuse of union funds, therefore the citizens of this town long to find comfort in the matter that their city is merely typical of the total national picture. But what happened in Seattle happened because the important citizens let it, because they shared in, prospered with, and never really challenged the whole deal.

The most damaging attack on Christian faith is not made by any violent atheists—there are not enough of these around really—the church can always resist that. But the most devastating blow to the life of the church is given when Christians become so ordinary that they give onlookers the impression that being a Christian doesn't make any difference on the quality of one's life.

We live in extraordinary times—this is, I believe the verdict of all who analyze our days—and ordinary people are not enough.

There are extraordinary people as they make their witness in the place where they stand at this moment in history.

All of us can't be part of communities like this, where the peculiar kind of witness is made, but as we look honestly and critically at our day we ought to see this moral swamp that is moving in on us at so many levels, threatening to engulf us, and make us ordinary people who do no different from anyone else who makes no profession of Christian faith.

Say what you will about Congressman Powell . . . but he put his finger on a question of great moral sensitivity for many Christian folks who do not separate themselves from the numbers game—which is a blight upon many a community.

I heard a preacher say once—*"Get your verticals straight man, and the horizontals will become straight too."* And he wasn't talking about numbers. He was too. He was saying that if we see really our relationship to God, then how we operate in and relate to, and serve and help our fellowmen and our communities will level off right. This is where the first century Christians began. And this is where we must begin too.

Whatever happened [with] the early Christians this much was sure—they were convinced sight unseen that God was alive—that he had called them by the power of the Holy Spirit to set the world straight—maybe by first turning it upside down—but to set it straight—and they set themselves to the task by putting the right price tags on the right values. *"Seeking first the Kingdom."* Placing number one where it belongs—not seventh or tenth, but first.

They knew they could only survive as they took on the character of extraordinary people who had come into a mind independent of the prevalent one—and in opposition to it.

It is no longer I who live, but Christ who lives in me?

To all who received him, who believed in his name, he gave power to become children of God.

Extraordinary men.

Are ye not behaving like ordinary men?

A loud resounding No—for one who has become a child of God has no business being ordinary.

§54 Reverend Will D. Campbell

Will D. Campbell is a self-described bootleg preacher. Born in Liberty, Mississippi on July 18, 1924 Campbell's ordination as a Baptist Minister took place at the age of 17 at the East Fork Baptist Church in Amite County, Mississippi. From 1941 to 1943 he attended Louisiana College but served in the army despite his exemption from the draft as an ordained minister. After his service in the armed forces, he attended Wake Forest University, Tulane University, and Yale University, receiving his B.D. from Yale in 1952. From 1952 to 1954 he served as a Baptist minister in Louisiana. In 1954 he accepted a position as director of religious life at the University of Mississippi, which promptly forced him out in 1956 for his civil rights activism. From 1956 to 1962 Campbell served the National Council of Churches as a race relations consultant. His duties in this regard included his participation as one of four ministers to escort the Little Rock Nine to Central High School in September 1957. In 1962 Campbell became involved with the Committee for Southern Churchmen, and he helped found the organization's journal, *Katallagete*, which means "be reconciled." While fulfilling these duties, he also wrote frenetically. He is an accomplished author, completing 17 works of fiction and nonfiction, and winning numerous prestigious literary awards. His 1977 memoir, *Brother to a Dragonfly*, won the Lillian Smith Prize, the Christopher Award, and garnered a National Book Award nomination. He currently lives with his wife Brenda in Tennessee. They have three children. His papers are housed at the University of Southern Mississippi in Hattiesburg.

Campbell begins the speech by identifying strongly with the southern cultural landscape. He feigns ignorance and refers casually to Yankee bastards, but even this epithet merely puts others on equivalent moral ground with him and his audience. His message is that southerners can still be southerners while their familiar world is crashing to a halt all around them. He assures the audience that people who do not understand them are overly sophisticated and inauthentic. Moreover, conflict is to be expected and realists must move forward even if progress means collision. He reminds his listeners that an authentic southern minister named David Lipscomb told them in 1878 that separate worship services for different races was an abomination, and he did not mind ruffling feathers when he said it. A corollary issue is a loss of membership and therefore tithing for southern churches. Campbell argues analogically that worrying about membership and tithes is akin to the fool who builds bigger barns instead of preparing his soul for heaven. He ends his message with his visionary call for radical forgiveness. Those who suffered for a righteous cause will be the victors in eternity. Those who tortured the innocent will be the vanquished in eternity. Both require the intervention of a merciful God.

Witnessing When the Cultural Landmarks are Down

Methodist Women for Christian Service, New York, New York
November 30, 1960

Frankly, I don't know what a cultural landmark is. But we are supposed to talk about it and then you are supposed to answer. I am supposed to apply the topic to the specific area of race relations. There was a time when I hesitated to speak to a national gathering on what appeared to me then to be largely a regional issue. But after moving about the north it didn't take me long to learn that yankees, being fully human, are bastards too. Hopefully, I believe that despite their being little different from southerners God still loves them just like he does those of us of the basement states.

Now if we are talking about how the *churches* might witness when the cultural landmarks are down we are engaged in a ludicrous pursuit and the question might be better phrased, not, "How we may witness when the cultural landmarks are down," but rather, "when in God's name will we stop being the *first* cultural landmark to go down when a crisis comes." (By the way, I work for the National Council of Churches from 9 til 5. I'm on my own time now. On my own time I'm free to say what I want to—I can even talk about the Methodist if I please and I do please). But look in city after city throughout America and you pick the crisis—the industrial revolution, McCarthyism, integration . . . what is virtually the first institution to be afflicted with spiritual laryngitis and who is the last usually to recover from this sudden loss of voice?

I have recently returned from a large American city where there is some bit of disagreement between the federal and state governments over the question of slavery. Little by little agencies, institutions and groups are crawling out of their shells. How many churches have spoken out? At the time of my departure, none.

Thus I am assuming that we are talking about how can the individual Christian witness in a crisis situation when the chamber of commerce, the merchants association, the PTA, the League of Women Voters, and such other cultural landmarks as the Daughters of the American Revolution and the Sons of Confederacy have fallen and I belong to all of them.

If this is what we are talking about then I have a few observations I should like to make and then we'll flip and rejoice and go back to propping up the cultural landmarks. WHICH IS WHAT WE DO MOST OF THE TIME ANYWAY! We try to *live* with the symbols. We try to fit them into our own strategy, our own methods, our own message. If we live in a culture, as we do, which, like the army, marches on its own belly, then we'll build the biggest and best kitchens and call Betty Crocker for the assistant minister to students.

If we live in a culture, as we do, in which there is great emphasis on entertaining the blessed youth then we build the biggest and best gymnasiums, dance floors and pool tables.

If we live in a culture, as we do in which all dimensions, theological or otherwise must read 36-24-36 we spend a great deal of time in seminars on love, courtship, marriage and sex. Well, that's one cultural landmark I don't know much about. 'Course I know prohibition didn't work.

All I am trying to say is that quite often we feel that we have failed when all the cultural landmarks are down and the reason is that we have identified ourselves with them. IT IS NOT THAT OUR TASK IS GREATEST when the cultural landmarks are down. It is then that our task can begin. Our message is that these landmarks are irrelevant. Let'em crumble. Quit trying to prop them up. The quicker they fall the sooner the Christian message might get a hearing.

We live in a world of bigness, of numbers and large ones. So we have mass revivalist movements and souls are saved all over the place. AND WE IN this room are terribly critical of that, aren't we? We read in the voice of prophecy, U.S. NEWS AND WORLD REPORT that church membership is up several percentage points. SO we talk about the tragedy of a popular religion and quote Kierkegaard's story of buying beer for five cents and selling it for three and making the profit on volume. And we question whether or not this religious revival reflects anything significant at all and we compare it to crime rates and unwed sorority mothers, and the constant threat of war and the starving masses and unemployment. I share this skepticism and try to join in sounding the alarm.

But though most of us in this room would be critical of the mass revivalist and their use of Madison Avenue techniques to achieve bigness, many of us in this room commit an even more dangerous act by using intellectually respectable methods to make the gospel intellectually respectable. The sophisticates *should* ride herd on the mass religionist because the mass religionists *do* reflect the symbol of bigness and success. But when we disagree we had better disagree on our knees because in adopting intellectually respectable methods we "touch up" the gospel too and this is one more effort to make it more palatable to those we are trying to reach. I FAIL TO SEE any difference between saying, "All you have to do is come on down this sawdust trail and give your heart to the Lord and your hand to this humble pastor and you'll be saved," . . . I don't see any difference between this and our saying, "Hey fellows, look, we're not a bunch of squares. We're really the latest thing in beatnikdom. Come on over to the pad and join us in art, drama and jazz."

Well we *are* a bunch of squares. The gospel *isn't* intellectually respectable and shrouding it in respectable art forms isn't going to make it intellectually respectable.

Many of the people to whom we minister may be offended if we proclaim verbally, "God was in Christ, reconciling the world to himself. He was born of a pleasant Jewish girl whose boy friend loved her enough to marry her even though he knew the baby she carried within her was not his own. The boy she bore was a wise guy who insulted the doctors, the professors, and doctors have long memories. They kept calm though. Even when this little smart aleck claimed to be the son of God they kept their heads." Tell them this. Tell them this was Christ and God was in him; and that he was crucified, dead and buried, and the third day he rose again from the dead; that he will come again to judge the quick and the dead, and that in all this they are sinners, in need of a Saviour, and this is their Saviour. Tell them this in verbal discourse and many of them will be offended.

But we must *communicate this gospel*, mustn't we? We told a man God was in Christ and he chuckled. He was sophisticated. He was one of the doctors and he chuckled. We'll show him that we are just as big an egghead as he is. So we turn to the respectable art forms. Art, drama, jazz. . . . Now he isn't offended. He listens and says sure enough they too are eggs and respectable.

But is he really convinced that God was in Christ? That here is his Saviour? Let's go back to what offended him in the first place. We have said that it was the package that offended him . . . the verbal proclamation of the word. If we are to assume that he is now convinced after we have *communicated* the message through other channels we must logically assume that it was the verbal form that was offensive to him. But strangely enough he isn't offended if his wife verbally proclaims, "Come to dinner. Here it is. It is for your sustenance." Or he doesn't chuckle if you proclaim, "FDR is in Kennedy." I suspect it really wasn't the form that he found offensive. It was the message. It was the same scandal, the same stumbling block for it still doesn't make sense. Thus we find that we are no different from the mass evangelist because he has employed the symbols of success of those he would win, those with whom we would *communicate*, and we have used the acceptable forms and symbols to *communicate* those to whom we would witness.

Our job isn't to communicate the gospel. Our job is to proclaim it. Well, how do we proclaim it? My job is to talk about how to proclaim it in the area of race relations. Thus far I have wandered far afield. During the next few minutes I will try to say that the way to proclaim the gospel in race relations when cultural landmarks are down is to proclaim it. There is no substitute for the sacrament of the word—to use a Lutheran term.

Let me read you this quotation: "We believe it is sinful to have two congregations in the same community for persons of different races. That race prejudice would cause trouble in the churches we know. It did this in apostolic days. Yet not once did the apostles suggest that they should form separate congregations for the different races. Instead, they always admonished them into unity, forbearance, love and brotherhood in Christ Jesus."

These words were spoken by a man representing a group far from notorious for its social liberalism. These are the words of a Church of Christ evangelist. The place was Nashville, Tennessee. The year was 1878. The preacher was David Lipscomb for whom the local Church of Christ college was named. All the cultural landmarks were down. He was in the middle of reconstruction; Yankees, scalawags and carpetbaggers were all about him.

Ah, but haven't we come a long way since 1878? Day by day in every way we're getting better and better. And give us time, patience, understanding; don't pass repressive legislation against us or try to cram *any*thing down our throats and we'll work this thing out. You bet your life we will!

Now there are two rather remarkable things about this statement in the light of which we would do well to view the last remains of a lot of alleged religious institutions today.

One, he did not appeal to harmony. Harmony is a chief landmark in our culture. He ignored it. He did not try to avoid conflict but admitted its existence and walked right into the face of it with his eyes wide open. Apparently this spokesman of a group, which is referred to by the sophisticates as "a fringe sect," had the idea that Christian behavior had nothing to do with what people *wanted* to do, or were *ready* to do, or what did not violate the local mores. Apparently he had the strange notion that Christian behavior had only to do with the uncompromising demands of Almighty God as revealed through the life and teachings of Jesus Christ.

Contrast this to our day when cardinal landmarks are harmony within the fellowship, peace, goodwill, program, every member canvass, building campaign, a million more in '54, standard of excellence and every Baptist a tither.

But when Mr. Lipscomb lived in an era when observers could say of the pulpit what Herman Melville said, commenting on the unusual pulpit of Whaleman's Chapel in Moby Dick, shaped like the prow of a ship with an open Bible resting upon a wooden scroll, fashioned like a ship's beak: "What could be more full of meaning," he said, "for the pulpit is ever this earth's foremost part; all the rest comes in the rear; the pulpit leads the world. . . . Yes, the world's a ship on its passage out, and not a voyage complete; and the pulpit is its prow. . . . "

Who says this of the pulpit any more? Contrast those words with these of Mary and Robert Lynd: "Middletown is building its religion in its own image; there is a tendency to appraise the fruits of religion by the same tangible material measurements which it applies to its other activities."

So, in a system as far from central authority as Oral Roberts from the Mayo Clinic, a leader in 1878 could say from Tennessee to a local church in Texas, "We mean simply this, a church which cannot bring such prejudiced individuals to see their rebellion against God must withdraw from that individual as one who with a heart full of pride, bitterness and treason fights against God." That's witnessing, brother. But today, in the name of harmony, they are more apt to be given the chief seats.

Almost a hundred years after David Lipscomb, laymen organize in church houses to tell the world and the bishop what the church is and what *their* church will and will not do. In another communion, an archbishop submits to the demands of a band of racists who say, "Pope or no pope, we ain't going to integrate our parochial schools."

What we are talking about is far more basic than desegregated schools. The churches have failed in this matter of race, partly, and perhaps primarily, because we have failed in the matter of authority and the meaning of the pulpit. While groups like Southern Baptists, to which I belong as all of you know, have moved more and more toward a system of centralized authority, those churches with established channels of authority have gone under in the wake of "creeping congregationalism."

The second remarkable thing about Mr. Lipscomb's statement, which seems now to have become a text, is that he made no appeal to law, another landmark, to the courts, an all time favorite, to democracy, the clincher among landmarks, to anything devised of man. His was a simple, yet powerful proclamation of "Thus saith the Lord." This despite the fact that the Emancipation Proclamation was as close to him and as controversial as the Supreme Court decision of 1954 is to us.

Now I am not suggesting that we are not making a witness in this crisis today. I think that we are. What I *am* suggesting is that the world is saying that we have failed, and since we are all in the family—whether all of us are legitimate or not—I think we should take a serious look at some possible reasons while we are in the family circle.

Campbell and Pettigrew talked of the failure of the church in Little Rock with regard to race. But it occurs to me that our failure does not really have to do with race at all. If we have failed, I am inclined to believe that it has nothing to do with what we have or have not done about race. Rather, it seems to me, it has to do with the manner in which we have dealt with the nature of God, with the redemptive power of Jesus Christ and with the judgment of God. Further, it has to do with our failure to proclaim the essentials of the Christian gospel and with our reluctance to proclaim categorically and with power and authority, "Thus saith the Lord, . . . 'I am the Lord thy God; . . . thou shalt have no other gods before me.'"

In short, our failure has to do not with the cultural landmark, the fourteenth amendment, but with the biblical landmark, the first commandment; it has not to do with constitution but with idolatry. And in this process race has become identified, not as an element of our culture, but as an element of our faith. Let me illustrate what I mean by race being a violation of the first commandment and becoming an element of our faith, of how we fail by making the cultural landmarks our own.

One of my earliest recollections is of sitting in a little rural church in the alleged state of Mississippi with my father one night and seeing the Ku Klux Klan file solemnly into that little frame building and the ceremony that followed. Being low church and not accustomed to vestments in the service, the hoods and robes made a lasting impression on my young mind, though I had no reason to question their presence. In that ceremony a large pulpit Bible was presented to the congregation and accepted by the revival preacher. On the back was stamped in brazen letters, KKK.

Several years ago, I was preaching in that same pulpit and as I held the back cover reading the Scripture, my fingers moved across those large, embossed letters. Later in the afternoon in conversation with several members of the congregation, I inquired as to their attitude toward having a pulpit Bible given by the Klan and wearing its symbol. Although these were people who had lived their entire lives in that community and who were present at the ceremony, each one stated that he had quite forgotten the incident and never knew that the letters, KKK, were raised on the back cover of the Bible in their pulpit.

This, I submit to you, is the greatest danger facing the Christian Church in the South today. The real danger, it seems to me, is not racism per se, but that racism becomes a part of faith. The Klan no longer exists in my community, but it has left its stamp, not only on the pulpit Bible, but upon the minds and hearts of generations yet unborn. Its modern counterpart will also pass away. But the seedlings they are planting will grow and thrive for a long, long time.

And these seedlings are essentially religious in character. Most of what is written and distributed by those groups subverting the laws of church and country has a religious theme. No subject has more religious relevance and arouses more religious support than the subject of race in the South today. And the segregationist man in the pew and pulpit who appeals to such support is not simply rationalizing. The stamp of racism has become a part of his religious heritage, and it is almost impossible to break through and reach him. If he would say, "Down with the church and Jesus Christ,

I like segregation and I am going to keep it forever," the task of the church would be simple. Instead he defends white supremacy in God's name. It is in the name of the church that he vows to keep segregation, and it is with Bible in hand and chapter and verse upon his lips that he offers his argument. When he, in the name of God, denies the love and mercy and justice and judgment of God, he is deviating from the faith in such proportion as to become a serious threat to the life of the church as the church, and the cultural concept of race has become a part of the faith all over America. In voting, employment, housing, marriage, basically there is no difference between the Mississippi planter denying the Negro the ballot and the New England industrialist taking certain precautions to make sure his debutante daughter does not marry a Negro. Both infer a hierarchy of creation.

The failure of the Protestant faith in America is not a failure to ask and answer the anthropological question, "What is race?" This question has been answered effectively and efficiently. Our failure, it seems to me, is that we have not succeeded in answering the theological question, "What is the Church, and what is the nature of the Christian faith?" And when the question is asked by such dark-skinned people as Elizabeth Eckford in a mob-possessed school yard when her only comforter and protector was a woman accused of being a communist by a congressional committee for surely no sane Christian lady would behave in such a strange manner. Or when it is asked by the spirit of Mack Parker as he is dragged from the waters of the muddy Pearl, or the residents of a Harlem ghetto. Or when it is faced in the light of the words of still another dark-skinned man who told those who considered themselves the church in his day that those who sold their bodies for pay and those who cooperated with occupying forces for pay—truly, I say to you, scalawags and whores enter the kingdom of God before you! When it is asked by those voices, it is more than an academic question to be considered in seminary halls and faith and order conferences. It is a question to be asked by anyone wearing the sign of the Cross.

But, they say, look at our amazing rate of growth. Look at the results of evangelistic crusades and the success of contemporary revivalists. Look at the souls we are bringing in. And it is so. Sometimes I wish it were not, for I see others, with no claim to being Christian, fighting for their very lives every step of the way, branded as communist, involved in law suits for the right to exist while we are growing by leaps and bounds. I do not know about your denomination, but in my Holy Mother Church, the Southern Baptist Convention, we do not have enough buildings to house those we are attracting in the midst of this crisis. We are forever building bigger and better barns . . . "Thou fool, this night thy soul!" This is a warning seldom heard. Nor is this one heard more often, "Beware when all men speak well of you."

And it is not enough to sit around and condemn the segregationist to the depths of hell. There are those who insist that a man cannot believe in segregation and be a Christian. I am not prepared to argue the point except to say that I am too much a part of the sin of the world arbitrarily to rule a man out of the Kingdom for any reason. I am convinced that this man is wrong and I believe that in this area someone else must be for him the church. But I cannot forget that tomorrow he may be for me the church. For tomorrow the White Council president or even the Klan leader may be for me the church, pulling me back into the fellowship of Christ, bringing me back into the community of the redeemed.

But a more serious point is that he is even now playing what seems to me to be a significant role. For he is constantly forcing us to defend what we consider the Christian position against what he considers the Christian position. It is troubling that we who consider ourselves the children of light in regard to race in the South are being much better humanists than we are Christian. Examine our resolutions, our statements, our actions. They speak most often of *law* and *order*, of *human* dignity, of man's rights, of democracy, of constitution and at best of the principle of the brotherhood of man and the Fatherhood of God. Instead of moving in with the message of a Saviour when all these landmarks go down, we panic and busy ourselves in propping them up.

And we are finding that more and more this is our most vulnerable point. And I believe we have left the door open for the attack of the segregationist Christian. This is not to quarrel with the humanist for he has played his role more than well. But for the Christian Church to assume this same role is to bet on the wrong horse. For, as Dr. T. A. Kantonen has suggested, the Christian view of race does not rest on the principle that all of us are brothers and ought to act like it. The Christian view on race is not the universal principle of the Fatherhood of God and the brotherhood of man, as important as that is. If the segregationist is told that the gospel is to obey the law, accept the Supreme Court, or open his lunch counters, he can see no gospel, no "good news" here. It must be elsewhere and he sets about to find it for this is only *bad* news.

But if he is told, as he *must* be told, that the Christian gospel was and is a message of redemption; that it was and is "God was in Christ, reconciling the world to himself . . . God was in Christ reconciling us to one another and thus to Himself . . . God was in Christ breaking down the walls of hostility that separate man from man and thus man from his God . . . God was in Christ loving man, accepting him, forgiving him . . . even if he cannot love and accept his brother yet . . . tell him this and if he hears it, believes it and accepts it, he is a lot closer to an integrated church in an integrated society than if he is told that he "ought" to be a good boy and obey the courts.

Some say there is no such thing as a Christian race relations—that we must take our cue from the social scientist. Indeed there is! And it might be that the racist will force us to see it anew. But it has to do with grace, not law, not order. And by this grace we are no longer Greek, African, Asian, but we are, in the words of the Pentecost story, "all together, in one place (yes, integrated) hearing the wondrous works of God." And all our resolutions, petitions, strategies, all our human engineering, all our propping up of the landmarks, will fail if we miss that simple point. We are the *tertium genius*—the third race. The Christian message on race is that race is irrelevant—that ours is a kingdom which asks no questions except one, and that has nothing to do with color or caste but only with redemption.

It would be ironic if history should prove that the present racists contributed more to the total company of the redeemed of all times by forcing us to re-examine the gospel than all the present righteous ones. God does indeed work in mysterious ways.

Well, all I have tried to say is that we have failed in our message on race insofar as we have failed in our message on redemption, and insofar as we have relied upon our culture to supply the landmarks.

Now, of course, the obvious converse of what we are saying about the message of redemption is the often neglected message of the judgment of God. Redemption has meaning primarily in terms of judgment. A great deal of our social action has the wrong subject and object. The suffering of the minority does not stand between him and his God, though God is certainly concerned with his suffering. Amos never proclaimed that the judgment of God would come to the Northern Kingdom because people were suffering. Rather God's judgment was to come because others of his children were causing them to suffer. In any concern for social justice the soul of the dispossessor must concern us as much as the suffering of the dispossessed.

But our weakness is that we timidly proclaim the message of redemption and apologetically proclaim the judgment of God.

A preacher of the deep South had labored long and hard with his middle class and lily-white congregation about their relationship with all men. For many years he had pounded the pulpit in his proclamation that God has created all men, loved them, and made no distinction between them. Finally there came what was inevitable from the beginning—a meeting of the governing body of his church which decided in the finest democratic tradition that it was clearly and unequivocally the will of God that the beloved pastor move on to richer fields of service. There came the last sermon for the preacher to this congregation to whom he had ministered for these many years. Obviously familiar with the homiletical techniques of Jonathan Edwards he meant to make this last shot count. His descriptive account of the wrath to come was vivid in every detail. "And you will be writhing and screaming in the bottomless pit of that eternal inferno and you will look next to you and see the seared and blistered skin of a black man, and on the other side you will hear the dreadful and eternal screams of a yellow man, and you will lift your eyes to paradise and there you will see, partaking of their everlasting joy, white men and black men and yellow men, and then it will occur to you that this ole preacher was right when he told you that God is no respecter of persons. And you will see God standing on the precipice of Glory with His hand on the big, forged door of eternity and you will cry out, 'Lord, we didn't know! We didn't know!' And then you will hear the clanging of the door, and the rattling of the chain and the snap of the lock and the last works of God to you: 'Wal, Ya KNOW NOW!!'"

Perhaps few of us in this room would look with favor on the scorched flesh policy of Jonathan Edwards' evangelism, but whether we would or whether we wouldn't, few of us would fail to hold some interpretation of the judgment of God.

And whatever our interpretation—whether we use the words to the hymn, "God, the All Merciful," or the more ancient ones, "God, the All Terrible," there has been a failure simply to point our people to the cemeteries.

Why, in God's name—any God—haven't we convinced our people by now of the simple truth with which the Bible is filled—that life is suffering and sorrow, that we all come forth like a flower and are cut down and are of a few days and full of trouble, and all flesh is like grass, and we are all here dying together. This takes the wind out of our sails and even a racist god must see that.

So that no matter how high we rise, no matter the legislation we engineer, no matter the investigating committees we chair, no matter how loudly we shout, "Never!", and no matter how much we invoke the blessings of Almighty God upon the work of our hands—the final outcome will be that of the mighty kings of Judah recorded in the Books of the Chronicles and the Kings—each one died and slept with his fathers and another reigned in his stead, and so will each of us die and sleep with our fathers and another will reign in our stead and history will record us in one sentence if we are terribly good or terribly bad, and we will all sleep in this giant sepulcher together and be judged by one God. The best text on race relations is not from Acts, "God hath made of one," but from II Samuel, "How are the mighty fallen!"

Our sin has not been in neglecting to tell our people that "red and yellow, black or white, they are precious in his sight"; we have told them that. Our sin is that we have not told them what Isaiah said: that man is as grasshoppers. We have told man of his worth and dignity and perhaps rightly so. But we have not told him often enough of his insignificance in the total scheme of things. "It is God that sitteth above the circle of the earth . . . that bringeth princes to nothing; that maketh the judges of the earth as vanity . . . he bloweth upon them and they wither; and the whirlwind taketh them away as stubble."

What, now shall we say? Is there a demon? Is there someone we can blame? Yes, I think there is and in testimony thereof, I make this final witness.

There is some virtue in honesty. And if prejudice is acquired in the manner described by the social scientist, then I am sure that within me lie the vestiges of as much racial pride and prejudice as there is within anyone. They tell us we do not rid ourselves of it simply by intellectual declaration and I have no reason to disagree. But this sends us racing back over the years to David Lipscomb who saw that there was a difference between feeling and behavior—between prejudice and discrimination.

And during the past few years as it has been my ministry to move about the crisis areas of the South, I have seen those vestiges of the savage fade and grow dim.

I went with a pastor into what is left of his church, after a sack of dynamite had been thrown into it in the dark of winter's night. And there are all the little brown faces outside, not allowed now into what is referred to as "their church." And I wonder what they are thinking as they see a white face crawl through the wreckage. And inside the debris, the pastor picks up a small chalkboard which still bears, prophetically, part of last Sunday's lesson, written in what is obviously the handwriting of a child—"God loves all the little children of the world." And remembering the faces outside for a moment I wonder about this "they are precious in his sight" business and if He really does have the "whole wide world in His hand." Maybe He is the demon to let this happen—to the children—to the little children. But then there are the familiar words, "Let the little children—all children—come unto Me, for of such is the Kingdom."

And somehow my Southern way of life seems like less than the Kingdom of God.

Or a mother is struck with a bottle as she takes her little girl to the school where the law of that city says that the child should go. And thinking for a moment as a Southern white man, I wonder why this is so important to her—to take her child and herself into the face of death and hell. And I am sorry for a mother who is hit with a bottle, but I recall some other words—"that men will come from the East and from the West and from the North and from the South and sit down in the Kingdom and the least shall be greatest. . . ." And I am no longer sorry for her for somehow I have the feeling that at that moment I am looking at one of the greatest.

And those vestiges of prejudice will grow still a little dimmer.

Or a pastor with the little brown hand of a six year old parishioner thrust trustingly in his is spit upon as he walks with her into the face of a screaming mob, and he makes no answer but enters as the crowd opens up. And again I am sorry for the man who is spit upon. But then the words, "If a man say to his brother 'racca' he is in danger of the judgment." And some have suggested that the word originally came from the noise made in the throat of one preparing to spit. H-a-a-r-c! And my sorrow for the man spit upon turns to stark terror and fright. But it is not fright for the man spit upon, but for the man who spit. But not fright for him alone now, but fright for all that has produced and now sustains him.

And I remember who I am and what I am. A white man, an American, a Protestant. And I pray:

> Lord, have mercy upon us.
> Christ, have mercy upon us.

§55 LeRoy Collins

Thomas LeRoy Collins's biography appears in the introduction to his March 20, 1960 speech in Jacksonville, Florida. On his way out of office in late 1960, Florida's Governor LeRoy Collins addressed the B'Nai Brith in south Florida. While some of the state's racial strife had been quelled in recent months, just days before his speech, on December 6 and 7, new boycotts had broken out in downtown Tallahassee. Picketers protested in front of Neisners, McCrorys, Woolworths, Walgreens, and Sears as negotiations to desegregate these stores' lunch counters had stalled.

Even though a progressive on racial matters compared to other governors in the deep south, Collins defines the conflict more on an individual basis than a collective one. He notes, "I frankly believe that very little progress in race relations can be forced by litigation or by public demonstrations. . . . Real progress in race relations depends much less on the desegregation of a school here or there or on biracial eating at lunch counters, than it does on meaningful changes in the hearts and minds of the people of a community." If people "accept the idea of the brotherhood of man and the dignity of the individual under the fatherhood of God," the civil rights revolution could and would indeed come to pass. Of course Collins's argument strategically omits the fact that without demonstrations, protests, marches, and sit-ins, white "hearts and minds" might never be convicted about the injustices of the Jim Crow South.

Speech to the Anti-Defamation League of B'Nai B'rith
Hollywood, Florida
December 10, 1960

I am deeply grateful for the award you have just presented to me. Without wishing to appear modest, I cannot but question that I deserve it. If my public record reflects tolerance and concern for human relations, this is no more than conduct in line with my public duty.

A public official's primary impulse should be one of obligation to every citizen he serves. And I believe very deeply that I was elected to serve every man, woman and child in this state, of whatever race, color or creed, whether rich or poor, influential or defenseless, whether a person of deep faith or a wandering lost soul.

My term as Governor is ending. It has been an experience more richly rewarding than I could have imagined. There have been some defeats and frustrations along with our successes. These years in which I served have not been quiet and serene ones for the ship of state. Maybe they could have been had we been content to lie at anchor indifferent to needs or had we been willing to run for the nearest port of compromise every time a stiff wind blew. But a forward moving ship must leave wake. Florida's needs have demanded that we move ahead—that we deal truthfully with the people and that we not be deviated by the squalls and anguish generated by those who would impede the state's progress for self-aggrandizement, or by those who did not have the vision to see the course of right. As we have moved forward we have at times left a backwash of currents in violent collision, squirming and frothing, but the simple truth is we could not have made the progress we have made without this.

We have made remarkable gains in this period in the physical progress of our state and our state government, particularly in the areas of providing more adequate institutional facilities and services—great new mental hospitals, modern correctional institutions, model institutions for delinquent and mentally retarded children, greatly expanded and entirely new institutions of higher learning, and we are leaving a road system which has been improved more in six years than in all the history of the road department prior to our administration.

These things will last and will continue to serve succeeding generations of Floridians. But the things which I most hope will survive and grow in the years ahead are the intangibles which we have sought to instill in the hearts and minds of our fellow citizens.

This has been a very difficult period for human relations in our state, our region and our nation. It has seen destructive suspicion and hysteria feeding on the threat of communism. There have been recurrent manifestations of religious bigotry. But most damaging of all has been the fear and hatred and violence aroused by racial antagonism and prejudice.

I have been greatly encouraged by the mature way in which many of our local communities in Florida have accepted the challenge presented by the highly explosive forces working for change in our traditional relationships between the races.

Some two dozen communities have established bi-racial committees or similar groups to open and expand channels of communication and provide the means for constructive consideration of legitimate grievances in the light of the local situation.

The State Fowler Commission on Race Relations has been remarkably successful in giving effect to my call for the settlement of differences around the table rather than in the streets.

Under the strong leadership of Mr. Cody Fowler, this hardworking state commission has gained the confidence of responsible leaders of both races. Where it could mobilize people of good will to recognize frankly that they have a problem in their local communities and that it is their responsibility to do something about it, the Commission has been able to end dangerous demonstrations and assist in the development of that atmosphere of mutual confidence so necessary for progress.

I wish I could illustrate for you how this has been accomplished in specific instances. But, unfortunately, to do so would compromise the work that has been done and perhaps jeopardize its efforts in the future. But, take my word for it: this Commission has prevented some potentially very ugly situations from developing in a number of Florida communities and it has ameliorated ugly situations in others.

In the broader aspects of its work, the Fowler Commission has carried on an extensive program of education—through its public statements, through consultations with merchants and others most directly concerned by demonstrations, through the formation of statewide advisory committees of religious leaders, educators and other responsible leaders, and through programs of specialized information for law enforcement officers to enable them to deal more effectively with threats to the public order.

In all of its work the Fowler Commission has not tried to promote integration or segregation. It has sought rather to make people aware of the realities we face in this area of race relations and aware of the simple fact that the responsibility for deciding what can be done to improve race relations in a particular community rests upon the responsible people of both races in that community.

There has been a tendency to measure progress in race relations by the number of schools and lunch counters desegregated or, from a different point of view, by the number of "outside agitators" jailed and the number of integration attempts thwarted.

But progress for our Negro citizens is not basically a matter of school admission policies or policies for service at lunch counters. Our Negro citizens need better homes, better employment opportunities, better education, higher health standards, more recreational opportunities, and a greater sense of being able to progress in American society according to their individual ability, diligence and standards of conduct.

They long to be treated equally before the law, and not have their worth measured solely by the color of their skin. And this is a goal the Constitution of the United States holds out assurance they can achieve.

The struggle toward it is no more their responsibility than ours if we accept the idea of the brotherhood of man and the dignity of the individual under the fatherhood of God.

I frankly believe that very little progress in race relations can be forced by litigation or by public demonstrations. But the opportunities for such progress also cannot be wholly neglected in our local communities without building up resentments and frustrations which are bound ultimately to find outlets in irresponsible acts, open aggressions and racial violence.

Real progress in race relations depends much less on the desegregation of a school here or there or on biracial eating at lunch counters, than it does on meaningful changes in the hearts and minds of the people of a community.

Meaningful progress in race relations takes place when people decide in their own minds that the attitudes of yesterday are not adequate for the realities of today, and when they realize that they share the responsibility for determining what kind of relationships will exist in their communities tomorrow.

I am convinced that the antidote to intolerance and bigotry and prejudice, is people—people learning about people who are different from themselves—learning about them as individuals—learning that they have common hopes and fears, common concerns and aspirations—and learning that the people we have classified under a single label are as different from one another as those we have long identified as our own "kind" differ among themselves.

We are beginning to realize, I think, that people of the whole world must get along together notwithstanding drastically different social, political and economic orders, if we are not to cease to exist in mutual desolation. We must also realize that we will have to learn to live more harmoniously and more constructively with people of different creeds and colors if we are to avoid spiritual desolation in the communities of our land.

The great American goal is freedom—both at home and through-out the world. We cannot be free if our minds and hearts are enslaved by prejudice.

I recall seeing a little report in a paper a few months back about a rather strange happening in one of our southern towns. A county was building a new jail. One of the workers on the project on the day it was completed was arrested in the jail he had built.

When we allow bigotry and prejudice to enter our lives we build the jails in which we are then imprisoned. We cut off communications. We can no longer be free.

And no one else can free us from our self imprisonment. We can only free ourselves from the bonds which constrict our spirits.

I do not pretend to any specialized knowledge of the psychology of prejudice and intolerance. But I have known them in myself, and I have seen their destructive work in our society.

I read recently that perhaps 10 percent of Americans are virtually free of prejudice. But I rather doubt that there is one among us tonight who has never felt—or who has entirely eliminated from his life—the emotional rejection of persons on the basis of pre-conceived notions.

I am not sure that this deep-seated feeling can be eliminated entirely in the make-up of a man. Some times I am even inclined to feel that a little prejudice—if it is consciously recognized—may be to the good as an energizing agent. The struggle to overcome in ourselves what we deplore when we see it in its grosser forms in others should strengthen us for the big battles against prejudice and intolerance in our society. And it should also make us more understanding and less self-righteous in our dealings with our fellowmen.

The human relations conflict in our society is going on within each of us—arraying traditions, religious teachings and other aspects of our inner lives against one another. This inner conflict can destroy the gains we have made in human relations in the past. It can destroy or cripple us as human beings.

But, if we face up to this inner conflict and seek better relationships with our fellowmen, we can make ourselves and our society more nearly whole and more truly humanistic.

I think each of us has two selves—one is an inner self or true self. This is the one that responds with love or hate—with assurance or fear—with patience or anger—with selfishness or unselfishness—with an instinctive evaluation of right and wrong.

The other is what I would call a pretending self—the one we seek to sell to others—the one we want to make people believe is the real or true self, whether it is or not.

It seems that we run into this more and more in politics these days. Politicians and their public relation agents worry about the "image" they are creating. He must look like a good family man, they say. He must appear candid and direct. He must always seem kind, courteous and understanding. So go the arguments of the image-makers. And in their unmitigated conceit they feel that regardless of what a man's inner self may be they can dress him out in a way that no one can see what is under the costume.

A person whose inner self is strong usually reacts instinctively and immediately. But if his pretending self is in control he waits to see what the popular thing will be to say or do before committing himself.

A person whose inner self is strong is motivated by right or wrong. The person whose pretending self is in control acts from expediency. A person whose inner self is strong has convictions, while one whose pretending self is in control has calculations.

This is not just true of individuals. Organizations are the same. They constantly strive to create images that are not the real thing. For example, bar associations loudly profess to uphold the dignity of the law—the strength of the Constitution. But this becomes an unreal image if the association by action or inaction actually encourages destruction of respect for law, or wrongly degrades courts charged with the responsibility to uphold it.

Cities go in for image-making in a big way. In almost all of them right now, large and small, the Christmas decorations shine up and down and across the streets. There are pretty bells that can't ring. Cardboard carolers that can't sing—blue trees, purple trees, yellow trees, that have one thing in common, they all sparkle. Now these aren't really put up to honor the birth of Jesus. They are actually a part of the hucksters' technique to sell merchandise, to make children want to go to town.

Even nations have great departments elaborately financed whose sole job is to create an image of something its true self is not.

We must, fellow citizens, individually through our families, through our business, through our governments, stop trying to sell ourselves as something we are not, and start making ourselves something better than what we are.

We must nourish our inner selves

It was an ancient Greek, I think, who, centuries ago, said, "Our greatest danger comes from those who try to please us, rather than serve us."

Today, as in every age, what is needed is not pleasing images, but men who, in the words of the motto of one of our sister states, will strive: "To be, rather than to seem."

1961

1961

§56 Dr. Haywood N. Hill

In this brief speech to a Sunday School class at Trinity Presbyterian Church, Dr. Haywood Hill offers up a confessional of sorts—what he prefers and why he prefers it. As a native of the south, he favors the racial status quo. But, as a Christian and as a scientist, Hill is compelled to reject his prejudices and preferences for his convictions and his conscience. The actions that follow from them include: treating every person as a child of God; paying a living wage to those who work for him and persuading others to do the same; providing equal opportunities in education; treating blacks with respect; allowing blacks to live in the same neighborhood if they so desire; ignoring politicians who want to stir up racial strife; and Hill must help blacks achieve their aspirations and so should the church. These are the actions that Hill (and presumably many other white southerners) are committed to based on the principles in which he believes.

This I Believe

Trinity Presbyterian Church, Atlanta, Georgia
January 1961

I am a Southerner. I was bred in the South where my forefathers were slaveholders and Confederate soldiers. I was born and raised in Southern towns with their rigid racial patterns and their typical Southern prejudice. I was away from the South for a few years, but I returned to live in the South by choice and intend to remain here for the rest of my life. I love the South and its people.

I like to have two black arms in my kitchen and two black legs pushing my lawn mower, to help take the drudgery out of living for myself and my family, and I like having them at a very minimum of cost to me.

I like choosing my own friends and associates, and I like eating in pleasant places with well bred people of my own race, class, and status.

I like to worship in a church which is composed of my friends and equals where I will be among my own group, racially, socially, and intellectually.

I like for my children to go to school with their own kind and with other children of their own racial, social, and intellectual level. I like for them to be shielded against poverty, ignorance, dirt, and disease.

I like to practice medicine among intelligent, cooperative people who understand what I am trying to do for them, who are friends as well as patients, and who pay their bills.

I like to live in a neighborhood composed of people of my own group who have pleasant, well kept homes, and where there is no conflict or strife.

I do not want my daughter to marry a Negro.

I like the racial status quo. I am a Southerner.

But, I am also a Christian. As a Christian, I must believe that God created all men and that all men are equal in the sight of God. I must believe that all men are my brothers and are children of God, and that I am my brother's keeper. I must believe that Jesus meant what He said when He commanded me to love my neighbor as myself and when He commanded me to do unto others as I would have them do unto me. I must believe that the church is God's house and that it does not belong to me, to the congregation of Trinity Presbyterian Church, or to the Southern Presbyterian Church. I must believe in the fellowship of all believers.

I am also a scientist and have devoted my life to the pursuit of objective truth. Therefore, I must know that while there are individual differences among people that there is no such thing as racial inferiority. I must know that within every group there are individuals with different potentialities, and that I cannot arbitrarily classify anyone on the basis of his race or color. I must know that poverty and ignorance and isolation, call it segregation if you will, breed feelings of inferiority, frustration, resentment, and despair and that these feelings in turn lead to misery, to immorality, and to crime which, in turn, not only depress the people and the communities involved but the community as a whole and the whole country.

Therefore, as a Christian and as a scientist I am obligated to act on the basis of what I know and what I believe and not on the basis of what I like. I must live by conviction and by conscience rather than by preference and by prejudice.

I must, therefore, regard every man, rich or poor, black or white, as a child of God and as a person, not as some kind of subhuman being or animal or even as an inferior. I must try to see to it that every individual gets equal rights under the law and in politics. This applies particularly to the right of equal justice in the courts and to the right of the exercise of political privilege; that is, the right to vote. If I fear the effects of bloc voting and voting from ignorance, then I must try to see to it that every man is educated to the point where he votes intelligently.

I am obligated to pay a living wage to every man who works for me and to do my best to see that others do the same. I must accord to every man the right to rise to the limit of his abilities in any job or profession, and I must make every attempt to see that no man is blocked because of his race or his social status. If any individual of any race rises to a position equal to mine, then I must accord to him the same privileges that I have and welcome him as an equal.

I must see to it that everyone has an opportunity for an education as good as my own children have. If this means, as the social scientists, the courts, and the Negroes themselves believe, that that education must be the same education as my children have, then I must accept it and encourage it.

I must try to see to it that no man be humiliated and rejected because of his color. If this means that the Negro eats where I eat, sits next to me in the theatre, or rides next to me in public transportation, then I am obligated to accept it.

I must see to it that every man has an opportunity for a decent home and decent surroundings, and if this means that he will live in my neighborhood or in the house next to mine then that is the way it must be.

If a Negro wants to worship in my church or join my church, then I am obligated to see to it that he is not only accepted but welcomed into that church, even if it be Trinity Presbyterian Church. I must not be led by false pride to try to judge his motives for coming into that church, and I must welcome him on the same basis that I would welcome any other individual.

I must try to overlook the selfish politicians who use the Negro for their own ends; the Communist agitators who delight in stirring up racial strife; the noisy, aggressive Negro who abuses his privileges and who makes life unpleasant for me; and even the Negroes who exploit their own race. I must ignore such irrelevant questions as which race settled this country, which race pays the most taxes, etc., and remember the basic principles on which I am trying to act and in which I believe.

I must not only accept the efforts of the Negro to achieve his legitimate aspirations, but I must try to help him achieve them, and I believe that the church must do the same if it is a truly Christian church. I must do this, even though it goes against my deepest prejudices and even though it threatens my superior and isolated position in the community and even though it entails the risk of intermarriage.

Basically, the problem is not one of what I like but of what I know to be right. I must not let my wishes determine my attitude to my associates, my school, my church, or even my own family, but if I am true to the principles which I profess, then I must act according to those principles. This, I believe.

§57 Colbert S. Cartwright

Colbert ("Bert") Scott Cartwright's biography appears in the introduction to his July 1959 sermon in Little Rock, Arkansas. In the following Race Relations Sunday sermon on February 12, 1961, Cartwright uses an anecdote from his father's childhood to illustrate a theological lesson in race relations. Near the close of Jesus' Sermon on the Mount, Christ intones, "Whoever shall say, 'Thou fool,' shall be in danger of hell fire." That judgment extends easily to Little Rock's race relations: "we white persons have got ourselves into a position of saying 'You fool' to members of the Negro race. When you boil our practices of racial discrimination and segregation down to their essence, we white people are saying very emphatically to Negro people, 'We are superior and you are inferior.' We are saying to the colored race, 'You fool!'" Why the harsh judgment of Jesus? Cartwright specifies two reasons: first, to continually emphasize someone's inferiority is to maim him—mentally, morally and physically; second, the attitude is perhaps more destructive to the person who holds it; it "maims and cripples" his soul. Cartwright closes by noting that Christ's judgment is followed by His command to leave the church until we are reconciled with our brother—and we "don't have forever to work this problem out."

Some Stern Words of Jesus
Pulaski Heights Christian Church, Little Rock, Arkansas
February 12, 1961

One day, when my father was a child, he was playing with one of the neighbor boys, and as it frequently happens, a misunderstanding arose between the boys. The boys had done something that my father did not like, and my father with anger cried out, "You fool!" Somewhat to his amazement his grandmother, who had been watching the boys, grabbed him and took him into the parlor, opened up the family Bible and read to him where Jesus said, "Whoever shall say, 'Thou fool,' shall be in danger of hell fire."

In relating this incident, my father has said that the reading of this terrible judgment scared the living daylights out of him. He could feel the temperature of the room getting decidedly warmer already. From that time on, so far as he was concerned, to call a person a fool was one of life's greatest sins.

Today the word "fool" is a common enough one and there are not many of us who have any qualms of conscience when we use it. Why was it that Jesus spoke so harshly about a person's saying to someone, "You fool!"

Jesus makes this statement in the portion of the Sermon on the Mount in which he reinterprets the traditional Jewish laws. He says: "You have heard that it was said to the men of old, 'You shall not kill: and whoever kills shall be liable to judgment.' (This was the standing law and practice of Judaism.) But I say to you that everyone who is angry with his brother shall be liable to judgment: whoever insults his brother shall be liable to the council, and whoever says, 'You fool!' shall be liable to the hell of fire." Jesus is saying that murder is something much more inclusive than just killing a physical body. There are attitudes one has which are deadly.

The attitude of regarding oneself as superior and some other person or group as inferior is as deathly as physical murder. The attitude which says, "I am a superior person and you are a fool" is deathly. Such an attitude is death-dealing to the one who is its object and it is death-dealing to the one who exhibits it. It harms the person who is regarded to be a fool, and it jeopardizes the eternal well-being of the one who by his attitude and actions says, "You fool!"

It is the teaching of Jesus that God created all men with an equal love toward them. In God's sight, regardless of individual differences, all his children are worthy of love and worthy of equal treatment. God does not divide his children into groups of superiors and groups of inferiors. They are all of equal worth—they were all worth dying for on a cross. Every living person is regarded as "special" by God. "He loves each one of us as if there were but one to love." This must be our attitude as well.

But we are always tempted to think that somehow we, ourselves, are special. It is easy to think of ourselves as superior and some other people as inferior. Perversely we succumb to the temptation to regard ourselves to be wise and others fools. Jesus in our Scripture says that when we do this we are sinning. We are in danger of God's harsh judgment.

This, of course, has a direct bearing upon our present racial problem. Through a complex of causes we white persons have got ourselves into a position of saying "You fool" to members of the Negro race. When you boil our practices of racial discrimination and segregation down to their essence, we white people are saying very emphatically to Negro people, "We are superior and you are inferior." We are saying to the colored race, "You fool!"

The key phrase in our talking about the Negro is that he must "keep his place" and this, of course, is a place of inferiority to ourselves. He must not put on airs and think he is as good as a white person. He must not seek the same rights and privileges of a white person. He must recognize his inferiority and humbly keep his place.

Most of our laws and practices in regard to the Negro have the primary purpose of keeping him aware that he is regarded by us as inferior. By segregating him we tell him he is mentally, morally and socially unfit to move freely about the city. There is something inferior about him which bars him from sitting just anywhere in a theater or at a football game. He must not contaminate our parks by his presence. He is shunted off into separate schools as though he had leprosy. He is arbitrarily excluded from jobs and occupations—on no other basis than color, which automatically labels him as incompetent. White Christians keep him out of their churches—letting him know he had best keep his place of inferiority. A Negro can prepare food for white persons, but must not sit down and eat with those white persons. In short, we brand the Negro as inferior by our laws, and we segregate him so he can be treated as an inferior.

Jesus just has one comment to make about all this: "Whoever says, 'You fool!' shall be liable to the hell of fire." These are stern and harsh words from the gentle Jesus. Why so? There are two main reasons which we need to look at in turn.

First, to continually din into the ears of someone that he is inferior is to severely maim that person—to thwart the development of that person's personality. We all know what happens when we constantly tell a person that he is no good.

As a parent I know what would happen to a child of mine if from his birth I dinned into his ears that he was not as good as other people. I know the tragic results if I daily told him not to do this or not to do that because he was "different" and not deemed worthy of the privileges that other people have. I would so destroy my child's spirit that in all likelihood the state would take him away from me, denouncing me as one who is unworthy of parenthood.

Yet this is exactly what we white people are doing every day as we continue to condone the practice of racial discrimination. We white people are in a vicious conspiracy to twist and contort the souls of countless children who become the objects of our destruction because they are Negroes. You and I are doing this in one way or another every day of our lives.

Under these circumstances we often retard a Negro's mental, moral and physical development. By our attitudes and institutionalized practices we crush his spirit in a thousand ways. And then, strangely enough, with our superior logic, after putting him through all these personality-shattering experiences, we point to him as an adult and say, "See, I was right. Just look at how inferior he really is. I told you so all along."

Somehow I am not impressed when someone says, "Bert, you just don't know colored people like I do. If you worked [with] them the way I have to, you'd know they're not much." We have dinned into the ears of these people from their birth in segregated hospital rooms or in segregated neighborhoods that they're inferior. They live up exactly to our expectations. Demanding that they recognize their own inferiority, we produce persons of limited ability and aspiration. Let us face the fact squarely that a Negro growing up in our community never has any way of knowing what his full potentiality might have been. He was never given an adequate opportunity to develop it.

It is no wonder that Jesus harshly and emphatically says, "Whoever says, 'You fool!' shall be liable to the hell of fire." To drum into people's minds and souls that they are inferior is to shrink their souls. Is this not the worst kind of murder?

There is a second reason why Jesus spoke harshly in regard to a person's saying "Thou fool!" to another: Jesus saw that this attitude is self-destructive. When you have this attitude it not only harms other people, but it maims and cripples your own personality—your own soul. In the process of our racial discrimination something tragic happens to us.

Booker T. Washington once said in essence that you cannot keep a man down in a ditch unless you stay in the ditch with him to keep him there. There is plenty of evidence to substantiate this observation. By insisting that the Negro be regarded as inferior we have as white people exhibited our own inferiority.

This attitude has dulled our sense of justice, stifled our feelings of compassion, filled our hearts with unfounded fears, and sapped our souls of courage. It has led us to lie with straight faces and to blandly justify shady practices. It has twisted our powers of reason and contorted our faith. One of the most disturbing effects of racial prejudice is that it has infected our very understanding of the nature of Christianity, the Church, and the ministry. Jesus' gospel of all-inclusive and humble love has been twisted to teach white supremacy. The New Testament church which knows no social or racial barriers has been transformed by prejudice into exclusive clubs for white members only. The basic Christian conviction that the ministry must fearlessly and without favor preach the gospel of God has been changed to mean the ministry must muffle God's voice if it would disturb the prejudices of too many people.

It is quite possible that our attitudes of superiority have done infinitely more damage to our own personalities than they have to those who have been the objects of our prejudice. This attitude is self-destroying. It kills the best within a person. In a very real sense we create our hell for ourselves. Possibly this is what Jesus really means when he bluntly asserts, "Whoever says, 'You fool!' shall be liable to the hell of fire."

Jesus will not let us go this morning until we see with him the urgency of our taking immediate action to put an end to racial discrimination. Jesus teaches, "Whoever says, 'You fool' shall be liable to the hell of fire." But he does not stop there. We must listen to the words which immediately follow. He goes on to say: "So if you are offering your gift at the altar, and there remember that your brother has something against you, leave your gift there before the altar and go; first be reconciled to your brother, you then come and offer your gift."

Jesus says that if a person comes with his sacrifice to the altar of the temple for the purpose of worshiping God, but knows he has said "You fool!" to someone, he must stop right then and there and go out to correct the offense. He says you have no business worshiping God till you get squared away with those whom you have offended. That makes it rather urgent, doesn't it!

Our colored brothers have something against everyone of us—you and me—because we have shared in perpetuating racial discrimination. We have not done everything we could to end the institutionalizing of this cry "you fool!" toward them. Complacently we continue to share in the respectable plot of our community and state to devaluate its colored citizens. We share in the present policy of our community leaders to let every Negro pupil know he still is regarded as inferior, whatever Christianity or the courts of our nation may say. We share in the policy of our community leaders to make no move whatsoever toward ending racial discrimination in public facilities.

Jesus drops a bomb in the midst of our complacency, saying, "Don't go to church again until you correct your offense against your Negro brother." It's just that urgent.

Well, I don't suppose any of us are going to take Jesus that seriously, but he does shatter our complacency. He reminds us that we don't have forever to work this problem out.

The time to do something is NOW.

§58 Reverend William O. Byrd

William O. Byrd was a native of Meridian, Mississippi. Born on October 12, 1916 Byrd received his education at Louisiana Polytechnic Institute and Southern Methodist University. From 1943 to 1945 Byrd served as an army chaplain, spending part of his time with the 82nd Airborne Division as parachute infantry chaplain, where he broke two vertebra skydiving into the European theater. After returning to the U.S., Byrd pastored the First Methodist Church in Arkadelphia, Arkansas; the First Methodist Church in Pine Bluff, Arkansas; and Methodist churches in Bonita, Farmersville, and Lake Charles, Louisiana. He was called to the First Methodist Church of New Orleans in June 1960. Reverend Byrd died on March 4, 1999.

In this moving and intimate sermon delivered before an interracial gathering in New Orleans, Reverend Byrd uses autobiography to indict an entire region and a way of life. "Hear my confession, please," punctuates many of Byrd's personal observations. But the confessions function rhetorically as the confessions of a hypocritical people who mouth American pieties yet practice segregation. And, in a climactic irony to the speech, black Americans have taken these pieties at face value: "We have made the terrible mistake of teaching the Negro these truths; so now it is the Negro who has the ultimate weapon which they provide: nonviolent love. Against such there is no defense." No institution in Byrd's past remains innocent: "This is my dilemma: my whole lifetime, country, family, community, school, church, have taught me to be a brother. But now they say I cannot act as a brother must act! Can I believe them? Hear my confession, please!"

———

Mistakes I Have Made in Race Relations

First Methodist Church, New Orleans, Louisiana
February 1961 (reprinted)

Proverbs 3. Matthew 7.

I have a confession to make. I must confess mistakes I have made in race relations. Mistakes of omission and commission. Will you hear my confession, please?

My first mistake was to be born in this time. Perhaps in the dear dim days beyond recall I would have never faced the problem, but I picked the wrong century in which to be born. I shouldered my wrinkled way into this world in 1916. I was weaned during *the* war, that shining crusade to make the world safe for democracy. Now, after forty-four years, with another World War and a Korean "police action" (strange—the casualties are just as dead whether we call it war or not) we are threatened with nuclear holocaust. This one, if it comes, may be the war to end all worlds, at least as we know them. Now the question is to make our much proclaimed but much less practiced democracy safe for the world.

And in such a world, shrunken into neighborhood by jets and our communication media, we must have brotherhood; we must act "Thy kingdom come" or we shall be blown to kingdom come. There is no place to hide.

This is a world in which Little Rock can be hissed by Indians in Peru and by Africans in the Congo. I have heard that hiss and I know that "no man is an island, no man lives alone."

And this is my sin, my mistake; for to be born in a time such as this is to know that I am a part of a world in which Little Rock and all the other symbols of man's inhumanity to man are possible. And I cannot ignore it, nor live with it comfortably any longer:

> "The time is out of joint;
> O cursed spite,
> That ever I was born to set it right!"

Who? Me? Reared on beautiful words; "World Safe for Democracy," "Four Freedoms," "United Nations," on these was I nourished. And I believed them, for the time demands belief. That was my first mistake in race relations. Hear my confession, please!

It was a mistake to be born of my particular parents. I should have chosen more wisely. They were of Scotch-Irish stock, with the sturdy Protestant faith. Rather ordinary, yet amazingly good and independent people, driven by an unrelenting Puritan conscience.

My "Mom" (bless her) really believed and loved everybody. She could master the stately language of the King James Version of the Bible but she never did learn how to pronounce the simple word "Negro." To her dying day she called them "Nigras" with a Mississippi accent, and loved them "in their place" with all of her Scotch-Irish heart. "Pop" was more lenient in law, if not in love. In fact, he could "bend" the law when it got in the way of his Scotch (and I don't mean blood). But others knew and understood and joined him in saying, "don't sell it to the Nigras—they can't handle it like us Southern gentlemen."

But both of them, Mom and Pop, taught me to know the virtues of honesty, fair play, and respect for others. I was warned never to cheat, not even a "Nigra"; never to take advantage of another, not even a "colored child"; and never to talk back to my elders, not even a "Nigra mammy." They saw that I attended Sunday school and that I learned to sing:

> "Jesus loves the little children, All the children
>   of the world,
> Red and yellow, black and white, They are
>   precious in His sight,
> Jesus loves the little children of the world."

And I sang the words and I believed them and that was my mistake. Hear my confession, please!

It was a mistake to be born in this particular country. No man who wants to remain exclusive should ever select America as his land of birth. Even deep in Mississippi, that "Magnolia Jungle" and later in Louisiana, the growing mind of a child could not help but be aware of the breath of freedom. For in those days, before the citizens came to their senses and gave their schools to the tender "protection" of the governor, a growing boy could hear such exciting words: "We hold these truths to be self-evident that all men are created equal, that they are endowed, by their Creator, with certain unalienable rights. . . . " And they told me that in America it was true and I believed them and that was my mistake.

Of course, I should have known better, for "Bubba," my almost constant playmate away from home and along the riverbank, wasn't in *my* school. His skin was darker than mine even when mine was dirty with Mississippi mud. But I ignored that and I believed the teachers because, you see, I really *wanted* to believe those beautiful words.

It was a mistake to be reared in a small Southern town. Perhaps here was where I really went wrong. No one, not even Mom, thought it strange to have me play during the hot summer days with Bubba and his friends, or to have "Aunt Cindy," Bubba's mother, walk with us across the hot pavements to buy penny candies for all, share and share alike, *not* separate, *but* equal!

For years I did not know that I was "better" and that while we could sit side by side on the curb and eat our candies, Bubba must never, never sit down in the house. And yet they said: "Son, always play fair, always be honest. Do unto others as you would have them do unto you." And I believed them and that was my mistake.

Of course, I *am* grateful for one saving grace. I could not join the Boy Scouts (my folks couldn't afford the uniform, they said) and so I never had to unlearn all the "impractical" words of the Scout Law. But my friends did and they said they believed them and that was *their* mistake.

So my sins pile up. Time would fail to tell them all. The tragic mistake I made, as a product of such a background, when I chose my life work, the ministry of a man named Jesus. How could I be comfortable any more, bothered by the words: "God so loved the world (and nothing about it being a black or white world) that he gave. . . ." "Come unto me, all ye. . . ." (who are white? or Southern?) "Inasmuch as ye have done it unto the least of these . . . (the least rich, least educated, least white?) ye have done unto me." So on and on, the demanding, impossible ethic of Christ. And I try to escape it and cannot and that is my mistake.

That ministry carried me into the army chaplaincy of World War II, to stamp out the last great prophet of "the Master Race" (that is, before Faubus, Eastland and their company). And deep in the Hurtgen forest, in the Belgium Bulge, I watched a Roman Catholic doctor give captured German blood plasma to a Southern Negro American rifleman and I looked as the Jewish medic assisted the doctor by cleaning the stump of what had been the Negro's leg. And the clean white teeth flashed up and demanded, "Look at it, my blood, it's *red*, you bastards!" And somehow it didn't sound like profanity at all, more like the echo of a Holy Book that says something about "He hath made of one blood all men to dwell upon the earth. . . ." And I saw and I believed and that was my mistake. For back at home the little hitlers, the supermen, still shout their patriotism and measure it by the hate they can arouse to insure elections.

Even so, I made a greater mistake. For I believed that when we saw what race hate could do in Dachau and Buchenwald and on a thousand battle-fields that the people who call themselves Christian would never rest until the big, beautiful words were translated into flesh. I turned to the church, the fountainhead of all these great Judeo-Christian truths men hold to be self-evident. And there in spite of the agony of many sensitive ministers and laymen, too often the church (or rather the caricature we make of his Holy Body on earth) became molded and shaped by pious prattle, mouth-ing its love of the Supreme Law Giver and Lover of all life while dragging behind the Supreme Court in human relations. Publicly it could pass great resolutions yet privately pass the word along, "Don't rock the boat, keep everybody happy, say nothing controversial, but say it beautifully." And the greatest of crimes is to offend one of these not least but loudest councils.

And I wonder if we ministers and members have become "killers of the dream" in our futile desire to avoid the cost of awakening. Aren't we haunted by the hymns we sing: "In Christ there is no East or West, in Him no South or North" and " Dear Master in whose life I see All that I would fail to be . . ."? And I awake in the night to ponder the words of the noted Ralph McGill, editor of the Atlanta Constitution as he writes about "The Agony of the Southern Minister." And I know the agony of which he writes, of the pressures brought to bear, of programs blocked, of silent curtains. And I know the truth of seeing my fellow ministers and my people being haunted by the presence of our brother whom we deny. We sing: "Faith of our Fathers, living still" and we try to believe it and that is our mistake. Hear my confession, please.

But the greatest mistake of all, the most terrible confession I must make (and here *you* must join me at the confessional), *our* greatest mistake was to teach the Negro that we believed this heritage of ours, this Judeo-Christian faith in the fatherhood of God and the brotherhood of man. And, believ-ing, we find ourselves bound whether we like it or not in unbreakable ties.

For the Negro *is* my brother, whether I like it or not, or whether I ever choose to act like a brother to him. He is *my* brother, for God *our* Father called him to life even as he did me. He chose him and me and you to be born in this particular time, of our particular parents, in this particu-lar land, to live as one people before him. And, whether I turn to ancient Proverbs (1–3) or to a later prophet (Matthew 5–7) I am reminded that it is not *my* opinion that counts but the inescapable judgment of God our Father. We have made the terrible mistake of teaching the Negro these truths; so now it is the Negro who has the ultimate weapon which they provide: nonviolent love. Against such there is no defense.

So I confess. I am hurt and puzzled and bewildered. This is my dilem-ma: my whole lifetime, country, family, community, school, church, have taught me to be a brother. But now they say I cannot act as a brother must act! Can I believe them? Hear my confession, please!

§59 Robert J. McCracken

Robert James McCracken was born on March 28, 1904 in Motherwell, Scotland. He trained for the ministry at the University of Glasgow and received an M.A. in 1925 and a B.D. in 1928. McCracken was ordained into the Scottish Baptist ministry in 1928. His first pastorate was at Marshall Street Baptist Church in Edinburgh that same year. In 1932 he began to teach systematic theology at the Baptist Theological Seminary in Glasgow while he served as the pastor of Dennistown Baptist Church. McCracken moved to Canada in 1938 to work as a professor of Christian theology and philosophy of religion at McMaster University in Hamilton, Ontario. In 1944 he became head of his department. The next year he was elected as president of the Baptist Convention of Ontario and Quebec. McCracken took over the pastorate of Riverside Church in Manhattan, New York in 1946, succeeding the legendary Harry Emerson Fosdick. Three years later he was invited to join the staff of Union Theological Seminary as a part-time lecturer in practical theology. He wrote several books during his time in New York. However, in 1967 he retired from both Riverside and Union although being named pastor emeritus. He died in 1973.

In this rather strong indictment of the white American church, McCracken begins in Africa—and the United States' resemblance to South Africa in its race relations. The principle problem with the church, as McCracken sees it, involves the chasm between Christian principle and Christian practice. Instead of more preaching, proclamations, and resolutions, the church must "discover the real outreach of their responsibility to minority groups." That outreach can and should be done on a daily basis, neighbor-to-neighbor—and guided always by brotherly love. Anything less would result in a "dreary intellectual exercise and nothing more."

———

The Christian Way in Race Relations
The Riverside Church, New York, New York
February 1961

The question of race relations is at the very center of the world crisis. In importance and urgency it should be bracketed with the threat posed to civilization by the manufacture of nuclear missiles. Recently a British news writer, commenting on the problems besetting his country in Kenya, predicted that if Western democracy continued to be based on the supremacy of the white man, that in itself might well be the precipitating cause of World War III.

In the nineteenth century the whites established an ascendancy over the peoples of Asia and Africa. Almost everywhere in some degree they abused their power. Now the subjugated peoples are striking at their shackles, are

filled with a fiery zeal for freedom from oppression, fear and want, for political freedom, for a better life. This may prove the most significant revolution of our age. Its implications for the future are becoming more and
more apparent every day.

Nowhere have all the traditional alignments of power undergone so
drastic a change in so short a period as in Africa. Whites there are haunted
by the perpetual fear that the blacks may bring their ascendancy to an end.
It is certain that that is going to take place, for it is inconceivable that two
and a half million whites can hope permanently to mold Africa with its
population of two hundred million to their pattern. This can only be done
by subjugation and the subjugated peoples are in revolt, with communists
ready to inflame and exploit them. Pandit Nehru has said that the African
problem is perhaps the most fundamental problem in the world today because it is the central issue of race relations, and because, in consequence,
the question of whether the next war will be a war between colored and
white people may be decided by policies pursued in the African continent.

With the aspirations of the African and Asian peoples Christians are
bound to sympathize. Many of them have done more than sympathize.
Christian missionaries in preaching the gospel and in teaching Christian
truth in their schools have bred and nourished those aspirations. Blantyre in
Nyasaland, was the scene of an uprising. It is not a fortuitous circumstance
that Blantyre, deriving its name from David Livingstone's birthplace, is a
long established center for missionary work carried on by the Church of
Scotland. Ministers and elders of the Scottish church have been vigorous in
protesting the wrongs done in British dependencies in Africa. How could
they do otherwise? There is no contemporary issue about which Christian
principle is clearer than the issue of race relations.

That in the matter of race relations Christian principle and practice
are often at variance is part of the tragedy of our times. The two countries where creed and conduct clash most are South Africa and the United
States. More than any other factor their record in race relations discredits
Christianity in the eyes of Asians and Africans. It is *the* objection repeatedly raised when Christianity is commended to them. American visitors,
when traveling in the Far East, seem always to be encountering people
sensitive to the race problem in the United States and raising questions
concerning the way Negroes, Indians, Chinese, Japanese, Mexicans, Puerto
Ricans, Jews are treated in this country. The communists, minimizing our
strengths and the notable and striking advances of the last decade, make
the most of our shortcomings in this area.

With race relations the crucial issue of these days, the Christian pulpit must spell out time and time again the Christian principle. The world
has no common conviction about which its life may unite and cohere. It

has forgotten, it has still to realize, that down below race, class, color there is a fundamental fact which is universal and everywhere the same. God is the Creator of all men. All men are equal in his sight. He cares for all men equally and intends that men should live in community with one another and love their neighbors as themselves. Racism is an affront to the native dignity of man and an insult to God. Think of Christ's parable of the Good Samaritan and the point of it; think of his attitude to the Samaritans, Greeks, Romans who crossed his path. Before his searching gaze racism cannot go unchallenged. A new world order is being built in our generation. In it whites will not be in the majority. They are less than a third of the world's population. The church of Christ will forfeit any moral right to leadership unless it stands unequivocally by its God-given gospel and declares that *all* men are made in "the image and likeness of God," and that in consequence each *person* is of infinite and eternal value.

Time and time again the Christian pulpit must spell all this out. But preaching is not enough. The proclamation of principle is not enough. Practically all the denominations in this country have passed resolutions in support of integration. Resolutions help in creating a climate of opinion and a conscience, but resolutions in themselves do not change race relations. There is ample evidence that they have little effect on local congregations. The rank and file of church people have yet to discover the real outreach of their responsibility to minority groups.

In the resolutions passed by church boards there is much talk about the churches "building bridges of understanding" around the world. That is a splendid vision and our Christian duty. Brotherhood, however, begins on a person-to-person basis at home. Without some practical manifestation, without deeds backing up words, it is idle talk. Christian relations with people whose color and class are not our own have to be cultivated here in the United States, in *this* state, in *this* city, in *this* neighborhood, in its housing, its schools, its clubs, in your job in shop or office. Louis Adamic, the author, charged, "On this point, most American Christians as such are frauds. The best that the best of them can do is to be tolerant." Something much more positive and dynamic than tolerance is needed. Tolerance may not issue in action. It may not take one step towards an improvement of race relations. What is required in our pluralistic society is acceptance, association, co-operation, joint undertakings.

Putting Christian principles to work—that is our task. The number of Christians who reject the myth of racial superiority is growing, but far too many find some reason why in their particular situation it is not possible or expedient to worship or work or associate with minority groups. The churches would materially assist the state in its attempt to establish integration if more of their members were willing and eager to act like

Christians towards their brothers of another color. About the remedying of some social problems we feel well-nigh helpless. They are so complex and vast; there seems so little that one individual can do. The encouraging feature of race relations is that it is an issue about which every Christian can do something, beginning where he lives, works, worships. Committing himself to belief in an unsegregated church and an unsegregated society, he can conform his personal, family, business and religious life to his belief. He can cultivate contacts and friendships with members of other races. He can invite them to his home and visit theirs, can press for the right to invite them to his club and golf course; Christian race relations begin in these immediate person-to-person contacts.

Beyond such contacts there is the challenge of the community. The evils of discrimination and segregation are mitigated through neighborhood self-surveys, interracial conferences, social action undertaken jointly by citizens—Protestant, Catholic and Jew—by churches and synagogues, by colleges and hospitals. Association and co-operation break down the emotional barriers among races from which discrimination springs. Work can then be done for the enactment and enforcement of fair employment practices, of the right of every person to acquire housing on the basis of personal preference and financial capacity without regard to race, religion or national origin. Churches and individual Christians square their practice with their profession when they recognize their responsibility for creating and maintaining the racially inclusive character of their communities. Of their communities *and their churches.* A Christian church should strive to make its fellowship inclusive of all types of folk. It is the weakness of Protestantism that its churches by and large are socially restricted. When the emphasis is on congeniality and sociability, membership confines itself almost automatically to one class, culture and color, and comprehensiveness is lost. Every church of Christ is intended to be a house of prayer for all of God's children.

What motive is strong enough to bring all this about, to spur us to live up to what we profess? H. N. Brailsford, pleading that the African be given the opportunities and rights which are his due, asks: "Why should we do that? Because we believe that sound economics point this way? Because we think that in the long run our own interests will be served? Never. Men who have no hotter fire than that in their bellies will stammer and wilt and yield, as soon as the battle looks doubtful. We shall do it for backward peoples and do it at some cost to ourselves, only if our motive is brotherly love. Whether we think of them as our fellow workers, or as our fellow men, it must be a warm [impulse] of fraternity that drives us to defend them and to aid them. If we have in us the faith and the love this great adventure demands, we shall succeed. If we lack this principle of action then our plans are a dreary intellectual exercise and nothing more." That from a journalist. It is precisely where the Bible puts the emphasis. "You shall love your neighbor as yourself." "If any one has this world's goods and sees his brother in need, yet closes his heart against him, how does God's love abide in him? Let us put our love not into words or into talk but into deeds and make it real."

In what is happening around the world, in what you see in your city and in your community, do you not hear God calling you to active participation in an enterprise that cuts across all dividing lines of culture, color and class? The most crucial field for the extension of the Kingdom of God in America today is the interracial church.

Said William Morris, "If these hours be dark at least do not let us sit deedless, like fools and fine gentlemen, thinking the common toil not good enough for us and beaten by the muddle; but rather let us work like good servants trying by some dim candlelight to set our workshop ready against tomorrow's light."

§60 Reverend Duncan Howlett

The Reverend Duncan Howlett was born May 15, 1906 in Newton, Massachusetts. He received his S.B. degree from Harvard in 1928 and an LL.B. degree in 1931. During that same year, Howlett was admitted to the Massachusetts Bar. In 1933 he returned to Harvard and was awarded the S.T.B. degree with honors in 1936. He resumed his religious passion and was ordained a Unitarian minister and during the years of 1933–1938, served as minister of the Second Church, Unitarian, in Salem, Massachusetts. Howlett transferred to the First Unitarian Church in New Bedford, Massachusetts until the mid-1940s and then continued to fulfill his minister's duties at the First Church in Boston for 12 years. He persisted in his preaching at the All Souls Church in 1958 until he retired in 1968. Howlett completed his impressive and influential career by dedicating his time and services to the environment, especially forestry.

Reverend Howlett was also active in public affairs. In 1968 Howlett served on the presidential campaign staff for Hubert Humphrey. He was deeply concerned with his role in Unitarian denominational affairs and was a member on several committees and boards, such as The Beacon Press, Historical Library and the Christian Register. His combination of religious zeal and civic duty made Howlett a vocal and influential supporter during the Civil Rights Movement. He passed away in May 2003 at the age of 97. A wife and four children survive. His papers are housed at the Bangor Theological Seminary in Bangor, Maine.

In a sermon before congregants at the Eighth Street Baptist Church in Lynchburg, Duncan Howlett offers a micro and local reading of the sit-in movements sweeping the south. His questions are several: what are the meanings of the sit-ins, what are the moral dilemmas faced by participants, and what is the motive for their participation? In answering these questions, Howlett looks no further than the demonstrations then taking place in Lynchburg. He makes clear that these college students have thought through with great care just why they are participating and towards what end. And it's clear by their own statements that the American political tradition and the Judeo-Christian tradition are the very ground of their actions. Borrowing from the Old Testament prophetic tradition, Howlett notes, "We will never understand the motive power of the sit-in movement until we recognize the fact that it is essentially religious. Most if not all of the sit-ins think of themselves as following the path of Christian discipleship." In addition, the great strength of the sit-ins involved the merger of thought and action, ideal and real. The students were not in it for glory or martyrdom, but for the fulfillment of a promise. "It [the sit-ins] is the story of American society moving in the direction of its own political and religious ideal."

The Untold Story of the Sit-Ins

Eighth Street Baptist Church, Lynchburg, Virginia
March 12, 1961

"The land was not able to bear all his words."
Amos 7.10

Long ago a shepherd boy named Amos, who lived in the little town of Tekoa in the Kingdom of Judah, went to the northern kingdom of Israel, to its capital city Samaria. He was profoundly shocked by what he saw there because it was utterly inconsistent with the teachings of the religion of his people. Amos spoke what was in his heart. He continued to speak until, we are told, "the land was unable to bear all his words." His preaching came to an abrupt end when by royal decree the king silenced him and sent him back to Tekoa.

There is a modern parallel to the feelings of the upper classes at Samaria under the impact of Amos' preaching. I speak of the sit-in movement that has developed in this country in the last few years and the jailing of young men and women of high vision and noble purpose that has often accompanied it. There have been many instances in many cities of the south and as you so well know there have been instances right here in Lynchburg.

You know the indignities these young people have suffered, for some of you have yourselves endured them. You know the patience these young men and women have shown, the self-restraint they have exhibited and the charity with which they have met the contumely that has been heaped upon them. You know they have been sentenced to jail terms normally reserved for serious misdemeanors and crimes of violence.

You are aware also of the attempted intimidation of some of those who have taken part in the sit-ins. That story too has been told. But its meaning does not always come home to us, and I would like to elaborate on the point for a moment. The following story, told me by Lillian Smith, is typical of what had happened in many places. Certain details in the story are changed or blurred in order not to disclose the identity of the person involved.

A young white woman—we will call her Mary—took part in a sit-in demonstration in a southern city. When asked to leave the premises, she did so. In the process she was asked her name, and convinced that she had nothing to be ashamed of she gave it. That was her mistake. Soon afterward two policemen, without authority from their superiors, visited her land-lady and informed her that Mary was a dangerous person, no fit occupant of her house, and probably a Communist. Mary had been exemplary in her conduct, both inside the house and out. She belonged to an old and cul-tured southern family. But all that made no difference. Her landlady asked her to leave, which of course she did.

Mary next found a room with an elderly and devoted churchwoman. Again the same two policemen made a call, again quite on their own and without authority. Again Mary was asked to leave, even though her land-lady was sympathetic to the integration movement. A barrage of telephone calls now began, some of them late at night, in the course of which an un-identified person would vilify her in obscene language.

Mary moved once more and no one now knows her address. When she wrote Lillian Smith recently there was no return address on the envelope or in the letter. "I am becoming afraid," she wrote, "and I have never been really afraid in my life before—not this way. Now I know what it is to be brave. And I find I'm not. But that isn't what matters. What matters is what is happening inside me.

"I took part in the sit-in at _____ out of feelings of love—Christian love, if that doesn't sound too self-important. I don't think seg-regation is Christian and I don't think it is constitutional. So I joined in the demonstration. And it really wasn't bad. But what has happened since then has left me aghast. I didn't know people could be so low. Those feel-ings of love—I still have them I guess but I find I am growing angry at the way people treat me and I'm afraid I'm beginning to hate." Lillian Smith says the letter shows no evidence of hate. It overflows with love for her fel-lowman. But what a dreadful anxiety do we implant in the hearts of our young people! What a price we make them pay if they choose to love their neighbor as themselves and their neighbor happens to be a Negro.

The decision to sit in is never casual and rarely impulsive. These young people know exactly what they are up against, and they know what they are doing and why. They have thought it through. The six students who were recently sentenced to thirty days in jail here in Lynchburg well illustrate this observation. Soon after their initial arrest, they published a statement to the *Lynchburg News* in which they made the following points:

> "Editorial comment thus far has failed to delineate three essential distinctions which separate our action of civil disobedience from the more familiar forms of law violation. These distinctions are as follows:
>
> 1.   Our action was not accomplished through threat, force or subterfuge. Instead it was executed by non-violent means.
> 2.   Although our action involved the violation of the 'law,' we have made no effort to evade the consequences. In fact we are willing and ready to accept the burden of our choice.
> 3.   Our action was taken in the belief that what is now the 'law' is not the law and is ultimately destined to become unlawful. It was a protest against a policy which is now protected by 'law.' "

Consider carefully what these young people have said:

There has been no violence, nor any threat of violence. They reminded the forces of law and order that they are not the kind of people against whom a community needs to protect itself. No one would be led into evil ways by them; no one would be injured by them; no one would be put in fear by them; no one would be corrupted or incited to evil by them. No one's life would be endangered, except possibly their own, if they were permitted to remain at liberty. To the students this distinction was perfectly clear, and for us to shut our eyes to it is willfully or blindly to fail to look at the realities in the case.

In the second place, the students pointed out they made no effort to evade the consequences of their allegedly "illegal" act. They did not flee after committing their "crimes." They are not purse snatchers or muggers, or hit and run drivers whom the police have to find and catch in order to prosecute. And once in the toils of the law they did not employ counsel to strive by every possible legal maneuver and stratagem to free them from the penalty they incurred. On the contrary, these young people submitted willingly to the regular process of the law.

Moreover, they declared their belief in law, in law enforcement, and in the need for a society ordered by law. Because of this belief they willingly accepted the penalty the law imposed upon them. When they might have appealed, they decided to accept their punishment instead. "We have chosen to withdraw our appeal and accept our sentences," they said. And when they were given thirty days in jail apiece, there was no outcry. They did not say the sentence was unduly severe. They did not beg mercy. They did not accuse the judge of injustice. They accepted their sentences without complaint.

Their purpose, they said was to show that the new Virginia trespass laws are unconstitutional and need not be obeyed. In their second statement, issued February 6 after they were sentenced, they said: "We believe more firmly than before that the 1960 trespass law, passed by the state legislature with the intent of 'keeping the Negro in his place' and preserving the 'purity' and 'sanctity' of the white race, is not in fact the law and is destined to become unlawful." You couldn't ask for a plainer statement of conviction than that. The Virginia law, they say, is not merely wrong morally, it is unconstitutional as well.

What do you do about such a law, they asked themselves. How do you prove that it is unconstitutional? You break it, they answered, and then carry the case to the Supreme Court. The Lynchburg students withdrew their appeal and accepted their sentences, they pointed out, because the constitutionality of the new trespass laws was already slated for a test under an appeal from a case in the Richmond courts.

Much has been made of the fact that the sit-ins have broken the law and in that sense have done wrong. But is not this what business does constantly in order to test statutes it thinks unconstitutional? When previously have we seen such moral indignation registered against someone who took this method of finding out whether or not a law belonged on the statute books under our system of jurisprudence? I confess that I do not know of an instance. It is our regular practice and we take it for granted. And have we forgotten that a law which is unconstitutional is so from the beginning and not from the time of the court decree? Should the new trespass laws turn out to be unconstitutional, the students who have broken them will not have been guilty of any wrongdoing at all.

I have said these young people are perfectly clear as to what they are doing and why. In many instances they seem to be clearer than their elders who criticize and challenge what they do. A New Orleans girl, Margaret Leonard, whom the police picked up after a sit-in demonstration, was queried at length but very courteously by the New Orleans police. As she tells her story in a recent issue of *Look*, she had the most difficult time persuading the authorities that she was not being paid by anybody for what she was doing and that nobody had talked her into it; that she had done it out of personal conviction at which she had arrived by thinking things out for herself. "I keep being surprised," she commented, "at people who talk about being starry-eyed and young and naïve. When it comes to choosing, most of them don't really think and choose; they just automatically think about themselves and call it 'judgment.'"

This college girl, younger than anyone who questioned what she was doing, is impressed above all else by the fact that those who think her naïve or impractical haven't really thought much about the situation for which she has risked a great deal. She finds that they react to it automatically and without thought. On the other hand, she and all the other sit-ins have thought long and hard about the problem. They know what it is, they know what can be done about it, and they know the risks to those who are willing to make the effort.

These young people have also squarely faced the fact that they confront a dilemma as to their own motivation. The first question a boy or girl who plans to sit-in must ask himself is, what are my real motives? Do I really believe in racial equality? Is the essential dignity of all men a truly central conviction of mine? Am I acting out of love for my fellowman? Or do I, perchance, seek excitement? Would I find a little notoriety pleasant? Am I coveting martyrdom?

These are not easy questions for anyone to answer. Who can ever be sure of his own motives? But these students are earnestly asking such questions of themselves and of one another. They have to for they are often accused of courting martyrdom. The six students who were sentenced to jail on February 6 here in Lynchburg, in the statement following their arrest, said: "Our cause was not the glory of martyrdom, nor was the action a mere publicity stunt. It was a different and far more real concern which moved us to involvement in what is a serious and potentially costly action. . . . We have taken seriously the most basic principles of our Judeo-Christian heritage—the sacredness and worth of human personality. These, we believe, represent a Higher Law than the law of governments."

Yet to look into their own hearts and to decide whether they sought publicity or wished to bring about a fundamental social change was really the least of the moral dilemmas that these students, so often called naïve and immature, have had to face and think through. The most serious of all their problems concerns their parents. What, they are forced to ask themselves, will be the effect of what I do upon my father and mother? The risk is particularly grave if the parents are southerners. And most of them are. The students have learned that a demonstration by southerners is far more effective than by northerners. Southerners will take another southerner seriously, where they will dismiss a northerner as meddlesome. Over and over again, Margaret Leonard was asked why she as a southern girl would do such a thing.

No student knows what the result of his participation in a sit-in demonstration will be. This is part of his dilemma. Reprisals through the White Citizens Council may be very great. They have been in certain instances, like the one I cited earlier. For the fathers of some sit-ins, the demonstrating of their children has meant loss of their jobs. A young man or woman of conscience will not usually jeopardize his or her father's livelihood. They know for how little cause such a person may be dismissed and how hard it then is to find another position.

Not many would willingly subject their parents to the less dramatic but equally real possibility of threats, abuse and intimidation which is becoming increasingly standard practice. Put yourself in the place of those who are threatened. Suppose your phone began ringing constantly. Suppose that it rang not only all day but all evening and on into the night and all night. How long could you stand it? Most of us would, I think, go insane. We can hardly endure the tyranny of the telephone as it is. But suppose added to that you knew when the phone rang that it was unlikely to be a friend calling you. Suppose you knew that when you lifted the receiver threats, obscenity and abuse would pour out upon you, all of it anonymous. Suppose your mail each day contained poison pen letters. Don't dismiss this as of no consequence unless you have received such letters. Until you have found them in your own mailbox you don't realize how such letters make you feel in the pit of your stomach.

Or suppose that as you walk across the street you never know when some person you never saw before will brush past you, breathe a threat in your ear and disappear in the crowd before you quite know what has happened. Even if your job were not threatened, could you stand up under such treatment without cracking? Not many of us could.

This is the moral dilemma of the sit-ins. They have not only to ask what sacrifices they themselves are willing to make. They have also to ask themselves what sacrifices they are prepared to exact from their parents, and perhaps their teachers and friends as well.

All these questions face the white students. The Negroes face one more because they are Negroes. Their parents are putting them through college at the greatest possible sacrifice. Their mothers may work at menial positions. Their fathers perhaps hold two jobs. It has been the ideal of the family since the children were born to give them the chance the parents never had. The sacrifices of the parents have been truly incredible because the Negro usually earns less than does the white man for a comparable job, and he all too often pays more for what he buys, particularly in housing.

Suppose you are a Negro student. You want to participate in a sit-in in order to help your people gain the chance to which they are entitled to play their part as full-fledged citizens of the United States. No sacrifice is too great for you personally to make if only you can help a little in bringing about racial equality. No sacrifice is too great for *you*. But what about your parents? They have said to you since you were small that it has been their hope and prayer that you might graduate from college. What do you do? What do you say to such parents? Do you sit-in and go to jail? They may not understand the niceties of moral as against legal principles, and laws that are constitutional or unconstitutional. Can they understand if you offer them a jail record instead of the college degree for which they have sacrificed everything? What would you do?

This is part of the untold story of the sit-ins, but it is not quite all of it. Nor, poignant as it is, can we say that the foregoing is the most important part of it. When these students have thought through their convictions and decided that they must act in spite of all the consequences, they have also consciously allied themselves with the best in our western tradition. They have taken the ideals their parents and their teachers have set before them and they have applied them in their own lives. They have brought together theory and practice. They have tested the validity of the ideal by applying it in the real world. They have united thought and action.

When, long ago, Amos, the shepherd boy of Israel, appalled at the difference between the faith and practice of his people, began preaching righteousness until "the land was unable to bear all his words," the king silenced him and sent him home. But his words rang in the hearts of his people for centuries after and they ring in our hearts today. "Let justice roll down as the waters, and righteousness as a flowing stream," he cried. So spoke Amos and Isaiah, so spoke Hosea and Jeremiah, so spoke Micah and the unknown prophet whose words are found in the latter half of our book of Isaiah. And so spoke Jesus of Nazareth. We will never understand the motive power of the sit-in movement until we recognize the fact that it is essentially religious. Most if not all of the sit-ins think of themselves as following the path of Christian discipleship.

What has happened here in Lynchburg is happening all over the south. It has wide application in the north as well. Of this we are aware. But how many of us are aware that what is happening in America today has happened throughout American history, and more especially throughout the Judeo-Christian tradition, whenever a fresh, young, unimpeded mind has measured the practices of his time by his ideals—the ideals taught him as a child, ideals that represent the best in his own tradition.

As a result of this searching examination by our youth, principle and practice are moving together. Last Friday night, as you so well know, at a great meeting of all the parties concerned, the Southern Christian Leadership Conference, of which Martin Luther King is the head, the Lynchburg Improvement Association, a member group of which the Reverend Virgil Wood is President, the NAACP, and all others concerned agreed to a 60-day moratorium on boycotts, sit-ins and other demonstrations, while the Lynchburg Interracial Committee, made up of eight respected business leaders of the community—four white and four Negro, proceed with desegregation.

And yet, it is not too much to say that the Lynchburg Interracial Committee would never have been formed and it would not be moving toward integration in the stores had the sit-ins never been held. We cannot forget that the Reverend Virgil Wood and the Lynchburg Improvement Association want a 30-day pre-Easter boycott now. They believe that no less a measure than this will produce an appreciable result in the integration struggle. In the interest of cooperation and harmony and an amicable working out of the solution to the problem, they went along with the 60-day moratorium. But they stand ready to act if the moratorium produces nothing. What has happened in the past and their readiness to act now, together with the good will of many people who do not say very much, is the motive power that is moving integration along.

All this is being accomplished without bloodshed, without violence and to a remarkable degree, without acrimony. When a fundamental social revolution can be brought about in this wise, inspired by the highest principles we know and guided by those principles as the change is made, we are witnessing something that is very, very new and very, very unusual. When and where before were the rights and privileges of a ruling class won for the common people under such circumstances?

The untold story of the sit-ins is the story of personal travail. It is the story of the searching of heart and mind and conscience on the part of the individuals who take part in these demonstrations. It is the story of young men and women who have thought these questions all the way through. It is the story of action motivated and carried out by the highest standards we know. It is the story of American society moving in the direction of its own political and religious ideal.

"The people that walked in darkness have seen a great light. They that dwell in the land of the shadow of death, upon them hath the light shined." To be sure, many of those who now see the light do so only because they have been made to see it. Many still do not see the light at all. But slowly we as a people are coming to see it. Slowly the Negro is taking his place as a full-scale citizen of the United States of America and a full-scale brother of the white man. And slowly, too, the world will come to know that segregation represents our past and not our future: that it represents what we once thought but now believe no longer.

And why? Because of the clean, strong conviction of young men and women throughout this land. Because they have courage that matches the clarity of their moral judgments; because they have found the Judeo-Christian tradition valid, and finding it valid have taken it seriously; because taking it seriously our young people have found that they can lift American society a little higher: a little nearer in practice to the ideals in pursuit of which the United States was conceived and established, the ideal of brotherhood, the love of God through the love of one's fellowman, which is the heart of our faith. "We have taken seriously the most basic principles of our Judeo-Christian heritage," wrote the Lynchburg students, "the sacredness and worth of human personality." So, too, may we.

§61 Rev. Ralph David Abernathy

Ralph David Abernathy was born in Linden, Alabama, in Marengo County on March 11, 1926. The son of a farmer, Abernathy served his country during World War II before being ordained as a Baptist minister in 1948. He studied at Alabama State University, receiving a B.S. in mathematics in 1950, followed by an M.A. in sociology from Atlanta University in 1951. Upon graduating, he returned to Alabama to lead the First Baptist Church in Montgomery. In 1955 Abernathy befriended Martin Luther King, Jr., as the two were instrumental in founding the Montgomery Improvement Association in response to Rosa Parks's arrest. For 13 years, where King went, so went Abernathy—including to jail. Perhaps the best "warmup" act in the movement, Abernathy's rhetorical role typically involved getting a civil rights audience ready for Dr. King's eloquence.

Shortly after King moved from Dexter Avenue Baptist Church in Montgomery back to Atlanta's Ebenezer Baptist, Abernathy followed, becoming pastor of West Hunter Street Baptist Church in 1961, where he delivered this address. Following King's assassination in April 1968, Abernathy took over the presidency of the Southern Christian Leadership Conference, preaching, teaching, protesting, and organizing until 1977. Once retired from active involvement in the movement, Abernathy continued to pastor West Hunter. He also ran unsuccessfully for Congress. He published his controversial autobiography *And the Walls Came Tumbling Down* in 1989. Abernathy died on April 17, 1990. His papers are housed at the King Center in Atlanta, Georgia.

Abernathy begins his speech giving a brief historico-biblical account of the struggle for freedom. Throughout our collective histories, freedom has always arrived through struggle. For those that deny freedom to others do not relinquish their control voluntarily, as evidenced by events in India as well as Africa. So too, African Americans must realize that "Pharaoh" is determined "not to let God's people go free." Abernathy then recounts a particular episode in the life of Christ. It occurred when Jesus was 12 years old when he, Mary, and Joseph went to Jerusalem for a Passover pilgrimage to the Temple. On their way back, Mary and Joseph had assumed that Jesus was in the large caravan returning from Jerusalem, when He actually remained in Jerusalem teaching the religious scholars. His parents eventually found Him after a several days of searching.

Abernathy draws three lessons from this biblical account. The first is that we must never assume that Jesus is with us. We must, daily, strive to make him an integral part of our lives. Abernathy argues that we have forgotten Jesus. Much contemporary strife and conflict is due to our neglect of making our Savior an integral and daily part of our existence. Second, when we seek Jesus, we must be good not just to family, friends, and acquaintances, but to the whole of humanity, regardless of race, religion, or creed. Finally, Abernathy argues that, like Mary and Joseph, to find Jesus actually, "we must go back." We must go back to our religious roots. Our society must seek to discover and know Christ, as intimately as possible. And once we find him, we must never let go. Because, for us to succeed in our callings and purpose on this earth, we must make Jesus the center of our existence. Only in that way will we realize, "Sometimes I am tossed and driven, Lord; sometimes, I don't know where to roam, but I've heard a city called heaven; I've started to make it my home. Yes, our home is higher than this wilderness, for sweet heaven is our home. But we can't get there without Jesus."

Trying to Get Home Without Jesus
West Hunter Street Baptist Church, Atlanta, Georgia
October 8, 1961

Our text gives an account of a visit made to Jerusalem by Mary, the mother of Jesus, and her husband, Joseph. They went up from Nazareth to Jerusalem to attend the feast of the "Passover." This was an annual visit, an integral part of their religious observances. Being Jews, they remembered the history of their struggle to gain freedom and the breaking loose from their Egyptian captivity.

You see, freedom is never won easily. All through history, you will find that the oppressors have never given up their privileged positions, without a struggle. Exploitation, denial of protection of the law, and the idea of a superior race are all sins; and sin is a disease—and no man has ever been cured of a disease without a doctor or some kind of home remedy. Every group of people who is free today will tell you that, "freedom comes only through the suffering and the struggling on the part of those who want to be free." Look, if you will to the birth of this nation. It gained its freedom from Great Britain only after the words of Patrick Henry, "give me liberty or give me death," became the spirit, the will and the determination of the people who made up the thirteen original colonies. The same must be said of India and the new emerging nations of Africa. Mr. Nehru, Mr. Nkruma, Mr. Ezekuiah, Mr. Mboya and all of the leaders of the new nations, which will control our world within the next fifty years, have all been in jail many times and forced to serve long prison sentences. Yes, it can be seen clearly that privileged ruling classes do not give up their positions without a struggle. It would be well if the Negro today would learn this lesson from history. For whether you turn to Indonesia, China, Costa Rica, Cuba or even Southern United States of America you will find that the Pharaohs are determined not to let God's people go free.

The same was the case with the Israelites in Egypt. God sent the leader, but the Pharaoh heard not His voice and he was determined not to free the people. So God had to move. His will must be done. Plague after plague troubled the land, but finally God got tired and decided to send the death angel through the streets with orders to take the life of the first born son in each Egyptian family. He was charged to cover the country, and to miss not a single home. But wherever he saw the blood on the door post, he was to "pass over." The sprinkling of blood on the door post was the method God instructed the Jews to use in identifying their homes. So the death angel moved through the streets; the blood was sprinkled on the door post; Egyptian sons died; the death angel "passed over" wherever he saw the blood and the children of Israel were freed. They never forgot this fact, and in appreciation for God's "passing over" their sons, they would make the annual pilgrimage to the temple in Jerusalem and engage in thanksgiving services and in feasting.

Let us pause here and say that we ought not forget the goodness of God. God has been good to us; He has brought us a mighty long way and we ought to thank Him and give His name praises. Oh, that I had ten thousand tongues. David said, "make a joyful noise unto the Lord." God freed us from the shackles of slavery and yet we can't hardly have a decent emancipation service on January 1. God broke loose from us the shackles of ignorance, but as soon as we get a little training, we feel that we are too important to be bothered with the Church. God lifted from us the yoke of economic oppression, but as soon as we get 15 cents in the bank and can write a check, even though we have to beat it to the bank to make a deposit, we then feel that we are so busy that Sunday must be used to go fishing, to play golf, or to stay at home and rest and look at the television. Instead of worshipping and praising God, too many of us whom God bless soon feel that religion is for the ignorant, untutored, and the poor. Our souls ought to be filled with thanksgiving to almighty God daily, and like the Jews we ought to remember God's goodness and celebrate our, "pass overs."

So, Mary and Joseph went up to Jerusalem. Jesus being twelve years of age and the oldest son, they took him up with them according to the Jewish custom. And when the festivals, religious services, and all were over their minds turned toward home and they set out on the journey, trying to get home. There was only one thing wrong at that point, they were trying to get home without Jesus.

There is no sweeter word in the English language than the word, "home." It brings to our minds loving thoughts and sweet memories. It recalls pleasant childhood experiences and the fields over which we first roamed or the streets and avenues we love to call our own. Mother is there and father too; sisters, brothers, kinsfolk, and people we once knew. It is just wonderful to go home. It is fine to travel on vacations, or to go abroad for a season; it is wonderful to visit with friends or to labor all day at a job; but the ticking of the clock to the second when we can go home, always brings a particular joy that no other event can possibly bring. I don't care where you've been or what you've been doing, I repeat, it is simply wonderful to go home. So it was with Mary and Joseph. They had completed their work in the temple; they packed up their belongings and got with the crowd and started out for home. But, they left Jesus behind.

So my Bible tells me that they went a whole day's journey without Jesus, simply supposing that he was in the crowd. And when they discovered that he was not with them, they sought him among their kinsfolk and acquaintances. But they did not find Him there. So they began to search everywhere for Jesus. They looked the first day and did not find Him. On the second day, doubtless the search was intensified, but they spent all that day seeking Him, and did not find Him. And only after the third day of searching, seeking, asking, agonizing, and praying did they find Him. And when they found Him, He was in the house of the Lord, doing the work of His Father. He had amazed and astounded the lawyers and the doctors by His profound answers to their questions, his knowledge of the scripture and his prophetic insight into the future. His reply to His mother was something like this, "Mother, the time has come for me to be about my Father's business. You didn't ask me to go home with you. But now that you tell me that you need me to make the journey and that you want me to go with you, how can I turn you down? If you really want me to go home with you, then I will go. I'll walk by your side, I'll be your friend. And with my youthful vitality and powerful strength, I will run ahead and prepare the way. Even though the crowd has left, there will be no need to worry about the robbers and thieves who may seek to destroy you. Because I will be there by your side." And Jesus got up and said to those important people, "I must go now because someone wants me to go home with them." And Jesus went home with Mary and Joseph.

Let us look at this text and see if we can lift it from the pages of our Bible and find a message in it for us today.

The first message which we may learn is the fact that they went a whole day's journey supposing that Jesus was in the crowd. It is a tragedy for anyone to try and take Jesus for granted. Let us never assume that he is with us, but let us know for ourselves that he is there.

C. Austin Miles says:

> I come to the garden alone, while the
> Dew is still on the roses, and the voice
> I hear, falling on my ear, the Son of God
> Discloses.

He speaks, and the sound of His voice
Is so sweet the birds hush their singing,
And the melody that He gave to me,
Within my heart is ringing.

Chorus

And He walks with me, and He talks with me,
And He tells me I am His own; and the joy
We share as we tarry there,
None other has ever known.

A day's journey is too long to go without Jesus. The dangers are too great; the road is too rough; the way is too dreary and the journey is too uncertain to attempt to make it for one day without Him. You need Him every day and every hour. "Every day and every hour, let me feel thy cleansing power." In fact Annie S. Hawks made it clear when she said,

I need Thee every hour, most gracious Lord;
No tender voice like Thine can peace afford.

I need Thee every hour, stay Thou near by;
Temptations lose their power when Thou art nigh.

I need Thee every hour in joy or pain;
Come quickly and abide, or life is vain.

Chorus

I need Thee, O, I need Thee; every hour I need Thee!
O bless me now, my saviour, I come to Thee!

Therefore, the Prophet says: "Remember now thy Creator." Start early in life. "This day." Jesus says, "The day and the hour that ye hear my voice, harden not your heart, but accept. For ye know not the day nor the hour when the son of man shall come. Therefore, be ye always ready." Don't try to make a day without Jesus. Every individual when he wakes up in the morning ought to thank God and ask Him to go with him through the day.

Can't you see that the world today has gone a whole day's journey without Jesus and as a result we have strife, conflict, and confusion on every hand. We have gone a day's journey without Jesus in the United Nations and we have uprisings among the nations of the world. We have gone a whole day's journey in human relations without Jesus and on every hand we have social revolutions and chaos. We have gone a whole day's journey without Jesus in the economic world, and because of this, we have more hungry people in the world than ever in history, yet there is more food in our world today than we have ever had before. Men are dying of starvation in Africa, India, throughout Asia, and even right here in the United States. Millions have no houses to live in; no heat for their bodies; or shoes for their feet; they do not have decent clothing or medical care for their feeble bodies. While all of this is happening, the rich is getting richer and the poor is getting poorer. The privileged are saying to their souls, "O soul, be thou at ease. Thou hast much in store. Eat, drink and be merry." They are so merry until they can't hear the knock of destiny on the door of time saying to them, "thou fools, this night, thy souls shall be required of thee."

We have gone a whole day's journey without Jesus in the family and as a result, we have more broken homes, unfaithfulness, divorces, and juvenile delinquency than ever before in the history of civilized man. If Jesus is not in a home, then it ceases to be a home and it becomes a house. Without Him, a mansion becomes a hell house. But with Him, a shack becomes a haven of peace.

We have gone a whole day's journey without Jesus in religion. What are the results? We have beautiful church buildings, but no spirit; we have many church members, but few Christians; we have singing, praying, and preaching but little worship; we give a little money, but have no love. Our churches are in court, or they are merely social institutions bowing to the whims and wishes of the world; having become nothing but sounding brass and a tinkling cymbal. You see where there is no Jesus, there can be no peace. And if He is there, you can have peace, even in the midst of a storm. I know what I am talking about. They went a whole day's journey without Jesus.

And, then they sought him among their kinsfolk and acquaintances. This is significant, for all too often when we discover that we have left Jesus behind, we feel that we can find him by being good to our mothers and fathers; sisters and brothers; wives and husbands; aunts and uncles; children and cousins; friends and the people we know. But this is not so. For Jesus says that, "If ye are kind only towards those who are kind towards you, then what have ye. For sinners are also kind towards sinners." But the "Jesus religion" must lead you to be kind toward, good to, and help all men. It will lead you across the barriers of races, creed, and color. It will lead you across denominational lines, to saints and sinners alike. It will lead you across the lines of friendship and cause you to even love your enemies. To do good to them that despitefully use you and say all manner of evil against you. The "Jesus religion" will cause you to pray for your persecutors, saying, "Father, Father, forgive them for they know not what they do." This religion will cause you to seek Jesus beyond the circle of the family, friends, and acquaintances.

Thirdly, the text convinces us that if we in this generation are to find Jesus at all, then we must go back. It is true, we are busy building skyscrapers, bombs, and missiles. Our minds and hearts are set on projecting a man into space and on being the first to get to the moon. But if we are to find Jesus then we must go back. We must go back and rediscover the family altar in the home, and fireside religion in the family circle. We must go back and reestablish prayer in the life of the church. We must go back and get that old time religion, that will make you "love everybody"; cause us to bear one another's burdens, participate in each others' joys and with tender sympathy share one another's sorrows. We must go back to the temple, the church, God's house, the place where Jesus promised to meet us. We must go back and say, "Lord here I am, use me in thy service. I don't have much to give, but use me. I can't sing like an angel, but use me; I can't preach like Paul, but use me. I have strayed away, but use me; like the prodigal son, I have spent my life in riotous living, but use me." Like Mary, say to him, "Master, I want to go home, please come on and walk with me" just as it was necessary for Mary and Joseph to go back, so it is with the world today. If we are to rediscover Jesus, then we must go back.

And finally, once you find Him, please never leave Him. For the text tells us that it takes longer to rediscover Jesus than it does to leave Him behind. They only went a day's journey without Him, but it took three days to find Him. It is easy to drift from His presence, to join with the gangs and the gangsters; it is easy to stop going to church and to start putting other gods before God; but it is more difficult to break away and get back in the straight and narrow path. All I am saying is that it is more difficult to break a bad habit than it is to form that habit. It is much easier to do wrong than to do right. Let us go back and find Him and never leave Him. He will take you home.

You see, this world ultimately is not our home. Every now and then we get the news that we are citizens of another world. We live in houses of clay, but our home is on high. Sometimes in our lives we experience a loneliness. We look around ourselves, and we don't feel at home anymore. This is why we cry out, "I am a poor pilgrim of sorrow, I'm tossed in this wide world alone. No hopes for tomorrow. But I've started to make heaven my home. Sometimes, I am tossed and driven, Lord; sometimes, I don't know where to roam, but I've heard a city called heaven; I've started to make it my home." Yes, our home is higher than this wilderness, for sweet heaven is our home. But we can't get there without Jesus.

§62 Marion A. Wright

Marion A. Wright was born on January 18, 1894 in Johnston, South Carolina. He attended the University of South Carolina, where he received his law degree in 1919. Prior to practicing corporate law in Conway, South Carolina, Wright taught public school and was a reporter for the *Columbia Record*. In 1916 he married Lelia Hauser. In Conway he was chairman of the Illiteracy Commission, as well as a member of the American Civil Liberties Union. From 1951 to 1958, Wright served as the president of the Southern Regional Council. He also served the council as vice president from 1958 to 1965. In the following years, Wright founded and became the first president of North Carolinians Against the Death Penalty (NCADP). Wright continued to fight for desegregation and the abolition of the death penalty, the two most important issues in his life, until his death on February 14, 1983.

As president and vice-president of the Southern Regional Council, Wright often delivered speeches and lectures on important human and civil rights issues, as Wright used his position to influence his audiences and promote equality. Wright also played a vital role on the board of directors for the American Civil Liberties Union, as he continued to speak out against segregation. His papers are housed at the Southern Historical Collection at the University of North Carolina in Chapel Hill, Winthrop University in Rock Hill, South Carolina, and the University of South Carolina in Columbia.

Before a group of ministers meeting in Goldsboro, North Carolina, Wright offers a unique, polyphonic blend of the Old Testament, Shakespeare, Sophocles, Aristotle, and James Joyce to urge ministers to specific action against North Carolina's Jim Crow system. One of the distinct features of religion, argues Wright, is that it resists and speaks out against tyranny. Wright seeks to establish two points: first, that it is the duty of the Christian minister to resist unjust laws; and, second, all of the world's "great religions" have historically taken part in fighting against injustice. Wright catalogues those injustices in North Carolina specifically: blacks hold very few jobs other than janitorial positions, and school segregation is still the order of the day. And while prospects for civil rights continue to improve at the national level, Wright warns Governor Sanford that he and others are being watched. "The heroes of the church," Wright concludes, did not dodge moral issues; rather, they "confronted corrupt regimes and risked the stake and the cross for what they knew to be right." A "measure of immortality" awaits the "North Carolina minister of today" who will but give himself to the cause of justice and equality.

The Minister as Citizen

Goldsboro, North Carolina
October 12, 1961

I appreciate the opportunity of meeting with you on this occasion. To tell you the truth, I think the Southern Regional Council likes for me to attend meetings of this kind so that I may observe how you have withstood the attacks made upon you. You remember that Thomas Carlyle, in his *History of the French Revolution*, tells of a clergyman who was asked "What did you do during the Revolution?" He replied, simply, "I survived."

Well, at times it is no small accomplishment to survive, I shall be happy to report to the Southern Regional Council that you have survived and seem quite hale, hearty and well-fed.

But surely, in times of revolution, mere survival is no cause for pride. One may survive, save his hide, by dodging the battle, by remaining neutral, on the sidelines. In the eye of such a man there will be no gleam when he tells his grandchildren that, in a struggle which involved their welfare and the welfare of all mankind, his major accomplishment lay in slinking away from the conflict.

One of Shakespeare's characters (I can't be sure which one because I do not have access to a public library), one of them told another, "Go hang yourself. A great battle was fought and you were not there." Surely none of us would want to have that kind of comment made about himself.

There are all kinds of revolutions. They do not all involve fire, brimstone and barricades in the streets. Perhaps the most enduring of all revolutions involves none of these. It involves, not introducing bullets into bodies, but introducing ideas into brains. I need not remind a group of ministers that Roman society was shaken to its foundations by a mere handful of men who carried no weapons except the truth and who sought no victories except over the minds of men.

Perhaps every age has presented mankind with a moral issue as to which only the coward may remain neutral. Slavery posed such an issue in the Nineteenth Century. Its offspring, segregation, poses such an issue in the Twentieth Century. Certainly no Minister of the Gospel can live serene with his conscience if he blinds his eyes and deafens his ears to the spectacle and clamor which rage about him.

Resistance to tyranny has always been a distinguished feature of religion. Tyranny means a denial of right, a suppression of the individual's instinct for growth and expression. Religion seeks, above all things else, the right of the individual to grow in stature and in grace. Hence, the age-old conflict between religion and tyranny.

Nebuchadnezzar made his great image of gold and set it up on the plains of Babylon. He issued his decree, directing that "At what time ye hear the sound of the cornet, flute, harp, sackbut, psaltery, dulcimer, and all kinds of music ye fall down and worship the golden image that Nebuchadnezzar the King hath set up." But Shadrach, Mechach and Abednego to his face told Nebuchadnezzar "Be it known unto thee, Oh King, that we will not serve thy gods nor worship the golden image thou hast set up." And so they walked unscathed through the fiery furnace.

But it would be mere vainglory for us to assume that resistance to unjust law is a peculiarly Christian doctrine. It was known to paganism. Five hundred years before the birth of Christ, Sophocles, in his great play *Antigone*, tells of an edict by the tyrant Creon, forbidding on pain of death the burial of a slain soldier, directing that the body be left to dogs and birds to devour. But the soldier's sister Antigone defied the order and gave decent burial to her brother. She was brought before Creon to have sentence of death imposed. Creon addressed her:

> "Now tell me thou—not in many words, but briefly—knewest thou that an edict had forbidden this?"
>
> "I knew it: could I help it? It was public."
>
> "And thou did'st indeed dare to transgress that law?"
>
> "Yes, for it was not Zeus that had published me that edict; not such are the laws set among men by the justice who dwells with the gods; nor deemed I that thy decrees were of such force that a mortal could override the unwritten and unfailing statutes of heaven. For their life is not of today or yesterday, but from all time, and no man knows when they were first put forth. So for me to meet this doom is trifling grief; but if I had suffered my mother's son to life in death an unburied corpse, that would have grieved me; for this I am not grieved. And if my present deeds are foolish in thy sight, it may be that a foolish judge arraigns my folly."

Within recent months many Magistrates and Justices of the Peace in Mississippi, Alabama and elsewhere, in imposing sentence upon brave ministers and college students, have told these offenders how foolish they were. Perhaps, in 1961, as in the days of Creon, a foolish judge sometimes arraigns folly.

Now, I have gone to all of this trouble to bolster two points, but these are points which seem to me to give significance and meaning to the career of a minister. They are that resistance to unjust law is historically and traditionally the duty of the Christian minister and that this is a duty which transcends the limits of any particular faith but is the hallmark of all of the world's great religions.

If we may move now from such lofty and philosophic considerations, let us come at once to the matter of the duty of the North Carolina minister in the year 1961.

Let us say that nowhere in the world is there a perfect society. One does not have to be cynical to observe the imperfections of the world in which he lives. Indeed, recognitions of these imperfections is the first step toward their elimination. Ministers have a duty, above and beyond that of ordinary mortals, to nudge society in the direction of the perfect state.

One would be bold indeed to attempt a definition of such a state but Aristotle hinted at it when he wrote: "Only he who has the power to take part in the deliberative and judicial administration of any state is said by Athenians to be a citizen of that state."

There is a phrase which I should like to see disappear from current speech. It is "second class citizen." Under Aristotle's view, there are no gradations of citizenship. One is a citizen or he is not. If he does not have the power to participate in the administration of a state he is not a citizen.

I have recently had occasion to examine some figures showing the extent to which Negro residents of North Carolina, composing 30% of the total population, participate in the formation of state policy under which they live. These figures, and the conclusion drawn from them, reflect the judgment of the North Carolina Advisory Committee to the Commission on Civil Rights. Neither the figures nor the conclusions have been challenged.

The North Carolina National Guard has approximately 12,000 members, every one of them white. Thus, a Negro, who may be drafted into the United States Army and become a general, under present law and practice, cannot be a buck private in the North Carolina National Guard.

The North Carolina Employment Security Commission, which spends five and a half million dollars of Federal funds each year, has in its central office in Raleigh only ten Negro employees, none above the rank of janitor-messenger, which means no typists, stenographers, clerks, bookkeepers, accountants or persons in administrative or executive capacity. In managerial and professional capacities within the Commission in the state as a whole there are 681 whites and 39 non-whites, and there are 264 white clerical employees and only 2 Negro clerical employees. So much for the staffing of an agency supported by Federal funds and, ostensibly, concerned with merit employment.

In the year 1959 this Commission secured jobs of a professional and managerial nature for 1,851 whites and 25 non-whites; in clerical and sales positions, 19,811 whites and 320 non-whites; in skilled positions, 12,824 whites and 1,315 non-whites. But in menial, or service jobs, it placed 8,109 whites and 29,376 non-whites.

A survey of the employment practices of all of the state's agencies shows the same picture—non-use of Negro employees in positions above the service level.

What a shocking waste of Negro talent and skill when we put men and women with college degrees to digging ditches and waiting on tables! How far are we from reaching Aristotle's conception of the ideal state in which every citizen has the power to take part in the deliberative and judicial administration!

While such discrepancies are matters of concern to every citizen, they are, I submit, of special and peculiar concern to ministers. They condemn people because of color to an inferior status. They tend to brainwash such people into a conviction of their inferiority. Religion is concerned with the development of the potential of every human being to the limit of his capacity. No religion worthy of the name will remain indifferent to social forces which consign men and women to low levels of living.

But it is in the handling of our school situation that the morals of state policy are drawn most clearly into question.

The Supreme Court on May 17, 1954, seven years ago, held that the segregation of public school pupils by race was a denial of their constitutional rights. Every public official in North Carolina has taken an oath to uphold that constitution. But seven years after the decision less than one-fourth of one percent of the Negro children enjoy the right the Court has said is theirs.

This deprivation has been accomplished by what is known as the Pupil Placement Law, North Carolina's peculiar contribution to legal skullduggery. That law has given us what is known as "token integration," by which we mean that we appear to be observing the law when actually we are not.

This is a form of obtaining credit by false pretense. It is a species of ethics which would be repudiated in an ordinary horse trade.

Let the state beware. It is an expert and omnipresent teacher. Its citizens will be quick to learn and they will practice what they have been taught.

In other states already chickens have come home to roost. The fulminations of Governor Faubus produced violence in the streets of Little Rock. The pronouncements of Governor Davis and the shenanigans of the Louisiana Legislature triggered New Orleans women to snarl and spit at little children on their way to school. And Governor Vandiver's solemn assurance—"During my administration not a single Negro"—inspired violence and obscenity around the girl's dormitory in Athens. The line of action runs straight from state capitols and highly placed men to mobs who move like puppets.

North Carolina, fortunately, has been spared that type of utterance. Our public figures, out of innate dignity and self-respect, have not stooped to vulgarity. But, upon the parliamentary level and behind their suave phrases, they have launched the state upon a massive effort to deceive the courts as to their real intentions.

Our leaders seem to be inspired by Mark Twain's advice: "In statesmanship get the formalities right; never mind about the moralities." The child deprived of a constitutional right will experience great comfort from the fact that those who robbed him behaved like perfect gentlemen.

The raucous and vulgar speeches of public officials elsewhere have logically and inevitably produced violence elsewhere. The clever and fraudulent maneuvers practiced here will inspire here [sic] the general practice of deception and misrepresentation.

Let us pursue the idea of token integration to its logical conclusion. As a token of my observance of law, I will stop at one red light out of ten. I will pay one-tenth of my income tax. I will serve one-tenth of my enlistment in the Army. And, as evidence of my devotion to a code of morals, I will observe one of the Ten Commandments.

In the class room the child painfully copies the ancient motto "Honesty is the best policy." But if he should raise his eyes and look out of the window, he will observe his native state laughing at him for being so naïve. What chance has the pure morality taught at school and Sunday school against the example set by men whom the state has exalted to high station?

Is it the role of the state to corrupt its youth, to contribute to the delinquency of minors?

I lay these matters upon the hearts and consciences of ministers, not white ministers, not Negro ministers, but ministers of the Gospel. They negate everything for which religion stands. Indeed, men of no religion— atheists and agnostics, if you please—have consciences, and conscience is offended by an immoral policy. Voltaire and Thomas Paine were not religious in any orthodox sense, but no two men ever lived who fought more valiantly for equal rights for every citizen.

So the path and the duty of the minister in the imperfect state are clear.

All of what I have said relates to the legal policy of a state. But a state's character and genius are revealed as much by its managers as by its laws. Emerson remarked: "Your manners are always under examination and by committees little suspected but are awarding and denying you very high prizes when you least think of it."

About a year ago Dr. Ralph Bunche was denied membership in a tennis club because of his race. More recently African diplomats, representing their countries at the United Nations, have been publicly insulted by waitresses. Perhaps the club and waitresses were within their legal rights. But their judgment was poor and their manners were atrocious. So ominous are the consequences of this kind of action that our State Department has requested the State of Maryland to adopt laws forbidding such discrimination. Mr. Edward R. Murrow, head of the United States Information

Service, has appealed to all Americans to treat all citizens alike in their provision of public accommodations.

You will remember that President Kennedy wrote to all Southern governors asking that they take precaution to see that foreign visitors were not subjected to indignity on account of their race. Governor Almond of Virginia warmly applauded the idea and suggested that such dignitaries wear some distinguishing insignia in order to guard against unfortunate incidents. This led the *Washington Post* to remark bitterly—and truthfully—that one had to establish that he was not an American citizen in order to be treated with respect.

We are at that juncture in history when the conduct of a waitress, or a ticket agent, or a real estate salesman, may determine whether mankind survives or perishes in the flames of nuclear war. But back of the waitress, the agent, and the salesman stands the state which tolerates a policy of denying service to people because of their color.

Now, it is, of course, pure snobbishness to distinguish between foreign diplomats and American citizens of humble station. If Dr. Bunche and a raw Negro freshman present themselves at a lunch counter, they pose precisely the same moral problem. If they are rebuffed, the suffering of the freshman would probably be more acute because he would not be sustained by Dr. Bunche's knowledge of his own impeccable status.

Cities and states adopt all sorts of laws and regulations designed to see that one does not become nauseated by eating a moldy slice of apple pie. There are no scales yet designed by which one may measure the suffering of a person temporarily nauseated as compared with one who has endured public humiliation. Only the purblind state may see its duty in the one instance and fail to observe it in the other.

Today the City of Charlotte becomes host to an international fair. African and Asian visitors will be guests of the city. Charlotte may set the moral tone for the country if it now takes steps to see that, not merely foreign diplomats and businessmen suffer no indignity, but that any citizen of North Carolina may experience that same even-handed and courteous treatment.

Let us recur for a moment to Aristotle—"Only he who has the power to take part in the deliberative and judicial administration of a state is a citizen of that state."

The American system of government is unique in that there are two citizenships. One is a citizen of his state; he is also a citizen of the nation. There may be a great gulf between the quality of these two citizenships.

As to his national citizenship, there is little, if anything, about which the Negro may complain. There his influence in the deliberative and judicial administration daily expands. In one week the Interstate Commerce

Commission outlaws segregation in bus travel and the President names Thurgood Marshall as a Circuit Judge. Events may hardly move more rapidly than that.

I should like to keep politics out of this—no doubt many good Republicans are in this audience—but it is only fair to remind you that, since the present administration took office, a Negro has been elevated to cabinet rank, Federal marshals aided the orderly opening of New Orleans schools: Vice President Johnson's Committee on Equal Employment Opportunity, of which North Carolina's John Wheeler is a member, has brought about the employment of thousands of Negroes at higher levels, and young Bobby Kennedy—bless his little heart—has resigned from the Metropolitan Club.

In all of these actions the President has shown the contempt, felt by all decent citizens, for the southern congressional bloc—I almost said block heads.

This progress has not come of itself, automatically. It has come because, on the national level, the Negro wields political power. Again, it is only fair to say that the NAACP, by its intelligence, skill and persistence, has channeled that power, brought it to bear upon the great issues of our times.

The moral seems plain. The imperfections of North Carolina's policy will yield only to political power, intelligently, skillfully, and persistently applied. For that application this organization is the ready, available and appropriate instrument.

For eight years the national executive stood inept, mute, paralyzed, while the human rights issue seethed and fermented. Dramatically, overnight, all of that is changed.

North Carolina, too, has had its period of masterful inactivity, its temporizing, its quibbling, its evasion, its puerile appeals for "voluntary segregation," its bland pronouncements from Raleigh that thirty per cent of our people were quite happy with their second class status and wanted only to be let alone.

Governor Sanford and the men who surround him should as well know now as later that they are being watched—their utterances, their policies, their appointments to boards and commissions. The times demand a change here as dramatic as the one which occurred in Washington. If that change should be made, those responsible will receive their reward in political currency—approval and votes. If we continue to hear the ancient platitudes and to observe adherence to the ancient traditions, swift, and certain and drastic will be the repudiation.

The heroes of the church were not men who dodged a moral issue. They were gaunt, shaggy, craggy men, who confronted corrupt regimes and risked the stake and the cross for what they knew to be right.

Every age has produced them. They are here now, in Montgomery, in Birmingham, in Charlotte, throughout the entire South.

To be sure they suffer, but they also follow the great example of the Founder of their faith and thereby secure a measure of immortality.

You recall the speech of the Irish patriot in Joyce's *Ulysses* in which he replied to an Englishman's appeal for Ireland to give up her independence. The patriot imagined a similar appeal by the Egyptians to the Israelites:

> Why will you Jews not accept our culture, our religion, and our language? You are a tribe of nomad herdsmen: we are a mighty people. You have no cities or no wealth; our cities are hives of humanity and our galleys, trireme and quadrireme, laden with all manner of merchandise, furrow the waters of the known globe. You have but emerged from primitive conditions. We have a literature, a priesthood, an agelong history and a polity. You pray to a local and obscure idol: our temples are majestic and mysterious, the abodes of Isis and Osiris, of Horus and Ammon Ra. Yours serfdom, awe and humbleness; ours thunder and the seas. Israel is weak and few are her children. Egypt is a host and terrible her arms.

But, ladies and gentlemen, had the youthful Moses listened to and accepted that view of life, had he bowed his head and bowed his will and bowed his spirit before that arrogant admonition, he would never have brought the chosen people out of the house of bondage nor followed the pillar of cloud by day. He would never have spoken with the Eternal amid lightnings on Sinai's mountaintop, nor ever have come down with the light of inspiration shining in his countenance and bearing in his arms the tables of the law.

The North Carolina minister of today will find little material inducement to volunteer his support for the cause of human rights. But, if he should steal himself against the seductions of those presently in authority and in majority, and give himself unreservedly to that cause he will enjoy the companionship of the elect spirits of the earth and have a part in elevating man an inch nearer to the stars.

§63 James McBride Dabbs

James McBride Dabbs was born on May 8, 1896 in Mayesville, South Carolina; he would die there 74 years later. He received his A.B. from the University of South Carolina in 1916 and his M.A. at Clark University in 1917 before serving during World War I in field artillery. He became a first lieutenant in the army during the war and after serving he spent several years in graduate study at Columbia University. He married his first wife, Jesse Clyde Armstrong in 1918 and they had two children. Following the death of Jesse, he married Edith Wells Mitchell in 1935; they had three children. Mr. Dabbs was something of an everyman: from

English professor, farmer, lecturer, writer, Presbyterian churchman and Sunday school teacher, and outspoken civil rights leader; he led a very rich and influential life. Dabbs authored several highly praised books on the subject of race relations in the South including *The Southern Heritage* (1958), for which he received the Brotherhood Award of National Conference of Christians and Jews, *Who Speaks for the South?* (1964) and the posthumously published, *Haunted by God* (1972). Dabbs was a member of the board of directors of the South Carolina Council on Human Relations from 1957 to 1963, served as president for the Southern Regional Council from 1957 to 1963 and served on its executive committee from 1963 up to his death on May 30, 1970. His papers are housed in the Southern Historical Collection at the University of North Carolina in Chapel Hill.

Dabbs's speech is a rhetorical inquiry into the South's character and composition. He begins by probing into the contemporary ideas about the South's identity. He argues that southerners have a strong identity, but he asks, what is that identity exactly? There is a sense of being "southern" but few ideas on what that is—at least none based on reality instead of false romantic notions. One aspect that identifies southern culture is segregation, which is quite unfortunate. He sees the South as gradually moving away from segregation but that movement is not over. Dabbs posits that the African Americans who have led the civil rights struggles understand being southern far better than they could ever admit or any white would ever acknowledge. Their attempt to democratize the South and bring about racial inclusion (integration) instead of seclusion (segregation) is the fulfillment of southern ideals. Southern identity is only found in the complex interracial tapestry of the South. The ties that bind southern blacks and southern whites, constitute their common culture—religion, manners, and most importantly, their history—and it unites them more than they realize. To move forward, they must recognize that fact. Only when they do, will the South be able to confront itself, solve its problems, and become a culture that offers the world something positive and unique. "It is possible, however, for the South to see more truly what it is: whites and Negroes who have suffered history together, and who in this enforced relationship have learned more wisdom than they know. The nation needs this wisdom."

Who Speaks for the South?

President's Address, Southern Regional Council, Atlanta, Georgia
November 9, 1961

OTHELLO, on the verge of taking his own life, begged of his lieutenant Cassio, "Speak of me as I am. Nothing extenuate, nor set down aught in malice." I should like to speak of the South as it is. I don't think it intends, like Othello, to commit suicide, though some of its gestures are rather frantic. I do think that in the modern world, into which it is rushing, it may lose its life without really having found it.

On the surface it seems to have found it. I came into the world with Plessy Ferguson and never since that, to me, halcyon day has the South been so aware of itself as now. The Southerner, like a true horseman, is forever mounting and charging off—into vacancy. Paul Revere without the message. We must set our backs to the wall, said a defiant South Carolinian recently. Sure, I said, and with our hands out: "Gimme, gimme."

We have the emotions, but what do they mean? We are aware of the South, but what is it we are aware of? I'm afraid it would be one thing for whites, another for Negroes. For the whites something to be defended, for the Negroes something to be attacked. The South cannot achieve greatness so long as it harbors such a basic division. There was a time when the voice of the Negro didn't have to be considered; in fact, he had no voice. That time is past. The world has now become for the Negro resonant; his voice reverberates beyond the region, beyond the nation, around the globe.

If the white South had ever really understood itself, it would be in a far better position now to hearken to this new voice and accommodate itself to it. The old South, however, was destroyed before it came to an assured sense of its identity. It is impossible, therefore, for us to go back, and, lifting into memory some moment of the past, say, Here is the image of what we were trying to do. Here is ourself. History holds no such moment.

With a strong sense of being southern, we lack a vision of what the South is. I imagine that the Negroes are less confused in this matter than the whites. Having never been received frankly into the life of the South, and having received directly from the Nation certain large benefits, the Negroes of the South are far less aware than the whites that they are southern. It is my belief that they are; that, often unknown to themselves, they are drawing sustenance from southern soil. If this is not so, if it should turn out that the Negroes of the South are simply Americans, with no regional ties and traits, then the possibility of the South's remaining a living region are slim indeed; the Negro population is relatively too great. For my part, I can imagine the South, under the impact of the modern world, ceasing to be the South, but I can't quite imagine this happening as a result of the Negroes of the South not being southern. How they are southern, we shall consider later.

All I have said indicates the need in the South for creative vision. It is hard for us to realize this. For we have lived largely by custom, as Tennyson said, "From precedent to precedent," and our chief concern has been to rally round the flag, boys, floating there above the battlements of the *status quo*. Speaking to my Aunt Alice, my uncle, a true Southerner who died too young partly perhaps from mixing too little branchwater with his bourbon—my uncle said, "Ideals are a sin, Alice, we should love God."

But there's a difference between ideals and vision. Ideals lie in the future; vision is of the present; this is the way things are now—though many may not see it. Vision reveals the truth, the pebble of quartz shining at the bottom of the well when the water is clear and the sun right. (But who looks into wells any more? We have filled them up. They are dangerous nuisances.)

We have already in the South one or two partial visions but nothing that encompasses the whole. What we need is insight into the total and unique South. I'm not speaking of the "solid South." Politically, there's none. In South Carolina next summer a Republican may make a good race for the United States Senate. Regardless of this, I still think it feels somehow different to be a Southerner.

Let's consider briefly two of the partial visions. The first—which I am disposed to call a nightmare, and from which we are at last happily awakening—the first is segregation, and all the racially discriminatory practices connected with it. Some Southerners have called this "our way of life." Even the southern historian, Francis Simkins, college-mate of mine, coming, interestingly, from the Ben Tillman section of South Carolina, suggests that if the present race pattern goes, the South is dead. So far as I'm concerned, then, the South is dead, and I, for all my present—what shall I call it? *Joie de vivre*—am a ghost.

However much the institution of segregation may have expressed at one time the vital life of the South—and I don't know how much it did—that time is gone. The life-blood seeps from the institution, Negroes cease to obey it, whites cease to enforce it. It is pathetic how some southern segregationists, admitting by their actions a dependence upon the nation that by their words they often deny, try to persuade other Americans to adopt segregation. The Editor of the *Charleston News and Courier* makes forays into the North, trying to sell segregation there. So far there have been no takers. There's plenty of segregation in the North, but not bought and sold across the counter; it's all bootleg stuff. It may be as common as bootleg liquor was under Prohibition, but it's still bootleg, without state or federal stamp.

Come to think of it, there's an added pathos about these northern trips. In spite of all the South's verbal defiance of the North, there is, deep down, a simple desire to have something to contribute to the Nation. We know we are Southerners; we want to be Americans; we can be sure we are Americans only when the Nation accepts and uses what we have to offer. And so, not realizing we have anything else, we offer the Nation the gift of segregation. This is the ultimate pathos of the Lost Cause, and perhaps should not be spoken about further.

The other partial vision I shall consider has much more vitality, but is still partial and unsatisfactory. This is industrialization. The vision that Henry Grady saw and that we are now realizing. This is the vision—if you can call it that—seen by politicians and chambers of commerce. I am in favor of further industrialization. Only thus can our standard of living be raised; and that standard is too low. However, the more we simply industrialize, the more we become thereby a copy of the rest of the Nation, and the more we may lose the chance of contributing, out of our history and our culture, something unique to the Nation.

Furthermore, as important as I think man's way of making a living is, I do not see industrialization as a cause that can command the devotion of the South. It's probably a good thing, we'll have more money to spend; but not only is it not rooted deep in our hearts, it is foreign to the non-industrial life we have lived so long; and, though we may not be clearly aware of this, much of our present uneasiness, which we are inclined to attribute to changing race relations, is really attributed to changing productive relations.

These changing productive relations are undoubtedly changing our race relations, in some ways bringing whites and Negroes together, in some ways pushing them apart. It therefore at least touches what I consider the heart of the South. What is this heart? The fact that whites and Negroes have lived together here for several centuries, each group somehow a burden to the other, each somehow a solace. If this is the heart of the South, industrialization touches it but glancingly. It cannot be truly called a vision of the South, because a vision must lay bare the deep desires of the heart. In some strange, and perhaps tragic fashion, in the heart of the South whites and Negroes are together.

How shall I describe this? What are the words? Fortunately, now, there are deeds. If I'm mistaken, the vision I'm trying to describe is already taking form. The question is, can we recognize the southern meaning of what is happening? Can both we the actors and we the observers say: "At last the heart of the South is speaking."

I am talking of course about the sit-ins, stand-ins, kneel-ins, and even—as Marion Wright has called them—the "drive-ins." This movement, with the possible exception of the "drive-ins," seems to me primarily and essentially a southern movement. I could be mistaken in this, and still be correct in my feeling that a true vision of the South must see whites and Negroes together. However, if I'm not mistaken, it means that we are closer to great possibilities than we had thought. For the vision necessary for such possibilities is already taking form.

Can we recognize the actions of these southern youngsters as an expression, however unconscious, of the dawning vision? As for the youngsters themselves, it isn't necessary for them to understand the deep significance of what they are doing, though it is advisable. I think they would be both inspired and hardened for the long pull if they realized the depth from which they draw their strength and the implications of their actions. I recognize that there might be strong resistance on the part of the Negro youth to accepting the view that they are also Southerners in their actions. A Negro leader said to me recently in regard to this suggestion, "I think they would tend to disagree with you in their minds, but in their hearts many would know what you are talking about." I should hope they would. I understand their disagreeing in their minds. Southerners have always been white people. The whites themselves said so. Therefore these young Negroes, protesting against the treatment accorded them by the whites, naturally think of themselves as protesting against Southerners. They are Negroes. They are Americans. They are not Southerners. I understand the protestations. I still feel that deep in their hearts, they are more southern than they think.

But if it's hard for them to admit that they are Southerners, it's far harder for white Southerners to admit it. It's the old cry, "Can any good come out of Nazareth?" Are we going to be led by what we've told ourselves for centuries is an inferior race? Well, if it comes to that, it won't be the first time that God has used the weak things of the world to confound the things which are mighty. Maybe we have the chance here, if we have the faith, to see God at work. But it's hard to have the faith. We whites didn't intend for it to come out this way; and we always understood God was backing us up. As a religious people, we should hearken to the voice of the prophet Jeremiah, as heard by Franz Werfel, "It is not good to be too sure of God."

Let's put it another way. I believe that there was and is something that may be called southern culture. I believe that a living culture is creative, not merely carrying on the past but continually remoulding the past to suit the needs of the present. I believe that the great creative moment of southern culture, perhaps within my lifetime, is the movement primarily of Negro students that began in Greensboro, North Carolina, on February 1, 1960. This is the growing edge of southern culture. I suppose I am selfish. I should hope that this moment is rooted in the total life of the South, the product somehow of Negroes and whites. Let us see how this may be possible.

But first, two cautions. I don't mean that these young people have been influenced by nothing beyond the South. Of course they have, as most of us have. I mean only that their main roots are in the South, that they have grown out of the South. Again, I don't mean that the several traits I shall discuss as southern are possessed by Southerners only. Of course they are not. It's a matter of greater or less emphasis and of the weaving of the several traits into the culture in question.

In the first place, then, these young people have shown great courage. The South has boasted, and with some reason, of its courage. It is a virtue we have stressed, as against prudence and planning. It is the virtue of a once aristocratic and still conservative society. The more showy part, of course, has been our military courage; and it is probable that the memory of Jeb Stuart of the sash and plume has blinded us to the more daily courage that Southerners have often shown. There's the story, told by Celestine Sibley, in *This is the South*, of the old country-woman, writing to her son after Appomattox: "Don't be shamed cause you got licked. You fit bettern you knowed how. And if ole Abe's folks offer you a mule, take it and come on home. It ain't too late to git a crop in the groun." This is moral courage: to face without flinching the problems of the day.

It is this moral courage—physical too—that our young people are showing. But they're bringing to it something new: the non-violence of its expression and the excellence of the cause. The South has been unfortunate in defending badly mixed causes. As regards the Civil War, it is indeed true that, after the invasion began, the South was fighting to defend its land and its homes. Many Southerners also felt that they were fighting to defend constitutional liberties. The fact remains that at the heart of the matter there was the enslaved Negro—the economic base of the plantation South, the cloudy fear of the nonplantation South—and Southerners were fighting to keep him under some sort of undemocratic control. In contrast to this moral confusion, the cause of our young Southerners today is just. Not absolutely just; there's no such thing, but largely.

When you compare their cause to that of the segregationists, you realize the moral edge they have. Many segregationists think they are as committed to segregation as these students are to desegregation—or, as they may say, integration. Since man is a moral being, and also to some degree a realist, this is impossible. The segregationist is fighting for supposed interest and for pride; and even his bad weather-eye tells him that the sky grows increasingly dark. Yet, being a Southerner, he may still feel committed; these young people, also Southerners, are committed more deeply to the purest cause the South has so far discovered.

In the second place, these young people have come out of a long defeat. So has the South been defeated. Vann Woodward points out that this is the distinctive quality of the South. We are that section of the United States that has been defeated, occupied, colonized. We are the Americans—the only Americans—who know how this feels. Because Southern Negroes were defeated for different reason than Southern whites—and indeed largely by these same southern whites—we are slow to realize that the wisdom that may come from defeat does not depend upon the cause of the defeat.

Southern whites have learned some wisdom from their defeat, but Negroes have learned more. Southern whites have learned, at their best, a healthy skepticism, a distrust for blue-prints, an abiding sense of the possibility of failure despite the excellence of the cause. But I'm afraid most of this knowledge is incidental; it has not been woven together to become an intrinsic part of our religion. For the Negroes generally it has. It is enshrined in the spirituals. Here all the harshness and frustration of life is woven together and presented to God, and the gist of the long argument is that if we admit and accept our troubles, He will give us strength and patience to bear them. And so these young Negroes, trained in the same harsh school as whites attended but trained better and perhaps better equipped to profit by their training, now, having settled their quarrel with God, sit down at lunch counters and open their quarrel with us. In this quarrel we haven't a chance. We're still quarreling with the Yankees about states rights: we haven't even faced God on the issue of human rights; and while we argue with the students, He's going to take us from the rear.

So these young Negroes, having understood better than we the deep implications of our common history, now stride toward a success which can come to all of us as we too understand.

In the third place—as I have just implied—these young people are religious. The South is religious. With the possible exception of California, which claims to excel in everything, the South is the most religious section of this country. As my reference to California implied, this doesn't mean the South is necessarily the best part of the country—though I think it is. Its religious quality may or may not be an asset. I simply say that Southerners tend to agree that religion has a place in life. Probably the Ku Klux Klan feels undressed without a chaplain.

The innovation is in the nature of the religion these young people have. They have been brought up in a world where the best people talked of kindness and mercy, and where, even interracially, the best white people revealed these virtues, but where few talked about justice for Negroes and fewer tried to achieve it. Yet the Christian religion, upon which they were nurtured, contains the writings of the Great Prophets—flaming evangels of social justice. These young people were brought up in a world where the name of love was used to cover injustice, and now, in a radical understanding of the Christian faith, they sit at lunch counters in the reality of love, seeking justice. They have taken the words of the South—a great land for words—they have taken *kindliness* and *love*, and now they say to the white people of the South, "See, you *said* you loved us. Well, we are showing that we love you; so much, indeed, that we can no longer let you be unjust to us."

Of course, this describes the best among them. Doubtless many are bitter, and for them this is just another form of power struggle. Regardless of these, I'm indicating the growing edge of southern culture, the present creative moment. It lies in the hearts and the actions of the best of these youngsters, who took what life gave them, the limited Christianity and the beautiful words of the South, poured meaning into those words and redirected, out of the Christian tradition itself, the religion of their childhood. This is social invention, this is cultural creation.

In the fourth place—as again I have implied—they haven't gone back on the words, they have kept the forms, they have revealed good manners. If this isn't southern, I quit. Even James Kilpatrick, editor of the *Richmond News-Leader*, and one of the most intelligent segregationists of the South, was impressed by this. As much as the presence of the Negro students at the white lunch counters disturbed him, the bad manners of white by-standers disturbed him more. The contrast seemed to him total. At the counter, quiet, studious, neatly-dressed youngsters, behind them, young gangsters. He felt so bad about it that he fell into Latin. "Eheu," he cried, which, as I remember my *Caesar*, means "Alas!"

Of course, this aspect of the matter is complicated by the fact that we have stressed in the South both manners and racial etiquette. The essential purpose of racial etiquette is to keep the two races apart no matter how close they come together. These youngsters are walking right through racial etiquette—or, more aptly, sitting down on it. The point is, however, that they're not doing this brutally, without any regard to the means used. They are doing it quietly, reservedly, in the best manners of the South. Again I say, race has little to do with it. These are our young people, created out of the hardship and the ease, the tenseness and the relaxation, the sorrow and the joy of the South. The culture which whites and Negroes created together is today expressing itself in the actions of these young people. This is the South speaking. Can Southerners hear the voice?

The essential problem suggested by all I have said is the problem of the relation of the spirit of life to the forms. No one can question the fact that the forms of life in the South are changing. It may be of course that the essential spirit too will change, the South will cease to exist, and Harry Ashmore's "Epitaph for Dixie" will be all we have. It may be, on the contrary, that the inner spirit, the style of life, may impregnate and master the new forms, and the South remain a living region still. There is one thing that we cannot change. Our history. So long as that has a living meaning for us—as surely it still has today, though most of us misread the meaning—so long will there be something southern in our way of life.

I said in the beginning that the South has a strong sense of its identity but only a confused understanding of it. I said also that we cannot fulfill one of our deepest desires until we know better what we are and what we have to offer. We desire to make our contribution to the Nation and the world. What is it we have to offer?

I have said so far that our culture is the product of the common effort of whites and Negroes. I have also shown how this common effort has found expression in certain traits and attitudes. Is it possible to generalize still further and find at the heart of these several traits one basic attitude? I do not know, but I will risk it.

Perhaps it is something about the value of personal life, the value of people. Just people. I know the critic can say immediately, if you Southerners value people, why did you set up segregation, which dis-values people? The answer is too long for the present occasion. But it is worth pointing out that even within segregation, which could have been made cold and completely utilitarian, personal relations were retained, though distorted and truncated. I believe the important fact is, not that the South established an institution that dis-values persons, but that it tried to retain even within this institution at least the shadow of personal relations. Maybe this was just a southern substitution of the form for the fact. I think it was more.

We live in a world where the position of the person grows increasingly precarious. Urban, industrial life tends to obliterate him; totalitarian government tends to obliterate him. Beyond these present dangers lies the ominous future, in which, if we do not destroy ourselves, we shall inevitably build units far greater than our national states, at the last perhaps a world state. What becomes of the person in such a comprehensive net?

The South cannot solve these problems. It is possible, however, for the South to see more truly what it is: whites and Negroes who have suffered history together, and who in this enforced relationship have learned more wisdom than they know. The nation needs this wisdom. We need the exhilaration that comes from sharing it.

1962

1962

§64 Heslip "Happy" Lee

Heslip Malbert "Happy"Lee was born in Polk County, Georgia on February 21, 1922 to a family of sharecroppers. He received the nickname "Happy" from his younger sister who had trouble pronouncing his name. Lee married Laura McClung in 1941. They had five children. Lee was ordained to preach in October of 1949 at Antioch Baptist Church in Cedartown, Georgia. Both he and his wife attended Truett-McConnell Jr. College in Cleveland, Georgia in 1951. In 1952 they continued their education at Mercer University in Macon, Georgia from which Happy received a B.A. in philosophy. During this time, he pastored at Belerma Baptist Church and Jenkinsburg Baptist Church. In 1954 Lee attended Colgate-Rochester Divinity School in Rochester, New York and while studying there pastored at York Baptist Church. He received his M.Div. from Colgate in 1957.

In 1961 he became a member on the board of directors of the Virginia Council of Human Relations and later was appointed executive director. He also joined the Virginia State Advisory Committee to the U.S. Commission on Civil Rights. As a consequence, the Kennedy administration called on Lee to help fight racism; this resulted in the integration of schools throughout the South. In 1964 Lee moved to the North Carolina State Advisory Committee as well as becoming a consultant for the U.S. Department of Health, Education, and Welfare. In 1966 he became a member of the board of directors for the North Carolina Council on Human Rights and was later appointed vice president. Since that time, Happy Lee has remained very active in the civil rights arena. In 2004 the Gandhi Foundation of USA chose Reverend Lee to be the first non-Indian recipient of the Gandhi Lifetime Achievement Award in recognition of his work in human relations. His papers are held at Virginia Commonwealth University in Richmond.

In his sermon to the First Unitarian Church of Richmond, Lee reminds his listeners that the racial climate is favorable to change, but also that there remains a condemnation and resentment among many whites over the "overaggressiveness" of some in the fight for better human relations. Throughout this address, Lee uses the term "human relations" to describe the civil rights movement. Such a strategic renaming makes the movement more rhetorically inclusive and perhaps less objectionable to many southerners. Lee offers three "basic persuaders," what he later terms "hidden persuaders," fundamental to any movement. The first and most important of these is commitment. Bound up intimately with commitment are motivation and the presuppositions underlying a movement's activities. The second hidden persuader involves the extent to which we are willing to have our presuppositions and motivations scrutinized by others—"and that means all others." If a movement's basic beliefs cannot stand up to careful critique, then that movement should, and will, wither and die. The final hidden persuader, and taking a page right out of Kenneth Burke's *A Rhetoric of Motives*, is "identification with our adversaries or even enemies." Such an identification lies at the heart of the Christian message that "God was in Christ." Through agape love, God identified himself "through man, through the Prophets, through Jesus Christ, and now through committed persons." Lee closes with his belief that human relations have moved to center stage in the problem of human survival.

Hidden Persuaders in Human Relations
First Unitarian Church, Richmond, Virginia
April 1962

I am indeed honored to be invited to speak to you for a second time, the first occasion having been a few months ago at the invitation of your former pastor while he was away speaking in Atlanta, Georgia. I still do not know the mind and internal workings of the Unitarian Church, but if this were a Baptist Church, some would be proud to have seen Eugene Pickett go. But I stand here as a Baptist this morning to tell you that I have truly missed the Reverend Mr. Pickett very much, and all of Richmond and Virginia lost something when Gene Pickett chose to go to my home state of Georgia. I say that with all sincerity.

At the same time no man is indispensable; Richmond and Virginia are both still with us, and it remains to be seen how many of us can stay with Richmond and Virginia. However, let's try to find our roles and responsibilities while we do. After eight months as Executive Director of the Virginia Council on Human Relations, I can report to you in truth that I feel that I am where I should be, and doing what I should be doing, during these days of anxiety for some, and complacency for most, within the Old Dominion.

I am told, and have been led to believe, that Unitarians are noted for their honesty, and their sincerity to seek truth from any source, as well as adhering to the policy of allowing persons within their midst to express themselves freely and in their natural manner. My mannerisms are no doubt remembered from my previous visit with you, and the way you responded following that service has led me to face this second speaking engagement with the feeling that you will now allow me to speak freely within the field of Human Relations to which I am devoting my life, using the subject HIDDEN PERSUADERS IN HUMAN RELATIONS. First, I would like to make some observations about the climate within the field of Human Relations between the White South and minority groups, and especially Negroes. I will limit these observations to four in number:

First, the racial climate is favorable to change. Here we can point to some progress in the field of Human Relations, and the increasing acceptance of the fact that further changes must, and will, take place. It would be absurd to think that resistance to change does not exist, but there is a growing feeling that the extreme reactionary who is opposed to all fundamental change is engaged in a losing cause. My brothers-in-law in North Georgia admit change is coming, but are dedicated to having history show that it came slowly and against their wills. Yet the dominant mood is that of expectancy of change.

Second, there remains a condemnation and resentment among many White people by what they call the overaggressiveness of Negroes in pursuit of their rights. Thus many Whites point out that many cooperative ventures, previously carried on successfully, have been dropped. Many Negro leaders regard some degree of change in White attitudes as a calculated risk.

Third, the climate presents a mixture of satisfaction and discontent. Satisfaction because of the progress that has been made; and discontent with what seems to be the slowness and limitedness of "token" advance. It seems to me that most of Virginia prides itself on the fact that since some change had to come, it has come without violence. Dissatisfaction comes to those of us working in the field of Human Relations when we see that many changes, although accepted by political authority, represent a token conformity to irresistible pressures, without any fundamental change of heart and mind, and with no real dynamic for further constructive progress. "Tokenism" may have merely provided a beach-head for further techniques and methods of resistance.

Fourth, with many people, there is disillusionment with moral appeals, persuasion and "education," and an increasing feeling that real progress will come only through mobilization of power or coercion expressed through the arm of the law or through pressures exerted by disciplined groups of citizens. If this disillusionment should continue to spread, there are some serious implications for which we must be prepared to face.

It may mean that "Law" then becomes the prime area of ethical effort. Ideas of goodness, brotherhood, and compassion become somewhat lost as they are embodied in law.

It could mean that the extension of suffrage, the ballot, and political action comes to be regarded as superior to, though not yet displacing, a place for education, discussions, moral teachings and much of the fiber necessary for real and true community.

It suggests that churches and other groups have not been successful in weaving into the religious fabric a social ethic which has power over the minds and hearts of men.

Whether or not my observations are correct remains for the interpreters of this vital period of the making of history to judge, and as has been the case throughout the ages, those who are involved within the actual events of history are perhaps too closely related to events to see things in their proper perspectives.

I now wish to turn to the heart of my sermon and give three basic persuaders which have influenced me more than any others, and I will dare to say that these are the hidden persuaders within any period or level of Human Relations. If we look for these, and discover them, we shall be most apt to see the course which any person, any group or any movement will take.

Commitment—The Ideal, the person or the cause to which a person, group or movement is committed, and the degree of commitment are the primordial factors, and the greatest persuaders, in Human Relations of any kind. This is basically a religious principle, regardless of what name it is given. This principle is basic and necessary for any movement to maintain itself. More important, however, for any movement to be of real stature, or to last beyond an exciting beginning stage, are the presuppositions upon which it is founded. Usually, only a few persons will fully understand these, and most adherents or disciples of a movement will soon be trying to debate the presuppositions without much degree of commitment; thus some of the fire and vigor begins to wane. When the presuppositions get written down as dogmas or rigid rules, then persons reading these are at least two steps removed from the commitment itself, and it becomes next to impossible for readers of movements to be a part, or to understand very much, of the movement itself. For example, Christian Faith Doctrines are far removed from experiences. No movement lasts after motivations have ceased, thus renewal of commitments are most necessary for motivation and continued strength to carry the movement. Anyone who identifies himself with a movement must consider the cost and unless he or she is willing to pay the price, which is usually high if the movement is for change, would do well to consider selling shoes or automobiles or insurance for a living. There is nothing wrong with any of these vocations unless it becomes just a job and not a part of any fulfillment of life.

Before we leave this discussion on commitment, I wish to say that I found meaning and purpose for my life in my commitment to the Christian Faith. It had certain presuppositions about God, man, history, and human relations. I still do not understand all of the terminology, theology, cosmology, anthropology, soteriology or doctrin-ologies which are a part of the churches, but very simply given, although perhaps very unorthodox, my commitment is to an understanding of life which says that I am not the center of the universe, my denomination, the Baptist, is not the center of the Kingdom of God, nor are White Southerners the chosen people of God. The message of the Church gave me this view.

At five years old they had me on a box singing "Red and Yellow, Black and White, all are precious in God's sight." The Church gave me the message that there was no East, West, North or South in the Kingdom of God. The Church gave me the message of the Fatherhood of God and the Brotherhood of man, and the Church gave me the message that if we were committed to this God who was the Creator of all things, the center of all things, above all things, beneath all things and within all things, then the gates of Hell could not prevail against or destroy my confidence in or commitment to, this commitment. I soon found that many who had preached this message did not really believe it, nor did they want me to practice it. I soon learned when my wife and I had a Negro lady eat at our table, and hold hands for Thanks before we ate, with our children, that, if we took too seriously this business of the church's message, I might be treated as the man of Galilee who became the Christ whom we call Lord of our lives. I soon learned that the price was great to live this out in life. It cost us my parents' good will and good relationship, although my Father is a Baptist Minister who preached and taught me these things. Certainly, my giving seven years of my life to study of the basic presuppositions of the Christian Faith caused most of my formulations of my understanding of the basic presuppositions to change in words and in meaning, but somewhere the basic commitment and motivation remained, and today, although most of my time is taken up outside the framework of a local institutional church, I feel none the less that I am more committed and motivated to the Christian Faith than I was in the beginning of my pilgrimage. Whether I am absolutely right, I perhaps can never be absolutely certain, but I shall remain within the framework of the Christian Faith until something else becomes more meaningful as the meaning and purpose of our existence.

I would like to suggest that another hidden persuader in Human Relations which will determine whether or not our commitments and presuppositions are solid, is that of being willing to subject our commitments, with presuppositions and motivations with everything we hold as dear, to the scrutiny or constructive criticisms of others, and that means all others. If North Georgia Christianity cannot stand up under the attacks or views of Southern Christianity, it is not worth being committed to. If Southern Christianity will not stand up under the attacks or views of Northern Christianity, it is not worth seven years of my life in pursuit of theological studies. If Christianity cannot stand up when confronted by sin, atheism, non-Christian religions including Communism, then it is not what I was told it was, nor is it what Christians claim it to be. If Christians who are White cannot sit together, discuss together, fellowship and worship this One God with Black Christians then it is not what Christ's dying on a cross was interpreted to be. If what Albert Schweitzer has done with his life in Africa cannot be done in America, then to use Schweitzer as sermon illustrations is mockery. White Missionaries have gone to Nigeria, Africa to preach, minister and teach the Christian Gospel. Recently a Nigerian Convert left his wife and four children for four years to come to Virginia to study, only to find that the church which sent the Missionaries would not allow him to enter its sanctuary and worship God. Christianity is ineffective as a world movement as long as incidents such as this prevail, and one wonders how long it can have any impact upon a broken, divided world which is hungry for an ideal, a movement, a religion which practices what it preaches and seeks to make whole a whole world.

One of the greatest sins spelled out in the Christian Faith is that of self-righteousness. That is absolutizing our position, believing we are right and everyone else is wrong, and acting as if the only way to bring about human relations is to have everyone else become an adherent of our way. This kind of thing is nothing short of putting ourselves in God's place and play-acting God.

Born in a poor home, I have learned something from the rich. Born in an uneducated home, I have learned something from educated people. Born in the South, I have learned something from the Yankees. Born in a Baptist home I have learned something from other broken bodies of the Christian Church. The Baptist church of which I am a member, learned something from a Catholic Priest five weeks ago when he spoke to a group of adults. This same group learned something three weeks ago when an Episcopalian spoke, and last Sunday night when Dr. Aubrey Brown, a Presbyterian and your speaker for next Sunday, spoke. However, there were those within the membership who didn't learn because they were unwilling to come and discuss. One of those who did not come said to this same group recently, and I quote him, "The Jews own this country, the Catholics run it, the Protestants do the work and the Negroes enjoy it." You see, this man already knows all about the whole situation and perhaps couldn't be taught even by Christ. Being born a White boy, I have learned something from the Negroes. I have every reason to believe that the American Negro community has a tremendous commitment and motivation which even the gates of Hell cannot prevail against, nor forever can the Byrd machine of the Old Dominion. I doubt very seriously if all of the commitment or motivation comes from the Christian Faith and the Black Muslims are dedicated to its destruction. But once again I say, that any gods they or the Communist can destroy need to be destroyed, and as I told the group within my church of which I spoke, if the Catholics take over this country it will be an indictment on the message of the Protestant Church, and if the Communist take over, it will be because neither Democracy nor the Christian Faith remained true to their founders but degenerated into movements which has disciples without commitment or motivation and who are unwilling to pay the price through involvement within their true framework. I am not predicting nor advocating that I, or we, or anyone, should be what North Georgians call "wishy-washy" or soft, or liable to infiltration of destructive forces, but instead I am saying that if Democracy and Christianity are what we claim them to be that we should be unafraid of freedom of speech, freedom of press and freedom of discussion.

The last hidden persuader for sound human relations is that of an identification with our adversaries or even enemies. This goes one step beyond becoming unafraid of those who seek us out but actually implies taking the initiative of going into all the world and fulfilling the role of suffering-servant for the cause of better human relations. This is what I think Theology says when it uses the term, "God was in Christ." That is, God did not elect to sit in his heaven on his golden throne, He did not choose to stand on Mt. Olympus and cry or laugh over the human situation, nor did He make the world and go off to sleep, but he committed himself, and out of LOVE, Agape love, not erotic love, to identify Himself with us within our situation. He chose to do this through man, through the Prophets, through Jesus Christ and now through committed persons. This idea works. Justice Douglas of the Supreme Court says that as far back as 1930 when he visited Russia, that the Russians were developing great numbers of trained agriculturists who were being sent out to underdeveloped countries to identify themselves with these people. For an ulterior purpose, no doubt, but this is why we must know the differences in the presuppositions and motivations of Communism and Democracy and Christianity. Arnold Toynbee said recently on TV that he had just come back from a three-month tour of Pakistan, Indonesia and that part of the world. While there, said he, "I could tell every American and European I saw. I could identify them by their dress, by the wheels on which they rode or the homes in which they lived. We knew Communists were everywhere within the countries, but they had so identified themselves with the people until we couldn't tell them when we saw them." What a tragedy! The idea of an ungodly, atheistic country using the same technique which the originator of the Christian Faith used over 2,000 years ago to identify himself with mankind—getting hungry, thirsty, tired, and even dying as they did in order to reveal the commitment of God as personally concerned with the welfare of humanity, with the purpose being proper human relations. To the church this is missions, to the Kennedy Administration this has become the Peace Corps. And to other movements it takes on other names. But the idea of identifying ourselves with those in need, where they are, with commitment, compassion and willingness to suffer for their sake are the hidden persuaders which will ultimately make its mark and win disciples. May God help us if we remain in our ivory towers of institutional churchism, in our self-righteous, status quo White supremacy Southernism, or in a state of isolationism from the suffering majorities of this world. But we need commitment with presuppositions which includes all of life and all life of this planet. We need motivation, and a willingness to pay the price for peace, brotherhood, goodwill and human relations.

In closing, I believe so strongly that any ideology has to deal with human relations at its core, and I believe that human relations have moved to the center of the stage of the problem of human survival and world peace.

§65 Reverend Fred L. Shuttlesworth

Reverend Fred L. Shuttlesworth's biography appears in the introduction to his June 4, 1957 speech in Birmingham, Alabama. In his sixth annual message to the ACMHR, Reverend Shuttlesworth adopts the voice of the Old Testament prophet Jeremiah. He warns Birmingham, Alabama and the nation that "judgment is at hand." Like "God's people of old," members of the ACMHR have righteously withstood police brutality, injustice in the courts, firings, beatings, and bombings. Like Babylon, Birmingham is ruled by mad men drunk "off the wine of the Southern Way of Life, and have become mad with power." Many share in the judgment: mad judges, mad politicians, mad governors, mad police officials, mad whites, and even mad blacks, who refuse "to speak or deal justly with other men whose color happens to be different from theirs." But Shuttlesworth saves most of his prophetic bile for the madness of the white church, "an incubator of classism and racism." The white pulpit is ashamed to speak out for "freedom, justice, equality and brotherhood." Shame, too, is on the Negro preacher who similarly does not speak out. Finally, the righteous army of Christ will prevail if its good soldiers will only keep their hearts and minds focused on Christ and his word.

A Call for Reason, Sanity, and Righteous Perseverance in a Critical Hour

Sixth Annual Message to the Alabama Christian Movement for Human Rights, Birmingham, Alabama

June 5, 1962

Jeremiah 51:7-10

> Babylon hath been a golden cup in the Lord's hand, that made all the earth drunken: the nations have drunken of her wine; therefore the nations are mad. Babylon is suddenly fallen and destroyed: howl for her; take balm for her pain, if so be she may be healed. We would have healed Babylon, but she is not healed: forsake her, and let us go every one into his own country: for her judgment reacheth unto heaven, and is lifted up even to the skies. The Lord hath brought forth our righteousness: come, and let us declare in Zion on the work of the Lord our God.

Jude, verses 20-21

> But ye, beloved, building up yourselves on your most holy faith, praying in the Holy Ghost. Keep yourselves in the love of God, looking for the mercy of our Lord Jesus Christ unto eternal life.

Alabama, Birmingham, and many other places in this Southland are fast coming face to face with their most dangerous, desperate, and critical hour. Dangerous, because what is done these days will either advance or hinder future progress; desperate because their political leaders are chained with race-baiting ideas, and seem to be fatally inclined toward tyrannical despotism; and critical, because the Christian Army in their midst—having lost both voice and leadership in racial matters—is neither lifting the voice nor sounding the alarm that judgment is near.

But judgment is at hand for our native state of Alabama and our lovely city of Birmingham. Six years ago, we started out upon a journey toward freedom and human dignity—an endeavor which was designed to gain us liberty or give us death. It is well known history all over the country how we faced the lions of adversity in their dens of iniquity, and how we—defenseless except for our faith in God and love for our country—stood like God's people of old against the worst that tyrants and evil men could visit upon our homes and persons. Time would fail me to give a recantation of police brutality, chicanery between county and city officials, injustice and abuse in all the city and state courts, as well as lack of jurisprudence for a long time in the federal courts, the firing of helpless people from their jobs, the abuse of Negroes on the buses, the bombings by Klansmen, and the beatings by mobsters in this state and city, and many others too numerous to mention.

God has His purposes! He still moves in mysterious ways to perform His wonders! Holy and reverend is His name. And if our walk toward freedom has brought our city and state closer to the day of judgment, it must still be said today as in Lincoln's day—yea, even in David's day, that "The judgments of the Lord are true and righteous altogether." (Psalm 19:9)

Babylon of old was warned by the prophets; but having become drunk off power and pride, and thinking that her powerful army and her wonderful swinging gardens would sway the future, she did not heed the voice of God when He said: "And thou Babylon, which art exhalted to heaven, shalt be cast down to hell"; and, "Behold, I am against thee, O thou most proud, saith the Lord God of hosts: for thy day is come, the time that I will visit thee. And the most proud shall stumble and fall, and none shall raise him up: and I will kindle a fire in his cities, and it shall devour all around about him." (Jeremiah 50:31-32) Truly, Babylon, which had "been a golden cup in the Lord's hand" had a chance to unify the world and lead men into the ideals of brotherhood and justice. But she got drunk and made the other nations drunk.

"The nations have drunken of her wine; therefore the nations are mad."

Can we discern any difference in today's Birmingham and yesterday's Babylon? Nay, except that Babylon's might was her army, and Birmingham claims her strength in the sinews of coal and steel. Babylon thought more of her swinging gardens than the God of the universe; Birmingham prides her zoo more highly than she values her Negroes. Babylon held God's chosen people captive and demanded of them mirth while inflicting misery; for it is written: "They that carried us away captive required of us a song; and they that wasted us required of us mirth, saying, 'Sing us one of the songs of Zion.'" (Psalms 137:3) Birmingham and Alabama persecute us because we fight segregation and [they] demand that we be happy, saying, "You ought to be happy in a white man's land, and content with any treatment a white man gives you."

But Negroes have read that the "Earth is the Lord's and the fullness thereof"; and we—even though persecuted and cast down—don't mind singing the Lord's song in strange circumstances; and for six long dreary years, we have walked and talked with Him who "giveth songs in the night."

Babylon became mad and was destroyed. Alabama and Birmingham have become drunk off the wine of the Southern Way of life, and have become mad with power. Not willing to sober themselves with the vitality of Twentieth Century light, they persist in 1860 standards, and thus, in their madness, are becoming vicious and pulling blinders over their own eyes.

Whom the gods would destroy, they first make mad. The tragedy of our city and state today is that madness has been substituted for sanity. Men who occupy seats of power appear to use passion and madness rather than calmness and reason. They continue to misread history and misjudge the future. They refuse to believe that the Civil War was lost, or that slavery was destroyed. They still believe that a Negro has no rights a white man is bound to respect; and still persist in judging a man by the color of his skin.

The bible is right; and it says that they are mad. And madness has never been an incentive to humanitarianism or progress. The people of Alabama and Birmingham must also bear their share of judgment, for they continually elect madmen to lead them. Birmingham has recently entrusted its destiny to three men whose acts and statements give evidence of madness. This state, just a few days ago, turned its back on reason and sanity and nominated a man for governor who is committed to leading and leaning backwards in a forward going age. So you see, we have been, and for some time will be, caught up in this whirlpool of mad thoughts, mad acts, and impassionate actions one toward the other. "It's nice to have you in Birmingham," they say; but what really is nice about being in Birmingham?

What's nice about being in any place where madness reigns and sanity and justice have taken a holiday?

It is only people who are mad who continually rebel against justice. Mad men have closed Birmingham's parks, and mad people allowed them to remain closed. Mad politicians still growl like fices at the governmental moon of power, knowing they cannot hold back the inevitable day of justice, integration, and freedom. Mad men growled at the Freedom Riders while allowing mobsters to beat them up; so in effect, it was madmen that caused federal marshals to come to Alabama in 1961. Mad governors make statements which they do not want to appear as reasonable; and mad police officials would rather have dogs than people on their police force. Mad judges, on the bench, will close their eyes to justice when any case involving the elimination of segregation comes before them. Mad citizens, of color, continue to walk the streets of Birmingham and Alabama, refusing to speak or deal justly with other men whose color happens to be different from theirs.

Perhaps the worst part of this madness is that the white church is for the most part an incubator of classism and racism. The white pulpit is captive—afraid to stand and speak to men's hearts on the issue of freedom, justice, equality and brotherhood (And it is a shame for any Negro preacher to be afraid to speak about freedom in this day). Is it not also a symptom of madness that the presence of the Negro in a white church will chill the spirit of the congregation when they are "hot" at worship? This is not to say that all whites are evil by any means; it is to say that now is the time for all good men to come to the aid of their country—be they white or black. It is to say more than this that all Christians—white or black—have the God-given charge to stand up and speak out for God and God's people; for justice and human dignity. And I believe that if we persevere in our struggle in a Christian way, the day will soon come when more and more white people will either join our ranks, or in their own way stand and speak the truth to Birmingham and Alabama.

Beloved, these are critical times—but times for love, reason, sanity and passionate actions, one toward the other. We must not become embittered by other men's hate, nor impassioned by their acts of madness and persecution. Let us "keep ourselves in the love of God; let us build up ourselves on our most Holy faith; let us keep on praying in the Holy Ghost; and let us forever keep looking for the mercy of our Lord God Jesus Christ unto eternal life." This has been, is now, and ever will be the object and purpose of the Alabama Christian Movement for Human Rights. We will not throw stone for stone; we will not curse and abuse those who curse and abuse us; we will not wish harm and evil upon those who spitefully use us.

We believe that if we stand as Christians, if we contend for our rights as righteous soldiers in the Army of Christ, if we endure the hardness and madness of this hour as good soldiers, and if we keep our hearts and minds stayed on Christ and His word, then in God's own time—here today or tomorrow—He will do that which is right and give us the victory so help us God!

Our battle is hard but the end is not yet. There is yet much more land to be conquered. The forces of evil and darkness have already caused us untold misery and suffering; but we are ready to suffer even more that freedom might reign. For if freedom is worth living in, it is worth dying for. Already, the unjust officials and courts have caused us to spend over $72,000.00 in six years for bonds, court costs, transcripts, lawyer fees, etc., and we are in debt even now thousands of dollars with several more cases which have to be filed.

But we are making great strides toward freedom. The parks decision has spoken plainly to Birmingham that "it's time to wake up." The buses are desegregated by law, and we must ride them up front so that they will be desegregated in fact. We must quit flocking in large numbers to the back of the buses or to the dark and dingy holes called waiting rooms and restrooms for Negroes. It is time for us to be first class in mind, in body, in position and everywhere else. Negroes are as good as anybody else; our problem is to believe that we are as good as anybody else and to act as if we are as good as anybody else.

A final thought: but for the trials, tribulations, and successes of the Movement, there would be No Progress in Birmingham. The selective buying campaign came about as a result of the parks decision and the jailing of Reverend Phifer and myself. It is led by the students and should be supported by every single Negro in this city and county. Let us support the efforts of our race to be free and stay out of town until the madness downtown gives way to sanity and reason. "Lift up your heads, Oh ye gates; and be ye lift up ye everlasting doors; and the King of Glory shall come in." He is our rock and our shelter; He is all we need and He will give us the victory. Amen.

§66 Robert H. Walkup

A graduate of Ole Miss and Louisville Seminary, Robert H. Walkup pastored the First Presbyterian Church in Starkville, home of Mississippi State University for 11 years between 1953 and 1964. He would later serve churches in Texas and Arkansas. But on the very afternoon that James Meredith took up residence on the Ole Miss campus, Walkup preached this message to his congregants. The sermon was later broadcast on radio to Starkville residents. In the incredibly charged atmosphere, Walkup tries to defuse some of the hostilities by meditating on the first chapter of James, specifically James's call to ask God for wisdom, should we lack it. The enthymeme is that, of course, Mississippians lack wisdom in this crucial hour. Cleverness they have plenty, but have they asked God to provide them with heaven-sent wisdom? Walkup also skillfully steers clear of the divisive state sovereignty versus national sovereignty question. Instead, he claims that there is "only one type of sovereignty and that's absolute sovereignty." This brief sermon illustrates how a southern preacher, thrust into the vortex of racial politics, could steer a third course between the Scylla and Charybdis of federal marshals and states righters, while simultaneously invoking a seemingly just solution.

Not Race but Grace

First Presbyterian Church, Starkville, Mississippi
September 30, 1962

These are difficult days. You know that without my telling you. You know how we've lived these last hours—prisoners of the news reports—hearing what we could hear and reading what we could read, and all of it seeming to us almost like a nightmare, a disquieting dream from some fantastic place unknown. And yet we've known in our hearts all along, that were it not for God's own mercy, what is happening a hundred miles away could just as well be happening right here. And we're involved! As a minister of Jesus Christ—indeed, as just a common garden-variety Christian—I'm troubled!

There is a word of Scripture which keeps haunting me: "What do ye more than others?" *We are Christians!* We are not politicians. We are not skilled to understand maneuvering—but we are Christians! For two thousand years now the gospel has been saturating our thoughts. Do we know any more than the others know? Is there any contribution that we can make that non-Christians cannot make? "What do ye *more* than others?"

Will you hear the text? "If any of you lack wisdom, let him ask of God, that giveth to all men liberally, and upbraideth not; and it shall be given him. But let him ask in faith, nothing doubting."

You remember that our good friend Martin Luther didn't care much for the Epistle of St. James. Martin Luther, who was given sometimes to extravagance of language, referred to the Epistle of James as an epistle of straw. You see, Martin Luther couldn't use the Epistle of James for what he was trying to do. He was in an argument, and while he was in an argument he was looking for what weapons he could find, and the Epistle of James didn't have any weapons. It's not a theological epistle. If you want theology, go to Romans. So Luther went to Romans. But what James is trying to do is just deal with the everyday problems of Christian living. He seldom touches any of the deep, profound, involved truths. Even so, he can speak to us; even so, he has a word we need today—or at least a word that helps me. Let's look at that text: "If any of you lack wisdom. . . ."

Now wasn't that a courteous way for James to put it? Wasn't that nice of James to put that "if" in there? Was there really any doubt in his mind about whether or not we lack wisdom? Wisdom to James did not mean learning or profundity of thought but the ability to use the trials of life—the ability to discern in life itself the will of God. Now, do we lack that? For all of our supposed learning . . . for all of our big talk . . . do we lack wisdom? There is no hope really for us as long as we think that we're wise. As long as we keep on believing that wisdom was born with us and that understanding shall perish with our going. Only men who confuse themselves with God will dare to pretend in this anguished and troubled day that they know the exact route to the Promised Land. Only men who take unto themselves the omnipotence that belongs to the Lord God Almighty alone will believe that they have in their own mind this day every answer and every truth.

Only Job's comforters will offer us now shallow answers to these questions. Do we lack wisdom? *Certainly* we lack wisdom! We've got cleverness in abundance, but cleverness is not what the Scripture's talking about—and it's not what we need. We need wisdom, and hope begins with our knowing that we need it! There is hope for us only if we realize that we don't possess wisdom. Only if we realize that we are desperately in need. "If any of you lack wisdom," says James, "let him ask God."

But that seems too simple. If any man lacks wisdom, ask God, that's—oh—we've grown past that, haven't we? Just ask? That simple! But the New Testament certainly puts it that way, doesn't it? And the Apostles believed it. St. Paul was quite sure, you know, that he lived by prayer. St. Paul was quite sure that his missionary journeys were guided by the will of God in answer to his prayers. And did not our Divine Redeemer himself spend much time in prayer? But we've grown beyond that, haven't we . . . or have we?

Do we really think we'll get wisdom these days *by sharing our common ignorance?* By pooling our misinformation? Or do we think, perchance, we'll get wisdom by asking God? That's the lesson of history that we have to relearn again, and again, and again; and we don't want to ask God. Sometimes we're afraid to ask God.

You will remember that one time there was an assembly of supposedly large men in Westminster Abbey. You will remember that the great bulk of these men were Englishmen—and the seasoning of the group was Scottish. They had met together to write a statement of Christian belief, which later became the Westminster Confession of Faith and the Larger and Shorter Catechisms. But this assembly was split, and there was in that assembly almost the most learned man in Christendom, a Dr. John Selden. He was the great champion of the Erastian heresy. You all know the Erastian heresy, you just don't know it by that name. That's the heresy which teaches the supremacy of the state over the church. It's still with us. And Dr. Selden, learnedly and persuasively, presented the position of the Erastians in the assembly. And the poor Presbyterians had about given up hope. They felt that what he said was heresy, but they didn't know where to grab it to grapple with it. A saintly young Scotsman, almost the youngest man there, named George Gillespie, got up to speak. They'd watched him while Dr. Selden was speaking and all the time he'd been writing on a pad before him. He got up and put his hand on that pad and began to speak. And he spoke for an hour! Dr. Selden, himself, said later that in that one hour George Gillespie destroyed ten years of study and work for him. And the whole course of that assembly was changed. So men rushed to that note pad. They wanted to see his notes—the outline from which he had spoken. And over and over again he'd written on that pad one Latin phrase: "Da lucem, Domine"—"Give light, O Lord."

"Give light, O Lord"—that could be our prayer. We could spend the rest of this Lord's Day praying—for wisdom—for light—for understanding! We need light today, not heat. What we need today is not men with hot heads and big mouths, but men with cool heads and warm hearts. We've talked on the street corners now to about everybody, haven't we? How much have we talked in the closet to God? We've talked about men—but have we talked to *God* about them? We have a solemn duty of prayer. "If any of you lack wisdom, let him ask of God." We've gathered our neighbors' opinions, but have we asked God's? He says, "But ask in faith, nothing doubting"— that's the condition. He promises wisdom if we ask for it, provided we ask in faith, nothing doubting. "Nothing 'wavering,'" the Greek really says. For God will do nothing for a double-minded man who says, "Yes," and then again, "No"; nor for a man who says, "I trust in God, but I trust in myself too." We must come dependent, wholly and completely dependent upon God's wisdom, God's mercy, God's providence.

Now listen to me carefully, because you're not going to like what I say, some of you! (That's all right. I've said it to God and I've already talked this sermon over with God. He likes it.)

I don't believe in state sovereignty!

I don't believe in national sovereignty!

All this talk about the United States government being sovereign is *fool-ishness!* And all this talk about the State of Mississippi being sovereign is *foolishness!* Sovereign means: "one who has power that is not diminished by anything anywhere." There is only one type of sovereignty and that's abso-lute sovereignty, *and that belongs to God!* And that's the only place it belongs. If we lack wisdom, if we lack understanding, if we are troubled in this day, we will turn back where we should have been, God pity us, all along—to the one who really owns us, to the one whose world this *really* is.

I read somewhere that Wendell Phillips frequently got discouraged. When he came home one day there was a large black wreath on the door. And when he came in, all the shades were drawn, and there was black all over the house. When his mother came to meet him, she was dressed in black and wearing a veil. He ran to her and said, "Mother! Who's dead?" And she said, "God." He thought she'd lost her mind; he called to her and said, "What did you say?" And she replied, "I said God is Dead! I know he must be dead, because you've lost hope and as long as he's alive there's no reason to lose hope."

And now I want to give you one statement from the book of Revelation: "Alleluia: for the Lord God omnipotent reigneth."

Prayer: We lack wisdom! We lack understanding! We're not men of good will. We have trusted in our cleverness. But now we trust in thee. Now we cry unto thee, O Lord God. Now we beg thee, O Lord God, take us and lead us through troubled days, for Jesus' sake. Amen.

§67 Robert H. Walkup

Robert Walkup's biography is in the previous section. On October 7, a week after preaching *On Race Not Grace*, Robert Walkup again preached on the situation at Ole Miss, but instead of wisdom, he asks the simple question, why? If God is a just God, why would he let this happen? Walkup, using Job as his exemplar, has three answers. First, God's providence is often retributive. Because of slavery, because of unpunished lynchings, mobs could terrorize with impunity. And a just God would not forget. Second, even as God punishes, that punishment also teaches, setting us on the right course if we allow God to speak to us. And finally, God's punishment can still be redemptive, drawing us closer to him even as we suffer. Perhaps ironically, redemptive suffering was also being preached from the other side of the "tracks," but it followed from a completely different set of actions.

————

Speech at the University of Mississippi

Oxford, Mississippi
October 7, 1962

When you consider the football scores, it was a great weekend for us in Starkville. But we had a weekend a week ago that wasn't a great weekend. Since we last assembled in this place something has happened that has hurt our whole state, and nation, and world. Many good weekends, but a week ago tragedy struck—and it's too familiar to need my description at this time.

I am a minister of Jesus Christ—a Presbyterian Calvinist minister, if you please—a child of the Reformation, a believer in the Confession of Faith, which has said always that all events alike are under the sovereign will of God; which says that God is working out his purpose in the lives and times of men.

Now, believing that, do I not find myself, and do you not find yourself, crushed down between the horns of a cruel dilemma? How can we put what has happened into line with what we know of *God?* Why? *Why?* WHY did God let this happen? Why did God let us come to this day? Look to the Bible.

I've spent some time on my knees this week. I've spent some time searching, searching again not only my heart but the Scriptures. What do they say? Well, I found my friend Job there. (Some of you were here Wednesday night and we looked at him then. Let's look at him now.) For Job had a question not unlike our question. It was the same one-word question. As we frame this word with our lips, "why," so did Job.

You remember him. He was the greatest man in the East, wealthy and upright before God. He had seven sons and three daughters, thousands of cattle and camels. And yet the day dawned when all of his sons were killed. His daughters were destroyed. His cattle were stolen and his camels were driven away. Why?

His friends came to sit with him and take counsel with him. And they sat, considerately enough, silent for a while. Then they began to say, "Job, did anything like this ever happen to an upright man?"

Then it must follow that this is punishment for sin. Now, that's not the right answer. That was not the right answer for Job, but it was a part of the answer to the problem of Job, and it's a part of the answer to our question today.

If we want to know why God let this thing come to us—if we want to know why we've been put through this day in our state—a part of the answer is . . . *sin!* A part of the answer is punishment for sin! Because the first thing I think we learn from the book of Job is that God's providence is *penal.* Or take it out of "theological" terms. Put it simply: there *is* such a thing as punishment. *Part* of the reason this has come to us is our sin.

It was a long time ago when men stole other men. It was a long time ago and very, very far away when men . . . when *men* went out to steal other men, and they brought them to our shores and they sold them in slavery.

That was sin!

You see, there was more to slavery than we remember. There was more to slavery than the magnolias and the mint juleps, more to slavery than the happy carefree people, more to slavery than the nice aspects of "ol' mastah" and "ol' missus" that we like to talk about. There were people being put through a wringer so severe that they cried out: "NOBODY KNOWS THE TROUBLE I'VE SEEN! NOBODY KNOWS BUT JESUS!" There were people being put through a wringer so severe that they cried out for a chariot to swing low and take them away from it.

That was SIN!

And we paid for that sin. We paid for it frightfully when this whole section of our nation was almost completely destroyed.

A year ago last summer I walked over the battlefields. The scars will always be on the face of Virginia and those states where the bulk of the war was fought. I walked over the battlefields, and I stopped to read at Chancellorsville and Fredericksburg and Appomattox and Manassas. I read the things they put up there on those bronze tablets. And every bit of work, every load that was lifted, every bale of cotton that was picked by the slaves, was *not worth that!*

Nothing could have been worth the carnage that swept over this nation. And our southland is not yet over it!

Now I know there are two sides. I know that more than slavery was involved. Certainly I do. If I hadn't known it, my grandmother saw to it that I understood there was another side. But *both* sides paid, because there is such a thing as the penal providence of God!

When I was a little boy in Senatobia (you know, I'm a Mississippian; I was surprised this week to discover somebody didn't know that—I thought I bragged about it!—but I'll tell you again), when I was a little boy in Senatobia, I came home from school one day at noon, as we did every day. After lunch we started back to school. When I got along there about where Mr. Jess French's hotel was, I saw a crowd of people watching. They were crowding into a store, so I crowded in with them. And because I was small, I wound and wiggled my way through the crowd to see what they were looking at in the store. And I saw . . . I saw a man on the floor dead! I saw a man who had been shot about five minutes [earlier]. He was "black."

I asked, when I got out of that crowd, I asked who shot him, and they told me—and it nearly broke my heart. It was the man who let me ride his Shetland pony. It was the man who only a summer or two before had put his Shetland pony in our yard and left him there all summer so John and I could ride. And I went running to my grandfather distraught. And I said, "Poppa! Will they hang him?"

He said, "No, now calm down, son."

"They'll hang him, won't they, poppa?"

"No, they won't hang him."

"Well, what *will* they do to him?"

He said, "Now let that alone, boy." And so when it came out in the paper, I learned my first legal term.

"Poppa, what does n-o-l-p-r-o-s spell?"

"It spells 'nol. pros.' Why, son?"

Well, that's what they did; they nol-prossed the case. What does that mean? It means *sin*, that's what it means. It was wrong! And my grandfather was the best man I ever knew! My grandfather was better than Job—but he didn't say a word. He didn't say a *word!* He didn't do a *thing!*

I'm his grandson, and I'm paying for that sin and the sins of others who were silent, and I have four children. I'm paying because we have allowed to grow up in our hearts contempt for other men. The long years of our semi-quasi approval of lynching did something to make the climate in which we could give way to mob violence. The long years that we went through left a contempt for law and order. And that's part of our trouble today. When we think God doesn't punish us, we're not really thinking. And part of the answer to "why" today is the punishment of God. God's providence is penal.

But God's providence, as Job found out, is also educational. God's providence does not only punish us, but it also teaches us.

I like ol' Elihu. Elihu was a young man and so he had to be silent until all the old men could talk. That must have been a terrible burden for Elihu to bear. But finally, when all the old men had talked forever and said nothing, Elihu began. In the course of his great speech he said, "But none says, ' . . . God my Maker . . . gives songs in the night'" (Job 35:10).

There's more than punishment for sins. There is also *learning* to be had. Men in all ages have learned from the experiences of Job. And this speaks to us. Why? Why has God let us come to this? That we may learn a more excellent way! That we may learn from this shame and from this heartache a more excellent way.

"All they that take the sword shall perish with the sword" (Matthew 26:52). It was a long time ago when our Lord Christ said that any man that calleth his brother a fool (*Raca*—one could translate it "I spit on you") is in danger of hell's fire. But we haven't learned it yet. What have we learned?

I picked up the paper and read quotations from students at Ol' Miss. And what did they say? Well, one of them said, "If I was sure I wouldn't get caught, I'd go kill that man now!" Two or three more affirmed their desire to kill somebody. Do we not know that there is in the Old Testament a *commandment against killing?* Do we not know that in the New Testament it gets *stronger?* That in the New Testament it is not only killing that is prohibited, it's the desire to kill? *Do we not know that if we have in our hearts a desire to kill someone, we have already committed murder and stand guilty before God?*

We've paid a frightful tuition for what we've learned. But wouldn't it be a dreadful thing to go through these days and not learn a thing? I pray that the good God will hasten our growth in grace. I pray that we'll know what we need to learn: *that we cannot keep on planting thistles and expecting to pick strawberries off of them!* Thistles yield thistles—and that's all they ever yield.

God's providence is educational and penal, but most of all. . . . (You know I don't like to preach like this. You know what I like to preach about; what I like to preach about is the grace of God.) I'm glad we've come now to where not only can I say God's providence is penal, God's providence is educational, but God's providence is redemptive. Redemptive! The very tragedy through which Job passed brought him close to God.

He could now say, "I know that my redeemer liveth." (Job 19:25). We, too, can be brought near to God.

Sin is a stubborn fact, but the cross is also a fact! The cross speaks of God's unfailing love. Here we see in spite of sin the *redemptive purpose of God.*

And now, let us repent, and now let us come to his table that we may receive the dear Sacrament of Holy Communion. Here in his broken body and shed blood God speaks the visible word: The word of reconciliation, of forgiveness, of health.

§68 Charles L. Stanford, Jr.

Few white Mississippi clergy were willing to speak out in 1962 against white segregationists. One such brave minister was the Reverend Charles Leo Stanford, Jr., who graduated from Mississippi State University and Louisville Presbyterian Theological Seminary. Ordained in the Presbyterian Church in 1958, Stanford first served the Vidalia Presbyterian Church in Louisiana. His second pastorate, in Meridian, Mississippi at the Jones Memorial Presbyterian Church is where he delivered this sermon. "After the sermon," according to R. Milton Winter, "Stanford noticed that one of the elders refused the Lord's Supper. Following the evening service, he happened to drive past the elder's home and realized that his session was meeting there secretly. The next week Stanford was given a resolution calling his sermon 'untimely' and the references to alleged sins of the congregation 'uncalled for.' Attendance dropped precipitously." Sixteen months later, Stanford received a new "call" to Kentucky.

While it might have been relatively safe to speak out against the Meredith Riots at Ole Miss outside of the Magnolia State, not so for a white minister. In this brief sermon on worldwide communion Sunday, Stanford lays the blame explicitly from the outset: "The horror at Ole Miss has been the result largely of Christian preachers who have not been preaching the whole counsel of God to the people of God." And yet Stanford also points the finger at his congregants: "if you have hatred in your heart toward anyone, you do not have love in your heart for God." But Stanford goes even further in his condemnation, pointing to some members "of this particular church" who counseled violence. Such people "are more at home with the spirit of violence and war. And to claim that such a spirit is a Christian spirit is to do blasphemy to the name of Christ."

————

Love Disqualified

Jones Memorial Presbyterian Church, Meridian, Mississippi
October 7, 1962

Almighty God, who dost say to us through thy holy word how thou wouldst have us live; but whose Word is often ignored or misunderstood by us; give us understanding minds and loving hearts, that we may hear and receive thy will for our lives; through Jesus Christ our Lord. Amen.

My dear friends and fellow Mississippians, this is a sermon that I really do not desire to preach and which I kept hoping would never have to be preached. But now I find that my hope was only wishful thinking, and my silence was only cowardice. And the result of that combination of coward-ice and childishness has been tragic.

The horror at Ole Miss has been the result largely of Christian preach-ers who have not been preaching the whole counsel of God to the people of God. Those of us who have remained silent on a great and grave moral issue have lent support to those who have spoken out on the side of error and evil. We are now reaping what we have sown—the violence that comes from hatred: a hatred that we have allowed to develop because we never said that it is wrong.

But, at the same time, we never should have had to say that it is wrong. The Bible says it and says it quite strongly. The Bible knows no cowardice. It knows no childish wishes. It knows only that which is true about God and about Man and it speaks that which is true.

And in this instance this is what it says: "If any one says, 'I love God,' and hates his brother, he is a liar; for he who does not love his brother whom he has seen, cannot love God whom he has not seen."

So the matter boils down quite simply to this: if you have hatred in your heart toward anyone, you do not have love in your heart for God.

During this past week we have seen the ugly head of hate reared in our state, and we have not liked what we have seen. Yet, we have not known that such a hideous monster has long been present here. We have not real-ized that he has been lurking beneath the surface for a great many years, rising now and again to give us a short, hurried view of his horror. But now at long last he has burst through into full sight, and we have seen the hideousness of his face. And there are only a very few who like what they have seen.

But there are some who like it, and there are many who have approved it, though not particularly liking it. And there are so many who have been saying, "This is what must happen if integration is tried here." So that is what did happen!

It is like any sin—if you think about it long enough and often enough, when it finally comes about you can enter into it joyfully and energetically because you have been doing it all along in your minds.

But the deeper tragedy is that of those who have approved it, of those who have been preparing for it, of those who have done it, many are members of Christ's church, and some are members of the Presbyterian branch of Christ's church, and some are members of this particular church.

In other words, by giving ourselves into the hands of Christ, we have pledged ourselves to be servants of the Prince of Peace. But when the chips have been down, and when the line has been firmly drawn, we find that we are not really the servants of the Prince of Peace at all. We find that we are more at home with the spirit of violence and war. And to claim that such a spirit is a Christian spirit is to do blasphemy to the name of Christ.

No! We have hated—all of us have hated to one extent or another during this past week. Some of us have hated Meredith for wanting to go to the university in the first place. Some of us have hated the Kennedys for attempting to force him into the school. And some of us have hated Barnett for disobeying the court order. But hatred has been in our hearts to one extent or another during this past week, and we have not tried to keep it from bursting forth. And the result has been tragedy and horror and, in many cases, blasphemy.

And now we come today to the holy table of our Lord. We come to this spot where we thank God for his goodness to us. We come to this table where we are reminded of the sacrifice which Christ made of his own body and blood because of the hatred and violence of men.

And we are not just coming to this table by ourselves today. This is World-Wide Communion Sunday.

We are approaching this table while people all around the world, people of varying hues of skin color and cultures and customs, are also approaching this table. We are coming to take the elements which mean to us that Christ has broken down the barriers which separate men from God and from one another.

And we come knowing that we do not love all these people—knowing that some of them we even hate.

But we come to the table saying, "O God, how much we do love thee. How much do we love thee for thy great goodness to us."

And the Bible says: "If any one says, 'I love God,' and hates his brother whom he has seen, cannot love God whom he has not seen."

If you come to this table today with unrepented sin upon your soul, you are doing your soul grievous damage. But if you repent of your sins and are profoundly sorry for them, then come joyfully to this table and learn of God's great love for you; and then go forth and share that love with your neighbors.

§69 Reverend Duncan M. Gray, Jr.

Duncan M. Gray, Jr. was born on September 21, 1926 in Canton, Mississippi. He earned a commission with the Navy after graduating from Tulane University with an electrical engineering degree. He completed his M.Div. at the University of the South, Sewanee, Tennessee in 1953 and was ordained a priest that same year. From 1957 to 1965 Gray served St. Peter's Episcopal Church in Oxford, Mississippi, site of the Meredith Riots in 1962. During this time, Gray also became active in the civil rights movement, working closely with NAACP leader, Amzie Moore. More than 20 years after being ordained as an Episcopal priest, he became the bishop of the diocese of Mississippi in 1974. His father and son were also bishops. He is a former chair and current member of the Mississippi Religious Leadership Conference, the Mississippi Council on Human Relations, and the Mississippi Advisory Committee to the U.S. Commission on Civil Rights. Gray was also a member of the Committee of Southern Churchmen and served on the editorial board of its publication, *Katallagete.* He has published articles in national and regional magazines, and in 1962 he won the national Speaker-of-the-Year Award from Tau Kappa Alpha, National Forensic Honor Society. An oral history conducted with Duncan M. Gray is available at the University of Southern Mississippi in Hattiesburg.

On the Sunday following the Meredith riots at the University of Mississippi, Reverend Duncan M. Gray addressed his parishioners at St. Peter's Episcopal Church in Oxford. His first task is leveling blame, and it's all around: the "thugs and toughs" who came from all over the state, the undergraduates, the press, legislators, and of course the governor Ross Barnett. But Gray saves perhaps his harshest invective for "us," the people who allowed the moral and political climate to be poisoned by racial hatred. Even as Gray looks to the future with faith and confidence, perhaps Robert E. Lee's example is the one white Mississippians should follow: when no one else would, Lee joined a kneeling black for communion. The accumulated force of Gray's indictment reaches a crescendo as he closes: "no university in the world would defend this position rationally, and no Christian church in the world would defend it morally." Moreover, Gray asks his audience to look Christ in the eye and tell him of the university's admission policy—with conviction.

Paranoia, Guilt, and Atonement

St. Peter's Episcopal Church, Oxford, Mississippi
October 7, 1962

I'm sure that all of us here today—a week after the tragedy—feel depressed, burdened, and sorrowful; as, indeed, we should. But, as Christians, we cannot let our reaction stop at this point. Fundamental to the Christian faith is the deep conviction that even out of worst tragedy, some good can come. What can we learn from tragic experience? (And God help us if we do not learn; for then we will only have it to go through again and again). But what can we do now? This is the real question.

The first thing we can do is to face up to our own guilt in the situation. You and I didn't go out there and throw the broken bricks and the bottles.

You and I didn't go out there and fire the guns. Yet you and I, along with every other Mississippian, are responsible in one degree or another for what happened. For we are responsible for the moral and political climate in our state which made such a tragedy possible. Maybe you and I didn't do much to create this climate, it is certainly evident that we did all too little to dispel or change it. The "things that we have left undone which we ought to have done" should bother us every bit as much as the "things which we have done which we ought not to have done." The decent, respectable, and responsible people of Mississippi have failed, when events like those of Sunday night can take place within our state.

What has been the climate in our state during the past several years? You know and I know that it has been one of fear and intimidation; one of defiance and irresponsibility. The official line of massive resistance to any form of desegregation and of last-ditch defiance of the federal courts was laid down, and anyone who dared to challenge it found himself in deep trouble. Calm and rational discussion of the matter was virtually prohibited, so that there was no chance for moderate men of both races to sit down in good faith and work out some reasonable and workable solution to the very real problems posed by the decisions of the Courts. Above all, the people of Mississippi were told by their leaders over and over again that the federal courts could be defied forever; that they would never have to obey the law of the land. And most of the people of Mississippi believed them. Mississippians have been thus deceived and misled by their leaders for nearly eight years now. Is it any wonder, then, that violence erupts when the issue becomes real, rather than academic, within our own state.

The freshman at Ole Miss today was only ten years old when the Supreme Court's decision on segregation was handed down. A senior today was only thirteen. Theirs is the generation exposed to the textbook and library censorship, mandatory essay contests on White Supremacy, and a massive propaganda campaign against the federal courts. Is it any wonder that they feel persecuted and oppressed? Seldom, if ever, have they been reminded that half of the people in Mississippi are Negroes and that they are people, too, with hopes, aspirations, and rights of their own. Think of the freshmen and upperclassmen as well who were out there throwing bricks and bottles the other night. Who could really blame them when the Governor of the state himself was in open rebellion against the law?

Think of the thugs and the toughs from near and far who did the most damage Sunday night and nearly all the damage Monday morning. What could you expect when supposedly responsible legislators were saying, "We will never surrender," and "The people of Mississippi know what to do!" What could you expect when so much of the Mississippi Press was voicing the same sentiment? It was an open invitation to every thug and tough for hundreds of miles around to come pouring into Oxford, for they had every reason to believe that the decent, responsible people of Mississippi would back up their action one hundred percent. There are thugs and toughs everywhere, but they come in such numbers and with such violence only where they think they are wanted.

The major part of the blame must be placed upon our leaders themselves; and upon you and me and all the other decent and responsible citizens of Mississippi, who have allowed this impossible climate to prevail. It is for this that we pray God's forgiveness this morning.

But true repentance means more than just remorse. We must now give our all to salvaging the situation; to bringing order out of chaos, peace out of strife. We must accept the fact that the color of a person's skin can no longer be a barrier to his admission to the University of Mississippi. I would hope that, as Christians we would accept this because it is just and right, whether we like it or not. But if we are not yet able to do this, at least we can be realistic enough and patriotic enough to accept this as the law of the land. To think and to act otherwise—to continue to breathe defiance and disobedience—will only bring more suffering and shame, violence and horror that has shocked us so deeply since we last came together as a congregation.

This is what worries me most about the efforts of so many Mississippians to pin the blame for last week's violence on the federal marshals. If we are not mature enough and secure enough to admit and confess our own guilt—if we continue to nurse and nurture our collective paranoia—then we will never get around to doing anything about the real root of our troubles: the moral and political climate in which we live. And we will have to go through again and again the horror of more violence and bloodshed. We will have learned nothing.

But I, for one, look to the future with faith and confidence. I am convinced that most of the decent and honest people of the Oxford-University community have learned the lesson we must learn from last Sunday's madness. And from the statement of those 127 Mississippi business men released last Tuesday it is apparent that others have learned also. The fact that many other Mississippians have not, and that many of our political leaders are still making every effort to keep them from doing so should only spur us on to better and greater efforts. By God's grace, some real good can come out of this tragedy, and it is up to you and to me to see that it does.

A little less than a century ago, our own southern forebears found themselves in the aftermath of a far greater tragedy. And there were those then who tried to redeem the times. Among them was our own L. Q. C. Lamar. Another, George Washington Cable, made his most memorable speech on the campus of the University of Mississippi. But, above all, there was the noble example of General Robert E. Lee. A devout Episcopalian, Lee was present in the Church shortly after the war, when a Negro Churchman came to the altar to make his Communion. The other people in the church, confused and resentful, stayed in their pews. Then General Lee quietly arose, walked up the aisle, and knelt beside the Negro.

This great man set a standard which has never quite been forgotten by the South. It is to this standard that we must now repair. For, ultimately, it will be through countless small words and small deeds, done in the name of Christ by Christians, that this University, this community, and this state will yet redeem herself for the tragic events of last Sunday and Monday.

I think we should ask ourselves, first of all, if we are really sufficiently aware of the deadly serious nature of our present predicament. This may seem like a silly question in the light of the anxiety and concern which has burdened us all during the past several days. But one wonders if it is so silly when we see legislators joking, wearing Centennial uniforms to the floor of the house, and students cheering and laughing in a situation where even the Lieutenant-Governor said someone might get killed. I am afraid that there may be many who seem to put this whole affair in the category of waving Confederate flags and singing "Dixie" at a football game; or standing up and proclaiming to the world that we are proud to be Mississippians.

As we all know, our University is on the verge of losing her accreditation along with all the other colleges in the state. But even if this is averted, the dignity and good name of the University have suffered damage it will take years to repair. For many years the University of Mississippi has been known as a venerable institution of sound learning, gentle manners and fond memories, and, more recently as the home of great football teams and beautiful coeds, neither of which hurt her a bit. Today, and perhaps for years to come, when Ole Miss is mentioned, the first image generated in the minds of millions everywhere will be one of lawlessness, racial strife, and reaction. The picture has been painted, and largely by native Mississippians who claim to love her. That picture will be hard to erase.

Of course, there are still those who talk of closing the University, as a last resort; and, again, this in the name of love and service to Mississippi. But, surely, we cannot be so blind as this. What greater disservice could we render to our beloved state than to close down her colleges and universities—we who need, perhaps more than any other state to raise our educational level, not lower it; we who need to keep and train our bright young people here at home, not drive them away to other parts of the country?

Even more serious than the threat to the University is the threat to our nation and our system of government posed by our continued defiance of the federal courts and the federal government. No government is perfect. But I sincerely believe, as I'm sure you do, that our system of government in this country comes closer to providing the Christian ideal of freedom and justice than any other system yet devised by the mind of man. So, then, it is as a Christian, as well as an American, that I want to see this system preserved. But we cannot long survive as a country if every state is free to decide which federal laws she will obey and which she will not. We found this out 100 years ago, and most of us thought the issue was settled then.

We know there are good laws and bad laws, good court decisions and bad court decisions; and, fortunately, under our system of government, we are free to protest the ones we don't like and to take every legal means to repeal or reverse them. We do not have the right to defy and disobey the law when it is established and in force. In trying to do this, we have brought upon ourselves the threat of anarchy, and, as Christians, we cannot and must not support this alternative to the democracy under which we live.

Finally, and most important of all, I ask you as a Christian people to consider the real moral issue which lies at the base of the whole crisis: are we morally justified in refusing to admit to the University of Mississippi any student who meets all the necessary requirements except for the color of his skin? Remember, the question here is not "What would I like?" or "What do I want?" The question is simply, "What is just and right?"

Our governor has said that the state's cause on this score is righteous and just; and I am sure he is sincere in his belief, as are many other Mississippians who share it with him. But in the name of reason and of Christian standards of freedom and justice, I ask you to consider the fact that no university in the world would defend this position rationally, and no Christian church in the world would defend it morally. And I do not believe that any one of us here today could stand in the presence of Jesus of Nazareth, look Him squarely in the eye, and say, "We will not admit a Negro to the University of Mississippi." For it was our Lord who said, "In as much as ye have done it unto one of the least of these my brethren, ye have done it unto me."

Brethren we need to pray, for our University and our community, our state and our nation. Perhaps, above all, we need to pray for ourselves. The seeds of anger and hatred, bitterness and prejudice, are already widely sown, and, as Christians we need to do our utmost to uproot them and cast them out. You and I have a heavy responsibility in the days and weeks to come. Let us pray daily, even hourly, for God's guidance and direction, that we may faithfully fulfill this responsibility to the end that God's will be done.

§70 Reverend George A. Chauncey

George A. Chauncey was born in Memphis, Tennessee in 1927. As a young man, he served in the U.S. army counterintelligence corps in postwar Japan. Chauncey earned a B.A. from Southwestern College in 1949 and an M.Div. from Yale Divinity

School in 1952. He served as a Presbyterian minister in numerous communities, including a congregation which asked him to leave Brownsville, Texas when he shared his views on *Brown v. Board of Education*. The University of Mississippi withdrew its invitation to him to participate in a religious conference held on campus once his views on race relations were known. His son, George A. Chauncey, Jr., endured a steady supply of harassment during his school days in the South.

While a minister in Arkansas, Chauncey signed a petition protesting Governor Orval Faubus's attempts to block integration. But Chauncey's testimony in Little Rock went far beyond merely symbolic action: along with Colbert Cartwright, Dunbar H. Ogden, Jr., and Will D. Campbell, he accompanied the Little Rock Nine to Central High School in September 1957. The sermon below takes place in Danville, Kentucky in 1962, two weeks after rioters killed two men when Ole Miss was forced to integrate its student body. The Danville congregation was especially interested in events at the University of Mississippi, because a local elder had just taken a faculty position there.

Chauncey's ministry eventually took a more manifestly global trajectory. He earned a D.Min. from Union Theological Seminary in 1972. In that same year John Knox Press published his introduction to Christian ethics *Decisions! Decisions!* From 1973 to 1989 Chauncey served as director of the Washington office of the Presbyterian church where he addressed world hunger, poverty and a more just U.S. involvement in Central America. His global and catholic orientation also led him to founding the ecumenical lobby Interreligious Taskforce on U.S. Food Policy, where he joined hands with Protestant, Roman Catholic, and Jewish organizations to urge U.S. policymakers to address global hunger and poverty.

Chauncey centers his sermon on Isaiah 58, where God tells the nation of Israel that he does not accept their worship because they are unjust, and urges the congregation to do what it can to make changes locally as the civil rights era gains momentum. He also urges his congregation not to think of events outside its town, such as the Mississippi riots, as realities external to their own. Arguing by analogy, Chauncey offers up the church and clergy in communist Russia and Nazi Germany as exemplars of an out-of-touch ministry whose vision only extended inward. Chauncey warns his listeners of the perennial "temptation to divorce love of God from love of neighbor." And his call, via question, is radically local: "what have we done together as a church—as this particular congregation set by God in this particular community—to be his instrument of reconciliation and healing among men?" The question also implies a temporal shift: that is, what will we do here in Danville to please God?

––––––––

The Worship God Wants

First Presbyterian Church, Danville, Kentucky
October 14, 1962

Apparently a religious revival was going on in ancient Israel at the time when Isaiah 58 was written. People were coming to church as never before. Every Lord's Day both priest and ushers took great pride in the fact that they had almost a "full house." The choir was the largest and finest it had ever been. The anthems were truly magnificent. The various programs of the church were running smoothly. Even the financial contributions, though not as large as they should be, were coming in pretty well.

It was a religious revival, all right. And everyone was pleased. Everyone, that is, except the Lord. In spite of all the evidence of interest in religion, in spite of all the services and meetings, in spite of all the prayers and praise—the Lord was not pleased at all. So he raised up for himself a prophet and told him to get the loudest public address system he could find (to lift up his voice "like a trumpet") and to declare to his people in the midst of their religious revival the living Word of God.

The living Word of God, spoken in that day under those circumstances, is what is recorded for us in Isaiah 58. It is a word of protest, a word of proclamation, and a word of promise. Let us attend to that threefold word.

The Word of God proclaimed to ancient Israel was, first of all, a word of protest. The God whom those people worshiped protested against their worship of him. He protested against their worship because these sincerely religious people had yielded to that perennial temptation of sincerely religious folk—the temptation to separate prayer from politics, communion from the common life, the service of God from the service of men. What had happened was this: In their enthusiasm about what was going on in the church, they had ignored what was going on in the world. In their concern for religious fasting, they had neglected their neighbor's need for food. In their zealous attention to God, they had completely disregarded their brothers. And the Word of God to them was, "I'll have none of it! Fasting like yours this day will not make your voice heard on high."

There is no evidence at all in our text that these people were deliberately trying to deceive the Almighty. Other people at other times apparently did try to fool God with their worship. But there is no note of this callous contempt of God in the word that is before us. For these people do not scorn God. They ask for his judgment. They do not worship as a duty. They worship as a delight. They do not ignore their Creator. They seek him every day. Yet the Lord through his prophet still protests! And he protests because although they do not attempt to deceive him, they have succeeded in deceiving themselves. They have come, honestly and sincerely, to believe that real religion is a matter of prayer and praise, church attendance and institutional activity; and for the sake of his own integrity and their ultimate salvation, God simply can't let this stand! So, in effect, God says to them:

"Listen, as much as I rejoice in your worship, your praise, and your prayers, I cannot accept them apart from your faithfulness in the life of society. My interest is not in religion, but in life. I am not the God of the church, but the God of the world. And service to me, divorced from service to your fellow man, is not real worship at all. Fasting like yours this day will not make your voice heard on high" (see Isaiah 58:2-4).

Such is the divine protest which the church needs to hear in every generation, for the temptation to which ancient Israel yielded—the temptation to divorce love of God from love of neighbor—is the perennial temptation of the people of God.

The church in Russia yielded to this temptation. On the very day in October 1917, when the communist party seized control of the revolution in Russia, some key leaders of the Orthodox Church gathered for a discussion. And do you know what they discussed? Proper liturgical dress for the clergy! The church was in the midst of a social revolution, and its main concern was what robes its ministers should wear in church.

The church in Nazi Germany yielded to this temptation. Hitler did not persecute the church at first because at first the church was not in his way. It played right into his hands, either by endorsing what he wanted to do or by ignoring him through a separation of "civil" affairs from "religious" affairs. The persecution of the church in Nazi Germany began only after a small minority of courageous Christians insisted that this compartmentalization of life was a lie.

Has not the church in our own nation quite unintentionally yielded to this same temptation? We are now living in the midst of the greatest social revolution our nation has known since the years of the Civil War. The bloody character of this revolution was tragically revealed two weeks ago tonight in Oxford, Mississippi, when two men were killed and seventy-five were wounded in the riot that followed the admission of James Meredith to the campus of Ole Miss. You and I were not there. We did not violently defy the court order. We did not hurl stones at the marshals. We did not yell obscenities at the man. We did nothing. We did nothing about the revolution at Ole Miss. We have done nothing about the revolution here. Nothing. We live in the midst of the greatest social revolution in a century. And as a church—as a congregation of the people of God in Danville, Kentucky—we have done nothing at all. Is not this—our failure as a church to do anything at all about securing the rights of every person in our community, regardless of his race—is not this failure a sin and transgression against which the Lord God Almighty, by his very nature as God, must protest?

We mean well. We are men and women of good will. There is not a person here this morning who rejoiced over the rioting in Mississippi or who takes pride in the shedding of blood. On the contrary, we are ashamed as Christians, as Americans, as those who love the South, over what happened there. But what have we done about it? What has First Church done—not in Oxford, Mississippi, but in Danville, Kentucky—to bring healing and reconciliation among men?

There are, I know, many individuals in this church who have a social conscience informed by our Lord Jesus Christ. These persons are ready and willing to accept criticism, economic loss, personal defeat, for the sake of God's Kingdom and his righteousness; and in the affairs of daily life they serve their Lord well. But what have we done together as a church—as this particular congregation set by God in this particular community—to be his instrument of reconciliation and healing among men?

God protested against the worship of the people of ancient Israel because despite their sincerity and good intentions they ignored the plight of the needy. What must he say today?

But we have in our text not only a word of *protest* but also a word of *proclamation*. God not only tells his people what is wrong. He also tells them what is right. He not only rejects the worship they offer but also specifies the worship he wants. God is a gracious God. He does not beat his people over the head with their sins, leaving them ignorant of his will for them. No, he clarifies for them in love and mercy just what he wants them to do.

> "Is not this the fast that I choose:
>   to loose the bonds of wickedness,
>   to undo the thongs of the yoke,
> to let the oppressed go free,
>   and to break every yoke?
> Is it not to share your bread with the hungry,
>   And bring the homeless poor into your house;
> When you see the naked, to cover him,
>   And not to turn your back on your fellow man?"
> (see Isaiah 58:6-7).

Now, there are many things in the Bible that I do not understand. I do not know how John the Baptist recognized Jesus. I do not know what to make of the demonic spirits that possessed ancient men. I do not know how to interpret some of the miracles of the Bible. Many parts of Paul's theology leave me confused. But this essential proclamation of the Lord is so clear that, try though I may, I cannot escape it. I can disregard it—and I do disregard it. I can disobey it—and I do disobey it. I can wish that it were not so—and I do wish, time and time again, that it were not so. But I cannot deny it or escape it; for I know, deep in my heart, that it is there, and that it is true and right. And in this essential proclamation God tells me that he has so identified himself with my neighbor that when I neglect or exploit or betray or turn my back on my neighbor, I am in that very same moment neglecting, exploiting, betraying, or turning my back on God.

Is not this word a call of God for us to *do* something as a congregation of his people? Is not this a divine demand that we take responsible action?

God knows the problem is difficult! But can't we do something? Can't we at least publicly declare that we know, and rejoice in the fact, that God intends for his church to be a house of prayer for *all* peoples? Can't we at least try to find some way in which we can come to know our Negro neighbors here in Danville, to learn from them what it means to be a second-class citizen in our town? Can't we at least protest against the most flagrant violations of human dignity in our midst?

As many of you know, I am chairman of the Council on Christian Action for our synod. There are three Negroes on the twelve-man council. Not long ago I wanted to have an overnight meeting of the council here in Danville. I called each of our three motels to see if I could get accommodations. I laid the request on thick! I told each person who I was, who the Negroes were (a college president, a Presbyterian minister, and the minister's wife), and what the meeting was all about. The manager of one motel said he would like to accommodate us, but was afraid to. If his were the only motel accommodating Negroes, he might lose business. The clerk at the second motel told me that, the owner being out of town, he could not make the decision. The manager of the third motel was insulted that I asked her to accommodate Negroes, but she could give me rooms for the eight whites!

> "Is not this the fast that I choose:
>> to loose the bonds of wickedness,
>> to undo the thongs of the yoke,
> to let the oppressed go free,
>> and to break every yoke?"

We have in this ancient Word of God to his people a *protest*, a *proclamation*, and, finally, a *promise* of the Lord.

> "If you take away from the midst of you the yoke,
>> the pointing of the finger, and speaking wickedness,
> if you pour yourself out for the hungry
>> and satisfy the desire of the afflicted,
> then shall your light rise in the darkness
>> and your gloom be as the noonday.
> And the LORD will guide you continually,
>> And satisfy your desire with good things . . .
> And your ancient ruins shall be rebuilt;
>> you shall raise up the foundations of many generations;
> you shall be called the repairer of the breach,
>> The restorer of streets to dwell in." (Isaiah 58:9-12).

Such is the promise of the Lord. This promise of God to the people who obey him is not a guarantee of peace and prosperity, of comfort and success. We need in all honesty to recognize that if we took our Lord's proclamation seriously and tried to be faithful, if we determined as a congregation to become a house of prayer for all peoples, if we obeyed our Lord's commandment to break every yoke, we would doubtlessly be criticized and abused, and our church might well suffer both numerical and financial loss.

But God does promise to those who obey him his presence in their midst, his light for their guidance, and his glory as their refuge and strength. If you obey him, "then you shall call, and the LORD will answer; you shall cry, and he will say, Here I am" (Isaiah 58:9). This is God's word of promise, and many a church in history, suffering from persecution for righteousness' sake, has found God to be as good as his word.

§71 James McBride Dabbs

James McBride Dabbs' biography appears in the introduction to his November 9, 1961 sermon in Atlanta, Georgia. In the following address to the Houston Council on Human Relations, Dabbs uses the events from just a month prior in Oxford, Mississippi to tell the anthro-historical tale of the South. The title of Dabbs's talk, "The Moving Finger," refers to the Rubaiyat of Omar Khayyam, which in turn, refers to the Old Testament prophet, Daniel. In the fifth chapter, King Belshazzar entertains on a grand scale. In drunken revelry, he orders his servants to bring in the gold and silver vessels taken from the Jewish temple in Jerusalem by his father, King Nebuchadnezzar. Upon drinking from the sacred vessels, "Suddenly the fingers of a man's hand emerged and began writing opposite the lampstand on the plaster of the wall of the king's palace, and the king saw the back of the hand that did the writing. Then the king's face grew pale, and his thoughts alarmed him; and his hip joints went slack, and his knees began knocking together." Dabbs does his best imitation of Daniel, interpreting the hand of God at work in Mississippi generally and Ole Miss specifically. King Belshazzar is slain on the night of Daniel's hermeneutic intervention. So, too, does Dabbs see an end to the profane ways of the old South.

————

The Moving Finger Writes in Mississippi
Houston Council on Human Relations, Houston, Texas
November 1, 1962

Houston being the cosmopolitan city it is—with its moon shot direction center putting it on the edge of the cosmos, indeed in the front yard of the moon—I don't know how many of you are born Texans. Perhaps it doesn't matter, Texas being a state of mind. Certainly I don't know how many of you remember the Puritans. Texas with its expansive air has come a long way from the constrictive Puritanism of early New England. I remember a phrase from Puritanism which some of you may have heard. It was called "improving the occasion." No matter how bad the occasion was, the Puritan felt you should improve it. That is, draw a lesson from it, especially if it was a bad occasion.

Well, as my title indicates, I should like to improve the occasion as regards Oxford, Mississippi. I think it isn't fair to talk about Oxford and the really tragic events that occurred there, unless you feel you can draw some meaning from it. Now, don't assume that because I took as my title the phrase, "The Moving Finger Writes in Mississippi," that I'm certain what the Moving Finger was writing in Mississippi. Doubtless you remember the source of the title: "The Rubaiyat of Omar Khayyam":

> The Moving Finger writes; and, having writ,
> Moves on, nor all our piety nor wit
> Shall lure it back to cancel half a line,
> Nor all our tears wash out a word of it.

But at least I'm going to guess what the happening in Mississippi means.

Two figures stand out in the Oxford affair: Governor Ross Barnett and student James Meredith. They stand over against each other. I suppose the meaning of the situation lies in the lives of both these men. Some Southerners—many of them perhaps—are inclined to emphasize Ross Barnett. Others—especially Negro Southerners—will emphasize James Meredith. I might as well say at the beginning that I think Governor Barnett represents a lost cause, and James Meredith a winning cause. In fact, there's some question as to whether Ross Barnett doesn't enjoy representing a lost cause. There's no doubt about it that over the years the lost cause of the Southern Confederacy has had an almost hypnotic effect upon white Southerners. A friend of mine once said, "you know what I learned in high school? I learned that the greatest days of the South were the heroic years from 1861 to `65 during which she was committing suicide." According to this, the most important image in Southern history is Pickett's glorious but ill-fated charge at Gettysburg. If you're going to fail, this is the way to do it. Failing thus, you will be remembered. And Governor Barnett may have, far in the back of his mind, the feeling that he too is engaged with Pickett at Gettysburg, and that his failure—which will come—will be a glorious one. Well, I wouldn't encourage him in this. He has failed, he will fail, but it doesn't seem to me very glorious.

What do we have represented at Oxford? In the first place, as many people have pointed out, we have evidence of the increasing concentration of federal power. There's no doubt about this. Little Rock showed it, and Oxford shows it. Usually the people who point this out, express tremendous concern, and suggest that this has happened recently, maybe since Kennedy got into office. Certainly, they say Kennedy's the worst one. Or they may go back beyond Eisenhower to Truman, beyond Truman to Roosevelt. Undoubtedly, the evidence of this concentration has become most clear in the last generation. But what about the Civil War?

It seems to me that the second thing that Oxford means is simply that the South lost the Civil War. Now, if you say, anybody ought to know that, yes, surely, anybody ought to know it, but very few white Southerners know it in their hearts. It may be different in Texas. Maybe the independent republic of Texas never lost a war. But I'm talking about the Deep South.

I think a good many white Southerners believe that story I saw posted over the cash register of a lunch counter somewhere in south Georgia. This was the true account of the close of the Civil War. Seems that Lee had concluded his heavy attack upon the Yankees at Gettysburg, where he really had shocked them and set them back on their heels. Now he'd retired to Virginia, somewhere down near Appomattox, and was getting his forces together again. He just about had his plans ready, and he intended—and he believed he had the power to do it—simply to roll up the Atlantic seaboard, moving north through Washington, Baltimore, Philadelphia, New York and EVEN Boston. Well, as he was putting the finishing touches to the plan, General Grant—I don't know how he got into the vicinity—stumbled into Lee's tent. You know how Grant dressed. Rough, like a private, may have had a star tucked away somewhere but it didn't show. Lee simply glanced up, saw a solider standing there, thought it was his orderly come to polish his sword, reached over on the table by his side, picked up his sword, and handed it to Grant. Grant, of course, thought that Lee was surrendering. And acknowledged it. Lee, looking up and seeing what he had done, but being a perfect gentleman, couldn't ask Grant to return the sword, so he surrendered, and the war was over.

Well, of course, that wouldn't end a war, and I think much of the white South has in its mind that kind of image, that the war never has been ended. Certainly, they talk that way. And they think that way. All this talk about the reserved powers of the Tenth Amendment. Of course, they were reserved, but a lot more of them were reserved before the Fourteenth Amendment got into the Constitution than after that amendment spelled out certain powers as belonging to the Federal Government. Since then the Tenth Amendment hasn't been what it used to be. But to hear Ross Barnett talk, this never happened. Of course, the Fourteenth Amendment was a direct result of the Civil War, but maybe the Civil War never happened. But the Fourteenth Amendment is there and the Tenth Amendment isn't what it used to be. It was the South, of course, which, challenging the power of the nation, so frightened and in the long run angered the nation, that, the war being over, almost inevitably the nation, using the military power it possessed, forced the Fourteenth Amendment into the Constitution. Maybe it wasn't legally or constitutionally adopted. Anybody who thinks he's going to change this after nearly a hundred years of water under the bridge is in my opinion sadly mistaken.

Another thing that Oxford means is that politics is still of tremendous importance in the South. The main theme of my talk is the over-emphasis, historically, upon politics in the South. Its recent importance can be seen by looking at what happened in Arkansas, Virginia, Louisiana, Georgia, Mississippi, and is about to happen in South Carolina. In each instance, the pattern is somewhat different. Is it different simply because the citizens of each state are different? To some degree, yes. But basically the pattern is different because the political power in each state is different, and is handled for different ends. And my assured guess is that no Governor of South Carolina, whoever he may be, will ever bring about in South Carolina, or permit to develop in South Carolina, the kind of situation which developed in Mississippi. Because South Carolina is South Carolina, and Mississippi is Mississippi. I haven't time to give you the background of the remark, but a friend of mine once described the difference between the two states as follows, "South Carolina fell into sin; Mississippi was conceived in sin."

In a region in which politics has always been of tremendous importance, the Negro now enters politics. You can see this in Oxford, Mississippi. The power behind James Meredith was in part politically motivated; it wasn't simply unbiased, formal, national power. It was power exercised by men who have a sense of what is going on in the country. They wouldn't be in the positions they're in unless they had some sense of what's going on in the country.

Why has the Negro entered the political arena? The first thing I would point out is, this is a somewhat delayed result of the Great Depression of the 1930's. The Great Depression created in Americans the determination that that kind of thing should not happen again if the country could prevent it. Also, because it made men aware of how many people were suffering, it also made them aware of underprivileged people. Among the underprivileged and discriminated against in America, the largest group is the Negro. Therefore, the humanitarian impulse set going by the 1930's included especially the Negro.

In the second place, the Negro has come to political power because of the movement of population, the tremendous outflow of Negroes from the South, beginning with World War I and running a mill-race during World War II and since, out of the countryside of the South, into the cities of the South, the East, the North, and the West. And because these incoming Negroes were pushed into ghettoes but were given at the same time—outside the South, that is—the right to vote, they have become political powers in the great cities of the East and the North, so great that they sway state elections and influence national elections. A part of this political power rests of course upon the economic power that Negroes have gained both in the North and in the South. It is very evident from "selective buying" movements that have occurred in the South that, even in the South, Negroes, if they desire it sufficiently, can hurt badly the pocket-books of white merchants.

Another thing that has brought the Negro to prominence in American life is the world situation: the challenge of Communism, and especially, the breakdown of colonialism and the rise of the colored peoples of the world. I don't need to emphasize this. It's clear that with news of these great movements in the daily press, with so many of them involving colored people, the Negro will make some kind of identification with these people around the world, and will receive strength here in America because of them. Indeed, the rise of the Negro in America indicates the breakdown of colonialism in the same way that the rise of the colored people of the world indicates the breakdown of colonialism.

Finally, one of the forces bringing the Negro into prominence is his education. Of course, the white South should have known that if you educate people, in America, you're finally going to give them an American education. The white South never intended that the Negro should read Patrick Henry's declaration, "Give me liberty of give me death," but like other American students the Negro did, and now he begins to demand liberty. Like Patrick Henry, political liberty. An increasing education, an increasing knowledge of what is going on in this country and in the world, has sharpened the Negro's mind and has sharpened his determination to have the same rights that other Americans have.

But the Negro's entrance upon the political scene is not merely the entrance of one more voter. It is the entrance of a voter with a particular historical background, and because of this background a distinctive voter. The Negro enters politics after a long experience of frustration, denial, and discrimination: through the centuries of slavery, through the three generations of segregation. During this long period, the Negro, being unable to argue effectively with men, that is, with the men in power, white men, being unable to quarrel with them—it was simply foolish—took his argument into his religion. He quarreled with God. Through the long years, he carried on with God the same kind of quarrel Job had. Job too had suffered, unjustly he thought, and he said, in effect, to the Lord, "Sit down here with me, face me, put the cards on the table, and tell me what the game's all about." The most striking evidence of the Negro's long quarrel with God is the spirituals, which sum up this quarrel. They tell of the hardships of life, the frustrations, the difficulties; they speak also of the hope that somehow

God will make all right in the end. For a long time, this was all the Negroes could do. But now, because of many circumstances, some of which I have just referred to, the Negro enters politics. Enters the quarrel with men. But he comes with a long quarrel with God behind him. He admits that life is hard, but he still has the religious convictions—I speak generally—that it has meaning, meaning for him now. He is going to use his political power to get more meaning into his life.

Indeed, strange as it sounds, the Negro is beginning to use John C. Calhoun's methods to attain ends which John C. Calhoun never dreamed of. This sounds shocking, for John C. Calhoun was the great leader of the conservative South, while today the Negro is taking a leading position in the liberal South. But consider for a minute the similarities. Calhoun was upholding the rights of a minority against the majority. His whole concern was to work out some scheme by which the Southern minority in the United States could hold its own against the Northern majority. For this purpose he offered the remedy of the concurrent majority, implemented the idea by nullification in South Carolina, and died a failure, his hopes overthrown by the hotheads who came to power after his death in 1850. For Calhoun was a great conservative, doing his best to save the Southern position within the Union, within the community of states. And though his doctrine in the hands of hotheads led to war, he had always sought, according to his biographer, Wiltse, "to direct Southern discontent into nonviolent channels."

And now today. Consider the best-known Negro leader in the South, Martin Luther King, Jr. He too, faced by a majority that uses the laws to hold the Negro minority down, but concerned to make real and hospitable to all, the communities of Montgomery, Atlanta, Albany, or whatever, leads his followers in civil non-violent disobedience. The purpose of this action is to force the white majority to pause, to consider, to confer before executing racially unjust laws or passing more such laws. In regard to Calhoun's hoped-for innovation of the concurrent majority, Scott Buchanan said recently, in a conversation with Joseph Lyford, "It seems to me that Calhoun was asking for the invention of an institution or a procedure that would formally admit civil disobedience, not only as a legitimate procedural step in government, but also as a pledge of a new faith in deliberation as the method of discovering political truth." Martin Luther King is inventing what Calhoun asked for, and with Calhoun's purpose of protecting a minority, but he speaks for a minority which in Calhoun's day had no political voice at all—although indeed its presence in the South affected almost every action and thought of the South.

But the Negro not only brings to American politics a new character, hardened in the fires of history, and a new concern for a group formerly unrepresented; it is possible that he also brings a notable temperament. I speak with some hesitancy, here, since anthropologists are not agreed as to the existence of racial temperament. But one of them, Herskovits, believes that the Negro possesses a striking combination of inner firmness and outer resilience. Of course, the American Negro may have learned from necessity this combination: to yield and not to yield. This, by the way, seems also a general Southern characteristic: to be pleasantly agreeable on the surface, and stubborn as a mule inside. As long as 1860, one of the leading sociological thinkers of the South, D. R. Hundley, said that the successful planter possessed outer resiliency and inner firmness. Perhaps he had to be that way in order successfully to work Negro labor. Perhaps Negro labor had to be that way in order successfully to "work" him. It is certainly evident to any dispassionate observer that each group has "worked" the other to a fare-you-well.

One other comment in this connection. Robert E. Lee has been practically worshipped in the South. A young Virginia lady remarked once, "We had heard of God; we have seen General Lee." This worship has been due in part to the fact that Lee has been the symbol of the Lost Cause. Perhaps it is also due to the fact that he was fitted to symbolize, not just the cause, but the people at their best. It is certainly true that Lee had all the outer suavity of the gentleman and all the inner strength of the soldier—and the Christian—or perhaps I should say, the stoic.

What all this may mean is that the Negro, now appearing on the political scene for the first time—Reconstruction was a sham—is perhaps as Southern as they come. We are beginning to say, "The Negro Southerner." The time may come when, referring to the Southerner, we may automatically include the Negro in the composite image. This is an outcome not to be feared but hoped for. If Southerners followed Lee to Appomattox because they trusted him—and some would have followed him to the mountains—it is hardly reasonable for their descendants to distrust that group which may show as a predominant characteristic the balance of traits that made Lee great.

The whole thing is highly ironic. Or, if you're religious, it may speak of the providence of God. Historically, the South never intended to produce this result: James Meredith, courageous and, what is more, modest—I mean that; read the statements he has made—representing the young Negro, suggesting by his situation the power the Negro may command in America today. Historically, the South never intended James Meredith. The South intended tobacco, and rice, and indigo, and sugar-cane and cotton—most of all cotton. "Cotton is king," said James Hammond of South Carolina, about 1860, and "the world bows before its throne." That was another ironic remark. But in order to produce cotton, the South had to be concerned with the Negro. As a matter of fact, the white South has spent a lot more time thinking about the Negro than about cotton even. How to control him, how to get along with him, how to make him happy. Remember we were Christians, and we wanted to make him happy in his place. Now, also as a matter of fact, the South never made much out of all its staples, including cotton. It's only since Texans have taken up cotton that it's amounted to much. We're buying cows back in South Carolina. If the South, therefore, couldn't succeed in producing the staple to which it set its mind, it's only fair that it should succeed in some of its efforts. To put as much thought and concern on the Negro as the white South has done and not have the Negro amount to something would be indeed disappointing. I think that James Meredith, and others like him, amount to a great deal. I am happy that the South is at last turning out a solid and valuable product. Of course, we don't know it yet. In fact, we'll hate to learn it. But we'll learn.

It shouldn't have taken legal, political, and even military power to get James Meredith into Ole Miss. Basically this is a human question, not a political football: the right of a citizen of Mississippi to attend the University of Mississippi. And Meredith is a citizen of Mississippi whether some people like it or not. In fact, and, most strangely, even in spirit. Born of the soil of Mississippi, son of a man who hewed his own farm out of forest, his heart is still bound to Mississippi. "If I ever leave Mississippi," he says, "I will be leaving the country."

But Southerners, as I said, have been prone to over-emphasize politics; and always there have been other Southerners who recognized this and cautioned against it, but with little effect. Here are several illustrations. I take them mainly from the history of South Carolina, but in its political emphasis South Carolina is highly Southern.

In the first quarter of the nineteenth century, Governor David Rogerson Williams, combating the political bitterness that was growing out of the tariff fight, urged the South to turn from its pre-occupation with cotton, build factories, and thus take advantage of the tariff. Suiting the deed to the word, he built a small clothing and hat factory, but to no avail. South Carolina was determined to remain agricultural and political. In a senatorial debate of 1837, according to Hesseltine and Smiley in *The South in American History*, Calhoun formulated a brief for the South. "Defying those who would industrialize the nation, Southerners thereafter took refuge in a doctrine of localism, and depended upon the constitution to protect their institutions from outside assault." Clement Eaton, in *Southern Civilization*, says "The neglect of social reform in the South was partly owing to the politicians' obsession with federal politics," and he quotes the South Carolina conservative leader B. F. Perry, in 1853, to the same effect: "What might not South Carolina now be if her Calhouns, Haynes, McDuffies, Hamiltons, and Prestons had devoted their great talents and energies to the commercial and internal improvements of the state, instead of frittering them away in political squabbles, which ended in nothing." On May 14, 1860, Thomas Ravenal made the following notation in his journal: "Our people do not reflect enough upon these things (for instance slavery in the territories) for themselves, but are led on by politicians, and made to think that safety, honor, self-respect and our very existence depend upon these issues." A present-day Southern historian, Ulrich B. Phillips, commenting upon the South today, said that we are again in the situation of a Southern writer of 1860, who declared that the region's problems were more than political, and not to be settled by the political wisdom of Webster, Calhoun, and Clay; but were social and industrial, raising such questions as these: "Is it just to hold the Negro in bondage? Is Negro slavery inimical to the rights of white men? Is it best for both the white and the black man?" Here and there men raised the questions, but the politically minded South did not pause to answer. By this time politics had become almost a religion, as the Alabamian Edgar Gardner Murphy realized in 1907. Speaking of antebellum beliefs about states rights, constitutional liberty, etc., Murphy said, "These faiths, however sacred to us, are today irrelevant. Slavery, secession, were ended at Appomattox." But as I said, a good many Southerners, in Mississippi certainly, apparently still figure that Lee gave his sword to Grant by mistake, and that therefore the war is still on.

Finally, as a humorous note, the University of South Carolina published in 1901 an alumni list entitled "Jewels of Carolina." This list included only generals, governors, congressmen, and senators.

If the South has over-emphasized politics, the question arises, Why? We can note briefly the main causes.

The first is the character of the people themselves. From the very beginning the Southerner tended to be a little different from the early New Englander. The New England settler was predominantly Puritan, with an intense interest in man's inner, private relationship with God. True, the Puritans set up a political state; but it was in the beginning a theocracy, controlled entirely by those who could prove they had had a religious experience. The Southern settlers, on the contrary, although strictly religious, were less inclined to be concerned about a man's inner life—they left that to God and the Episcopal Church—and more inclined to be concerned about his public appearance and his political action.

The second cause of the emphasis upon politics in the South was the existence of a landed aristocracy. An aristocracy must always be concerned about political power because of the privileged position it holds. This is especially true when the aristocracy is open, as it was in early America.

It was continually gaining—and losing—members from and to the lower classes. Especially in the increasingly democratic temper of America, an aristocracy was on the defensive.

The third, and perhaps the strongest cause of the Southern emphasis upon politics was the defensive position of the South in relation to the North. Virginia—together with South Carolina—had offered superb political leadership in the formation of the nation and during its early years. The South had seen New England threaten secession before and during the war of 1812. Yet, in sympathy with the difficulties of New England brought on by the embargo, the South was willing to aid the young industries there with a reasonable tariff. But when the tariff became as the South thought unreasonable, she fought against it politically, in South Carolina even to the point of nullification. And when to this economic pressure was added the moral pressure of abolitionism, the South threw all its weight into the political scales. It was an unhappy contest. It was a contest never really drawn in full debate but shoved, almost undiscussed, onto the battlefields of the Civil War. For when Calhoun claimed constitutional rights—which were clearly the South's—William Lloyd Garrison replied with moral invective—which certainly had a reasonable basis. It would have been well if the North had been more political, and the South had been more moral, or perhaps religious. But in thus following Jefferson, who believed that religion was a private affair and that man's destiny was encompassed in politics, the South stuck to politics until, as we have seen, it made its political slogans articles of faith.

But what happens then in defeat, in such an absolute defeat as befell the South in 1865? The religious faith of the South, if not destroyed by this defeat, was seriously damaged and warped. Really to prove this would demand that we understand exactly what the religious faith of the South had been, and we simply haven't time for that here. I can only suggest that the exclusive, individualistic, forward-looking Protestantism of the South offered a poor support for the inclusive, community-centered, backward-looking social order of—not the entire South—but the ruling South. It was perhaps because of this deep flaw in its religion that the South turned so energetically to politics, trying to cover up by its brilliant manipulation of means the fact that its ends were vague and divided. Unlike its Negro population, who, as we have seen, had to carry their frustrations to God, and like Job, quarrel with Him, the South—the white South—always had the Yankees and the Puritans to quarrel with, and always had a chance of winning, a good chance in the early years of the quarrel.

Men seldom take their troubles to God when they can lick the world without him. Even today, the white South, still over-concerned with politics, finds it hard to raise the more fundamental questions. The human questions. The religious implications of the fact that James Meredith, a citizen of Mississippi, in a great democratic country, has to call upon the power of that country to gain admission to his own state university. But who considers these implications? Not Ross Barnett. Why should Ross Barnett quarrel with the Lord when he's got the federal government to quarrel with twenty-four hours a day? But there's less and less percentage in a state's quarreling with the federal government. In fact, there's been no real percentage since 1865. But—Southerners have always seen gamblers—and usually have lost.

Let me say in passing that the South's refusal for one hundred years to accept the facts of life, her absorption in a mythical past of heroism and splendor, indicate what I've been saying: that the South never really understood itself, never found a religion that was deeply rooted in its culture.

But now comes James Meredith. Now the Negro appears in public, and therefore in Southern eyes, as I have pointed out, becomes a man; for a man is largely what he appears to be. Does he bring just one more vote to the polling place? In a democracy, even that would be significant, but the Negro Southerner brings more. The essential thing he brings is an understanding clearer than that of the white of the relation between politics and religion.Southerners are a great people for emphasizing the home, family, kinship, home-ties, at-homeness. From the beginning they easily made themselves at home in the New World because they were not too ill-at-ease in the Old: they were Englishmen living abroad. Apparently the Negro who, at urgent invitation, came to live among them, also has a remarkable tendency to make himself at home. He was often referred to as "our people," the white Southerner thereby saying much more than he knew, as perhaps the coming days will prove. But the Negro was permitted to be at home in the South in such a limited way—in such a sadly limited way—that he sought and in his spirit found an other worldly home beyond the River Jordan, which he longed to cross over into campground.

Perhaps we have no patience with this other-worldliness, this quality of at-homeness in a universe that offers no real home here. But when the Negro's cosmic at-homeness, through the passage of time and the concatenation of many circumstances, eventuates in the NAACP, the sit-ins and the voter registration drive, we sit up and take notice.

The white Southerner did remarkably well at making himself at home in this world—still does, easy-going, hospitable, offers a stranger pot-luck and—if he's a Texan—this is the myth—also gives him a Cadillac to go on his way in. But for all his local at-home-ness, the white Southerner is not, and has never really been, truly at home in the universe. Houston today is a cosmopolis, are Houstonians cosmopolitans?

It is the sense of this larger at-home-ness, induced in him by history itself, that gives to the Negro the calm assurance he has shown in the last few years; an assurance in marked contrast to the feverish efforts of the whites, from Klansmen to governors. The Negro, having settled his quarrel with God—of course, it's never settled. Let's say, then, having wrestled like Jacob with the angel through the long dark night, now sits calmly at lunch counters and conference tables, meeting the whites with steady democratic eyes. Except for a bitter few, who learned their lesson too well, they do not assert, as they might well do, black supremacy; they do the much more difficult thing of rising to a certain point and stopping, thereby indicating the kind of moderate, reserved people they are. Remember Lee. They assert democratic equality.

Aside from generalities, there is one specific thing the Negro brings into politics that is new in America life. This is the quality of his liberalism. That he is predominantly a liberal goes without saying. As an underdog he has to be either liberal or radical; and as I have just indicated—and as the Communists have found to their discomfiture—he is not a radical. But he is the one American liberal who has learned—not in a foreign country but here in America—what he is fighting against. He knows what feudalism is.

Louis Hartz wrote a book recently entitled *The Liberal Tradition in America*. He began it by a quotation from de Tocqueville: "Americans are born free." Speaking in the 1830's, de Tocqueville was referring only to whites. Hartz, developing this idea, points out that the American is born into a world where no feudal institutions have ever existed. He does not, therefore, have to overthrow them. In his Revolution, the American simply cut loose from overseas government and set up a similar government here. In Europe, on the contrary, eighteenth, and nineteenth century liberals had to fight long and bitterly against feudal oppression. This has given to the European liberal a stern, revolutionary quality the American liberal lacks. So far Hartz.

But now the American Negro is coming to power, fighting his way step by step against feudalistic oppressions. For the antebellum plantation South looked backward toward feudalism, attempted, however unsuccessfully, to adopt it, and, partly to prove the existence of what had such a flimsy hold, in its leisure time read Sir Walter Scott and ran tournaments in honor of "My Lady." We have quit running tournaments—we still do in South Carolina, occasionally. I have ridden in them—but in the countryside of the Deep South the Negro still belongs, in a way, to the peasantry. He is fighting against this. He is fighting his way out of feudalism toward democracy. Perhaps, more strictly, he is fighting his way out of colonialism toward democracy. He therefore knows what he is fighting against. Like the European liberal, he has to overthrow before he can build. He even has to break off the old, one-way, paternalistic communication before he can establish a two-way democratic communication. Also, like the early European liberal, he wants the government—the state governments—first of all to let him alone.

But—and in this he is like other American liberals today—he wants the national government to help out. I don't want to get into the conservative-liberal argument here. But what the liberal says is, the government, in the spirit of Hamilton, has always helped out the Big Boys, with tariffs, rebates, and bonuses; we should like some help too.

So the Negro is opposed to feudalistic state governments and in favor of a democratic national government. But the main point is, he knows through bitter experience what he is against. He was not born free. He has had to fight, he is having to fight, for his freedom.

This brings me to my last point. The American Negro is, in general, a part of the world-wide struggle, mostly by colored people, against colonialism. America did not need land for colonial exploitation. In the long run, it stole land so easily from the Indians it has never felt it stole it. I believe you folks did bring on a little tiff with Mexico over Texas. What we lacked was not land to exploit but people to exploit it. Therefore, while European nations were going to Africa—for instance—to obtain land for exploitation, we went there to obtain people. Nationally and internationally, then, the Negro in America occupies a position somewhat similar to that of the other colonialized and colored people of the world. His rise to power in America is a part of the breakdown of world-colonialism and the rise to power of the colored people of the world. His struggle for freedom matches in time and somewhat in nature theirs.

One of the basic problems of the United States today is how to speak to the new nations struggling out of colonialism into freedom. Who can understand them better, who will speak to them better than the American Negro, especially the Southern Negro, the conditions of whose life have most closely resembled theirs? Alone among American liberals, the Negro has had to fight for his freedom. He can understand, therefore, these freedom-fighters scattered around the world, can speak to them and can be understood by them. We have Ralph Bunche. There will be others like him.

Thus—to conclude—we have "improved the occasion" of Oxford, Mississippi, deciphering, I hope not too inaccurately, the Moving Finger, pointing out some of the meanings of that situation, stressing the positive meanings. They lead outwards, as we have seen, to the ends of the earth. If that is not enough for wide-skirted Texas, and Houston, perhaps these meanings also lead, through your own moon-shot direction center, to the moon itself, where, whenever men arrive there, they will have to live together, if they live, with resiliency and reserve.

§72 James McBride Dabbs

James McBride Dabbs's biography appears in the introduction to his November 9, 1961 sermon in Atlanta, Georgia. In this complex, theo-philosophico-historical exploration into the mind and heart of the South, James McBride Dabbs seeks to answer the question," What defines the South's love?" One key flaw is emotion. The South has always been too emotional. The "reins" have been "too slack." Accompanying that attitude has been an easy acceptance for the way things are—not the way they ought to be. Perhaps it was the climate. Perhaps it was the soil. But the South became an accepting people, all too willing to accept the American institution of slavery, only to be remade by it. Similarly, the "individual white of good will" sees his relationship with the individual black "as a personal relationship; seeing it thus, he sees himself as expressing the great Judaic-Christian tradition of the ultimate value of the person." The problem is that the relationship does not extend "to the public arena, where the Negro like any human being has to live, [therefore] he does not really value the Negro personally as he proudly feels he does." But what does the South love? It is easy to see the hatred, but if who we are is a function of what we love, the task of definition remains. Until the South cultivates a good mind in a good heart, its easy acceptance and emotionalism will lead to more hatred and death.

––––––––––

To Define Our Love

Presidential Address, annual meeting of the Southern Regional Council,
Atlanta, Georgia
November 20, 1962

Years ago, our oldest daughter, then a child of four, growing up in New York City, out of some deep well of wisdom made a little prayer: "O Lord, give us a good mind in our hearts." Though she was a long way from home, she voiced a peculiarly southern need: the need to know what we want. "What will you have?" quoth God. "Take it and pay for it." Mississippi is now paying for it. Does it really want it? Hasn't it paid too much for its whistle? Hasn't it really bought a tin horn? I'm not referring to the Governor.

Especially do we of the South need to define our love. To define it and to affirm it. We have stressed emotion; we are people of feeling, of sentiment; we are proud—and with some reason—of our ability to commit ourselves to a cause regardless of the cost, sometimes apparently unaware of the cost. During the terrible battle of Shiloh, in the spring of 1862, along one section of the line the Confederates advanced doggedly through a peach orchard where the bullet-clipt petals were floating down. "They went forward," says one commentator, "with their heads bowed as against a snow-storm." Outside of Homer, there's nothing better than this.

But what were they fighting for? Even a hundred years later we don't know. Certainly, the cause was far more mixed, far less pure than that pure image of the farm boys moving with bowed heads into the deadly snow. But what am I asking for? That we should not act until we find pure causes? Then we would never act. There are no pure causes. And, lest we become proud, no pure hearts. Except, perhaps, momentarily, fleetingly, when, as we have it on good authority, the pure in heart see God.

The danger of emotion is, it runs away with us; though, without it, we don't move. To speak in the almost forgotten language of my boyhood, without the horse the buggy doesn't leave the yard. But the horse may run away. The South still has a horse, a good horse in spite of Fords and Chevies. The South always had a horse. But we've always driven him with too slack a rein; and, upon one most disastrous occasion, he ran away, smashed the buggy and crippled the driver.

Let's leave the horse-and-buggy—it's too slow for this occasion—and take a jet plane, out of the Atlanta airport, back through American history. I doubt if any first-class historian would risk such a flight. But, then, I'm not a first-class historian, I've just failed on this year's cotton, and I don't give a hang!

From the jet's altitude, the main thing we see is the blue, enveloping air. The charm of the South was, very early, the relaxed easy nature of Southerners. Disaster overtook the South partly because this quality was over-indulged, and this disaster brought to many white Southerners a tautness and bitterness that now overlies or mixes uneasily with the early acceptance.

In fact—to telescope my argument so that we shall have a better chance of understanding what I'm rather vague about myself—the predominant mood of the South moved from a rather relaxed acceptance of life to a rather intense denial. This is, in part, simply the swing of the pendulum. However, the two extremes of the swing have a common characteristic: the emotional, unintellectual, blurred quality of the attitude. Whether our hearts have been right or wrong, we have trusted them too much, our minds too little.

Though the men who originally settled the South were as religious as those who settled New England—men were frankly religious then—they were religious in a different way. The Southern settlers were more in-clined to accept the world with its customs, to accept themselves as citi-zens of the world, and to leave traffic with another world and with God to an established church, the Episcopal. Of course, every man had also his own traffic with that other world, for these people were predominantly Protestants, but it was a purely private traffic, not of the highways at all, but only of the secret paths of the heart.

Moreover, these Southern settlers were encouraged in their relaxed, acceptive attitude by the climate and soil of the land they settled. It was in sharp contrast to the rocky soil and bitter climate the New Englanders faced. When the New England Puritan denied the world, he wasn't doing much. Seeing for months a snow-clad landscape, he might well turn away from the window and seek God in the private recesses of his mind. But the Southerner! Even the New Yorker Whitman hailed in living words the Virginia air:

> Again Virginia's summer sky, pellucid blue and silver,
> Again the forenoon purple of the hills,
> Again the deathless grass, so noiseless, soft, and green,
> Again the blood-red roses blooming.

In such an open, sunny land, really to believe in the utter wickedness of the human heart took more energy than most Southern settlers had brought with them, certainly more than they had left after they'd been burned by several Southern summers—not to mention debilitating fevers.

I'm not saying that these Southern settlers relaxed completely in this open, sunny land. They never have. You can find today in the South—but of course much water has run under the bridge—men who, for concentrated drive, match any American. Indeed, Riesman comments that if you find in the North a man whose eye is set steadfastly on the peaks, you are apt to find a man recently from the South, where men have been starved for success. It takes physical energy to conquer a frontier anywhere, and until recently much of the South has been frontier. I am only saying that the Virginians and the Carolinians were less concerned with the private, personal implications of the struggle than were the more puritan New Englanders. They raised fewer questions; they were more inclined to accept the whispered suggestions of the situation. In a sense, they were more poetic, less practical.

But, again, don't be misled. They were also hardheaded businessmen. In the 18th century, there were combined plantation and mercantile men in South Carolina, ship-owners, who traded on an equal footing with any Yankee; and, indeed, the host of Scotch-Irish, who poured across the piedmont of the South from 1717 to 1776, were called "the Yankees of the South." (I might say here that the Scotch-Irish confused the picture considerably, both hardening the mellowness of the Anglican South and softening the contours of Puritan and Presbyterian Ulster.) On the whole, Southerners tended to be an accepting people. Along with the insoluble mystery of life, they accepted the fact of their freedom in a new world, they accepted the good chances of life and made the most of them.

As for that great evil of the South, slavery, they accepted this not as Southerners but as Americans; as Americans also they extended and developed it because they thought it paid. But having really adopted the system, they became in a sense its creatures. Without slavery, the South would still have been a distinct region; but having adopted a "peculiar institution," Southerners became a peculiar people.

The presence of the slave relaxed the white South still further. Patrick Henry, reflecting of course the liberal spirit of the Revolution, admitted that slavery was wrong and that the wrong must be grappled with, but, alas, he said, we find it so comfortable. This is in part what Cotton Mather, the New England Puritan, had said: he thanked God for the *comfort* that the gift of a slave brought him. So the ideal of leisure, fostered by the Southern sun, grew. The Negro, impressed by the white man's leisure and having no interest in the white man's work, stole what leisure he could. As a result, the entire South was deeply influenced by this anti-puritan gospel of leisure. I don't recommend the Southern attitude; and I surely don't recommend the Northern. Wisdom lies between. The South, hell-bent now for production at any price, may be hellbent indeed. For in a way, we are the original Madison Avenue boys. Suave. We just never had Madison Avenue. Now we've got Peachtree. Won't be long now, we'll be selling shoes to the Yankees.

I distract myself from my theme. This is a Southern habit. Just as I have permitted myself to be distracted from my attempt to define our love, so historically the South permitted itself to be distracted by outside pressure and attack from its attempt to develop a culture. It was also distracted by inner conflict; by the fact that its citizens were also Americans, carrying within them many Yankee and Puritan traits. But it was, I think, not this inner conflict but the outer pressure that stamped the Southern character.

How did we oppose this pressure? Mainly by a public, political fight, which, partly because neither side spoke the language of the other, had to end in war. In focusing upon politics as a means of defense, we were expressing the frank, open, non-private, public sense of the early Southerner, the feeling that the important things take place in the open air; we were expressing Thomas Jefferson's belief that man's destiny is encompassed by politics; we were expressing the natural emphasis of an aristocracy, which, because of its privileged position, must always be ready to defend itself politically.

But what were we defending? Our peculiar institution, said the frank Calhoun. Our way of life, said others, meaning a plantation system using slave labor, like all plantation systems both an economic and a social complex. But this economic and social complex was anathema to the industrial and the puritan North; and the more Calhoun defended it on political grounds, the more the North attacked it on economic and especially on moral grounds.

(The South, by the way, still stands on the Constitution; the North on Morality with a capital M. They don't hear us any more than they heard Calhoun; and we—I don't mean us here—we don't hear them any more than Calhoun heard Garrison.)

How else could we have defended ourselves? How else can we defend ourselves? The answer is in both cases the same: by understanding who we are, and what, therefore, we must defend in order to save ourselves. Who we are is, most deeply, what we love, what we cherish, what in the final analysis we trust and must have in order to live. We need to define our love.

As I have already suggested, the South has been long on feeling, short on understanding. This is the nature of a conservative society. Such a society does not have to consider where it is going; to analyze, to plan; it has only to hold fast where it is. It needs loyalty, not understanding.

But the conservative society of the South had within it from the beginning strong seeds of progressivism, of drive toward the uncharted future. Furthermore, it had to the north a growing community whose emphasis was almost entirely upon the future; it was going there like an exile going home. I have never known just what it was looking for there. Indeed, it has never known. The early Puritans, so they said, came into the American wilderness to find God. In this natural wilderness they have constructed an urban, industrial wilderness; I think they haven't yet quite found God. Currently they—and, God save us, we—are looking for Him on the moon, which I understand is more wilderness than anything in our West. Maybe the wilder the wilderness the greater the chance of finding God. Maybe. Maybe not.

Well, I return from another diversion against the enemy. The South has always had such grand enemies, such clear and perceptible devils to fight against, it didn't need to ask what it was fighting for. But now, with the troops in Mississippi, it looks as if we'd better ask what we're fighting for. If we know this, we shall know more surely what we are against. I give you Walt Kelly's comment here. Surely the creator of Pogo should know what he's talking about. "There is no need to sally forth," he says, "for it remains true that those things that make us human are, curiously enough, always close at hand. Resolve, then, that on this very ground, with small flags waving and tinny blasts on tiny trumpets, we may meet the enemy, and not only may he be ours, he may be us."

Indeed, the Southerner's worst enemy is himself. More than this, it's his very goodness. This is what makes change so hard. The goodness of the South lies essentially in the temporal and physical ties men have established here. The ties to space and time. Here is an area of the earth's surface that its inhabitants generally have come to love. They tended to love it from the beginning, because it was a sunny land and they a frank and open people, accepting without question the gifts life put in their hands. They have come to love it more intensely because they—all of them—have suffered defeat here. This is recognized by white Southerners, who defended, and fruitlessly, these woods and fields against the invader. It is not generally recognized by Negro Southerners, but I think it will be. When, out of their confusion and occasionally their bitterness, there shall have been pressed, through time, the wine of wisdom, they may well recall with love the places where they learned it. Wisdom may arise from joy but more commonly it arises from sorrow; and those who have borne the burden and heat of the day may on a more fortunate morrow remember with a strange happiness the fields which by their labor they made truly their own. James Meredith's father cut his own farm out of Mississippi forest. "If I ever leave Mississippi," says James Meredith, "I will be leaving the country."

It's a good thing to love a place, to have roots there. It's a good thing to belong in time, to feel that today is important, not merely the future or the past. The trouble with the Southerner is that he has been rooted in time and place without being conscious of what this means, what goodness lies in it, and what danger. He has felt these attachments, has fought for them, and has felt them with increased intensity. But the ties of sentiment, unconsidered, tend to become the wrappings of sentimentality.

What the South has lacked has been poets. And philosophers. But first of all poets. I don't mean writers of verse. I mean men of imagination; poets in the largest sense. In the last generation they have come with a rush, Faulkner the best known and perhaps the greatest. But their trouble is, so much evil has grown up in the South, and has been so interwoven with the good, that they must employ dynamite, they must demolish before they can build.

Wordsworth said that poetry is emotion recollected in tranquility. The poet must be detached, by time or his own effort, from the experience. It is this detachment that permits the poetic creation to be a criticism of life: it presents life, you get the feel of life, but the scene appears in a "light that ever was on sea or land," the light of the poet's mind.

The Southerner felt he didn't need to think about life. Didn't need to contemplate it. He liked it, it was a good thing, that was enough. And so he not only committed himself to it, to his time and his place, he became all entangled in it. If he had thought about it sufficiently, he would have realized that there is past time and future time, and ceaseless change, and yet out of moving time there rise occasionally eternal moments. He would have realized also that a place is to be loved and a man's place in society is important, for all men seek a place, all men seek to belong; but, as St. Augustine suggested centuries ago, earthly place is finally significant because it implies something beyond earth: "Thou hast made us for thyself, and we are restless until we find rest (our place) in thee."

The South has needed more mind in its heart, a better understanding of its devotion. When we got around to being publicly religious, in the frontier revivals of the 19th century, we went in for emotionalism pure and simple. Even in our general life, we emphasized love, kindliness, courtesy. Our stress upon manners is a stress upon good will. For manners serve not only as a protective device for an elite group, like the aristocracy or the military, but more fundamentally as the earnest of good will. Like the open hand in greeting, they say, "I expect to get along with you." At the very opening of any meeting, they indicate that the people involved intend some friendliness for each other.

But what is this friendliness the South has intended? What is this kindliness, this love? We don't think about it. We don't define it in the sense of separating it in our thought from the things about it, into which it moves imperceptibly, taking another color as it moves; nor do we define it in the sense of placing it in the total picture. This second form of definition may be called affirmation; we do not affirm it.

As a consequence, the white's so-called love for the Negro turns into hatred, or at least lack of concern for this Negro as the member of a race. Because this "love" is little concerned for the Negro in the world, it does not flower in justice; and the fact that it bears no fruit of justice proves it is not real love but a mere sentimental wish. The individual white—the individual white of good will—sees his relationship with the individual Negro as a personal relationship; seeing it thus, he sees himself as expressing the great Judaic-Christian tradition of the ultimate value of the person; but because he does not extend this concern to the public arena, where the Negro like any human being has to live, he does not really value the Negro personally as he proudly feels he does. Failing to define his love, he lets it drift away through a miasma of indifference into a stagnant pool of dislike.

As for our failure to affirm our love, our lack here is perhaps even more serious. There are two main ways to live: you may deny the world, condemn it as evil, and retreat to the desert; the trouble is, you're still alive and the evil of the world is still with you. This is the way of the ascetic. In modified form, this is the way of your typical modern man, who is an acolyte of business; I refer to the devoted organization man—or woman. The other way is to accept the world. This has been mainly the way of the South. If you deny the world in modern fashion, you will reduce its rich complexities to abstractions, the use of which will permit you to control, even to enslave the world, in the long run unintentionally enslaving yourself. Thoreau remarked a hundred years ago, "The division of labor is finally the division of the laborer." If you accept the world, you will be less inclined to reduce it to abstractions since you have a strong liking for it just as it is. One of the distinctive marks of the recent generation of Southern writers is their emphasis upon the concrete. Related to this is Robert Penn Warren's remark that Southerners fear abstractions.

But what we haven't realized is this: if it takes a good mind to get away from the world, either to sit abstracted upon the tower of St. Simon Stylites, or, more importantly, to sit, also abstracted, in the control towers of Wall Street or Madison Avenue, it takes an even better mind to stick with the world and not be swallowed by it. The South tried to stick with the world; it seemed pleasant and harmless; the South has been nearly swallowed by it. "It is not enough," said Nietzsche, "to accept fate; you must love it." Substitute *life* for *fate*. The South was too acceptive. Too easygoing. Too relaxed. Not taut enough. In the true sense, not passionate enough. Either you flee from the evils of the world or you passionately affirm the excellence of the world. The classic illustration is Dante, who affirmed his love for Beatrice until he had seated her near the throne of God; the single rose had become, in the words of Yeats, "the rose of the world." Of course, Dante was one individual, and a genius; even Italy could not follow him. But, if I mistake not, his is the ideal for a people like ourselves. We feel that life itself is good. Then, by God, and in God, we'd better affirm it.

We have not done so; we have not followed our own original light. Accepting life too easily, without sufficient understanding and determination, we have come, across a tragic century, into an intense rejection of what we do not like: the outside, the threatening world. It's always easy to see, in stark outline, however falsely, what you hate. It's hard to see what you love. For hatred separates you from the hated object; while love unites subject and object and blurs the outlines. Hate as separative is symbolized by death. The dead hands lie folded within themselves, cut off from the world, meaningless. The living hands caress the object of their love.

It's easy to hate. Hard to love. Love demands not only the good heart—which, after all, no one has—but also the good mind in the heart. Love demands the student. And this may be the basic significance of the student movement in the South today. I saw these young people in Chapel Hill last year in the process of desegregating a movie theatre. They were thoughtful, they were cautious, they moved prudently. Why? Because they desired an integrated theatre set in a true community, where men worked together because they were in basic agreement. They weren't fighting simply for justice; in a sense they weren't even fighting. They had a good mind in their hearts. They were defining their love for the community of Chapel Hill. They were also, but incidentally, knocking into a cocked hat Charles Kingsley's injunction. "Be good, sweet maid, and let who will be clever."

They had to be clever in order to be good. They had a good mind in their hearts.

Which is what I still lack. For I have not only spoken about the South's failure to define its love, I have also illustrated that failure: every time I made a sally against the Yankees—and the Puritans—I did so because it was easier to attack them than it was to define myself—and the South. I didn't plan it this way. It just happened that way. I call it to your attention in order to assure you that, whatever you may have heard in the last half-hour, you have at least heard a Southerner.

§73 Marion King

On Monday, July 23, 1962 Marion King, with her two children, drove from her home in Albany, Georgia to the Mitchell County Jail in nearby Camilla. Her maid's daughter was incarcerated there following mass arrests during a protest march two days earlier. She had brought food for the daughter and fellow incarcerated protestors. While standing and singing freedom songs outside near a chain link fence, King did not move back fast enough for the sheriff and his deputy. As the sheriff slapped her hard across the face, sending her three-year old daughter Abena flying to the pavement, the deputy kicked her in the shins, knocking her to the ground, whereupon he kicked her several more times as she lay on the ground. Marion King was six months pregnant at the time of the assault. She later miscarried the child. Charges were never pressed.

Typically it was Marion King's husband, Slater, a real estate broker and civil rights activist, who delivered the speeches. But during the Thanksgiving holiday of 1962, the Student Nonviolent Coordinating Committee (SNCC) invited Ms. King to speak, recounting the Albany protests as well as the death of her unborn child. While praising SNCC for starting what would become the Albany movement, particularly Charles Sherrod and Cordell Reagon, King briefly contextualizes the loss of her child. While not privy to any "divine revelation," she nonetheless claims that her spiritual strength had grown. And while she saw "pure, unadulterated hatred of the two persons who attacked me," she also sees a God at work among some white southerners.

Reflections on the Death of a Child

Student Nonviolent Coordinating Committee Meeting, Nashville, Tennessee
November 1962

My husband has said that he cannot always buy non-violence and that had he been present when the incident occurred at Camilla, he would have had to die trying to protect me. But let me say that we have both learned many lessons in non-violence during the past year, and we are still learning.

As I stand here now and look into your faces I feel that we are attending a homecoming, for I see so many people whom we have had the pleasure of having in our home at some time or other during the last critical year in Albany. And I know the names of others of you who have visited in our home, although we didn't know you were there at the time, because we were in jail and you were out, and later you were in and we were out, and we didn't have the chance to meet!

I would like to take this opportunity to thank you of the Nonviolent Coordinating Committee for what your coming to Albany has meant to us, and for what it will mean to the world. You may feel discouraged because things are not happening as fast as you thought they would, because you think you don't see any change in a place where they are still excluding Negroes from the dignity, opportunity and liberties of life in Albany, and where Negro citizens are still put in jail for peacefully petitioning for redress of our grievances, for asking for a share in our government and public places and for walking in orderly non-violent demonstration on our wide streets.

But I would thank you young people of SNCC for starting something that will not die and that cannot be stopped. You have given my children something that cannot be taken away from them. Even my little three-year-old knows many of the Freedom songs we have sung in Albany and that you have sung here tonight—word for word. Many, many other children have seen the struggle for freedom in the marches on the streets of Albany. Thousands of children have seen pictures of it on television and have heard about it on the radio. And they will not forget. This vision cannot be taken from them and I know that the fight you have started will go on and on.

There has been more publicity for the Peace Corps, but let me re-emphasize a statement of Bill Weatherby, correspondent for the *Manchester Guardian*: you are the real Peace Corps, the unsung heroes who will be the salvation of America.

So, may I say that I am happy that Charles Sherrod and Cordell Reagon of SNCC saw fit to come down to the "bushes" of Albany, 170 miles southwest of Atlanta, to help us start this movement, this struggle, this vision and this faith in freedom that will not die and cannot be stopped.

As to the loss in our family, I cannot say that I have received any "divine revelation" out of the whole ordeal. There are a few things, though, that stand out in my mind and feelings.

First, I cannot forget the pure, unadulterated hatred of the two persons who attacked me and my children. I say they attacked my children because I was holding one child in my arms and had the others right there with me. I really feel that in the eyes of those policemen we were much lower than human beings, not to mention fellow men. I have asked myself and my

God "why" a few thousand times. It would be easy to give a ready-made answer, such as that they are products of an evil system which has brutalized them, and that we must forgive them and get rid of the system. But I cannot be completely satisfied with this, and I wonder again and again what is the matter with the white people of Albany.

Second, I have been amazed at the strength that has come pouring into me from some source outside myself. Despite the many days and the sleepless nights of labor, even when I knew for sure that the baby would not make it, I felt literally physically strong. I could hoe a few rows in my yard in the bright autumn sunshine and I gradually grew spiritually stronger, too.

Third, the love which we now share with our little children seems newer and stronger than ever and compensates more than enough for any loss that we might have sustained. It is probably natural that we should be more dear to each other.

So, even though we don't understand why the incident happened or all of its implications, and even though I have had some moments of real despair, I do feel that there is some master plan, some purpose for it all. I have had more moments of real hope than of despair. I see in some white Southerners of just and generous spirit "Signs of the coming of the Lord," and I know that "His truth is marching on."

1963

1963

§74 Reverend J. Claude Evans

Rev. J. Claude Evans was born on February 5, 1917 and grew up in Anderson, South Carolina. He graduated in 1937 from Wofford College and received his B.D. from Duke University in 1940. As a seminarian, he preached in the colored ward of Duke University Hospital. The experience impressed on him the tremendous potential of the African American church. He was especially impressed by how actively the congregation participates in shaping the sermon. Like many civil rights era ministers, Reverend Evans served in World War II, but his chronology is fairly unique. Because of his prophetic prescience, he experienced the intransigence of the south prior to his World War II service.

In July 1942, while an associate pastor at Washington Street First United Methodist Church in Columbia, South Carolina, he gave a sermon on racial justice while the senior minister was on vacation. The senior minister, J. Owen Smith, was a Yale graduate who would soon be a Methodist bishop. Smith saw the sermon in advance and saw nothing wrong with it. Immediately upon delivering the sermon, a prominent church member told Evans angrily that the 25-year-old minister had ruined his career. Reverend Smith was called back from vacation early, and Evans had to face a hostile board of stewards. By a vote of 87 to 3, the board voted to ban Evans from the pulpit. The three members to support him were Carlisle Roberts, a former Rhodes Scholar and attorney; H. B. Trull, an Efird's department store franchise owner; and A. L. Humphries, a hardware wholesaler. The following excerpt from Reverend Evans's unpublished memoir allows us a look inside his mind as he faced the hostile board in 1942:

"I was there Tuesday night, shaking in my shoes. . . . Member after member spoke. 'This pulpit has been desecrated.' 'Bishop Capers (buried beneath the pulpit) has been dishonored.' Etc. etc. The pastor defended me on the basis of my youth and inexperience. I tried to explain the intuitive origin of the sermon. . . . The Board voted 87–3 that I should be barred from the pulpit 'until Conference.'" Ironically, the board allowed Evans to continue his ministry with youth for the duration of his time at Washington Street. Many of those young people participated actively in the civil rights movement in the 1950s and 1960s.

Evans next served three churches in rural McCormick County (SC), where they were so grateful to have a young minister, they said he could say anything he thought. After two years in McCormick, he served as an army chaplain in the South Pacific during World War II. Returning to civilian life took him to Walhalla and Clemson, South Carolina. He then served as editor to the South Carolina Methodist Advocate from 1952 to 1957. From 1957 to 1979 he was the chaplain at Southern Methodist University. Upon his retirement he was active in family counseling and is still a member of the South Carolina Methodist Conference. In 1994

Washington Street United Methodist Church invited him to return to the pulpit and he accepted the invitation.

The sermon took place during his tenure at Southern Methodist University. Early in the sermon, he dismantles traditional arguments about scriptural support for slavery. Towards the middle of the sermon he catalogs historically grounded interpretations of Scriptures that support integration. He ends the sermon with a concrete ethic of pragmatism for people who are not yet persuaded: think what you think, but be a decent person as the new world emerges.

The Christian Faith and Race

Southern Methodist University, Dallas, Texas
February 1963

Lillian Smith, southern-born author of *Strange Fruit, Killers of the Dream* and *The Journey*, was asked about her interest in racial justice in the South. She replied by telling this story out of her childhood.

A new colored family moved into her town with its adopted white-skinned child named Janie. Janie's presence disturbed the white community. "They must have kidnapped her," said one of the ladies in Mrs. Smith's book club. The clubwomen investigated, and finally the town marshal took the child from her adopted family and moved her into Lillian Smith's home. Janie shared Lillian's room, clothes, and toys, and a bond of love soon grew between them. But one day a telephone message came from an orphanage and after hurried conversations all around, Lillian was told that Janie would have to leave. "Why is she leaving?" asked Lillian. "Because," Mother said gently, "Janie is a little colored girl. . . . You have always known that white and colored people do not live together."

Thirty years later the memory of this experience gave Lillian Smith a motivation for open opposition to segregation. She did not come to this position by sociological study, or by philosophical thought, or by an abstract study of the Bible. She came to it through concrete, real life events in her own experience which radically changed her understanding of the meaning of life. One of the reasons the race problem has been so troublesome to us is that we have approached it abstractly rather than concretely. We have made up our minds as to proper principles of race relations and then sought to make life conform to these principles. So the slaveholding South went to the Bible and found proof texts for slavery, the cursing of Ham's son in Genesis, whose sons were to be slaves and presumably black. It did not bother many to discover that it was not God who cursed Ham's son, but his grandfather Noah with a hangover. One abstraction can always twist another abstraction into line when the compulsion is strong enough. And today, segregationists are again quoting the Bible to support one abstraction, the theory of segregation, by another abstraction, Scripture quoted and interpreted out of context.

Actually, the Bible says little or nothing about race as race. But it has much to say about human life under God and human relationships under obedience to God in concrete ways, which have more concrete meaning and application to the race problem than a thousand abstractions.

The Bible views all human relationships, including race relationships, through creation. The Old Testament traced the origin of man back to a common origin in two creation stories in Genesis with Adam and Eve as the figurative prototypes of all men. Liston Pope tells of a rabbi who was asked why God created only two people in Genesis. He replied, "So that nobody could say, 'I come from better stock than you do.'" In the concrete event of creation, God created man "in his own image" and placed him on earth to live responsibly in obedience to his Creator. Man, therefore, has a sanctity, not in himself, but in the source of his being—God. Old Testament man is every man with every man called to be obedient to God as creature to Creator.

The New Testament view of creation illuminates what is implicit in the Old Testament. Paul, preaching in Athens, before a crowd of many nationalities, perhaps conscious of the prejudices and hostility felt by many, faced up to the problem in his sermon. Present before him were Jews and Samaritans. The Jew hated the Samaritan, and the Samaritan hated the Jew. Also present were Greeks and Romans. The Greek despised the Roman as a pretender of culture, while the Roman looked at the Greek with a personal sense of intellectual inferiority for which he compensated by arrogant military aggression and domination. Of course, these are not examples of modern race prejudice, which is a phenomenon of the last two centuries, but they are examples of problems in human relations, close kin to modern race problems. It was to this crowd, with these kinds of divisive emotions present, that Paul said: "And he made from one every nation of men to live on all the face of the earth."

But this God was now known as the God who revealed himself as *agape* love in Jesus Christ. The Creator God is the God and the Father of our Lord Jesus Christ. So man is concretely created for concrete obedience to the God who is love. This means that every man of every race and nation was created by God for purposes of existence-in-community, of love-in-being. The application can be seen in the Parable of the Good Samaritan. What should be the proper relationship between people that would exemplify neighbor love? Who is my neighbor? The Parable of the Good Samaritan gives the answer: Any man in concrete need that crosses your path.

But, just how do you love your neighbor? The answer is easy. You love your neighbor as you love yourself. Whatever right of creation you demand for yourself, you must demand for everybody else. Politically, this means that every man from creation has political rights. If creation has placed you concretely in a democratic frame of government and given you the vote, then concrete love of neighbor demands that this right be given your neighbor also. If creation has placed you in a capitalistic economy, then neighbor love demands that the right of equality of opportunity be sought for every man. You cannot understand the race problem apart from the Christian view of creation.

The Bible views all human relationships, including race relations, from the viewpoint of human sinfulness. And, again, the Bible is very concrete. In Genesis 3, sin is not an abstraction but a concrete act of disobedience. Adam and Eve were forbidden to eat of the fruit of the tree of life, but they ate it anyhow. And when God appeared in the Garden they hid from him, revealing by their actions that they were already hearing in their consciences what they were to hear from the mouth of God: "What is this that thou hast done?"

It is sin that separates us from God and from our fellow man. It is the real, concrete leap of self-centeredness in each one of us that violates God's intention for us. It is true that the Bible knows little about race in the modern sense of the word, but it knows about the sinful separation of man into prideful groups of superior versus inferior. You cannot understand the radical act of Jesus in sitting down and talking to the woman at the well in Samaria until you recognize that he was violating at least three customs of his society. First, he talked to a woman as an equal, on the subject of theology too. Second, she was a bad woman at that, and Jesus knew it. Third, she was a Samaritan and he was a Jew. And proper Jews didn't sit and talk in public with women, and especially bad women, nor with Samaritans, and especially Samaritan women! So the Bible may not know much about race segregation as such, but it knows plenty about religious, nationalistic, sexual and other forms of separation rooting in man's self-centered rebellion against God.

It is sin, too, that explains the racial conflicts in the South and in the world today. And much of the confusion lies in our refusal to face the concrete reality of the meaning of slavery. While the southerner, with the help of New England slave traders, wrenched the Negro from his African culture, which was concrete enough, he plunged the slave into a new and abstract world of caste, of superior white versus inferior slave. The agriculture of the South with its hunger for cheap labor obliged the southerners, who were also Christians, to turn slavery into an abstraction. Man is driven, say the psychologists, to give what seem to him to be rational answers for his irrational acts. So began the long history of the emotional defense of slavery. The emotions of the South soon became the logic of the South.

James McBride Dabbs describes the growth of slavery in the South as "an actual situation eventuating in a theory." Thus it was that slavery produced its own rationalizations just as did the sin of Adam and Eve. Out of the caste differences in slavery between the whites and the Negroes came the superior-inferior divisions of segregation and the patterns of white supremacy which haunt us today. You cannot understand the race problem apart from the Christian view of human sinfulness. Just as sin separated our first parents from God and produced the first direct aggression of the one person upon another, so it is sin as slavery, as obligatory segregation, as white supremacy, that evidences our aggression against one another today.

The Bible views all human relationships, including race relations, from the perspective of the life and death and resurrection of Jesus Christ, which is a concrete way of describing what we mean abstractly by the Incarnation and Atonement.

In Christ Jesus there is no such thing as race. His life and death and resurrection are for all men of faith, regardless of race, or class, or nationality, or sex. We are all one in him. Every man is loved of God in Jesus Christ. This is the place that belongs to every man regardless of human differences. This is the guarantee of the Incarnation and the Atonement. We belong to God, who loves us despite our sins, and who wants to be related as Father to son to every man.

But we deny this with our rigid placing of men into segregated areas of life. This is the falsity behind the view that a Negro has "his place," with the unspoken assumption that the white man has his place too, which, of course, is a place of privilege and superiority. Dr. Dabbs, himself a southerner, helps us here: "Apparently there is something attached to every Negro which is not attached to every white man; the idea of place. . . . We like him in his place. We like him for staying in his place. The liking is a bonus for staying there. We don't have to give the white man any bonus for staying in his place, the place itself is the bonus. The Negro's place, being unattractive, has to carry a bonus with it. Consequently, white people like or dislike other white people for purely individual and personal reasons. With one exception: if a white man, for some fool reason, gets out of his place—fails, that is, to keep the Negro at the proper distance, in the place he belongs in, where he can be liked—we bestow upon him our deepest dislike. We like any Negro, then, just so long as he remains in the inferior position to which he has been assigned, as actual or potential servant. We do not like him as a man; indeed, we seldom see the solid, living man beneath the abstraction servant."

So from the love of God in Christ we know there is no such thing as an abstract Negro, or an abstract white, whom God loves. There is only the concrete Negro, the concrete white, the concrete person of any race or class or nation or sex whom God loves and whom we should love. And this is the only place of selfhood for any person in community.

The Bible views all human relationships, including race relations, from the perspective of the church and the coming kingdom of God. It was out of the life and death and resurrection of Jesus Christ there came a new community composed of every nation and race. At Pentecost, which is usually thought of as the beginning of the New Israel, the Church, fifteen nations are reported to have been present and involved. And the only requirement of membership is to be found in the words of Peter's sermon: "And it shall be that whoever calls upon the name of the Lord shall be saved" (Acts 2:21).

This new community paid no attention to race. Paul was commissioned by a group of Christians at Antioch which included a black man, presumably a Negro. Peter's experience with the centurion in the Roman army led him to declare to the officer: "You yourselves know how unlawful it is for a Jew to associate with or to visit any one of another nation; but God has shown me that I should not call any man common or unclean" (Acts 10:28). And the Parable of the Last Judgment describes the King judging membership in the kingdom on the basis of whether or not the hungry were fed, the naked clothed, the prisoners and the sick visited, the stranger welcomed, and the thirsty given drink. The judgment is made simply on the basis: "as you did it to one of the least of these my brethren, you did it to me" (Matt. 25:40). So in the church, the beloved community—which in its life of loving and being loved, forgiving and being forgiven, experiences the kingdom by foretaste and looks to its ultimate fulfillment beyond death and history—there ". . . cannot be Greek and Jew, circumcised, barbarian, Scythian, slave, free man, but Christ is all, and in all. . . . And above all these put on love, which binds everything together in perfect harmony" (Col. 3:11, 14).

Admittedly, this inclusiveness of the church poses a problem for Protestants. Our theology of the church has come to be that of a congenial club or a fellowship of middle class friends. The Protestant Reformation with its emphasis on individualism has obscured for many a modern doctrine of the church as a community.

Dr. John Deschner of the Perkins School of Theology warns that we latter-day Christians and the members of the church should pay close attention to this early church inclusiveness. For we are not charter members of the Christian faith. We were once outsiders "separated from Christ, alienated from the commonwealth of Israel, and strangers to the covenants of promise, having no hope and without God in the world" (Eph. 2:12-13). But God's love in Christ, in a sheer act of grace, broke down the walls and grafted the wild shoots of the Gentiles into the New Israel. So we are not to set ourselves off from others in the church, but become the servants of others in our obedience to Christ.

What does this mean? Says Dr. Deschner:

"It means that a local congregation is not an association of those Christians who happen to like each other, and who can therefore set their own exclusive rules for admission. When that happens, the congregation has not simply omitted a moral implication of the Gospel; it has allowed a fundamental question to arise as to whether it belongs to the Church of Jesus Christ. It is no good trying to solve the race question by asking where people 'feel at home.' The Church is not our club; it is God's holy instrument, in which we have been permitted a place—but a place which has room only for God's task, and no room for our conditions and preferences. He created this people. He set its task: to bear witness to the good news of reconciliation. He set the essential rule: that not only this People's word but its very existence should shine like a light in the world (Matt. 5:14 ff)."

You cannot understand the race problem apart from a Christian view of the church and the kingdom of God!

Where does this leave us specifically and concretely? Where will these concrete biblical insights lead a modern Christian?

The Bible warns us that it is easy to be a Christian in the abstract. It is easy to solve the race question in propositional form. But this is not the call of God. It is not the purpose of the Christian faith merely to hold defensible views on this or that question of theology. Rather it is the purpose of the Christian faith to bring men into a relationship of faith and obedience to God concretely. This puts the race question right back where it came from—in the concrete events of our lives. This is where we shall be judged whether or not we were obedient to God's will in our neighbor, some of whom will be members of other races, "even these least."

Surprisingly, some people will be found obedient whose abstract views may be highly irrational. I have a friend, a farmer in South Carolina, who is a "states righter" of the first order. He believes the Supreme Court usurped legislative functions in its 1954 decision outlawing legal segregation in the United States. He belongs to one of the citizens' councils in his area organized to oppose integration in any form in the public schools. He is literate, educated, and a little on the "egghead" side. We have had many long arguments on these issues, always ending in disagreement. One day I asked him, "Tom, what are you going to do the day a Negro walks into your church some Sunday during morning worship and takes a seat by you?" Tom hesitated a moment and then said, "I'd offer him a hymn book." I hope the day will come when this will happen to Tom. And in one concrete act of obedience all his abstractions on race will collapse.

For, mind you, this abstract Negro coming into our churches, our schools, our colleges, our downtown lunchrooms has become a concrete person. Will you, and I am talking to the concrete "you," you sitting right there, will you be ready to "offer him a hymn book" of acceptance and let all your abstract theories of race collapse in one act of obedience? If you do, a miracle will take place. For you will find that you have not simply accepted a person of another race. In reality, the "really real" reality of the life of faith, you will have "offered a hymn book" to Christ Himself.

§75 Reverend James A. Pike

Reverend James A. Pike's biography appears in the introduction to his April 30, 1957 speech in Detroit, Michigan. In this closing speech to a church and race relations conference, Pike employs his acerbic wit to excoriate the church, its parishioners, and those who would wait for hearts to change. Pike diagnoses two confusions that plague the church: first, reconciliation cannot and should not precede law. "First JUSTICE . . . then Reconciliation . . . we should act and then pick up the pieces. That is Christianity. Not a soft kind of love that does not face the calling of justice." The second confusion is the inability to change people's hearts by legislating. That's fine, says Pike. Don't bother then. But do go ahead and "change their external conformity, [to law] which is what gives the rights and protection to others." Let God do the judging for it is "his clear light that sees evil and hate, and bias." By changing the laws, this also forces a role switch: "as long as the law is on the side of evil then the reformers and all are way out . . . they're radicals . . . they're rocking the boat." So changing laws will force changes of perception. Pike closes with more ironic blasts at the church in its reluctance to act, as he thanks God for the "atheists and unbelievers who are doing the work of God when the pious folk just won't do it, because they are afraid something might happen to their property values."

Speech at a Church and Race Relations Conference

Grace Cathedral, San Francisco, California

May 5, 1963

The Church has been in a very ambiguous relationship to an important aspect of social change with which we are all familiar in all parts of the country—the matter of the provision of equal rights for all persons regardless of their color or ethnic origin.

On a recent trip to Houston I was sitting by a gentleman who asked me what I was going to do there and I told him that I was going to speak out at the parish day school of St. John the Divine. He said "Oh that's fine. We're developing wonderful new schools, fast. We'll continue to, of course . . . as long as they continue to push that integration business on us they'll continue to spread. You know we can always count on the Church!"

I'm afraid that's about the truth too. I was on that plane sitting by an emergency exit. I almost opened it and left right then, very embarrassed I even had a collar on. I know this is not malicious on the part of the Church. I know only one, or possibly two clergy who are demonically in league with the forces of the devil on this. I know of no bishops who for a moment do not want the fulfillment of the doctrine of this Church as implemented by resolution at every level of the Church on this subject, but what does confuse us? Why is the Church not in the fray in the lobbying for social change in communities where there is housing discrimination, for example? I am chairman for California of the U.S. Civil Rights Commission and have held hearings throughout this state under the Federal Government on this very matter, and I can tell you that there is a very segregated situation here. San Diego is more segregated than Atlanta on housing, and San Francisco has nothing to brag about. Why are not our Church people like a mighty army ready to rip limb from limb any legislator that does not do what is the will of God, what is the will of our Constitution, the will of our government? Why? Why is it we still have segregated schools and hospitals in the Church itself? Why are we not the strongest social force in the Church itself, in Alabama, with all these troubles, to make right what is wrong, to provide the freedom that must be provided, and is being demanded, sometimes incautiously, perhaps, and sometimes rebelliously . . . but representing a genuine upsurge of the desire for the rights of American citizens? Why are we not there?

I have come to the conviction that our embarrassing weakness and flabbiness—letting our Lord down—are twofold. There is confusion about two things. And it is very good that this is LAW day. For we have to think of the relationship of law to redemption; law and grace; of outward conformity and the hearts and motivation of men. I don't think that the actual practicing church has thought this through very well and I'm not sure we thought it through very well in the various resolutions we have adopted; some of which I have gone right along with without having thought this through myself.

I think there are two great "bugaboos."

The first is that the role of the Church is Reconciliation. . . . We are to be the ones who in situations like this keep love and peace and smoothness. We are to help heal the wounds of those who are irritated that they have to sit down by a negro. We have to make them feel better about it. Make the negro feel better about the fact that his children can't go to a decent school for ten more years . . . that's our task "reconciliation." This is utter bunk.

JUSTICE COMES BEFORE MERCY, LAW BEFORE GRACE . . . WE HAVE NO RIGHT TO TALK ABOUT RECONCILIATION UNTIL THE THING IS DONE.

The law is a schoolmaster to bring us unto Christ, said Paul. Until you confront yourself with the evil and wretchedness of a situation and change it, you have no right to say let's leave the evil ferment and keep everybody kind, and happy and charitable. Our first task is NOW to do all we can do . . . immediately and politically to bring into equality all the sons of God. If some people are bruised by that then let them take that up with God or come to us for pastoral counsel. We have lots of ministers willing to talk to bruised people. . . . Because the rights are there whether people like it or not, whether they are hurt by it or not. . . . Look at those who have the rights who have been injured all this time. Even northerners are gullible about this line. "That the South does not want such and such, or Alabama does not want such and such." Who is Alabama? They mean White Alabama, they don't mean all of Alabama. Let's give them their rights now and if other people don't adjust, well that's on their conscience. God will judge them. And, by the way, not necessarily send them to hell either. Because he knows the many roadblocks that have been built-in by the flabbiness and weakness of a Church that has often supported this evil system in the Name of Jesus Christ . . . God knows that the Church has deceived people, that the Church has compromised, that the Church has lulled people into a sense of making black into white . . . so God isn't going to send these people to hell. Let justice work for those who have a right to it and let God take care of the rest. Then let the Church be the instrument of reconciliation, and interpretation and understanding. Let the Church also be concerned with the adjustment of minority groups who when given rights can act badly and flaunt it in a way that is hurtful to others—or who can be difficult. . . . But let's get on with it . . . and we have no right to wait even for a day. The collect for today makes this clear:

> "Almighty God who showest to them who are in error the light of thy truth to the intent that they may return to the way of righteousness, grant that ALL those who are admitted into the fellowship of Christ's religion may AVOID those things that are contrary to their profession and follow all such good things as are agreeable to our profession."

What's our profession? We profess Jesus Christ with whom there is neither Jew nor Greek nor bond nor free nor slave . . . and our actions and our inactivity is contrary to our profession. What does profession mean? I analyzed that carefully in a little book of mine that has just come out this week, which represents the Rosenthal lectures at the Northwestern Law School last winter. Profession means what you hold yourself forth to be. We hold ourselves forth to be Christians, and it is contrary to that holding forth for us to put up with for one day evil and injustice contrary to the clear manifest will of God and contrary to the law of our land and the spirit of our

Constitution and institutions. First JUSTICE . . . then Reconciliation . . . we should act and then pick up the pieces. That is Christianity. Not a soft kind of love that does not face the calling of justice.

THE SECOND CONFUSION that has taken in Church and Church people: YOU CANNOT BY LAW CHANGE THE HEARTS OF PEOPLE.

That's the cliché. You cannot by legislation change morals. You cannot by the law change hearts. There are two answers to that.

The first answer to this is: THEN YOU DON'T CHANGE THEIR HEARTS! . . . You change their external conformity, which is what gives the rights and protection to others. The problem of their hearts and minds is something God will judge with his clear light that sees evil and hate, and bias. All right, we DON'T change their hearts . . . we get the thing done. That's the first answer.

I might be very resentful of the police that I can't drive ninety or a hundred miles an hour when I am in a hurry to get to a confirmation visitation. But when he comes up with that ticket, he could not care less about the state of my heart, even if I practically have a heart attack on seeing him. There's the ticket! Conformity because other people's lives are at stake. If I hate him—all right—he's used to that! He's been given indoctrination in that in his training school. He's a guy that's going to be hated by a lot of people. . . . "But there's the ticket Bud!" Go on hating him and let God judge that evil in you. So we don't change the hearts of people . . . we give them their rights. You love or you perish as Smiley Blanton has pointed out. . . . But that's not the final word, but that's what Christianity must say FIRST or everything else becomes sentimental twaddle or consciously devised rationalization. Surely we want the hearts of people changed. We're in that business very much. And a change in the law does indeed tend to change the interior motivations and intentions of people. Here's what it does. And here I rely quite a bit on a secularist, strangely enough and I give him more space in my book than I give some Christian writers. "The children of darkness are wiser in their generation than the children of the light." Our Lord reminded us.

Once you have changed what the legal situation is, what the external structure is, you have changed the labels (in terms of Westerns you have seen on T.V.) as to who are the bad guys and who are the good guys. You see, as long as the law is on the side of evil then the reformers and all are way out . . . they're radicals . . . they're rocking the boat. But when you change the legal situation then those who are trying to protect the existing mores become the bad guys. They're on the defensive, and people do become accustomed to that which the law has brought about.

Take for example fair housing laws. When people become accustomed to living with persons on the same street and community, going to the same church and schools with those who happen to be of another color, the time comes when they judge people as individuals and not by color. That does not mean they are going to like everybody who happens to be of another color. One of the tragedies of this transition is that we can't tell any of those good jokes any more. . . . There are some awfully good Jewish and negro jokes. But in this period of sensitivity now it looks like you have some kind of race prejudice. I want the time to come when we can tell these things and laugh about them and tell that there isn't any race prejudice, but that the flavor that comes out of a particular background or dialect adds to the delight of our response. And also you know every negro now has to be described as a good guy—a fine, fine man. I'll be glad when the day comes when I'll be able to say of a negro person: "I cannot stand John Jones!" When that day comes we'll be very close to the millennium. The only thing needed more is that I am thus enough redeemed that I can find something good in him as a person, of course. But I would like to have the time come when we are so much taking people on their merits that we can expect a negro to have as much right to be disliked as anyone else!

These things ARE conformed by the external social structure. Here in this chart, it is pointed out that where the notion of the good seems excessively abstract the good in law can provide projection by virtue of drama. The very fact that it is the law gives it a liturgical flavor. It projects that abstract good so we can see it vividly.

Where the notion of good seems excessively vague, the good in law can provide precision.

Where the notion of good seems excessively neutral or irresolute the good in law can supply intervention and decisiveness.

Where the notion of the good seems excessively utopian the good in law can supply responsibility.

The trouble with our lofty statements, even at a conference like this, is that in the end there is no vehicle for direct responsibility. The law sets the framework for that. In that context we can act and say: "Here we go, let's clean it up. They DID do it; get them arrested." Then talk to them in jail about the state of their souls. We've got chaplains for that . . . who can work with these people who defy both the law of God and man.

"The law is a schoolmaster to bring us to Christ . . . when that faith comes you no longer need the law."

It will always be the shame of the Christian Church in this country that we DID need the law. This was Christian country all along in the sense that we had a lot of people who could have been politically active and effective in their personal lives in getting things done without the need of any secular forces. . . . We could have changed everything ourselves. Our principles are perfectly clear. And we didn't do it . . . and secular forces put it over. . . . Thank God for the atheists and unbelievers who are doing the work of God when the pious folk just won't do it, because they are afraid something might happen to their property values. Those who are supposedly committed to the Eternal Kingdom of God! . . . They will be among those, who at the Great Assize, as is pointed out in the Gospel, will be addressed by our Lord: "Come here at my right hand . . . you did these things; took care of the oppressed . . . the least of your brethren."

It will always be to our shame that it was too little and too late on our part. For those, who in the Church have fought the battle, taken a position, spoken up, acted often to their hurt; all praise and thanksgiving. But we have been confused; our witness has been blurred. The salt has lost its savor by and large, except for certain specialized movements like ESCRU and works of such conferences, because of a genuine or feigned confusion. First that our task is reconciliation, and second that you can't by law change people's hearts. . . .

I may sound [like] I have no love and charity for those who act in a segregated way. I do. I am called to have Christian love and concern for the spirit and make-up of every man. But when a man has broken into my house, I am not at that moment thinking of my role as pastoral reconciliation. I would do all I could to stop him . . . and then talk about the state of his heart and soul. This is the time order . . . for the LAW IS A SCHOOLMASTER TO BRING US TO CHRIST THAT WE MIGHT BE JUSTIFIED BUT AFTER THAT FAITH HAS COME WE NO LONGER NEED A SCHOOLMASTER. . . .

§76 Edler Garnet Hawkins

Reverend Edler Garnet Hawkins's biography appears in the introduction to his October 1960 sermon in Bronx, New York. Hawkins delivered the following eloquent appeal to his fellow Presbyterians at their 175th general assembly. Ostensibly a report of the Standing Committee on Christian Education, Hawkins's message throughout is inspired by James Baldwin's "God gave Noah the rainbow sign; no more water the fire next time." That is, without resources and concerted, planned action, "terror in the heart of our whole world" will continue to reign. And without such action, the Black Muslims and other leaders skeptical of the church's commitment will be right: "the church is only a place for hypocritical jargon that makes a travesty of the temple." Yet Hawkins remains sanguine. With a church "on the firing line of racial activism," the "kingdoms of this world," can be made to resemble "the kingdom of God."

This Is the Mood and This Is the Time

175th General Assembly, Report of the Standing Committee on Christian
Education, Des Moines, Iowa
May 20, 1963

Through the kindness of the general secretary of our Board of Christian
Education, and with the encouragement of our Stated Clerk, and as a part
of the report of this Board, which bears a major share of the work of our
church in the area of race, I have been asked to try and say some of the
things that are upon the hearts of many of us as we face the concern of race
in our church and our society.

Let me say at the very beginning what I can only do at the end—express
the prayerful hope that our church will consider a serious involvement in
this critical area of race relations, beyond anything we have ever done, an
involvement that will capture the spirit and meaning as well as the opportunity of this present period through which we are passing.

When I say present period, I have no intention of centering on
Birmingham, ugly as it is, and filled, as it is, with the tremendous possibility of arousing passions and indeed some immediate action that might
ease the ugly situation. To play up Birmingham unduly would be to miss
the point. The dogs and the hoses and the brutality of local police did but
one thing for a large segment of white America, a segment that might still
secretly hope that the Negro not press quite so hard, but that knows now
that the Bull Connor and all who support him are wrong, and can't win,
and that the Negroes are right—however hard they press. Birmingham
has helped to excite the moral indicator as to who was right and who was
wrong, but apart from what it has done for white America, Birmingham is
only a manifestation of a deeper mood, and the deeper mood is the thing
to which the church must respond. It must understand, though, what it is.

There are a number of facets to this deeper mood, but several are very
clear and definite. One is that the Negro has accepted primary responsibility in his push for freedom rather than delegating it to others, however
friendly or liberal, for neither of these attributes in the lives of others will
be the occasion of his freedom apart from his own involvement.

Secondly, the Negro is saying now what he has for so long withheld,
even though it hurts some of his best friends and saying it with an honesty
and integrity that was not characteristic of an earlier period when he just
did not say what he really felt, even to his friends.

And thirdly, because of the inevitability of the issue, the Negro is staking
almost his life in it, as he realizes, even without admitting or sometimes even

not caring about its deep religious implications, that a freedom that is so necessary is also a freedom for which he must suffer, and perhaps even die.

This is no use of dramatic words for effect, for no words can be as dramatic as the reality of the mood that the Negro is not only expressing, but acting out in a period when no cause is more urgent, not only for him but for the very survival of our culture. However one may differ with some of the nuances of James Baldwin's thought, he is eminently right, as with an artist's heart he uses the language of Scripture, after he has so thoroughly rejected its institution, to predict the catastrophe we all face if we cannot match with understanding and courage the demands of our time. "God gave Noah the rainbow sign; no more water the fire next time."

And the interesting thing is that neither Baldwin nor the Negro personality will be the one, necessarily, who will light the torch that will destroy us. It will rather be lit by those who do not comprehend the nature of our times nor the course of history, but who in their bitter prejudice will destroy everything in the American dream rather than give up an unmerited privileged position in a society that must relate brother to brother in simple and equal human relationships.

This is the mood, and no one understands the real nature of the Negro protest unless he acknowledges that the Negro is right as he articulates his basic requirements for freedom and equality now and not later.

Those who counsel "wait" and "later" only confirm the words of the great jurist who said, "A justice too long delayed is a justice denied." Freedom is so precious that no one who has achieved his own freedom has the right to set a delayed time-table for another man's freedom. The Negro sees breaches in the dike, a gleam of light at the end of the long, dark tunnel in which his life has been lived, and as he sees that glimpse of light, you've got to understand his impatience as he rushes towards the full light at the end of the tunnel.

And when a Birmingham is selected as the testing ground for what he knows to be right, it does not mean that Birmingham is the only personification of evil and the only place at which the struggle is joined. The evil is in many other places, as our retiring moderator said so well . . . North, East, West, as well as South. As a matter of fact, one of the most vivid descriptions of the very heart of the problem was one I read about, a Morgan Park, up North, where the inhumanities of a man against his black brother start. I wish I could remember all the things that described this Morgan Park—"the other side of the tracks of human dignity . . . an ink-blot of black poverty that breeds ever greater crimes in the filthy cradle of the gutter. A black shantytown up North, where the whites look down their noses and shut their ears to the blues crying up and down the middle of this one way street of misery." This was the black Babylon into which kids were born who became the victims of a society that scorned then and turned them down.

Hundreds of black ghettoes are all over this country. If we can win at Birmingham, it will help those who are thousands of miles away to break out of these ink-blots of black poverty—not just the poverty of being poor in things, but a worse poverty, a poverty of spirit of those who no longer have hope that they can be a part of the American dream. But what the people of Birmingham are saying to these kinds of kids everywhere, even if they say it from jail, is: "You are part of the American dream—or will be—and nothing can stop you. Indeed the dream will not be fulfilled without you."

Having said that, leadership within the race recognizes that the structure of society that has inflicted the kind of injustices that the Negro community has endured does not have the ability to adjust to eliminate these abuses immediately. That's why, really, in terms of demands, the demands of the Negro community are minimum ones, but the one issue that the Negro will not give up on is the conviction that the course of history is on his side, and that he is morally right in pressing for these demands.

I might add that the one thing that the present political administration has not done, nor the one before it, is to act as if the moral imperatives of race are more important and basic than any other considerations of carefully-timed announcements, or troop deployment, for to see this would have required a more forthright [reckoning] with the racists before the periods of intense crisis.

It is in response to this mood that the church has no alternative, really. Our hope is that our church will see it and lift both our policy and our practice to new levels of human dignity that will involve all God's children. Many of us in the Negro community who also stand in the life of the church are under constant pressure to forsake our faith and admit that it is no longer relevant to this fight for freedom. Many are saying quite moderately that the church has failed, and the issue will be joined outside the church and despite the church. Others, the Muslims, go many steps further and say that the church is only a place for hypocritical jargon that makes a travesty of the temple, concerned only about how a people in power can keep in servitude its slaves.

Some of us are not asking the church to fight this battle, within the racial structure, for us. We know that the church has not risen up to this present moment, but we hope we can help people see the difference between an institution that has lacked the courage of its true witness and a great faith that sits in judgment upon the institution and still calls upon it to discover the courage that is the real measure of its faith. For the church to do this—and this is our hope—it must go behind every pronouncement on race it has ever made and put the whole machinery of the church to work on it.

We must go beyond everything we have done in Church and Society, and make it, really, the conscience of the church rather than something into which we syphon our resolutions with neither the money nor the staff to get them up off paper. This is the time to express the hope that you, as a General Assembly, will follow the present leading of the Holy Spirit, as it is represented in our Boards, and put sufficient resources to work as the symbol of the church's intent to provide real leadership in the challenge of Religion and Race.

I do not know all the machinery by which the church grinds out its witnesses, but I would speak with pleading for this aspect of the report of our Board of Christian Education, with which the other boards concur, as we behave as one church. The action gives high visibility to the concerns of race, as a sign of the church's integrity and intent, as, in the rather common phrase, it "puts its money where its mouth is."

I can think of innumerable ways in which this action would put our church out on the firing line, involved in conversation as well as in works in the areas where our witness will count. This and other reports will spell it out in far better ways than I can for all those areas in the world in relation to race where our obedience is required. Let me add just a few things that are equally as pressing, which the church must do within its fellowship and do it as fast as it can.

It must look with great care to its own house—its homes for the aged, its hospitals, its schools, all of the institutions that bear the name of the church—and it must make clear its conscience and its practice in these matters. And if it continues to talk about an integrated church, it must look carefully at what it is talking about. It cannot continue to be a truly integrated church that moves in one direction only, without ever, or rarely ever, providing the opportunities for a Negro to lead an integrated fellowship except when we know it will be but for a while. And when we talk about an integrated school, here again, the image of minority members on school faculties, as a challenge and stimulation to minority youth everywhere, must not be left out as an important responsibility of the whole task of education. And if we embark upon a capital funds program that builds across the country, every single church that builds can look at its own house. It does not have to wait for a state FEPC to operate, but can see to it that written into every contract is a clause that speaks to the integrity of the church at the level of equal employment opportunities.

I could go on, but these are indicated in the report, which expresses the many ways in which, as a church, we respond to this present mood and work at the tasks, however difficult they may be, of making the kingdoms of this world something like the Kingdom of God in the crucial concerns of race.

My own faith is that all that we would suffer in this regard will be woven into a final plan that shall give us no regrets at all, even as those who have suffered have felt themselves to be in the hands of one who is utterly good. His purposes may be delayed by evil men but will not be defeated. All of their dreams will come true, even the American dream, for the cause of which some are in jail today.

Let me close in this wise. Dr. William Edward Burghardt Dubois is 95 years old, and spends his last years away from the country from which he has become estranged. He had been hurt, and he is reacting to that hurt. But even away, in a posture that many of us could not take, he gives us a vivid and indeed classic way to describe something not unlike our times. It was in 1906—almost 60 years ago—that he was a member of the faculty of Atlanta University. That was the year in which the mobs of Atlanta took over control of the city. Negroes in that city were assaulted and killed by the hundreds. Dr. Dubois was riding into Atlanta on a Jim Crow train during the height of the riot, and he wrote his "Litany of Atlanta," one verse of which goes like this:

> "Listen to us Thy children;
> Our faces dark with doubt; are made a
>   mockery in Thy sanctuary.
> With uplifted hands we front Thy heaven,
>   O God.
> Crying, we beseech Thee to Hear us, Good Lord.
> Surely, Thou too are not White, Lord,
> A pale, bloodless, heartless thing.
> But whisper, speak, call, Great God.
> For Thy silence is White Terror to our
>   hearts."

What the mood of the Negro is saying now—almost sixty years after his terror, and as it happens again in Birmingham, New York, Chicago, or any place—is that for the church not to speak and not to act—leaves a silence that is terror to the hearts of those of us who being Negroes were yet born into the life of the church, and will die in it, and, one hopes we could add, die for it.

If it means agonizing to find the money to speak and to act and to enlist the staff to serve, if it means bringing the church to the place where it accepts whatever cross it is called upon to bear, so let it be. It may be that the only way we can keep from striking terror in the heart of our whole world is to become what we really ought to be—a church that enters the world where its obedience is, and does it even if it has to do it in terms of its suffering. And if we are ever able to sing "We have overcome," it will only be because as a church we are willing to act, speak, and maybe suffer in the areas of race in the certain knowledge that in the fulfillment of the American dream for all people we have rendered our obedience to God in this our day.

For the church so to speak, so to act, and so to suffer is to believe that in the personal relationships of love and brotherhood and justice, we touch not only what ought to be, but even more, what is the deepest truth about the God of Jesus Christ, from whom we have said nothing can separate us—neither principalities nor powers, height nor depth, nor any other creature—for this is the very ground of our faith.

We submit this report for your prayerful consideration in the hope that if it meets your acceptance, we shall inch some steps further towards that love that died for us and in which we are kept.

§77 Reverend Wyatt Tee Walker

Reverend Wyatt Tee Walker was a nationally and internationally influential champion of civil rights. Walker was born on August 9, 1932 in Brockton, Massachusetts. After completing primary and secondary schooling in New Jersey, he attended Virginia Union University, where he earned a bachelor's degree in 1950. He later completed a doctorate from Rochester Theological Center. One of Reverend Walker's most notable characteristics was his gift for music. As a composer of sacred music, his appreciation spread to researching the historic implications of music in the African American church and as an exhibiting artist he developed the name "Harlem's Renaissance Man." Walker traveled widely, studying at the University of Ife in Nigeria and the University of Ghana. These visits gave fuel to Walker's campaign throughout the civil rights movement.

Reverend Walker achieved great acclaim in his career as a pastor, theologian, cultural historian, and prominent civil rights leader. Walker and Martin Luther King became intimate allies and partners in the battle against segregation in 1960. Replacing Ella Baker, Dr. King quickly positioned Walker in Atlanta as the Southern Christian Leadership Conference's first full-time executive director in 1960. The organization grew into a national power under his leadership. Reverend Wyatt Tee Walker also served as the president of the local chapter of the NAACP and state director of the Congress for Racial Equality. Walker did not satisfy himself with national achievements. In 1978 Walker organized the International Freedom Mobilization to bring attention to the atrocities of apartheid in South Africa. Walker's beliefs in equality and tolerance were felt in the public arena and also from his pulpit at the Canaan Baptist Church of Christ in Harlem New York, where he remained senior pastor from 1967 until 1991.

Walker's fame grew in no small measure to his work organizing Birmingham's Project C (confrontation) in the winter and spring of 1963. Created largely for the express purpose of focusing the nation's eyes on racial violence in the south,

Walker and the SCLC leadership targeted Birmingham for two main reasons: Reverend Fred Shuttlesworth had already organized many in the city; and, his arch-nemesis, Theophilus Eugene "Bull" Connor had a short fuse. Pushed to confrontation, Connor, the SCLC predicted, would snap. And so he did. In choreographing SCLC's strategy and tactics in Birmingham, Walker wasn't without his critics. The Student Nonviolent Coordinating Committee's (SNCC) Executive Secretary, Jim Forman, witnessed Walker's elation at police brutality: "They said over and over again, 'We've got a movement. We've got a movement. We had some police brutality. They brought out the dogs. They brought out the dogs. We've got a movement!' It was a disgusting moment for me."

In this, one of his first speeches after the successes of Birmingham, Walker addresses a sympathetic San Francisco audience. In the 33-minute address, Walker tells the story of Birmingham, from laying the initial groundwork to the final negotiations. He contextualizes Birmingham as a "leavening process," one that began in 1955 with the Montgomery bus boycott, gathered momentum with the student sit-ins and the freedom rides, continued on despite the ups and downs of Albany, and reached its apotheosis in Birmingham. With the movement's successes there, the practice of nonviolent protest, Walker claims, had achieved full maturity. Not surprisingly, that nonviolence is "religiously oriented," and Walker details for his listeners the "cosmic companionship" that typified so many of the events in Birmingham.

————

Broadcast on KPFA, Los Angeles May 28, 1963
San Francisco, California
May 1963

To the president of this nation, let them know that you felt a sense of involvement with them. You have suddenly been very patient and it has been a kind of a grueling two days for me here on the West Coast. There have been just a couple of moments when I wished I was back in Birmingham and only working 20 hours a day.

Birmingham, Alabama in many ways is symptomatic of what's wrong all over this country. And it is but by the grace of God that Birmingham, Alabama has not happened to San Francisco, California because many of the problems that we face in an overt and blatant way in the South in many ways are present here in subtle and covert forms, and it is only right and proper that you have a concern about us. But I am sure I am just repeating what you already know when I say you can't be free here in the bay area until we are free down in Birmingham, Alabama.

It is unfortunate that most of the inside story of Birmingham is never told in the wire reports, nor in the news report squibs that appear on the television shows such as Walter Cronkite and Chad Huntley and David Brinkley. But I would like to share with you perhaps some little tidbits of what made Birmingham, Alabama perhaps [sic] one of the most heroic and unusual civil rights stories perhaps in the history of the nonviolent movement.

I suppose many of you wondered, as others have wondered, why was it that we picked Birmingham. Birmingham has been known to us in the civil rights movement in the South and very literally as the Johannesburg of America. We have said many times it was the last stop before you got to the union of South Africa. When you review the tragic history of Birmingham, Alabama it is but a catalog of man's inhumanity to man.

In the last 24 months, there have been 22 bombings, none of which has ever been solved by the police authorities there. It is not an uncommon occurrence for a Negro woman to be accosted after dark in her automobile by police officers and taken off to some secluded spot, criminally assaulted, and then under the threat of death, her lips sealed so that she would never say anything about what happened. The Intercitizens Committee of Birmingham has a record during the last year of 56 documented cases of police brutality. Within the last several months it was still possible for a Negro to be maimed or killed in Birmingham, Alabama without anything ever happening to the people who were responsible for it. It is in a very real sense the last stop before Johannesburg, South Africa.

We wouldn't want you to think that Birmingham just happened as some spontaneous sociological phenomena that occurred in the spring of 1963, but for more than a year the executive committee and the administrative staff of the Southern Christian Leadership Conference has been concerning themselves with what could be done about Birmingham, Alabama because it was the bastion of segregation in the deep South. Mississippi and Louisiana and Alabama and South Carolina remain as the four hard core states. And of all of these perhaps, as far as cities are concerned, Birmingham, Alabama is the worst of the lot. And so we felt that there ought to be a confrontation in Birmingham with the Negro demands for self respect and human dignity, for the rights of peaceful protestors guaranteed under the 1st and 14th Amendments.

And yet when we finally decided in late summer that Birmingham would be our next target city we knew full well and had resigned ourselves to the fact that some of us would never come out of Birmingham alive. And I assure you with all sincerity that it is by the grace of God that Bernard Lee and Wyatt Walker and Ralph Abernathy and Shuttlesworth and King and the others are alive today out of the Birmingham circumstance. We moved into Birmingham shortly after our annual convention in September, planning then to lay the groundwork for a nonviolent campaign. Between then and April 3rd when we finally did launch our campaign, I suppose all the members of my staff and myself were in Birmingham 13 or 14 different occasions laying the groundwork for the necessary mobilization of the community. Because, you know, we have not only opposition from the opposite side of the color spectrum but there are also some people in the Negro community who are segregationists, unfortunately. And so we felt that this task had to be done.

We suffered four postponements. There was the Governor's race and, of course, there are always the calmer and wiser voices in quotation marks who say that this is not quite the time. Maybe we ought to let the heat of the Governor's race get over with before we launch a nonviolent campaign. And so we did. We waited. And then there were some little negotiations that took place and the business community said that they would do certain things. One, two, three, four. And two weeks before Christmas nothing had been done about implementation and we learned then that we had been deceived. And then, following Christmas we began to organize toward the Easter buying season for the nonviolent movement with its parallel method of an economic withdrawal must use these two seasons of the year if we are going to have our greatest impact. And they somehow engineered a change of city government referendum and they said, "Well, let's get this out of the way." And we postponed a second time. And then Bull Connor threw his hat into the mayoralty race and they said, "Well, we don't want to cloud the issues. Let's let Bull be excluded from the primary election and then move." And we postponed a third time. And bless my bones if Bull didn't get into the run-off and we had to postpone a fourth time. And so it was the run-off was scheduled for April 2nd. And Bull Connor lost the mayor's race by a scant 10,000 votes which was exactly the number of Negro registered voters. And on April 3rd we launched our nonviolent campaign.

Friday that week, we had lain what we thought was the necessary groundwork, prepared for an injunctive proceeding, which we knew would inevitably come. We had 350 persons, 240 adults, and 110 youngsters, who had signed up and we had their names, addresses, and phone numbers, who had committed themselves to stay in jail ten days. But there was something else that occurred that we had not anticipated: they began after the arrests to have the trials the next morning or that afternoon or that night and if there were going to be an appeal bond posted it had to be posted in five days so that shot holes in our program to keep people in jail 10 days or more. And, of course, this curtailed the opportunity to build up over a period of time the national climate of opinion that we sought.

But, of course, somehow there's always the genius to the nonviolent movement that at the very moment that we have expended our resources and strategized to the limit of our human resources that somehow the opposition always does exactly the thing that is calculated to give new life and dynamism to the movement. And this is when old Bull brought out the dogs and the water hoses. We were enjoying that after about two weeks and three days of activity we had 400 people in jail. They enjoined us, cited us for contempt of court, tried us, and convicted us and sentenced us for the sentences to start sometime three weeks prior; and the next day we had 45 people arrested and visited 38 churches the following Sunday. And since that time, we haven't heard a single word about contempt so I guess we have just about beaten down the illegal use of the judicial process to bog down the civil rights of the Negro in the state of Alabama.

And so it is. You have I'm sure kept track that by last weekend more than 2,700 people have submitted to arrest. Old people, young people, men, women, children, people from eight to eighty. Some crippled, some halt, some lame, and even one blind man, Al Hibbler. And so it was that we were able to cut across the entire cross section of the community of Birmingham and have an impact that was felt around this nation.

Now, I suppose the first thing that would come to minds, how is it that in a city that traditionally had been absolutely segregated from top to bottom and from center to circumference, where you had all kinds of diverse strains of the Negro community, where there were 41 different geographical pockets of Negro residential neighborhoods, how on earth was it that you were able to mobilize a movement that has such dynamism and vitality that it caught the fancy of, not only the nation, but also the entire world? And I say this as no exaggeration because the day that the settlement was announced we had 178 correspondents from all over this world. We had one man, interestingly enough, who had come from, where do you suppose, Moscow, Russia. And another from Stockholm, Sweden. And a TV crew from West Germany. And five or six men from France. Two reporters from a TV outfit in Tokyo, Japan. Somehow, what was going on in Birmingham was symptomatic of a cancerous disease that is a part of the body politic of America which has not yet been resolved. How does this come to be?

Well, I would say it has been a part of the leavening process that began with Montgomery, Alabama which later evolved into the sit-ins of 1960, and then the freedom rides of 1961, and then the eruption of the entire community of Albany, Georgia in the summer of 1962. And out here in 1963 Birmingham, Alabama. And to a very large degree a certain part of it must be attributed to the fact of the new sense of self respect and dignity that the Negro has of himself. You know, in the midst of all of our anguished moments and the precarious circumstances that the Negro suffers out of his compounded frustration dealt to him by 244 years old childhood slavery and 100 years of quasi-freedom, in the midst of all of this somehow the Negro community has maintained the ability and the stance to laugh at himself in the midst of the most trying circumstances. And in the civil rights field we have there is a whole repertoire of interracial jokes that go the round of the movement which illustrates that even in our lighter moments we can laugh at some of our anguished circumstances.

I suppose the most recent one that has come to me is the one about a Negro who went up to heaven, as I remember, after he died and he knocked on the door. Saint Peter came to the door and discerned that he was a brother of color and motioned to him that he would have to go around to the side entrance. He drew himself up to his full height with his shoulders squared and said, "What the hell you mean, the side entrance?" And he said, "Well, that's the colored entrance." He said, "Well, wait a minute, you don't know what's going on down in the United States of America. Don't you know the Supreme Court unanimously decreed that segregation in public schools is illegal? And they had the sit-ins in 1960 and in 210 cities across the South the barriers are down at the lunch counters? And they had the freedom rides in 1961? The Negroes are riding almost anywhere they want all over the South interstate and intrastate. And John Kennedy just signed into law an executive order outlawing discrimination in federally financed housing. Why we're making progress, man. I'm from Mississippi and I just moved into an integrated neighborhood. I joined a white church and I got a white pastor. He took me down to the river the other day. . . . That's funny, that's the last thing I remember."

Well, you have illustrated by your response that even in the midst of the moment by moment and the day by day anguish and burden and the illness of being a Negro in America, particularly in the South, and we can look back at some of these moments and in lighter moments laugh at them. And this is the thing that has given the Negro the sense of balance which has kept his cup of endurance from running over into bitterness and into vengeance and turning not only himself and our nation into a more terrible state than that which we now find ourselves.

And then the Negro has looked at himself and discovered a new sense of somebodyness, as Dr. King describes it. For over a hundred years we have been shackled by the plantation song we used to sing, you know. "I'm coming. I'm coming. And my head is bending low. I hear their gentle voices calling, Old Black Joe." The image of the Negro who hung around the courthouse and in the presence of a white person would snatch off his hat and start scratching where he wasn't itching and grinning when he wasn't tickled has passed from the scene. And there's a new Negro in the South now who stands tall with his shoulders square and his eyes clear demanding all of his rights right now. And he has paraphrased the meaning of the old plantation song. And he is saying, "I'm coming. I'm coming. And my head ain't bending low. I'm walking hard. I'm talking loud. I'm America's New Black Joe."

And then I suppose the second thing which has contributed to the dynamism and the vitality of the Birmingham movement and other movements is that the Negro community has lain hold upon this new world that is a household word now, nonviolence. A nonviolent discipline that was spawned in the Montgomery bus protests of 1955 and '56, where Negroes 50,000 strong banded themselves together and rather than to ride in disgrace and humility decided that they would walk with dignity and with self-respect. And then it spawned, of course, as I indicated the sit-ins and the freedom ride in Albany and now in Birmingham. And it was interesting to note that sociologists and some prophets of doom said of Montgomery, "Well, this is just one of those sociological freaks, a phenomena that will never happen again. Nonviolence can't have its effect in America because we're too westernized. Our chromium-plated push button society won't take it." Or, "This discipline comes out of an Eastern culture where people are meditative and reflective and we're too busy ripping and running, trying to make a living instead of trying to make a life."

And yet we have had the catalog of the last four or five years. And Birmingham, if it does nothing else, it marks perhaps the nonviolent revolution in the South finally coming into maturity. I have said so many times that there was a revolution afoot in the South, but it was an infant trying to make its first feeble steps in the transition from the crawling stage to the walking stage. Perhaps Birmingham indicates to us that now the nonviolent revolution can really be mounted. And it's a strong young athlete now, ready to stand and run the race to the promised land of freedom. And yet in the midst of all of this, the Negro community, and I would be the first to admit to you, not everyone is committed to nonviolence as a way of life. But at least the tenor of the movement in the South is one which respects the discipline of nonviolence.

If you could have been in Birmingham during the hours and the days that Terry François has described to you, where these state troopers, who are literally maniacs, itchy with their trigger fingers, itching for trouble, trying to precipitate any kind of incident by which the Negro community would retaliate with some kind of violence and then sabotage all that has been done in the four or five weeks prior to that. And this against the backdrop of all of the experiences that the Negro community has had in Birmingham and in the South. Where the symbol of a police uniform on a white face has always been one that they associate with brutality and mayhem. Then it is a marvelous thing to see that the Negro community has practiced as much restraint as it has practiced. And it is a marvelous thing that somehow the message of loving your enemies has gotten to the pool rooms and the skin houses and up and down the avenues of our southern cities so that Negroes who admit to bitterness and yet say that, "Well, I'm not with this nonviolent bit, but I'll go along for the sake of the move-ment." This is commendable in itself. For, I suppose there are many of you who do not face the trying circumstances that a Negro faces in the South. And when someone suggests to you that you are to love your enemy, that you are to be understanding to people who oppose you that you say, "This is at best most difficult." Because, I suppose if your experience is like mine, I've got some friends who it's difficult to like. We're saying love your en-emies. Understand your opposition.

But it's something like what happens in the natural realm. It is a pro-gressive development. Last winter, the scientists tell us that the winter solstice passed December 21st, and when the winter solstice passes, two minutes of daylight is added to each days around of 24 hours each which doesn't really seem like very much. But these two minutes which are suc-cessively and persistently and progressively applied. But after awhile, what happened? The earth's crust began to thaw and little blades of grass began to push their way up through the sod and the trees and the flowers took on the green verdeaux of springtime and we heard the voice of the turtle throughout the land. And someone said to us without our scarcely per-ceiving it that spring has come. Stepping in at the lunch counters, in the city jail, let those two minutes of love be persistently and consistently and successively applied. And after awhile it is our hope and faith that little blades of grass of freedom will, one day, begin to sprout, and the trees and flowers will begin to take on the green verdeaux of the American ideal of democracy. And we shall, one day, see the springtime of the fatherhood of God and the brotherhood of man. We shall see the prophetic meaning of every valley being exalted and every hill and mountain brought low and the rough places made plain and the crooked made straight. And see the day when every man shall sit down under his own vine and fig tree and none shall be afraid because the mouth of the Lord hath said it and all because of two minutes of love in your life and in mine.

And then a final thing, for which as a religionist, I will make no apology that in the nonviolent movement in the South understandably it is reli-giously oriented. It follows in the Hebraic Christian tradition of our church and of our church community. For the Negro church is the only thing that the Negro really owns and operates without anybody having anything to do with it. It has been his only forum. It is the site of his protest meetings. The Negro minister is the intentional leader of his civil rights protests. It is the one place where they can go unshackled by any controls whatsoever.

And I have been persuaded in the years that I have been a participant that at so very many critical moments of the struggle there is no way to rationally explain what happens to give the movement continued life or to find another watershed by which the movement makes another progressive step. I've seen it happen over and over again. I saw it in the contagion of the sit-in movement of 1960. I saw it with what was the apparent demise of the freedom ride at the Mother's Day Massacre in Birmingham in 1961. I saw it pick up again in Montgomery, Alabama. I saw it continue itself in the freedom ride at the end of the line in Jackson, Mississippi when in the jails they tried to dehumanize us. And I've seen it over and over again in Birmingham, Alabama in the last six weeks.

But perhaps the most poignant memory that I have of how this sense of cosmic companionship, of what we call the presence of God, what I would describe as the mystique of the movement, which you somehow cannot explain, which gives new life to the thrust, happened a few Sundays ago, two Sundays to be exact, when after we had 2,400 people in jail and the police had decided that to break up the demonstration they would use these pressure hoses and put the dogs on the demonstrators. And what an inspiring sight it is to see old men, young women and old women, and young men going to face the dogs without any apparent fear. Yes, with tremblings within, but going nevertheless. Displaying a courage that was operative in spite of their fear. Facing the water hoses. Being knocked down. Clothes torn from their body by the pressure. Their bodies driven up and down the concrete pavements by the force of the water hoses. Regrouping themselves, tattered and torn, soaked to the skin. Regrouping and going back to face the water hoses and the dogs again. And on this Sunday, 2,000 strong, we decided that the 2,000 or more people in jail should hear some word from the community.

We left the New Pilgrim Church on 6th Avenue South and started the six-block trek to a park that was just across the street from the city jail. We knew this would be in earshot. One block short of our destination, Bull Connor threw up his police lines with his water hoses and with his dogs. We went as far as we could and then stopped. We knelt and we prayed. Then, when Reverend Billups, the leader of the line, stood up and decided that we would move on, Bull Connor yelled out in his raspy voice, "Turn the water on Billups." And I saw with my own eyes the fireman in charge of the lever that would turn on the power hoses reach forward and then freeze and then drop his head in his hands and shake his head. He couldn't do it. Somehow the discipline of the nonviolent movement had gotten through to his basic morality and basic humanity and he could not turn the clamp on that would release the water pressure. And I heard Captain Walker say to Captain Evers, "Let them pass." And 2,000 of us walked over the very water hoses that had been put there to stop us. Walked within touching distance of the dogs who were to maim and injure our bodies.

How else can you explain it except to say somehow that the presence of the divine spirit in the hearts of and minds of determined and dedicated people that they want their freedom and they want it now. And so I could say to you in a few words, as far as the sentiment of the people of Birmingham, Alabama and of many other points South, that there is this groundswell of determination and activity in the Negro community that we hope is going to spread all over the Southland.

One of the things that you here in the bay area can do is to needle your city officials, your county officials, your state officials, your congressmen, your senators, yea, even the federal government, the Kennedy brothers to somehow make them realize that this problem cannot be resolved until the nation begins to seriously grapple with this problem which is a national dilemma. It is always a sad, sorry tale of the federal government arriving with too little that's too late. They're always there at the crash, but they're never there at the take-off. Do not be mistaken and think that the demonstrations here in San Francisco and in Buffalo, New York and in Los Angeles and New York and a thousand other places does not have its effect on the federal government in Washington, D.C. It helps us so very much in the Deep South to let them know that attention is focused on what is a national problem.

And somehow the federal government must be needled into the position that they will work out a hard-headed program that will deal with the problem and come to grips with that thing which threatens to embarrass and humiliate our great nation in the world community of nations. How can we extend to them economic aid and lend lease and a thousand other kind of helping hands and we've got a non-free Mississippi, Alabama, and Louisiana? The time has long since passed when the federal government can stand on the sidelines and be a spectator to what's going on. They must come down out of the stands and become participants in this struggle to make this nation what it ought to be.

I say to you that the sincere sentiment of the Negro community by and large in the South is one of dogged determination. At many moments our cup of endurance is tempted to run over, but we're committed to the nonviolent method and despite the dynamiting of our homes, the bombing of our houses of worship, the physical and economic intimidations that they place upon us, the Negro community in the South has made up in its mind that it's going to be free. And in the moments, in the sober moments when we would feel like giving up and wonder what's the use, perhaps there is a strain of the message of Langston Hughes's poem, "Mother to Son," which somehow gives us the tenacity to keep on with our dogged determination to see this thing through to the end.

He portrays an old Negro woman who has taken in washing, as it were, to see that her son had a chance better than she had had. And he gets into trouble with some of his studies and comes home on a weekend and wants to give up because he's going to punch out. She takes the kerchief from her head and betrays that her brow has been kissed by the snow of many winters. She looks at her gnarled hands and thinks of the hours of sacrifice that she has made for this boy now and he wants to throw it all down the drain. And in Langston Hughes's words she says to him, "Well, son. I'll tell ya. Life for me ain't been no crystal stair. It's had tacks in it, boards torn up, places with no carpet on the floor, bare. But all the time, son, I's been climbing and reaching landings and turning corners and sometimes going in the dark where there ain't been no light. So don't you sit down now 'cause things are kinda hard 'cause all the time, son, I's been climbing and life for me ain't been no crystal stair."

Deep in our hearts we have made the solemn resolve that if we can't get reservations on the jet flight to freedom, we're gonna go by train. If we can't go by train, we're gonna get in a carpool and ride. If we can't ride, we're gonna run. If we can't run, we're gonna walk. If we can't walk, we're gonna crawl. If we can't crawl, we're gonna drag. If we can't drag, we're gonna keep inching along. We're gonna be free by and by.

§78 Reverend J. V. Cosby Summerell

In June of 1963, Fayetteville, along with so many other southern cities, erupted with demonstrations and violence. In the midst of the chaos, Revered J. V. Cosby "Bing" Summerell delivered this sermon to his parishioners at First Presbyterian Church, a congregation he had served for less than two years. While he begins with considerable fear of offending many, his authority to speak out derives from "God's will." Two stories lie at the heart of the sermon: a bus trip that Summerell took where he witnessed first-hand the cruelty and humiliation of Jim Crow laws; and a story related to him by a local businessman involving the fact that, despite serving together in World War II to defeat the Germans and the Japanese, citizens of the former axis powers were free to go places where the American Negro, in his own country, could not. Both lessons elicit the Apostle Paul's declaration that Christ had reconciled any barriers between Jews and Gentiles. Summerell closes by offering three "guideposts." First, change is inevitable and ought rightly to be embraced. Second, the divisiveness of the world contrasts sharply with the oneness to be found in Christ. And finally, the white attitude toward black worshipers is wrong and inconsistent: motive is not the point, but true repentance is.

––––––––

The Testing of Our Faith
First Presbyterian Church, Fayetteville, North Carolina
June 23, 1963

This cannot be an ordinary hour of worship. This is no routine ordinary day. It is a time of stress and strain, of tremendous problems that touch every life and affect us all. What I say to you today I must say. There are some among you who know that as your minister a heavy burden has been upon my heart. If I tell you that I am convinced that to evade the deep and depressing issues of these times would be an evasion of the holy vows I made when I became an ordained minister of God, perhaps you will understand. It is good to remember that when I was invited to become your minister, I was assured of the freedom of this pulpit to preach the gospel as God leads me to understand it. I have tried not to abuse that responsibility and sacred trust. It is a mark of my confidence in you as a congregation concerned with seeking and finding the word and will of the Lord that I speak as I shall this morning.

This is very difficult for me because I know that what I shall try to say to you may be disturbing to many, and I would not want that. Some may be offended, and I do not want to offend anyone. Others quite conscientiously feel that I am abusing the privilege and responsibility of the pulpit. If this is true, I pray that God will make me aware of it, but with all my heart I have prayed about this, and I believe that this is his will. I am encouraged by the fact that so many of you have already expressed to me your compassionate understanding of the difficult place the ministry holds today. A number of you have come to talk with me about these things, and I am grateful. You have assured me of your prayers, and this means more than I can say. I want to discuss with you forthrightly—"The Testing of Our Faith."

I am a southerner by birth. I was born and educated in Virginia, and came to North Carolina a year and a half ago from a pastorate of six years in Alabama. There is in my heart a deep affection for the Negro race—an affection shared by true southern people. It bothers me quite a bit, as I know it bothers you, to know that these bonds of devotion between the white and Negro races are being tested and strained by the problems of today. Many of you have said warmly and sincerely, "Some of my best friends are Negroes." But obviously something is wrong. What is it? I would not presume to have the full answer to that. Wiser men than I are grappling with that—sociologists, anthropologists, statesmen, and politicians. But I can see clues to the answer. Unforgettable events have a way of stirring the complacent man to deeper thought and more purposeful action.

Several years ago I flew from Florence, Alabama, to Birmingham. Bad weather grounded the return flight, and I rode a late afternoon bus on the return journey. The bus stopped about 6:30 at a small crossroads community, and the driver announced that this was a fifteen-minute rest stop and that food was available here. A small hot dog stand was the only eating place in sight, and immediately it was crowded. I was one of the last to be served. I noticed that a young Negro couple were standing outside, and I watched them. Obviously, the young man was waiting until all others had been served. Then I saw him walk to the screen door, open it, and look at a waitress with a wordless question. I watched as she shook her head "no," and he shut the door and went back to his companion. It was time to eat and they could not eat. Impulsively, I bought two hamburgers and Coca-Colas and took them outside to the Negro couple. They thanked me profusely and he was anxious to pay, but I did not accept his money. Frankly, at that moment I was not proud of my race. When a white man came up to me and gruffly said, "What are you tryin' to do, mister, start trouble around here?" I was more confused, hurt, and ashamed than before. But I was glad that all of us on the bus, not just some of us, had had something to eat as we continued our journey.

The other incident happened more recently and here in Fayetteville, and was related to me by a leading businessman of our city. A leader of the disturbed Negro community sat in his office and talked about the place of the Negro in our society. He was making demands, and demands are rarely made or received graciously. The businessman was angry, but controlled his anger, and as he related the experience to me, he said, "That man had enough truth on his side to keep me from throwing him out." Interesting. What was the truth he was speaking of? The Negro said to the businessman something like this: "When World War II came, Americans white and black were drafted into the service of their country to defend it. We fought the Germans in Europe and the Japanese in the Pacific, and together we defeated them and the war was won. They were our enemies seeking to destroy us. Today a German or a Japanese can eat in any restaurant, sit anywhere he desires in any theatre, find employment in places where I, an American citizen and a Negro, cannot go. Is that fair?"

No, something is wrong. Our Negro friends grow weary of hearing the white man say, "I love the Negro. Some of my best friends are Negroes . . . but. . . ."

Are you surprised when I say that this same wrongness, these same tensions were felt deeply and painfully in the early church? We read this morning of a raging controversy centering around Paul's dealings with both Jews and Gentiles in the church.

Paul had arrived in Jerusalem at the time of Pentecost. The Jews had become suspicious of Paul, thinking that he had encouraged Jews to forsake their cherished customs and traditions. He had never done this, of course, but it is true that he had insisted that Gentile Christians need not observe ancient Jewish rites and ceremonies. To satisfy the Jews in this instance, Paul consented to sponsor four men who were taking their Nazirite vows. This was expensive and probably distasteful to Paul, but he did it in order to show his respect for Jewish law. For him it was merely a gesture. Since his conversion such distinctly Jewish acts had lost their relevance, but he did it because it meant much to Jews and did not violate his Christian convictions. Trouble arose, however, when the Jews, still not satisfied that Paul was with them and not against them, were persuaded by a mob of Asian Jews that Paul had taken Trophimus, a Gentile, into the sacred precincts of the Temple—a direct violation of Jewish law. The record says that the whole city was disturbed. Violence erupted. Paul was dragged outside the Temple, and the angry mob was about to kill him, when soldiers rushed in to restore peace and order. Does all this have a familiar sound to you? The commander of the troops asked who Paul was, and the crowd shouted back contradictory answers. How like a mob! Then, when Paul was being led to the safety of the barracks, a violent mob still following, shouting, "Kill him!" Paul asked the commander for permission to address the crowd. As a Christian, Paul used the time of crisis to preach the power and love of Christ.

He told them of his Jewish birth and of his higher education as a rabbi. Then of his miraculous conversion and of his becoming a new man in Christ, reborn, remade, the follower of a living religion with a living Lord. They listened in silence until he declared that God had led him to preach also to the Gentiles, and at this, the crowd became a mob again, shouting, "Away with such a fellow from the earth!"

There is much more about Paul's trial and ultimate deliverance. But the point is that Paul's conversion brought down the traditional barriers of race which he had been taught to recognize and respect. With Christianity, there came new and broader visions. It was from his experience as a man remade that Paul declared, "There is neither Jew nor Greek, there is neither slave nor free, there is neither male nor female; for you are all one in Christ Jesus" (Galatians 3:28).

So, you ask me what this means for us today, and I confess that I cannot tell you clearly and finally. We cannot superimpose Paul's situation on our own, obviously. And yet, there are guideposts here to help us find our way.

For one thing, *there is before us the inevitability of change.* How thankful we should be for that! Paul's travail was the growing pains of an expanding and maturing religious community. But change does not come easily. Human progress has come about by revolution that was painful, difficult, and dangerous. Thank God that there was a Paul to address the mob. My concern for the church in these times is that when the day of challenge and opportunity has come, the church by its silence and lack of Christian commitment will not lead. Many people have lost faith in the power of the Christian community to influence the world by its preaching and its witness toward peace and brotherhood. I have not lost that faith, and yet I am greatly concerned and deeply disturbed that apparently so many in the church feel that the problem of race is not a legitimate Christian concern, that the church should not "meddle." But Jesus said to us, "Ye are the light of the world" (Matthew 5:14). The whole world is the concern of the Christian!

Secondly, I fear and am disturbed by *the modern tendency to see no dishar-mony between the oneness of Christ's gospel and the divisiveness of the world.* How can we do this, when the New Testament directs us to unity of faith and life? We cannot ignore the prayer of Jesus, "That they all may be one; as thou, Father, art in me, and I in thee, that they also may be one in us: that the world may believe . . ." (John 17:21). We cannot evade the great commandment, "A new commandment I give unto you, That ye love one another" (John 13:34). Nor can we escape the stern and hard saying, "If you are offering your gift at the altar, and there remember that your brother has something against you, leave your gift there before the altar and go; first be reconciled to your brother, and then come and offer your gift: (Matthew 5:23-24). Most of all, we cannot disobey Christ's Great Commission, which makes the preach-ing of the gospel to the world our responsibility. How inconsistent that we should send missionaries to win black men in Africa and be so fearful that the black man will come into God's house here! Our Lord crossed traditional barriers of race and kind to minister to and to save a lost humanity. Can we, his church, hold the lines and refuse to overleap the barriers?

Thirdly, I am disturbed by *our unworthy attitudes toward others, and the suspicions we seem to cherish.* Suppose that the motive of a Negro going into a white church is not what it should be? How many of us could stand the test of honest and pure motive as we come into God's house? Do we not make jokes about those who come to church at Christmas and Easter to show off their fine clothing? Do we deny them entrance because their mo-tives are not the best? Of course not. Rather, we take our cue from Christ who said, "I came not to call the righteous, but sinners to repentance" (Luke 5:32). Let sinners come! Negro or white, the church is for the winning of souls and the remaking of men, all men. "My house shall be called a house of prayer for all peoples" (Isaiah 56:7; Mark 11:17).

Not as mere men, but as Christ's men must we face the tensions of our times. These times are for the testing of our faith. They are times for pray-ing and for our *being* an answer to prayer. The Negro and the white together bear the guilt and share the blame for today's problems. Right is not on one side, nor is wrong. But this we have in common, we all need to stand in the presence of the Lord and Father of Jesus Christ and to confess: "All we like sheep have gone astray; we have turned every one to his own way; and the LORD has laid on him the iniquity of us all" (Isaiah 53:6).

§79 James Bevel

James Bevel was born on October 19, 1936 and grew up in the tiny Mississippi Delta hamlet of Itta Bena. After a stint in the service, Bevel enrolled at American Baptist Theological Seminary in Nashville. Though a reluctant recruit to James

Lawson's nonviolence seminars, Bevel eventually became one of the most outspoken, eloquent and effective advocates of nonviolent protest. After helping to desegregate Nashville in 1960, Bevel participated in the first Freedom Rides, landing in the notoriously brutal Parchman Farms Penitentiary in the Delta in 1961. Not long after, Bevel shocked many movement activists when he married Diane Nash, a leader of the Nashville movement. As Taylor Branch notes, the "chicken-eating, liquor-drinking, woman-chasing Baptist preacher," had won over the Catholic girl from Chicago who had earlier participated in beauty pageants. The couple had two children before their relationship ended.

After the Freedom Rides, Bevel worked with Bob Moses and Amzie Moore in Mississippi voter registration. But his main claim to fame in the movement came in April and May 1963 during Project C (confrontation) in Birmingham. Working behind the scenes, Bevel recruited hundreds of school children, some as young as six, to march and be arrested. Of course when "Bull" Connor turned his water fusillade on the young people, the nation watched in righteous revulsion. Bevel would later play a key role in bringing the voting rights campaign to Selma, Alabama. In more recent times, Bevel remained an active presence in black civil rights, though from the unusual platforms offered by Lyndon LaRouche and the Reverend Sun Myung Moon. John Blake's book *Children of the Movement*, offers a fascinating glimpse into Bevel's private world.

Always a spellbinding and hyper-kinetic preacher, Bevel was sent to Savannah, Georgia in July 1963 by King's SCLC to bring order to the budding movement there. While Hosea Williams had been incarcerated for several days, marches and protests continued, resulting in violent clashes with police. The NAACP was so vehemently opposed to the protests that local churches had even closed their doors to movement activists. They resorted to holding their meetings at a local nightspot, the Flamingo Club. As if the club's symbolic bravado as an overt challenge to prudish gossip were not enough to electrify the ambience, congregants arrived perfunctorily armed. As Bevel delivered this speech, assistants circulated buckets among the audience to collect any and all weapons. Perhaps more importantly, Bevel incited the audience to make a very dangerous night-time march, which resulted in Andrew Young's (of SCLC) first trip to jail. Dr. Robert Spike of the National Council of Churches was also in the audience for Bevel's speech. He later noted, "This is the first time in my life that I experienced this [fear] to be a physical fact and not just a figure of speech. . . . I had the strongest feeling that I was in Egypt on the night of Passover." This transcription is taken from an audio recording from the Pacifica Radio Archives.

Speech at the Flamingo Club
Savannah, Georgia
July 12, 1963

[*Andrew Young*]: There are many of you who know the gentleman that I'm about to introduce to you. You've heard him preach before. But I want to remind the others and I want to tell you all that you're listening or you will listen to one of the pioneer freedom fighters in the whole southern struggle. This is a man that comes to you with no little bit of experience because back in 1960 when the sit-ins first had their beginnings he was the chairman of the Student Nonviolent Coordinating Committee group in Nashville, Tennessee that desegregated the lunch counters and many of the downtown facilities in the city of Nashville. But there were many students that took part in the sit-ins back in 1960. But after the lunch counters were desegregated and you could go downtown and get a cup of coffee, they went on back to their flirting and their football and their studies and they forgot all about freedom. But this young man didn't forget about freedom because he realized that even though the lunch counters were open, we still didn't have enough jobs to make enough money to go get a decent sandwich but once in awhile. And so the lunch counter desegregation was really just starting.

This group stuck together and in 1961 when another group of people started the Freedom Rides and, you remember the Freedom Rides came down from New York and they came on through, they got as far as Anniston, Alabama and then the Ku Klux Klan and the White Citizens Council or somebody over there burned down the buses. Well, you'd think that that would discourage people from wanting to freedom ride. But this young man and the other students in Nashville, Tennessee got a bus of their own and came right straight on down through Birmingham into Montgomery and on into Jackson, Mississippi. And it was their faith in the nonviolent movement and their understanding of the fact that when God is with you and you're right, you don't have to worry. You can go through any obstacle. Now, they took the freedom ride bus on into Jackson, Mississippi but, you see, the white folks made another mistake because they arrested everybody and they made them stay around there for trial. Well, while he was around there waiting on his trial they started up another little movement in Jackson, Mississippi and another one spreading on down around in McComb, Mississippi and on up into the Delta of Mississippi. He finally ended up marrying another freedom rider and making Mississippi his home.

And so for the last two years at least, he has been working on the staff of the Southern Christian Leadership Conference in Mississippi. Now when folks tell you that Mississippi is bad, they ain't telling you no lie. And for a man to live and stay alive in Mississippi when he's been shot at, when folks daily harass him and intimidate him, you have to know what the movement is all about and you have to have a strong faith in God. But, you see, it wasn't enough to live in Mississippi because I say that since 1960 every significant movement across the South since 1960 James Bevel has had something to do with. Now, I think that deserves a hand.

I was with him last summer in Albany. We were just complaining that we haven't had a vacation in about three or four years 'cause every summer when other folks going on vacation, it seems like we get caught up in somebody's movement. Last summer, the whole month of July and all of August we were together in Albany, Georgia. This spring we were together in Greenwood, Mississippi. Then earlier this year, this summer, it was largely the work that James Bevel did with the students of Birmingham, Alabama that turned this whole nation out.

Now, I don't know whether you remember back in the early days of this movement but, you see, even though we've come in and out there have been several significant occasions and I think we've been around for most of them. You remember when we brought the 75 students from Birmingham up here? And went around in the streets singing freedom songs? Those were some of the kids from Birmingham. Now, we've had to go back and forth to work with them because things are still going strong there. And since they left here, they've registered about 4,000 voters and we've been working with them while we haven't been over here with you. So what I'm trying to say is that if there's anybody, anybody, and this includes Martin Luther King, Ralph Abernathy, Roy Wilkins, Wyatt Walker, anybody you want to name that knows what's happening in the South and that has given his life to freeing you people and my people and me, 'cause I'm not free.

It's a shame to admit it in this day and age, but I'm not free. Just last Sunday my wife and two children and I were put out of the Holiday Inn in Atlanta 'cause we thought it was supposed to be integrated. We're trying to go back this Sunday if we can get back in time. I don't know. But I want to say to you that if anybody knows what's going on in the South and can see this whole thing in perspective all the way from New York City to Greenwood, Mississippi, it's the Reverend James Bevel and I want you to give him a rousing vote of applause.

[*James Bevel*]: I want to thank Andy for that fine, kind introduction. It's sort of like a lady who was working for a white lady, an old maid, she's about 50 or 60 and she had never been married. So she went to work and when she got to work her boss lady says, "Mary," says, "I understand you about to get married." She says, "No, Ma'am," says, "I ain't about to get married, but thank God for the rumor." I don't know about all of that what Andy said, but anyway, thank God for the rumor that I've done those things.

Now I think tonight we stand at a very crucial period in the Savannah movement and I'm happy to see so many young men out, so many young men, because usually young Negro men don't like to fight for freedom, but here in Savannah we have a lot of them in the freedom movement. And that makes us feel real good. And to see so many people out here giving themselves, their time, their energy and money to free themselves and this makes me feel real happy to see so many people over here in the freedom struggle. And when I see folks over here in Savannah fighting for freedom, then I know it won't be long before people everywhere have their freedom.

Now, there are some serious problems that I want to discuss with you tonight and I want every Negro in here, now the white folks here can talk because I don't worry about them. I'm talking to the Negroes. I want all of y'all to be quiet. I want every Negro in here particularly to be quiet because I don't like to pussyfoot around in a town. I like to do business and be on my way. And so I don't want no talking and I don't want you to go out not understanding what I'm saying. I want you to hear everything because I believe in freedom and I think I'm getting old now, and I don't plan to die without getting my freedom. And I don't suspect I'm going to live that much longer, so, you see, we don't have but a little while to do a lot of work, is that right?

Now there are some things that disturb me and there are some things that I'm never disturbed by. I suppose you heard about the white people in Birmingham turning dogs loose on people. You heard about that, didn't you? Well now, that didn't disturb me.

You heard of last year of the city putting Negroes in jail by the hundreds over there in Albany, Georgia. You heard about that, didn't you? Well, that didn't disturb me.

You heard about Medgar Evers getting shot in the back while he was going home. You heard about that, didn't you? Well, that didn't disturb me. You see, anything the Klan or the Citizens Council or the mayor or the police department do in any town or country or county or state, this is not the thing that disturbs me because it really doesn't matter. But the thing that disturbs me is what Negroes do. This is the thing that disturbs me.

When I hear white people shooting up Negroes, I know that's a part of their tradition; they've always shot up people. And I know that. Always shot up people. And in fact, all of their heroes are someone who's killed up a lot of people. I know that. So you see, that doesn't disturb me.

When I heard about the city arresting Hosea Williams and putting him in jail and then the white folks get together and go down and find out some kind of fool law that they dug up from 1861. And put him in jail and I understand that his bond is now $30,000 and by morning it's supposed to be a million. But that doesn't disturb me. That doesn't bother me at all.

When they put Dr. Martin Luther King in jail in Alabama and in solitary confinement and locked him away from everybody else, that didn't disturb me. When I was over here the other day they had Ben in jail locked up over there, but that didn't bother me. For I knew that if Ben was in jail and if King go to jail, if Hosea go to jail and if his bond becomes ten million, that's all right. But that's not the thing that will make us lose.

But I'm concerned about winning and I'm a poor loser and I don't like for some Negro in any town, any place to set the movement back. And I understand that there are Negroes over here in Savannah, Georgia who are in the process of almost destroying the movement. I want you to hear me and I want you folks in the back to hear me, too. For, you see, you need to understand how this movement works and how it has been working for three years.

And, you know folks, you've heard Negroes get on their knees and talk about how Jesus is so good and he's never lost a patient. You've heard'em prayed that, haven't you? We've been in this movement for three years and we haven't lost a case yet. Did you understand that? And we don't plan to lose a case because we plan to remain nonviolent and as long as we remain nonviolent in our movement we will never lose a case.

And there have been some people over here who've gotten the movement all mixed up with something else. And as some of us go out and demonstrate to show to the world that there is an evil going on here in Savannah, we've walked the streets and we've kneeled and we've done a lot of things to tell the world and to the city officials and to the power structure downtown that there is something definitely wrong here and that's the issue we're trying to get out to the world. That's the message we're trying to get out. And that's the whole purpose of people marching in the first place, to tell the world that there's something wrong in Savannah.

But then, when you, on the other hand, get out and resort to the hoodlum tactics of somebody from I don't know where, the kind of stuff Hitler would do, throwing bottles and cutting up folks' tires and cussing and breaking out folks' windows—then when you resort to those tactics, can the world know what you're doing then? This is the issue. And you can never have a movement, a nonviolent movement, when there are those of us who resort to violence because in the first place it obscures a situation and you don't know what's going on.

When I picked up the paper this morning in Atlanta, Georgia the headline said, "Negroes rioting in Savannah, Georgia." It didn't say you had a nonviolent movement going and a few folks threw bottles. It didn't say that. It said the Negroes were rioting. And from the reading of the paper, I thought every Negro over here had a stick and a bottle in his hand. So, you see, when one Negro throws a bottle in Savannah, Georgia, he endangers the whole movement. So we, you can't move like that.

You see, in a nonviolent movement you can't move when half of the people are trying to project Christ and the other half is projecting the Devil. You can't do that. You can't move effectively like that. In the first place, when you resort to throwing bottles and cussing and fighting on the street, you are falling directly where the city wants you. That's what they want you to do. When you get out here and throw bottles, you are helping nobody but the Klan and the Citizens Council. That's exactly what they want you to do. Because they don't want the world to know that they are discriminating against you. They want to tell the world that the reason they got the police beating you is because you've gone mad over here. Bless my soul, some of us gave them such a great opportunity to take the offensive away from the movement and put the movement on the defensive and now the city's on the offensive. They said, "We need a lot of policemen to curtail all these rioting Negroes." Because a few people threw bottles.

Now, in the first place, I think you have to understand that in a nonviolent movement we never attempt to humiliate or beat anybody down; but the whole problem, you see, is the problem of hate and fear. And what we're doing in the process is trying to reconcile people. There are some Negroes over here who don't quite understand that and I know it's easy to hate white folks because I live over there in Mississippi where white folks are so mean they make these white folks look like little boys. You think these white folks over here know how to beat up Negroes? Them white people over there have electric blackjacks. That's right and they stick Negroes with electric blackjacks. So these are not the meanest white folks in the world over here.

But I just want those of us who have been resorting to the jungle tactics to forget all about that. And that as long as there are those of us who are going to throw bottles, hide in the dark and throw at policemen, throw rocks in people's windows and cut people's tires, there cannot be an effective movement here.

Now, I want to ask the question here: do you want to be free? Now, in the first place, as long as there are any of us who resort to violence in any way, you lessen the effect of the movement. I guess you know that, don't you? Do you Negroes in the back know that? You don't know that. Well, I'm telling you that. That as long as you throw bottles or fight or do anything, this is what the police department wants. And you are playing right in the hands of the police department.

I was in Birmingham one Saturday about three or four o'clock in the afternoon and it was about 80 degrees over there. Negroes had been drinking good wine and beer, you know. And they were standing around and talking and having a good time and the police came up and decided that they was going to put dogs on the Negroes. Well, the whole point in putting dogs on the Negroes was to get them to start a riot, you see. And that's all they wanted to do was get the Negroes to rioting so they could have an excuse for beating up Negroes. And that's precisely what some of the police officials want to do here in Savannah.

It is no accident that when you were marching downtown quietly that they threw tear gas in the midst of you. They did that to cause confusion so you would resort to breaking out windows. What I'm saying here is that I'm no coward, but I'm never going to let the southern white man make me play into his hands and make me defeat my own movement and I don't think you all would do it either.

So we have the problem of violence. Now this means that everybody here, every man, woman, boy and girl has to rededicate himself to the proposition that he is not going to humiliate, disrespect the property or life of anybody else. That's what it means. You can't go around talking about the white folks mistreating you and then you hiding behind a tree and throwing a bottle at them. Then what are you doing for them? You are resorting to their tactics and you can't teach anybody how to respect you by disrespecting them. That just won't work.

So that means that everybody here must discipline himself and, not only that, he must discipline everybody around him when a demonstration is in process. That you can't sit up and see somebody throwing a bottle and say, "I hope he hit that policeman." But you got to get out there and tell him, "When you throw a bottle, you are damaging this movement."

What would Hosea Williams look like out on the street throwing bottles? What would Ralph Abernathy look like out on the street throwing bottles? Would Dr. Martin Luther King recommend that you go out and throw bottles? And that's where the power lies, you see. And that's what some of us need to understand. So maybe we've got some of that cleared up.

Now, let me go on and discuss something else with you and I want you to hear this, that in Savannah, Georgia you have a sort of complex situation here. There are a lot of white people who think they can't be taught. There are a lot of white people who think they are saved. There are a lot of white people who think they can hide their heads in the mud. There are some who are stupid enough to believe that by bringing in policemen, that's going to make Negroes stop wanting freedom. Now, I would have the city officials and everybody else to know they can bring in the whole United States Army. They can bring in Red China on me. They can bring in the National Guard. They can bring in the Russian Army and that doesn't make any difference. I still want freedom. Bringing in troops doesn't mop out the desire for freedom and the only way they are going to stop demonstrations and anything else in this town, is that they are going to have to face up to the problem of justice and fairplay.

They're talking about that law and order business, law and order business, and I'd like to let you know that when Hitler killed six million Jews in Germany, he was being lawful. I want you to know that. That when the white people worked men day in and day out as slaves, they were being lawful. And I'm not interested in law and order necessarily. I'm interested in justice and I'll never let law and order supercede justice for me.

A lot of white folks who go around talking about what we need is peace and quiet for a few days. And I let them know that since 1865, they've had peace and quiet all day. Back in the 1930s and 1920s when they were lynching Negroes, they had peace and quiet. And in the 1940s when they was lynching Negroes and in the 1950s when they were lynching Negroes and then a few weeks ago in Mississippi they lynched a Negro, they had peace and quiet. Don't you let anybody tell you that the white folks got to have some peace and quiet and they can't work because you threatening them. That's a lot of foolishness.

But the Negroes must let them know nonviolently that we are no longer going to be your slaves. And this is all that means: it simply means standing up straight and walking straight and nobody can ride your back any longer. And the Negroes have to let people know that without reservations.

You know, I'm a Christian preacher. I reckon I am. I seldom get a chance to preach in churches because preachers always putting out and making us preach in a place like this but I guess I'm still a Christian preacher. But one of the things that disturbs me so is these Christian folks who go around telling this story about, and it's a fact it's in the Bible, about Mary and Joseph not having a place for Jesus to be born and all that and he had to go out and get in the stable and then you'll hear white folks say, "Poor little Jesus boy." That's a fine story, isn't it? Well, now the man at least had a legitimate excuse, didn't he? He said that his place of business was full and he couldn't take anybody else in, didn't he? Now, you try to drive from here to Atlanta tonight and stop on the highway by a motel that says "Vacancy" and because you're black and your wife can be pregnant and carrying twins and they won't let you in there. And I say that the Negroes in Savannah, Georgia and Negroes everywhere must demonstrate.

Now, I'm not against it and I think you ought to demonstrate sometime all night long. But you must have nonviolent demonstrations. I was talking to a white man in town today and he's talking about, "But Reverend, you see law and order." And I just looked at him. Here I am being robbed of everything that's good. Man stealing in Alabama from Negro people. The white people last year stole $439 million and he's talking about some law and order. In Mississippi last year there wasn't hardly 1,000 Negroes going to accredited schools, and they talking about law and order. They want law and order. And I said, "Well, you know, the Americans dropped bombs on folks for their freedom, they say." And he said, "Oh, yes sir. But that was a war." And I told him, "We're in a war, too." And then he goes on to and talks about some little boys who go up and sit in the street and hold up traffic. He said, "What y'all going to do about it?" I said, "When I find out who they are, I'm going to give them a tip and tell them to go back and do it again."

What I liked about the report I got on those little boys, no one said they cut anybody's tires, nobody said that they'd damaged anybody's automobile, except they got in the street they didn't hurt anything. They didn't hurt the street and they didn't hurt anybody's car. But they was just out in the street. Making a witness against the system. For they themselves were exposing themselves to danger. They weren't exposing anybody else to danger. And that's what we say in the nonviolent movement, is that I suffered to save you. Not I'm going to make you suffer to save yourself. And this is the psychology that Jesus has. That I'll go to the cross to save you. To redeem you. This is what those of us in the nonviolent movement must say to America. We will suffer in order to save you. So we can never resort to violence.

But just for those folks who always talk about this little marching y'all doing down here. Well, I don't think there's been any marching in this country yet. I was reading Mr. Kennedy's bill the other day, this so-called Civil Rights Bill. But I've got news for you; it ain't no Civil Rights Bill. It's nothing but some foolishness. Ain't nothing in that bill that's going to help Negroes in Georgia, Alabama, Louisiana and South Carolina. There's nothing in the bill.

Now, Mr. Kennedy, what he's trying to do is trick all the Negroes to make Negroes think he's looking out for them. Kennedy ain't looking out for nobody. He says that you have to, you know they got one place in the bill that says, "Anybody who will go register have [sic] a sixth grade education in an accredited school," and James Meredith [is] the only Negro in Mississippi in an accredited school. So [there is] only one Negro that can register to vote. So you have to watch Mr. Kennedy. He's not looking out for anybody.

But I'll tell you what we can do. I'll tell you what we can do. We can write up our own Civil Rights Bill. We can do that. And we going to take our own Civil Rights Bill to Congress. And we're going to present our own Civil Rights Bill. And they haven't seen any Negro marching, have they? We're going to close down everything black and get in the streets. We're going to close up Washington, Philadelphia, and New York. They haven't seen any marching yet.

Walking around here, grown folks, over 21, got families and they can't even stop on the highway and use the toilet. Now, that wouldn't be so bad if that was over in Africa but that's in America, the leader of the free world. That's the tragedy of it. Christian nation, educated folks, and supposed to be civilized—and folks can't even stop and use the toilet.

See we're going to have to get some basic things straight in this country, but we're going to get'em straight nonviolently. Now in a few minutes, Andy going to come and talk and CARE going to come up and talk about what they got from Mr. Williams and all of that. But I just want the Negroes to know here that you cannot conduct a campaign for your advantage if you going to be violent. I want to leave that with you. And that every place I've been in Nashville, when we had folks who resorted to violence, it wasn't the white folks who called it off. We called it off because we said we cannot demonstrate in violence.

I wish you could read the papers all around the world today and now the white folks sitting back just laughing because "Yes, we've got them throwing stones. We've got them now." Well, I was in Albany, Georgia when folks threw some bottles, we stopped and had two days of prayer meetings. In Birmingham when we resorted to violence we had to call off demonstrations. But you can't have a nonviolent movement while people are throwing bottles because you get the issues mixed up.

So don't worry about the mayor. Don't worry about the state troopers downtown and don't worry about the police and the jailhouse and don't worry about the people who go to jail and they put a million dollar bond on them. Don't worry about that but when you see Negroes resorting to violence and hate, you start getting worried. That's an important thing and that's more important than having a demonstration itself.

For, you see, let me tell you something: the Lord always is with a man if the man is right. But, you see, when you start throwing bottles and bricks and breaking out windows and cutting tires, then God has nothing left to do with that, see, and as mean as these white folks are in Georgia, you can't beat them unless God's helped you. That's right. 'Cause if they lock you up in jail and made you think of all the nasty mean tricks that you can do in a hundred years, you couldn't think up the nasty mean tricks that these white folks on the police department can do here in Savannah. You couldn't think up enough nasty stuff to do. So you can't beat them at being nasty.

But there's one thing you can beat them at: loving and nonviolence; they don't understand that. So we going to change the city here in Savannah by being nonviolent in the first place. Dr. Martin Luther King, somewhere right now wanting to come to Savannah, but he can't come when you out throwing bottles. No. No. He can't come down here. In Savannah, Georgia, Negroes out on the street fighting. That ain't the way we win the war. No. Can't do that.

And like I tell you when I see some coward Negro out hiding and pretending like he's so mean and bad, that he can't help but throw that. He's a coward. That's why he's hiding when he throws it. I don't like to see some Negro hide in the shadow and throw at white folks and then hide behind women. Now, that's nothing but a coward that would do a thing like that. And we don't need cowards. We need strong men, brave men who can stand up to anything here in Savannah.

That's what I like about Hosea Williams. Hosea Williams is a brave man. He's a courageous man. That's what I like about Ben Clark. He's a brave man. We cannot let the cowards who would hide in the dark destroy Hosea Williams and Ben Clark by throwing bottles at people.

Now I think we ought to have a time for prayer. We need to call off and have a prayer meeting and pray for those who are weak and fall by the wayside. I don't believe in condemning folks. I believe in praying for people. When a man gets so weak that he has to throw bottles and stones at people, he needs praying for.

I want you to know this is God's movement. In Albany, Georgia, this is God's movement. You know something? I look at a lot of Negroes in Mississippi and they said, "you know, I'm scared to get in that movement." You know, we don't get many folks killed in this movement. More Negroes get killed fighting on Saturday nights than they do in the nonviolent movement. Every now and then somebody gets killed, but by and large, because the fact that we do move nonviolently, because we do love people, nobody gets hurt too much in this movement.

And I'm going to be around here for several days. And I came here to do business. You know, I'm a doctor. I'm not a medical doctor. Sometimes the white folks see me putting out my knife, getting ready to operate, and I'm just like a surgeon. I'm not going to kill anybody. Just trying to get the cancerous cells out of the system here in Savannah. So Savannah can live and a lot of people might get disturbed when they see us come to town and say, "What are they doing in town?"

We didn't come to kill Savannah. We didn't hurt Birmingham. We operated over there. We didn't come here to hurt the mayor of the city. We didn't come here to destroy anybody's business. We came here to teach men how to live and love black folks. I'm proud to be a black man.

You know, I look around at the white folks now and I'd hate to be white now. You know, it's bad to lie and steal for 300 and some years and then get caught in it, isn't it? That's right. But the worst thing could happen to us and that is if we start lying and stealing and fighting like they do. That's the worst thing could happen to us. That's the worst. You know, it would be bad, wouldn't it? 'Cause I'd hate to have to pay the white folks' debts. In Georgia they done stole enough, robbed and beat up enough Negroes to have to pay for a million years and I don't want to have to pay that debt. So I don't want you guys beating up white folks and throwing at them. You'd become worse than they are. And we gonna do business here in this town. That's right and the mayor and them and the businessmen, they think they gonna get away. They got a few troops over there that supposed to be mean white folks. I understand they go out on the peanut farms and get the meanest white peanut pickers they can get. And they give them a test. You know, Georgia believes in giving folks tests. They get about two thousand and ask them, "Do you hate niggers?" And the ones who say "Yes" the loudest, those are the ones who get the job. I understand they got new ones coming in town. But that's not disturbing me at all. 'Cause they can go on, go over and get Bull Connor and bring him over here. Doesn't make any difference. But I tell you if we remain nonviolent in Savannah, we can be free in Savannah. And nobody, we say it like the song that started it all in Albany, "we ain't gonna let nobody turn us around."

Now I'm happy to be here. And we gonna have to start settin' up some nonviolent workshops. Teachin' folks about nonviolence. That's the best weapon we can have, and that's the biggest weapon. And that's the weapon that'll change the whole structure of the south. And it's changin' it. And I was so happy, you know, when I went back to Birmingham the other day, and the students brought out a report, where they had registered 4,000 people. And I said, now these are people who can dedicate to something. You know a lot of Negroes, they'd get in a demonstration, but they won't go out and help nobody get registered. And you know, the only way we gonna get folks like the Sheriff of the county out. I understand he's up for election next year. I understand he's a pretty mean white man. Well I understand that he ought to be somewhere on his farm next year after the election. That mean, a lot of folks gonna have to knock on doors to get him outta there, because we gotta get everybody registered. We gotta lot of work to do here in Savannah. And I just want to tell ya, I don't wanna see no more headlines where Negroes threw anything. The only thing I want to see in the headlines is that the Negroes threw the sheriff of Chatham County out because they voted for somebody better. Thank you.

§80 Bruce William Klunder

The Reverend Bruce William Klunder holds a special place in civil rights history: he is one of only 40 names to appear on the Civil Rights Memorial in Montgomery, Alabama. Born and raised in Oregon, Klunder graduated from Oregon State University in 1958. Three years later he completed his theological training at Yale. Moving to Cleveland in 1961, Klunder was associate executive secretary of the Student Christian Union, ministering to students at both Case Institute of Technology and Western Reserve University (now unified in the Case Western Reserve University). Klunder also served as assistant pastor of Church of the Covenant in Cleveland.

On April 7, 1964 Klunder, along with other activists organized by the Congress of Racial Equality (CORE), was protesting the building of a new school in one of Cleveland's black neighborhoods. That school, activists believed, would simply reify Cleveland's pattern of school segregation. To block the use of heavy construction equipment, two people lay down in front of a bulldozer. Klunder lay down behind it. The driver did not know Klunder was behind him. To avoid the protestors, the driver backed the bulldozer away, crushing Klunder to death and triggering a new round of violence in the city. He is survived by a wife, Joanne, whose oral history of the event can be found in the Ralph J. Bunche Oral History Collection of the Moorland-Spingarn Archives at Howard University in Washington, D.C.

Klunder's sermon, delivered in July of 1963 in his hometown of Baker City, Oregon, masquerades as an Easter sermon. Why? Because Klunder's message is about "a death and life matter. Life for the Christian is life which does not deny or ignore pain, suffering, and death. It is life which emerges victorious from the pain of our dying to what we once were." In other words, the Christian message of a reconciled life through death on the cross means that we must "suffer with and for those who are oppressed by those structures of injustice which we have described." Most of Klunder's sermon is spent describing some of the structures of injustice—what the United States Civil Rights Commission called "the iron ring" of law and custom—he discovered upon moving to Cleveland. Beginning with housing, Klunder deftly moves his way through the complexities of public finance, schools, and employment to illustrate just how insidious the iron ring of racism can be in but one northern city.

Untitled Sermon

Baker City, Oregon
July 1963

> The glory which thou hast given me I have given to them, that they may be one even as we are one . . . so that the world may know that thou hast sent me and hast loved them. (John 17:22, 23)

Strange as it may seem, I have chosen today to preach an Easter sermon. Thus, I have read as the Scripture lesson for the day portions of the Passion narrative as recorded by John. We have read from the prayer that Jesus offered with his disciples before his betrayal. We have read of the crucifixion itself, and finally, we have read of the presence of Jesus with his disciples in the post-Easter community. This is the stuff of which Easter sermons are made, and to make it complete we shall sing a very familiar Easter hymn at the conclusion of our worship.

I hope that it will become clear as we progress why the sermon of the day must be an Easter sermon.

Now, while the title I have put to the sermon—"A Death and Life Matter"—is no mistake, I would like first of all to turn it around and address our attention to what must necessarily be termed a *life* and *death* matter. At this point I want to attempt to interpret certain of my own experiences and feelings about an issue which can no longer be ignored by any of us.

It is no secret to anyone that the past few years and especially the last few months have been for our nation a period of turmoil and finally a test of courage and purpose, the result of which cannot be seen with any great certainty at this point. Since the Emancipation Proclamation of one hundred years ago now, we have been faced with the problem of conscience which is posed by the disparity between an official policy of universal human freedom and the daily observation that *in fact* for many of our fellows this proclamation of freedom is a hollow thing indeed. We are faced with the discrepancy between the American dream of unlimited upward mobility for each person and the fact that the American Negro lives surrounded by walls and covered with a nearly immovable ceiling.

These last two years, since I have settled with my family in Cleveland, Ohio, has been a period of real confrontation for us with the many ways that the Negro in America finds the American dream to be a hollow one for him. It has also been a period of increasing personal involvement and identification with the movement that is protesting radically against the closed door which our Negro brethren confront as they seek to enter the mainstream of our society and economy.

It seems that the thing we most readily think of as we ponder the scandal of American race relations is the fact that some white persons are prejudiced and, therefore, discriminate against colored persons; or conversely, the fact that some whites are not prejudiced, have Negro friends, and thus treat these friends and other Negroes justly and equitably. We then try to think of ways that might work to change those who are prejudiced to be more like those who are not. But to view the major problem in race relations in this fashion—that is, to try to change the attitudes of individual prejudiced people—could have no result, I should think, other than to leave one baffled by the current tactics of the Negro freedom movement with its demonstrations, marches, sit-ins, and freedom rides. It is obvious that such measures do little to make the prejudiced person less prejudiced. In fact, the opposite is most often the case. Prejudiced people in the face of such tactics have something real to retaliate against, and most often that is precisely what they do.

If, however, the experience of living two years in a city with a Negro population of over 300,000 has taught us one thing, it is that the issue of race relations must be approached much differently than this. It can no longer be a question of strictly interpersonal relations, as if my responsibility ended with my attitudes toward those five, ten, twenty, or fifty Negro individuals with whom I come in contact in the course of a week. I must, of course, be concerned with personal attitudes, but finally the problem is one which involves institutions. It involves questions about the structures of society; it involves my behavior in the voting booth, the apportionment of my tax dollar, my buying and selling habits; it involves these things in a profoundly important way whether or not I can claim to have any Negro friends or even any Negro acquaintances to my name.

Now the question of whether the bulk of white America can see this difference becomes the life and death matter. It is the question of whether we can cease hiding behind the all-too-familiar expression, "Some of my best friends are Negroes," and begin seeing the issue in terms of the structures which serve as the imprisoning walls for all too many Negro citizens. This is the question which the rapidly moving freedom movement forces us to answer.

It is my intention then to lay bare as far as my limited experience makes possible some of these institutionalized structures which continually add up to the keeping of the white man's foot on the neck of his Negro brother. After this I would like to return to the original title, which I think captures the essence of the Christian faith's direction for this issue.

The United States Civil Rights Commission has issued a report documenting the full range of racial discrimination in this country. It is because they look at discrimination in terms of the structures of our society that they can preface the entire report with a section entitled "the iron ring"—the iron ring of law and custom that forces an *inferior status* upon its victims. What are some of the elements of that iron ring? The interesting and important thing is that you can't pick out any one element without already implying all the other elements. This is what makes it a ring, or in more common language, a vicious circle.

Since we must start somewhere, let's start with the question of where Negroes live in a city like Cleveland. Cleveland, like almost every large urban community, is a cluster of cities. Cleveland is made up of some sixty separate municipalities. The largest of these, of course, is Cleveland, but the other fifty-nine together have as many people as does the city of Cleveland. Some of these communities are among the nicest, most prosperous residential areas in the country. Many new schools have been built to serve developments made possible by FHA and VA insured loans. But are these areas for the Negro? The answer is an overwhelming No! A recent census count found that all these suburban communities were by actual count 99.44 per cent white. Why is it that 300,000 of Cleveland proper's 800,000 residents are Negro, living in a rapidly deteriorating community? Why is it that they crowd themselves into overcrowded, run-down flats and apartments in areas where trees and grass are all but unknown? Is it because they like so well to live so closely together? Hardly! Is it because the 800,000 whites in suburbia have discriminated against them? Most of these would deny it vigorously. It is primarily because of certain structures which have grown up for which few people take any personal responsibility. It is because the FHA and VA housing developments that mushroomed in the late forties did so as consciously segregated communities with the blessing and guidance of these agencies. Now, while policy has changed, the legacy remains. It is because integrated neighborhoods have appeared to be poor financial risks, and therefore, the policy of all the major banks in Cleveland prohibits the making of loans to Negroes, regardless of collateral, if they wish to buy or build in a predominantly white neighborhood. It is because real estate agents and brokers refuse in a unanimous way to make such sales even if the money is available. It is because until recently renters and sellers advertised blatantly in the major newspapers "white only" or "colored only." It is structures like this, not individual acts of discrimination, that lead to the fact that of Cleveland's 300,000 Negroes probably less than fifteen or twenty families are the first occupants of the homes in which they live. New homes are built by the dozens, but they are *not* for Negroes.

What is the result? Quite obviously the result is a Negro ghetto made up of inadequate and anything but low-cost housing. In one of the really deteriorated slum sections of Cleveland the average monthly rent is seventy-eight dollars. This is for three or four rooms to house large families.

And so around the ring we go. The fact that we have Negro ghettos in our inner-city neighborhoods has meant necessarily that we have had segregated schools—schools where close to 100 per cent of the pupils were Negro. What kind of schools are they? They are in areas cut off from the tax revenue of the prosperous suburbs. Thus the schools are crowded—often they are on half-day sessions. They are understaffed, and facilities are inadequate. It is just here where special remedial and individualized programs are needed most that they are usually not present at all. In one area the only accelerated program is for children from several different schools who have to walk through two classrooms in order to meet in an attic. And for what? For instruction with the standard curriculum of most suburban schools.

High rents and low incomes lead to frequent moves to find better housing or to avoid rents that cannot be paid. Consequently many of the schools experience close to 100 per cent turnover in their student body in the space of a year. And another thing, even where all students are Negro nothing is read in the textbooks about Negroes in America because these books are written on the assumption that all people in America are white. Inferior education, therefore, with a lack of any personal interest leads many to drop out of school prior to graduation.

What about the employability of these school dropouts? Of course it is low, but the depressing thing is that it is not very different from the employability of all Negroes; thus the incentive to finish school is not high. Here we have come to a third element of the ring of discrimination, the element of employment. If there were ever a crucial issue it is this one, for without steady employment one can hardly hope to be a member of mainstream American society. What are the facts here? The American economy has been compared to a "train in which the Negro is the caboose and the number of cars between the engine and the caboose is constantly being increased."

The fact that the Negro is in the caboose can be illustrated in a few striking ways. In our economy we have learned to live with a certain amount of unemployment. Still we must remember that America's Negroes have had to learn to live with an unemployment rate between two and a half and three times as large as the whites. One summer in a section of Cleveland with a population of over 60,000 Negroes a group of college students voluntarily tutored junior-high students. They had to learn that as a fact of life in this community, unemployment for men sixteen to twenty-one years old is about 85 per cent. For the rest unemployment runs around 50 per cent and of those who are full-time employees few are making more than fifty dollars a week. Partly it is because education and skills are lacking. But, on the other hand, it has been ten years since a large technical high school there has placed anyone in a job. This is not because of the lack of skills, but because the unions do not accept Negro apprentices and because semiskilled jobs are rapidly disappearing due to automation.

Then try to sense the mounting frustration of many highly educated Negroes who have taken what was available to them and year after year either carry the mail or drive buses, while displaying M.A. or Ph.D. degrees at home.

We are beginning to have large communities of those who could be termed permanently unemployed. These are those who live in a culture of poverty which guarantees that the ring of oppression will continue—in housing, in education, and in the world of work.

We also see the breaking up of home life which further guarantees a continuation of the vicious circle. In Ohio mothers can receive aid for dependent children only if no father is present at home. This means that for many unemployed, unproductive fathers the only altruistic act is to desert, thus making the family eligible for this aid. We find in many areas that only about a third of the families have any father figure present.

This may all sound like a horror story from somewhere far away. It is not at all intended as such. These are the facts with which millions of people live daily. And my point is that they are the responsibility of every American regardless of where he lives, for they are consequences of structures which we through our disbelief, or apathy, or smugness have allowed to develop and to continue for far too many years.

It is a life and death matter for all who exist as oppressed people. It is a life and death matter for all of us, for our times are explosive. None can claim the luxury of not having to decide. The structures are being radically attacked, and each of us must respond even if it is only a personal response to the reading of a newspaper account of some action somewhere. It is an American dilemma.

How did you respond to the freedom rides or lunch counter sit-ins as they challenged the structure of separate facilities? How would you respond to the sit-ins in which I participated in a governor's office and in a state legislature protesting inaction on a pending fair housing bill? How do you respond to the idea of thousands of students boycotting their schools in protest against schools which are all Negro because neighborhoods are all Negro? How do you respond to massive boycotts of certain brands and certain products in an attempt to force employers to be non-discriminating in their hiring practices? These are the questions which every newspaper is forcing us to answer.

Now where does the Christian faith, especially the faith based on the Easter event come in? Let us ponder for a moment the nature of this central event in our faith. At its core, to participate in the Easter faith is to affirm that, in spite of—in spite of—our rebellion against God who is our Father and to whom we owe our total existence, we have been accepted. We have been reconciled to this God not because we turned to him, but because he continued to turn to us. He loves us not because we are lovable, but because he chooses to suffer with us in our very unloveliness. His love for us as expressed for us in its supreme form in the agony of Jesus in the garden and on the cross is not a sentimental, comforting, warming thing. It is a love which pursues us relentlessly and finally causes us to become radically new creatures. It is a love which challenges much more than it comforts and which finally wins its victory in its willingness to suffer even the death on the cross. This kind of love is at the center of our faith, and because it is we cannot avoid involvement in the crisis which I have attempted to describe. Our central affirmation is that through Jesus Christ we are all one—one with God and one with each other, But this is not the oneness of jolly good fellowship. This instead is the oneness of suffering *with* and *for* one another. If it seeks to be anything less it ceases to be the oneness of Christian faith. Thus, we see what I mean by the title—a death and life matter. Life for the Christian is life which does not deny or ignore pain, suffering, and death. It is life which emerges victorious from the pain of our dying to what we once were.

What this suggests as a guideline for me is that we must—each in his own way—suffer with and for those who are oppressed by those structures of injustice which we have described. This will mean that we must learn to feel their pain as *our own* and that we must be willing to bear personally some of the cost of that pain's removal. The policy of many of us has been that justice is fine if it doesn't cost us anything—economically, socially, or politically. That time is past. Changes are taking place which will inevitably cost us all something. Are we willing to bear this cost, with a realization that it is only a small part of what many have been forced to pay for many years? We must learn to feel the injustices of the structures of our society as do those who are oppressed by them. We must know what it is like to be a man for whom our economy has no use and who thus can be of no use to his family. We must try to know the feelings of one who has spent a lifetime hearing, "No, not here; not for you; you're not wanted," and we must learn to repent to those who come to believe our charges of inferiority.

Finally, I think we must identify with those in the freedom movement who are acting on the faith that suffering love can overcome hate. We must understand the depth of feeling expressed in a statement by a veteran of the freedom rides with whom we talked in Nashville. Still bearing the marks of numerous stitches on his face, he replied when questioned why he could say he did not hate his attackers, "Would you hate a blind man if he stepped on your foot?" This person and this movement are willing to endure pain without hating in return; yet how long is this possible, and what can we do to support it?

To understand suffering and to make it your own will not dictate a particular strategy of action, but it will throw you into the battle to make your own decisions as a follower of him who suffered all that we might be one. Our Lord is risen! In him we have peace and life. Amen.

§81 Eugene Carson Blake

Sometimes referred to as the Protestant pope, Eugene Carson Blake was born on November 7, 1906. His lifetime dedication to the Christian church began through the influence of his profoundly religious parents. Blake received his undergraduate degree from Princeton University, where he graduated cum laude, majoring in philosophy. After teaching for a year at Forman Christian College in Lahore, India (now Pakistan), Blake then spent a year at New College, Edinburgh, where he was inspired by Professor Hugh Ross Mackintosh, a leading voice for neo-orthodoxy. After graduating from Princeton Theological Seminary in 1932, Blake began his ministry at St. Nicholas Church in New York City. Over the next 19 years, Blake continued to preach as a senior pastor of the First Presbyterian Church in Albany, New York, and as a pastor of the esteemed Pasadena Presbyterian Church in California. Blake furthered his dedication to the church as he served as the stated clerk of the Presbyterian General Assembly from 1951 to 1966, president of the National Council of Churches from 1954 to 1957, and general secretary of the World Council of Churches from 1966 to 1972. Blake used these powerful positions to argue frequently and publicly for the cause of civil rights.

Blake quickly entered into the public eye as a committed civil rights leader after an arrest brought him worldwide attention. Blake was taken into custody, as he and several members of the Congress of Racial Equality (CORE) gathered to protest the opening of Gwynn Oak Amusement Park in Baltimore. The park anticipated opening as a segregated amusement park, allowing admittance only to white customers. Blake's arrest received favorable reaction from the black church community because a powerful, white pastor was fighting for its cause. Blake continued his public battle against racism as a speaker at the historic March on Washington and later through his position in the World Council of Churches. Blake died on July 31, 1985. He was survived by a wife, Jean Ware Blake, who passed away in 1997.

In this sermon just three and a half weeks before the March on Washington and more than a month after his arrest in Baltimore, Blake uses that arrest experience in concert with biblical precedent to warrant breaking unjust laws. His speech to a predominantly white Christian audience also relays the message of change, which is inevitable in the community and in the church, but the medium for change is solely determined by the participation of the members. That change was needed is highlighted by Carson's bold indictment: "Frankly, the Christian church in America does not look much like a Christian church as far as race is concerned. We look like a religious club for our own kind, the religious embroidery on a secular culture. . . ." If members of the churches do not reach out to their fellow Negro brothers, then violent change is foreseeable. Blake relays the message that Christians have a moral obligation to fight for equality, even if it means disobeying regulations. Through his arrest, Blake argues that the only way racial equality will spread voluntarily is by demonstration. He points out six different ways to get involved and show support for a unified, racially equal Christian church. Blake closes his message with the reminder that there's a Christian duty to serve God and love one another. And through that service and love, "the Church of Jesus Christ will be his church. Thus will the church witness to its Lord."

Law and Order and Christian Duty

First Presbyterian Church, New Canaan, Connecticut
August 4, 1963

> But Peter and the apostles answered, "We must obey God rather than men." Acts 5:29

The United Presbyterian Church is a church of law and order. The standard and authority for what Presbyterians believe and for their moral duty is the Bible, consisting of the Old and New Testaments as they witness to Jesus Christ, the very Word to Man from God. Our Confession of Faith tells Presbyterians that it is not only their civic duty, but also their Christian duty to honor civil law and the civic magistrate.

> "It is the duty of people to pray for Magistrates, to honor their persons, to pay them tribute and other dues, to obey their lawful commands, and to be subject to their authority for conscience sake." (C. XXXII, 4)

From this you can see why I feel it important to preach to you about "Law and Order and Christian Duty," since this is my first sermon since I was arrested just outside Baltimore, Maryland, for having, with others –ministers and laymen, Negro and white—broken deliberately the trespass law of that state. The occasion was a demonstration organized by the Congress of Racial Equality (CORE) designed to protest the standing indignity offered the large Negro community by a private amusement park which regularly advertises that it is open to the public (it even appears in Rand McNally maps) and just as regularly has refused admittance to all dark-skinned Negroes.

One of the most distinguished Presbyterians of Baltimore, Mr. Furman Templeton, an elder, the director of Baltimore's Urban League, was with me. He is a Negro. We approached the gate of the amusement park together. The guard stopped us, saying that we could not enter. I protested. The guard said that I could go in but Mr. Templeton could not. I protested again. The trespass law (in digest form) was read to us. We were asked to leave the private property. We refused, continued our protest, and were arrested. Scores of others were arrested too, including six Roman Catholic priests, a Jewish rabbi, a dozen Protestant ministers and many young people of both races. I was there as acting chairman of the commission on religion and race of the National Council of Churches. Three others went with me from New York, representing the National Council of Churches, including Bishop Daniel Corrigan of the Protestant Episcopal Church. The question is: Is this kind of action right, or is it wrong? The fact that the demonstration was successful, that the owners of the park have promised to stop their discrimination this month and that the charges against all of us have been dropped is not really relevant to my question. When, if ever, is it right to break the law? That is the question that I want you to think about with me this morning.

First, let me make it perfectly clear that breaking [the] law is not something to be done lightly. Anarchy is a terrible thing. Disorder makes civilization impossible. I have already noted that Presbyterians have the tradition of honoring law, both civil and ecclesiastic. Anyone who has lived through a riot or revolution knows how much all of us ought to appreciate civil order and the police who enforce it for us all.

But let us be entirely clear that law is not God. It has always from the first been a basic Christian conviction that there are times when a Christian ought to break law. Let us look at a New Testament precedent. Peter and some of his fellow apostles had been officially and legally ordered not to preach publicly that Jesus, the Christ, had been raised from the dead. They were in and out of jail several times, refusing to obey the injunction established by the church and state officials (high priest, council and senate).

As Christians, Peter and the apostles believed that they must not obey any order, however legal, which would stop them from making their witness to the Lord Jesus Christ. They said, "We must obey God rather than men."

I do not believe that any of you would argue in general that it is never right to break a law. What about Christians or Jews under Hitler? What about the Boston Tea Party? What about the whole series of arrests in the New Testament when Christians regularly refused to obey some laws even when they were taught through the Apostle Paul that "The powers that be are ordained of God"?

But has the present-day effort by American Negroes to win equality *now* in voting, in education, in job opportunity and advancement, in housing, and in public facilities—even amusement parks—anything to do with witnessing to Jesus Christ, as in the first century?

It is quite clear that all of the highest authorities in the Church of Jesus Christ do so believe. Our own general assembly has repeatedly made it clear that the white man's treatment of the Negro in our free nation is morally wrong and that our normal treatment of the Negro even in the church itself is morally wrong and a betrayal of Christ. The pope has made it clear that this is also the Roman Catholic understanding. The presiding bishop of the Protestant Episcopal Church spoke most eloquently and officially this spring in the same vein. So all the major churches in the whole world!

The World Council of Churches has been willing to lose from its membership several South African churches rather than weaken its witness to the Christian importance of racial equality and justice.

The general board of the National Council of Churches, in the same way as our own general assembly, has asked us all to begin now to act in harmony with our Christian profession. But why just now? Why do we act now, apparently encouraging an increasing lawlessness on the part of the Negro community? It is clear enough that we should have begun to witness our convictions in this matter much sooner, but there are at least two reasons why I plead with each of you today to consider what may be your Christian duty in this battle for justice and equality in 1963 in the U.S.A.

First, the nation faces a crisis. It is not a sectional crisis; it is a national crisis. For one hundred years since their fathers were freed from chattel slavery the Negro community has on the whole followed Christian nonviolent leadership in trying to win a place of dignity and equality according to our American Constitution.

In some states Negroes do not yet have the right to vote, either because of intimidation or unjust local laws. Due to interrelated discrimination in getting jobs, finding housing and good opportunities for education, most Negroes find it almost impossible to move out of the lowest social and economic strata of our society. It was not too long ago in California that we had in my town Negro college graduates operating garbage trucks because they were discriminated against in jobs for which they were prepared at great effort and sacrifice. Is it then surprising that many other Negroes drop out of high school when they see how hard it is to get ahead, even if you are good? Is it surprising that there are not enough Negroes ready for good jobs when some do open up? Then why are we surprised that Negroes generally are forced into crowded housing—high priced—because they do not qualify for other communities as "our kind of people."

I say these inequalities are all interrelated; a push towards solving them all together, along with the right to vote everywhere and the right to public accommodation everywhere, is the only solution. And the people who are preventing this national and Christian solution are not the Governor Faubuses and the Governor Wallaces away off in Arkansas or Alabama. The responsible people for the stalemate in August, 1963 are we white Christians who have isolated our bodies from the realities of the city by living in the suburbs, and our minds from the realities of the injustice our laws and social patterns impose upon Negroes by forgetting all about them whenever they become quiet and patient. We have a national crisis which may lead to all sorts of violence and even revolution if we do not now decide to throw our persons and our influence into changing the segregated pattern of American life. For the Negro community is tired of being patient under a century of excessively slow progress. They have seen what less qualified peoples of their own race have done in Africa to become free, and they don't intend to wait any longer. If there is increasing violence in the United States it will not be the fault of Negroes striving for fairness and justice, it will be the fault of all of us who, in apathy and ignorance, let injustice continue. I might say here that if any of you are worried at the lack of popularity of our American way of life in Asia, Africa, and even in Europe, you could do more to make "the free world" strong by helping establish justice and dignity in our land for the colored people in it than in any other way I know. Communism makes worldwide progress with each headline of violence in Alabama, Mississippi, New York or Illinois.

But that is merely the national crisis. The second reason why you and I must act now in 1963 to establish justice—and this second reason is of first importance for any Christian—is that there is an equally grave crisis in the Christian church. A part of the crisis we face in the church is that Negro Christians have now largely lost their faith in the sincerity of the professions of white Christians in the matter of race. If we do not act the way we have talked, the Negro community will turn increasingly from the Christian church to which up until now Negroes have been amazingly loyal.

But there is a greater crisis yet in the church. It would be my conservative estimate that there are at least five thousand Presbyterian pastors who have a bad conscience about what they are doing to help right Negro wrongs. And this is because they are fearful that you would not support them if they simply obeyed the gospel and led their congregations to take the lead in this contest for human dignity for all men for whom Christ died. I estimate that five thousand Presbyterian ministers hesitate to lead in this effort because they are afraid of their jobs. And they have good reason. Again and again congregations all over this land have made it clear that they do not want their pastors to be "controversial" even when that controversial position is clearly based upon the gospel of Jesus Christ.

This leads us to a further crisis in the ministry of our church. I am sure you know that the recruitment of the ablest young men for the pastorate has fallen off in recent years. I am sure that one of the chief reasons why the ablest of our dedicated young men do not look forward with joy and enthusiasm to becoming pastors is that they do not want ever to find themselves in the embarrassing position in which too many sincere and conscientious pastors are today. Despite all the attractiveness of the pastorate and its daily opportunity to serve Jesus Christ, these young men do not see congregations willing to follow truly Christian leadership.

I dare not estimate how many of the three and a quarter million United Presbyterian members like you have bad consciences too. You know that we all have allowed our own comfort, our own prosperity, our own tears and our own conscious and unconscious prejudices to guide us in our actions—and equally in our lack of actions—rather than our professed Christian faith.

Frankly, the Christian church in America does not look much like a Christian church as far as race is concerned. We look like a religious club for our own kind of people, the religious holy embroidery on a secular culture which is essentially more and more selfish and fearful the wealthier and more comfortable we become. I say then that the reason people like you and me should stand with our Negro brethren in their effort to achieve equality is that if we do not we shall reveal ourselves at last as hypocritical and we shall fail in our day to witness to Jesus Christ whom we proclaim to be the Savior of the world.

One of my correspondents since July 4 wrote me to inquire if I thought Jesus Christ would ever demonstrate and cause violence. I wrote him that that was entirely too simple a way to put the question. I am sure that the white and Negro school kids who have gathered in churches all over the South and then gone out to sit in physical danger in protests at lunch counters are nearer to the Kingdom than most of us.

What then can you do? May I conclude this sermon by suggesting some very concrete actions:

First, you can try to get Congress to pass stronger civil rights legislation. If you believe in *upholding the law*, will you not do your part to get the laws in this matter strengthened? Write your two senators and your congressman today. Tell them that you believe civil rights to be a moral matter, that you want good legislation passed this summer and that you do not want your representatives to make this a partisan issue nor will you countenance their allowing a filibuster to prevent this needed legislation. This effort will cost you fifteen cents and an hour's time to write good letters.

And come and meet me and the thousands of others in Washington, D.C. on August 28, where there is to be the greatest orderly demonstration of concern that the capital has ever seen. The invitation is to you. Unless people like you begin to demonstrate it is now freely predicted that no civil rights legislation will pass, and if the Congress is unable or unwilling to legislate, it is freely predicted that a new and more violent phase in civil rights demonstration will then begin.

Second, tomorrow join the National Association for the Advancement of Colored People and make a whopping big contribution to its legal and defense fund. Again let me appeal here to any of you who really would uphold the law. For the N.A.A.C.P. has, for a quarter of a century and more, pressed in court after court trying to honor the law by seeking justice and equality for all under the Constitution.

On Tuesday join the Urban League, a national organization that has been working for years to make a break for Negroes in getting jobs and being advanced according to merit. Make a contribution to the Urban League and add to your charities (all by the way, are not deductible) the Southern Leadership Conference of Martin Luther King, the Congress of Racial Equality, headed by James L. Farmer, the Student Nonviolent Coordinating Committee. These are the organizations that are leading this effort for justice and equality now. If you are unwilling to give to them, give then to the National Council of Churches or to your own United Presbyterian Church and earmark the funds for their commissions on religion and race.

What else can you do besides writing letters and joining organizations and supporting them?

Third, you can make it your project where you work to see that jobs are open to Negroes who are qualified and that your business will train unqualified Negroes the same way you train and upgrade presently unqualified white people. If you don't work, but are a stockholder, write the management and tell management or owner that you want your company to be leaders in enlightened employment policies as to race. You may lose a bit of your popularity if you really take this seriously, but you must begin where you have influence.

Fourth, you can pray each night for the Negro community and its leaders; you can pray for the people who are in Mississippi jails under excessive bond and have been there for weeks and months. You can pray for any of us who day by day have to make hard decisions, realizing that we may be wrong in them but must nevertheless try to make them as Christians.

Fifth, you can begin an effort to make it possible for anybody who has the money to buy and rent in your town. I know I am moving into a touchy subject here. I do not speak only to you. I speak to myself as a resident of this lovely spot of isolation and retreat. Ah, but this is the place that you have found for your own family's peace and development. "Don't make us ruin our hometown!" But suburban living by the power structure of our society is one of the causes of the racial crisis. I have driven off and on from New York to this area of Connecticut for thirty years. I noticed that recent racial disturbances on the Boston Post Road in the Bronx are in a part of the city I used to drive through. But I have not been on that road for twenty years. We have thruways and expressways now which make it possible to isolate ourselves almost completely from any ugliness. And in these twenty years more and more Americans are driven from rural to urban life, and all those who are poor live in increasingly crowded cities. You will find that you will not increase your popularity in your town if you really mean to back the housing program already begun by the churches of New Canaan.

Sixth, you can protest every time you hear anyone blaming Negroes for agitation or saying they ask too much. Some do ask too much and some ask for the wrong things. But the cause of extremism is justice delayed and we, not they, are responsible for that.

What you can do is to begin to act your faith even if it may lead you to arrest, ridicule, or poverty, or even physical danger. The widely publicized July 4 demonstration in Maryland will not be important unless it symbolizes and encourages the members of our churches to act in a new pattern of witness to Jesus Christ with regard to racial equality and justice. If this happens widely, not only among a few ministers and members, it will go far to mark the very renewal of our church by the Holy Spirit of God in faith and in hope and in love. It is time for us all to stand up and be counted.

"We must obey God rather than men," said Peter and the apostles, and that simple decision became the foundation of the church of Jesus Christ and the reason for its winning the world to him. It is not easy always to know how to obey God. But no one who is failing to try to find the way to change the racially segregated pattern of American life can claim these days to be trying very hard to obey God. And then when we have done our best we will still be sinners, as the gospel reminds us, and we will need each other's fellowship and prayers, as sinners who are forgiven freely when they do repent of evil and turn to God through Jesus Christ. For the Christian gospel is a power for reconciliation of sinners to God, and of all men to all men. In worship here or in any Christian sanctuary we need to be helped to be agents of that Divine reconciliation, loving one another even when we deeply disagree, loving the enemies we make and those, too, who make us their enemies. Thus the church of Jesus Christ will be his church. Thus will the church witness to its Lord.

§82 Francis Gerald Ensley

Francis Gerald Ensley was born on August 12, 1907. He received his educational training at Ohio Wesleyan University (A.B.) and Boston University (S.T.B. and Ph.D.). From 1938 to 1944 Ensley was a professor of homiletics at Boston University. Later he became pastor for eight years at the North Broadway Methodist Church in Columbus, Ohio. In 1952 Ensley became a bishop in the Methodist church, first in Iowa and later in Ohio. Married to Eunice Ensley, he passed away in 1976.

Before a large gathering of Methodists in Chicago, just two days prior to the March on Washington, Ensley delivered a thoughtful exegesis on Matthew 19:19: "You shall love your neighbor as yourself." Ensley rejects what he terms a *quantitative* interpretation of the text; after all, this could mean simply more separate but equal. Instead he favors a *qualitative* reading, in which we project onto our neighbors an "imaginative sympathy." Like the feeling a parent has for a child, so too should we have for our neighbors—including our black neighbors. Ensley notes that the "power of fellow feeling dies for so many of us at the color line." This fellow feeling is not a rigid equality akin to mathematics, but more like a "fabric of unity." How then might we acquire this feeling? Ensley suggests three possibilities. First, we need to project ourselves imaginatively onto others. Second, we need to associate consciously and more frequently with blacks. And third, if we fully realize the love of God, we will in turn project that love onto others.

On Loving One's Neighbor as Oneself

Second Methodist Conference on Human Relations, Chicago, Illinois
August 26, 1963

"You shall love your neighbor as yourself."
Matt. 19:19

Broadly speaking there are two ways of interpreting our text. The first is what we may call the *quantitative*: "You shall love your neighbor as *much as yourself.*" I will give as much concern for the other man's welfare as I do for my own. I shall seek his happiness with the same earnestness as my own. I shall endeavor to screen him from what may hurt him as truly as I seek to escape hurt myself. I shall treat the other man's good as intrinsically as valuable as my own good. The guiding principle is equality—50-50 all the way around.

This conception means—laudably—that my neighbor's rights are quite as worthy of regard as my own. But it could mean also "separate but equal" facilities! If the community spends as much on Negro schools as on white, then my conscience need not be troubled about segregation. If the Jim Crow car is as modern and well-furnished as my own I do not need to ride with my Negro brother, for I can tell myself that I am doing as well by him as I am by myself. Certainly "love" in this quantitative sense—really justice—still far exceeds our attainment. But is this what Christ died to make real?

There is a second possible interpretation of our text which I should call the *qualitative*: "You shall love your neighbor as yourself"—not as much as yourself, but *as though he were yourself*. It means tying my sensibilities to my neighbor's nerve endings so that I feel things as he does. It means crawling under my neighbor's skin and experiencing the world as he does. It means endeavoring to look at the world through his eyes. It means trying to comprehend *his reasons* for doing what he does. We tap people's telephones. Christian love presupposes the imaginative power necessary to tap what the other fellow is saying to himself. It means tuning in on the other man's aspirations. Christian love presupposes an imaginative sympathy with the joys, the pains, and the hopes of every man who crosses our path.

Christian love does not signify that we feel the same toward the casual acquaintance that we do toward our own flesh and blood. I do not imagine that Christ on the cross felt the same tenderness toward his enemies as he did toward his mother. Christian love does not mean that we approve of the other man or that sentiment makes law and discipline unnecessary. Christian love doesn't mean that we are candidates for marriage with anyone we meet—that putrid old herring that is always being dragged out when race is up for discussion. Christian love means, as Paul put it, being members one of another. By the power of imagination we are to share in the inner life of every human being with whom we deal. "You shall love your neighbor as yourself"—as though he were yourself.

Every true parent understands the meaning of what I am saying. A parent, physically speaking, is a distinct entity from his child. But nothing hurts the child that does not hurt the parent, because spiritually they are one organism. Did you ever sit through a piano recital when one of your youngsters was performing—and a bit shakily? Every bad note hits you as though someone were striking your spinal column with a mallet! Two bodies but one unit of sympathy! A great teacher has this imaginative power. As a recent biographer has put it with regard to "Copey" Copeland of Harvard, "He never needed to be told; he always sensed his pupils' difficulty." A great artist has this power. Isn't it interesting that we know so little about Shakespeare's life and personality despite his voluminous writing? He entered so skillfully into the mind of his every character, from Falstaff to Macbeth, that we do not know what his own philosophy was. How wonderfully Lincoln possessed this power to feel with the other man! When the Battle of Shiloh was at its height he hastened to the War Department, where he found the brother and sister-in-law of General Lew Wallace, who was in the thick of the fight. "Oh!" the sister-in-law exclaimed, with a sense of relief in her voice. "We had heard that a General Wallace was among the killed, and we were afraid it was *our* Wallace. But it wasn't."

"Ah," Lincoln replied, looking down into her face with sad eyes, "but it was *somebody's* Wallace." Everybody's Wallace belonged to him! "You shall love your neighbor as yourself"—love every person as though he were your very own.

I advance this interpretation of Christian love because it is so conspicuously absent when it comes to the question of race. We "feel for" the other person in our family or among our friends, or perhaps among our social class, but somehow the power of fellow feeling dies for so many of us at the color line. I don't think that we of the white race understand the burden of spirit which our Negro brethren carry. Have we ever projected ourselves into the Negro's place and asked how some of the experiences which are almost daily for him would feel to us? Have you ever thought how it would feel to be driven from a restaurant or a market when you had the money to pay just because your color was not right? What would it be like to be a world-famous scientist like George Washington Carver and to be required to ride on a freight elevator to address a learned society? How would you feel if you were required to live in a sixty-year-old house in need of repair and decoration, cold in winter and hot in summer, in a deteriorating neighborhood conveniently located to a smoking factory or the animal smells of a stockyard, because custom will not permit you to live elsewhere? I wonder how many of us appreciate in the most remote way the aspiration of the colored people of the world for the advantages that we take for granted. Did you notice the article in *Time* magazine a while ago which told of an international ink manufacturer who found that his African sales were skyrocketing and native retailers were asking for gallon bottles? The company finally discovered that its popularity was due to a thirst for education. Pregnant mothers were drinking ink in the hope their children would be born with the capacity to write! Can anyone of us really comprehend such a fact?

"You want to know what it's like being colored?" asks Waring Cuney.

Well,
It's like going to bat
With two strikes
Already called on you—
It's like playing pool
With your name
Written on the eight ball.
Did you ever say
"Thank you, sir,"
For an umbrella full of holes?
Did you ever dream
You had a million bucks,
And wake up with nothing to pawn?
You want to know what it's like
Being colored?—
Well,
The only way to know
Is to be born that way.

The Master wasn't "born that way," yet he had the power to feel with the other man. He lived in a segregated society. "Jews have no dealings with Samaritans." Yet, he could make a Samaritan the hero of a parable. He lived at a time when Rome and all her lackeys were hated as were the Nazis by the Europe they subdued a quarter century ago. Yet, he healed a centurion's servant and called a publican—a Roman henchman—down out of a tree to eat with him. He lived in a day when every orthodox priest offered a Temple prayer, thanking God that he was not a woman. Yet, the Master responded to the touch of a woman's pain upon the hem of his garment and forgave a guilty woman in Simon's house before the icy self-righteousness of the Pharisees. "You shall love your neighbor as yourself"—as though he were yourself, whatever your race.

Let's consider what this qualitative view of Christian love means.

Let's begin by noting that *this kind of love bypasses altogether the question of equality*. If my heart is tinged by Christian love I don't ask if my neighbor is my equal. I only put myself in his place and ask how he feels. I don't ask whether the foot is equal to the hand, to use Paul's figure—both are essential to the body's well-being. I simply make sure that nothing the hand does hurts the foot. Equality is in essence a mathematical category. It does not truly apply to human qualities. Human beings are different; they are not equal or unequal. To ask whether white is intrinsically superior to brown is like asking whether the name Smith is intrinsically better than Jones. Is straight hair superior to curly hair? I am told that some Negroes believe it is, while a whole host of white ladies spend their husbands' and fathers' money trying to make theirs permanently curly! Is one sex superior to another? (Some time ago a pompous male made the public statement that men had proved themselves superior to women in all the professions. To which the president of one of our women's colleges replied, "No wonder, the poor women don't have wives to look after them!" It was a sufficient answer, because equality in the strict sense does not have a place in the human equation.)

I sometimes wish we could superannuate the notion of "equality." It is the silent partner of so much of our prejudice. Gordon W. Allport in his notable study of prejudice says there are two ingredients of prejudice. First is the notion that other groups are not the equal of our group. The white man is superior to the Negro; the Gentile is superior to the Jew; the Protestant is superior to the Catholic. (I do not know how you would ever prove such judgments to an impartial jury.) The first ingredient of prejudice is the belief that other groups are unequal to mine. The second ingredient of prejudice, Allport said, is the belief that within the inferior group all members are equal. That is, all Negroes are equally Negroid; all Jews are sly and materialistic; all Indians are lazy, et cetera. Again, such judgments have no standing in fact. As most anthropologists acknowledge, the average Negro has as much white ancestry behind him as Negro. Most whites, too, are mixtures, and no race has a monopoly of good or evil. As Will Rogers once observed with a sly wink, "I'm 1/8 cigar-store Indian; I have just enough white blood in me to make my honesty questionable!" Away with equality! When the good Samaritan came upon the bruised and bleeding man beside the Jericho Road he didn't stop to inquire whether the unfortunate fellow was his equal. He merely sensed that he was in need. He intuited by the power of imaginative sympathy how it must feel to be in that condition. Then he picked him up and took him to an inn and cared for him. He bypassed altogether the notion of equality. "You shall love your neighbor as yourself"—the antidote to the spurious notion of equality.

In the second place, when this qualitative conception of love is accepted we'll bring *race relations in America in line with the twentieth century*. Human relationships resemble everything else in an evolutionary world. Things that were good in one age cease to be in the next. I hear some of my friends proclaiming the virtues of segregation. Well, confessedly there was a day when segregation was good, when it represented a step forward. Certainly segregation is good compared with slavery, as slavery is good compared with the killing of one's captives, as primitive men did. Now the time has come, however, when segregation is out-of-date.

A study of Henry Ford and the Ford Motor Company was published by distinguished Pulitzer-Prize-winning historian Allan Nevins. The book makes this judgment about Henry Ford. It says that for sixty years he was ahead of his time and for the last twenty years he was behind his time. For six decades he was an industrial pioneer. He introduced the assembly line, the five-dollar wage, and a cheap, useful product that set America on wheels. But he refused to keep up with the developing world, and at last his time passed him. He refused to style his cars. He fought the rising labor movement. He insisted on the same autocratic, one-man rule when he had 100,000 employees that he had enjoyed when he had 100 employees. The consequence was that by 1933 General Motors had overtaken him, and by 1943 he was on the threshold of destruction, spared only by the rising up of the Ford family itself to take away his power. That is a parable of what happens at every level of experience when we fail to keep up with the calendar.

Our present racial situation is out-of-date. There is a new Negro. There is a rising professional class—the Negro doctor, for instance—who nets 500 dollars a week, drives a Cadillac, and lives in a ranch-style house. He is not going to take the treatment that a sharecropper would. The Negro of today is not the field hand of Civil War days; he is capable of producing from his ranks a Ralph Bunche, with his Ph.D., his Harvard professorship, and his Nobel Prize. The Negro is not an indigent class as it was in the days of Reconstruction. According to the *New York Times* Negro purchasing power in this country is now equal to our total foreign exports.

There is a new world. Time has marched along. The colored peoples of the world are in the majority, and in nation after nation they are sitting in the driver's seat. In land after land they are evicting their erstwhile masters. Can we put our heads in the sand and pretend it isn't so? So often we hear it said by defenders of the old order, "Now don't push us. This thing must be done gradually." No one likes to be pushed, but have we forgotten that the Emancipation Proclamation was enunciated a hundred years ago? And nullification was smashed, not by the Supreme Court in 1954, but by a Tennessean, Andrew Jackson, in 1833. How slow is slow? How near to the absolutely motionless may one be and still be gradual?

There is a new conscience in the world. Many a white person is chagrined that we have come so little way in a hundred years. No, it isn't pleasant to be pushed, but it isn't pleasant to be hobbled either when the Christian conscience speaks. Christian love means not only that we shall sympathetically feel with the Negro, but also that we shall sympathetically feel with the white conscience that feels with the Negro.

"You shall love your neighbor as yourself." When we begin to think in terms of the brotherhood of unity we shall forget altogether about time; yet strange to say, we'll find ourselves up-to-date.

Well, how do we acquire this ability to feel with other people? Let me make three brief suggestions. The first is that we "take thought," as the Bible puts it. Let us project ourselves imaginatively into the place of others. Let us ask *why* they do as they do. The papers not long ago reported a unique school in Britain which endeavors to teach sensitivity to others. For a day the children are blindfolded and must get around without eyes, which teaches them to appreciate the blind. For a day their ears are stopped; this multiplies their understanding of the deaf. Perhaps there ought to be a day when we could take on the complexion of the other race and see how it feels. At least this is possible in imagination. Instead of looking out we might look within. This was Jesus' suggestion in the Golden Rule. Let us ask how this feels to me, and I have a clue to the way others feel it. A woman said the other day that she felt very much like everybody else at the center but different around the edge. This was her way of saying she was a human being at heart and an individual on the circumference. Take thought then; consult your heart and you will understand the pulsing heart of your neighbor.

Secondly, if we would learn to love the neighbor we *will associate with him*. Association does not *guarantee* love; indeed, some of the hardest persons to love are one's neighbors! Practically all the studies of prejudice show that acquaintance lessens prejudice. In the Army the white and Negro soldiers who fought in the same platoons had the least objection to one another, according to the tests. Instead of familiarity's breeding contempt, experience shows that it begets a sense of value. This is why segregation is such an iniquitous thing. It not only poisons the relations of the present, it builds a wall of hindrance that prevents a better relationship that ought to be. We white people have discovered these last few months that we did not know our Negro brethren as we thought we did. Their resistance has surprised us. Their willingness to risk danger for their cause has been a marvel. But it would not have happened, I surmise, if we had been in brotherly fellowship with one another. Segregation has destroyed the very access to each other which might have saved the tragedy we have been going through.

Finally, we achieve love for others *by realizing the love of God*. Love begets love. Love, believed in, produces love. The law of human nature is that we love in reply to love. "We love because he first loved us." "Beloved, if God so loved us, we also ought to love one another." If a person believes that God really loves him he will find it impossible to hate those whom God loves. When we lose sight of God's love, on the other hand, the heart sours and men no longer seem worth the loving. Let a person ponder the great love God has for him, unworthy though he may be, and he can never treat others with disrespect.

In the long run, human rights rest upon community of feeling. American history is instructive on this point. The American Constitution is the basic body of law and right. What is behind it? The War for Independence, climaxing in a Declaration of Independence. What is behind that? A sense of unity residing in the thirteen colonies, transcending their differences. Historians tell us now that months, years, before Paul Revere rode that night to Concord and Lexington to warn of the British advance, he and other bold riders had been moving up and down the Atlantic seaboard carrying messages to and from the patriots. Like shuttles they sped back and forth, weaving a fabric of unity. They did their work so well that when the crucial hour came and the British attacked Massachusetts distant Virginia felt it was an attack on her, and George Washington went at once to her aid. Out of that community of feeling came independence, and finally a new and greater unity.

Well, the first task of the church is to weave a fabric of sympathy by which our minority brethren may lose their bonds and be united in a stronger and closer fellowship. When love becomes *qualitative*, a feeling for the other person's feelings, racial exclusiveness in the church will cease.

§84 Eugene Carson Blake

Eugene Carson Blake's biography appears in the introduction to his August 4, 1963 speech in New Canaan, Connecticut. The March on Washington would prove to be the single, most important march of the twentieth century. As representative of the Commission on Religion and Race of the National Council of Churches, and a cosponsor of the march, Blake earns his place on the speaking dais. In an event completely overshadowed by King's "I Have a Dream" anthem, Blake begins by calling for the unity of all Christian denominations to rally together in the name of obtaining the rights due all American citizens regardless of skin color. He expresses what a privilege it is to be a part of the movement striving for this worthy cause, yet Blake conveys his disappointment in the churches of America still remaining segregated—this despite the church saying "all the right things." Moreover, white churches are "partly" to blame for the unfulfilled promise of the nation's founding documents. Unlike many black leaders who have "mirrored the suffering of the cross of Jesus Christ," "Late we come" expresses Blake's hope that, in fact, it isn't too late to redeem and reconcile the white church community to the cause of civil rights. This transcription is from the Moses Moon Audio Archive at the National Museum of American History in Washington, D.C.

Late We Come

March on Washington for Jobs and Freedom, Washington, D.C.
August 28, 1963

I wish indeed that I were able to speak for all Protestant, Anglican, and Orthodox Christians as I speak here today in behalf of full justice and freedom for all who are born or living under the American flag. But that is precisely the point. If all the members and all the ministers of the constituency I represent here today were ready to stand and march with you for jobs and freedom for the Negro community, together with those of the Roman Catholic Church and of the synagogues in America, then the battle for full civil rights and dignity would be already won.

I do however, in fact, represent officially the commission on religion and race of the National Council of Churches, and I am honored to be here in the highest tradition of that council and of the churches which constitute it, thus to represent one of the sponsoring bodies of this march for jobs and freedom. For many years now, the National Council of Churches and most of its constituent communions, have said all the right things about civil rights. Our official pronouncements for years have called for a non-segregated church in a non-segregated society. But as of August 28th, 1963 we have achieved neither a non-segregated church nor a non-segregated society. And it is partly because the churches of America have failed to put their own houses in order that, that one hundred years after the Emancipation Proclamation, 175 years after the adoption of the Constitution, 173 years after the adoption of the Bill of Rights, the United States of America still faces a racial crisis.

We do not therefore come to this Lincoln Memorial in any arrogant spirit of moral or spiritual superiority to set the Congress or the nation straight, or to judge or to denounce the American people in whole or in part. Rather we come late. Late we come, in the reconciling and repentant spirit in which Abraham Lincoln of Illinois once replied to a delegation of morally arrogant churchmen who came to see him. He said, "Never say God is on our side. Rather pray that we may be found on God's side." We come in the fear of God that moved Thomas Jefferson of Virginia, whose memorial stands across the lagoon, once to say, "Indeed I tremble for my country when I reflect that God is just." Yes, we come to march behind and with these amazingly able leaders of the Negro Americans who, to the shame of almost every white American, have alone and without us mirrored the suffering of the cross of Jesus Christ. They have offered their bodies to arrest and violence, to the hurt and the indignity of fire hoses and dogs, of derision and of poverty, and some death, for this just cause. We come, and late we come, but we come to present ourselves this day, our souls and bodies, to be a living sacrifice, holy and acceptable to God, which is our reasonable service, in a kind of tangible and visible sacrament, which alone in times like these can manifest to a troubled world the grace that is available at communion table or high altar.

We come in prayer that we in our time may be more worthy to bare the name our tongues so fluently profess. We come in faith that the God, who made us and gave his Son for us and for our salvation, will overrule the fears and hatreds that so far have prevented the establishment of full racial justice in our beloved country. We come in hope that those who have marched today are but a token of a new and massive high determination of all men of religion and of patriotism, to win in this nation under God, liberty, and justice for all. And we come. Late we come. We come in that love revealed in Jesus Christ which reconciled into true community all men of every color, race, and nation, who respond in faith and obedience to him.

§84 Archbishop Patrick O'Boyle

Patrick O'Boyle was born on July 18, 1896 in Scranton, Pennsylvania. He attended St. Thomas College in Scranton, Saint Joseph's Seminary in Yonkers, New York and the New York School of Social Work. In 1921 he was ordained as a priest in New York City and served parishes there. In 1947 O'Boyle was installed as the Archbishop of Washington, D.C., a position he held for nearly 20 years. He was named a cardinal in 1967, a position he held until he retired in 1973. O'Boyle died at the age of 91 on August 10, 1987.

Archbishop O'Boyle delivered this invocation at the March on Washington for Jobs and Freedom. That historic march, sponsored by the major civil rights organizations, and organized largely by Bayard Rustin, would become the signature event of the civil rights movement. O'Boyle would play a major role in the March before it even started by objecting strenuously to John Lewis's speech, which had been circulated a day earlier. He went so far as to state he would not participate in the March unless the speech was changed. Largely because of the influence of A. Philip Randolph, Lewis, working with SNCC colleagues Jim Forman and Courtland Cox, changed parts of the address. As with many clergy before him, O'Boyle links the "ideals of freedom" with democracy and religion. O'Boyle departs from convention, though, in asking God to send his Holy Spirit—the third and often unacknowledged aspect of a triune God—"to open the eyes of all to the great truth that all men are equal in your sight." These remarks were transcribed from the Moses Moon Audio Archive housed at the National Museum of American History in Washington, D.C.

Invocation for the March on Washington for Jobs and Freedom
Washington, D.C.
August 28, 1963

In the name of the Father, and of the Son, and of the Holy Ghost, amen. Our Father who art in Heaven, we who are assembled here in a spirit of peace and in good faith, dedicate ourselves and hopes to you. We ask the fullness of your blessing upon those who have gathered with us today, and upon all men and women of goodwill, to whom the cause of justice and equality is sacred. We ask this blessing because we are convinced that in honoring all your children, we show forth in our lives the love that you have given us. Bless this nation and all its people. May the warmth of your love replace the coldness that springs from prejudice and bitterness. Send in our midst the Holy Spirit to open the eyes of all to the great truth that all men are equal in your sight.

Let us understand that simple justice demands that the rights of all be honored by every man. Give strength and wisdom to our president and vice president. Enlighten and guide the Congress of these United States. May our judges in every court be heralds of justice and equity. Let just laws be administered without discrimination. See to it, we implore, that no man be so powerful as to be above the law, or so weak as to be deprived of its full protection. We ask special blessing for those men and women who, in sincerity and honesty, have been leaders in the struggle for justice and harmony among races. As Moses of old, they have gone before their people to a land of promise. Let that promise quickly become a reality, so that the ideals of freedom, blessed alike by our religious faith and our heritage of democracy, will prevail in our land.

Finally, we ask that you consecrate to your service all in this crusade who are dedicated to the principles of the Constitution of these United States. May we be sensitive to our duties towards others, as we demand from them our rights. May we move forward without bitterness, even when confronted with prejudice and discrimination. May we shun violence, knowing that the meek shall inherit the Earth. But may this meekness of manner be joined with courage and strength so that with your help, O Heavenly Father, and following the teaching of Christ your son, we shall now and in the days to come live together as brothers in dignity, justice, charity, and peace. Amen.

§85 John Lewis

John Lewis was born to Alabama sharecroppers on February 21, 1940. Growing up just outside of Troy in Pike County, Lewis often entertained himself as a young boy by preaching—to the family's chickens. Lewis joined the civil rights movement upon moving to Nashville where he enrolled at American Baptist Theological Seminary. As with many Nashville student activists, James Lawson mentored him in nonviolent protest and in creating the beloved community. In addition to helping desegregate downtown Nashville, Lewis volunteered for a hazardous mission in the spring of 1961. Sponsored by the Congress of Racial Equality (CORE), Lewis signed on to test desegregation in interstate transportation facilities. That small group of men and women—the Freedom Riders—would be brutally beaten in both Birmingham and Montgomery and thrown in the notorious Parchman Farms Prison in Mississippi.

Lewis was elected chairman of the Student Nonviolent Coordinating Committee (SNCC) in June 1963. He held that position until 1966 with the contested and controversial election of Stokely Carmichael. Many, including Lewis, left SNCC in 1966 as the organization moved further towards Black Power and with the organization's exclusion of whites. Part of Lewis's lasting fame as a civil rights advocate came on March 7, 1965, as he and Hosea Williams led marchers across the Edmund Pettus Bridge in Selma, Alabama. Later that evening, Americans watched the "Bloody Sunday" assault as Alabama law enforcement officials brutalized the peaceful marchers.

Once Lewis parted with SNCC, he worked as associate director for the Field Foundation and later as the director of the Voter Education Program. In 1981 Lewis was elected to the Atlanta City Council. Five years later he defeated good friend and fellow SNCC activist, Julian Bond, in a bitterly contested race to represent Georgia's Fifth Congressional District in the U.S. House of Representatives. He has been elected nine consecutive times to this post. Lewis's wife, Lillian, works in Atlanta. The couple has one child, John-Miles. Lewis's memoir of the movement, *Walking with the Wind*, was published in 1998 and has garnered several awards.

Only one speech at the March on Washington generated much controversy— the Lewis/SNCC joint creation. Archbishop Patrick O'Boyle objected to the address on religious grounds, specifically a paragraph denouncing patience as "a dirty and nasty word." Others were upset about a reference to a "scorched earth policy." Still others more politically inclined were angry about references to the Kennedy administration's lack of leadership. And finally, there were some who disdained the use of terms such as "black masses" and "revolution." A. Philip Randolph eventually convinced Lewis to amend the speech—literally at the last minute, in the shadow of Lincoln's Monument.

There is but one mention of God in Lewis's speech. As a group, SNCC was split on whether nonviolent resistance was a Christian witness or a secular strategy to foment legal and economic changes. That said, Lewis's mention of God—which does not appear in the earlier draft of the speech—is extremely significant. Whether it was inserted to placate O'Boyle or other leaders we do not know. What's clear is that SNCC, like so many others, still held fast—albeit tenuously perhaps—to a civic faith in solving the problems of the "segregated South." In addition to the brief theological moment, the speech is an important example of how Judeo-Christian ideals momentarily weld the clashing pipes of ego and political ambition. The transcription of this address comes from the Moses Moon Audio Archive housed at the National Museum of American History in Washington, D.C.

Speech at the March on Washington for Jobs and Freedom

Washington, D.C.
August 28, 1963

We march today for jobs and freedom, but we have nothing to be proud of, for hundreds and thousands of our brothers are not here, for they are receiving starvation wages or no wages at all. While we stand here, there are sharecroppers in the Delta of Mississippi, who [are] out in the fields working for less than three dollars a day, twelve hours a day. While we stand here, there are students in jail on trumped-up charges. Our brother James Farmer, along with many others, is also in jail. We come here today with a great sense of misgivin'. It is true that we support the administration[s] civil right[s] bill. We support it with great reservation, however. Unless Title Three is put in this bill, there is nothing to protect the young children and all women who must face police dogs and fire hoses in the South, while they engage in peaceful demonstration.

In its present form, this bill will not protect the citizen of Danville, Virginia, who must live in constant fear of a police state. It will not protect the hundreds and thousand[s] of people that have been arrested upon trump[ed] [up] charges. What about the three young men, SNCC field secretar[ies] in Americus, Georgia, who faced a death penalty for engaging in peaceful protest? As it stand[s] now, the voting section of this bill will not help the thousands of white people who want to vote. It will not help the citizen[s] of Mississippi, of Alabama, and Georgia, who are qualified to vote but lack a sixth-grade education. "One man, one vote," is the African cry. It is ours too. It must be ours. We must have legislation that will protect the Mississippi sharecropper, who was put off of his farm because he dared to register to vote. We need a bill that will provide for the homeless and starving people of this nation. We need a bill that will ensure the equality of a maid who earns five dollars a week in a home of a family whose whole income is 100,000 dollars a year. We must have it, this FEPC bill.

My friends, let us not forget that we are involved in a serious social revolution. By and large American politics is dominated by politicians who field their career[s] on immoral compromises and alliance to the open forum of political, economic, and social exploitation. There are [ex]ceptions, of course. We salute those. But what political leader can stand up and say, "My party is the party of principles"? For the party of Kennedy is also the party of Eastland. The party of Javitz is also the party of Goldwater. Where is our party? Where is a political party that will make it unnecessary to march on Washington? Where is the political party that will make it unnecessary to march in the streets of Birmingham?

Where is a political party that will protect the citizen of Albany, Georgia? Do you know that in Albany, Georgia, nine of our leaders have been indicted, not by the Dixiecrats, but by the federal government for peaceful protest? But what did the federal government do when Albany deputy sheriff[s] beat Attorney C.B. King and left him half dead? What did the federal government do when local police officials kicked and assaulted the pregnant wife of Slater King, and she lost her baby? Those who have said,

"Be patient and wait," we must say that we cannot be patient. We do not want our freedom gradually, but we want to be free now!

We are tired. We are tired of being beaten by policemen. We are tired of seeing our people locked up in jail over and over again, and then you holler "be patient." How long can we be patient? We want our freedom, and we want it now! We do not want to go to jail, but we will go to jail if this, this is the price we must pay for love, brotherhood, and true peace. I appeal to all of you to get in this great revolution that is sweeping this nation. Get in, and stay in the streets of every city, every village and hamlet of this nation, until true freedom comes, until the revolution of 1776 is complete. We must get in this revolution and complete the revolution. On the Delta of Mississippi, in southwest Georgia, in the black belt of Alabama, in Harlem, in Chicago, Detroit, Philadelphia, and all over this nation, the black masses are on the march for jobs and freedom.

They're talkin' 'bout slow down and stop. We will not stop. All of the forces of Eastland, Barnett, Wallace, and Thurman will not stop this revolution. If we do not get meaningful legislation out of this Congress, the time will come when we will not confine our march into Washington. We will march through the South, through the streets of Jackson, through the streets of Danville, through the streets of Cambridge, through the streets of Birmingham. But we will march with the spirit of love and with the spirit of dignity that we have shown here today.

By the forces of our demand, our determination, and our numbers, we shall splinter the segregated South into a thousand pieces, and put them together in the image of God and democracy. We must say, "Wake up America, wake up!" for we cannot stop, and we will not and cannot be patient.

§86 Charles Morgan, Jr.

Charles Morgan, Jr. was born on March 11, 1930 in Cincinnati, Ohio. He received his B.S and LL.B. from the University of Alabama. He married Camille Walpole on September 5, 1953 and they had one son, Charles Morgan III. In 1964 Morgan created and became the director of the American Civil Liberties Union's Southern Regional Office. Eight years later Morgan became director of the Washington National Office. As a lawyer, Morgan defended several controversial cases including the appeal of Muhammad Ali and the army's court-martial of Captain Howard B. Levy and Green Beret Captain John J. McCarthy. He has also authored books and various articles for national publications.

Morgan contributed to major civil rights litigation throughout the South. He was a key trial attorney in several important cases involving the notion of "one man, one vote" and the omission of women and minorities from serving on southern juries. In addition, Morgan served as a special counsel for the National Association for the Advancement of Colored People (NAACP). An Episcopalian, his book, *A Time to Speak*, is considered a significant document of the civil rights movement.

Prior to the church bombing, "The Magic City" was a city in great crisis. Just months prior, in April and May, in the Southern Christian Leadership Conference's (SCLC) Project C (confrontation), Birmingham had been targeted in part because of the likelihood for violence. Of course Birmingham is now etched indelibly in civil rights memory for its marching children, "Bull" Connor's orders to turn fusillades of water aimed at children, and for snarling German Shepherds loosed on unsuspecting bystanders. After the apparent defeat in Albany, Georgia, the victories of Birmingham greatly buoyed King and the SCLC.

Morgan's speech to the Birmingham Young Men's Business Club comes just a day after the bombing of the Sixteenth Street Baptist Church, which killed four young African American girls. Morgan condemns all the residents of Birmingham, Alabama, including himself, for the tragedy. He emphasizes the hypocrisy of those who want to point the finger at one individual for the bombings, while denying their own involvement in perpetuating racial hatred. As a white man, Morgan is disgusted by the apathetic nature of the white community in Birmingham. He explains why the African American community has good reason to suspect the all-white police force of not working as hard as they could to solve the bombings of the past. He reserves particular disdain for Birmingham's clergy, noting that "the police chief and the sheriff in the school crisis had to call the local ministers together to tell them to do their duty." Among others, he directly denounces the governor, the newspapers, the mayor, and the business community. Morgan stresses the idea that anyone who has assisted in promoting racial hatred in the past is just as guilty as the individual who ignited the dynamite the day before. He ends his message poignantly by asserting that Birmingham is dead until it evolves as a city.

Who Is Guilty in Birmingham?

Young Men's Business Club, Birmingham, Alabama
September 16, 1963

Four little girls were killed in Birmingham yesterday. An aroused, remorseful, worried community asks, "Who did it? Who threw that bomb? Was it a Negro or a white?"

The answer should be, "We all did it." Every last one of us is condemned for that crime and for the bombing before it and for the one last month, last year, a decade ago. We all did it.

A short time later, white policemen killed a Negro and wounded another. A few hours later, two young men on a motorbike shot and killed a Negro child. Fires broke out and, in Montgomery, white youths assaulted Negroes. And all across Alabama an angry, guilty people cry out their mocking shouts of indignity, and they say they wonder "Why?" and "Who?" Everyone "deplores" the "dastardly" acts.

But, you know, the answer to "Who did it?" is really rather simple. The "who" is every little individual who talks about the "niggers" and spreads the seeds of his hate to his neighbor, to his son. The "who" is the jokester, the crude oaf whose racial jokes rock the party with laughter. The "who" is every governor who ever shouted for lawlessness and became a violator of the law. The "who" is every senator and every representative who, in the halls of Congress, stands and with mock humility tells the world that things back home aren't really as they are. The "who" is the courts that move ever so slowly, the newspapers that timorously defend the law. The "who" is all the Christians and all their ministers who spoke too late in anguished cries against the violence. The "who" is the coward in each of us who clucks admonitions.

We are the result of ten years of lawless preachments; of ten years of criticism of law, of the courts, of our fellow men; of a decade of telling school children the opposite of what the civic books say. We are a mass of intolerance and bigotry and indictments shouted before our young people. We are cursed by the failure of each of us to accept responsibility, by our defense of an already dead institution.

Yesterday while Birmingham, which prides itself on the number of its churches, was attending worship services, a bomb went off and an all-white police force moved into action, a police force which has been praised by city officials and others at least once a day for a month or so, a police force which has solved no bombings, a police force which many Negroes feel is perpetrating the very evils we decry.

And why should Negroes think this? Well, after all, there are no Negro policemen, no Negro sheriffs or deputies. Few Negroes have served on juries, few have been allowed to vote, few have been allowed to accept responsibility or granted even a simple part to play in the administration of justice.

Do not misunderstand me. It is not that I think that white policemen had anything whatsoever to do with the killing of these children or with the previous bombings. It's just that Negroes who see an all-white police force must think in terms of its failure to prevent or solve the bombings, and must think perhaps Negroes would have worked a little bit harder. They throw rocks and bottles and bullets and we whites don't seem to know why the Negroes are lawless. So we lecture them.

Birmingham is the only city in America where the police chief and the sheriff in the school crisis had to call the local ministers together to tell them to do their duty. The ministers of Birmingham who have done so little for Christianity call for prayer at high noon in a city of lawlessness and, in the same breath, speak of our city's "image." Did those ministers visit the families of the Negroes in their hour of travail? Did any of them go to the homes of their brothers and express their regrets in person or pray with the crying relatives? Do they admit Negroes into their ranks at the church?

Who is guilty? A moderate mayor elected to change things in Birmingham and who moves too slowly and looks elsewhere for leadership? The business community which shrugs its shoulders and looks to the police or perhaps somewhere else for leadership? A newspaper which has tried so hard of late, yet still finds it necessary to lecture Negroes every time a Negro home is bombed? A governor who offers a reward but mentions not his own failure to preserve either segregation or law and order? And what of those lawyers and politicians who counsel people as to what the law is not, when they know full well what the law is?

Those four little Negro girls were human beings. They had lived all their years in a leaderless city, a city where no one accepts responsibility, where everybody wants to blame somebody else, a city with a reward fund which grew like Topsy as a sort of sacrificial offering, a balm for the conscience of the "good people"—the people whose ready answer is for those "right-wing extremists" to shut up, the people who absolve themselves of guilt, the liberal lawyer who told me this morning, "Me? I'm not guilty," then proceeded to discuss the guilt of the other lawyers, the ones who told the people that the Supreme Court did not properly interpret the law. And that's the way it is with the southern liberals; they condemn those with whom they disagree for speaking, while they sit in silence.

Birmingham is a city in which the major industry, operated from Pittsburgh, never tried to solve the problem. It is a city where four little Negro girls can be born into a second class school system, can live a segregated life—ghettoed into their own little neighborhoods, restricted to Negro churches, destined to ride in Negro ambulances to Negro wards of hospitals and from there to a Negro cemetery. Local papers, on their front and editorial pages, call for order and then exclude their names from the obituary columns.

Who is really guilty? Each of us. Each citizen who has not consciously attempted to bring about peaceful compliance with the decisions of the Supreme Court of the United States; each citizen who has ever said, "They ought to kill that nigger"; each citizen who votes for the candidate who hoists the bloody flag; every citizen and every school board member and school teacher and principal and businessman and judge and lawyer who has corrupted the minds of our youth; every person in this community who has, in any way, contributed during the past several years to the popularity of hatred is at least as guilty, or more so, than the demented fool who threw that bomb.

What's it like living in Birmingham? No one really has, and no one ever will—until this city becomes part of the United States.

Birmingham is not a dying city; it is dead.

§87 Reverend George H. Woodard

George H. "Jack" Woodard graduated from the University of Texas and was an engineer for 12 years before entering the ministry. After graduating from the Episcopal Theological Seminary of the Southwest in Austin, Woodard became rector at All Saints Episcopal Church in Galena Park, Texas. He later served as rector at Meade Memorial Church in Alexandria, Virginia.

In this sermon delivered the week after the bombing of the Sixteenth Street Baptist Church in Birmingham, Alabama, Woodard attempts to delineate the difference between the murder of four black girls and the murder of two white Houston women. He notes "vast differences" between the crimes. First, racial hatred is the "reason" for the crime rather than race being incidental to the commission of the crime. Woodard confesses his guilt in the Birmingham deaths because he refused to speak out when he might have. As a white minister, he is complicit of a corporate, rather than an individual, crime. Second, the effects of the crimes contrast starkly. America and the south would receive negative publicity for the Birmingham murders. Not so with the Houston murders. Third, the Birmingham murders compel Woodard to see the problems of race in his own community. Finally, the effect of the crimes for whites and blacks might actually improve the situation: blacks might reevaluate some of their strategies, while whites might realize the "extreme danger" of defying court orders and forcing blacks to wait to receive their just due.

After the speech Woodard takes the unusual step of soliciting immediate reaction from his parishioners. Ninety-five percent of his listeners agreed with the substance of the sermon; 74 percent said the church was not doing enough work for racial justice and understanding; and, only 11 percent were against the public accommodations section of the civil rights bill.

———

Some Important Differences

All Saints Episcopal Church, Galena Park, Texas

September 22, 1963

This past week's issue of our church bulletin, the *Outpost*, carried the following memorial box on its last page:

In Memoriam

Killed while worshipping God in Birmingham,

Sunday, September 15, 1963

Carol Robertson	Cynthia Wesley
Addie Mae Collins	Denise McNair

> May Almighty God be merciful unto us
> and grant them eternal rest.

Thursday, the discussion in two of our parish groups centered around the question of why I did not also have a memorial in the *Outpost* dedicated to the memory of the two Houston women killed last week by a Negro man. When I was asked this question I tried to answer it, but I was not satisfied with my answer and it has been much on my heart since then. The fact that several of our parish family are wondering about the difference between the Birmingham tragedy and the Houston crime makes it necessary, as I see it, for me to deal with the question this morning after much Bible study and careful thought and prayer. If I were to say nothing about such an important question, I would have a hard time ever walking into this pulpit again with any self-respect. So I shall attempt quietly to discuss this with you in the love and understanding that has grown up between us in the two and one-half years of our ministry together.

First let me say that I am sure no one would be so silly as to think I would defend in any way the criminal assault and murder of the two Houston women by the Negro criminal or the same crime on a white girl for which a white man was given twenty years last Friday at the courthouse. There is certainly no question of the terrible evil of such crimes and those who commit them must be punished in due process of American law and justice. Also, I am sure that no one would question the terrible evil of the bombing in Birmingham last Sunday morning and the death of those four children, or the necessity of identifying and punishing the bombers in due process of American law and justice. All these crimes are hideous and evil and wrong. That is not our question: Our question is whether there is any difference in these crimes that justifies a church bulletin recognition of one of them and not the others.

I submit to you that there *are* vast differences, and I want to talk with you for a few minutes about those differences and what they mean.

First, *any* killing of innocent people is wrong. But I think there is an important difference between the crime of a Christian man being killed by a soldier in a street-corner brawl and that same Christian man being killed by being shoved into an arena by that same soldier for the reason that the Christian is a Christian. There is a difference between a Jewish woman being murdered in Germany by a burglar and that same woman being put into a gas chamber at Auschwitz or Dachau because she is Jewish. There is a difference between the accidental execution of an innocent man in the electric chair and the crucifixion of Jesus Christ by the leaders and society of that day and this.

These are the same differences that we would see between the murder of one of the children in this congregation—God forbid—by a criminal on the street and the death of that same child from a bomb thrown into this church right now because someone hated all Episcopalians and had been encouraged to express that hatred.

What are those differences? I suggest they have to do with the differences between the sins of someone as an individual and the sins of a whole group of people or nation or race. Clearly in the Bible there is such a thing as individual guilt and sin and there is corporate sin and guilt. I do not ask God to forgive me for the death of a Christian man killed in a tavern brawl over on the waterfront. There is no need because I did not kill him and am not guilty of his death. But I *do* ask God daily to forgive me for my share in the crucifixion of Jesus.

In the same way, I am not guilty of the death of those two Houston women. But I *do* share the guilt of the death of those four girls in Birmingham last Sunday in church. One thing that shows I am guilty is the difficulty I have had in answering the question about the difference between these crimes. This indicates I had not sufficiently thought out my responsibility. I am guilty also because there have been times when I have kept quiet when speaking out would have been too costly or controversial. When we keep quiet like that, someone is likely to think we agree with them when we do not. I am also guilty for having often said that we must be patient with injustice—that time will heal everything. This is false. Actually, it is men and women of goodwill and determination and Christian faith in action by the power of the Spirit that heal and change where there needs to be healing and changing—not people sitting around doing nothing but hoping that the turning of the clock hands will somehow miraculously make a difference. When I have done this, I have contributed to the church in our time being a taillight rather than the headlight she is supposed to be for the world. I am guilty for not providing enough leadership on this whole subject. I am even guilty for laughing at "nigger" jokes.

So one important difference between the death of the Houston women and the Birmingham girls lies in the fact that one is the crime of an individual, a crime such as individuals have been committing since Cain slew Abel. Only the individual is guilty of a crime like that. The other is the crime of a whole people against a whole people.

Another important difference has to do with the effects of the crimes. I have heard no governors offering rewards for the capture of the Houston murderers, no senators making speeches about them. I have seen no newspaper editorials in this country or around the world, no special television programs. But I have seen and heard of all these things in regard to the bombing of the Birmingham church. You remember Alexander and Betty John who were our guests and speakers from India last year. They are in England now and you may be sure they know nothing about the Houston crimes and much about the Birmingham bombing. The same is true of their families in India. Why? I think it is because of the effect of the Birmingham crime. First, there is the effect on the position of the United States in the whole world. I love America and her greatness and the best of what she has stood for in the hopes and dreams of men everywhere for almost two hundred years. I don't want to see her good name smeared with hate and blackened with shame, and I think that is what is happening right now.

Second, there is the effect on the position of the South. I am by birth and by pride a southerner. My forefathers were changed overnight from wealthy aristocrats to poor tradesmen and farmers when their plantations were burned by General Sherman's Yankee troops on the march to the sea. All or most of my relatives now live in Alabama and Tennessee. I was born in Florida of Alabama parents and brought up in Texas and I love the Southland. I value the graciousness and culture and hospitality and fine literature she has produced in the best of her heritage. All this makes me the more ashamed of the effect on her good name when hate mongers and demagogues kill innocent people and preach hate and claim to be good southerners. They are not good southerners. They are traitors to the South. Their evil work has destroyed the position of great southern moderates and great southern leaders in the Congress of the United States. Instead of southern senators and representatives being able to debate civil rights legislation rationally, with some hope of intelligent legislative procedure, they are now in the position of being either for federally enforced civil rights laws or for murder. They are defeated before the debate even begins. The racial problem belongs to the whole nation and not just to the South. On this question the linen of the North is just as dirty as that of the South. But how can any southerner win any argument about that after what happened last Sunday?

Third, there is a difference between the two crimes because of the difference in me and perhaps in you. I was already aware of other kinds of injustice right here in Houston. For example, a sheriff's deputy told me just last Thursday morning that a teenage boy from Tanglewood or River Oaks is more than six times *less* likely to be sent to reform school than a boy from the Ship Channel area for the same crime. Then again, it doesn't take many trips on the streets in this area, such as Clinton Drive, and then out in the southwest part of Houston to see how an unbalanced share of tax money for good streets and other improvements gets spent in one part of the county. It doesn't take much experience with the political squabbling over the city-county charity hospital to see how the quality of humane medical care a person gets depends far too much on his bank account. All these things are examples of injustice being practiced right here in Harris County, and we Christians are responsible for working and voting to change these things. But last Sunday in Birmingham has made me realize more than ever that these are not the only injustices here in Harris County that cry out for the attention of Christian men and women of good will. I don't think it's too farfetched to say that many of the elements that led to the Birmingham tragedy are all around us here, and now is the time to work on them, not wait until there is a tragedy here too.

Finally, there is a difference in the two crimes because of the effect the death of the four girls will probably have on race relations and the revolution that swirls around us in these days. I suggest this may prove to be a turning point in the whole situation. I pray both sides may realize things they need to realize from this shock. The Negro leadership may realize the extreme danger of some of the tactics which have been used and re-evaluate their strategy with caution. The white leadership may realize the extreme danger of encouraging defiance of court orders and the law and wild speeches made for political gain and expecting the Negro to wait and wait for a long time to get what the Constitution has said for a long time is already his.

I will close by saying these things which have come out of my prayer and Bible study and deep thought during the past days.

I am convinced that the racial problem in our day is not just a matter of complying with court orders and living orderly lives as obedient citizens. It is clearly God's Word that hatred between races and discrimination because of the color of men's skins—men who bleed the same red blood—is morally wrong and is against the core of meaning for which Christ's church stands.

I do not condemn, nor love one bit less, anyone who disagrees with me on any of this or all of it. I have said I am a southerner, and I know first-hand how deeply these things run in us. I also know Jesus loves all of us as much as he loves any of us.

I intend to do these things:

1. Pray daily for the realization of the brotherhood of men in Christ and for the victims and the criminals.

2. Ask God to wash me clean of hate and prejudice and cowardice and the immaturity that fosters them.

3. I have already written Senators Tower and Yarborough and Congressman Thomas in support of civil rights legislation, including the section on public accommodations. I tell you this simply as what I as one citizen have done. You must do what your own conscience requires of you.

4. Unless love should require it, I will not again by keeping quiet let someone think I agree with him when I do not.

5. As I try to exercise the best judgment and wisdom of which I am capable, I shall work openly to make this parish and this diocese more effective forces in removing the practice of prejudice and injustice from this community and this nation.

I pray your love and understanding as together we try in all that we do to be faithful to the God who loves all men in the world enough to give up his Son on the cross that together we might have the victory.

Usually you have no real opportunity to reply to my sermons, but this time you do. The ushers will now pass out a questionnaire which will give you a chance to let me know what you think. Please do not sign it unless you want to, and if for any reason you should not want to fill one out, then I suggest you join me in silent prayer for the next five minutes while those who do want to reply work on their paper. Just leave the questionnaires in the pews when you leave the church, and I will appreciate it.

§88 Dick Gregory

Dick Gregory was born on October 12, 1932 in St. Louis, Missouri. Born into poverty, Gregory excelled at athletics, eventually earning a track and field scholarship to Southern Illinois University. After being drafted into the army in 1954, Gregory later returned to SIU but never completed his degree. Having practiced stand-up comedy while in the service, Gregory got his big break in 1961 as a last minute fill-in at the Chicago Playboy Club. He quickly earned a three-year contract and was on his way to a national following. In 1963 Gregory enthusiastically joined the civil rights movement, raising money and demonstrating in places such as Greenwood, Birmingham and Selma. Gregory's much-heralded autobiography, *Nigger*, also was published in 1963. To date the book has sold more than seven million copies. While Gregory remains a very popular speaker on the college circuit, he continues to write. He also markets nutrition products. His second memoir, *Callus on My Soul*, was published in 2000. Gregory and his wife of more than 45 years, Lillian, live in Plymouth, Massachusetts. The couple has ten children.

The Student Nonviolent Coordinating Committee (SNCC) had targeted Selma and the Dallas County area for voter registration activity in 1963. The Reverend Bernard Lafayette and his wife Colia, both 22 years old, had arrived in February. After surviving assaults and harassment, SNCC called a mass meeting in May led by Executive Secretary Jim Forman, which had been surrounded by armed whites. That first major meeting of SNCC's Voter Registration Project, went until 1 a.m., until the armed group of whites dispersed. Sheriff Jim Clark, perhaps the second most feared southern lawman next to "Bull" Connor, frequently intimidated and abused local Selma blacks.

In September, Forman's assistant Worth Long replaced the Lafayettes in Selma and things immediately heated up. On September 15th, five high school students sitting-in at several lunch counters were arrested and beaten. Later that day nearly 100 black high school students marched in protest. They, too, were arrested. Long was also arrested (even though not demonstrating) and beaten in the county jail. Into this maelstrom came Forman, who began conducting frequent mass meetings at Brown A.M.E. Chapel, the same church to which badly beaten civil rights marchers would retreat in March 1965. His aim was less on demonstrating and boycotting, and much more on registering people to vote. The slogan for the project was "One Man, One Vote" with the climactic goal being a massive turnout of local blacks at the Dallas County Courthouse on Freedom Day, October 7th. Forman called in the advance guard: John Lewis was arrested along with 27 Selma University students on September 25th for leading a picket at the courthouse. Two days later, Dick Gregory's wife Lillian was arrested. Dorothy Height of the National Council of Negro Women flew in for the demonstrations. And on October 7th, the celebrated author and civil rights activist, James Baldwin addressed a large gathering at Brown Chapel. As Forman notes in his memoir, "The inclusion of personalities from the world of entertainment, from the arts, was a tactic we developed from our analysis that many people in the nation identified with them. Whatever they did, other black people would in a sense feel it."

In order to maximize participation for the Freedom Day on October 7th, Forman was able to coax Gregory into coming to Selma and addressing would-be registrants. On Friday, October 4th, Gregory delivered a scathing satirical rebuke of the "white southern man." Whether Gregory had even planned to address the topic is not known, but it is clear that his caustic humor was propelled by a lone white mole taking notes in the audience. Gregory in turn uses the outsider's presence as synechdochic of the southern white man's arrogance, ignorance, and general stupidity in dealing with the southern black man. But at the close of the lengthy address, Gregory turns serious, going after both the white and black clergy and their cowardly, abysmal failure to do God's will. Perhaps Forman had given Gregory a copy of Bernard Lafayette's June field report. It began, "In spite of the deep fears among the Negro community, we have been able to move along with some degree of success. We have been able to get very little cooperation from the Negro ministers and church leaders, as a whole."

The following evening, Saturday, October 5th, Gregory again addressed a mass audience. But in 24 hours his tone had changed dramatically. From the dozens-playing satirist from Chicago, Gregory had become the New Testament hermaneut. Gregory attempts to convict the adults in his audience that their timidity to get behind the jailed children parallels what happened to Christ's followers when he was crucified. And like Judas, they are willing to sell out their own kids, who they raised to be strong and patriotic. The contrast from Friday to Saturday night is indeed striking, so we have paired the addresses. While Selma would largely remain out of the civil rights limelight for another year and a half, the Monday Freedom Day was a success as more than 250 black Selmans braved Clark's posse of lawmen and lined the street leading to the courthouse.

———

Speech at Brown Chapel A.M.E. Church
Selma, Alabama
October 4 and 5, 1963

Friday, October 4, 1963

I say thank you very much. I can't tell you what a pleasure it is being here, I'm just sorry I had to show up ten days late. But I think I was able to see my all-time first, see a white southern dumb cop writin'. I've never been able to see one writin,' he's writin' like so. Every time I've seen 'em in the meetins they've always had tape recorders, but this one must have a little piece of education he got from somewhere or he just. . . . That's the first one I know have enough intelligence to write and I still don't believe he got anything on that paper. Then again, I think we'd better not put him down too much nor laugh at him too hard cause on one 'dem old good songs I caught him kinda shakin' his finger der a lil' bit. So that's wonderful when man comes to spy on us and end up shakin' wid' us for a few minutes. That mean he can be saved, too.

Yeah that's, uh, a great thing. It always amazed me to wonder how southern white folks will knock theyself out, pose as all kindsa everything but a cop to slip in a Negro meetin' and we haven't got around to wantin' to slip into a Ku Kluck Klan rally. So I think it speaks for itself, the whole world wants to slip in and be around right and good and godliness, but only fools wanna be around filth.

'Cause it just knocks me out to see white folks talk about how much they dislike us, how they can't get along wit us. And I'm glad they was in here tonight to witness two Negro women that one of 'em and I don't even have to put 'em together, anyone of 'em probably even have more education and more intelligence than this whole police department put together.

Now these are the people that don't wanna be around us. These are the people that complain 24 hours a day. These are the peons, these are the idiots that do the dirty work. These are the dogs that get paid to do all the bitin'. These are the ones that have become big men among small people. These are the ones that need something like that and many southern white men need the job of bein' a southern cop 'cause when you sit down put yourself in a southern white man's shoes. Think about it for a minute. Just think about it for a minute. A southern white man. Only thing you have to identify with is a drinkin' fountain, a toilet, and the right to be able to call me nigger. And before we really put him down, put yourself in his shoes. Think. That's all you have to identify with the world is a toilet. Then you know why they got toilet ways.

Put yourself in this southern white man's shoes and you'll understand why he would blow up one of yo' churches. You'll understand why he will fight you the way he will fight you. Everyone was so upset over a white man dynamitin' a church. And you forgot John Brown put forty sticks of dynamite in his white mammy's luggage and blew her plane out the sky.

Put yourself, put yourself in this southern white man's shoes for just a few minutes and you'll almost get out there and wanna hit your own self in the head with a stick. Put yourself in this southern white man's shoes. Just think. Never owned anything new, ignorant, can't read, can't write. But when I wanna feel superior to you, I can walk into my own toilet. That's the difference. And when he lose that toilet, baby, and we plug up one dem fountains and when he call us nigger we fix it way he have to say it a lil' bit pretty, he lost it all. He have lost it all.

This is a heck of a thing to be a white man in America, and when you threatened about losin' your toilet, you ready to kill. This is a heck of a thing to be a white man in America, and when you find out you can't call me nigga no more, not like you used to call me nigga, because he's almost 'bout to find out who that nigga really is. He's almost about to find out. Every white man in America know we are Americans, know we are Negroes and many of 'em know us by our name. And when he calls us a nigga, he's callin' us something that we not, so it must exist in his mind. So if nigger exists in his mind, who is the nigga?

Now let's take it a step further, let's take it one step further. We know this is a Bible, we know this is a book. Now when I sit here and call this a bicycle, I have called this something that it's not. The bicycle must exist where? In my mind? I'm the sick one, right? So that's why we really don't have to worry 'bout these folks. We don't have to get mad when a white man call us boy. He knows how old we are. That means he got doubts about his own manhood.

If you think white folks in this country hate us, they need us. You think these redneck crackers down here hate us. I just wish it was some kind of way, I just wish it was some kind of way that we would lay down and go to sleep tomorrow night, and when they wake up through the grace of God we would all be gone. They would go crazy lookin' for us. Where are they? Please ya'll come back.

If they could wake up and every Negro in America would be like, gone baby. Oh, I would give a million dollars just to slip back and watch Huntley and Brinkley report. I'an just see it now. "There's no clues to where the Negroes are." Ah, the news would be wild that day. "Klu Kluck Klan have announced due to all the Negroes gone in America they are moving to Alaska and now are gonna 'en lynch the Eskimos."

Ah, can't you just hear the news? "Governor Wallace decided that due that all the Negroes are gone and he have nothing else to campaign for, he's still gonna stay in politics and campaign against keepin' Jews outta pizza joints." Yeah, we could just wake up one day and all of us be gone, baby. Oh, it'd be some wild news that night. I can just see the headlines back north, "Seven Chitlin Manufacturers Found out the Negroes was Gone then Committed Suicide."

Yes, if we could only leave here for three days. Three days. Let's leave 'em down here by deyself so they can find out who da nigga is. Be all we would need. But look like we gone have to do it the hard way, and stay here and educate these folks. An' we gone educate 'em, baby, we gone teach 'em how to live and teach 'em how to act. And when you hear all this talk, talkin' about we don't know how to live and we don't know how to act and when the Negro can act like him, he'll accept us. I would rather be accepted by a elephant first if I had to act like him.

To be accepted. Here's a man here, and thank God this white man have always had a conscience, but he's always wondered what's wrong with the Negro. People say, "Well, they've had slaves before." No slave in the history of the world had to go through what the American Negro slave had to go through. Because we had a master that was lower than us. Never in the history of slavery had you had a white man that would go out in the barn and have a sex affair with all the slave women like this dog did.

Ah, you always had masters that would go out once every so often and pick the Liz Taylor out the group and bring her in the house. But the slaves were proud. We had a master that we couldn't even respect. No slave have ever had to go through that in the history of the world. We had a master that was so much below us and knew it, he said, "Sure, let 'em ride on the same bus. Just put 'em in the back." No master in the history of slavery have ever wanted to be with his slave, front or back.

But we had a man that was so low down and so ignorant he didn't even qualify to have slavery. 'Cause if he'd qualified, he would have set it up right. He set it up wrong. The biggest fool in the world know if you wanna segregate me and keep me down you don't put me in the back where I can watch you for 200 years. The biggest fool in the world know if you wanna keep me down, you don't keep me under conditions where I can become stronger than you.

And this is his greatest mistake whether he know it or not: he do not represent strength. He represents a gun, he represents crooked ways, he represents dirty, trampy dealing. That's why we can let him in here, 'cause we stronger than he is. And if you don't believe it, watch a demonstration, when they round up a bunch of Negroes and all they have to do is say "you under arrest" and pull the wagon up and we'll walk into the car, watch what happens. Watch what happens. A little baby could arrest Negro demonstrators 'cause we intend to go to jail so it's no big thing when they knock. It's no big thing at all, baby, because we know when the man say "you're under arrest," we goin'.

Now I don't know who they tryin' to impress, their little white kids at home that still is young enough to believe that they somebody or what. But they haven't been one demonstration in America this year that caused for a Negro to be knocked down 'cause when we go out we intend to go to jail.

Ah, when a man slips so low he forgets about God. The dirtiest hoodlums have ever lived and you're lookin' at it now, on television. They got this chump up here in Washington, D.C. on the Senate investigation. These people have talked about all types of murders, all types of everything. And as I sit everyday and look at this hoodlum testify of a hundreds thousands of millions of dollars and the amount of dope they slipped in. I can't help but feel kinda happy for them. Feel sorry for these fools like this that would throw tear gas in a church. The dirtiest hoodlums in the world still haven't lost respect for God's church, black or white. Here's a man that have become so insane and so bitter on the hate pill, if it means losin' God to keep this thing away from him, he'd do it. And you know why he would do it? Because he had a little bit of doubt in him, had a conscience.

And he had to tell himself for a long time that you was inferior to him. He knew better but he had to keep telling himself that because God gave him a little piece of conscience in order for him to rest at night, he had to convince himself beyond a shadow of a doubt that he was better than you and it ran him crazy. Livin' a lie for a hundred years and you would go dynamitin' a church. Live in hate for a hundred years and you would tear gas this same crowd.

This man had to sleep and he had to say that he was better than you. And he said that and he wake up every now and then and he look around and he still can't believe it. And he sits up little hurdles, sits up little roadblocks in front of you, so he can still tell his warped mind that he must tell himself this and he must believe this. Because he had to leave here tonight and go back to a shack. That cop on the street got to knock you down and hope he can whoop you for five hours, 'cause he got to go home to something less than what you have to go home to because the truth is in your house.

There's a man here that's human. We fought wars wit' him. We've helped him plant his crop and we raised his kids. And even went so stone crazy he tear gassing ours. But we raise his kids. And that black woman never told him that she raised that white boy of his that lynched her black son. Never told him that. Said the Lord gone take care of him for us. Well that's right. That's the Lord out there in that street, that gone be the Lord out there in that street Monday goin' down to register to vote. They're gone take care of him. See, we don't have to be violent. We have the three most violent things man could ever use on our side. We have truth, we have justice, and we have the United States Constitution. And with those three things, baby, we can't lose.

We can't lose with those three things. This chump might kill you wrongly, but he'll never win. Because he hasn't got the truth on his side. And if you don't think that three things on your side creates a winner. If the south today wanted to raise the educational standard of the dumb, southern white boy, it would be a simple matter. But he do not have the intelligence to know, so we got to tell him. If he wanted to raise the educational standard of his dumb, stupid son, then you know what he would do? He would pull the Negro teachers out of the Negro schools and put 'em in the white schools and take the white teachers and put 'em in the Negro schools. And his boy would learn from it.

Now I know I don't have to break it down to you, but I got, I don't, I can't trust his intelligence so just give me a few minutes to break it down to him. All I'm really tryin' to say is that I want to prove to him beyond a shadow of a doubt that ninety percent of the southern Negro teachers are much better equipped and better qualified than these white teachers. Now the reason hold it, hold it, hold it, hold it, hold it. The reason for it, don't want to disturb him now 'cause we got him concentratin' for a few minutes. The reason that the Negro teacher in the south would be better qualified and better equipped to teach his dumb son is simple. We were denied the pleasure of going to a bad University of Alabama. We were denied the pleasure of going to a bad University of Mississippi. Consequently we went north to Harvard, Yale, NYU, Howard, UCLA, University of Chicago. We went to the best universities in the world and then came back home.

So due to the facts that we as Negroes was denied the privilege to go to one 'dem bad, low-grade, white colleges we had to go up north and go to a good school. Thank God, it backfired on them again.

Through this man's dumb, stupid mistakes and hate, he have made the American Negro the strongest man in the world today. And he knows it and he don't know it. That's why he gets his little cattle prods and he gets all his police out. Because what he realized, we strong, he don't wanna believe it. There's two basic things that go in to build up a strong man: joy and pain. Joy makes you wanna live, pain teaches you how to live. There's not a race alive on the face of the earth has had as much, both, as the American Negro. So that makes us the number one strong man in this country.

And what makes it so beautiful is here's a man sitting over here that due to he have so much hate for me, he don't understand that I decide the fate and the destiny of this country today. Because the Negro in America is the number one strong man and you southern Negroes is stronger than us all. He's gonna learn this one day. He's gonna learn it when he comes up to you one day sayin', "It wasn't none of me." This southern white man is gonna come to you on his knees because he's too much of a fool to know the only friend this southern, tramp, red neck got is you because the northern honky hates his guts. Hates his guts! And if he don't believe it, let him go up to New York and tell one 'dem white cops what he do down here and they'll bust his head wide open.

The only friend, the only friend this man and people like him have is the southern Negro and he do not know it. How can a man walk in a church like this every time you have a meeting and see what goes on and still can't wake up to the fact of who's winning? Can one group of individuals be that stupid? Well baby if for no other reason than to be on the winning side you ought turn traitor tonight and get wit' us. You southern Negroes, whether you know it or not, you will free yourselves. Then you will free the northern Negro. Then together we will free this American white man.

Every now and then, every now and then you hear this southern white man say, "You niggers want mo' than what the white folks got." He feels what we gonna do for him, but he really don't know. We gonna free this southern white man because every southern white man haven't got a damn thing. That's what we gon' do for this southern white man, that's what we gon' do for this southern white man. Every time we integrate a golf course in the South, it was 10,000 white folks that didn't know that golf course existed. I dare say how many cops on the police department didn't know where to go where to register to vote until we started and they had to come down and arrest us. Every time we integrate a library in the South there was 20,000 white folks that didn't know where that library was.

In the southern white man, you got two fireman standing out there that they have some northern friends. Just check up north and find out what you make compared to your northern brother, driving the same truck and fighting the same heat. You get a dollar hour less. Well baby we fixin' to get you your money so you can be somebody. The white man that has a job down here in the factory, he makes a dollar less an hour than his same white brother in Philadelphia but they give him the privilege down here of calling me nigger, of having his drinking fountain, of having his own washroom. But, baby, when I take his washroom away from him, plug up one of his fountains, and make him call me a nigger a little bit sweeter, he gon' ask for his other dollar a hour. And when he ask for that other dollar a hour, he gon' get it. And you'd figure he'd been working eight hours a day, we gon' give him eight more dollars a day times five. That'll be forty dollars added on to that little peanuts they giving him now. Then he won't have to hate me as hard then 'cause he has forty dollars, go on and have some fun, extra. He has some money to get some insurance for the family and send his kids to some of them good schools we sendin' our kids to.

We gon' get him some rights, whether he know it or not. Just God bless him, and hope God let him hang on long enough so we can educate him and get that monkey off his back and straighten things out for him. 'Cause there ain't nothin' wrong with this southern white man that a little education won't help me, just don't know. Southern white man will call you a monkey, they've called you monkey before 'cause they don't know. If he just stop before he called you monkey and, dawned on, a monkey got straight hair. If this man would just think before he called you monkey, that a monkey has thin lips, his mouth is cut wide, but a monkey got thin lips. If he would just think for a few minutes before he called you monkey, he would find out a monkey got blue eyes. You know, by God, if would go on and look at his folks, he might could see that monkey.

So you see, when you stop and think about it, there's nothing wrong with this man that all we got to do is sit and stop and teach him. That's all. He don't mean to act like this, but we haven't taken time out to teach him how he's supposed to act. Every time you look around you hear him talking about Negro women with illegitimate kids. And he living in a neighborhood where they got abortion credit cards. You ain't talking about Negroes on relief and he . . .

[cut in tape]

And this air base right over here we might have to take the commander out of there and put another one in because that's gonna be off-limits.

[cut in tape]

And we gon' say white folks keep your nigger ways, but we gon' mess with your money.

[cut in tape]

Plus, he said a couple of things about Bobby Kennedy and vicious as Jimmy Hoffa is, Hoffa never said anything about Bobby, you know. Said you might have a couple of old tricks and we might meet him in jail one day. Said he might be sitting wit' us, singing, "We Shall Overcome." Well, I don't want to give too many secrets away but, uh, let me tell you one thing, gon' be some changes in a few days, baby. Gon' be some changes in a few days. You people just keep your head up, keep fightin', go on down there and register to vote.

You got a whole lots of protection in this town now. You got more protection coming. They not going to be able do a whole lots of these things that they been doing and getting away with it. Go ahead downtown, register, walk on in there, execute your right to vote. Execute your right to vote. A lot of these white folks think when we get the power to vote down here, that we gon' put them out of office and put us in. But that won't be necessary because when we get the power to vote down here, them gon' be out doing us, to help us. Like one thing about this southern white politician, he knows how to roll with the punch. Ten years ago he just said nigger any way he wanted to say it, now a couple of us vote, and he don't say it too loud. And we threaten to go down and vote again, and you don't hardly hear him use that word no more. So we gonna straighten him out, but it's left up to you. We've let him try to straighten out himself too long, you understand? Too long we've let him win.

Man gave us everything, bless his little heart. Gave us religion and now we got to show him how it work. Gave us the word nigger, now we got show him who the nigger really is. Now he gon' be alright one day cause he been around soul too long for none of it to have rubbed off on him. Oh, he get off by theyself and act colored. He slipped tonight over there. Oh, he was really going with it. You know, Al Lingo probably sits down to a plate of them good chitlins every now and then. But they so busy worrying about being nobody, he's just going through this light change right now. He got to knock us down. This makes them big in the eyesights of man, but I wonder how small it makes 'em in the eyesights of them other folks.

So we don't have to worry. You have the main things on your side that you need. You are the strongest group of people on the face of the earth today. We decide the fate and the destiny of this country and to top that off, we don't hate him. That's the beautiful thing, we don't hate him. Matter of fact, we've bent over backwards with this clown, trying to go along wit' him. Hundred years ago he told us, when you get like me baby you can come on in with me. We didn't argue with 'em, we tried to get like him hundred years ago. Slaves didn't wear shoes or nothing. We've put on his shoes, put on his socks, put on his drawers, put on his shirt, put on his tie, put on his suit. We had this cat covered from the ground to the Adam's apple and he still didn't give it to us. Eighty year period, he said get like me and we tried, this had him right down. And we didn't get mad at him.

Some cat decided well man made us this big lip and we grew a mustache for him so we could hide that lip from him. In a eighty year period, baby, we have gone from the bottom of our feet to the bottom of our nose trying to pacify whitey. And he still didn't give it to us and 20 years ago, some cat decided, wait a minute, "Let's still be fair with 'em." Must be this nappy, kinky hair and we processed our wig. Now in a 100-year period we have gone from the bottom of our feet to the top of our head trying to get like this man wanted us to be. And he still didn't give it to us. Now we gon' have to take it from him. And we gon' get it too, baby. 'Cause every time we snatch we get a piece of it and this whole thing [inaudible]. Nah, he gon' [inaudible] watch you [inaudible] they ain't doing no snatchin', they ain't doing nothin' but hitting. We doin' all the snatchin' and when they hit, they break off a little piece for us, and we hold onto it.

Don't forget, Monday, walk out and show 'em for every time they threw the tear gas in here made you stronger. Show 'em for every time they knocked your kids down in the street, it made you stronger. Show 'em for everything they get out there and do and use against ya, it'll make you stronger. Not weak because one weak man cannot make a strong group, as this American Negro, weak because he thinks weak. Monday is the day to prove to 'em. He has a lot of weapons on his side. He has all the lies. Turns around and he calls us, outside agitators. Here we went, American Negro, went all the way over to Germany to fight the war, and Hitler didn't call us outside agitators. We went all the way to Japan to fight a war, and the Japs didn't call us outside agitators. And you know why? Because as vicious, as ignorant, as Hitler was, he still had more sense than these clowns to know that when a man was fighting for what he believed in and what he believed in was right wat'nt no way in the world he could make us outside agitator over there.

That's what this man is gonna have to wake up to. Calls us communists, if he would just stop and visualize his own actions, then maybe he could find the parallel between himself and the communists. Let's take a peep into it. Now you had so many people in East Berlin that wanted freedom, they was leaving, going over to West Berlin, that the communist folks decided to put up a brick wall. You have so many people that's hungry for the truth, we have to spend hundreds of millions of dollars for radio-free Europe.

Now let's look at this situation down here. You got so many of us that want freedom, the man had to bring in the cattle prod, the Lingo's, the firehoses. I see no difference in this type of action here than what the communists are doing. So who acts more like the communists, us or 'dem? We have to spend hundreds of million dollars a year for radio-free Europe because the communist newspapers is not going to tell the truth. How many times have you picked up one of these southern newspapers and read the truth? So who acts like more like the communists, us or them? Who acts like more like the outside agitators? These cats act like foreigners down here. They act like a bunch of Moon folks. They just got here, it's gon' knock everything down. Who acts like the outside agitator? When he stole me from Africa and brought me over here, he didn't call me no outside nothin'. But he charged me first-class taxes over here, and he wants to keep me a second-class citizen over here. And that arithmetic have never work right nowhere.

So he's in trouble now. He is definitely in trouble. He didn't realize he gave his animals more protection than he gave me. They got a deer season, a hunting license, a fishing license, even got a game warden. And I'm sure that game warden that they hire, care a little bit 'bout them animals. But they just run a Lingo in here on us in and a Clark that don't even like people. So I guess we gonna have to get us some colored sheriffs. That's right get us some colored sheriffs that comes in these churches every Sunday, get 'em some heart, get 'em some soul. It's not gonna go out there and knock little white kids down.

So only way we can do this is gon' out there Monday. If you go out there strong enough they'll know what you gon' do and give you one. You don't even have to elect them. So I can't tell you how beautiful you are. I can't tell you how shook up you got these people here, ah, they shook up, baby, shook up. Anytime you see fireman standing in our doors, make sure that our lives will be safe and protected and the exits won't be blocked, they shook up, baby. Anytime whitey gets up off his Friday night fish fry to come out here and watch us, they shook up, baby. Now, just keep 'em shook up.

I don't know why this clown hadn't been able to figure out that we gon' win it. I heard Governor Wallace say the other day, "We winning" and that made me know Governor Wallace must be colored or something. 'Cause I know we winnin' and when Wallace said, "We winnin'," that mean he must be us. It would be awkward if ole Wallace could go home and find out his mother was colored. But it'd be awkward if he went home, knocked on the door, said, "Mother, mother" and she came to the door and said, "Who dat out dere?" It probably would be just our luck that we get something that low down and filthy and end up, it'd have to be one of us.

But everything gon' be alright. This cat's fighting hard and the worst thing in the world is lose a battle the way they losin'. They played this game by all the crooked rules, invented the game, played it crooked. And we played him fair and we gon' outplay him being fair than he is with his own game, being crooked. And haven't got too much more time left and then he's gon' be in trouble. 'Cause man it's a heck of a thing when today he can borrow a dime and go sit down there in the drug store, Walgreen's drug store, and say, "Give me a cup of coffee," looking all bad and everything.

And in a couple of more years, he gon' borrow that same dime and go sit in there but we gon' be on the scene then. And teach the owner how you supposed to look when you come in the drugstore to get a cup of coffee, and he gon' throw him out this time. Tell him, "Boy, you can't come in here drinking coffee with no tie on, look at my colored friends." Gon' throw him out the door. Throw him out the door. He's in trouble 'cause his own white brother's fixin' to change the rules on him. Told him 100 years, said, "Baby, all you need is that white face, you superior to them," and he ate it up. That's what his Yankee brother made a deal with him, you boss the Negroes, we'll boss the money, and he thought he had something bossing us. And his brother don' stole him blind. Got all the money from him he wanted and fixin' to tell him, "I was playing about them, man. They alright." Now, he gon' find out the little, ole white face didn't make him so superior. Matter of fact, it hurt 'em. 'Cause had he known he wat'nt no better than me, he would've got him a little bit more education. Had he known that he wat'nt no better than me, he would've been a little better man. But he in trouble now. Ten years from now, he gon' run up there, looking for a job, talking about, "You remember me, I . . . I. . . ." And when we take things over, we ain't gon' be too hard, we've gonna give 'em 40 points cause they were hung up in that trick for so long. And they still couldn't pass it.

So Monday, dis is the day, the day is over to be scared. Too late to be scared, they'd already blew your church in, in Birmingham. Just so happen that they didn't kill everybody in it, but it wat'nt they fault. Blew it in, and I flew into Birmingham, and I walked to the side of that church and I looked at that window with that picture of Christ wit' his face blown out. And I told my wife, I said, "Honey, I want you to look at that window there because that is one of the greatest pieces of artwork that exists on the face of the earth. Because it took 100 years of hate to produce an artist that could produce that picture the way it looks now." No artists in the history of the world have had to go to school that long, have had to paint that long, to produce anything. But whoever threw that dynamite was the artist of that piece of glass still in that window down in Birmingham. There's a heck of a price they had to pay to produce an artist that can produce a masterpiece.

So we can't be afraid anymore. The days of being scared is over. And it kills me when a Negro is scared. Because he gets scared in so many funny ways. Preacher say, "Well, I don't want ya'll having no rallies at my place, not that I don't dig the cause, but this is a place of Holy Communion." That same Negro that would tell you that, would tell Christ's mother if she approached him about having that kid in his place today, she'd still end up going to a manger if it was left up to him, talking about Holy Communion. Lord, these preachers, white and black, would ever wake up in this country. If the religious leaders in this country, white and black, would ever wake up, we would never sit and watch a thing like that because it would have been impossible for them to exist. That's why we halfway understand him. If religion had played its part down through the years, if you would have talked about this thing on Sunday, we wouldn't have to be in here on Friday night. But you were so busy talking 'bout them other things because, ah, this thing here might have heard about you and something might have happened to you.

That church that was dynamited, there in Birmingham, 90 percent of that blame goes on religious leaders in America—white and black. Because they sit right up in these churches and let hate go on and it's a funny thing, they let it go on in the church and it had bounced back on the church.

These clowns out there that threw the tear gas in here on ya, they went to church. They went to church and that white preacher didn't teach 'em when he could have. And the Negro preachers didn't teach us when he could have to be honest with the folks and tell them what they need to hear instead of telling them what they wanted to hear. If the religious leaders would wake up, the Bull Connor's and the Lingo's and the Wallace's, would either wake up or go to sleep forever.

When you got a religious leader that's walking the line and pushing it and playing two sides to a middle and afraid to speak up to a local mayor when his boss is supposed to be up there, then there's something wrong with his religion. When a religious leader is not willing and not ready, black or white, to die for my cause because he knows my cause is right and if he think my cause is not right, then get on the other side with them. 'Cause we know where we're going. It's an awful day; it's an awful day in the church, people, when a swimming pool will integrate in Atlanta, golf course will integrate in Mississippi, taverns and bars and nightclubs are integrating all over the country, and the churches still haven't opened up their doors. That's a disgrace.

And you can't blame it all on them white boys neither. Got to blame it on both of 'em, got to get both them cats together. Can't blame it on no colored cops cause we ain't got no colored police down, that's all whites. But you gotta get that white preacher and that colored preacher all over in one bowl and just put it down on all of 'em, and say, "Baby, you have failed us. And if you failed us, you've failed the man upstairs. And if you've failed him, we really can't use ya no more." Oh yeah, horrible things happen. Sit up and look where they kicked that woman out that Catholic church in New Orleans last year and everybody thought that was good, and I felt sorry for the woman. 'Cause when the Pope can go along with a racially segregated school 'till the year one thousand nine hundred and sixty-two, then let that woman go along with it 'till her daughter graduates. Church have failed.

You better wake up, you better wake up somewhere down the line. And if you don't believe this church have failed just listen to the way people talk today, just listen. Had the church been doing their part in this great struggle, today everyone in America would be saying, "Thank God," instead of "Thank the United States Supreme Court." If we had to wait on our religious leaders, we still wouldn't a had it. Nine Supreme Court justices, that we wouldn't even guaranteed that they had ever gone to church, reached up and got that thing for us. And religious leaders all over this country, they still running and dodging and hiding and Tomming. And the worst type of Tom is a white Tom. 'Cause he ain't supposed to Tom. Go to World

War II and fought for what he believed in and came back home and can't even teach it. So somebody's gonna have to wake up the religious leaders and hope that, that we way ahead of 'em now, but they might wake up and run around here and catch up with us 'cause we wanna give it back to 'em some kind of way, if they let us. This week, God bless you. Thank you.

———

Saturday, October 5, 1963

I'd like to say thank you very much and again good evening. I guess it's 'bout the first time in my life I ever requested a church song, 'cause I usually listen to all of them. Some I like and understand and some I don't like. But I asked for 'em to sing that song because as I sit back there and wondered, had we been livin' in that day in era of the crucifixion of Christ, when it was taking place, when it was going on. And had we turned and ran the other way, I wonder how we would've felt, 20 years later, 30 years later, knowing that we weren't there and could have been there. If I could honestly prove beyond a shadow of a doubt that I had some kinfolks in that same area, in that same location, and they didn't show up to say no more than "I'm wit you, baby," I would be ashamed of them, and ashamed of myself.

We goin' through an era today equally as important. So amazing how we come to church everyday and cry over the crucifixion of Christ, but we don't cry over these things that's going around among us. When if he was here now he would cry and take those nails again, for this problem. Just so happened that his day and time, religion was the big problem. Today same situation only it's a color. What do you think would happen to Christ tonight if he arrived in this town a black man and tried to vote Monday? What do you think would happen? Would you be there? Then how come you not with these kids? Because he said, "whatever happens to the least, happens to us all." And I wonder one day when this final push is over, when the whole world know that this was the work of God. When they sit back in the nineteen's and sing, "Were You There," I wonder how many of us have to hang our head in shame? How many of us will have to hang our heads in shame?

Let's analyze the situation. We not saying let's go downtown and take over city hall. We not saying let's stand up on the rooftops, and throw bricks at white folks. We not saying let's get some butcher knives and guns and make 'em pay for what they've done to us. We saying we want what you said belongs to us. You have a Constitution, me as a black man goin' to a black school, you make me sit down and take a test on the United States Constitution. You have never made me take a test on this Bible. Mama had to give that to me at home. You have kept me in a segregated school, but you make me take a test on a Constitution that haven't worked for no one but you. And you expect me to learn it from front to back or you gonna flunk me. So, I learned it when I didn't even wanna learn it and I passed it.

You made me stand up as a little kid and sang, "God Bless America," "America the Beautiful," and all those songs the white kids were singing. I pledged my allegiance to a flag. That's what I'm askin' you for today. No Negro had anything to do with sittin' down and writing the Constitution so no white man can say we tricked him. He wrote that himself and he told the whole world about it. He said it was fair, he said it was just, and he's carried your son to war to die for it. And when you tell me a white man, with his corrupt beliefs can come and get your boy and send him to Korea, send him to Germany to die for something you not gonna to be a part of. And a man can't get your daughter, can't get your son, can't get you to go to jail. It's unbelievable his system have warped our minds this much. It's unbelievable you would let your son go and fight in a foreign country for a neighborhood he can't even live in.

But you won't let your kids march, demonstrate, and you won't demonstrate for what's yours. This I can't understand. That's why I'm here. That's what really made me make up my mind. If America went to war in the morning, I'm going 'cause as corrupt as the system is, I dig it. But I'm going. And then I had to stop and think. If I can subject myself to going to some foreign land and take a chance of being away from my wife, my family, my loved ones and take a chance on losing my life to guarantee some foreigner, that's livin' some place I can't even spell, a better way of life than I can my own brothers and sisters, there must be somethin' wrong with me. That's when I made my decision to come into the South, knowing when I stepped off the plane I could be killed. Knowing that getting involved might mean I wouldn't eat. Knowing that I might go to jail.

But I tell you what, I think jail is the best place. Jail is the best place. When a man can take a police that's supposed to be upholding the law and use them against you, then I think jail is the best place. We've talked about bandits and villains all over the world, but we know of none on record that have blown up a church. Do you realize the incident that happened in Birmingham, the incident that have happened in many places in the South, if that same incident would have happened in North Korea, in West Berlin, or South Vietnam, America would have been at war. And you ready for this? You would've been upset. Had you read about the communists blowing up a church, you would've been upset. This one you scared to even talk about around white folks. This you scared to even talk about around white folks. They had to tell you that Monday how sorry they was, and I dare say how many of you made like you didn't even know it had happened.

This is the problem we have. This is the problem that we faced with. It's in our hands now. You are the soldier, whether you wanted to be the soldier or not. For some reason, you kept saying, "Turn the other cheek." You kept praying to God every time something happened to you and for some reason or 'nother, He believed ya. And as He looked down, out of all the peoples in the world, He had to probably nudge His daddy, and say, "I've been checking 'em, pa, for 100 years, they're the ones." "How do you know?" "Well, look what they've been going through. Let's look at the books. Look at the lynchings; they haven't fought back. Look at the shootings; they haven't fought back. Look at the bad things, papa, they've gone through." "Yes, Son, kinda makes me, remind me of your story."

In 1963 He probably nodded His head and gave you the ball. And the best thing for us to do is get ourselves together and either take it or give it back to Him. Take it or give it back to Him. I can't believe a parent would worry about a kid being in jail over night, and then again I can believe, I guess. But how can you worry about a kid bein' in jail over night and can live with him under the system you have to bring him up in. I can understand a white man worrying about his kid being in jail because he's missin' something, missin' something. For 50 years they've been telling us about a Negro crime rate, telling us we do all the crime. Never came to your house once, and said, "Mrs. so and so, would you talk to your kids and keep 'em out of jail." Not only once, they wanna talk to you in the middle of the night. Because there's somethin' that happens to a white man when he have to look at a black man in jail for right. There's somethin' that happens to a man's conscience when he have to look at your kids in jail at night. But nothing seems to happen to this man when he looks at the horrible things that've happen to your kids in growing up because it happens so subtle and we have accepted it so nicely he really can't see it.

And the bad part about it is we really can't see it. When is the last time you felt your ears growing? But they growed. When is the last time you could feel your little feet growing into big feet? But they growed. When is the last time you felt your hair growing? But it grows. And as these things happen to us, this problem slips up on us. Slips up on us in a way you can't tell. Or in a way you don't wanna tell because every man knows when he need a haircut, every man knows when his feet's too big. But in a 100-year period, we seem not to know what this problem is doing to us. Because we've accepted it. Did we accept it because we wanted to do somethin' about it? Or did we accept it because we felt this is all we could do?

We have everything to work with. It's a difficult thing when a man says, "Make me some biscuits, Mama," and he didn't bring nothing home for you to make biscuits with. It's a heck of a thing. When he has everything there and the biscuits aren't done, maybe he'll look elsewhere or maybe he'll give up completely. There's a funny thing that happened in 1963, and the sooner we wake up and realize it, the better off this whole world is gonna be. Because for some reason, God has put in your hands the salvation of not just America, this thing is bigger than this, the whole world. And if you don't believe it, check the papers, check the records. Khrushchev and Kennedy never sit down and made a deal 'till you people in the South started rising up. The monks in Vietnam never started striking back for religious freedom, until we had a Greenwood and a Birmingham.

Peoples looking at you all over the world because they come over here, they see the situation, and they gave you up. Gave ya up and they couldn't understand that. The Negro in America has the highest standard of living, the highest educational standard, the highest medical care of any black man in the world over and most white. And we got backward countries that's getting more respect from this white man than you could ever command. Because we've grinned when he want us to grin. We've cried when he's want us to cry. We've spent money when he want us to spend money. And we've done without when he said, "Do without." He owns all the missiles in the whole world, and then he talks about you owning a switchblade, and you get ashamed of it. He's started all the wars, and he talks about you cuttin' somebody. He don't give us anything else to do. He don't occupy my time, he makes me feel small, he calls me everything on the job but my name. So I'm aggravated before I get home.

Then he tells me about my education, he tells me about my education. Well, if it took education his style to produce a clown that would thrown some dynamite in a church, I hope we never get that. If it took education to produce an American white man that would neatly lay 40 sticks of dynamite in his mother's luggage and blow a jet plane out the sky for a, for some insurance money, I hope we never get that. The greatest education in the world he can get from us if he only look back. We could teach him the most important thing in the world today. It's teach him how to live, teach him how to live.

I have a paper, and I wish I would've brought it with me tonight. I have a paper I keep with me because it's embarrasses me so many times, so many times. I have a paper from 1848, the New Orleans morning paper, 1848. And if you turn to that back of the paper, you'll see where white folks was running ads offering rewards to get their runaway slaves back. Can you believe that? Not can you believe that a white man would run a ad to get his slave back, but can you believe in 1848 we were running away, rebelling, and didn't have no place to run to? 1848, slaves were running away. Can you imagine what this ol' Negro had to go through? Can you just literally imagine a parent, a Negro woman coming to a black man and saying, "Honey, I'm pregnant," and the both of 'em fall on their knees and hope the baby is born deformed. Hope the baby is born cripple, or born with one leg. Can you imagine this is what a Negro had to go through? Because if they was born that way, he would have less chance of being a slave and more chance of having freedom.

Think about it. Think about the woman you love coming to tell you she's pregnant with your baby, and you cross your fingers and hope that baby's born cripple. Because you know if he's born healthy and strong. Can you imagine what it must have felt like to get on your knees and pray to your God and ask Him, "Please let it be cripple." This is what the slaves went through. A man would pray that his own son would have one arm, so maybe he could get some freedom. And 100 years from then, we have parents that worry about their kids being in jail over night. Many parents that didn't even know where their kids were for the first time, they know where they are 24 hours a day. Twenty-four hours a day, and there for a good cause and a good reason.

How can a parent let a son play football when all he can do is help his team win a victory today that's gonna be forgot tomorrow. But you can't let your son fight for freedom, somethin' that the whole world will profit by. Sometimes I wonder how much have this system corrupted us. Sometimes I wonder when will we be able to see that the day is over now that we can say we not involved. Those four kids that was killed in that church, they were not demonstrating in Birmingham. You don't have to participate, just be black. Or be white for our cause, and that bomb was thrown at you. Somebody's gonna have to get killed, we know this.

Fifty percent of the killing's our fault because we let this man get crazy on us, instead of bringing him around when we should've brought him around, we scratched our head five years too long for 'em. Tomming was good once upon a time. That's how we got here. The old folks knew that the only way they could raise you. What we call Uncle Tom isn't today was nothing but finesse and tact. The old folks had to scratch their head and grin their way into a man's heart that wouldn't accept them any other way. But I bet if they could peep out the grave and see us still Tomming, they'd be ashamed they even invented it. Ah, they had to Tom then, that's before they had federal aid, relief, and AFDC selling milk bottles. They had to Tom. But they knew how to Tom, they watn't shucking and jiving. And they helped the whole situation because they laughed their way into a man's heart that wouldn't accept 'em no other way. And what did the old folks do about Tomming? They learn him frontwards and backwards, and they taught him to us. That's why every Negro in America can think like a white man, but few white men can think like a Negro. They gon' start Tomming now.

At what point do we stop, at what point? A Negro is better off goin' to a foreign country, fighting for America than he is coming to the South, fighting for the Negro's cause because when you go to a foreign country, you have all of America behind you, white and black. When you come here, you have a few, a few. I could've stepped out of show business, joined the Peace Corps, been sent to South Vietnam, and every Negro in America never would've questioned my intentions. But join the army and fight for the black man, even Negroes walk up and ask me, "Are you doin' it for publicity?"

There's a young man here, probably one of the most underrated fighters in the country. He is one of the most brilliant comedy writers the world have produced. His salary per year is equal to that of President Kennedy. He don't have to be here. He don't have to be here at all. Here's a man who went into the South with me when I went into Greenwood, Mississippi, and he found the same thing I found. He's been with me ever since. And last week, when I was called and asked could I come in town, I was so sick, couldn't. I said, "You can have my wife. She's never been in the South without me, never been to jail without me. But she had two kids, and she feels the same way I feel. I just soon be dead in my grave than have my kids grow up under the same system I had to grow up under. And I was fortunate enough to break through mine, but at the expense of how many other Negroes had to fall by the wayside that one would be able to break through. I would rather die trying to sit my people free than be alive half free and half enslaved.

Here's a man here who flew in town last week that he like myself had never heard of Selma, Alabama. That's what you do when that thing is workin'. You hear about things and you feel things all over the world that you never heard about before. That is the beauty in right. That is the beauty in right. If 20 Negroes took pistols and got in a crap game and killed 10,000 people in this town, I still wouldn't have known where Selma, Alabama at. There's a funny thing about right, funny thing. Here's a man flew in last week who's gonna get married Saturday. Said James, "I have no guarantee that you'll be back in time for your wedding." Said, "Okay." He was here, Thursday it rained, Thursday, right? Rained real hard that Thursday, I wat'nt here but I know what goes on in Selma. So I say, "Alright, we'll pull you out of there, let you get on a bus. Go into Montgomery, catch a plane, go on back to Detroit." He says, "Well, I'll stay." I said, "Well, we don't know how long it's gon' rain." He got out that morning, and got put in jail that evening. He gave up a wedding for ya, and it might have not never been able to happen.

Every day you get more and more people the world over that's joining you with your battle. But every day when you get around these white folks and talk this crooked, filthy, dirty, foul, against the movement talk, you killin' a potential friend and making a potential enemy that might kill your own kids. Now let me run it down to you real quick, and show you what this man needs. It's nothing new. He knows what's happening is wrong.

He wanna believe it's right. So I wait for Uncle Duglow to come to work in the morning and we'll, ask him, "Is he happy?" We'll ask him 'bout these nigger, outside agitators. I won't tell ya, I'll let him tell ya. And you tell him too, baby. And you tell him. And when you tell him, that's all he needs to confirm it.

Well, let's take the same situation, let's go back. You had a guy that hit town that was raising so much hell as far as the white folks was concerned, they didn't know what to do with him. Bugged everybody, that was Christ. Now you tell me, they didn't know what he looked like. Do you believe they had to get that punk to kiss him? You mean to tell me a man that didn't hide from nobody, and they didn't know what he looked like? Nah, don't you never believe that. They did the same thing with him they gon' have to do with you. They said, "Baby, we can bump him off tonight. Tell me he don't even believe in fighting." That wat'nt no big thing to get Christ. Nah, that wat'nt no big thing to get him. He knew how they felt. Man going all over, telling 'em, "Love your enemy." Well, man, if I'm your enemy, and I hear you telling a cat to love me and I think it's a big thing to get, ah, ain't no big thing. But they had to make it big. And the only way you can make it big, I got to get one of they own. I got to get one of they own. Then it'll stand up. "Come here, Judas boy, come over here. What's this cat doing, you with?" "Oh, He's doin' wonderful things. He's doin'. . . ." You realize if Christ came back here today, he'd make a lot of people mad. Don't you know that? The man came to America healing people, the doctors would shoot him. They didn't even want you to get no Medicare, you know what they'd do if he came by here, healing everybody. Not charging no money. If he took a loaf of bread and fed everybody, the farmers would kill him. If he went out there to that river and got some water and made some wine, they'd bust him for being a bootlegger. Man, he wouldn't stand a chance today. He wouldn't stand a chance today.

Ah, the man had to go through some things. People that claimed they loved him 24 hours a day he had to keep proving things to them. "God, we know you God, we know you, but here's a piece of bread, do somethin' with it, we gon' watch." They say, "Yeah, that's alright, man, that's really, really somethin'." Then somebody threw a fish up just to be dirty. "What you gon' do with that?" Ah, they knew what he looked like. But they had to confirm the conviction. So they brought Judas in. Said, "Look here, boy. This guy you with, he's pretty nice, pretty nice guy, huh?" "Yessir, he's alright. He's really turned some wonders." He said, "Look, I got a crooked finger here, can you straighten out?" Said, "Oh no, sir." "I bet Peter and Paul could." "Sho'could." "Well, how come he not teaching you no tricks?" There it was right there.

You give a man the biggest piece of the pie, another man could come up and show him where he's wrong because you not lettin' him cut it. And he was bought, simple. Said, "Look here boy, you go out there, you see him comin', you kiss him." You mean to tell me Christ, didn't nobody know him, all that beard, that robe, the way He stood straight. You got to have somebody to spot him out for you? No, but we got to get his own to do it. We got to get his own to confirm it. Then the folks won't be too mad at us because we can always say, "Wat'nt us." That's what white folks tell you now in this town. "Ah, those Negroes won the vote, how come they don't come out?" They don't understand it goes a little bit deeper than this. But you have to come out anyway. "And, and they wanted freedom, they send them black kids overseas to die for 'em. You can't let 'em stay in jail overnight for 'em, they must not want it."

You got to check yourself one day and find out what do you want. If you want it, get over here on this side. If you don't want it, go on over there with them. Yeah, if my mother would've sold some secrets to the Russians, Mama would've been a traitor. Okay, Mom, get on over there wit 'em. You still Mama. Still dig ya, but get on, on the other side, Mama. 'Cause you messin' round with gettin' me killed. So this is 'bout what it's boiling down to, now. It's boiling down to it right now. That you got to commit. And you goin' through the same thing today I guess the folks went through when they crucified the boss. "Who else is with 'em?" And everybody just stood there and prayed silently for the first time. Then go back and said, "I prayed." Didn't see your lips moving, sister. Then, ah, the funny thing, captain wanna come to your house and say the blessing and fold his hands, and say the blessing, but the minute he get caught up in one of those old webs, gotta stop and mumble it.

Boy, I wish really, I wish I coulda been there when Nero was feeding the Christians to the lions. I bet that was a beautiful sight to see. See, they didn't run, didn't run. Can you believe that? They didn't run from what they believed in. Feed me, turn the lions out, feed me. And what happened, who won? Christianity still here, Nero's not. It's hard to destroy the right thing. But a man can destroy a lot of the right because basically all men are right. So they have that little element to work with. When you walk into one of these white churches and you get put out, there's a whole lots of people lose sleep over that. Whole lots of people lose sleep over that. So we have problems, we have many problems. This is something that has hit us so fast and we've gotten hung up in it so quick, that whether you want freedom or not, you've got to accept it. Whether you want freedom or not, you've got to accept it.

And these young Negro kids have to knock you down and force it down your mouth, we gon' do that. And you know who taught us that? You did.

Well, you gave us castor oil that we didn't even want, but you knew it was good for us and you held our mouth and poured it down in. You cooked up some home remedies for us that the man would've put you in jail for giving it to us, but you knew it would help us. You made us eat food we didn't even want because you knew we had to eat certain types of food to grow up strong. And you held us, and you forced us, and you put it down in our mouth. The black woman in this country have made and produced one of the strongest black men the world have ever seen because you forced things on us that if every man would've had forced on him.

Because you black women was only ones really knowing what was goin' on in Miss Ann's kitchen. And we come back home, them folks had baby food 20 years fo' we had it. Twenty years because baby food was selling a nickel a jar and potatoes was selling eight pounds for four cents, and you had a family to feed and not a baby. So you went to the store and you bought them potatoes and came home and chewed it up and spit it in the spoon and put it down that baby's mouth. Only God know how we survived all them germs and bacteria, but we survived it, baby. I watch Mama chew up a orange and spit the juice out and pour it down in us. You held us for right and shoved it down our throat, and as they say, what go around, come around. So you might as well get with this taste of freedom, baby. 'Cause we gon' hold you and shove it down your throat.

And you know the frightening thing, the thing that has this white man scared all over the world, all over the world. Have you ever noticed how right this thing must be because right tonight, if 700 persons walked out there and got arrested. When the newspapers release it all over the world, what is it gonna say? "Seven Hundred got Arrested," right? They will never talk about the Negroes that didn't get arrested. Itn't that funny? If going to jail was wrong, they would say, "We had 10,000 Negroes that didn't go." Because you that don't go, you don't even count no more. Ain't that a funny thing? You don't even count no more. People walk up and had the right to talk to you because they'd been to jail and all you got to do with this day and age is get behind the movement and go to jail if you have to. And for the first time in your life, somebody invite you up here and say, "Talk to 'em." Isn't that funny? Ain't nobody invited you up here yet though, have they?

Those are the problems we have tonight. Those are the problems you have. In this one little county here, you are being watched because what you do will determine. See people haven't got much help up north. You send all your kids up north. They got sophisticated and don't like to be around snuff dippers no more. Don't want to be 'round nappy head folks no more. Check 'em out, if you don't believe. Pack a bag and go up there and catch 'em throwing a cocktail party. You in trouble. They'll introduce you to everybody but they mother. They always say, "Mama, I'll be home to see you."

Very seldom do they bring you up there. So, ya'll got this battle to fight all by yourself. All by yourself down here. So you gonna win it down here, and when you win it down here, not until then, will we win ours up there.

Will be simple winning ours after you win yours 'cause up north, we think we better than you. I guess you know that, I don't have to tell you that. We think we better than you. Every time a man call us a nigger up north, we, we say he's talking about you. 'Cause we give you credit down here for having all the big lips, all the kinky hair, all the big jaws, and bustin' all the verbs. Yeah, we feel if we can get rid of you southern niggers, we'd be alright up there. That's the attitude we have. Did you know that? That's the way we feel about ya. That's why you all got it made in the shade, baby. 'Cause when you get yours down here, we gon' get ours up there for nothing else but spite and envy. They ain't start jumping up north 'till ya'll start jumping down here. They don't even know how to vote up there. Here, a guy got put in jail in Chicago for selling his vote for a dollar. Yeah, for a dollar. Sold his vote for a dollar. They don't know what's going on up there.

All them Negroes up north, and they ain't never elected a Negro mayor in none of them places, never had a Negro governor in none of them places. That white man up there is doing us worse than he's doing ya down here cause at least he tell you what he's doing to you down here. He got us believing up there that we alright wit' 'em. But if you had to write down 20 of the top Negro leaders in America today, 19 of 'em would be a product of the South, 19 of 'em would be a product of the South. 'Cause this is where it is. This is where it is. This is where God is still with you here.

[break in tape]

. . . this big job. So all you can do now is if you don't want it, stand over there with the white folks and march against us. And if you do march it, want it, march wit' us. But we got to have you out here in the street now. Because when you don't come out, you lead him to believe that you didn't want it. So if you gon' make him feel you didn't want it, then get wit' him. I would rather see a Negro when I come to Selma, Alabama marching with the white police if they're not gonna march with me. Because there's one thing, I got, I don't mind dying but I'd hate to die asking, "Where was my folks now?" Either be here on my side or be in front of me, just let me see ya. Let me see ya. Where was my folks? That's all. Like they ask, "Where you there when they crucified the boss?" That's a nice song to sing now, but you have opportunity this time. I don't know what song's gonna come out of this one, they gon' have some. And it sho' would be a heck of a thing when they start singing 'em when your grandkids and great grandkids can stand up and sing. Yeah, he was there, baby. He was there. And 20 years from now and 30 years from now, people gon' be asking ya, "Where were ya?"

I'd like to tell you this story and then leave. I talked to one of the fathers of one the kids that was in that church in Birmingham that lost their life. That's a frightening story, half the, the stuff out there never did get out. There's a woman upstairs, been upstairs in the operating room for two hours praying with God that they could save her daughter's eyesight. And after the operation was over the doctor told her he did the best he could. And she said, "Thank God," only to turn around and find out they'd been looking for her for two hours to tell her about her dead daughter downstairs. I talked to the gentleman that lost his daughter. You know the thing that seemed to have moved him the most? He said, "Gregory, this girl of mine begged me to let her demonstrate. And I told her, 'No.'" That watn't the thing that bothered him. He told her she was too young, and she looked at him and said, "Then you do it, Daddy." That's what he got to live with for the rest of his life.

'Cause had Birmingham had enough Negroes behind 'em, there wouldn't have been no bombing. Two hundred and fifty thousand Negroes and all King could get was 2,000 to 1,500 every day. Uh-umm, that's not enough. That's not enough. So all I say, if you not for me, get over there with them, at least being wit 'em you know when they fixin' to blow up my church. You might can slip back and tell me. Or if I see you not coming to church, I know somethin' gon' happen. And I can stay out of it myself. This is what it's coming to. If you want to be on the winning team, get on this one. 'Cause this one's going all the way, all the way. That's why this man is scared. All at once, he realize, "I'm not dealing with a dog." A dog you throw him meat. But all at once, he was dealing wit' a man, and they make tear gas for men, baby. That's what they make tear gas for, for men.

The sheriff would never gon' out and got him a posse for somethin' he knew he could handle. And they never been able to get a posse this large. 'Cause he dealing with the truth, and when those boys finish grabbing, there still gon' some to overflow because the truth ain't nothing but God. So here's the problem we have. Just thank God we got strong enough people that can deal with 'em. And we strong. Two hundred and fifty thousand Negroes in Birmingham. Had the leaders decided, give me 2,000 Negroes to demonstrate and you other 248,000 stay at home. And at twelve o'clock Sunday, turn all your water on and flush your toilet, the firemans wouldn't had enough pressure for the hoses. That is nothing but pure strength and raw, naked power.

Twenty-two million Negroes in America and the United States has the greatest postal system the world have ever known. And if every Negro decided we gon' start a letter writing campaign, and on any given day, drop ten letters first class for every Negro in America. That would be ten times 22 million letters in the mailbox at the same day. We have just paralyzed the greatest postal system the world have ever known. And if you put the wrong address on it, you've paralyzed it twice for the same nickel. That's strength, and that's power. This is what we dealing with today. These are the problems we have. These are your problems, these are everyone's problems.

And when you walk across that line and commit, you drag ten of those white people across that line wit' ya. 'Cause it's a whole lots of white folks that wanna go, but they haven't missed you out of their kitchen. And they love you, they afraid of you because they know good and godly you are. And the day you don't show up that would be the day they might get religion. 'Cause they say, "You know if you got some Negroes down South make the white man jump off the Empire State Building, if you asked him to." Yeah, you've raised him, you've loved him, you've made him what he is. And all he doin' is sitting there, seeing what Aunt Sue Lou gon' do. "She didn't show up today, uh-oh. Maybe they right." 'Cause he ain't never known you to be wrong.

Yep, think ya'll did a wonderful job on feeding us and getting us strong. But all these kids is trying to tell you now is, "Mama, we take freedom over food. We take freedom over food. Because we sick and tired of ya'll raising these milk fed janitors. We sick and tired of ya'll raising these home-grown, no politicians 'cause they won't let us run. We saying, "Mama, get away from the pot because you making us strong for nothing." You should come home one day and if you got anything in that pot, put some freedom in there and say we gon' march, we gon' march. And check on your kids and find out what did they do for freedom before you lay a couple of that good stuff on 'em. And starting cooking you some march juice at home.

Jail ain't gon' hurt nobody. Them white folks wouldn't hurt one of them Negroes never, nothin' in the world, baby. 'Cause he know how right that is. Them Negroes in jail got more white folks watching 'em all over this world than you have sitting out here, and you supposed to be freer than they are tonight. Don't you know the ones the white folks hate are the ones they lock up in jail and a honkey would blow up a church before he'd blow up one of them jails with us in it? 'Cause he know he getting pure right over there in that jail. He don't know what he gettin' when he blow up one of these churches. That a sick thing in hell when a man would blow up a church 'fore he would blow up a jail and know we in there.

You know, how white people in the South have just broke in to jails and taken anybody out, anybody they want [inaudible]. The man just killed a Negro. He in jail, you remember that story, do ya? Killed him dead and gave him to the Negro undertaker and buried him. Don't nobody know too much about it, you know what I'm talking about? In jail, just walkin' in and killed him. So they been doin' that. But they not doin' it to us. Because all this man want to do is be able to lock up the truth for a few minutes. He know he can't kill it. Know he can't kill it. And everybody in there is comin' out. So when you have to go to jail, go.

Go ahead. Take your sugar diabetes and your lumbago and your polio and wrap you a little ol' snuff up in your pocket if you have to. Go on in there. Go on in there. You get more F.B.I. agents over there. Bobby Kennedy can't sleep while ya'll in jail down there. Did ya know that? People calling him every five minutes tellin' him what's happening. How else you gon' get the president's brother to have your name on his desk. I dare you to go over to jail, name be on his desk in the mornin'. But it's, it's, you haven't impressed nobody down here but these white folks here. You haven't impressed the world because they look down there and don't see nothin' but kids. Nothin' but kids. And whitey's going around tellin' 'em, "Oh, them niggers happy. They just got some devilish kids they can't control."

And you know what I wonder, when you think about these kids going to jail, and you have your reasons for not going, if this town busted open tomorrow mornin' and the white man walked up and said, "We want to make you the first Negro detective," would you take it? Or would you use the same excuses with him you're using now? Would you take it? These kids get through goin' to jail and taking all this talk and they walk up to you and say, "We want to make you the first Negro woman salesman." Would you take it, or would you tell them you don't qualify because you didn't get out there and get your head whooped?

These kids aren't doing anything for themselves. Freedom will run all over this town. If they wanted to keep it for themselves they couldn't. Nothin' selfish 'bout what they doin' for ya. But you got to get behind 'em 'cause it's too many of them white folks in front of 'em. And when a man looks back, and he sees somethin' behind him, he don't feel like running. Because he hadn't got no place to run, he'd bump into his mother back there and might hurt her. Get behind your kids in this town. Will ya? Please get behind 'em. God bless you. Goodnight.

§89 Dr. Arthur E. Shelton

Arthur Edwin Shelton was born on May 29, 1922. He earned his B.A. from Emory in 1943 and his B.D. from Emory in 1946. Four years later Shelton earned his doctorate in Theology from Boston University. For twelve years he served the Virginia Conference of the Methodist Church, including his appointmentt at Norview Methodist Church in Norfolk, Virginia, where he gave the following sermon. He left the pastorate in 1966 to pursue a career in higher education. He taught sociology at Claffin College, Belmont Abbey College, and Catawba College. He died on December 9, 1993 at the age of 71. His papers are housed at the Pitts Theology Library Archives at Emory University in Atlanta, Georgia.

In this brief, but powerful, sermon to the congregants of Norview Methodist Church in Norfolk, Virginia, Shelton uses Christ's example of going through Samaria to urge them to take the unfamiliar and the difficult way on race relations. Given his background in sociology, Shelton employs a bevy of statistics to illustrate the extent to which the 1960s and after will find white Christians in a decided minority. And, "Unless the love of Jesus Christ permeates those people, . . . then we will find ourselves overwhelmed by the revolution of the ignorant, illiterate, non-white, and non-Christian forces of the world's population." Presently, the communists are winning this revolution. Moreover, the Methodist response to the revolution has been abysmal, with more administrators "pushing pencils," and "too few proclaiming the gospel of Jesus Christ to the needy of the world." The Methodist clergy is not exempt, either. In fact, they seemed to Shelton to be far more concerned about the color of each others' skin than in doing their jobs.

Let's Face the World

Norview Methodist Church, Norfolk, Virginia
November 3, 1963

At the beginning of 1960, I made a prediction which I have become more firmly convicted of than ever before. The decade of the sixties is the era of American and world history when we must learn to live together as brothers, or else we will destroy ourselves in the process of trying to live otherwise. In the face of this, we can realistically ask if the church of Jesus Christ has a message for the world. We find the scripture for our thinking today in a little read story of the incident of Jesus taking a trip from Judea to Galilee. As he began the walk across the country, he was faced with the decision of the route he would take. Most of his fellows had a peculiar route which went around Samaria. All of the caravans traveled in this circuitous route in order to avoid the possibility of marauding bandits. The ancient bitterness between Samaritans and Jews went all the way back to Ezra and Nehemiah. The Jews despised the Samaritans, would have nothing to do with them, and even avoided traveling in their land. But Jesus, being what he was, chose to walk right through Samaria. He could have gone around, but he chose to go through, and the scripture gives us a sort of imperative which he felt in saying, "He must need to go through Samaria." This, beloved, is where we stand today. We must need to face the world in which we live, and find some route by which to travel, though not necessarily familiar or easy, yet one which will bring us a vision of the future.

Let us look at some factors of contemporary history which are both shocking and provoking. Of every thousand people in the world, sixty of them are Americans. Those sixty Americans out of every thousand in the world control half of the world's property, and half of its income. The rise of the scientific age, and the prosperity which it has brought to the average American is not felt in most of the world, because one-half of all the world's people are underfed, while we have surpluses. A bread line of the world's hungry this morning, beginning at the doorway of our church, would encircle the world twenty-five times before every hungry man could pass by. You and I, beloved, may be living in relative prosperity (despite our complaining of the high cost of living), but what you throw into the garbage can after your lunch today will be more food than half the world's population will see during the next thirty days. If these factors do not shock you very much, then let us turn to another facet of today's world. Most of you with children between the ages of one and fifteen are concerning yourselves as to just how you will manage to give that child a college education, and preparation to face the competition of tomorrow's world. But did you know that the millions of American children like yours who look hopefully toward going to college, are but a small minority of the world. Over half of the people in the world cannot read or write!!

Lest we settle back with thanksgiving for our own small prosperity as white Christian Americans, let me jar your minds with some even more startling facts. Though everything looks as if it is in our favor today, we must face the fact that the world's population is only one-third white, and only about twenty-five per cent Christian. In another forty years, less than twenty per cent of the people of the world will be Christian, and seventy-five per cent of the world's people will be non-whites! Unless the love of Jesus Christ permeates those people, and the technology of our affluent segment of civilization is spread to other peoples of the world, then we will find ourselves overwhelmed by the revolution of the ignorant, illiterate, non-white, and non-Christian forces of the world's population.

Ah, beloved, we must go through Samaria. We have no other choice. Revolution is the natural outcome of people who are hungry, illiterate, and seeking. If we wonder sometimes why it is that other nations seem to bite the hand which feeds them, such as has just happened in South Vietnam, or Korea, or in Africa, let us realize that these people—the poor, the ignorant, the hungry—have come to expect that the blessings of our civilization are their inherent rights also. Whether by the sincere efforts of democratic aid to the world's needy, or by cunning promises by the Communist leaders, the fact remains that the Arab in North Africa, the Buddhist in Vietnam, the Hindu in India, all expect and demand the same freedoms and scientific advances which the Americans and Russians have developed. And these people will get these things, too, either by broadening of our sense of mission to the world, by the collective materialism of Communism, or by the revolutionary uprising of their own kind which will take away from both

America and Russia what we have and make us the slaves of the future, the colonies of the former down-trodden.

If we are not aware of the rise of nationalism in the world, just look at the map. No, you can't do that, because the map of the world changes today faster than the printers can print up new ones. In the past eighteen years, almost one-third of the world's population has won its independence. Political power in the world has shifted since 1945 to the point that over 800 million people have changed from being subjects of a foreign government to living in an independent country of their own. And the startling fact is that this revolution has taken place among the non-Christian peoples of the world, and the non-whites. The effects of Communism upon the rise of the common man is significant, also. They have, either by force or persuasion, swallowed up more people in the past fifty years than the Christian church has won in all its missionary programs since the time of the Apostle Paul.

Where do we stand in all of this frightening picture of the world in turmoil today? Beloved, one-tenth of all the Christians in the world today are Methodists! Yet only 1100 of the 58,000 missionaries all over the world come from the Methodist Church. We have less than fifty per cent of the number of missionaries in the field today than we had thirty years ago, but the administrative personnel of the various agencies of Methodist missions in the United States has increased by nearly three hundred per cent in the same period of time. We have far too many executive-type Christians pushing pencils in an office somewhere making the program of missions go around, and far too few proclaiming the gospel of Jesus Christ to the needy of the world. But this is only symptomatic of the total lack of vital piety in our community. How many of you in this congregation have witnessed for Christ during the past seven days? How many of you have given any evidence by your actions, thoughts, or prayers, that Jesus Christ means anything to you at all, or that you really believe in One God for all mankind? Has it occurred to you that the future of your faith lies in your ability to suffer for it? Are you willing to put the church of Jesus Christ before all else, and hold her up as an answer? Until you find such a faith in God as compelled Jesus to go through Samaria, or Paul to preach to every people, then the complacent indifference will continue to dominate the church in this community as well as over the world. Do you realize, beloved, that more time has been spent by Methodists in the past twelve months in Virginia trying to figure out ways to keep the Negroes out of our white churches than has been spent in the past three years discussing missions and evangelism! How can we expect to win the world for freedom and democracy, for Christianity and the church, when we can't even bring ourselves to a point of Christian fellowship in our own community? I went to a meeting in Richmond the other day to plan the Pastor's School for Virginia Methodist Ministers in September 1964. We spent thirty minutes talking about the needs for Christian challenge in the people and subjects which would be on our program—and over three hours arguing whether to allow about five or six Methodist Preachers with black skins to attend the meetings next fall. Even we preachers have some serious praying to do, some repenting, and some soul-searching.

> Arise, ye prisoner of starvation
> Arise, ye wretched of the earth!
> For justice thunders condemnation,
> A better world's in birth.
> No more tradition's chain shall bind you.
> Arise, ye slaves! No more in Thrall.
> The world shall rise on new foundations,
> You have been naught; you shall be all!

No, beloved, I am not quoting some new missionary hymn of the Christian Church. I am quoting there the words of the "International" hymn of Communistic fervor! What have you to offer the world which sounds better than that? What have you to say to Norfolk as a Christian or Methodist which can stir the souls of men? Can you lift up the cross of Christ to other men? No, not until you have fallen before it and taken it on your back. Not before you have put the Christ on that cross in front of everything else. Not until you have elected to walk squarely thru Samaria and stopped to speak of Christ by whatever wells of Jacob you may pass. I am fully persuaded that while we must make progress in the exploration of space, in the long run, beloved, America's contribution to mankind will be judged not by the billions of dollars we spend in putting a man on the moon nearly so much as by the service we render to the millions of hungry, naked, and diseased people right here on earth. When we find the faith to walk with Christ, then He will give us the means by which to win the world. God is not dead, nor does He sleep! When men of good faith gather before Him, He shall give them power to become His sons.

Which is your way? Christ, or Chaos? When the church becomes a voice for that which is popular only, then it has lost its mission. When the pulpit strives never to offend in the Gospel, then it has lost its conviction. We like to adjust to society, but there are some areas where we must proclaim something greater than adjustment. The Answer? Ah, beloved, high on a hill, there stand two pieces of rough wood, nailed together to form a cross. From here, and here alone comes the proclamation which can save the world—proclamation that God is love, that man must love God and each other, that God alone can save men's souls, that Jesus Christ died for men's sins! This is still the answer to a troubled world, but it takes men of greater faith, deeper sacrifice, and nobler devotion then we have yet produced in Norview, in Methodism, or in Christianity as most of us now know it. Let us face the world, find this new faith, and God will show the way!

> Our crosses are hewn from different trees
> But we must all have our Calvaries;
> But may climb the height from a different side,
> But we each must go up to be crucified.

§90 Frank T. Wilson

Frank T. Wilson was born in Maxton, North Carolina and grew up in Wadesboro and Greensboro, North Carolina. After graduating from Lincoln University and Columbia University, Wilson became the national student secretary of the YMCA. Later, he returned to Lincoln to serve as Dean of men and teach in the education and psychology departments. From Lincoln, Wilson moved to Howard University where he was appointed dean of the school of religion. Wilson's expertise in education engendered travels around the globe. He wrote this sermon while in Jakarta, Indonesia.

Wilson uses the name of the location of Christ's crucifixion to begin this morality tale about the church's failure in race relations; so bad is it that Wilson deems it "the most embarrassing chapter in the history of the church in the United States." Part of the problem stems from some who seek to find grounds for racial separatism in the pages of the Bible. Others fancy themselves as the "churchly elite" who "magnify the formalities" of church membership to create divisions in the body of Christ. Wilson also urges his listeners to adopt a more international outlook on race relations, whereby believers can be selective in neither morality nor ethics. Across the globe, Christians must recognize "the image of the Creator in every member of the human family, in all places of God's creation." Wilson concludes with optimism, noting that the "wisdom of God" will temper the "madness of man." But if the church continues in its prejudicial ways, it will betray the mission of Christ and it will be judged accordingly.

Golgotha 1964

November 7, 1963

> And when they were come to the place, which is called Calvary, there they crucified him, and the malefactors, one on the right hand, and the other on the left. Luke 23:33

He was rejected, tormented, afflicted. In the moment of his deepest agony, he was ridiculed, reviled, forsaken. They nailed him to the cross. He died.

Those who cared most ran away. Those who cared least have bequeathed a legacy of hostility to all for which he lived and to all for which he was willing to die—the incarnation of the love of God in the heart and life of humanity.

The most embarrassing chapter in the history of the church in the United States of America is the record of its behavior in the matter of racial discrimination and segregation. The more respectable the congregation, the more ingenious the devices of racial bigotry. The more affluent the pillars of the church, the more efficient the screening of "undesirables." In this process of preserving the purity of the faithful, race and color have been touchstones of acceptance or rejection.

Some voices are heard today, speaking in the name of religion, arguing that the easily distinguishable marks of race and color were established in creation and that these are badges of separation fully sanctioned in the design of the Creator. It is argued, furthermore, that anyone who attempts to alter the design tampers with the handiwork of God and is subject to his wrath. The absurdity of this contention is matched by the avidity with which it is absorbed by many who rummage through the Scriptures for Biblical justification of bigotry and racism.

Barely less pathetic are the more genteel and sophisticated rationalizations of the "churchly elite." This embraces the rank and file of American Protestantism who flee to the inverted ghetto of suburbia or extend a grudging crumb of tokenism within the stable, old-line urban churches. In either case the etiquette of human association is narrowly conditioned by restraints and taboos which magnify the formalities of membership without deepening and extending the experience of unqualified community within the fellowship of those who profess the Lordship of Christ over the totality of human life.

In many ways there is coldness and blindness and hardness within the church which exceeds the more crass and unpretentious rejections and humiliations of the secular world. This is felt more deeply because the idea of participation in the body of Christ has suggested a kind of relationship in which there is nothing which prevents the outgoing of the human spirit in a complete sharing of life at its most fundamentally significant levels. The witness to the world is validated by the living testimony before the world.

But the disastrous consequences of our faltering over the stumbling block of race is a sin so deeply engrained in the structures to which we pay allegiance and to which we make so many concessions that the way of deliverance appears to require more drastic measures than we can bear. Segregation and discrimination as manifestations of racism have so corroded the human spirit and so tarnished the soul that the acids of redemption threaten the very existence of the structures which they are designed to save.

The major tragedy of many Christian churches and individual Christians in America is not that they have denied membership to blacks and not welcomed them into their pews and pulpits and choirs and homes, but that these denials have issued from a basic *negation* of *life* and a willful *rejection of a portion of God's creation*. This negation has been so deep and so thoroughgoing that the church has been reluctant in seeking the way of repentance and in fulfilling the conditions of forgiveness and reconciliation.

The testimony of the church at one point on the globe conditions its capacity for revealing and mediating the love of God at any point on the globe. If fear, prejudice, and arrogance have rendered the church in America incapable of being the redeeming society in which black Americans share its full life in decency, quality, and full community, then it is unlikely that a spirit so distorted can bring health and healing to that which is deepest in the hearts of black, brown, red, yellow people in any part of the world. Charity, humanitarian services, and passionate evangelism may bring temporary relief and a measure of hope to persons in distress and physical anguish. But love that knows no bounds, that enriches our companionship with every child of God, is the only power that touches one's deepest yearning, the only force that reaches one's deepest need.

The church as a "community in mission" is composed of all those in every land who have professed allegiance to Jesus Christ as Lord and Savior and who have committed themselves to the fulfillment of the ethical and moral imperatives of the gospel. The church as an instrument of redemption in the world is confronted with the unavoidable demand to demonstrate in its own life that depth and breadth of fellowship and communion which destroys all walls of separation and which rejects all artificial and arbitrary barriers to human association.

In the mission of the church morality cannot be selective, ethical concern cannot be partial, zeal for freedom, equality, and justice cannot be conditioned by considerations of class or ethnic origins. Neither can Christians in America "play safe" or compromise on the issues of racial segregation and discrimination in this country, in our own communities and churches, without losing spiritual insight and moral courage so necessary for a sincere and genuine witness in the total world community.

There is a law of the spirit and a law of the mind which makes it impossible for integrity to grow out of duplicity. I cannot at one and the same time be true to my neighbor in Asia and betray my neighbor in Africa. I cannot disrespect the dignity of my brothers and sisters in North America and honor the inherent worth of my brothers and sisters in Latin America.

There is no selective morality for the Christian which exempts one from recognizing the image of the Creator in every member of the human family, in all places of God's creation. It is a great illusion to suppose that the church or the individual Christian in the United States can live in convenient accommodation to the patterns of racial estrangement at home and then, or at the same time, participate with full conscience in building up the "beloved community" in Asia or Africa. There are evidences that evasiveness and cowardice in one situation undercut the capacity for resolute action in other situations containing similar factors. The obedience of the church as an instrument of reconciliation and unity in the world is dependent upon the preservation of its capacity for integrity in every local and national situation.

The mission of the church in America and in the world is indivisible. There is an underlying unity in life which is violated whenever offense is done to any segment of life. The yearning of the human spirit is not merely for houses and jobs and food and schools and votes, but basically for affirmation of worthfulness and identification with fellow human beings in all the high endeavors for fullness of life. The church is called to incarnate this ideal and to lead the way in America and to the end of the earth.

The madness of man is being tempered by the wisdom of God. The Holy Spirit is working in the affairs of this nation and in the life of the church as a mighty, moving wind and as a still, small voice. Men may hesitate, resist, and turn aside from the divine purpose, but what has been created in love and sustained by the indomitable will of the Maker of heaven and earth cannot be destroyed nor permanently defeated by the powers of evil at large in the world.

Where the church has conformed to the divisive forces in society, where it has made cowardly concessions to pride or prejudice or bigotry, it stands under the judgment of Him who has made man in His own image and it betrays Him who looked upon the people of God with the agonizing prayer "that they all may be one." The possibility of the redemption of the church in its mission to the world becomes most apparent when all who profess faith in Jesus Christ as Lord recognize that we are no longer aliens or strangers, but fellow citizens with the saints and members of the household of God.

Every crucifixion is a universal event. Yet His love is boundless and His kingdom is an everlasting kingdom. The people of God *will enter their inalienable heritage.* Although the powers of hell may be arrayed against it.

§91 Dave Dennis

Dave Dennis was a vital, but largely forgotten, organizer and activist in the early 1960's. Raised in New Orleans, Dennis was expelled from historically black Dillard University for his activism. An original Freedom Rider, Dennis later became the Congress of Racial Equality's (CORE) Mississippi field organizer in 1962. Simultaneously he served as the Council of Federated Organization's (COFO) assistant program director in Mississippi. He worked intimately with program director Bob Moses, to organize numerous voting-related projects in the state. Dennis also actively participated in Jackson boycotts and protests during May and June 1963. Beyond movement protests and voting projects, Dennis was a firm believer in economic independence. Toward that end, he helped organize the Home Industry Cooperative in the Delta community of Ruleville, a North American variant of the Andean arpillera movement. Eighteen local women made quilts, aprons, and rugs in their homes to be sold to movement supporters in the North.

Along with Moses, Dennis helped lay the planning and organizational groundwork for what would become Freedom Summer in 1964. After the murders of Chaney, Schwerner, and Goodman, as well as the failures of the Mississippi Freedom Democratic Party (MFDP) in August 1964, Dennis left Mississippi largely disillusioned. He would later get a law degree from the University of Michigan and a political science degree from Yale. In the 1990s Dennis reconnected with Bob Moses, and today Dennis is the director of the Southern Initiative of the Algebra Project, a program Moses initiated to teach algebra to at-risk black youth.

Dennis was a masters of ceremony for several Freedom Vote rallies held around the state of Mississippi in October and November 1963. The Freedom Vote, created by COFO leaders, was designed to show the nation that, if given the franchise, black Mississippians would turn out in large numbers to vote. It also had more local designs: perhaps blacks would see first-hand the power of the vote to effect change in their communities. As it turned out, the Freedom Vote was also a very important stage in the formation of the MFDP. At the head of the Freedom Vote ticket for governor was Clarksdale pharmacist and NAACP stalwart, Dr. Aaron Henry. Moses asked white Tougaloo College chaplain Edwin King to run as lieutenant governor. The Vicksburg native and Methodist activist eventually relented, despite significant opposition among clergy and his own family.

Always an impassioned and fiery orator, Dennis implores his Jackson audience not just to vote in the upcoming election, but he also has some sharp words for Mississippi whites. Perhaps more interesting is Dennis's invective against the clergy (which clergy is not clear). It is clear, though, that an integrated society should not have to wait for heaven—not when blacks and whites in Mississippi frequently interact, even if on unequal terms. Given his impressive energy stores, Dennis's frequent refrain of "we're tired" is probably less a function of physical exhaustion and more of a righteous anger with white Mississippi hypocrisy—from the governor on down.

Speech at the Freedom Vote Rally

Jackson, Mississippi

November 1963

We've come to the stage that usually at most of our mass meetings we call for collection. Tonight, we don't want your money really. Just your participation. We've had too long people marchin' around a table and givin', givin' a dollar or somethin' like that and goin' home and getting' in bed and sayin' they done their part. We don't need that, because your dollar is not gonna buy a vote tomorrow, Sunday, and Monday.

We've [been] havin' questions bein' ask'd all over this particular place as to why we havin' a freedom election, and what it stands for, and a lotta people all around, especially our good white folks and other people who just too dat-blastin' lazy to get up [off their] behinds and go out and try to participate, sayin' that it's stupid and silly. I remember the times when we used to stand up here and the certain person used to stand up and he would say, "Boycott downtown," and he would say, "Let's demonstrate, let's picket," he'd say, "Because we all want to be free." And I knew some of the same people used to say he was silly too. They're all green. Won't call no more names, but, he died for it.

On this particular weekend we only askin' people to participate and write on the ballot to mark an X and put it in a box, and say you want [Edwin] King and [Aaron] Henry.

People are out canvassing, people are out participating and working 24 and 36 hours at a time, people are up here running, putting their lives on the front line. They're doin' it because they're tired. We're all tired. We tired of people smilin' [at] us outta one side [of] their mouths and cursin' us out the other. We've had just about enough, you see. The young people are tired, the old people are tired, we're tired of you tellin' us day in and day out 'bout the fact you don't want to eat with us, you don't want to worship with us, you don't want to talk with us, but when you want somebody to cook your food, you get my black mammy to come and do it for you, you see. He's a sick man: he doesn't want his children to play with me; he doesn't want his children to go to school with me; he doesn't want his children to have anything to do with me; but when he wants a baby-sitter, he calls my black mammy again, you see. He's a sick man, you see.

He goes to church on Sundays and tellin' the other people and be preachin' on television and tellin' how we should love one another because we all brothers and children of God, he says. And he comes outside, and he hates me, you see. He comes about and we talk about goin' to this one particular land called heaven or hell, you see, where we all be able to live together happily ever after, you see, or in complete misery, you might say. He tell us that and he preach over somebody's body at some church, he lines us up in the beautiful flowers and put us in a casket and a hearse and ship us on out to a graveyard and he still preaches about how we're gonna go to that land of God one day, you see. Preachin' this stuff at a segregated church, carryin' us down a segregated road, you see, buyin' flowers from some segregated place and buryin' us in a segregated cemetery, and again hollerin' out, "We goin' to an integrated heaven." He's bad, he's wrong, he doesn't know what's happenin', does he? He's a mixed up person, you see.

We're movin' on, and this particular movement is somethin' that will never be stopped. It's a powerful thing, you see. It's like the mighty sea that God stepped out on one day and calmed down with the touch of a toe, you see. Yet it's that big thing that one of these days is gonna be crashed against the walls of segregation, and one day those walls will have to come crumblin' down, you see. It's a mighty wave. It's like that wave that dashed against the shores of every beach, and washes away all the loose sa-sand to be dissolved into nothing but that mighty running water, you see. It's there no more. This is what this movement is. It's a very powerful movement. And this is what the votin' is. It's sorta of an expression from the hearts of each and every individual. It's tellin' them, I'm tired. I'm tired, I'm tired, I'm tired, I'm damn tired, you see! Excuse me, brother ministers.

We've got to do somethin'. I'm tired of Barnett tellin' me what I like, you see. When I first came to Jackson last year, last summer was when I first came into Jackson to work. I'd been here on the Freedom Rides and things, but when I first came to Jackson to make it my home and live and work for freedom, I had a conference with Barnett, and all he could say, he looked into me, my eyes, and he kept sayin' over and over again, "All we want to do, son, is preserve these here races," he said. "We don't want to have no mongrels," he said, "We want to preserve the races," he said. And I looked at Mr. Barnett, I became quite angry, and I held up one hand like this, and I told him that no two black people got in bed and made a gray-eyed, bright, kinky-haired nigger like me, you see. There was another la-, there's a lady in California who claims to be a second cousin of Governor Ross Barnett. I saw a picture of her, and she's not white, you can believe me.

See we've not, we, we've not, this particular thing that they are standing on, only thing I'm tryin' to prove tonight is that it's nothing but a myth, and it's just something that's deep down inside that they're tryin' to prove that has been disproven a long time ago, you see. We're big segregationers in the daytime, but doggonit, we can sure do great at night, you see. You'd be surprised at the number of limousines they drive in the back alleys, you see, and pickin' up the black women and takin' them behind the wooded areas, you see. You'd be surprised at the number of nice looking girls off the streets who are picked up by the police and taken down and threatened with arrest, or somethin' like that if they don't do a little bit, you know. See we tired of that, you see. Not gonna talk anymore.

See, you hate us, you hate us, you hate us, and still you love us and you love us and you love us, you see, in your own sneaky way, you see. These are the things we are about tired of, and we want to bring the truth to light and let it shine, you see. And you men folk, you see, and ladies too, you see, stop lookin' up and lettin' that insurance man come in and sweet talkin' and stuff like that, you'd be surprised at all that too. Well, we are in a mixed up place, you see, got a lot of changes we got to make, you see. That's what we doin', we tellin' the world we are tired, you see. We're tired! We're tired! We're tired, you see!

Now we have one of our own gentlemen here, who will have to say a few words just before we have our main speaker, our next governor of Mississippi. Want to hear now our old friend and our man who has stood by us, and stood by Mr. Evers, and I think he really deep down inside, he always talks about how he regret that he wasn't there that particular night, and I feel sorry for him because he keeps suffering about it, but it was something he couldn't help buyin'. He's a man who has worked diligently for us and worked us, worked here before I got here and was, since I've been here, I been tryin' to run to keep up with him he's still workin' so hard. Mr. Sam Bailey.

§92 Dave Dennis

Dave Dennis's biography appears in the introduction to his earlier speech, also in November 1963 in Jackson, Mississippi. In the speech below, he introduces Robert Parris Moses, a legend among civil rights workers. Educated in New York and at Harvard, Bob Moses went into what editor P. D. East called "The Magnolia Jungle" in 1961. Working for the Student Nonviolent Coordinating Committee (SNCC) and later COFO, Moses was instrumental in the attempts to organize black voter registration drives throughout Mississippi. Along with Dave Dennis, Moses helped organize the Freedom Vote in 1963, Freedom Summer in 1964, and what would become the MFDP in 1964. Diffident and very soft-spoken, the charismatic Moses was insistent that local people take responsibility for their own liberation. Leaders must be indigenous. So, even while Dave Dennis introduces Moses in this brief speech as "the modern day Moses," he quickly counters the biblical comparison with an emphasis on the locals' actions to secure their own deliverance. This introduction is transcribed from the Moses Moon Audio Archive at the National Museum of American History in Washington, D.C.

A Modern Day Moses

Freedom Vote Victory Rally, Jackson, Mississippi
November 1963

The old saying around in Jackson, Mississippi is don't get weary. Don't get weary. We've been waiting for freedom for 300 years. We have come together tonight at 1072 Lynch Street in the auditorium part of the Masonic Temple to sort of see just how much progress we have made in this particular freedom struggle. We are making a step forward. We may never get a black man to sit in the capitol here in Jackson, Mississippi but one thing is for true, it is something that I believe from within my heart and it's something that each and every individual out there and people across the state of Mississippi tonight have demonstrated, is that it won't be long before man will get into office who is going to represent the people, is gonna be in there by the people and is gonna be there for the people. Because tonight we are showing our desire to participate in the political structure of Mississippi; tonight we are showing the nation that we are dissatisfied with the present system here.

Many, many centuries ago there's a man by the name of Moses and one day he was walking along and there was a little bush that they said was burning. They said Moses was frightened. They said Moses got a message. They said that the boss came out and told Moses to go and tell Pharaoh to "Let your people go!" I guess Moses felt [inaudible] that we stand out tall and walk. But the people said, "There's the sea over there and we can't go that way." But Moses kept on and he went and he told Pharaoh to let his people go. He was oppressed. He was probably followed around by Pharaoh's men just as the people here are followed around by the police department. He was probably looked upon and cast aside by Pharaoh's people. He walked the hot burning deserts and he went without food but he kept saying, "Pharaoh, let my people go," and finally the people began to believe in Moses and they began to stand up and they began to cry, "Pharaoh let us go!"

Moses did not stop crying out. The more pressure that was put upon Moses the more he stood up and said, "Let's go!" The people began to come one at a time. At first they were afraid. They said, "Thou would not get food. Pharaoh can take my food away from me." Say, "My job, my home, my children. What would they do, what will they eat, where will they go?"

And Moses said, "Trust in the Lord. But the Lord is not gonna deliver you unless you show the Lord that you want freedom yourselves and stand up and hold your heads up high." The people looked, they said, "But how can I hold my head up high with a hungry stomach? How can I hold my head up high when my children are crying?" Some say Moses looked at them and said, "Why, how?" he said, "What is it? What is a man fed by? Is he fed by food of the earth or is he fed by Lord, and trust, and understanding from the soul and heart." He said, "Believe!" And some of the people looked at Moses and said, "You're a fool man!" But they kept coming one at a time and Moses kept working. And then God saw Moses was so determined and that the people were so oppressed and that they were determined too. Until he began to give a little aid. The locusts came. Pharaoh's people began to stall. The angel came and destroyed some of Pharaoh's children, the firstborn. Pharaoh became, began to suffer but not because that God came down and said, "I'm gonna help you people, just wait!" but because of the fact God saw that the people were willing to do something for themselves and because of the fact they had a man who was so determined, by the name of Moses.

And then there came the big day when they did begin to flee across the land of Pharaoh. Pharaoh's army was behind in hot pursuit. Aligned in front of Moses was the big sea. And the people were in between. Some say it was a stick that Moses had. Some say it was the hand of God that split the sea. Some say that the sea was just shallow. But I say that it was the willingness of the people who said that, "We must be free," and also there was the courage that, and the faith and belief of the people had within themselves that they were able to accomplish something that split the sea. It was not only the rod, it was not only the hand of God. Because God has said himself that he helps those who help himself. The sea split. And Moses and his people walked across and Pharaoh's army was destroyed. The moral of the entire story is that: have faith, have courage, but most of all do something for yourselves and then help will come, you see.

Go get Bob Moses. Go get Bob Moses. Bob Moses, go get him. Bob Moses, go get him.

We in the state of Mississippi, the people for years and years who've been known the world over to hold our heads low. People for years and years who have not had the courage to stand up. People for years and years who were oppressed and afraid to move because we felt that we might lose our food, because of the fact that we felt that we might lose our lives, because we wondered what would happen to our children if they did not have a father and a mother. We in the state of Mississippi, for years and years did not really believe that we could do it but today we find out that we can and we stand together.

We'll answer the call in the state of Mississippi to another type of Moses, a Moses that we call a modern day Moses. One who has stood in this particular state and came in here at a time when no one was in here but he and Mr. Medgar [Evers]. Standing strong and tall, telling Bob, Ed and all the others, "Let my people go!" They walked together with their feet burning from the hot sun, their heads felt parched, their mouths were thirsty for freedom, their guts were hungry for justice, their eyes starved to see equality, their hearts overflowed for the people with sorrow. They walked in places like Belzoni, they walked in places throughout the state like Yazoo City, telling the people, the mayors of the city, the chief of the police, the mayors, the commissioners, the board of directors, the white segregationists, Barnett and all the others, "Let my people go!"

One of these men cannot walk with us today but in his footsteps there walks another, a man who has been beaten, a man who has been shot at, a man who has cried out from the bottom of his stomach, a man whose every word whose every snoring in his sleep, whose every thought is for "Freedom for my people!" A man who has not no concern for himself. A man who does not seek publicity and other things for we barely hear about his name unless they try to smear it in the *Jackson Daily News* or the *Clarion-Ledger*. He stays in the background, worrying because he has hundreds of people out here he must worry about, people who work with him. He's a man who has spent many sleepless hours worrying and planning and figuring out, "What can I do next?" To tell Barnett and Shawn that, "My people must be free and want to be free!" I'm proud to say tonight, as I think all the fellow workers in the house are proud to say, that in our hearts and in our minds, in our everyday life, and within our state there walks with us a modern day Moses, Mr. Bob Moses of the Student Nonviolent Coordinating Committee. Would you come up here please?

§93 Dr. Aaron Henry

Aaron Henry was born to Mississippi tenant farmers on July 2, 1922. Upon graduating high school, Henry was drafted into the U.S. Army where he served in the Pacific theater. Upon his discharge from the army, Henry enrolled at Xavier University in New Orleans where he earned degrees in politics and government, as well as pharmacy. Henry returned home to the Mississippi Delta town of Clarksdale in Coahoma County in 1950 where he opened the 4th Street Drug Store. The store would serve as a vital place for local activists to plan civil rights projects in and around Clarksdale. In 1952 Henry helped organize the Coahoma County NAACP, and by 1959, Henry was elected president of the state conference of the NAACP. In 1963 he ran for governor on the Freedom Vote ticket. He received nearly 80,000 votes from heretofore disenfranchised Mississippians. He also bridged the gap between conservative elements of the NAACP and the radicalism of SNCC in his capacity as chairman of the Council of Federated Organizations (COFO) in 1964. That same year he also served as president of the Mississippi Freedom Democratic Party (MFDP) and traveled to Atlantic City to pursue a seat as delegate to the

Democratic National Convention. Arrested more than 30 times, he later served 16 years as a congressman in Mississippi's House of Representatives beginning in 1979. Henry died on May 19, 1997. His papers are housed at the Labor History Archives at Wayne State University in Detroit, Michigan, Tougaloo College in Jackson, Mississippi, and the University of Southern Mississippi in Hattiesburg. His memoir, *Aaron Henry: A Fire Ever Burning*, was published posthumously in 2000. This transcription is from the Moses Moon Audio Archive at the National Museum of American History in Washington, D.C.

Equal parts stumping and revival meeting, Dr. Henry calls his Jackson listeners to *agape* love, to hate the act but love the man. That idea comes less from Bob Moses of SNCC, Charles Evers of the NAACP, or Dave Dennis of CORE, but from the "third K": Martin Luther King, Jr. In one brief but brilliant rhetorical gesture, Henry unites under the Freedom Vote banner nearly all of the major civil rights organizations. He also creates a space for the Freedom Party by raising several political questions that both Republicans and Democrats cannot and will not answer. On the other hand, he and Reverend Edwin King have answers in areas such as tax reform, a minimum wage, school integration, the justice system, and voting rights for black and white Mississippians. Many of Henry's reforms redound to class, and he in fact directs his remarks to "the kind of people that we are": poor whites and poor Negroes.

Speech at the Freedom Vote Rally

Jackson, Mississippi
November 1963

I certainly want to thank Al Lowenstein for this wonderful introduction, and I appreciate the part of it that reminisced about college days, when he was as spunky then as he is now as a leader. And I'm proud of the fact that the friendship that we gained as students has lasted all this time, and I'm sure that Al will be my friend forever, and I certainly intend to be his.

This campaign has had perhaps several unique experiences. Some have been joyful, and some have not been so joyful. I believe, perhaps that the meeting in Greenville, that Reverend Edwin King spoke about, where one of the places where he, where our trails crossed on the campaign trail, that I think that the meeting in Greenville, from a positive point of view, was perhaps the campaign that I have enjoyed the most.

Of course, I have enjoyed those that have had negative aspects, too. And perhaps the one in Hattiesburg the other night, wherein the police of the city set off their sirens and the firemen came into the house, looking around as if they thought there were fire, and they stood inside with their fire regalia to intimidate the crowd. And as we announced to them, there, as we say here tonight, that there certainly is a fire going on, gentlemen, but water won't put it out.

And then last night in Biloxi, as the Reverend R. L. T. Smith, who is a member of our executive committee, spoke in behalf of the freedom campaign ticket, and to have the house surrounded by a white mob, infiltrated with several members of the, of the Biloxi police department and to have the house pelted with rocks and, and, and, and steel pieces and iron to the extent that today there is not a window left in the Back Bay Mission where the banquet was held and to have the police there, looking on, condoning this kind of activity, and to ob-observe those who they arrested, bringing them back through the mob so that their, their cause could be pelted again with rocks and windows broken and eggs thrown at them.

Now, these kinds of demonstrations say certainly a lot to us. The thing I think that they say most clearly is that this is the death rattle of a dying and never to be revived again society. They would not be so content upon trying to do us harm if we were not in a position of winning, and of course that's what they realize.

I do want to express appreciation to the entire campaign team for all of the work that all of us have done, and are yet to do. Perhaps the most significant thing about this campaign has been the comradeship of men and women who perhaps have allegiance to one or [an]other of the major civil rights organizations, but yet in this particular campaign, we have joined together with our eyes on freedom, and that's the only thing that matters. The campaign manager for this campaign is a gentleman that I have the utmost respect for, Robert Moses. Of course his allegiance primarily is to SNCC, but when it comes to freedom, he is on the same team as the rest of us. Serving as speakers' bureau chief is Charlie Evers, the new field secretary of NA[A]CP. Serving as chairman of the policy committee is Dave Dennis of CORE. Also aboard the team is Reverend R. L. T. Smith, who is just about everything to everybody. Henry Briggs of Tupelo, and of course Allard Lowenstein serves as general advisor for the entire executive group. And we certainly want to express our appreciation to the students from Yale and other universities that have come in to help us [and] the students from the colleges and institutions here in our state. And we think that with this kind of cooperation, that victory will ultimately be ours, sooner than a lot of people think.

Now, if, uh, we go into a speech tonight, I think that we should direct our brief remarks to the kind of people that we are: the poor people. And of course, we think that the poor people are the ones that are really most concerned about freedom and they are the ones who stand to gain perhaps the most from the freedom campaign, from the standpoint of participation. Many of us who live on Snob Hill now figure that, that we have again attained a certain amount of freedom, and to some of us a Cadillac car is freedom. To some of us a job in a classroom where we sit thirty days and have salary is freedom. And to others of us, being patted on the back by the white man down the street and saying, "You know, if all Negroes was like you, everything'd be alright." But the main thing about directing our remarks to the poor people is that we recognize a division among the poor people. And this division, however, finds itself divided, finds us divided in this way. That we are divided into poor Negro people and poor white people. That's the only difference.

And those who are following this campaign, I'm sure, recognize the fact that the only issue that is being raised by both the Republican and the Democratic standard bearer[s] is the issue of maintaining the Mississippi way of life. Now, I know that many of us through the years have thought about the Mississippi way of life and we've had dreams about it. We've had desires to do something about it. And we often have had these d-desires and these dreams delayed or postponed by some fate of luck that we never got exactly around to experiencing the dream that we had. And I think that Langston Hughes somehow captures the sentiment of many of us in the lyrics or the words of his favorite dream poem when he says, "What happens to a dream deferred? Does it dry up like a raisin in the sun, or does it fester like a sore, and then run? Does it stink like rotten meat, or does it crust and sugar over like a certain sweet? Maybe it just sags like a heavy load, or does it explode?" And because of the possibility of the dreams that we have had delayed for so many years exploding into an activity and into a situation of violence is largely the main reason why we have become engaged in the Freedom Vote Campaign. To re-accentuate that there is hope, that there can be victory, by following the course that has been laid out for us by people who have observed the world as it is today and by people who are also not only concerned about espousing a particular philosophy but about a philosophy of saving this world from damnation.

Now, ironically or perhaps coincidentally, we feel that the three most important figures in this world today are men whose last name starts with K. In Soviet Russia, there stands Khrushchev, the ruler of a dialectic materialist country that negates the deity and says there is no God, that all things that we are to expect happen here on earth. There is no hereafter. Only the material counts. And on the other side of the world, ruling over a western civilization democracy, is a man named Kennedy. Wherever we find western culture or western democracy invoked, we also find the system of white supremacy. Take America, England, France, Italy. Wherever you have western civilization and western culture, parallel with it is the existence of white supremacy. But thank God between Khrushchev and Kennedy, there stands another man whose name begins, last name begins with K: Martin Luther King, saying there's another way. Pray for your enemies. You who live by the sword shall perish by the sword.

He teaches a philosophy of love that has captured the spirit of the movement. And when we say that we think that we, sh-we, when we advocate, that we have got to go away from this building tonight and continue to love the white people who abuse us everyday, we're not speaking about some kind of an affectionate, romantic activity. And we rely upon our knowledge of the Greek language to define the word that we want to use when we say, "love." And the Greeks used three words in defining love. The first word they used is a word called *phileo*, and this is a reciprocal kind of activity. One who is loved because he is loved, and certainly we cannot say that on this basis must we love our fellow white brother because he certainly doesn't act like he loves us. The second word they use, the Greeks used, is a word called *eros*. And *eros* is yearn of the flesh for the realm of the good, a syncopating, s-sensual kind of activity that results in boy meets girl, that kind of activity. And it is certainly not from the standpoint of *eros* that we espouse the cause of love for our white brothers. The third word that the Greeks used is a word called *agape*. And when we arise to love on the *agape* level, we love men, not because we like them, but because God loves them, and that makes a difference. When we arise to love on the *agape* level, we are able to hate the act that a man commits and yet love the man. Now, we admit that this is a very tedious, psychological activity, but we are going to have to be able to do it. We're gonna have to be able to learn it if we are going to be able t-to persevere, until freedom comes without the dreams that have been so long delayed exploding.

Mr. [Lyndon B.] Johnson says that the real danger in Mississippi is the rise of a two-party system. He says we only need one political party. And with one political party we will retain the conservative white vote and thus keep the Negro down in this manner. Mr. Phillips says we gotta have two parties. One to watch the other to be sure that neither does anything about the Negro's progress and in that matter both parties will keep watch on the Negro to be sure that he's kept down. They have two other slogans. One is, "Bury the GOP scallywags." The other is, "K.O. the Kennedys." But they've got all the same theme: how to keep the Negro down. Course, we would like to advise these two gentlemen that they are really wasting their breath because the Negro is now on his way up.

What these two candidates need to be telling us, though, is how much money are we making in Mississippi or how much money are we not making. Why is it that the politicians simply refuse to talk about the problems that affect Mississippi and its people? Why is it they never talk about the terrible shacks that many of us live in and have to call home? Why is it that they never discuss the question of a decent wage? Why is it they never explore the fact, why is it that a worker in Mississippi earns an average of 62 dollars and 57 cents a week, when the average wage of this nation is a 102 dollars and 18 cents a week? Why is it that they never talk about, with all of their discussions of the Balance Agriculture with Industry project and all of their discussion about their Ri-, their Right to Work laws, why is it they never tell us anything about the average factory worker in Mississippi today [who] earns 30 dollars less than the average factory worker throughout this nation? Why is it they never tell us anything about 51 percent of the families of this state [who] earn less than 3,000 dollars a year and 37 percent of the families of this state [who] earn less than 2,000 dollars a year. And in the Mississippi Delta, where I come from, over 50 percent of the people earn less than 1,000 dollars a year, hardly enough to keep body and soul together. They don't talk about the fact that we generally have no paid vacations, no sick leave, unemployment compensation, nor retirement benefits. They say nothing at all about the, the fact that automation and chemical weed control is putting thousands of people out of work every week. They say nothing about the fact that the sales tax places a heavy burden on the low wage earner. Why is it that none of our politicians say not one word about an income tax that would provide taxation from the more wealthy people and thus provide revenue for the building of better schools, better hospitals, and better roads?

Now I could talk on and on about what our politicians find convenient to ignore. Of course, there's a reason for it. They are remaining silent on these issues because the politicians of this state only represent the favored few. They never say one word about the fact that the present administration that we live under was elected by six percent of the people 21 and over in this state. Now, of course, that is somewhat a compliment to the other 94 percent of us, because at least 94 percent of us didn't vote for Barnett. Only six percent of us have to bear the burden of that responsibility.

There are three reasons, however, for the fact that only six percent of the people went to the polls and elected the present administration. The first reason is the one-party system where only one set of ideas is tolerated. Not only are Negroes so circumscribed that many of us are reluctant to talk about issues that the White Citizens' Councils would not like discussed. But thousands of white people are more afraid of the Citizens' Councils than Negroes ever dared to be. Now we were telling 'em a long time ago that the Negroes that were afraid of the white people down here are already gone to Chicago, that the rest of us are here for the duration, as long as it takes.

The second main reason why there was a six-percent vote that elected the present administration was the existence of the poll tax. And not only do the poll, does the poll tax disenfranchise Negroes, but a whole lot of white folks don't have that two dollars when [the] time come[s] to pay them poll taxes.

And of course, the last reason is the disenfranchisement . . .

[cut in tape]

. . . that we don't hear our politicians talking about any of these problems, really is because they don't care. And the reason that they don't care is because the victims, those of us who are inconvenienced because of the existence of these problems, are mostly, but not always, but w-they're mostly Negroes. Our politicians do not care about poor people, black or white, because the politicians themselves are, number one, they're usually the plantation owners. Senator Eastland owns one of the largest plantations in this state. And the white man usually finds himself as the boss man, and so it is to his convenience to develop a society on our cheap labor. It is to his convenience to have worked us all of our lives for nothin'. You know, we've felled the trees, we have drained the rivers, we have cleared away the debris, and the time has just come, ladies and gentlemen, where we are now calling for our payday. It's long overdue. Ever since 17 and 66, we have been a part of this nation and have remained loyal to it, and they're talking about Negroes don't pay taxes. But we have said before, that if they gave us a tenth of the money that they beat my grandma and my grandpa out of all these years that we could live forever, tax free.

Now there's not so much that [the] blatant noise of the bad people that gives us so much concern, that we are so disturbed about, but it's the thundering silence of those that call themselves good. The surest way for evil to triumph is for good men to do nothing. And I'm sure that most of us remember the biblical story that we've told so many times about when Esther became the queen. And she didn't want to do anything to disturb her position with the king, and how Mordecai finally told her, as we say to the church and to the leaders of this movement and to all of those who want to be free, that if we continue to remain silent at a time like this, God's gonna find another way to deliver evil.

When I'm elected governor of Mississippi, I will institute a tax reform that will see to it that the persons with the greatest ability to pay taxes will pay 'em. I will see to it, to the best of my ability, that sales taxes are removed from such items as food. Now, how inconsistent can we be when a mother has to pay taxes on the food that she gives her baby to keep him alive? That should be no sales taxes on food. How inconsistent can we be when we subscribe, prescribe a sales tax on medicines that are used to nurse the body back to health, to earn the funds to keep this country going? How wrong it is to have a sales tax on educational supplies, and how wrong it is to have sales taxes on the house that we call home, the temple that we rear children in, to try to be as thankful and as appreciative to God our heavenly father who have given us these children to promise him that we will give them back to him one day, rearing them in the homes. And yet, these very homes are subject to the taxation that supports this state.

We should also take into cognizance and into consideration a discussion of the black market tax in this state. Now, how are we ever going to get leaders of this state to comply with the law when they make a law saying whiskey is illegal, and turn around and collect taxes on the commodity? Now, it's our position that whiskey should be left to a statewide referendum or to local action and let the people decide what they want. But certainly, we need to get rid of the hypocritical black market tax that places our government in a defenseless position, that places Mississippi where it usually finds itself.

The only reason we are not 51st in a lot of things is because there are not 51 states. When there were 48 states, we were 48th. When we added the 49th state, we became 49th. When we added the 50th state, we became 50th. And the only reason why we're not 51st, when they add Puerto Rico, we're gonna go down to the 51st position, because of such stupidity as this.

Now you know, the story's told about a minister one day that was very much disturbed when Russia landed a satellite on the moon a couple years ago. And he was bemoaning the fact that Russia had captured the moon and was now going to begin [to] charge the world for the light that came from the moon. And as he was bemoaning this fact about how terrible it was that they were gonna have to begin to pay for their light from the moon, one of his deacons told him that, "Don't worry about that, Brother Parson," he said, "You see, we used to payin' for our moonshine."

Now to compensate for the revenue loss (if there would be revenue loss) by exempting what we consider crucial commodities from the sales tax, this could be overcome by a graduated income tax on all families, all persons earning 7,000 dollars a year and more. Now, when we Negroes get to the point where we earn 7,000 dollars a year, we won't mind paying the taxes, will we? We pledge to ensure every citizen o-of this state a decent wage. We advocate a dollar and a quarter an hour for every hour's work done in an establishment where five or more people are hired with a net income of 10,000 dollars a year. Now we think that's reasonable. We advocate a dollar an hour for an hour's work for all other citizens that are employed, whether they are pickin' cotton, washin' dishes, sweepin' the streets, or whatever chore that they find themselves engaged in. But we feel that when we use the body that God gave us, God's temple, as a vehicle to earn a living, that we are entitled to be paid for it, and that nobody has the right to make a slave of us anymore.

We feel that the government of this state has an obligation to see to it that its people are employed. However, we know that there are federal programs that are available, the Area Redevelopment Act, Urban Renewal, and many other federal programs that could be used to retrain and employ the unemployed and the untrained worker of our state. But because most of these people will find themselves divided into the nation's poor—poor whites and poor Negroes—the politicians of our state give little if any attention to it. Employment should be gained, we think, by taking advantages of the state's resources, rather than by the offer of cheap labor, free operations, no unions, and no Negroes. Now you know there are a whole lot of factories here in Jackson and throughout the state of Mississippi that have come in from the east and the west, that have come in with gentlemen's agreements: "We will give you 20 years rent-free if you just don't hire the niggers." And the factories have come in and they have bowed to these agreements. We believe that employment, as we said before, should come, certainly. We think that in the state that's the poorest state in this country that we are very stupid indeed not to take advantage of the public work projects that are available through a cooperative adventure with the federal government. And when Ed King and I get to be governor and lieutenant governor, you can rest assured that we are going to do a whole lot about the unemployment of poor people in this state.

We have already mentioned that six percent of the people of this state elected the present administration. We would like to elaborate on that phase of our campaign for a little while, but first let's explore currently two other planks of our platform. We are now becoming engaged tonight, largely in a discussion of economics, which is one of the things that the other politicians are refusing to talk about. Let's get in a little bit about education. When we realize that Mississippi, the poorest state in the country, trying to operate two school systems, put 'em both together and th-they won't make one good one. Mississippi has, Mississippi has the lowest academic attainment of any state in this nation and the reason for that is largely because the white person in Mississippi is not really concerned about affording the best education the state can afford to the white children. Their main desire is that the white school in a given community is better than the Negro school in that same community. And as long as we've got school boards that are all white (and they gonna be that way until we break the barrier) as long as we have school boards that are in control of the finance, all the money is going to continue to go to the white schools and what's left, if anything is left, is going to the Negro schools. The only way to fix this white man so he can't discriminate against us, is to fix him so he can't, see? And by fixing him so he can't, we mean by placing Negro children and white children in the classroom together. That's the only way we gonna ever be able to do it. And when we do that, whatever he does for his little blonde-eyed Mary, he's got to do the same thing for my little kinky-headed Rebecca.

Then there's the question of justice in this state. We feel that we have no real opportunity of successfully defending ourselves when we are charged with a crime, by any member of the white community, or any member of the police department. Now, I am as much opposed to crime by Negroes against whites as I am opposed to crime by whites against Negroes. But none of us have to think very carefully or very long, and remember the great number of Negroes that we've known that have paid the supreme penalty for a crime against white people. But think all night and the rest of this year, if you will, and find one white man that has paid the supreme price for a crime against a Negro: not one. We are still living in a situation, ladies and gentlemen, where we have no rights that the white man is bound to respect—and that's what the freedom campaign is all about: getting rid of this kind of carrying on.

We shall endeavor to see to it that every citizen 21 years of age in this state, get[s] the right to vote. We think that there are only two require-ments that a citizen ought to have to meet in order to get the right to vote. Number one, that he's 21 years old, and number two, that he's a citizen of Mississippi. Now this is not really a boring idea, because when we realize that it is possible, with teeth in it, when we remember the fact that we do have a law in this state that compels the registration of every, every boy when he becomes eighteen years of age. We never hear anything about a local boy denying a Negro boy the right to register to serve his country. Not one word! And such a law is possible, and such a law ought to have been here before t-the Armed Service Act, to give every person the right to vote, simply by going down and registering. Now they can't, the federal government can't tell us we can't do that, because they've already done it in another instance. And the federal government spends more time tellin' us what they can't do then they do findin' ways tryin' to do it, and I am ap-preciative to the federal government but, for all that it does, but I'm tired at lookin' at FBI agents and Justice Department agents comin' down here and not doin' a darn thing but take notes.

You know, since the beginning of this country, 1766, nine of its first presidents were from the South, mostly from Virginia. And since that time the South started down the road of racial bigotry and racial hatred—keep the nigger down, keep him in his place. And since that time, not another southerner has become president. And the moral of this story is, as long as you keep us from voting, we'll keep you from being president.

With the right to vote, we can span many waters and irrigate many des-ert lands and, as Al Lowenstein has said, instead of signs all over this state reading "Kill the Kennedys," the signs will then begin to read, "O.K. the Kennedys," because we're strictly for 'em. With the right to vote, we can make Senator Eastland and Congressmen Williams and Coleman do the

Mambo. We can make of them another Javitz , we could make of them another Douglass, and another Seller. And so [in] doin' this, we will unwrite a legacy that our white brothers have retained for so many years. We will unwrite the legacy that where a white man feels in his heart that he's better than any Negro God made. We will do it to some degree with the lyrics of another well-known play and it's from the great play *South Pacific*. For Hammerstein says:

> You've got to be taught to hate and fear,
> you've got to be taught from year to year,
> it's got to be drummed into your dear little ears-
> you've got to be carefully taught!
>
> You've got to be taught to be afraid
> of people whose eyes are oddly made,
> of people whose skin is of a different shade-
> you've got to be carefully taught.
>
> You've got to be taught before it's too late,
> before you are six, seven, eight,
> to hate all the folks your relatives [hate]—

[cut in tape]
. . . hate the act, and yet love the man. In these trials and tribulations we have learned well, from the knees of our parents, and from the knees of our grandparents that in the area of freedom, similar to the days of t-the early birth of the Christian church, that had there not been the people who went through these difficulties, there would never have been the victory that we now have today.

You know, every Good Friday, as we've mentioned before, must ultimately give way to the triumph and beat of the drums of Easter. That history may so shape events, that Caesar may occupy the palace, and Christ the cross for a day. But one day that same Christ will rise up and split history into A.D. and B.C., so that even the birth date of Caesar must be dated by his name. All we have to do is keep on down the freedom road. Keep on in the trenches as long as it takes. If we'll do that, before too long, perhaps on November 5th, we'll see a brighter day born here in our state. Thank you, and may God bless you.

§94 James McBride Dabbs

James McBride Dabbs's biography appears in the introduction to his November 9, 1961 speech in Atlanta, Georgia. Dabbs's approach in the following eloquent address before the Southern Regional Council is equal parts folklore, sociology, history, and religion: the Myth (the grand antibellum South), the Movement (civil rights protests of the 1960s), and the American Dream (the ideal that all people are free to make the most of themselves) are reconfigured along the twin axes of insider and outsider. Dabbs presents the idea that southerners, himself included, throughout history have thought of themselves as independent (and superior) from the rest of the world, thus insiders, and that their problems are a private matter.

Yet race-relations in the South are a public, not private matter. To think of blacks as outsiders is misguided thinking: because of slavery and peonage, blacks have the greatest connection to the land and, therefore are the true insiders. Similarly, blacks have tilled religious soil, cultivating a far better Christianity than those from whom they inherited its traditions. For the southern white Christian, religion is but a mechanism for repentance for the twin sins of slavery and segregation. Dabbs's final plea is for whites to embrace their black neighbors and think of them as extended family. He closes his address with a call to the old white South to combine its myth with the movement so there would be no need to worry about the American dream since the equality it espouses is inherent in the combined myth and movement.

———

The Myth, the Movement, and the American Dream

President's Address, annual meeting of the Southern Regional Council,
Atlanta, Georgia
November 26, 1963

The title comes from a suggestion at the close of an interesting article in *New South* for July-August, "The Movement, Negro Challenge to the Myth," by James H. Laue, of Emory University.

The Movement is of course the direct-action movement of the 1960's. The Myth is in general the whole myth of the South, that poetic creation which still haunts, though perhaps with decreasing effectiveness, the imagination of the Western World. The special aspect of the Myth I wish to consider is that which deals with insiders and outsiders, which distinguishes the anointed from the barbarians. The American Dream is the dream of a land where everyone may rise to the top—in brief, be president—and yet somehow be equal. It's all suggested by the old Jacksonian aphorism: "Every man is as good as every other man—and maybe a darned sight better."

I'm only pushing a little further the argument I began in these circumstances two years ago. I raised then the question, "Who Speaks for the South?" A year ago I tried, as I said, "To Define Our Love." Today I continue asking what is it we want?

Years ago my older brother, summing up his judgment of me as a Sunday school teacher, said I didn't have more than one or two ideas. Apparently he was correct. My only comfort is that so many people don't have—well, you know what I'm thinking!

The question of insiders and outsiders was also called to my attention by a remark of Franklin Hamilton, Alabama General Manager for
Southern Bell Telephone and Telegraph Company, as reported in the
Atlanta *Constitution* of last September 24. Mr. Hamilton was referring to
interference by "outsiders" in the affairs of Birmingham. "It is the ancient
and cherished tradition of the South," he said, "that everybody is an intrud-
er who is not invited." Since I'm always looking for ancient and cherished
traditions of the South, this really intrigued me. It also has a noble ring to
it, suggesting southern hospitality. Feeling as I do that we are "guests of the
universe" in our brief stay here, I am happy when any man speaks in terms
of hosts and guests.

The South has always had strong and, for a century now, confused ideas
about insiders and outsiders. It was always set on handling its own affairs;
and yet from the very beginning its affairs were world affairs. The South
was not planned as a land of self-contained, subsistence farmers but as a
land of producers of staples for the world market. The first ship for the
South Carolina settlement carried seeds of various kinds that might become exportable products. But the quality of life which developed in the
South increasingly marked the region off from the world, until finally it
came to think of itself as separate and independent—Alabama is still sovereign, says George Wallace—though tied by trade and even by sentiment
to the rest of the world.

There's a scene in lower South Carolina which symbolizes this conflict
between the inner and outer. I quote from my book *The Southern Heritage:*
"You turn off U.S. 17 and drive slowly along winding roads, sometimes
clay-surfaced, sometimes the old track where in earlier days 'the slow wheel
poured the sand.' You pass by fields and along great unkempt hedges left
to break the sea winds, through deep woods sweet with myrtle and open
spaces covered only with pines—the 'pine-barrens' of the early settlers. The
sun shines, the sand spins under the car wheels, slowly you get the sense of
being in a strange world. The road turns again and widens out, and there,
spread before you on a slight rise, is a great grove of moss-hung live-oaks
surrounding a plantation house, and, beyond, shining between the trunks
of the trees, the quiet waters of the Waccamaw.

"The men who lived in scenes like this—or even faintly resembling
this—behind a barrier of woods, in sunny glades on the banks of quiet
rivers, had instilled in them the sense of being alone, masters of their own
affairs, kings of little kingdoms. Yet the river ran by the doorstep; and from
these secluded plantations, from these magic kingdoms, curtained, perhaps, oh so delicately by Spanish moss, and along these quiet rivers, the
planters traded with the world. Isolated from the world and apparently in-

dependent, they were really bound to it by the periodic arrival and departure of the boat. They became accustomed, therefore, to living their own
lives without realizing how dependent they were. The South developed the
psychology of a folk society and the needs of an industrial society."

It developed, therefore a strong sense of insiders—the homogeneous
fold—together with a great need for outsiders. It was defeated in the Civil
War partly because of this need: it wasn't prepared to defend itself against
the outsiders. Defeated, the South—the white South, that is—developed
a unanimity and an intensity of insidedness such as this nation has not
elsewhere seen; but now, more than ever, it needed the outsiders for its
material salvation.

So, as some South Carolina senator said several years ago pleading for
resistance—it sounds like one of those we have now—"We must get our
backs to the wall." A beautiful southern image, symbol of the Resistance,
but incomplete: Backs to the wall and hands held out, crying "Gimme,
gimme." Are we mice or men?

The question is wrongly put. No such draconian choice is necessary.
We quarreled with the outsiders once before and got licked. I'm not exactly in favor of "jining 'em": I'm still suspicious. But I think we ought
to carry on some high level conferences with them—we're even talking
with Khrushchev now—and come to some agreement. But first we need to
come to some agreement with ourselves.

Don't get me wrong about the insiders. I smile at them because I love
them. I'm an old insider myself. This is discouraging to some of my segregationist friends—and enemies. I live in my grandfather's Winter House,
completed just before the late unpleasantness began. Years ago, while I was
visiting my aunts at its counterpart, the Summer House, one of them said
to me, "Had you noticed, James, that the sun isn't setting quite where it
used to. It used to set, on the first day of September, right down the avenue. Now it's setting a little to one side." That's insidedness for you. Sun
moves around the Summer House, and it had better report on time in
place. Really, this is the true insidedness: to be always at the center of the
universe, to see its farthest stars from our windows. It's the only way to see
them and not be chilled by them. Only by the handle of a community, said
W. B. Yeats, can we pick up the world. To be inside a community is to be,
at least potentially, inside the world. To be a Southerner is to be, at least
potentially, a man. You've got to stand on some earth. What's wrong with
the earth of South Carolina?

I've said before, speaking to Georgia audiences, the man we need is the
universal man, with the red clay of Georgia on his shoes, the strength of
Stone Mountain in his heart, and the mists that forever swirl around the
Atlanta airport in his eyes.

But you don't have to be chauvinistic about it. Isn't it possible to love Georgia without hating Massachusetts?

So far I'm mainly having fun. But I'm circling my subject. It's about as hard for a Southerner to get hold of a subject as it is for anybody to get hold of a Southerner. Grant found this out around Richmond in 1864. A Southerner doesn't like to be pinned down, even for his own good. He's afraid you're going to make an exhibit of him. He's not a deep thinker, but he's a maneuverer. And I'm maneuvering now trying to surround my subject.

Let's make another beginning. Let's take Senator Russell of Georgia. Some time ago, the Senator is reported to have said in opposition to that part of the President's civil rights package having to do with hotels, etc.: "If you can tell a man who can eat in his dining room (the context indicates "public dining room"), you can tell him who can eat in his private dining room and who can sleep in his bedroom." This is interesting logic. I suppose the bedroom gets in because if often leads off the dining room and because we go to bed after supper, or maybe, simply because it's in the house, and once an outsider gets his foot inside the door, he's likely to go anywhere. But how did Senator Russell get this outsider's foot inside the door? On the grounds, I suppose, that eating takes place in both the public and the private dining room, and therefore a guest in one would necessarily be a guest in the other. There are two errors here. One is materialistic: that dining rooms are for nothing but eating, and since you eat in both public and private dining rooms, there is no difference between them. The other is, I believe, a typical southern error. Senator Russell thinks of a business as a personal matter. This is the gentleman's view and is rather strong in the South. This view is supported by the fact that the paying visitor in a hotel is called a guest. But he is still the guest of a hotel, not of a private home. Now, I'm for keeping life—business life included—as personal as possible, but it does seem to me we can distinguish between a hotel and a home.

Senator Russell is all for protecting hotel managers against those who are not invited—as if the establishment of a public eating and sleeping place were not in itself an invitation to the public. Since those who are not invited are, as Mr. Hamilton said, intruders—he was replying to a question about outsiders—Senator Russell is for protecting hotel managers against outsiders. And since we know that the whole ruckus is about the Negro's acceptability in hotels, we came to the conclusion that the Negro is an outsider. This ought to make a horse laugh. And this, by the way, is the heart of my subject. We are now on page 9 and I have arrived.

One more digression, however, before we settle down. Many of these hotel people came from outside; many of these still live outside. How did they get to be insiders? They invested money here. So, it isn't absolutely necessary that one's grandfather should have fought on the right side at the Battle of Atlanta. It does seem necessary, however, that one should not make disrespectful remarks about the Stars and Bars. But clever outsiders soon learn that if they have money to invest and hold their mouths right, they can do as they please.

Mr. Hamilton is also reported to have said that outsiders were welcome if they intended to be "useful." He didn't say useful to whom, but I should guess to the establishment, the successful insiders, not the nondescript "outsider insiders" rioting in the streets.

Maybe all the Negro needs to do to become an insider is to have money to invest, thereby becoming useful to the establishment, and to refrain from making uncomplimentary remarks about the Stars and Bars. This won't bother him, because any Negro who has made enough money to invest won't have time even to think about the Stars and Bars.

But I doubt if it's as simple as this. What we have is the ironic situation that the man who is most truly inside, nearest our hearts—and in a sense this is true—is treated as an outsider. Here we have that gap which Eugene Patterson pointed out in a recent editorial in the Atlanta *Constitution* on "The Mind of the South": the gap between the heart of the South and the fictions its mind has created.

If it's an invitation to come that makes a man an insider, then the Negro is the most inside American we have. We needed him. According to David Ramsay, author of *History of South Carolina from the First Settlement to the Year 1808*, that state had to have him to become the leader she had become. We invited him as compellingly as did the host in the parable, who sent out into the byways and the hedges and dragged the guests in. We gave him a pretty rough meal, but nobody can say we didn't ask him to come.

And then, when we got him here, we gave him the richest land to plant, and, in order that he might be even more intimately associated with the earth, we took away from him the profit motive, and suggested that he be satisfied with the sheer poetry of earth itself. More completely than any other group, he has mixed with this earth his blood, and sweat and tears, his dreams and fancies, his joy and his despair. More than the rest of us he owns it; it is his own; he has loved it and hated it more than we. Its long furrows are preeminently his, its shade trees, its myrtle thickets, its hot, high pine barrens, and the long drink of cold water from the spring, or the cold water sweetened with molasses from the jug in the high cotton.

I am not trying to romanticize slavery and peonage. I'm simply saying that the meat closest the bone is sweetest, and this was the only meat we left him. He had to live close to the bone, close to earth, close to life which is close to death. And now when we act as if he were an outsider, we are simply fools. I fear that life has little patience with fools. Bad men it can abide. The spirit of life is at least active in them though misdirected.

But bumbling people, who cannot see their hands before their faces, or their neighbors before their eyes! Stupid politicians, turning and turning in dead and dying myths! If only they would look at the myths, and translate them into modern language.

They said—we said—that the Negroes were "our people." Far more than legal ownership was implied. The patriarchal life was implied, the sense of the expanded family. The sense of spiritual kinship was implied. Physical kinship wasn't really talked about. We spoke of the loyalty of "our people." This is another one of the myths which needs looking into, as Bell Wiley has done, especially in Chapter III of *The Plain People of the Confederacy*. The truth about the much vaunted loyalty of slaves to their absent masters during the Civil War is suggested by a story Wiley tells of a conversation between two Negroes during the early days of the war. To the one who insisted they should run away and enlist in the Union forces, the other replied with the question, "Did you ever see two dogs fighting over a bone?" "Yeh, but what's dat got to do wid dis?" "Did you ever see the bone fighting?" In brief, the Negro like Brer Rabbit "lay low." There were of course instances of beautiful loyalty, but the general attitude was more realistic.

But what of the "loyalty" of "our people" today? In all honesty, I think they are the best Southerners we have. Most loyal to the truest things in the South. They are of course bent on scrapping a johnny-come-lately institution called segregation. They are tired out with our talk about superiority, with nothing but police billies and cattle prods to support it. How could they live in the modern world and not be? And they live in the modern world. The winds of the 1960's blow through their open windows. The men who try to sit on top of them may be good Southerners, but of the vintage of 1880, and the wine has turned sour. They too are the South, but the South at its worst, poor, ignorant, scorned, defeated. Yet, let's be fair: many of them are good people—when they're not trying to act like Southerners. But as Southerners, dead. Galvanized into action by short-circuits in their cattle prods. Troublesome. Dangerous. But dead. And the living wave moves on, and sweeps them out to sea.

Thank God for this living wave from inside the South. Men and women who have been inside the South so long that they know, perhaps better than the whites who planned it, what we were trying to do. They weren't busy fighting outsiders. They weren't busy fighting anybody; it wasn't any use. When they finished their tasks in the cotton, they quarreled with God, and were defeated, and accepted. When they finished their earthly tasks they went home to Him. Meanwhile, they helped the South to develop its distinctive characteristics. They had a sense of form, of manner, of hierarchy, of place. They have this still in Africa. Read Noni Jabavu's *Drawn in Color*. The southern aristocrat, or aristocrat-on-the-make—and most of them were on the make, and many didn't get made—these men also had this. The Negroes encouraged it both because they liked it, and because the more form they could develop, the less work they had to do. You see, this was poetic form they were developing. The whites had taken the profit motive from them, and had left them no desire, therefore, to develop productive form. So, as far as they could, they made a game out of work, and made game with the boss, sometimes with his knowledge, sometimes behind his back. Life was too serious for them to take it too seriously. The southern white Christian, holding slaves, had a problem he couldn't face; the slave had a problem he couldn't face. Therefore he often diverted himself, and the white man too.

Which leads us from the play of life to its serious undertone. Without characterizing its religion, it is safe to say that the South is the most religious section of the Nation. Why? Largely, though not solely, because of the presence of the enslaved and discriminated against Negro. White Southerners had to get religion to repent of owning slaves. Of course, they didn't say this. They repented of too much wine, women, song, and cards. But they had to get rid somehow of that big backlog of sin connected with slavery and, later, segregation. They usually had these big revivals after the cotton was laid by, and before the picking began. This was the season for repentance. The rest of the year was open season for sin. And the cotton was full of sin.

It's clear why Negro Southerners had to get religion. They had to get along with these whites—these strange Christian Anglo-Saxons and Scotch-Irish, with one season for cotton and another for repentance. Only the grace of God gave them the strength to do it. It's possible he planned for them to Christianize their strange white neighbors. Anyway, they got the feel of the whole thing even better than their teachers had it. They understood what the cross meant, and whole-souled commitment, and laying one's life on the line, one's body in the jailhouse; and most creative of all, they understood the Great Prophets and the ideal of social justice.

And now they come, scorning the whole structure of segregation, and bringing to its overthrow the best manners and the deepest religious hearts of the South. They are insiders, speaking inside our hearts, undermining the foolish things our brains have thought. They speak to our hearts for two reasons. First, because they speak from the human heart with its deep vision of life's tragedy and its possible glory, and so speak to human hearts everywhere. But, second, they speak to us, because now for a hundred years, through our own defeat, subjection, colonization, exploitation, frustration, and disappointment, life has been whispering to us what it really is; and their voices put in words what life has put in deeds. We and they have been defeated for different reasons, but we have all been defeated. Wallace still thinks it's the Yankees, and hopes that at last under his leadership we may hold Cemetery Ridge. Martin Luther King, Jr. knows it's life.

I was thinking the other day about the plaintive quality of so many Negro songs. "Sometimes I feel like a motherless child." Then I remembered the plaintive note in pioneering America; the homesickness for old streets, and settled ways, and village lights at dusk. Translated into religion, this became such a song as

> I've wandered far away from God,
> Now I'm coming home . . .
> Open wide thine arms of love,
> Lord, I'm coming home.

And I wondered how the plaintive note of the pioneer crossed with the plaintive note of the Negro slave, and how perhaps we southern whites have a double sense of nostalgia. For we too were pioneers. We too left the seaboard and moved inland . . . and moved inland. And we carried with us, sometimes willingly sometimes unwillingly, these dark neighbors of ours whom even more than we could not be at home.

And now we have the gall to act as if these people, many of whom taught many of us the first words of love and courtesy, told us the first stories, conjured up for us Brer Rabbit and Brer Fox, shook us with gales of laughter and filled our hearts with the "tears of things"—we have the gall to act as if these people were outsiders. What does God do with such stupidity?

Are there no Southerners left among the whites to match these colored Southerners? Have we been so minimized, so belittled, by the last hundred years that we do not remember greatness of spirit? Courtesy, magnanimity, devotion? I do not believe it. We have been confused by false leaders, by fictions; we have been frightened by the great revolution of the world. Why should we who survived the greatest defeat Americans have ever suffered be bothered by this passing tempest? Especially when we know it had to come and moreover that its winds are blowing the cobwebs and even some dead flowers out of our hearts. The South is filled with good men. Are they good enough for 1964?—and I don't mean just the election.

We began with the Myth, the Movement, and the American Dream. If the Myth and Movement combine as they should, and as they may, we need not worry about the American Dream. As the Negro gains power in the South, the South becomes more American and democratic. It may well become more southern at the same time, for now there appears among us a Southerner who is not southern because of an old hatred but only because he has lived, laughed, and suffered here, and because he helped to make the region what it is.

§95 Reverend Duncan Howlett

The Reverend Duncan Howlett's biography appears in the introduction to his March 12, 1961 sermon in Lynchburg, Virginia. In this profoundly moving and image-laden sermon to his congregants at All Souls Church, Reverend Howlett begins with the archetypal image of the sea, specifically the "broad river of racial prejudice." As an "evil-smelling and sludge-laden" river, it calls to mind the countless murders and lynchings of black Americans, where rivers capriciously hid and exposed corpses. Howlett asks his listeners to see from both sides of that river, from the "prosperous" side as well as the oppressed side. The basic problem, though, is not in privilege or its opposite, but in the "mists" of prejudice that rise from the river and "distort our vision in both directions." Such mists cause us to see what we want to see, thereby creating even greater distances across the river. Even so, Howlett thinks he hears a new song, emanating from the heart of the black man and heard in the white community. The emerging river ballad is a song of love, a song of a better future, and a song of faith. It is also a patriotic anthem paying white America the ultimate compliment, for it says to them I believe in your Constitution, I believe in your capacity for love and for justice. "Can we not see that upon his shoulders, bent with the toil of centuries, we are lifted up? Can we not see that it is given to us in this century to rise to moral greatness, albeit on the back of those we have miserably oppressed?" Howlett closes his sermon by adopting the prophetic voice, beseeching his fellow white Americans to cross the river, to build the bridge and to honor God by so doing.

———

The Two Way Barrier

All Souls Church (Unitarian), Washington, D.C.
November 1963

President Kennedy recently declared that the civil rights struggle now in process in the United States is a "two way street." Thus he summed up, in an almost offhand remark, the most fundamental and perhaps the least noticed aspect of the entire civil rights movement. Today the Negro and the white communities stare at each other across a broad river of racial prejudice, flowing down from the most remote regions of man's history, swollen to a flood by the great tributary of American slavery and the pattern of discrimination and segregation that followed upon it.

The landscape of either side of the river looks quite different from that on the other side. What you see depends on where you happen to be when first you raise your eyes to look across it. Many, on both sides, have not done that as yet. They have never even been to the banks of the river. They do not really know what segregation means. A few hardly know the river is there at all, although this number has been sharply reduced within the last few years. More have looked upon the river, or across it, and yet have not quite realized what they saw. They have realized that the river was wide. They could see that is was slow-moving; they knew it was evil-smelling and sludge-laden. They have known its eddies and currents were treacherous. They have seen there was no bridge across it. They are aware that a few hardy souls have crossed the river, both ways, many more from the Negro to the white side than the reverse.

The islands in the river have made convenient and necessary stopping places. There, the dwellers on both sides have often met and helped each other on their way. But many have drowned trying to cross the river. More have been beaten back from the white side as if they have come as enemies and invaders rather than as friends. All this is known and not known, understood, misunderstood, suppressed, hidden away or forgotten entirely on both sides of the river. For the dwellers on both sides have sought to do what all men and all times have done—to make their peace with their lot, to get along as best they could, however difficult or distasteful it might be.

The river of racial prejudice has a character all its own that reinforces the separation it engenders. From there it rises a mist which creates the most extraordinary illusions for those on either bank. And what is most remarkable, these illusions are not the same. The mists of prejudice are such that they endow the dwellers on the prosperous side of the river with the illusion that their material comforts make life a constant delight, that they alone are happy, moral and to be envied. They overlook the great wrongs they have done and are doing, the massive evil that has marked and still marks their culture, the syndicates of crime that have fed and still feed upon it. They forget the corrupting, corroding, pervasive evil in their culture that seeks out both the great and the humble, and eats away their native honor.

Those on the prosperous side of the river of prejudice think of themselves as not merely more accomplished, they also think they are better by nature. And so they come to believe that the dwellers on the opposite shore are inferior, not merely in achievement but in ability and in native endowment as well. In this way they justify to themselves the severe measures of oppression they adopt by which to keep the dwellers on the opposite bank "where they belong." No doctrine is more insidious, but none, it seems, is more deeply rooted in the nature of man. The Hindu caste system exhibits this philosophy in the East as does the Judeo-Christian tradition in the West. We should not forget that the idea of the chosen people, the elect of God, is at the heart of both the Old and New Testaments.

And so, if we stand on the shore of plenty and look through the mists of prejudice toward the shore of want, we see degeneracy and violence. We see stupidity and sloth. We see lust and brutality. We hear no laughter, for we are too far away and the noise of the river drowns it out. We see no joy, no love, no honor, no fidelity.

And yet at the same time, we do. For when we look through the mists of prejudice, we not only see what we want to see, we also often see what is really there. These things may not register upon our conscious minds. We perceive them subliminally, as it were. But the knowledge enters our subconscious and, lodging there, haunts us, as in an evil dream. And so we know, while yet we do not know that we know, the misery that life on the other shore forces upon those who dwell there. Through the mists of prejudice we look and see yet do not see. We know but do not know because we do not want to know.

Now let us move to the other side of the river of racial prejudice. There we shall find the view of the opposite shore is no less distorted but the distortion is different. The victim of prejudice sees only arrogance, hypocrisy, greed and hate. He cannot understand how good men can blind themselves with their own prejudices. If they subject their children to what amounts to brain-washing in race prejudice, the victim of the process cannot but believe that the end result, by which he suffers, is intentional in the most literal sense.

This is the heart of the problem. The mists that rise from the river of racial prejudice distort our vision in both directions. Because of it, we do not know each other and do not know ourselves. This the American people must learn to do, as we are learning to do it here in this church. For we are learning here, each one of us, Negro and white, bit by bit, to accept each other as people, as individuals, on our merit as persons, and quite apart from our particular racial background.

I say we are learning. But we have at the same time to face the fact that no matter how high our intent, and no matter how hard we may try, we are doomed to fall short of our goal, at least for the present, and probably for the lifetime of most of us. As the civil rights movement gains momentum in this country, as we steadily move toward achieving the social revolution that is now under way, we are doomed to become not less but more conscious of our individual racial identity, whether we will or no. As the integration movement mounts, the fact of the difference between us will increasingly be emphasized and under these circumstances it will be increasingly false for us to try to treat each other as if there were no difference between us.

For this reason, we should believe in integration, we who would, if we could, treat each other as people and not as members of this or that race; we are called upon now, in our time, to take an intermediate step in the integration process. Because of the prejudices that still exist and lie so deep between us, because of the need to take calculated steps toward integration, because we ourselves are beset by prejudices we so not even realize we possess, I a white man have got to learn to say to you a Negro, looking you

straight in the eye, "I am white, you are Negro, and this is our problem."
And you a Negro have got to be able to look me in the eye and say the same
thing: "You are white, I am Negro: this is our problem." It is our common
problem because the society in which we dwell makes it so, quite apart
from any personal feelings you and I may have. We cannot begin to solve
it for ourselves or for society, until we begin to face it in ourselves, openly,
both acknowledging together that it is our problem. This is the two-way
street on which we must meet. This is the two-way psychological barrier
we must overcome.

Suppose we are able to take this intermediate step, you and I. Suppose
that thousands and later millions like us are able to do it. Suppose that then
we find we can begin to treat each other as people and to forget to what
race any of us belongs. Suppose that American society increasingly does as
we have done in this church, elevate people to office on the basis of merit,
with race offering no barrier whatever, in the choice we make. Can we hope
to succeed?

Our problem is as old as man, for man, whatever color he may be, is a
creature of greed and avarice. He is a creature of cruelty. He can be utterly
insensitive to the sufferings he inflicts upon others. Whenever and wherever he can lift himself up above his fellow men. Standing upon their backs,
he cares not whom he hurts, to what race they may belong, or what color
their skin may be. These accidental differences only provide the excuses by
which he seeks to justify to himself what he knows in his heart is wrong.
He knows it is wrong because he knows he would object if the roles were
reversed. He knows he would cry out, and the despair that would seize him,
if he were enslaved and his servants became his masters. So he seizes upon
any excuse by which to explain the mastery over others he proposes to
enjoy for himself. His real purpose is mastery. It is comfort, ease and luxury
for himself. Man who has lifted his eyes to the stars still grinds his fellow
man beneath his feet. Will he not always do so? Is color more than a convenient device by which men strive to perpetuate a pattern of oppression?

There are those who would have us think so: the men of theology who
tell us that man is lost in sin, helpless to save himself, and that he can only
fling himself on the mercy of Almighty God. There are others who think so:
the men of sociology and psychology who tell us that man is beset by self-
centered drives he is powerless to control to any degree and that however
he may design his social program it will be corrupted, twisted and broken
by evil men. These are comfortable teachings if good fortune or hard work
or both have landed you in a comfortable place in the social scale where
most of your needs are provided for by the labor of others. If God or man's
psychological makeup have ordained him for evil and we cannot do much
about it, then presumably we are excused from trying.

Lowest of all on the scale of rationalizing segregation is the use of the Bible for this purpose. It is beneath contempt. The habit the ancients had of enslaving a fallen foe recorded not merely in the Bible but in all ancient literature is not to be canonized as the law of God. It is to be repudiated as one of the evil ways of men.

But there is another kind of response to man's tendency toward evil as it expresses itself through our racial differences. A song is beginning to be heard in our land. It rises from the hearts of the Negro. It is a song of hope. It rises out of the night of their despair. It passes from ear to ear, from lip to lip and from heart to heart. This song is also heard in the white community, but there it is more a song of recognition than of hope, more a song of commitment than of expectation. I am thinking of no particular song, although there are many I might mention. I speak of singing that rises from somewhere deep within us and expresses who we really are. I speak of a song that sings in the spirit of men whose hope has become faith, and whose expectancy of a better future has become the trust that that future will come to pass.

The song I hear people singing is no mere whistling in the dark. It is no mere hope based upon unfilled desire. The song I hear people singing rises out of the deepest yearning a man may know—the yearning for companionship, the yearning to love and be loved. The song I hear people singing, though it might have been a song of hate, is a song of love. Though it might have called for vengeance, it calls for forgiveness; though it might have been a call to arms, it is a call to peace; though it might have been a call to terror, it is a call to conscience.

In the song that he now is singing, the American Negro has paid the American people the greatest compliment a person has ever been paid by an oppressed minority. The Negro is saying to his fellow Americans: I believe in you. I trust you. I think you mean what you say in our Constitution. You have not lived up to your own ideals. You do not even seem to know you have not. But perhaps you will if I make my case clear. Perhaps you will if I am able to press my demands upon you in a manner you cannot ignore.

I often wonder why I have to go to such lengths to get my point over, the Negro says to his fellow Americans. I ask myself why I must sit-in, kneel-in, pray-in, and march by the thousands in our streets, just to get your attention. I ask myself why I must fill up your jails and risk my life just to get a hearing. Yet I still believe. I believe in our Constitution and I believe in you, the white majority. I believe you want to enforce the law of the land, for me as well as for yourself. I know man's sin as well as you do. I know all too well that man will oppress his fellow man if he can. But I also know he has lifted his eyes to the stars: I know he is capable of justice as well as oppression, of love as well as hate. I believe man has a conscience and I know that in our American society, constructed as it is, I am able to speak to the conscience of men. For when I speak, I am heard.

All these things the Negro is saying to his fellow Americans. He has chosen the path of reason and peace by which to win the rights the Constitution guarantees to him. Can we not hear what he is saying, both in word and deed, as he asks to take his rightful place among us? Cannot we see how noble is his appeal? Cannot we see that he is appealing not to the worst but to the best in us? Can we not recognize that because he appeals to our better nature, he brings that side of us to the fore in a period of moral disillusionment? Can we not see that upon his shoulders, bent with the toil of centuries, we are lifted up? Can we not see that it is given to us in this century to rise to moral greatness, albeit on the back of those we have miserably oppressed?

Our question as a nation is the question that has now to be faced by the white majority of the nation. Are we ready to accept the compliment our Negro citizens have paid us? Are we equal to their expectations of us? Are we really the men of high conscience they have supposed us to be? We shall soon know. We shall soon know whether an oppressed minority can ask for justice and get it in this country, or whether as in most places and times, they shall get only what justice they may wrest from us by fire and sword.

Today the Negro is the suffering servant of America. The words of Isaiah written so long ago seem to have been written for him and the relationship he has had to American life.

> "He was despised and rejected of men
>   a man of sorrows and acquainted with grief
> And we hid as it were our faces from him
>   He was despised and we esteemed him not.
> Surely he hath borne our griefs,
>   and carried our sorrows
> Yet we did esteem him stricken
>   smitten of God and afflicted,
> But he was wounded for our transgressions
>   he was bruised for our iniquities:
> The chastisement of our peace was upon him
>   and with his stripes we are healed."

O thou my country! How often hast thou stood at the crossroads of history. How often hast thou faced a moral choice and taken the high road of conscience, of justice and liberty! O thou my people! Look where we stand today. Behold the choice before us. A great revolution is at hand. The oppressed in our midst ask for freedom. They ask it in the name of right, of decency and love. They offer us the chance to give it to them out of our belief that all men stand alike before God and must so stand before men. O Thou my people, are we worthy—are we equal to the honor that has been done us?

Or shall we take the other road, the one that leads back to oppression? Shall we go on denying to a segment of our people the rights with which our Constitution and their manhood has endowed them? Are we not to be worthy of the trust they place in us? Are we not to prove ourselves lesser men than they are ready to think? Are we now to be false in our history and false to our destiny as a people? Shall we begin now to close the door of freedom which we have opened so wide?

O thou my country! I tremble for thee, tremble lest thou shouldst choose the lesser part: lest at the crossroads of history where we stand today, thou shouldst choose the way of oppression, for it has ever been the way of strife and bloodshed, and it will not be different with us. Before us stand our Negro citizens, their hands outstretched not in supplication but in entreaty. They do not kneel before us: they stand like men. They say to their nation and ours, Give us these rights and privileges you have taught us to prize as American citizens. Give us these rights, as you have declared they belong to all men. *Give* them to us. Don't make us force them from you. Give them to us because you believe they are ours.

No nobler call was ever made to a people than this. No greater honor was ever done a people than this. This is how we shall overcome the two-way barrier that now divides us from each other. Here is the bridge over the river of racial prejudice upon which we shall meet, the bridge of our common tradition of love for our fellow man rising out of the heart of God.

§96 David G. Colwell

David G. Colwell was born on December 19, 1916 in St. Louis, Missouri. He attended Yale University, receiving a B.A. while also distinguishing himself as a fullback on the football team. He then attended Harvard University where he earned an M.B.A. before returning to Yale to earn a B.D., which he completed in 1943. After his schooling, Colwell served as an army chaplain, where he survived the horrors of war including tending to survivors of the Holocaust after the liberation of Ohrdurf on April 5, 1945. After the war he served congregations in Colorado and Washington, D.C. Colwell was a coordinator of the March on Washington in 1963, participating in the event along with 40 members of his church. From 1967 until his retirement in 1982 he served as senior pastor at the Plymouth Congregational Church in Seattle, Washington. In addition to his activism, he was a family man with a wife, Catherine, and six children. He died on September 22, 2001 at the age of 84.

The sermon below urges his Washington, D.C. congregation to give an offering for the Church of Christ's "Racial Justice Now" fund, which would coordinate civil rights activities such as the 1965 march from Selma to Montgomery where Unitarian minister James Reeb was killed. Colwell compares the atrocity of events in the South to the events that had puzzled him in Ohrdurf, Germany. Like Nazi Germany, southern churchgoers risked violent pogroms if they dared to gather. Like Nazi Germany, destruction of property accompanied violence. Like Nazi Germany, an unbearable silence follows the violence because no one wishes to risk the consequences of speaking the truth. Like Dietrich Bonhoeffer, Colwell believes that obedience to God requires bearing the cost of discipleship, whether this entails merely material investment or the more expensive loss of life and liberty.

As if in a Foreign Country

First Congregational United Church of Christ, Washington, D.C.
November 1963

We must obey God rather than men. (Acts 5:29)

In the late winter of 1945—it must have been Lent—I found myself at a concentration camp outside the little German city of Ohrdruf. A few days earlier American troops had first entered the area, and the concentration camp had been liberated. This was a kind of minor-league concentration camp, not one of the big ones like Buchenwald. A few days after the liberation some of us went to the camp, taking with us some of the leading citizens of that little German city, including the burgomeister. They had told us that they had no knowledge of what had been going on inside the walls of that camp. Yes, they had used the labor of some of the people in the fields, a few of them had worked in the factories from time to time, but they really didn't know anything about the conditions under which the prisoners lived—and as it turned out, died. On this particular morning, seeing the shock and revulsion on their faces, I had to believe that they spoke the truth when they had said they didn't know. A couple of days after that, the burgomeister, confessing his failure as a Christian and as a citizen, took his life.

That was a long time ago, and in a foreign country. I remember wondering how it was that good people—basically decent people—could not know, and how a nation, a city, could allow such things to happen in its midst. I remember wondering how a Christian-oriented people could be the agent of so much death, suffering, and persecution directed to those of a different race; how the Church of Jesus Christ with only a few exceptions could keep silent in such a time. I also remember, now with quite vivid guilt, how critical some of us were of the church in Germany because of her silence, and how critical we were of the solid mass of the German people who through their silence and their indifference seemed really not to care about the persecutions. That was a long time ago, and in a foreign country.

On October 30, 1963, I spent the late afternoon and evening in Plaquemine, Louisiana. This, you will remember, is the city where James Farmer, the National Director of CORE, was imprisoned [at] the end of August, at the time of the March on Washington. I had gone there with five others, staff and directors of the Board for Homeland Ministries of the United Church of Christ, which was meeting in New Orleans. We had been asked by the board to go to this beleaguered community as evidence that we knew and cared about what was happening there. In that little city the Negroes hadn't been able to hold a public meeting for some time because there had been too much violence and bloodshed on the past two occasions when they had gotten together. Because we were coming, however, that night seemed to be a good time to try it again. They got out some handbills around the town, and in other ways spread the word that some Christians from outside were coming to be with them. So we gathered in the Plymouth Rock Baptist Church. The last time folk had gathered there to talk about freedom and their civil rights and to confess their faith in the Lord of Creation, the local police had ridden horses up into the vestibule, and indeed, one of them into the church, and had fired tear gas into the building. The medical repair bill for that little exercise in freedom had been over 800 dollars. It included the repair of very serious second-degree burns from tear gas fired at point blank range and repairs to flesh and bone and muscle injured by iron shoes on the hooves of the horses ridden by the sheriff's men. Most of these injuries were on feet and ankles and lower legs, but at least one of them was on the chest of a man. This bill also included treatment to injuries of vital and sensitive parts of the human anatomy inflicted by the cruel and abusive use of cattle prods.

What was it like in Plaquemine, Louisiana, in this year of grace? The overpowering sense that one got was that of being in a foreign land. There was really nothing familiar, and the dependable things that you and I have unconsciously based our lives upon were all absent—the verities, the principles which structure all solid communities—they just weren't there. In communities like this one the police are not your protector; they can be your enemy, the specific instrument of your torture. The community is not your friend; it becomes a kind of battleground. The six of us rode together in a rented car the sixty miles from New Orleans. Because Archie Hargreaves, a Negro, was with us, we were followed many of those miles. The law there is not that majestic protector of the rights of citizens which we like to believe it to be; it becomes one of the instruments for persecution in the hands of a few. It is twisted and distorted to suit the desires of one group. Ideas like justice and freedom and decency—these cornerstones of any community where I had ever lived—are gone. They just aren't visible when the white community meets the Negro.

But above all was the incredible silence—that massive, depressing, awful silence in which so few white voices are raised to cry out against brutality, against discrimination, against persecution. The deadening pall over all of this, however, is the incredible silence of the Church of Jesus Christ. If one really wants to express himself on the issue of obedience to God's will in this racial struggle the only place he can safely do it in this town of 8,000 people is in one little Negro church, and even there, there is no safety. There is no place else. Massive intimidation against those who stand for racial justice is so great that it takes great courage and real faith to serve the Lord obediently in that place.

In war-torn Germany most of the people were not cruel persecutors; they just didn't want to know what was happening. When Nazism began its rise it played upon little prejudices, and the people said, "This is all right. I really don't like Jews anyhow." Then the monster began to devour and to destroy, and they couldn't stop it; they just sat silently in their fear. Now, most of us are not cruel persecutors either. We have our little prejudices, and we try to tell ourselves that it doesn't make any difference. But we have in this country police states like those we so hated in Nazi Germany and in some places like the Soviet Union today. They exist because we just sit silently.

"But Peter and the apostles answered, 'We must obey God rather than men.'"

For America, it seems to me, the crisis is very clear. Can democracy—this cherished form of government—give justice to the oppressed, the persecuted? Can the national government act to protect its citizens from brutality, from injustice delivered at the hands of elected and appointed officials of the states, counties, and towns. Documented evidence of brutality has been forwarded to the Department of Justice over and over again, but somehow it seems powerless to act in the protection of citizens of this land who are only seeking their Constitutional rights. Can the federal government prevent state and local governments from persistently keeping certain citizens from voting through the exercise of various means of intimidation, beginning with outright violence and running through various more subtle forms of persecution and discrimination, and down to a failure to apply impartially the voting registration rules? Can the whole people do something about a school system in which the Negro school has no equipment for its laboratory, no maps on the walls, and miserably few textbooks that are hopelessly out-of-date. This last happens to apply also to the District of Columbia, you know.

These are not academic questions. These are the crucial questions which face this nation—our future hangs in the balance. Can this nation, can American democracy, act for justice?

Can the Congress of the United States rid itself of the unreality and the ritual that keep it bound to dead traditions and act to give justice to the whole people?

What about the Church of Jesus Christ? Can it overcome its sin and its sloth and resolutely and courageously speak the word of truth to this generation? Some time ago I placed a large poster on the bulletin board near the Chapel entrance. The text on the poster asks, "Shall we betray our Lord?" And then it says, "Racial Justice now." During the past days someone has crossed out the "Now" and scrawled in the word "Never." I have left it just that way. It is still there, a proper, poignant reminder to all of us that the church is called to obedience. This is not just pious language. It means enough that someone feels so threatened that he has to fight back. At least that unknown person was startled into action—betrayal action though it was—and left the great morass of neutrality into which most of us comfortably sink and prepare to die. The question of course is: "Is the Church of Christ on the side of Racial Justice Now?" Or is it content to keep its mind and its energies directed toward safe and inconsequential things? God calls for a decision.

Peter and the apostles had been jailed for preaching the word about Jesus Christ. Now out of jail, they were again hauled before the authorities and charged to keep silent—this is revolutionary teaching, this Gospel. But Peter and the apostles answered, "We must (there is no option here) obey God rather than men."

In the providence of God the time has again come for the Church and for Christian men and women to face precisely the same question of obedience. In some places the risks again are jail and violence. For most of us, however, it is not jail and violence, but a kind of social ostracizing and uncomfortable stares. For some maybe this is worse than going to jail, but it doesn't make any difference. The question still is being pressed upon us by the Lord of the church.

What are some of the things that you and I can do in the midst of the revolution? First I think, we can recognize that we are in a revolution. Whether we like it or not is immaterial. This is where we are. As in any revolution the great, uncommitted, neutral middle ground is the most irrelevant piece of real estate in the United States. I mean by this that in this revolution we are called to stand on one side or the other. God does not call his people in this day to silence; God does not permit us to sit by silently and uncommittedly pretending that it is really none of our concern. Mark this well! In this day and generation the silent man is really on the side of injustice, of persecution, of segregation; whether he wants it that way, once again, is immaterial here. This is the nature of our time.

Secondly, we cannot all go into the crucial areas to testify. But we can thank God that we are called into membership in a denomination that has committed itself to real and faithful involvement. But, it can't do this unless we give the kind of support, financial and otherwise, to make it possible for the United Church of Christ not only to maintain its commitments, but also to penetrate new fields of testimony with the truth of Jesus Christ. In short, we can give generously in the special offerings for Racial Justice Now.

Thirdly, we as persons who have confessed that Jesus Christ is Lord can take steps to become members of the "Fellowship of the Committed" (which is a denominational project to bring together the people who are willing to take a stand for racial justice now). This is not an easy commitment to make, nor an easy one to live up to. No man should do it lightly and without due counting of the possible sacrifices that might be demanded of him. But insofar as I can see these matters, in our time this is the call to Christian discipleship and obedience. You will note that a part of this commitment is to press for civil rights legislation. I should earnestly hope that each member of this church would today write to his representatives in the Congress. If he doesn't have a representative—if he is one of the disenfranchised residents of the District—he should write to the leaders of both the House and the Senate. In these letters, I trust that you will confess your commitment to justice, to the American principle of democracy, to your faith as confessing Christians who are called to speak that Word which God gives you to speak. I hope also that in some of these letters the idea will get through to the respected members of the Congress that the people are tired of their stalling; and that they are becoming failures through their refusal to overhaul their structures.

Finally, I trust, that God will give to each one of us the grace to join the great company of Peter and the apostles that we may testify to the nature of our obedience in clear-cut language, "We must obey God rather than men."

§97 Robert W. Spike

Dr. Robert Warren Spike was born in 1923 in Buffalo, New York. Educated at Denison University, Union Theological Seminary, Columbia University, and Colgate-Rochester Divinity School, Spike pastored the Judson Memorial Church in Greenwich Village in the late 1940s, reviving the social activism of this famous urban church. In 1958 he was appointed general secretary of the united church board for homeland ministries. In 1963 Spike became the executive director of the National Council of Churches' Commission on Religion and Race (CORR), an important arm of the civil rights movement's machine. In that capacity, Spike quickly organized Protestant churches to participate in the March on Washington. In 1965 Spike wrote *The Freedom Revolution and the Churches*. In January 1966 Spike took a position as director of a new program, Doctors of the Ministry, at the Divinity School at the University of Chicago. Less than a year later, on October 17, Spike was murdered in Columbus, Ohio. His body was discovered in a guest room in a new ecumenical Christian student center at the Ohio State University. No one was ever tried for his murder. His widow and two sons courageously survive their loss. Below they share from their files the condolences of a whole nation:

[Western Union Telegram, 1966 OCT 18 PM 1 05]

DEEPLY SADDENED TO LEARN OF THE DEATH OF OUR DEAR FRIEND BOB SPIKE. HIS DEATH COMES AS A GREAT LOSS TO THE NATION AND TO THE FELLOWSHIP OF THE COMMITTED. HE WAS ONE OF THOSE RARE INDIVIDUALS WHO SOUGHT AT EVERY POINT TO MAKE RELIGION RELEVANT TO THE SOCIAL ISSUES OF OUR TIME. HE LIFTED RELIGION FROM THE STAGNANT ARENA OF PIOUS IRRELEVANCIES AND SANCTIMONIOUS TRIVIALITIES. HIS BRILLIANT AND DEDICATED WORK IN THE NATIONAL COUNCIL OF CHURCHES WILL BE AN INSPIRATION TO GENERALS YET UNBORN. WE WILL ALWAYS REMEMBER HIS UNSWERVING DEVOTION TO THE LEGITIMATE ASPIRATIONS OF OPPRESSED PEOPLE FOR FREEDOM AND HUMAN DIGNITY. IT WAS MY PERSONAL PLEASURE AND SACRED PRIVILEGE TO WORK CLOSELY WITH HIM IN VARIOUS UNDERTAKINGS. AS WE CONTINUE TO GRAPPLE WITH THE ANCIENT EVILS OF MAN'S INHUMANITY TO MAN, WE WILL BE SUSTAINED AND CONSOLED BY BOB'S DEDICATED SPIRIT. PLEASE KNOW THAT WE SHARE YOUR GRIEF AT THIS MOMENT AND YOU HAVE OUR DEEPEST SYMPATHY AND MOST PASSIONATE PRAYERS FOR STRENGH AND GUIDANCE IN THESE TRYING MOMENTS

MARTIN LUTHER KING JR

[Western Union Telegram 1966 OCT 20 AM 11 48]

MAY I EXPRESS ON BEHALF OF THE NATIONAL ASSOCIATION FOR THE ADVANCEMENT OF COLORED PEOPLE AND ON MY OWN PERSONAL BEHALF ESPECIALLY OUR PROFOUND SHOCK AND GRIEF AT THE TRAGEDY WHICH HAS STRUCK YOU AS COLLEAGUE AND FRIEND AND DEVOTED COWORKER BOB SPIKE HAD A PLACE IN OUR HEARTS SHARED BY ONLY A TREASURED FEW WE SHALL MISS HIM GREATLY

ROY WILKINS

[Western Union Telegram 1966 OCT 19 PM 5 38]

I WAS DEEPLY GRIEVED AND SHOCKED BY THE NEWS OF THE DEATH OF DR ROBERT SPIKE. I KNEW HIM FROM ASSOCIATION

IN THE CIVIL RIGHTS STRUGGLE. THE CIVIL RIGHTS MOVEMENT
HAS LOST ONE OF ITS MOST VALIANT WARRIORS. THE COUNTRY
HAS LOST A GREAT AMERICAN, A GREAT MORAL STATESMAN
AND A GREAT MAN. I JOIN YOU IN SORROW OVER THIS GREAT
LOSS

A PHILIP RANDOLPH PRESIDENT BROTHERHOOD OF
SLEEPING CAR PORTERS

[Western Union Telegram 1966 OCT 28 AM 11 30]

DEEPLY REGRET IMPOSSIBLE ATTEND MEMORIAL SERVICE
ON BEHALF OF THE STUDENT NONVIOLENT COORDINATING
COMMITTEE PLEASE ACCEPT OUR HEARTFELT SYMPATHY IN
YOUR LOSS WHICH IS A LOSS FOR ALL OF US

STOKLEY CARMICHAEL CHAIRMAN IVANHOE DONALDSON
DIRECTOR NEW YORK OFFICE

[Western Union Telegram 1966 OCT 28 AM 11 30]

I AM SHOCKED AND GRIEVED AT THE NEWS OF YOUR
HUSBANDS DEATH HE WAS A FINE FRIEND AND A CONSTANT
SOURCE OF STRENGTH FOR THE THINGS THAT ARE RIGHT. ALL
OF US WHO HAD THE PRIVILEGE OF KNOWING HIM WILL MISS
HIM SORELY. MY DEEPEST SYMPATHY TO YOU AND YOUR TWO
SONS.

NICHOLAS KATZENBACH

[Western Union Telegram 1966 OCT 19 AM 11 56]

MRS HUMPHREY AND I WANT YOU TO KNOW HOW MUCH
OUR THOUGHTS ARE WITH YOU AND YOUR SONS. BOB WAS A
GOOD AND DEAR COUNSELOR TO SO VERY MANY. HIS HELP,
STRENGTH AND FIRM CONVICTIONS WILL CONTINUE IN
THOUSANDS OF WAYS IN THOUSANDS OF LIVES. WE WISH THAT
THERE WERE MORE MEANINGFUL AND HELPFUL WAYS TO
EXPRESS OUR SORROW. THE PEOPLE OF THIS COUNTRY FIND
THEIR GUIDANCE AND THEIR LEADERSHIP IN THE STRONG
DEDICATION OF THE SELFLESS MEN OF BOB SPIKE'S STATURE.
THIS IS THE LOSS THAT WE CAN ILL AFFORD. OUR PRAYERS ARE
WITH YOU AND YOUR FAMILY.

HUBERT H. HUMPHREY

[Western Union Telegram 1966 OCT 18 AM 11 59]

THE TRUSTEES AND STAFF OF THE NATIONAL URBAN
LEAGUE JOIN ME IN EXTENDING DEEPEST SYMPATHY TO YOU
AND YOUR FAMILY. THE TRAGIC AND UNTIMELY DEATH OF
YOUR HUSBAND ROBERT SPIKE HAS CUT SHORT A BRILLIANT

CAREER AND DEPRIVED THE NATION OF AN INDEFATIGABLE CHAMPION OF INTERRACIAL JUSTICE. THE CIVIL RIGHTS MOVEMENT HAS LOST A NOBLE SOUL

WHITNEY M YOUNG JR EXECUTIVE DIRECTOR

Many of Dr. Spike's papers are housed at the University of Chicago in Chicago, Illinois.

In the speech below, Dr. Spike addresses the National Council of Churches general assembly in Philadelphia on December 2, 1963. The speech is a pastiche of perplexing questions: How do we react to slander about communist associations? How do we survive ordinary hatred? How do I maintain friendships with black and white friends who do not understand one another? How do I run a fair job search for a business in an integrating city? These perplexing questions have no simple answers. We are assailed in a storm of impossibilities. But that frightening truth stands alongside the gleeful reverence for the moment we have with the tear-gas-stained and the curfew violators. The demands of the times are no different than those our ancestors knew among the catacombs.

Division of Home Missions

National Council of Churches of Christ in the U.S.A., Philadelphia, Pennsylvania
December 2, 1963

The American nation stands immersed in the most traumatic period of its history since the Civil War. We have had our wars, bloody and lengthy. We have lost other leaders. Never, however, have we stood in the intersection of so many powerful emotions, with so much at stake—national and international; and we have had cut down the very flesh of our national purpose, our President.

We search back and forth across the pattern of our life as a people looking for some reason, some meaning that will restore us to the complacent self-possession of a few weeks ago. But it will not come. The screen on which has been projected our image of ourselves as a people, confident, rational, generous is blurred and distorted. Nearly every commentator on the national scene has something to say about the wildness and extremism that suddenly seem manifest. Most reflect on the fact that it has been growing—that it is not something confined to Texas and to the specific events of the week. Some say that it is all of a piece with the McCarthy madness which began over a decade ago.

Nearer in time, however, it cannot escape our notice that 1963 has been a year of sudden violence, erupting like a gas jet here and there, consuming Medgar Evers and the postman Moore, and six children in Birmingham. All those who now belatedly call for a cessation of hatred are surely right. You cannot accuse and distort truth, you cannot make defiant stands against the federal government and then not expect to reap the whirlwind.

It is against such a backdrop that we must look at the task of the laity in its mission in race relations. How different a context with which to begin our thinking from what would have been expected not many years ago. We cannot begin with propositional theology—"God is our father, all men are brothers. Now brethren, white brethren that is, go forth to practice a little more kindness, a little more charity to those less fortunate than you. Things are getting better and better for our colored brothers, slowly, of course, so as not to disturb the white power structures."

No, now we stand in the midst of a generation that has experienced a genuine freedom movement. The incline of action is not from white beneficence to Negro supplication. It is from an awakened Negro people who take the initiative and say to the white man, what are you going to do about it? A day or two ago, I heard one of the leading white churchmen of this country state this profound truth with much feeling. "Negroes have to take the lead in this struggle," he said. "I am firmly convinced that henceforth this always has to be true."

Thus, the most important factor in any understanding of a lay movement for Christian mission on race relations is that one exists. It is a fact across broad sections of the nation. Rosa Parks was one of its sparks when she took her stand near the front of that bus in Montgomery.

Hosea Williams in Savannah, Aaron Henry in Clarksdale, and countless other Christian men have taken their stand at great personal cost. Death is a constant possibility. Life continually fraught with minor and major emergency is what they have come to expect. And as usual, the students, north and south, are the real dynamos of the movement. They teach us by their abandoned sacrificial way of living what we do not want the gospel to tell us. Man after man goes to work for SNCC on a subsistence salary of $10 a week. The only fringe benefits he can count on are constant harassment by the police, a few stray bullets, and the love and gratitude of an embattled Negro community.

I am not trying to sentimentalize or glorify the Negro freedom movement out of proportion. But I have been privileged to see enough of it from close up that I am impressed by its authenticity. These are not saints, who march and try to negotiate, and go to court endlessly, and sing the freedom songs, and lose their jobs because they want to vote. That is, they are not saints in the popular use of the word—perfect human beings with no sin. But in the truer sense they are saints—the people of God who see clearly a destiny, and are willing to put aside the immediate claims of bread and butter to participate in that destiny. In the delta of Mississippi, many a man has to choose between a job which will keep bread in his children's mouths, and continuing to participate in voter registration programs.

I would be willing to test the validity of all our other lay movements by this one. Somehow, our programs and study themes, our banquets and rallies, and yes, even our theological study groups seem a bit contrived alongside a movement where whole loaves are demanded. I suggest this is the surest place to begin to understand the lay mission in race relations—in the freedom movement itself, fed and nourished by the gospel, watered by the spirituals and hymnody of the Christian church.

I have been this past summer in some places that seemed to be close to the life of the early church itself. I think of a rally in Savannah during the height of the struggle there in July. It had to be held in an abandoned night club just outside the city limits. Hundreds of people were in jail, including most of the indigenous leadership. In order to get into the meeting, you were carefully questioned and looked over. Inside was as sorry a group of people as I have ever seen gathered in one place. Here were women stained on their dresses and on their person with tear gas burns. Here were young men bandaged and bruised. All had relatives and friends in jail. All knew that when they left to go back up the hill into the city they would probably be arrested. It was a night when no one knew what sort of sniper lay hidden in the darkness. In fact, when I left the place later, I was given a guard of young men, Negro and white, who searched behind all the buildings and on the hills until I left the district.

But inside there were singing and preaching and witnessing. In desperation there was hope, and no hate at all. There was prayer for all who were caught in the struggle on both sides, and there was unbelievable dedication. I felt I could just as easily have been in the catacombs in the first century.

I do not wish to imply that only Negro freedom fighters qualify for the Christian mission in this crucial hour of destiny. Heroic white Christians, often in places of lonely witness, both north and south, keep their trust as well.

Nor do I believe that the long struggle for integration in terms of equality and justice will take its fullest shape in wave after wave of demonstrations. The complicated network of Negro-white relationship in this country means that social and economic freedom of opportunity will have to be struggled for even after the civil rights have been won.

But the essential characteristic of the Christian mission in this area of race relations is seen essentially now in the freedom movement. It is a struggle to transform the shape of society in obedience to the will of Christ. It is not an advisory operation whereby certain people called Christians comment on how people ought to believe and behave. It is not a course in personal character building with the pious hope that changed hearts may sometime be moved to act for justice.

The mission of Christians to the world always involves immersion in the human struggle—wading deep into the heart of the web of human sin, there to do the generally unpopular thing of standing by the side of the aggrieved, proclaiming God's justice as the Bible reveals it, and seeking reconciliation around the specific shape that justice may take in that particular instance.

This is the fundamental challenge to Christian laymen in this country. Are they willing to change the habitual ways of doing things which perpetuate white supremacy? Deeper than that, are they willing to take a good hard look at their communities, their businesses, their churches, their carefully guarded social enclaves, and try to see them through the eyes of a Negro neighbor? In many instances, this can only happen when there is actually a Negro neighbor to help.

There has been a decade or more of steady hoopla about the renewal of the lay witness. Theological study for the laity has been thought by many to be the key by which a culture is bound. American laymen would have their eyes opened to the universal and disturbing claims of the gospel.

All the theological study that can be managed surely ought to be encouraged. Questions, however, have to be raised about the nature of the theological study. I personally know of men who are whizzes in Biblical studies in their Sunday school classes, who also head units of the white citizens' councils. There is something drastically wrong with theological study that perpetuates an heretical doctrine of man based on racial superiority.

Christian theological study is not defined alone by its content—that is doctrines, and expositions, spun in a vacuum.

Christian theological study is basically an attempt to find an answer to two questions, "What is God doing in the world?" and "What should my brethren and I be doing in response to his deeds?"

The awakening that is needed among many laymen is the awakening to the fact that God is moving in these moments of history. He is in the struggle for freedom in every corner of the world. He is shaking the nations. He is in the anguish that besets our own country right now, trying to find some meaning in the results of our sinful disregard for truth and for the oppressed. The Bible can really only be read when it is read as commentary on our times as well as ancient Judea. Isaiah and Jeremiah cry out for an America whose heart is fattened.

We need the most faithful kind of theological and Biblical study—study that is forced upon us because we desperately have to know what is going on in our world. What is God up to?

Sometimes voices completely outside our familiar circles speak more prophetically than we know. Harry Golden, writing just this past week about our land, says that "The affliction of America is that we are so careless. So positive we are right, so sure of ourselves we can let the petulance of infants and madmen change our destiny, corrupt it, twist history until we ourselves are out of shape."

The challenge to Christian laymen is the challenge to change the structures of society before our blindness leads us into disaster.

There is in some quarters the mistaken impression that Reformation theology is simple proclamation of what God has done—a flat propositional affirmation of God's mighty acts, letting the chips fall where they may. Any study of our early forefathers, particularly our Calvinist influenced ancestors, reveals the utter over-simplification of such a view. God's mighty acts proclaimed, set anxious sinners to ordering their common life, to building a society that seemed consonant with those acts. Both Calvin and Luther were mightily concerned with the ways in which faithfulness became structured and embodied.

This is the only kind of lay theology that is of any consequence. How do we change this town where negroes have dwelt in their own little enclave across the tracks for a hundred years? How do I cope with the problem of job training and recruitment in my business, now that our policy is an open one?

What are the responsibilities of my corporation in a city where gross segregation still prevails, and where our economic power could make a difference in influencing the city fathers?

What about my working for the passage of civil rights legislation, when I find any kind of political activity slightly reprehensible?

What can I do about the lies that are circulated about Communist influence in the civil rights movement and even in the National Council of Churches?

And most of all, how do I stay close enough to some Negro or white friends with whom there can be candid talk in perfect freedom?

Wrestling seriously with these questions in the light of Christ's kingship over our common life, constitutes the real theological task of the laity.

It is good that we can report the increased number of Christian men and women who are so deeply engaged. One finds them everywhere in government, in the professions, and often among the lowliest. What is disturbing, however, is how seldom they recognize that they are engaged in Christian mission. They are overcome by the urgency of the hour, their vision of the just society is clear, their competency serves their passion. But in a strange way we in the church often so define Christian mission so as to exclude them, even those who in some other compartment of their life have church affiliation. Church sponsorship is not a guarantee of Christian mission, nor is its absence either.

What is becoming clearer by the day is that the authenticity of the Christian view of life is being increasingly judged by performance of this land in race relations.

We do not like this. It doesn't even fit our most accepted theological categories. The church is supposedly above nation. We cannot be judged by what the United States does. Unfortunately, we can and are, and in many ways quite rightly. No other nation has such a peculiar interweaving of church life and public life. Nowhere else either does the church still have so much influence in the common life. Christian profession is rightly judged by Christian action here.

The overseas mission of American churches begins in Mississippi and Chicago, and is rendered almost ludicrous if we cannot bring our faith and our talents to change forms of racism in either place.

More than that, the fate of the worldwide Christian enterprise is deeply involved here. That is why next week I will ask for help from churches of other lands at the World Council meeting in Mexico City in meeting our crisis. For years we have assumed that we have all the superabundance of resources which other churches need. Now we are in need—of personnel and funds to heal our wounds.

What of the future? Will the laymen of this land rise up in a great movement like the foreign mission movement of a century ago?

My belief is that many will, that we will begin to reinforce one another in terms of skilled professionals who can help in community racial conflicts; that we will form cadres of men of both races to stand together against the onslaught of hatred and intransigent white supremacy.

And we will need this. For any honest look at the future sees also the hardening of resistance, the defensive, vicious lashes of violence which we have begun to experience this year. And in these movements will be men who also call themselves Christian and who often use the same theological vocabulary. Let us not be beguiled into thinking that we mean that same thing, or even worse, put harmony in the church ahead of justice in the world. That is perhaps the greatest temptation.

The only way through is the strengthening of ties between those who know deep in their hearts that God cannot be mocked. "Love your neighbor as yourself" cannot be qualified with compatible adjectives. "Inasmuch as ye have done it unto the least of these, ye have done it unto me," cannot be evaded. It is Christ who meets us in the eyes of the wronged and the brutalized. It is Christ who bids us keep faith with every lost son and man as unto him.

The dike of delusion is being torn from America's shores. We are not some super people with a special kind of moral protection. The sea of trouble, that engulfs the world, washes over us. God grant that Christian men may find a good footing to stand the storm.

§98 Reverend Lawrence Campbell

Some of the bloodiest, though least publicized, moments of the civil rights movement took place in Danville, Virginia in June of 1963. While we remember "Bull" Connor's firehoses in Birmingham, we have no recollection of Police Chief McCain's fire hoses. Police dogs defended their white master's hydrants and elaborate web of drinking fountains. One of the founders and leaders of the Danville Christian Progressive Association (DCPA) throughout the 1960s was Lawrence Campbell, a young black minister. Born in 1930, Campbell remains a very visible Christian presence in Danville, as he leads the Bibleway Worldwide Church of God.

In this speech at a DCPA meeting in December 1963, Campbell recalls a humorous sit-in story before reminding his listeners that God is working through the movement. He also briefly touches on the events of June 10th, the racial violence that forced even battle-hardened Martin Luther King to send a telegram to Attorney General, Bobby Kennedy, complaining of "the beastly conduct of law enforcement officers at Danville." The transcription is from the Moses Moon Audio Archive at the National Museum of American History in Washington, D.C.

Speech at the Danville Christian Progressive Association
Danville, Virginia
December 1963

We give honor to the Lord for being here and to our most esteemed, uh, president, uh Reverend [Lendell W.] Chase and to Mr. Avon Rollins, national executive officer of the Student Nonviolent Coordinating Committee, and to all of the, all of the freedom fighters that are here today. Uh, Reverend Chase, uh, commending me he also needs a hand of applaud for, uh, an applaud rather for the very fine report that he gave, uh, on the air. I would like to see how many of you heard the report. If so, raise your hand. Let's give Reverend Chase [inaudible] was very well done, very well done. And I trust that you will continue to listen because he will be giving in a number of reports to sorta keep you informed about the things that have already happened in terms of achievements that the DCPA and other groups have made in Danville.

Uh, first of all I would certainly like to talk about the tremendous spirit that we have seen in the jail of the kids that are there. I've been down three times and on a third time I was admitted to go into the jail and we talked to the fellas, and we couldn't see the girls because they were raising so much noise, uh, and singing freedom songs and they were really singing. The jailer and everybody else the, uh, disturbed because they had been singing for hours and the fellas say the girls just sang practically all night just keeping things going and I know all the concrete that they have in that jail but and I'm not exaggerating, that jail was rocking when I got down there and those girls were beating on the bars and everything else. Cynthia likes that, uh, they were really having a glorious time and we talked to the fellas there and some of the parents had been down to bond them out and they don't want to come home. They said they were willing to stay in there until Tuesday to see what we're going to do, uh, that is the citizenry of Danville if you are gonna get involved and go down in the form of a demonstration or try to sit-in at some restaurant or hotel or motel and they're willing to stay there until Tuesday.

And it really encouraged me when I was talking to Mr. Bennett's grandson and he has an opportunity to get out and he said that he didn't want to go and they are other parents that have been down and their children just don't want to leave. They're not disturbed, they are not uneasy, and they are just walking around there having a big time for freedom. So that made me feel good, it made me feel like going in jail myself. I sat in this week, this past week, at the Verdanne Restaurant and I thought that, uh, we were gonna get arrested. We anticipated that. I know that there are some people that don't feel that ministers should wear overalls but I think most of the ministers that believe that, are ministers that have not been to jail.

But I'm not going to wear a suit to jail because it is kinda rough in jail and you just wear your clothes out so this does not make me lose the Holy Ghost or nothing else. I don't think that your religion is in your clothes; it's in the heart, it's in the, uh, in the heart and you can, it can't rub off in your clothes and it can't rub off just because you sit-in or something. I think that once our religion becomes so rigid, uh, so great until we can't intermingle with other people I don't think it's very much to what you have. I believe that the Lord intends for us to go and to get other people to share in this what He has already given to us.

So we sat-in at Verdanne's and, uh, I think it was on Tuesday and while we were sitting there the man came over, there were five of us and J .V. Henry was one of the five and J. V. Henry you know is a white boy and, uh, the restaurant owner came and told J. V. that he had to go. But the Negro people, the four of us, could stay and, uh, he said that J. V. Henry was nothing but poor white trash and scum. Looked at me and said, "You're better than J. V. Henry" and I said, "No I'm not better than J. V." I said, "We all the same." I said, "We are trying to fight for equal rights and we're trying to show that all men are the very same and that we are not esteemed higher than any other person!" So he told J. V., "Well, I'm tired of you, you poor white people going around here living off of the NAACP"! And that really got me because they're not living off the NAACP. And I said, "Well this young man is a college student." And he said, "No, if he was a college student he wouldn't be sitting there." And I said, "Well his father is a prominent business man." "I don't want to hear that! I feel like taking my fist and hitting him in the nose."

So I had my back to the man and I heard him say something about "let's get some hot coffee and pour down on 'em." Well that really upset me because I didn't want him to scald me you see and I wanted to get in the position where I could see what they were doing to me. And so I told the young people I said "Now if they hit J. V. we got to get on top of him so that he won't take all of the licks." And so he came around and said, uh, since you won't leave this is the time when I must sweep up. And so they got the broom and start sweeping, they pulled the table out and I didn't pay much attention to that and a few moments later they came back and, uh, with a great big, uh, mop bucket with a big mop in it.

And I didn't pay much attention to that. Until I looked over at J. V and I saw tears running down from his eyes and I said "Ah what's wrong?" And by the time that I got in my mouth to say "what's wrong with him," it hit me too. And the man had a whole bucket of ammonia. Now you can, you can probably imagine stronger than ammonia so we had to be nonviolent and I sat there and I cried like a baby. I stood there, uh, shaking in my shoes and trying to, you know show the man that we were strong. And that we weren't going to leave. And J. V. was crying. So there was one little boy, a young man sitting over there, they called him Snake. His, uh, Brakeley is his last named but they called him Snake. And that's one time that that Snake wiggled out of there. 'Cause that brother, he wiggled his way out of that place. He said "I can't stand it, Reverend, I got to go." So that boy left the four of us there to suffer all that ammonia.

But the thing about it, you cannot, a man that, uh, is a hater finds that he is so engulfed with his own hatred until he finds himself more offensive to himself than he is to other people. He is a victim of his own hatred in that he was, he was trying to get us out of the restaurant by using ammonia, he was also losing a lot of trade, too. Because just as he used it on us, nobody could come in and those that were in there wanted to go out. So he found that he was losing a lot of business too by trying to treat us in this very unjust way. So I say that to really say this, we are willing to take the abuses that have and are afflicted upon us because we believe that the Lord is with us! Now this is the thing that continues to keep me going on.

There are times when we talk so much about the various organizations that we are working with in terms of the NAACP, SNCC, CORE, and, uh,

SCLC and [inaudible] and various organizations until we focus so much attention on them until we somewhat forget about God. But on the, the Sunday following the death of the president, a thought came to me which is as follows that says that the kid at King Urzy died, I saw the Lord. And I believe that they are times in our lives that God permits things to happen to us that we might be able to see God.

We get so involved in getting many material gains because we work and because we have some finance. There are some of us, uh, you that are teachers and in other professional capacities, that you have gained so much through your own resources until you have forgotten about God. Then you say these things were gotten by faith. But I don't believe that you can really say that these things were done by faith when you have got them from your own efforts. There are times when God puts you in a position where you must depend upon God and depend on Him alone.

That's why God permitted the children of Israel to get to the sea when there was no escape and God did not tell them to turn around but God told them to go forward. There was a man that was blind from his mother's womb but God knew that man's extremity was God's opportunity. Now God realized that we have limited faith, but God believes in unlimited faith. That's why when Jesus permitted Lazarus to die, a very good friend of his, and when Mary and Martha saw Jesus they said "Master, if you had been here Lazarus would not have died." And Jesus said, "If thou shalt believe, thou shalt see the glory of God." Now what Jesus was disturbed about, Jesus was disturbed because Mary and Martha had limited faith. They believed if Jesus could have been with Lazarus then he would not have died. But Jesus wanted them to realize that even though this man is dead, my faith or your faith in me should not stop because the man is dead but you should believe that I am able to raise him up after he's dead.

We only see God in a limited way or in a limited perspective, but God is a great God. He is the King of Kings and the Lord of Lords. He is the Father of all fathers. He's the Guardian of the universe. I believe that this man called Jesus can do anything. Someone wrote a song that said, "God can do anything but fear." Many times when we sing that song, I believe that we don't really believe it as the songwriter intended that song to be taken. I believe that God can do anything!

Who is Mayor [Julian] Stinson in the eyes of God? Mayor Stinson was made from the dust of the earth and saved when God blew, God blew the breath of life into his nostrils! And Ole Stinson became a living soul. God is able to trouble this man while he lies upon his bed of rest. God is able to trouble him so forcefully and disturb the consciousness of his thinking, until he gets down to his office and he intends to make an unjust law. God is able to change him until he will make a just law. I believe that "God can do anything but fear." I am reminded a few, uh, Scriptures, I'm reminded of a few Scriptures and one in particular when there was a man by the name of King Nebuchadnezzar. As he lied upon his bed of rest and as he was sleeping God troubled him in his mind.

And I believe that God works in mysterious ways and wonders to perform. God has a hand in this society of ours, even though we cannot recognize the hand of God, but I believe God is moving. How do you know Reverend Campbell that God is moving in the city of Danville? I have seen the Danville Christian Progressive Association down to its lowest egg, but some kinda way God came to us when we needed him most. There was a time when we needed money and we didn't know where it was coming from, but God stretched his hand out of the heavens up in Bannockburn, Maryland.

Touched a woman by the name of Anne Carroll, told her pay your money and get on the bus and go to Danville because somebody needs you there. She came to Danville, nobody said to her "Mrs. Carroll demonstrate," but one night I remember she walked into the Northview Hope Baptist Church, a white lady standing beside a little girl by the name of Karen Cunsler. And she said, "Ladies and Gentlemen, whatever you want me to do, I will do it." You can't tell me that God is able to take nothing and make something out of it. God is able to take what you throw away and make something out of it. God took this little lady, Anne Carroll, and brought her to Danville. And she went to jail for eleven days, and went back to Bannockburn and aroused that community and she aroused that community, it stimulated their thinking, it converted even [inaudible]. There were those who didn't understand demonstrations, but when she got through with them, that they knuckled around her and said, "We will go to Danville, too!"

Yeah, God works in a mysterious way and wonders to perform. I remember when we've had hundreds of people in the jail, when Reverend Chase was down in Halifax, Mrs. Chase was over in Chatham, Virginia and Patricia was there, too. And there was no one in Danville but me. And Reverend Dunlap was in North Carolina and Mr. Adams and others were here and we were struggling trying to make a way. I've seen God step in when people say I didn't have clothing. I've seen hundreds of clothing, pounds of clothing coming from New York, Chicago, coming from North Carolina and other cities, pouring into Danville to help us in Danville. I tell you this God we serve is a great God. God can make a way out of no way. He can put clothes on your back when you are naked. He can put shoes on your foot when you don't have any.

Yeah, when it seems like all hope is gone, God knows how to step in! I have seen God turn the darkness into light. I have seen him turn our failures into success. I have seen God take our disappointments of actions and turn them into roses of great advancement. Yeah this is a great God that we serve. Somebody said that God is like fire shut up in my bones. There was a prophet that said that I looked and I saw a mountain and there was a stone that was hewed out of a mountain and this stone came tumbling down. Ezekiel said he's like a wheel in a middle of a wheel. David said, "Oh, taste and see that the Lord is good." Yeah, the joys of God will take us through. [inaudible] things that God has done for us.

I have seen not only these things, but I have seen God even do greater things. The night of June 10th, when we told the people to go down and to demonstrate, to go down to the jail and to pray for those that were in prison. Even there that night when [Police] Chief [Eugene] McCain said, "I'm tired of you niggers eating off of me like leeches, eating off this community like leeches." They put the hoses on them and hosed them down with high-pressured hoses. The water was so forceful, until it washed human bodies down the street like trash. The water was so powerful until it knocked bark off trees. Amen! And it was so powerful until people were screaming in the midst of the water as though they were caught in a fire without any escape.

But God worked a wonder there. Yeah, you might think that all hope was gone, but one thing God didn't do. God didn't let nobody become blind. God did not let nobody die. God did not let nobody get discouraged, but God took those little people and raised them up until the next day they walked down the streets again. Even with bursted heads, with bruised arms, lacerations across their breasts, they walked with dignity, they walked with courage. And I believe tonight that that is recorded on the roll book of God. Somebody said when I get to heaven, when every posse there will be one of the prophets that I seem to remember that no man can remember coming up to their trials and tribulations and have their garment washed in the blood of the lamb. One day children it's going to be good when we get to heaven. When we can sing the songs, "How I got over, how I got over! Yeah my soul looks back, Hallelujah! How I got over!"

1964

1964

§99 Ella Josephine Baker

Ella Baker was born on December 13, 1903 in Norfolk, Virginia. Raised in Littleton, North Carolina on land her grandparents had worked as slaves, Baker came of age under the careful guidance of her activist and deeply religious mother, Anna. Upon graduating as valedictorian from Shaw University in Raleigh, North Carolina in 1927, Baker headed north to Harlem. She would cut her organizing teeth in the city, working for the Young Negroes Cooperative League and other poverty relief organizations. Baker began working for the NAACP in 1940 and quickly earned a reputation as a nonpareil organizer of black youth. From 1943 to 1946 Baker worked as national director of NAACP branches; later she served as president of the New York City branch and led the fight to desegregate the city's schools. In 1956 Baker, along with two of Martin Luther King's closest confidantes Stanley Levison and Bayard Rustin, formed In Friendship, a fundraising organization designed to aid victims of discrimination in the South. Such was her organizing acumen, that Levison and Rustin persuaded King to bring Baker to the fledgling Southern Christian Leadership Conference's (SCLC) headquarters in Atlanta. She would serve as executive director of the organization for a year.

During her stint at SCLC as well as her earlier work in the NAACP, Baker grew suspicious of a leader-centered approach to civil rights, especially among glory seeking black preachers. Instead, she favored a grassroots model of vigorous and active local participation. Such an ethos was at the very heart of the Student Nonviolent Coordinating Committee (SNCC), a group she helped to found. In April 1960, while the student sit-in movement was in full ferment, Baker called a conference of youth leaders at Shaw University. Sponsored by the SCLC, Baker steered the students away from formally aligning themselves with the black clergy-dominated group. "Miss Baker," as she was known among SNCC workers, was a civil rights free agent throughout the 1960s, working seemingly wherever organizing work needed to be done. Baker is also credited with helping to create and organize the Mississippi Freedom Democratic Party (MFDP), leading its Washington, D.C. office. An activist to the last, Ella Baker died on her birthday in 1986. Her papers are housed at the Library of Congress in Washington, D.C., the Schomberg Center at the New York Public Library in New York City, and the Wisconsin State Historical Society in Madison.

Like so many other women active in the movement, precious few of Baker's speeches survive despite her constant presence on the civil rights battlefield. But this brief address at the Hattiesburg Freedom Day voter registration event, transcribed from the Moses Moon Audio Archive, captures something of Baker's approach to the movement—including a reproach, though gentle, to the man who introduces her, Clarksdale's Dr. Aaron Henry. Baker refuses to be characterized as having a "fling" with civil rights even as she emphasizes her radical independence. She is neither flirtatious nor tied down. Baker also develops the organic connection of her Christian spirituality with the aims of the movement: the perfection of individual freedom is simply the logical outcome of being a child of God. Presently, those blocking blacks' attempts to gain that freedom represent the darkest of forces in Baker's view. As the speech progresses, the freedom that Baker seeks is intimately bound up with peace, with economic security and with education. Moreover, such freedom isn't isolated to Hattiesburg, nor Mississippi, nor even America. Rather, Baker speaks of a freedom of the human spirit that transcends geography.

Address at the Hattiesburg Freedom Day Rally

Hattiesburg, Mississippi
January 21, 1964

This is rather unusual. Aaron Henry said that I had had my fling with all the civil rights organizations. Well, my greatest fling has still to be flung, because as far as I'm concerned I was never working for an organization. I have always tried to work for a cause, and the cause to me is bigger than any organization. Bigger than any group of people, and it is the cause of humanity. The cause is the cause that brings us together, the drive of the human spirit for freedom.

You know, I always like to think that the very God who gave us life, gave us liberty. And if we don't have liberty it is because somebody else has stood between us and that which God has granted us. And so we have come here tonight to renew our struggle, our struggle for that which we are entitled by virtue of being children of the Almighty. The right to be men and women, to grow and to develop to the fullest capacity with which He has endowed us.

And as I have listened here tonight, my spirit has roved over a long period of years and I can think of a number of things I would like to say, but if I had anything at all to say tonight it is to remind us of something that occurred to me, something that came into focus in a conversation on the night that Medger Evers's body came through Atlanta. A group of people were down at the station among us; we were there for the purpose of identifying with the great tragedy that had occurred in his being shot to death. And after the ceremony, the little ceremony in the station, one of the leading civil rights leaders (I won't name any because leadership is one of those things, you know, I won't talk about them too much) but this person said, "We are in the final stages of the freedom struggle." And I challenge that.

We are not in the final stages of the freedom struggle. We are really just beginning. We are just beginning the freedom struggle. Let me tell you why. Because even tomorrow if every vestige of racial discrimination were wiped out, if all of us became free enough to go down and to associate with all the people we wanted to associate, we still are not free. We aren't free until within us we have that deep sense of freedom from a lot of the things that we don't even mention in these meetings.

And I'm not talking about Negroes, I'm talking about people. People cannot be free until they realize that peace—we can talk about peace—that peace is not the absence of war or struggle, it is the presence of justice. People cannot, pardon me, people cannot be free until there is enough work in this land to give everybody a job. Tomorrow, tomorrow if we were able to vote our full strength and we still voted our full strength, until we recognize that in this country in a land of great plenty and great wealth there are millions of people who go to bed hungry every night. That tomorrow if we were to call up all the able-bodied men in our country, who could do some work, we wouldn't have work for them to do.

And unless we see this thing in its larger perspective, unless we realize that certainly we must sing, we must have the inspiration of song, the inspiration that comes from songs like this one that was created and demonstrated here tonight, but we also must have the information that comes from lots and lots of study. And so we must come to grips with a lot of problems. We must also know that we are, in the final analysis, the only group that can make you free is yourself, because we must free ourselves from all of the things that keep us back.

And so in conclusion let me quote one of my favorite or improvise one of my favorite thoughts in scripture. And it has to do with the whole struggle I think because it says, "For now we are nearer than when we first believed." I forgot the exact quote, but let us "cast aside the works of darkness and put on the armor of light."

I love to hear us sing. I've heard a lot of singing in my day. I've been a part of a lot of singing, but I know, and you must know, that singing alone will not do it for us. And we are going to have to have these freedom schools and we are going to have to learn a lot of things in them. We are going to have to be concerned about the kinds of education our children are getting in school, and all of this has to be done along at the same time that we also recognize that our white brothers, the very white brothers in Hattiesburg and in other parts of Mississippi who have kept us in bondage, that they did it because they did not know any better.

They have been fooled, and they have been fooled by those who told them the "big lie." The "big lie" was to the effect that they could do what they wanted in Mississippi with the Negro question. And you know what? The rest of the country for a long time tacitly agreed. That is, they didn't do anything about it.

And so all of us stand guilty at this moment for having waited so long to lend ourselves to a fight for the freedom, not of Negroes, not of the Negroes of Mississippi, but for the freedom of the American spirit, for the freedom of the human spirit for freedom, and this is the reason I am here tonight, and this is the reason, I think, that these young men who have worked and given their bodies in the movement for freedom. They are here not because they want to see something take place just for the fun of it, they are here because they should know, and I think they do know, that the freedom which they seek is a larger freedom that encompasses all mankind. And until that day, we will never turn back.

§100 Reverend Edward W. Harris

Edward W. Harris was born on August 22, 1910 in Shreveport, Louisiana and spent most of his childhood in Texarkana, Arkansas. He attended Texarkana Junior College from 1927 to 1929. On August 26, 1929 Reverend Harris was licensed to preach in the office of First Methodist Church in Texarkana. In 1931 he received his B.A. from Emory University and in 1933 he received his M.Th. from Candler School of Theology, also at Emory. He later enrolled in graduate school at Garrett Biblical Institute at Northwestern University and Union Theological Seminary in New York. While a student, he also played baseball, basketball and ran track. On November 13, 1933 Reverend Harris was admitted to the Little Rock annual conference at First Methodist Church, Hot Springs. He retired on May 29, 1981 after 48 years of service to the Methodist church in Lockesburg, Stamps, Fordyce, Monticello, Conway, Texarkana, El Dorado, Baton Rouge, New Orleans, Pine Bluff, St. Louis, and Little Rock. In addition to his distinguished career, Harris was a dedicated family man. On October 2, 1941 he married Mabel (nee Martin), with whom he had a daughter, Elizabeth. Mabel and Elizabeth were both educated at Hendrix College in Conway, Arkansas.

The following sermon by Reverend Harris may be one of the most careful theological and practical discussions of race relations of its era. The sermon took place on February 9, 1964, well after the antics of Orval Faubus, but several months before the mayhem that took place in Mississippi that summer. Despite the fact that this sermon occurred during a calm before the storm of Freedom Summer, Reverend Harris's words met strong resistance. Stubborn and fearful ushers resigned. They assumed they would soon have the uncomfortable task of seating the integrated flood of multiracial worshipers. The young men who volunteered to replace the ushers lost their jobs or were harassed at work.

The board of stewards met the following week and decided not to support Reverend Harris, with the exception of one local physician, who opined that white and black blood were both red. The Women's Society of Christian Service also voiced its disapproval, urging members to withhold pledges to ensure that Reverend Harris would not receive a renewed appointment. The bishop promised to support Harris, but the bishop, the conference, and the clergy, if supportive, maintained their positions silently. This silence felt like a betrayal, but Harris did not speak on this issue for the remainder of his life. He also discouraged his wife Mabel from speaking publicly on the matter. She has only come forward on the matter to speak and write publicly at the encouragement of friends and family members since her husband's death in 2004. Mrs. Harris recalls the fear of that era. The White Citizens Council actively harassed her family with death threats and other unwelcome phone calls. Despite the tumult, Mrs. Harris recalls the continual support of faithful friends and the Gibraltaresque friendship of Father Joseph Kehrer, a German (Roman Catholic) priest assigned to the local black parish. Reverend Harris's only Methodist recognition for his courageous stand came in 1979, when Philander Smith College conferred upon him an honorary doctorate. This lack of support from his ecclesial home resulted in depression, nightmares, and Post Traumatic Stress Disorder, which accompanied him for the remainder of his 94 years.

Even so, Reverend Harris served the Methodist church loyally and fully throughout his life. The sermon gives us considerable insight into his stoic acceptance. His able reading of the Methodist Conference Discipline makes it clear that an important choice was upon his congregation, and the responsibility for making that choice was his, and his alone. The text clearly indicates that he understand that he is not in a position to withstand the pressure of his influential board of stewards. Yet he makes a stand knowing full well what it would cost him and his family. He is able to take that stand because he also understands what the alternative would cost not only his family, but his local congregation and his global denomination as well.

A Methodist Pastor and Race Relations: Luke 4:16-30

Pine Bluff, Arkansas
February 9, 1964

The second Sunday in February has a dual significance for this Methodist pastor. It is Boy Scout Sunday, and it is Race Relations Sunday. As a Boy Scout of many years, I have devoted both morning services of worship for the past three years to the full recognition of The Boy Scout Movement, with special emphasis on our fine Troop Number 95. This year we have devoted a full page of "The Columns" to the recognition of Troop 95, but the sermon for Race Relations Sunday will be on the theme: "*A Methodist Pastor and Race Relations.*"

Inserted in the Sunday bulletins are two pamphlets, placed there by your pastor. One is "The Bible and Race." I commend this pamphlet to every thoughtful person as an opportunity to re-examine their own views in the light of The Word of God. The other pamphlet contains an expression of gratitude from Philander Smith College for the gifts we make annually for the support of this outstanding Negro Institution of Learning.

You will understand, I am sure, if I confine myself to the use of a manuscript in this message, in order that I may be quoted correctly on a subject that most people consider highly controversial. Copies of the message will be available for any who wish them. My purpose in this message is to interpret to my people the teachings and practices of Methodism in the area of Race Relations and the responsibility that these teachings place upon a Methodist pastor. Obviously, the limitations of time and space will not permit an exhaustive study of all areas in which the Methodist Church has spoken. For those who wish to pursue further such a study, I recommend a copy of *The Methodist Discipline of 1960*, which contains the statements of the last General Conference, the final authority in defining the position of Methodism in all areas of teaching and practice. The most recent interpretation of the teaching of Methodism in the area of Race Relations is found in a statement adopted by The Council of Bishops of the Methodist Church, in a meeting November 13, 1963, held in Detroit, Michigan. For practical reasons, I have chosen as an outline for my message only those portions of the statement that relate directly to the Local Church and the Local Pastor's leadership in the Local Church and the Local Community. Hence, the outline of this message will present, in as brief a form as possible: (1) A statement of The Methodist Heritage in the area of Christian Social Concern; (2) The Application of Christian Principles to Community Life; (3) The Application of Christian Principles to Church Membership; (4) The Application of Christian Principles to Public Worship.

Our Methodist Heritage

There are those who ask the question: "Why does Methodism feel compelled to speak concerning the social needs of people instead of confining its teaching and preaching to a gospel of personal redemption?" The answer is that Methodism does not consider it to be a question of "either or," but of "both and." We preach both a personal and a social gospel, and we do not separate them one from the other. The Methodist Social Creed begins with a statement concerning our Methodist Heritage: "The interest of The Methodist Church in social welfare springs from the gospel, and from the labors of John Wesley, who ministered to the physical, intellectual, and social needs of the people to whom he preached the gospel of personal redemption. In our historic position we have sought to follow Christ in bringing the whole of life, with its activities, possessions, and relationships, into conformity with the will of God. As Methodists we have an obligation to affirm our position on social and economic questions."

The recent statement of our Bishops, directed to layman and ministers, was altogether in keeping with the heritage that belongs to Methodism as a leader in the total area of Christian Social Concern. The opening paragraph is a statement of "Equal Rights," the substance of which is taken from paragraph 2020, of the Methodist Social Creed, found in the *Methodist Discipline of 1960*: "The Methodist Church stands for the equal rights of all racial, cultural, and religious groups. We confess with deep penitence that our performance as a church has not kept pace with our profession. The right to choose a place of residence, to enter a school, to secure employment, to vote, or to join a church, should in no way be limited by a person's race or culture." These words of our Bishops and of the Methodist Social Creed are forthright, clear, and need no explanation. As a Methodist pastor, I share the rich heritage of Christian Social Concern that belongs to Methodism. It is my purpose to give myself in renewed dedication to the task of implementing the teachings of my church, by identifying this heritage with the present needs of society especially as it relates to the White and the Negro races.

Applied to Community Life

Most communities such as ours are forced to admit that the existing relationships between the White and the Negro races should be given priority as our number one problem in every area of community life. Many, however, are willing to discuss the question in general terms, but shrink from the practical application of Christian principles in every area of community life. Our Bishops are responsible for the general oversight and promotion of the temporal and spiritual interests of the entire church. With this in mind, their statement constitutes a charge to pastors and laymen to assume the responsibility for carrying into effect the rules, regulations, and responsibilities prescribed and enjoined by the General Conference. This charge reads: "The Methodist Church must build and demonstrate within its own organization and program a Fellowship without racial barriers. The church must also work to change those community patterns in which racial segregation appears, including education, housing, voting, employment, and the use of public facilities. To insist that restaurants, schools, business establishments, and hotels provide equal accommodations for all people without regard to race or color, but to exempt the church from the same requirements is to be guilty of absurdity as well as sin."

There are many sincere people who feel that the local church should not involve itself in the application of Christian principles in the life of the community, especially with respect to Race Relations. It might be the part of wisdom to examine this viewpoint in the light of practical experience. In many communities such as ours the church has left the area of Race Relations entirely to the leadership of non-church groups. The number and variety of groups, both amateur and professional, that have moved in to fill the moral and spiritual vacuum left by the inactivity of the churches are known to all of us. They often become divisive forces in the life of the community. There is also the constant danger of violence lurking just under the surface in any movement engaged in social reform, unless that movement is motivated by love of God and love of fellow man. When immature or unworthy leadership appears in such movements, it is difficult for the church to criticize the quality of leadership that has been supplied in the absence of church leadership. It is my sincere conviction that the Christian Gospel alone can supply this motivation for any movement that aims at changing the pattern of community life. It is also my firm conviction that the church which preaches the Gospel of Love cannot, like Pilate, wash its hands in a basin of water and thereby avoid their responsibility by dismissing the problem that lies on the community doorstep. Any church that refuses to assume any responsibility for applying Christian principles to the problem of Race Relations in community life, may have to answer to the youth of the community concerning the relevance of religion to any part of life.

Applied to Church Membership

In the area of Church Membership, our Bishops selected a vital target: "We urge our pastors upon whom rests the responsibility of receiving persons into the church, to receive all who are qualified and who desire to be received without regard to race, color, or national origin, and we individually and collectively pledge them our support as they do so. The Methodist Church is an inclusive church."

You will note, I am sure, that our Bishops have not recommended any change in the rules for church membership. So far as I know, Methodism has never had any rules for church membership that exclude any race or color, and its invitation to church membership has always been, "Whosoever will, may come." During slave days, the names of Negro slaves were carried on the church rolls, along with those of the masters. It is true that they sat in a different section of the church, but so did the women sit apart from the men. The absence of their names from our church rolls since emancipation is due to several reasons: (1) their own preference; (2) strained relations between Negro and White, due to the Civil War and Reconstruction Days; (3) customs, traditions, community mores that demanded absolute separation of races and colors in the religious, social, and economic areas of life. The third reason listed is the dominant factor that perpetrates absolute segregation in white Methodist Churches today. On the Mission Fields, there is no color line with respect to church membership, yet we use the same rules for church membership that American Methodism uses. The truth is that we could not possibly operate on any mission field today if we did not apply the rules for church membership as our Bishops have asked us to do in our local Methodist Churches. As. Dr. E. Stanley Jones has said: "There is a spiritual 'groundswell' that is stirring the nations of the earth." All races are demanding freedom, respect as persons, and equality of opportunity in every area of life, and, first of all, in the Church of Our Risen Lord. If the words of our Bishops come as a shock to some of our members, we should remember that they are leaders of a World Church, not a Provincial Church. They know what all the world is beginning to recognize, namely, that no church can survive this generation that does not project and main-tain a World Outlook by making any person of any race or color an accept-able candidate for church membership. This is in keeping with the position of every other Christian denomination that claims to be a World Church, and whose message and life are relevant to the twentieth century.

It is not difficult to understand what our Bishops meant when they spoke of the principle of inclusiveness in church membership. They were looking to the Local Methodist Pastor as the "key person," and saying: "Thou art the man!" The responsibility rests upon the local Methodist pas-tor, where it has always rested. Methodist congregations do not vote on the admission of new member, as some churches do. The only exception to this rule is made for those who are unable to be received in a church service, and must be received elsewhere, presumably in a hospital, prison, or in the home. Only in this case, is the approval of the Official Board needed. In all other cases, the pastor is the sole judge as to whether the applicant is a proper candidate for church membership. The disciplinary rule that guides the pastor is found in paragraph 107 of the 1960 Discipline. "All persons seeking to be saved from their sins and sincerely desiring to be Christian in faith and practice are proper candidates for membership in the Methodist Church." Further, any person received into a local Methodist Church is a member of The Methodist Church in its worldwide meaning. Therefore, there can be no distinctions made in color or race in one part of the world that will not hold in another part of the world.

Any Methodist pastor whose hearing is sensitive enough to hear the "cries of race and clan" that echo in the streets of our cities knows that the racial tensions that accompany such cries often move into the life of a local congregation. Although they need not control the words or actions of a pastor who is in possession of his own soul, it does make him keenly aware of the heavy responsibility that rests upon his shoulders at the point of church membership. Some may wish for a congregational form of gov-ernment, where laymen would share in the decisions concerning church membership. I, personally, do not anticipate any change in this area of church life by legislation at the forthcoming General Conference. As your pastor, I am prepared to follow the leadership of our Bishops, and have been prepared for some time to do so. I have had no applicant for church membership from those of another race or color, and I do not anticipate a rush of applicants when my attitude becomes known to our Negro friends. However, for the large numbers of the Negro people who do not apply, the knowledge that they are free to choose and are not excluded from a church because of race or color, there will come a new and immeasurable sense of worth to their personalities and a new sense of assurance as professing Christians. For White Christians there will also come a cleansing of conscience and the removal of unspoken and unrecognized fears that rested heavily upon our hearts.

To be fully honest with my congregation, there are many ways to evade, by letter and spirit, the difficult decisions that will inevitably confront any local Methodist pastor. The simplest method of evasion is to change the traditional invitation to church membership which Methodist pastors generally extend before the singing of the closing hymn in the service of worship—or omit it altogether. In lieu of the public invitation, some churches are using a card in the pew. The applicant signs the card and indicates whether he would like to talk with the pastor in the study or in the home. Then, if the person is acceptable, the applicant's name is announced on Sunday from the pulpit or published in a bulletin as having been received. The policy of your pastor is easily understood. It is to be found in the printed invitation which appears in parenthesis beneath the invitational hymn which is sung at the close of each service of worship. It reads: "Those who wish to unite with First Methodist Church will please come forward during the singing of this hymn." As long as I am your pastor, this will continue to be the approach to the matter of church membership, namely, "to receive all who are qualified and who desire to be received without regard to race, color, national origin." I say this to you this morning, knowing that, although you do not have a vote as to who is qualified to be members, you have a great deal to say about who is qualified to be your pastor. However, I hope that you will not mistake my absolute frankness with you this morning for a change in the deep, abiding affection in which I hold every official and member of First Methodist Church, Pine Bluff.

Applied to Public Worship

Since I am confining my message chiefly to the responsibility of the local Methodist pastor in the area of Race Relations in the local church, I will quote only one other paragraph from the statement of our Bishops—the portion which has to do with the admission of those of any race or color to the services of worship: "We decry, on legal as well as Christian grounds, the denial of any person of any color or race the right of membership or the right to worship in any Methodist Church. Further, to move to arrest any persons attempting to worship is to us an outrage."

Here, again, the chief responsibility rests upon the pastor, although it is shared to some extent by ushers, church officials, and members of the congregation. In this local church, this subject has not been discussed at any meeting of the Official Board during my four years of ministry. I have been told by each of the three very fine Chairmen with whom I have served that this is by common consent of the group, in order to preserve unity and peace in the congregation. In the absence of any statement of policy on the seating of visitors in services of worship, the decision rests entirely upon the pastor. Obviously, the only account of his stewardship in this area would be given by his personal announcement from the pulpit. If the peace and unity of the congregation has been served by this policy, then I am happy to carry such a load. If my message appears to any official or member as a move on my part to break that peace and unity, I should like for you to remember that the emphasis placed by our Bishops and The Methodist Discipline is at the point of pastoral responsibility for making all decisions concerning the use of the property for worship. Therefore, a local Methodist pastor stands as a free moral agent when he is faced with the decision whether to admit or exclude any worshipper.

So far as I know, no person of another race or color has asked to be admitted to a service of worship in our church except our friends from India, who often worship with us, because of the mutual love and esteem that exists. This may be due to the fact that our Negro friends have not felt welcome. Also, during the periods of greatest tension in the past, when demonstrations and unpleasant incidents were happening daily, their leaders may have felt that a visit to the churches of the city would be unwise. Whatever the reasons for their failure to appear, we may anticipate, in my opinion, visits of some nature in the future. How or when they will come, I do not know. I do know that it will be a testing time for us, as White Methodist Christians. I have every confidence that this great Missionary-Minded Congregation will demonstrate at such a time the willingness to practice the true spirit of Christian brotherliness by receiving such visitors in a spirit of Christian fellowship.

When the Rev. Ed Matthews, our fine Methodist Missionary to the Congo, spoke from our pulpit Sunday, July 21st, I fully anticipated that we might have Negro visitors to hear a Missionary who was serving Negro natives in distant Africa. I made a personal request to our fine chief usher that he and his ushers seat any visitor of another race or color, and place the full responsibility upon the pastor. This he agreed to do, without opposing his pastor. Because of the mutual respect and understanding between us, he felt free to tell me what I had realized already, namely, that the ushers were unanimously opposed to the idea. In spite of this, I still believe that they would have granted their pastor's request. It was simply inconceivable to me that we should turn away some person whose racial origin was found in Africa, and forbid him the opportunity of worshipping with a Missionary who was sent to Africa to witness for our Christ. Such news would have been flashed to the Congo within twenty four hours, and would have cancelled much of Ed and Pat's Christian witness there.

One never knows fully the results that follow the rejection of a worshipper of another race or color. Many years ago, in Africa, when a young lawyer, Mahatma Gandhi, was transacting business for a client, he attempted to worship in an Established Church. He was turned away at the church door because of his color. He never forgot this experience. Later, he came to admire greatly Jesus, the Prince of Peace, and he fashioned his Non-Violent movement of passive resistance to British rule in India upon the teachings of Jesus. But he never became a professing Christian, chiefly because the Church that claimed to follow Jesus would not include a man of his color in its worship services or extend to him the right hand of Christian fellowship.

Your pastor has continued to make unshared decisions concerning the use of our church facilities for services of worship open to all races. Recently a request came to your pastor from The United Church Women of Pine Bluff for the use of Wheeler Memorial Chapel for the annual Business Men's Prayer Service on Friday, February 14, The World Day of Prayer. On the day the request was made the leaders of The United Church Women had voted by a large majority to open their services for The World Day of Prayer to those of all races and colors. Knowing this, I granted permission for the use of our facilities for the service requested. I do not know whether those of other races will attend, but they are welcome according to the permission granted by your pastor. Some have referred to this service as "the opening wedge" in the wall that has separated absolutely the races in the church life of the city. I, personally, think of it in terms of the discharge of my responsibility as a Methodist pastor in a local church that is known as a "Missionary-Minded" Church whose time to testify at home has arrived. It will be our own way of saying that we can practice at home what we expect our missionaries to practice in other lands where they give their witness for us.

Here let me express to the officials and membership of First Methodist Church my sincere appreciation for the "free Pulpit" in which I stand this morning. Never, during my four years as your pastor, has any person sought to tell me what to say or what not to say. By the same token, I have tried never to abuse the privileged position that this sacred desk affords me as a minister of the Gospel. There are times when your pastor has spoken to you on controversial themes, always after long periods of prayer and soul searching. Today is one of those times. I have been told by members, some of whom are leaders in "key" organizations of the church, that a large majority of our members and officials differ strongly with the position of The Methodist Church on the subject of Race Relations, and, therefore, with the views that your pastor has expressed in his endorsement of those views. From my personal knowledge of my people, I have no reason to question the size of the majority. Knowing this, some may feel that their pastor has deliberately measured himself for a "Martyr's suit." This may be true. If so, some spiritual alterations in my makeup may be needed, chiefly in the shoulders, since my shoulders have never carried a fraction of the burden for the Kingdom that The Christ has carried through the years for this "ransomed sinner." I trust that The Holy Spirit will give that needed strength to these shoulders, so that whatever burdens rest upon them may be borne with joy and thanksgiving.

Whether you agree with my conception of A Methodist Pastor's responsibility in the field of Race Relations or not, I trust that you will remember me as a pastor who always dealt with the theme of Race Relations in terms of God's Love for every child of His, in terms of a Christ who died for every man, and in terms of the work of The Holy Spirit, who is no respecter of persons. Within a Methodist Church there is, and always has been, a place for differences of opinions concerning the methods of solving the problems that exist between the races, but there is no place for differences in spirit. Within First Methodist Church, the answers to the problems that confront us will come through the guidance of the Holy Spirit as we apply Christian principles to these problems, and through the cultivation of the fruits of The Holy Spirit. These fruits are: Love, Joy, Peace, Longsuffering, Gentleness, Goodness, Faith, Meekness, Temperance. If our people maintain such a spirit in all that they do and say, then First Church will have its best and brightest days as the future unfolds. Above all, remember that you have a group of fine leaders in your Official Board who are worthy of your loyal support. Strengthen their hands and keep strong the life of First Church, for it is much easier to maintain the strength of a church than it is to rebuild it.

First Methodist Church, Pine Bluff, is set on a corner of a busy thoroughfare in the heart of the city. It has been a channel through which God has permitted His Stream of Grace to flow through the life of this great city for almost a century and a half. What it does and says, or what it does not do or say, on the subject of Race Relations will influence greatly the heart and life of the city of Pine Bluff. As your pastor, I have spoken without apology in presenting to you what I believe to be the voice of The Methodist Church and the voice of my Lord and Saviour. I trust my words in your hands, and I surrender them completely into the hands of God. If they are of God, they will abide. If they are not of God, the testing fires that burn in our world will consume whatever dross they contain and will refine whatever gold of truth they may contain.

The clearest words I have heard spoken on the responsibility of the local church in the area of Race Relations were spoken by Pat Matthews, the lovely wife of Brother Ed Matthews, missionary to the Congo. At the close of her recent message to the joint meeting of the Woman's Society of Christian Service and the Wesleyan Service Guild, January 28th, Pat listed four things that the local church could do to support the missionary on distant fields of service. The fourth point, the most important in her opinion, she described in these words: "To create in your family, home, church, and community a spirit of love and understanding, not only for the people of Africa, but for people of all the world—for your actions hinder or help the cause of the church in the world." I pray that such a spirit of love and understanding in the life of First Church and the city of Pine Bluff may grow day by day, until our city may truly become the city of our God.

My closing plea is for spiritual unity in the life of the church. It is easy to remain united when our race, our color, and our background are the same. When we ask others whose skins are of another color to share a service of worship in our own church then we quickly discover whether "the Love of Christ constraineth us" or whether we are ruled and divided by our prejudices. When faith demands that we cross that line which separates words and actions, we may truly become "broken bread and poured out wine" for our Christian convictions and for Christ's sake. These are days when the divisive forces of prejudice, hatred, greed, selfishness, and secularism threaten the very life of the Christian Church from the local to the ecumenical level. In the midst of such days, I would counsel church members and officials to remain united at all times in spirit and life. To that end, I urge you to study the seventeenth chapter of The Gospel of John, which contains the matchless prayer of Jesus for spiritual unity: "That they all may be one; as Thou, Father, art in me, and I in Thee, that they also may be one in us." My prayer for First Church is that Jesus may be Lord in all of its life and that we may be one in Christ.

§101 Reverend L. Wilson Kilgore

Reverend L. Wilson Kilgore was born in Elmira, New York on February 25, 1917. He earned his B.A. from Colgate University in 1939, and his M.Div. from Colgate Rochester Divinity School in 1942. From 1943 to 1953 Reverend Kilgore served as senior minister at First Presbyterian Church in Hartford, Connecticut. From 1953 to 1964 he served as Minister at Lakewood (Ohio) Presbyterian Church. And from 1964 to 1972 he served as Minister to Cherry Hill Presbyterian Church in Dearborn, Michigan. The final 14 years of his service were to Valley Presbyterian Church in Scottsdale, Arizona. Reverend Kilgore is a father to five children and six stepchildren. He is a husband for the third time after being twice predeceased in loving marriages. Reverend Kilgore is still a vocal advocate in neighborhood association politics.

This sermon takes place at Lakewood Presbyterian Church, a predominantly white suburb of Cleveland. Employing an extended metaphor from space travel, he begins the sermon with a clear understanding of the fleeting power of empires in Europe, Africa, Asia, and America built on undervalued human worth. America's "countdown" began 2,000 years ago, when St. Paul declared the end of distinctions such as "Jew and Greek, circumcised and uncircumcised, barbarian, Scythian, slave, free man. . . ." The countdown would have been short indeed had civilizations not so desperately sought out scapegoats. Getting beyond these scapegoats would be difficult were it not for the possibility of being a new creation. As to the very sticky issue of the salvation of racially prejudiced white congregants, Kilgore deftly refers to such people as "partial birth" Christians, as opposed to the unsaved, imposters, or hypocrites. Kilgore ends the sermon by identifying the Magna Charta of new creation: "Here there cannot by Greek and Jew. . . ." Later that year, Reverend Kilgore left the Lakewood congregation to assume responsibilities at Cherry Hill Presbyterian Church in Dearborn, Michigan. The relevance of the ideas he developed in Lakewood persisted stubbornly. In 1967, during the Detroit riots, a revised version of this sermon was broadcast and published under the title, "Soul Brother."

Countdown on Human Worth

Lakewood Presbyterian Church, Lakewood, Ohio

February 1964

A new word has become familiar to all of us in this age when missiles are sent aloft from their launching pads. Before the launching there is elaborate preparation on the part of all the scientific and service personnel. After this preparation the final checking out of all the systems takes place. This is called the "countdown." Excitement reigns as the control officer begins the final count: "Ten, nine, eight, seven, six, five, four, three, two, one, zero." With a blast-off the mighty missile is in motion.

It does not take a wise person to note that this is not man's only "countdown." The countdown in the field of scientific space age is nothing in comparison to what is happening in the relations between human beings, especially in the field of race relations. All over the world human beings are being held in check, kept back, held down, deprived of their rights and made to feel and to be less than human. And all over the world there is abundant evidence that the countdown on this kind of situation has begun. The count is getting less and less as time and events and human desire acting as the "control officer" call off the decreasing numbers. Explosions have already occurred which have changed the whole course of history. England is no longer an empire; France has lost her colonies and now strives to keep Europe for herself; the Europeans have gone home from all of Africa; and all over the Orient there is unrest.

America herself has not escaped this countdown. In the past few years since the historic Supreme Court decision concerning segregation in the classrooms we have heard the control officers call out decreasing numbers disguised as events—"Little Rock"; bus boycott; lunch counter sit-ins; freedom riders; and James Meredith trying to enter the University of Mississippi while the Governor of that state placed himself and his state against the law of this land.

Every once in awhile I pause to read and ponder over one of the newspaper centennial accounts of the Civil War. We read these accounts as if the war were long since over. Well, one part of it is—that part to preserve the Union intact. But that other cause for the war—to free the slaves—is still going on.

Long ago in Egypt some of God's people were held in bondage. "Let my people go!" cried Moses. Now, centuries later, another great part of the people of God has been held captive by custom, by mores, by law, by decree and by downright degrading of people to a subhuman level. "Let my people go!" is the cry once more in Little Rock, in Birmingham, in Nashville, in Oxford, Mississippi, and in Cleveland.

St. Paul never heard of "the land of the free and the home of the brave" when he cried out as the result of what Christ did to man and to life, "Here there cannot be Greek and Jew, circumcised and uncircumcised, barbarian, Scythian, slave, free man, but Christ is all, and in all." Paul put his finger on the beginning of the countdown—when God in Christ revealed to all of us the worth of a man to God and thus to all men.

Of course there is nothing new about prejudice. It has a long, long history. The other tribe, those people over the mountain, those funny folk across the river—these have always been the object of prejudice throughout history. When to these former geographical "differences" which marked man, physical differences of color, size, hair and ways of living are added, prejudice is given a new additive to fuel its fires. Then came man the conqueror, and he made those he conquered to be a subject people. Thus the idea of the slave was born and with it the man who was the master. We have never lost this idea that some are made "to order" and others are made "to obey." All sorts of excuses are used and even Bible references are brought up to prove the point that this seems to be the way God made the people.

To this must be added another historic reason for prejudice. There seems to be something in man which requires that he feel superior. We all have this basic nature which drives us to be better than the other fellow. If we cannot be better then we want to think that we are. So we bring custom and even law itself to support us in our feelings of superiority over someone of a different race or class. The origin of the Jim Crow law rests in this cause as much as in the white man's fear that since he was outnumbered he had to protect his difference and his power. With such laws and customs supporting the white man of the South in his prejudice, he could, therefore, feel "superior." No matter how low on the social or economic ladder, no matter how steeped in ignorance he might be, such a white man could feel "superior" to a Marian Anderson, to a Ralph Bunche or to a Jackie Robinson.

Another historical reason for prejudice has been the frustrations which we have encountered in life. Frustration makes for hostility. Hostility must be expressed. Often we cannot express the hostility toward the proper person, so we seek a scapegoat. The wife, the husband, the child, the dog becomes the object of our misplaced hostility. However, if you can blame everything on the Jews or the Negroes you have something bigger to take it out on!

Hitler convinced almost an entire nation that all the troubles of the nation had come upon them because of the Jews. When this blood bath of prejudice was over, some six million Jews had been placed on the altar of prejudice and slain! The most terrible thing about this historical root for prejudice is that the more a person or a culture or a nation is frustrated the greater becomes the need for a scapegoat. And in this age of anonymity in cities, meaninglessness in vocation, unemployment because of automation, this need is increasing all the time. This kind of countdown can only result in explosions of prejudice, race riots and mass condemnations of whole peoples because of misplaced hostility.

All through history there has been this separation of the sheep from the goats. All through history there has been the "in-group" and the "out-group." Between the two there have existed the ill winds of racism, prejudice and even at times open warfare. "The Jew had his gentile; the Greek had his barbarian; the Roman had his non-Roman; the crusaders had their infidel; the fifteenth-century Roman Catholics had their heathens; the English had their Irish; the Lutherans had their Anabaptists; the Nazis had their non-Aryans; and now the white man has his Negro. Every 'in-group' has an 'out-group' upon which it projects all that is by its standards abhorrent and in which by contrast it sees its own glorification reflected."

Such a history seems to make dark the outlook for the solution to the problems of human relations. Yet, I cannot help but feel that a new era is dawning. Although pride and prejudice will forever remain a problem of man, there is hope for control, for understanding, for a more healthy direction for all our hostilities. Obviously, the Christian church must put its own house in order. It must do this as well as be in the vanguard of improving the relations between people and nations.

The church through the years has contributed to prejudice. In recent centuries she has of course been the "in-group." By that very fact she has helped to create and foster prejudice. Moreover, in the South, the "white" church helped to divide Christianity further by creating the "colored" church. Two causes worked this result. One was the desire of the southerner to evangelize the Negro that he might be a proper subject! The other was the desire of the Negro for a church of his own where—at least here—he could bow before just one Master, Jesus Christ! Interesting, isn't it, that this very "colored" church has turned out to be the most forceful instrument of racial equality in the South.

Happily, there are movements for union between white and colored churches and denominations. There is a greater spirit of brotherhood than has existed for a long time. White pastors have voluntarily joined their colored brethren in the South to share their burden. What a tragic situation it is that while one branch of the Christian church in the South is a force against segregation and for total freedom of the colored man, another branch of the church is heavily in favor of keeping things as they are and enforcing segregation! The Christian church will never put its own house in order unless and until all the members and all the branches realize and accept the fact that all are children of the same God and all are equal before him. It is the Christian doctrine of man which must unite us, and this union must come not only in the sanctuary where we worship the God of all men, but in the fellowship hall where we break bread together!

Would that it were just our own problem—that is, the problem of the churches. But it is the problem of society, and the church is influenced by what happens in society. Do you think for one moment that the southern church can come clean on this matter of race relations until the customs, mores and laws of the South are altered? These customs, mores and laws which help to reinforce prejudice also reinforce the church's color line. The southerner's prejudice is reinforced in the church because of the laws and customs outside the church. This gives him the comfortable feeling that what he cannot admit in the church does not matter, because "God's laws" are so obvious in his society.

Let us try this in reverse now. Is our church a so-called "white church" simply because the members believe in segregation? Or do we have this color simply because of what has happened in society and because of the laws and understandings which compel the Negro in Cleveland to live where he does and deny him the privilege of living with us and we with him? No amount of integration in this church could change the fact of our color, because of the social situation which prevails. The same is true in the South.

Therefore the church, to put its own house in order, must move on a broad front. This has doctrinal and ecclesiastical implications. But it also implies that if we believe what we say we do about the equality of man and the worth of all men in the sight of God, then we must do everything possible to educate all men, to make fair the economic practices and pay for all men. It means that we must give to all men the right to live where they can afford to live—even in Lakewood! Then they could worship with us and break bread with us in our fellowship groups. Otherwise, without this kind of thrust of the Christian gospel into the social, economic and political life of our world, what we do inside the church about segregation is frustrated.

So the countdown on human worth not only involves the church in what she does in and to her own structure and order but it involves her in what she does in the social order, which affects the life of the church as well as the lives of the children of God.

What about the individual Christian and this matter of race relations? It seems to me that here is where the case for society and the church must finally rest. For if the individual Christian is not convinced that there is something wrong about prejudice and segregation, then court order and legislation will avail little in the end. For always, in the end, the individual will manage to change law and change custom unless he himself is changed. And if the individual Christian is not convinced that there is something socially, morally and religiously wrong about degrading any other human being for any reason, then who else will be expected to feel this wrong and want to do something about it?

As Dr. Haselden has reminded us: "If we press toward the exact center of the concentric circles of inclusion and exclusion we find there the lone individual in proud and splendid isolation from the rest of mankind." It is this individual who wants to be different, who must have evidence that he is superior, who must have some object or person for his scapegoat. It is this individual who must be so changed and altered in his ways as to see every person as a child of God.

For some people prejudice becomes almost a way of life. It is the way by which they feel their existence and have a sense of being. Take away the negative feeling such a person has about another race, or another person, or another religion and such a person seems to dissolve.

It seems to me that the Christian religion has a special answer for this kind of person. It is an answer that goes beyond our common humanity and our common fear. It is an answer that links us to all men because we are linked to the God that gave us birth. But the wideness and the vastness of this idea is lost—completely lost—on that person who is filled with his own self-importance. Filled with such self-importance, this person has no room for any other person.

Further, such a person has no room for God. This is the tragedy of the whole matter. If such a person had room for God in his life he could then find room for the needs and feelings of any of God's children. Dr. Haselden has opened the problem to its core when he writes of this self-centeredness which, "carried to its logical and final extreme, must exclude God. Racial prejudice is an externalized and objectified form of that self-centeredness, visible part of that invisible pride which must subdue all rivals and whose last rival is God."

Let me illustrate: I have in mind two or three persons who have loved the church and they have professed a love of the God whom they see in Christ. The only problem with these people was this—when the chips were down, their prejudice against Negroes was greater than their love for God! Which simply means that this "new being in Christ" just really never came into being! It was only partially created. To be born "after the Spirit" is to see all men as the children of God; it is to see all men as made in the image of God; it is to understand that no man in the sight of God has any preference over another because of race or class. The "new being in Christ" must be a complete birth of the spirit—not a partial birth—and such a complete birth of the spirit as to move us to see all as children of God and as our brothers.

This implies in its practical aspects that we will not deny to any man because of his race or religion what we would not deny to ourselves. This implies that we would desire for all men and women what we desire for ourselves. This implies that there will be no walls, no barriers, no fences, no signs, no invisible agreements, which will prevent any man from being a complete child of God.

The countdown on human worth is being heard all around us. When did it begin? It began back in that time when God so loved the world—and all the men in the world—that he "sent" his Son to be our Savior. God's love and God's salvation is for the white man and the black man. St. Paul caught this vast idea early in Christian history and wrote these words which have been called the Magna Charta of Christian human relations: "Here there cannot be Greek and Jew, circumcised and uncircumcised, barbarian, Scythian, slave, free man, but Christ is all, and in all."

§102 Reverend Duncan Howlett

Reverend Duncan Howlett's biography appears in the introduction to his March 12, 1961 speech in Lynchburg, Virginia. Reverend Duncan Howlett's Report from the South is an update from one of the most volatile regions of the nation. He compromises in this speech by balancing broad issues with detailed stories of prejudice against blacks and dilemmas faced by Unitarian churches. Howlett's concern for the future of the nation, especially in terms of racial equality and integration reveals itself in his formal accusation that segregation is only a justification for the nation's treatment of Negroes. He mentions several ways Americans try to rationalize the current status of a divided country. Howlett claims that the shame and guilt of the American people is hidden behind the mask of racism and discrimination. In other words, white supremacy is but sublimation of a guilty conscience: "It is his only defense against himself and against you. Without it he becomes a monster. Without it, he must go mad, for no such man could bear such guilt." Howlett not only pleads for governmental justice but for all individuals to look within themselves to crush intolerance and arrogance. Reverend Duncan Howlett reports from the South, that bigotry is prevailing, but perhaps not for long.

Report from the South
All Souls Church, Washington, D.C.
March 8, 1964

As many of you are aware, I was in the South a week ago, visiting Unitarian churches and fellowships there, and speaking on various university campuses. It was an experience both heartening and disheartening; heartening because of the movement toward real integration that is under way in all but one of the groups I visited, but disheartening because of the intransigence in the white community in the South generally, toward any meaningful integration. I might add that my observations were confined to Alabama, Georgia and northern Florida.

And in case any of you thought I was having a vacation 'neath warm southern skies, I might also add that it rained through most of my stay in the sunny South and it was always cold. At Atlanta they hauled the plane on which I was riding into the hangar for de-icing before take-off. In thousands of miles of flying in the North, that had never happened to me before. I looked longingly at the swimming pools at each of the motels where I was housed, but I never saw anyone in any of them. And in the cold and the rain, I never felt like going in myself.

Except for a tour of the Space Agency at Huntsville, Alabama, my one excursion was to the Killearn Gardens at Tallahassee, where the camellias were magnificent, and the trees hung heavy with moss. They told me the azaleas there are beyond belief, but none were yet in bloom. They urged me to come back next year the second week in March which is azalea time for them. But for a New Englander, who thinks of March as the most drab of all the months in the year—in fact the only drab month, when the snow has gone, but no blossoms have yet opened—for a New Englander March in Washington is too exciting a time to be away.

I returned to this city March first, to find snow drops in bloom in my front yard and pussy willows at the back. Crocuses are popping up everywhere about the city today and the second week in March has only just begun. No, March is not the time to leave Washington, either for azaleas or swimming in Florida. You see, I am becoming a convert to the Washington climate, of which I had very low opinion before coming here. As a former New Englander, I could do with a little more white snow in winter, and a little less heat and humidity in summer—indeed, who could not—but I have learned to treasure the long mild autumn, and the long glorious spring now just beginning.

But I shall not bore you with travelogue. I was on serious business in the South and I had serious questions to ask. The purpose for which the trip was designed was to lend what strength I could to Unitarian churches and fellowships in the South, both on and off university campuses. But as you can imagine, I was as much concerned with questions of civil rights as with the development of our own movement. As a matter of fact, in the South, the two are inextricable, as they are with us. Unitarians and Universalists who disagree on just about everything else, are virtually unanimous on the question of integration. To ask how a Unitarian church or fellowship in the South is succeeding is also to ask how they are dealing with the integration problem. None is doing as well as it would like to, and many are deeply divided as to how to proceed.

Our Unitarian churches in the South today know what they want to do, but they are not able to do it, and for many reasons. They want to de-segregate the economic and social life of their communities as rapidly as possible. They want to integrate their churches, their schools, in fact all of the economic and cultural life of the South, again as rapidly as possible. Let alone, they would do it. But they are not let alone. They are frustrated at every turn. Every conceivable obstacle is set in the path of those who would advance the cause of the Negro. Whoever participates in the civil rights movement, or supports it, even though without any overt act, is subject to widespread social pressures of the most powerful and subtle sort.

Let me take the Unitarian Church at Birmingham to illustrate the point. Organized only twelve years ago as a fellowship, the group grew so rapidly it became a church in two years. Soon they bought land and had a capital building fund drive. Today they occupy a beautiful new plant all their own. It was in the Birmingham church, as some of you know, that our theological school intern, Mr. F. Jackson Zylman, decided to enter the Unitarian ministry. While I was in the city, I asked to be taken by the Sixteenth Street Baptist Church which was bombed last fall, killing four pupils, for whom an offering of nearly $500 was taken up in our church the following Sunday. I am glad to report that the Sixteenth Street Baptist Church is now in the process of being repaired.

It may surprise some of you to learn that the Unitarian Church at Birmingham is integrated. Not only do Negroes attend its services and activities, they are welcomed into membership. From time to time Negroes are scheduled as speakers at the church exactly as they are here, not because they are Negroes but because they are people with something important to say and the competence to say it effectively.

I hope you realize what this means. I hope you appreciate the courage such an arrangement takes in Alabama today. The Unitarian church is located in an all-white suburb. On more than one occasion, the Board of Trustees has seriously considered whether to proceed with a program that had been planned. They have had to ask themselves whether they were ready to run the obvious risk of bombing their going ahead entailed. The minister, the Reverend Alfred Hobart, on more than one occasion considered having his telephone taken out as the only means of avoiding a constant succession of telephone threats. In the end he did not, having resolved to see it through, and eventually the harassment subsided.

The Birmingham Church has a Sunday evening public forum in addition to its Sunday morning service. Negroes attend this program, as they do in the morning, and occasionally they have been scheduled as speakers. One evening a Negro whom several members of the congregation had heard at the Sixth Avenue Baptist Church was scheduled to sing at the Sunday Evening Forum. A small group in the church, critical of this action, brought the matter before the Board of Trustees which overwhelmingly voted not to interfere with the program.

At first I was quite unable to grasp why this matter was taken to the trustees. It seemed to me the precedent of having Negro speakers was already established by the church in practice. Furthermore, Negro singers have long been accepted when speakers were not. And then, through a chance remark, it all became clear. Those who had brought in the Negro singer had undertaken to advertise the event widely. Thus, all the white citizens of Birmingham were directly informed that on a given Sunday night a Negro would give a concert to a white audience, in a church in an all-white neighborhood.

This, in turn, subjected the people of the church to reprisals of all sorts, both openly threatened and implied, and it subjected them also to very real anxiety that their church would be bombed. The question under debate in the church was very real, and I think quite properly one for the trustees to decide on behalf of the congregation as a whole, provided that it affected a major policy issue. As a member of the church I would stand with those who invited the Negro singer to the Sunday Evening Forum, who advertised the event, and were ready to take personal abuse and their chances with the church building. But I would also argue that if this had been a true departure from the established policy of the church, the trustees should first have been consulted and they should have been prepared to act on behalf of the entire congregation. In this case the trustees decided no departure from policy was involved. But through this incident we can see the deep dilemma faced by our Southern churches. How best shall they proceed with the integration in which all believe, but on the means toward which they differ so widely.

Another of our Unitarian groups in the South is in a deep dilemma over picketing and boycotts. In this instance, a well-organized group of students had picketed a particular store which would not integrate, until it finally closed and the owner went out of business. The event was hailed as a great victory for the civil rights movement. You and I would agree. If the man would not integrate he deserved to be driven out of business, we would say.

But I found one of the leaders of this particular group in a deep dilemma. It was a woman, and she had been at the forefront of the civil rights movement, ready for direct action, until she met Dr. and Mrs. Clarence Jordan. Years ago they had established Koinonia Farm at Americus, Georgia. Many of you, I am sure, are familiar with it. Koinonia is a twentieth-century experiment in Utopianism, like Brook Farm and other similar attempts of the nineteenth century. The Jordans had established their farm on three basic principles in which they deeply believed: 1. pacifism 2. integration and 3. Christian communism or mutual sharing. This was before the Second World War.

The farm at first was a great success. Its products were highly prized and eagerly bought because of their quality. The members of the farm were peaceful and caused no trouble to anyone. But pacifism, integration and communism, however Christian any of them might be supposed to be, were not to be tolerated, and the people of Georgia struck back in every way they could. They set up a boycott against buying the farm's products, a boycott against transporting its goods, and a boycott against selling the farm raw materials. The boycott has succeeded. Koinonia Farm has been paralyzed and as an enterprise it is nearly dead.

The Unitarian leader who had so recently met and talked with the Jordans still found herself quite shaken by the experience. For the Jordans, who were among the first to attempt integration in the South, now tremble at the growing use of the boycott in the civil rights movement, because of its potential for evil as well as good. They have learned from personal experience how powerful a weapon it is. They are asking, and so now is this Unitarian leader who had upheld the practice, what will happen when the weapons of picketing, boycotts and the rest are taken up by the segregationists and used to enforce their demands.

Let me give you another example of the problems with which high-minded Unitarian leaders in the South are struggling. They are not rationalizing. Some are, of course. But most of those with whom I talked care very much. But they are deeply troubled as to what, under all the circumstances, is the best thing to do.

In setting up the trip, I had offered several topics to the various groups, and asked them to choose what they liked. "Civil Rights" was one of the topics. To my surprise, but one group chose it, and I think they regretted the choice. Not that I was too hard on them: I did not call them to account for what many would say were their shortcomings. I think we have problems enough here in the District, without my going to the South to tell them how to handle their problems. The real truth of the matter was that they regretted the public discussion of an issue many of their members would have preferred to discuss in private. They are timid, you will say. So said some of their own members who were glad the discussion was public. But with some of these latter, you had the feeling they were not above embarrassing their fellow members.

Who was right? I do not profess to be able to make a judgment. I wish I were wise enough to, or charitable enough to do it. But I know many who do not seem to me to be wise, and who are not charitable, who would be swift to pass such judgment. In any case, my purpose this morning is different. My emphasis today is rather upon the dilemma in which any such group finds itself, and the dilemma in which all but the most extreme individuals find themselves, when they face the complex problems of the civil rights movement in the South. Is it the business of a group to survive, they ask, even though at the price of compromise? If they do not survive, as some groups have not, then who is to carry the banner, they ask. But if they are to compromise, then how much?

In the Southern churches and fellowships I visited all agreed that integration for their own group is the break-off point. On that there is no compromise. With them all, Negroes are genuinely welcome. But after that, the questions start—for the group, and for the individuals who make it up. What further steps should they, and should they not, take? What will advance the cause of integration and what will impede it? These are real questions for them; and how they despise the Northerners, who, from their safe little islands of self-righteous integration, and leaving their own back yards unattended, undertake to tell the South what it must and must not do. And may I add my hearty concurrence. This, above all else, is what I learned on my tour of our Southern churches and fellowships: their very deep concern with the integration movement, coupled with a very practical hardheaded concern as to how best to go about it. One of their problems is the finding of Negroes who will attend their churches, much less participate in their activities. By our standards, none of them have achieved more than token integration, and some, none at all.

Each of the campus-connected groups for example is confronted by a university where integration is token indeed. The University of Alabama has but one Negro student out of 12,000; the University of Georgia has four; the University of Auburn only one; Emory has two undergraduates and Florida State two. In each case the student body as a whole is numbered by thousands. These figures are not official. Nevertheless, all those with whom I talked felt the first break was the most difficult. Now that it has been made, they felt the pace of integration in the universities will rapidly accelerate. This I believe will depend upon the determination with which they press for it.

Let me illustrate with one final story how difficult the situation is, as our Southern liberals meet it and are called upon to deal with it. A leader in one of the churches I visited is a member of the local Council on Human Relations. He is deeply concerned at the intransigence of the white community in the face of increasing and well-justified Negro demands. Like many others, he sees strife ahead unless some measurable progress can soon be made. Hoping to help, this man went to see another member of the Council on Human Relations, a city official, with segregationist leanings, but one with whom he felt he could talk.

He believed the Negro demands were not only right, he told the official, and that therefore they should be met, but also, he said, those demands are like a rising tide, the force of which must be released or it will burst all bounds and a floodtide of trouble will follow. The Negro leadership in their city is now moderate, he explained, at least measured by the spectrum of Negro demands. But the moderates will lose control if they are not able to accomplish anything, he continued. Should moderate leadership be rejected by the Negro community, he cautioned, advocates of force and violence, now waiting in the wings, will step to the center of the stage. At this point the city official leaned forward across his desk, his eyes narrowed, and he said,

"Are you threatening me?"

"No," said the leader of the Unitarian church sadly, and left, his heart heavy, his anxiety for the peace and good name of his city markedly increased. The white community in that city and the cities all over the South will not yield. The white community will not face the facts about itself, and it will not face the facts about the Negro, either.

How is this possible, we ask. The people of our American Southland are honorable. They do not wish to do wrong. They wish to be upright and moral, as do we all, or most of us. But how can they, when they look at their race policies? We know the answer. They protect their innocence by a theory which is now as fixed as Gospel. They do it by the ancient theory of racial superiority. They defend it on anthropological grounds (which the anthropologists have proven false) and on Biblical grounds (which Bible scholars say are absurd). They support it by the statement that Negroes like to live as they live in the South.

If you have seen how they live, as I have, and as I did again last week, you might be moved to agree with the Southerners, who ask, "Why would anyone live like that unless he wanted to?" You would, perhaps, until you recalled the generations of economic, social and cultural deprivation that created the people who live in the hovels you see. You are ready to agree, until you realize those who advance such arguments are themselves responsible for what they condemn. And then you understand. Then you understand how the white segregationist is able to believe what he says he believes about the Negro. It is his only defense against himself and against you. Without it he becomes a monster. Without it he must go mad, for no man could bear such guilt.

No man can do to another man what the segregationist, South and North, does to the Negro and keep his sanity. As the Nazis based their pogroms on the theory of a super-race, and as the Middle Ages based its Inquisition on the theory of Christian superiority, so the segregationist does the same. He lives with himself by creating and enforcing the conditions that make the Southern Negro the kind of limited person that seems to support his theory of race superiority, and thus justify what he does.

This is how he is able to live with himself. So he is able to keep his self-respect. This is how he frees himself from guilt. And this, I think, is the explanation of the intransigence of the South. As the South moves toward civil rights, it must begin to shoulder blame for the misery in which the Negro has been kept. And this guilt is too great for a righteous man to bear.

But is it very much less so with any of us? Does not every man, north, south, east or west, share the guilt American society bears for the degradation of the Negro in the South, and to a great extent in the North as well? Do not those Negroes who have taken their place in American middle-class society also bear the guilt that falls upon us all? Who but those who are still the victims of the system we have inherited from slavery, is free of taint? Who is guiltless but the victim himself? We all might have done better than we have. We all have profited, directly or indirectly, from the misery and poverty in which so many of our Negro citizens have been kept.

If we could see, as a people, that the South's problem is the nation's problem and that the South's guilt is the nation's guilt, then perhaps we could make the Southerner feel that he does not stand quite so isolated and alone as he faces the question of integration. Perhaps integration would become tolerable to him if we could make him feel that he no longer needed the doctrine of race supremacy to hide his own shame: that his shame is known, and that it is borne by us all. If we could let him see the kind of superior being the Negro can become when he has been set free and given the same chance the white man is given, perhaps then the Southerner would feel that he could make concessions. Perhaps then he would begin to yield.

How then shall we proceed, you and I, who believe in integration? How shall we who are ready to confess the corporate guilt of the American people for the problems the Negro faces in our culture, set about making amends? In the first place, we must realize that sectional differences are surface differences. Basically we all face the same problem. Our problems differ greatly in degree, but the fundamental issues are the same. We will understand one another better, and we will be more charitable in our judgments if we remember this.

There is another point we might well keep in mind. We are accustomed to contrast courage and fear, wisdom and stupidity. But when we do, we show our own lack of wisdom and our lack of courage, too. For the real tension we face is between courage and folly, between caution and common sense. When is it foolish to be bold and when is it wise? That is what we need to know. When will our valor, loudly though it may be praised, thwart the very purposes toward which it is directed? Yet into what quicksand do we slide whenever we ask ourselves such a question? Fear so easily wears the mask of common sense. And courage, bold, thoughtless courage, that only pursues its goal and counts not the cost—courage, committed to high purpose so often carries the day, just because it is bold and fearless. These are the real dilemmas within which we are caught. And none of us escapes them.

The real answer to all these questions does not lie in barren philosophical principles. Your answer and mine is not to be found in the elements of law and order society must state in order to guide its own practice, although we are always involved in them. Your answer and mine will rise from somewhere deep within us where the conflicts society must resolve begin. As I face and try to help resolve the multiple problems of the integration movement, I am sometimes clear as to what we must do and then am able to speak with seeming boldness. But often I am far from clear as to what it is best to do. Some say this is timidity. And isn't it the same with you? Sometimes perhaps I am wise, but surely more often I am foolish. This too must be so for you. For such is the lot of man. His decisions must ever lie somewhere between the ideal and the possible.

Then since we are creatures of both courage and caution, of both fear and common sense, let us in our personal decisions weigh out as best we may the principles that apply in whatever social reform we would undertake. Let us be sure, insofar as we can, that what we do really advances the cause in which we believe. Let us not forget that often it takes more courage to stand against a seemingly high-minded proposal that may offer short-term victory but long-term defeat. Society, whatever its present wrongs, must hold together and maintain a modicum of order. With anarchy come wrongs far greater and far more terrible than any an ordered society will tolerate.

And yet in the face of great wrong, when society itself supports injustice, and misery is hidden from mercy, then it is wisdom to call for justice and noble to seek out mercy. And if this seeking needs courage then let courage come. No society was ever destroyed by the bold demand for justice. No nation has perished because the government was merciful to its citizens. Then let the cry for justice ever be heard in our land. Let it roll down the halls of government, and let it echo through every university and in every church. Let the cry for justice and mercy be heard until the people awake, until the fetters are cast off every man upon whom they have fallen, and the disinherited are claimed as our brothers and granted the privileges the rest of us enjoy.

§103 James McBride Dabbs

James McBride Dabbs's biography appears in the introduction to his November 9, 1961 speech in Atlanta, Georgia. In the following speech before his fellow Presbyterians, James McBride Dabbs raises the question of what work God is doing in the world just now? If God is ever-present, how is he involved in the ongoing world racial revolution? For Dabbs the answer lies no further than the young students sitting in at lunch counters. He sees in them the reclamation of a social order long denied. That order is but one manifestation of God's providence. Moreover, their method of nonviolent resistance reflects the best traditions of the South: a deep religiosity and good manners—both of which, for Dabbs, represent the grace of God. In performing such actions, black students also challenge and redefine the rhetorical codes of the South: "For they were engaged, however quietly, in a revolution. And perhaps the essence of this revolution is a redefinition of the great words of the South. We have been a people of great words: courtesy, honor, integrity, truth, courage, love. We are being asked to look at these words and see what they mean for today." But the key to understanding the powerful testimony of the students, claims Dabbs, lies in their commitment to social justice. Love, without a concomitant concern for justice, smacks of sentimentalism—and this has been the sin of the white South. For this reason blacks, finally, are showing their white brothers and sisters what God's grace really means—in word and deed.

Christian Response to Racial Revolution

Cherokee Presbytery, meeting at Acworth Presbyterian Church, Acworth, Georgia
April 21, 1964

Alfred North Whitehead has remarked that two lines of one of our great hymns sum up man's perennial response to the world:

> Change and decay in all around I see;
> O Thou who changest not, abide with me.

I would call your attention especially to that first line: "Change and decay in all around I see." We tend to equate change with decay. We are poor creatures, frightened by the vastness of the world, holding on to the scenes and the faces we have known, wrapping the roots of our being about particular things and people. It is man's way "to hold on with the heart." But as Christians we also recognize that God is somehow in the world now, in these changing places and faces, that he is the God of the living, an ever-present God, that as Jesus said, "My Father is working still, and I am working" (John 5:17). The creation of the world still goes on.

It is the duty of the Christian then to ask, What is God doing in the world now? And particularly, What is God doing in the revolutions of our time? Looked at superficially, the world is going to pieces, around the globe, even here in the South. Looked at more deeply, it may be merely shaking itself; that is, God may be shaking the foundation, to make clear to us which structures are built upon sand and which upon the rock. And though such periods are always periods of disorder, new structures arise, through which men create and find order. The old structures give way, not because men are essentially chaotic; we do have chaos in us, but we are essentially social creatures, creatures of orderly institutions, and the old structures give way because, for all their apparent orderliness, they rest upon spiritual disorder.

Consider our racial situation in the South. In recent years we have seen or we have heard much of Negroes sitting at lunch counters reserved for whites, requesting service. Though these people, usually young, sat there quietly, many of us said their actions were disorderly. We meant that they were not in accordance with the accepted order and custom of the South.

The Negro was getting out of his place, and in the South this by definition is disorder. But who made the order—of segregation, of the Negro kept permanently on the bottom rung of the ladder? Did the world-rejuvenating spirit of democratic America make it? I know there are those who argue that God was the first segregationist. I am not going to try to refute them. You can prove anything from the Bible, if you take only chapter and verse. The devil, too, can quote Scripture. That's one reason I hesitate to quote it. I can only say of those who argue like this, I pity them; nor do I understand how their spirit is any reflection of the compassionate spirit of Jesus and the redemptive love of God. So far as I am concerned, segregation denies the basic historic thrust of American democracy. Therefore I oppose it as an American who believes in democracy. It also denies the compassionate, universal spirit of Christianity. Therefore I oppose it as a Christian.

But let us come back to those young people sitting quietly at the lunch counter. These young people, though quiet, are committing an officially disorderly act. It's always dangerous to guess what may be in people's hearts and minds; but my guess is that, beneath the excitement, the fear, the tense nerves, there has been in these demonstrators a sense of order and quiet which previously they had seldom known. They had never agreed to be segregated, to be shunted out of the mainstream of our culture. Nobody asked them. We white people had the power, and we used it. We said that we were using it to preserve the peace, but they knew we were using it because we thought we were better than they. Put yourself in the Negro's place, and imagine the disorder this stirs up in your mind. When, therefore, these, young people rose against the social order, they were expressing an inner sense of order that had been denied and trampled upon for a long time.

Segregation is going now for many reasons, but most of all because it rested upon spiritual disorder. The physical and social world in which our fathers lived was so confused and threatening, so close to chaos, that they were induced to hammer out some kind of order regardless of what it did to their spirits. We today have no such excuse. So far as the local problems of the South are concerned, we live in far happier times. (I do not forget the atomic cloud.) Being therefore less constrained by circumstances to enforce an iron order, we are better able to sense the inner disorder that this outer order causes. If now, simply out of complacency or out of selfish desire to maintain our privileged position, we refuse to consider and weigh the inner disorder, we shall surely be condemned. In the past, God may have winked at our racial misdeeds; but now he is looking at us. We continue the disorder at our peril.

The racial revolution, which is showing its influence even in the South, is world-wide. We ought to remember this when we are prone to blame a few individuals for the radical changes which are taking place. I do not say that because it is world-wide it is necessarily God's direct will. But if we believe in God's providence, I think we could hardly believe that such a world-wide movement was taking place in opposition to providence.

The world racial revolution is primarily a revolt of so-called "natives" against imperial control. They are now demanding freedom, respect, and a fairer share in the goods they have helped to produce. As Christians how can we deny them this? Indeed, we should be pleased, both as democratic Americans and as Christians, that these millions are coming of age, and are asking to be treated like men.

The Negroes of the South, and of America, are strictly a part of this revolution. In a certain sense the Negroes of America are colonials. When the structure of colonialism collapses throughout the world it is at least appropriate, if not inevitable, that it should collapse here.

In spite of the resistance with which many southerners and indeed many Americans greet this inevitable collapse, the will to defend segregation steadily grows weaker. Why? Because year by year we move further from its bitter causes in Reconstruction. We have less reason to support it. Also, because we, too, are moved by a zeal for democracy, and cannot support from the heart this undemocratic practice. Finally, because the will with which men support any institution is directly related to their hope of maintaining it. Daily the hope of maintaining segregation grows less.

I do not need to emphasize the fact that this racial revolution is occurring throughout the United States. It may have begun in the South; its chief locus may still be the South; it is certainly evident now in the big cities across the nation; but there are good grounds for believing that the South will resolve this problem before the rest of the nation does. The reason, simply, is that southerners, white and colored, have all lived with it, and with one another, and in the process have learned far more of the answers than at the moment they realize.

There are the answers evident, for example, in the non-violent nature of the Negro's revolution. It is true that the Negroes may have adopted the strategy of non-violence partly because historically the South has been prone to violence and quick on the trigger. Non-violence seemed the most practicable method of challenging the system. But they have adopted it also because they have learned a patience which is rooted in the Christian religion, and they have a Christian—and a southern—faith in their white neighbors. This non-violent revolution is occurring not solely because we have been both undemocratic and unchristian in our treatment of Negroes, but also because we have been, however limitedly, Christian. Many southerners have talked as if the southern way of life was simply segregation, discrimination, and the Negro "in his place" at the bottom. This is to sell the South sadly short; this is to make ourselves out far worse than we are.

As selfish, as complacent, as proud as we have been, there has also been God's grace working among us. It is the presence of grace that gives to this revolution its peculiar character. As Christians we should ponder this. Is not grace the key word in Calvinistic theology? And yet today we look around us and are disturbed, irritated, angry, frightened. Let us trust God and look closer. We shall find in the Negro movement qualities and attitudes which neither the Negroes nor the whites intended, but which have simply grown out of the life of the South. If these unplanned attitudes are commendable, I should say they illustrate the grace of God.

Let us consider again those young people sitting at lunch counters in the first faint dawn of their movement. Everybody has noticed their excellent manners, often in such contrast to the unmannerliness of the white delinquents who stood around. Is not good manners the quality on which the South, justly, or unjustly, has prided itself most? Were not these Negro youngsters, then, by this standard, good southerners?

But ah, you say, they were violating racial etiquette. Well, they were. In the democratic world into which they had been born, stirred by the wind of freedom which at long last had blown to them across the pages of the Bible, they saw no place now for racial etiquette. They did not declaim against it; they simply discarded it. For they were engaged, however quietly, in a revolution. And perhaps the essence of this revolution is a redefinition of the great words of the South. We have been a people of great words: courtesy, honor, integrity, truth, courage, love. We are being asked now to look at these words and see what they mean for today. Maybe now, in this revolution, the South will not be lost but found. Found for its place in the modern world.

These Negro youngsters came with good manners and also with a religious heart. As I read the history of the South, we are generally a people of deep religious convictions and of good manners. But time and again I sense a flaw, a gap, between the manners and the religion. There is always some gap between culture and any world religion, Christianity most of all. In the South, however, the gap was too great. There was a complex social culture, a rich web of manners, covering the surface of life, shutting off from daily view the mystery, the violence, the terror of life. It was hoped that individualistic Protestant religion would take care of this, but a highly social life and a highly individualistic religion hardly go together.

Look again: here, in these well-mannered, quiet-spirited, committed youngsters the gap is closed. They are at home in this world and in another. They are at home in this world because they are at home in another. Just as they adopted southern manners but discarded racial etiquette, so they combined with the deep piety, the personal religion of the South, a sense of social justice drawn straight from the great prophets but never stressed in the South before. They are not revolutionary in being religious; the South is religious. They are revolutionary in combining with the religious piety of the South a religious demand for social justice which the South could never make.

Why could it not make it? Because of slavery, and, afterwards, of segregation. We may have been hypocrites—all men are, more or less; but we weren't such hypocrites as to preach social justice while maintaining slavery and segregation. What did we do then? We stressed love, with all its variations: kindliness, courtesy, good humor. Though I think love is the root and the fruit of the universe, in this world love needs justice to support it. Try to express it without at the same time striving for justice, and you get sentimentality. Southerners are admittedly sentimental. We like the songs at twilight, the Carolina moons, the sunset all misty through the Spanish moss; but we ought to know when we are sentimental, saving the mood perhaps for those moments when day fades into night, not trying to use it at high noon. We southerners try it at high noon, and in regard to our perennially most urgent problem, race. We see the Negro through a haze; we had to see the Negro like this; we couldn't bear to see him as he was.

And now he comes, in the best manners of the South, *redefined*, with the religiously committed heart of the South, *redefined*, trying to unite courtesy and Christianity, piety and justice.

Is not this God's most gracious Spirit giving us at last what we tried so long unsuccessfully to get? But giving it to us in a form nobody had planned or even dreamed of? The Negro was brought here to speed the production of tobacco and cotton. In our last desperate defense of slavery we said—our own Dr. Thornwell said it—that God had brought the Negro here in order that he might receive the message of salvation. Maybe Dr. Thornwell was right. Maybe the Negro has received through us, by God's grace, a clearer realization than we ourselves had. This may be another case of the stone the builders rejected. If it is, it is a sharp rebuke to our pride. For we shall have gained what we always strove for, but by a means we neither desired nor planned, so that we find it hard now to accept. It is hard, brethren, to accept the grace of God.

As I see the racial revolution in the South, then, it is the Spirit of God working for freedom against bondage, and it is the spirit of the South discarding old evils, creating new goods. We should welcome the revolution, both as Christians and as southerners—as southern Christians. If we cannot welcome it completely, we should at least not fear it. "All things work together for good to them that love God." Though our world is changing it is not necessarily decaying. "My Father is working," said Jesus, "and I am working." Let us work with him.

§104 Mildred Bell Johnson

Born to a former slave, Mildred Bell Johnson was raised in Middlesboro, Kentucky. After receiving a B.S. from Kentucky State University, Bell Johnson moved to Birmingham, Alabama in 1926, where she taught nursery school until 1936. That same year she married Robert C. Johnson, a Birmingham high school principal. They had two daughters, Barbara and Alma. The latter would marry a Jamaican immigrant by the name of Colin Powell.

A dedicated community activist, Bell Johnson started the first Girl Scout troop for African American girls in Alabama. She was also actively involved in the United Church of Christ (UCC), where she served as a representative of the UCC to the National Council of Churches, and vice president of the National Fellowship of Congregational Christian Women. Bell Johnson later became the first African American woman to hold high elective office in the UCC as she became assistant moderator of the Fourth General Synod in 1963. In this capacity, she traveled and spoke extensively with UCC audiences, often on the theme of improving race relations.

In her address before a Minnesota UCC gathering, Bell Johnson speaks at length about the United Church of Christ's duty in the volatile climate of 1964. Employing the extended metaphors of roots, trees, branches and soil, Bell Johnson argues that the Negro Revolution has come to full flower in spite of 350 years of abuse. Only a deep and abiding faith in God had prevented withering, decay, and death. But even as this faith sustained Black Americans, Bell Johnson castigates many nameless members of the UCC for not participating actively in its Racial Justice Now campaign. As such, the speech provides a unique window on race relations in the spring of 1964, while simultaneously a uniquely powerful black woman offers a very pointed critique of United Church of Christ racial politics and participation.

Deep are the Roots

Minnesota Conference, United Church of Christ

May 12, 1964

A play on Broadway, New York some years ago had as its title Deep Are The Roots. It was a problem play which dealt with the American Dilemma . . . the Negro. Seeing the play proved to be a redeeming influence upon my understanding, if not acceptance, of racial prejudice with which I have lived through the years since; and the lessons it taught stand me in good stead as I seek to develop a saving philosophy toward current events in race relations.

The underlying causes for the existing resistance to the eradication of segregation in our national life, including the rationalization of many who oppose the implementation of civil rights legislation, are to be found in the deep roots of racial prejudice. Any efforts to rid our nation of the resulting effects must take this root system and its far- reaching enmeshing into the soil and soul of our nation into account.

It has a growth history of three hundred fifty years and presents a formidable outgrowth, a tree of gigantic proportions. Utter discouragement prevails for those of us who care, until we come to realize that there are other root systems with the same growth history.

One such concern is that which dwells in the heritage of our United Church of Christ. Its devotion to Christian ideals as they related to freedom and a determination to separate itself from any forces which deny freedom surely began years ago. A small band set sail from Leiden for a new land, but surely too this root system stretched forth in concern over an incident of one hundred twenty six years ago when in 1839 a group of African slaves, captured on the coast of West Africa, were brought across the ocean chained to the hull of a ship called the Amistad. They were sold at auction in Cuba to a slave merchant who proposed to sell them again in America.

En route from Cuba the slaves mutinied, murdered the captain and set sail on a course which they believed would return them to their home.

An error of navigation carried them to the proximity of New England where they were arrested, jailed, and awaited what they and most people believed: inevitable death. In Connecticut a group of businessmen (we have always believed them to have been Congregational laymen) formed a committee (proof enough!) for their defense. At long last the case was brought to the Supreme Court of the United States. The lawyer for the defense was John Quincy Adams, former president of the U.S., who in his defense summary pointed to the wall of the courtroom saying as he pointed to the Declaration of Independence hanging there, "Are these the principles upon which the United States will stand before the world?"

The slaves were acquitted.

This same document hangs on the walls of thousands of school rooms across our country; and today one hundred twenty six years since the acquittal of the slaves of the Amistad, the children of twenty million Negroes ask the same question as they contemplate the meaning of these words, "We hold these truths to be self evident. . . ."

Concurrent with the events of the Amistad, the abolitionist movement was growing in New England. Ministers and laymen of the Congregational Church become involved in the movement, they were active in the Underground Railroad (an illegal, nefarious and meddlesome occupation in the minds of its critics) but nevertheless they were busy helping, hiding, healing—active in a movement to the extent of forming a cadre for an emancipation. There your ancestors and mine joined in becoming America's first non-violent protest movement! May our tribe increase!

Through one hundred twenty six years these roots of concern for justice, humanity and love of fellowman spread and deepened and sent forth a tree which spread its branches in many directions, until in Denver, Colorado at the Fourth General Synod of the U.C.C. this tree came to magnificent flower as it took action—precedented by that of the laymen of Connecticut. A committee was formed!

Hear new the words of the president of the United Church of Christ as he sets the stage for the forming of the Committee for Racial Justice Now: "This General Synod will not adjourn without speaking out prophetically and boldly, courageously and in compassion, so that in the minds of the members of the United Church of Christ and in the Negro community there will be no question as to where we stand. Not only will we call this people to law and order, but to justice and brotherhood. We shall back our pronouncements with our lives. To do less than this would be to forsake our responsibilities, and to be unworthy of our Lord."

So there in Denver, Colorado, July 1963, The United Church adopted a Call for Racial Justice Now and by so doing fulfilled again its promise.

Yet another root system I would expose for you, but before I do there is a pertinent story: In my garden there grows a pecan tree; several years ago it was a shabby little tree, ridiculed by the family because it had failed after several years of maturity to perform its promise. It was taking up space enough for a fruitful tree but it bore no fruit. The decision was made to dig it up and plant another; but a friend came along who asked if he might try to make it bear. We promised him not half the pecans but all if he could make the tree bear.

So one day he came, carrying not the correct instruments for tree culture—spray, plant food, pruning shears—but carrying a gunny sack in which were a baseball bat, an ax and a large supply of lime and lye.

In amusement we watched as he climbed the tree with his baseball bat, beat upon its branches, scarring the bark and shattering off leaves. When he climbed to the ground he took out the ax, cut the surface roots, dug a trench around the tree and threw in lye and lime, then topped off his brutal treatment by pouring boiling water around the base of the tree.

The family shrugged and went inside the house saying, "Well that's an inexpensive way of getting rid of an unwanted tree."

Later we knew that in our cynicism we had overlooked an established fact in horticulture, in nature, and in the way of all life. For while we were ignoring the effect of the ill-treatment given the tree, it was responding to the treatment after a manner God has made. In its struggle to survive, it put forth a gigantic effort, so great that the best within it came to fruition. When fall came we noticed it again. . . a tall and stately tree with abundant foliage . . . new shiny bark and a bumper crop of pecans.

Analogous to this tree is the Negro revolution, with three hundred fifty years of persecution, of being defiled, flayed, beaten, spat upon, disfranchised, disinherited, this root system comes at long last to flower in the fulfillment of its promise. A promise of faith engendered by deep religious orientation to life, by a monstrous struggle to survive, and its only hope for survival being a faith and trust in God. By the simple acceptance of the Christian gospel through tears, through prayers, clinging to the preached word of God, this race composed songs of the spirit: "I'm gonna tell God how you treat me." "One of these days I'm gonna lay down this heavy load." "O Lord, My good Lord keep me from sinking down," striving to live, to put forth branches—this tree comes now in 1964 to full stature as a redemptive influence in our democracy. Offering America a new moral strength, the race comes singing a new song, "We shall overcome." It is at this point in our church's history that again you and I are joined again in a non-violent protest movement as we seek to work for Racial Justice Now.

Since the forming of the Committee for Racial Justice Now, it has been about its delegations. Our publications are full of reports of the committee, and I hope you have read them all. But I am a group worker and know all too well that printed materials circulated by an organization are sometimes not read and that even when they are their message is never so effective as person to person communication, so without any hesitancy I am pleased to delineate the work of the Committee for Racial Justice Now.

This is the program launched last summer at the General Synod in response to the racial crisis in our country. The Committee for Racial Justice Now with eleven members, under the direction of Dr. Garry Oniki, has really accomplished much in these nine months. Let me give you the outline of the story: First, in the last half of 1963, $147,000 was collected in special offerings and gifts to bear the cost of Racial Justice Now. The amount was $170,988.24 by April 1st 1964. Second, during this time up to August 20, 2,790 churches declared themselves to be open membership churches. This represents 33.2 percent of the churches within the United Church of Christ. More than 4,100 persons have committed themselves as a part of the Fellowship of the Committed. These people are pledged to do five things:

1. I commit myself as a Christian: to work now for inclusive membership in my church;

2. To seek now the enactment of appropriate civil rights legislation in the areas of education, employment, housing, public accommodations, and in voting at every level of government and to protest the evasion of such laws;

3. To engage now in persuasion, in negotiation, in reconciliation and in non-violent demonstrations when such actions are necessary for racial justice;

4. To establish now at least one friendship across racial and cultural lines;

5. To fortify myself and deepen my commitment to racial unity and justice by daily prayer, by study and by sharing my experience with others.

Actually, this organizational part of the Committee on Racial Justice Now is but a framework. Let me give you a few examples of the kinds of things that it has been engaged in.

The Committee has worked out a program of counsel and financial aid to ministers who might incur difficulties because of a witness for racial justice. They share this work with the Council for Church and Ministry.

For example, a minister in a mid-western city was fired because of his vigorous insistence that the church he served minister to the newcomers in the neighborhood; the newcomers happened to be predominantly Negro. Ironically, after he had been dismissed, a city wide civic organization granted him its annual brotherhood award for his leadership in furthering good human relations. The Committee has provided counsel and financial assistance to this man while he was seeking a new position. The Committee has also worked out criteria for support of individuals who have been arrested while witnessing for racial justice. This support is based on the right granted by our legal system that bail is available when one is charged with a crime. Bail does not excuse one from trial, even when local laws are in violation of one's constitutional rights. Setting of excessive bail has been used in many cases against those who struggle for racial justice as an instrument of punishment against them.

For example, a young white woman who was trained as a director of Christian Education, went to work for a civil rights group which was engaged in a voter registration drive in Mississippi. She witnessed a policeman beating a Negro man; she testified to this fact before a grand jury. The man was forced to withdraw his complaint and she was in turn charged with perjury. Bail was set at $5,000. She is a member of the United Church of Christ.

The Committee has also worked as an enabling force to undergird the various units of the United Church of Christ as they work to be a more vigorous witness for racial justice now in and to the world.

For example, the Committee has joined with the Board for Homeland Ministries to provide a film which will serve as a vital tool for stimulating citizens to register to vote in spite of personal hardships which may be inflicted on them and in instances where an apathy has developed resulting from long deprivation of this basic citizenship right.

For example, the Committee has provided scholarship aid to economically deprived Negro students in predominantly white colleges. One such grant made possible the registration of the first non-white day student in one of our church-related colleges in the south.

For example, the Committee extended aid to the Washington-North Idaho Conference for a denominational contribution to CURE (Christians United for Racial Unity) where eight denominations joined together to attempt to mobilize support of the churches for housing referendums in Tacoma and Seattle, Washington. In this way our churches in the area were able to involve themselves directly in the struggle for racial justice now.

A complete report of money expended for each of the projects in which the Committee has been engaged is to be found in FACTS.

Is it a good report? Does the amount given reflect the limits of our concern? Well, as one of the millions for whom justice is sought I must say that I surely hope that this amount of money given to carry out the work which has been delegated to the Committee for Racial Justice Now is not a reflection of the concern of the church. Perchance the concern evidenced is in direct proportion to the knowledge owned as it is related to current history. If there should happen to be any one here who can help bring enlightenment to those who need it, be patient with me for a few minutes and I will speak of just some of the reasons for crying out that racial justice is needed, and my speaking will not be because I have watched television, or read the news magazines as most of you have but because of personal experiences.

[Bell Johnson lists personal experiences with the KKK, inferior schools, local bus travels, closed cafes and motels, police brutality, house bombings, dangers in church, and church bombings].

These experiences should validate my prerogative to say to you that the denomination's emergency appeal has not been successful.

We had hoped for $300,000 for the appeal in October 1963; but we have received as before stated through March 1964 only $170,988.24.

We are 7,000 churches; 1,928 have contributed. This is a fact that hurts. I ask you to which of the two root systems do you think the other 5,072 churches belong? To that system rooted in soil of concern for justice, or to that system rooted in the deep earth of prejudice or unconcern which is of course loss of justice by default.

It is wrong to pass judgment, and I do not. I simply conclude that many churches have not understood many things—among them the background of the Negro Revolution in America. This is understandable. Many people have not thought about the problem; it makes one uncomfortable to have full knowledge of unpleasant events. These people turn the page or flip off the T.V. or engage in various activities to keep a peaceful mind.

Some have questioned where the money goes any way. Some have taken issue with the sit-ins, etc., or have misunderstood bail bonds promised. Some have felt that human rights cannot be legislated any way so why all this dither about writing Senators? Some have alleged that such a program stiffens the southern opposition and negates all that we hoped to accomplish in that area. Still others have felt that the church should not become involved.

The answers to some of these assertions and questions are again to be found in at least one of our church publications but also again perhaps I can lift up some of these for further clarification.

Why sit in, march and make an undignified spectacle of ourselves? The protest in many places is an organized one which has 4 steps: (1) the collection of facts to determine if injustice exists; (2) go to the people who are in position to make some changes in community affairs and try to negotiate with them; (3) self-purification; (4) direct action.

In gathering facts across the country the movement has had adequate assistance. Documented facts, some of which you heard if you listened to the former president of the U.S. on June 11. "Every American ought to have the right to be treated as he would want to be treated as one would wish his children to be treated but this is not true. The Negro baby born in American today, regardless of the section or the state in which he is born, has about one half as much chance of completing high school as a white baby, born in the same place on the same day. 1/3 as much chance of completing college; 1/3 as much chance of becoming a professional man; twice as much chance of becoming unemployed; about 1/7 as much chance of ever earning 10,000 dollars. If any American, because his skin is dark, cannot eat lunch in a restaurant open to the public; if he cannot send his children to the best public schools available; if he cannot enjoy the full and free life which all of us want, then who among you would be content to have his skin changed and stand in his place?"

Who of you, which of the members of the 5,072 churches would not react in a similar manner under leadership which interprets to them that this sitting in—wading in—marching—praying—etc., will make some impact upon the conscience of the nation and create a climate for change?

Many sources furnish facts-documentaries for study. One, an Inter-Citizens Committee of Birmingham furnishes affidavits of Negroes whose stories of police brutality lift up a need for the hiring of Negro police in that area. Voices are lifted up by conscience, [members of the] white community. And after many instances, bonafide information has been assembled, the people are called and an educational process begins. Prayer meetings, voter registration classes. Then business and local government are informed that, beginning at a stated time, demonstrations will begin. Direct action takes place.

This is a strategy and it is not new; it is an American tradition. There are calculated risks taken in such demonstration . . . injury, death, failure of demonstrators to maintain non-violent attitudes, participation in demonstrations by untrained· groups . . . irresponsible trouble-makers, exploitation of the idea by unscrupulous leaders.

But notwithstanding all risks and justification of much constructive criticism, the protests have had an impact.

Question: Does not this stiffen resistance of southerners and thus mitigate against the things the movement seeks?

Answer: Yes—this is likely.

But history records slim chance of positions of established privilege being abdicated except as a must.

Take a look from the banks of the Thames River, Surrey England 1815. King John is confronted by representatives of under-privileged people of England. There, not by persuasion or negotiation, did he recognize the drawn Magna Carta and set his royal seal upon it, but by realization that he had no choice. Stand beside the Column of July in Paris, France; remember the Bastille that stood there prior to July 14, 1789; know that it symbolizes the winning of freedom and equality by the French People. Live again in our own history with the spirit of '76. Why does the Battle Hymn of the Republic thrill you? Because a thing as precious as Freedom is worth any price.

Winston Churchill voices the determination of the British people for victory and for the continued holding of their freedom. His words can be translated into the Negro slogans of 1963: "Victory in spite of terror; victory however long the road may be, for without it there is no survival." Thousands of Negro young adults have no desire to live any longer without dignity.

They would borrow further the language of Churchill. They would say, "We shall not flag or fail . . . we shall protest with our bodies on the streets of Alabama, march on the streets of Mississippi, sit in restaurants, wade in beaches, kneel in churches . . . with growing confidence and with increased support from others who see our just cause. We shall contend for freedom whatever the cost. We shall never stop as long as America is free and 20 million of her local citizens are less than free."

When historians record the Fine Hours of many peoples, The March on Washington will stand among their selections.

To the question, why use the word NOW in the Racial Justice emphasis?

I would say that the use of the adverb NOW takes away the possibility of transporting the work needed to be done into the outworn channels of verbiage—where pronouncements, resolutions, empty promises, long range plans for action exist. Someone has rightfully asserted that one of the ways to get any desired action out of the way is to appoint a committee. The General Synod evidently recognized this danger so it attached the simple word NOW.

One of the persons questioned in the survey made by the *Newsweek* magazine, which throws much light upon the meaning of the Revolution, had this to say about NOW versus gradualism. "If a man is choking me I want his hands off my throat Now—not gradually."

And again "my definition of today is yesterday."

Another question to which many churches desire an answer before they participate in the appeal is a typical one and tragically is it a typical one.

Why should the church become involved?

This question is a summation of perhaps the whole sad state into which the church has allowed itself to wander. It highlights our reluctance to see The Church as a community of believers who are charged not to come into the church but to go out of the church into all the world.

Many of us would have responded generously and promptly to any appeal if it had only been far enough geographically from our doorsteps.

We could have taken real satisfaction in having given to right the wrong being done to any persons if only we could take consolation in having given alms, failing to remember that gifts of rings and jewels and money are not truly gifts at all but often they are apologies for the only real gifts of ourselves.

Some reluctance to relate the lives we live as butchers, bakers, candlestick makers, doctors, lawyers, Indian chiefs is a reluctance to truly accept Jesus Christ in his supreme Lordship and to listen to his commandments that we go into all the world—and not a general world in this instance but a very particular and a very specific world of 1964.

An America of which the Swedish sociologist a generation ago said in speaking of America's dilemma, as he observed that the fundamental clash between the abiding faith of white Americans with their creed of liberty and justice for all and their certain knowledge that they are denying the Negro this democratic heritage is a breach that should be and must be closed for the future welfare of the nation, both at home and in its relation to other nations.

If Gunnar Myrdal's conclusion had any validity a generation ago before the tremendous knowledge of and success in exploration of outer space, before the emergence of 28 new independent African nations, before the threatening prospect of 2/3 of the earth's people of color consolidating their grievances against the white 1/3 of the earth's people . . . if this conclusion had food for thought 20 years ago how much more does it have truth today?

Much as white people wish to continue to ignore it the problem will not go away. Racial injustice is an economic waste and a danger and a threat to all we believe. Not to become involved then is more than willful blindness; it is sheer foolishness; it is a line for our epitaphs.

I wish there was time for me to answer all of the questions of all the 5,072 churches of whom I hope no one is in the Minnesota Conference, but of course I cannot. There is one more that I feel compelled to address myself, that of the request from the General Synod that churches declare themselves to have OPEN MEMBERSHIP. What an easy request with which to comply. But as of March 20, only 2,326 of 7,000 churches had done so. The resistance to this request reflects a healthy obstinacy typical of our democratic and complete autonomous church life. I admire the spirit which says, "don't ask me if I am good," "mind your own business," "don't you dare suggest that we are not open," and can only conclude that most of our churches fail to see the importance of supporting racial justice to this extent. Such a request was not idly made, but so that by example the many might influence the few who are adamant about open church membership. Also there is the minority in our southern conferences who would like to have the support of the majority elsewhere; it would give them courage to take the step away from such a church as I know where the deacons asserted their policy one Sunday morning as a group of kneel-in protestors went to their door. "This church was built by and for white people." Thousands of churches making such a declaration would point the way for the few, among which I know have one member who is a member of the state legislature and has presented a bill which gives police power to the officials of the church in order that arrests, or whatever measures are needed, will be taken if Negroes seek to worship in a white church.

Are the roots of your church entangled with these deep roots?

I do not really believe that our hesitancy to do so is any thing more than failure to see the urgency of the matter.

Finally I would speak boldly to you concerning your involvement in this issue in terms of your personal and corporate relation to the gospel. Have no fear, I shall not attempt to interpret these passages of scripture. But do try them on as you think about the work of the Committee for Racial Justice Now and as hopefully you seek to winnow the truth from the perhaps too emotionally charged remarks I have sought to make. Two scriptures, Micah: "And what doth the Lord require of Me?" The other Esther: "Think not with thyself that though shalt escape in the king's house more than all the Jews. For if thou altogether holdest thy peace at this time then shall enlargement and deliverance arise from another but thou and they father's house shall be destroyed; and who knoweth but thou art come into the kingdom for such a time as this."

Deep are the roots of hate and prejudice.

But also deep are the roots of the faith and hope and determination of America's Negroes.

Deep are the roots of our United Church heritage in the areas of racial justice.

"A cause can never be lost or stayed that takes the course of what God has made that is not trusting in walls or towers but silently grows from the seed to flower. There by itself like a tree it shows how high it reaches as deep it grows and when the storms are its branches shaking . . . it deeper root in the ground is taking."

§105 Ralph David Abernathy

Ralph David Abernathy's biography appears in the introduction to his October 8, 1961 sermon in Atlanta, Georgia. Less than two months before Lyndon Johnson would sign the Civil Rights Act of 1964, Abernathy's speech to the American Baptist Convention showcases his considerable preaching talents. Invoking biblical passages typically associated with Martin Luther King, Jr., Abernathy skillfully and frequently links the successes of the freedom movement with the prophetic and apocalyptic. Note that Abernathy was not addressing the National Baptist Convention, a huge organization of black Baptists whose loyalties King (and Abernathy) coveted. Led by the "black pope," Reverend J. H. Jackson, the rivalry for control of the NBC was so inflamed that a riot broke out at the 1961 convention, resulting in the death of Reverend A. G. Wright of Detroit. Only after his failed takeover bid did King return prominently to the civil disobedience theater.

Abernathy's rhetoric in Atlantic City displays a marked physicality. The story of the Negro in search of freedom in American is one of bloodshed, of tears, of brutal toil and broken backs, and of course physical death. In this corporeal struggle had the Negro earned his freedom. Four centuries of suffering had vouchsafed full and equal rights. Yet in another sense, Abernathy states emphatically that the quest for freedom is less about suffering and far more about being "children of God." Being made in his image and likeness, Abernathy claims, "has caused the Negro to keep pushing on in this revolution." Only a revolution sanctioned by God could sustain the physical devastation wrought by white racism.

Even so, Abernathy chides the church for its inactivity and silence—presumably both black and white. Abernathy impugns the church by contrast: "for too long the church has not been a voice, but rather an echo; it has not been a light, but rather a reflection; it has not been a city on a hill, but rather a suburb in the valley; it has not been a tank out in the front of the battle, but rather it has been an old ambulance in the rear, picking up the wounded and caring for the dying."

Abernathy closes the speech by emphasizing the work that remains to be done in economics, politics, housing, and education. While the ends were purely secular, the means were not. The "philosophy of love manifested by Thoreau, Mahatma Gandhi, and Jesus Christ" ensured both a just and a nonviolent outcome.

Love and Race Relations

American Baptist Convention, Atlantic City, New Jersey
May 19, 1964

Thank you. Mr. Chairman; the Honorable Harold E. Stassen, President of this distinguished body; fellow Pastors and Ministers of the Gospel; officers, members and my dear friends.

First, I wish to express my profound thanks and appreciation to you for inviting me to address this session of our great Convention. You may be assured that I count this among one of the highest moments of my life and I will treasure it until I enter the silent halls of eternity.

"The Spirit of the Lord is upon me, because He hath anointed me to preach the gospel to the poor; He hath sent me to heal the brokenhearted, to preach deliverance to the captives, and recovering of sight to the blind, to set at liberty them that are bruised. To preach the acceptable year of the Lord."—St. Luke 4:18-19.

Truly, for me this is a mountain-top experience and like the prophet of old, I must say "it is good for us be here." But, as I stand here this evening on top of this mountain and take a look back into the pages of history at the long, rough and rugged road over which our civilization has come; as I survey the trash, ruin and decay which encompass the church and Christians as we meet here; as I gaze into the future and see the many obstacles which must be removed before the kingdom comes; and as I look into the faces of these who are chosen by God to save the world, I must confess that I cannot speak in joyful sounds, but I must do so in fear and trembling. This I do, for I am well aware of the fact that a hand is writing on the wall and the clock is fastly ticking toward the hour of man's doom and his utter destruction. Time is absolutely running out, and on your shoulders and mine rest the responsibility of running through the streets and crying as did the mighty prophet Amos, "Let justice roll down like waters and righteousness like a mighty stream." Yes, in our hands the future of the nations of the world rest. So, when I think of the task which is mine this evening, that of reminding us of our duties and responsibilities as ministers of Jesus Christ and disciples of the lowly Nazarene, the joy which I had anticipated for this hour leaves me, and seemingly I hear a strange voice saying, "pull off thy shoes, for the ground on which thou standest is holy."

Almost three long centuries and a half ago now, our forefathers landed on American soil. They were kidnapped and brought here from the sunny shores of Africa against their wishes and their will. They sailed the tempestuous seas bound in chains and shackles, and upon their arrival, like cattle of the field, they were branded with hot irons. Robbed of their country, their culture, their language, their families, their relatives and friends. They were forced to start life anew as poor pilgrims of sorrow. They were denied freedom, their rights and the bare necessities of life. The Negro was compelled to face the future in a strange land, helpless and even sometimes hopeless. Yes, my forefathers were compelled to launch out in the dark and dim unknown even as a ship without a compass, or a boat without a sail; a fox without a hole or a bird without a song. But today, hope has been restored by the radiating light of the promised land which flashes every now and then on the horizon; direction is now found by a chart and compass which come from the eternal and everlasting God and music has returned to the soul and is even heard according to the freedom fighters, in the air. It is a true fact, the movement is moving and God's truth is marching on.

Beyond a shadow of a doubt, the current movement in this country to gain total freedom for the Negro can accurately be called the most moving drama of the twentieth century. The main characters in this magnificent drama are Negroes themselves and the stage is the entire country, with most of the acting taking place in the southern section. As one of the participants, I wish to say that we are now in the final act of this civil rights drama and it will not be long before the curtains will fall. You see, the Negro has been denied his civil rights ever since he first landed here in 1619. It is true that he has known 244 years of the long, bitter and desolate night of slavery and then 101 weary years of man's inhumanity to man under the so-called, "separate but equal" system. But today, a restlessness is found in the Negro community. It is present in every section, every state, every city, every village and even the rural areas of this nation. This restlessness is expressed in sit-ins, wade-ins, kneel-ins, freedom rides, marches, picketing, boycotts, selective patronage campaigns and many other forms of demonstration. The participants come from every walk of life and include adults, young people and even children. These Americans are determined to win their civil rights. These rights are guaranteed all citizens by the Bill of Rights, the Declaration of Independence and the Federal Constitution.

But the continued denial of these rights to some citizens by certain states solely because of their race has brought us to this critical hour in the life of our nation and made "race" one of the most foremost problems of our time. You see, for the first time in the history of the Negro in America, he is rising up demanding his freedom. He has been cured from the paralyzing disease of intimidation and emancipated from the crippling shackles of fear. Thus, his head is high, his shoulders are up and his back is straight, and people can only ride on your back when you are bent over.

The desire for freedom on the part of Negroes did not come about only after the 1954 Supreme Court's public schools desegregation decision. This desire for freedom is as old as the Negro himself and he has always prized it more dearly than life. Our trail is well marked by the blood of brave men and women who took death because they were not given liberty. Let it be known that there is much truth in the words of our spiritual, "Before I'll be a slave, I'll be buried in my grave, and go home to my Lord and be free." The sentiment expressed in these words pervades the air and everywhere there is heard Freedom, Freedom, Freedom, Now!! Yes, the people who tilled the fields and cleared the new ground, who dug the ditches, cared for the sick and helped to build this nation with their sweat, blood and tears wish now to enjoy the fruits of the land. We have made a noble contribution to the life and welfare of America. For two centuries and a half, our fathers worked in the fields and made cotton king. They were treated not as persons, but rather as things. Beaten and bruised by mean and cruel taskmasters, they never lost faith in themselves, their fellowman nor the almighty God. Hear them singing in the cotton patches of Mississippi, Alabama, Georgia, Louisiana and all over the South, "Keep inching and inching along, we'll get there by and by," "I'm so glad troubles don't last always," "Soon I'll be done with the troubled world." They had faith.

Even when they were sold down the river to the highest bidder, husbands separated from their wives, fathers from their sons and mothers from their daughters, they could envision a reunion in a land just beyond the river where the wicked will cease from troubling and the weary will be at rest; and from their sun-parched lips and burdened souls, they would cry out, "My Lord, what a morning."

James Weldon Johnson has well said:

> Stony the road we've trod, bitter the chastening rod, felt in the
> days when hope unborn had died,
> Yet with a steady beat, have not our weary feet, come to the place
> for which our fathers died.
> We have come over the way that with tears have been watered,
> We have come treading the path of the blood of the slaughtered,
> Out of our gloomy path, till now we stand at last
> Where the white gleam of our bright star is cast.

So, you see the record is clear. This race, the Negro race has suffered much in our land and history must record the fact that his contributions far exceed his sufferings. Yet in spite of his lot, he has remained loyal to the nation. He has participated in every war and he has given his life defending our homeland. For all the way from Boston Commons, when Crispus Attucks, the first to give his blood in the revolution to bring this nation into being, you can trace the course of American wars down to the present time by the shed blood of black men. For whether it was on the beaches on Normandy or that sad Sunday morning at Pearl Harbor, our fathers and sons fought and died. Yes, on the fields of France, the hills of Italy and throughout the Pacific and European Theaters of operation, black and white men died side by side in order that Democracy might live. Their bones are bleaching this very evening in every national cemetery and from their graves their silent cry to the pharaohs of the Egypts of injustice, inequality, segregation, discrimination and bigotry is, "let my people go."

But the demand for freedom is not based solely upon the fact that the Negro has earned a right to it through his generations of suffering and his marvelous contributions. For we realize today as never before that the future of our nation will depend to a very large degree upon the speedy solution of the race problem. It is a true fact, "a house cannot stand divided against itself." And just as it was true in the days of President Abraham Lincoln, when the nation could not survive half slave and half free, so it is today, we will all be saved together, or we shall all perish separately. The nations of the world are saying to America today in no uncertain terms, "We can't hear what you say about liberty and justice for all, for seeing how you practice Jim-Crowism and inequality for some—you must practice what you preach." So you see, in spite of our wealth, our vast mineral and natural resources, our scientific and technical advancements, our might and power, we shall soon become a second rate nation, losing our goods as well as our souls, unless we learn to respect the worth and dignity of all human personality. For the people of the world know now that, "man cannot live by bread alone." So our love for this country will not let us stand idly by and see it destroyed by its own wickedness, ignorance and barbarity. But rather, we seek to redeem the soul of America, and create a society built on love and brotherhood. Segregation is evil. Segregation is a sin. Segregation is a sickness—a disease which will eventually destroy the segregators as well as the segregated.

But there is another reason why the Negro is engaged in the present nonviolent revolution. This reason is more basic than either of the first two I have already mentioned, and might I add, it is more fundamental and important. This reason is, we are all children of God. God is our Father and we are all brothers, made in the image and likeness of Him. This being true, then God loves all of His children, and He loves them alike. A realization of this fact must lead us all to know that there is but one race and that is the human race. For, "out of one blood, God has created all nations to dwell upon the face of this earth" says our Holy Bible. It has been an awareness of this eternal fact that has caused the Negro to keep pushing on in this revolution. In 1955–56, it caused fifty thousand Negroes in Montgomery, Alabama, the cradle of the confederacy, to sacrifice tired feet for rested souls and walk the streets for freedom 381 days; it has caused hundreds and thousands to fill up the jails and prisons of the South; and it has sustained a people as their homes and churches were bombed, dynamited and burned, and even their bodies were beaten, bruised and killed. So there can be no turning around, no cooling off or slowing down, because our investments are too great, our love is too strong and our God says, "keep marching, I am with you, even unto the end of the world."

Because of the love which Christians possess for God and for their neighbors, they cannot possibly keep silent during this crucial hour. I call upon the church to make a more active stand in supporting the movement to build better race relations through love. It is a tragic fact that for too long the church has not been a voice, but rather an echo; it has not been a light, but rather a reflection; it has not been a city on a hill, but rather a suburb in the valley; it has not been a tank out in the front of the battle, but rather it has been an old ambulance in the rear, picking up the wounded and caring for the dying. I would have you know that our responsibility is not just to help those who are robbed, stripped and beaten on the Jericho Road, but we must seek to straighten out the curves, exalt the valleys, hew down the mountains and change the Jericho Road into a super highway so that it may not be so convenient for thieves and robbers to hide along the way and attack other travelers. It is an old but still true maxim that eleven o'clock on Sunday morning is the most segregated hour in America, and that the Sunday school is the most segregated school of the week. Let us join hands and overcome the barriers that stand in the way of building a good society and a strong nation characterized by brotherly love.

The first barrier which we must overcome is economics. There can be no resolution to the race question in America until we bring about economic justice. We must put an end to the exploitation of minorities or any person in this country. There is too much food in our nation for so many to go to bed hungry at night and get up hungry in the morning; and all too many have no beds to retire in at night. We must concern ourselves with the poverty in our midst, aid in the program and help President Johnson do even more to feed the hungry of the land. It is a fact that the annual income of the average Negro family is only about half of that of the average white family. In my native state of Alabama, the average Negro family earns $2,008 per year, while the average white family earns more than $4,500 annually. Unemployment among black Americans is doubled and in our big cities tripled that of white Americans. Remember, "Lord, when saw we thee an hungered, or athirst, or a stranger, or naked, or sick, or in prison, and did not minister unto thee? Verily I say unto you, inasmuch as ye did it not to one of the least of thee, ye did it not to me?"

Then there is the political barrier. The vast majority of the Negroes of the South are still denied the use of the ballot, and in many counties of Mississippi there are no Negro voters at all. This is also the case in at least two counties in Alabama, and it holds true in parts of Louisiana. Nearly a half of the people of Mississippi are black, but how many Negroes are members of the Legislature of that state? This holds true for all the states of the Deep South, with the exception of Georgia, where it became front-page news all across the nation when one lone Negro was elected to the Senate of that state quite recently for the first time in one hundred years. When we look at the nation as a whole, with its twenty million Negroes, we do not see a single black face in the United States Senate and only five in the House of Representatives. Yet, we call ourselves a political democracy; "a government of the people, by the people and for the people."

It is not enough for us to be shocked, appalled and say that there are people in certain southern states that deny Negro citizens their voting rights. But those of us who live in the North, East and West must insist that this intolerable violation of the constitution be stopped. This political disfranchisement not only enslaves the Negro, it is responsible for the enslavement of the democratic process. The control of Congress by southern reactionaries means that legislation to aid our booming metropolitan centers is crippled; it means that committee appointments are controlled by southerners and that a junior Senator from the North or West must bargain with Senator Eastland or Senator Russell if he is to represent his people. It also means that federal contracts are subject to regional preferences due to the inordinate southern power. It is no coincidence that Boeing Aircraft in Seattle, Washington is laying off men while Lockheed Aircraft in Georgia is booming at peak production. Senator Russell, as Chairman of the Senate Armed Forces Committee has a lot to say about that. Our silence, lukewarmness, our merely fitful interest is really at fault. We must call upon the Senators and Representatives from the North, East, and West—the section that we are from—to refuse to seat so-called Representatives who come to our national Congress from areas where we know so very well that so many people are disfranchised. If we fight wars to preserve democracy in Korea and Viet Nam, we must be willing to enforce Democracy in Mississippi and Alabama.

Closely associated with the political and economic barriers is the housing problem. The church should take a firm stand for open occupancy. It must be our position that a man may purchase a home on any street and in any neighborhood or section he chooses. We must also call upon our members and citizens of the community to stay there when Negroes move in and welcome them with open arms.

But above all, let there be religious equality and integration in our churches, the houses of God. We all know that many Negroes have been arrested for attempting to attend religious services in the South where the pastor and congregation happen to be white. Also, this has happened to white friends who sought to worship in these churches with Negroes. This is most unfortunate indeed and to the rest of the world this may be unbelievable. But let me add, that it is equally as bad when a church moves out, closes its doors or sells the sanctuary simply because the community around it changes. We would do well to take a lesson from another faith and stay there and serve the people. It is sad to say, but as our parishioners have fled from the inner city, so have our churches. Let us all remember that more than any prayer or statement on race: Yes, more than any ritual or pronouncement, resolution or declaration, what the church does is the measure of its force for religious brotherhood.

We must make more progress in the field of education if we are to solve the problem of race. Integration in the public schools lags so very far behind. Let me illustrate what I mean: Now, ten years after the Supreme Court's historic decision in which segregation in the public schools based on race was declared unconstitutional, only 153 Negro high school students out of 14,159 are attending classes with white students in my hometown, Atlanta, Georgia. Not a single Negro child attends a desegregated elementary school. Recent statistics reveal that in Gary, Indiana a city in the North, ninety seven percent of the 23,000 students attend segregated schools. This is a shame before almighty God.

These barriers will only be overcome when churchmen become an active part of the campaign to rid our nation of the evil system of segregation, discrimination and injustice. The very first item on the agenda is to work untiredly and unrelentingly for the passage of the civil rights bill in its present form which is now before the Senate of the United States. The Bill must not be weakened—the filibuster must be broken and the Bill must be passed. But the passage of this bill will depend upon the stand taken by men and women like you.

We can relieve these ends through love in race relations—for love is the most powerful force known to man and it is life's unfailing quality. It is greater than faith and hope. If it is found perfect, then it will cast out fear. I am happy to say that ours is a nonviolent movement, rooted in the philosophy of love as manifested by Thoreau, Mahatma Gandhi and Jesus Christ. We will not turn to violence; we will not even retaliate with violence. No, we will not resort to arms, nor will we turn to bitterness or hate. We will keep on loving and always remain obedient to the words that He gave to Peter, "Put down thy sword, for he who fighteth with the sword will perish by the sword." We know very well that if the philosophy of, "an eye for an eye and a tooth for a tooth," is followed to its ultimate conclusion that we will eventually end up with a blind and toothless society. And I ask you, can the blind lead the blind? But you may be assured that there will be no turning back, until the victory is won. This we must do for ourselves. This we must do for our children, for already they want their freedom too. I saw and felt this very clearly when I was released from the jail in Birmingham, Alabama last summer after several weeks of confinement. Upon my release I rushed to Atlanta to see my two daughters, my son and my wife. Upon my arrival, I was greeted so very warmly by all of them. After the kissing and hugging was over, my youngest daughter, just five years of age, looked at me and asked, "Daddy, are you out of jail now." I then assured her that this was so. She then said, "Oh, I am so happy, for we are now free." I said to her, "No my darling, we are not completely free yet." My child then said, "Well, daddy you go back to jail and stay until you win us freedom. For I want to be free." What could I say to my innocent child? What can we say to our heavenly father? Remember, "Men will soon forget what we say here, but not what we do here."

The task is not easy, but neither is it insurmountable. Let us not give up in hopelessness and despair. May we keep the faith knowing that the words of Isaac Watts are as true as the dawn:

> Jesus shall reign wher-e'er the sun, does his successive journeys run;
> His kingdom spread from shore to shore, till moons shall wax and
>   wane no more.
> From North to South the princes meet, to pay their homage at His
>   feet
> While Western empires own this land, and savage tribes attend His
>   word.
> People and realms of every tongue; dwell on His love with sweetest
>   song,
> And infant voices shall proclaim; their early blessings on His name.
> Blessings abound wher-e'er He reigns; the prisoner leaps to lose His
>   chains;
> The weary find eternal rest; and all the sons of want are blest.

Then the races of the world will cease to be but one race—the human race. And "men will beat their swords into plowshares, their spears into pruning hooks and study war no more. The Lion will lie down with the Lamb, and the Calf and Fatling together." Confident of this fact, let us go out this evening from this place knowing that, "every valley shall be exalted, the hills and the mountains shall be made low, the crooked straight and the rough places plain, and the glory of the Lord shall be revealed; and all flesh shall see it together, for the mouth of the Lord has spoken it."

For His truth then shall cover the earth, like the waters cover the sea.

§106 Reverend Fred L. Shuttlesworth

Reverend Shuttlesworth's biography appears in the introduction to his June 5, 1957 sermon in Birmingham, Alabama. In the following annual address to the Alabama Christian Movement for Human Rights, Reverend Shuttlesworth takes stock of the past year and the iconic status that Birmingham now occupied in the nation's imagination. Borrowing from President Kennedy, Shuttlesworth employs the "But for Birmingham" phrase to great effect. And while he recounts with no small degree of pride the steps which the city has taken, hate and fear still grip many in Birmingham. It is by no means an integrated city. But Shuttlesworth also places the Birmingham movement in a larger context, one in which the Civil Rights Bill of 1964 and a complete rethinking of blacks' role in the larger society are its tangible results. Indeed, Birmingham blacks "have forever left the Egypt of discrimination and inequality, and have set their sights upon the promised freedoms of Canaan." The Birmingham movement also has enabled an important opportunity for religion to be made "real in the lives of men." Perhaps "Deep South pulpits will no longer be captive; but that from them will sound the Word of God to the Hearts of men."

The National Civil Rights Crises and Our Relationship To It

Eighth Annual Address to the ACMHR, Birmingham, Alabama
June 5, 1964

The occasion of our Eighth Anniversary as a Movement for Freedom, Justice, and Human Dignity, finds us still deeply engaged with the opposing forces of darkness. We dare not let up in our struggle lest these forces of reaction roll back our gains and turn the hands of the clock back past the horrors of the Slave Period when there was no hope for a man with a "black skin." We are today more determined that there be no let-up in the struggle, no cowardice in the non-violent battle, no cooling off period in a hot age, and no retreat from the front lines. Each one of us must be Christian, vigilant, consecrated, courageous, and full of faith that he who fights on God's side is assured of victory.

The gains which ACMHR has accomplished in this the most notoriously segregationist stronghold are numerous, and give us cause for rejoicing, and hope for a brighter future. We rejoice that we can ride buses up front; that Negroes and Whites can visit baseball parks and play ball together; that Negro children can play at Kiddie-Land and the Zoo; that golf courses are open to Negroes; that train terminals, and bus facilities are equally available to all; that doors to all Birmingham public schools are being pried open for Negroes; that segregation signs have bitten the dust all over the city that some stores downtown have desegregated facilities and hired Negro personnel; that Negroes can now eat at the Airport Restaurant and sleep at the Airport Motel; that Negroes can now sit anywhere in our courthouses without fear, and have a right to be called "Mr." and "Mrs." by the judge, prosecutor, policemen, or anyone else. We can picket, we can march, and will demonstrate if we must!

God forbid that we glory save in the Cross of Christ which has sustained us through eight literal years of hell and terror. Only God really knows— and history will someday tell—the miseries, the sufferings, the jailings, the persecutions, the untold and unsolved bombings, the mobbings and beatings; yea, the humiliations and frustrations suffered by Negro people. The gains we have made only prove that Birmingham is partially desegregated by law; it cannot now by any measure be called an integrated city. There is still too much hate and fear here; too much hesitation and too much unwillingness to face the future.

Our goal is integration—the moral and brotherly acceptance of Negroes as human beings and citizens in the mainstream of American life—in Birmingham, in Alabama, and all over the United States. This is our National problem, America's gravest crisis, and somehow Birmingham bears a peculiar and special relationship to it. It is true that the Negro drive started years ago by aiming at legal prohibitions against Segregation and Discrimination, and then in 1960 enlarged by grasping at hamburgers and cups of coffee at public lunch counters. But we have long since surpassed this dimension.

Since the Birmingham Demonstrations of 1963, our nation has been in crisis, as its creaking and unequal social structure seeks to strike a balance between a maladjusted past and an uncertain future. At a July White House Conference—one of the many racial meetings hastily summoned by President Kennedy in 1963—the President made the terse but profound statement: "But for Birmingham, we wouldn't be here today." What a tribute to be paid to your 7 years of ordeal and hardship! What an acknowledgement that Birmingham through the joint efforts of SCLC-ACMHR, had so stirred itself that it had shaken up the nation. How little did we know or even dream in 1956 that we would carry on and discipline ourselves as a Movement that destiny would use the Birmingham Movement as a vehicle to make America come to grips with its conscience! In this city over 3,400 had filled the streets and overfilled the jails. Water hoses tried in vain to drench a fire that wouldn't go out; dogs and police lines failed to stop the masses of Young People and Adults who meant it when they sang, "Ain't Gonna Let Nobody Turn Me Around." School children suddenly became freedom soldiers, and old men and women found themselves feeling young and useful again.

But for Birmingham! Sparks from Birmingham fell in Boston, New York, San Francisco, Houston Texas, Chicago, Detroit, and other cities were catching afire with the flames of freedom! The young and vigorous President saw that there would be open warfare and untold bloodshed unless he, as the Chief Officer of this so-called Christian Country, came up quickly with a law which would be a national expression of our supposedly moral order. Mr. Kennedy, with the voice of a modern prophet, told the nation via television that the issue was more a moral than legal one; and that we must cease being a nation of many creeds and few deeds.

But for Birmingham the Civil Rights Bill would not be before Congress today! Let no one be deceived: it was neither church prayers nor conciliating committees which brought about the Civil Rights Bill. It was non-violent demonstrations—marching feet, praying hearts, singing lips, and filling the jails, which did it. Mr. Kennedy sensed the deep needs of the hour and sought to find a lasting remedy for the illness of his nation. Alas! His exalted head is fallen, his body lies molting in the clay, but his spirit and his works will forever inspire men of courage to greater duty and greater consecration.

There is good reason to be happy that President Johnson has so far given unqualified support to the Civil Rights Bill in almost every speech he has made. There is also concern that the Justice Department will be more vigorous as it did under Mr. Kennedy in prosecuting Policemen and Officials who assaulted or allowed others to attack Negroes as they seek their freedom. Once the Civil Rights Bill is passed, as the Election is over, we are hopeful that he will be as forthright in its enforcement.

Birmingham served dramatic notice that Negroes have forever left the Egypt of discrimination and inequality, and have set their sights upon the promised freedoms of Canaan. "We shall overcome" has become almost as famous as the "Star Spangled Banner," and today's marching feet will be as important to historians as the hoofbeats of Paul Revere's midnight ride. Negroes rose up against a system in which some men who did not hesitate to kiss dogs were allowed to curse and kick Negroes; a system in which demagogues propelled bombs at Negroes while their scientists were shooting rockets at the moon.

But for Birmingham there would not today be the agonizing reappraisal of the entire structure of the American system; one which was planned without Negroes, built without Negroes—except for their unrequited labor, operated without Negroes, and designed to forever exist without Negroes being a part of its mainstream. It cannot be credited either to American goodness or an unexplainable accident that Negroes suddenly began appearing in T.V. movies and advertising media; and whoever heard of the cry, "find qualified Negroes" in government, in business, and in industry?

Progress is always met by reaction. The struggle still goes on in Birmingham as we walk picket lines today in an effort to collect yesterday's promises. Practically no effort has been made by City Hall to meet the needs of the Negro community. Governor Wallace has made himself popular by defying the government, championing the cause of bigotry and backwardness in the North, cursing the Supreme Court, and leading Alabama further down the road of racial hatred. Governor Wallace makes much of his great love for prayer and the need for prayer in our schools since the Court ruling on Prayer; but one wonders if he ever really prays as he experiments with ignorance, and traffics in human misery. An earnest, sincere, prayer meeting at the Alabama Governors' Mansion and the Capitol would be a great help to America. The Civil Rights forces would be glad to participate both in the arrangements and in the prayers. Worse than this, Mr. Wallace has become the mouthpiece and chief spokesman for the radical right wing, the ultra-conservative element, and all those forces of hatred, suspicion, mistrust, and abuse, who parade under the guise of super-Americanism, and think that the best things America could do is kill the Kennedys, impeach Earl Warren, and the Supreme Court, despise the federal government, keep control of the metropolitan cities in the hands of rural counties, shout "states rights" while imposing states wrongs, and honor the great loss of the Civil War by flying the Confederate flag along beside the Stars and Stripes. Majoring in madness, they have forgotten that "Whoever is angry with his brother without a cause shall be in danger of the judgment."

The crisis for our country will remain for a while in Alabama and Mississippi. God has his purposes; and from the wrongs of this age, He will wring some good. Birmingham cannot shirk its duty, for Birmingham remains the chief battleground and focal point in the nation's struggle to cleanse itself. We must meet and defeat Mr. Wallace and the things he stands for. Let the word sound forth here and now that the non-violent battle will go on until good politicians will have no place to go, and the goodness about which America sings will be crowned with Brotherhood!

But for Birmingham! We welcome back to Alabama that wonderful organization, the NAACP which was outlawed 8 years ago. We would urge every ACMHR member to take out membership and give active support as soon as its machinery is set up. But for a long time to come, ACMHR, as the strongest Civil Rights Organization in the State, must carry on in a massive way its efforts to make America think right and to act right in a thinking and acting age.

In a real sense, ACMHR and the Civil Rights Organizations of the country have given the Christian Church its greatest opportunity in centuries to make religion real in the lives of men. Thank God for the awakening of the Religious forces! Let us pray that Deep South pulpits will no longer be captive; but that from them will sound the Word of God to the Hearts of men. God give us men for times like them! And what is this badly needed word? That of "one blood God hath made all men for to dwell on the face of the earth" . . . that "the Earth is the Lord's and the fullness thereof" . . . "Let justice run down as the waters and righteousness as a mighty stream." As ye would that men would do unto you, do ye ever so unto them.

Finally, I wish to thank Vice President Gardner, the Executive officers, various committees, the ACMHR Choir and Ushers, and especially the loyal following for the wonderful support they have given. And I must remind that there is yet much more land to be conquered. We have come too close to the top of the hill to linger at its crest; and it is our task to sail the stormy seas—not to lie in the harbor. We note with sadness the recent passing of our beloved Treasurer, Mr. W. E. Shortridge. Let us remember his widow and child with our support, and make a living tribute to his memory of the Shortridge Memorial Scholarship Fund. He has done his work well.

> What are they doing in Heaven today?
> Where friends and loved ones are all gone away
> Where Peace abounds, like a river, they say
> Oh what are they doing there now?

We may be certain that those who reach heaven are free from strife, turmoil, and unrest.

We are left here in Birmingham to carry on. Thank God for the Birmingham Movement, which has made weak men strong and strong segregationists weak. It has brought hope for the hopeless and help for those feeling that no help could come.

The national crisis demands that we be always on our best behavior as Christians and as citizens of a great land. Let us be always against the wrong and for the right. Let us be concerned without being frustrated, angered without becoming embittered, determined without becoming desperate, reviled without reviling others, persecuted without being cast down, rebuffed without losing our heads, misused without losing our self respect. Let us carry on knowing that the God of Heaven will do right. We've come this far without violence. We've come this far by faith—leaning on the Lord. Faith of our fathers, living still, we will be true to thee till death.

> Beams of Heaven as I go
> Through this wilderness
> Guide my feet in useful ways
> Turn my darkness into day.
> I do not know how long t'will be
> Nor what the future holds for me
> But this I know, If Jesus leads me
> I shall be free someday.

§107 Thomas Merton

Thomas Merton was born on January 31, 1915 in Prades, France to Owen and Ruth Merton. Both artists, Merton's parents led something of a nomadic existence, shuttling between England, France, and the United States. By the age of 15, Merton had been orphaned: his mother died when he was six, and his father passed away from brain cancer nine years later. Entering Cambridge in 1933, Merton's grades were poor as he drank heavily and tended to an active social life. Before moving to the United States to live with his maternal grandparents in 1935, Merton had a child out of wedlock—a fact that was conveniently excised by his superiors in his bestselling autobiography *The Seven Storey Mountain*, published in 1948. Merton entered Columbia in 1935 and studied literature, where he earned an M.A. in 1939. Three years after converting to Catholicism, Merton entered the Abbey of Our Lady of Gethsemani Order of Cistercians of the Strict Observance near Louisville, Kentucky. The monastic life in this Trappist order was characterized by strict silence and intense introspection.

At Gethsemani Merton was encouraged to cultivate his literary talents. His autobiography not only brought acclaim and revenue to the order, but it also more than tripled the number of monks. While the increasingly famous Merton often chafed at the abbot's strict discipline, the ascetic life engendered a vast literary corpus: presently, more than 70 volumes of Merton's writings are in print. Not content to write merely about esoteric doctrinal and scriptural matters, Merton's was an influential voice in many social justice movements, including the civil rights movement. That "voice" was almost always bound to the printed page, though the Trappists at Gethsemani did record many of Merton's lectures to his fellow monks. During one of his very few trips away from the Abbey, Merton traveled to a conference in Bangkok, Thailand. After delivering a lecture on December 10, 1968, Merton went back to his room to rest where he was electrocuted to death by a fan's faulty wiring. That day marked the 27th anniversary of Merton's entrance into the brotherhood at Gethsemani. Merton's papers are housed at Bellarmine University in Louisville, Kentucky.

As noted, Merton frequently lectured to his fellow Trappists at Gethsemani. In a 30-minute lecture delivered on June 10, 1964, the staccato-speaking Merton used the Birmingham demonstrations of the year prior to draw out lessons useful at the Abbey. Using the "ten commandments" of Birmingham as his text, Merton explores the unity of brotherhood exemplified by such commandments. He emphasizes that Birmingham was action oriented. Similarly, monks must understand the difference between merely thinking something and what it means to be involved. The self-sacrifice of the demonstrators also invites monks to meditate on their own vows and how God might use them in very specific, concrete ways. Finally, while the material gains of Birmingham were very few, Merton sees far bigger victories. First, the visibility of violence in Birmingham was a "great moral victory." And second, the citizens of Birmingham, by changing the world, understood their own importance to the cause of justice. Before the classroom bell rings, Merton urges his brothers to be non-violent in tongue and thought as well as aware of the sacrifice they are all making to the larger world.

The transcript of the conference reproduced here has been done with the minimum of editing so as to keep as closely as possible to Merton's spoken word while, however, omitting certain repeated words and phrases which were characteristic of Merton's lecturing style but which would have distracted from his overall message.

These conferences involved a certain amount of dialog with the novices Merton was teaching. As a rule Merton's questions to the novices are audible, but their replies are not. As with many of Merton's lectures at Gethsemani he ends abruptly when the monastery bell rings.

Delivered in the 1960s, in an all male environment, Merton observed the linguistic conventions of his day in regard to gender. If Merton were writing today he would, no doubt, be using inclusive language. The inclusivity of his message in this lecture rises above the exclusivity of his language.

Some Points from the Birmingham Nonviolence Movement
Abbey of Our Lady of Gethsemani, Trappist, Kentucky
June 10, 1964

Well, I've got some interesting stuff today, a little unusual, but I think you have to get something unusual once in a while to get a good sense of perspective as to what we're doing in the religious life and to see other people who have a dedicated approach and who get into things that require a great deal of virtue and perfection. Remember last year this time, in Birmingham, they had this terrific series of demonstrations. The Negroes were going out and they were getting attacked by police dogs and getting attacked by hoses. Of course something like this had to be planned. This wasn't one of these things where everybody just decided they were going to go out and do it. It was planned very carefully beforehand. And the people who were in it had to be trained. And they had to have a very definite idea of what they were going to do and they had to have very definite motives as to why they were doing it. And very clear ideas, basing their actions on definite principles and oriented in a certain way so that this would really be possible to do, and to do well.

So, anybody who wanted to get into this thing had to sign a pledge promising to carry out the following program. Of course, the idea of the program is to get them so that they've got this full grasp on what they're doing and so they're really going to be dedicated in this thing. So they promise to do these various things, to live in this way while carrying out these demonstrations. Now, just from the monastic point of view this is very interesting indeed.

What do you suppose they're going to have on this list of things? What kind of things do you expect to find? Take a few guesses. I think you probably aren't going to hit high enough. Well, what do you mean, general humanism? I promise to look at this from the general love of man, or something like this. In other words, there's going to be some love that's going to get in there. That's important. They're going to have to make this a question of love and not politics. That's extremely important. That's the basis, that's the cornerstone of the whole thing. It was not simply political action. It was religious action. It was spiritual and it was based on love.

Well now, supposing you are organizing this, how are you going to form people so that they're going to be able to go into a thing like this without too much fear and they're going to have to have some kind of a religious basis. What would we do? Supposing you're going to go out of here and you're going to walk down to New Haven or go down to the distillery here and protest against the way the distillery is making a mess out of the moral atmosphere of Nelson County or something like that. You know they're going to get you with a hose or something. So how do you steel yourself for this ordeal? In other words, you're bringing God into it and you want to get God into it as close as possible to you, so that you are in this with God and it isn't just a question of you going down there with a political gripe and you're going to start some action. You want to get God into this. That's another thing that they want to get.

Well, let me just read through this. These things are relevant for us. The things that these people did, we should be doing. Not quite in the same way. We're not engaged in this kind of particular social action, but we should be in this with people who are going through this kind of thing. If you stop and think, this time last year we were sitting here giving conferences and talking about spiritual effects, and while we were sitting here talking about this jazz, down South, probably about this time of day these things would be hottest, down South, people were being bitten by police dogs and thrown into jail and bowled over by fire hoses and everybody was saying that they were all criminals and this was very bad and it was undermining the American nation. And they're getting treated bad and they're accepting this treatment for the love of God, which is a big thing. So in other words, a real profound Christian activity was going on at this time. We're supposed to be united with people who do this sort of thing, so we should have in our hearts very much the same kind of ideals and outlook.

Let me read the thing and then we'll talk about it. So if you were going to go into this now, you would have to sign this: "I hereby pledge myself, my person and body, to the nonviolent movement. Therefore, I will keep the following ten commandments."

And here are the things that they have to do:

1. "Meditate daily on the teachings and life of Jesus." See, so that right away they sign up for a daily meditation.

2. "Remember always that the nonviolent movement in Birmingham seeks justice and reconciliation not victory." This is putting it on a completely disinterested basis.

3. "To walk and talk in the manner of love, for God is love."

4. "Pray daily to be used by God in order that all men might be free." Now, look at that. That's a terrific statement. It isn't just a question of "pray that we may win," or something like that, but pray and that's a very personal thing.

5. "To sacrifice personal wishes in order that all men might be free."

6. "To observe with both friend and foe the ordinary rules of courtesy."

7. "To seek to perform regular service for others and for the world."

8. "To refrain from the violence of fists, tongue, or heart."

9. "To strive to be in good spiritual and bodily health." This is a very important thing, too. Think of all these things in connection with this movement.

10. "To follow the directions of the movement and of the captain on a demonstration." That's where the obedience part comes in; it comes in at another place there above, too.

"I sign this pledge having seriously considered what I do and with the determination and will to persevere." And then you sign and you put the address of your nearest relative and their phone number so that if you get conked, why, they can come pick you up. And then it says: "Besides demonstrations I could also help the movement by: run errands, drive car, fix food for volunteers, clerical work, make phone calls, answer phones, mimeograph, type, print signs, and distribute leaflets." So right away, you are in contact with real life. We get so much into the way of sitting around thinking about the spiritual life and occasionally we get up and do something but most of the time it's all up here. We're thinking about it all the time. We're reading about it and here are these people. This stuff had to be practical. They didn't just promise they were going to think about these points. They said they had to do them.

Well now, it seems to me that this is right up the alley for monks. I mean, this is a monastic program. These people were committed to a kind of monastic program in the civil rights movement. So, comment on that a little bit. What does this have in common with the monastic life here?

Think of the different points. While you're thinking about it, think of some of the things we haven't thought of. What's one of the things here that we perhaps neglect? [inaudible reference to the "ordinary rules of courtesy"]. You've got to face the fact that a lot of the monks who have been around for a long time have become, so to speak, ossified as regards to the ordinary rules of courtesy. There is such a thing as some of the senior professed and so forth who just don't see novices. Well, this is a pity but it's not their fault. They've lost interest in novices and I don't see particularly why they should be terribly excited when they see you coming along but still they should. It would be nice, but you've got to face the fact that a lot of them [have] kind of just lost the habit of paying too much attention when you go by. It's true. What's the purpose of this? Think of the context please—"Observe friend and foe the ordinary rules of courtesy." What's the situation where this is going to arise for these people? When they're getting clubbed and they've got to observe ordinary rules of courtesy when they're being hit over the head. This is not too easy. It should be relatively easy. It should be relatively easy around here to observe ordinary rules of courtesy when nobody's hitting you over the head. This is a program of heroism. The people who signed up and followed this out had to act heroically. A person who would sign up on something like this and carry it out for fully Catholic motives and hang on with the thing would be canonized. You're canonizable if you do this. Here you've got people who did it in ordinary life and people also got killed for doing it, not too many but some and children, six-year-old kids.

So anyway, the first thing is it's based on meditation. We meditate. There's no problem about that, except it has its own problems. They meditate on the teachings and the life of Jesus. That's their first point. Everything starts with that. So that means to say that the thing is a basically Christian program. It's a fundamentally Christian program meditating on our Lord. We've got only one source of strength and this whole thing is based on the theological principle: you've got no strength except from God and from our Lord, and you can't do these things without him. These people are putting themselves into this position because they feel that our Lord wants this of them and that he's going to give them the strength to do it and down here it says, "To pray daily to be used by God." Now look at the ideal of that. That's the ideal of the religious life. A religious is a person who prays to be used by God, who wants to be used by God. Now, what does that imply? What's that got to do with our vow of obedience, for example? Is there any connection between this and religious obedience? Does there seem to be any? [inaudible] If I ask God to use me, how's he going to use me? How's he going to make known the ways in which he uses me? Through superiors, through obedience. Of course, in this particular case, they don't have a vow of obedience, but still, if I'm asking God to use me, I'm saying, "Alright, I've put myself in Your hands, now use me." And then, I say this understanding that it's not going to be done through the means of an angel. It isn't going to be an angel [who] is going to appear in the Father Master's room and say, "Now, you've got to give this conference today," or something like that. It comes through superiors. The superior appoints you to this job or the superior gives you this thing to do or you're sent to this work, or circumstances arise and this is demanded. So if we pray God to use us, it means that we're going to remain open when He starts using us and sometimes we forget. We ask God to use us, and then all of the sudden, it's nice in the morning meditation, we've asked God to use us and so forth and all of the sudden someone comes up and says, "Hey, wash the dishes." "But it's not my turn to wash the dishes. I'm off this week," or something like that.

There is such a thing as what they call an examine of prevision which I don't recommend. I don't recommend all these stereotype methods and so forth, but there is such a thing. Look, we're here to be used by God. We've given ourselves to God, therefore he's going to use us for something or other, so it doesn't hurt to look ahead a little bit and say, "Well now, I've asked him to use me. What's likely to happen today so that I won't miss?" What is coming up today and so forth? What are going to be the possible indications of his will? And then, of course, I'm going to be ready always for indications that I haven't expected because there are always going to be unexpected things. They're going out looking for it. That should be the monastic idea. Of course, actually, in a community, when you've got a well-run community, there isn't exactly an awful lot. If you run a foundation, there would be more. That's one of the things about a foundation. If you're in a community like this it's understood that most of it goes like clockwork. It's kind of automatic because it's a big community and everything is set up but, nevertheless, you're liable to be called upon to be used and if you're living the kind of life [of] a dedicated person around here, you're going to be used. And you want to look out sometimes that you don't stick your neck into too many things because that can happen, too. But if you're dedicated at all, you're going to be used, in some way or other. If you ask God to use you, he'll use you. There's no question about that. The only thing is, don't start asking if you don't mean it. If you want to be used, ask. If you don't want to be used, well stay out of it until you can get at it really from your own heart.

What about this second point of "remembering always that the nonviolent movement in Birmingham seeks justice and reconciliation, not victory?" What's that got to do with the monastic life? Has this got anything to do with our kind of monastic spirituality? [inaudible] Not looking for a personal gain, definitely, and of course, especially, the thing I'm emphasizing is this idea of remembering. Remember what you're here for. Remember what you're doing. Now this is a very important psychological and spiritual point that they bring up here. 'Cause when you're in a thing like this, you get into something, remember what you're doing. So, remember your aim and you've got to have an aim and keep it in mind and of course the aim [is] not a selfish aim. You have to remember that your aim is not for yourself. "We're not in this," they say, "for ourselves." This isn't just to win. This isn't just to defeat these other people. It's to seek justice and reconciliation because this is good for everybody.

Of course, this is the basic principle that you get in Pope John's *pacem in terris*. He's saying that the world problems have to be settled by people who are willing to seek justice and seek reconciliation and unity on a higher plane and not just be seeking that our side's going to win. We've got to defend ourselves against evil and all that sort of thing but on the higher plane we have to seek unity and reconciliation and universal justice.

So, well now, we should be in this. We should be in this. Here's an aim that isn't just something for these individuals. It's for everybody. These people are in this for everybody. They want everybody to have what's coming to them. Justice. Okay, we should be thinking of that. Any other points that has struck anybody here particularly? Well, you've got this idea, for example, "sacrifice personal wishes in order that all men might be free." See this is kind of a corollary for this business of being used. This is basically monastic. What are we in the monastery for? We're here to give up our wishes for the good of others, for the good of all men. It's sacrificing our way, our desires, and so forth, in order that all men might be free. And you see they say all men. This is just Birmingham but they're thinking of everybody, thinking of the whole world. That, of course, gives you a powerful motive.

What happened in Birmingham? What actually was gained in Birmingham, really? What came of it? [inaudible] What did they actually get out of it? They got that agreement that a lot of things were supposed to be integrated. They haven't been. Materially speaking, they got very little out of it. But they got a great deal out of it, from two points of view. First of all, it was a great moral victory because it made the real meaning come out in the open. Hitherto, what had happened would be one Negro would get taken in jail and beat up and nobody ever hear about it and another one would get beat up and nobody would ever hear about that either. It's all in this, isolated, but nobody said anything about it. Now, these people in the thousands went out and stuck their necks out and for about a week the police tried to be nonviolent about it and finally they got out the police dogs and then it was all over the country. And it was absolutely clear and everybody saw it. Since that, the whole situation is different. And this had a big effect on a lot of white people in the South, too. It couldn't help but.

But the other main thing that it had was that it gave the Negroes this realization that they're important, the realization that they can come out and do something and it mean something. That when they get out there and do something it has a meaning and it had a meaning for everybody and this is tremendously important, this having been done. Once this corner's been turned, it's never going to be the same again because now you've got the Negroes in this country [who] are aware of the fact that they mean something and that what they do cuts ice all over the world.

So, that's another thing. So, if a person has the conviction that when he's sacrificing his own wishes, this can have meaning for everybody in the world. This could have meaning for somebody in Africa and for somebody in China, and so forth. Well then, he's doing this in a totally different way, than if he just believes, "Well I do it because I got to do it." So, therefore, [the] conclusion for us is to renew in ourselves this kind of motive because this can sort of get lost in a monastic life. You know, the kind of a feeling that "well it's all a very nice thing. Somebody preaches a sermon about it and it sounds great but, really, does it mean anything? Are the sacrifices that I make of my own wishes, are they really meaningful?" Seeking "to perform regular service for others and for the world," again, you've got this worldwide aspect. These people have the courage to say, "What I am doing, the little act of service that I do, isn't just for these people, it's for the world." Again, this is most important for the monastic life. See this is monastic spirituality. That's one thing that keeps a monk going, the realization that the service that he performs isn't just something to make himself look like a good monk in the community. This is a real service. This is my contribution to the human race. And, again, we have to feel this.

See, all this is so important just from the ordinary psychological point of view. If you stop and think, when things get bogged down with us, we feel that, what's the meaning of it all? And what am I here for? And I'm wasting my time and that kind of thing. What it usually amounts to is that you've lost the sense that it can mean anything to anybody else. And then, of course, it gets to be individualistic. Finally it gets watered further and further down. You get down to the point of, "what am I getting out of it from the point of view of perfection? And what's the merit that I'm getting out of it?" Then finally, after that, you cease to be interested in the merit and you're looking for what's the immediate, how do I cash in on this here and now?

If I work in the refectory well maybe I'll be able to get a glass of milk on the side, or something like that. When it gets down that far, it's really gone too far. When it's way down to that level, you're in trouble. You ought to start getting back up because there it's necessary to get this realization that what I do has a real meaning for the world.

Now, get this one too. What does this got to do with us? "To refrain from the violence of fist, tongue or heart." Well, there's not much violence of fist in the monastery but there can be. There has been in the past. It's possible. What strikes you as particularly useful for us? [inaudible] Violence of the heart. You see, this we don't bother with too much. I think there's a fair amount of it in the monastery. Tongue, well, usually we don't. That can happen. Violence of the tongue can burst out every once in a while, and so forth. Even in choir that has happened. No reference to any recent history, but I know in the past somebody in choir was telling his neighbor a few things about what he was going to do to him if he didn't shut up and so forth. So this can happen. Violence of the tongue can crop up in the monastic life. But especially violence of the heart and this is very important; it's a real obligation for us. If we're looking for perfection and we're thinking about these things and we're thinking about these people who have to face this sort of thing. We can contribute something to this whole business of peace in the world by working very hard to be nonviolent in our hearts. And that is to say, not having aggressive thoughts about people. Now, that calls for really a whole conference actually. Because what does it mean? It means to say you've got to give this a little thought. How are we aggressive towards people? What is the violence that we have in our hearts? It isn't just necessarily cussing him up and down or anything like that. What are some of the standard forms of violence that we don't recognize as violence and that are violence of the heart, really? [inaudible] Well, it's rejecting. See, rejection is a form of violence. I mean to simply out of hand reject the person or even reject it before he says it, before he proposes it, "no." The answer's going to be no because it comes from this fellow. Or, especially taking him apart. Really, just systematically, everything he does. "That's wrong. That's wrong. Look, he did it that way," and so forth. See this is a form of violence. This is a form of aggression on the person. In a certain sense, destroying his works. You can destroy what he does mentally. He gets up to sing. You say, "Ah, he's flat." He goes to do something. "He always does it the wrong way. Why does he do it that way? That's not the way it's supposed to be done," and so forth. You take him apart. So, in your mind, what has happened is that if your mind were the whole world and if you were God, by the time that poor guy got through there wouldn't be anything left. You would have completely destroyed the man. You have mentally destroyed the person. So, I would say this is a tremendously important thing: to learn not to be destroying people in our hearts; not to be taking them apart so that when we're through with them, there's just nothing left. And this is something as monks, we should know. You don't expect people outside to think about this too much. Although they probably think about it more than we do sometimes, but as monks this should be part of the program.

And then, finally, "strive to be in good spiritual and bodily health." Now, what's that got to do with anything? Is that important for the monastery? Why would you say that's important in the monastic life? What's the good of that? Has this got any reference, is it just a counsel for yourself, or what? [inaudible] You owe it to other people. You owe it to other people to be functioning properly if you can. If you're not functioning properly, somebody else is going to have to carry you. It's a question of both spiritual and bodily. They go together. It doesn't mean to say, you've got to be constantly worrying about your health or anything like that, but you've got to keep yourself in trim because you've got your job to do and if you don't do it somebody else is going to have to do it. Now, we're getting to the point where you begin to realize that. During the old days if somebody didn't show up for the dish washing it didn't make too much difference. But now, if somebody's missing, nobody eats. So, it's getting to the point where we have to be able to handle the thing. You've got to be there and we've got to be in good spiritual health. That means, especially, I think we've got an obligation to the community to keep ourselves in trim from the point of view of morale. From the point of view of keeping up our spirits a little bit. We don't have to be corny about it, but there is such a thing as keeping ourselves a little bit on a more or less happy level. We have to keep ourselves a bit happy. You can't keep yourself totally happy, it's impossible. But if a person's morale is down and he's dragging around in the community, what happens? Again, he's got to be carried. Other people are going to have to put up with this. If a person is constantly down and constantly griping and constantly with a long face and so forth, if a person is constantly down like that, it's going to be a drag on everybody and everybody has to bear up with it and it's a weight on everybody. So, you see that something can be learned from these wicked people out in the world after all.

§108 Robert W. Spike

Dr. Spike's biographic information appears in the introduction to his December 2, 1963 speech to the National Council of Churches. Spike addressed the breakfast for ministers at the annual convention of the NAACP in his role as executive director of CORR. Spike begins the brief speech by first noting the Senate passage of what would become the Civil Rights Act of 1964. He also heralds the publication of James Silver's *Mississippi: The Closed Society*, a book that would rock Ole Miss even as it breathed new life into the first few weeks of Freedom Summer. Spike uses Silver's book to foreground his main point: hope and danger are in the air. As to the former, Spike notes the seismic shift in corporate hiring practices, the role of students in the freedom movement, and most importantly, a new and vital ecumenicism among the nation's churches and synagogues. As to the dangers, Spike warns of increasing black militancy even as he prophesies of "dramatic violence" by whites in the "sick" state of Mississippi. Though he makes no mention of it, only two days earlier, on June 21st, James Chaney, Andrew Goodman, and Mickey Schwerner had been abducted and then murdered by a Klan/police cabal in Neshoba County. Finally, Spike warns his fellow ministers that they might need to inject into their speeches a "prophetic understanding" of the freedom movement such that utopic dreaming or cynical despair do not result from a dynamic reality. "If religious leadership does not assist its interpretive role here, other voices will be heard and these will be voices that echo fundamentally simplistic, utopian dreams which can only end in disaster." But to do this kind of interpretive work, Spike warns that society will heed only "those who have stood in the midst of struggle." Preaching from the "safety of a comfortable pulpit" will not secure the prophetic understanding of a God at work in the world.

Address to the 55th Annual NAACP Convention
Washington, D.C.
June 23, 1964

This past week has seen two remarkable events in the Civil Rights struggle.

Of enormous importance, of course, was the passage of the long awaited bill by the Senate. For a year, some of us have lived and worked for the bill, so that now there is a curious feeling of unreality in our lives. We were determined that it would become the law of the land—so obviously necessary and yet so bitterly fought by men like Senator Goldwater. On the day of the cloture vote, people wired and called from all over the country. Yet I could feel no elation, only a sense of, "This is where we should have been a year ago." Nonetheless, it is important not to let our impatience with its belated appearance obscure what a great difference this will make. It provides for the first time substantial grounds for the federal government to act in behalf of citizens whose constitutional rights and guarantees have been abused by the blatant misuse of states rights.

It says clearly and unmistakably that no ancient "tradition" of social inferiority and social superiority by race can be allowed to contravene the civil rights of all Americans in any part of this free land.

It attacks for the first time in any serious way, the legal hypocrisies masquerading as states rights, while fully maintaining all the safeguards of abuse that might creep in.

The other event I want to mention may not seem as momentous as the bill. In itself, it is not, but is symbolic of something perhaps even more important. It is the publication of *Mississippi—The Closed Society* by James Silver. Professor Silver, at the University of Mississippi since 1936, documents for the first time all the incredible events and distortions of truth that make Mississippi a paranoid society.

It is not that the material Dr. Silver presents is new, but here it is, all spread out in full documentation, by someone who has lived on the inside of that society. It is a book that symbolizes hope in that it has been published. Heretofore, people would have discredited much of it as too bizarre. The dark doors of what lies behind the magnolia society are really swinging open. It is a disturbing book in that you realize the full impact of a system where discrimination is built into the very marrow of the people through a continuous process of perverse indoctrination. It will not die easily.

In many ways, the publication of this book is a sign of the times—the early summer of 1964. It is a time of incredible hope and incredible danger.

The hope really springs from the important changes that have occurred in the past few months in this country in the field of human rights. Despite hysteria about white backlash and all the rest there has been a decided swing in the great uncommitted middle class of this country toward the opening up of all areas of our life to all people regardless of race. It is belated and in some places, not very spectacular, but this shift of the center of gravity ought not to go unnoticed. There are so many signs. The large corporations of this country are moving from the top down to revise all their policies on hiring, particularly at the executive level. There is at long last a strong student response to the freedom revolution. It has been the students through the past few years who have really ignited the fires in strong Negro protest. We have much to be grateful for in their courage and commitment. But now the passion of a relatively small cadre of students has expanded. The thousand students going to Mississippi this very month is a testimony to the way this commitment has caught fire.

Perhaps the most important new factor leading to hope is the way in which the churches and synagogues have moved into the heart of the struggle. The very existence of the agency I serve as director, the National Council of Churches Commission of Religion and Race, is a good illustration. In one short year, we have been able to move on many fronts, taking a significant place in the successful struggle to pass the Civil Rights Bill, establishing a massive rehabilitation program for Mississippi, moving in many places of direct racial conflict to affect changes for justice, helping to train the young volunteers going South this summer, coordinating and advising religion and race movements in many northern cities. We have also gone a long way toward the desegregation of the life of the church itself. The other great religious traditions in this country have also made rapid strides. And most significantly, we have had unprecedented cooperation between the religious communities. Protestant, Orthodox, Roman Catholic, and Jewish leaders think and often act as one in this crucial hour. Probably true ecumenicity has been as much advanced in this country by shared participation in this fight, as by any one other single thing.

And then the bill itself is the single greatest monument to the movement of the middle toward a greater freedom in fact in American society.

What we are witnessing is the beginning of a major social revolution in America—the changing and shaping up of our most basic traditions of freedom to make them consonant with the technological changes that have already swept the country. We will either bring a greater opportunity for mobility from region to region, economic level to economic level, more flexibility in employment and use of time freed by automation, or we will have a bloody revolution of discontent. The gross sins of segregation and discrimination have been the most blatant evidences of a hypocrisy in American life that is now being attacked. Let us not think that this freedom revolution is racial alone. The redistricting rulings of the Supreme Court are of great consequence in the total picture of opening up our common life, so that all the people will be more adequately represented, according to where they live now and not where they used to.

These are great grounds for hope in 1964. The blood of the martyrs of the past months has not been spilled in vain. It never is.

But like most periods of revolutionary change, it is an incredibl[y] dangerous time for the country. And the most serious danger is not that there may be racial violence. This is a kind of bug-a-boo that certain forces in the country like to keep before us to retard change. There may indeed be the enlargement of discontent in the Negro community as the gap between where we are and were we ought to be narrows. As Negro leadership becomes more aggressive, some opportunists may push militancy to the extreme. It is to be expected that when the hostility against white arrogance and cruelty is at last openly allowed expression, there will be displays of it. White people ought to expect it. But these are not the real dangers. They come, rather out of the boiling pot of a new freedom itself. They have to do probably more with the unconscious than the conscious changes that are taking place. These dangers cling to the myths by which people live. A myth, you know, is not necessarily a bad thing. It is the interpretation of the meaning of human history that gives individuals rationale for their own lives. Human beings need not only bread and butter, not only equal opportunity, but also a sense of their own destiny, in order to live. Even the ordinary man, and perhaps he most of all, needs a cause larger than himself to live by.

That is what is sick about Mississippi. The myth of the southern way of life is so frail a reed, so unmoral a vessel that it cannot sustain people without frequent resort to dramatic violence to feed it.

James Silver writing in his new book says, "Like other southerners, Mississippians are obsessed by their sense of the past, but this does not insure the accuracy of their historical picture; they see legend rather than history." It is not accident that in Faulkner's *Light in August* the Reverend Gail Hightower's life is shaped by his vision of galloping horses and slanted lances, whereas his confederate grandfather had been in fact killed by a shotgun blast while raiding a henhouse. The southern myth is too unsubstantial, too unchristian if you will to sustain people.

But in a time of shifting roots, there are many frightened people who grasp at the most spurious parts of the past and try to make them their guide. The Goldwater boom is the attempt to reverse time. "Goldwater for President in 1864" is a good bumper banner I have seen. In revolutionary times, there are always those who want to close their eyes and move backward. And that can cause a terrible human traffic-jam, as the great mass of the population moves in another direction.

But there are other problems with life-serving myths that we ought to take a look at. Those of us who give our energies to the freedom movement must also check the reality and validity of our myths against history and truth.

Perhaps the greatest single problem that has ever faced revolutionary movements has been a belief in the inevitability of human progress theory or in another version of it—the innate goodness of man. The Marxists have been the great victims of this idea. But good Christian, humanitarian Americans are equally susceptible. Right now many of us may believe that the day of true brotherhood is about to dawn. We hear it in our speeches. We may be tempted to take Martin Luther King's dream speech too literally.

This false hope in an immediate utopia is exceedingly dangerous. It leads people either to relax their energies just at the time when real vigilance is needed, or it turns into cynicism when the Kingdom of God has not dawned on the morrow.

The long struggle for freedom in which the Negro people have been engaged has not been characterized by this faulty myth. There has always been hope, but also the sturdiest kind of doctrine of man, which expects people to rise above their natural instincts to self preservation, but is never surprised when it doesn't happen.

This is essentially a Biblical understanding of what human nature is like; it is prophetic understanding.

Now with the sudden burst of change that is at long last sweeping the country, we must not lose the basic reality. It may indeed be the minister's role to inject this into the struggle. People who have had less opportunity to understand some of the real complexities of history, particularly new adherents to the movement are very susceptible to a superficial view of what is happening.

Ministers and indeed Christian laymen must bring a historical perspective into the midst of the struggle—pushing always for concrete expressions of justice—in compliance with the new Civil Rights Act, new breakthroughs in education and housing, but at the same time alert to the possibility that reactions and fears may grab ahold at any time. Only an even, mature appraisal of the Old Adam in all men, black and white, can keep us on guard against the hysterical reactionary right or the bitterness of the discovery that good allies can be weak.

In the late 30's and 40's, Reinhold Niebuhr provided this kind of Christian wisdom about limited goals, strategy and action for a whole generation of political thinking. People like Adlai Stevenson, Arthur Schlesinger and many others not so well known acknowledge their debts to this thinking.

We need a new kind of interpretative ministry in the midst of the movement today. Events are moving so rapidly that there is a vacuum of theory and philosophy to undergird the events. The ethical and political theory of the 40's and 50's will not do.

If religious leadership does not assist its interpretative role here, other voices will be heard and these will be voices that echo fundamentally simplistic, utopian dreams which can only end in disaster.

But—and this is a big *but*, this kind of interpretation, for which so many hunger, cannot be given through a megaphone from the safety of a comfortable pulpit. Only those who have stood in the midst of the struggle, with all its ambiguities, all its misunderstandings, all its pain, will be listened to.

In fact, preaching of any kind, "at" people, exhorting them how to behave, condemning them for immaturity or some other defect, perpetuates a gulf between organized religion and the freedom movement.

If one believes that Almighty God, the shaper of all human history, is at work in these tumultuous times, then we must be at work where our decisive action counts. We must not be afraid to take ahold of the "hot" issues, not afraid to deal with new leadership, sometimes less than secure or mature. We must be willing to risk losing our acceptability with the power structure of our city or state, if the solution of a knotty problem requires us to take a stand that offends that structure. It is in the midst of the demonstration, in the midst of a struggle over schools, in the midst of a battle over job opportunities that we will have our opening for a basic ministry of interpretation, or we will not have it at all.

I do not mean that there will come perfect openings for slipping in an appropriate Bible verse, or a little homily straight from Heaven. In the quality of our leadership, in the choices of acts, and sometimes even in direct conversation, will be revealed what is the life giving myth of Christian faith—and you note I use the word "myth" positively here—historical truth enlivened by decision—God cares for human events—men can be summoned to decisive goodness in behalf of others, but they can never be

God. God alone judges. The calling of man is to give ourselves to human justice with skill and courage.

These hopeful and dangerous days need seasoned leadership. The seasoning comes from constant experience and exposure to risk. If God is trusted, and not our own feeble aims we will move into a new era of society in this nation.

§109 Albert D'Orlando

Reverend Albert D'Orlando's biography appears in the introduction to his September 25, 1955 sermon in New Orleans, Louisiana. Exactly one week after the disappearance of civil rights workers, Andrew Goodman, Mickey Schwerner, and James Chaney and four days before President Johnson's signing of the Civil Rights Act of 1964, Reverend Albert D'Orlando sermonized on the meaning of "the long, hot summer" (Freedom Summer) to his fellow Unitarian parishioners in New Orleans. In response to the questions, how did we get to "the long, hot summer" and how will we get through it, D'Orlando offers four answers. First, the summer of 1964 did not just happen. Rather, the extensive push for freedom in Mississippi was long in coming. And it was not just the result of the murders of Emmett Till and Medgar Evers, but the accumulated suffering of centuries. Second, D'Orlando calls on the South to admit the truth: its culture was one of white supremacy vouchsafed by violence should the concept of "place" get violated. Third, as any smart activist might, D'Orlando diminishes expectation. The problems in Mississippi will not be solved by northern college students overnight. And while he places these workers in the noble tradition of nonviolence, he reassures his listeners that they will be armed—with knowledge, conviction, courage, enthusiasm, dignity and self-respect. Finally, D'Orlando reminds his fellow southern Unitarians that they are in the midst of not just a southern civil rights struggle, but a far broader, countrywide revolution for human rights. As such, they are all important participants in that revolution.

The Long, Hot Summer
First Universalist Unitarian Church of New Orleans, New Orleans, Louisiana
June 28, 1964

Undoubtedly, you are aware that usually, with the final sermon of the year the mood tends to be somewhat mellow. During the proceeding months, we have explored a wide range of interests and ideas. There have been sermons designed to meet personal needs, others have dealt with the moral and ethical side of important issues. Some have suggested the need for reflection within, others have called for expressions of responsibility through action. Ultimately, we come to a time when we speak about the need for renewal, the need to relax a bit from our hectic pace that we might re-charge our batteries for the year ahead.

Certainly, I feel the need for this, as I know you do, and I look forward to it with much anticipation. In my study there is the usual pile of books waiting to be read; in my files are suggestions of ideas I wish to pursue. Hopefully, I shall find time, at least during the Blue Ridge Institute in the beautiful mountains of North Carolina for some contact with nature, feeling as I do with Thoreau that "we can never get enough of nature." All in all, many pleasant things come to mind this morning; and I know that you will understand when I acknowledge the tendency to deliver this final sermon with "one foot on vacation."

Having acknowledged that tendency, I must now move to restrain it for, this is no ordinary year. This is a time when apprehension fills the air, when the issue is joined and, when the human conscience is aroused. The daily skirmishes at St. Augustine and the disappearance of three Civil Rights Workers in Mississippi leave us troubled, even alarmed, at the prospects ahead. Moreover, as hundreds of college students continue to arrive in our neighboring state to participate in Mississippi Freedom Summer, sensitive and conscientious people sense the growing tension, a tension which is underlined by the news media as they constantly refer to this as the beginning of "a long, hot summer." I suggest that in this situation, to indulge the typical sermon on pleasantries would not only be to offer a convenient escape from our own responsibility in this matter; it also would be a gross contradiction of that concern for human dignity which has always been the heart of my ministry.

In view of this, it seems to me that it is not necessary for us to dispense with the concept of renewal this morning; instead, we can agree that it must now take on a broader meaning, and that it must be considered in another context. At this point in the making of significant history I need to ask myself whether renewal comes only, or at least primarily, from external sources or whether this is not a time when it is best inspired from the very depths of one's own being. And, the answer is obvious, for this is a time when I must seek renewal within the strength of my own resources, within the courage of my own convictions, and as an expression of my own experience. I must do it by re-evaluating my own place in the present struggle by re-considering everything I have done in the past and by re-affirming my commitment to the future.

During the next two months, I shall of course be on vacation from my usual activity. Needless to say, I hope you all will find time to do the same. Yet, I cannot go on vacation from my mind and soul, for they remain ever with me—active and sensitive, compelling me to pose some pertinent questions and urging me to strive for meaningful answers.

How do I really feel about this situation?

What do I really believe about it?

Am I doing enough? And, how can I know whether it is enough?

Am I sensitive to the feelings of people who have been too long persecuted? Can I really say that I feel what they feel? That I know the tragedy of
persecution? That I am able to articulate their needs and their hopes?

Have I thought enough about the people of Mississippi? About how
they think and feel? Am I aware that Mississippi, like the rest of the South,
like the rest of the country, is made up of people who hold various opinions on this subject, emotionally and intellectually? Am I aware of how
difficult it is for people of moral conviction to express themselves, to free
themselves, that they might function as they would rather than to be controlled by the local mores?

Perhaps I am only thinking aloud this morning. If so, then it is because this is something I must do. I must share my thinking with you, and
hope that you will share your thinking with me. For, in this very critical
period it is increasingly urgent that each person among us, without exception, rethink his role as a religious liberal, in a religious tradition which has
moved from authoritarian control to freedom of mind and of soul, as an
American, whose entire history has been a continuing struggle for freedom
and, whether by birth, or by choice, as Southerners whose regional growth
has brought us to the point where we now witness the dying gasps of what
borders on feudalism—all the while, standing on the verge of a new burst
of freedom, not only for the Negro, but for the white man too.

Now the question is: "What does this mean to us? And what shall we do
about it?" Or, to put it in the context of the moment: "How did we come to
this long, hot summer? And, how shall we get through it?"

Well, if we are sufficiently concerned about this and if we hope to understand it then, it seems to me that there are several things we ought to
bear in mind.

1. First of these is the realization that this long, hot summer didn't just
happen. In a sense it had to happen; indeed, I fail to see how it could have
been otherwise for, it has long been in the making. Now it comes as a legacy
of that system of exploitation, which has been sanctioned in the name of
State's Rights.

You can say, of course, that this is the inevitable result of a year in which
the climate of fear has been considerably intensified. There was the murder
of Medgar Evers; the murder of four Negro girls in the bombing of a church
at Birmingham; the reprisals on thousands of Negroes in Mississippi, who
have attempted to register that they might exercise their right to vote. You
can point to them as but a few examples of widespread persecution that
has been building up to a crisis. Then remember that in the state courts of

Mississippi, as the Emmett Till case revealed, it is virtually impossible to obtain a conviction in such cases while in Birmingham in the past six years alone there have been at least 18 racial bombings, and not less than 50 cross burnings by the KKK. There can be no question but what each of these incidents, added to the many that go unreported, have further intensified an already intolerable situation.

But, as you know, the beginnings go back to a time long before any of this, to the creation of a system which has not only stripped the Negro of his inalienable right to personal fulfillment, which has short-changed him in education, as well as in economic opportunity, but, a system which has fostered various forms of reprisals when he dared to "forget his place."

There is no need to review this in detail this morning; its history is generally well known. You are aware of the terror that has been imposed over the years, the lynchings, the numerous bombings that have gone unsolved, the deliberate use of power hoses, howlings dogs, and electric cattle-prods that have been used to quell demonstrations, and the disappearance of Negroes never to be heard from or seen again.

Add to these items, two others: the common practice of limiting the Negro to low-grade jobs opportunities and the fact that in the present rise of automation he is its prime victim, not only by virtue of being the first to be displaced, but also because there is less likelihood of his being employed elsewhere. Take the total effect of all this, multiply it over and over again and you begin to understand what Edward Brooke meant when he called it "a constantly mounting pressure." Mr. Brooke is the Negro Attorney-General of Massachusetts who recently pointed out that this pressure has been smoldering for a long time. "This," he says, "is a justifiable impatience."

What Mr. Brooke didn't say is that this impatience is not limited to the Negro alone; it also is felt and expressed by many white people everywhere. The long, hot summer is happening in this year of 1964 because the country demands it; it demands an end to discriminatory injustice; it demands an end to brutality, official and unofficial; it demands an end to enforced suppression, to organized persecution, and to the sanctioning of violence. Today, this country demands an end to terror, an end to an American Apartheid, an end to behavior which can only be characterized as sub-human. This has already been reflected in the passage of the Civil Rights Bill. Now it is articulated in a further extension of what A. Philip Randolph meant last summer, when he said of the March on Washington: "Something is underway in this country, which cannot be stopped."

2. Another thing we must bear in mind, is the emotional factor involved in this matter. This aspect of the problem has now reached the point where the only thing that can save the South is the truth, and the only way that truth can be known is for the South to have the courage to face it.

Psychology has taught us how important this is with regard to personal problems. Whenever a person is in trouble, the only thing that can help is his willingness to face the truth about himself; to see himself as he is, as others see him, then to do something about it.

The same principle applies to society as well. As a people, we see ourselves, mirrored in the eyes of others and, what we see is an image, which tells us that we are in trouble. It is an image which tells us that violence and terror are sanctioned on the basis that it is the business of this area, and not of anyone else. Whether or not we wish to know it or to admit it, this is an indication of emotion distress.

This is the importance of Sargent Shriver's comment the other day, when he pointed out that the Peace Corp had sent many young people to work in under-developed countries, in all parts of the world without even one incidence of violence. But, it was unfortunate that we could not send young people into Mississippi with the same assurance.

Here, Mr. Shriver was telling us once again that we are in trouble. The interesting thing is that he was speaking not as a foreigner from some far-away land; on the contrary, he was speaking as a member of the family, speaking to other members of the family as only one can who enjoys such a relationship. He was pleading with them to see what is so obvious to everyone else, and to do something about it, while there is yet time.

If we will understand this, then we will know that the period of waiting is over. This is the great confrontation we can no longer avoid. Undoubtedly, it will be a traumatic experience for many among us. Nonetheless, we must now come to grips with the issue. We can no longer continue to play the part of the ostrich with his head buried in the sand, hoping the disturbance will go away. Now we know that as with any sick person the only way our society can get well is for us to acknowledge the confrontation, and to act accordingly.

3. A third factor to bear in mind, is that students now moving into Mississippi are making a contribution whose effectiveness cannot be measured in terms of whether they solve this problem overnight. They are well aware that this will not happen; they know, as you do, that the problem is much too complex to lend itself to an easy solution. Yet, they come with what we sometimes call "The courage of the young," the courage to believe that the seemingly impossible can be resolved, if men will but set themselves to the task, the courage to show by their own example that their belief need not be but an idle dream.

This courage compels them to act at considerable sacrifice either of earning power during the summer months, or of personal pleasure in a variety of ways. It fills them with a sense of being vital at a crucial turning-point in history, and it brings them to an area where they know they will meet hostility, possibly even danger to their lives.

They will learn, as many others have, that in the movement for Civil Rights violence is almost exclusively the instrument of the frustrated white man. This is not only because the movement itself is founded on the principle of non-violence. Instead, it is because violence is bred into the very being of a person; it is not something he learns, but something he absorbs as a way of life. It is what growing young people, living in a violent society, see and hear as the accepted mores of their community; it is all they know and ultimately, it is the only response they can trust.

It is into such an atmosphere that the students are coming, completely unarmed, without weapons to defend themselves, in the knowledge that violence might flare up at any moment of the day or night. They come trained in one of the most precious qualities of the movement, the Gandhian tradition of non-violence, that spirit which meets hate with love and which meets force with understanding. It might be that on some occasions their patience will be sorely tried, but, with all that, they have been attracted to the movement by this great and wonderful spirit, and their objective will be to keep it that way.

This tradition of non-violence is a very delicate thing, currently challenged both by the Black Muslims and the White Citizens Councils. Meanwhile, it is often questioned by many sincere people, liberals who weigh its motives, and who fall easy prey to charges that it is but another extremist movement. It seems to me that if there is one thing we need to know today, it is that this movement is the very essence of moderation. The students going to Mississippi are the moderates who deserve our support and the call now is for us to give our support, that the movement might secure its identity.

I said that they go unarmed. This isn't quite true, is it? Of course they are armed. They are armed with knowledge, and with some knowledge of how to transmit that knowledge to others. They are armed with conviction, with courage, with enthusiasm, with dignity and with self-respect. They are armed with postponed promises of the Declaration of Independence and with a belief in freedom the only condition under which men can grow to maturity and hope to attain their fulfillment. They are armed with the living example of what it can mean to be free. Above all, they are armed with assurance and reassurance to the Negro that he has not been abandoned, that someone does care about what is happening to him and that someone is willing to help him to help himself to freedom.

This is the threat to the segregationist. This he cannot tolerate; for to expose the Negro to this assurance is to give him new hope for himself, yes, but more important, for his children.

If the Mississippi Freedom Summer can succeed in doing this it will have given the Negro a new sense of his own dignity; one which will enable him to become a person. Not only that, it also will have disarmed the hostile native thus investing him with a new sense of his own humanity. And, in the long run, it will have helped to rescue the white man from his own self-destruction.

4. A fourth factor to be considered is that whether we like it or not, today the entire nation is in the midst of a revolution for human rights. The plain fact is that an era of docility and silent degradation is ending; it is ending not only in the South but in the North, too and in the East and in the West. The point is that we can hasten the process or we can inhibit it. Very likely, what we do will be influenced by our willingness, or our lack of willingness, to acknowledge what the rest of the world already knows; that henceforth, our nation will either become a Western Hemisphere version of South Africa, or that it will move to fulfill the promises of the Declaration of Independence and of the Constitution of these United States. There is no other alternative. On this there is no middle ground.

Which way will it be?

Essentially, this will depend on the extent to which the Civil Rights Bill is accepted and implemented. Governor Wallace has already announced that he will not enforce that law in Alabama. If this is so, then let him bear the responsibility for any consequences that might follow. And, let him recall that last September, when the church was bombed in Birmingham, the Editor of *The New York Times* felt compelled to write: "This is the sixth bombing since May and not one has been solved. How long can such barbaric abuse go on without a mass uprising by men and women who see in the forces of law only a shield for their bloodstained oppressors. Birmingham is reaping the whirlwind sown by its governor's own contempt for legal process. Only the superhuman forbearance the leadership of the Negro community has exhibited and communicated to its rank and file, has prevented a civil war of incalculable proportions."

Undoubtedly, this is a Federal matter. And, as Dean Erwin Griswold of the Harvard Law School, Senator Wayne Morse, and Congressman Emmanuel Cellar, among others, all have pointed out, the President and the Attorney General have plenty of authority to act, even without the Civil Rights Bill.

Nevertheless, the present situation calls for more than needed Federal courage in enforcing the Constitution for every citizen. It calls for a realization by every person that the momentum now underway cannot be stopped, that there is no turning backward, that even as the time has come for the nation to make a choice as to the direction it will take, so too each must do the same; each one must do it knowing that there no longer is a time for uncertainty, that the time has come to decide one way or the other. Then he must act on that decision, recalling the words of James Baldwin, when he said: "Today we are reaping a fortune in human wreckage. I believe that since this society is created by men, it can be remade by men. The price for transformation is high. Every white citizen of this country will have to accept this fact; that he is not innocent of those dogs, and those hoses, those crimes being committed in your name whether in Birmingham, in St. Augustine, or in Mississippi. For, actually, there is no moral distance between the place where the crimes are committed, and you."

Mr. Baldwin, along with Martin Luther King, and many other leaders, is placing the blame exactly where it belongs: with each one of us. Moreover, he is calling us to know that it isn't necessary for us to be in Mississippi in order to act. Some young people have gone there because they have picked this as the one spot on which they preferred to concentrate their energy. They might have picked Louisiana, Alabama; they might have picked New York or Chicago. Nor is it necessary for us to believe that we are on the sidelines, while others are making the effort. Actually, there is no place where people are on the sidelines. Each person can make his own contribution in his own community. We all have any number of opportunities to do this each day, in the office, on the street, in the home.

How often do you have an opportunity to quash the lie, to tell the truth, to neutralize the cliché, to clear a misunderstanding?

If I may be permitted a personal note, such an opportunity presented itself several days ago as I waited in line to purchase stamps at the post-office. It is no secret to anyone who frequents the post-office with any regularity that in recent weeks there has been a marked deterioration of service. Several of us were commenting on this when the lady standing behind me ventured her opinion: "It's just those niggers they have put at the windows, what else would you expect?" Whereupon I pointed out to her that the clerk at the window had been on that assignment for at least two years and that I had always found him to be courteous and efficient. Furthermore, if she would look about her she would see that several windows formerly opened for service were now closed, and that the personnel had been reduced by at least 50% from what it had been. Obviously, this reflected an economy move by the Post-Office Department, a fact, incidentally, which the Postmaster General has since confirmed in testimony before a Congressional Committee, and that it had nothing to do with the color of anyone's skin. On the contrary, it seemed to me that the clerk in question was carrying more than his normal work-load; perhaps we could help him by being a bit patient.

Of course, she hadn't thought of it that way, but she guessed that I was right, although I am under no illusions about having converted her in one easy lesson.

I cite this example only because it seems to me that often when people speak this way, they assume they are in friendly company and are seeking confirmation of what they themselves do not necessarily hold as a firm belief. If this can happen often enough, then perhaps the way we perform in such a situation, will help to mold public opinion in this area.

And, why not make the effort? When you come right down to it, we have everything on our side. We have our religious traditions; we have our moral convictions; we have the approval and support of government; we have the mass media; but, above all, we have segregation on the defensive. Now is the time to face it and to dispose of it, once and for all, that we might be free to go about the business of welcoming other free men into a free and open society.

These, it seems to me, are the conditions under which renewal will take place in this year of "the long, hot summer." Allow me to close this morning with these words of James Baldwin, which echo my own conscience at this hour: "It is the responsibility of free men to trust and to celebrate what is constant: birth, struggle and death and love. It is our responsibility to apprehend the nature of change, not on the surface, but in the depths, change in the sense of renewal. But renewal is impossible if one supposes things to be constant which are not; safety, or money, or power. The price of the liberation of the white people is the total liberation of the blacks, in every city and town, before the law and in the mind."

§110 Reverend Fred L. Shuttlesworth

Reverend Fred L. Shuttlesworth's biography appears in the introduction to his June 5, 1955 sermon in Birmingham, Alabama. On the one-year anniversary of Medgar Evers's murder, Shuttlesworth delivered this brief address at a memorial service. One of the few major civil rights leaders who managed to maintain fairly cordial relations with many organizations, Shuttlesworth is expert at praising the work of the NAACP—the organization that Evers worked for in Mississippi. Shuttlesworth claims that the nation is on the threshold of its greatest changes: business, labor, education, religion, and even the federal government had made sweeping reforms in response to the freedom movement. Why these changes? Always the activist, they weren't the result of some "silver tongued orator," but because people had risked, and in some cases, given their lives for the cause—from Crispus Attucks, Mack Parker, and Emmett Till to the marching children of Birmingham. But Evers, Shuttlesworth closes, was the movement's "martyr of our age."

Address at Medgar Evers Memorial Service

June 1964

We stand tonight upon the threshold of some of the greatest and significant changes ever to be made in our country. These may well be changes in our way of thinking about democracy without acting so, and of giving song and lip service to our principles without making conscientious efforts to build upon them. These forthcoming changes may be best reflected in the way America accepts the Negro—north and south—into its mainstream of life.

The day is fast approaching when a Negro will be able to enter any public place anywhere in this country and be accorded the very same courtesy, respect, and privileges as any other person. The day is dawning in which no plant manager or businessman hopeful of success would dare turn away a Negro with the oft used phrase "We don't hire Negroes here." Labor unions, which have aided and abetted the cause of the little man, the forgotten man, the helpless man, are now in a soul searching period—being called upon by the country and this crisis age to return to that pure humanitarianism which made the labor movement great.

The Educational system of the country is having second thoughts about its structure, its purpose, and its design, as more and more people are found to be misfits in a maladjusted society.

The Organized Church is stirring itself as it views the morning rays of an era in which it must more effectively communicate with men's hearts, or see it more powerless in an age where power is magnified. Never before have so many church bodies searched their hearts and asked, "Lord what will thou have me to do?" And it doth not yet appear what they can do.

The day is already here my friends when the three Branches of the Federal Government have nearly gotten in step on the question of whether or not a man is a man, and if so, should he not be respected by his fellowmen. We are witnessing the day when the government is concerned with efforts for freedom; and whether or not a man can seek his rights without other men bashing in his head. This is why Governor Bryant of Florida today sent in State Police to St. Augustine to oversee police protection in that city.

The Supreme Court has spoken with emphasis; the Executive Branch has become vigorous, and the Congress is at last awaking to the sense of its duties to effectuate laws to enforce our Constitution. All is not yet well; nothing is nowhere perfect in the field of race relations anywhere in this country. But the brilliance of a new day is now being seen upon the American Scene.

But why these changes? And why the swiftness and urgency of the tempo of our times? Did these things come from Political pronouncements from the mouths of some silver tongued orator? Did they happen as the result of Church prayers or recitations of loyalty to Christ? Did they happen because America is a beautiful sweet land of goodness to and for everyone? Did they come because of this atomic and hydrogen bomb age?

No my friends; the basis of a better tomorrow was laid by those who gave their all that others might live. They are coming because thousands have died and hundreds of thousands have suffered that this society might redeem the time and purify itself before it is too late. The Civil Rights Bill in Congress is the direct result of Praying lips, uplifted spirits, and marching feet.

Freedom and the better day for all have always been costly—from Bunker Hill to the plains of Boston Commons, when the red blood of a black man flowed freely with that of his white brothers. It was costly as the NAACP has spent millions of dollars and many days in laying groundwork and winning legal victories for this day and the tomorrows which must follow. Freedom is costly, and justice comes slowly and hard in the bayou-land of Louisiana, and the swamps of Mississippi. The bodies of Mack Parker and Emmett Till give mute testimony to the inequalities of a system of segregation and discrimination. Freedom is costly as jails overflowed in Birmingham; and little children marching and singing suddenly gave new light to the old scripture which said: "A little child shall lead them."

But every now and then a star must fall; and our generation can claim Medgar Evers as its star of destiny, its martyr of our age. For Medgar helped in a dramatic way to bring about the changes he will never see. Like Moses, he saw from afar that Promised Land into which his people must enter. A foul hand brought him down.

Some day—Dead men tell no tales—I say men who die for truth insure truth shall live. Medgar Evers is not dead. He lives in ideas he expounded. He lives in things—in us.

§111 Robert W. Spike

Dr. Spike's biographic information appears in the introduction to his December 2, 1963 speech to the general assembly of the National Council of Churches in Philadelphia, Pennsylvania. In the sermon below, Spike delivers his consistently unflinching lucidity to a New Hampshire congregation. The message of Christ, he reminds us, is conveyed in symbols of blood, agony, sacrifice, and crucifixion. Comforting notions of neutrality and retreat from conflict are seductive misdirections.

Sermon at Deering Community Church
Deering, New Hampshire
July 12, 1964

Indeed, according to the Law, it might almost be said, everything is cleansed by blood and without the shedding of blood there is no forgiveness." —Hebrews 9:22.

Last week, flying out of Jackson, Mississippi, on my way to New Orleans, I sat across the aisle from a nun. Having just come from a visit to the headquarters of the Mississippi summer project and to our National Council of Churches' ministry there, I pricked up my ears when I heard her discussing the students in Mississippi this summer with her seat companion.

She was decrying their presence in Mississippi on the grounds that their misplaced idealism would only provoke violence on the part of the local white supremacists. She said she wasn't questioning their dedication nor even the rightness of their position, but surely it was a bad thing to stir up people who felt differently and thereby create danger and turmoil. All the time she was speaking she was fingering a very large crucifix which hung around her neck.

The terrible irony of what she was saying, of course, escaped her— namely, that the one whose sign she held most precious would never have set his face to go to Jerusalem, would never have hung upon that cross if he had believed the thesis she was expounding.

It is not my intention to berate the unfortunate nun. What she was so innocently doing, others, and all of us do much less dramatically. We venerate a religious faith that we fail to recognize in the acts of those around us or cannot bring ourselves to consider.

The lesson of the morning from the Book of Hebrews reveals to us how profoundly the Christ event is centrally about this relationship between ceremony and actuality, and even more importantly it is about the sacrificial giving of life.

It is probably a long time since any of us listened to a sermon on the text, "Without the shedding of blood there is no remission of sins." Perhaps many of us here never listened to such a sermon. It is connected in our minds with a certain kind of fundamentalist preaching which makes us uneasy. There is something offensively unreal about a theology which is transfixed by the blood of Jesus. The doctrine of the Atonement, which seems to say that God required a sacrifice in order to forgive men, is offensive; and almost all variants on this theme seem to be insulting to the Holiness and Majesty of God or to the complexity of his creating man. It just isn't that simple. It is a messy little metaphysic that embarrasses us and seems totally irrelevant to the most basic issues that haunt our lives. So be it.

But it cannot be left there. Rejecting a narrow little Jesus is not the same thing as understanding the analogy the author of the Book of Hebrews uses in such a sustained way. It is right to reject a mechanical blood-of-the-lamb theology, but it is not right to assume that the Christian faith is a bloodless, inoffensive philosophy about noble living. What the New Testament writers were seeking to describe was an unflinching, honest view of life as they saw it through the experience of Christ's life and death.

That view of life simply casts up the observation that "almost everything is purified with blood, and without the shedding of blood there is no forgiveness of sins."

Hear this comment from the first century not as an abstract theological theory which has to be imposed by a struggle of the will upon life as it is normally experienced. Hear it not as a religious commandment to believe that a supernatural bargain was reached over the Crucifixion.

Hear it as a profound fact of life that under the law—which is the balance of society—only the self-giving sacrifice redeems men from the infection of their worship of themselves and their security.

Only the outpouring of life impulsively beyond what is expedient can create a new start in life.

All the religions of the world are caught up with the idea of sacrifice. Somewhere inherent in most primitive religion is nearly always the sacrifice of animals as expiation for the lack of the sacrifice of human life. The mysterious power of God, the giver of all life, can be adequately worshipped only by the gift of life in its most final form—the death of the living. Most religious practices really based on the evasion of the ultimate sacrifice by the substitution of representative sacrifices—animals, ceremonies, signs and symbols of that ultimate gift.

What the author of Hebrews is saying to us is that the coming of Christ means really the seconding of the religious ceremonies of sacrifice. He does not condemn them; he simply says that Christ's sacrificial life and death points a way beyond the sanctification of the religious ceremonial of sacrifice. "The first covenant indeed had its ordinances of divine service and its sanctuary, but a material sanctuary. . . .But now Christ has come, high priest of good things already in being. The tent of his priesthood is a greater and more perfect one, not made by men's hands—that is, not belonging to this created world. The blood of his sacrifice is his own blood, not the blood of goats and calves; and thus he has entered the sanctuary once and for all and secured an eternal deliverance."

In other words, Christ's bold life of breaking the bonds of tradition for the welfare of humans releases men from the necessity of religion. It does not mean that men will not from time to time need symbol and rite to speak to them of truth beyond their rational comprehension. But the life of sacrifice—the life lived for others, the life spilled recklessly for justice and freedom of the human spirit—is itself the authentic sacrament. What is announced in the New Testament is not the abandonment of blood sacrifice, but a far more radical and pervasive blood sacrifice—human beings who become priests and sacrifices for one another.

That is why Christ again and again says that he has not come to counteract the law but to fulfill it. The true power of the Christian gospel lies not in its advancing beyond some more primitive religious understanding, but the completion of a limited idea of what is demanded of human beings, if they are to be truly human, and thus truly obedient to God—namely, the passion of a whole life poured out rather than just a libation, the daring of death for the life of another rather than just risking a taboo of some sort.

Now why, you may ask, on a pleasant Sunday morning in July, in a chaste New England church, should I choose to talk about blood, and only an hour before dinner too?

It is because church people are so susceptible to a bloodless, spirity kind of gospel; and it is because this past year's experience for me, in the midst of the civil rights struggle, has shown me how many people out-Christ the Christians.

The most pervasive temptation to Church people who hear the powerful words of truth about life in Biblical language is to use that language and that experience as a soporific—as a lulling antidote to the rough edges of life.

We slip back again and again to the first covenant as Hebrews describes it. "It is only a matter of food and drink and various rites of cleansing—outward ordinances in force until the time of reformation."

But now Christ has come, and the tent of his priesthood is a greater and more perfect one. This tent is likely to be found pitched in unexpected places by people who may not even be sure what is going on inside.

You cannot spend very much time in Mississippi with people who daily risk their lives for the sake of their brethren without being struck by the authenticity of such sacrifice. At the Oxford, Ohio, orientation program for students going to Mississippi, one of the new volunteers asked the tall, handsome young Negro where he had learned to sing Freedom songs the way he did. He replied without hesitation, "Standing for 24 hours with my arms tied above my head to the bars of my cell, looking into the eyes of my jailer."

It is not that the people involved in this struggle are not afraid often—that they are superhuman. They sin and falter. They think up ways to evade the encounter from time to time. They give way to hatred and to jealousy. They do not differ from any of us who sit comfortably here this morning, except that they have been purged by their suffering so that they are freed more and more to move forward toward their goals—a free society in which the color of skin is no overt or subtle barrier to any part of that society.

And as more and more of the anxious fear is burned away from them they see more clearly what it is they struggle for—not just racial equality, but a whole society in which old and outworn hypocrisies are attacked and demolished.

I do not want to engage in hero worship, but we are seeing developed in the civil rights struggle a generation of young leaders who have been through toughening times. As Americans we ought to give thanks for this new infusion of the pioneer spirit—the disciplined realism that emerges from a struggle to change what others say is unchangeable. Places like Mississippi are changing despite the cries of, "We'd rather die before we give up the southern way of life." and "You outside agitators only make it worse."

Well, the people who are dying are not the staunch defenders of an outworn and evil social caste system, but the young, the innocent, those naive enough to believe that this caste system is not unchangeable.

"Indeed, . . . it might almost be said, everything is cleansed by blood and without the shedding of blood there is no forgiveness."

Without the awkward and embarrassing act of courage where fear seems more appropriate, without the gesture of neighborliness—an afternoon's trip to visit the people whose church has been burned, just to reassure them that the larger fellowship still is with them—these simple acts so infuriating to those who want to stay wrapped in the comforting lies of their superiority that they hurt and kill—without these acts, individually so simple and collectively so unassailable, there can be no break in the stalemate of hate; there can be no forgiveness; no penance.

These deeds purify the land; these gifts of self are all we have to wash away the horror of our arrogance and violent self-protecting fear.

And what of the body that bears Christ's name while other bodies so frequently bear his ministry?

Rather slowly and rather belatedly, we are coming to recognize our Lord's real presence. Somehow he seems to have escaped our genteel white boxes without our noticing. We felt a vague uneasiness that something was missing, but we thought it was probably our youthful idealism. But it was Christ. He had slipped out the door and gone somewhere else.

Yet many of us still do not want to admit that we have let him get away, or worse, that he might be dwelling with outlanders—with many who are his companions rather than his followers, who call him only nicknames. Whether we like it or not, he cannot be contained or disguised. He is where blood is being spilled for others. And it is his blood.

This whole business of identification terribly rocks us as a church. Can he be where people may not know he is? What is the role of the church which bears his name, if others bear his cross?

Sometimes I hear people say that the church ought not to get mixed up in this struggle—that its job is reconciliation after it is all over.

This idea has to be rejected on two counts:

Some kind of neutral compromise arranged after the cost has been borne is a totally foreign idea of what reconciliation means in the New Testament. The only reconciliation that Christ knows is that which is bought through suffering—through the agony of involvement in the struggle. The holiness of Christ comes not from his abstinence from the corrupting touch of decision but from his transcendence won and struggled for.

There is a second reason why this must be rejected. No one will listen to a body that has ducked and hid to avoid pain. It will have abdicated his right to speak to the contenders.

In the 10th chapter of Hebrews we find these words, "So now my friends, the blood of Jesus makes us free to enter boldly into the sanctuary, by the new, living way which he has opened for us through the curtain, the way of his flesh."

This is the great promise of the gospel. It is not just that we are commanded to be obedient, to love our neighbors. It is that this human path toward the relief of bondage and the casting off of chains is a gateway to God. Not by turning our backs on men, nor by cultivating serenity, but by plunging recklessly into the struggle do we move toward the mystery of life—that which haunts us until we can barely stand it.

It is, of course, a road beset with many temptations too—as misleading as monasticism and self-worship. These are frantic activism, unthinking reaction, rather than clear-eyed commitment.

But we do have a great priest who has gone before us, whose life and death and coming again redeem us from futility. It is in this sense that the blood of Jesus redeems us.

This is not a sermon designed to urge us all to go to Mississippi. It does suggest, I hope, that—wherever we live or work—in the present struggle for fuller humanity, Christ may be present and may be met.

Nor do I want to denigrate these chaste periods of remembrance and praise. They fulfill a hunger deep as history. But let us keep in our minds the awareness that they are not the whole worship of God, nor even the guaranty of our living respectable, clean useful lives—that the life poured out in agony and in the midst of violence is still the measure of our faith, and it cannot be evaded.

§112 Dave Dennis and Reverend Edwin King

On August 4, 44 days after their disappearance, the bodies of Mickey Schwerner, James Chaney, and Andrew Goodman were discovered near Philadelphia, Mississippi. Buried fifteen feet deep under an earthen dam, their disappearance had sparked massive attention on Mississippi and the Council of Federated Organization's led (COFO) Freedom Summer project. Dave Dennis, who led the Congress of Racial Equality's (CORE) operations in Mississippi, was asked to speak at CORE worker James Chaney's funeral. The charismatic and excitable Dennis could very well have been the fourth civil rights worker executed by the Klan on June 21. He had lent his station wagon to the three men, and save for a bad case of bronchitis, the CORE leader might very well have been along to investigate the burning of Mt. Zion Methodist Church in Longdale, Mississippi. Captured on video, Dennis's unscripted speech is one of the most impassioned and powerful addresses of the entire movement. The speech is also fairly well known because of its inclusion in the civil rights documentary, *Eyes on the Prize*. So inflamed and overwrought was the young Dennis that he collapsed into the arms of the Reverend Edwin King, unable to complete the conclusion. Dennis was led outside where he leaned against a tree and sobbed.

Dennis used the eulogy, not "to do the traditional thing," but rather to question the commitment to change to which members of his immediate audience were committed. Dennis eloquently fuses the salvation of the Mississippi movement with the salvation of his listeners' souls in the dramatic climax of the address: "If you do go back home and sit down and take it, God damn your souls!"

Into this rhetorical maelstrom the Reverend Edwin King stepped. Born to a prominent white Vicksburg family in 1936, he quietly assumed his place of privilege among the better families of Vicksburg. This changed during King's senior year of high school when, after a destructive storm, he volunteered to assist in the black area of town. He was stunned to see such deprivation and poverty. A graduate of Methodist Millsaps College in Jackson, King went north for his graduate theology training at Boston University. He returned home to Mississippi in the early sixties to work in the movement, particularly with Medgar Evers and John Salter in organizing blacks in Jackson.

As the chaplain at historically black Tougaloo College, King became prominent in civil rights circles in the fall of 1963, when Bob Moses asked him to run for lieutenant governor on the Freedom Vote ticket with Clarksdale's Dr. Aaron Henry. That campaign put the young white chaplain in the media spotlight for nearly a year, culminating in his delegate status during the Mississippi Freedom Democratic Party's (MFDP) invasion of Atlantic City during the 1964 Democratic National Convention. Pictures of King during this time period typically show a tall blonde man in clerical garb with a heavily bandaged jaw. The injury was the result of a near-fatal car crash on June 18, 1963 in Jackson, when the son of a staunch segregationist ran a car he was in off the road. His face lodged in the windshield, local whites gathered at the scene and laughed at the activists' mangled car and bodies. King recently retired from the University of Mississippi medical school and is a frequent speaker on college campuses. His papers are housed at Tougaloo College in Jackson, Mississippi.

King ably fills the void left by Dennis by picking up where the overwrought CORE worker left off—namely venting his anger at the F.B.I. and the federal government for being so slow to respond. Later in the address, King also gives approval to anger, what he deems "the righteous anger of Jesus," the same type of anger that enabled Christ to wreak havoc among the moneychangers in the temple. King closes his message by contrasting the charred crosses of the Ku Klux Klan with the blood-stained cross of Christ—a living blood that will engender freedom and forgiveness even in this life. Both speeches are transcribed from audiotapes at the Pacifica Radio Archives.

Address at the Funeral Service for James Chaney
First Union Baptist Church, Meridian, Mississippi
August 7, 1964

I'm not here to do the traditional thing most of us do at such a gathering. And that is to tell of what a great person the individual was and some of the great works the person was involved in and etc. I think we all know because he walked these dusty streets of Meridian and around here before I came here. With you and around you. Played with your kids and he talked to all of them. And what I want to talk about is really what I really grieve about. I don't grieve for Chaney because the fact I feel that he lived a fuller life than many of us will ever live. I feel that he's got his freedom and we are still fighting for it.

But what I want to talk about right now is the living dead that we have right among our midst, not only in the state of Mississippi but throughout the nation. Those are the people who don't care, those who do care but don't have the guts enough to stand up for it, and those people who are busy up in Washington and in other places using my freedom and my life to play politics with. That includes the president on down to the government of the state of Mississippi, you see. In my opinion, as I stand here, I not only blame the people who pulled the trigger or did the beating or dug the hole with the shovel. I bury the people . . . not bury, sorry. But I blame the people in Washington, D.C. and on down in the state of Mississippi for what happened just as much as I blame those who pulled the trigger. Because I feel that a hundred years ago, if the proper thing had been done by the federal government of this particular country and by the other people, responsible people or irresponsible across the nation, we wouldn't be here today to mourn the death of a brave young man like James Chaney, you see.

As I stand here a lot of things pass through my mind. I can remember the Emmett Till case, what happened to him, and what happened to the people who killed him. They're walking the streets right now and the brother of one is a police officer in a place called Rulesville, Mississippi. I remember back down here, right below us here, a man by the name of Mack Parker and exactly what happened to him and what happened to the people who beat, killed him, and drug him down the streets and threw him in the river. I know that those people were caught, but they were never brought to trial. I can remember back in Birmingham of the four young kids who were bombed in the church and had just went to service and I know what has happened to the people who killed them—nothing. Remember the little 13-year-old kid who was riding a bicycle and who was shot in the back? And the youth who shot him, who was a white guy from Birmingham, got off with three months. I can remember all of that right now. Or I can remember the Medgar Evers case in Beckwith. The person who was governor of the state at that particular time going up and shaking his hand when the jury said that it could not come to a verdict. I can remember all of that. And I can remember down in the southwest area where you had six Negroes who'd been killed, and I can remember the Lees and all these particular people who know what has happened to those who have been killing them. I know what is happening to the people that are bombing the churches, who've been bombing the homes, who are doing the beatings around this entire state and country.

Well I'm getting sick and tired! I'm sick and tired of going to memorials! I'm sick and tired of going to funerals! I've got a bitter vengeance in my heart tonight! And I'm sick and tired and can't help but feel bitter, you see, deep down inside and I'm not going to stand here and ask anybody here not to be angry tonight.

Yeah, we have love in our hearts, and we've had it for years and years in this country. We've died on the battlefield to protect the people in this country. We've gone out in World War I and in 1942 millions of us died too, you see. Meanwhile you understand there are people in this country with no eyes, without a leg, without an arm, to defend this country and to come back to do what? To live as slaves you see, and I'm sick and tired of that. Yeah, I'm probably supposed to stand here . . . got a lot more I want to say.

You see, we're all tired. You see, I know what's gonna happen! I feel it deep in my heart! When they find the people who killed these guys in Neshoba County, you've got to come back to the state of Mississippi and have a jury of their cousins, their aunts and their uncles. And I know what they're going to say—not guilty. Because no one saw them pull the trigger. I'm tired of that!

See another thing that makes me even tireder though, and that is the fact that we as people here in this state and the country are allowing this to continue to happen. Even us as black folk. So I look at the young kids here—that's something else that I grieve about. For little Ben Chaney here and the other ones like him around in this audience and around on the streets. I grieve because sometimes they make me feel that, maybe, they have to go through the same thing, you see. And they are gonna have to go through the same thing! Unless we as individuals begin to stand up and demand our rights and a change in this dad-blasted country, you see. We have to stand and demand it because tomorrow, baby, it could be you or your child.

And one thing that I'm worried about is just exactly what are we going to do as people as a result of what happened, for what this guy died for and the other people died for. We're going to come to this memorial here, say, "Oh, what a shame," go back home and pray to the Lord as we've done for years. We go back to work in some white folks' kitchen tomorrow, and forget about the whole God-blasted thing, you see.

Don't applaud! Don't applaud! Don't get your frustrations out by clapping your hands. Each and every one of us as individuals is going to have to take it upon ourself to become leaders in our community. Block by block, house by house, city by city, county by county, state by state throughout this entire country. Taking our black brothers by the hand, one at a time, stepping across with our feet through the mighty oceans to the mighty country of Africa. Holding our hands up high, telling them that if they're not ready for us, "Too bad, baby, 'cause we're coming anyway." So we have to do as people.

We can't take it any longer and be wiped off of the face of the earth. I look at the people of grey hair down here, the tiredness in the face and I think about the millions of bolls of cotton that you picked, the millions of actions it took to chop it for $10 a week, $25 a week, or whatever you could get to eat. I watch the people here who go out there and wash dishes and you cook for them. For the whites in the community and those same ones you cook for, wash and iron for, who come right out and say, "I can't sit down and eat beside a nigger," or anything like that. I'm tired of that, you see. I'm tired of him talking about how much he hates me and he can't stand for me to go to school with his children and all of that. But yet, when he wants someone to baby-sit for him, he gets my black mammy to hold that baby! And as long as he can do that, he can sit down beside me, he can watch me go up there and register to vote, he can watch me take some type of public office in this state, and he can sit down as I rule over him just as he's ruled over me for years, you see.

This is our country too. We didn't ask to come here when they brought us over here, and I hear the old statement over and over again about me to go back to Africa. Well, I'm ready to go back to Africa, baby, when all the Jews, the Poles, the Russians, the Germans and they all go back to their country where they came from too, you see. And they have to remember that they took this land from the Indians. And just as much as it's theirs, it's ours too now. We've got to stand up.

The best thing that we can do for Mr. Chaney, for Mickey Schwerner, for Andrew Goodman is stand up and demand our rights. All these people here who are not registered voters should be in line Monday morning from one corner of this county to the next, demanding, don't ask if I can become a registered voter. Demand! Say, "Baby, I'm here!"

People, you've got relatives in places like Neshoba County, talk to them. They're at a disadvantage. They only have 12 percent of the population that's black over there. So that man thinks he's going to run over us over there. But we're going in there, baby! We're going to organize in there, and we're going to get those people registered to vote and organized. I don't care if we are just 12 percent, because that 12 percent is part of the almost 50 percent of this whole entire state you see.

Don't just look at me and the people here and go back and say that you've been to a nice service, a lot of people came, there were a lot of hot-blasted newsmen around, anything like that. But your work is just beginning. I'm going to tell you deep down in my heart what I feel right now. If you do go back home and sit down and take it, God damn your souls!

Stand up! Your neighbors down there who were too afraid to come to this memorial, take them to another memorial. Take them up and take them down there. Make them register to vote and you register to vote. I doubt if one fourth of this house is registered. Go down there and do it.

(Pause)

Don't bow down anymore! Hold your heads up!

(Pause)

We want our freedom now! I don't want to have to go to another memorial. I'm tired of funerals, tired of 'em! We've got to stand up.

REVEREND EDWIN KING:

I'm glad Dave got angry tonight. Any of you who are not angry in your heart will not find the strength to go on. You have to hate this thing that has been done. And then have to somehow be able to forgive the people who have done it. But I don't think we start off by automatically forgiving. If we cannot admit when we feel pain, when we feel anger, when we feel hate then we are not using the feelings that God gave us. Our hatred should be to destroy the system, but is destroying the souls and the bodies of men.

Dave and I have been to several funerals together. I think I know how Dave feels. I don't know that I can know fully ever how another brother feels. What Dave did not say I must say as we begin. We're not here talking about a crime that has just been committed in Mississippi. We are not here to talk about the love for one who will not walk again in our midst in this life. This murder was not just done by sick white Mississippians. You and I know, and we're probably not supposed to say it out loud, but these men would not be dead if the U.S. government cared. The government may care now, the lives of other people may be protected because of this sacrifice, but if the Justice Department and the FBI had done the minimum that we requested, going to Philadelphia when we first asked them, these men might not have died. Of course, people are killed frequently in Mississippi and we do not say that our government could protect every person who believes in democracy from being murdered by those who don't. But the U.S. government must bear part of the responsibility along with the murderer who sits in the governor's mansion in Jackson, and the rest of the murderers who tolerate murder in this state. And the American people must examine themselves for allowing a government to allow white Mississippians to kill black Mississippians at will, and now because white blood has been shed also our country is looking for the first time.

I come before you now, some of you know me, some of you don't. I'm a Mississippian. I'm the chaplain out of Tougaloo College. I ran for lieutenant governor with Aaron Henry last fall. My wife is from Jackson, Mississippi. My parents used to live in Mississippi before they were run out of Mississippi. By the same kind of people who do this kind of thing, and the silent people who I think are just as guilty and are more damned in their souls because they know it's wrong. But I've said enough about the country, we'll just talk about Mississippi.

I come before you to try to say that my brothers have killed my brothers. My white brothers have killed my black brothers, and somehow you have the greater burden to be able to forgive the people who do this and through your forgiveness bring salvation to them, for they are in a living hell and will not admit it. Their souls are being destroyed by the hate and fear they bear towards all of us. I was not surprised when a black man and white man fell together this summer because in the past five or six months many black men and women have been murdered in this state, and as the spring wore on we began to have attacks on the people at Tougaloo, white people and black people. Someone tried to kill me this spring and it wasn't the first time my white brothers had tried to kill me. They want to kill me because I am saying that I have white brothers and I have black brothers and I am a man, no more no less, who would be Christian and still believes there is hope for America.

For the first time bloody Neshoba has had the red blood of black men and the red blood of white men enrich its soil. I don't think we will ever forget this. Too often in Mississippi in these last 300 years Negro mothers, Negro wives, Negro brothers and sisters have had to cry alone, have had to go into the white kitchen and wipe away the tears so that nobody would know it mattered when a person died. But we are now saying that no longer will a person die in Mississippi and the world not know it, and this country and the people of this world not grieve with us. If we can die together in Mississippi surely we can find a way to live together, to grow together, to learn together, to love together. This will take great strength, great courage that God alone can give.

I met Andrew Goodman only in Ohio. I remember him as a person who seemed to be full of love for himself and for his fellow man. A quiet, easy-going, friendly fellow—I wish I could have known him better.

I know James Chaney a little better. But here in Mississippi people like Edwin King from Vicksburg, and James Chaney from Meridian, are not supposed to be able to know each other as brothers. And people killed James Chaney so that we could not live in a society where white men and Negro men in Mississippi could know each other. I had met James when he was with the Schwerners. I had heard Mickey Schwerner say wonderful things about James Chaney. I have heard Rita Schwerner this summer say wonderful things about James Chaney. James Chaney helped support the Schwerners to give them strength when they came as strangers to this community, but full of love for this community. James befriended them and worked with them and truly, they were brothers. Rita has often talked this summer of how important James was to this project. She said he was willing, just as Mickey was willing, just as she was willing to give all to this project, for this freedom.

I'd like to read several things to you tonight before we close. They're not from the Holy Scriptures because I believe God can speak through men and women who are writing and revealing and living his word today. Monday morning after they first disappeared, when you and I already knew in our hearts what had happened but we couldn't say it, we couldn't say it, but we knew, we tried to pretend and this kind of pretending is hope, and hope is good. I've got a newspaper from a peace organization which had two letters in it from Rita Schwerner and although this is a funeral to memorialize James Chaney tonight I knew you people from Meridian would appreciate tonight these letters from Rita written after she and Mickey, the both of them, came to the community. It was strange I got them on the day I knew Mickey was dead.

The first is written from Meridian on March 30, to a friend in Vermont: "The community center is growing beautifully. We started a new program about two weeks ago," and then she describes the programs that went on in the community center. She says, "Now we've run out of material, I've been begging for more. The need seems so great that I don't know if our contacts up North are going to be able to keep us supplied, but down here we just keep begging. I've lost all feelings of personal pride about begging because the need is so very great, and some people don't seem to do anything until you plead with them. At any rate the program is truly exciting and there are tangible results. The library continues to grow, more and more people hear about it and send what they can. We've been able to get an old phonograph to play records on and children are coming in for classes, and adults are starting to overcome their fear about registering to vote. I believe our experiences are showing that a community center can work, and that people do want this project."

And the second letter written in April 12, she says a little more about what she and Mickey were thinking: "I tend to think a lot of projects which never go beyond the thought stage in my brain. When the two of us, Mickey and me, came down to Mississippi we said we would leave and return to social work in New York in the fall, we still want to, yet our feelings are ambivalent. It's hard to leave Mississippi. There's so much to do here and there's so few people to do it, that leaving seems like deserting it. Still, there's no way to live a normal life while living and working in the Movement. Life is so uncertain here in Mississippi that I wouldn't even obligate myself to the care of a puppy let alone an infant. There is little more that I can tell you about the Freedom Summer except that preparations are underway. Workers all over the state are busy looking for housing. The Negroes will open their homes to white men this summer. We will try to establish meaningful programs. Here in Meridian we hope to have a number of people in the Freedom Schools and an intensified voter registration campaign we will go into the surrounding tough counties." I wonder if she even knew the name Neshoba back in April? "We anticipate increased police harassment throughout the state, but we also hope for the chance to drive a meaningful wedge into the system of segregation. We can use people with specific skills, but most of all we want people in Mississippi with an overwhelming desire to get a nasty job done. From Mickey and Rita Schwerner in Meridian Mississippi."

Rita has lost a husband. People here have lost a son that they had known through 20 years. You have lost a friend. The tragedy of a time like this is, that like me many of you realize I never came to know James Chaney. What a wonderful person he must have been. I wish I could have known him better. But I will remember James Chaney and I will remember his friends, and I will remember what he gave his life for. James Chaney and Michael Schwerner knew what they were facing when they went up to Neshoba, and Andrew Goodman probably knew when he went with them, and yet they did what they had to do—a dirty job that had to be done. Working for freedom is never easy. "Freedom is never free," as we said yesterday at our convention in Jackson.

Two days after our friends disappeared Rita came to Jackson to plead the cause for all three men. Now I met Rita and went with Rita to the governor's mansion. We tried to see the governor in his office and they would not give Rita Schwerner an appointment. You can imagine what they would have done if Mrs. Chaney had tried to see the governor of Mississippi about her son. They would probably have jailed her and her grief. They did not dare lay a hand on Rita, but they almost did. We went to the governor's mansion; they had been told we were coming, and by coincidence the governor of Mississippi and Governor Wallace, who helped perpetrate the murder of children in a church, were talking on the front porch of the governor's mansion; we did not know they would be there. We walked up and Rita Schwerner was introduced as the wife of Mickey Schwerner to Governor Johnson of Mississippi who had just finished mouthing statements about how concerned he was and how hard he would work. And Governor Johnson said, "I have no time for her," quickly stepped into the governor's mansion and literally closed the door of the mansion of the governor of the state of Mississippi, shut the door in her face, and two armed policemen stepped in front of her with guns, and blocked her path.

Our path to freedom does not lie through the door of the governor's mansion, although one day soon, and I say within four years the next governor of Mississippi, if he is not a Negro, will be a white man elected because he believes in the things that you and I believe in. We will not tolerate another racist murderer like Paul Johnson. And I say murderer because I believe as a Christian he is morally responsible for murder. This state will either cease to be a state, or we will not tolerate that kind of man contaminating the office of governor in a free society in the United States.

The greatest tragedy that has occurred here is not just these deaths, but the failure in the white community that brought this about; that has brought this about, that has tolerated it. Many white people talk of being Christians. They are afraid of Christianity as much as they are afraid of you. And they are afraid of you. They are afraid because of a guilty conscience. Afraid that you would treat us as we have treated you. I don't believe it will be that way, but that is what they fear. So their fear allows a few men to commit murder. But it doesn't matter if a few men do the murders and burn the churches, the rest of the people are responsible. The white Christians of the city of Meridian who are not grieving with us tonight, here, need your prayers because God almighty sees them and knows in his eyes that every white Christian who did not come to this church is no Christian!

You can help save them. You must try to rededicate yourselves to helping them. Not just forgiving the people who beat and murdered our brothers, but our other brothers who ran and hid from this. I know so many people who said "that is a hoax." Ask Mrs. Chaney what mother would want her son to have a hoax. Ask Mrs. Goodman and Mrs. Schwerner in New York, you saw all three of these mothers on television and the news. What has happened to the white people of Mississippi who could say after seeing three broken mothers and a widow that this is a hoax? The only hoax is that these people think they have found the prize, the Christian way. That these people think that their religion, which is a religion based on white supremacy's southern way of life first, and Americanism and Christianity second. This is the hoax. That these people think they have a faith that can support them, that these people think that they are part of a democracy, that these people call us communists, but please I beg you try to forgive. Do not let your anger die. Make it the righteous anger of Jesus who turned over the evil things in the temple, and we may have to turn over everything in this state in the way Jesus did in the temple, and that may be what faces us.

We do not know yet if all of us try to vote that the American government will let us vote, and it is now the responsibility of the United States because Mississippi has proved it will not let us vote. We do not know what the future will hold.

Please do not turn back, your white brothers need to be free. They need to be free to come before God and not try to pretend that they did not know what was going on, to try to say that every Negro I know is happy. Those of you who work in white homes, who meet white people, if you will tell them the truth. You may lose your job, but you will help save their souls. God has placed a great burden on you, the burden of grief on a few, the burden of the pain of not seeing John [James] Chaney, of not seeing Mickey Schwerner, of not having Andrew Goodman return home alive from Mississippi. This is a pain I cannot know. You cannot really enter into this mother's pain, this family's pain, but let us say we will try to take all the sorrow, all the pain of this family, and of the families of those who did the murder, and of the families of those white Christians who wanted to be here but were afraid. Some afraid that they would be murdered, but others afraid that someone would not speak to them. They need freedom.

When freedom comes to one half of Mississippi it will bring freedom to the other half and we will not be free just to vote, just to have justice, we will be free to break bread together on our knees. We will be free to kneel before the ruins of burned churches, bombed homes, and newly dug graves and hold hands, black and white together and say, "We are brothers in Christ despite all that there is to keep us from being brothers." The love of God can overcome even Mississippi.

The symbol of white Mississippi today is a burning cross as it has always been. A symbol of destruction of the Christian faith. A symbol of destroying the thing they say they are upholding, and it is very interesting that they must burn the cross and leave it only a charred ruin, a thing with no power. But our cross is not a burned cross, it is the one cross of Calvary that is stained with the blood of Jesus, God's son. God gave his son for all of us and this is the cross that we follow, the cross that means victory not emptiness and decay. The cross that means victory over death, but victory in this life. The cross that means we can forgive. God will help us to love.

The cross that means we will have a new beginning, a new resurrection, a new birth. That over this blood which is mingled with the blood of the children of Birmingham, the people killed by the Klan in southwest Mississippi, of Medgar Evers, John Kennedy, and of Jesus Christ and all whom have died for the love of their brothers in service to their brothers, this blood can free us all and we must share this freedom and forgiveness with the white people of Mississippi, and from Mississippi with all of America.

§113 Fannie Lou Hamer

Fannie Lou Hamer was born Fannie Lou Townsend on October 17, 1917 in Montgomery County, Mississippi. She was the youngest of 20 children born to sharecroppers. In 1919 her family moved to the Delta where they worked on the E. W. Brandon plantation. Fannie Lou was forced to quit school after the sixth grade. Baptized in the Quiver River, she was a devout Baptist all of her adult life. In 1944 Fannie Lou married Perry "Pap" Hamer and the two settled on the W. D. Marlow plantation just outside of Ruleville, Mississippi in Sunflower County. Fannie Lou picked cotton and was a timekeeper for most of her 18 years on the plantation.

Hamer became a civil rights activist only when she was 44 years old. At the invitation of her friend, Mary Tucker, she attended a mass meeting at the Williams Chapel Missionary Baptist Church in Ruleville on August 27, 1962; it was the only church in Ruleville willing to host the meeting. The Council of Federated Organizations (COFO) in concert with the Student Nonviolent Coordinating Committee (SNCC) had sent Charles McLaurin into the area to canvass for its voter registration program. By late August, McLaurin had convinced only three locals to attempt to register to vote. At the August 27th, meeting, Hamer listened to Bob Moses, Jim Forman, and Reginald Robinson. But perhaps she was most inspired by James Bevel's sermon entitled, "Discerning the Signs of Time." Hamer would later make use of this sermon in her own speechmaking. Fannie Lou Hamer became a convert to the cause on August 27, as she volunteered, along with 17 others, to attempt to register at the county seat of Indianola that Friday. The events that transpired on August 31, would appear frequently when Hamer told her story to audiences all over the country.

Hamer proved to be the perfect embodiment of SNCC's civil rights philosophy. Instead of a top-down, hierarchical model, the organization favored leadership at the grassroots, where local leaders were cultivated to sustain the movement long after civil rights organizations had left the area. Bob Moses recruited Hamer to become a field secretary with SNCC and she obliged in November 1962. From then on, her life as an activist was cemented. She was a frequent speaker and singer at SNCC conferences and local meetings, and almost always Hamer would highlight her voting story of August 31, 1962 and the Winona jail story of June 9, 1963. The latter story is a brutal account of rape-like torture of Hamer and other activists arrested on their way back from a Charleston, South Carolina workshop. The beating, while part of her rhetorical repertoire, stayed with her the rest of her life as her vision was affected and a limp from polio exacerbated.

Hamer's fame outside of the movement grew exponentially in August of 1964. As part of the elected delegation of the Mississippi Freedom Democratic Party (MFDP) that traveled to the Democratic National Committee meeting in Atlantic City, Hamer testified on live television before the Credentials Committee. In that brief speech Hamer so captivated the country that President Lyndon Johnson called an impromptu press conference to preempt her address. She would be a candidate for public office many times, though never winning.

With the radicalization of SNCC in the late 1960s, Hamer dropped out of the organization and helped run Freedom Farm, a Delta food cooperative as well as a small garment factory. As the 1970s began, Hamer remained active in Mississippi politics, the burgeoning feminist movement and of course day-to-day life in Ruleville. Plagued by poor health for much of her life, diabetes, heart disease, and later cancer slowed Hamer's frenetic activism. She died on March 14, 1977. Her papers are housed at the Amistad Research Center at Tulane University in New Orleans, Louisiana.

Precious few of Fannie Lou Hamer's speeches survive from her early years in the movement. Of all the scores of speeches she delivered in Mississippi prior to 1966, we're aware of only one that survives, which we have transcribed below. Delivered in the late summer of 1964 in her home county of Sunflower, Hamer speaks in the local vernacular to local people. And while the audiotape reveals that Hamer begins haltingly as if reading from a prepared text, she quickly finds her voice and her pace. The speech offers a dizzying array of personal narrative, local humor, biblical quotations, grassroots theological precept, and of course, her urgent appeal to get registered to vote. Hamer's voter registration story and her beating in the Winona jail are dramatically rendered, and she emphasizes the gendered nature of that beating with subtle yet profound pathos. Though the two could not have been more different in upbringing and formal education, Hamer and Dr. King preached similar messages based on similar texts: love, not hatred, for one's enemies would convince and convict Americans that civil rights was, above all else, a profoundly Christian call.

Untitled Speech

Indianola, Mississippi

September 1964

I am here for the first time in Indianola, Mississippi to speak in a mass meeting, and you just don't have a idea what a pleasure this is to me. 'Cause we been workin' across for the past two years and Mr. Charles McLaurin work very hard tryin' to get a place here durin' the time that I was campaignin' and he failed to get a place. But it's good to see people wakin' up to the fact something that you should've been awakened years ago.

First I would like to tell you about myself. As McLaurin say, my name is Mrs. Fannie Lou Hamer and I live at 626 East Lafayette Street in Rulesville [Ruleville], Mississippi. It was in 1962, the 31st of August that 18 of us traveled 26 miles to this place, to the county courthouse to try to register to become first-class citizens. When we got here to Indianola, to the courthouse, that was the day I saw mo' policemens with guns than I'd ever seen in my life at one time. They were standin' around and I will never forget that day. One of the men called the police department in Cleveland, Mississippi and told him to bring some type of big book back over there. But anyway, we stayed in the registrar's office, I'm not sure how long, because it wadn't but two allowed in the room at the same time.

After we got out from the registrar's office, I was one of the first persons to complete as far as I knew how to complete, on my registration form and I went and got back on the bus. During the time that we was on the bus, the policemens kept watchin' the car, the bus, and I noticed the highway patrolman watchin' the bus. After everybody had completed their forms and after we started back to Rulesville, Mississippi, we were stopped by the highway patrolman and the policeman. And was ordered back to come to Indianola, Mississippi. When we got back to Indianola, the bus driver was charged with driving a bus the wrong color. This is the gospel truth, but this bus had been used for years for cotton choppin', cotton pickin', and to carry people to Floriday to work to try to make enough to live on in the winter time to get back here to the cotton fields to get here the next spring and summer. But that day the bus had the wrong color.

After we got to Rulesville, about 5 o'clock, Reverend Jeff Sunny, drove me out into the rural area that I'd been workin' as a timekeeper and a sharecropper for 18 years. When I got there, I was already fired. My children met me and told me, say "momma, this man is hot." Said "He said you will have to go back and withdraw. Or you will have to leave." During the time [s]he was talkin', it wadn't too long before my husband came, and he said the same thing. I walked in the house, sit down on the side of my little daughter's bed and then this white man walked over and said, "Pap, did you tell Fannie Lou what I said?" He said "Yes sir," and I walked out. And he said, "Fannie Lou did Pap tell you what I said?" I said, "He did." He said, "Well Fannie Lou," said "you will have to go down and withdraw or you will have to leave." And I addressed and told him, as we have always had to say "Mister," I say, "I didn't register for you," I say, "I was tryin' to register for mahself." He said, "We're not ready for that in Mississippi." He wadn't ready, but I been ready a long time.

I had to leave that same night. On the tenth of September in 1962, sixteen bullets was fired into the home of Mr. and Mrs. Robert Tucker for me. That same night two girls was shot at Mr. Herman Sisson's in Rulesville. They also shot in Mr. Joe McDonald's house that same night. Now, the question I raise: is this America? The land of the free and the home of the brave? Where people are bein' murdered, lynched, and killed because we want to register and vote?

When my family and I decided to move back in Sunflower County in December, the car that we had been payin' on for the last three years, it was taken. We didn't have many things and part of them had been stolen. But just to show you that God want people to stand up, so we began at this address 626 East Lafayette Street.

Last Febeyary, my husband was arrested because I said I don't believed I've used 9,000 gallons of water, and don't have a bathtub or runnin' water in the house. Can't you see justice in disguise? Can't you see justice in disguise? One mo'nin' about five o'clock, my husband got up to use the washroom; there was a knock on our door. He said, "come in." That was two policemen. "What are you doin' up this time of night, five o'clock in the mo'nin'?" Can you see how justice is workin' in Mississippi?

You see, the point is about this and you can't deny it, not either one of you in this room, not Negroes, we have prayed for change in the state of Mississippi for years, and God made it so plain, he sent Moses down in Egypt-land to tell Pharaoh to let my people go. And he made it so plain in here in Mississippi, the man that has the project his name is Moses. Bob Moses. And he sent Bob Moses down in Mississippi, to tell all of these hate groups to let his people go.

You see, in this struggle some people say that "Well, she doesn't talk too good." The type of education that we get here, years to come you won't talk too good. The type of education, the type of education that we get in the state of Mississippi will make our minds so narrow it won't coordinate with our big bodies.

This is one of the next things that I don't like. Every church door in the state of Mississippi should be open for these meetings. But preachers have preached for years what he didn't believe hisself. And if he's willin' to trust

God, if he's willin' to trust God, he won't mind openin' the church door. Because the first words of Jesus' public ministry was "the spirit of the Lord is upon me, because he has anointed me to preach the gospel to the [inaudible]. He has sent me to proclaim and bring relief to the captive." And you know we are livin' in a captivated society today. And we know the things we done is right. The 37th of Psalms says, "Fret not thouselves because of evildoers. Neither be thy envious against the workers of iniquity. For they shall be cut down like the green grass and whither away as the green herb. Delight thouselves in the Lord and verily shalt thou be filled." And we are determined to be filled in Mississippi today.

Some of the white people will tell us, "Well, I just don't believe in integration." But he been integratin' at night a long time. If, if he hadn't been, it wouldn't been as many light-skinned Negroes as it is in here. The 17th, the 17th chapter of Acts and the 26th verse says, "Hath made of one blood all nations." So whether you black as a skillet or white as a sheet, we are made from the same blood, and we on are way.

We know, we know we have a long fight. Because the leaders like the preachers and the teachers, they are failin' to stand up today. But we know some of the reasons for that. This brainwashed education that the teachers have got, he know if he had to get a job as a janitor in this missile base that they'll be buildin', he probably turned somethin' over and blow up the place because he wouldn't know what it was.

Righteousness exalts a nation, but sin is a reproach to any people. Sin is beginnin' to reproach America today, and we want what is rightfully ours. And it's no need of runnin', and no need of sayin', "Honey I'm not gonna get in the mess," because if you are born in American with a black face, you are born in the mess. Do you think, do you think anybody would stand out in the dark to shoot me and to shoot other people, would you call that a brave person? It's a shame before God that people will let hate not only destroy us, but it will destroy them. Because a house divided against itself cannot stand. And today America is divided against itself because they don't want us to have even the ballot here in Mississippi. If we hadda been treated right all these years, they wouldn't be afraid for us to get the ballot.

People will go different places and say, "The Negroes until the outside agitators came in was satisfied." But I been dissatisfied ever since I was six years old. I remember my mother has worked for one measly dollar and a quarter a day. And you couldn't say that was satisfaction.

But to be truthful to you tonight, I first wished I was white. Some of you have wished the same thing. The reason I wished that they was the only people that wadn't doing nothin' but still had money and clothes. We was workin' year in and year out and wouldn't get to go to school for four months in the year because two of the months we didn't have nothin'.

Now you can't tell me you trust God and come out to the church every Sunday with a bunch of stupid hats on seein' what the other one have on and payin' the preachers way to hell and yours too. Preachers, preachers, preachers is, is, is really shockin' to find them out. You know they like to rear back in the corners and over the rostrum and say "what God has done for Meschach, Shadrach, and Abednego." But what he didn't know, God has done the same thing for Fannie Lou Hamer, Annelle Ponder, and Lawrence Guyot. And I can tell you now how this happened.

After I had been workin' for eight or ten months, I attended a voter educational workshop in Charleston, South Carolina. On the ninth of June, in 1963, we was returnin' from the workshop. We arrived in Winona, Mississippi about eleven o'clock. Four of the people got off of the bus, to use the restaurant. Two of the people got off the bus to use the washroom. At this time I was still on the bus. And I saw the four people rush out. And I got off of the bus. And I said, "What's wrong?" And Miss Ponder, south-wide supervisor of the Southern Christian Leadership Conference said, "It was a chief of police and a state highway patrolmen, ordered us to come out." And I said, "This is Mississippi for ya." She said, "Well, I think I'll get the tag number and we can file it in our report." And I got back on the bus. One of the girls that had used the washroom got back on the bus and that left five on our side.

When I looked through the window, they was gettin' those people in the car, and I stepped off of the bus again, and somebody screamed from that car, and said, "Get that one there." And a man said, "You are under arrest." When he opened the door, and as I started to get in, he kicked me. And I was carried to the county jail. When I got to the county jail with the two white fellows that drove me to jail, they was callin' me all kinds of names. And they was askin' me questions. And as I would try to answer they would cut me off.

And as we got to the county jail there, when we walked into the bookin' room, one of the policemens walked over to one of the young men, and jumped up with all of his weight on one of the Negro's feet. And then they began to place us in cells. I was placed in a cell with Miss Euvester Simpson from Itta Bena, Mississippi. And during that time they left some in the bookin' room. And I began to hear screams. And I began to hear howls. And I began to hear somebody say, "Can't you say 'yes sir' nigga." And I could hear Miss Ponder's voice say, "Yes, I can say 'yes sir.'" "So, say it." She said, "I don't know ya well enough." And I would hear when she would hit the floor again. And during the time they was beating Miss Ponder, I heard her when she began to pray. And she asked God to have mercy on those people, because they didn't know what they was doin'.

I don't know how long this lasted. But after awhile and Miss Ponder passed my cell. She didn't recognize me when she passed my cell. One of her eyes looked like blood. And her mouth was swollen. And she was holdin' up by proppen' against the back of the brick cell.

And then three men came to my cell, a state highway patrolman and a police and a plain dressed man. The state highway patrolman said, "Where you from?" I said, "Rulesville, Mississippi." He said, "I'm gonna check that out." And it wadn't too long before he was back. And he used a curse word and he said, "You are from Rulesville alright," said, "we going to make you wish you was dead."

I was led out of that cell, into another cell, where they had two Negro prisoners. Three white men in that room and two Negroes. The state highway patrolman ordered the first Negro to take that blackjack; it was a long leather blackjack and it was loaded with something heavy. And they ordered me to lay down on my face on a bunk bed. And the first Negro beat me; he had to beat me until the state highway patrolman give him orders to quit. Because he had already told him, "If you don't beat her, you know what I'll do to you." And he beat me I don't know how long. But after awhile he was exhausted and I was, too. And it was a horrible experience. And the state highway patrolman told the second Negro to take the blackjack. And I aksed at this time, I said, "How can you treat a human being like this?" The second prisoner said, "Move your hand lady; I don't want to hit you in your hand." But I was holding my hand behind on the left side to shield some of the licks. Because I suffered from polio when I was six years old. And this kind of beatin', I know I couldn't take it. So I held my hands behind, and after the second Negro began to beat me, the state highway patrolman ordered the first Negro that had beat, to sit on my feet, to keep me from workin' my feet. And I was screamin', and I couldn't help but scream. And one of the white men began to beat me in my head, and told me to "stop screamin'." And the only way that I could stop screamin' was to take my hand and hug it around the [inaudible] to muffle out the sound. My dress worked up from this hard blackjack, and I pulled my dress down, taking my hands behind me and pullin' my dress down. And one of the city policemens walked over and pulled my dress as high as he could. Five mens in this room while I was one Negro woman bein' beatin'. And at no time did I attempt to anything but scream and call on God. I don't know how long this lasted. But after awhile I must've passed out. And when I did raise my head up, the state highway patrolman said, "Get up from there, fatso." But I couldn't get up. I don't know how long, but I kept tryin' and you know God is always able, and after awhile I did get up and I went back to my cell.

That Tuesday when they had our trial, the same policeman that had participated in the beatin, was on the jury seat, people. And I was charged with disorderly conducted and resistin' arrest. And I want to say tonight, we can no longer ignore the fact, America is not the land of the free and the home of the brave. When just because people want to register to vote and be treated like human beins'. Chaney, Shriner [Schwerner], and Goodman is dead today. A house divided against itself cannot stand. America is divided against itself and without they considering us as human beings, one day American will crumble because God is not pleased. God is not pleased with all the murderin' and all the brutality and all the killins' for no reason at all. God is not pleased at the Negro children in the state of Mississippi sufferin' from malnutrition. God is not pleased because we have to go raggedy each day. God is not pleased because we have to go to the fields and work from ten to eleven hours for three lousy dollars. And then how can they say, "in ten years time, we will forced every Negro out of the state of Mississippi."

But I want these people to take a good look at theyselves. And after they sent the Chinese back to Chiney, and the Jews back to Jerusalem, and give the Indians their land back, and they take the Mayflower from which they came, the Negro will still be in Mississippi.

We don't have anything to be ashamed of here in Mississippi, and actually we don't carry guns because we don't have anything to hide. When you see people packin' guns, and is afraid for people to talk to ya, he's afraid that something is goin' be brought out in the openin' on him. But I want the people to know in Mississippi today the cover has been pulled back off of ya, and you don't have any place to hide. And we are on our way now. We are on our way and we won't turn around. We don't have anything to fear. I don't know today, I don't know tonight whether I'll actually get back to Rulesville. But all that they can destroy is the Fannie Lou that you meet tonight.

[break in tape]

. . . will keep on livin' day after day. Righteousness exalts a nation, but sin is a reproach to any people. The beatitude of the Bible, the fifth chapter of Matthew said "blessed are they that moan." We had moaned a long time in Mississippi. And he said, "The meek shall inherent the earth." And there's no race in America that's no meeker than the Negro. We are the only race in America that has had babies sold from our breasts with this slavery time, and had mothers sold from their babes. And we are the only race in America that had one man that marched through a mob group just to go to school, which was James H. Mary [Meredith]. We don't have anything to be ashamed of. All we have to do is trust God and launch and out unto the deep. You can pray until you faint, but if you don't get up and try to do something, God is not gonna put it in your lap.

It's very plain today some of the things that you have read in the Bible, when this man looked out and saw the number and said these are day from every nation. Can't you see these things coming to pass today when you see all of these students comin' here to help America to be a real democracy and make democracy a reality in the state of Mississippi?

Can't you see the fulfillin' of God's word? He said, "A city that sat on a hill cannot be hid. Let your light so shine that men would see your good works and glorify the father which is in heaven." He said, "Blessed are ye when men shall revise you and shall prosecute you, and shall set almighty evil against you falsely for my sake. Rejoice and be exceedingly glad, for great is your reward in heaven. For so they prosecuted the prophets which were before you." That's why I tell you tonight that you have a responsibility. And if you plan to walk in Christ's footstep and keep his commandments, you are willing to launch out unto the deep and go to the courthouse, not come here tonight to see what I look like, but to do something about the system here.

We are not, excuse me, we are not fighting against these people because we hate 'em, but we are fighting these people because we love 'em and we are the only thing can save 'em now. We are fighting to save these people from their hate and from all the things that would be so bad against them. We want them to see the right way.

Every night of my life that I lay down, before I go to sleep, I pray for these people that despitefully use me. And Christ said, "The meek shall inherit the earth." And he said before one tenth of one dot of his word would fail, heaven and earth would pass away, but his word would stand forever. And I believe tonight that one day in Mississippi, if I have to die for this, we shall overcome "We shall overcome," means something to me tonight. We shall overcome mean[s] as much to me tonight as, "Amazing grace how sweet the sound that saved a wretch like me." Because if grace has saved a wretch like me than we shall overcome. Because he said, "Seek and ye shall find. Knock and the door will be opened. Aks and it shall be given." It was a long time but now we see. We can see, we can design the new day. And one day the little Negro children, the little Negro boys and the little Negro girls, won't be afraid to walk down the street because of so much hate that will make a police jump on the kids. And one day, by standin' up, goin' to the courthouse try to register and vote, that we can get people this concerned about us. Because anytime you see a Negro policeman now you can rest assure he is a Tom. Because, because if he wadn't a Tom, if he wasn't a Tom he would be elected by the people, not just a handful of folk. And he'll get out on the street and beat your brains out and afraid to go down the corner and arrest a white man.

We want people, we want people over us that's concerned about the people because we are human beings. Regardless of how they abused us for all these years, we always cared what was goin' on. We have prayed and we have hoped for God to bring about a change and now the time have come for people to stand up and as something real, real peculiar but still is great. There used to be a time when you would hit a Negro, a white man would hit a Negro, the others would go and hide. But there's a new day now. When you hit a Negro, you likely to see 1,000 there.

Because God care, God care and we care, and we can no longer ignore the fact that we can sit down and wait for things to change, because as long as they can keep their feet on our neck they will always do. But it's time for us to stand up and be women and men. Because actually I'm tired of bein' called "Aunty." I, I wondered, I wondered in life what actually time are they allowed for me to be a woman? Because until I was 36 I was a girl. "Girl this." And now I'm 46 and it's "Aunty." But I want you to know tonight, I don't have one white niece or nephew. And if you, and if you don't want to call me Miss Hamer, just call me plain Fannie because I'm not your aunt.

You know, people had said for years and years, "The Negroes can't do anything." That's the report that they were sending out about the people of Mississippi. "The Negroes are ignorant," but just who's actin' stupid now?

I heard a preacher say one night, I heard a preacher say one night that people could look at the clouds and say it was going to rain, and it would rain. And still now they can't discern the signs of time. We can see the signs, people, the signs of time. And the time now is to stand up. Stand up for your constitutional right and one day if we keep on standin' up, we won't have to take this literacy test to copy a section of the constitution of Mississippi we had never seen, and interpret it too. When if he had the same test, he couldn't. One day we won't have all of this to do. We'll keep right on walkin', and we'll keep right on talkin', and we'll keep right on marchin'.

And when your minister say, "Well, it's all right to stand up, but don't march. . . ." [cut in tape] And when he says this it make me sick, because he's tellin' a big lie. Because every dollar bill got a politician on it and the preacher love it. And if this man, and if this man don't choose to be a shepherd, he can be a sheep and follow the shepherd. Ya know, actually I used to have so much respect for teachers and preachers, I would be nervous when I'd be around 'em, but since I found out that that's the scariest two things we got in Mississippi. How, how can you, how can you actually trust a man and have respect for him, he'll tell you to trust God but he doesn't trust him himself?

We want leaders in our community, and what people will say, say well, "If we can get rid of Fannie Lou," say "we can get rid of the trouble." But what they don't know freedom is like an Eden council: if you kill me, it'll break out all over the place.

We want ours, and we want ours now. I question sometime, actually, as any of these people that hate so, which is the white, read anything about the Constitution. Eighteen hundred and seventy, the 15th amendment was added on to the Constitution of the United States that gave every man a chance to vote for what he think to be the right way. And now this is '64 and they still trying to keep us away from the ballot. But we are determined today. We are determined that one day we'll have the power to ballot. And the sooner you go to the courthouse the sooner we'll have it.

It's one thing, it's one thing I don't want you to say tonight after I finish—and it won't be long—I don't want to hear you say, "Honey, I'm behind." Well move. I don't want you back there, because you could be 200 miles behind. I want you to say, "I'm with you," and we'll go up this freedom road together.

Before I leave you I would like to quote from an old hymn my mother used to sing, "Should Earth against my soul engage, and fiery darts be hurled. When I can smile at Satan's rage and face this frowning world."

Thank you.

§114 Father Theodore M. Hesburgh

Theodore Martin Hesburgh was born on May 25, 1917 in Syracuse, New York. He attended the University of Notre Dame and received his bachelor of philosophy degree from Gregorian University (Rome) in 1939. He received his Congregation of the Holy Cross ordination at Notre Dame's Sacred Heart Basilica on June 24, 1943 from Bishop Noll of Fort Wayne. Father Hesburgh received his doctorate in sacred theology from the Catholic University of America in 1945, and joined the Notre Dame faculty later that year. In 1952 he became Notre Dame's 15th president, at a time when the university had already begun its commitment to racial integration.

In a recent phone interview, Father Hesburgh recalls that there were no African American students or staff members when he was a student in 1934. He remembers thinking it seemed strange, and asking about it. Honest administrators told him it would be uncomfortable for southern students, whose tuition and residential fees were integral to the college. When he returned from Gregorian University to join the Notre Dame faculty, he remembers that there were African American students after 1945. An archive photograph shows integrated basketball players on campus in 1950, and by the time future Minnesota Supreme Court Associate Justice Alan Page was a consensus all-American football player for the Irish in 1966, many in the university community realized they had done no altruistic favors.

Hesburgh's life of public service started unexpectedly: he began getting Sunday afternoon phone calls from General Dwight D. Eisenhower's aide de Camp, Robert L. Schulz, in 1947. The first request was that he join a panel of physicists at the

National Science Foundation (NSF), which would receive a formal charter in 1950. He received similar requests in 1952 and 1954. In 1957 the Eisenhower administration asked him to serve on the first ever United States Commission on Civil Rights. The intent was to have a commission evenly split ideologically (three Democrats and three Republicans) and geographically (three from the North and three from the South). Eisenhower said that Father Hesburgh would count as a Republican, despite his Independent auto-identification. Hesburgh's service as a charter member (1957–1968) and chair (1969–1972) of the U.S. Committee on Civil Rights show traces of his global leadership style. He exudes commanding power and knowledge of the political plate tectonics convulsing the nation simultaneously with local, individual concerns.

In this rather stunning and erudite speech to the Academy of Arts and Sciences, Father Hesburgh addresses the nation's intellectual elite on the moral dimensions of the civil rights movement. Readers with minimal social scientific training will recognize the names of a handful of still active members of the academy who would have been part of the intended audience in 1964: Robert Dahl (1960), Maurice Duverger (1962); David Easton (1962), John Kenneth Galbraith (1952), Claude Levi-Strauss (1963), Seymour Martin Lipset (1962), Lucian Pye (1962), and Henry Kissinger (1959). In his address Father Hesburgh appeals to the abstract lines of thought developed by Jacques Maritain, Socrates, Aristotle, Augustine, Aquinas, Henry David Thoreau, and Mohandas Gandhi. But the logic of these abstractions is only clear relative to each case of humiliation and violence. When principles are disconnected from human well-being, the principles have been misused. After carefully delineating the moral dimensions of human beings via a detailed and scholarly exegesis on metaphysics by way of political theory, Hesburgh concludes, with many of his predecessors, that these principles "are all too often assumed rather than demonstrated." It remains for the nation to put into practice equality in education, equality before the law, equality in the franchise, equality in opportunity and equality in public accommodation. Without a concomitant program of action, these sacred principles will do nothing to alleviate the despair of the ghetto. Importantly, Hesburgh's foundations are shot through with New Testament theology, which leaves him with but one conclusion as to civil rights: if we are created equal; if we are all members of the body of Christ; if we are all redeemed by Christ's death; if we have a common rebirth through baptism; if we are striving for heaven; and, if we do to him what we do to the least of these, "any form of racism is tantamount to blasphemy."

The Moral Dimensions of the Civil Rights Movement

Meeting of the American Academy of Arts and Sciences, Boston, Massachusetts
November 1964

Several years ago I attended a lecture by a distinguished South African scholar at Capetown University on the subject: "The Moral Justification of

Apartheid." After the lecture, we were driving down the Cape to his home university of Stellenbosch when he asked me: "What did you think of my lecture?" I told him that he had convinced me that there was no moral justification of apartheid. "I had hoped to do the opposite," he replied.

It might be said that I hope to do the opposite today: to show that the civil rights movement here and about the world is not just another economic, political, social, or ethnic movement, although it is all of these, too. There is a deep moral dimension to the whole concern for civil rights in our times. In fact, the moral dimension is the most fundamental aspect of it all. Without it, the movement loses much of its vital dynamism and ultimate thrust. Also, without the moral dimension, the civil rights movement will never be completely understood, or completely successful either.

Even our political leaders have understood this truth. Many of them have said that we should try to achieve full civil rights for all of our citizens not simply because it will be helpful to our cause in the international field, or because it will make American life more peaceful and productive, but because it is right that this should happen.

As he signed the Civil Rights Act of 1964 into law, President Johnson said:

"Our generation of Americans has been called on to continue the unending search for justice within our own borders.

"We believe that all men are created equal—yet many are denied equal treatment.

"We believe that all men have certain inalienable rights—yet many Americans do not enjoy those rights.

"We believe that all men are entitled to the blessings of liberty—yet millions are being deprived of those blessings, not because of their own failures, but because of the color of their skin.

"The reasons are deeply imbedded in history and tradition and the nature of man. We can understand without rancor or hatred how this all happened. But it cannot continue.

"Our Constitution, the foundation of our Republic, forbids it. The principles of our freedom forbid it. Morality forbids it. And the law I will sign tonight forbids it. . . ."

"The law says," President Johnson continued, "that those who are equal before God shall also be equal in the polling booths, in the classrooms, in the factories, and in hotels and restaurants and movie theaters, and other places that provide service to the public.

"We will achieve these goals because most Americans are law-abiding citizens *who want to do what is right.* . . .

"Let us hasten the day when our unmeasured strength and our unbounded spirit will be free to do the great works ordained to this nation by the just and wise God who is Father of us all."

If you ponder upon these words, you will see that this is at base a moral statement of the problem. The appeal is directly to conscience, to justice, to equality before God, to inalienable rights, to responsibility in freedom, to the law of basic human dignity as ordained by a wise and just God and echoed in our Constitution and the laws that specify the civil rights that our Constitution proclaims. The appeal of our President is most forceful because one cannot reject his conclusions without rejecting his moral principles which are at the base of what it means to be a human person in the good society.

I am reminded of what often happened during the hearings of the United States Commission on Civil Rights here and there about the country. We would come to a particularly difficult moment when any kind of consensus seemed impossible, either because of the complication of the problem at hand or the hostility of the audience or witnesses. At this point, one of the staff would slip me a note scribbled on the inevitable long sheet of yellow legal paper, saying in effect: "Better give them some theology." All of us can legitimately differ about ways and means, about possible solutions to seemingly impossible problems. But ultimately, anyone who understands anything of the Judeo-Christian tradition at the base of Western Culture must hold some common principles about the nature and destiny of man which alone validate the society in which we live. It is characteristic of our ambivalent age that all too few people ever consciously consider these fundamental philosophical and theological principles, but yet, consciously or unconsciously, they are there, and in a time of great conflict they will be recognized, appealed to, and, however incoherently, understood.

It has always been to me a curious reality that among the multitudinous books that our age produces one finds so very few that address themselves to the moral foundations of democracy, or correlatively, to the moral dimensions of human rights. Professor John Hallowell of Duke University has written such a book. He justifies it in a few words: "Our democratic institutions require a philosophy of life to sustain them . . . Without a clear understanding of why the institutions exist, we shall have neither the means of defending them intellectually, nor the resolution to defend them by force when the occasion demands it." And again, "Democracy rests upon a faith in man as a rational, moral, and spiritual creature, and it is as much aspiration as it is fact. The ideals of democracy never have been and never will be achieved with perfection—they are goals constantly to be striven for, but never perfectly realized. In the last analysis, democracy is 'a venture of faith in the moral and spiritual possibilities of men when entrusted with freedom.'"

Sir Richard Livingstone, one-time Vice Chancellor of Oxford University, made the same point, on both the philosophical and theological level, in a book he wrote during the last war. He was addressing himself to another crisis, but I find his words relevant today as we face the major crisis of our own times, the drive towards a more complete realization of civil rights. Sir Richard says:

> "We shall not understand ourselves and our predicament unless we realize what has happened during the past fifty years. Every civilization grows up round and with a system of beliefs and values, which are its vital principle, the nerve which feeds and keeps it healthy. If that principle perishes, if that nerve is cut, then the structure of society which depends on it still remains, but the life has gone out of it, its self-renewing power is gone, and it declines first into decay and then into death. Those who have lived through the last fifty years have witnessed the steady and progressive destruction of the soul of Western civilization. . . .
>
> "The soul of Europe is partly Greek and partly Christian. The vital force of our civilization comes from two sources, beyond which no others count seriously, from Palestine and from Greece. We may not believe in Christianity. We may not like it, but whether we deplore it or not, the main source of Europe is Christianity . . . the mass of people drew and still draw the best part of their beliefs and standards in life and conduct from Christianity, however confused and diluted the channels through which they pass. To attack Christianity was to attack the spiritual life of Europe, to weaken it was to weaken that life . . . and so we got our modern civilization—a civilization of means without ends, with ample body, but with a meager soul, with a rich inheritance, but without clear values or a ruling principle. . . . There is a phrase in Plato which exactly describes our condition . . . the danger of living 'by habit without an intellectual principle.'"

I take it that what Hallowell and Livingstone are telling us is that moral dimensions are historically, philosophically, and theologically discernible, but often taken for granted except in time of crisis, when we come running to them to justify our cause, to inspire heroism, to bolster courage, and to convince ourselves that the battle is really worth fighting. The deeper the crisis, the deeper our principles should run, the more clarion-like they should sound, the more clearly should they be enunciated. The last three Presidents have told our nation that the present crisis in civil rights is the greatest and most important domestic problem facing our nation. Clearly, then, it is again a time for basic principles.

While the principles at issue have recently been enunciated often enough, and clearly enough, as for example in the statement of President Johnson quoted above, the foundations of the principles are all too often assumed rather than demonstrated. Even our Founding Fathers held these truths to be self-evident: That man is endowed by his Creator with certain inalienable rights and that among these are life, liberty, and the pursuit of happiness. This is the tradition, rightly enough, but there is more to it than the mere statement and what it assumes, and wrongly assumes to be philosophically self-evident. It is not self-evident apparently to those who rule a third of the human race today and hold in practice that man has only those rights conceded to him by the State.

Where does one begin then? Since we are talking about human rights and the problems incident to our common humanity, we might well begin by considering more deeply what a human person is, for it is the human person who alone is the subject on earth of these inalienable rights which somehow originate in his nature. It is the human person, too, who bears the responsibility to respect these human rights. It is likewise the human person who is endowed with that inherent dignity and destiny that make a denial of these rights not merely a bad political, economic, or social situation, but a devastating spectacle of the inhumanity of man to man.

To consider the human person is to enter the realm of metaphysics, the mystery of being as uniquely realized in the inner sanctuary of the individual human being. The metaphysical tradition of the west defines the person in terms of individuality and independence. The person exists not as migrant bird against the Fall sky, the sound of wings, the flash of light against color, but as a reality which subsists spiritually, constituting a universe unto itself, a relatively independent whole within the great overarching whole of the universe and deriving from the Transcendent Whole which is God. A person lives in self-possession, a master of himself, capable of containing himself, thanks to intellect and freedom. This same tradition sees in God the infinite essence of personality, since the very existence of God consists in the infinite and absolute superexistence of knowledge and love.

The individuality of the human person is not like the individuality of other corporal beings, because personality is not directly related to matter, man's body, but has its roots in spirit, man's immortal soul.

The best description of human personality that I know of comes from Jacques Maritain's *Principles d'une politique humaniste*,

> "What do we mean precisely when we speak of the human person:
> When we say that a man is a person, we do not mean merely that he
> is an individual, in the sense that an atom, a blade of grass, a fly or
> an elephant is an individual. Man is an individual who holds himself
> in hand by intelligence and will. He does not exist only in a physical

manner. He has spiritual super-existence through knowledge and love; he is, in a way, a universe in himself, a microcosm, in which the great universe in its entirety can be encompassed through knowledge; and through love, he can give himself completely to beings who are to him, as it were, other selves, a relation for which no equivalent can be found in the physical world. The human person possesses these character-istics because in the last analysis man, this flesh and these perishable bones which are animated and activated by a divine fire, exists 'from the womb to the grave' by virtue of the very existence of his soul, which dominates time and death. Spirit is the root of personality. The notion of personality thus involves that of totality and independence; no mat-ter how poor and crushed he may be, a person, as such, is a whole and subsists in an independent manner. To say that man is a person is to say that in the depths of his being he is more a whole than a part, and more independent than servile. It is to say that he is a minute fragment of matter that is at the same time a universe, a beggar who communicates with absolute being, mortal flesh whose value is eternal, a bit of straw into which heaven enters. It is this metaphysical mystery that religious thought points to when it says that the person is the image of God. The value of the person, his dignity and his rights belong to the order of things naturally sacred which bear the imprint of the Father of being, and which have in Him the end of their movement."

The moral conscience of the human person tells him many things: what is morally right and morally wrong, a knowledge, more or less developed, of what is generally called the natural law, and the rights that any human person possesses simply because he is a person, an independent whole who is master of himself and his acts, who can know his destiny, what is to his ultimate good, who is not a means, but an end. The natural law means nothing if it does not say that the human person has a right to be respected for what he is, and what he is for. As Maritain has said, there is by virtue of man's ontologically unchanging human nature, an order or disposition which human reason can discover and according to which the human will must act in order to attune itself to the essential and necessary ends of the human being.

There is, of course, progression in the sensitivity of man's conscience and in his perception of the full meaning of the natural law, the full exten-sion of the rights of man. The fact is that during ancient and medieval times, more attention was often paid to the obligations, than to the rights of man. The Eighteenth Century finally saw more emphasis on human rights, although, at times, somewhat exclusively. Now today the wheel has come full round. One of the most stirring documents of our times, Pope John's *Pacem in Terris*, is totally cast in the framework of rights and duties. The transitional paragraph, following the opening outline of human rights, bears quoting here:

> "The natural rights with which we have been dealing are however inseparably connected, in the very person who is their subject, with just as many respective duties; and rights as well as duties find their source, their sustenance and their inviolability in the natural law which grants or enjoins them. Therefore, the right of every man to life is correlative with the duty to preserve it; his right to a decent standard of living with the duty of living it becomingly; and his right to investigate the truth with the duty of seeking it ever more completely and profoundly.
>
> "Once this is admitted, it also follows that in human society, to one man's right there corresponds a duty in all other persons: the duty, namely, of acknowledging and respecting the right in question. For every fundamental human right draws its indestructible moral force from the natural law, which in granting it imposes a corresponding obligation. Those, therefore, who claim their own rights, yet altogether forget or neglect to carry out their respective duties, are people who build with one hand and destroy with the other."

There is one more basic consideration which must be studied here: that of human equality in regard to rights, or, as it is often more specifically stated: equality before the law. Historically, this basic truth, a necessary consequence of all that has been said of human dignity, natural law and human rights, has been honored more in the breech than in the keeping. Philosophically, there have been those who could easily rationalize slavery in all its multitudinous forms: the great slave class of the Greeks and Romans, the lower caste untouchables of India, the millions enslaved and transported from Africa in the name of white superiority, the economically enslaved of the Industrial Revolution, the millions enslaved today in the name of the Marxist-Leninist myth to promote the eventual millennium of the Proletariat. As was declared by a Nazi at Nuremberg, there was in their judgment "a greater distance between the lowest forms still called human and our superior races than between the lowest man and the highest monkey." This noxious poison of racism is still with us in many forms today, and often enough science is prostituted in an attempt to make it intellectually respectable.

Human equality has an almost equal enemy in those who confuse equality with egalitarianism. The human person is not an abstraction; he lives as an individual in time and space. Individually human persons are unequal in many ways, both natural and acquired: in talent, ability, virtue, intelligence, beauty, grace, energy, and health. To all of these natural or acquired inequalities, one must add those that result from long generations of injustice, persecution, exploitation, the whole weight of sorrow that re-sults from bad men and bad institutions. These inequalities of time and place do not create a new species of man, or produce a man less entitled to his rightful equality before the law and equality of opportunity for all things human. The basic mistake of the idealistic egalitarians is that they refuse to look at the reality of the human situation. They are disturbed by any hierarchy of values. Everything must be leveled. Mediocrity must be the order of the day. There is no place for the superior, no matter in what context it is achieved. Creative genius of any kind must be put into their preconceived straight-jacket. Culture must be, and really is in their society, horribly drab. There are no mountains to valleys among men, only plains. All this is a perversion of human equality, is again an over-emphasis on rights at the expense of obligations. Egalitarians may indeed speak the right words at times, and engage in good causes, but their music is disso-nant when one considers that equality in rights is only a moral beginning. Performance differs from person to person. All should have an equal op-portunity, but then if history is any guide, within the democracy of equal men there will always be the aristocracy of excellence.

Once more, I believe that of all the philosophers I have read on this sub-ject, Jacques Maritain best puts the whole problem of equality in clearest perspective:

> "If you treat a man as a man, which means if you respect and love the secret he bears within him and the good of which he is capable as an individual person, then to that extent you make effective in yourself his equality or unity in nature with yourself.
>
> "In the experience of misery, in the sorrows of great catastrophes, in humiliations and distress, under the blows of the executioner or the bombs of total war, in concentration camps, in the hovels of starving people in big cities, in common necessity, the doors of solitude fly open and man recognizes man. Also man knows man when the sweetness of a great joy or a great love for a moment makes the eye pure. In helping his fellows or being helped by them, in sharing the same elementary actions and the same elementary feelings, in beholding his neighbor, the humblest gesture shows him, in others and in himself, human na-ture's common resources and common goodness, a goodness that is primitive, rudimentary, wounded, unconscious, and repressed. At one stroke the real equality and community of nature is revealed to him as a most precious good, an unknown marvel, a fundamental stratum of existence, of more worth than all the differences and inequalities grafted onto it."

Theology adds new dimensions to this philosophical concept of the unity of the human race. One of the mysteries of iniquity is how a Christian people can ever espouse racism in any form when professing to believe that we are all created equal in the same image of God; that we are all members of the same Body of Christ; that we are equally redeemed by Our Lord and Savior; that we share His same divine life through our common rebirth in Baptism; that together we are striving to possess Him unendingly in the same Kingdom of Heaven; that whatsoever we do to one of these, His least brethren, we do to Him. Against this central belief of Christianity, any form of racism is tantamount to blasphemy.

Every great moral system, philosophical or theological, is in reality an effort to ask man to rise above the human condition, in one way or another. The concrete realization of human equality, especially in the social order, requires great human effort, intelligence, and virtue, since in historical fact man is engaged in a progressive conquest over his nature and himself. Human equality may well be a philosophical postulate, but in human society it will be assured by the dual dynamism of human law and human understanding. Equality in the social context is, like liberty, a goal to be won, a battle never ending. Pope John summarized it briefly:

> "The order which prevails in society is by nature moral. Grounded as it is in truth, it must function according to the norms of justice, it should be inspired and perfected by mutual love, and finally, it should be brought to an ever more refined and human balance in freedom."

This now brings us to a question which I have been asked before. When appearing once before a hearing of the Senate Judiciary Committee, Senator Eastland asked me: "What are civil rights?" On that occasion, which was less friendly than this, since my appointment to the Civil Rights Commission was in contention, I answered more briefly: "Civil rights are the rights granted to every American citizen under the Constitution." Even in the short seven years since that day, the specificity of civil rights has grown appreciably, but the basic principles are the same.

It appears to me that we avoid some of the deviations mentioned above, and place ourselves in the most propitious moral stance, if rights are placed in the context of equality of opportunity to exercise both one's rights and one's responsibilities. Fundamentally, what we are seeking for everyone is the equal opportunity to have free access to everything that bears upon the full development of all of our human capabilities. This means many things in modern American society. First and foremost, it means the right to life. In one county in Mississippi, there was a murder, several shootings, whippings, and beatings during the first five months of this year, without a single indictment of the guilty parties. In one city of 10,401 people, McComb, Mississippi, there have been 35 bombings, burnings, and beatings this year without punishment, even of the parties who admitted guilt.

A Negro citizen of that State told me that his right to life was as tenuous as the good will of every White citizen, since any one of them could take his life with impunity. To develop oneself humanly, one must first live.

Then there is the right to become involved with the political life of the city, the state, the nation. This today is abridged in many ways, first, by the denial of voter registration, then by the denial of the vote to those registered, and, finally, by fraudulent miscounting of the votes cast. All of this is further vitiated by the lack of representation, indeed the misrepresentation, of many Negroes in the South, and by the inability of many to take any personal part in the political life of their community by holding office.

Next consider the equality of educational opportunity. Juridically, this was settled more than ten years ago by the *Brown* decision of the Supreme Court. In fact, only 1.2 percent of the Negro population in the South has been integrated in the past ten years, and in the North, the great majority of Negro children are condemned to inferior segregated schooling because of the pattern of segregated housing. Here we have the perfect vicious circle: Negroes are poorly educated because Negroes are poorly educated. The products of inferior schools staff the schools that gave them an inferior education to produce another generation of poorly-educated children and so *ad infinitum*. The simple moral mandate here is to break the vicious circle, and on every point of its circumference. This will involve radical educational reorganization in the South and a change of housing patterns in the North, but again, equality is a mercurial element that must be captured by the continued dynamism of a drive for human progress in any society. This must be done without impairing the quality of education for anyone, and it can be done if we prize equality enough to give it a chance to operate in the life of every American. It will be costly, but the moral imperative is deaf to financial considerations. It must be done because it is right. If we can afford to spend fifty billion dollars every year for defense, we can afford to spend whatever is necessary to elevate the quality of life in America. This, after all, is what we are defending. Without equal opportunity for education on all levels, the door to every other opportunity is automatically closed. We cannot appeal to the weight of past negligence to foreclose the opportunities of the present and the future. We have had enough of conversation. What we need now is imaginative plans and action.

Another large area of opportunity that remains to be opened to minorities in America is housing. Anyone with the money can buy the highest priced car on the market. However, the Negro pays twice as much for his house as the White purchaser, and to compound his problem, he is restricted for the most part to buying only those houses that the White citizen no longer wants in neighborhoods that Whites have deserted. Whatever one says of rights, there is a vast and silent conspiracy to keep this immoral situation as it is. Bankers, builders, and realtors, often aided and abetted by public federal financing, close the normal housing market to Negroes and other minorities. Again, the moral imperative is clear. Every American should have equal opportunity to buy a decent home in a wholesome neighborhood, wherever his heart desires and his means permit. Our moral blindness in this situation has given us a divided America, an ugly America replete with black ghettoes. We can spend forty billion dollars to get a man on the moon where no life exists, and yet we continue to condemn millions of human beings to substandard, unsanitary, and dilapidated housing. We allow children to grow up in city jungles, to attend disgraceful schools, to be surrounded with every kind of physical and moral ugliness, and then we are surprised if they are low in aspiration and accomplishment. Some say: "Why don't they move?" And I ask you, "Where?" of the hundreds of millions of dollars of FHA assisted private housing, less than one percent has benefited the Negro, because of the closed market. The moral judgment is clear enough. First grant equality of opportunity and then criticize poor performance, if indeed there is then poor performance. But poor performance in an impossible situation is no reason for withholding the equality of opportunity to improve the situation.

Equality of economic opportunity is likewise on this list. This, of course, is meaningless without the educational opportunity to qualify oneself. Here, too, we face the vicious circle of denial. Negroes have historically been educated only for menial jobs because only menial jobs are available to Negroes. In times of economic crisis, the Negro is the first fired, naturally, since he was the last hired. Because he makes on the average only half as much as the White citizen, many other opportunities that cost money are closed to him. He presents a dismal picture of personal failure to his children; his wife must work which further corrodes his family life. Thus, each new generation, reared in failure, has no great aspiration to the success that appears impossible. Failure breeds failure and misery begets more misery.

Then there is the matter of the administration of justice, equality before the law. I think it a fair appraisal of history, ancient and modern, to say that the poor have always fared badly with the instrumentalities of justice. Perhaps the many injustices that often accounted for their being poor made them troublesome and sometimes violent, but, once more, the fruits of injustice are no excuse for further delaying justice. If the poor happen to be highly visible, as the Negroes are, then they fare even more badly.

Think of your chances for justice in a county where no member of your race is on the police force, or among the jail personnel, or on the judge's bench, or in the jury box. Add to this situation that of a state where there are only four Negro lawyers and they are intimidated from handling civil rights cases, and there is only one White member of the bar who will promote this kind of justice until he is summarily disbarred.

We have a magnificent record of federal enforcement in many difficult areas like kidnapping, espionage, and inter-state auto theft, but somehow the area of infringement of basic civil rights, even the murder of those promoting their own and other's rights, has generally eluded all of our electronic expertise. What do we do? Perhaps tighten the blindfold on the figure of Justice so that justice indeed is color blind and all men are equal before the law. We might also promote a new passion for justice in all of our law schools. A former president of the American Bar Association has just recently perpetrated a monumental intellectual fraud in misrepresenting the meaning of the proposed Civil Rights Act in an effort to defeat its passage, financed incidentally by public money from his State.

Lastly, there is the matter of equal access to public accommodations, now clearly a matter of civil rights. Have you ever imagined what it would be like to be insulted ten or twenty times a day? To travel and not know whether you would be able to find a place to wash or eat or rest or sleep, despite the fact that you were surrounded by facilities apparently open to the public? To be looked upon as something unclean when all you wished was a haircut or to try on a suit you would like to buy? To have to drink from a special fountain, to sit in a special seat, the worst one? To be always the last served, if you were allowed to be served at all, to be made to feel inferior even amidst people who were clearly your inferior as person, to have to do all the menial work, to always be the servant if not the clown, to expect nothing and generally get what you expected? This is the life of second-class citizenship to which we have generally subjected our Negro brethren until most recently. When they began finally to resent it, we were the most surprised people in the world. They actually wanted to eat in the same places where we eat, to swim where we swim, to rest where we rest, to pray where we pray, even to be buried where we are buried. The fact that they surprised us by the vehemence of their desire to enjoy the same human rights and the same human dignity that we claim for ourselves is perhaps the measure of our own moral blindness. Had we not heard for centuries: "Do unto others as you would have others do unto you." What is our moral obligation as a nation? To make possible basic human dignity at the very least; to judge human persons for what they are and how they perform when given an equal chance, not by their color, a fact over which they have no control or no choice; to make equality of opportunity a reality in the whole spectrum of human development; this at least would begin to open up the closed society.

The litany of inequality might go on, but I believe that we have at least said enough to establish the depth and range of the moral dimension of the civil rights movement. One more point should be emphasized. Morality is not just one decision; it is a system. The problem of civil rights in America today is an organic problem of many closely articulated parts. The total problem cannot be solved by tinkering with a solution to one of the segments of the problem. We must have an integral moral solution, across the whole spectrum of the problem, if equal opportunity, human rights, and human dignity are to be realized in our times.

The equal opportunity to vote creates further problems without equal opportunity for education. Equal opportunity for education is an empty phrase without equal opportunity for housing. Equal opportunity for housing is meaningless without economic opportunity, which, in turn, is an empty promise without educational opportunity. Justice before the law is chimerical without participation in the instrumentalities of justice. And, none of this will come to pass in a truly humane fashion until each American is convinced that he cannot detach himself from the problem at hand, for each one of us is involved, and every part of our nation is involved. No man is an island in this total sea of inequality. When one man's dignity is cruelly wounded, every man suffers indignity. When one man is denied equality, none of us is really free. And when all of this happens on a wholesale scale, the whole quality of our life as a nation is debased.

How did we arrive at the ugly impasse we so often see today? President Johnson said in the statement quoted at the beginning of this paper that: "The reasons are deeply imbedded in history and tradition and the nature of man." A brief look at history might help us understand the agonizing rise and fall of tension, the fluctuations in the moral relationships between Whites and Negroes in this country. This is, of course, a two-sided history, increasingly so in recent years and months.

We must begin with the state of slavery, more or less passively accepted by both sides for about two centuries, mainly because the Negro could not do very much about it and the Whites did not want to do much about it because of economic considerations. However, America's stated morals finally came to the surface under the pressure of abolitionists. There was a bloody war, Lincoln's Emancipation Proclamation, and the 14th and 15th Amendments to bring the Constitution up-to-date.

After an initial good start, there appeared the original White backlash— a reaction to the excesses of the carpetbaggers. The thrust of this backlash was, as institutionalized for the next eight or nine decades, to keep the Negro in his place, definitely a place inferior to that of the Whites. The *Plessy* decision of the Supreme Court further silenced any moral inquietude regarding the "separate but equal" situation that resulted. Thus, for almost a century after the Emancipation Proclamation, what was proclaimed did not come to be, and one finds all too little moral concern from any public or private source during this whole period. At best, the Whites were paternalistic; at worst, they were oppressive and morally insensitive for the most part.

What was the turning point, the new day for civil rights? First, there was World War II which meant greater mobility for Negroes in service or war industries, greater employment opportunity under the stress of labor shortages in the North, East, and West, a breath of new interest from President Roosevelt—but still, for most Negroes, depressingly servile work in industry and the Armed Forces. President Truman began the work of integration in the Services, the *Brown* decision of 1954 reversed the earlier Supreme Court decision of *Plessy*, outlawing separate but equal in education. The walls began to crumble.

President Eisenhower signed the first Civil Rights Bill in eighty years, and established the Civil Rights Commission. Shortly after its first biennial report, another and stronger Civil Rights Bill appeared.

About this time, less than ten years ago, the real birth of the Negro's civil rights movement took place. In Montgomery, Alabama, Mrs. Rosa Parks, who had many times moved to the rear of the bus when told to do so, one day refused to move. When the driver stopped the bus and threatened to call the police, she said, "Then just call them." The second key event came in North Carolina when some young Negro students staged the first sit-in. No one would have guessed that these two Negro actions would result, within a few short years, in another federal law outlawing for all time what had been the accepted, although immoral custom, of many generations. What was the thrust of the movement that grew from these two seemingly unimportant events?

Philosophically, the roots go deep. In the pre-Christian era, there was the action of Socrates, more than two thousand years ago, that first lit the flame. Socrates drank hemlock rather than concede the right we grant our citizens in the First Amendment. Aristotle quoted Antigone to argue that "An unjust law is not a law." The two greatest intellects in the Christian tradition, Augustine and Thomas Aquinas, agreed that any human law contrary to natural or divine law ought not to be obeyed. In the American tradition, we have Henry Thoreau's essay on *Civil Disobedience*, that inspired Gandhi's doctrine of non-violence. Together they provide the best descriptive name for the Negro civil rights movement of the past few years: non-violent civil disobedience. It has many dangerous offspring, some clearly illegitimate, but this should not distract us from the inherent moral dynamism that, from the first, characterized the best part of the Negro civil rights movement.

To return for a moment to its most recent forebears: Thoreau and Gandhi. In 1846, Sam Staples, the town jailor, interrupted Thoreau's tranquil life at Walden Pond and put him in jail because he refused to pay his poll tax to a government that imprisoned and returned runaway slaves, thus upholding slavery. He was somewhat upset to be released the next day because apparently his Aunt Maria paid the tax for him. Thanks to Aunt Maria's action, we have Thoreau's personal protest in print today. It is the text by which all the world best knows Thoreau.

I shall only give the headlines of his thesis, the bare bones of Thoreau's argument: "Can there not be a government in which majorities do not virtually decide right and wrong, but conscience? . . . Must the citizen ever for a moment, or in the least degree, resign his conscience to the legislator? . . .The only obligation which I have a right to assume is to do at any time what I think right . . . a wise man will not leave the right to the mercy of chance, nor wish it to prevail through the power of the majority. . . . Unjust laws exist: shall we be content to obey them, or shall we endeavor to amend them, and obey until we have succeeded, or shall we transgress them at once? . . . If the injustice is part of the necessary friction of government, let it go, let it go, perchance it will wear smooth . . . but if it is of such a nature that it requires you to be the agent of injustice to another, then I say, break the law. Let your life be a counter friction to stop the machine. I think that it is enough that they (The Abolitionists) have God on their side . . . any man more right than his neighbors constitutes a majority of one already. . . . Under a government that imprisons anyone unjustly, the true place for a just man is also a prison." True to his word, when Emerson asked Thoreau what he was doing in jail, Thoreau replied, "What are you doing outside?" Thoreau concludes: "A minority is powerless while it conforms to the majority . . . but it is irresistible when it clogs by its own weight. If the alternative is to keep all just men in prison, or give up . . . slavery, the state will not hesitate which to choose."

This was heady doctrine, even back in 1846, but its relevance did not later escape either Gandhi or Martin Luther King. Gandhi saw civil disobedience as a constitutional form of persuasion, as a way to reach the minds and hearts of people and thus to mold the law. Thoreau, in one brief phrase, gave Gandhi an insight to a new element adding greater moral weight to the doctrine of civil disobedience. "How much more eloquently and effectively he can combat injustice who has experienced a little in his own person."

Gandhi made an eloquent plea to his countrymen for this new element of non-violent, suffering civil disobedience, implicit in Thoreau:

"Non-violence in its dynamic condition means conscious suffering. Rivers of blood may have to flow before we gain our freedom, *but it must be our blood.* Things of fundamental importance to people are not secured by reason alone, but have to be purchased with their suffering (what else characterized the early Christian martyrs in the face of an all-powerful Roman Empire?) *Suffering is infinitely more powerful than the law of the jungle* for converting the opponent and opening his ears, which are otherwise shut, to the law of reason." Gandhi concludes: "The appeal of reason is to the head, but the penetration of the heart comes from suffering. It opens up the inner understanding of man."

One last footnote is in order to show how this theme is reflected, most recently, in Pope John's *Pacem in Terris.* Once more, as in Thoreau, the focal emphasis is on conscience.

"As authority rests chiefly on moral force, it follows that civil authority must appeal primarily to the conscience of individual citizens, that is, to each one's duty to collaborate readily for the common good of all." Pope John then makes the point that only God can ultimately command the human conscience, and adds:

> "those, therefore, who have authority in the state may oblige men in conscience only if their authority is intrinsically related with the authority of God and shares in it. By this principle, the dignity of the citizen is protected.
> "Since the right to command is required by the moral order and has its source in God, it follows that, if civil authorities pass laws or command anything opposed to the moral order and consequently contrary to the will of God, neither the laws made nor the authorizations granted can be binding on the consciences of citizens, since 'God has more right to be obeyed than men.'"

I have already said that this is heady doctrine and, as such, can easily lead to abuses. Arnold Toynbee, in his monumental study of human civilizations, wonders at the patience, forbearance, and good will of America's Negro citizens, despite their cruel human lot. Martin Luther King's "Montgomery Improvement Association" gave American Negroes a way to begin to redress their wrongs in an open, non-violent way through civil disobedience. The many other movements that followed were predicated more or less on the same Gandhian premise that voluntary human suffering in the cause of justice would most effectively and eloquently change the pattern of injustice. The passage of the 1964 Civil Rights Act is ample demonstration of the effectiveness of non-violent civil disobedience, especially in the most difficult area of public accommodations. So much for history.

Now the whole civil rights movement seems to be entering into a new phase which may well reverse the gains of the recent past, since the moral foundations outlined above are being more and more abandoned in many of the latest manifestations of the movement.

Most unfortunately, non-violence is often giving way to violence which loses the moral force and persuasion so essential to Thoreau, Gandhi, and King. Civil disobedience must also consist in direct non-compliance with what is essentially an unjust law, so that there is clearly established an open, honest protest that has some direct relationship with injustice. Opening water faucets to deplete a water supply, clogging highways to the World's Fair, or booing the President who was at the moment championing a new Civil Rights law is simply another form of injustice, insensitivity, or in-humanity—alienating friends and confirming enemies. Looting, inane destruction of property, hooliganism and violence, personal injury, and irresponsibility are as far from the moral foundations espoused by the true promoters of civil rights as injustice is far from justice, order from disorder, humanity from inhumanity. As Martin Luther King said, commenting on the race riots of Harlem, Brooklyn, and Rochester:

"My position on non-violence and my continued adherence to non-violent philosophy are well-known. I do not think violence can solve the problem in New York, nor can it solve the problem in Mississippi."

Or as Gandhi said earlier: "Suffering is infinitely more powerful than the law of the jungle."

Suffering there has been, and violence has not only risen in the North and among Negroes. Between June 12 and September 19 of this year, in 14 counties of Mississippi, there have been 32 Negro churches burned or bombed. Imagine the reaction if this had happened to White churches or synagogues in Boston, New York, or Chicago. Clearly violence is no answer.

We might then summarize the moral case for non-violent civil dis-obedience as legitimate only when all legal redress has failed to change an unjust law. The Lutheran Church in America, at its 1964 biennial conven-tion, stated this clearly: "If and when the means of legal recourse have been exhausted or have been demonstrably inadequate, Christians may then choose to serve the cause of racial justice by disobeying a law that clearly involves the violation of their obligations as Christians."

However, the disobedient person must be non-violent to preserve his moral stance. He must engage in meaningful protest, not indiscriminate demonstration, and he must be willing to accept the legal penalty for his action. Moreover, the basic aim of non-violent civil disobedience is always the same as regular litigation, to challenge the law and to bring it to a test under the regular legal procedures, only in this case by disobeying it and suffering the consequences.

Who can predict the future, who can forecast further progress if the waters are continually muddied by a perversion of civil disobedience? At best, we can assume that the patience, forbearance, and good will of which Toynbee wrote are apparently wearing thin, even at a time that seemed to be the dawn of victory. All of these symptoms, however, ultimately point to a profound malady that I suspect has only one great geographic focal point in modern America—the dismal slums of our great cities that can only produce, as long as they are allowed to exist, a continuous caldron of pent-up human frustration, born of miserable living conditions, blighted neighborhoods, over-crowded rooms, broken marriages and promiscuity, education all in the wrong direction, unsanitary, unhealthy, and dilapidated living conditions, playgrounds only in crowded streets, children perverted by all around them, poverty, crime, rape, dope, and drunkenness. Everything here speaks of human failure and perpetuates a primordial, primitive human misery. Again, how to break out of this basically immoral and inhuman circle of frustration?

If we can spend forty billion dollars to put a man or two on the moon, and fifty billion annually on defense, then I take it that our affluent society can afford a similar amount to bulldoze our slums into oblivion and to recreate the hearts of our cities. I fully realize that more than physical conditions must be recreated, that there is needed a new moral revolution within the deprived Negro community itself, based on a new pride in what human dignity and human equality can mean in America. As the late President Kennedy said, "Let us make a beginning."

I said earlier that every great moral system asks man to go beyond his natural condition. The human condition of the world today is ambiguous, to say the least, in the whole area of civil rights. The situation in our own beloved land, the so-called showcase of democracy, is one of great and growing tension. If the great moral tradition we have inherited says anything to us today, it must say this: we are free to deny the human condition, but it will remain what it is despite our denial. We can try to forget it, by indulging in the multitudinous distractions that our age offers. Or, we can accept the human situation for what it is: a great moral challenge to demonstrate in these our times that man is growing, not standing still or falling back; that human dignity means so much to us that we wish to share it with all our fellow countrymen, indeed with all the world; that human equality need not be a bitter and frustrating travesty, but a bright reality to which all of us are committed in the depth of our hearts and souls; and, finally, that all of us recognize each of these tasks as a deeply human moral obligation to which we, too, are willing to pledge today, as our forefathers did in their day, our lives, our fortunes, and our sacred honor.

§115 Reverend Robert J. McCracken

In this widely anthologized sermon, Reverend Robert McCracken urges his Riverside Church parishioners to get involved in the civil rights movement. To date, the "big religious bodies" had preached more of rights than of duties; some had not yet preached of these rights. McCracken quotes Martin Luther King, Jr. at length to prove, first, that the white clergy had been wrong in urging delay, and second, that Governor Ross Barnett's (and many others') charge of communism was simply a purposeful and incendiary misreading of the movement's basic message of non-violent love. McCracken also adopts the prophetic voice in noting the "ominous signs" about him that if the church didn't act quickly, large-scale violence might well erupt. Violence did erupt, but not in the South, and not until Watts in 1965. McCracken closes his sermon with a call to get involved and to do it at the most local of levels. That involvement was both "a civil obligation [and] a Christian obligation. We take pride in our rights. What do we intend to do about our duties?"

———————

Civil Rights and Christian Duties
Riverside Church, New York, New York
1964 (republished)

> Have we not all one father? Has not one God created us? Why then are we faithless to one another, profaning the covenant of our fathers? (Malachi 2:10)

We are hearing a great deal these days about civil rights. The subject is headline news in the press, is prominently featured on television and radio, is without a doubt *the* national issue facing Congress. While a political issue, it is prior to that a moral and spiritual issue. A preacher would be guilty of dereliction of duty if he said nothing about it.

Americans have affirmed repeatedly their belief in human equality. The belief has often been called the American Creed. It is written into the Declaration of Independence and the Bill of Rights. It is reflected in the claims made for the United States—"the land of the free," "the land of opportunity," "the cradle of liberty," "the home of democracy." If I had a black skin and had to go through an experience like that of James Meredith I am sure I should find it hard not to be cynical about those slogans.

In the matter of civil rights the churches are inescapably involved. There is no social issue on which their charter is clearer. The belief in human equality has biblical origins. The biblical principle is unambiguous and emphatic. Underlying race, class, color there is a fundamental fact which is universal and everywhere the same. God is the creator of all mankind. In His sight we are all equal. He cares for us equally and it is His will that we should live in community with one another and love our neighbors as ourselves. The explicit teaching of the Bible is that there are no inferior races, no second-class citizens, that God has no favorites, that Christ died for all and in Him there is neither Jew nor Greek, neither bond nor free, neither male nor female; all are one in Him. Racism is an affront to the native dignity of man and an insult to God. The Church of Christ will forfeit its leadership unless it stands unequivocally by its God-given gospel that we are all made "in the image and likeness of God" and that in consequence every human being is endowed with inalienable rights.

There was a day when Jesus rose in a synagogue, opened the Scriptures, and read: "The Spirit of the Lord is upon me, because he has anointed me to preach good news to the poor. He has sent me to proclaim release to the captives and recovering of sight to the blind, to set at liberty those who are oppressed, to proclaim the acceptable year of the Lord." The Church came out of that. The Church must keep going back to that as a mandate and directive. What concerned Jesus must concern it. He was concerned for all that affected the well being of men and women, and we must be no less concerned.

Where my brother man has a right I have a duty. Every civil right carries with it a civil obligation, a Christian obligation. Rights are not merely privileges, prerogatives, ends in themselves; they are opportunities, instruments, trusts. The value of any human right lies in the use to which it is put. Freedom does not consist in having rights but in fulfilling them. Mazzini, when people were insisting on the Rights of Man, came forward with a list of the Duties of Man to balance the account. This is where we have been at fault. We have made more of rights than of duties. A distaste for the very idea of responsibility is widespread. It is part and parcel of the weakness of democracy and of our moral confusion and futility. We complain loudly enough that things are not what they should be, but we are not morally sensitive about them to the extent that we feel an obligation to do something personally and specifically about putting them right.

There are Negro leaders who are saying to the churches, "You have stopped justifying racial wrongs but have you begun to rectify them?" It must be acknowledged that we have been tardy in rectifying them. We have been tardy even in recognizing them. An adult class in a church school was studying the booklet, "Jesus Christ the Light of the World" in anticipation of the Third Assembly of the World Council of Churches. One of the discussion questions asked, "What, in your own life and your local community, are the forms of opposition to Christ?" When the teacher raised the question the members of the class sat racking their brains, trying to think of one genuine foe to the Gospel. Finally, someone said, "I read in a recent issue of the *Saturday Evening Post* about Bishop Pike. He thinks the story of the Virgin Birth is a myth." That was as big an enemy as anyone in the class could come up with.

The extension of full and equal rights to all citizens goes on under the direction of government, under the pressure of the courts, under the determined prodding of minority groups (with churchmen often in their leadership), but the big religious bodies in America have been slow in getting into concerted action. So much so that Martin Luther King was constrained to write a letter from a jail in Birmingham to clergymen who protested that the Birmingham crusade was ill-timed: "I must confess," he wrote, "that over the past two years I have been gravely disappointed with the white moderate. I have almost reached the regrettable conclusion that the Negro's great stumbling block in his stride toward freedom is not the White Citizen's Councilor or the Ku Klux Klanner but the white moderate who is more devoted to 'order' than to justice; who prefers a negative peace which is the absence of tension to a positive peace which is the presence of justice; who constantly says, 'I agree with you in the goal you seek, but I cannot agree with your methods'; who paternalistically believes he can set the timetable for another man's freedom . . . and who constantly advises the Negro to wait for 'a more convenient season.' Shallow understanding from people of goodwill is more frustrating than absolute misunderstanding from people of ill will. Lukewarm acceptance is much more bewildering than outright rejection."

A conscience-probing statement! One sentence in it puts a finger on a common attitude: "I agree with you in the goal you seek, but I cannot agree with your methods." The methods—the sit-ins, the freedom marches, the prayer vigils, the non-violent protests—merit more consideration, as to their nature and purpose, than some of us are giving them. Leaders of the Negro churches see their Christian duty in regard to civil rights in the light of the teaching of the Sermon on the Mount. They have forsworn violence as immoral, as profaning the sanctity of the human spirit and outraging the innate dignity of man. The have reiterated as a cardinal principle of the non-violent movement any blood shed should be Negro blood. In classes for the training and discipline of volunteers they stress such rules as these: "Walk and talk in the manner of love, for God is love." "Refrain from the violence of fist, tongue or heart." "If you are arrested, go to prison quietly; if assaulted, bear it cheerfully; if shot, die peacefully."

Recall the injunction of Jesus: "You have heard that it was said 'You shall love your neighbor and hate your enemy.' But I say to you, Love your enemies and pray for those who persecute you, so that you may be sons of your Father who is in heaven." This is the spirit in which Martin Luther King makes his stand for civil rights. Governor Barnett on Friday denounced him and resorted to the old McCarthy tactic—the Communist smear. It is extraordinary how so much that is essentially Christian is condemned as Communist. Bearing in mind the injunction of Jesus, listen to the words of Dr. King! "To our most bitter opponents we say: 'We shall match your capacity to inflict suffering by our capacity to endure suffering. We shall meet your physical force with soul force. . . . We cannot in all good conscience obey your unjust laws, because non-cooperation with evil is as much a moral obligation as is cooperation with good. Throw us in jail and we shall love you. Bomb our homes and churches and threaten our children, and we shall still love you. . . . But be assured that we will wear you down by our capacity to suffer. One day we shall win freedom, but not only for ourselves. We shall so appeal to your heart and conscience that we shall win *you* in the process and our victory will be a double victory.'" Does that strike you as Communist teaching?

The man who makes a stand like that never stands alone. Ministers, teachers, students, teenagers have rallied in support. Many of them have been arrested and lodged in jail—William Sloane Coffin, Chaplain at Yale, Robert McAfee Brown, Professor of Theology at Stanford, Eugene Carson Blake, executive officer of the United Presbyterian Church who will preach here in September. The consensus is growing in the churches that the Negro must not be left to bear the whole brunt of the struggle. The Secretary of State has said that if he were a Negro he would demonstrate. He has put the weight of his office behind the demonstrations. If I were a Negro I would want to say to the White: "Don't leave us to demonstrate alone. Take your stand alongside of us." Pledged to non-violence he is attempting to further the cause of human rights peaceably. It would be an evil day for this country if instead there should be an eruption of raw force. There are ominous signs that patience is growing thin and that leadership could pass into other and belligerent hands. One wonders whether white people who criticize the strategy of non-violence realize what the alternatives are. The American Negro is determined to gain his rights by *some method*. Either the struggle for justice will proceed peaceably or it will break out in violence. Those are the alternatives and there are no others.

In these turbulent days, days of peril, days of opportunity, what should be the role of the churches? They must get out from behind closed doors. They must be social action institutions. They must move from the rear to the forefront of the crusade *for* civil rights legislation, *against* segregated schools, segregated housing, discrimination in employment. They must take a strong stand against the indignities and injustice imposed on minorities. They must follow the lead taken last month by the General Board of the National Council of Churches and support negotiations and demonstrations and direct action in areas of particular crisis.

The call is to members of local congregations and not only to denominational executives and ministers. About the remedying of some social evils you may feel well-nigh helpless. They are so vast and complex; you do not know where to take a hold; there seems so little that one individual can do. The encouraging factor in regard to civil rights is that it is an issue about which every Christian can do something. He can begin where he lives, where he works, where he worships. Committing himself to belief in an unsegregated church and an unsegregated society, he can conform his personal, family, church, business, and social life to his beliefs. He can cultivate contacts and friendships with members of minority groups. He can invite them to his home and visit theirs. We reject the myth of racial supremacy. We believe in integration. Are we putting our belief into practice in everyday relationships? Christian race relations begin with these immediate person-to-person contacts.

But that is only to make a start. These are days that demand more than fraternization. Members of a church like this, living in a city like this, ought to identify themselves with school problems, community problems, recreation, the enactment and enforcement of fair employment practices, the right of every citizen to acquire housing on the basis of personal preference and financial capacity without regard to race, religion, or national origin. It is not enough for the minister to preach about such matters or a social study committee to survey them. The whole church should face them. City concerns ought to be church concerns, and not abstractly but specifically, situations known at first hand, people involved in the situations known by name. Here the vital consideration is not program promotion so much as it is personal identification and involvement.

Last Sunday I preached on personal religion and social concern. On Monday I received a letter from a member of the congregation. He is white, married and the father of one child. He expressed regret that in what I said I had not struck closer home to Riverside Church members. He shared with me his conviction about the challenges confronting church members in the present crisis. Here, as he sees them, are the challenges: (1) To welcome Negroes and Puerto Ricans into our social and civic clubs; (2) To hire and advance minority group members in business firms; (3) To welcome Negroes and Puerto Ricans into our residential areas and stay there ourselves so that the areas may not be resegregated; (4) To keep our own children in public schools with minority children. Those are some of the specific challenges confronting us as church members. Where our brother man has a right we have a duty. That needs to be sharpened, made specific. Where a Negro or Puerto Rican has a right we have a duty. Every civil right carries with it a civil obligation, a *Christian* obligation. We take pride in our rights. What do we intend to do about our duties?

God is known in many ways, in churches and out of them, and especially "where cross the crowded ways of life, where sound the cries of race and clan." Religion has well been defined as Ultimate Concern. Mahatma Gandhi, with all his emphasis on private prayer, stated in his autobiography that God was never so real to him as when he was actively identified with the struggles of the poor farmers in the north of India. Social concern is not only the inevitable consequence of personal religion; it validates and deepens and enriches personal religion.

1965

1965

§116 Kelly Miller Smith

Reverend Kelly Miller Smith was born on October 28, 1920 in the all-black community of Mound Bayou, Mississippi. Raised and educated in this southern town, Reverend Smith continued his higher education by entering Tennessee Agricultural and Industrial State College in 1938. He transferred to Morehouse College in Atlanta when he felt called to the ministry, earning his bachelor's degree in 1942. He continued on to Howard University, where he earned an M.Div. in 1945. Howard later conferred on Smith an honorary doctorate degree in 1976.

Between 1946 and 1951 Reverend Smith presided as pastor of Mount Heroden Baptist Church in Vicksburg, Mississippi. In May of 1951 he became the pastor of First Baptist Church, Capitol Hill, Nashville's first black Baptist church. Smith would serve First Baptist for the rest of his life, working locally as well as nationally, lending his hand to civil rights activity. First Baptist would become temporary home to a generation of activists—notably John Lewis, James Bevel, Bernard Lafayette, Diane Nash, and Marion Barry—as Smith allowed James Lawson to use the facility to hold workshops in nonviolent protest. At the time of the 1954 *Brown vs. Board of Education* ruling, Reverend Smith was president of the Nashville NAACP chapter. In 1955 he joined with 12 other black parents in a federal lawsuit to desegregate Nashville's public schools. He was involved in the founding of the Southern Christian Leadership Conference (SCLC) in 1957 and founded the Nashville Christian Leadership Council in 1958 (NCLC), serving as president until 1963. This organization encompassed Reverend Smith's ideals of nonviolent tactics in desegregating Nashville's public facilities. He served in many organizations, notably as president of the National Conference of Black Christians and was a member of the board of directors for Morehouse College's School of Religion. He delivered the Lyman Beecher lecture series at Yale University in 1983, which served as the basis for his 1984 book, *Social Crisis Preaching*. He was appointed assistant dean of Vanderbilt's Divinity School in 1969 and served until his passing in 1984. His papers are housed at Vanderbilt University in Nashville, Tennessee.

Reverend Smith's unique transformation of a newspaper photo to a Sunday message calls his congregation to consider their willingness for genuine concern in doing the will of God. In this sermon Smith poignantly moves the argument that Christians should be responsible in taking the call to action. Through convincing arguments, Smith shows how equal rights can be brought about by a "misfit," one who must creatively fit into the mold of a Christian by fitting outside the mold of society. Reverend Smith calls for more misfits as many white and black churches merely give allegiance to the status quo, especially on the issue of segregation. He sheds light on the hypocritical position of churches that echo the sentiments of society's unwillingness to desegregate. Moreover, Smith cautions his First Baptist parishioners against the tempting allure of gradualism and tokenism. Smith closes by challenging his audience to become one of God's creative misfits and to see race beyond the lens of segregation to include issues of war and poverty.

The Misfits

First Baptist Church, Nashville, Tennessee
January 1965 (reprinted)

"Adapt yourselves no longer to the pattern of this present world, but let your minds be remade and your whole nature thus transformed. Then you will be able to discern the will of God, and to know what is good, acceptable and perfect." Romans 12:2

During the nonviolent demonstrations for the desegregation of the theaters in Nashville a few years ago, there appeared a striking photograph in one of the daily papers. It showed a group of students standing in line at the hastily closed theater under the marquee which bore the title of the picture then playing—*The Misfits*. This was uniquely descriptive of the young students whose very presence there was a protest against the status quo. By their action they were saying that they were no longer willing to fit into the slot an evil society had prepared for them. They were misfits.

In an even more profound sense, the people of the church are, properly, misfits. When they are true to their heritage and fulfill their mission they will find it impossible to adapt to much in the society about them. The great apostle bids us "Adapt . . . no longer to the pattern of this present world" or, as J. B. Phillips presents this passage: "Don't let the world around you squeeze you into its own mold, but let God remold your minds from within." Those who fit too well are unfit for kingdom service.

Ours is no accommodative, Casper Milquetoast religion. It is a disturbing and disruptive faith. Its adherents do not fit well into an evil system—and they never did. The prophets in our heritage were divinely ordered to "pluck up, break down, destroy and overthrow"; they lived on the periphery of society at best. They would have won no popularity contest in their day. They were considered to be everything from impractical idealist to raving maniacs. When Paul and Silas got their work underway at Thessalonica, someone went to the city authorities and told them, "The men who have made trouble all over the world have now come here." Once, because Jesus did not fit into the established patterns of a certain community, it was written that "they begged Jesus to leave the district." Jesus was a true misfit.

It should be made clear that our world needs creative misfits, not just odd people. To be sure, some of us of the church are a strange lot. But there is no virtue in being odd for the sake of being odd. Irrelevant preaching is no asset to the kingdom of God, even if the particular preacher does have a curious, unenlightened slant on certain passages of scripture. We do not need the kind of misfits who wage major battles over minor issues. We have our fill of the experts in the infinitesimal and of the crusaders against the inconsequential.

The misfits who can rescue us are those who are able to "discern the will of God, and to know what is good, acceptable, and perfect." This is what makes them misfits! Those who have the audacity to express a genuine concern for the will of God are the oddballs. Our richly upholstered generation seems concerned least of all about what that will of God may be. There is a rather gripping ethnocentrism which has us in its thrall. Our concern is not as general or as broad as the will of man, but the will of certain men: those who represent a rather neat extension of ourselves. Those who are "our kind of people" come first.

The tragedy of it all is that the church, that agency which should make a difference, accentuates the problem. Instead of crying out against this preoccupation with "our kind of people," the church, in far too many instances, has simply reflected the evil which it should be condemning. As E. Stanley Jones has made clear, the church should be a prophetic voice, yet it is but a resounding echo. Although the courts have required the public schools to desegregate, the Sunday Schools have been under no such requirement. In some communities efforts are being made to remedy *de facto* segregation in schools, but *de facto* segregation in the churches is quite accepted. In Nashville, some church-sponsored schools remain segregated while most of the others have ended this senseless practice. The ironic fact is that the church has become the custodian of the status quo. One Nashvillian was heard to say recently, "I go to church now more than ever before. You know, it's about the only place you can go and not hear something about the so-called 'race problem.'" Underlying this statement is the fact that here more than almost any place else, one can find the kind of ethnic homogeneity which feeds racial prejudice.

To discern and adhere to the will of God is to recognize that there is no liturgical substitute for the prophetic demands of our faith. Amos makes this clear in presenting the message of God to the people of Israel: "I hate, I despise your feast days. . . . Take thou away from me the noise of thy songs . . . but let judgment run down as waters, and righteousness as a mighty stream."

The clear, ringing voice of Micah confronts us, unequivocally, with the purposes of God: "He hath shewed thee, O man, what is good; and what doth the Lord require of thee, but to do justly, and to love mercy, and to walk humbly with thy God?"

The need is for this kind of misfit.

Those who are creative or prophetic misfits are likely to engage in disruptive acts. They will turn up on the "wrong" side of the most delicate issues. They will espouse the most unpopular causes. They will be subjected to the worst kind of criticism and, at times, persecution.

Of course, this is not new in the annals of the Christian faith. There is a moving hymn which optimistically extols the "Faith of our fathers! living still, In spite of dungeon, fire and sword."

In his book, *The Black Muslims in America*, Charles E. Lincoln points out that there are three basic types of response to a constant environment of prejudice and discrimination: avoidance, acceptance and aggression. While he mentions these responses as being characteristic of the oppressed minorities, they also say a good deal about the conduct of those on the other side of the picture. As our Nashville friend has indicated, there are those churches which use the technique of avoidance. They avoid coming to grips with the problem in a conscious manner. (Of course, no one can truly avoid it, whether consciously or unconsciously). And there are those who accept whatever prevails at the time. No challenges are offered, no radical action is taken or recommended. This, perhaps, is the route the church has followed more than any other. On the matter of the violence of war, C. Wright Mills has said that the preachments of the church are irrelevant. They may be heard or ignored and it will make no real difference. Christians have gone to war against other Christians and have killed them and have been praised by still other Christians for doing so. This is the fruit of acceptance. The people of the church, as such, have rarely ever challenged the city authorities regarding the practices in the arena of racial problems. The truth is that we have lagged behind the civil authorities in most instances. This is another way of saying that we have simply fitted too well.

The way of the misfits, however, is the way of aggression. To be sure, the technique of aggression shelters both those who operate within the context of proper ethical concerns and those who operate outside such concerns. It includes both those who adhere to a philosophy of nonviolence and those who believe violence is the only way. Both those who recognize the radical demands of the Christian faith and the Black Muslims are misfits. It is important, then, that the terms of the rebellion be set. The Judeo-Christian faith, by virtue of its nature and its history, sets the direction. When men have become misfits on the basis of the lofty motives of this faith they have been blessed with startling fruits for their labors. The prophetic insights of Jeremiah led him to break with established patterns of his day, and the nation experienced a new morality. After his ecstatic vision in the temple, Isaiah uttered the kind of pattern-breaking message which gave birth to a new holiness among the people. When Amos spoke with flaming tongue before the people of Israel a new sense of social justice was born. A spiritual emancipation resulted from the aggressive stand of Martin Luther, and John Wesley preached until slaves burst forth with the hope, "I'm so glad, trouble don't last always." Martin Luther King lived and applied the tenets of Judeo-Christian tradition and fifty thousand of the black and tan children of God in Montgomery, Alabama, marched during the day and prayed at night until the walls of bus segregation fell. Further, because this man was aggressively opposed to the status quo, because he was a creative misfit, there is a movement under way in America which may still redeem the soul of our nation.

I received a letter from one of our most frequent correspondents— "Anonymous"—saying that those of us who have been involved in demonstrations and the like cannot properly represent God, for "He is a God of order, not disorder." But we should know that whenever our actions can cause the forces of evil and the forces of good to war with each other we are following in the footsteps of him who came, not to cause an artificial peace to exist, but to bring a sword of discontent with evil. The truth is that we do not represent God properly when we fail to challenge evil.

The creative misfits are never satisfied with tokenism, whether in social action or in our religious professions! They can assume no "a-little-dab'll-do-you" attitude. Perhaps this is why we have not created more of a furor just being Christians. It may be that we have had such a tiny "dab" of what our faith is all about that it does not affect our fitting into the patterns of our day. We are more conformed than transformed.

Very often our growth as Christians is stymied at the point where the faith calls for a breaking with established patterns. Everyone wants to be accepted—to be a good fellow. We take on enough to get identified by our fellows, but not enough to make any real difference. We apply a little of the vaseline of Christianity as balm occasionally, but we are not willing to have the surgical knife used to perform the major surgery necessary.

In dealing with the most pressing social problems of our day the disciples of acceptance pitch their tents in the fields of tokenism. A little progress is sufficient for now. "These things cannot be done overnight." How often do we hear these words! The misfit says, "Maybe they can't be done overnight, but let's try it anyway." A negotiating team went to a merchant in Nashville in the fall of 1959 and requested that the practice of racial segregation be terminated by "nine o'clock tomorrow morning." The startled and somewhat angered merchant told us that this was ridiculous. The group made him understand that this was our goal and that we wanted to come as close to that goal as possible.

When token progress is accepted, it gives a false sense of "having arrived." In many communities aggressive effort stopped when a few concessions were granted. Frequently the membership of a single Negro on a municipal board is considered significant enough to be hailed as a great accomplishment. One community gave a testimonial banquet for two Negroes who had been named to important boards. A token achievement is no occasion for victory celebration but rather an indication of how far we have still to go. To speak of Negro "representation" on boards and committees is to admit that we have a society which is largely pagan, and that the human family has been artificially divided by men and that, rather than correct this evil, we would honor it.

Tokenism is too meager to cure the malady which afflicts us. Ours is a segregated society which, far too often, promotes inferiority rather than equality; divisiveness rather than fellowship; stigma instead of dignity; prejudice and bias rather than mutual respect and goodwill; pretense and hypocrisy instead of sincerity and good faith.

Changes have been made in many communities because some misfits have had the audacity to challenge the status quo. Such disrupters have been involved in the favorable court decisions and the Civil Rights Act of 1964. We hope that their number is growing and that their sphere of concern is also growing. Perhaps some day they will include all of those who call themselves members of the church. Perhaps the misfits will also have something to say about the violence of war and about the problem of poverty and the other problems which beset men. Perhaps they will help transform our nation and our cities—and our churches!

§117 Hearings before the United States Commission on Civil Rights

The United States Commission on Civil Rights held hearings in Jackson, Mississippi in February 1965. The hearings come in the wake of Freedom Summer, the death of three civil rights workers and several dozen church bombings. The last panel to testify at these hearings involved eight local clergy—Richard O. Gerow, S. Leon Whitney, John M. Allin, Commissioner Rankin, Perry E. Nussbaum, Edward J. Pendergrass, William P. Davis, and Joseph B. Brunini, each of whom discussed the role of the church and its major denominations in negotiating racial strife in Mississippi. The panel, guided by Notre Dame President Theodore Hesburgh, was broadcast by local Jackson television stations. Early in the testimony, Reverend Davis read part of his statement into the permanent record. The statement documents his role as chairman of the Committee of Concern, an interfaith organization created on September 9, 1964 to help rebuild many Mississippi churches burned during Freedom Summer.

While each of the eight clergy speaks in general support of one another, the hearings reveal clear tensions, perhaps the most notable occurring between Bishop Pendergrass and Reverend Whitney. "In the fullness of time God will do this thing [total integration] and He will help us to do it in the way that we are trying to do it to the very best of our ability," states Pendergrass. To which Whitney later responds, "to say that God is going to work this thing out—but you see God's not going to work it out apart from us. He will work it out through us. We are the instruments through which God will solve this problem. I think it is good to put it in the hands of God, but I think our lives must be dedicated to the proposition that we are going to do the will of God in our day and in our time." As with many clergy, the issue came down to performing the will of God actively or waiting on God to make his will manifest. Whitney, a black clergy in the African Methodist Episcopal Church, echoes King's "Letter from Birmingham Jail," in advocating for an activist clergy. While the themes of communication and perspective serve as guiding themes to the testimony, Father Hesburgh's idealism meets with frank and critical rejoinders from a Mississippi clergy many of whose parishioners were active adherents to the doctrine of a biblically sanctioned white supremacy.

Religious Panel, February 20, 1965
Jackson, Mississippi
February 16–20, 1965

Commissioner HESBURGH. Reverend gentlemen, and ladies and gentlemen, we come to our final panel, a group of religious leaders from the community. I would like to begin by introducing each of them. On my far left and your right, we have the Most Reverend Richard O. Gerow, Bishop of the Catholic Diocese of Natchez-Jackson, Mississippi. Next to him we have the Reverend S. Leon Whitney, Pearl Street African Methodist Episcopal Church, Jackson, Mississippi. Next, the Right Reverend John M. Allin, Bishop Coadjutor, Episcopal Diocese of Mississippi, Jackson, Mississippi. On my immediate right and your left, we have additional help for the Presbyterian Church because Commissioner Rankin is an elder in the Presbyterian Church in North Carolina. On my immediate right and your left, we have Rabbi Perry E. Nussbaum, Temple Beth Israel, Jackson Mississippi. Next to him we have the Reverend Edward J. Pendergrass, Bishop of the Jackson area Methodist Church, Jackson, Mississippi. And next to him we have the Reverend William P. Davis, President of the Mississippi Baptist Seminary, Jackson Mississippi. And, finally, we have the Most Reverend Joseph B. Brunini, Natchez-Jackson Diocese, Jackson, Mississippi.

I think I should say on behalf of the panel and on behalf of the Commission, that in coming to Mississippi, as in coming to many of the other States we have visited as a Commission on Civil Rights, we have, without exception, in our public hearings called upon all segments of the community which we thought could bring some vision, some imagination, and some courage to bear upon the vital problem of civil rights, which three successive Presidents have said is the most pressing domestic problem in the United States. We have received great help all over this country from the religious segments of our society, which in conjunction with other segments of our society—the businessmen, professional men, lawyers, doctors, leaders of industry and people of good will everywhere—take responsible action within the community to bring the full weight of their good will and the full courage of their leadership to bear upon this problem. We are delighted this morning to have all of these gentlemen with us. We are here to hear from them primarily, not from me.

I would like to make one or two primary observations which have grown out of the hearings thus far. The first observation is that we have found one of the most necessary elements in the moving forward in society—and this is not something unique to Mississippi, it is unique to this problem throughout the united States—that is the element of communication. I think it is simply a matter of history that in the whole life of this Nation, as well as in the life of many other great nations, it is the religious sector of society—the religious leaders of society—who have been able to facilitate that communication, who have been able to draw together separated parties within a community and have been able to stand up clearly, forthrightly, and courageously for that which is just against that which is unjust and erroneous and deleterious to the building of a great society. I think, also, that it is the duty and obligation of religion in our time, as in any time, to be relevant. We have had some serious criticism in many of our hearings, including these, to the effect that there have been times when religion was not relevant. It followed rather than led. It has seemed to follow the course of expediency rather than the course of courage. It has not been clear in outlining those principles which are at the base of our society, which are derived, as you know, from the strong religious base of Judeo-Christian culture.

I believe that many of you have heard the leaders of the business community today. They indicate, as did the leaders of the legal community yesterday, that there seems to be a turning of the road in this State, as there is a turning of the road throughout this country, and that people today are beginning to see the importance—the moral importance—the moral imperative of solving this problem. I think it is particularly relevant to this panel that it makes very little sense to say that half of the education system, for example, in Africa, which is a continent of colored peoples, that half of the education in elementary and secondary schools is provided by missionaries from this country and then to say that in our own country we have problems that are not being solved.

So, I'm delighted to be associated with all of the gentlemen on this panel this morning. I would like to begin by setting up, as we have in our other panels, one or two questions to which each of you may address yourselves. The first question I would like to ask—and I think everyone on the panel should have an equal opportunity to answer these questions—the first question I would like to ask is this: What is the religious community doing to make manifest to this Commission, to this whole State, and to each particular community of this State what they think should be done about this most pressing problem—the problem which has brought us to Mississippi?

The lawyers have come out with several statements and the business leaders have come out with several statements. The governor and the attorney general this past week have made statements on this problem. I think it is important that we hear from all of these religious leaders regarding their statement or what statement they might make, either separately or collectively, about the possible answers to this problem. I would like to begin with Bishop Gerow, and just let them take turns in saying whatever they might wish to say.

Bishop GEROW. Yes. I'm very happy to speak on this question. During the year 1963 there gathered in St. Andrews Rector, or St. Andrews Hall, a small group of religious leaders, and we discussed what we should do. This group then grew, it grew to the point where our meeting place was not sufficiently large. So we moved to our diocesan chancery where we have ample accommodations. And about once a month we had a meeting consisting of prominent religious leaders. Each meeting would consist of about 10 white leaders, religious leaders, and about 10 colored religious leaders, one of whom was Dr. Whitney here beside me. In these meetings we found a beginning of communication amongst ourselves. We learned to understand each other. We learned to appreciate each other, to respect and really love each other.

I enjoyed these meeting. We would sit around and in an informal way we would talk. We finally came up with this thought. The question of communicating between the races was an important question and we resolved to do something about it. So the group of us arranged to meet with one of our prominent local organizations of men. I would prefer not to mention names or identify organizations. Somehow or other we didn't get very far on that occasion. They just didn't understand us, and we didn't understand them. We tried again to get communication with one of the civic officials. We didn't get very far there. And we felt that if we would establish communication, if we could get together and sit down and talk things over in a very cordial, friendly, and informal way, we might come up with something that would better the situation.

Those conditions that I speak of were conditions that existed probably a year or little less than a year ago. I think things have grown a little bit better now, but still they are far from being what they should be. Now does this answer your question?

Commissioner HESBURGH. Thank you very much, Bishop Gerow. Now, I would like to ask Reverend Leon Whitney to say a few words on the same subject.

Reverend WHITNEY. Yes. I think that perhaps with Bishop Gerow and the rest of the members of the community, we have had some communication. But there is no communication with the Negro and white church *per se.* This is definitely a fact. I think of reevaluating what Mr. Ezelle said a few minutes ago, his categorizing of the Negroes' need. I think perhaps the first thing we need is communication across the line. These must be all inclusive and the question as to when we should start, we start now. We work on all these things as we go along. Unfortunately in Mississippi we have extended the invitation to any ministers in the white community to just come and talk with us about the problem, but even this has been not done. A few of us, as stated by Bishop Gerow, have talked about it but we have not gotten beyond the point of talking about it. But the church has not faced up to its moral responsibility in solving the race problem in Mississippi.

Commissioner HESBURGH. Thank you. I would like to ask the Right Reverend John M. Allin, the Bishop of the Episcopal Diocese, to speak.

Bishop ALLIN. The key word has been communication as Bishop Gerow said. We started more than 2 years ago, and found that in the worst of circumstances there are some benefits and good fruits. One of these was the discovery of the persons, and perhaps many more religious leaders have come, as the Bishop said, to know each other and maintain communication throughout this period of 2 ½ years or more under great difficulty. It was difficult, for example to find a place to meet. I remember at the outset in speaking to one of the public officials we were told that the white clergy exercised perhaps a 10 percent influence and the Negro clergy a 90 percent influence. I rather think that was an accurate estimate and it was a good lesson in humility, too, which we learned.

In terms of how confused or how scattered the people were, we debated and discussed at length the matter of making pronouncements. There were a great many pronouncements. I remember the feeling expressed on a number of occasions that to make a statement simply presented something that was then to be placed amidst the confusion and the lack of communication to be distorted and misused by those whose efforts sought to separate us. As the Bishop said, we made an appeal to a prominent board. Some of the men on that board received us and heard us. There were some who would have moved to remove us immediately. But our whole purpose at that point was to find some way to communicate. I might add that one of the problems of communication which I think is perhaps still before us is that of pressures from both inside and outside. These have changed in some regard, but I remember listening to one of the city officials respond to our request by saying we are never sure whom we are talking to on the other side. If we could talk to people in our own community—now I'm fully aware that the argument has been presented many times that we don't want outsiders and I'm not referring at this point to that. But I am saying people with common problems many times come closer to solving them if given a chance to discuss them and I could appreciate—I couldn't entirely agree with him—but I could appreciate his fear and the anxiety that was expressed.

I think in addition to communication the greatest need we had was for perspective. There are many blind spots in the picture. We could spend a long time in talking about our failures and, as I know the men that are present here and others who have met with us, I don't know anybody who has made any boasts about our accomplishments. But in trying to get the perspective to understand a very complicated problem that faced us, there was a move, for example, by one group—an appeal to the laymen in churches that said in effect, "If your clergy doesn't behave we will meet with you and show you the means of reforming the church."

I remember 2 ½ years ago making what I thought was a rather innocuous speech to a civic club to which I was asked to speak on prophecy. I talked about the need to gather around a problem, to attempt to define a problem, to isolate the factors, to coordinate an attempt to solve it. I was told later by one of our layman that on the way down somebody said to another man on the elevator, "You know, if he had been one of our boys, we would have cut off his groceries." You know, this gives pause for thought. But the greatest need, I think, still is communication and perspective. While I'm willing to admit that in the face of all the difficulties and the complications I never have lacked real hope, I felt there have been many things that have been bad. It could have been worse, and the reason it wasn't worse is because there were many factors and indeed many, many people in the State of Mississippi who are concerned with seeking the truth and are concerned with fair play.

Under the pressure of group anxiety, under the pressure of blown-up fears of what might happen, these people frequently retreat. But I have seen too many times that when persons do meet, there is a courtesy that comes through. And I don't think this should be discounted. So we make no claims for great accomplishments, sir, but we at the same time must say we feel deep concern. There has been what feeble effort we could make to reach out and communicate with one another.

Commissioner HESBURGH. Thank you very much, Bishop. I would like to ask Rabbi Nussbaum to say a few words.

Rabbi NUSSBAUM. Mr. Chairman, I'm often disagreeing with my very good friend Bishop Allin when we get together, and I'm disagreeing again.

Bishop ALLIN. It makes it an official meeting.

Rabbi NUSSBAUM. It makes it the kind of meeting that we have been having over the past 2 years at the Catholic Diocesan office. I don't think the key word is communication. I think the key word is brotherhood, and I mention that deliberately because we are beginning a brotherhood week. This whole idea, this concept, is still missing from so many parts of our country and from these parts. I think that not until religion in general will go from the preaching in the pulpit to implementing in the pews what the fatherhood of God means and the brotherhood of man also means in the real sense, will we ever accomplish more than this creeping progress.

Yes, we have made some progress. But it has been my feeling as a Jewish teacher that not until we rise to our responsibilities, religiously speaking, will this basic problem of our times, this crisis in human relations in our time, ever be met. I think it was Mr. Patterson who asked a question in the last panel to the industrialist and others who were here. He wanted to know is it good economics? Now, the question that I have been asking for years, "Is it good religion?" I am one of those naïve people who think that religion is at the core of our life—our national life, our State life, and our community life—and that it should not be on the fringes. Bishop Allin's quotation from a very distinguished public official, I think, expresses the attitude of most people. But I do not agree. I think that if we can call ourselves worshipers of one Father, then this must be part of our life and every facet of our living.

Now, your question is what are we doing. You have heard what we have tried to do in the past years. I think we have made certain progress, but much more has to be accomplished. There's no question. We need interfaith programs. We are just beginning that in this State and for most of the State the idea is unknown. We need to make understood what the word "brotherhood" means in terms of various religious groups, in terms of the racial groups. If religion is to be a force in this State, we need councils and committees and organizations on human relations which will not be afraid of the term "human relations." For too long a time we have run away from the canards about the concept of human relations. We have run away from these rhetorics, these distortions of all of the ideas and the values which, as religious people, we believe in and we are called upon to teach. I am very hopeful for our State. We have made progress. But if patience is a virtue, I think procrastination is very much of a vice and a religious sin. And since 1954 there has been a good deal of procrastination in this whole area of the brotherhood of man under the fatherhood of God.

Commissioner HESBURGH. Thank you, Rabbi Nussbaum. As you can see, this is like a lawyer's panel. We are getting a little disagreement. But that is all to the good because it is out of this basic disagreement that we find a common unity. Next we have the Rev. Edward J. Pendergrass, Bishop of the Jackson Area Methodist Church.

Bishop PENDERGRASS. Mr. Chairman, ladies and gentlemen. Thank you very much for the privilege of coming. I have no desire to disagree with anyone. I'm a Johnny-come-lately to Mississippi. I only came last August. I came from the State of Florida, and I came with my eyes open and my heart heavy and my hopes high. And I have found here one of the finest groups of people with whom to work that I have known.

I represent a church that is connectional. We number more than 10 million people, if that means anything at all. We meet every 4 years to develop our program for the denominational group. I came in light of the fact that much of the program of the church had been enacted this year that was controversial. It affected some of the churches in Mississippi as it has affected some of the churches elsewhere who are in disagreement. While the program was enacted in a democratic way, it was not fully accepted. Our people are Episcopal in their form of government. Some of them have not learned that fact, even though they have avowed themselves to the principles of the church. They want to be congressional in their worship and, therefore, are doing some things that are not in keeping with the total program of the church.

With the things we are attempting to do here, we are in the process in our religious community of trying to effect communication between the races. There is, out of the four conferences representing the white and the Negro races in Mississippi, committees in each of these conferences to communicate with each other. This is, as you can see, a biracial group to discuss our problems and how we can solve them among ourselves. Then the second thing that we have done is to try to thwart the purposes of those who come in and try to tell us how to do our job. We have had a number of people come into areas of our work in Mississippi that have frustrated our people, who have not understood their problems, who have been in some instances hindering the work that we could do if this interference had not taken place. We developed the missionary program that will take effect. This is biracial in that the committee who forms the program will be both from the central jurisdiction, which is the Negro division of our church, and the southern jurisdiction, which is the white, until such time as this can be rectified. These will develop a program to help us in our missionary activity in the Delta system that has created such a great problem for all denominational groups in Mississippi.

In addition to that, within the last several hours, we have at our State, denominational schools, signed Federal compliance on education, which I think is a tremendous step in doing something here to meet the issues that confront us.

Now we do have pressure from within. We have people who are differing with those who are attempting to follow the patterns of the church as a whole. These have created a great deal of problems both for the bishop and his cabinet who work out the affairs of our Methodism in Mississippi. But I think in many, many instances we made progress. We tried as best we could, and I hope the others would say the same thing, to be as faithful and even more so if we can, to cooperate with the denominational groups in this State as they have with us. These gentlemen who are here with us on the platform today have given me the privilege of chairing the Committee on Concern. And I have had delightful experiences in that and have had an opportunity to share any sort of ability that I have and any sort of influence that I have to ask people to share in that. I think, Mr. Chairman, if I were to analyze things in Mississippi from August of 1964, until this moment, I think that great progress has been made, notwithstanding the fact that much information has been to the contrary.

Commissioner HESBURGH. Thank you very much, Bishop Pendergrass. I want to say a special word of thanks to the next gentleman who is going to speak since he was very helpful in getting this panel together this morning. Also, although he was officially scheduled for a much longer statement I would like to ask him to make this statement as a matter of record. I am very happy to present to you the Reverend William P. Davis of the Mississippi Baptist Seminary.

Reverend DAVIS. Mr. Chairman, I would like for the printed copy to become a part of the official record. The press has a copy and will handle it as it thinks best.

Commissioner HESBURGH. It will be copied into the record as if read.

Statement of Rev. William P. Davis
Mississippi Baptist Seminary

I have been invited to discuss the Committee of Concern—its background, when and how it was formed, what it has accomplished, and its purpose for the future.

The tragic background has been told by news media in many ways. But the concern of a small group of religious leaders has been overlooked. The leaders of that group have met from time to time for many months to seek some way out of the confusion and misunderstanding and to offer guidance for the common welfare. Some who expressed their concern resigned their places of leadership and left the State because of pressure. Many other religious leaders courageously challenged their people to consider the judgment, justice, and mercy of God in every movement of history. They restrained the surging tides of brutality and death, thus making it possible for leaders on the battlefront to make advances in good will for better human relations. These have been Jewish, Catholic and Protestant.

Since 1957 many of these leaders have sustained my place of leadership as Secretary of the Department of Work with Negroes of the Mississippi Baptist Convention Board and President of the Mississippi Baptist Seminary and have enabled me to have biracial communication throughout Mississippi. The small group of religious leaders inspired me with their confidence. Their concerns as early as 1960 gave me the idea of a Committee of Concern to help resolve racial tensions.

The Mississippi Baptist Seminary was organized in 1942 with an interracial faculty and board of trustees. Constant growth has been its history. It is now operating a system of 22 schools with 15 extensions. The enrollment last year was 1,923. Through these 22 schools and 15 extensions, the Sophia Sutton Mission Assembly, Baptist student work on college campuses, scholarship aid for college students, Bible institutes, conventions and conferences, I have had biracial lines of communication with thousands of people. This vast work has been made possible by the concerned leadership and support of the Mississippi Baptist Convention, and hundreds of National Baptists leaders as well as by many other religious and civic leaders in Mississippi. This work is jointly financed by the Mississippi Baptist Convention, which allocated $80,166 for this work, and the National Baptists in Mississippi, which gave $34,804. White Baptist churches gave $15,192. Teachers donated $1,124 in professional services. Allocation of MBC for 1965 is $94,386.

Naturally, the burning of crosses and churches and other injustices and indignities heaped upon Negroes became my supreme challenge, likewise my greatest problem. How I have thrust myself into the midst of the struggle for the welfare of all people is well known in every section of the State.

On July 18, 1964, I stood in the ashes of a burned church. The smoke of burning Bibles, hymn books, the playthings of little children, pulpit and communion furniture drifted over my head. I said, "I must and I will challenge the religious leaders of my State, my Nation and my world to create beauty from ashes by building a community of good will."

A few days later two of my best friends, Dr. Chester L. Quarles, executive secretary-treasurer of the Mississippi Baptist Convention Board, and Dr. Joe T. Odle, editor of the *Baptist Record*, called me for a conference. They expressed their concern and discussed how best to challenge Mississippi Baptists to manifest their concern. On August 9, 1964, Dr. Odle wrote a lead editorial, "Smoke Over Mississippi," that stirred concerned people to action. Shortly, in a second editorial and a news release, he announced that the Department of Work with Negroes would receive funds to help rebuild the burned churches and made an appeal for funds. Other religious journals called upon their people to support this worthy cause.

On September 9, 1964, the most important step was taken in helping to rebuild the burned churches. The Committee of Concern was formed in the chapel of the Baptist Building to "make it possible for men, women and children of good will to respond to violence, hatred, and destruction with concern, compassion and construction." The committee was interfaith and biracial—Jewish, Roman Catholic and Protestant.

The Friends Committee for Church Construction and Reconciliation (Quakers) and the Mennonites had been working in Mississippi making an on-the-scene study of the burned churches. Members of the committee offered to cooperate with the Committee of Concern in helping rebuild the churches. The Committee of Concern welcomed their offer. The Society of Friends of Philadelphia and New York sent Lawrence Scott to work with the Committee of Concern. The Mennonite Disaster Service sent volunteer workers. Contributions from individuals, organizations, churches, and synagogues have been received from almost every State of the Union and from 16 foreign countries. Contributions since October 5, 1964, have totaled $58,099.54. Over half of this amount has come from Mississippians. The Mennonite Disaster Service has contributed $15,000 of skilled labor. Many others have donated labor and materials, both inside and outside of Mississippi. Architects in Jackson have donated their services. The Council of Churches of Southern California has raised the money to rebuild and furnish the St. Matthews Baptist Church. Eighteen of the 38 burned churches are under construction. The Christian Union Baptist Church was dedicated January 24, 1965. Six churches are almost completed. The Committee of Concern will help the remaining 20 burned churches, if funds are available.

Students from Oberlin and other colleges, in cooperation with the local congregation, rebuilt the Antioch Baptist Church and raised the money for the construction and furnishing of the building. Students from Queens College, New York, spent 2 weeks, from January 29 through February 12, working on three churches. A number of college students, both inside and outside of Mississippi, have indicated a desire to help. At the YWA House

Party, Gulf Shore Assembly, over 400 high school and career girls gave $184.30 and expressed a deep concern in helping rebuild the churches. If the remaining 20 burned churches are to be rebuilt, the Committee of Concern must have an additional $100,000.

The immediate and future purpose of the Committee of Concern was clearly stated by a spokesman for the Quakers in explaining their role in the church construction program:

> "As we see it, the most important thing about this entire effort is not so much the buildings being replaced as the manner and fact of their reconstruction. Thus, we have endeavored to explore the opportunities which a cooperative building program might provide for bringing the white and Negro communities into a more meaningful relationship. We have chosen to work with the Mississippi Committee of Concern because we have felt this constructive new response to violence and hatred might serve as an appropriate vehicle for the establishment of new bridges of interracial understanding."

In addition, let it clearly be added that anarchy, bigotry, demagoguery and violence shall not be allowed to prevail in Mississippi—that we, the people of Mississippi, will not stand for it. A new sunrise of interfaith and biracial good will stand at the gate of the morning in Mississippi "to bind up the brokenhearted and give unto them beauty for ashes, and to build the old waste places, the desolations of many generations. Let no man's heart fail." Indignities and injustices shall not prevail. Tyranny must go! A power structure designed to deprive citizens of their voting rights and to discriminate in the administration of justice because of race or creed is tyranny. It is not treason to challenge tyranny. It is the highest act of patriotism and obedience to the eternal command of Almighty God: "Let My People Go."

Any citizen worthy of the name is entitled to his civil rights. Intimidation or discrimination used to deny a citizen his civil rights should not be tolerated in Mississippi or anywhere in the United States of America. There should be no place for such practice in the wide, wide world. Human beings matter more than empty tradition.

Reverend DAVIS. I would like to say that I am not a Johnny-come-lately. I have spent most of my life in Mississippi with the exception of about 14 years during which time I was abroad visiting our mission fields and other places of interest—studying humanity. I returned to Mississippi in 1948 and have been officially connected with interracial mission work in Mississippi almost since that time. I have seen this work grow from infancy to a position which today covers a State like—as one of the newspapers described its spread—the dew. We have 1,900 students enrolled in our seminary system, 22 schools, 44 extension centers of those schools. So it was easy for the department, which I am trying to lead, to become identified with the leadership of the Committee of Concern which was organized September 9, 1964, in the Baptist Building of the Mississippi Baptist Convention.

It has been, since its beginning, interracial and interfaith. There isn't anything fraternalistic about the Committee of Concern. Presently we are engaged in rebuilding 18 of the 38 burned churches. Six of the churches have been completed and if we have the money we intend to rebuild or help rebuild the remaining 20.

I think that because of the efforts of the Committee of Concern, we have created a different situation in Mississippi. The lawyers supported the Mississippi Baptist Convention, the convention board, the executive committee. And these gentlemen here on the panel with me and thousands of Mississippians not here this morning, but who probably are listening to this panel discussion, have been most helpful in making this work a reality.

Commissioner HESBURGH. I think we ought to give him a cheer.

Reverend DAVIS. I thank you and I think you ought to give me a lot of prayers too. These gentlemen have helped me so sacrificially in bringing these things to pass. I claim no credit for myself. The committee in return has received contributions from every State in the United States and 17 foreign countries, $58,000. You have it on the record there. Please put it in the press. We need a hundred thousand dollars more, though.

Commissioner HESBURGH. I think these good people in the audience would expect that now is the time to pass the hat, but we are not going to.

I would like to ask Bishop Brunini if he would like to add a few words to this.

Reverend BRUNINI. Mr. Chairman, I would like to accept all the fine things that have been said up here this morning and early afternoon. It has been a pleasure for me to be associated with all the men of religion of this panel. You ask what we should do. First of all we must basically continue to teach the Christian principles for the dignity of all men as children of God and brothers of Christ. We must move into actual integration. The time of talk is past. We say with protection of the law and the courts there should be no difficulty. We do have communications of course in the Catholic Church, Negro priests, Negro sisters and brothers in Mississippi and over 6,000 devoted self-sacrificing Negro Catholics. We are happy to assist all races in attaining full citizenship rights both as citizens of this world and as members of the church.

This is a moral problem. This racial problem, this problem will be with us in our part of the world for many years. We are keenly aware of the deprivation, the suffering, the hardship of our Negro citizens and indeed of our white citizens, also, here in Mississippi. Thirty years ago, I believe, President Roosevelt said that the South is ill-fed, ill-housed and ill-clothed. We can hardly say in 1965 that there is much progress that the South is well-fed, well-housed, and well-clothed. We are very much interested in the antipoverty program and all programs to benefit all of our people. We have many very, very poor people, white and Negro, here in Mississippi. The situation is desperate. The Catholic Church has gathered priests, brothers, sisters and money here in Mississippi from various parts of Europe and from all parts of the United States to teach Christian principles and to educate the Negro and our white people also.

The Catholic Church is not a Johnny-come-lately in helping the American Negro. And I might add that like the authority of J. Edgar Hoover, the reputation of our Catholic institution in keeping out communistic influence is well established. Here in Mississippi at the present time we operate 28 Negro schools, educating over 5,000 students. Our interest is not limited to our Catholic people. Sixty-five percent of these students are not of the Catholic faith. We have assembled 170 teachers. And besides this program on the elementary and secondary level we operate a seminary in St. Louis. Bishop Gerow and myself, these men there, have assisted in educating and ordaining over 40 Negro clergymen. At the present time, according to public school costs, the cost of educating in our Catholic schools is $1,154,515, not including the cost of the land and buildings involved. The amount of this money, 65 percent representing those who are not of the Catholic faith, would come to about $700,000. So we are happy to have this panel here in Mississippi and that you came, Father Hesburgh—and the other members. It has been rather salutary. We are ready to roll up our sleeves and make progress. God bless all of you.

Commissioner HESBURGH. Thank you. Now, Commissioner Rankin said he wants to put in a plug for the Presbyterians, and I think we ought to give him that opportunity.

Commissioner RANKIN. I am completely out of place up here. I should be down with you because each Sunday I listen to men like these. But I think we have a secret insofar as really making better race relations. They preach to me and tell me, "Do unto others as you would have them do unto you." If we members of the different churches represented here really followed that admonition, we could solve most of these problems that we have. It's not a question of a gap in a civil rights law. It's really a question of treatment. It's really carrying out this admonition that is given us.

The other day I was down in eastern North Carolina attending a Presbyterian Church that had very fine race relations. I asked this young minister how he accomplished this. He said, "Well, I added a new tenet to the Presbyterian doctrine. To election and predestination I added reincarnation. I preached a sermon not long ago in which I said, 'All of you are coming back to the Earth, and you are coming back as a cotton cropper out on the plantation here, earning $2 a day with inadequate medical attention, education not further than the fourth grade, and so on and so forth.' And it really worked. It started those people thinking. I find that here in my church, race relations have been much better." So all I can say is to remember the admonition of these men, "Do unto others as you would have them do unto you," and most of our race relations problems will be solved.

Commissioner HESBURGH. Thank you very much, Mr. Rankin. I think everyone has had a chance to say something. I would like to put a hypothetical question to this group since it represents a wide sweep of the religious element in Mississippi. We have heard a number of times during the course of this week and, of course, on other occasions—and we heard it from the good Bishop Allin this morning when he spoke about getting the groceries cut off—what would happen to the clergyman of this State if they really came out for the things that have been spoken about this week—the things Mississippians yearn for in this new day.

If they came out with the statement that every registrar in the State of Mississippi should act on what has been said by the business community and by the legal community and by many of your fine leaders who have spoken here, including your Governor; if they said that they believe every capable citizen of this State should have the right to vote, not 20 years from now, not 50 years from now, but right now, even if we have to keep the registration places open all night long to register people who are qualified; if every single religious representative in this State came out and said he believes that equal opportunity in education is important because no State moves forward without education and he thinks we all ought to put our shoulder to the wheel and come out for adequate education right now so that every single citizen of this State would have a much greater opportunity to be educated to the full extent of his talents; if they said they think that every citizen of this State should have an equal opportunity to a decent place in which to live, so far as that is possible, and should be accepted as a human being on his own personal capability and his own personal dedication, his performance as a human being, not his color; if they went beyond that and said they are going to try to invigorate aspiration among all people, white and colored, that they are going to make of this State a kind of new South which people haven't seen before. And are going to do it quickly, ignoring those people in their congregations who think this is a bad idea. Because part of religion is prophecy, and part of prophecy is having the courage to stand up and say what is right, what is right today, not next year or when it is easy to be right, not what is right because it is popular or what is right because it is profitable, but right because this is the will of God for His people, and we are His people. What would happen if every religious person in this state would sign such a statement?

They can't drive all the ministers and all the priests from the State. There wouldn't be any religion here, and I think there is a great deal of religion here. As a matter of fact, I think there is a lot more religion here in Mississippi than in many other States of the Union. We have heard some wonderful people during this past week who said, "I'm afraid to go into that booth alone, but I am not really alone because I have prayed, and God is with me. But I have been afraid. And yet I realize all I can do is die. And if something is right, you should be willing to be a martyr for it as evidenced by others who have gone through great indignity and great injustices." Vice chairman Patterson asked one little old lady about 80 years old, "Do you like the white people."

And she said, "Of course I likes them. I loves them. I wouldn't be Christian if I didn't."

I think I would like to ask the panel this question, and I would like a little open discussion on it. What would happen if every religious leader in this State came out in one swoop and said, "This is our manifesto, and this is what we believe. We are going to begin preaching this doctrine day in and day out. We are going to live it in our church associations and our church activities. And if you don't like it you are going to have to drive out every one of us." I just don't think that's going to happen.

Reverend WHITNEY. Mr. Chairman, I think this is hypothetical.

Commissioner HESBURGH. That is all right.

Reverend WHITNEY. But I think really that you have a situation here which is much deeper than most people recognize because there are a lot of persons who preach the Gospel who don't believe it, who really believe that God made several groups and put some groups here and other groups there and there should be no communication between these groups. I don't think you could get the ministers of this State to really come out with a statement stating that this is the will of God, and we should follow it. I think Mr. Golden, in his book, *Mr. Kennedy and the Negroes,* talks about it very beautifully when he says the society is sort of moving on the middle class and most of the ministers are no longer leading the people but the people leading the ministers.

I think this is the problem we have, for example, in our congregation. I have said to the people when a white man or woman cannot come into our congregation and worship with us, then I am not going to accept this church as my pastorate. I am not going to work with you. This is my conviction, that any person who wants to come to X church can. A person comes to worship God and I don't think we should deny him the right. I believe this, but I'm not sure whether or not the men in the other denominations really believe that we should be together as children of God.

Commissioner HESBURGH. Well, I think we have that problem confronting us when the good Lord says, "Whatsoever you do to one of my least brethren, you do to me." Bishop Allin, I think you have been doing some scribbling, and I would love to hear what you have on that paper.

Bishop ALLIN. I think that if the supposition you said came about that we would be able to adjourn and have harp practice. I think we would all be in heaven at harp practice. A man of my color skin has no right to ask for patience or for delay and there's a keen awareness of how little we understand the longer we live in this situation.

But, by the same token, to attempt to wish in something or oversimplify something or to ignore the facts is meaningful. Let me put it this way. Gradualism as a doctrine or a theory is here identical and doesn't make sense. To oppose it from a governmental situation is no longer reasonable. But by the same token the literal meaning of the words, steps, conditions, stages, are processes which cannot be ignored. When you find yourself lost, to the degree that in a sense we have been lost or confused, it simply takes steps to get back. These are tedious; these are painful. I wish it were not so. I wish it were possible to say what you have said. But one of the illusions which we the clergy have labored under in many periods in this country's history is that somehow we are the only voice or the infallible voice.

You said that if all of the clergy were driven out then we would have no religion. You didn't really mean that. I have always remembered the question that a theology professor put to me in the seminary. He said, "Gentlemen, if the garbage collector and all of the ministry went on strike at the same time, which would the society ask to come back to work first?" We have a voice and a voice of reason, and we have a responsibility to reach out. There is such a thing as integrity and sometimes integrity means that you have to admit that you're identified with people who may hold the wrong position.

Now, to say I no longer agree with you and I won't have anything to do with you any longer I think oversimplifies it. I become very leery of anyone who begins a sentence with "It's simply a matter of fact. . . ." There's nothing simple about it. Indeed, the fact of complexity requires that as one race or one group of people or one church we cannot alone solve the problems.

It would be a great deal easier if we could look to one person to answer the question and that's why the—indeed we have got to develop within this community and within this country and I think in this world, strength enough to disagree without becoming violent about it. True, it is only through disagreement and maintaining communication that we learn. And so while I wish, sir, it were possible to say, "yes," and I sincerely think that the majority of the clergy do say or would say what you say. There's also the question of hearing. And we have been concerned with the hearing and tried desperately at times to keep so many people from adding to the confusion by one more pronouncement.

I would say just in conclusion that very many times I have felt the deepest pain, indeed have admitted cowardice in not speaking. But by the same token I have discovered that the clergy are not the voice of the community alone but that you only have a voice when it is a voice in concert in the same sense as you only have a whole community when the various agencies and people, businessmen, labor, government agencies as well as clergy come and speak together. And I think this is where we must continue to struggle. It's not going to be tomorrow. We have had some casualties, incidentally, in our clergy ranks. But, I still think that it's an attempt to talk with one another, and to do this honestly and realize it is not going to be solved simply—if we are going to find our way out. And I am convinced we are going to find our way out.

Commissioner HESBURGH. I am certainly glad to hear it. Rabbi Nussbaum?

Rabbi NUSSBAUM. He has seen me scribbling. And you will excuse my theological difference here, but the Episcopalian said we would be in heaven if everything happened according to your long rhetorical question.

Commissioner HESBURGH. All my questions are long.

Rabbi NUSSBAUM. My answer is that we have a little heaven on this earth, and this is what we need.

As you always point out, we agree with each other; we say it a little differently. I should have wished—and I don't think it's too late—we are doing it now by our very presence on this panel because this is the first time this has happened, and Heaven help some of us, perhaps—

One or two of us are not the bosses. This is the first time it has happened. I don't think it's too late for united religions to speak out. Now, it has happened in other parts of the Deep South. This isn't the business of just going on in the North. And wherever it has happened in the Deep South, whether it has been on a State level or a community level, where the voice of religion has said, "This is what I believe in. This is what we think is the teachings of our Bible," there has been encouragement for people. And there are thousand of similar people in this State who have been looking for some kind of leadership.

Mr. Chairman, this morning—and this is the first time I have been here because I have been out of town—this morning I heard certain industrialists say some things about what's going to happen and the hopefulness now. Mr. Owen Cooper, who is the past president of the Mississippi Baptist convention board, tried not to talk religion but was talking religion all the way through here. He was trying to talk as an industrialist. And Mr. Cooper, I think, reflects the dilemma that has been in existence here for many, many years, and not just since 1954—the exact role of religion in the going problems of living, and this is every facet of living.

I think the time has come for teachers of religion to say this is what we believe in. This is what we think is God's word. Now, Bishop Brunini said that. I think the time has come for us to say that in a united voice—if only for the sake of somebody like myself because that old song about hanging together or hanging separately is very true—if only for the sake of the Negro preacher on this issue. And to me, it's the greatest challenge that has confronted our State and our Nation and it's a challenge that we all know is going to be with us for the rest of our lives. In this issue we as religious leaders must do some teacher work, and if you please, then some leading without deprecating all the fine sacrificial efforts that people on this panel here—that people in this room have been engaged in for all these years.

If there is one thing that I resent—and I'm going to say this in public—I don't think Bishop Allin was strong enough and here I agree with you, John. I resent the image that has been created by our colleagues in other parts of the country that we are the weaklings, that we have accepted the status quo. I resent it. I resent the type of clergymen who have come into Mississippi and on an overnight investigation has become an expert on the problems of Mississippi and all of these areas in which this Commission is concerned. I have the highest respect in the world and I have met hundreds of those who have come into the State to make witness, and to make witness is something else besides coming in and becoming an expert on a 24-hour basis. I had a young rabbi come this past summer. He called me up on Monday morning with one foot on the plane and said to me he came in on

Sunday. And he had come down to have a look-see. And he had seen and he called me up and said, "Rabbi, I admire you. I know what you are going through." My answer to him was—Well, I can't give it in public.

You haven't the faintest idea what is happening in Mississippi. There have been too many such clerical experts who have come down into our State. Come down and share with us—not as the voice of the North telling us simple-minded folk of the South what to do.

Commissioner HESBURGH. I think one thing is coming through. They aren't dead yet.

I would like to wind this up in about 10 minutes. I don't want to arbitrarily say who should speak or not speak, but I think we have something rolling here and I think it's terribly important. Would you like to say something again, sir?

Reverend DAVIS. Well, I would like to say, sir, that the role of the minister is in behalf of the welfare of all the people of the State and of the Nation. That is his primary concern. The concern of God is not for things but for people. And, our concern likewise becomes a concern for the total welfare of humanity in this State. I think that more ministers and more leaders have been aware of that and working in that direction than we have recognized. We are fellow laborers in a common cause; I see no defeat—I see victory. I think that we will resolve our tensions. We will settle our disputes and difficulties. We will come through to victory. I don't think we are going to do it tomorrow, but I think we will do it. I think we shall do it.

Commissioner HESBURGH. Thank you very much, sir. Now, would you like to say something again, Bishop Pendergrass?

Bishop PENDERGRASS. May I say this. Since 1940—these are facts that people do not altogether understand—the church that I represent has been totally integrated at the upper level. We have representatives on the major boards of our church. We have bishops in the Methodist church. And when I spoke a moment or two—and this is in rebuttal—that I'm a Johnny-come-lately, I meant by that, that while I have come to Mississippi as a Johnny-come-lately, I have not been totally unaware of the problems that exist. And with my deep and sincere appreciation for Rabbi Nussbaum's presence here, if he will permit me, I would like to say just this one word. Almighty God has never done anything overnight. In the beginning he made a world and spoke unto chaos and said, "Let there be light, and there was light." He put a perfect man and a perfect woman in a garden and they could not deal with the problem—there were problems of disobedience and an unwillingness to abide by the principles of God. Then He gave us the patriarchal fathers, but they were not enough. He then gave us the law giver, but he was not enough. He then gave us the prophets but they were not enough. And then He reached in the coffers of love, as we Christians say—and for this I apologize to my friend here.

Rabbi NUSSBAUM. Why apologize?

Bishop PENDERGRASS. I do it in deference to my own faith and to the position I hold. He gave us his Son. The scripture says, "in the fullness of time," it is upon that principle that I build my hope for total integration. In the fullness of time God will do this thing and He will help us to do it in the way that we are trying to do it to the very best of our ability. I do not apologize for any of the ministers in my connection.

We have had them to do exactly what our chairman has said to do, and they have done it without fear. Fear is being hungry. Some of them have left the State because of that. I do not think simply for the group of ministers represented here today to stand up and make any sort of pronouncement that we will do so and so is the answer to this problem. Because what good will it be to try to lead a parade if you have nobody following it? And that's exactly what would happen to us. We have got to win them by love. And I think we are doing it. And I think we are doing it with some degree of success. And while I'm sure that my Negro friends are impatient with us, I hope that that impatience will not be destroyed or destroy our hope. And make us understand that we are trying to be as faithful as we can. God knows that the things that have been represented by this panel in the discussions that I have been in with them have been an eagerness to do what we believe is the right thing under God to do. And Mr. Chairman, I think that that's the thought that all of us have.

Commissioner HESBURGH. Thank you, Bishop Pendergrass. Who else would like to speak?

Bishop GEROW. I want to agree with Bishop Pendergrass that the religious leaders of this locality are doing everything possible. Now, fortunately I occupy a position somewhat different from the position of the Rabbi and some of the others. I'm not going to lose my job when I speak. And this is what we have done briefly. We have worked from time immemorial upon the principle that the church building is the house of God and—anyone who comes sincerely to worship Almighty God is welcome. And in our Catholic churches it is not unknown or uncommon to see a Negro or small group of Negroes—I'm speaking of what you might call white churches. I don't like to call them by that name, but you'll understand better when I speak of them that way. It is not all uncommon to see a Negro or a small group of Negroes attending Mass or another devotion and coming to the Communion rail with the rest of the congregation to receive Communion.

There was an occasion on which I was very, very happy. On the day of the burial of President Kennedy we had a memorial service to which we invited leading ministers of the city and the high officials of the city, county and State. We had a nice congregation. In fact, someone who couldn't get in, told me there were over a thousand turned away who couldn't get in. But we did have a nice representation of ministers and civic officials. What pleased me most at that time was when Communion time came there was a nice group of Negroes that came up to receive Communion and knelt at the Communion rail right beside the rest of the congregation. There was no resentment. It was just a normal thing because it had been normal in the past.

Now, I feel that then another thing, we have integrated our schools, as Bishop Pendergrass said, not entirely, but on a gradual basis. We sent out word last year that our schools were to be integrated starting with the first grade this year, and, of course, an increase in years to come, because we felt we had a problem there that we had to solve and if we tried to take too great a step at one time we might be set back. I was surprised at the fine reaction I got from a number of our Catholic people I can't say that that same reaction was found in all cases. I did get some pretty bad reaction. In fact, a few, not many, of our parents were withdrawing their children from the Catholic school. However, this was to be expected.

But, I feel we are making progress. Now, I feel that I say this because I think this represents the intention and the desire of the ministerial body of Mississippi—at least of Jackson. I know, I have gotten to know these people. We have been meeting together. We have gotten to know each other and trust each other. And I know them and they want to do the same thing. And they are doing a good job, I think. And they are trying their best to do it. And I want to tell them I appreciate what they are doing. May God bless you.

Commissioner HESBURGH. Yes?

Reverend WHITNEY. One word. I think that perhaps among the many things the people misunderstand is that the segregator is more victimized than the segregated, and the religion here seeks to save the total man. And that as long as the Negro is not really free, then none of us is free. This is the problem we are grappling with. And to say that God is going to work this thing out—but you see God's not going to work it out apart from us. He will work it out through us. We are the instrument through which God will solve this problem. I think it is good to put it in the hands of God, but I think our lives must be dedicated to the proposition that we are going to do the will of God in our day and in our time. We can't just say, "Well, it will happen after a while." We must be the instruments through which God must work.

Commissioner HESBURGH. Ladies and gentlemen, we have used up our time but I promised Rabbi Nussbaum I would let him close with an aphorism famous among the rabbis.

Rabbi NUSSBAUM. Well, everybody has gotten in a lick for their religion and I want to say something in behalf of mine. When the children of Israel came to the Red Sea and they heard about the Egyptian hordes pursuing them, as we are all aware, they got scared and started crying to the Lord. And according to a rabbinic comment, the Lord said, "Moses, you tell those people to get up from their knees and stop praying and let them do something." This is what we have to do. We have a rabbinic aphorism that says, as I remember most of it, "The day is short, the work is much, the matter is urgent. It's not up to you to complete the work. But, neither are you free to desist from it." And I say thanks to the Commission for being here to give us the kind of encouragement that we need to continue with this work that has gone on for many years in this State of Mississippi which we all love.

Commissioner HESBURGH. Ladies and gentlemen, on behalf of all of you and, I presume, on behalf of all those who are seeing us on television, I want to thank each and every one of these gentlemen for the wonderful hour they have given us. I think it has taken courage on their part to say what they have said. I think we have tried to blend courage with realism, but also with idealism which, after all, will get us where we are going. It is customary at both the beginning and the close of Commission meetings to have an official statement from our Chairman who, as you know, is Dr. John Hannah, president of Michigan State University.

Chairman HANNAH. Thank you, Father Hesburgh.

As we bring this Mississippi hearing to a close the Commission on Civil Rights extends its appreciation to the U.S. District Court in Jackson. And then I want to say a few words about the hearing. First we want to express our appreciation to the Federal district judges who made possible the use of the Federal courtroom for the last week's executive session. We are very grateful to the director of the Veterans' Administration Center and his staff members whose cooperation greatly facilitated the conducting of this week's public sessions. We are also grateful to Chief U.S. Marshal Jack T. Stuart and his deputies who have ably assisted us during all sessions of the hearings.

A special measure of appreciation must go to the members, past and present, of the Mississippi State Advisory Committee to this Commission who have worked so patiently and courageously to help awaken the consciences of their fellow Mississippians. Their work has been performed under conditions which have sometimes been extremely trying. It is reassuring that so able and dedicated a group of Mississippians will remain in constant communication with us and will be continuing their important work long after the Commission has left Mississippi. We thank the many members of our own staff who have worked so hard in making this hearing possible. In the view of all the Commissioners, they have done very well indeed.

Most of all, we should like to express our appreciation to all those who have appeared before the Commission during these hearings. It was encouraging to us that the Hon. Paul B. Johnson, Governor of Mississippi, not only came before the Commission to discuss the problems and progress of his State but urged other responsible Mississippians to seize upon this hearing as an opportunity to put the facts about Mississippi in perspective. We are grateful to State Attorney Joe T. Patterson and Mayor Allen C. Thompson of Jackson and to the scores of other private citizens and public officials from whom we have sought information during the past 2 weeks.

For some of these, it was not an easy experience to testify before the Commission, but we would assure them that our sole concern has been to elicit facts, not to cause any person discomfort or embarrassment. We are aware, too, that some of those who testified here had already paid a substantial price in physical suffering or economic loss for speaking their convictions or attempting to exercise their rights. It is a tribute to Mississippi that such citizens have been willing to appear at this hearing and the Commission hopes, with them, that the climate of opinion in Mississippi is now such that people can speak the truth as they see it without risking reprisals or abuse.

When the commission opened these hearings 2 weeks ago, we announced that we intended to call a broad range of witnesses so that we might examine allegations of racial discrimination in voting and law enforcement objectively and in context. We have conscientiously sought to do this, both in the executive session and in the public session. Since the beginning of the hearings, the Commission has heard the testimony of some 100 Mississippians of both races, representing a wide spectrum of experience and opinion. The hearing itself was the outgrowth of months of preparation and research, including many field trips by staff members and the sifting of voluminous records and complaints in an earnest attempt to examine as fully as possible the conditions which produced civil rights problems, in certain parts of this State, of a kind and intensity rarely encountered elsewhere. It was determined long before the Commission arrived here that our major interests would be the present status and future prospects of civil rights in Mississippi rather than an exhaustive and largely profitless review of past injustices.

We have not presumed to come to Mississippi either as sanctimonious critics whose own home States are perfect havens of racial equality or as all-knowing physicians equipped to prescribe instant cures for Mississippi's social ills. We are simply attempting, as best we can, to fulfill an obligation which has been ours since 1957 when the Congress first charged us with finding and evaluating facts and recommending corrective action in the complex and difficult field of civil rights. Though final decisions must wait till a later time, it is probable that the Commission, after it has studied the transcripts of this hearing, will issue a report, including recommendations, to the President and Congress. A somewhat broader gauged report on the status of civil rights in Mississippi will follow at a later date.

It is too early to assess fully the testimony we have received here, but some tentative observations may be in order. First, it seems clear that, despite some encouraging signs of change, many of Mississippi's Negro citizens continue to face extremely serious and unwarranted denials in voting and law enforcement. In most parts of the country citizens of both races take the fundamental right to vote for granted. It has been very disturbing to realize that there are still places in Mississippi where merely seeking to register, much less to vote, requires considerable courage. Some white Mississippians in far too many counties are still seemingly bent on denying the vote to Negro citizens by the application of discriminatory standards, intimidation, and violence. It is hoped that thoughtful and conscientious white leaders in this State will take every necessary step to guarantee the free exercise of this fundamental citizenship right throughout Mississippi.

The Commission has been heartened during this hearing by signs of a developing consensus among many responsible white Mississippians that it is poor economics, poor law, and poor morality to encourage or permit racial violence and injustice. Physical security is basic to all other rights and the Commission is appalled to find that there are many citizens in some Mississippi communities who fear for their lives.

The people of Greenville, Mississippi have been able to develop a community in which Negroes as well as whites feel that they will receive fair and just treatment and adequate protection from law enforcement officials in their town. What was possible in Greenville we are sure is possible throughout this State. Business and political leaders of other communities from which we heard testimony would find it no less beneficial to insist on well-trained, impartial officers of the law. Violence and disorder are certainly less likely to occur in any community, North or South, where fair and equal administration of justice acts as a curb on distrust of, and contempt for, the law.

Although education was not a primary field for consideration at these hearings, the testimony of witness after witness pointed to the need for improved educational opportunities as a key to many of Mississippi's problems. Certainly Mississippi cannot achieve the economic growth so many of her leaders see as a crucial requirement in the decades ahead without a determined effort to increase the amount and quality of training available to her young people—especially those coming from Negro and poor white families. Attempting to maintain a segregated system that results in lower quality and higher cost will not advance the long-term best interests of any group of Mississippi citizens. It is encouraging to note that school authorities in some Mississippi communities have apparently recognized that Mississippi can ill afford to shortchange its children by rejecting Federal aid to education as it becomes available in ever larger amounts.

On these and other matters the best decisions for Mississippi are likely to flow from frank and open discussions, shared in by Negro Mississippians who constitute almost half of the State's population. It is a matter of common sense, as well as simple justice, that Negro citizens be allowed a larger voice in the decision-making process. More than one witness indicated the need for free and open exchange between white and Negro citizens of Mississippi. It would seem that the possibilities for improved communication between the races are better now than at any time in the past 10 years. Hopefully, the voices of moderation now being heard, after a long silence, will begin speaking clearly and forcefully for a progressive Mississippi.

As Governor Johnson said in his appearance before the Commission, Mississippi is, and must be, an integral part of America. It is no good for this state or for the rest of the Nation to assume that Mississippi is a place outside the normal flow of American life and culture. As Mr. Leroy Percy of Greenville said yesterday, sitting in the chair, which I now sit, "The people want to be in the mainstream of America and not in the backwater. They are tired of being led by the dead hand of the past . . . they want a change and I believe they are going to get it."

And finally, 10 days ago, at the opening session, the Commission announced that it hoped to conduct the hearings that we now close in a manner which would assist Mississippians in finding solutions to the problems of their State. We have tried as best we know how to keep that pledge. We sincerely hope that we have in some measure succeeded.

These hearings stand adjourned.

§118 Charles F. Wittenstein

Charles F. Wittenstein was born on January 16, 1928. He received his B.A. from Columbia University in 1949 and his J.D. (also from Columbia) in 1952. That same year he married Elinor (nee Heyman), with whom he raised their three children. Wittenstein began his career in Atlanta at the law firm of Heyman, Abrams and Young, where he practiced for five years. The remainder of his career he devoted to the civil rights movement, serving in numerous roles for the Anti-Defamation League and the American Jewish Committee.

The following speech takes place at the Hungry Club, a weekly gathering of black elites at a local YMCA in Atlanta. Wittenstein makes deft use of voting data to convince the audience that Jewish businessmen have embraced the civil rights agenda despite their ostensible similarities to segregationist commercial elites. While constructing a plausible interest-based profile for local Jewish concerns, he deftly outlines the different roles the American Jewish Committee plays in contrast with prominent civil rights umbrella organizations such as the NAACP, SNCC, and the SCLC. While those representative groups may take legal action because of their aggrieved constituencies, Jewish groups are more useful ushering in the new era once the courts enfranchise the aggrieved. Implicit in this analysis is Wittenstein's critical stance toward Martin Luther King, Jr.'s and the SCLC's strategic failures in Albany, Georgia, where organizational movements were not properly aligned with necessary litigation. This analysis also identifies the Kennedy administration's Tuscaloosa strategy (litigation with mobilization) as a model approach to civil rights progress.

Jews, Justice and Liberalism
Hungry Club of Atlanta, Atlanta, Georgia
February 1965

After the last General Election, a Republican candidate for Congress in Memphis, Tennessee, who had gone down to defeat with Barry Goldwater was bemoaning his fate: "I had hoped against hope that the Jewish group would see things my way. I am a businessman. They are businessmen. Apparently I didn't succeed. I am amazed that I couldn't. If ever there was a group that should be conservative, they should." It is not difficult to see where this misguided man went wrong. He correctly identified the Jews of Memphis with a certain economic class, then incorrectly assumed they would behave like other members of that economic class. But Jews are different, and it is this difference—its extent and cause—that I want to discuss with you this afternoon.

In that same election, Jews voted about 90% for Johnson and against Goldwater—more than any other white group, whether defined by income, region, religion, or ethnic character, and almost as much as the Negroes.

A recent article in *Commentary Magazine* by Milton Himmelfarb of the American Jewish Committee's staff makes this point. Mr. Himmelfarb goes on to say that earlier in 1964, in the Maryland Presidential Primary, the Jews of that state voted against Governor Wallace of Alabama more than any other white group. Going back to 1960, at each income level, proportionately many more Jews voted for Kennedy than did anyone else, including Catholics.

The *Commentary* piece tells us also that half or more of the white young men and women who went down to Mississippi in 1964 to work with Negroes and risk their lives were Jews. And the proportion of rabbis who have come South and been jailed or beaten is greater than that of white clergymen of any other faith.

You all remember Proposition 14, the anti-Negro constitutional amendment which repealed California's Fair Housing Act. Two-thirds of the voters were for it, but two-thirds of the Jews were against it.

In civil liberties, both the Gallup and Roper polls registered a significant difference in the attitude of Jews toward McCarthyism. While only 31 % of the Protestants were expressing "intense disapproval" of the late Senator Joseph R. McCarthy, 65% of the Jews stated those sentiments.

So far I have been talking about the political behavior of Jews nationally or in places other than Atlanta, Georgia. I turn now to our local scene. Four years ago we had a run-off in the mayoralty election between Ivan Allen and Lester Maddox (celebrated segregationist restaurateur). Lester got a majority of the white votes, but I seriously doubt that a single Jew voted Maddox, with the possible exception of Charlie Leb (another restaurant owner and holdout against integration). And you know these restaurateurs can be clannish.

From my experience I'm confident that Charlie Weltner (Fifth District Democratic Congressman) had a substantial edge among Jews over Jim O'Callaghan (Republican candidate) and Jim Mackay (Fourth District Democratic congressman) probably had better than 95% of the Jewish vote in the 4th Congressional district when he beat Roscoe Pickett (his Republican opponent).

I have referred several times to a "Jewish vote" and perhaps that phrase needs to be clarified. It means, as I have been using it here, the collective expression of Jewish voters, but it is in no sense a "bloc vote." Bloc votes can be delivered. Jews are highly individualistic and, even though their political behavior shows a pattern, no one can "deliver" their votes or tell whom they must support.

One frequently advanced explanation for the political liberalism of Jews which I have been describing, is that they are a minority.

"Last year (says Himmelfarb) was a good year for testing the proposition that minorities naturally sympathize with each other. The commentators singled out, above all, Polish backlash and Italian backlash within the general category of white backlash. Governor Wallace and Senator Goldwater were not strikingly unpopular with ethnic minorities who, in the referenda across the country, were almost solidly against open housing. These differences between the Jewish and other minorities just possibly could mean that when the Jewish minority behaves well, it does so less because it is a minority than because it is Jewish."

What is the explanation for this behavior pattern? I think it can be found in the Jewish passion for justice. Not all Jews have it, but I believe it does exist and that it is firmly rooted in our religion. "Justice, justice shalt thou pursue." "For I the Lord love justice." Many of us take these words seriously. We were repeatedly warned by the Prophets of old that ritual and professions of faith would avail us nothing if we dealt treacherously with our fellow man. The entire history of the Jewish people has served to reinforce the Biblical injunction to do justly and to love mercy. Over three thousand years of persecution have been more than enough to teach us the folly of bigotry. The commitment to social justice which grew out of our years of slavery and oppression in Egypt has been validated by the pogroms of Eastern Europe by the mass murders of Nazi Germany, and now by the cultural and religious genocide of Soviet Russia.

It is not enough to love your neighbor. We have seen that in the South, which is full of people who profess to love Negroes and at the same time strive to segregate them. This kind of love is nothing more than sloppy sentimentality at best, and sheer hypocrisy at worst. I don't love all Negroes any more than I love all Jews. But I concede to every man his right to human dignity, whether I love him or not. This is social justice—that is what it takes to make "love" meaningful.

As for constitutional rights—all Americans are born with them. The laziest bum in town is entitled to the equal protection of the law. It is not something that has to be "earned" or "deserved." It belongs to him because he is an American citizen. I'm tired, and you must be too, of the sanctimonious snobs who say they will "let" the Negroes in "their" schools when the Negro has "earned" it through self-improvement.

In human relations, we are always talking about communication. So often that is at the nub of a problem. All issues would not be resolved if we knew more about each other and understood each other better, but many of them would. And I am sorry to say that communications between Negroes and Jews in Atlanta leave a lot to be desired.

How many Jews do you think are in Atlanta. One hundred thousand? That is what the last Christian businessman I asked told me. Well, in this city of 1,100,000 people there are only about 15,000 Jewish men, women and children—less than 1 1/2%. But you couldn't tell that by looking at the list of sponsors of the recent testimonial dinner for Martin King. About 20% of those sponsors were Jewish, and Jews comprised 28% of the white sponsors. I think that's a pretty good showing, but most Negroes don't know it.

I suspect everyone knows that Charlie Leb is Jewish, and that he has rejected and abused Negroes who sought service at his restaurant. But I suspect few of you know that when he did that, he lost virtually all of his Jewish customers. There was never any organized boycott of Leb's in the Jewish community. There didn't have to be. Most Jews, on their own, instinctively stayed away from his place of business.

There is a good reason why these things are not better known. The explanation is that much of the contact between Negroes and Jews in a big city is contact between tenant and landlord, or employee and employer. Those are not peer relationships and they are not conducive to mutual understanding. If by chance I have given the impression up to now that I think all Jews are good men sold on social justice, let me take this opportunity to correct it. We have our share of exploiters. Too often these are the Jews most likely to come in contact with the Negro community.

Every man must be judged on his own merit. I refuse to be judged a hustler by someone who knows a crooked Jewish pawnbroker. Because a Negro robs a liquor store, that doesn't make another Negro untrustworthy. But too many people stereotype a whole group because of the behavior of a few individual members of it.

I couldn't kid you if I wanted to. There are Jewish bigots, although to me those terms should be mutually exclusive. There are not many of them but unfortunately they do exist. As an educational agency working within the Jewish community, the American Jewish Committee is trying to bring our people to an understanding of race that would eliminate bigotry from our midst. But I know we still have a way to go.

Just as I frankly concede the existence of prejudice against Negroes among Jews, I believe there is prejudice against Jews among Negroes. Anti-Semitism is a fairly common phenomenon among Christians and most Negroes are, after all, Christian. Most religious leaders now recognize that anti-Semitism has important roots in Christianity. It is for that reason that the World Council of Churches, The Vatican Council, the Episcopal and Lutheran denominations as well as others have recently made explicit efforts to destroy the canard that Jews generally are responsible for the death of Jesus. But slander dies hard, and this one is both old and hardy.

Before I close, I want to say something about my agency's role in race relations in the South. We are rarely the initiators of social change. The initiative for social change in the South comes mostly from Negroes. It may be spontaneous student demonstration, or a carefully planned legal assault on some bastion of white supremacy by CORE or the NAACP. We do not see ourselves, by and large, as the appropriate group to start the ball moving. Indeed, from a legal point of view, it would be impossible in many instances where the courts insist that one must be a Negro to have standing to challenge segregation.

We see ourselves as a catalytic agent in the process of social change. After the initiative has been taken by NAACP or SCLC, we then seek to assist the community in accepting change in an orderly manner. We are catalytic in the sense and to the extent that we accelerate the process.

We serve as a professional channel for enthusiastic volunteers banded together in groups such as HOPE (Help our Public Education), OASIS (Organizations Assisting Schools in September) and Partners for Progress. Under certain circumstances, we may be, and often have been, a resource for public officials and business leaders seeking professional assistance in inter-group relations problems. One of the byproducts of the consultative role, however, is that it often must be played largely behind the scenes. Otherwise we couldn't carry it off. But this lack of publicity, while it often enhances our effectiveness, has an important drawback. Our work is little known and appreciated sometimes even by our own constituency. If you hear little or nothing about us, please don't assume we are standing aloof from that struggle.

I should point out that when we are promoting compliance with court ordered desegregation, or with the new civil rights laws, we are serving Jewish interests as well as the general, civic interest. We know that when a community has a traumatic desegregation experience, such as with buses in Montgomery or schools in Little Rock, that a consequence of the tension created is an increase in overt anti-Semitic activity. The smoother the transition and the more orderly the compliance, the less anti-Semitism. It is apparent, therefore, that in the course of progress, Negro interest and Jewish interest coincide with each other and the best interests of the entire community.

Another way to differentiate our role from NAACP, CORE, SNCC or SCLC is to characterize them as the fathers of social change, and us as the midwives. When we help to deliver, we are earning our keep as a human relations agency.

§119 Reverend Duncan Howlett

On the evening of March 9, 1965, three Unitarian ministers: Orloff Miller, Clark Olsen, and James Reeb were walking from Walker's Café in Selma, Alabama to Brown Chapel AME Church. The men were in Selma in response to Martin Luther King, Jr.'s call for clergy to participate in the march to Montgomery. Each of the men had witnessed the brutal and unprovoked assault on the Edmund Pettus Bridge just two days prior. As the clergymen passed the Silver Moon Café, several whites assaulted them from behind. Reeb was struck in the back of the head by a baseball bat. Two days later, the 38-year old minister was dead. He left behind a wife and four children. Less than a week later, Lyndon B. Johnson, in his famous March 15th Voting Rights Address praised his efforts. King also praised Reeb in a eulogy, but he also used the occasion to blister the church, stating, "James Reeb was murdered by the indifference of every minister of the gospel who has remained silent behind the safe security of stained glass windows. He was murdered by the irrelevancy of a church that will stand amid social evil and serve as a taillight rather than a headlight, an echo rather than a voice."

Reeb was born on New Year's Day, 1927 and grew up in Colorado. After graduating from St. Olaf College, Reeb attended Princeton Theological Seminary. Upon converting from Presbyterianism to Unitarianism, Reeb served until 1964 as assistant minister under Duncan Howlett at All Souls Church in Washington, D.C. So strong was his affection for Reeb that, following Reeb's death, Howlett immediately went to work on a biography, *No Greater Love: The James Reeb Story*, which was published by Harper & Row in 1966. At the time of his death, Reeb was working for the American Friends Service Committee in Boston in the area of urban housing. The men who killed Reeb and assaulted Miller and Olsen, Elmer Cook, Stanley Hoggle, and O'Neal Hoggle were acquitted in April after jurors took 90 minutes to reach their verdict.

Reverend Duncan Howlett's biography appears at the introduction to his March 12, 1961 speech in Lynchburg, Virginia. Just four days after Reeb's death, Howlett preached the following sermon at All Souls. It is less a eulogy to Reeb and more a condemnation of George Wallace and law enforcement officials. Even as Howlett levels his opprobrium at the Alabama Governor and Al Lingo, his sermon also emphasizes that "the wind has changed." In Alabama and Mississippi white people are "beginning to see that change is here." Whether that change had been induced by the Civil Rights Bill of 1964, economically driven boycotts, or a deep sense of shame at witnessing the brutal violence, white southerners were now aware that the lid of secrecy had been lifted. Perhaps more importantly, Howlett reveals his keen understanding of the visual: the "whole civil rights movement" had been reduced to but one thing, "We are exposing to the eyes of the nation and the world the subjection in which the American Negro has been held by the American people. . . . We lay it bare that we may cut it away. We bring it into the light of day to eliminate it. We reveal it to destroy it forever." Howlett closes the sermon by rephrasing parts of Lincoln's Gettysburg Address to glimpse a future in which blacks will be free citizens of full stature.

Report from Alabama and Mississippi
All Souls Church (Unitarian), Washington, D.C.
March 14, 1965

We meet this morning under the shadow of over-arching tragedy. It is the second time in less than two years we have done so, the third in less than a decade. It is not ten years since A. Powell Davies died suddenly, while still in the prime of life. We shall never forget the Sunday we gathered here not two years ago to face together the fact that a man with evil in his heart had slain President John F. Kennedy, forty-two years of age and still in the full vigor of early maturity. Today as we gather again in this place, we have to face together the fact that another man with evil in his heart has slain the Reverend James J. Reeb, first Assistant, then Associate Minister of this church from 1959 to 1964. He was but thirty-eight years of age, and still had about him the freshness, the vitality, the zeal and the idealism of youth. To face his passing is more than we can do. Really to believe that it has happened is still impossible.

The temptation to make our service this morning into a memorial to James Reeb is overwhelming. There would seem to be no reason why we should resist. But there is just one. And it is enough. It is too much. Jim was our own. He is our own. He always will be.

Memorial services for him are being held all across this land today in churches of every denomination. Three official services have, however, been arranged. The first will be in Selma, Alabama, at Browns Chapel, to which Jim was going to attend a freedom rally when he was struck down. Martin Luther King and other civil rights leaders will conduct that service. It will be what you might call the official civil rights service. It centers in the civil rights movement and the immortal place James Reeb now holds within it.

Another of the three official services we have set up, through which to express the dimensions of James Reeb's life and the place he now occupies in the hearts of the American people, will be held next Thursday at 12:15 p.m. in Boston, where Mr. Reeb has been working this year. It will be held at the Arlington Street Church and will be interfaith in character. It, too, will center in his work in the civil rights movement, but more particularly in the role he had increasingly come to play in the rehabilitation of the poor in our American urban centers, and the manner in which the general problems of the city aggravate the difficulties faced by the Negro under all circumstances.

Of the three official services we have set up, the one that is of greatest moment to us will be held here at All Souls Church next Tuesday at 2:00 p.m. Like the other two, it will be a memorial service in the strict sense, for Jim's ashes have already been flown to Wyoming. But in the more general sense, the service here will come closest to the traditional funeral. For when we gather here on Tuesday afternoon we shall not, as most will do, pay tribute to someone whom we did not know but who has now become a symbol for a great movement. He is indeed such a symbol, and when we gather here the wider dimensions of his life will not be forgotten. But we who come here will also meet to mourn the loss of a beloved friend. Not forgetting his larger role in life, we shall gather and call to mind a man we knew and loved, who greatly loved us.

Dr. William Stuart Nelson, Vice President of Howard University, Dr. Dana McLean Greeley, President of the Unitarian Universalist Association, and I will conduct the service here. Mrs. Reeb will return to Washington for the service, accompanied by Mr. Reeb's father and mother and other members of the family.

This morning, with religious people throughout the land, we turn our attention to the movement for which James Reeb gave his life. It is a movement and a great one. Remembering this we realize, almost with a sense of shock, that others have given their lives in this struggle too, a fact James Reeb would be quick to point out. The list is a long one. His name is but the latest to be added to it. Where does the list begin? Not with the three civil rights workers murdered at Philadelphia, Mississippi, last summer. Not with Medgar Evers. Does it perhaps begin with John Brown, who died over a hundred years ago at the beginning of the movement to make the Negro an integral part of American life?

There is a sense, perhaps, in which our active participation in and total commitment to the movement here at All Souls Church began with the bombing of the 16th Street Baptist Church in Birmingham and the death of the four Sunday school children that resulted from it. The following Sunday, September 22, 1963, our bulletin board was draped in black, as it is today. That Sunday a march originated here, as a march will originate here today to go down 16th Street to Lafayette Square where a service will be held. The march and the service were then, as they will be today, interracial and interfaith.

Today's march begins at 1:00 p.m. By prior arrangement with the police, we will use the sidewalks on both sides of 16th Street. We will not sing. We will wear black armbands rather than carrying signs, and we will observe traffic lights. This auditorium will be the point of assembly for the 16th Street procession. Others, such as the group from the Roman Catholic

Church of Saints Paul & Augustine, led by Father Baroni, will join us as we proceed. Other marches will follow other radials to Lafayette Square.

Of course, this church was identified with the civil rights movement long before the great upsurge of feeling that has occurred just recently. When most churches in this city were still segregated, All Souls Church was integrated both in theory and in fact. When there were few to speak out, A. Powell Davies, from the pulpit in which I stand this morning, sought to rouse the American conscience to the plight of the American Negro. That was why this church honored the Birmingham children—because our thought and practice in these matters had long been established. This tradition was among the things that drew James Reeb to us in the first instance, back in 1959 after he had decided to leave the Presbyterian Church and to enter the Unitarian ministry.

Meanwhile, Governor George Wallace of Alabama has come to this city to talk to the President and gone quietly home again. The air somehow seems a little less oppressive since his departure. He is holding a press conference shortly after we conclude our service this morning. I shall not be hurrying off to a TV set to take it in. There is nothing the Governor can say to redeem himself short of granting Negroes the right to vote in Alabama, and I don't expect him to do that.

In my mind, Governor Wallace bears a burden of guilt that should have left him prostrate. His club-wielding state troopers, a week ago today, set the pattern for the club-wielding civilian who felled James Reeb. The President gave Wallace three hours, it is said. I don't think he deserved five minutes. I believe, of course, that the opposition ought always to be heard. But we heard all George Wallace had to say when he was campaigning in this area some months ago. We saw last Sunday what his principles mean translated into practice. That the President heard him at all is an indication of Lyndon Johnson's determination to find a solution to the racial turmoil that now rocks Alabama.

Governor Wallace, in asking to see the President, said defiance of lawful authority and the preservation of lawful society was the issue, not voting rights. I myself believe deeply in law and order. So did Jim. Human society cannot function without either. But to launch a tear gas attack upon defenseless marchers and then, while they are rendered helpless by the gas, to club them to the ground and lash them with bull whips may be to maintain lawful authority and to preserve lawful society, but it is also to deny human rights. It is to revert to the methods of governmental oppression this country was founded to escape.

In medieval Europe, law and order was maintained by means of brutality and terror exercised by lawful authority. Governor Wallace would do the same. He looks upon the Negro as a monarch of the Middle Ages looked upon his subjects. For Wallace, as for all racists, the Negro is not a citizen, he is a subject. He has no rights, only obligations. Through the use of arbitrary power the state may, if it can, bend the Negroes' will to its own. If the Negro does not like what the lawful authorities do to him, he has no redress. He has no voice, no right of appeal, no hope. He can only suffer.

Wallace has capsuled the issue of the civil rights movement in his phrase "lawful authority." That is the question. What is lawful authority and how do you maintain it in a land where men, by law, are free? The problem arises in the civil rights movement because Wallace and the men of the South whom he symbolizes still try to pretend that for the Negro lawful authority applies, but not freedom. For three hundred years, since slaves first were brought to our shores, men have rationalized their treatment of the Negro by telling themselves that he is not a man—by telling themselves that the Bill of Rights does not apply to him. This is a free country, they would say proudly. But if forced to, they would add that in this country there live a number of dark-skinned individuals who look like people and act like people, but who really aren't people and ought not to be treated as if they were. They have therefore only a secondary place in society which they must learn to accept. One of the purposes of lawful authority, they would say, is to keep the Negro in his "place." That is the word. Then there is no trouble. The Negro is cared for by the Southern whites, they remind us—even loved. But always and only when he knows what his place is and how to remain in it. That is their shameful doctrine.

For the Negro in the South the Bill of Rights has traditionally been replaced by devices of tyranny as old as the civilizations of man. In the South the Negro who does not know his place and keep it is terrorized into doing so. And if, made desperate by the suffering and degradation to which he is subjected, he cannot be driven back to his "place," he is killed: not always, of course, but often—usually, we might say. It used to be by lynching. From this outrage the South has been forced to retreat by the conscience of the nation. But Negroes are still killed, as were Medgar Evers, Jimmy Lee Jackson, and a number of others we might name. Tragically and unbelievably, the list is too long even to read.

Now, however, there is a difference. The wind has changed. The lynchings have been given up. The Civil Rights Bill is the law of the land. The civil rights movement is on the march, and today, while the nation as a whole mourns for James Reeb, George Wallace comes to see the President almost alone. Regarding this change, I know whereof I speak. I returned only last Monday—not yet a week ago—from an eight-day stay in the State of Mississippi. I had planned to report to you this morning on the situation there. On returning to Washington, I went back almost immediately to Alabama to be with Jim and Marie Reeb, returning to Washington again Friday after he died. Although I never left the University Hospital in Birmingham throughout that time except for a few hours of sleep, I talked to a wide variety of people in Alabama while acting as a kind of public relations officer for the family. I saw and heard the expressions of sympathy, shock, and shame that came to Mrs. Reeb from the Birmingham community.

While in Mississippi earlier, I talked to people all over the state, in all walks of life: civic leaders, newspaper editors, civil rights workers and ordinary citizens. I talked to many civil rights workers who had come in from the outside, but I made a particular point of talking to the people who lived and worked in the State of Mississippi itself in order to understand, if possible, what they are thinking and what they propose to do. I say to you without hesitation that the white people of the South are slowly waking. They are beginning to face the fact that a major social change is upon them. Whether they like it or want it, they are beginning to see that the change is here. Generally speaking, they face the fact that they no longer have a choice. The question now is not whether, or even when, but how best to bring that change about.

Many Southern whites have for some time seen the change coming. Many have long wanted it and sought to bring it about. This number has been steadily increasing. Right now it is increasing very rapidly. There are many reasons for this. The Civil Rights Bill, passed by the Congress last summer, is one. Another is economic. The South is now beginning to see how greatly the debasement of the Negro has debased its entire economy as well as its mores. Another economic factor is the boycott. Those that have already been held have been very effective. There is widespread anxiety over boycotts now threatened. There is an increasing readiness to sign the H.E.W. compliance agreements in connection with the receipt of special grants for school aid.

There is also a very real sense of shame at the violence perpetrated by whites against Negroes and Northern civil rights workers outside of lawful authority. There are now but few to defend the rampage of church burnings and bombings that took place in Mississippi last summer. Almost no voice is lifted in defense of the killing of Negroes who have been active in the civil rights movement. Yet but a generation ago whites on every hand would have been found saying of a Negro who had been killed, "You may not think it is right, but he deserved what he got. He didn't know his place." What is more, you would not even have been able to ask why he had been killed, for you would not have known about it. Few, if any, papers would have reported it even if they had had the story. Only the Negroes who wept with each other would know. Only the men and women who burned with helpless indignation, yet trembled in fear of further reprisals, would know.

What you might have known a generation ago and what you as a Southern white would still know, but would seldom mention, would be the fact that the chief means of suppressing the Negro in the South is the law itself and its enforcement officers. The acts of violence on the part of self-appointed individuals are but a small part of the pattern of oppression by which the Negro has been held in subjection. You as a Southerner would now know that officers, sworn to uphold lawful authority, were the very men who most harassed, threatened, beat, imprisoned, and generally terrorized the Negro people.

The great change that is now taking place lies in the fact that the lid of secrecy is being lifted from the system of subjugation of the Negro that has so long prevailed in the South. The North is beginning at last to face what has actually been going on. As a matter of fact, the North too bears the same guilt, though by no means to the same degree. For we too have now begun to see how different has been, and in some areas continues to be, the pattern of justice met by the Negro and that met by the white man in our Northern cities. But having seen it, we have happily begun to change it. Here in the District of Columbia, for example, we have been making rapid progress along this line.

This is what the struggle in Alabama right now is all about. This is what the whole civil rights movement throughout the land is all about. We are exposing to the eyes of the nation and the world the subjection in which the American Negro has been held by the American people. We expose it, not to wallow in our own sin and shame or in a paroxysm of repentance to seek forgiveness. Our aim is far more practical than that. We now seek to expose and expunge every aspect of the system of degradation under which the American Negro has lived. We lay it bare that we may cut it away. We bring it into the light of day to eliminate it. We reveal it to destroy it forever.

The nation: all the world, saw in Selma, Alabama, last Sunday how the system works. On Tuesday when white ministers from all over the country, answering the summons of Martin Luther King, joined with the Negroes of Selma in their second march, we saw it yet more clearly. For then there was no violence. This was by previous arrangement, I am told. And perhaps it was. If so, then my point is further strengthened. Governor Wallace guessed that the conscience of white Alabama might accept the vicious attack of his state troopers upon the Negro marchers. But he did not think the people would support him in such an attack when both Negro and white stood together facing him, even though the white men were Northern "trouble makers," as he calls them. And there could have been no doubt in his mind that if he set upon such a group with gas, bludgeons and whips, fifty thousand Northerners would have poured into Selma the next day to stand with the Negroes in their protest.

Governor Wallace has come to Washington to talk to the President about lawful authority. Let us ask: Lawful authority for whom? Governor Wallace came to Washington out of the past. He came from a day that is dead. He offers us a philosophy of government the whole free world has rejected—a philosophy that permits the government to tyrannize over men, provided it is duly constituted under law. Wallace represents a group of white people in the South and elsewhere who would maintain, if they could, the ancient pattern of tyranny and terror by which the Negro has been subjugated since the Emancipation Proclamation set him free. Wallace was not worthy of the time and attention of the President, although, I repeat, the President is to be commended for seeing him.

Four score and many more than seven years ago, our fathers brought forth upon this continent a new nation, conceived in liberty and dedicated to the proposition that all men are created equal. The war that we later fought to preserve the union and bring slavery to an end in accordance with that principle was successful. But we replaced the legal bondage in which the Negro had been held with civil, economic, and psychological bondage. Today we are engaged in a new civil war, in the North as well as the South, throughout the length and breadth of this land. In this new civil war the Negro is a participant with us. We are not fighting for him so much as we are fighting with him. And as the fight goes on, the emphasis shifts, as it should, so that already the leadership, and the troops, to continue the analogy, are more Negro than white. When this war is over, Negroes as a people will be free, as many individual Negroes already are. They will be citizens of full stature, as many already are. And they will no longer be a minority group.

When this, the new civil war is over; when the rights to which the Negro is entitled as a citizen and as a man have at long last been given to him, there will be those who have fallen in the struggle because of whose sacrifice we who remain will know victory. At the front rank of this group James Reeb will stand. Today the civil rights movement has suddenly surged forward, catching through his tragic end the quality of his valiant spirit. His life, by that magic alchemy through which men and movements merge, is now the life of the movement itself. His soul is its soul. And one day his sacrifice will be transmuted from tragedy into victory—the victory of right over wrong and good over evil. In him, and in the movement for which he gave his life, hate one day will be transfigured by love.

§120 Albert D'Orlando

Reverend Albert D'Orlando's biography appears in the introduction to his September 25, 1955 sermon in New Orleans, Louisiana. The sermon below occurs the week after D'Orlando's house was firebombed with gasoline. D'Orlando begins the sermon with his common take on ethics: as decent human beings we are all responsible for world events and suffer with innocent victims at the hand of oppressors. Thus, fellow Unitarian minister James Reeb's death was harm to all of us. While it is tempting to think of Reeb's death as the result of his own youthful zeal or the excesses of "know nothing" thugs, there is a deeper logic to James Reeb's martyrdom—he had to stand up to sanctioned murder. Emmett Till, Medgar Evers, the four Birmingham girls, the three Freedom Summer workers, and others had been similarly murdered. Yet lawless people murder almost everywhere. The unique quality of these murders is that no indictments ensued. Until the decent people of these states reestablished judicial norms, activism like James Reeb's would have to persist. D'Orlando closes his sermon on a note of cautious optimism: "The great hope in the present situation is to be found in the apparent resurgence of the church as a leader on this issue. . . . It is our hope this is but the beginning of a trend in which the prophetic quality of religion will reassert itself, and find expression in all the moral issues of our time."

In Memoriam . . . James Reeb

First Universalist Unitarian Church of New Orleans, New Orleans, Louisiana
March 14, 1965

When the Rev. James Reeb died on Thursday evening, a piece of each one of us died with him. It is that part deep down within us which dies a bit more, each time a fellow human being is the victim of wanton cruelty; it is that part of us which dies a bit more at each instance of man's inhumanity to man. The vicious attack on Mr. Reeb was also a vicious attack on all decent, honorable people everywhere. Its immediate victim might have been any one of us: it might have been you or, it might have been me or, it might have been any one of the many thousands of individuals throughout the country who have been demonstrating for the full emancipation of the American Negro.

But, it wasn't you or me or, anyone of the many who now raise their voices in protest. It was James Reeb, Unitarian minister, colleague, husband, father, a person of deep conviction, of dedicated conscience, deeply committed to the enhancement of human dignity, prepared to leave at a moment's notice to make his witness where it was needed, and where it might count.

When Martin Luther King issued his appeal for ministers to come to Selma, following the police brutality of last weekend, Jim Reeb was quick to respond. He must have been aware of the potential danger involved in going into this tension-ridden community; yet, he went there in the belief, as well in the hope, that his presence, added to that of 2,500 other clergymen, might help to relieve the situation.

This response was entirely consistent with a philosophy of life that had its origins when he was a student in theological school, and, which evolved as he went on to work with people who, in trying to find their way of life, were forced to cope with the elements of discrimination; fear, intimidation, rejection, frustration, confusion and uncertainty. One of his professors tells about the beginning as there unfolded before him the implications in the long human struggle for worth and dignity. The leader of a YMCA where he worked, tells how he implemented his ties by bringing together young people of all backgrounds, regardless of race. Dr. Duncan Howlett, minister of our church in Washington, D.C., with whom Jim Reeb served as associate for 5 years, describes him as one of the finest persons he has ever known; a man of high integrity, deeply committed to the cause of human justice.

It was out of this background that he evolved into a person who could be deeply moved by the events at Selma, and, who went there to make his witness.

Incidentally, shortly before his death the newspapers quoted Mrs. Reeb as saying that her husband was prepared to give his life for the cause. I don't know whether that was a direct quotation. But, assuming that it was: I do not believe that James Reeb intended it in terms of offering himself as a sacrificial lamb nor, do I believe that he sought out or welcomed the martyr's role. There are many ways for a person to give his life to a worthwhile goal, without inviting premature death. He can consume his energy, his talent, his enthusiasm in supporting what he believes to be right. He can spend his strength in unwavering devotion to its fulfillment. History is full of individuals who were the moving force behind causes that were dear to them, though not popular at the time, people who literally made this the focal point of their life. And, I believe that if Jim Reeb thought in terms of giving his life for a cause, it was in this sense that he meant it.

The fact that he was so prematurely struck down deprives us of a colleague in the continuing struggle against human oppression. Perhaps even now we are not fully aware of the extent of that loss. But, this much we do know: that this senseless murder deprives a devoted wife of her husband and companion, and it deprives four growing children of their father. They are the ones who shall bear the heavy burden of this loss for many years to come. In bearing this burden, they join the vast throng of sad and lonely families, both Negro and White, who return at the end of each day to empty homes, who go on without loved ones who were lost in this same way: husbands, fathers, brothers, sons, in some cases, daughters, sisters and mothers, too, victims of hatred, prejudice, brutality and inhumanity, who sometimes have simply disappeared, never to be heard from again.

Much of this has been sanctioned under the heading of what some people like to call "our southern way of life," a way of life that often is regarded as a sacred privilege for all who will live by its principles but, which does not recognize the sacred quality of any person who will question its principles. It is a way of life, which claims the rights granted by the American Constitution while refusing to accept or to discharge its concomitant responsibilities. It is a way of life that is breeding a new generation of "Know Nothings" responding to conditions quite similar to those of their counterparts of a generation ago.

You might remember the historical background, which accounted for the "Know Nothings" of the mid-19th century.

One winter night in 1854, a band of masked men broke into a shed within sight of the White House. They searched for what one of them called "that blasted stone from Rome," a beautiful block of marble from the Temple of Concord, a gift from the Vatican to be used in constructing the Washington Monument. The masked men rolled the block onto a wagon and dumped it into the Potomac River.

The vandals were "Know Nothings." They belonged to a secret order whose members were pledged to do exactly as told and to reply to all questions asked by non-members: "I know nothing."

But, the point that must be underscored is that their theft of the papal gift was a protest against profound social change then stirring the nation. Prior to that time, waves of Catholic Irish and German immigrants had been brought here to dig the canals and build the railroads that were to make of this a great nation. Now these same immigrants were in the process of gaining political power. Then, in 1844 "Native Americans" rioted in Philadelphia, burning two of the old and most famous Catholic Churches. They initiated a movement to have naturalized citizens banned from public office and they sought to extend the waiting time for citizenship to 21 years. A decade later, the "Know Nothings" had grown into a movement powerful enough to elect governors in seven states.

As the magazine "Progressive" put it, "The seeds of Know-Nothingism lie deep in the American soil, and periodically crises occur which stimulate the seeds to force up shoots." Examples of this are the Ku Klux Klan of Reconstruction days and the Klan's revival in the 1920's.

Today the seeds are forcing up shoots once again: the Ku Klux Klan and other groups are at work in the same way, they are the contemporary "Know Nothings," and, for essentially the same reason: they set out to resist social change which inevitably must come, and as with their predecessors, they destroy if necessary, in their effort to prevent change.

For some time now, they have bombed schools, synagogues, churches, and private homes. Many Negroes have disappeared under circumstances that no one can or will explain. Today they are intimidated as they attempt to register in Selma; tomorrow it could be something else.

In part, this reflects a national uncertainty about ourselves. As one foreign visitor discovered, our faith in ourselves and in our destiny is seriously shaken. Prof. D. W. Brogan of Cambridge University, wrote in the Manchester *Guardian* of a steady "deterioration in American self-confidence . . . and of a decline in trust in the American way of life." To a considerable extent this same influence is felt here as elsewhere in the country. But, beyond that, he pointed out that here in the south many people are alarmed at social change brought about by integration, and in saying this, he put his finger squarely on the issue at hand.

Today this resistance to social change has created an environment in which violence is encouraged by the "Know Nothings" of our time. They know, but they do not know. And, as they maintain their silence, they give sanction and support to continued unrest and confusion. Meanwhile, each additional victim of violence is possible because nothing was done in the cases preceding his to bring to justice the ones who were responsible for them.

James Reeb died as a result of having gone to Selma. But, this is not the reason for his death nor, does it explain the attack on him as well as on two colleagues who were with him at that time.

James Reeb died because when Emmett Till was brutally murdered ten years ago that murder was sanctioned by the community. Two men were arrested; they were indicted; they were acquitted. As I recall, they later acknowledged their part.

James Reeb died because when Medgar Evers was murdered two years ago, his murder was sanctioned by many people in that community. Available evidence still points in one direction, but twice now juries have disagreed. Meanwhile, the defendant has been rewarded by being made a deputy in the city's safety department.

James Reeb died because when four young girls died in the insane and murderous bombing of a church in Birmingham less than two years ago, that act was sanctioned by too many people in that community. It was that act which prompted the late playwright, Lorraine Hansberry to say: "I am terrified at the death of the heart which is happening in my country. The white people have become moral monsters." It was that same act which prompted *The New York Times* to write, editorially, "This is the sixth bombing since May and not one has been solved. How long can such barbaric abuse go on without a mass uprising by men and women who see in the forces of law only a shield for their blood stained oppressors."

Last summer 3 Civil Rights workers were killed in Mississippi. Their murder was sanctioned by a community whose people accept this as a lesson to other COFO workers coming into the state. To be sure, a grand jury did return indictments—not for murder, but for a violation of Civil Rights. But, even these indictments have been dissolved.

A prominent Negro educator was murdered in Georgia toward the end of the summer as he drove through the state on his way to his home in Washington. Yet, the jury could find no reason to convict the men who were charged.

James Reeb died because over and over again violence has been fostered, and murder has been sanctioned, as a natural consequence of that violence. Now four men have been charged with his murder, and all four have been released under individual bonds of $25,000.00. Selma Public Safety Director, Wilson Baker explains their release this way (and, this is a direct quote from the *Times-Picayune*): "Under Alabama Law, bond is permitted on a murder charge if there is indication that a jury will not return the death penalty," a statement which not only confers on him the combined roles of prosecuting attorney, judge and jury but, which raises the further issue of a double standard of justice by posing the simple question: "What might have been that decision if the four men charged with murder had been Negro?"

Incidentally, for those among you who know my views on Capital Punishment, let me say that I have not changed my thinking on this issue. I continue to be unalterably opposed to Capital Punishment, in this case, as in any other. At the same time, I do not believe that justice is served by giving these men their freedom until all the evidence at hand shall have been weighed by a grand jury.

Moreover, I would hope that the day will come when crimes of this nature will be treated not as crimes against a particular state, but as crimes against all humanity. There is good precedence for this in the Nuremberg trials that followed the second World War, when Nazi War Criminals were tried for having committed crimes against humanity rather than against one state or nation. There has been some difference of opinion as to the justification of the trial but, it is my understanding that this difference is over the question of whether such law should have been created after the fact and not on the nature of the offense itself. What did emerge from that trial is an awareness that murder is a crime against all humanity and we would hope that this principle might pertain in our own situation. Perhaps, then, we shall make broader efforts to uphold justice and thus we shall create a living and meaningful memorial to James Reeb, as well as to the many others who have met a similar fate.

When I reached this point in my sermon, late last evening the quiet of the night was suddenly shattered by an explosion under my window. It was a result of a gasoline bomb which had been thrown at the house by some individual or group of individuals.

Only paint damage, nobody injured.

But it did serve to remind us that the struggle for civil rights is at hand, here in New Orleans, as well as in distant Selma, Alabama. We too must make our witness, in our own way, in our own situation.

In any case, I had intended a shorter sermon today for reasons I shall mention during the announcement period.

The great hope in the present situation is to be found in the apparent resurgence of the church as a leader in this issue. You know that this is long overdue. This is also reflected in statements from leading churchmen:

Methodist Bishop, Gerald Kennedy of Los Angeles: "The church is under judgment, and out of these revolutionary times will come great things. But, one thing is certain . . . freedom is standing up and starting to march."

The Right Reverend John E. Hines, recently installed as Presiding Bishop of the Episcopal Church: "The majority of the segments of the church's life in times of social crisis have been weighed in the balance and found wanting."

Now, most branches of the church, and in this I include all faiths and religions, whether they worship in a church, a temple, or a synagogue, most of them sent their best men to Selma. It was a moving experience, not only to see them pour into Selma but, to put aside all theological differences, all organizational hierarchies, to march side by side, and ready to go all the way to Montgomery if possible.

Eric Severeid summed it up this way: "Here we see that the church which has long lent itself to accommodation . . . is now becoming the church militant."

It is our hope this is but the beginning of a trend in which the prophetic quality of religion will re-assert itself, and find expression in all the moral issues of our time.

Thus we honor the memory of James Reeb. Thus we extend our love and sympathy to his wife and their four children. And we trust that his witness, designed to serve the brotherhood of man, may reach even beyond his utmost dreams.

§121 Roy Wilkins

Roy Wilkins's biographic information appears at the introduction to his speech on May 22, 1955. On March 7, 1965, Bloody Sunday in Selma, Alabama, one of the nation's most powerful civil rights leaders didn't know James Reeb from James Bond. That all changed in less than a week, with Reeb's assault and murder four days later. So, too, with Lyndon B. Johnson, who at government expense, had James Reeb's wife Marie flown immediately to a hospital in Birmingham, Alabama. There were some in the media critical of all the attention James Reeb received; after all, why hadn't Jimmie Lee Jackson, gunned down just outside of Selma on February 18, gotten such attention and adulation? Was this 1965's version of Goodman and Schwerner, two white activists murdered in Neshoba County, Mississippi in June 1964?

Wilkins's eloquent eulogy to the fallen Unitarian minister in Casper, Wyoming, reprises the Good Samaritan story of Luke, though in his twentieth century version, the stricken man is black. James Reeb "went straight into the gully of darkness and strife and hate. He offered his great spirit, his unadorned goodness, his unselfish love, to his stricken neighbor."

Of course Wilkins also had a political message for his Wyoming audience—that James Reeb understood the campaign for voting rights in Alabama and that Johnson's pending voting rights legislation would hasten the day of the black franchise in the Deep South. The following evening, in his Voting Rights Address to the nation, President Johnson began thus, "At times history and fate meet at a single time in a single place to shape a turning point in man's unending search for freedom. So it was at Lexington and Concord. So it was a century ago at Appomattox. So it was last week in Selma, Alabama. There, long-suffering men and women peacefully protested the denial of their rights as Americans. Many were brutally assaulted. One good man, a man of God, was killed." So it was that James J. Reeb entered the American pantheon of martyrs.

Eulogy at Memorial Service for James Reeb

Casper, Wyoming
March 14, 1965

The priest in whose memory we are gathered here today did not pass on the other side.

James Reeb heard the anguished cry against injustice and heeded it—with his warm concern, with his prayers, with his bodily presence at the place of evil, and with his life. It is difficult to realize that only last Sunday—a short week ago—he preached at his services in Boston and ended his day, as did many of us, by viewing the nightmare TV film of the Selma Sunday.

The sight of fully-armed state troopers beating down and gassing unarmed men and children who were staging a peaceful marching demonstration to secure the right to register and vote sickened and angered America.

But the inhumanity called to Reverend Reeb.

These were his neighbors, beaten and robbed. These were those of the great downtrodden of the world in whose behalf a manger in Bethlehem became a cradle so many years ago.

And James Reeb, a disciple of that Savior, felt impelled to go to Selma.

Of course, Selma was a challenge to the principles of our United States Constitution, to government.

Of course, Selma was a challenge to the disciplines of civilized society, to its carefully built checks and balances and restraints.

But more than all these, Selma was a challenge to the religious teachings upon which James Reeb had built his life. The great precepts of love of God and man, and of brotherhood, were cruelly dared in that ugly attack of last Sunday.

James Reeb rose to that Challenge unhesitatingly and unflinchingly.

He knew about the underlying issue, the facts in the right-to-vote campaign. Yesterday, Governor Wallace, in connection with his interview with President Johnson, sought to shift the blame from Alabama's original sin of denying the vote to Negro citizens, to the protests against that denial. By the Wallace formula, all would be peaceful and everything would remain undisturbed if the demonstrations were forcibly halted. The Governor had a dream that he could "sell" this Alabama idea to the President and that the Federal Government would help him halt the demonstrations.

President Johnson and the Federal Government know better about the Alabama voting situation.

They know that in 33 out of the 67 counties in Alabama, less than 15 percent of the Negroes of voting age are permitted to register to vote.

There is only one right way to solve this problem, to have peace and dignity and that is to remove the barriers to the participation of Negro citizens at the ballot box.

There is every reason to believe that the legislation to be offered will empower the Federal Government to register persons to vote, will do away with literacy tricks masquerading as tests, and will include all elections, not just Federal ones. President Johnson has made it clear that the determination of his Administration is that no man shall be deprived of the right to vote.

James Reeb knew this wrong had to be righted by government, but he knew that a necessary ingredient to the solution of any human stress is concern.

"Come over into Macedonia and help us" is more than a call for technical and legal aid, more than a plea for formulas.

It is a call to conscience, to faith, to belief, to universal humanity—a plea for ministration to the human spirit in an hour of trial, a call to neighbors.

James Reeb knew his neighbor and followed, with a fidelity rare in these practical days, the Biblical admonition to love God and "thy neighbor as thyself."

His neighbor was every man, everywhere. Geography, religious compartments, nationality and skin color were to him but labels covering hearts and souls related, like his, to the God of all mankind.

There was a man, a black man, off the highway of life, in the gully by the side of the road where he had been left to die by robbers. The thieves stole his dignity, they took away his rights as a man and as a citizen in the land. When he sought to recover his possessions, they struck him down, they trussed him up with all manner of restraint, both crude and subtle. And they left him.

A priest was going down that road in the middle years of the Twentieth Century—a priest named James Reeb—and he did not pass by on the other side.

He went straight into the gully of darkness and strife and hate. He offered his great spirit, his unadorned goodness, his unselfish love, to his stricken neighbor. He sought to share the neighbor's misfortune, to minister to his wounds, to lighten his burden and to comfort his spirit.

Today, here among his loved ones and the people who watched him grow to manhood, I come as but one spokesman for a sorrowed and grateful people to thank God and to thank his family and all those who shaped him for James Reeb.

All of us, black and white, from the North, East and West—and from the South, are poorer for his going. But the nation he served is better for his underscoring of her weaknesses in being a just government.

The faith by which he lived is richer for his devotion and his supreme sacrifice. May that sacrifice speed the day when love shall conquer even those who struck him down and make men brothers.

§122 Robert A. Reed

Robert A. Reed was a longtime friend of James Reeb. During the spring of 1944, Reed was a mechanic at the air base in Casper, Wyoming. Reed and Reeb met while attending services at the First Presbyterian Church. Reed organized the North Casper Boys Club and when he shipped out in January of 1945 with the military, it was Reeb who took over the club for him. Reed and Reeb kept in contact throughout the years via letter-writing. Reed entered Wheaton College after his service. Both Reed and Reeb desired to enter the Presbyterian ministry after completing their education. In 1959 Reed was ordained as a Unitarian minister at the Unitarian Church of Arlington.

Reed's sermon/eulogy depicts James J. Reeb as a martyr for the Negro cause. He informs the audience of its obligation to understand the meaning of Reeb's life and death in order to grow as spiritual beings. Reed explains how Reeb was not simply concerned with voting rights for African Americans, but also world peace and justice for all. Reed is hopeful that Reeb's death will be vindicated by the

advancement of voting rights legislation. He also provides biographical information on Reeb to demonstrate how Reeb, even at a young age, desired to act in accordance with God's plan. In addition, Reed quotes from American essayist Ralph
Emerson, Indian poet Rabindranath Tagore, Catholic novelist Morris West, and
Swedish statesman Dag Hammarskjöld to underscore James Reeb's noble character and supreme sacrifice. Reed closes by drawing a parallel between the nation's
present state of affairs with the biblical story of Palm Sunday: "As on that Palm
Sunday long ago a time of crisis has come to a nation. Jim Reeb was not silent. He
lived and died in obedience to the cross."

To Be a Man
First Presbyterian Church, Casper, Wyoming
March 21, 1965

During the past ten years, in every part of the nation, there have been editorial tributes, memorial services, marches and eulogies; literally hundreds
of thousands of Americans of every faith and every political persuasion
have expressed the agonized sorrow and the profound respect of an awakened nation for the martyrdom of Jim Reeb. The President's message on
Monday night and the overwhelming support of both political parties for
the voting rights legislation indicate that history will show Jim's sacrifice
a major turning point in the nation's struggle to secure justice for all her
citizens.

But we have not come to this house of worship for another eulogy. We
are here as men and women of faith to seek the comfort, the strength, the
direction of God. You and I who loved Jim Reeb have a sacred obligation
which must begin in these moments of worship. We must open our hearts
at the deepest possible level as we seek to understand the full meaning of
Jim's life and death. For it is only in such a search for understanding that we
can find the courage to live our own lives in obedience to the cross.

Jim loved life more than most people do. He was always ready with a
story, a stunt or a smile. He was quick to laugh or clown. His enthusiasms
and exuberance were contagious. He never met a stranger; he never met a
human being he did not try to like. His spirit was as big as the mountains
and the out-of-doors he loved so well. Emerson said: "Let the measure of
time be spiritual, not mechanical. Life is unnecessarily long. Moments of
insight, of fine personal relation, a smile, a glance—what ample borrowers
of eternity these may be." There are men who live and give and feel more in
ten minutes than others do in ten years. Jim was one of these.

Jim not only enjoyed life more than most men; he was also more serious than most. Even in his teens he thought more, cared more, believed
more. He found many things about this world which he wanted to change,

for they were things he believed God wanted changed. Frequently in those years we talked together about the end of the war and what might be done to justify the awful suffering and sacrifice in human life. We spoke of the dreams of brotherhood and freedom for which so many young men had given their lives. It was during this period, while he was so active in this congregation, that Jim began to consider the ministry as a vocation.

There is a verse from the Indian poet Rabindranath Tagore which defines the difference between the true man of God and the rest of mankind:

> We cling to our seats and never stir,
> We allow our flowers to fade in peace,
>   and avoid the trouble of bearing
>   fruit.
> Let the starlights blazon their eternal
>   folly,
>   We quench our flames.
> Let the forest rustle and the ocean roar,
>   We sit mute.
> Let the call of the flood-tide come from
>   the sea,
>   We remain still.

Jim Reeb did not remain still or silent. He did not quench his flame. He did not turn away from the trouble and the suffering that are the price of bearing fruit in life. Jim met life with open arms and open heart.

Two weeks ago when Jim packed his things for Selma, Alabama, he was a mature man. He was fully responsible, fully conscious of all the possible consequences of his actions. Twenty years had passed since he had been moderator of the youth fellowship at First Presbyterian Church here in Casper. He had been an infantry staff sergeant in Alaska during the closing months of World War II. He had graduated from college and seminary and earned a graduate degree in counseling at Temple University.

Jim never wanted an ordinary parish in the safety of the suburbs. As a chaplain in the charity wards of a huge metropolitan hospital, as "Y" director and inner city minister, he spent his life on the front lines of human need. He worked with the sick, the underprivileged, the delinquent, the friendless and the poor. Going to Selma was simply one expression of a lifelong concern for the suffering and oppressed. Jim was concerned with much more than the right to vote, basic as that is. He cared about the shame and hopelessness of those who must spend their entire lives in grinding poverty. He cared about world peace in this age of nuclear terror. Most of all he was disturbed by the violence and injustice still so common in our day.

What the world needs is not a gigantic leap into space, but a gigantic leap into brotherhood. Those who work for a breakthrough in human relations are required to undertake risks no less great than those who pioneer in outer space. There is a high price to be paid by all who would overcome the insanity of hatred and the folly of indifference to the suffering of other men.

Conventional Christians have missed Bonhoeffer's insight that to be a Christian is first of all to be a man! Jim's lifelong struggle was to be a full, free and compassionate human being. He died as he lived, seeking to take some meaningful action on behalf of brotherhood and justice. To become a man is the first business of life. These words of Morris West, the Catholic novelist, describe for me the kind of man Jim had become:

> "It costs so much to be a full human being that there are very few who have the enlightenment, or the courage, to pay the price. One has to abandon altogether the search for security, and reach out to the risk of living with both arms. One has to embrace the world like a lover, and yet demand no easy return of love. One has to accept pain as a condition of existence. One has to court doubt and darkness as the cost of existence. One needs a will stubborn in conflict, but apt always to the total acceptance of every consequence of living and dying."

In a few weeks Christians around the world will celebrate Easter. We need to be reminded that the first nonviolent march calculated to stir the conscience of a nation was the procession of rough peasants and simple Galilean hill people led by Jesus of Nazareth into the city of Jerusalem on Palm Sunday. What a demonstration that was! A multitude of men and women and children—shouting, singing, shattering the silence of the city as they proclaimed allegiance to another King and another kingdom. Caiaphas and Pilate were more subtle than Governor Wallace and Colonel Lingo. They did not meet the multitude with bull whips and clubs and tear gas. Yet then as now many objected to any spiritual force that directly challenges the kingdoms of this world. The Pharisees demanded that Jesus rebuke his disciples and command them to keep silent.

The world still resists the knowledge that there is another King and another Kingdom. The response still comes, "If these were silent, the very stones would cry out." As on that Palm Sunday long ago a time of crisis has come to a nation. Jim Reeb was not silent. He lived and died in obedience to the cross.

Dag Hammarskjöld wrote in his personal journal: "He who has surrendered himself to it knows that the Way ends on the Cross—even when it is leading him through the jubilation of Gennesaret or the triumphal entry into Jerusalem. Do not seek death. Death will find you. But seek the road which makes death a fulfillment."

§123 Reverend Duncan Howlett

Reverend Duncan Howlett's biography appears at the introduction to his March 12, 1961 speech in Lynchburg, Virginia. In the important and perceptive sermon below, less than two weeks after the murder of his friend and former coworker, James Reeb, Reverend Howlett links the suasory power of the movement to its explicit links with the Judeo-Christian religion. More specifically, Howlett fears for the movement in part because of signs of militancy. And if militancy wins the upper hand, the persuasive appeal of the movement will immediately die. In this sense does Howlett limn the contours of why the movement has moved so many. For one, the movement's nonviolent ethos has appealed to the best in Americans: "The civil rights movement does the American people honor it can ill afford to ignore. The movement treats us as if we were a morally mature people. It appeals to the best in us." And second, the appeal of the movement is fundamentally linked with the Judeo-Christian religion and its command to love our God and love each other.

The Moral Stature of the Civil Rights Movement
All Souls Church (Unitarian), Washington, D.C.
March 21, 1965

When we are caught up in the swirl of great events, we have from time to time to stop and take stock of ourselves. We need to know where we are, where we have come from, and where we are going. Such a time for us is now.

More than three years ago, I traced for you the legal development of the civil rights movement culminating in the Supreme Court decision of 1954. The story begins with the Emancipation Proclamation, grows during the Reconstruction period, dies out in the Southern reaction that followed and the Northern neglect that accompanied it, and begins again in 1896 with the famous dissent of John Marshall Harlan in *Plessy v. Ferguson.* "Our Constitution is colorblind," he declared, "and neither knows nor tolerates classes among citizens." Harlan's dissent has proved to be one of the most historic in the long line of dissenting opinions that distinguishes the Supreme Court of the United States.

This morning I want to trace the activist as contrasted with the legal antecedents of the civil rights movement. Opinions would vary as to when this particular phase of the story ought to begin, but most would probably choose the Montgomery, Alabama, bus boycott organized by Martin Luther King in 1955. Seeking for the origin of this effort, many would think of Gandhi, for Dr. King was and is an exponent of the Gandhian doctrine of nonviolent resistance. It was with Gandhi too that the idea of the march began. In 1930, during the struggle for the political independence of India, he resolved to dramatize the movement by defying the government's salt monopoly. Accordingly, he and his followers walked all the way from his ashram near Ahmedabad to the sea at Dandi. There, in deliberate defiance of government regulations, they made salt by evaporating sea water. This march had a great effect upon public opinion, helping to consolidate resistance to British rule. Nevertheless, the form the civil rights movement has taken is, not surprisingly, American and not Indian in character. It remains nonviolent, but its techniques, specifically those of the sit-in and the demonstration march, are derived not from the Indian drive for political independence, but from the drive for decent pay and working conditions for the American workingman. In short, the activist pattern of the contemporary civil rights movement is derived from the American labor movement.

Labor established itself as a force in American life during the long period of peace that followed the Civil War, just as the civil rights movement sought to do in the peaceful period following World War II. Labor made further gains in the 1920s and 30s, after the First World War. Today it is part of the American way and wields enough power to be considered a major factor in our economic life. But the beginnings of the labor movement go back before the Civil War, when small craft unions were organized in an effort to give some protection to the worker against the ravages of laissez faire capitalism. But they were local and of little effect. The conditions faced by the workers were intolerable, but there was little they could do. The flood of immigrants, who had known even worse conditions in Europe, kept the labor supply market full and the worker at the mercy of the employer.

As industry grew in size it became further depersonalized and dehumanized. In the textile mills of New England, men, women, and children— whole families—often worked twelve or more hours a day, except in winter when they worked from dawn till dusk, and earned barely enough to keep alive. Working conditions were appalling. When the Northerners began agitating for freedom for the slaves in the South, the Southerners, with full justification, pointed to the economic slavery of mill workers in the North. They pointed out that Negro slaves on many a Southern plantation were far better off than Northern mill workers. The Northern rationale for this state of affairs was no less elaborate and pious than that of the Southerner for slavery. It was the order of nature, they said. They liked to quote Herbert Spencer, who had written, "The poverty of the incapable, the distresses that come upon the imprudent, the starvation of the idle . . . are the decrees of a large and farseeing benevolence."

Like the civil rights movement, the first lesson that labor learned was that to succeed it must become national in scope. Small local victories might be won, but to be effective they had to be part of a national effort. American industry after the Civil War was already becoming national in scope. That put a new weapon in industry's hands. The employer could then exploit the labor market where the demand for jobs was greatest. He could close down a plant where workers, because they were fewer in number, could demand higher wages. A local union was utterly helpless against such a national concern.

By 1866, the National Labor Union had been established. It was a combination of craft unions and other groups, organized on the principle of federation. But the Panic of 1873 brought its life to an abrupt close. It proved powerless to meet the wage cuts introduced almost everywhere at that time. A second national labor union, the Knights of Labor, followed, but it too soon faltered. Then came the American Federation of Labor, a strong national federation of national craft unions, and the labor movement was launched as a force in American life. Would there were time to trace this little-told but thrilling chapter in American history.

Beginning in the 1870s, the theoreticians and the utopians of the pre-Civil War period in the labor movement gave way to more practical men who sought more immediate goals. Jay Gould had once said, "I can hire one half of the working class to kill the other half." And he was right when he said it. The "Know-Nothing Party" was an instance of the way the workers in the early days turned upon each other to fight for the crumbs the employers offered them. The unions sought to draw them together to fight side by side against a common enemy. Their weapon was the strike. But the problem, particularly in the early days, was to enforce it.

Out of this effort grew the practice of picketing, marches, great rallies, and protest meetings. Out of it came the use of injunctions and a series of court decisions granting to labor the right of peaceful picketing. Out of it also came club-swinging police, the use of state militia and federal troops. The martyred dead who gave their lives in the struggle to free the American workingman from a terrible bondage are too numerous to count. The very names of many of them are unknown or forgotten. But their monument is the elimination of child labor in this country and the establishment of decent working conditions and decent pay wherever the labor movement has gone.

These techniques, developed by the labor movement, have been taken over by the civil rights movement, with one important exception, and it is fundamental. Labor always fought back, with every means at its disposal. The civil rights movement to date is nonviolent in its philosophy and in its actions. I say this only as a matter of fact, not to pass judgment upon the labor movement. For who shall say now that it too should have been nonviolent in its methods? What was labor to do, confronted by the violent means used by the employers to keep labor in subjection? In those days there was usually no recourse through government, as there is today for the civil rights movement. Then, business virtually owned politics, as it does not now.

We learned in India, where the philosophy and technique of nonviolence was first developed, that it works only against a civilized and basically humane opponent to whose sense of decency and compassion it is possible publicly to appeal. A nonviolent resistance movement never appeared in Nazi Germany. It was unthinkable there except to theorists living elsewhere, protected by power they themselves would not use. The fierceness of industrial competition in the nineteenth century left even the most humane employer with little, if any, choice. To survive, each had to squeeze the last hour out of the workman, under the worst conditions at the lowest pay. But once the system was established, it continued out of its own momentum for no other reason than to fatten profits further. Few appeals to human kindness made any impression. The use of force alone was effective.

We pass no judgment upon labor for the methods it used then, but we remember, if we are to be realistic, that the techniques now employed by the civil rights movement were evolved in violence by the labor movement. They are by their nature always potentially violent. Furthermore, as James Reeb pointed out almost prophetically in his last sermon to this congregation, the temptation to violence lurks in every one of us, even the most peaceful. For this reason, it is the more remarkable that the civil rights movement was established as a nonviolent movement and that is has thus far remained so.

There was a genuinely religious quality about the labor movement, but it was seldom if ever church-oriented, and it was seldom that clergymen were identified with it. This fact hardly stands to the credit of the churches, which we know were preaching the brotherhood of man during this period. But the activist arm of the civil rights movement *is* church-oriented. It was born in a theological school and has been led from the beginning by churchmen. Some who have come in more recently are not churchmen. But the movement is still largely controlled by churchmen and dominated by their standards and attitudes.

Martin Luther King, who is still its acknowledged leader, got his basic ideas in theological school, first at the Crozer Theological Seminary and later at the Boston University School of Theology, where he took his Ph.D. Men who influenced him at this time were Reinhold Niebuhr of the Union Theological Seminary, and Dean Walter Muelder and Professor Allen Knight Chalmers of the Boston University School of Theology. He speaks of many others as well. A turning point in his life came on a Sunday afternoon when he heard President Mordecai Johnson of Howard University speak on the life and teachings of Gandhi. All these men showed him that the church has a fundamental role to play in the reformation of society. Martin Luther King, as a churchman himself, appeals to churchmen, works through churchmen, and, except for the students, it is largely churchmen in the white population who have responded to his call. What we see in Alabama today is religion in action. But it is religion. And in no small part it has succeeded because it is religion.

I have said before and I say again that Martin Luther King is the conscience of this country just now. The civil right movement does the American people honor it can ill afford to ignore. The movement treats us as if we were a morally mature people. It appeals to the best in us. The movement is addressed to our minds and hearts. It seeks to call attention to the wrongs that we as a people have done to our Negro citizens, with the implicit assumption that once the people have seen and faced what has been going on, they will back the demands the movement has made. The question we face as a people is whether we are worthy of the compliment we have been paid. Can we be reached at the moral level? Or will we yield only to force and violence? If our affections are not touched by sympathy, then our complacency will be tested by force.

This morning I ask you, as the civil rights movement asks the people of America, to look upon the suffering and deprivation American Negroes endure today for no other reason than because they are Negroes. Open your eyes to the conditions under which many of them are forced to live for no other reason than that their skin is dark. Open your hearts to them. See their need. Then close your eyes if you dare. Close your heart if you can. But if you look, and really see what you are looking at, you will not close them. You will feel the privation you behold. Love for a people who have suffered long and silently will rise about you like the tide until it has covered the dry rocks of your self-sufficiency.

Martin Luther King and the other civil rights leaders have aimed the movement at the heart of the nation, and I believe they have struck it. The movement has not yet reached the hearts of all the people, to be sure, but it has already reached the hearts of many who had not been touched here-tofore, and the number goes on increasing. The President himself, address-ing the Congress and the nation last Monday night, spoke in the terms in which the civil rights movement talks: he asked that the Negro be given a vote in the South, not for reasons of expediency, but because it is right. Dr. King has never departed from this elevated moral principle. He knows that what he seeks for the Negro is right, and he never ceases to say so.

Furthermore, since it is an altogether righteous end he pursues, he in-sists that it must always be pursued by righteous means. The trouble is, not everybody agrees with him. There are those who say that social progress can be made only through social disruption. This does not mean communists or fascists, the two chief advocates of social disruption in our time. Neither does it exclude them. Any militant movement invites their attention. This we have always known. The civil rights movement has had to be on its guard against this danger from the beginning. Nevertheless, loudly as some Southerners and groups like the John Birch Society may shout, there is no danger from communist infiltration, at least at the moment. Of this I can assure you from personal knowledge of the inner workings of the movement.

But there is another danger, and it is very real: that is the natural militancy in all of us and the feeling on the part of some leaders that we ought to capitalize on it. No one has yet openly advocated violence. Only the Black Muslims have done that, and they are not a part of the movement. But many advocate measures that can only be called provocative. If an agreement is made with a safety officer, they are quite prepared to break it, if necessary, in order to register a protest. They do not think it important to relate their manner or place of protest to what they are protesting. They measure what they do by its nuisance value, thinking it important because it gets attention. If anyone suggests that the measures they propose will not further, but will rather defeat their own ends, they are not impressed. They want to do something, and often it seems to matter much more that they are doing it than that it will achieve a particular purpose.

Of course, nothing like perfection can be achieved in a movement so resurgent and so loose-knit. The vitality and commitment of the participants is one of its most important ingredients. But its leaders can and must keep to their moral purpose, both in the ends they pursue and the means they adopt. I know, again from firsthand experience, that the means adopted by some of the lower echelon leaders have not always conformed to the standards of the movement as a whole. Well-publicized instances are the White House sit-in and the Pennsylvania Avenue lie-down of last week. Such departures are to be expected. But the top leadership must continue to state and enforce as far as possible the unquestioned moral ends and means of the movement. If they do not, overnight we shall have quite a different phenomenon on our hands.

Whenever the police indulge in violence, the hand of the militant group in the civil rights movement is strengthened. Whenever the police deal with the situation with restraint and understanding, the hand of leaders like Martin Luther King is strengthened. But the contest goes on in spite of both. It is for this reason that rapid progress toward reform represented by the President's bill for voting rights is so essential. Here the analogy with labor is exact. On the whole, labor did not strike where its legitimate demands were met by the employers. By the same token, the demonstrations can easily be kept constructive while progress toward civil rights continues. If this progress stops, then the militants in the movement will take over. Should this happen, the great rising tide of public opinion in favor of granting full rights to the Negro will turn. What is now support will become opposition. What is now progress will turn into retrogression.

Do not think I am calling for moderation. Do not think I am saying we ought to slow down. Do not think I want to let up on the pressure. The pressure should be increased, the process speeded up, and the demands expanded until every member of American society is a first-class citizen. We must not slacken the pace until every American citizen is given an equal opportunity to make of himself what he can.

I am not calling for moderation this morning but I am calling with all the clarity and power at my command for the continued commitment of the civil rights movement to its own high principles. Martin Luther King is, and must remain, its acknowledged leader. He has never departed from the principles he laid down at the outset, no matter how great the pressures were upon him. The same may be said for the Reverend Walter Fauntroy, his representative here in Washington. I have developed great admiration for this young man as I have seen him and worked with him under the greatest pressures from people of the widest variety of opinion. He is a man of both courage and sound judgment, who never takes his eyes off the goal, and, in pursuing it, never departs from the moral standards of the movement.

For this reason I have responded to Dr. King's call for a massive demonstration of moral force in Alabama next week. I shall be away for as short a time as practicable, for I have much work to do here. But I am going because I believe the cause is just and this is a valid way to advance it.

We are doing two things in the civil rights movement, both at the same time. First, we are seeking full rights for all our citizens. But secondly, we are also saying something about how you organize and govern human society. We are saying something about how human society moves forward. No social structure can be perfect. When the fight for civil rights has at last been won, there will remain as much still to do. Injustice, inequality, misery, human suffering will remain. We shall only have eliminated its racial aspect. But in gaining this particular victory, if we hold to our ideals throughout, we shall have shown to ourselves and the world that human society can go forward without going through the violent revolutions we have always associated with major social change. This achievement, should it occur, will be a major revolution in and of itself.

When the struggle is over and the victory has been won, our movement will have paid its price. We here at All Souls have already paid a higher price than we were willing to pay, as I said a week ago. But the personal loss we have suffered must not be multiplied by hundreds or by thousands, as it surely will be if we depart from our ideals and resort to the age-old methods of violence. We who would keep James Reeb's memory green can do that much for him, for all he stood for and all that we ourselves believe. We can lend our strength to holding the civil rights movement to its non-violent ideal and to its basic appeal to the conscience of America. We can oppose every advocate of nuisance demonstrations, every participant in demonstration for demonstration's sake, every suggestion that we not keep the agreements we make, and every act of violence.

The civil rights movement is a moral movement. That is why I believe in it and why I have supported it with all the strength at my command. It is also religious. It grows straight out of the Judeo-Christian tradition, as have we all. It is rooted in a belief in the dignity of man, in the doctrine of human brotherhood, and in the faith that the life of every man is meaningful in a cosmic sense. For must of us, to say this is to root the whole movement in the two basic commandments Jesus of Nazareth laid down: "Thou shalt love the Lord thy God with all they heart, with all thy soul, with all thy mind and with all thy strength. And the second is like unto it. Thou shalt love thy neighbor as thyself." For some, the second commandment alone is enough. For me, both are essential, and both are the same.

Let us conclude with a prayer of President Johnson's, carried by the newspapers of the nation this morning:

> "It is my prayer—a prayer in which I hope all Americans will join me earnestly today—that the march in Alabama will proceed in a manner honoring our heritage and honoring all for which America stands.
>
> May this, the conduct of all Americans, demonstrate beyond dispute that the true strength of America lies not in arms, and not in force, and not in the might of the military nor in the police nor in the multitudes of marshals and state troopers, but in respect and obedience of law itself."

§124 Morris B. Abram

Morris Berthold Abram was born on June 19, 1918 in Fitzgerald, Georgia. A highly educated man, Abram, attended school at the University of Georgia, the University of Chicago Law School, and Oxford University, where he was a Rhodes Scholar. His educational background positioned him for career that included terms as chairman of the United Negro College Fund, chairman of Cardozo Law School, president of Brandeis University, president of the American Jewish Committee, and chairman of the Conference of Presidents of Major American Jewish Organizations. President Ronald Reagan also appointed Abram to the U.S. Civil Rights Commission. Perhaps Abram's most profound influence on American society came as founding chairman of the United Nations Watch Group, a facet of the United Nations that focused on maintaining human rights throughout the world.

After completing U.N. work under four presidents, the first President Bush named him America's permanent ambassador to the United Nations in Geneva. Abram also authored two books, *How to Stop Violence in Your Community*, and *The Day is Short, an Autobiography*. Abram was also very active in Georgia civil rights: in 1960 he secured Martin Luther King, Jr.'s highly politicized release from jail. Later in the decade, he successfully challenged Georgia's sedition law, which was used to arrest civil rights demonstrators and hold them without bail. Morris Abram died from leukemia in 2000. His papers are housed at the Robert W. Woodruff Library at Emory University in Atlanta, Georgia.

Morris Abram begins his address to the Fifth General Synod of the United Church of Christ by acknowledging the atypical situation of a Jewish man addressing members of a Christian church. He quickly reveals his strong relationship with religion by linking prejudice and discrimination to the lack of communication between people of differing religious faiths. His constructive stance on interreligious equality provides the faith-based white community with the moral and religious responsibility for ending discrimination against people of color. For Morris Abram, the different beliefs and teachings between Christian denominations and Judaism are obvious, but he is quick to draw upon certain comparisons in the two religions that emphasize tolerance. He concludes by orchestrating several ideas that churches and synagogues can employ to improve communication, which for Abram, is a key prerequisite to ending prejudice.

Address to the Fifth General Synod of the United Church of Christ

Chicago, Illinois
July 5, 1965

This is a rare and an appreciated occasion. It is not customary even in this so-called ecumenical age for a Jew to address the general assembly of a great Christian church. In fact, this may even be a first occasion for this body.

Of course, we speak to one another on increasingly frequent inter-religious programs, and we attend one another's houses of worship on special days for planned events. We engage in dialogues and trialogues—and I have attended many.

But this afternoon, I feel particularly, the responsibility of this opportunity.

As you may have guessed, I am Southern born, and until three years ago, had never lived permanently outside Georgia.

Since I was 16, I was in substantial disagreement with the racial mores of the society in which I lived. I mention 16 as the watershed year for my racial attitudes. I can do this with some precision because I recall the evening of the event. I was home from college, on a summer evening, standing in front of my father's small store on East Pine Street, Fitzgerald, Georgia. The sidewalks were teeming with farmers mostly sharecroppers, black and white—shopping, lounging and visiting after a week of toil in the cotton, corn and peanut fields. I found myself silently contesting the idea, then very new, that segregation of the races was not right. I thought: "How many of these illiterate, unwashed and unkempt Negroes would you, Morris Abram, want in your home for a meal and a visit?"

My unspoken answer was unequivocal: "None." Somehow, for some reason, out of somewhere, however, another question percolated into my consciousness: "How many of these illiterate, unwashed, unkempt *Whites* would you, Morris Abram, want in your home for a meal and a visit?" My answer still was "None." Then, for the first time in my life, I realized that I had never judged white Baptists, Methodists and Presbyterians as a group, but selectively as individuals; that neither I nor any white man adopted the principle that all whites of a particular group had to be acceptable before any *one* could be accepted. Yet in the case of one identifiable minority, at least, we had set up unattainable standards by which a *whole group* must be 100% acceptable before normal relations were possible with *any* of them. I resolved never to do this again. For now I saw the nature of prejudice—it's really a mental trick by which the majority accepts the fact that it's unworthy members are exceptions, but judges the minority all too frequently by its least attractive examples. Thus, too many have said: We believe in Negro rights—when *they* are ready for them.

Rights, however, are in your ethic and mine, derived by birth as gifts of God, not granted by man or state, but rightfully protected by both.

I have held these views for a very long time and had practiced them in the South. However, I was and am indebted to your church for making me aware of how out of touch I frequently have been with the racial inequalities and discrimination in American life. I was so struck by your protest to the renewal of the Jackson, Mississippi television station license that I reacted by a letter to *The New York Times* in April 1964. I said then—and I say now—that a re-education of white America is desperately needed. For although I lived as an adult in the South for 25 years and knew first hand that the radio and TV broadcast bands which belong to all the people were being essentially used by and for the benefit of the white community, and frequently against the Negro community, I had never raised my voice against this important discrimination. It was not a case of my agreeing with the policy or a fear of speaking out. I now realize I was simply anaesthetized by local custom and tradition to the point that I did not focus on and recognize this evil. Until the majority of Americans become more sensitive to such wrongs to other Americans, we shall not rid ourselves of our most acute national problem. For we will not even be aware of many of the forms in which it exists.

In a fundamental sense, the problems of prejudice, misunderstanding, insensitivity to the needs and wants of others, as well as outright discrimination are the result of a failure of communication between the various racial, ethnic and religious groups of this country. I believe this, because I have faith in the innate goodness of our people and their instinctive preference for justice and fair play. It is interesting to note that the most persistent and deepest discrimination is against that segment, the Negro, with which the majority has had the least communication. The Negro has never really been a part of the American public schools and the satellite social system which revolves around the neighborhood school. Frankly, the Negro and the white don't know what they would find in each other in a normal setting of equality, for most of us have seldom met on such a plane. The great contribution of the desegregation process is the chance that we may soon know Negroes and Negroes shall know us in the ordinary course of growing up, being educated, working together and playing in the same places.

However, such structural changes in society will not eliminate prejudice. As a Jew I know this, and so do white Catholics and white Protestants too. We also know that frequently what is described as deep piety and religiosity do not produce the understanding, charity and love of one's fellow man which is the proclaimed goal of all religions. Recent studies sponsored by the American Jewish Committee at Protestant, Catholic and Jewish university centers have shown that the very text books used by each faith fail to serve the ideals of these religions, either because of serious omissions or because of invidious references or outright prejudiced statements about other religions. It is as unfortunate as it is amazing that the streams of good will have been polluted at one of their sources—the church school. It is good and hopeful that this problem is being attacked by all faiths today. Such efforts at reform must not falter or fail.

Some have said, including some rabbis, that what one faith teaches is not a concern of another. Others say that the inter-religious dialogue is a matter only for theologians, ministers, priests and rabbis, and that ecumenicism is the prerogative of the religious elite.

I say that a man's conscientious opinion, religion and belief—theistic, non-theistic or atheistic—is a matter for himself and his God or whatever authority he recognizes. But the evil one does to another and teaches about another in the name of religion or outside—that is the proper concern of the victim, lay and clerical, and of all mankind. Thus the charge of deicide against Jews is not the exclusive concern of those who in ignorance parrot this canard. It is the rightful concern of Jews—rabbis and laymen—as well as of such bodies as the United Church of Christ, as you in the World Council of Churches so clearly recognized as long ago as 1961.

It is true that prejudice against the Negro is in a sense the white man's problem, but no thinking, feeling person believes the Negro should not struggle to change the white man's attitudes. Similarly, it is true that the deicide tradition is a matter which must be dealt with by Christianity. Thus, when the Catholic Vatican council confronts this matter, as well as the matter of religious liberty, Jews as well as Protestants—men of decency everywhere—are legitimately concerned and particular efforts may be required to see to it that the overwhelming sentiment of the Catholic fathers in Rome shall not be stifled by a tiny minority which prefers to remember only the past and which strives to strangle the future at its birth.

So I say I am concerned and involved in many of the manifestations of *your* work at this Synod, you and I are properly interested in what goes on at Rome this fall, and I hope you are interested in the manifestations of my faith.

I think we must learn to communicate at all levels—not just in churches and synagogues—not just in structured programs—but on every conceivable occasion. Some may fear this. Some may prefer the five o'clock curtain that falls on America and separates many people particularly Christians and Jews, after the working hours. Some may be willing to stretch their contacts to include formal occasions such as those arranged during Brotherhood Week. Some Catholics, Protestants and Jews really are worried about such contacts. Some even fear loss of their group strength if the barriers were to come down and an open society prevail—with competition in religious as well as political ideas.

For my part, I choose freedom. I believe in pluralism, theologically as well as sociologically. My faith has survived 5,000 years under every conceivable hardship, society and condition. It can stand on its own—and will. The open society of vigorous, vital dialogue will require—and I predict it will stimulate—the better education of young Jews, Catholics and Protestants. I predict further that the clash of ideas will refresh every congregation.

Once Moses established Judaism twelve convinced and committed men built Christendom. Twelve hundred thousand selected at random in synagogue and church at weekly services could not have done the same. It is the *quality* of those who bear the life force of the faith that counts—not the quantity.

I hope that we shall learn to talk and to know one another at all the customary places—and at new ones too, before five o'clock and after, realizing that in these contacts each faith not only will influence the other, but each will survive and perhaps even be strengthened in its own uniqueness.

But it is not sufficient that we meet more and we talk more. We must learn to talk to each other in more significant ways—and at deeper levels. I am weary with dialogues which communicate only platitudes, with Jewish meetings which exhibit a Christian of goodwill, and with Christian meetings at which a special Jew is presented—and each tells how much unites us and how little divides us; how we share a common testament and are part of the Judeo-Christian tradition. Of course this is all true, and no one in his right mind denies it and that's just the point—it is all so true.

But there is so much else that's true—interesting, topical, controversial and therefore seldom mentioned.

Catholicism, Protestantism, and Judaism differ substantially in many respects. Each faith adheres to certain beliefs either rejected or not adopted by the other. No one faith can prove the truth of its core by scientific demonstration and, except to its adherents, that it is better than another. But the differences are illuminating not only in themselves but, properly understood, they add a dimension to the comprehension of each man's own faith.

Your faith lays great store by the Golden Rule—"Do unto others. . . ." The sages of Judaism stated the concept differently—"Do not unto thy neighbor that which is hateful unto thee." Now the two precepts on first impression sound quite similar but they are significantly different. If one compares and analyzes each statement, one can come to grips with a central approach in the two systems each of which encourages man to do justice. The Christian statement of [the] Golden Rule to me is an idealistic goal to which exception cannot be taken. But to me, the Jewish version appears a more practical and attainable standard. Few, if any, can treat all exactly as one's self—but all can strive to avoid doing deliberate hurt to another and many may succeed.

What a useful discussion we might have over these ideas if we let down the barriers and dealt with one another in honesty and with mutual respect! Discussions which evade the heart of what each regards as important are evasions rather than courtesies. Such evasions indicate not respect but contempt for the other man's views. The evasion may be a way of saying: "your views are not worthy of honest discussion." Or it may reflect a fear that one's own beliefs cannot stand examination. I plead for a dialogue between the religions in which each in candor evaluates its own successes and failures, admits its past errors and resolves to work cooperatively for a better society.

Our major opportunities and shortcomings are all so similar that joint discussion, and perhaps action might prove dramatically productive. For example, many of our churches and synagogues have been relocating away from the heart of the central city taking along with them institutions and resources needed most desperately at the teeming and blighted city core. Can we not work cooperatively to ensure that when the well-to-do leave an area, God's institutions are not also withdrawn?

If we will learn to discuss candidly with one another the substance of our beliefs and work cooperatively towards a better world, we possess today remarkable instruments to carry out these purposes. I am as distressed as you must be by the tendencies of American commercial radio and television, i.e., by the sketchy news, by the approach to the public as a consumer, by the elevation to the level of a hero, of the gangster who operates outside the law, and by the infantile, trite, if not empty, programs which have become the steady diet of adult and children alike for hours in each day.

But the fault is not all with the broadcasting industry. Time *is* made available on most bands to churches and religious organizations. More frequently than not, though, a broadcast church service amounts to no more than the extension of the dialogue between the minister and his congregation into the ether waves. Most of the institutions which use this facility have failed to comprehend that this medium provides a vast audience— not only of people committed to their faith or belief, but also many of different persuasions. From this point of view, the whole use of broadcasting needs radical change and recasting on the part of our religious institutions, geared to the reality of *who* is being talked to and what message is relevant to this unseen audience.

Out beyond the walls of the church or synagogue from which the broadcast originates, lie rich homes, poor homes, middle-class homes, thinking people, feeling people, religious people, irreligious people. Ask yourselves what the founders of any religion would have done with such an opportunity. Would they have downgraded it? Or would they have used it to the fullest extent? One thing is central: no matter how enticing the form of any program, it will never be more than a parochial appeal unless its substance fits within the framework of honest dialogue, in which the needs and sensitivities and aspirations of *all* men are taken into account, rather than merely those church pews in front of the speaker.

As the father of five, I know that today's young are remarkably realistic and deeply committed to the building of a better society than that in which we live. They may be children, but they will not fool themselves and they will not permit themselves to be fooled. The happiest and most productive youths I know today are those who are engaged in the civil rights struggle, frequently under religious auspices. Some have even been martyrs.

The youths I know believe this action is relevant and meaningful, and those who are religious accept this activity as the ultimate and supreme manifestation of their religion in today's world. They have undertaken to deal with their fellow men no longer as objects, but as subjects, as human

beings. They have sought to establish and are establishing an I-Thou relationship, not only with their fellow man, but with their God. They are
communicating, not only by means of words, with human beings whom
they hold in respect, but also by means of deeds, with the dignity which
the human personality deserves. They understand what many of an older
generation have forgotten, that a dialogue requires not only that we speak,
but that we *listen* as well.

Strangely enough, this idea is encompassed in an ancient chant of my
people, which is heard at every service, and has been heard at every service
for 5000 years wherever Jews have worshipped: "Hear, O Israel, the Lord
our God, the Lord is one," and the word, "hear," the Rabbi says, means
"listen!"

§125 Jonathan Daniels

Jonathan Daniels was born on March 20, 1939 in Keene, New Hampshire. His
father was a physician and his mother was a schoolteacher. After graduating from
high school, Daniels attended Virginia Military Institute and graduated as valedictorian. Daniels enrolled at Harvard University in the fall of 1961 with the intention
of studying English Literature. In 1963, after a religious awakening, he decided to
attend the Episcopal Theological Seminary in Cambridge, Massachusetts.

In March of 1965, Daniels responded to Martin Luther King Jr.'s plea to join
the voter registration drive in Selma, Alabama. After participating in the Selma
to Montgomery march, Daniels decided to stay on in the area and work with the
Student Nonviolent Coordinating Committee (SNCC) primarily in voter registration work in Lowndes County, known among activists as Bloody Lowndes. While
in Alabama, Daniels assisted in integrating the local Episcopal church. He also
helped assemble a list of federal, state, and local agencies that could aid those in
need and he worked with poor local residents to apply for aid as well. He served as
a tutor to children and worked to register voters.

On August 13, 1965, Daniels went with an integrated group to picket white-
only stores in Fort Deposit, Alabama. The following day, all the protestors were
arrested and jailed in Hayneville, Alabama. On August 20, after a surprise early
release from jail, Daniels and Reverend Richard Morrisroe along with two African
American women, Ruby Sales and Joyce Bailey, walked to the Cash Store to buy
soft drinks. When the group was asked to leave, Daniels protested. Tom Coleman,
a white man from a prominent local family and friend of store owner Virginia
Varner, shot Daniels in the chest at point-blank range with a 12-gauge shotgun .
Despite several witnesses, an all-white jury later found Coleman not guilty for the
killing. They rendered their verdict in 91 minutes. In 1991 Daniels was designated
as a martyr of the Episcopal church.

The paper, read by Reverend William J. Wolf at Daniels's funeral, is an intensely
personal and philosophical reflection of Daniels's civil rights work in Alabama.
In the paper, Daniels explains what led him to Selma. He discusses his initial

excitement at hearing Dr. King's request for volunteers and later his disinclination to travel south. Daniels states that it was only after an Evening Prayer ceremony that he dismissed his prior hesitation. He also highlights his experiences at a week-long, rain-soaked vigil where he felt, at one moment, his defensive and self-righteous nature creep out. He explains how he made a conscious effort to retract back to modest behavior, but it was a struggle in the face of his opposition.

Upon leaving Selma and driving north, Daniels recalls his realization that instead of defending himself against those individuals who considered him an "Alabama white," he was required to absorb the guilt as part of the covenant, "part of the price a Yankee Christian had better be prepared to pay if he goes to the black belt." But even more, his experiences across the color line forced a radical synechdoche: "We were 'standing in' for the rector at Selma and for the whole parish family at St. Paul's, for the white men of the black belt. Their guilt was ours, and ours, theirs." He accepts the status as a "white nigger" and understands more fully the "the harsh tenderness of the cross," the fact that Christ died to atone for the sins of all—white and black. By being baptized as both a "white nigger" and an "Alabama white," Daniels had a far greater appreciation for the inheritance of sin and guilt endemic to the human condition—and what it means to try to redeem that inheritance.

———

Paper Written by Jonathan Daniels and Read Posthumously

Funeral Service at St. James' Episcopal Church, Keene, New Hampshire
August 24, 1965

Reverend William J. Wolf reading:

Many times since my reconversion three years ago I have been asked (with varying degrees of outrage and pain), "Why?" I have found that the best way to answer has been to tell a story, to sing a "song of myself," which, like that of the singer, finally modulated to the Song of Songs: the Eternal Word of God. Intellectual history had to wait for flesh to tell its tale. That in itself was a great lesson for me.

Before I left for Selma the second time, a kind friend asked me someday to "theologize my experience in Selma." At the time the phrase meant something to me: *self-righteousness*, though I had yet to learn that. I was, of course, delighted. Since then a kind of song has sung itself in Selma (and in Cambridge), as a consequence of which the phrase now seems unmanageably abstract. I shall therefore sing the song instead, a few bars of it—and hope the Truth will out.

At two o'clock in the afternoon of March eighth, I dashed into the T.V. room of the Episcopal Theological School for an Executive Committee meeting. As I grabbed a cup of coffee and found a seat, I had just time to overhear one of the brethren say that his wife planned to fly down before the chairman called the meeting to order. At some point on the agenda past yawning, the brother whose wife was flying was encouraged to make his pitch. There was trouble in Selma, as we all knew from Huntley-Brinkley, and Dr. King has asked for northern volunteers. *That* was where his wife was flying, and he was trying to raise money for her travel expenses. A strategy was speedily devised for that purpose, and as we went our several ways there was excited talk about the possibility of sending other members of the community. . . .

I raced back to Lawrence Hall, flew up the three flights, and hurled myself into the room of a friend. The friend had been asleep, but graciously composed himself for what was visibly my latest insanity. I delicately reminded him that he had invited me to go south with him over the spring holidays (to talk with Bishop Allin of Mississippi and others) and suggested that we *go now*. My friend was not free to go, and I went off to study, a little disconsolate. From time to time I mused: could I spare the time? Did I want to spare the time? Did He want. . . . Reluctantly I admitted to myself that the idea was impractical, and, with a faintly tarnished feeling, I tucked in an envelope my contribution to the proposed "Selma fund."

"My soul doth magnify the Lord, and my spirit hath rejoiced in God my Saviour . . . ." I had come to Evening Prayer as usual that evening, and as usual I was singing the *Magnificat* with the special love and reverence I have always felt for Mary's glad song. "He hath showed strength with his arm. . . ." As the lovely hymn of the God-bearer continued, I found myself peculiarly alert, suddenly straining toward the decisive, luminous, Spirit-filled "moment" that would, in retrospect, remind me of others—particularly of one at Easter three years ago. Then it came. "He hath put down the mighty from their seat, and hath exalted the humble and meek. He hath filled the hungry with good things. . . ." I knew then that I must go to Selma. The Virgin's song was to grow more and more dear in the weeks ahead. . . .

After a week-long, rain-soaked vigil at the "Berlin Wall," we still stood face to face with the Selma police, who were flanked by the sheriff's posse and backed by five or six ranks of state police. The President had not yet addressed the nation, and we were not a foot nearer the Dallas County Courthouse. I stood, for a change, in the front rank, ankle-deep in an enormous puddle flooding one side of the street. To my immediate right were high school students, for the most part, and further to the right were a swarm of clergymen. My end of the line surged forward at one point, led by a militant Episcopal priest whose temper (as usual) was at combustion-point. Thus I found myself only inches from a young policeman. The air crackled with tension and frustration and open hostility. Emma Jean, a sophomore in the Negro high school, who had been standing next to me before the line moved forward, called my name from behind. I reached back for her hand to bring her up to the front rank, but she did not see.

Again she called, a note of growing concern in her voice, and asked me to come back before I got hurt. My determination had become infectiously savage, and I insisted that she come forward—I would not retreat! Again I reached for her hand, this time successfully, and pulled her forward. The young policeman spoke: "You're dragging her through the puddle. You ought to be ashamed for treating a girl like that." Flushing—I had forgotten the puddle—I snarled something at him about whose-fault-it-really-was, that managed to be both defensive and self-righteous. We matched baleful glances and then both looked away. And then came a moment of shattering internal quiet, in which I felt shame, indeed, and a kind of reluctant love for the young policeman. I apologized to Emma Jean. And then it occurred to me to apologize to *him* and to thank him. Though he looked away in con- tempt—I was not altogether sure I blamed him—I had received a blessing I would not forget. Before long the kids were singing "I love ——," filling in with the badge numbers of the policemen standing in front of us. The young policeman had apparently forgotten his badge, so one of my friends asked another for his name. His name was Charlie, which for some reason (Steinbeck, perhaps!) endeared him to me all the more. When we sang for him, he blushed and then smiled in a truly sacramental mixture of embar- rassment and pleasure and shyness. Soon the policeman looked relaxed, we all lit cigarettes (in a couple of instances, from a common match), and small groups of kids and policemen clustered to joke or talk cautiously about the situation. It was thus a shock later to look across the rank at the clergymen and their opposites, who glared across a still unbroken "Wall" in what ap- peared to be silent hatred. Had I been freely arranging the order for Evening Prayer that night, I think I might have followed the General Confession directly with the General Thanksgiving—or perhaps the *Te Deum*.

I was prepared for a tiresome crop of sermons as I entered St. Paul's Episcopal Church in Selma on Good Friday for the interdenominational "Seven Last Words." Most were as bad, in fact, as I had expected. One, on the other hand, was unforgettable. Dr. Newton, the pastor of the largest Presbyterian Church in Selma, himself an integrationist, preached about the word, "I thirst." The point of his meditation was that Jesus had had the humility and the freedom to ask for water *from His enemies.*

We were made to sit in our pew at the rear of St. Paul's Episcopal Church in Selma on Easter Sunday (yards from the nearest communicants) until everybody else had communicated and returned to their seats. When finally we were allowed to approach the altar, the looks and gestures of hostility we encountered on the way were palpable. Though I had tried to make careful and foresighted preparation, I found myself falling prey to the reigning dynamics. Then it occurred to me that if I could not go to the altar in genuine charity, in chaste compassion, then I would go only to my peril. For by my very presence I had assumed responsibility for "the weaker brethren." I had heard—and probably made—scornful remarks about the "validity" of *any* celebration at St. Paul's. Now "validity" was an existential and decisive question: but the validity in question was entirely my own. I could not make my communion without sorrow under the circumstances. But I had begun to taste joy and perhaps the triumph of the Cross.

The night before Judy Upham, my fellow student from the Episcopal Theological School, and I left for the North we were the dinner guests of the priests and brothers at the Edmundite (Negro) mission. After dinner we withdrew with Father Ouellet, the pastor, to his living room. Our friend began to talk deeply and openly of his experience and of his life in Selma in particular. We were stunned at the honesty, the integrity, and the beauty of this saintly man. Though he graciously provided opportunities for us to talk, to share with him our concerns and beliefs and observations, it became increasingly clear to us that we could have little to say to the pain and the quiet glory of that life except that we revered and loved him. He said that after twelve years in Selma, he had finally stopped hating. Perhaps it was merely because he was nearing forty . . . but his bitterness had gone. Though (as a "white nigger") he had been repeatedly rebuffed by the white Protestant clergymen in town (and, presumably by the pastor of the white Catholic Church, as well, though Father Ouellet himself is white), he thought it was time to try again to establish some sort of relationship with them all.

Father Ouellet said at some point early in the evening that he had discovered what the ecumenical movement was all about when he had begun to notice our faces in the congregation at Mass each Sunday (we had gotten into the habit of picking up the kids in the Negro family with whom we stayed after early Communion at St. Paul's Episcopal Church and taking them out to St. Elizabeth's Roman Catholic Church). As we knelt for his blessing before we left and he placed his hands on our heads, we knew that, from almost any perspective, a miracle had occurred.

As we packed the car our last day in Selma to return to seminary, my eye caught a number of times on the Alabama license tag. Each time, it occurred to me that—at some point on our route—it might be expedient to dig out Judy's Massachusetts plates. Yet I could not bring myself to remove the blue-and-orange tag which, in an ambivalent fashion, I had come to love. It may have been only that my first memories are of the towns in Kentucky and Arkansas where my family lived during World War II, and the fact that I had been graduated from a college in Virginia. At any rate, I could not remove the tag.

When we left Washington on the Baltimore Belt, an attractive Negro couple in a glistening new black Chevy pulled out behind us and shot by.

As they passed, they both turned and stared. I nodded to them and tried to return their gaze. But instead I found myself flushing under their cool stare, and I quickly looked away. In their eyes, my identity was painfully clear. I wanted to shout to them, "No, No! I'm *not* an Alabama white. I'm on *your* side." We rode for a few miles in deeply troubled silence. There were no words that could dispel the pain and the shame and the vicarious guilt we both felt. Then, gently, illumination came. Of course, I could not shout, "No, no . . ." That would be cheap, cutting a knot that, in the ambiguous conditions of fallen creation, is far too sacred for minor surgery. To be a Christian, to be baptized into the Death-and-Life of the Cross, is not that simple. Whether we had known it or not, whether we liked it or not, whether it made any difference or not, we were *in His Name* and *for His sake* on the Baltimore Beltway, in Cambridge, Massachusetts, in Keene, New Hampshire with "the Heart of Dixie" branded on our flesh and buried in our hearts. We were "standing in" for the rector at Selma and for the whole parish family at St. Paul's, for the white men of the black belt. Their guilt was ours, and ours, theirs. That was part of the covenant we had silently made with them when we had discovered that our "presence" in Selma meant listening and absorbing before it meant talking. We now knew that "chaste compassion" meant more than absorbing the suspicion and the fear and the hostility of our white brethren in Selma, though all that was part of the Covenant, part of the price a Yankee Christian had better be prepared to pay if he goes to the black belt. It meant absorbing their guilt as well and suffering the cost which they might not yet even know was there to be paid. If, in Selma, our baptism made us "white niggers" we now knew that it also made us "Alabama whites." I suspect that knowledge lies very close to the heart of the harsh tenderness of the Cross, the costly, puzzling, eucharistic glory of the Tree of Life. It is certainly part of what Christians mean by "Atonement."

The discovery of all this has lead to some unexpectedly beautiful moments. At the conclusion of my talk to the Churchwomen of my home parish in New Hampshire some weeks ago, a militant liberal expressed the wish that I would stop calling the parishioners of St. Paul's, Selma, "Christians"—"churchmen" would make her happier. Instinctively, I felt defensive for the people of my adopted "parish family," recalling the painful ambivalence and anguished perplexity I knew some of them were beginning (belatedly, it is true—for all of us) to feel. Then I recalled some of the self-righteous insanities I permitted myself to indulge in, early in my life in Selma. Before I delivered a gentle blast I could not help thanking Him for the gift of delicious irony. "He chasteneth whom He loveth."

It was my great privilege during graduation this spring to help host the family of a very dear friend from the deep South. For some reason, whether blessed or demonic I am still not entirely sure, they were bombarded by the language of civil rights, which seemed to be a theme in the week's festivities. During the sermon the afternoon before graduation—a particularly massive assault, it seemed—I became so uncomfortable for them that I stole to their pew to sit with them. I shall never forget the community which existed between us in that moment. The unspoken "wall" which had subtly divided us until then suddenly afforded a narrow path, and a thread of genuine affection ran through the fabric of our mutual disagreement and suspicion. Atonement is objective, indeed.

All of this is the raw material for living theology. And yet in as deep a sense, from my point of view, it is the *product* of living theology. The doctrines of the creeds, the enacted faith of the sacraments, were the essential precondition of the experience itself. The faith with which I went to Selma has not *changed*: it has grown. Darkening coals have kindled. Faith has taken wing and flown with a song in its wings. "My soul doth magnify the Lord, and my spirit hath rejoiced in God my Saviour. . . ."

I lost fear in the black belt when I began to know in my bones and sinews that I had truly been baptized into the Lord's Death and Resurrection, that in the only sense that really matters I am already dead, and my life is hid with Christ in God. I began to lose self-righteousness when I discovered the extent to which my behavior was motivated by worldly desires and by the self-seeking messianism of Yankee deliverance! The point is simply, of course, that one's motives are usually mixed—and one had better know it. It occurred to me that though I was reasonably certain that I was in Selma because the Holy Spirit had sent me there, there nevertheless remained a fundamental distinction between my will and His. ". . . And *Holy* is His Name." I was reminded by the Eucharist, by the daily offices, by the words of confession, by the healing judgment of the Spirit, that I am called *first* to holiness. Every impulse, every motive, every will under heaven must attend first to that if it is to be healthy and free within the ambiguities and tilted structures of a truly fallen Creation. "*Worldly* holiness," a dear friend of mine would rightly insist: but the *holiness*, the "chaste compassion" of the One in Whom all life, all love, all truth are grounded. Of the ubiquitous Kingship of the eternal Word, through Whom all things were made, I found very real if ambiguous confirmation in that beloved community who ate and slept and cursed and prayed in the rain-soaked streets of the Negro "compound" that first week in Selma.

Another kind of organicity has dawned upon me more gradually. As Judy and I said the daily offices day by day, we became more and more aware of the living reality of the invisible "communion of saints"—of the beloved community in Cambridge who were saying the offices, too, and sending us carbon copies of their notes (and a thousand other things as well!), of the one gathered around a near-distant throne in Heaven—who blend with theirs our faltering songs of prayer and praise. With them, with black men and white men, with all of life, in Him Whose Name is above all the names the races and nations shout, whose Name is Itself the Song Which fulfills and "ends" all songs, we are indelibly, unspeakably *one*.

§126 Daniel Berrigan

Daniel Berrigan was born on May 9, 1921 in the northern Minnesota town of Virginia and grew up in Syracuse, New York. Through his father's union work and exposure to Dorothy Day, Berrigan's interest in matters of social justice blossomed. In 1939 Berrigan enrolled in a Jesuit seminary in Poughkeepsie, New York; he was ordained as a priest in 1952. For six years beginning in 1957, Berrigan was associate professor of dogmatic theology at Le Moyne College in Syracuse. His "call" to militant activism came in 1965 when Dr. King urged clergy to come and march in Selma. Berrigan answered the call. Three years later Berrigan became famous as one of the Catonsville Nine, a group that broke into a Catonsville, Maryland draft headquarters, stole hundreds of draft files and then burned them in a parking lot with homemade napalm. His actions earned him 18 months in a federal prison. In 1980 Berrigan along with his brother Phillip, cofounded Plowshares, a group committed to radical action in defense of peace. A prolific writer, Berrigan has written more than 50 books, including many volumes of award-winning poetry.

In this eulogy for Jonathan Daniels, slain just days before in Hayneville in Lowndes County Alabama, Berrigan ruminates on the meaning of Daniels's death in the context of the blood of man and the blood of Christ. For the Christian, death promises immortality. But borrowing from Paul's letter to the Corinthians, Berrigan also uses the occasion of Daniels' passing to reflect on brotherhood and reconciliation, and their resolution in Christ's sacrificial blood. "But the blood of Christ summons us to all men. When I have drunk his blood, I may not ever again question the blood which runs in the veins of other men; of men of color, of men who worship in another Church, of men whose blood runs violated in the streets. . . . A universal bloodstream joins man to man, religion to religion, race to race, sex to sex." Ultimately, the truth of Jonathan Daniels's death and the truth of God's word calls us to a "life in public," a life not of comfort and easy repose, but of hard discipline, perhaps even martyrdom.

Dear Friends in Christ

Jonathan Daniels's Memorial Service, St. Andrew's Church, Yonkers, New York
August 1965

When a good man dies, there is no mistaking the loss. We know it in our bones and in our flesh. We know it as if we had awakened one morning and, turning to rise, come upon a bandaged stump in place of a whole limb. We know our loss, as the price of being awake at all. We know it, when we have loved another, his voice and face and living thought; when death has left us only a photo upon a wall, and silence, and a life of secret grieving.

Indeed death does not always have the same sting. It comes easily to the old; it thins their blood to water; then like a midday sun, it draws them into the atmosphere, leaves the veins dry, like a vine cut down in autumn. We can understand the word of the King to Hamlet: "you must know, your father lost a father, that father lost, lost his. . . ." But the death of the young is another matter: When it occurs in circumstances of injustice and brutality, it cleaves us to the bone; it challenges faith with manifest absurdity, it leaves us appalled and dismembered. How could such a thing occur? What is the meaning of this death? Or, indeed, does it have any meaning at all? And if the violent death of the young is meaningless, what are we to say of this absurd universe, of this absurd God? Our faith has accepted the fact of death, has made it at least remotely bearable. The word of God penetrates the appearance of death, blesses our hope of immortality, gently quiets our protest and rebellion. Those we love, it assures us, are not taken from us; their lives are changed for the better. A mystery breaks through the universal fate of death, which the Greeks saw as iron necessity and the Romans softened with a gentle longing for immortality in the memory of man. The Christian word is both rigorous and merciful; it assures us that love of others is more than a temporal blessing, that we shall see again those whom we have loved in both flesh and spirit. "We shall all rise again." To be man is to be immortal, as man.

The words of Paul to the Christians of Corinth imply a universal release from slavery of death. His words profoundly alter not only our view of the afterlife but our view of the world, our understanding of what human community is, of what our duties of piety toward others are, of what the simple world "brother" means. But the word of God is one thing; our understanding of it is surely another. Awareness of our brother, a living awareness that accepts the price and task of reconciliation, does not come easily to men. Such an awareness dislocates our loyalties; it demands that one go beyond the blood, beyond the tribe, in order to come upon the will of God. Family loyalties, family professions, family status, family ethics, are placed into question. When the Gospel is in the air, all, all other loyalties are heard only with extreme reservation; for their summons is often intoxicating . . . and sometimes poisonous.

But the blood of Christ summons us to all men. When I have drunk His blood, I may not ever again question the blood which runs in the veins of other men; of men of color, of men who worship in another Church, of men whose blood runs violated in the streets. When the blood of Christ is upon the altar, there is neither Greek nor Jew, freeman or slave, male nor female standing about the altar. There is only one New Man, Jesus Christ, of whom we all are members, limb for limb. A universal bloodstream joins man to man, religion to religion, race to race, sex to sex. The family of man is once and for all created in Christ; a delicate web of life joins me to the race of man, in Him. The constricting curse of nationalism, tribal loyalties, racial frenzies, class injustices, is lifted; in Christ the call of the blood is heard at last for what it is, in the manifest intention of God. It is a call, as old as the blood of Abel, as young as the blood of Jonathan Daniels; it cries out from the earth, I am your brother.

We have all been moved to the heart by the death of this man. Unworthy of the blood of Christ, we are unworthy of the blood of such a brother. We cannot easily claim him, we come only reluctantly, and with a kind of dread, to the truth in which this man's sacrifices implicates us. It is not easy to be brother to such a man; our understanding depends in fact on the most electric and ironic change of heart.

How can we know *my* brother, Jonathan Daniels, without knowing as well all the brothers whom he recognized as his own? How far will this death stretch us upon the rack of the world? We are not merely celebrating a new friendship this afternoon, as though I, a Roman Catholic, had come suddenly to understand in the death of a Protestant, the presence of a brother. Jonathan Daniels did not win me so easily. Nor can I welcome him easily to my own heart. Indeed this young death has called me further than I had thought, or even wished. How could I have gained this man for friend, and not have gained you? How could I grasp the hand of the dead, without seeing that this hand was closed, with the rigor of its final choice, upon white hands and black, Jew and Catholic, the defeated and the persecutor, the Vietnamese, the Congolese, the Russian—all men, all intractable and strained and unworthy hands—even my own?

No, we celebrate something far more than a new friendship this day. The word of God tells us so. The word of God says that the death of this man is martyrdom, a drama, a crisis, a summons to change of heart, a death and resurrection, mysteriously joined to the destiny of Christ, and the destiny of all men; a death that sucks us into its vortex, its moment of truth, its bloodletting and cruel defeat, its terrifying call to conversion. The truth of such a death comes hard to us. We are unready for it; we are used to an easy faith: which is to say, to easy lives and easy deaths. We expect faith to bless our somnolent hearts, to reduce our suffering, to prosper our bloodline. But the Bible has another message for us; it calls us to a universal existence, to life in public, to responsibility for, and to, all men. And in order that a man may be a universal man, he must overcome the call of the blood and all it implies; its insularity and fear, its adoration of idols, its dread of life. The call is as old as the murder of Abel, the exodus of Abraham, the vocation of Moses, the call to the New Testament mission. The disciple must leave all things; he must leave father and mother and flocks and good repute and secure lodgings, and presuppositions and prejudice and false hope, and the cheap grace that flows tranquilly in the veins of the tribe. He must go out from himself; into exile or bondage or prison. And this is not all.

The New Testament summoning to faith may be a call to martyrdom. Blood will have blood, we are told; the blood of Christ lays claim on the blood of man. All the idolatries and paganisms consecrated by the worship of blood, by the superiority of the blood, by the blood that visits the unthinking brain and the unconverted heart—all these are destroyed, the unholy fevers are stilled, the inhuman chill is warmed, when "a man lays down his life for his friend."

A transfusion of blood. The blood of Jonathan Daniels, flowing in the dust of an obscure southern town, has joined the great stream of the blood of Christ, blood of martyrs, the blood of good men. Despite the call of the blood, the call of clerical peace and clerical immunity, unexpected and undeserved like the blood of Christ, Jonathan Daniels is joined to the bloody witness of black man and white, of Jew and Gentile, of man and woman, crying out from beneath the throne of the Lamb; "those who had been killed for the sake of the faithfulness of their witness."

Such a witness indeed sternly forbids all other calls. Before the spectacle of the martyrs, their moral splendor, their incorruptible gift, heaven and earth stand transfixed. We know with the best part of us, which the blood of heroes has quickened, that martyrdom is neither to be explained nor explained away. Before the martyrs our conceits fall silent, our human expectations wither; the web of nature, in which man has been ensnared, is torn asunder and the fact of martyrdom becomes a miraculous crossroads, a place crisis, a place of drama. No one can come upon it, and come away unchanged. The unbeliever is shaken by a mystery for which neither logic or cynicism had prepared him; the believer is shaken from his paltry security, from a faith which had taken into account neither the omnipresence of tragedy nor the rigorous call for love.

A martyrdom is a crossroads and a place of meeting; it is also a place of worship. We know that in the early church, men spontaneously set their altars up at the place where good men had died in witness. Where the blood of good men had run, the Eucharist was celebrated, the blood of Christ was drunk. And in that place, men came to know their brother for the first time; slave and free, Jew and Gentile became one in Christ, drawn one to another by the blood that lay warm upon the altar. In such a way, the witness of blood is a supreme witness to human unity. It is a hard saying; our blood runs cold at the price exacted in order that the simplest of human recognitions may have place, that man may know his brother. But who is to instruct us in a better way?

Dear Friends, in the geography of our land, the rivers of the South may yet flow north. It may be that the land has imperceptibly tipped, that the blood sacrifices of one hundred years shall now turn in our direction; to ease our moral impasse, to shed light upon our path. Our own blood flows tranquilly in our veins; its untroubled murmur, its childish complaints, the fear that lies in it like a biotic, the dread that sends us fleeing change, fleeing sacrifice, fleeing neighborhoods, fleeing our brothers—who can speak to this death? Indeed, a few have stood in the breach, have conquered their dread, have put their bodies where their words were. In the letting of their blood, such men have been freed of the cowardice that plagues the blood of the living. And such men may yet help to free us of the imperfection to which life itself condemns us. Being white, we cannot be black; being Episcopal, we cannot be Catholic; being affluent, we cannot be poor. But when a man has given his blood, he has literally given everything; more, he has been transformed into his gift. So he becomes a universal man in the gift of his manhood. His blood has reached further, and cried out more truthfully, than ever his word could, so a gift that is normally postponed until the end of things, is brusquely placed in our hands. A man of the last day becomes the man of our day. We may now, if we will, take in our hands the life blood of Daniels where the gunshot released it. The living blood is offered to God, and to men, to transform our pusillanimity into heroism, our denseness into moral clarity, our dead words into prophetic speech, our inanity into faithful deeds. In this blood, may we take heart; may we take up with new heart the task of the living: one nation, one mankind, one Body of Christ.

§127 Reverend Ralph David Abernathy

Ralph David Abernathy's biography appears in the introduction to his October 8, 1961 speech in Atlanta, Georgia. At the time of the following speech Abernathy was serving as vice president of the SCLC. This speech, given to a northern audience less than two months after the Voting Rights Bill had become law, looks back at the successes of the movement and foreshadows the SCLC's northern agenda. That agenda goes "far beyond racial segregation" to include the far more intractable problems associated with class. Abernathy also expands the rhetorical parameters of the movement to include world peace, a peace for which Dr. King had been criticized for speaking out on "by all of the powers that be." A Christian movement, Abernathy memorably notes, "must be as concerned about the poor in India as we are about the poor of Indiana."

After praising the movement for its successful merger of Old Testament hymns and prophecies with the New Testament's command of unconditional love,

Abernathy outlines three challenges: political reform in the South, economic reform throughout the nation, and the establishment of peace and freedom throughout the world. He advises his audience that the United States' greatest contribution to world peace would be to demonstrate to the world that "democracy can work and that men of different colors and national origins can live together." But in order to bring further positive change to the nation and to the world, Abernathy explains that we must first remember that God is a revolutionary God and that he will help us overcome the evil that has produced racial prejudice.

A Christian Movement in a Revolutionary Age

Rochester, New York
September 28, 1965

When Moses walked into the courts of Pharaoh and thundered forth the call to "Let my people go," he introduced into history the concept of a God who was concerned about the freedom and dignity of all his children and who was willing to turn heaven and earth that freedom might be reality. Throughout the history of Israel as recorded in the Old Testament, we see God active in the affairs of men, struggling relentlessly against the forces of evil that beset them and seeking to mold a people who will serve as his children, as partners in the building of His kingdom here on earth.

The God of our fathers is a God of revolution. He will not be content with anything less than perfection in His children and in their society.

It is this strong biblical tradition which has been the foundation of the freedom struggle for the past three centuries. As far back as the early days of slavery, black men heard the story of Moses and learned of this great God who would lead his people to freedom, and so they sang, "Go Down Moses." They sang of a "Balm in Gilead" that would "heal the sin-sick soul" and "make the wounded whole." They sang of Ezekiel's dry bones and prophesied the day when the dry bones of the valleys of our land would rise up and become men and stand tall for freedom and dignity.

The past ten years have seen the blossoms of freedom come near to full bloom, and they soon will bear fruit; for the masses of people across the Southland have translated the songs and prophecies of their forefathers into stirring campaigns of action and have taken the Old Testament call for righteousness and justice flowing down like waters in a mighty stream and merged it with the New Testament call to love one's enemies and to bless one's persecutors and formed the most creative and constructive revolutionary force that our world has known for many a decade.

I say that this is the world's most creative and constructive revolutionary force for it has brought changes without destruction; it has established justice in areas once dominated by the terror and lawlessness of the Ku Klux

Klan; and yet it has not destroyed the person or the property of our enemies; and communities which yesterday toiled with tension between the races are now moving forward to new heights of brotherhood and understanding.

This is revolution in the very best biblical sense of the word. This is God making all things new.

The past ten years have been but our beginning, and like infants we have stumbled as we learned to walk through the valleys and shadows which encompass us. We have gone out like Abraham into a land which we know not and by faith carved not only our destiny but perhaps the destiny of our entire world. We have groped for words and sung songs of faith when we had no words. We have blindly tread in faith through the injustices of our society seeking hot dogs when we needed jobs, standing in at movies when we needed education, arguing over bus rides when we needed houses, and staging boycotts for jobs which would soon be nonexistent when we needed political rights to shape and structure our own destiny.

And now we have come to the threshold of the Promised Land. We have shattered the legal barriers of segregation and discrimination, but there are new giants which await us in the land. These giants not only threaten us as Negroes, but they threaten the structures of our entire society. The challenge which the Movement undertakes at this point in history is its most serious challenge indeed. I see this challenge coming in three main areas, the first two of which we are seeking to meet head on with all of the resources at the command of our Movement; but the third, while equally important, is not our primary responsibility. It is an area, however, in which men of freedom must speak the truth. These three aspects of the challenge are political reform in the South, economic reform throughout the nation and establishment of a community of peace and freedom around the world.

The passage of the Voting Rights Bill of 1965 gives us a new opportunity to reform the political structure of America and make democracy a reality. Already we have begun to see Congressmen change their tunes. Former Congressman Weltner of Atlanta voted with liberals of the Johnson Administration on all but one issue, the repeal of the right to work laws. Talmadge, whose name is synonymous with racism and bigotry, has offered to nominate Negroes to the military academies and he has entertained Senator Leroy Johnson at his Lovejoy, Georgia, plantation. Mayor Ivan Allen of Atlanta, who ran as a segregationist for Governor of Georgia only a few years ago, was the only elected official to testify in behalf of the public accommodations section of the Civil Rights Act of 1964. These occurrences and many more fulfill the maxim of Frederick Douglass: that this is a struggle to save black men's bodies and white men's souls. We are going to see many more southern Congressmen "get religion" and start thinking about their Black Brothers.

There are also now ten Negroes sitting in the Georgia Legislature, and the next election will certainly triple the number of Negro elected officials across the Southland.

But the job is only beginning. These represent merely token changes which affect at best only a few of the ten million Negroes of the South. Conditions in the Black Belt of Alabama remain virtually unchanged, except in the counties which now have or have had federal voting referees. The other counties are even beginning to show a more determined resistance to change. The Klan still intimidates people who are attempting to register by taking their pictures at the entrance to the courthouse and threatening prospective voters with loss of jobs and other economic reprisals. We have seen a resurgence of violence, and to date not a single person has been brought to justice for violence and murder against persons engaged in nonviolently seeking their constitutional rights. Southern states continue to make a mockery of justice in an attempt to maintain their hold on political power and the special privileges which go with it.

The only way that voters will be registered and the political reform which was promised in Selma completed is through a concerted, organized campaign of voter registration, community organization, and political education. This process was begun by the SCLC with more than eight hundred college volunteers in our SCOPE Project across six deep South states two summers ago, but the delays in passage of the Voting Bill meant that their work had only begun when it was time to return to school in September.

The completion of these reforms in the South is not only of the utmost urgency for the Negro, but our ability to place in the Halls of Congress men of justice where racists now dominate may determine the passage or failure of numerous bills which are necessary for our nation to cope with the changing times. Many of the key committees in our Congress are headed by men like Richard Russell of Georgia and James Eastland of Mississippi, and the decisions of, "peace on earth, good will toward men," are too often subject to their power.

Another half million Negro voters by the next General Presidential election would go a long way toward making democracy a reality, not only in Mississippi but in Massachusetts as well; for Massachusetts will never have adequate programs of urban transit or education as long as the power in our Congress is held by an old-line, power-ridden southern block.

A Christian Movement in these times must take seriously the realities of political power. The blessings of God's Kingdom must become incarnate in the institutions of our society, and the laws of our land must be made to reflect justice and mercy for all men.

As soon as we began to see our way clear in the South the shock and horror of northern and even southern riots exploded before our eyes, and we were made to see that the problems of the Negro go far beyond mere racial segregation. The recent catastrophes in Los Angeles, Cleveland, Chicago, Tampa, Atlanta, Montgomery, Louisville, Rochester are a result of seething and rumbling tensions throughout our nation, and indeed, throughout the world. It was a quite similar set of internal convulsions which brought down the walls of the mighty Roman Empire. But unlike Rome, the United States has the material resources and technical competence to deal with these problems positively. The question confronting us now is whether we have the moral, spiritual, and intellectual resources. The incidents of Chicago's west side, Harlem, Watts, Atlanta and Montgomery should not be considered race riots. Rather, they are rumblings of discontent from the rejected people of our society; it is a cry for jobs from the unemployed and a call for justice for the under-employed who are in no way touched by the present federal minimum wage law. They are voices of anger from the children who have grown up in fatherless homes, because their fathers are unable to find work and often have to leave home so that their families can qualify for Aid to Dependent Children. It is a seething bitterness from the people who share in none of the benefits of our great society and who are reminded of that fact daily by the humiliation they receive from police, welfare workers and city councils.

All of the progress of the recent movements in the South has passed them by. Two civil rights acts have only served to widen the gap between the masses of Negroes and the new Negro Middle Class. These are more class riots than race riots, and they seriously threaten the very survival of our nation.

The challenge to the Nonviolent Movement is now to provide the creative methods of nonviolent direct action for northern cities which have worked so well in the South. Instead of sitting in at lunch counters, we must sit in at employment offices. We must stage work-ins at some of the places in our community where work is desperately needed but where landlords and government officials refuse to make funds available. We must organize the unemployed to help themselves. Automation is now replacing most unskilled workers. Unemployment in the Negro ghettos of the North is about twenty per cent. In a city like Chicago, this means something like sixty to one hundred thousand people in need of work.

For the past ten years we have been preaching throughout the nation that black men are God's children and that as God's children they are entitled to certain basic human rights. These often exceed existing constitutional rights. God's children should not have to live with rats and roaches when there are resources for adequate housing in our land. A movement which is concerned about "the least of these, my brethren" must find ways to so dramatize and mobilize people around the issue of decent housing for all that our entire society may be moved to act to legislate these basic human rights, even as they have legislated our constitutional rights in the Civil Rights Act of 1964 and the Voting Rights Bill of 1965.

This will not be easy, but the people are there, their needs cry out to us; and in the words of their beautiful folksong, "How many ears must one man have before he can hear people cry?" We have heard the cries of our people, and we pray that God will lead us into new forms of action and new avenues of truth-force to overcome the evils of the northern ghetto and continue this revolution in its present nonviolent tradition.

We must bring our nation to see that American life must be an integrated life; integrated racially and culturally as well as economically. The day must come when we will build apartments with all scales of the economic ladder present in the same building rather than building a thousand units of low income housing in one area and middle income housing some place else.

Our suburbs must be willing to absorb some of the low income families and build them into their community life, rather than section the poor off in a poverty-stricken corner of the inner city. This is not only morally right, it is a social and economic necessity.

The challenge of the North and the South are in themselves too great a burden for our Movement to bear, but added to them we find still another area which demands our attention, for as my friend and colleague, Martin Luther King, has said, "What does it profit a man to gain a seat at an integrated lunch counter only to be served a glass of milk filled with Strontium 90."

Now this is a difficult issue for us, for there are many of our friends who feel that it is all right for Dr. King to speak out on injustice in Mississippi, but they say we must not speak of injustice in Viet Nam or Santo Domingo or the Belgian Congo. The minute Dr. King steps into the arena of world power politics, he must be suddenly criticized by all of the powers that be. In the South I am known as a man who likes to set the record straight, and I must say to you fine people here today that behind the criticisms of Martin Luther King's role in international affairs is the assumption that foreign policy is a white man's business. But when I look around and see the mess that the white man is making of this business, I must encourage men of good will and sound judgment, whatever their color may be, to call our nation to her senses and not allow us to be driven down the road to international disaster by allowing all the decisions in regard to human life and destiny to be made by military men in the Pentagon, and under-cover politicians in the Central Intelligence Agency.

A Christian movement in an age of revolution cannot allow itself to be limited by geographic boundaries. We must be as concerned about the poor in India as we are about the poor of Indiana.

This does not mean that the Movement will abandon its emphasis on the problems of the Negro, North and South, in order to devote time to organizing demonstrations around the issue of world peace. Our most important contribution to world peace can be made as we finish the political reforms of this nation and demonstrate to the world that democracy can work and that men of different colors and national origins can live together and work together and play together. Nevertheless, this is no time for good men to be silent, and the prophetic words "Thus saith the Lord" must be spoken in the United Nations no less than in the legislature of the state of Mississippi.

There are those who look out upon this world in all of its revolutionary turmoil and predict that the end is near at hand; but there is one message which a Christian Movement must continue to make clear, and that is that this is still my Father's world, that God is a revolutionary God, and that he can overcome the forces of evil and destruction in our midst.

> Darker yet may be the night,
> Might may often conquer right
> But if I am right, He will fight my battles
> And I shall be free some day.

§128 Kelly Miller Smith

Kelly Miller Smith's biography appears in the introduction to his January 1965 sermon in Nashville, Tennessee. In this his final sermon of 1965, Smith proposes a radical idea: the merger of two Baptist churches in downtown Nashville: First Baptist Church Seventh and Broad, and First Baptist Church, Capitol Hill. While the latter petitioned to be separated from the former back in 1865 on the grounds of skin color, Smith asks that, 100 years later, "can we any longer justify a separation that is based upon such a triviality as skin color?" Smith makes his appeal in epistolary form; that is, instead of preaching a sermon to his primarily black congregants, Smith addresses a letter to his "Brothers and Sisters in Christ Jesus." Rhetorically, a letter perhaps mimicking the Pauline tradition of the New Testament, functions less as a mandate and more as an inspired suggestion. In addressing perhaps the most pressing fear of his congregants—that the white church is not the "social cosmos" that it is for the black church—Smith claims that a Baptist merger would "address itself to all of the concerns of man," including maintaining an active "social consciousness."

––––––––––

Trek Toward The Dawn

The First Baptist Church, Capitol Hill, Nashville, Tennessee
December 26, 1965

The year now closing has been a momentous one. It has been filled with drama and drudgery and has been characterized by triumph and tragedy. All the way from the blood soaked fields of Viet Nam to the dark and broken streets of Nashville, there have been events which have commanded our attention and required our concern.

The blessings of the year of 1965 have at times been so great and so obvious that we have cried out with the psalmist: "The Lord hath done great things for us; whereof we are glad." And there have been times when the problems have been so critical and devastating and the solutions have appeared so remote that from the depths of our troubled spirits we have exclaimed: "My God, my God, why—WHY hast thou forsaken me?"

Nineteen Sixty-five has been a year of reflection for us at First Baptist Church, Capitol Hill. We have taken an eight month look over one hundred years of our existence as a church. With grateful appreciation and awesome wonder, we have reviewed our dramatic history. We saw how men—still taunted by the unhealed sores of slavery—set out on the venturesome journey of independence and dignity. To be sure, the road was hard and steep. They traveled over mountains that were rough and rugged and through valleys dangerous and dreary. Inspired by the Word of God and by the prophetic words and deeds of their consecrated leaders, and singing their moving spirituals, stately anthems and inspiring hymns, they marched together through the fires and the floods.

In our Centennial observance, persons from many walks of life have joined us. We have been applauded by the mighty and by the humble. Congratulatory messages have come to us all the way from the White House in Washington, D.C. to the unlettered porter in downtown Nashville. The achievements of our Church have been heralded in both the local and national press. In fact, I venture to say that we have even patted ourselves on the back a little.

The great danger is that we may be tempted to conclude that we have done enough now that we can settle back and relax. But, there must be no attitude that "the battle is fought and the victory is won." We must not confuse the way-station with the destination. That which is the closing hymn of an exciting era must be but the prelude to an even more exciting and daring level of existence. There is a creatively disturbing word which Moses heard and which comes ringing down through the windswept corridors of time to us in this hour: "Ye have compassed this mountain long enough." The suggestion is that the first hundred years is but the first lap in our holy pilgrimage—our trek toward the dawn.

In order to suggest an answer to the question "where do we go from here—toward the dawn?" I would like to address a letter to two churches which bear the relationship of mother and child.

The epistle is addressed to the congregation of First Baptist Church, Seventh and Broad, Nashville, Tennessee and the First Baptist Church, Capitol Hill, Nashville, Tennessee.

Dear Brothers and Sisters in Christ Jesus,

I praise God for the witness you have made in the Nashville community. You have helped mend broken lives and have given a sense of hope to many who have come under your influence. Both churches have served to make Nashville a better community.

In spite of the faithful service you have both rendered and in spite of your unquestioned influence in the community, there is a troublesome matter with which we must deal. The good news we both profess demands that we face it.

More than a hundred years ago, on March 16, 1865, the following letter was written to the First Baptist Church of Nashville: "We, the colored members of the First Baptist Church of Nashville, Tennessee, do hereby petition to your honor for a separate and independent Church to be known by the name of the First Colored Baptist Church, Nashville, Tennessee. . . . We, your brethren in love and respect, done by order of the Church, at its regular meeting for business the 7th day of March, 1865."

The reasons Negroes sought to be separated from the predominantly white congregation of which they were a part are fairly well known. When they prayed "Our Father," they were addressing the same God professed by the members of the church from which they were departing. The same Ancient Book of Inspiration called the Holy Bible was a "lamp unto their feet and a light unto their paths" and they claimed redemption through the same divine act and the same Son of God. They pledged allegiance to no kingdom save the Kingdom of God and of His Christ.

Yet, for these one hundred years these congregations have gone their separate ways. In the name of the Christ of Calvary, can we any longer justify a separation that is based upon such a triviality as skin color? Do we not hear the words of Almighty God Himself saying to us "Ye have compassed this mountain long enough?"

In the name of all that is high and holy, is it unthinkable that you two great congregations of Christians begin conversations on the topic of a merger of these churches?

Here you two congregations are, only five blocks apart. Both of you are planning gigantic building programs and both of you are trying to minister to the same part of the same city. Each of you receive telephone calls and mail intended for the other. More important than that, you are kin. You have the same spiritual ancestors. Your relationship is that of mother and child. And still more important is the fact that we are all the children of God and, by virtue of that fact, we are kin:

And all men are my kin,
Since every man has been
Blood of my blood;
I glory in the grace
And strength of every race,
And joy in every trace
Of brotherhood.

You have already made a start. The church which once had the char-tered name "First Colored Baptist Church" is now the First Baptist Church of Capitol Hill. The racial reference has been left out. Both congregations have had persons of different ethnic identities worship together with them. The Capitol Hill Church no longer has a uniracial membership. Yes, you have already made the start. The question is whether or not you are ready to take the first giant step in your trek toward the dawn.

In his history of First Baptist Church, Nashville, *The Spiritual Conquest of the Second Frontier*, P. E. Burroughs calls it the "fruitful mother of church-es." The Capitol Hill Church was separated from First Baptist purely on the basis of color—race. Regardless of whose initiative it was that effected the separation, the result was the same. More than between any of the other children of the "fruitful mother of churches," serious discussion of merger between First Baptist, Seventh and Broadway and the First Baptist, Capitol Hill would speak eloquently and convincingly to a world whose faith and interest in that which we call the Church is seriously waning.

Some among us recognize the importance of the Church to worldly dis-inherited children of God and who know that for Negroes the church has been the "social cosmos"—the answer for all that was lacking everywhere else. Some will look at the social role played by the Capitol Hill Baptist Church and, fearing that this social consciousness will be lost, will object to merger. The fact is, however, that we are not suggesting that we should become less than the Church. To the contrary, the proposal is that we will become *more* the Church. If we talk, we must do so with an awareness of the fact that the Church of the living God must address itself to all of the concerns of man.

This letter is written with full awareness that some will point to "nonra-cial" problems which help keep predominantly white congregations from uniting. While admitting that the major reason for this continued sepa-ration of the people of God is prejudice, Kyle Haselden has listed other problems in his *The Racial Problem in Christian Perspective*. These other problems should be honestly faced if you two congregations decide to talk to each other after all these years.

While the Church should be the leader in movements that make for righteousness and right, we must confess that sometimes we *react* when we should have *acted*. Sometimes we are an echo when we should be a voice. But when the initiative has been taken by other forces and the course is right, why should the church not at least participate? Further, the church can and ought to give depth of meaning and direction to these trends toward right and justice. Certainly, we can never afford to do less than that which we call "secular" life is doing.

Many of our children go to public school together; why can they not go to Sunday School together? Members of the two congregations work together, why may they not worship together? In Nashville and in other parts of the country we eat together in the restaurants; may we not feast on the Bread of Life together?

If you two great congregations agree to talk, please begin with the premise that the ground at the foot of the Cross is level. Begin with the realization of the fact that the Kingdom of God is a Kingdom above caste; ours is a faith which transcends race. We are all one in Christ. Those who were once a dependent mission must come in the spirit of interdependence and brotherhood.

The suggestion which I am now making to these two congregations is not for "migration" but merger. Both congregations have something to contribute to the work of the Church and these resources should be combined. There is much in the long history of the church at Seventh and Broad which will enrich those who comprise the Capitol Hill Church. There is something in the courageous action and social awareness in the tradition of the Capitol Hill Church which will enhance the church at Seventh and Broad. Whether we are willing to face it or not, we need each other, and God wills us one.

If there are those in either congregation who feel that such a proposal should cause them to lessen their support of the building programs now underway by both churches, it must be said that they do not understand the meaning of building *for Christ*.

We are living in an age when great and harsh criticisms are being hurled at the Church. Some have severed connections with it because they have felt that we are not doing that which is obedient and relevant. This move would, perhaps, restore the confidence of some.

In the meantime, we should not only have our doors open in the spirit of "whosoever will, let him come." We should go out into the "highways and hedges" and seek until we find those who have heretofore been excluded either because of official policy or the general practice of both congregations.

There is much that we can do in downtown Nashville if we are willing to walk together as the people of God. There is unparalleled strength awaiting, should these two congregations decide to respond favorably to the mandates of God.

When we do our best in this direction, the words of Ralph Walker may well be applied to us:

> God bless the church on the avenue that hears the
> city's cry;
> the church that sows the seed of the Word where
> the masses of men go by;
> The church that makes, midst the city's roar, a
> place for an Altar of Prayer,
> With a heart for the rich and a heart for the poor,
> and rejoices in their burdens to share.
> The Church that's true to the call of Christ who
> wept o'er the city's need,
> And who sent His disciples to labor for Him
> where the forces of evil breed,
> The Church that gives and the church that lives,
> as seen by the Master's eye –
> God bless the Church on the avenue that answers
> the city's cry.

But we must not postpone being virtuous. We need not wait for this glorious and long awaited day if we are to march in accordance with His commands. There are things for us to do even now. Our hearts and our spirits must be prepared. Our eyes have grown so accustomed to the darkness that they are likely to be hurt by the true Light. In all that we do, let us remember that he has required of us that we continue our trek toward the dawn. He says to these congregations, "Ye have compassed this mountain long enough."

> He has sounded forth the trumpet
> that shall never call retreat;
> He is sifting out the hearts of men
> Before his judgment seat;
> O be swift, my soul, to answer him;
> Be jubilant, my feet!
> Our God is marching on!

I close, with the words used by the great apostle when he wrote about love to the Church at Corinth. "The grace of our Lord Jesus Christ be with you. My love be with you all in Christ Jesus." Amen

§129 Gardner C. Taylor

Gardner C. Taylor was born on June 18, 1918 in Baton Rouge, Louisiana. Taylor's father was a black Baptist preacher but his son didn't come into religion until 1937 when he was involved in a car accident in which a white man died. That same year he enrolled in the Oberlin Graduate School of Theology where he met his wife, Laura Bell Scott. He began preaching at Bethany Baptist Church in Oberlin, Ohio while he was still in school. He graduated Oberlin in 1940. After serving churches in Elyria, Ohio, New Orleans and Baton Rouge, Taylor began a 42-year tenure at Concord Baptist Church of Christ in Brooklyn. After losing the presidential race for the National Baptist Convention, Taylor formed the Progressive National Baptist Church Convention. Taylor was active in New York City's race relations, serving as a member of the Board of Education and the New York City Commission on Human Relations. An orator of great renown, Taylor was named in 1993 by *Ebony* magazine as one of the 15 greatest African American preachers. In 2000, Taylor was awarded the nation's highest civilian honor, the Presidential Medal of Freedom, by Bill Clinton. Taylor remains a preacher in great demand around the nation and world.

In this brief sermon on racism, Taylor grounds his call for a religious solution in the story of the Good Samaritan, the psalms of David, and the death and resurrection of Jesus. But he begins ambivalently: "the church has been a scourge on racial comity just as it has inspired the rebellions of John Brown, Denmark Vesey, and Nat Turner. Similarly, on the subject of racism, Taylor reminds his listeners that race hate flows in both directions—and that the same Christian God will judge whites and blacks for their hatred. That hatred cannot alone be solved by nonviolent protest, by boycotts, by "amalgamation," racial separatism as espoused by Elijah Muhammad and the Black Muslims, nor yet interracial marriages. No, the problem of race hatred will only be solved by a threefold religious recognition: first, since all of us are made in God's image, we are kin to him and thus "authentic nobility"; second, Christ's sacrifice at Calvary proves that each and every human soul is worthy of God and thus us; and third, we "share an august destiny within and beyond this time sphere which belongs to every human being." In other words, Gardner closes by emphasizing the divine and mysterious Great Chain of Being that links us all, one to another.

Some Comments on Race Hate

Unknown location
1965 (reprinted)

Then saith the woman of Samaria unto him, How is it that though, being a Jew, askest drink of me, which am a woman of Samaria? For the Jews have no dealings with the Samaritans.

Race hate is an old and persistent disease in the bloodstream of society. It has divided Jew and Samaritan, Greek and barbarian, black American and white American. Race hate is not a one-way street. It infects the hater and the hated, since the hated learns to hate the hater. Prejudice and bigotry produce prejudice and bigotry. The church's supreme consideration must be that such hatred of people, for whatever reason, and most especially on the basis that they are physically different from us, offends heaven and shuts so many out from God. This is the ultimate danger in any sin and makes race hate eligible for consideration and concern by the church. It may, rather it does, shut men from God.

This nearly happened in the well-known meeting of Jesus with the Samaritan woman. A long and bitter enmity had existed between Jews and Samaritans who, in truth, had a common ancestry. The basis of the ancient rift had been religious, but was also compounded with difference of race. When Jesus appeared at Jacob's well with Mount Gerizim in the background the woman of Samaria of whom he asked water was blinded by her prejudice. Now, let us leave out of the matter the divinity of our Lord. Even then we must say that there was force and thrust in his words of wisdom and insight, but race hatred blinded this woman to that wisdom and insight. He was full of compassion, and an infinite sympathy for people rested like a holy light upon his countenance. Again and again it is said in the New Testament by those who watched as he dealt with the people, "He was moved with compassion." Bigotry blinded this Samaritan woman to the sight of that deep and pervasive sympathy which beamed forth from his face. There were in his voice the accents of conviction and tones of authority, so that people hearing him went away saying, "No man ever spoke like this man." Race hatred deafened this woman's ears to those notes of blessed assurance that sounded forth when he spoke. She said to him, "How is it that thou, being a Jew, askest drink of me which I am a woman of Samaria?" Bias of race blinded this woman's eyes and deafened her ears. Such prejudice can prove fatal.

The pulpits of this land must point out that this hatred—this deep, angry, bitter animosity which we call racial prejudice—warps our thinking in this country and is a cancer eating at this nation's vitals and dooming it to failure. In addition to the acts of hatred aimed at black men, there are depths of hatred and bitterness in the Negro community toward white America which would shock and shake this land if they could be plumbed and beheld.

The Church of Jesus Christ might well bow its head in America, for it, North and South, led in promoting the ceremonies and rituals which institutionalized and shaped the contours of this evil. Kyle Haselden in

The Racial Problem in Christian Perspective has pointed out that segregation in public facilities in this country goes back only to the 1870's and in many places only to the early 1900's, even in the South. This is true as far as the secular institutions are concerned, but in 1795 in New York City, in the John Street Methodist Church, free black men found so much embarrassment because of race that Peter Williams, a former slave who had purchased his freedom, led the Negro members of that church forth to form the African Methodist Episcopal Zion Church. In Philadelphia at the turn of the century, Richard Allen who started the A.M.E. Church was pulled from his knees while praying in old St. George's Church. In reality the church set the pace, established the pattern, and provided for segregation in this country. For this the church must bow its head in shame.

At the same time, the gospel of Jesus Christ agitated and prodded and disturbed and distressed some Christians so much that they, black and white, made their protest, some in their own blood, against the evils of racism that existed and still exist in this country. John Brown whose raid on Harper's Ferry helped light the fires of civil conflict was religiously motivated. On the side of the slaves, the gospel of Christ helped to motivate the uprisings of Denmark Vesey in Charleston, South Carolina, in 1822 and Nat Turner in Southhampton County, Virginia, in 1831. It is to the credit of the gospel and its releasing power for freedom that these incidents led the Virginia legislature to decree that, "No slave, free Negro, or mulatto shall preach, or hold any meeting for religious purposes day or night." The publication is a badge of honor for the gospel. For where Christ truly is, man must and will be free.

There are those who constantly assert that morality cannot be legislated, and that people's acceptance of one another must be a matter of religion and not of law. This is palmed off as religious insight. But this is only a half truth. Our Christian faith recognizes the place which law must hold if man will not obey grace. Paul Tillich, the theologian, has put it aright: "If law is not internalized in conscience, then conscience must be externalized in law." Christians must press for laws that restrain the wild, primitive, savage lunges of race hatred and bigotry. Paul speaks of the law as a schoolmaster who brings men along, trains them, and restrains them until the power of Christ can go to work.

We must dismiss the idea of a Christian faith that is all sweetness and light and patience and niceness. There is judgment with God, swift and awful. A cry is heard in the midnight chill, "Behold, the bridegroom cometh," and the wise are by that sudden summons divided in judgment from the foolish. Every man's work is judged. Every nation's work is judged. We mourn in this country the necessity for the long bitter campaign that goes forward to make the deeds of the land fit its words. We lament the traumas and shocks and pains and deaths suffered in the cause of liberating the nation. But we would have reason to wonder and to doubt God if this season of trouble and tension, hatred and violence had not come upon the nation. This country could have solved this problem with double ease a hundred years ago. It is doubly hard a hundred years later. It will continue to be hard because hatred, suspicion, and bitterness are all through the land. This is the judgment of one who has said, "Whatsoever a man soweth, that shall he also reap." In our lifetime we shall not know peace between the blacks and the whites in this country. It is because not enough blacks are so dedicated to liberty that they are ready to confront the nation in love with every resource at their command, including their own death. It is because not enough whites believe sufficiently in the Christian religion, the Jewish faith, or the Constitution to make them living reality.

This matter of men disliking each other because of color is basically, like everything else in life, a religious problem. False gods cannot finally save us because they cannot solve our problems. Elijah Muhammad, the Black Muslim, and his followers are understandably angry, and it must be said that he has given to his disciples a sense of identity and dignity. But the doctrine of separation has already failed when sponsored in the white community. It is doomed to the same failure when sponsored by the black community. We, black and white, have irrevocably and indelibly influenced each other and cannot be separated in the land, as James Baldwin has pointed out with classic eloquence.

List the cures and they are all partial. Nonviolence is an attractive, but only a partial answer to the problem of race, since it must be attended by the force of boycott in a situation where boycott will hurt. In addition, it presupposes a goodness in man which may be alien to our true nature. Many speak of amalgamation as the full and sufficient answer to the problem of race in this country. This is to think in terms of centuries rather than years, since the rate of amalgamation in the country is perhaps slower today than ever before. The new status of personhood makes Negro women less vulnerable to the clandestine trespasses of the white male, and the Negro male is better equipped to defend his hearth against the sexual adventures of the white man. In addition, interracial marriages face the severe strains of a society grievously sick at this point of race. In my own fifteen years in Brooklyn, I have performed more than a thousand weddings. Fewer than fifty of them have been interracial.

No, the problem of people accepting one another is religious. James Baldwin, honest, bitter spokesman of the current American scene, has stated the religious consideration, though he doubtless would not admit the religious nature of his thesis. "It is not a question," he said, "of whether the white man can love me, it is a question of whether he can love himself."

The same may be said of the black man as he faces the white man. I can accept other people only as I have accepted myself. I must first identify myself before I can tell who you are. I must first be delivered from self-loathing before I can regard you with reverence and respect. I must first have my own center of loyalty established before I am eligible to offer loyalty to you.

The reason I owe respect and reverence for every human person is ultimately religious, and roots in my faith about my origin, status, and destiny and, in turn, about every man's. What is it that gives preciousness to every human soul, never mind the color, the creed, the previous condition of servitude, as we like to say? It is our origin, our worth, and our destiny that we find the price tag which belongs upon every man. There is no satisfying word about when and how we started other than that contained in the Hebrew-Christian Bible. God! Our beginnings are no meaner, no more parochial than that! The psalmist, looking back upon the high, brave assumptions of his fathers, exclaimed with a gasp in his voice, "It is he that hath made us, and not we ourselves; we are his people, and the sheep of his pasture." There lies our origin, in the words "It is he that hath made us." So! Every man is kin to God. However much we may differ from him there is something of us in him. However defaced the likeness there is in every man the image of God himself. This is every man's origin, and the nature of his beginning marks every man as authentic nobility.

There is in every man a worth attested by God. Again, the psalmist looks at man and remembers admiringly that God is mindful of him in the face of the vast stretches of his creation and his divine prerogatives and responsibilities. Never was a more extravagant paean of praise sung to man under God than by this ancient Theist, "What is man, that though art mindful of him? And the son of man, that thou visitest him? For thou has made him a little lower than the angels, and hast crowned him with glory and honor." This is the biography of every human soul.

The New Testament contains a still sublimer proof of worth. There is the act at Calvary and the vast mysterious transaction which occurred there involving us men. All that God means by that hill and that Cross and that man on it we cannot pretend to know. But this one thing we do know: There God placed his price tag, his estimate of value, on every human soul who walks the face of the earth. And if God so assesses, so gauges worth, then I have an obligation to every man who means as much to God as Calvary.

There is a third element in the constitution of the human spirit which mandates my respect and enlists my regard. There is some august destiny within and beyond this time sphere which belongs to every human being. I sense that awareness in myself and in other men. Wordsworth was spokesman for all men, black and white, when he wrote:

> Though inland far we be,
> Our Souls have sight of that immortal sea
> Which brought us hither.

I hear that same cadence of destiny in the mysteriously compelling words of the music of my fathers. Black backs glisten with sweat in the moonlight after a long and cruel day of unrequited toil. If ever there was a dead-end street this is it. They have been snatched from Mother Africa and planted in a cold and hostile land. Their customs have been wrenched from their lives by the alien culture with which they are surrounded. Maybe 30,000,000 of their people died in the iniquitous Middle Passage. They were "motherless children a long ways from home," and yet there is in their music that theme of a high and lofty destiny.

> Before I'd be a slave
> I'd be buried in my grave
> And go home to my Lord
> And be free.
> I looked over Jordan
> And what did I see?
> A band of angels coming after me.

That sense of destiny in every man, given body and substance by the New Testament, demands in me respect and regard for every man. It is in this sense that religion, alone, is the answer to our deep chasms of tension and mutual hate which afflict white and black people in this land. God grant us his grace that we may be equal to this issue with which our lives are met.

§130 Theodore Parker Ferris

Reverend Theodore Parker Ferris was born in Port Chester, New York on December 23, 1908. He graduated with an A.B. from Harvard University in 1929 and a B.D. from General Theological Seminary in 1933. From 1933 to 1937 he stayed on as fellow and tutor at General while assisting the rector at Grace Church in New York City. From 1937 to 1942 he served as rector of Emmanuel Church in Baltimore, where summaries of his sermons enjoyed broad distribution. From 1942 until his death in 1972 Reverend Ferris served as rector of Trinity Church in Boston. His weekly sermons were printed in full and enjoyed both nationwide and internationally. In addition to his duties as a rector, he taught homiletics, served as delegate to the World Council of Churches, and served as a deputy to the Episcopal church's General Convention. His sermons served as a basis for numerous book publications. Ferris was an accomplished pianist and served as trustee for the Boston Symphony. Ferris died on November 26, 1972.

The sermon below comes in the wake of the March on Washington on August 28, 1963. Six civil rights groups coordinated the march, which featured speeches by prominent civil rights leaders and celebrities, and included songs led by famous artists. President Kennedy discouraged organizers, but eventually supported the event while simultaneously activating 15,000 paratroopers in case of rioting. The main stage for the event was in front of the Lincoln Memorial, and the event occurred several weeks shy of the centennial anniversary of the Emancipation Proclamation. The assembly of some 200,000 people abided by its program and dispersed within a half hour of its closing anthem. The participants wore dress clothing and the event took place on a Wednesday, so weekend revelers would not breach the integrity of the sober, yet joyful event. While many pro-civil rights ministers took the stance that biblical directive clearly indicates equality and justice, Ferris admits that no clear indicators emerge. But he finds more powerful indicators than contextually limited fiat would allow. Jahwist and Christian narratives emphasize the emancipation of slavery on a consistent basis. Whether we are brickmaking Hebrews, Samaritans, lepers or tax collectors, we need people to set us free from our slavery. The Christian narrative ends slavery by association with the outcast. Ferris takes this notion to its logical conclusion: some day people will marry across racial boundaries. What will happen then? He answers that interracial marriages will happen, and if problems arise we will address them at that time.

Civil Rights from a Christian Point of View

1965 (reprinted)

On Wednesday, August 28, 1963, 200,000 people marched into the city of Washington, D.C. Most of them were Negroes; many of them were not. It was a demonstration for equal rights. The amazing thing about it was that there was no disorder, no violence. On the following Friday James Reston wrote about the March in his column. He is one of the interpreters of events whom I admire most and to whose mind I turn most confidently. Some of you may not, but I do.

The first sentence of his article struck me like a blow. This was it: "The first significant test of the Negro March on Washington will come in the churches and synagogues of the country this weekend." It was quite clear that the implication was that if nothing happened in the churches nothing would happen in Congress. He went on to say, "As moral principles preceded and inspired political principles, as the Church preceded the Congress, so there will have to be a moral revulsion to the humiliation of the Negro before there can be significant political relief."

Then I stopped to think about this church. What happened in this church on that weekend? Nothing. At least nothing was said that had anything to do with the March or its purpose. I did not intend to say anything about it at that particular time, for reasons that I need not go into now. I am not sure that something had not already happened in this church and in many other churches, and I wonder whether James Reston fully appreciated how much has been happening in the churches. Granted, the churches have not done all that they should, but they have done infinitely more than that particular article of his would lead an outsider to guess.

I am not sure that preaching in and by itself will change anybody's mind, but Reston's article has lain heavily on my conscience, and for better or worse I am going to say now what I think about civil rights from a Christian point of view.

First, there are no specific directions about this particular matter in the Bible, none whatever. Slavery is taken for granted in both the Old Testament and the New Testament. Words like integration, segregation, desegregation, interracial do not appear anywhere in the Bible, for the situation to which they refer did not exist then as it does now. The first thing that I would like to make as plain as I possibly can is this: You can neither defend nor oppose the idea that the colored and white are separate on the basis of some particular passage in the Bible. Many people have tried to do it. Some have tried to defend the idea that the colored and white are separate, and some have tried to oppose it, on the basis of a fragment, a scrap, taken out of its biblical context. You cannot do it.

You cannot defend or oppose the idea that the earth goes around the sun on the basis of any particular passage in the Bible. The Bible is too early for that idea, and it is likewise too early for the particular social revolution which is now raging full tilt.

There is something much more powerful in the Bible than specific directions. There is in the Bible a movement toward the emancipation of men and women. That is the important thing about the Bible. From the first page to the last page the Bible is the story of a movement toward the freedom of a man to be himself and to live his own life within the limits of his human condition.

The movement began at the Red Sea when one small tribe broke loose from bondage to another people. It was the beginning of the movement. It ends supremely on Calvary where Jesus, one single human being in whom the fullness of God revealed itself, was free to be himself and as a consequence frees other people to be themselves. It is liberty born out of sacrifice. It's the only real liberty there is.

During his brief ministry Jesus never spoke about Negroes or said anything that has anything to do with the problem that we are now dealing with. For one thing there weren't many Negroes in his neighborhood. There were, however, a great many Samaritans, and the Samaritans were as thoroughly segregated from the Jews as Negroes are from the whites.

Segregation was a habit peculiarly congenial to the Jewish people. Yet as far as we know Jesus never talked about integration or segregation in principle or in theory. One time he told an unforgettable story about "a certain Samaritan" who helped a Jew who was in a bad way—the last person in the world you would expect to stop to help a Jew. And when ten lepers ran to him for help he healed them all, but only one went back to thank him, "and he was a Samaritan."

In his own behavior Jesus treated people like human beings no matter who they were, whether they came from the aristocracy or from the gutter, and no matter what they had done, whether they had a magnificent record or whether they had only the record of failure. Regardless of their present status, he treated them like human beings. The essential thing is that in his dealings with people he brought them into the presence of God, the same God from whom they all originally came, from whom they all derived their lives, in the sight of whom they all failed, and by whose tender, understanding love they could all be made new. He brought them all into the presence of that God, and the equality they had was the equality that he gave them as he drew them into the presence of his Father.

There on Calvary stands Jesus. I wonder if you can see it clearly as you look back across the centuries. I know that some think that the images of Christianity will have to be changed in a radical way. The years go by, the generations pass, and the fashions of thought change, but Jesus remains on Calvary. There he stands, the center of human dignity and integrity, where the cross-purposes of life are accepted and saved from desperate remedies.

Gradually people begin to see what it means to be associated with him. They don't see it all at once. Even Paul didn't see it completely; he saw the great thing, but he didn't have time to work out the details. But gradually people see that to be associated with Jesus means to treat other human beings the way he treats you. It's quite a thing to see! If you once see it, you won't always be able to do it, but you will never be the same again.

Copernicus declared that the earth went around the sun, and to his satisfaction he proved it. It took a hundred years for the plain people of the Western world to take in that idea, and they are still working out the implications of it. Jesus declared that every human being revolves around God. It took a long time for people to take in that idea; they were so used to thinking that God revolved around them. He began a movement toward freedom, and it took some people a long time to see that that movement toward freedom includes, and this is very important, not only freedom from hell, but also freedom from humiliation. It is much easier to reach for one than the other.

Let me tell you something that happened as I was working on these notes in the rectory. A great many people go to Mass in the Roman Catholic Church just up Newbury Street, and they park their cars all around the rectory. Across the street from the rectory was parked a small foreign car in which was a little French poodle. While the owner of the car was in church praying for salvation from hell the poodle spent the entire time yelping to be saved from the humiliation of being locked up in a car for three quarters of an hour. If the door had not been locked I would have opened it; at least I would have been tempted to. Jesus began a movement to do something for the people who are crying for help.

This movement has now reached a new front. In this country Negroes have never been treated like human beings, by and large. I know that that is a general statement, and I know that some of you will take exception to it. I stand by the statement, however, that Negroes in this country have never been treated before the law as human beings. Many of them have been dearly loved and treated with great kindness—the way you would treat a child—but when they wanted to vote they were treated another way.

In the last few years two things have happened. The first is that the Negroes in this country now demand to be treated as human beings. Some of you would prefer that they didn't, but they have the numbers and the intelligence to demand it, and they will continue to demand it until they get it. They have waited for one hundred years, and they might well say to us, "We've waited long enough." The longer they wait, the more insistent their demands will become.

The other thing that has happened is that some white people, many white people, sincerely want this. They are people who have caught up with the movement of Jesus. Nominally they may not be Christian, but they are a part of this movement toward freedom, and I am proud to claim my association with them. The Christians who want this see the difficulties involved if they have any eyesight at all. They are enormous. Imagine what is involved in changing a whole social pattern; for many people it's like an earthquake. They see the difficulties, but they cannot deny the principle, and they begin to move bravely toward it.

Take, for example, one of the many difficulties. If you give Negroes equal social rights, they may intermarry with whites. A great many people believe that this is highly undesirable and that the intermarriage of white and colored people causes all sorts of difficulties. Their solution is not to give them equal social rights. If equal social rights encourage intermarriage, and if intermarriage is not good, then withhold the rights. Keep them in their place.

The Christian, I believe, takes a different position. The Christian says, "Give them equal social rights because it is right." If there are undesirable consequences as a result you deal with those as well as you can when they arise. This is essentially what we said in another situation fifty years ago. You give labor the right to organize because it is right; if there are undesirable consequences, and there certainly have been, you handle those as they arise as well as you can.

We are now standing on the new front, and as we stand there we can see real gains in every direction. As we look toward the South we can see real gains in many Southern cities and towns, gains that have been made quietly, white and colored people working together, both realizing how difficult it is, with patience, intelligence, and loving-kindness. Right here in our own state the gains are easy to see. We see a Negro in the office of Attorney General of the Commonwealth of Massachusetts. We see a Negro on the staff of the Cathedral.

Looking more closely at our own parish, we see that there are Negroes— not many, but there are some who belong to this church, with all its rights and privileges. They have been accepted as members of this parish for years. We see that there are white people in this church who are working for this movement, quietly, not necessarily talking about it, but working for it, to give to people who crave to be treated as human beings the right to live as human beings in a community which includes both white and colored people.

There are some in this church, I am sure, who think that this whole movement is in the wrong direction. There are some who think that it is contrary to the Bible, and a few who think that it is inspired by Communism. And there are some, I am sure, who are in sympathy with the article that David Lawrence wrote about the March, which he called "The Day of Disgrace." I welcome those people to this congregation. We will never all be of one mind. I do not agree with them. I think they are wrong, but I love them, and I want them to be here.

I am speaking only for myself and for those whose consciences are stirring, for those who know that Christians belong to a movement begun originally by God, brought to a head by Christ, and worked out imperfectly by individuals like you and me.

I am speaking for all those who see, even though dimly, what Paul was aiming at. He didn't see it himself, but he was aiming at something great, the fullness of which he never attained. I am speaking for those who see what he was aiming at when he wrote, "There is neither Jew nor Greek, there is neither bond nor free, there is neither male nor female; for you are all one in Christ Jesus."

BIBLIOGRAPHY

Ralph David Abernathy

Primary

And The Walls Came Tumbling Down: An Autobiography. New York, NY: Harper & Row, 1989.

A Black Preacher Looks at the Black Manifesto. Chicago, IL: The Christian Century Foundation, 1969.

with Howard Levy and J.H. O'Dell. "The G.I. Movement vs. the War." *Freedomways* 10 (1970): 358–368.

Secondary

Chase, Robert T. "Class Resurrection: The Poor People's Campaign of 1968 and Resurrection City." *Essays in History* 40 (1998): n.p.

Cotton, Dorothy. "A Conversation with Ralph Abernathy." *Journal of Current Social Issues* 9 (1970): 21–30.

Fairclough, Adam. "The Preachers and the People: The Origins and Early Years of the Southern Christian Leadership Conference 1955–1959." *The Journal of Southern History* 52 (1986): 403–440.

"The Fortieth Anniversary of the Freedom Rides." *The Journal for Blacks in Higher Education* 32 (2001): 7.

Morris Abram

Primary

The Day is Short: An Autobiography. San Diego, CA: Harcourt, 1982.

"Is Strict Separation too Strict?" *Public Interest* 82 (1986): 81–90.

The Jewish Case for Extending Nazi Prosecutions. New York, NY: American Jewish Committee, 1965.

"Liberalism and the Jews: A Symposium." *Commentary* 69 (1980): 15–82.

The Paradoxes of Freedom. New York, NY: American Jewish Committee, 1968.

The Second Vatican Council's Declaration on the Jews. New York, NY: American Jewish Committee, 1965.

Ella Jo Baker

Secondary

Elliot, Aprele. "Ella Baker: Free Agent in the Civil Rights Movement." *Journal of Black Studies* 26 (1996): 593–603.

Grant, Joanne. *Ella Baker: Freedom Bound.* New York, NY: Wiley, 1998.

James, Joy. "Ella Baker, 'Black Women's Work' and Activist Intellectuals." *Black Scholar* 24 (1994): 8–15.

Payne, Charles. "Ella Baker and Models of Social Change." *Signs: Common Grounds and Crossroads: Race, Ethnicity, and Class in Women's Lives* 14 (1989): 885–899.

Ransby, Barbara. *Ella Baker and the Black Freedom Movement: A Radical Democratic Vision.* Chapel Hill, NC: University of North Carolina Press, 2003.

Ross, Rosetta E. *Witnessing and Testifying: Black Women, Religion, and Civil Rights.* Minneapolis: Fortress Press, 2003.

Daniel Berrigan

Primary

A Book of Parables. San Francisco, CA: Harper, 1984.

Absurd Convictions, Modest Hopes: Conversations after Prison with Lee Lockwood. New York, NY: Random House, 1972.

America is Hard to Find. New York, NY: Doubleday, 1972.

And the Risen Bread: Selected Poems 1957–1997. New York, NY: Fordham University Press, 1998.

Block Island. Oakland, CA: Unicorn Press, 1985.

The Bride: Images of the Church. Maryknoll, NY: Orbis Books, 2000.

Consequences: Truth And… New York, NY: Macmillan, 1967.

Daniel: Under the Siege of the Divine. Farmington, PA: Plough Publishing House, 1998.

The Dark Night of Resistance. New York, NY: Doubleday, 1971.

"Dear Friends in Christ." *Katallagete* 1 (1965): 84–86.

Discipline of the Mountain. New York, NY: Seabury Press, 1979.

Encounters. New York, NY: World, 1971.

Ezekiel: Visions in the Dust. Maryknoll, NY: Orbis Books, 1997.

The Geography of Faith. New York, NY: Bantam, 1972.

The Geography of Faith: Underground Conversations on Religious, Political, and Social Change. Woodstock, VT: Jewish Light Publishing, 2001.

Genesis: Fair Beginnings then Foul. Lanham, MD: Rowman & Littlefield, 2006.

"International Life And Peace: What Way is Reality?" *Katallagete* 1 (1966): 32–37.

"Journey to Hanoi: A Poetry Reading." *Liberation* 13 (1968): 26–35.

Jubilee: Fifty Years as a Jesuit 1939–1989. Oakland, CA: Unicorn Press, 1991.

Laurel. Ithaca, NY: Cornell United Religious Work, 1968.

Night Flight to Hanoi. New York, NY: Macmillan, 1968.

No Bars to Manhood. New York, NY: Bantam, 1971.

No One Walks Waters. New York, NY: Macmillan, 1966.

"Open Sesame: My Life and Good Times." *Katallagete* 2 (1968): 19–25.

Portraits of Those I Love. New York, NY: Crossroad Publishing, 1972.

Prison Poems. Greensboro, NC: Unicorn Press, 1973.

Stations: The Way of the Cross. San Francisco, CA: Harper & Row, 1989.

Testimony: The World Made Fresh. Maryknoll, NY: Orbis Books, 2004.

They Call Us Dead Men. New York, NY: Macmillan, 1966.

Time Without Number. New York, NY: Macmillan, 1957.

To Dwell in Peace: An Autobiography. San Francisco, CA: Harper & Row, 1987.

The Trial of the Catonsville Nine. Boston, MA: Beacon Press, 1970.

Uncommon Prayers: A Book of Psalms. New York, NY: Seabury Press, 1978.

"Values and the University." *Katallagete* 2 (1969): 8–11.

We Die Before We Live. New York, NY: Seabury, 1980.

The Words Our Savior Gave Us. Springfield, IL: Templegate Publishing, 1978.

The World for Wedding Ring: Poems. New York, NY: Macmillan, 1962.

Mary McLeod Bethune

Primary

"The Adaptation of the History of the Negro to the Capacity of the Child." *The Journal of Negro History* 24 (1939): 9–13.

"The Association for the Study of Negro Life and History: Its Contribution to Our Modern Life." *The Journal of Negro History* 20 (1935): 406–410.

"The Torch is Ours." *The Journal of Negro History* 36 (1951): 9–11.

Secondary

Bennett, Carolyn LaDelle, ed. *An Annotated Bibliography of Mary McLeod Bethune's Chicago Defender Column's 1948–1955.* Lewiston, NY: Edwin Mellen, 2001.

Broadwater, Andrea. *Mary McLeod Bethune: Educator and Activist.* Berkeley Heights, NJ: Enslow Publishers, 2003.

Cummings, Melbourne S. "Mary McLeod Bethune." In *African-American Orators.* Ed. Richard W. Leeman. Westport, CT: Greenwood Press, 1996, 1–9.

Halasa, Malu and Coretta Scott King. *Mary McLeod Bethune: Educator.* New York, NY: Chelsea House Publications, 1988.

Hanson, Joyce Ann. *Mary McLeod Bethune and Black Women's Political Activism.* Columbia, MO: University of Missouri Press, 2003.

McCluskey, Audrey Thomas. "'Most Sacrificing' Service: The Educational Leadership of Lucy Craft Laney and Mary McLeod Bethune." In *Women of the American South: A Multicultural Reader.* Ed. Christie Anne Farnham. New York, NY: New York University Press, 1997.

————. "Representing the Race: Mary McLeod Bethune and the Press in the Jim Crow Era." *Western Journal of Black Studies* 23 (1999): 236–245.

————. "We Specialize in the Wholly Impossible: Black Women School Founders and Their Mission." *Signs* 22 (1997): 403–426.

McCluskey, Audrey and Elaine Smith, eds. *Mary McLeod Bethune: Building a Better World, Essays and Selected Documents.* Bloomington, IN: Indiana University Press, 1999.

Meltzer, Milton. *Mary McLeod Bethune: Voice of Black Hope.* New York, NY: Penguin, 1987.

Perkins, Carol O. "The Pragmatic Idealism of Mary McLeod Bethune." *Sage: A Scholarly Journal on Black Women* 5 (1988): 30–36.

Ross, B. Joyce. "Mary McLeod Bethune and the National Youth Administration: A Case Study of Power Relationships in the Black Cabinet of Franklin D. Roosevelt." *The Journal of Negro History* 60 (1960): 1–28.

James Bevel

Primary

"Caught Not Praying." *Katallagete* 2 (1968): 8–11.

Secondary

Blake, John. *Children of the Movement.* Chicago, IL: Lawrence Hill, 2004.

Branch, Taylor. *At Canaan's Edge: American in the King Years, 1965–1968.* New York, NY: Simon & Schuster, 2006.

Halberstam, David. *The Children.* New York, NY: Fawcett, 1999.

Eugene Carson Blake

Primary

The Church in the Next Decade. New York, NY: Macmillan, 1966.

He is the Lord of All. Philadelphia, PA: Westminster Press, 1958.

with William P. Thompson. *Presbyterian Law for the Local Church: A Handbook for Church Officers & Members.* New York, NY: United Presbyterian Church, 1975.

Secondary

Brackenridge, R. Douglas. *Eugene Carson Blake: Prophet with Portfolio.* New York, NY: Seabury Press, 1978.

Buchanan, John M. "Eugene Carson Blake: The Pastor." *Journal of Presbyterian History* 76 (1998): 265–274.

Findlay, James. *Church People in the Struggle: The National Council of Churches and the Black Freedom Movement, 1950–1970.* New York, NY: Oxford University Press, 1993.

Steinhilber, August. "The U.S. Supreme Court and Religion in the Schools." *Theory into Practice* 4 (1965): 8–13.

Toy, E. V., Jr. "The National Lay Committee and the National Council of Churches: A Case Study of Protestants in Conflict." *American Quarterly* 21 (1969): 190–209.

Marion A. Boggs

Primary

What Does God Require in Race Relations? Richmond, VA: Covenant Life Curriculum, 1964.

Horace Mann Bond

Primary

Black American Scholars: A Study of Their Beginnings. Detroit, MI: Balamp Publishing, 1972.

The Education of the Negro in the American Social Order. New York, NY: Prentice-Hall, 1934.

Negro Education in Alabama: A Study in Cotton and Steel. Washington, D. C.: Associated Publishers, 1939.

The Star Creek Papers. Athens, GA: University of Georgia Press, 1997.

Secondary

Fairclough, Adam. "Forty Acres and a Mule: Horace Mann Bond and the Lynching of Jerome Wilson." *Journal of American Studies* 31 (1997): 1–17.

———. "Washington Parish and its Black Community: Horace Mann Bond's Study of 1934–1935." In *A Fierce and Fractious Frontier: The Curious Development of Louisiana's Florida Parishes, 1699–2000.* Ed. Samuel C. Hyde, Jr. Baton Rouge, LA: Louisiana State University Press, 2004.

Norton, Rita. "The Horace Mann Bond Papers: A Biography of Change." *The Journal of Negro Education* 53 (1984): 29–40.

Urban, Wayne. "The Black Scholar and Intellectual Testing: The Case of Horace Mann Bond." *Journal of the History of the Behavioral Sciences* 25 (1989): 323–334.

———. *Black Scholar: Horace Mann Bond.* Athens, GA: University of Georgia Press, 1994.

———. "Philanthropy and the Black Scholar: The Case of Horace Mann Bond." *The Journal of Negro Education* 58 (1989): 478–493.

————. *The Rise and Fall of a University President: Horace Mann Bond and Lincoln University, 1945–1957*. Atlanta, GA: Georgia State University Press, 1987.

Charles P. Bowles

Primary

The Unfinished Pyramid. Nashville, TN: Parthenon Press, 1967.

Chester Bowles

Primary

Africa's Challenge to America. Berkley, CA: University of California Press, 1956.

The Conscience of a Liberal. New York, NY: Harper and Row, 1962.

The New Dimensions of Peace. New York, NY: Harper & Brothers, 1955.

Promises to Keep: My Years in Public Life 1941–1969. New York, NY: Harper and Row, 1971.

A View from New Delhi: Selected Speeches and Writings, 1963–1969. New Haven, CT: Yale University Press, 1969.

Secondary

Dauer, Richard P. *A North-South Mind in an East-West World: Chester Bowles and the Making of United States Cold War Foreign Policy, 1951–1969*. Westport, CT: Greenwood, 2005.

Schaffer, Howard B. *Chester Bowles: New Dealer in the Cold War*. Cambridge, MA: Harvard University Press, 1993.

Sarah Patton Boyle

Primary

The Back Together Heart. New York, NY: Forward Movement Publications, 1966.

The Desegregated Heart: A Virginian's Stand in Times of Transition. New York, NY: William Morrow, 1964.

The Desert Blooms: A Personal Adventure in Growing Old Creatively. Nashville, TN: Abingdon Press, 1983.

For Human Beings Only. New York, NY: Seabury Press, 1964.

Secondary

Egerton, John. *A Mind to Stay Here: Profiles from the South*. New York: Macmillan, 1970.

Hobson, Fred. *But Now I See: The White Southern Racial Conversion Narrative*. Baton Rouge, LA: Louisiana State University Press, 1999.

Dierenfield, Kathleen M. "One Desegregated Hearth: Sarah Patton Boyle and the Crusade for Civil Rights in Virginia." *Virginia Magazine of History and Biography* 104 (1996): 251–284.

Ritterhouse, Jennifer. "Speaking of Race: Sarah Patton Boyle and the 'T. J. Sellers Course for Backward Southern Whites.'" In *Sex, Love, Race: Crossing Boundaries in North American History*. Ed., Martha Hodes. New York, NY: New York University Press, 1999.

J.R. Brokhoff

Primary

Advent and Event. Lima, OH: CSS Publishing, 1980.

As One with Authority. Luton, UK: Good News Books, 1989.

The Case of the Missing Body: Messages from the Gospel Lessons of the Easter Season, Series C. Lima, OH: CSS Publishing, 1982.

Christian Strategy. Philadelphia, PA: Muhlenberg Press, 1954.

Cross Purposes: Sermons for Lent and Holy Week. Lima, OH: CSS Publishing, 1976.

Defending My Faith. Philadelphia, PA: Lutheran Church Press, 1966.

Grace Words from the Cross. Lima, OH: CSS Publishing, 1991.

If Your Dearest Should Die. Lima, OH: CSS Publishing, 1987.

Introductions to the Lessons. Austin, TX: Church Management, 1992.

Jesus . . . Who? Lima, OH: CSS Publishing, 1977.

Lectionary Preaching Workbook: Revised for Use with Common, Episcopal, Lutheran, and Roman Catholic Lectionaries. Lima, OH: CSS Publishing, 1994.

Lectionary Preaching Workbook: Series IV Cycle A. Lima, OH: CSS Publishing, 1992.

Lectionary Preaching Workbook Series B: Revised for Use with Lutheran and Common. Rev. ed. Lima OH: CSS Publishing, 1984.

Lent: A Time of Tears. Lima, OH: CSS Publishing, 1984.

Luther Lives! Preaching Resources for the 500th Anniversary of Martin Luther's Birth 1483–1983. Lima, OH: CSS Publishing, 1983.

Old Truths for New Times. Lima, OH: CSS Publishing, 1983.

Pray Like Jesus: An Exploration in Prayer P Discussion. Lima, OH: CSS Publishing, 1995.

Pray Like Jesus: Sermons and Bible Study On Prayer. Lima, OH: CSS   Publishing, 1995.

Preaching the Miracles: Cycle C. Lima, OH: CSS Publishing, 1992.

Preaching the Parables. Lima, OH: CSS Publishing, 2002.

Preaching the Parables: Cycle A Texts. Lima, OH: CSS Publishing, 1989.

Preaching the Parables: Cycle C Texts from Common, Lutheran and Roman Catholic. Lima, OH: CSS Publishing, 1988.

Preaching the Parables Series B. Lima, OH: CSS Publishing, 1987.

Read And Live: A Study Dealing With How to Use the Bible. Philadelphia, PA: Muhlenberg Press, 1953.

Renewal of the New: Sermons for Sundays after Pentecost Second Half: Cycle B First Lesson Texts. Lima, OH: CSS Publishing, 1990.

Table for Lovers. Lima, OH: CSS Publishing, 1975.

This is Life. Old Tappan, NJ: Fleming H. Revell, 1959.

This is the Church. Philadelphia PA: Lutheran Church Press, 1964.

This You Can Believe: Faith Seeking Understanding. Lima, OH: CSS Publishing, 2001.

This You Can Believe, a New Look at the Apostle's Creed Leader's Guide and Participant's Book. Lima, OH: CSS Publishing, 1994.

Why? The Weekend Church School Series, Grade X. Philadelphia, PA: Muhlenberg Press, 1952.

Wrinkled Wrappings: Sermons for Advent and Christmas. Lima, OH: CSS Publishing, 1999.

with Barbara Brokhoff. *Faith Alive.* Lima, OH: CSS Publishing, 1978.

James R. Bullock

Primary

Heritage and Hope: A Story of Presbyterians in Florida. Orlando, FL.: Synod of Florida, 1987.

Whatever Became of Salvation? Atlanta, GA: John Knox Press, 1979.

Will D. Campbell

Primary

". . . and the Criminals with Him . . ." Luke 23:33: A First Person Book About Prisons. Costa Mesa, CA: Paulist Press, 1972.

And Also With You: Duncan Gray & the American Dilemma. Franklin, TN: Providence House Publishing, 1997.

Bluebirds Always Come on Sunday (Father Thyme). Franklin, TN: Providence House Publishing, 1997.

Brother to a Dragonfly. New York, NY: Seabury Press, 1977.

Cecelia's Sin. Macon, GA: Mercer University Press, 1993.

Chester & Chun Ling. Nashville, TN: Abingdon Press, 1989.

The Convention: A Parable. Atlanta, GA: Peachtree Publishers, 1988.

Covenant: Faces, Voices, Places. Atlanta, GA: Peachtree Publishers, 1989.

The Failure and the Hope: Essays of Southern Churchmen. Ed., Will D. Campbell. Grand Rapids, MI: Eerdmans, 1972.

"The Faith of a Fatalist." *New South* 23 (1968): 53–57.

Forty Acres and a Goat: A Memoir. Reprint ed. Oxford, MS: Jefferson Press, 2002.

The Glad River. Macon, GA: Smyth & Helwys Publishers, 2005.

"If We Should Get Serious." *Katallagete* 1 (1967–68): 1–2.

"Law and Love in Lowndes." *Katallagete* 1 (1965): 11–14.

"Milestones into Millstones." *Katallagete* 1 (1966–67): 2–4.

The Pear Tree That Bloomed in the Fall. Franklin, TN: Providence House Publishing, 1996.

Providence. Atlanta, GA: Longstreet Press, 1992.

Race and the Renewal of the Church. Philadelphia, PA: Westminster Press, 1962.

Robert G. Clark's Journey to the House: A Black Politician's Story. Jackson, MS: University Press of Mississippi, 2003.

"The Role of Religious Organization in the Desegregation Controversy." *Union Seminary Quarterly Review* 36 (1961): 187–196.

"The Sit-Ins: Passive Resistance or Civil Disobedience?" *Social Action* 27 (1961): 14–18.

Soul among Lions: Musings of a Bootleg Preacher. Louisville, KY: Presbyterian Publishing, 1999.

The Stem of Jesse: The Costs of Community at a 1960's Southern School. Macon, GA: Mercer University Press, 1995.

Sugah and Doops (Father Thyme). Franklin, TN: Providence House Publishing, 1997.

"Vocation as Grace." *Katallagete* 4 (1972): 80–86.

"Which Way for Southern Churches: Footwashing or the Hermeneutic?" *Katallagete* 1 (1966): 1–6.

"The World of the Redneck." *Katallagete* 5 (1974): 34–40.

with James Holloway. "Can There Be a Crusade for Christ?" *Katallagete* 4 (1972): 2–6.

with James Holloway. "An Open Letter to Billy Graham." *Katallagete* 3 (1971): 1–2.

with James Holloway. "The Good News from God in Jesus is Freedom to the Prisoners." *Katallagete* 4 (1972): 2–5.

with James Holloway. "Our Grade is 'F.'" *Katallagete* 2 (1970): 3–10.

with James Y. Holloway. *Up to Our Steeples in Politics,* 2d ed. Eugene, OR: Wipf & Stock Publishers, 2005.

Secondary

Egerton, John. *A Mind to Stay Here: Profiles from the South*. New York: Macmillan, 1970.

Hobson, Fred. *But Now I See: The White Southern Racial Conversion Narrative*. Baton Rouge, LA: Louisiana State University Press, 1999.

Connelly, Thomas L. *Will Campbell and the Soul of the South*. New York, NY: Continuum, 1982.

Hawkins, Merrill M. Jr. *Will Campbell: Radical Prophet of the South*. Macon, GA: Mercer University Press, 1997.

Powledge, Fred. *Free At Last: The Civil Rights Movement and the People Who Made It*. Boston, MA: Little Brown and Company, 1991.

Paul N. Carnes

Primary

For Freedom and Belief: A Manual for Unitarians. Boston, MA: Beacon Press, 1952.

Longing of the Heart: Prayers and Invocations. Boston, MA: Unitarian Universalist Association, 1979.

Colbert S. Cartwright

Primary

Candles of Grace: Disciples Worship in Perspective. Atlanta, GA: Chalice Press, 1992.

Chalice Worship. Atlanta, GA: Chalice Press, 1997.

He Taught Them, Saying. St. Louis, MO: The Bethany Press, 1956.

The Lord's Prayer Comes Alive. St. Louis, MO: The Bethany Press, 1973.

People of the Chalice: Disciples of Christ in Faith and Practice. Atlanta, GA: Chalice Press, 1987.

with Susan L. Adams, & Daniel B. Merrick. *Chalice Hymnal: Worship Leader's Companion*. Atlanta, GA: Chalice Press, 1998.

Secondary

Campbell, Ernest Q., and Thomas F. Pettigrew. *Christians in Racial Crisis: A Study of Little Rock's Ministry*. Washington, D. C.: Public Affairs Press, 1959.

Goddard, Terry D. "White Southern Social Justice Advocate: The Rev. Colbert S. Cartwright and the Little Rock School Crisis." *The Pulaski County Historical Review* 51 (2003): 30–42.

George A. Chauncey

Primary

Black Power. Louisville, KY: Presbyterian Church, 1967.

Decisions! Decisions! Louisville, KY: John Knox Press, 1972.

Evangelism: Communicating the Gospel: A Leader's Guide for a Course on Evangelism. Glen Allen, VA: Division of Evangelism, Board of Church Extension, 1960.

How to Go to School and Learn at the Same Time. Louisville, KY: John Knox Press, 1972.

Serving God Through Worship and Work: Five Bible Studies. Louisville, KY: Board of Women's Work, Presbyterian Church, 1964.

Theological Reflections on an Ecumenical Effort to Influence Public Policy. Washington, D.C.: Center for Theology and Public Policy, 1978.

Violence in the Streets and the Judgment of God. Louisville, KY: Presbyterian Church, 1967.

The Worship and Service of God: Three Bible Studies. Louisville, KY: Office of Women, General Assembly Mission Board, Presbyterian Church, 1982.

LeRoy Collins

Primary

The Civil Rights Movement in Florida and the United States: Historical and Contemporary Perspectives. Tallahassee, FL: Father and Son, 1989.

Forerunners Courageous: Stories of Frontier Florida. Tallahassee, FL: Colcade Publishers, 1971.

"Foreword." In *Your Public Relations Are Showing,* John Newton Baker. New York, NY: Twayne Publishers, 1958, n/p.

Freedom and Responsibility in Broadcasting. Evanston, IL: Northwestern University Press, 1961.

The Mazes of Modern Government: the States, the Legislature, the Bureaucracy, the Court: An Occasional Paper in the Role of the Political Process in the Free Society. Santa Barbara, CA: Center for the Study of Democratic Institutions, 1964.

The South and the Nation. Atlanta, GA: Southern Regional Council, 1960.

Secondary

Chappell, David L. *Inside Agitators: White Southerners in the Civil Rights Movement.* Baltimore, MD: Johns Hopkins University Press, 1994.

Coffy, Cecil. *Florida's LeRoy Collins.* Nampa, ID: Pacific Press, 1958.

Cornett, John Michael. "A Study of Disposition in Selected Speeches of LeRoy Collins on Race Relations 1954–1964." M.A. Thesis, Florida State University, 1965.

Karl, Anne Marie M. *Governor LeRoy Collins: Lesson in Leadership and Citizenship.* Tallahassee, FL: Florida Law Related Education Association, 1995.

Lucoff, Manny. *Leroy Collins and the National Association of Broadcasters: Experiment in the Public Interest.* Iowa City, IA: Lucoff, 1971.

Norris, Hoke, ed. *We Dissent.* New York: St. Martin's Press, 1962.

Wagy, Tom. *Governor LeRoy Collins: Spokesman of the New South.* Tuscaloosa, AL: University of Alabama Press, 1985.

David G. Colwell

Primary

"Toward More Effective Community Action: The Minister Guides the Manager." *The Harvard Business School Bulletin* 35 (1959): 17–23.

James McBride Dabbs

Primary

Civil Rights in Recent Southern Fiction. Atlanta, GA: Southern Regional Council, 1969.

"From the President." *Katallagete* 1 (1966–67): n.p.

Haunted By God: The Cultural and Religious Experience of the South. Richmond, VA: John Knox Press, 1972.

The Road Home. Philadelphia, PA: The Christian Education Press, 1960.

"Robert Frost, Poet of Action." *The English Journal* 25 (1936): 443–451.

"Southern Church Men: Fellowship to Committee." *Katallagete* 1 (1965): 7–11.

The Southern Heritage: A Classic Statement of the Enlightened Southern View of Race Relations in the Long Perspective of History. New York, NY: Alfred A. Knopf, 1958.

"Southern Indirection: the Southerner and Time." *Katallagete* 1 (1965): 22–23.

"The Tragic Sense of Life in the South." *Katallagete* 1 (1967): 37–38.

Who Speaks for the South? New York, NY: Funk & Wagnalls, 1967.

Secondary

Egerton, John. *A Mind to Stay Here: Profiles from the South.* New York: Macmillan, 1970.

Hobson, Fred. *But Now I See: The White Southern Racial Conversion Narrative.* Baton Rouge, LA: Louisiana State University Press, 1999.

Hobson, Fred. *Tell About the South: The Southern Rage to Explain.* Baton Rouge, LA: Louisiana State University Press, 1983.

Johnson, Thomas Linderman. "James McBride Dabbs: A Life Story." Ph.D. diss., University of South Carolina, 1980.

Martin, Neal A. *The Library of James McBride Dabbs: An Inventory.* Florence, SC: James A. Rogers Library, Francis Marion College, 1980.

Norris, Hoke, ed. *We Dissent.* New York: St. Martin's Press, 1962.

Jonathan Daniels

Secondary

Eagles, Charles W. *Outside Agitator: Jon Daniels and the Civil Rights Movement in Alabama.* Chapel Hill, NC: University of North Carolina Press, 1993.

A. Powell Davies and Muriel A. Davies

Primary

American Destiny. Boston, MA: Beacon Press, 1965

America's Real Religion. Boston, MA: Beacon Press, 1965.

The Faith of an Unrepentant Liberal. Boston, MA: Beacon Press, 1965.

The First Christian. Seattle, WA: Signet, 1957.

The Language of the Heart: A Book of Prayers. New York, NY: Farrar, Straus and Cudahy, 1956.

The Man from Nazareth. Summit, NJ: The Community Church of Summit, 1937.

Man's Vast Future: A Definition of Democracy. New York, NY: Farrar, Straus & Young, 1951.

The Meaning of the Dead Sea Scrolls. Seattle, WA: Signet, 1956.

The Temptation to Be Good: A Book of Unconventional Sermons. New York, NY: Farrar, Straus & Young, 1952.

The Ten Commandments. Seattle, WA: Signet, 1956.

The Urge to Persecute. Boston, MA: The Beacon Press, 1953.

with F. Forrester Church. *Without Apology: Collected Meditations on Liberal Religion.* Boston, MA: Skinner House Books, 1998.

Secondary

Douglas, William O. *The Mind and Faith of A. Powell Davies.* New York, NY: Doubleday, 1959.

Marshall, George N. *A. Powell Davies and His Times.* Boston, MA: Skinner House Books, 1990.

Dave Dennis

Secondary

Erenrich, Susie, ed. *Freedom is a Constant Struggle: An Anthology of the Mississippi Civil Rights Movement.* Montgomery, AL: Black Belt Press, 1999.

Fairclough, Adam. *Race and Democracy: The Civil Rights Struggle in Louisiana 1915–1972*. Athens, GA: University of Georgia Press, 1999.

Umoja, Akinyele K. "1964: The Beginning of the End of Nonviolence in the Mississippi Freedom Movement." *Radical History Review* 85 (2003): 201–226.

P.D. East

Primary

Editorial Reprints from the Petal Paper, Petal, Mississippi, and Personal Comments. Hattiesburg, MS: P. D. East, 1959,

The Magnolia Jungle: The Life, Times, and Education of a Southern Editor. New York, NY: Simon & Schuster, 1960.

Secondary

Huey, Gary. *Rebel with a Cause: P. D. East, Southern Liberalism, and the Civil Rights Movement.* Wilmington, DE: Scholarly Resources, 1985.

Francis Gerald Ensley

Primary

John Wesley, Evangelist. Nashville, TN: Methodist Evangelistic Materials, 1958.

The Marks of Christian Education. Peterborough, UK: Methodist Publishing House, 1958.

Paul's Letters to Local Churches. New York, NY: Methodist Church, 1956.

Persons Can Change. New York, NY: Abingdon Press, 1964.

J. Claude Evans

Secondary

Lechtreck, Elaine A. *White Pastors and the Civil Rights Movement: South Carolina's Courageous Few.* Copyright by the author, 2003.

Theodore Parker Ferris

Primary

Book of Prayer for Everyman. Greenwich, CT: Seabury Press, 1962.

For Adults Only. Cincinnati, OH: Forward Movement Publications, 1965.

Go Tell the People. New York, NY: Scribners, 1951.

The Image of God. New York, NY: Oxford University Press, 1965.

The New Life. Greenwich, CT: Seabury Press, 1961.

A Positive Way: Christian Affirmations on Faith and Life. Cincinnati, OH: Church Congress of the Episcopal Church in the United States, 1943.

Selected Sermons. Boston, MA: Trinity Church, 1976.

The Story of Jesus. New York, NY: Oxford University Press, 1953.

This Created World. New York, NY: Harper Brothers, 1944.

This is the Day. River Grove, IL: Wilcox and Follett, 1951.

What Jesus Did. New York, NY: Oxford University Press, 1963.

When I Became a Man. New York, NY: Oxford University Press, 1957.

D. Perry Ginn

Primary

A Study of the Old Testament. Nashville, TN: Broadman Press, 1963.

Frank Graham

Primary

The Faith and Hope of an American. New York, NY: Spiral, 1952.

Secondary

Ashby, Warren. *Frank Porter Graham: A Southern Liberal.* Winston-Salem, NC: J. F. Blair, 1980.

Drescher, John. *Triumph of Good Will: How Terry Sanford Beat a Champion of Segregation and Reshaped the South.* Jackson, MS: University Press of Mississippi, 2000.

Egerton, John. *Speak Now Against the Day: The Generation Before the Civil Rights Movement in the South.* Chapel Hill, NC: University of North Carolina Press, 1995.

Pleasants, Julian M. *Frank Porter Graham and the 1950 Senate Race in North Carolina.* Chapel Hill, NC: University of North Carolina Press, 1990.

Schulman, Bruce J. *From Cotton Belt to Sunbelt: Federal Policy, Economic Development, and the Transformation of the South, 1938–1980.* Durham, NC: Duke University Press, 1994.

Duncan M. Gray

Secondary

Barrett, Russell, H. *Integration at Ole Miss.* Chicago, IL: Quadrangle, 1965.

Shattuck, Gardiner H. *Episcopalians and Race: Civil War to Civil Rights.* Lexington, KY: University Press of Kentucky, 2000.

Dick Gregory

Primary

Callus on My Soul: A Memoir. Athens, GA: Longstreet Press, 2000.

Code Name Zorro. New York, NY: Pocket Books, 1978.

Dick Gregory's Political Primer. Ed. James R. McGraw. New York, NY: Harper & Row, 1972.

From the Back of the Bus. New York, NY: Avon Books, 1966.

Nigger: An Autobiography. New York, NY: Pocketbooks, 1967.

No More Lies: The Myth and the Reality of American History. Ed. James R. McGraw. New York, NY: Harper & Row, 1971.

"Non-Violence from Strategy to Karma." *Katallagete* 6 (1974): 12–14.

The Shadow That Scares Me. New York, NY: Pocket Books, 1968.

Up From Nigger. New York, NY: Stein & Day, 1976.

What's Happening? New York, NY: E.P. Dutton, 1965.

Write Me In! New York, NY: Bantam Books, 1968.

with Mark Lane. *Murder in Memphis: The FBI and the Assassination of Martin Luther King.* New York, NY: Thunder's Mouth Press, 1993.

Secondary

Ellis, Catherine and Stephen Smith, eds. *Say It Plain: A Century of Great African American Speeches.* New York, NY: New Press, 2005.

Green, Robert L. *Dick Gregory, Daring Black Leader.* Arlington, TX: Franklin Publishing, 1974.

Nachman, Gerald, ed. *Seriously Funny: The Rebel Comedians of the 1950's and 1960's.* New York, NY: Pantheon Books, 2003.

Fannie Lou Hamer

Primary

"Life in Mississippi" (interview with J. H. O'Dell). *Freedomways* 5 (1965): 231–42.

"Sick and Tired of Being Sick and Tired." *Katallagete* 1 (1968): 19–26.

To Praise Our Bridges. Jackson, MS: KIPCO, 1967.

Secondary

Bramlet-Solomon, Sharon. "Civil Rights Vanguard in the Deep South: Newspaper Portrayal of Fannie Lou Hamer, 1964–1977." *Journalism Quarterly* 68 (1991): 515–21.

Bridges, Flora Wilson. *Resurrection Song: African-American Spirituality.* Maryknoll, NY: Orbis Books, 2001.

Carnes, Mark, ed. *Invisible Giants: Fifty Americans Who Shaped the Nation but Missed the History Books*. New York, NY: Oxford University Press, 2002.

Carter, Stephen L. *God's Name in Vain: The Wrongs and Rights of Religion in Politics*. New York, NY: Basic Books, 2000.

Chalmers, David Mark. "'A Tremor in the Middle of the Iceberg—From a Stone that the Builders Rejected': Black and White in Mississippi." *Reviews in American History 23* (1995): 535–44.

Chappell, David L. *A Stone of Hope: Prophetic Religion and the Death of Jim Crow*. Chapel Hill, NC: University of North Carolina Press, 2004.

Egerton, John. *A Mind to Stay Here: Profiles from the South*. New York: Macmillan, 1970.

Ellis, Catherine and Stephen Smith, eds. *Say it Plain: A Century of Great African American Speeches*. New York, NY: New Press, 2005.

Hamlet, Janice D. "Fannie Lou Hamer: The Unquenchable Spirit of the Civil Rights Movement." *Journal of Black Studies 26* (1996): 560–576.

Hu-DeHart, Evelyn. "Writing and Rewriting Women of Color." *Journal of Women's History 13* (2001): 224–33.

Jordan, June. *Fannie Lou Hamer*. New York, NY: Crowell, 1972.

Kling, Susan. *Fannie Lou Hamer: A Biography*. Chicago, IL: Women for Racial and Economic Equality, 1979.

Lee, Chana Kai. "Anger, Memory, and Personal Power: Fannie Lou Hamer and Civil Rights Leadership." In *Sisters in the Struggle: African American Women in the Civil Rights-Black Power Movement*. Eds. Bettye Collier-Thomas and V. P. Franklin. New York, NY: New York University Press, 2001, 139–70.

Lee, Chana Kai. *For Freedom's Sake: The Life of Fannie Lou Hamer*. Champaign, IL: University of Illinois Press, 1999.

Litwin, Laura B. *Fannie Lou Hamer: Fighting for the Right to Vote*. Berkeley Heights, NJ: Enslow Publishers, 2002.

Marsh, Charles P. *God's Long Summer: Stories of Faith and Civil Rights*. Princeton, NJ: Princeton University Press,

Mills, Kay. *This Little Light of Mine: The Life of Fannie Lou Hamer*. New York, NY: Plume Books, 1994.

Nies, Judith. *Nine Women: Portraits from the American Radical Tradition*. Berkeley, CA: University of California Press, 2002.

Reed, Linda. "Fannie Lou Hamer: New Ideas for the Civil Rights Movement and American Democracy." In *The Role of Ideas in the Civil Rights South: Essays*. Ed. Ted Ownby. Jackson, MS: University Press of Mississippi, 2002.

Ross, Rosetta. *Witnessing and Testifying: Black Women, Religion, and Civil Rights*. Minneapolis, MN: Fortress Press, 2003.

Smith, Jessie C. *Epic lives: One Hundred Black Women Who Made a Difference*. Detroit, MI: Visible Ink Press, 1993.

Young, Billie Jean. *Fear Not the Fall: Fannie Lou Hamer: This Little Light.* Montgomery, AL: NewSouth Books, 2004.

Edler Hawkins

Secondary

Adair, Thelma C.D. "I Remember Edler." *Church & Society* 78 (1987): 5–9.

Cave, Clarence L. "Pastor of St Augustine Church, Leader in the Community." *Church & Society* 78 (1987): 26–46.

Cave, Clarence L., J. Oscar McCloud, and Robert T. Newbold, Jr. "The Witness of a Prophet." *Church & Society* 78 (1987): 47–59.

Choy, Virstan, compl. "Testimonies of Friends and Disciples." *Church & Society* 78 (1987): 82–99.

Gunn, Lenton, compl. "Edler Hawkins Speaks." *Church & Society* 78 (1987): 100–118.

Hanson, Geddes W. "Edler G. Hawkins: The Princeton Years." *Church & Society* 78 (1987): 74–81.

Livingston, Michael, E. "Done in Love: Edler G. Hawkins." *Church & Society* 78 (1987): 10–25.

Ramos, Jovelino P. "A Tribute from the Council on Church and Race." *Church & Society* 78 (1987): 3–4

"Strong Stands." *TIME* Magazine 81 (1963): 58–60.

Thompson, William P. "Edler G. Hawkins: Ecumenist." *Church & Society* 78 (1987): 68–73.

Wilmore, Gayraud. "CORAR: The First Five Years." *Church & Society* 78 (1987): 60–67.

Aaron Henry

Primary

"Foreword." In *A Black Physician's Story: Bringing Hope in Mississippi*, Douglas L. Conner with John S. Marszalek. Jackson, MS: University Press of Mississippi, 1985.

with Constance Curry. *Aaron Henry: The Fire Ever Burning.* Jackson, MS: University Press of Mississippi, 2000.

Secondary

Dittmer, John. *Local People: The Struggle for Civil Rights in Mississippi.* Urbana, IL: University of Illinois Press, 1995.

Sinsheimer, Joseph A. "The Freedom Vote of 1963: New Strategies of Racial Protest in Mississippi." *The Journal of Southern History* 55 (1989): 217–244.

Theodore Hesburgh:

Primary

And They Called it the University of Notre Dame du Lac. Notre Dame, IN: National Campaign Committee, Campaign for Notre Dame, 1979.

The Challenge and Promise of a Catholic University. Ed., Theodore Hesburgh. Notre Dame, IN: University of Notre Dame Press, 1994.

Directory: Theodore M. Hesburgh Civil Rights Collection. William R. Valentine, comp. Notre Dame, IN: Notre Dame Law School, Center for Civil Rights, 1976.

Foreign Policy & Morality: Framework for a Moral Audit. New York, NY: Council on Religion and International Affairs, 1979.

"Foreword." In *Catholic Education Faces its Future,* Neil G. McCluskey. Garden City, NY: Doubleday, 1968.

"Foreword." In *Deepening the American Dream: Reflections on the Inner Life and Spirit of Democracy,* Robert Bellah. San Francisco, CA: Jossey-Bass, 2005.

"Foreword." In *Revolution from the Heart,* Niall O'Brien. New York, NY: Oxford University Press, 1987.

"Foreword." In *The Intellectual Appeal of Catholicism and the Idea of a Catholic University*, Mark W. Roche. Notre Dame, IN: University of Notre Dame Press, 1994.

God and the World of Man, 2d ed. Notre Dame, IN: University of Notre Dame Press, 1960.

God, Country, Notre Dame: The Autobiography of Theodore M. Hesburgh. Notre Dame, IN: University of Notre Dame Press, 2000.

The Hesburgh Papers: Higher Values in Higher Education. Kansas City, MO: Andrews and McMeel, 1979.

The Humane Imperative: A Challenge for the Year 2000. New Haven, CT: Yale University Press, 1974.

Letters to Service Women. Washington, DC: National Catholic Community Service, 1952.

The Nuclear Dilemma: The Greatest Moral Problem of All Time. New York, NY: Carnegie Council on Ethics and International Affairs, 1989.

"On the Streets of a Fragile World." In *Walking with God in a Fragile World.* Eds., James Langford and Leroy S. Rouner. Lanham, MD: Rowman & Littlefield, 2003.

"Preface." In *Veil and Cowl: Writings from the World of Monks and Nuns.* Ed. James B. Simpson. Chicago, IL: Ivan R. Dee, 1994.

"The Relation of the Sacramental Characters of Baptism and Confirmation to the Lay Apostolate." Ph.D. diss., Catholic University of America, 1946.

"Roots and Reform." In *Why am I Still a Catholic?* Eds. Kevin Ryan and Marilyn Ryan. New York, NY: Riverhead Books, 1998.

Travels with Ted and Ned. Ed. Jerry Reedy. New York, NY: Doubleday, 1992.

Secondary

Ames, Charlotte A., and Thomas Stritch. *Theodore M. Hesburgh: A Bio-Bibliography.* Westport, CT: Greenwood Press, 1989.

Connelly, Joel R. *Hesburgh's Notre Dame: Triumph in Transition.* Portland, OR: Hawthorne Books, 1972.

Gallin, Alice. "Hesburgh: A Biography." *The Catholic Historical Review* 85 (1999): 673–674.

Karam, Thomas J. "A Rhetorical Analysis of Selected Speeches on Higher Education by Theodore M. Hesburgh." Ph.D. diss., Louisiana State University, 1979.

Lungren, John C. *Hesburgh of Notre Dame: Priest, Educator, Public Servant.* Lanham, MD: Sheed and Ward, 1987.

Mueller, Thomas J. and Charlotte A. Ames, compls. *Commitment, Compassion, Consecration: Inspirational Quotes of Theodore M. Hesburgh, C.S.C.* Huntington, IN: Our Sunday Visitor Publishing Division, 1989.

O'Brien, Michael. *Hesburgh: A Biography.* Washington, D.C.: The Catholic University of America Press, 1998.

Padilla, Arthur. *Portraits in Leadership: Six Extraordinary University Presidents.* Westport, CT: Praeger, 2005.

Pruett, Robert E. *Words Have Meaning: The Selected Speeches of Father Theodore Hesburgh.* Bloomington, IN: AuthorHouse, 2002.

Haywood Hill

Primary

This I Believe. Atlanta, GA: Southern Regional Council, 1961.

Secondary

Heimburger, Susan West. "Of Faith and Fact: Haywood N. Hill's 'This I Believe.'" *Young Scholars in Writing: Undergraduate Research in Writing and Rhetoric* 2 (2004): 29–37.

TRM Howard:

Primary

"Foreword." In *Time Bomb,* Olive Arnold Adams. Mound Bayou, MS: Mississippi Regional Council of Negro Leadership, 1956, 6–7.

Secondary

Beito, David T. "Black Fraternal Hospitals in the Mississippi Delta, 1942–1967." *The Journal of Southern History* 65 (1999): 109–40.

Beito, David T., and Linda Royster Beito. "T.R.M. Howard: Pragmatism Over Strict Integrationist Ideology in the Mississippi Delta, 1942–1954." In *Before Brown: Civil Rights and White Backlash in the Modern South*. Ed. Glenn Feldman. Tuscaloosa, AL: University of Alabama Press, 2004.

Dittmer, John. *Local People: The Struggle for Civil Rights in Mississippi*. Champaign, IL: University of Illinois Press, 1995.

Duncan Howlett and the Estate of Duncan Howlett

Primary

An Interpretation of Jesus the Man. Washington, D.C.: Unitarian Church, 1943.

The Consecration Ceremonies of Life. Washington, D.C.: All Souls Church, Unitarian, 1963.

The Conspiracy Against the Poor. Washington, D.C.: All Souls Church, Unitarian, 1965.

The Critical Way in Religion. New York, NY: Prometheus Books, 1984.

The Essenes and Christianity: An Interpretation of the Dead Sea Scrolls. New York, NY: Harper and Brothers, 1957.

The Fatal Flaw: At the Heart of Religious Liberalism. Amherst, NY: Prometheus Books, 1994.

The Future of Man: A Sermon. Washington, D.C.: All Souls Church, Unitarian, 1964.

The Fourth American Faith. New York, NY: Harper and Row, 1964.

Is Unitarianism Really Different?: A Sermon (Washington Unitarian Pulpit Subscription Series 1964–65). Washington, D.C.: All Souls Church, Unitarian, 1964.

John Fitzgerald Kennedy Memorial Address, Sunday, November, 24, 1963. Washington, D.C.: All Souls Church, Unitarian, 1963.

The Legacy of Servetus: The 400th Anniversary of the Great Controversy with Calvin. Washington, D.C.: Division of Publications, American Unitarian Association, 1947.

Man against the Church: The Struggle to Free Man's Religious Spirit. Boston, MA: Beacon Press, 1954.

Man's Search for Meaning. Washington, D.C.: All Souls Church, Unitarian, 1962.

No Greater Love: The James Reeb Story. Boston, MA: Skinner House Books, 1993.

The Unitarian Movement: Projections and Realities. Washington, D.C.: Unitarian Information Department of the General Assembly of Unitarian and Free Christian Churches, 1985.

What about the Dead Sea Scrolls? Boston, MA: First Church in Boston, 1955.

What is Unitarianism? Boston, MA: First Church in Boston, 1958.

The World Around Us. Boston, MA: First Church in Boston, 1955.

James Hudson

Primary

Diamond Anniversary Symposium. Edited by Charles U. Smith, James Hudson, and Charles J. Stanley. Tallahassee, FL: Florida A&M University, 1962.

Secondary

Rabby, Glenda Alice. *The Pain and the Promise: The Struggle for Civil Rights in Tallahassee, Florida.* Athens, GA: University of Georgia Press, 1999.

William Lloyd Imes

Primary

The Black Pastures, an American Pilgrimage in Two Centuries; Essays and Sermons. Nashville, TN: Hemphill Press, 1957.

with Paul F. Swarthout, James H. Burckes, Artemas P. Goodwin, R. Earl Pettingill, William H. Thomas, Josheph Feyrer, and Frank E. Reed. *The Hills Beyond the Hills.* Utica, NY: North Country Books, 1971.

Secondary

Jenness, Mary. "A City Pastor." In *Twelve Negro Americans.* Freeport, NY: Books for Libraries Press, 1969, 35–52.

Wilson, Frank T. "William Lloyd Imes—Urban Pastor/ Educator." *Journal of Presbyterian History* 51 (1973): 359–361.

Mordecai Johnson

Primary

An Address on Abraham Lincoln. Manchester, CT: Allied Printers, 1959.

Opening Address of Mordecai W. Johnson: First Negro President of Howard University, at the beginning of the Autumn Quarter, Wednesday, September 29, 1926. Washington, D.C.: Washington Tribune, 1926.

Secondary

Georgiady, Nicholas Peter. *Mordecai Johnson: American Negro Scholar.* Arlington, TX: Franklin Publishing, 1969.

McKinney, Richard I. "Mordecai Johnson: An Early Pillar of African-American Higher Education." *The Journal of Blacks in Higher Education* 27 (2000): 99–104.

———. *Mordecai: The Man and His Message, the Story of Mordecai Wyatt Johnson.* Washington, D.C.: Howard University Press, 1997.

Edwin King

Primary

"Foreword." In John R. Salter, Jr. *Jackson, Mississippi: An American Chronicle of Struggle and Schism.* Hicksville, NY: Exposition Press, 1979.

"Of Elections in India and in the South." *New South* 26 (1971): 70–74.

"SNCC and Dr. Lohia." *New South* 26 (1971): 57–62.

Secondary

Marsh, Charles. *God's Long Summer: Stories of Faith and Civil Rights.* Princeton, NJ: Princeton University Press, 1999.

Newman, Mark P. *Divine Agitators: The Delta Ministry and Civil Rights in Mississippi.* Athens, GA: University of Georgia Press, 2004.

Dr. Martin Luther King, Jr.

Primary

"Don't You Turn Back." *Liberation* 13 (1968): 13–15.

"Honoring Dr. Dubois." *Freedomways* 8 (1968): 104–111.

A Knock at Midnight: Inspiration from the Great Sermons of Martin Luther King, Jr. Eds. Clayborne Carson and Peter Holloran. New York, NY: Warner, 1998.

"Letter from Birmingham Jail." *Liberation* 8 (1963): 10–16, 23.

The Measure of a Man. Minneapolis, MN: Fortress Press, 1988.

"Never Let Them Rest." *Liberation* 13 (1968): 11–12.

"The Nobel Prize." *Liberation* 8 (1965): 28–29.

"Our Struggle." *Liberation* 1 (1956): 3–6.

The Papers of Martin Luther King, Jr. (5 volumes). Ed. Clayborne Carson. Berkeley, CA: University of California Press, 1992–2005.

"The Social Organization of Non-Violence." *Liberation* 4 (1959): 5–6.

Strength to Love. New York, NY: Pocket Books, 1963.

Stride Toward Freedom: The Montgomery Story. New York, NY: Harper & Row, 1958.

A Testament of Hope: The Essential Writings and Speeches of Martin Luther King, Jr., Ed., James Melvin Washington, San Francisco, CA: HarperSanFrancisco, 1986.

"A Time to Break Silence." *Freedomways* 7 (1967): 103–117.

"We Are Still Walking." *Liberation* 1 (1956): 6–9.

Where Do We Go From Here: Chaos or Community? Boston, MA: Beacon Press, 1968.

Why We Can't Wait. New York, NY: Harper & Row, 1964.

"Who Speaks for the South?" *Liberation* 3 (1958): 13–14.

Secondary

Albert, Peter J. and Ronald Hoffman, eds. *We Shall Overcome: Martin Luther King, Jr., and the Black Freedom Struggle.* New York, NY: Pantheon Books, 1990.

Baldwin, Lewis V. *Between Cross and Crescent: Christian and Muslim Perspectives on Malcolm and Martin.* Gainesville, FL: University Press of Florida, 2002.

———. *To Make the Wounded Whole: The Cultural Legacy of Martin Luther King, Jr.* Minneapolis, MN: Fortress Press, 1992.

Bass, S. Jonathan. *Blessed are the Peacemakers: Martin Luther King, Jr., Eight White Religious Leaders, and the "Letter from Birmingham Jail".* Baton Rouge, LA: Louisiana State University Press, 2001.

Bazelon, David L., Charles L. Black, Jr., Stanley H. Fuld, William T. Gossett, Earl Johnson, Jr., Louis Lusky, William D. Rogers, Albert J. Rosenthal, and J. Skelly Wright. "Symposium in Memory of Dr. Martin Luther King, Jr." *Columbia Law Review* 68 (1968): 1012–1048.

Beifuss, Joan Turner. *At the River I Stand: Memphis, the 1968 Strike, and Martin Luther King.* Brooklyn, NY: Carlson, 1985.

Berry, Edward I. "Doing Time: King's 'Letter from Birmingham Jail.'" *Rhetoric & Public Affairs* 8 (2005): 109–131.

Branch, Taylor. *At Canaan's Edge: America in the King Years, 1965–1968.* New York, NY: Simon & Schuster, 2006.

———. *Parting the Waters: America in the King Years, 1954–1963.* New York, NY: Simon & Schuster, 1989.

———. *Pillar of Fire: America in the King Years, 1963–65.* New York, NY: Simon & Schuster, 1998.

Burns, Stewart. *To the Mountaintop: Martin Luther King Jr.'s Sacred Mission to Save America, 1955–1968.* New York, NY: HarperSanFrancisco, 2004.

Calloway-Thomas, Carolyn and John Louis Lucaites, eds. *Martin Luther King, Jr. and the Power of Sermonic Discourse.* Tuscaloosa, AL: University of Alabama Press, 1993.

Carson, Clayborne and Kris Shephard, eds. *A Call to Conscience: The Landmark Speeches of Dr. Martin Luther King, Jr.* New York, NY: Warner Books, 2001.

Carson, Clayborne and Peter Holloran, eds. *A Knock at Midnight: Inspiration from the Great Sermons of Martin Luther King, Jr.* New York, NY: Warner Books, 1998.

Chappell, David L. "Religious Revivalism in the Civil Rights Movement." *African America Review* 36 (2002): 581–95.

Chernus, Ira. *American Nonviolence: The History of an Idea.* Maryknoll, NY: Orbis Books, 2004.

Colaiaco, James A. *Martin Luther King, Jr.: Apostle of Militant Nonviolence.* Reprint ed. New York, NY: Palgrave Macmillan, 1992.

Cook, Anthony E. "Beyond Critical Legal Studies: The Reconstructive Theology of Dr. Martin Luther King, Jr." *Harvard Law Review* 103 (1990): 985–1044.

Daynes, Gary. *Making Villains, Making Heroes: Joseph R. McCarthy, Martin Luther King, Jr., and the Politics of American Memory.* New York, NY: Garland, 1997.

Dyson, Michael Eric. *I May Not Get There With You: The True Martin Luther King, Jr.* New York, NY: Free Press, 2000.

Echols, James, ed. *I Have a Dream: Martin Luther King Jr. and the Future of Multicultural America.* Minneapolis, MN: Augsburg Fortress Publishers, 2004.

Ellis, Catherine and Stephen Smith, eds. *Say it Plain: A Century of Great African American Speeches.* New York, NY: New Press, 2005.

Erskine, Noel Leo. *King Among the Theologians.* Cleveland, OH: Pilgrim Press, 1994.

Frady, Marshall. *Martin Luther King, Jr.* New York, NY: Penguin Group, 2002.

Frank, Gerold. *An American Death: The True Story of the Assassination of Dr. Martin Luther King, Jr. and the Greatest Manhunt of our Time.* Garden City, NY: Doubleday, 1972.

Fulkerson, Richard P. "The Public Letter as Rhetorical Form: Structure, Logic and Style in King's 'Letter from Birmingham Jail.'" *Quarterly Journal of Speech* 65 (1979): 121–36.

Garrow, David J. *Bearing the Cross: Martin Luther King Jr., and the Southern Christian Leadership Conference.* New York, NY: William Morrow and Company, 1986.

———. *The FBI and Martin Luther King, Jr.: From "Solo" to Memphis.* New York, NY: W.W. Norton and Company, 1981.

———. "King's Plagiarism: Imitation, Insecurity, and Transformation." *The Journal of American History* 78 (1991): 86–92.

———. *Protest at Selma: Martin Luther King, Jr., and the Voting Rights Act of 1965.* New Haven, CT: Yale University Press, 1978.

Gregory, Dick and Mark Lane. *Murder in Memphis: The FBI and the Assassination of Martin Luther King.* New York, NY: Thunder's Mouth Press, 1993.

Hansen, Drew D. *The Dream: Martin Luther King, Jr., and the Speech that Inspired a Nation.* New York, NY: Ecco, 2003.

Hendrick, George. *Why Not Every Man?: African Americans and Civil Disobedience in the Quest for the Dream.* Chicago, IL: Ivan R. Dee, 2005.

Herman, A. L. *Community, Violence, and Peace: Aldo Leopold, Mohandas K. Gandhi, Martin Luther King, Jr., and Gautama the Buddha in the Twenty-First Century.* Albany, NY: State University of New York Press, 1998.

Hoffman, Scott W. "Holy Martin: The Overlooked Canonization of Dr. Martin Luther King, Jr." *Religion and American Culture* 10 (2000): 123–148.

Ivory, Luther D. *Toward a Theology of Radical Involvement: The Theological Legacy of Martin Luther King, Jr.* Nashville, TN: Abingdon Press, 1997.

King, Coretta Scott. *My Life with Martin Luther King, Jr.* New York, NY: Henry Holt, 1993.

King, Dexter Scott and Ralph Wiley. *Growing Up King: An Intimate Memoir.* New York, NY: Warner Books, 2003.

King, William, M. "The Reemerging Revolutionary Consciousness of the Reverend Dr. Martin Luther King, Jr., 1965–1968." *The Journal of Negro History* 71 (1986): 1–22.

Kirk-Duggan, Cheryl A. *Refiner's Fire: A Religious Engagement with Violence.* Minneapolis, MN: Augsburg Fortress Press, 2000.

Lischer, Richard. *The Preacher King: Martin Luther King, Jr. and the Word that Moved America.* New York, NY: Oxford University Press, 1995.

Lokos, Lionel. *House Divided: The Life and Legacy of Martin Luther King.* New Rochelle, NY: Arlington House, 1968.

Long, Michael G. *Against Us, But For Us: Martin Luther King, Jr. and the State.* Macon, GA: Mercer University Press, 2002.

McKnight, Gerald. *The Last Crusade: Martin Luther King, Jr., the FBI, and the Poor People's Campaign.* Boulder, CO: Westview Press, 1998.

Melanson, Philip H. *The MURKIN Conspiracy: An Investigation Into the Assassination of Dr. Martin Luther King, Jr.* New York, NY: Praeger, 1989.

Miller, Keith D. "Martin Luther King, Jr., and the Black Folk Pulpit." *The Journal of American History* 78 (1991): 120–123.

———— *Voice of Deliverance: The Language of Martin Luther King, Jr., and its Sources.* New York, NY: Free Press, 1992.

Moldovan, Russel. *Martin Luther King, Jr.: An Oral History of His Religious Witness and His Life.* San Francisco, CA: International Scholars, 1999.

Mungazi, Dickson A. *The Journey to the Promised Land: The African American Struggle for Development Since the Civil War.* Westport, CT: Praeger, 2000.

Nojeim, Michael J. *Gandhi and King: The Power of Nonviolent Resistance.* Westport, CT: Praeger, 2004.

Paris, Peter J. *Black Religious Leaders: Conflict in Unity.* Louisville, KY: Westminster John Knox Press, 1991.

Pearson, Hugh. *When Harlem Nearly Killed King: The 1958 Stabbing of Dr. Martin Luther King, Jr.* London, UK: Seven Stories Press, 2004.

Pepper, William. *An Act of State: The Execution of Martin Luther King.* New York, NY: Verso, 2003.

Phillips, Donald T. *Martin Luther King, Jr. on Leadership: Inspiration & Wisdom for Challenging Times.* New York, NY: Warner Books, 1999.

Posner, Gerald L. *Killing the Dream: James Earl Ray and the Assassination of Martin Luther King, Jr.* New York, NY: Random House, 1998.

Ralph, James R., Jr. *Northern Protest: Martin Luther King, Jr., Chicago, and the Civil Rights Movement.* Cambridge, MA: Harvard University Press, 1993.

Richards, David A. J. *Disarming Manhood: Roots of Ethical Resistance.* Athens, OH: Swallow Press, 2005.

Roberts, J. Deotis. *Bonhoeffer and King: Speaking Truth to Power.* Louisville, KY: Westminster John Knox Press, 2005.

Schlueter, Nathan W. *One Dream or Two?: Justice in America and in the Thought of Martin Luther King, Jr.* Lanham, MD: Lexington Books, 2003.

Schneier, Marc. *Shared Dreams: Martin Luther King, Jr. and the Jewish Community.* Woodstock, VT: Jewish Lights, 1999.

Stull, Bradford T. *Amid the Fall, Dreaming of Eden: DuBois, King, Malcolm X, and Emancipatory Composition.* Carbondale, IL: Southern Illinois University Press, 1999.

Sunnemark, Fredrik. *Ring Out Freedom!: The Voice of Martin Luther King, Jr. and the Making of the Civil Rights Movement.* Bloomington, IN: Indiana University Press, 2003.

Tilove, Jonathan. *Along Martin Luther King: Travels on Black America's Main Street.* New York, NY: Random House, 2003.

Watson, Martha. "The Issue is Justice: Martin Luther King Jr.'s Response to the Birmingham Clergy." *Rhetoric & Public Affairs* 7 (2004): 1–22.

Weisberg, Harold. *Frame-Up: The Martin Luther King – James Earl Ray Case.* New York, NY: Outerbridge and Dienstfrey, 1971.

———. *Martin Luther King: The Assassination.* New York, NY: Carroll & Graff Publishing, 1993.

Wilson, Kirt H. "Interpreting the Discursive Field of the Montgomery Bus Boycott: Martin Luther King Jr.'s Holt Street Address." *Rhetoric & Public Affairs* 8 (2005): 299–326.

James Lawson

Primary

"The Wounds We Hide: The Silent Scars of Racism are not Limited to Communities of Color." *The Other Side* 39 (2003): 10–17.

with W. Stuart Towns, compl. *"We Want Our Freedom": The Rhetoric of the Civil Rights Movement.* Westport, CT: Praeger, 2002.

Secondary

Ackerman, Peter, and Jack Duvall. *A Force More Powerful: A Century of Nonviolent Conflict*. New York, NY: Palgrave, 2000.

Carson, Clayborne. *In Struggle: SNCC and the Black Awakening of the 1960's*. Cambridge, MA: Harvard University Press, 1981.

Chappell, David L. *A Stone of Hope: Prophetic Religion and the Death of Jim Crow*. Chapel Hill, NC: University of North Carolina Press, 2004.

Sumner, David E. "The Publisher and the Preacher: Racial Conflict at Vanderbilt University." *Tennessee Historical Quarterly* 56 (1997): 34–43.

Williams, Juan, ed. *My Soul Looks Back in Wonder: Voices of the Civil Rights Experience*. New York, NY: Sterling, 2004.

Heslip "Happy" Lee

Secondary

Shivadas, H.V. *Happy Warrior: The Legend of Happy Lee*. Baltimore, MD: PublishAmerica, 2005.

John Lewis

Primary

"Foreword." In *Atlanta: An Illustrated History*, Andy Ambrose. Athens, GA: Hill Street Press, 2003.

"Foreword." In *Challenges to Equality: Poverty and Race In America*, Chester Hartman. Armonk, NY: M.E. Sharpe, 2001.

"Foreword." In *The Coming Free*, David Rubel. London, UK: DK ADULT, 2005.

"Foreword." In *Highway Robbery: Transportation Racism & New Routes to Equity*. Eds., Robert D. Bullard, Glenn S. Johnson, & Angel O. Torres. Cambridge, MA: South End Press, 2004.

"Introduction." In *Bus Ride to Justice*, Fred D. Gray. Montgomery, AL: River City Publishing, 1994.

"Introduction." In *Traveler's Guide to the Civil Rights Movement*, Jim Carrier. San Diego, CA: Harvest Books, 2004.

"The Last Integrationist." *The New Republic* 215 (1996): 19–26.

"The Nashville Lunch-Counter Sit Ins." *American Educator* 22 (1998): 24–30, 46–49.

with Michael D'Orso. *Walking With the Wind: A Memoir of the Movement*. New York, NY: Simon & Schuster, 1998.

Secondary

Allen, Archie E. "John Lewis: Keeper of the Dream." *New South* 26 (1971): 15–25.

Brown, Amy B., and Karen Poremski, eds. *Roads to Reconciliation: Conflict and Dialogue in the Twenty-First Century.* Armonk, NY: M.E. Sharpe, 2005.

"Congressman John Lewis: An American Saint." *Journal of Blacks in Higher Education* 21 (1998): 42–43.

Egerton, John. *A Mind to Stay Here: Profiles from the South.* New York: Macmillan, 1970.

Fairclough, Adam. "Civil Rights and the Lincoln Memorial: The Censored Speeches of Robert R. Moton (1922) and John Lewis (1963)." *Journal of Negro History* 82 (1997): 408–416.

Halberstam, David. *The Children.* New York, NY: Fawcett, 1999.

Hill, Christine M. *John Lewis: From Freedom Rider to Congressman.* Berkeley Heights, NJ: Enslow Publishers, 2002.

Mayer, Robert, ed. *The Civil Rights Act of 1964.* San Diego, CA: Greenhaven Press, 2004.

Meachem, Jon, ed. *Voices in Our Blood: America's Best on the Civil Rights Movement.* New York, NY: Random House, 2001.

Mills, Nicolaus. "Heard and Unheard Speeches: What Really Happened at the March On Washington?" *Dissent* 35 (1988): 285–291.

Pauley, Garth E. "John Lewis's 'Serious Revolution': Rhetoric, Resistance, and Revision at the March on Washington." *Quarterly Journal of Speech* 84 (1998): 320–340.

Pomper, Gerald M. *Ordinary Heroes and American Democracy.* New Haven, CT: Yale University Press, 2004.

Ritter, Kurt and Garth E. Pauley. "John Robert Lewis." In *African-American Orators.* Ed. Richard W. Leeman. Westport, CT: Greenwood Press, 1996, 226–38.

Sessions, Jim and Sue Thrasher. "A New Day Begun." *Southern Exposure* 4 (1976): 14–24.

Carlos Martin

Primary

Turning the World Upside Down: How to be a Radical Witness for Jesus. Nampa, ID: Pacific Press Publishing, 2000.

Benjamin Mays

Primary

"The American Negro and the Christian Religion." *Journal of Negro Education* 8 (1939): 530–538.

Born to Rebel: An Autobiography, Reprint ed. Athens, GA: University of Georgia Press, 2003.

The Christian in Race Relations. New Haven, CT: Promoting Enduring Peace, 1952.

The Church Amidst Ethnic and Racial Tensions. Louisville, KY: Division of Christian Relations, Presbyterian Church in the U.S., 1954.

"The Color Line Around the World." *Journal of Negro Education* 6 (1937): 134–143.

"Democratizing and Christianizing America in this Generation." *Journal of Negro Education* 14 (1945): 527–534.

Disturbed About Man. London, UK: John Knox Press, 1969.

"Foreword." In *Daddy King: An Autobiography*, Martin Luther King and Clayton Riley. New York, NY: Morrow, 1980.

"Improving the Morale of Negro Children and Youth." *Journal of Negro Education* 19 (1950): 420–425.

"A Look at the Black Colleges." *Foundations* 17 (1974): 237–246.

Lord, the People Have Driven Me On. New York, NY: Vantage, 1981.

"The Moral Aspects of Racial Segregation." *Journal of Blacks in Higher Education* 31 (2001): 118.

The Negro's God as Reflected in His Literature. Princeton, NJ: Scribner, 1969.

A Pictorial Life and Times. Eds., Carrie M. Dumas and Julie Hunter. Macon, GA: Mercer University Press, 2006.

"The Present Status of and Future Outlook for Racial Integration in the Church-Related White Colleges in the South." *Journal of Negro Education* 21 (1952): 350–352.

"Progress and Prospects in American Race Relations." *Journal of Ecumenical Studies* 16 (1979): 128–132.

Quotable Quotes of Benjamin E. Mays. New York, NY: Vantage Press, 1983.

"The Religious Life and Needs of Negro Students." *Journal of Negro Education* 9 (1940): 332–343.

"The Role of the Negro Community in Delinquency Prevention Among Youth." *Journal of Negro Education* 28 (1959): 366–370.

"The Role of the Negro Liberal Arts College in Post-War Reconstruction." *Journal of Negro Education* 11 (1942): 400–411.

Seeking to Be Christian in Race Relations. Cincinnati, OH: Friendship Press, 1965.

"Segregation in Higher Education." *Phylon* 10 (1949): 401–406.

"The Significance of the Negro Private Church and Church-Related College." *Journal of Negro Education* 29 (1960): 245–251.

"Veterans: It Need Not Happen Again." *Phylon* 6 (1945): 205–211.

The Virginia Papers on the Presidency. Washington, D.C.: University Press of America, 1982.

with David H. Stevens, A.E. Manley, Rufus E. Clement, and Florence M. Read. "Life and Work of Trevor Arnett." *Phylon* 16 (1955): 127–140.

with Joseph William Nicholson. *The Negro's Church.* New York, NY: Beaufort Books, 1975.

Secondary

Beckner, Chrisanne. *100 African-Americans Who Shaped American History.* San Francisco, CA: Bluewood Books, 1995.

Carter, Lawrence E., ed. *Walking Integrity: Benjamin Elijah Mays, Mentor to Martin Luther King Jr.* Macon, GA: Mercer University Press, 1998.

Colston, Freddie C. "Dr. Benjamin E. Mays: His Impact as Spiritual and Intellectual Mentor of Martin Luther King, Jr." *Black Scholar* 23 (1993): 6–15.

———. *Dr. Benjamin E. Mays Speaks: Representative Speeches of a Great American Orator.* Washington, D.C.: University Press of America, 2002.

Cook, Samuel D. *The Wisdom de Profundis of Benjamin E. Mays, Black Colleges, and the Good Life.* Nashville, TN: United Methodist Publishing House, 1995.

Dorrien, Gary. *The Making of American Liberal Theology: Idealism, Realism, and Modernity, 1900–1950.* Louisville, KY: Westminster John Knox Press, 2003.

Gavins, Doris L. "The Ceremonial Speaking of Benjamin Elijah Mays: Spokesman for Social Change, 1954–1975." Ph.D. Diss., Louisiana State University and Agricultural and Mechanical College, 1978.

Huff, Archie V., Jr. "The Black Hero in South Carolina." *South Carolina Review* 4 (1972): 20–28.

Jelks, Randal M. "Benjamin Elijah Mays and the Creation of an Insurgent Professional Negro Clergy." *AME Church Review* 118 (2002): n.p.

Lindsay, Leon W. "The Views of Benjamin Mays." *Integrated Education* 8 (1970): 50–53.

Matthews, Verner R. "The Concept of Racial Justice of Benjamin Elijah Mays and Its Relevance to Christian Education in the Black Church." Ph.D. Diss., New York University, 1991.

McNeil, Pearl L. "Baptist Black Americans and the Ecumenical Movement." *Journal of Ecumenical Studies* 17 (1980): 103–117.

Preskill, Stephen. "Combative Spirituality and the Life of Benjamin E. Mays." *Biography* 19 (1996): 404–416.

Rovaris, Dereck J. "Developer of an Institution: Dr. Benjamin E. Mays, Morehouse College President, 1940–1967." Ph.D. Diss., University of Illinois, 1990.

Teel, Leonard R. "Benjamin Mays—Teaching by Example, Leading Through Will." *Change* 14 (1982): 14–22.

Tuck, Stephen G. *Beyond Atlanta: The Struggle for Racial Equality in Georgia, 1940–1980.* Athens, GA: University of Georgia Press, 2001.

Willie, Charles V. "The Education of Benjamin E. Mays: An Experience in Effective Teaching." *Teachers College Record* 84 (1983), n. p.

Robert J. McCracken

Primary

American Protestantism and Roman Catholic Power: A Sermon Delivered at the Riverside Church October 28, 1951. New York, NY: The Riverside Church, 1951.

Bibles for the Millions: A Sermon. New York, NY: Riverside Church in the City of New York, 1966.

The Church: Diagnosis and Prescription. Lynchburg VA: Lynchburg College, 1956.

"Foreword." In *Best Sermons 1968*. Ed., G. Paul Butler. Naples, FL: Trident Press, 1968.

The Legacy of the Reformation. New York, NY: The Riverside Church, 1953.

Man's Right to Knowledge and the Free Use Thereof: A Sermon Preached in the Riverside Church, New York. New York, NY: Riverside Church, 1954.

National Radio Pulpit. New York, NY: National Council of the Churches of Christ in the United States of America, 1960.

Putting Faith to Work. New York, NY: Harper & Brothers, 1960.

What Does "Believing on the Lord Jesus Christ" Mean? New York, NY: Riverside Church Publications, 1962.

What is Sin? What is Virtue? New York, NY: Harper & Row, 1966.

Thomas Merton

Primary

The Assent to Truth. New York, NY: Viking Press, 1951.

Bread in the Wilderness. New York, NY: New Directions Publishing, 1971.

Cables to the Ace; or Familiar Liturgies of Misunderstanding. New York, NY: New Directions Publishing, 1968.

"The Church in World Crisis." *Katallagete* 1 (1967): 30–36.

Conjectures of a Guilty Bystander. New York, NY: Image Books, 1968.

Contemplations in a World of Action. South Bend, IN: University of Notre Dame Press, 1999.

Contemplative Prayer. Garden City, NY: Image Books, 1971.

The Courage of Truth: Letters of Thomas Merton to Writers. New York, NY: Farrar, Strauss, and Giroux, 1993.

Dancing in the Waters of Life: Seeking Peace in the Hermitage. San Francisco, CA: HarperCollins, 1998.

Elected Silence: The Autobiography of Thomas Merton. London, UK: Hollis and Carter, 1949.

"Events and Pseudo-Events: Letters to a Southern Gentleman." *Katallagete* 1 (1966): 10–17.

Faith and Violence: Christian Teaching and Christian Practices. South Bend, IN: University of Notre Dame Press, 1968.

Gandhi on Nonviolence. New York, NY: New Directions, 1965.

Intimate Merton: His Life from His Journals. San Francisco, CA: HarperCollins, 2001.

"Is the World a Problem?" *Katallagete* 5 (1974): 28–33.

The Last of the Fathers. New York, NY: Harcourt Brace & Co., 1954.

Learning to Love: Exploring Solitude and Freedom. San Francisco, CA: HarperCollins, 1997.

Life and Holiness. New York, NY: Image Books, 1964.

The Living Bread. New York, NY: Farrar, Strauss, and Cudahy, 1956.

Love and Living. Orlando, FL: Harcourt, 1985.

The Monastic Journey. Kansas City, MO: Sheed, Andrews and McMeel, 1977.

Mornings With Thomas Merton: Readings and Reflections. Ann Arbor, MI: Charis Books, 1998.

My Argument with the Gestapo: A Macaronic Journal. New York, NY: Doubleday, 1969.

No Man is an Island. New York, NY: Image Books, 1967.

On Peace. London, UK: Mowbray, 1979.

The Other Side of the Mountain. San Francisco, CA: HarperCollins, 1999.

Passion for Peace—The Social Essays. New York, NY: Crossroad, 1997.

Praying the Psalms. Collegeville, MN: Liturgical Press, 1956.

Raids on the Unspeakable. New York, NY: New Directions Publishing, 1966.

A Search for Solitude: Pursuing a Monk's True Life. San Francisco, CA: HarperCollins, 1997.

Seasons of Celebration. New York, NY: Farrar, Strauss and Giroux, 1965.

A Secular Journal. London, UK: Catholic Book Club, 1959.

Seeds of Contemplation. New York, NY: Dell Publishing, 1960.

The Seven Storey Mountain. New York, NY: Harcourt, 1948.

The Sign of Jonas: The Journal of Thomas Merton. New York, NY: Doubleday, 1959.

The Tears of a Blind Lion. New York, NY: New Directions, 1949.

The Waters of Silence. London, UK: Hollis and Carter, 1950.

The Waters of Siloe. New York, NY: Harcourt, 1949.

The Way of Chuang Tzu. New York, NY: New Directions, 1965.

What are these Wounds? Milwaukee, WI: Bruce, 1950.

What is Contemplation? Springfield, IL: Templegate Publishing, 1981.

The Wisdom of the Desert: Sayings from the Desert Fathers. New York, NY: New Directions, 1970.

with Robert E. Daggy. *Introductions East and West: The Foreign Prefaces of Thomas Merton.* Oakville, ONT: Mosaic Press, 1981.

with William S. Shannon. *The Hidden Ground of Love: Letters on Religious Experience and Social Concern.* Washington, D.C.: Farrar, Strauss and Giroux, 1985.

Secondary

Adams, Daniel J. *Thomas Merton's Shared Contemplation: A Protestant Perspective.* Collegeville, MN: Cistercian Publications, 1979.

Baker, James T. "Thomas Merton: The Spiritual and Social Philosophy of Union." Ph.D. Thesis, Florida State University, 1968.

Barbour, John D. "The Ethics of Intercultural Travel: Thomas Merton's Asian Pilgrimage and Orientalism." *Biography* 28 (2005): 15–26.

Bryant, Jennifer Fisher. *Thomas Merton: Poet, Prophet, Priest.* Grand Rapids, MI: Eerdmans, 1997.

Carr, Anne E. *A Search for Wisdom and Spirit: Thomas Merton's Theology of the Self.* Notre Dame, IN: University of Notre Dame Press, 1990.

Cashen, Richard A. *Solitude in the Thought of Thomas Merton.* Collegeville, MN: Cistercian Publications, 1981.

Collins, David R. *Thomas Merton: Monk with a Mission.* Cincinnati, OH: St. Anthony Messenger Press, 1981.

Cooper, David D. *Thomas Merton's Art of Denial: The Evolution of a Radical Humanist.* Athens, GA: University of Georgia Press, 1989.

Cunningham, Lawrence S. *Thomas Merton and the Monastic Vision.* Grand Rapids, MI: Eerdmans, 1999.

Dell'Isola, Frank. *Thomas Merton: A Bibliography.* Kent, OH: The Kent State University Press, 1975.

Del Prete, Thomas. "Education and Being: A Reflection of Thomas Merton's Life." *Religious Education* 87 (1992): 459–470.

———. *Thomas Merton and the Education of the Whole Person.* Birmingham, AL: Religious Education Press, 1990.

DeWaal, Esther. *A Seven Day Journey with Thomas Merton.* Ann Arbor, MI: Servant Publications, 1993.

Farrell, James J. "Thomas Merton and the Religion of the Bomb." *Religion and American Culture* 5 (1995): 77–98.

Forest, James. *Living with Wisdom: A Life of Thomas Merton.* Maryknoll, NY: Orbis Books, 1991.

———. *Thomas Merton, a Pictorial Biography.* Costa Mesa, CA: Paulist Press, 1980.

———. *Thomas Merton's Struggle with Peacemaking.* Erie, PA: Benet Press, 1975.

Givey, David W. *Social Thought of Thomas Merton.* Quincy, IL: Franciscan Press, 1984.

Grayston, Donald. *Thomas Merton: The Development of a Spiritual Theologian.* Lewiston, NY: Edwin Mellen Press, 1984.

Griffin, John H. *Follow the Ecstasy: The Hermitage Years of Thomas Merton.* Maryknoll, NY: Orbis Books, 1993.

Hart, Patrick. *Legacy of Thomas Merton.* Collegeville, MN: Cistercian Publications, 1986.

———. *Thomas Merton, Monk: A Monastic Tribute.* Collegeville, MN: Cistercian Publications, 2005.

Herron, Fred. *No Abiding Place: Thomas Merton and the Search for God.* Lanham, MD: Rowman & Littlefield, 2005.

———. "To Be Who We Really Are: Thomas Merton's Appeal to Today's Students." *Momentum* 31 (2000): 42–43.

Higgins, John J. *Thomas Merton on Prayer.* New York, NY: Doubleday, 1975.

Higgins, Michael W. *Heretic Blood: The Spiritual Geography of Thomas Merton.* New York, NY: Stoddart, 1998.

Hourihan, Paul. *The Death of Thomas Merton.* Redding, CA: Vedantic Shores Press, 2003.

Inchausti, Robert. *Thomas Merton's American Prophecy.* Albany, NY: State University of New York Press, 1998.

Kramer, Victor A. *Thomas Merton: Monk and Artist.* Collegeville, MN: Cistercian Publications, 1987.

Labrie, Ross. *The Art of Thomas Merton.* Ft. Worth, TX: Texas Christian University Press, 1979.

———. *Thomas Merton and the Inclusive Imagination.* Columbia, MO: University of Missouri Press, 2001.

Lipski, Alexander. *Thomas Merton and Asia: His Quest for Utopia.* Collegeville, MN: Cistercian Publications, 1983.

Macchiarola, Frank J. "Reflections on Thomas Merton on the 25th Anniversary of His Death." *Cardozo Studies in Law and Literature* 5 (1993): 265–280.

Malits, Elena. *The Solitary Explorer: Thomas Merton's Transforming Journey.* San Francisco, CA: Harper & Row, 1980.

Nouwen, Henri J.M. *Encounters with Merton.* New York, NY: Crossroad, 2004.

————. *Thomas Merton: Contemplative Critic.* Reissue ed. Liguori, MO: Liguori Publications, 1991.

O'Connell, Patrick. "Thomas Merton's Vision of the Kingdom." *Logos: A Journal of Catholic Thought and Culture* 3 (2000): 195–216.

————. *Vision of Thomas Merton.* Notre Dame, IN: Ave Maria Press, 2003.

Padavano, Anthony T. *The Human Journey—Thomas Merton: Symbol of Century.* New York, NY: Doubleday, 1984.

————. *A Retreat with Thomas Merton: Becoming Who We Are.* Cincinnati, OH: St. Anthony Messenger Press, 1995.

Rice, Edward. *The Man in the Sycamore Tree: The Good Times and Hard Life of Thomas Merton.* Orlando, FL: Harcourt Press, 1985.

Seitz, Ron. *Song for Nobody: A Memory Vision of Thomas Merton.* Liguori, MO: Liguori Publications, 1995.

Shannon, William H., Christine M. Bochen, and Patrick F. O'Connell. *The Thomas Merton Encyclopedia.* Maryknoll, NY: Orbis Books, 2002.

Shannon, William H. *Silent Lamp: The Thomas Merton Story.* New York, NY: Crossroad, 1992.

————. *Something of a Rebel: Thomas Merton—His Life and Works.* Cincinnati, OH: St. Anthony Messenger Press, 1997.

————. *A Retreat with Thomas Merton: Becoming Who We Are.* Cincinnati, OH: St. Anthony Messenger Press, 1995..

————. *Thomas Merton's Dark Path: The Inner Experience of a Contemplative.* New York, NY: Farrar, Straus, and Giroux, 1981.

————. *Thomas Merton's Paradise Journey: Writings on Contemplation.* Cincinnati, OH: St Anthony Messenger Press, 2000.

Sussman, Cornelia and Irving Sussman. *Thomas Merton: The Daring Young Man on the Flying Bell Tower.* New York, NY: Macmillan, 1976.

Teahan, John F. "A Dark and Empty Way: Thomas Merton and the Apophatic Tradition." *The Journal of Religion* 58 (1978): 263–287.

————. "The Place of Silence in Thomas Merton's Life and Thought." *The Journal of Religion* 61 (1981): 364–383.

————. "Solitude: A Central Motif in Thomas Merton's Life and Writings." *Journal of the American Academy of Religion* 50 (1982): 521–538.

Voigt, J. Robert. *Thomas Merton: A Different Drummer.* Liguori, MO: Liguori Publications, 1972.

Waldron, Robert G. *Walking with Thomas Merton: Discovering His Poetry and Essays.* Costa Mesa, CA: Paulist Press, 2002.

Webster, Robert. "Thomas Merton and the Textuality of the Self: An Experiment in Postmodern Spirituality." *The Journal of Religion* 78 (1998): 387–404.

Woodcock, George. *Thomas Merton Monk and Poet: A Critical Study.* New York, NY: Farrar, Straus, and Giroux, 1978.

Charles Morgan, Jr.

Primary

"Dual Justice in the South." *Judicature* 53 (1970): 379–384.

"Negroes as the New Force in Southern Politics." *New South* 21 (1966): 69–73.

One Man, One Voice. New York, NY: Holt, Rinehart and Winston, 1979.

"Politics, Race, and the Law: The Southern Strategy." *Black Politician* 1 (1970): 8–12.

A Time to Speak. New York, NY: Harper & Row, 1964.

Secondary

Epstein, Joseph. "Two Southern Liberals." *Commentary* 38 (1964): 73–74, 76, 78.

Father Patrick O'Boyle

Primary

"Foreword." In *Theology and Race Relations*, Joseph T. Leonard. Milwaukee, WI: Bruce Publishing, 1963.

Sex in Marriage: Love-giving, Life-giving. St. Cloud, MN: Diocese of St. Cloud, 1968.

Sex in marriage: Love-giving, Life-giving, Questions Asked Since the Encyclical Humanae Vitae. Washington, D.C.: Archdiocese of Washington, 1968.

Secondary

Fairclough, Adam. "Civil Rights and the Lincoln Memorial: The Censored Speeches of Robert R. Moton (1922) and John Lewis (1963)." *The Journal of Negro History* 82 (1997): 408–16.

James A. Pike

Primary

Beyond Anxiety: The Christian Answer to Fear, Frustration, Guilt, Indecision, Inhibition, Loneliness, Despair. New York, NY: Charles Scribner's Sons, 1953.

Christianity as Perspective (The Partridge Lecture on Christianity). Middlebury, VT: Middlebury College, 1952.

The Church, Politics, and Society: Dialogues on Current Problems. New York, NY: Morehouse-Gorham, 1955.

Doing the Truth: A Summary of Christian Ethics. New York, NY: Doubleday, 1955.

Facing the Next Day. Basingstoke, UK: Macmillan, 1968.

The Faith of the Church (The Church's teaching). New York, NY: Seabury Press, 1956.

"Foreword." In *One Bread, One Body*, Nathan Wright. Greenwich, CT: Seabury Press, 1962.

If This Be Heresy. New York, NY: Harper & Row, 1967.

If You Marry Outside Your Faith: Counsel on Mixed Marriages. New York, NY: Harper, 1954.

Man in the Middle: Conversations of a Tempted Soul with Two Voices on the Seven Deadly Sins. New York, NY: Seabury Press, 1956.

A New Look in Preaching (The George Craig Stewart Memorial Lectures). New York, NY: Scribners, 1961.

The Next Day. New York, NY: Doubleday, 1957.

The Other Side: An Account of My Experiences with Psychic Phenomena. New York, NY: Doubleday, 1968.

Our Christmas Challenge. New York, NY: Sterling, 1961.

Our Faith & the Church: A Leader's Guide Based on the Faith of the Church (The Church's Teaching). New York, NY: Seabury Press, 1959.

The Place of Religion in a University. New York, NY: Columbia University Press, 1949.

Roadblocks to Faith. New York, NY: Morehouse-Gorham, 1954.

A Roman Catholic in the White House. Westport, CT: Greenwood Press, 1973.

Teen-agers and Sex. Upper Saddle River, NJ: Prentice-Hall, 1965.

A Time for Christian Candor. New York, NY: Harper & Row, 1964.

What is This Treasure? New York, NY: Harper & Row, 1966.

You & the New Morality: 74 cases. New York, NY: Harper & Row, 1967.

with John H. Hallowell. *Modern Canterbury Pilgrims: And Why They Chose the Episcopal Church*, 2d ed. New York, NY: Morehouse-Gorham, 1956.

Secondary

Friedland, Michael. *Lift Your Voice Like a Trumpet: White Clergy and the Civil Rights and Anti-War Movements, 1954–1973*. Chapel Hill, NC: University of North Carolina Press, 1996.

Pike, Diane K. and R. Scott Kennedy. *The Wilderness Revolt: A New View of the Life and Death of Jesus Based on Ideas and Notes of the Late Bishop James A. Pike*. New York, NY: Doubleday, 1972.

Robertson, David M. *A Passionate Pilgrim: A Biography of Bishop James A. Pike*. New York, NY: Alfred A. Knopf, 2004.

White, Larry A. "Rhetoric of James A. Pike: A Humanistic Criticism." Ph.D. Diss., Southern Illinois University, 1975.

Adam C. Powell

Primary

Adam by Adam: The Autobiography of Adam Clayton Powell, Jr. New York, NY: Kensington Publishing, 1971.

Secondary

Alexander, E. Curtis. *Adam Clayton Powell, Jr.: A Black Power Political Educator.* New York, NY: ECA Associates, 1983.

———. "Three Black Religious Educators: A Study of the Educational Perspectives of Richard Allen, Elijah Muhammad, and Adam Clayton Powell, Jr." Ph.D. Diss., Columbia University Teachers College, 1980.

Capeci, Dominic J., Jr. "From Different Liberal Perspectives: Fiorello H. LaGuardia, Adam Clayton Powell, Jr., and Civil Rights in New York City, 1941–1943." *Journal of Negro History* 62 (1977): 160–173.

———. "From Harlem to Montgomery: The Bus Boycotts and Leadership of Adam Clayton Powell, Jr., and Martin Luther King, Jr." *Historian* 41 (1979): 721–737.

Clark, Shelton Leroy. "The Black Clergy as Agents of Social Change: With an Emphasis on the Life of Adam Clayton Powell." Ph.D. Diss., Rutgers University, 1978.

Daniels, Lee A. "The Political Career of Adam Clayton Powell." *Journal of Black Studies* 4 (1973): 115–138.

Greenberg, Cheryl. "God and Man in Harlem." *Journal of Urban History* 21 (1995): 518–526.

Gunther, Lenworth Alburn, III. "Flamin' Tongue: The Rise of Adam Clayton Powell, Jr., 1908–41." Ph.D. Diss., Columbia University, 1985.

Hamilton, Charles V. *Adam Clayton Powell, Jr.: The Political Biography of an American Dilemma.* New York, NY: Maxwell Macmillan International, 1991.

Haskins, James, ed. *Keeping the Faith: African-Americans Sermons of Liberation.* New York, NY: Welcome Rain Publishers, 2002.

Haygood, Will. *King of the Cats: The Life and Times of Adam Clayton Powell Jr.* Boston, MA: Houghton Mifflin, 1993.

Hickey, Neil. *Adam Clayton Powell and the Politics of Race.* New York, NY: Fleet, 1965.

Kilson, Martin. "Adam Clayton Powell, Jr.: The Militant as Politician." In *Black Leaders of the Twentieth Century.* Eds., John Hope Franklin and August Meier. Urbana, IL: University of Illinois Press, 1982.

Kinney, John William. "Adam Clayton Powell, Sr. and Adam Clayton Powell, Jr.: A Historical Exposition and Theological Analysis." Ph.D. Diss., Columbia University, 1979.

Pollock, Art. "My Life's Philosophy: Adam Clayton Powell's 'Black Position Paper.'" *Journal of Black Studies* 4 (1974): 457–462.

Polsby, Nelson W. "Washington Monuments." *Congress & the Presidency* 19 (1992): 75–79.

Reeves, Andrée Elizabeth. "Burden to Powell to Perkins: Leadership and Evolution of the U.S. House of Representatives Committee on Education and Labor, 1951–1984." Ph.D. Diss., Rice University, 1990.

Rigsby, Enrique D. "Adam Clayton Powell, Jr." In *African-American Orators*. Ed., Richard W. Leeman. Westport, CT: Greenwood, 1996, 276–83.

Snipe, Tracy D. "The Role of African American Males in Politics and Government." *Annals of the American Academy of Political and Social Science* 569 (2000): 10–28.

Williams, Lea. *Servants of the People: The 1960's Legacy of African-American Leadership*. New York, NY: St. Martin's Press, 1996.

Wilson, James Q. "The Flamboyant Mr. Powell." *Commentary* 41 (1966): 31–35.

Woodard, Maurice C. "The Legislative Record of Adam Clayton Powell Revisited." *Black Politician* 3 (1971): 36–38.

Zelizer, Julian E. "The Constructive Generation: Thinking About Congress in the 1960's." *Mid-America* 81 (1999): 263–296.

Edward H. Pruden

Primary

Interpreters Needed: The Eternal Gospel and Our Contemporary Society. Valley Forge, PA: Judson Press, 1951.

A Window on Washington. New York, NY: Vantage Press, 1976.

Robbins Ralph

Primary

Only Yesterday 1974–1986. Quakertown, PA: First United Church of Christ, 1985.

A. Philip Randolph

Primary

The Negro Freedom Movement. Lincoln, PA: Lincoln University Press, n.d.

with Norman Thomas. *Victory's Victims? The Negro's Future Based on a Radio Discussion*. New York, NY: Socialist Party, 1943.

Secondary

Anderson, Jervis A. *A. Philip Randolph: A Biographical Portrait*. Berkeley, CA: University of California Press, 1990.

Bracey, John H., Jr., and August Meier. "Allies or Adversaries?: The NAACP, A. Philip Randolph, and the 1941 March on Washington." *Georgia Historical Quarterly* 75 (1991): 1–17.

Cwiklik, Robert. *A. Philip Randolph and the Labor Movement.* Minneapolis, MN: Lerner Publishing Group, 1993.

Davis, Daniel S. *Mr. Black Labor: The Story of A. Philip Randolph, Father of the Civil Rights Movement.* New York, NY: E.P. Dutton and Company, 1972.

Harris, William H. "A. Philip Randolph as a Charismatic Leader, 1925–1941." *The Journal of Negro History* 64 (1979): 301–315

———. *Keeping the Faith: A. Philip Randolph, Milton P. Webster, and the Brotherhood of Sleeping Car Porters.* Urbana, IL: University of Illinois Press, 1977.

Miller, Calvin C. *A. Philip Randolph and the African American Labor Movement.* Greensboro, NC: Morgan Reynolds Publishing, 2005.

Neyland, James. *Philip Randolph: Labor Leader.* Los Angeles, CA: Holloway House Publishing, 1994.

Panetta, Edward M. "Asa Philip Randolph." In *African-American Orators.* Ed., Richard W. Leeman. Westport, CT: Greenwood, 1996, 294–301.

Patterson, Lillie and John A. Scott. *A. Philip Randolph: Messenger for the Masses.* New York, NY: Facts on File Inc., 1995.

Pfeffer, Paula F. *A. Philip Randolph, Pioneer of the Civil Rights Movement.* Baton Rouge, LA: Louisiana State University Press, 1996.

Reef, Catherine. *A. Philip Randolph: Union Leader and Civil Rights Crusader.* Berkley Heights, NJ: Enslow Publishers, 2001.

Taylor, Cynthia. *A. Philip Randolph: The Religious Journey of an African American Labor Leader.* New York, NY: New York University Press, 2006.

Branch Rickey

Primary

Branch Rickey's Little Blue Book: Wit and Strategy from Baseball's Last Wise Man. Ontario, Canada: Sportclassic Books, 2004.

with Robert Riger. *The American Diamond: A Documentary of the Game of Baseball.* New York, NY: Simon & Schuster, 1965.

Secondary

Chalberg, John C. *Rickey and Robinson: The Preacher, the Player, and America's Game.* Wheeling, IL: Harlan Davidson, 2000.

Kirwin, Bill, ed. *Out of the Shadows: African American Baseball from the Cuban Giants to Jackie Robinson: The Best of NINE.* Lincoln, NE: University of Nebraska Press, 2005.

Lowenfish, Lee. "When All Heaven Rejoiced: Branch Rickey and the Origins of the Breaking of the Color Line." *NINE: A Journal of Baseball History and Culture* 11 (2002): 1–15.

Mann, Arthur. *Branch Rickey, American in Action.* Boston, MA: Houghton Mifflin, 1957.

McCue, Andy. "Two out of Three Ain't Bad: Branch Rickey, Walter O'Malley, and the Man in the Middle of the Dodger Owners' Partnership." *NINE: A Journal of Baseball History and Culture* 14 (2005): 41–46.

Polner, Murray. *Branch Rickey: A Biography.* New York, NY: Penguin Group, 1983.

Puerzer, Richard J. "Engineering Baseball: Branch Rickey's Innovative Approach to Baseball Management." *NINE: A Journal of Baseball History and Culture* 12 (2003): 72–87.

Fred Shuttlesworth

Secondary

Cosby, Camille O., and Renee Poussaint, eds. *A Wealth of Wisdom: Legendary African American Elders Speak.* New York, NY: Atria, 2004.

Eskew, Glenn T. *But for Birmingham: The Local and National Movements in the Civil Rights Struggle.* Chapel Hill, NC: University of North Carolina Press, 1997.

Houck, Davis. "Ed King's Jaw—Or, Reading, Writing, and Embodying Civil Rights." *Rhetoric & Public Affairs* 7 (2004): 67–90.

Manis, Andrew M. *A Fire You Can't Put Out: The Civil Rights Life of Birmingham's Reverend Fred Shuttlesworth.* Tuscaloosa, AL: University of Alabama Press, 1999.

White, Marjorie L. *Walk to Freedom: The Reverend Fred Shuttlesworth and the Alabama Christian Movement for Human Rights.* Birmingham, AL: Birmingham Historical Society, 1998.

White, Marjorie L., and Andrew M. Manis, eds. *Birmingham Revolutionaries: The Reverend Fred Shuttlesworth and the Alabama Christian Movement for Human Rights.* Macon, GA: Mercer University Press, 2000.

Kelly Miller Smith

Primary

Social Crisis Preaching: The Lyman Beecher Lectures 1983. Macon, GA: Mercer University Press, 1984.

Secondary

Halberstam, David. *The Children.* New York, NY: Fawcett, 1999.

Morris, Aldon. "Black Southern Student Sit-in Movement: An Analysis of Internal Organization." *American Sociological Review* 46 (1981): 744–767.

Robert W. Spike

Primary

The Freedom Revolution and the Churches. New York, NY: Association Press, 1965.

In But Not of the World: A Notebook of Theology and Practice in the Local Church. New York, NY: Association Press, 1957.

Safe in Bondage: An Appraisal of the Church's Mission to America. New York, NY: Friendship Press, 1960.

To be a Man. New York, NY: Association Press, 1961.

Secondary

Findlay, James F. "Religion and Politics in the Sixties: The Churches and the Civil Rights Act of 1964." The Journal of American History 77 (1990): 66–92.

Spike, Paul. Photographs of my Father. New York, NY: Alfred A. Knopf, 1973.

Gardner Taylor

Primary

How Shall They Preach? Elgin, IL: Progressive Baptist Publishing House, 1977.

The Words of Gardner Taylor. Comp., Edward L. Taylor. 6 vols. Valley Forge, PA: Judson Press, 1999–2002.

Mamie Till

Primary

"Foreword." In 101 Ways to Know You're "Black," in Corporate America, Deborah Watts. Wayzata, MN: Watts-Five Productions, 1998.

with Christopher Benson. Death of Innocence: The Story of the Hate Crime that Changed America. New York, NY: Random House, 2003.

Secondary

Feldstein, Ruth. Motherhood in Black and White: Race and Sex in American Liberalism, 1930–1965. Ithaca, NY: Cornell University Press, 2000, 86–110.

Wilkie, Lauri L. The Archaeology of Mothering: An African-American Midwife's Tale. New York, NY: Routledge, 2003.

Everett Tilson

Primary

The Conscience of Culture. Nashville, TN: National Methodist Student Movement, 1953.

Decision for Destiny. New York, NY: Women's Division, Board of Global Ministries, United Methodist Church, 1975.

Segregation and the Bible: A Searching Analysis of the Scriptural Evidence. Nashville, TN: Abingdon Press, 1958.

Should Christians Drink? An Objective Inquiry. New York, NY: Abingdon Press, 1957. Cole, Phyllis and Everett Tilson. *Litanies and Other Prayers for the Revised Common Lectionary: Year A.* Nashville, TN: Abingdon Press, 1992.

with Phyllis Cole. *Litanies and Other Prayers for the Revised Common Lectionary: Year B.* Nashville, TN: Abingdon Press, 1993.

with Phyllis Cole. *Litanies and Other Prayers for the Revised Common Lectionary: Year C.* Nashville, TN: Abingdon Press, 1994.

with Phyllis Cole. *Prayers for One Voice: 180 Prayers Based on the Revised Common Lectionary.* Nashville, TN: Abingdon Press, 1993.

with Catherine G. Gonzales, Ben Witherington, and Gayle C. Felton. *How United Methodists Study Scripture.* Nashville, TN: Abingdon Press, 1999.

Channing H. Tobias

Primary

"The Passing of William Francis White." *Phylon* 16 (1955): 243–45.

Secondary

Johnson, F. Earnest, ed. *Wellsprings of the American Spirit: A Series of Addresses.* New York, NY: Harper & Row, 1948.

Mjagkij, Nina. *Light in the Darkness: African Americans and the YMCA, 1852–1946.* Lexington, KY: University Press of Kentucky, 1994.

Wyatt Tee Walker

Primary

Gospel in the Land of the Rising Sun. Morriston, NJ: Aaron Press, 1991.

Road to Damascus: A Journey of Faith. Atlanta, GA: Martin Luther King Press, 1985.

Somebody's Calling My Name: Black Sacred, Music and Social Change. Valley Forge, PA: Judson Press, 1983.

with James Abbington. *Spirits That Dwell in Deep Woods: The Prayer and Praise Hymns of the Black Religious Experience.* Chicago, IL: GIA Publications, Inc., 2004.

with Marti Hefley and Harold Carter. *The Black Church Looks at the Bicentennial.* Montgomery, AL: Progressive National Baptist Publishing House, 1976.

Roy Wilkins

Primary

40 Years of the NAACP. Baltimore, MD: National Association for the Advancement of Colored People, 1949.

"Adult Education Program of the NAACP." *Journal of Negro Education* 14 (1945): 403–406.

The Conspiracy to Deny Equality. Baltimore, MD: National Association for the Advancement of Colored People, 1955.

Deep South Crisis. Baltimore, MD: National Association for the Advancement of Colored People, 1957.

"The Future of the Negro Voter in the United States." *Journal of Negro Education* 26 (1957): 424–431.

Integration Crisis in the South. Baltimore, MD: National Association for the Advancement of Colored People, 1957.

"Letter from Roy Wilkins." *Annals of the American Academy of Political and Social Science* 360 (1965): 224–225.

The Meaning of the Sit-ins. Baltimore, MD: National Association for the Advancement of Colored People, 1960.

Negro History or Mythology: The "Black Heritage Series" Controversy. Baltimore, MD: National Association for the Advancement of Colored People, 1969.

"The Negro Wants Full Equality." In *What the Negro Wants.* Ed., Rayford W. Logan. Chapel Hill, NC: University of North Carolina Press, 1944, 113–132.

"Next Steps in Education for Racial Understanding." *The Journal of Negro Education* 13 (1944): 432–440.

"Rape": A Case History of Murder, Terror, and Injustice Visited Upon a Negro Community. Washington, DC: The Committee of 100, 1949.

The Reminiscences of Roy Wilkins. Glen Rock, NJ: Microfilming Corp. of America, 1972.

"The Role of the National Association for the Advancement of Colored People in the Desegregation Process." *Social Problems* 2 (1955): 201–204.

The Roy Wilkins Column: Selections from Mr. Wilkins' Nationally Syndicated Columns published during 1972 and 1973. Baltimore, MD: NAACP Special Contribution Fund, 1973.

Search and Destroy: A Report by the Commission of Inquiry into the Black Panthers and the Police. St. Paul, MN: Metropolitan Applied Research Center, 1973.

Stalin's Greatest Defeat. Baltimore, MD: National Association for the Advancement of Colored People, 1951.

Talking it over with Roy Wilkins: Selected Speeches and Writings. Compls., Helen Soloman and Aminda Wilkins. Norwalk, CT: M & B Publishing, 1977.

Where We Stand: An Address by Roy Wilkins. Baltimore, MD: NAACP Special Contribution Fund, 1966.

with Tom Mathews. *Standing Fast: The Autobiography of Roy Wilkins.* New York, NY: Viking, 1982.

Secondary

Jonas, Gilbert. *Freedom's Sword: The NAACP and the Struggle Against Racism in America, 1909–1969.* New York, NY: Routledge, 2005.

Miller, Calvin Craig. *Roy Wilkins: Leader of the NAACP.* Greensboro, NC: Morgan Reynolds Publishing, 2005.

Wilson, Sondra Kathryn, ed. *In Search of Democracy: The NAACP Writings of James Weldon Johnson, Walter White, and Roy Wilkins (1920–1977).* New York, NY: Oxford University Press, 1999.

Marion A. Wright

Primary

Facing Facts in South Carolina. Columbia, SC: South Carolina Division of the Southern Regional Council, 1945.

"Firm Foundations for Democratic Advance." *The Phylon Quarterly* 20 (1959): 297–303.

Human Rights Odyssey. Durham, NC: Moore Publishing Company, 1978.

Making Democracy Work in South Carolina. Columbia, SC: South Carolina Division of the Southern Regional Council, 1951.

Segregation vs. the Space Age. Atlanta, GA: Greater Atlanta Council on Human Relations, 1958.

Shall We Reactivate the Gas Chamber? Carrboro, NC: North Carolinians against the Death Penalty, 1973.

The Sit-in Movement: Progress Report and Prognosis. Detroit, MI: Wayne State University Law School, 1963.

You Can't Go Home Again. Washington, D.C.: Institute of Religion, 1961.

INDEX

Permissions Acknowledgments

The editors of this anthology and Baylor University Press are grateful to the following people and groups for their kind permission to reprint texts.

Abernathy, Ralph David (§61, §105, §127): Courtesy of the Ralph David Abernathy family.

Abram, Morris (§124): Courtesy of the Morris Abram family.

Baker, Ella Jo (§99): Courtesy of the Moses Moon Audio Archive at the National Museum of American History.

Berrigan, Daniel (§126): Courtesy of Will D. Campbell.

Bethune, Mary McLeod (§5, §13): Courtesy of the Dr. Mary McLeod Bethune Papers, Bethune-Cookman College, Daytona Beach, Florida.

Bevel, James (§79): Courtesy of Pacifica Radio Archives (www.pacificaradioarchives.org).

Blake, Eugene Carson (§81): Copyright © 1963 *The Christian Century*. Reprinted by permission from the November 1963, Vol. 34, issue of *The Pulpit*.

Blake, Eugene Carson (§83): Courtesy of the Moses Moon Audio Archive at the National Museum of American History. Reprinted with the permission of Scribner, an imprint of Simon & Schuster Adult Publishing Group, from THE CHURCH IN THE NEXT DECADE by Eugene C. Blake. Copyright © 1966 by Eugene C. Blake.

Boggs, Marion (§37): Courtesy of the Southern Regional Council.

Bond, Horace Mann (§23): Courtesy of the Horace Mann Bond Papers, University of Massachusetts, and Julian Bond.

Bowles, Chester (§43): Courtesy of the Southern Regional Council.

Bowles, Charles P. (§2): Copyright © 1954 *The Christian Century*. Reprinted by permission from the July 1954, Vol. 27, issue of *The Pulpit*.

Boyle, Sarah Patton (§9, §10, 19): Courtesy of the Sarah Patton Boyle Papers (#8003), Special Collections, University of Virginia Library.

Bradley, Mamie Till (§17): Courtesy of the AFRO-American newspapers Archives and Research Center (AANARC).

Dennis, Dave (§91, 92): Courtesy of Dave Dennis and the Moses Moon Audio Archive at the National Museum of American History.

Dennis, Dave (§112): Courtesy of Pacifica Radio Archives (www.pacificaradioarchives.org).

D'Orlando, Albert (§15, §109, §120): Courtesy of Dr. R. Catherine Cohen.

East, P. D. (§28): Courtesy of Mary Cameron East Cowan.

Ensley, Francis Gerald (§82): From "On Loving One's Neighbor as Oneself," by Francis Gerald Ensley," in *The Pulpit Speaks on Race*, edited by Alfred T. Davies (New York: Abingdon Press, 1965). Used by permission.

Evans, J. Claude (§74): Copyright © 1963 *The Christian Century*. Reprinted by permission from the February 1963, Vol. 34, issue of *The Pulpit*.

Ferris, Theodore Parker (§130): From "Civil Rights from a Christian Point of View" by Theodore Parker Ferris, in *Pulpit Speaks on Race*, edited by Alfred T. Davies (New York: Abingdon Press, 1965). Used by permission.

Ginn, D. Perry (§27): Copyright © 1956 *The Christian Century*. Reprinted by permission from the November 1956, Vol. 27, issue of *The Pulpit*.

Graham, Frank (§4): Courtesy of the Frank Porter Graham Papers #1819, Southern Historical Collection, Wilson Library, University of North Carolina at Chapel Hill.

Graham, Frank (§52): Courtesy of the Southern Regional Council.

Gray, Duncan M. (§69): Courtesy of the Southern Regional Council.

Gregory, Dick (§88): Courtesy of Dick Gregory and the Moses Moon Audio Archive at the National Museum of American History.

Hamer, Fannie Lou (§113): Courtesy of Charles McLaurin and the Moses Moon Audio Archive at the National Museum of American History.

Harris, Edward W. (§100): Courtesy of Mabel Harris.

Hawkins, Edler G. (§53, §76): "Behaving Like Ordinary Men" (October 1960), Box 5 Folder 34; "This is the Mood and This is the Time" (May 20, 1963), Box 5 Folder 55, Edler G. Hawkins Collection, Robert W. Woodruff Library of the Atlanta University Center.

Henry, Aaron (§93): Courtesy of the Moses Moon Audio Archive at the National Museum of American History.

Hesburgh, Theodore Parker (§114): Courtesy of Rev. Theodore M. Hesburgh, C.S.C.

Hill, Haywood (§56): Courtesy of the Southern Regional Council.

Howard, TRM (§16, §25): Courtesy of the AFRO-American newspapers Archives and Research Center (AANARC).

Howlett, Duncan (§60, §95, §102, §119, §123): Courtesy of All Souls Church, Washington, D.C.

Hudson, James (§12, §24): Courtesy of James L. Hudson and the Florida A&M University Black Archives Research Center and Museum.

Imes, William Lloyd (§8, §11): Courtesy of Special Collections Research Center, Syracuse University Library.

Johnson, Mildred B. (§104): Courtesy of National Park Service, Mary McLeod Bethune Council House National Historic Site, National Archives for Black Women's History, Mildred Bell Johnson Papers, MAMC 93.

Johnson, Mordecai (§1, §31): Courtesy of the Mordecai Johnson family and Moorland-Spingarn Research Center, Howard University, Washington D.C.

Kilgore, J. Wilson (§101): Copyright © 1964 *The Christian Century*. Reprinted by permission from the July-August, 1964, Vol. 35, issue of *The Pulpit*.

King, Edwin (§112): Courtesy of Pacifica Radio Archives (www.pacificaradioarchives.org).

King, Martin Luther (§29): License granted by intellectual properties management, Atlanta, Georgia, as exclusive licensor of the King estate.

King, Marion (§73): Courtesy of the Southern Regional Council.

Klunder, Bruce W. (§80): From *The Pulpit Speaks on Race*, edited by Alfred T. Davies (New York: Abingdon Press, 1965). Used by permission.

Lawson, James (§49): Courtesy of Rev. James Lawson.

Lee, Heslip "Happy" (§64): Courtesy of Special Collections and Archives, James Branch Cabell Library, VCU Libraries, Virginia Commonwealth University.

Lewis, John (§85): Courtesy of John Lewis and the Moses Moon Audio Archive at the National Museum of American History.

Martin, Carlos (§46): Courtesy of Rev. Carlos E. Martin.

Mays, Benjamin (§6, §51): Courtesy of the Moorland-Spingarn Collection, Howard University.

McCracken, Robert J. (§59): Copyright © 1961 *The Christian Century*. Reprinted by permission from the February 1961, Vol. 31, issue of *The Pulpit*.

Merton, Thomas (§107): Transcription of a talk by Thomas Merton at the Abbey of Gethsemani, June 10, 1964. Used with permission of the Merton Legacy Trust and the Thomas Merton Center. #118:1.

Morgan, Charles, Jr. (§86): Copyright © 1962 *The Christian Century*. Reprinted by permission from the October 2, 1963 issue of *The Christian Century*.

O'Boyle, Father Patrick (§84): Courtesy of the Archdiocese of Washington D.C.

Pike, James A. (§30, §75): Courtesy of Diane Pike.

Polier, Shad (§36): Courtesy of the Shad Polier family.

Powell, Adam C. (§32): Courtesy of the Adam C. Powell family.

Ralph, Robbins (§18): Courtesy of *Chicago Defender*.

Randolph, A. Philip (§33): Courtesy of the A. Philip Randolph Institute, Washington, D.C.

Reed, Robert A. (§122): Copyright © 1965 *The Christian Century*. Reprinted by permission from the April 14, 1965, issue of *The Christian Century*.

Rickey, Branch (§20): Courtesy of the Branch Rickey family

Shelton, Arthur E. (§89): Courtesy of Martin A. Shelton.

Shuttlesworth, Fred (§34, §42, §65, §106, §110): Courtesy of Rev. Fred Shuttlesworth.

Smith, Kelly Miller (§116): Copyright © 1965 *The Christian Century*. Reprinted by permission from the January, 1964, Vol. 36, issue of *The Pulpit*.

Smith, Kelly Miller (§128): Courtesy of Will D. Campbell.

Spike, Robert W. (§99, 108, 111): Courtesy of the Robert W. Spike family.

Stanford, Charles L. Jr. (§68): Copyright © 1963 *The Christian Century*. Reprinted by permission from the February 1963, Vol. 34, issue of *The Pulpit*.

Summerell, J. V. Crosby (§78): Courtesy of Donald Shriver, editor, *The Unsilent South: Prophetic Preaching in Racial Crisis* (Richmond: John Knox Press, 1965).

Taylor, Gardner (§129): From "Some Comments on Race Hate," by Gardner Taylor in *The Pulpit Speaks on Race*, edited by Alfred T. Davies (New York: Abingdon Press, 1965). Used by permission.

Tilson, Everett (§50): Copyright © 1960 *The Christian Century*. Reprinted by permission from the August 1960, Vol. 31, issue of *The Pulpit*.

Tobias, Channing H. (§35): Courtesy of the Kautz Family YMCA Archives, University of Minnesota.

Walker, Wyatt Tee (§77): Courtesy of Pacifica Radio Archives (www.pacificaradioarchives.org).

Walkup, Robert H. (§66, §67): Courtesy of Donald Shriver, editor, *The Unsilent South: Prophetic Preaching in Racial Crisis* (Richmond: John Knox Press, 1965).

Wilkins, Roy (§14, §26, §121): Courtesy of the Roy Wilkins family

Wilson, Frank T. (§90): From *Black Preaching* edited by Robert T. Newbold, Jr. © 1977 The Geneva Press. Used by permission of Geneva Press.

Wittenstein, Charles F. (§118): Courtesy of the Southern Regional Council.

Woodard, George H. (§87): Copyright © 1964 *The Christian Century*. Reprinted by permission from the February, 1964, Vol. 35, issue of *The Pulpit*.

Wright, Marion A. (§39): Courtesy of the Southern Regional Council

Wright, Marion A. (§62): Courtesy of the Marion A. Wright Papers #3830, Southern Historical Collection, Wilson Library, University of North Carolina at Chapel Hill.

4375471